# Design Strat

This major practical handbook bridges the gap between strategy and design, presenting a step-by-step design process with a strategic approach and extensive methods for innovation, strategy development, design methodology and problem solving. It is an effective guide to planning and implementing design projects to ensure strategic anchoring of the process and outcome.

Built around a six-part phase structure that represents the design process, covering initial preparations and project briefing, research and analysis, targets and strategy, concept development, prototyping and modelling, production and delivery, it is a must-have resource for professionals and students. Readers can easily dip in and out of sections, using the phase structure as a navigation tool. Unlike other books on the market, *Design and Strategy* addresses the design process from the perspective of both the company and the designer. For businesses, it highlights the value of design as a strategic tool for positioning, competition and innovation. For the designer, it teaches how to create solutions that are strategically anchored and deliver successful outcomes for businesses, resulting in appreciative clients. It includes over 250 illustrations and diagrams, tables and text boxes showing how to move through each stage with clear visualisation and explanation.

This book encourages all designers in product design and manufacturing, service design, communication design, branding, and advertising, to think beyond shape and colour to see design through the lens of strategy, process and problem solving, and all business managers, innovators and developers, to see the value in strategic design outcomes.

**Wanda Grimsgaard** is Professor of Visual Communication at the University of South-Eastern Norway, USN Business School.

# Design and Strategy

A Step-by-Step Guide

Wanda Grimsgaard

LONDON AND NEW YORK

Cover image and book design: Lars Høie
Illustrations: Lars Høie and Wanda Grimsgaard
Typeset by: Bøk Oslo AS, Norway

First published 2023
by Routledge
4 Park Square, Milton Park, Abingdon,
Oxon OX14 4RN

and by Routledge
605 Third Avenue, New York, NY 10158

Routledge is an imprint of the Taylor & Francis
Group, an informa business



Translated and fully revised second edition from the Norwegian language:
*Design og Strategi* by Wanda Grimsgaard
© Cappelen Damm Akademisk 2018
ISBN: 978-80-02-49055-3

British Library Cataloguing-in-Publication Data
A catalogue record for this book is available from the British Library

Library of Congress Cataloging-in-Publication Data
A catalog record has been requested for this book

ISBN: 978-1-032-12290-8 (hbk)
ISBN: 978-1-032-12291-5 (pbk)
ISBN: 978-1-003-22395-5 (ebk)

DOI: 10.4324/9781003223955

Typeset in Type
Mériva by Armin Brenner and Markus John
(New Letters)
Domaine Text by Kris Sowersby
(Klim Type Foundry)

This book has been prepared from camera-ready copy provided by the author.

PREFACE

Preface by Bård Annweiler III
Preface by Wanda V
Acknowledgements VII

INTRODUCTION

How to use the book? VIII
What is design? X

PHASE 1 INITIATION
P. 1–40

Introduction 1

1.1 Initial preparations 5

1.2 Project brief 9

1.3 Initial meeting 10
1.3.1 Before the meeting 11
1.3.2 During the meeting 12
1.3.3 After the meeting 13
1.3.4 Meeting administration 13

1.4 Initial workshop 16
1.4.1 Purpose of initial workshop 16
1.4.2 Workshop preparation 17
1.4.3 Workshop invitation 17
1.4.4 Workshop facilities 18
1.4.5 Workshop management 18
1.4.6 Workshop execution 18
1.4.7 Workshop report 19
1.4.8 Workshop process 20

1.5 Project description 22

1.6 Progress schedule 24

1.7 Price quotation 26
1.7.1 Price request 28
1.7.2 Price setup 28
1.7.3 Terms and conditions 28
1.7.4 Negotiation 29
1.7.5 Hourly rate 29

1.8 Contract 31

1.9 Team collaboration 32
1.9.1 Control loop 35
1.9.2 Gameplan 37
1.9.3 Agile process management 39

PHASE 2 INSIGHT
P. 41–170

Introduction 41

2.1 Understanding the company 50
2.1.1 Value creation 51
2.1.2 Decision making 51
2.1.3 Organisational culture 53
2.1.4 Organisational development 53
2.1.5 The company's universe 54

2.2 Situational study 55
2.2.1 Situational study process 56
2.2.2 PIPI workshop 56
2.2.3 Where are we – where will we? 57

2.3 Problem statement 58
2.3.1 Problem 60
2.3.2 Problem statement process 61
2.3.3 Problem definition 61
2.3.4 Problem statement formulation 62
2.3.5 Problem statement delimitation 63
2.3.6 Problem statement analysis 65
2.3.7 Problem statement requirements 67
2.3.8 A good problem statement 67
2.3.9 Wicked problems 68

2.4 Method selection 70
2.4.1 Qualitative method 70
2.4.2 Quantitative method 71
2.4.3 Method triangulation 73
2.4.4 Research question 73

2.5 Research process 74
2.5.1 Problem statement (Step 1) 76
2.5.2 Research design (Step 2) 76
2.5.3 Choice of method (Step 3) 78
2.5.4 Choice of units (Step 4) 79
2.5.5 Data collection (Step 5) 80

2.5.6 Data analysis and discussion (Step 6) 80
2.5.7 Data interpretation (Step 7) 81
2.5.8 Report preparation (Step 8) 82

2.6 Research 82
2.6.1 Survey 82
2.6.2 Interview 90
2.6.3 Observation 97
2.6.4 Focus group 102
2.6.5 UX Research 104
2.6.6 Experiment 106
2.6.7 Scientific research 108
2.6.8 Artistic research 112
2.6.9 Design research 113

2.7 Analyses 115
2.7.1 Situational analysis 117
2.7.2 Internal analysis 119
2.7.3 Value chain analysis 121
2.7.4 Competitor analysis 122
2.7.5 Positioning analysis 125
2.7.6 Target group analysis 129
2.7.7 Brand analysis 137
2.7.8 Visual analysis 142
2.7.9 PESTLE analysis 146
2.7.10 SWOT analysis 148
2.7.11 Gap analysis 153

2.8 Mapping 155
2.8.1 Mapping methods 156
2.8.2 Moodboard 156
2.8.3 Storyboard 159
2.8.4 Customer journey 160
2.8.5 GIGA mapping 160

2.9 Testing and measuring 164
2.9.1 User testing 165
2.9.2 A/B testing 166
2.9.3 Funnel 167
2.9.4 Zero-point measurement 167
2.9.5 Why do we measure? 167
2.9.6 KPIs and metrics 168
2.9.7 Qualitative indicators and metrics 169
2.9.8 Mental availability measurements 169
2.9.9 Category entry points 170


PHASE 3 STRATEGY
P. 171–336


Introduction 171

3.1 Strategy development 176
3.1.1 Different approaches 177
3.1.2 Strategic management tool 181
3.1.3 TOP 5 182
3.1.4 Strategic workshop 182
3.1.5 Workshop process 182
3.1.6 Strategic workshop report 184
3.1.7 Workshop template 185

3.2 Overall strategy 186
3.2.1 Purpose 187
3.2.2 Mission 187
3.2.3 Business idea 187
3.2.4 Vision 189
3.2.5 Core values 191
3.2.6 Value proposition 196
3.2.7 The value pyramid 198
3.2.9 Strategic narrative 201

3.3 Goals and subgoals 201
3.3.1 Business goals 202
3.3.2 Big hairy goals 203
3.3.3 Development of goals 204
3.3.4 Goal hierarchy 204
3.3.5 Qual vs. quant goals 207
3.3.6 Measurable goals 208
3.3.7 Goal achievement 208
3.3.8 Sustainability goals 209
3.3.9 Goals for design project 210

3.4 Business strategy 211
3.4.1 Competitive strategy 211
3.4.2 Porter's generic strategies 212
3.4.3 Sustainability strategy 215
3.4.4 Blue Ocean Strategy 215
3.4.5 Transient advantage 217
3.4.6 Distinctive asset-building strategy 219
3.4.7 Agile strategy management 222
3.4.8 Is the right strategy chosen? 223
3.4.9 Strategy implementation 224

3.5 Business model 225
3.5.1 Business model canvas 227
3.5.2 Sustainable business model 227

3.5.3 Business model innovation 228
3.5.4 Lean start-up 229

3.6 Market strategy 230
3.6.1 Markets 230
3.6.2 Marketing tasks 231
3.6.3 STP marketing strategy 232
3.6.4 Customers' needs 233
3.6.5 The four Ps 234
3.6.6 The four Cs 236
3.6.7 Content marketing 238
3.6.8 Inbound marketing 239
3.6.9 Digital strategy 241

3.7 Brand strategy 245
3.7.1 Brand platform 251
3.7.2 Brand architecture 251
3.7.3 Brand positioning 260
3.7.4 Brand story 271
3.7.5 Brand identity 276
3.7.6 Brand assets 280
3.7.7 Brand name 289
3.7.8 Brand perspective 296
3.7.9 Brand refresh, redesign, rebranding 299

3.8 Communication strategy 300
3.8.1 Communication audit 304
3.8.2 Identifying the target group 307
3.8.3 Communication goals 309
3.8.4 Desired reputation 311
3.8.5 Communication platform 315
3.8.6 Communication elements 318
3.8.7 Communication development 321
3.8.8 Channels and media 325
3.8.9 Communication measurement 329

3.9 Design strategy 332
3.9.1 Design strategy compass 333
3.9.2 Design strategy development 333
3.9.3 Design strategy content 334
3.9.4 Design goal 334
3.9.5 Operational strategy 335
3.9.6 Design platform 335
3.9.7 Visual assets 336
3.9.8 Elements and surfaces 336
3.9.9 Design strategy vs. design brief 336

PHASE 4 DESIGN
P. 337–528

Introduction 337

4.1 Design brief 345

4.2 Strategy><Design 348
4.2.1 Mapping as a link 349
4.2.2 Visualise strategy 350
4.2.3 Visualise name 352
4.2.4 Distinctive brand assets 352
4.2.5 Idea as a bridge 353
4.2.6 The fifth element 353

4.3 Design methodology 354
4.3.1 Human-centred design 355
4.3.2 User-experience 358
4.3.3 Emotional design 359
4.3.4 Innovation 360
4.3.5 Iterative method 363
4.3.6 Divergence and convergence 366
4.3.7 Sprint 368
4.3.8 Scrum 370
4.3.9 Kanban 371
4.3.10 Lean and agile 371
4.3.11 Design thinking 374
4.3.12 Customer journey 376
4.3.13 Need-finding 378
4.3.14 Service blueprint 380
4.3.15 Co-design 381
4.3.16 Business design 383
4.3.17 Strategic design thinking 385
4.3.18 Systemic design 386
4.3.19 In retrospect 389

4.4 Concept development 390
4.4.1 Foundation and framework 390
4.4.2 Creative problem solving 392
4.4.3 Brainstorming 396
4.4.4 Idea development 398
4.4.5 Conceptual directions 409
4.4.6 Verbalisation and visualisation 410
4.4.7 Prototyping of ideas 410
4.4.8 Testing of ideas 410
4.4.9 Presentation of ideas 411

4.5 Design development 412
4.5.1 The three-direction principle 412

4.5.2 Design sketches 413
4.5.3 Concrete design 417

4.6 Design elements 421
4.6.1 Shape 421
4.6.2 Colour 426
4.6.3 Texture 430
4.6.4 Space 430

4.7 Composition 433
4.7.1 Perception 433
4.7.2 Principles of composition 434
4.7.3 Unity/whole 436
4.7.4 Focal point 440
4.7.5 Proportions 441
4.7.6 Balance 442
4.7.7 Rhythm 445

4.8 Surface and format 448
4.8.1 Surface 449
4.8.2 Format 451
4.8.3 Aspect ratios 455
4.8.4 The A series 459
4.8.5 The golden ratio 463
4.8.6 Golden rectangle 464
4.8.7 The golden spiral 466
4.8.8 Fibonacci 467
4.8.9 The rule of thirds 469

4.9 Identity development 470
4.9.1 The identity principles 471
4.9.2 The identity elements 474
4.9.3 Logo 476
4.9.4 Symbol 489
4.9.5 Identity colours 494
4.9.6 Typography 498
4.9.7 Distinctive assets 515
4.9.8 Identity management 516
4.9.9 Grid system 517

PHASE 5 PRODUCTION
P. 529–584

Introduction 529

5.1 Implementation 532

5.2 Model 533
5.2.1 Dummy 534
5.2.2 Sketch model 535
5.2.3 Wireframe 535
5.2.4 Mockup 536
5.2.5 Prototype 536
5.2.6 Data model and simulation 538
5.2.7 Presentation model 538
5.2.8 Blueprint 539
5.2.9 Production model 539

5.3 Material selection 539
5.3.1 Materials 539
5.3.2 Functionality 540
5.3.3 Material insight 541
5.3.4 Material properties 541
5.3.5 Material life cycle 542
5.3.6 Product life cycle 543
5.3.7 Product life extension 543
5.3.8 Incorrect material selection 544
5.3.9 Sustainable materials 544

5.4 Paper and cartonboard 544
5.4.1 Paper 544
5.4.2 Paper construction 545
5.4.3 Paper production 545
5.4.4 Paper properties 546
5.4.5 Paper selection 548
5.4.6 Cartonboard 550
5.4.7 Green packaging 551
5.4.8 Packaging materials 553
5.4.9 Ecolabelling and certification 554

5.5 Colour management 556
5.5.1 Colour models 558
5.5.2 Colour gamut 559
5.5.3 Colour profiles 560
5.5.4 Select colour profile 562
5.5.5 Colour channels and tone depth 565
5.5.6 Workflow 566
5.5.7 File types 568
5.5.8 PDF for printing 569
5.5.9 Colour reference systems 572

5.6 Production for digital media 573

5.7 Production for printed media 575
5.7.1 Press techniques 576
5.7.2 Printing methods 577
5.7.3 Raster 578
5.7.4 Four colours (CMYK) 579

5.7.5 Printing inks 580
5.7.6 Printing effects 580

5.8 Installations and constructions 582

5.9 Quality assurance 583


PHASE 6 MANAGEMENT
P. 585–622

Introduction 585

6.1 Intangible assets 588

6.2 Legal protection 590
6.2.1 Copyright 590
6.2.2 Trademark 591
6.2.3 Domain name 593
6.2.4 Company name 593
6.2.5 Exclusive rights in social media 594
6.2.6 Design rights 594
6.2.7 Patents 594
6.2.8 Counterfeiting 595
6.2.9 Marketing rights/ unfair competition 595

6.3 Design management 596

6.4 Design effect 597
6.4.1 Design ladder 598
6.4.2 The value of design 599
6.4.3 Design-driven company 600
6.4.4 Design impact awards 601
6.4.7 Visual impact 602
6.4.8 How to measure the design effect? 602

6.5 Design manual 604
6.5.1 Purpose and target group 604
6.5.2 Foundation 605
6.5.3 Scope 605
6.5.4 Digital design manual 605
6.5.5 Contents 606
6.5.6 Unbranding 611

6.6 Design templates 612

6.7 Operations manual 614

6.8 Further development 615

6.9 Sustainable management 615
6.9.1 Sustainability development 616
6.9.2 Corporate sustainability 616
6.9.3 Circular economy 617
6.9.4 Net zero 618
6.9.5 The trendsetters 618
6.9.6 Greenwashing 618
6.9.7 The designer's impact 619
6.9.8 High complexity 621
6.9.9 Sustainable font choice 622

References 624

Index 638

List of figures 644

List of tables 647

Planning tool 648

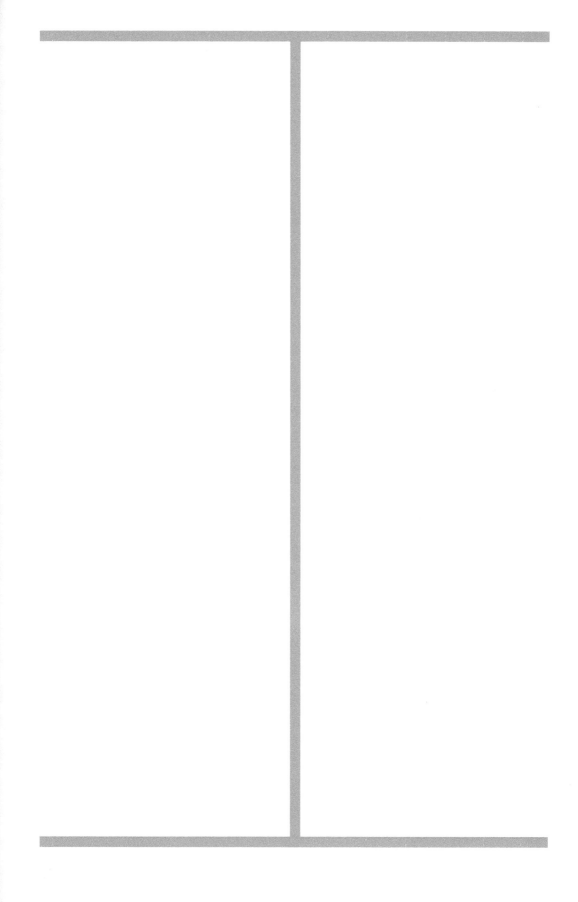

Bård Annweiler is one of the two co-founders of the award-winning Norwegian brand consultancy Mission, which opened in 2001.

Bård is the author of *Point of Purpose*, an essential book for modern leaders and global brand strategists. *Point of Purpose* introduces purpose as the fundamental reason for why today's companies and brands are successful in business.

He has more than 20 years of experience leading branding projects from strategy to implementation across sectors including lifestyle, technology and professional services.

Drawing on his experience with clients, existing and previous board positions, he helps some of the leading Scandinavian businesses reimagine how they interact with their customers and employees. Bård is used as a sounding board to ensure long-term strategic perspectives.

He has a Master of Science in Marketing from BI Norwegian Business School, and has a background of various positions on the client side before he transitioned to consulting.

# Preface
# Bård Annweiler

Design is a highly strategic profession, a fact we have all heard and experienced. So why has no one written a book that unites the two topics, design and strategy? There are tens of thousands of books in the design field and numerous ones about business and strategy, but not one of them hit the sweet spot interlinking the two fields.

Until now, no author has filled the gap. As a professor of visual communication and graphic design, Wanda Grimsgaard has, over the past ten years, diligently gathered world-class ideas, theories and processes from the field of strategy and adapted that logic into the field of design. Her academic background, and her more than 25 years of experience as a practising designer, have given her extraordinary expertise in both areas. It is at this intersection between design and strategy she focuses her writing.

Designers are visual problem solvers who try to find patterns in business problems. Therefore, strategy as a concept is essential to create a framework to help solve and articulate design issues. Experienced designers can make use of this rare combination to make logic and intuition come together. Designers will benefit significantly from this book, as they now have an excellent resource to use in their work.

Grimsgaard provides a timeless classic that gathers all the tools and thinking that make design strategic.

I first met Wanda Grimsgaard 15 years ago, when she was chair of the board at the Norwegian organisation for visual communication – Grafill. Her professional attitude made both her and her work an outstanding resource for others in the design community. Openness, curiosity, compassion and trustworthiness are all characteristics I would use to describe her – she is a true Scandinavian design explorer.

This first handbook combining design and strategy will soon be on the desk of every professional designer.

Wanda Grimsgaard is a professor of visual communication at the University of South-Eastern Norway, USN School of Business, and author of the book *Design and Stategy*, which was first published in Norwegian in 2018.

Grimsgaard was educated at the Oslo National Academy of the Arts as a graphic designer. Her background consists of many years' of experience in the design industry. The core business has been development of identities for companies, products or services, with the aim of increasing brand awareness, competitiveness and other value creation. Her clients includes both start-ups, medium-sized companies and large, well-known branded businesses. Besides working as an executive designer, Wanda has always been interested in sharing knowledge, as a lecturer, course leader and examiner for various course organisers and design schools.

In her teaching she is passionate about conveying to designers and their clients that every project should be aligned with the company's goals and strategies, so that the outcome can contribute to achieving the company's goals. She finds it equally inspiring and fun to work with strategy and design which she sees as two sides of the same coin.

Grimsgaard's core area of research is at the intersection of strategy and design, aiming to bridge the two. 'The challenge lies in integrating strategy in design, and vice versa. This is where the key to success is found. Herein lies the gold', according to Grimsgaard.

# Preface
# Wanda Grimsgaard

My father, Wilhelm Lefevre Grimsgaard, made his career in advertising, and he taught me early on how to use what he called a work platform, which in reality was a strategic platform. That is how I started working strategically, without being aware that's what I was doing. After a few years of practice in a design agency I experienced a great strategic 'aha' moment when one of our marketing consultants organised a strategic workshop with one of our clients. I then thought, 'I can do this, too.' This was the beginning of a number of strategic design processes and an exciting professional development, which has led me to write this book on design and strategy. A triggering factor was my need to share knowledge, something I have been doing ever since I held my first Mac course in the late 1980s. I was then an experienced Mac user as I bought their very first model back in 1984. So, design and teaching became my thing besides running a design business for many years, until I was appointed a full professor and went all in.

Teaching is a great responsibility that constantly requires acquiring new knowledge. As time went by, I realised that the more I learned, the less I knew. It became essential to put the knowledge into a system and gradually improve it. I started writing compendiums for the students and organised them into a system of phases based on the progress of the design process. This way, I got the idea of writing a book on processes and methods based on the framework of this phase structure. Writing this book has been a challenging and interesting journey. I have interviewed designers, strategists and social science experts, dived into old and new literature, and read literally tons of research articles and online stuff. Through this extensive research, I have refined the phase structure in order to ensure that it can work across design disciplines and have filled it with professional content. It turned out to be a demanding task that required a lot more effort than I had ever imagined. Not least because over the past decades there have been some major changes in the way we work with design, which have led people to perceive design differently. Design thinking, iteration and user-experience are among the many recent methods businesses and designers adopt in order to create attractive products and services. Large corporations see the advantages of design thinking, not only for creating visual solutions, but also as a key factor in problem solving and business development.

Design and strategy are inextricably linked. For a long time I have been aware that there is not one single answer when it comes to design. I have now also learned that there are no such thing as a single solution when it comes to strategy. Both strategy and design are major disciplines, and within these fields there are numerous underlying disciplines and executive professions. I have tried to identify the basics of some of the different areas you might encounter in a strategic design process. My greatest challenge has been to limit myself, to stay true to my initial concept, and remember that the main process is the most important thing to explain. At the same time, I have also dived a bit below the surface, offering some special treats throughout the book. Everything you will read about in my book can be explored further in specialised literature, articles and online. I leave it to you, the reader, to dive deeper into the areas you find most fascinating. I have not emphasised explaining how to design a finished product for a client, however, I have laid the groundwork for it by showing the processes and methods that can be used regardless of the specific task you have to tackle. My choice of content in the different phases is influenced by my background as a graphic designer, where identity development and branding are key. This knowledge will hopefully be useful for most companies across various design disciplines. The overall strategic design process I have developed can be used in any project.

Having written this book I feel a tremendous desire to know more, read more, and discover more. I feel like I have opened a treasure chest full of knowledge, processes and methods. Many will recognise traditional methods, some will recognise new ones, and yet others will find something missing. Some may also disagree with something. If so, it's actually a good thing because by disagreeing, you become more aware of what you personally think. Besides, some interesting debates might ensue. I bring a voice in through what I have included in the book, and through the way I have defined the strategic design process.

Alexander Fjelldal
Alf Bendixen
Alina Wheeler
Anders Tangerud
Anette Brekke-Bjørkedal
Anine Heitun
Anita Grimsgaard Loe
Anna Tokle Amundsen
Anne Cecilie Hopstock
Anne Holter
Annie Myhre
Arild Tofting
Arne Simonsen
Ashley Booth
Audun Farbrot
Bård Annweiler
Benedicte Wildhagen
Birger Opstad
Birger Sevaldson
Birgitte Appelong
Birgitte Hvidsten
Bjørn Rybakken
Brita Bergsnov Hansen
Camilla Martinussen
Carl Gürgens
Carl Tørris Christensen
Cathrine Røsseland
Dag Einar Thorsen
Eirik Faukland
Eivind Arnstein Johansen
Eivind Eide
Elisabeth Holmberg
Elise Kaspartu
Endre Berentzen
Erik Bakkelund
Espen Johansen
Frode Helland
Geir Skomsøy
Gillian Warner-Søderholm
Grace Harrison
Henning Karlsen
Henning Rekdal Nielsen
Henriette Scharning
Hilde Honerud
Hølje Tefre
Ina Brantenberg
Inger Renate Moldskred Stie
Ingunn Elvekrok
Inki Annweiler
Jacob Rørvik
Jakob Thyness
Jan Henrik Wold
Jannicke Øiaas
Jon Hovland Honerud
Jonas Aakre
Jonas Fredin
Jonathan Romm
Kai Victor Myrnes-Hansen
Kaj Clausen
Katrine Malmer-Høvik
Kjell Reenskaug
Lars Christian Gamborg
Lars Høie
Lars Olsen
Leif Friman Anisdahl
Linda Lien
Lise Feirud
Malene Loe Grimsgaard
Mathias Haddal Hovet
Matthew Shobbrook
Morten Throndsen
Nicholas Hermier
Nils Jørgen Gundersen
Nina Furu
Nina Lysbakken
Øivind A. Grimsgaard Loe
Ole Lund
Øyvin Rannem
Per Farstad
Rachel Cooper
Rory McGrath
Rune Døli
Sidsel Lie
Simon Manchipp
Skule Storheill
Sophie Moss Kravik
Steinar Killi
Susann Vatnedal
Søren Obed Madsen
Thea Ørneseide
Theo Sikkes
Thomas Hvammen Nicholson
Thomas Lewe
Tom Tysbo
Tone Bergan
Tor Paulson
Tora Aasen
Torbjørn Sitre
Tore H. Wiik
Torunn Mehus
Ulf Winther
Wegard Kyoo Bergli

# Acknowledgements


### Perpetual gratitude

I send some grateful thoughts to my father Wilhelm Lefevre Grimsgaard (1932–1995). His last message to me was: 'Remember to work strategically with design'. And, to my beloved children, Øivind, Anita, and Malene, for encouraging me 'Mom, be brave, think large'. And, a huge gratitude to my man in love and life, Audun Farbrot: 'Every word you write brings you closer to the target.' My deepest thanks to *Grace Harrison* at Routledge who saw the potential in the Norwegian 1st edition of this book and wanted to bring it out into the world.

Updating this book for an international audience, as well as adding new material, has been quite a job. I have been fortunate to have many professional people around me who have contributed, first with the Norwegian edition of the book and now with the English edition. Several people have followed me closely either throughout the whole process or during part of it. Others have lined up for interviews and talks, read and commented on scripts, shared their processes and methods with me and contributed generously with their knowledge.

Special thanks to: Lars Høie (book designer), Inki and Bård Annweiler and their team at Mission AS (my editorial team), Susann Vatnedal, and her colleagues at Bøk Oslo AS (text and design editing), Nicholas Hermier, and his team at Languages Power International (translation) and Gillian Warner-Søderholm, at the University of South-Eastern Norway, USN School of Business, for generous support.

## How to use the book?

The book you are holding presents a wide range of processes and methods for strategic development of design. The key concept is a phase system that represents a complete strategic design process.

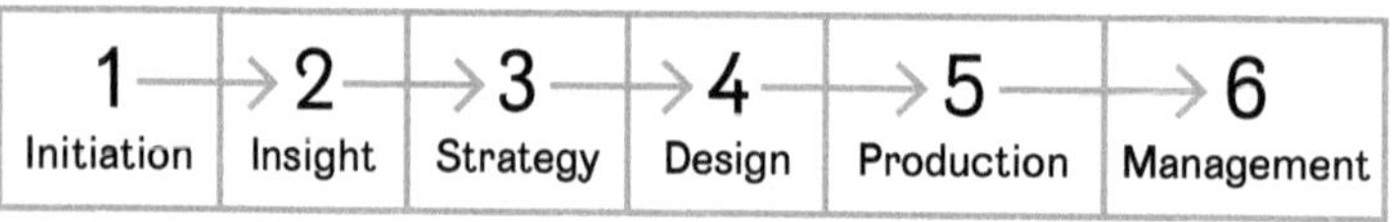


Fig. 0.1 Phase structure

The phase system is displayed on the right side of the book, as a navigation structure, so you always know where you are in the process. The book is first and foremost a handbook. It works across digital and manual platforms. You should use it as a tool in the planning and development of design projects and pick out what you need at any given moment. For this reason, the different phases and underlying steps are presented as independent units. Many of the topics, methods and models in the book are available online and in the source literature, if you decide to dig deeper. Figures 0.1 and 0.2 show the six main phases: initiation, insight, strategy, design, production and management. Figure 0.6 shows examples of how underlying levels appear in the navigational structure and how to navigate.

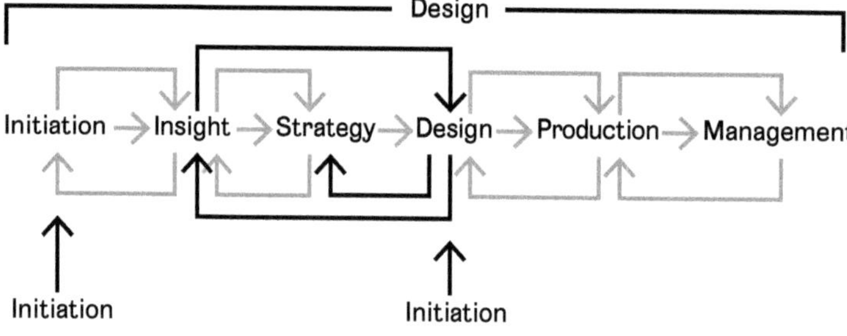


Fig. 0.2 Linear and circular

First and second levels: The navigation structure consists of four levels. Table 0.1 shows an overview of the first and second levels. Navigating around these levels and picking out what is relevant for different assignments is easy for an experienced designer. A design student might find it overwhelming at first. They might benefit from a lecturer or tutor breaking down the content and putting it in context with various tasks and other literature. If you learn to understand the phase structure and its logic, it will be much easier to navigate. The emphasis of the different phases will vary depending on the type of project in question. For example, in one project it may be necessary to work 10 per cent with strategy and 90 per cent with visual design, while in another project it may be the opposite. The names and order of the phases can be changed as needed.

Fig. 0.1 These phases are also the main phases of a strategic design process. The process is presented here linearly, but also works circularly.
© Grimsgaard, W. (2018)

Fig. 0.2 The figure shows the design process as a linear phase structure and the way we navigate back and forth and circularly in the phases. The initiation of a design project can take place in phase 1 or phase 4, depending on the need for insight and strategy development.
© Grimsgaard, W. (2018)

Tips for the reader
Phases 5 and 6 are no less important because they come last. You might as well start reading here. Why not start with 6.9 Sustainable management?

Level 1

1 Initiation
2 Insight
3 Strategy
4 Design
5 Production
6 Management

Level 2

1. Initiation
1.1 Initial preparations
1.2 Project brief
1.3 Initial meeting
1.4 Initial workshop
1.5 Project description
1.6 Progress schedule
1.7 Price quotation
1.8 Contract
1.9 Team collaboration

2. Insight
2.1 Understanding the company
2.2 Situational study
2.3 Problem statement
2.4 Method selection
2.5 Research process
2.6 Research
2.7 Analyses
2.8 Mapping
2.9 Testing and measuring

3. Strategy
3.1 Strategy development
3.2 Overall strategy
3.3 Goals and subgoals
3.4 Business strategy
3.5 Business model
3.6 Market strategy
3.7 Brand strategy
3.8 Communication strategy
3.9 Design strategy

4. Design
4.1 Design brief
4.2 Strategy><Design
4.3 Design methodology
4.4 Concept development
4.5 Design development
4.6 Design elements
4.7 Composition
4.8 Surface and format
4.9 Identity development

5. Production
5.1 Implementation
5.2 Model
5.3 Material selection
5.4 Paper and cartonboard
5.5 Colour management
5.6 Production for digital
5.7 Production for print
5.8 Installations and constructions
5.9 Quality assurance

6. Management
6.1 Intangible assets
6.2 Legal protection
6.3 Design management
6.4 Design effect
6.5 Design manual
6.6 Design templates
6.7 Operations manual
6.8 Further development
6.9 Sustainable management

Table 0.1 First and second levels

Table 0.1 The table shows the two first levels of the navigation structure. A planning tool with an overview of all the phases can be found at the back of the book. © Grimsgaard, W. (2018)

**Main characters in the book:** There are three main characters in the book. They are the designer and the company that the book is aimed at, and the user, who is the object of their attention. The company is the design buyer.

The term company is here used as a common term for both commercial and non-profit organisations, as well as private and public. The designer is the professional who carries out design assignments for the business. The designer can be an individual designer, a design agency or another kind of design company, regardless of design profession. The user refers to the person or target group the company wants to reach with their products and services, and whom the designer is aiming towards when creating user-friendly and attractive solutions. The user is the most important person. Without the user there will be no assignments and no design.

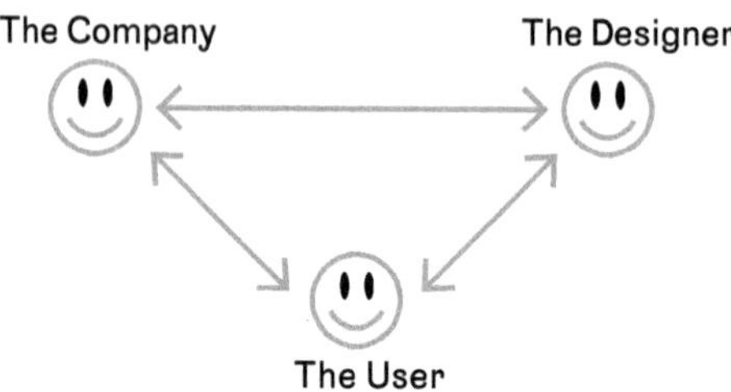


Fig. 0.3 The main characters of the book

Fig. 0.3 The figure shows the book's main characters: the company (the design buyer), the designer (the professional) and the user (the customer). © Grimsgaard, W. (2018)

Fig. 0.4 The figure illustrates where strategic design is located between the extremes of art and business. Which is close to business. The direction of art is often more individual, while the direction of business operations is more client-driven. © Grimsgaard, W. (2018)

Fig. 0.5 The figure shows strategic design at the core of tackling business challenges in the company's internal and external environment. © Grimsgaard, W. (2018)

Fig. 0.6 The figure illustrates how the navigation structure works. © Grimsgaard, W. (2018)

## What is design?

Design is a positively charged word. To most people, it stands for aesthetics, good shape, good function and identity. Therefore, there are many who wish to own the word 'design' and use it in different contexts. As a result, the design concept has a wide reach and might be perceived as ambiguous. What a lot of people do not consider is that design is not necessarily something visual or physical. Design is first and foremost about problem solving, and the result can be just as much an idea for improving a service as a tangible visual result. 'The designer's strength is solving problems, and is not primarily about shape- and colour, but about putting things in system so that new opportunities arise.' (Sevaldson, 2011). This means considering the problem-solving process as design. In other words, design is not just the end result, it is the entire process as shown in Figure 0.2. At the same time, design is a way of thinking, which is referred to as design thinking and systems thinking (4.3.11 Design thinking, 4.3.18 Systemic design), ways of thinking and working that can help solve complex problems, lead to innovation. Back to: What is design? A good way to view design is found in Bason (2017)[1] according to which design can be seen as:

1) a plan for achieving a particular result or change, including graphics, products, services and systems.
2) a practice with a particular set of approaches, methods, tools and processes for creating such plans.
3) a certain way of reasoning, underlying, or guiding these processes.

This is equally relevant for all design disciplines and for assignments across both public and private sectors. The design profession is particularly sensitive to the changes around us and adapts quickly to them in order to meet new requirements. Designers nowadays face increasingly demanding challenges in a technologically complex world with ever-increasing societal and global challenges.

1 Christian Bason: *Leading Public Design, How Managers Engage with Design to Transform Public Governance* (2017).

Even in small projects, the complexity can be high, and it is becoming increasingly important for the designer to use systematic and strategic tools and methods. (Phase 4 Design: Introduction, p. 337).

Design is a large multidisciplinary area that oscillates between free art on the one hand and business operations on the other. Between the extremes there is a range of disciplines that can be used to produce creative and target-oriented solutions. The designers going for free art are more likely to create solutions based on intuition and gut feeling than business-oriented designers. The latter will be more concerned with creating strategic and targeted solutions. This is a general observation and a lot of interesting things can come into being in the meeting between the extremes. Read more about *design* in the introduction of phase 4.

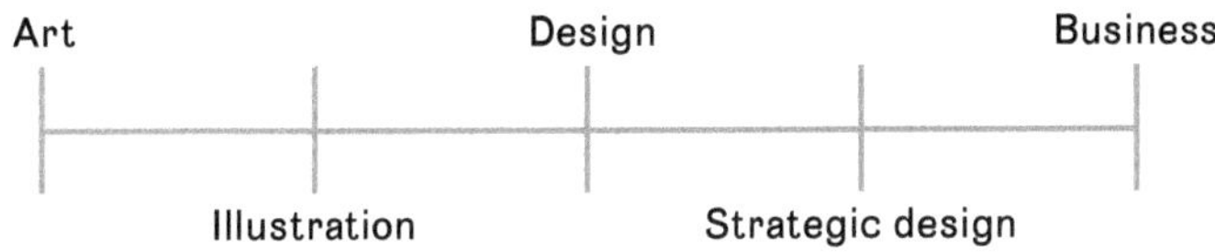


Fig. 0.4 Strategic design

**Strategic design development:** Strategic development of design can be explained as a way of developing and using design that is rooted in the company's overall strategy, and which should help the company build its position and reputation, achieve its goals and strengthen its competitiveness or other value creation. Strategic use of design can also be driven by a clear design ambition, i.e. design is part of the company's overall strategy. In strategic design, the design process has aims that go beyond the form and colour of a profile or a product. Strategic design development means solving problems and opening new opportunities that lead to creating value for the company. It can be anything from organisational changes to developing new business concepts. Strategic design links design and marketing together and brings design into the company's management and boardroom as part of corporate development and branding. Strategic design development requires the right methods for insight, analysis and strategy development, and the ability to incorporate this strategy into the design process and thus complete a task or solve a problem.

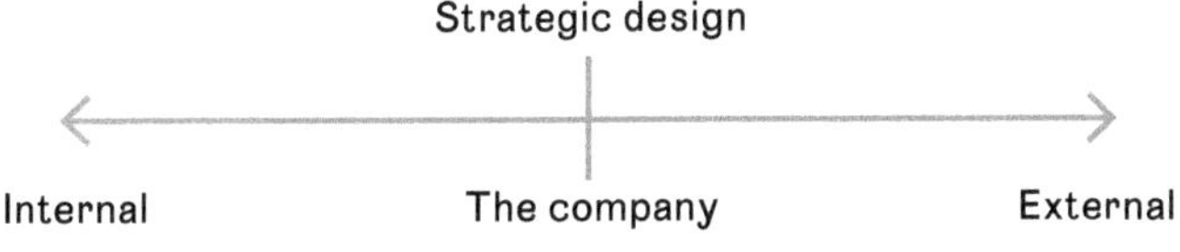


Fig. 0.5 At the core

**Strategy><Design:** For a strategic designer, all design projects will start by defining the problem, and in the further work will be about solving it in a creative and innovative way through a strategic approach. Central to this work is the use of processes and methods for insight, analysis, strategy, idea development and design work, and the conscious focus on the user. The challenge is to link strategy and design, where the success factor lies in the intersection between analytical and creative thinking

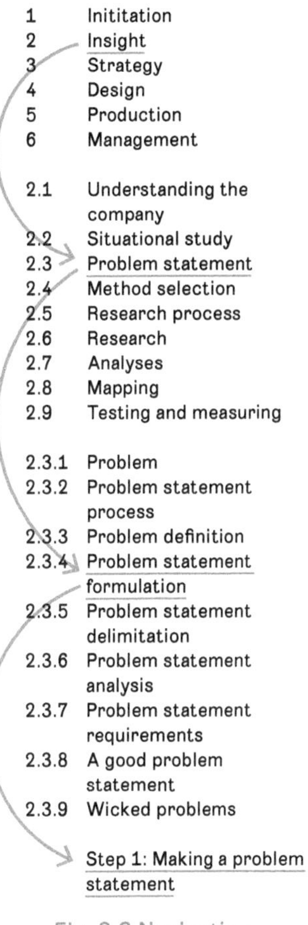

1 Inititation
2 Insight
3 Strategy
4 Design
5 Production
6 Management
2.1 Understanding the company
2.2 Situational study
2.3 Problem statement
2.4 Method selection
2.5 Research process
2.6 Research
2.7 Analyses
2.8 Mapping
2.9 Testing and measuring
2.3.1 Problem
2.3.2 Problem statement process
2.3.3 Problem definition
2.3.4 Problem statement formulation
2.3.5 Problem statement delimitation
2.3.6 Problem statement analysis
2.3.7 Problem statement requirements
2.3.8 A good problem statement
2.3.9 Wicked problems
Step 1: Making a problem statement


Fig. 0.6 Navigation

(4.2 Strategy><Design). There is no one-size-fits-all solution in a design project; the possibilities are endless. Strong insight, goal setting and planning, combined with solid idea processes, user insight and repeated testing and evaluation are all a prerequisite for success. Sustainability goals should be set and met (3.3.8 Sustainability goals). See the planning tool on page 648 Planning tool as well as Table 0.2 Example of use of phases.

**Package design**

1. Initiation
1.2 Project brief
1.3 Initial meeting
1.5 Project description
1.6 Progress schedule
1.7 Price quotation
1.8 Contract

2. Insight
2.2 Situational study
2.3 Problem statement
2.7.5 Positioning analysis
2.7.6 Target group analysis
2.7.8 Visual analysis

3. Strategy
3.5.2 Sustainable business model
3.7 Brand strategy
3.8.5 Communication platform
3.9 Design strategy

4. Design
4.1 Design brief
4.4 Concept development
4.5 Design development
4.7 Composition
4.8 Surface and format
4.9 Identity development

5. Production
5.1 Implementation
5.3 Material selection
5.4.9 Ecolabelling and certification
5.7 Production for printed media

6. Management
6.2 Legal protection
6.9 Sustainable management

**Corporate identity**

1. Initiation
1.2 Project brief
1.3 Initial meeting
1.5 Project description
1.6 Progress schedule
1.7 Price quotation
1.8 Contract

2. Insight
2.2.3 Where are we – where will we?
2.3 Problem statement
2.7.1 Situational analysis
2.7.4 Competitor analysis
2.7.5 Positioning analysis
2.7.10 SWOT analysis
2.9.8 Mental availability measurements

3. Strategy
3.1.3 Top 5
3.2 Overall strategy
3.3 Goals and subgoals
3.4.6 Distinctive asset-building strategy
3.7.5 Brand identity

4. Design
4.1 Design brief
4.4 Concept development
4.5 Design development
4.9 Identity development

5. Production
5.1 Implementation
5.9 Quality assurance

6. Management
6.2 Legal protection
6.3 Design management
6.5 Design manual

Table 0.2 Example of use of phases

Table 0.2 The table shows examples of planning from two different projects based on the book's phase structure. See *Planning tool* at the back of the book.
© Grimsgaard, W. (2018)

Tips for the designer
Check out the planning tool at the back of the book

Eight interviews from the research phase of the Norwegian version of this book (2017) are available online. Professionals from different design disciplines talk about their processes and methods. They also share their thoughts and reflections on design, and describe the opportunities and changes they see in the future. The interviewees are Mathias Haddal Hovet (Heydays), Torbjørn Sitre (Sopra Steria), Henning Rekdal Nielsen (EGGS design), Kjell Reenskaug (Cognizant), Nina Lysbakken (University of South-Eastern Norway), Carl Gürgens (Bold Scandinavia), graphic designer Lars Høie and interior architect Birgitte Appelong. The interviews are available at designandstrategy.co.uk.

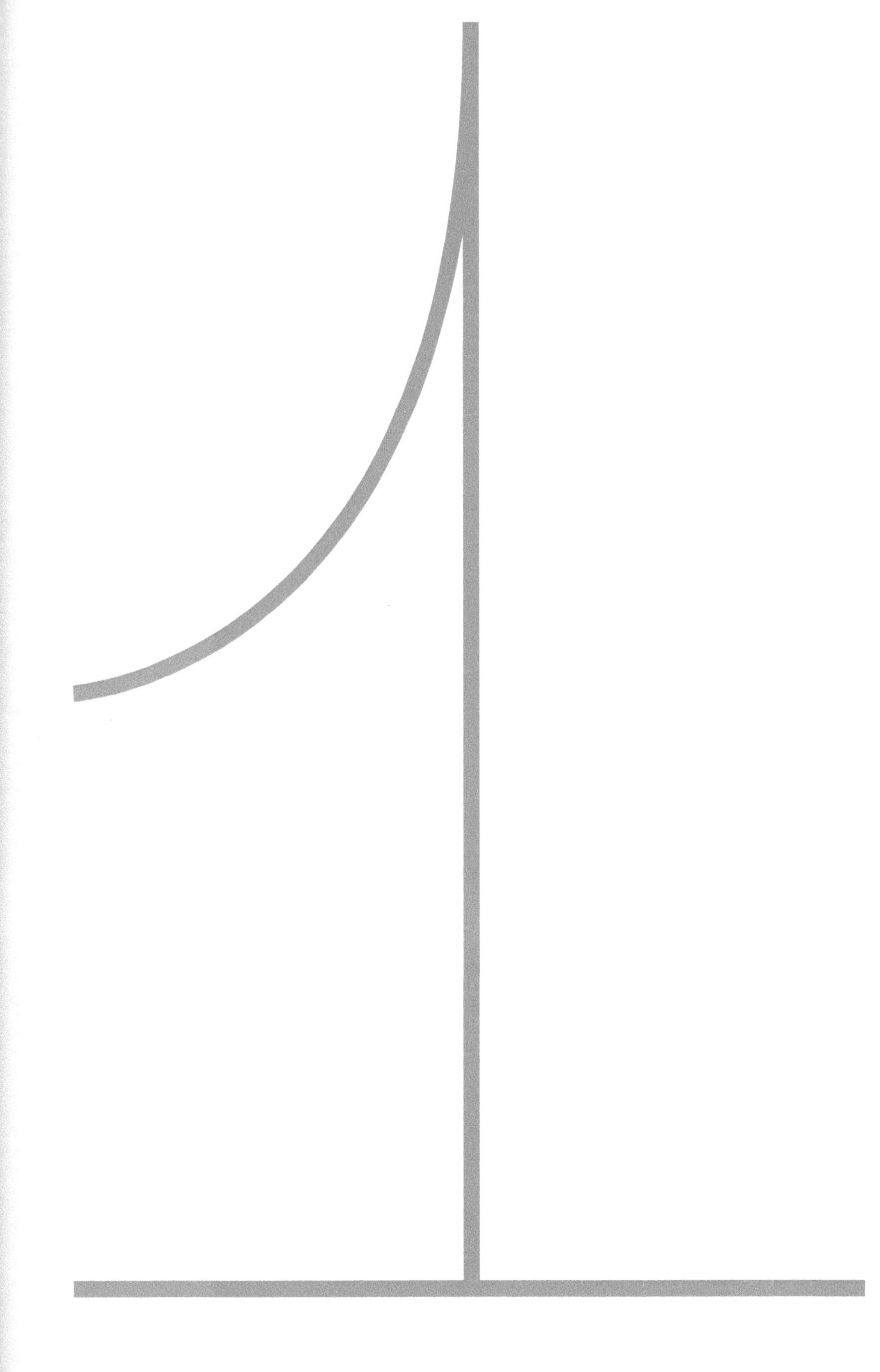

1.1 Initial preparations 5

1.2 Project brief 9

1.3 Initial meeting 10
1.3.1 Before the meeting 11
1.3.2 During the meeting 12
1.3.3 After the meeting 13
1.3.4 Meeting administration 13

1.4 Initial workshop 16
1.4.1 Purpose of initial workshop 16
1.4.2 Workshop preparation 17
1.4.3 Workshop invitation 17
1.4.4 Workshop facilities 18
1.4.5 Workshop management 18
1.4.6 Workshop execution 18
1.4.7 Workshop report 19
1.4.8 Workshop process 20

1.5 Project description 22

1.6 Progress schedule 24

1.7 Price quotation 26
1.7.1 Price request 28
1.7.2 Price setup 28
1.7.3 Terms and conditions 28
1.7.4 Negotiation 29
1.7.5 Hourly rate 29

1.8 Contract 31

1.9 Team collaboration 32
1.9.1 Control loop 35
1.9.2 Gameplan 37
1.9.3 Agile process management 39

Initiation is the first of six phases. It is about ensuring a good project start and facilitating a positive and predictable collaboration between the client and the designer. It involves clarifying which task is to be solved and defining clear frameworks and conditions. Meetings and workshops help start the dialogue, discuss the project, and develop a basis for quotation and contract. For the designer, this means making a good sales pitch and asserting oneself as a professional and competent partner. For the client, it involves choosing a designer who has all the necessary qualifications and the right mindset. Initiating a project is always about setting up a competent team to complete the given task, and ensure a good working climate.

Everything that happens from the first contact between the client and the designer until a contract is signed and work can begin, we call the initiation phase. When initiating the project, the foundation for the project's content, scope and progress is laid. The qualifications necessary to solve the task and all applicable conditions are also clarified. In this phase, it can often be challenging to predict the scope of the assignment and the competence needed. A strategic designer will clarify which problem or need the assignment is to solve while ensuring strategic alignment. If no goals or strategies are defined, it is natural to start with them. If the assignment is to create a website, it might be necessary to develop a communication strategy and a visual identity before starting to design the website. A seemingly small assignment may thus turn into a larger and more complex project than what the client initially imagined. Multidisciplinary expertise might often be necessary, especially in larger projects. Design agencies tend to have a broad range of expertise in their staff, while individual designers can connect with competent partners.

A project usually starts with the designer receiving a project brief from the client before or during their first meeting, referred to as the initial meeting. The project and collaboration are discussed at this meeting while also establishing a mutual understanding of what task to solve. If the task is not sufficiently clarified at this meeting, it may be helpful to conduct an initial workshop to clarify the company's situation and needs. Based on the information that emerges, the designer prepares a project description, a debriefing with suggestions for the work process, progress, and budget. The parties sign a contract before the project starts. If the project is clearly defined and aligned with the company's goal and strategy, project initiation can begin in Phase 4 with a design brief. If more insight is deemed necessary, in addition to setting goals and developing strategies, the project starts in Phase 1 with a project brief, see Table 0.1. (1.2 Project brief, 4.1 Design brief, 1.3 Initial meeting, 1.4 Initial workshop, 2.2 Situational study, 2.3 Problem statement, 1.9 Team collaboration).

Tips for the client

**How to choose the right designer?**
**– Look for the right qualifications.**
**– Look at value as well as price.**
**– Look for a good match.**

Tips for the designer

**Examine how the company presents itself and its products or services. Visible weaknesses can be good sales arguments, such as the logo or website seems outdated, the company's communication is not in line with how their product or service is experienced, their service or product is perceived as cumbersome and not user-friendly, the product packaging does not seem environmental friendly, that the company's behaviour does not seem to be in line with its identity, etc.**

**Initiation process**

**Project brief:** The client's description of the project.
**Initial meeting:** First meeting between the client and the designer.
**Sales pitch:** The designer's presentation of qualifications and portfolio.
**Workshop:** Initial workshop to clarify the assignment and establish a targeted and strategic anchoring.
**Project description:** The designer's description of the task and recommendation for work process.
**Progress schedule:** A plan for the project and deliverables within the given time frame.
**Price quotation:** The designer's quote or estimate for the project.
**Contract:** A signed agreement between the designer and the client.
**Collaboration:** Establishing a project team and facilitating a good collaboration within the team and with the client.

**Terminology**

**Designer:** Provider of design services, e.g. design agency or freelance designer.

**Client:** Purchaser of design services, e.g. a company or an organisation.

**Company:** A business, undertaking, enterprise, organisation, etc. producing and offering goods or services. Here we use company as a term also for private or public, commercial or non-commercial, as well as non-profit or NGOs.

**Assignment:** Allocation of a project.

**Project:** A project or task to be carried out for a client.


1 Initiation
2 Insight
3 Strategy
4 Design
5 Production
6 Management

1.1 Initial preparations
1.2 Project brief
1.3 Initial meeting
1.4 Initial workshop
1.5 Project description
1.6 Progress schedule
1.7 Price quotation
1.8 Contract
1.9 Team collaboration

– Preparations
– Presentation


## 1.1 Initial preparations

A business might be looking for a designer for a defined project, or the designer might seek contact to offer their services. When the designer receives a request for a new project, the initial preparations are crucial. First and foremost, it is about presenting their services and expertise to the company to prove that they have the competence needed for the assignment. It's an initial sales situation.

When a designer gets a new project, from a regular or a new client, the designer should regard this as an initial sales situation. The designer can never take for granted that they 'own' the client. Competition is fierce given the numerous enterprising players involved. Before you know it, other designers have made their advances and shown something new and different that may be more tempting. As a designer, you find yourself in a continuous competitive situation, where it is about being perceptive, alert, and up to date at all times. It is often a design buyer's market, but the situation can also be reversed, where a company has to pitch its way to a designer with whom they wish to collaborate. Among other things, it can be a matter of presenting the project so that the designer believes in it and wants to be part of it under the defined terms.

### Preparations

For the designer, an initial sale is about offering design services to the company to help them achieve their short-term or long-term goals. For commercial businesses, it can be a matter of standing out from the crowd in the market to strengthen their position and increase their competitiveness. For non-commercial organisations, it can be a matter of getting across their message and service regardless of profit. No matter who the designer is selling their services to, it is essential to prepare well for the sales pitch. A good approach is to consider the

Further reading

It can be a good start to read the chapters 2.1 Understanding the company and 6.9 Sustainable management.

company's situation and visible problem areas. The designer's goal should be to offer something appealing and relevant to the company, meeting their needs and qualification requirements. In order to do this well, it is not enough for the designer to know all there is to know about design. The designer must also know a bit about the business area and how it works, and typical challenges. This will simplify the conversation between the two and make it easier for the designer to identify the needs of the business, which can lead to a project. It is an excellent start to understand the company's situation by examining its website and social media presence. Gain knowledge of what they do and how they present themselves and their products or services. Try to track their values, attitudes, and measures to meet environmental or societal challenges. Look for potential for improvement. Furthermore, by examining the company's financial performance, one can determine whether they have a positive or negative development in sales, indicating whether they are doing something right or vice versa. It can also reveal whether they are creditworthy and able to pay for the design services they order.[1] Just as important as getting to know the company in question, is taking a look at its competitors and any news in the relevant business area. This will provide a more comprehensive picture of the field in which the company operates. This way, it becomes easier to understand what the client addresses at the meeting and ask the right questions. It will also make it easier to prepare a presentation for the meeting and know what examples from the portfolio may be relevant to showcase (2.1 Understanding the company, 2.2 Situational study).

Tips for the designer
**It is a good idea to keep an eye on the client during a sales pitch and assess when enough is enough. It is important not to oversell. Facial expressions and attitudes quickly reveal whether something is interesting or not. If someone starts to fidget and check their phone, it may be time to round off the presentation, and instead spend some time on setting up a new appointment and then end the meeting.**

> Ask questions, then poke, prod, and probe until you get people talking. Ask follow-up questions like: 'I really like what you said about ______, can you go a little further?', 'What do you mean by that?', 'Why do you feel that way?' (Norman, 2019)

### Presentation

For the designer, a good approach at an initial meeting may be to present some projects the company can identify with, for example, from the same business area, or something that can inspire them and urge them to think in new and different ways. This can also lead to additional sales. Being able to show measurable results such as increased sales, increased attention, increased awareness, or the like, is the best proof that a design can have a positive effect and be a sound investment. While it may be tempting to show the best projects, this should not be done uncritically. For example, it can be risky to show projects perceived as competitive or about something completely different and irrelevant, like presenting a book design to a company that wants help with packaging design. There are always exceptions, and it is nice to highlight great success stories that bring praise and honour. Demonstrating processes and methods can also be helpful, both to establish an understanding of what a design project entails and what is required in terms of time and resources for both parties. In this context, it is crucial to know the company's experience as a design buyer to avoid being too instructive. The main focus should be on pitching expertise related to the company's needs and advantageously referring to dedicated collaborators relevant to the project (1.3 Initial meeting).

Time is always an essential aspect. Dealing with the management, as is the case when pitching design services, they often have very little time. How much time they have set aside should preferably be clarified

1 There are several companies that offer such services online, such as experian.com and Dun&Bradstreet.com.

**Pitch Perfect**

A pitch is a short and sharp sales presentation. Here are five tips for a successful pitch, based on Amundsen (2015):

1) **Prepare well**
   - What is unique about you, your idea, product or service?
   - What needs do you meet? What is the market potential?
   - Any challenges? Why bet on you?
2) **Create a script**
   - Write down what you intend to say.
   - Review the text, edit, and see where you can put a full stop more often. This can help you get your message across more accurately and clearly.
   - Be concise, objective and precise. Put forward one thing at a time.
   - Make your message highly informative and vibrant.
3) **Practise your presentation – practice makes perfect**
   - It is not enough to talk through the presentation in your own head. Say it out loud. Then you will hear whether it works or not.
   - Test your presentation before a friend or colleague to get constructive feedback.
   - Practise until you know it by heart.
4) **Be yourself – do it your own way!**
   - Do not compare yourself to others.
   - Tell yourself that you are going to present something unique (to you).
   - It does not matter if you are nervous, as long as you are sure of what to say and how to say it. No one but you can do that better than yourself.
5) **Watch the time**
   Stick to the schedule and practise this beforehand as well. Make sure you can actually keep within the timefreame. It can be quite annoying when this is not taken into account.



in advance or at the beginning of the meeting. The designer may also request in advance that a decision-maker attend the meeting so that those present at the meeting would not have to 'resell' the designer's message. Those who are not designers themselves may have challenges expressing or conveying the designer's message, unique advantages, and expertise.

Business executives are not a homogeneous group: they come from many different industries and cultures. This applies to designers too, who span business and art. There may be diverse interests, specialist languages, terms, jargon, focus areas and last but not least, reality perceptions between the design buyer and the designer. One success factor is reaching out to each other and engaging in a good discussion, focusing on the opportunities in collaboration. The designer's ability to identify problems, think analytically and creatively, to see both the big picture and the details, and be able to work with both structural

Further reading
**Show Your Work!: 10 Ways to Share Your Creativity and Get Discovered by Austin Kleon (2014).**

### Five tips for a good argument

You may be a designer, but when it comes to introducing yourself or pitching an idea, you have to act like a salesman. To really convince a client, nothing beats a good fact-based argument. Based on (Hoekman, 2016):

1) **Listen and repeat their words:** The client often tries to tell you things they do not know how to express. Your job as a designer is to read between the lines and extract the truths, they are not clear about. Before you can develop any kind of solution, you need to know what the problem is. And that means listening. It helps you identify what the client's concerns and goals really are. Repeating what you hear makes the person feel more receptive to your recommendations and ideas. By listening, you show respect.
2) **Ask questions:** A designer asks questions – about the users, the business, the concerns, the needs, the previous decisions, the goals, and so on. Good designers want to see the big picture. They ask questions because they are curious and because the answers can help them make good design decisions. Asking is as important as listening. It helps form arguments for and against.
3) **Give reasons for your views:** Spend some time explaining and justifying your views, arguments, and recommendations. This is how you gain more attention and respect, and your ideas and views create more impact.
4) **Present your presentation as a story:** If you can explain your arguments through a presentation, by applying an essay-like structure to your communication, you do not have to spend so much time arguing. Ask those present to wait until you have finished your presentation before asking questions. In a worst-case scenario, questions along the way might steal your most important points. Instead, allow some time for questions after the presentation. You can almost guarantee that someone will ask you something you have not thought of.
5) **Point to the evidence:** One way to argue is to come up with facts and evidence. Proof can be found anywhere. It could be something you have read, a user survey you have conducted, it could be results from a similar project with similar issues where you can refer to measurable results. Be sure to have good sources, data and facts at hand to substantiate your claims. The last thing you want is to get caught making false claims if you are pinned up against the wall. If you have all the facts at hand and you can prove their validity, people will believe you. This is not only an advantage at the meeting in question, but with such an approach you may find over time that your customers see you as a reliable source and they will trust your arguments more than their own assumptions.

Tips for the client

**The designer standing in front of you, can be the key to your success. You are thinking that designers only create logo designs and décor? Well, some do only that, but many designers solve large complex tasks, which intervene in how the company thinks, performs its tasks, develops and sells its products or services, and how they approach a more sustainable and environmentally friendly way of doing business. The designer is first and foremost a problem solver with a creative way of thinking that can lead to increased value for the company and their customers.**

Tips for the designer

**Acquaint yourself in advance with the company you are meeting with. Think your argument through. Decide what impression you want to leave the company with, such as excited, impressed, convinced. Plan your efforts based on that. Be sure not to oversell yourself or offer easy solutions. Study negotiation techniques and avoid overpricing. Think smart. Be forward-looking and take interest, show commitment, be curious, ask questions, and take notes. All notes will come in handy in your further work if you get the job. Good luck!**

and visual solutions, makes the designer an important partner for businesses pursuing growth and value creation (2.1.1 Value creation, 2.3 Problem statement, 3 Strategy, 4.3 Design methodology, 4.4 Concept development, 4.5 Design development).


1 Initiation
2 Insight
3 Strategy
4 Design
5 Production
6 Management

1.1 Initial preparations
1.2 Project brief
1.3 Initial meeting
1.4 Initial workshop
1.5 Project description
1.6 Progress schedule
1.7 Price quotation
1.8 Contract
1.9 Team collaboration

– Project brief template


## 1.2 Project brief

The project brief is the client's first presentation of an assignment to the designer. It should provide a short and clear description of the project to serve as a starting point for their first meeting. The designer uses the project brief as a basis to draw up a more detailed project description or project plan.

When a designer receives a project brief from a client, it might be incomplete. The designer will seek to clarify matters that are unclear through initial meetings and workshops. Based on this, the designer writes a more comprehensive project description or project plan (1.5 Project description). The project brief should provide a clear presentation of the company, the project to be carried out, the reason for initiating the project, the problem to be solved, and the project goals. Furthermore, it is a plus if the client also describes what deadlines, frameworks and requirements that apply, as well as necessary qualifications needed to solve the task. This is also something that can be cleared through the introductory discussions. It is important for the client to be aware that the project may take a completely different turn after the initial meeting and workshop, where the designer asks in-depth questions to shed light on the real problems and needs of the company.

The layout, content and designation of a project brief may vary, but the structure can be quite similar. Here is a template that the designer can send to the client as a basis for preparing a project brief at the beginning of a project. The client fills in the items about which it is possible to say something initially. It may be difficult to have a clear idea about some of these items at an early stage of the project, such as for example, problem statement and project goals. Much can be sorted out during the initial meeting and in the workshop, as well as in further studies, research, and surveys. If the goals and tasks for the project are already clearly defined, and necessary studies and strategy development has been carried out, a design brief may be prepared, which is a more complementary briefing (4.1 Design brief).

Presentasjon online

Test the presentation in advance at the same type of digital meeting platform that will be used during the meeting with the client. Keep your slides simple. Limit the amount of text. Highlight important information and use quotes. Capture attention by showing beautiful images and video slides to break up the speaking. Avoid talking for too long in one stretch. Give your audience a chance to share their opinions. Interact with your audience. Enable participants to pose questions, clarify ideas, and solve any misunderstandings. Limit the time you spend sharing a screen; instead show your own face when talking. Reflect live after the presentation or use for example Mentimeter to ask how the attendees felt during the session and how useful it was. Based on Hanifan (2021), mentimeter.com

### Project brief template

**Client:** Company name and contact person.*
**Date:** Date on which the brief is prepared.*
**Project name:** Work title of the project.*
**The company:** Brief description of the company, product and/or service.*
**Problems and needs:** Brief description of the company's position, challenges, problems and opportunities, and what problems or needs the project will help solve.*

**The project:** Short introduction to the project, including background, what tasks should be carried out and why.*
**Project goal and ambition level:** Short description of the preliminary plan, goal and ambition level of the project, as well as how the project is intended to contribute to achieving these goals.
**Target groups:** Description of target groups relevant for the project and their order of priority; primary, secondary and other stakeholders.
**Strategic anchoring:** Short explanation of how, the project is or will be anchored towards the main goals and strategy of the company. Relevant strategy documents attached, if available. For example, short version of the main strategy, business strategy, any sub-strategies, such as brand strategy and communication strategy, etc.
**Deliverables:** Explanation of what activities, tasks and final deliverables are envisaged, such as visual identity, packaging design, service design, website, advertisement or the like. See also 4.1 Design brief, for a more complete briefing on the delivery.
**Time frame:** Delivery date*, and dates of sub-deliveries.
**Evaluation:** Any plan for measuring and evaluating results, and the measurement tools to be used.
**Budget framework:** Total budget, partial budget or budget estimate for the project.
**Qualification requirements:** Any other requirements or demands for inter- or multidisciplinary competence.
*The items that the client should answer as a minimum are marked with an asterisk.*

Tips for the designer
**Listen, ask questions, and show measurable results.**

Tips for the client
**The project brief should ideally be written and sent to the designer before the initial meeting. Alternately, you can give an oral briefing at the initial meeting. Designer provides a more specific project description after the meeting, which must be approved by you before the work can begin.**

A project brief is a short description of key elements of your project. Think of it as a quick summary for project stakeholders and cross-functional collaborators (Martins, 2020). The project brief is a key document at the initiation of a project, in that it brings everyone together to serve a common end (Landau, 2021).

## 1.3 Initial meeting

A successful initial meeting is essential in getting the project off to a good start. The purpose is for the client and the designer to establish a common understanding of the project, the client's objectives and level of ambition, the designer's qualifications and suitability, budget framework and delivery time.

The first meeting between the designer and the client in connection with the start-up of a new design project is described here as an initial meeting. This meeting is an opportunity for both parties to discuss what the client wants from the designer and what the designer can contribute with. The client usually selects a designer based on their qualifications and suitability, and quite often consider several designers for the project. Therefore, the initial meeting is also a sales pitch meeting for the designer.

If there is a question of whether the meeting should be held physically or digitally, there are advantages to both solutions. If the first meeting can be held physically, the communication might go more successfully. One might understand more easily each other's personality and determine whether the chemistry is right if it is a good match. When it is difficult to meet physically, meeting digitally can have its benefits. It

**Terminology**

**Project brief:** Written by the client when initiating a new design project, before research and strategy work is carried out. The project brief should give a short introduction to the project and should be followed up by the designer with a project description and price estimate.

**Project description:** Written by the designer based on the project brief and the information obtained during the initial meeting and the initial workshop. The project description should provide a clear description of the project, as well as tentative or final goals, framework and conditions.

**Design brief:** Written by the client when initiating a new design project, after research and strategy work has been carried out. It can also be written by the designer who has participated in the strategy development and must later be approved by the client. The design brief should describe the task to be solved, the purpose of the task and which deliverables will be included (4.1 Design brief).

**Creative brief:** Written by the designer to provide the basis and direction for the creative work. A creative brief is most often used internally by the designer or design agency. Some use the term 'creative brief' for the 'design brief'.

**What is a brief?:** A brief is a set of instructions given to a person about a job or task (Brief, n.d.). It should include a summary of facts, findings, and objectives, and provide the reader with a short and concise overview of a study, plan, situation, etc.

**Why do we need a brief?:** The designer/team and the client must have the same understanding of the project and its framework. This applies to time spent, finances and level of ambition for the job (Myhre, 2017).

blurs geographical boundaries and makes the designer and the client less dependent on being located close to each other. It can also be time-saving, as one does not have to spend time travelling. That again can be valuable in terms of lowering costs and saving the environment. Regardless of whether the meeting is digital or physical, many of the same principles apply to preparation, implementation, and follow-up after the meeting.

### 1.3.1 Before the meeting

The designer prepares for the initial meeting by reading the project brief and studying the client's company. This includes checking what products or services the company sells, what the market and the competitive situation looks like, how the company appears in different arenas, such as retail outlets, in the public space, office facades, web and social media, car decor, uniforms, advertisements, etc. Is the profile consistent and clear? What associations do the name and logo express? How is communication perceived? How do customers and users experience their products and services? Such information is often available online. It may also be a good idea to take a look at competitors, to find out how they appear compared to the company's product or service. What are the current trends? What is innovative in their category? It might be useful to make a simple visual analysis of the competitive picture from an early stage, in order to obtain an overview of the different market players' assumed position and be able to discover their possible differentiation potential. Is there a gap or niche that the company can fill? In general, it is important to look for obvious deficiencies, problems or needs (1.1 Initial preparations).

Both the designer and the client must decide who should attend the meeting, and what roles and areas of responsibility are required to be represented. The designer might have an opinion on which of the client's representatives should attend the meeting and communicate it to the client. If the design assignment will affect the strategy and business development of the company, it is a prerequisite that representatives of the owner and the management attend the initial meeting. Project leaders and decision-makers should always be present, but in general it is natural to consider the number of participants in relation to the scope of the project. In large projects the designer might consider to have two or more people present in order to be able to allocate roles and tasks during the meeting. In some projects it may be relevant for the designer to also involve external collaborators in order to satisfy requirements for the desired expertise.

Tips for the designer

**The client may consciously or unconsciously emphasise qualities other than professional skills, such as how the designer stands and communicates; whether the designer is perceived as open, inclusive, safe, engaged, confident, empathetic, with good communication skills and good at conveying thoughts and ideas.**

'Consistent' means that something is marked by harmony, regularity, or steady continuity: free from variation or contradiction (Consistent, n.d.).

### 1.3.2 During the meeting

If it is the client who has organised the first meeting, it may be natural for them to chair the meeting. In later stages, when ideas and drafts are to be presented, it is common for the designer to take up this role. During the initial meeting, it can be an advantage if the client is the one to open the meeting by presenting the company and the task to be carried out, before the designer gives their presentation. Thus, the designer can better adapt their presentation to the needs and problems emerging, as well as to fulfil the role as consultant and adviser. In order to do this properly, it might be a good idea to take notes and ask relevant questions along the way. A relevant question will often be: Will the task you want us to solve actually meet a need or solve any problems? For example, if the project is to create a new website, it would be natural for the designer to ask why the company needs a new website and what has triggered this need. What is the problem? If the problem turns out to be a decline in sales, the designer may suggest investigating the situation further to find out what the reason for the decline in sales is, and in the next round consider what steps should actually be taken to resolve the problem. Through questions and consultation, the designer demonstrates their own competence and qualifications. Clearing things up at the beginning of the project can help ensure that the time and the resources of both the company and the designer are used more expediently in the project. As a result, the project might become more comprehensive, strategic and exciting than originally envisaged.

Price is something that is often brought up at the first meeting. Naturally, the client is often concerned with getting a quote on the table as quickly as possible, but here the designer should show restraint and not suggest any prices during the meeting. Only when the content, scope and level of ambition of the project have been sufficiently clarified, the work on drawing up a project description and preparing a budget may begin. If the client is open with their budget framework, it could save time for both parties, because the designer can calculate time and resources within the set limits. The designer should consider whether the level of ambition of the project to be carried out is realistic in relation to the budget framework. High levels of ambition can mean more thorough processes and more time spent, resulting in a higher total price (1.7 Price quotation). Experience shows that many businesses purchasing design services, have little experience of what a designer can offer, what a design process involves in terms of time and resources, what it costs, and what results they can expect. To a certain extent, the designer can make this more predictable by presenting similar design projects and demonstrating successful outcomes, such as increased attention, greater awareness or increased sales, alongside explaining how a design process is normally carried out (Phase 4 Design; Design process, 4.3 Design methodology).

At the end of the meeting, a summary should be made of the questions and conclusions reached, and hopefully a plan for a new meeting and further progress. The designer may ask if the company has received sufficient information and when they will choose a designer. If the decision is not already taken at the meeting, a deadline should be agreed.



### 1.3.3 After the meeting

The designer should record their own meeting minutes, even if the client does too, and should ask the client to approve the minutes in writing. This way, the designer will have confirmation that both parties are unanimous on the matters and decisions taken during the meeting. The designer follows up after the meeting by sending the meeting summary, drawing up a progress schedule and drafting an agreement. It is the designer who will provide the service and make arrangements, thus facilitating the client. The designer should never take it for granted to be chosen for an assignment, even if it may seem that way during the initial meeting. The designer is constantly in a sales situation, and even after the project has been assigned, the designer will be continuously assessed on what is being delivered (1.6 Progress schedule).

### 1.3.4 Meeting administration

A successful meeting requires a good structure for planning and administration. Detailed level of preparation, implementation and follow-up must be considered in relation to the scope and complexity of the project. Whether it is the designer or the client that will act as the meeting chairperson may vary in the course of the design project. Here is an example of an outline for a good meeting plan.

**Purpose:** What is the purpose of the meeting? Clarify the purpose of the meeting and what you expect to achieve with it.

**Participants:** Who will attend the meeting? Clarify who the decision-makers are and other project participants/contributors.

**Invitation:** Who convenes the meeting and what matters should the meeting include? Usually, the person who initiates the meeting sends out

5 expert tips to boost your online presentation skills (Hanifan 2021, mentimeter.com)

1. Engage the audience and build a connection.
Get the audience involved. Give the audience a chance to share their opinions!
2. Add stunning visuals to capture attention.
Capture attention by showing beautiful images and video slides to break up the talking.
3. Interact with your audience.
Use Q&A session to enable participants to pose questions, clarify ideas, and solve any misunderstandings.
4. Keep it simple.
Keep your slides simple. Limit the amount of text and avoid talking for too long in one stretch. Highlight important information and use quotes.
5. Reflect afterwards.
Reflect live or use e.g. Mentimeter to ask how the attendees felt during the session, and how useful it was.

a meeting invitation, arranges the meeting venue, does the preparation, and acts as the chairperson. The invitation should be sent out in a timely manner and should include the time, duration and venue of the meeting, title and purpose of the meeting, names of participants, agenda and contact details, as well as the meeting location as well as an address or a link to a digital meeting platform. Ask for confirmation on who will be attending the meeting and, if necessary, send out a reminder.

**Agenda:** What should the agenda include? The agenda should describe each item, who is responsible for it and how much time has been allocated for each item. The agenda may follow as an appendix to the invitation. At the initial meeting, an agenda could look like this:

1) Opening remarks and introduction by the chairperson
2) Presentation of the client's company by the general manager
3) Presentation of the project brief by the market manager
4) Presentation of the design agency and its qualifications by the designer
5) Discussion about the project, level of ambition, time and budget framework
6) Questions about qualification and choice of agency
7) Summary and further progress
8) Miscellaneous

If there has been a previous meeting, the agenda may start with follow-up matters from the previous meeting. If someone is to prepare something, this should be stated in the invitation. Draft decisions may, where appropriate, follow the agenda.

> **Full digital meetings:** Ensure that all participants see and hear, and are included in what goes on in the meeting.
> **Combined meetings:** Combining digital and physical meetings might be successful if it is properly prepared (Norman, 2019).

**Before the meeting, the chairperson must:**
Make sure that the necessary equipment is available. For a physical meeting this might be a projector, video transfer, extension cord, whiteboard, flip charts, pens, etc. Check in advance what kind of serving and meeting facilities project participants would need or want. For a digital meeting there might be a need for digital boards, charts and teamwork facilities.

**Before the meeting, each meeting participant must:**
Prepare by reading the invitation and the agenda, checking out the roles and profiles of the participants, practise their own presentation, write down questions and comments, and so on. For physical meetings one should bring suitable equipment for presentation and notes, remember the correct dress code and allow plenty of time for travel and parking. For digital meetings one should pre-test the digital platform, trial run one's own presentation and remember to log in some minutes before the meeting.

Tips for the designer

**Think carefully about the purpose of the meeting, what you would like to get out of it, what impression you want the client to be left with after the meeting, and what feeling you want to leave the meeting with yourself. Do you want the client to be enthusiastic and perceive you as a skilled qualified person? If so, you must do both the mental and the practical preparations, which are necessary in order for the client to actually perceive you as such. It is about being conscious of your behaviour and clothing style, how you talk, listen, and argue, how you appear as professionally competent, engaged and trustworthy. All in all, being yourself is an advantage. A lot of things are about chemistry – good chemistry.**

**During the meeting, the chairperson must:**

- Consider the tone and style of the meeting (formal or informal?).
- Turn the attention away from oneself and focus on the role as chairperson.
- Start with some small talk before the meeting begins if there is time.
- Start the meeting on time. Delay is misuse of everyone's time. Manage time generously throughout the meeting.
- Clarify the purpose of the meeting, agenda, time frame, time for breaks and selection of the minute taker.
- Write clear notes, preferably based on the agenda layout.
- Create dialogue and debate by asking questions and challenging claims.
- Manage discussions, make sure everyone's opinions are expressed.
- Repeat important comments to emphasise.
- Ensure that discussions end in a conclusion by repeating decisions along the way and asking if everything is properly understood.

**During the meeting, the meeting participant must:**

- Present their input according to the agenda.
- Comment, ask questions, participate in discussions.
- In formal meetings raise a hand to speak.
- Take their own notes.

**After the meeting, the chairperson must:**

- Briefly summarise the items and conclusions.
- Clarify whether meeting participants have a common understanding of items and conclusions.
- Review which items are to be followed up, as well as their deadlines and who is responsible.
- Check if the purpose of the meeting has been achieved or if there is anything unclear.
- Did the client receive sufficient information to be able to choose a designer?
- Should the choice of designer be made during the meeting or after, and, if relevant, when?
- Has the designer received sufficient information about the project to be able to write a project description and submit a quotation?
- Are more meetings or a workshop necessary? If relevant, when?
- Suggest further progress and date for a possible new meeting.

**Minutes:**

The chairperson is responsible for the minutes being written and distributed. The minutes of the meeting must include the date and name of the meeting, the purpose of the meeting, the names of the participants, items and conclusions, the persons responsible and deadlines for the follow-up of items and, where appropriate, the date of a new meeting. Minutes of meetings should be sent out shortly after the meeting. Meeting participants are given a short deadline to make adjustments to the content. If the designer is the minute taker, they should request written approval of minutes from the client, preferably by email.



Tips for the meeting leader

Give people a warm welcome

*Physical meeting*: Shake hands with meeting participants when they arrive, look them in the eye, break the ice with small talk, for example. 'I see you've had a lot of press coverage in the past few days,' or: 'Did you find a parking space?'. Make sure everyone hang up their jackets, is given a drink, and finds a seat at the meeting table.

*Digital meeting*: If the meeting is not too formal and you have time before the meeting starts, you can say hello to each of the participants as they appear on the screen. Say their name, ask how they are, where they are, what the weather is like in their city or country, or give a positive comment about something they have achieved or shared recently.

## 1.4 Initial workshop

A workshop is a work meeting where a group of people gather to solve tasks together through brainstorming and creative processes.

An initial workshop is very useful during the initial phase of a design project. The purpose of such a workshop is to clarify the project to be carried out and establish targeted and strategic anchoring. An initial workshop may be held instead of, in addition to, or as part of the initial meeting.

If a new project has not been sufficiently clarified in the project brief and during the initial meeting, the designer may propose conducting an initial workshop with relevant participants representing the company and the designer. It is also possible to start a design project with a workshop. A workshop is a work meeting where a group of people gather to solve tasks together through brainstorming and creative processes. Using workshops is a great way to activate the client and make the company participate in the work process, which is a key factor to ensure a successful collaboration further on in the process. A workshop is also a strong tool for anchoring change processes internally in the company, by involving people from different areas of the organisation in the various phases of the process. There are no limitations as to what can be resolved at a workshop, or how a workshop can be conducted, nor by whom or where. It might be facilitated by the designer for the company or carried out by the company internally, in conjunction with a design project or any project. The need for a workshop is assessed based on the nature, scope and time of the project. We distinguish here among:

- *Initial workshop*: clarify project goal and task.
- *Strategic workshop*: gather insights and develop strategy.
- *Creative workshop*: develop ideas and solutions.

If there is time and budget to conduct only one workshop, an initial workshop could for example be combined with a strategic workshop. (3.1.4 Strategic workshop).

An initial workshop is a sound investment for the client since it makes the project clearer and more targeted. It should be carried out before the project description and quotations are drawn up, and the contract has been signed. The designer can give a separate price for an initial workshop, as a preliminary project independent of the price of the project in general. It is not necessary for the client to choose a design partner before the workshop is carried out. The workshop will in any case be useful to clarify the task to be solved in the project. The results of the workshop are compiled in a simple report with clear conclusions and recommendations, which will serve as a tool in further work.

### 1.4.1 Purpose of initial workshop

The main purpose of an initial workshop is for the client and the designer to have a common understanding of the project to be carried out and of what the mandate of the project is. Firstly, it involves identifying the company's needs or problems to be addressed as a starting point for defining a Problem statement (2.3 Problem statement). Secondly, it is about clarifying the project goal and connecting this to the company's main goal and strategy. It is also a plus to establish as early as possible a clear framework, scope and level of ambition for the project, as well what conditions and prerequisites will apply, although some of these may be clarified at a later stage. The design project, as presented in the original project brief by the client, can change in nature and scope after an initial workshop when the needs and situation of the company become clearer. Several workshops may also be necessary during the initiation phase, and here a smooth transition to a strategic workshop is possible, the purpose of which is to work out the necessary objectives and strategies (3.1.4 Strategic workshop, 2.2.2 PIPI workshop, 2.2.3 Where are we - where will we?, 2.7.10 SWOT analysis: SWOT-workshop).



### 1.4.2 Workshop preparation

When the designer proposes an initial workshop, the opportunity is there to take a central role in convening, planning and directing the workshop, as well as preparing a report. Good preparation is essential for a successful workshop. It involves thinking carefully through a number of questions. What is the purpose of the workshop? What is unclear? What should we know more about, which can be revealed through a workshop? Is the company's product/service and business strategy clearly defined? Are there clear overall objectives? How is the project rooted in the company's main goal and strategy? What challenges or problems does the company face, externally in the market and internally in the company? Which of these problems should the project help solve? Do they know their competitive situation? Do they have a clear position in the market? How does the communication of the company, product or service take place? Is it clear and easy to understand? How do they appear visually? Do they have a strong and distinct identity and image? How do their products or services work in terms of buyer expectations and user needs? Which of these or other questions can be answered during the initial workshop? Relevant questions are prioritised according to the importance of obtaining an answer and are part of an outline, which is used to steer workshop activities and serves as the basis for a simple report.

### 1.4.3 Workshop invitation

The invitation to an initial workshop does not require details of its content. A list of what results are desirable would suffice; for example, to clarify the project goal and framework. If the client does not prepare before the workshop, it is an advantage, because it is often the spontaneous and intuitive input that yields the best results. The client should have at least two representatives or as many as the client wishes to include, preferably not more than eight, who together represent a breadth of knowledge and experience in areas related to the company. The invitation should encourage the client to include people from different parts of the organisation, such as from marketing, production, technical or any other relevant areas.

Further reading
Check out the book: *Designing & Leading Life-Changing Workshops: Creating the Conditions for Transformation in Your Groups, Trainings, and Retreats* (2020) by Nelson et al.

An initial workshop brings clarity to the problem to be solved by the project.

### 1.4.4 Workshop facilities

It may be a good idea to hold the workshop at the designer's premises to get the client away from familiar surroundings. On the other hand, it can be an advantage for the designer to meet the client on their home turf, and it might be more convenient for people attending from the company. In any case, the designer must ensure that the necessary equipment is available, for example, a flip chart, heavy duty tape (for hanging up flip chart sheets), thick markers in different colours; Post-it notes are also a 'must', and 'brain food' in the form of chocolate, biscuits and fruit, or anything else that can give a good energy boost. The workshop might be conducted digitally using Miro Board,[2] Padlet or other digital platforms offering workshop facilities. Choose a digital platform that is easy to learn and use and has the necessary functions and tools for interaction. Anyway it might be necessary to calculate time for a short introduction of the digital tool to be used, for the participants that are unfamiliar with it.

Tips for the designer

**An initial workshop is suitable as input. It is a good way to uncover the client's situation and needs, and a favourable occasion to pitch one's own expertise. In other words, it is useful to both parties. Do not forget to get paid.**

### 1.4.5 Workshop management

Conducting a workshop involves many tasks. If more than one person from the design agency participates, tasks may be delegated. The designer may also handle all the tasks alone. The most important tasks are to engage and encourage people to participate, be open, join in on brainstorming and discussions. More practical tasks are also important, such as serving coffee/tea and something sweet, steering the workshop, taking notes of everything that is said, highlighting priorities and results that emerge, and finally making sure flip charts are brought and/or photographed. It may be helpful to include a photo of the entire team at work to include in the report or a subsequent presentation of the results.

### 1.4.6 Workshop execution

There are many ways to conduct a workshop, and it depends to a large extent on its purpose, the type of project and the nature of the company. An initial workshop may take place as follows: The workshop leader introduces the purpose of the workshop and explains that it will be carried out through drills, tasks, brainstorming and discussions, without going into detail about the content. The leader starts quickly with the first task. All participants receive pens, paper and Post-it notes, and are asked to respond to the task individually. The leader stands by the flip chart to record the results that emerge. Answers are sorted and processed together until there are some responses that everyone agrees on.

During an initial workshop, there are (almost) always three questions that can be used to clarify the current situation and project: a) What does the company do? b) What challenges do you face? c) What is the goal of the design project?

**a) What does the company do?** The first question may seem rather trivial: What is the company doing/offering? Most people would probably think that all businesses know what they do, and what they offer, and

2 Miroboard is an online collaborative whitoboard platform (miro.com), suitable for interactions in workshops and co-creation.

that everyone who works in the company has a common understanding of it. However, the designer should assume that the reality is different, that employees do not share an unambiguous perception of what the company does. Managers and owners in the same company might often explain the company and its product or service in widely different ways and have different opinions without really being aware of it, and without thinking that it leaves an unclear picture of the company. If you ask ten people from the same business to describe what the company does in one sentence, you will probably get ten different answers. When initiating a design project, it is important for the designer to have a correct understanding of what the company does, and it should be consistent with the client's perception.

1 Initiation
2 Insight
3 Strategy
4 Design
5 Production
6 Management

1.1 Initial preparations
1.2 Project brief
1.3 Initial meeting
1.4 Initial workshop
1.5 Project description
1.6 Progress schedule
1.7 Price quotation
1.8 Contract
1.9 Team collaboration

1.4.1 Purpose of initial workshop
1.4.2 Workshop preparation
1.4.3 Workshop invitation
1.4.4 Workshop facilities
1.4.5 Workshop management
1.4.6 Workshop execution
1.4.7 Workshop report
1.4.8 Workshop process

**b) What are their challenges and problems?** The second question is one of the most important ones to be answered. What challenges or problems does the company face? Such a question is often met with some resistance. Similarly, to people who perceive their problems as personal, the company perceives its problems as both personal and confidential and does not share them with just anyone. It can therefore be challenging to get the company to open up and share their problems (here it is important to assure them that all information they share will be confidential). In addition, experience shows that the vast majority do not use the word 'problems', or have no problems, but that they may face some challenges. Nevertheless, when the client initiates a design project, the cause is usually a problem, whether conscious or unconscious. A successful project is measured based on whether the solution has resolved the problem. No problem, no solution. In uncovering the problem, many other problems, both internal and external, may be raised. When problems are listed, they should be categorised, weighed and prioritised. This work is done during the workshop in collaboration with the company, and it constitutes the basis for the clarification and formulation of a problem statement (2.3 Problem statement).

**c) What is the project goal?** The third question comes as a natural continuation of the previous. Once the problems have been recorded and ranked, participants discuss which of them the design project should help solve, what results are envisaged, and what should be the project goal. Without a clear goal on which the parties agree, it will be difficult to plan how the project should be carried out and the results measured. In this context, it is also important to talk about how the design project should help the company in achieving its long-term overall objectives. Not infrequently, the need for development or adjustment of the goals and strategies of the company is revealed when initiating a design project. The designer may propose to work on this before the design task is defined and initiated (3.3 Goals and subgoals, 3.3.9 Goals for a design project).

'It is crucial that designers are good at handling complexity in order to take advantage of their unique abilities for visual thinking and problem solving. Design activities and processes are moving closer and closer into our customers' core structures. This creates an even greater need for information processing and stakeholder management. Keeping the right people, who are involved, at the right level and at the right time, creates basis for strong ownership of the process and the ideas it brings out' (Sevaldson, 2011).

### 1.4.7 Workshop report

The report should include the project name, date, purpose of the workshop and names of client and designer representatives. It should begin with a brief description of the project, what has been accomplished, and what has been concluded. Questions and results are then presented in a clear and structured manner. It is a good idea to record the results at the top of each item so that they are easy to find. Any unanswered matters are highlighted for further processing. If there are many words and phrases from the brainstorming, they may be included as an appendix to the report. The report should include suggestions for conclusions and further action. It is explained how the results affect the project to be carried out. The report may be included as part of the continued work on situational study and strategy development.

After the workshop activities have been completed, the report approved, and the assignment clarified, a project description, progress schedule, budget and contract can be prepared. If needed, a new workshop is proposed, along with suggestions for alternative dates and price. A second workshop can be expanded with questions from situational studies or situational analysis or combined with strategic workshop (2.2 Situational study, 2.2.2 PIPI workshop, 2.2.3 Where are we – where will we?, 2.7.1 Situational analysis, 3.1.4 Strategic workshop).

Tips for the designer
A small or medium sized enterprise is often led by an entrepreneur who has the whole business strategy in their head, and who believes that all the employees can read their mind. It is essential that everyone in the company has the same perception of what the company should be doing and that everyone communicates the same things to those around them. If you as a designer are to develop a visual identity or contribute with other services to a company, it is absolutely necessary that they know what the company offers, and that you and your client have the same perception of it. It should be clearly worded in a business concept, as part of an overall strategy (3.2.3 Business idea).

### 1.4.8 Workshop process

Below is an example of initial workshop process based on three main questions:

1) What does the company do/offer?
2) What problems/challenges does the company have?
3) What is the project goal, level of ambition and expected result/effect?

**Question 1:** What does the company do/offer?
Say in a sentence what your company is, does, or offers?
Select either a, b or c:

a) Business: Say in one sentence what you do/offer.
b) Product: Describe the product in one sentence.
c) Service: Describe the service in one sentence.

The purpose of the question is to arrive at a clear explanation of what the company does, so that the client, designer and everyone involved will have a common understanding of this.

**Proposed approach:**
1) The participants sit around a table. Everyone is given pen and paper. The chairperson stands up and gives guidance.
2) The chairperson asks each person to write a sentence describing what the company does without talking to the others.
3) Each person may write several sentences, but reads out only the one they are most satisfied with. (Feel free to have leaders/decision-makers read out their answers last, as their words and opinions often determine what colleagues dare to say.)

3 The question can advantageously be asked and elaborated in a strategic workshop. Workshop model suggestions: 3.1 Strategic workshop, 3.2.6 Value Proposition, Figure 2.15 AEIOU Empathy map.

4) The meeting leader records all the sentences on a flip chart and asks if anyone has anything to add. The flip charts are taped to the wall (numbered).
5) Each participant marks out, with a post-it note or marker, the word among all the sentences that they think best describes the company.
6) The selected words are rewritten on flip chart sheets, and everyone works together to find synonyms, or come up with new words that describe, explain, and express the company. The words should sound good, be easy to pronounce and easy to understand.
7) Participants are instructed to write down new sentences using the selected words to describe what the company does. This can be done individually or as a brainstorming session.
8) The best sentences are recorded on flip chart sheets. Steps 5, 6 and 7 can be repeated until there is a result that everyone is satisfied with.
9) In conclusion, the result can be used to clarify: 1) What the core business is? For example: A grocery store sells groceries. 2) In which industry does the company operate? The grocery business.
10) The chairperson praises everyone enthusiastically and emphasises that everyone now agrees on a description of the company.

Then it is time for the chairperson to explain why this is so important: a) it is essential for everyone to have a common understanding of what the company does before the design project is started, b) it is a success factor to be able to communicate the company verbally and visually to the outside world in a clear and consistent way, c) it is a good starting point for defining or adjusting the business idea (3.2.3 Bussiness idea). However, it is important to underline that the results of the workshop must be allowed time to mature, and that they can be edited in the further process. If there is time, a follow-up question can be asked: What problems does the product/service/business solve for the target group.[3]

**Question 2:** What problems does the company have?
Mention some clear problems/challenges the company faces associated with its business operation, product and/or service, internally within the company, and externally in the market. Start with a, then b:

a) Internal issues/challenges (resources, expertise, product, finances, culture, etc.)
b) External problems/challenges (external communication, market, competition, visibility, etc.)

Use the same process as described in question 1 above. Each participant answers individually on their own paper.

1) Each participant writes down as many internal problems as they can think of, and ticks the most important one.
2) Each participant reads out the most important internal problem.
3) The chairperson lists the most important problems on flip chart sheets.
4) Everyone goes up and puts a Post-it note on, or underlines, the problem they consider most important.



Further reading
*The Workshop Book* (2016) by Pamela Hamilton.

Project description = description of the project, problem and project goal.

5) Everyone contributes to the preparation and completion of the list. The three main problems are highlighted.
6) The chairperson lists the main internal problems in order of priority.
7) Once internal problems have been clarified, the process is repeated in order to clarify external problems.

NOTE: Another option is to bring up all the problems first, and eventually sort them into internal and external. The results of this exercise provide good basis for a simple SWOT analysis (2.7.10 SWOT analysis).

**Question 3:** What is the project goal, level of ambition, and expected results or impact?

1) Use the prioritised problems from question 2 to answer this question.
2) Discuss this across the table: Which of the problems the design project should help solve?
3) Clarify the project goal through new questions or brainstorming.
4) Clarify whether or not there are guidelines regarding name, logo, visual identity or anything else that the designer must take into account in the project. And discuss what opportunities for possible changes the project offers.

Tips for the designer
Remember to enter the title and number on the flip chart sheets. Take photos of them for the record. It may be a good idea to keep them. You can hang them on the wall or lay them on the floor, stand on them and walk on them, while you work on processing the contents and write the report.

Tips for the client
Sustainability considerations should be taken from the project launch. Read more in 6.9 Sustainable management.

A project description is an overview of what the project should include and why it should be conducted, without delving into how the project should be solved. (Eby, 2021)

## 1.5 Project description

A project description is an overview of what a project should include and why it should be conducted, without saying anything about how the problem should be solved. The project description serves as basis for setting up a progress schedule and a price quotation.

Preparation of a project description is absolutely crucial in the start-up of a project so that the client and the designer can agree on what the project should include and why it should be conducted. The project description is written by the designer based on an initial meeting, workshop and project brief from the client. Dividing the project into phases makes it easier to explain the content of the process and provides a good starting point for preparing a price quotation. The task, the designer is to help solve, must be clearly outlined in the project description. It should preferably be based on a specific problem clarified in the project brief or during the initial meeting or workshop. Studies, surveys and strategy work may be required before the problem statement can be formulated. The result may have implications for the design process and deliveries (2.3 Problem statement, 1.7 Price quotation).

The project goal and how it is anchored in the overall strategy of the company should be stated in the project description. It may also be advantageous to describe the methods that are going to be used for measuring results. For example, if one is to measure whether the project has led to increased knowledge, it will be necessary to measure knowledge both before and after project completion in order to compare results.

**Project description outline**

The content of the project description of a design project will vary for different projects. Here is an example of an outline that can be used as a disposition.

**Project title:** Work title of the project. Date.
**Introduction:** Company name and contact person. Design team and contact details. Brief explanation of why the designer was contacted, and what meetings and activities have been carried out.
**Overview:** Explanation of the project and tasks to be carried out. About the company: Brief description of the company, their product or service, and their current situation.
**Project justification:** Explanation of what the problem or opportunity is and why the project is necessary.
**Strategic basis:** Connection to the main goal and strategy of the company.
**Goals:** Define one or more project goals. A project goal should be S.M.A.R.T.: specific, measurable, achieveable, relevant, time-bond (3.3.6 Measurable goals: Smart-goal).
**Project plan:** Divide the project into phases according to the nature, needs, scope and timeframe of the project. Include proposals for research, strategy development, creative processes, design deliverables, implementation, etc., as well as description of the desired outcome for each phase. Explain your methodology, any key technologies or project management techniques you will use and why they are needed (Eby 2021/ smartsheet.com).
**Progress schedule:** Outline the timeline for each phase, including the basic tasks that you will accomplish, with start and end dates. Include meetings, presentations, partial deliveries and milestones up until the final delivery date.
**Deliverables:** Identify the project deliverables.
Metrics for evaluating: Include the metrics you will use to measure and evaluate the project's success.
**Estimated budget:** Include the budget, price estimate or quotation for the entire project or part of it, preferably specified for each phase.
**Reservations:** Make reservations about changes to deliverables, phases and content of work after research activities and strategy processes have been completed. Clarify payment terms and other conditions.

If the content, framework, and scope of the task have not been sufficiently clarified, reservations should be made for any changes to the process and budget. If necessary, the project description can be adjusted during the project in collaboration with the client, and supplemented with a design brief defining what tasks are to be carried out in the design phase (4.1 Design brief).

**A strong project description provides a roadmap for stakeholders and communicates the vision without getting bogged down in details. (Eby, 2021)**

## 1.6 Progress schedule

The progress schedule follows the project description and is a management tool to get a good flow in the work process, and ensure timely delivery.

Fig. 1.1 The figure shows an example of a Gantt chart, which is a type of column or bar chart. There are many varieties. The chart illustrates the start and end time dates of the various tasks in a project and shows an overview of the entire project.

Example progress schedule outline

*Introduction*:
- Project name
- Date
- Brief description of the project, or reference to the project description.

*Chart*:
- Timetable
- Tasks
- Distribution of responsibilities
- Priorities
- Presentations/meetings
- Partial deliveries
- Production
- Final deadline

At the beginning of a project, it is always necessary to create a progress schedule, regardless of the time frame or scope of the project. The progress schedule is prepared by the designer and presented to the client along with the project description and budget. The purpose of a progress schedule is to obtain an overview of the work to be carried out, and to create a schedule that ensures continuity and progress in the project up to the delivery deadline. The progress schedule also provides a good indication of the resources needed in the various project phases and is a good starting point for allocating tasks and responsibilities.

An ambitious timetable is an advantage for getting the project off to a good start, but progress should be realistic, and sufficient time should be allocated for the proper implementation of various parts of the project. In order for the progress schedule to be of any significance, it must be followed up and adjusted in the event of changes or delays along the way, which is usually the responsibility of the project leader. The progress schedule should therefore be easy to supplement and update. Using digital solutions to create a progress schedule can make it easy to update, share and interact with it. There are lots of different tools online, tailored to various needs for planning and scheduling. The progress schedule may be made simple or detailed depending on the complexity of the project, and the number of people involved. It may be limited to a simple time schedule or may take the form of a project plan with an overview of tasks, highlighting of interim milestones, partial deliveries and distribution of responsibilities.

When preparing a progress schedule, it should be structured in line with the phases set out in the project description in order to ensure good synchronisation. It should be stated how the various tasks in the project are emphasised in relation to the allocated time and resources. How the designer emphasises and prioritises resources in the progress schedule can show the client how the designer has understood the task, and whether the designer is qualified to do it. For example, if the designer has set aside 5% of the time for strategy, and the rest for design, even though it is stated in the project brief that strategy development should be emphasised, this may at worst indicate that the designer does not have a realistic relationship to the use of time and resources in the project.

A good method of scheduling time in a project is to start with the delivery deadline and calculate backwards, just as one does when planning a flight, starting with the departure time, calculating when to be at the gate, when to leave home, and so on. Time and the use of resources set out in the progress schedule should be consistent with the allocated time and resources defined in the price quotation. For example, if in the progress schedule only one day is set aside for field research while in the price quotation it is budgeted for one week, there will be a clear discrepancy (1.7 Price quotation).

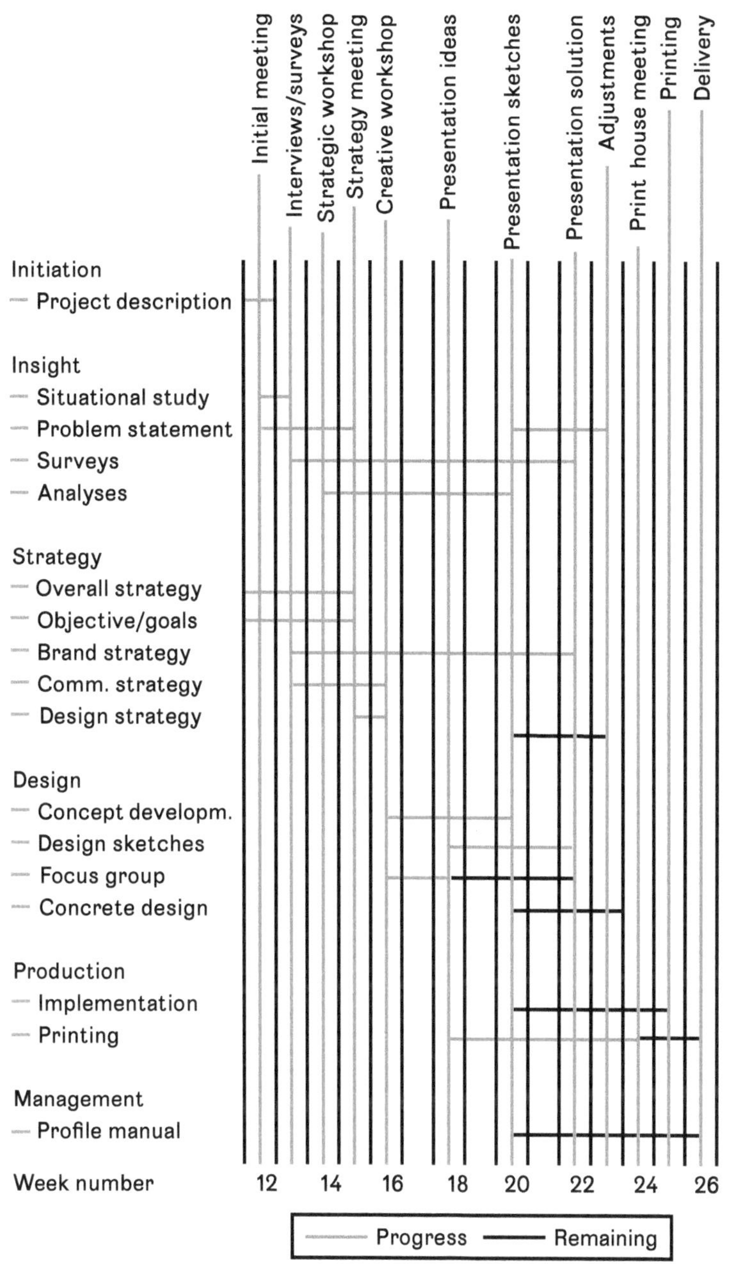


Fig. 1.1 Gantt chart

1 Initiation
2 Insight
3 Strategy
4 Design
5 Production
6 Management

1.1 Initial preparations
1.2 Project brief
1.3 Initial meeting
1.4 Initial workshop
1.5 Project description
1.6 Progress schedule
1.7 Price quotation
1.8 Contract
1.9 Team collaboration

**Progress schedule outline:** There are many ways to draw up a progress schedule: Here, the designer has the opportunity to use their creative abilities to prepare a visual, structured and navigable schedule. A Gantt chart is a visual, transparent and effective method for drawing up a progress schedule, and it is also well suited as a project management tool; see Figure 1.1. Here, it is important to bear in mind that the time spent on drawing up the progress schedule should be proportional to the scope of the project. Regardless, finding a suitable digital schedule template online might be a good start, where you can also get an idea for a good setup if you want to make your own version.

Tips for the designer
**Wait until the assignment has been clarified to prepare price quotations for design work and production. Instead, give a price for a workshop or preliminary project to investigate the assignment. Results from initial investigations and strategy work may often lead to changes in the design project beyond what was originally intended.**

Price quotations are the designer's price proposal to the client used as basis for negotiating the final pricing of a project or service. The quotation estimates the use of time and resources and defines applicable payment terms and conditions. In case of quotations in procurements, pre-defined assumptions and frameworks usually apply.

The price quotation is prepared after the designer and the client have clarified the project during an initial meeting or workshop. The price quotation is often based on a project description and progress schedule and shows the price of the various phases and tasks of the project based on estimated time and resource use. The quotation should show the terms and conditions set by the designer. A price quotation signed by the client may serve as a work agreement, but it is recommended to sign a work contract in addition in order to address areas of interest other than those related to the price quotation. Once approved, the price quotation helps create predictability for both parties in the work relationship.

Having too little information at the beginning of the project is not uncommon, which means that it may be difficult to calculate the price and provide a binding quotation. In that case, a good alternative

**Tips for the designer**

When you receive an inquiry, there are a number of questions you should take into account before preparing a price quotation:

- Do you understand the project? What is important? What is unclear? Ask questions!
- What is the client's experience of purchasing design services?
- What is the scope of the assignment in terms of time and resource use? Is it realistic for you to take on the assignment? Do you have the capacity, time, expertise and desire to do so?
- How important is it to you to get the assignment? Does the assignment give any opportunity for additional sales and good references?
- Are there any other designers that have been approached?
- Is it a competition? Do you have the capacity to participate? What are the criteria? Do you get paid to participate?
- Do you need to invest time to get the assignment, or can you charge from start-up?
- Is the fee amount set? Is it proportional to the workload?
- Does the client expect you to submit a quotation for the entire project? Is it sufficient to prepare a price estimate or budget?
- What are the client's creditworthiness and ability to pay like?
- What terms and conditions should you set?
- Consider whether the task is in conflict with your own beliefs, such as environmental considerations, equality, politics, fair trade, etc.
- Is the project sustainable for you, i.e. is the payment proportionate to effort and time spent?

**Price quotation template**

**Main page:**
Client: Name of client/company: Document type: Price quotation. Sender: Name, business name and logo. Project: Name of project. Highlighted.
**Introduction:**
Designer/Design agency: Brief information about us and why we have been chosen.
Design team: Names and roles. Project leader and contact person.
Client: Brief information about the company, product/service.
Project group: Names and roles. Project leader, decision-maker and contact person.
**Background:** Brief description of the company, current situation and the challenges or needs that have prompted the initiation of the project.
**Project description:** Summary of the project description. The project description may be attached or integrated fully.
**Price quotation:** Price quotations are prepared according to the phases in the project description. It should be made clear which tasks are included in each phase, without going into too much detail. An amount is set for each task in the phase, possibly only one amount for the entire phase.
*Explanation of the price quotation*: For example: The budget is prepared based on the phases in the project description.
**VAT:** VAT (or GST) is added to the final amount if you are subject to VAT.
**Confirmation/agreement/contract:** Signature on the price quotation, or written confirmation by email, is to be considered a binding agreement. In case of larger projects, a contract should be drawn up and signed before project start.
**Progress schedule:** The progress schedule is included in or attached to the project description, and the price quotation.
**Note:** Price quotations for small projects can be simplified.



is to price some of the services separately, such as initial workshop, a preliminary project, individual studies, necessary strategy development or consulting, and postpone preparing a full quotation until the scope and framework of the project are more clearly defined. If the client nevertheless wants a price quotation for the entire project, the designer may propose preparing a price estimate or budget. Such a suggested price can provide the client with an indication of the total costs to assess in relation to its own cost framework and makes it possible to compare prices if there are other providers in the picture. If a price estimate is provided, the price may not significantly exceed the specified amount. However, this does not apply if another price limit is expressly agreed, or the designer is entitled to a surcharge for additional work, extra materials or other unforeseen circumstances.

It is important that the designer has understood the client's level of ambition for the project as a starting point for assessing the scope and size of the project. The same applies to the client's ability to pay. For example, creating a new logo for a bank will be a larger and more comprehensive process than creating a logo for a small business, because designing a new logo/visual identity for a bank is likely to require more extensive research and strategies, more extensive design process with more idea concepts and sketching rounds, more meetings with more decision-makers, and so on (1.5 Project description).

Tips for the designer
**You should consider declining a project with unrealistic framework and assumptions, rather than risking delivering something that you will not be proud of.**

### 1.7.1 Price request

The client is often concerned with price, which can also be a decisive factor for the client's choice of designer. Therefore, it can be tempting for the designer to propose a price quickly in order to get the assignment. Rather than rush, it may be wise to explain to the client that it is necessary to acquaint yourself properly with the nature of the project in order to submit a realistic quotation. A good approach for the designer is to give a price at an initial workshop in the first place and come back with a quotation once the scope of the project has been clarified. Many clients have little experience in buying design services and knowing little about what to expect in terms of price, result and quality. Therefore, it is important that the designer provides information about what a design process entails, what is required in terms of time and resources for creating good results, and how the process itself can be instructive for the parties involved (1.6 Progress schedule).

### 1.7.2 Price setup

There are infinitely many ways to set up a quotation. How detailed the price quotation is to be, must be considered in the context of the nature, scope and level of ambition of the project. The quotation may be preceded by a summary of the project description and concluded with a short version of the progress schedule. A good alternative is to provide a project description, price quotation and progress schedule together. The price quotation can be set up in phases, with a brief description of each phase, and the tasks involved in each phase. An aggregate sum should appear for each phase, with an aggregate sum at the end. In larger project meetings, project management and reporting should be specified for each phase. The number of phases may vary. The same applies to what one chooses to call the phases, how detailed the price specification in each phase should be and whether a specification of hours should be provided. The most important thing is that the client understands what the phases entail, and what they cost, besides the project's conditions being met. If adjustments are made to the quotation, the front page should state that it has been revised, its version and date.

### 1.7.3 Terms and conditions

Terms and conditions should be stated in the introduction or at the end of the quotation.

*Conditions* should describe what requirements are made for the maturity of the invoice, collection requirements, the validity of the price quotation, etc., and what is not included in the price. There should not be too much surcharge in the price. The client should normally have as much predictability as possible. Here are examples of how conditions can be formulated: All prices exclude VAT, shipping, travel, production, printing. Purchase, rental, or development of an illustration or photo is not included. Purchase of fonts, dummy development, continuous costs for materials and tools, or other unforeseen expenses are not included. Phase 1 is invoiced when the project is assigned. Furthermore, 50% of each phase is invoiced at the start of the phase in question, and the remaining 50% is invoiced at the end of the phase. Invoices fall due with 10 days' notice. We reserve the right to adjust the price quotation in case of changes/additions to the agreed starting point. Work and meetings outside the budget are invoiced by the hour. Strategic advice is calculated by the hour at fixed hourly rates. Budget meetings are up to two hours long. The price quotation includes two rounds of editing/proofreading; additional editing entails a price surcharge. We will keep you posted on any additional costs for the prices to be approved in advance. The price quotation is valid for four weeks from this date.

*Terms* apply to circumstances under which one wishes to make reservations or insure against. Here are examples of how the terms/reservations can be formulated: We reserve the right to adjust the prices for phases 4, 5 and 6 when the scope and basis for the work has been clarified in more detail. Revised quotations for these phases will be prepared after the strategic process has been completed. We reserve the right to ownership of all work undertaken until payment is received as per agreement. Please also refer to the signed contract (1.8 Contract).

### 1.7.4 Negotiation

If the designer and the client disagree on the price, they can negotiate in order to reach a joint decision or agreement. It is important for both parties to listen and ask questions in order to understand the other party's position. If the negotiations become too demanding, or the parties fail to reach agreement, there may be no further collaboration. In some cases, it may be an advantage to seek legal advice in order to ensure that both interests are best served.

### 1.7.5 Hourly rate

Most designers use their hourly rate to calculate a price or quotation. The hourly rate is calculated mainly on the basis of the designer's or design agency's production costs, which cover salaries, overheads and estimated profit. Fixed costs such as premises, equipment, software and other operating costs are usually higher for a larger design agency than for an individual freelancer, which will affect the hourly rate calculation. Furthermore, an experienced designer or a profiled design agency will often be able to charge more for their services, based on reputation and demand. Other factors that matter are competence, efficiency as well as the designer's ability to negotiate good terms by conveying the value of their services. An example of that is the value of a logo. Rated as a piece of graphic work, it will have lower value than if it is rated by virtue of its brand value and scope of use.



Invoice

Invoice/bill is a sales document. Invoice number, invoice date, buyer's name/address, seller's name/company reg. number, description of the goods, specified price + VAT if applicable, and due date are added to the bill.

## Terminology

**Price:** Price is a payment for output or service. The use of the phrase 'price' signals that there is a price without specific basis for negotiation, as opposed to wordings such as price quotation or suggested price, which leave room for negotiation. The agreed price and the invoice sent to the client after the project has been completed must be consistent. Make reservations.

**Price quotation:** Using the wording 'quotation' may signal that the price implies a price reduction or discount, which makes acceptance of the price more attractive.

**Price suggestion:** Using the phrase suggested price or price estimate, you clearly state that prices are an indication of what it may cost. It can be useful when the pricing basis has not been defined, such as when the scope (number of pages and level of detail) of a web page or brochure has not been determined. This will affect both the price of design and production (programming/printing).

**Draft price:** When using the wording 'draft price' or 'price estimate', to a great extent you open negotiations. When drawing up a price estimate, it is important to make the necessary reservations provided that the price is not to be perceived as binding.

**Budget:** A plan to show how much money a person or organisation will earn and how much they will need or be able to spend (Budget, n.d.). Budget in a design assignment means that you prepare a statement of expected costs related to the design project over a specific period. The purpose of a budget specification is for the client to get an overview of the costs associated with your services and to implement it in its business budget. State clearly whether the prices in the budget are merely an indication or estimate and make the necessary reservations about changes and any additions to the price. If relevant, you can call the budget provisional (Sending, 2007).

**Budget estimate:** Temporarily calculated budget. When preparing a price estimate it is important to take necessary precautions if the price is not supposed to be experienced as binding.

**Tender:** Tenders are offers in connection with a procurement. Pursuant to public procurement regulations, tendering is required for procurements above a certain threshold. In a procurement, negotiating the tender or amending it after the closing date for submission of tenders is prohibited. Sometimes tenders are commonly referred to as a price offer.

**Dispute:** If the parties fail to reach an agreement, the matter may be referred to the Conciliation Board or to the Consumer Council.

**VAT:** It is common to specify a price on design services exclusive of VAT (or GST).[4] Design projects are usually B2B, i.e., the designer sells their services to businesses and not consumers. Companies liable for VAT receive VAT refunds on incoming invoices. Therefore, it is the price without VAT that is the amount they actually pay. VAT is calculated as a percentage of the price and added to the invoice.[5]

**Invoice:** VAT or GST number and company registration number are added to the bill.

Tips for the client

Pushing the price too much might compromise the quality of the product you receive. The price reflects the time the designer estimates for project completion. If relevant, you can negotiate the hourly rate, or reduce the scope and level of ambition of the project, which can mean fewer sketches, fewer meetings, etc.

4 VAT vs. GST: 'VAT stands for Value Added Tax and it is a consumption tax applied to the purchase price of goods and services. GST stands for Goods and Services Tax and it is a consumption tax that is imposed upon the cost of goods and services. Both GST and VAT are taxes that share the same characteristics but have different names. The only differences between these taxes derive from the specific rules that each country apply on the taxes themselves such as: tax rates, items exempt from tax and the requirements of registration' (Global VAT Compliance, globalvatcompliance.com)

5 Professional organisations for designers, such as AIGA (The American Institute of Graphic Arts), ICoD (International Council of Design), GDC (Society of Graphic Designers of Canada), Design Council of UK, as well as similar associations in other countries, provide advice and guides to copyright, as well as standard forms of agreements that may also be available online i.e. 'AIGA Standard Form of Agreement for Design Services'.

6 Competition Act or competition Law is a general term used relatively similar in different countries for a law that promotes or seeks to maintain market competition by regulating anti-competitive conduct by companies. Taylor, Martyn D. (2006). Competition law is implemented through public and private enforcement. (Cartel Damage Claims, CDC).

Supply, demand and market price are factors affecting the value of most goods and services, including design services. Design services are among the services that are generally sensitive to market economy fluctuations, where a decline in the market economy may result in less willingness to pay compared to when business is doing well. That is an example of why designers can experience great competition and price pressure at times, and one may feel pressured to lower the price. The designer should avoid offering too low a price, as this might contribute to giving buyers of design services an incorrect picture of what a design service should cost and what quality to expect. Price and quality are interconnected. Creating good quality work requires time and resources. In order to maintain a proper price level and ensure the quality of the design deliverables, it is important for the designer to maintain a correct hourly rate, and instead propose to reduce the scope or level of ambition of the projects in question, than lower the hourly rate. Dumping price levels is also an ethical matter, a responsibility towards our own industry.

**Calculating your hourly rate.**

a) Salary: The annual or monthly income the designer must calculate for housing, eating and leisure.
b) Operating expenses: Fixed expenses related to premises, equipment, software, materials, etc.
c) Profit: The surplus that remains when salary and expenses are paid.

Divide the sum by the number of working hours in the year that are billable. The result is your hourly rate.

It can be difficult for established as well as for recently graduated designers to know what they should charge. Some choose to ask others what they charge or leave it up to the negotiations in each individual project. Many look for indicative hourly rates for design services, but this could hinder free competition under the Competition Act.[6] Nevertheless, a good indicator may be to use salary surveys conducted by stakeholders for different design professionals as a basis.

The hourly rate can also easily be calculated by making an overview of what you actually need to cover: salary, expenses and get an acceptable profit. There are various price calculators online, which can be helpful.

## 1.8 Contract

### A signed contract is a good starting point for predictable designer-client collaboration.

First and foremost, a contract helps safeguard the legal rights of both parties in the event of disagreement. What should be included in the contract may vary depending on the project.

A contract addresses issues related to the delivery that has been agreed on and the conditions that apply in the event of changes. 'A well-written agreement clarifies expectations, prevents common misunderstandings, and helps avoid potential legal problems' (Aiga Standard Form of Agreement for Design Services 2020).[7] Here are some key factors that should be included in a contract between the designer and the client:

**The parties:** Name and data of both parties of the agreement.

**Delivery:** Specific description of what the assignment concerns and what is to be delivered. Consequences concerning a change in delivery, resulting in additional or reduced work for the designer. Consequences if the designer does not deliver as per agreement.

**Price:** Specific description of the agreed price, VAT (or GST), payment deadline, late payment claims, conditions for additional work for the designer, unforeseen costs and other payment terms.

**Deadline for delivery:** Specific description of the time of delivery. Consequences of changes in delivery deadline by the client, or delayed delivery by the designer.

**Complaints:** Specific description of the criteria applicable to a complaint about the designer's work and consequences thereof.

**Legal ownership:** Specific description of the legal ownership of the final product. The designer's rights under the Copyright Act[8] are clarified, and any transfer of ownership to the client is confirmed.

**Duties and responsibilities:** Specific description of the duties and responsibilities of both parties.

**Disputes:** Specific description of the circumstances of a dispute, and how the parties are to proceed in order to resolve the dispute.

**Signing:** Both parties sign two copies of the contract, one for each party.

Tips for the designer

**You should avoid working for free to qualify for a design assignment. If sketches are needed at an early stage you might argue that insight is necessary to create something of value. Suggest an initial workshop as a start. It can provide some insight and strategic anchoring. You might also suggest an initial quote for the workshop and sketches. Get a written confirmation of what you have agreed on and at best sign a contract.**

## 1.9 Team collaboration

In a design project, assembling a team with the right qualifications is a success factor, as well as embracing diversity and differences.

It is crucial to create a good working environment in the team, and help make each other better, so that everyone can unlock their greatest potential. It is just as important to establish an open and trustful collaboration with the client. Good team dynamics and a common level of ambition are required for a group of people to function well and essential for the quality of the results that can be achieved together. A prerequisite is careful goal formulation and planning, as well as a conscious allocation of responsibilities and quality assurance during the various phases of the project.

A design project can be completed by one person alone, or it can be carried out by several people in collaboration. Working together can have many advantages, including bringing more expertise, views and ideas to the project. Assembling a good project team is first and foremost about ensuring that the right qualifications are represented among the project participants. These qualifications may be present within the design agency, school environment or one's workplace, but they may also be

7 AIGA (The American Institute of Graphic Arts) is a professional organisation for design, including communication design, including graphic design, typography, interaction design, user-experience, branding and identity.

8 A copyright Act is the body of law that governs the protection of the ownership and usage rights for creative works including works of art and books, among other types of media. Each country has its own domestic copyright laws that apply to its own citizens, and also to the use of foreign content when used in one's country (copyrightlaws.com).

9 'How Diverse Teams Produce Better Outcomes', Beilook 2019, Forbes

10 'Diversity wins' is one of three reports from McKinsey investigating the business case for diversity.

acquired externally. Project teams that gather together to complete a task may be people who know each other well and have good experience of working together, or they may be people with little to no knowledge of each other. Some may initially feel unsafe working with people they do not know, while others may experience this as inspiring and motivating. Either way, it is a good start to begin a team collaboration by creating predictable and secure relationships, with a high degree of trust and empathy. A good team collaboration will also have a positive effect on the relationship with the client. Inviting the client to collaborate in the project can be beneficial as well. By involving the client in the project work it might be it easier to speak together about ideas and the client will more easily stand behind the solution that is promoted. As a consequence, it will also simplify the implementation of the solution in the company.



### Inclusive and diverse

How do we define who the right people are when assembling a team? Having the right team of people to help generate ideas to propose is critical. Studies show that a diverse selection of people in a team can be more successful. 'From the classroom and the workplace, to the laboratory and the playing field, research shows that diverse groups of people often make better decisions' (Beilock 2019, Forbes).[9] According to studies conducted by McKinsey, being inclusive and assembling a team with diversity can be an essential factor in achieving a successful project delivery, as it has been proven that diverse teams produce better outcomes. We also see such an effect on a company's management, where there is a relationship between diversity on executive teams and the likelihood of financial outperformance (Dixon-Fyle et al., 2020, McKinsey).[10]

### Qualifications

When starting to build a team, getting to know each other's skills and work experience will always be a good start. It is important to allocate plenty of time for this so that everyone can get an idea of what opportunities the competence of the others provide. It will also serve as a good foundation for building respect and trust. In addition to professional knowledge, there are several responsibilities or roles to be distributed within a team. These include fixed roles such as project leader and the minute taker, and more specific roles such as creative manager, strategic manager, etc., depending on the nature of the project. In large projects, the project team may be able to handle tasks such as writing reports and sending meeting invitations outside the group, but usually the project staff themselves have to allocate these tasks and responsibilities among themselves. A good place to start could be to talk about the roles needed in the project and which of these each person feels good about. Are you a good leader? Are you good at writing reports? Are you good at research and mapping? Are you good at thinking and getting ideas? Are you good at leading brainstorming and creative processes? Are you good at strategic work? Are you tech-savvy and great with digital tools? Are you good at drawing, shaping, creating? Are you good at manufacturing techniques and materials? Are you good at quality assurance, etc? The point is not just to do what you are good at. A good start would be to map out the different qualities of the group. This can simplify the work

Further reading
***101 Team Building Exercises: To Improve Cooperation and Communication*** **(2020) by Mr. Herman Otten.**

on planning how the roles are to be distributed within the group. One person is often suitable for several roles. Roles can also go hand in hand, although in a design agency it is most common for individual project participants to deliver on their top expertise.

### Level of ambition

Each person's level of ambition is another important aspect to clarify when assembling the group. Level of ambition in this context means how much time and resources you want to put into the project. It is about the personal goals you have in the project, what you envisage that you can contribute, and what significance the result has for you. This depends on the effort you want to put in. Some will stretch a little extra to achieve the best possible result, while others may be satisfied if it is good enough. In those projects where each person is paid according to effort, it can create a good balance. This is not always the case in projects where profits should be shared equally, or in a school setting where everyone in the group gets the same grade, or if your salary enters your account every month regardless of effort. Having differing levels of ambition in a group can lead to collaboration problems, because some may feel they work more than others. Often you have no options to choose from. The group is what it is. In other words, you are put in a group. Group members might not only have different levels of ambition, but also different levels of energy. Some function on high gear, others on low gear.

People are different, and having a high level of ambition is not necessarily the same as sitting and working until 2:00 in the morning. It may as well be working within normal work sessions, but with the right work methodology, high concentration, and good workflow. If you have the opportunity to put together people with roughly the same level of ambition, it can be a success factor, where everyone is equally eager and will do their best. In school projects and in job contexts where groups are put together by others, doing so is not always possible. It is about finding a way to work together that creates security, where people do each other good, and which allows everyone, regardless of their level of ambition and qualifications, to contribute as much as possible. It is about tolerance, openness and security. These are qualities that are necessary in all collaborative projects, and especially in projects where you put in a lot of yourself, as well as in creative projects where exchanging and building on each other's thoughts and ideas is essential. In addition to the level of personal ambition, we have the client's level of ambition. Deadlines and cost framework do not always allow the project team to develop the 'perfect solution'. The group should discuss early whether it is realistic to complete the project within the given time frame and budget. One possible approach is to reduce the number of design sketches or suggest a higher price and deadline extension.

### Goals and tasks

Goals and level of ambition go hand in hand. In a collaboration, it is always important to clarify early on what people should collaborate on. What is the goal and which problem needs to be addressed? In some projects, the goals and tasks have been clarified by the project owner, who can also be the client. In other projects, this is something the project team

Fig. 1.2 The figure shows a control loop, a project management tool based on Westhagen (2008). Goal formulation: Decide and describe what the project will result in. Planning: Break down the goals into elements, which can ensure that we perform the task expediently. Execution: Management, communication, resource use, team, motivation. Follow-up: Record what is happening in the project and compare with plan and goals. Manage necessary corrections in goals, planning and execution.

> Walk the talk:[11] It is OK to fail. It is OK to have ambitions. What you pay attention to grows. Leave your comfort zone.

11 The phrase 'Walk-the-Talk' means putting words into action, i.e. implement in practice the things you say you will do.

needs to work on in order to establish. The project may have one main goal and several subgoals, or the project may be divided into several tasks and responsibilities. In any case, it is important for group dynamics and collaboration to move more or less in the same direction, towards a clear and well-defined goal (3.3 Goals and subgoals). The project leader has a central role in leading the group, but it is the individual's responsibility to lead themselves. Once the meter is in place, the planning and distribution of work tasks can begin. It is through the tasks that the execution of the project takes place. The project leader must ensure that the tasks are evenly distributed and that everyone has a relevant task to complete. One problem that can arise here is that activities are often based on each other, as a result of which not everyone will have the same amount of work at the same time. A pitfall may be that the project leader is tempted to start activities before the prerequisites are available, which may result in additional work by having to redo the work. Follow-up and quality control are important in all project phases, right up to the delivery of the completed solution, to ensure that the achieved result complies with the goal. A good way to do that is to define checkpoints as part of the project plan so that any non-compliances or errors can be followed up along the way and adjusted at an early stage (5.5.6 Workflow).



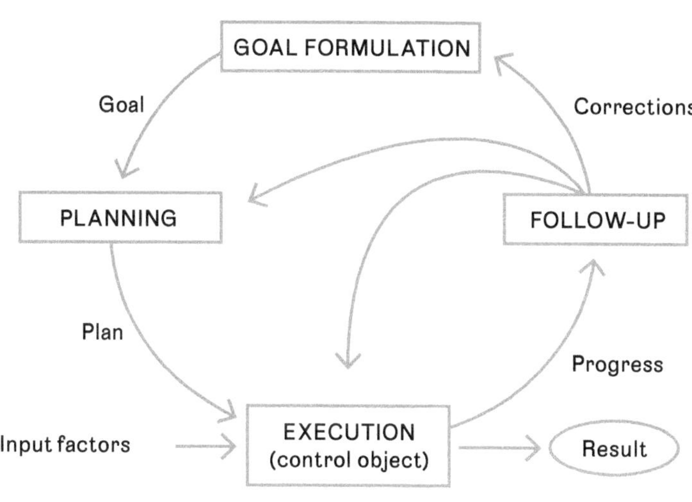


Fig. 1.2 Control loop

### 1.9.1 Control loop

Westhagen's control loop (Westhagen et al., 2008, p. 31, Wiik 2015) is a good management tool for project planning and follow-up. It contains four main elements in a circular process. These are goal formulation, planning, execution and follow-up, see Figure 1.2. *Goal formulation* is about describing the project deliverables and what the project should result in. *Planning* is about outlining what should be done in the project, and the activities needed to create the project deliverables. *Execution* is about implementation. *Follow-up* is about, among other things, frequently following up and correcting the implementation. Sometimes you have to change your plans. This may involve adding more resources and working more efficiently. Other times it is necessary to change the project deliverables and thus change the goal formulation. The term loop indicates that we must go through this loop many times during a project. Every time we follow up on a project, we usually have to go in and correct something. Projects do not have a static implementation plan but are carried out dynamically. This is also called agile implementation (4.3.5 Iterative method, 4.3.10 Lean and agile).

**Progress schedule:** Initially, create a progress schedule, which includes all work phases. The progress plan could be updated in the event of delays. Where schedules fall short, it is important to put in extra effort and make up for the lost time. Lagging behind wears everyone down. All experience suggests that you need all the time you can get in the end (1.6 Progress schedule).

**Collaboration agreement:** Being well-organised and preparing an agreement at the beginning where, among other things, the goals of the collaboration are described will be a good resource for the rest of the project. Such an agreement should contain some information on mutual expectations between the participants, level of ambition in relation to the project input, 'traffic rules' for roles, responsibilities and division of labour.

**Planning of meetings:** The project leader should prepare a plan before each meeting and a goal for what is to be accomplished during the meeting. Before a meeting, clarify to everyone in the group what should happen and sum up at the end of the meeting to see if everyone has done what they intended to. Writing logs and meeting minutes is good project management.

**Common methods:** A good way to bring the group together is to agree on common methods. 'If the project staff do not work according to common methods, but according to their own individual arrangements, this can weaken the collaboration in the project, and reduce the opportunity for exchange of experience. The project leader's freedom of action could be reduced, and it becomes difficult to transfer people from one project activity to another' (Andersen et al. 2012) (see also 4.3 Design methodology).

**Sustainable principles:** Make sure to identify a set of common principles for sustainability, to ensure diversity and equality in the collaboration, as well as common attitudes, ethics and values for sustainable processes and solutions (3.3.8 Sustainability goals: Oslo Manifesto, 6.9 Sustainable management).

**Group climate:** The work environment in a group can have a lot to say both regarding the professional benefits and the implementation of the project. How do we communicate? Care, respect, responsibility, and constructive criticism are important. If everyone has a certain ceiling of blunders, this improves the climate of collaboration. It is recommended to allocate time to exchange experiences about the climate and the work of the group. This way, each member of the group can gain experience in giving and receiving feedback.

**Communication:** Good feedback and constructive criticism can provide opportunities for awareness-raising and further development. Positive communication among group members means that everyone participates, and everyone receives support. Active listening involves listening attentively to the other(s) and giving a response that shows that you have understood.

Fig. 1.3 **The figure shows gameplan (based on Aakre and Scharning 2016/The Grove Consultants International). Gameplan is a dynamic project management tool that the project team creates together, manually or online by for example using Virtual Strategic Visioning Templates Pack – Digital Download, grovetools-inc.com. © Grimsgaard, W. (2018)**

12 Miro board: miro.com. Grove Tools: grovetools-inc.com, thegrove.com. Figma: figma.com. Padlets: padlet.com

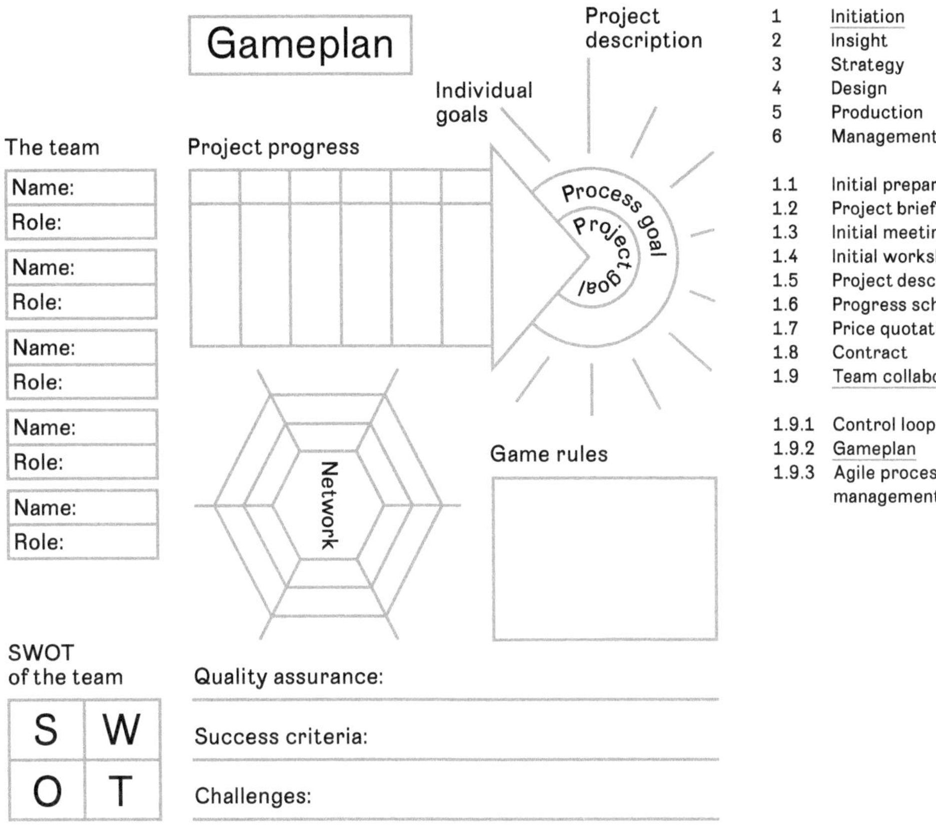


Fig. 1.3 Gameplan

1 Initiation
2 Insight
3 Strategy
4 Design
5 Production
6 Management

1.1 Initial preparations
1.2 Project brief
1.3 Initial meeting
1.4 Initial workshop
1.5 Project description
1.6 Progress schedule
1.7 Price quotation
1.8 Contract
1.9 Team collaboration

1.9.1 Control loop
1.9.2 Gameplan
1.9.3 Agile process management

**Work visually**: Use flip charts, mapping methods, images, and sketches in the process. This simplifies the transfer from strategy to visual solutions (2.8 Mapping).

### 1.9.2 Gameplan

Gameplan is a tool for mapping and planning a project. 'The purpose of the tool is to provide the team with a solid common basis for starting the actual work on the project. When the gameplan is completed, everyone should know who does what, when, how and why. The gameplan makes it easy for everyone to keep track of things along the way as the plan is updated daily. The overview also works well as a checklist to keep an eye on whether everyone is working towards the right goals, cooperating well and having the desired momentum' (Aakre and Scharning 2016, The Grove Consultants International). The project team can design a physical gameplan or a digital version using a platform suited for interactions, planning, workshop and co-creation, e.g. Miro board, Grove Tools, Figma, or Padlet.[12]

**1) Start by laying out a roll of paper** or a large sheet/poster that you will use to draw and fill in the items, or choose any online gameplan tool. When working with gameplan, one can work digitally or with pen and paper. There are digital game plan tools that make this process seamless

A good work environment in the group is a success factor for good results.

(good tools are often free), and the principle of the process is the same. One option is Grove Tools.[13]

**2) Project description:** Start by entering a concise and precise version of the project description/problem you will be working on, in the upper right corner of the gameplan, see Figure 1.3 (1.5 Project description).

**3) Project progress:** Define the name, time frame and order of the phases you will be going through in the project. Enter the name of the phases in the top fields of the project progress (action plan). After that, fill in the different tasks belonging to the different phases. You may want to prioritise the order and importance of the tasks. Use Post-it notes for this section since you are likely to change and move the notes during the project (1.6 Progress schedule).

**4) SWOT analysis:** Identify each person in the team (for example in terms of competence and personality) using a SWOT analysis. Summarise each individual SWOT into a common team-SWOT, which is registered on the gameplan (2.7.10 SWOT analysis).

**5) Roles:** Define the different roles and responsibilities that are necessary to cover in the project and team, and give the roles appropriate names/titles. Identify the tasks that should be assigned to each role. Distribute the roles (according to each person's competence, desires, and motivation). Also, discuss your expectations of each other and the project in relation to your roles.

**6) Goals:** Define specific goals for the project (project goals), the team process (process goals) and individual learning (learning goals). Fill in the goals overview on the right of the tool template (3.3.9 Goals for design project).

**7) Network:** Considering what you need for your project, create a network map of contributors and contacts that can be used. Enter name, contact info, and what they can contribute with. Also write down what you may need and what you must try to obtain through the others' contacts.

**8) Challenges and success factors:** Identify critical challenges and success factors for the different phases of the project. Be specific about what to do to secure successful collaboration and project results, and what to do to prevent and resolve the challenges that may arise.

**9) Game rules:** Agree on a set of game rules (procedures, decision techniques, etc.) on how you will cooperate during the project. Use experience from previous collaborations and how you have worked together so far, as a basis to identify a good way for you to work together in the project, to perform, learn, and thrive - individually and as a team.

**10) Quality assurance:** Agree on some simple measures/procedures as to when and how to quality assure the product and collaboration in each individual phase so that you can develop both along the way (5.9 Quality assurance).

**11) Project leader:** The project leader is responsible for the progress and finances of the project, and ensures that the project is managed and delivered according to the goals and requirements agreed with the client (1.6 Progress schedule, 1.7 Price quotation).

**12) Process leader:** In larger projects, a process leader may be needed in addition to the project leader. Process management may also refer to the responsibility of the project leader, or to a task that is done in turns. Process management is the art of guiding people through processes toward common goals in a way that supports participation,

'Gameplan not only helps your team plan the project, but it also helps you implement and evaluate the project' (Aakre and Scharning 2016).

13 Grove Tools: grovetools-inc.com/collections/graphic-gameplan

creates ownership, and triggers creativity for everyone involved. It is all about quality management and continuous improvement. The process leader is responsible for creating a room for interaction and discussions where everyone involved is given the opportunity to create new solutions, acquire new understanding and make decisions. The process leader plans and directs design processes and actively participates in all phases of a project, from planning to implementation of the finished product. The process leader has a key role in interdisciplinary teams, working with insight, concept development, prototyping and testing. The process leader is in their element when they can create a vision and realise it by inspiring, motivating and challenging others when needed. Self-motivation is strong, and the process leader can mark out the course and bring others along, even when things are at their worst (Myhre, 2017) (6.3 Design management, 6.9 Sustainable management).



> When presenting your status updates, focus on the process instead of the people. This way you will make sure that progress is actually being made (Kanbanize.com).

### 1.9.3 Agile process management

In order to have regular status updates, stand up meetings can be beneficial. Gameplan can be used as a reference (1.9.2 Gameplan). A stand-up meeting is a short meeting between a team while standing on their feet, commonly used in agile process management. The goal is to go over important tasks that have been completed, are in progress or are about to be started. During the daily meeting each person in the team, with no exception, must be able to answer 3 fundamental questions regarding their workflow (kanbanize.com):

- What did I accomplish yesterday?
- What will I do today?
- What obstacles, if any, are impeding my progress?

For this type of process management, digital tools such as the Kanban board are well suited and can be combined with meeting physically. A Kanban board is a physical or digital project management tool for workflow visualisation. Using a Kanban board, the advice is to schedule a meeting at the beginning of the workday and aim for a length of 5–15 minutes. This will allow you to sync your plan for the day and avoid mistakes caused by a lack of communication. When meeting at a Kanban board, it is not necessary for each individual to explain what they have done the day before, since the progress of each task is visible and only updates are necessary.

For teams that need to visualise their work when meeting, it will be necessary to set aside more time for the meeting. Either way, keep it short and within the agreed time. Raise the alarm. In a design project, such meetings can be a good way to keep up with the progress, but in addition it will be necessary for the team to gather in workshops, brainstormings and meetings for ideation and sharing visual mapping, sketches and design solutions (4.3.10 Lean and agile, 4.3.8 Scrum, 4.3.9 Kanban).

Further reading
***Agile: An Essential Guide to Agile Project Management, The Kanban Process and Lean Thinking + A Comprehensive Guide to Scrum*** **(2018) by James Edge.**

**Team contract**

Without good rules, the chances of frustration and conflict increase during the project. The purpose of a team contract is to agree on the rules of the game. Here is an example of a team contract based on Aakre and Scharning (2016). See also 1.8 Contract.

**Yes, to differences:** Utilise each other's differences and qualities as a strength and resource. Respect one another - even when you have different opinions.

**Knowledge sharing:** Challenge each other to take on tasks you are not entirely confident in, in order to learn something new. Help each other in that role and in the tasks assigned to you. Ask for help and help others when someone is stuck. Support each other.

**Working hours and workplace:** Meet at scheduled times and locations. Notify the project leader in case of delay. Schedule the workday between 9 AM and 5 PM if possible. Be good at making the work situation more varied. Seek inspiration and impulses outside the workplace as well.

**Stand up meetings:** Have regular status updates. Stand up meetings[14] can be beneficial, during which you summarise what has been done, how the team and each and every one of you has worked, what tasks need to be carried out in the future, and what changes can be made to the working methods in order for things to flow even better. Gameplan can be used as a reference .

**Feedback:** Give each other honest and constructive feedback so you can grow as much as possible. Most things can be said, if we say them properly and have a good intention behind it.

**Get inspired:** Get inspiration by visiting digital platforms such as SoMe, advanced Google searches, blogs, discussion forums, etc., as well as different physical environments, watching films, reading books, magazines, newspapers, etc. that can give us ideas and insights.

**The creative process:** Use different processes and methods in the creative process, so that we get as many different ideas as possible. All ideas must be explored - even those that are not immediately perceived as good. Let the person most passionate about an idea have the opportunity to sell it to the rest of the team and motivate team members who are more introverted.

**Sustainable management:** Talk together about how sustainability can be included in processes and solutions (3.3.8 Sustainability goals, 6.9 Sustainable management).

**Guidance:** Quality assure the solutions along the way by using both advisers and external resources around you. In order to get the best guidance and input, make sure to come well prepared with a good pitch and questions.

**Have fun along the way:** Surprise each other with rewards along the way when everyone thinks it is necessary. Everyone works better when there is a good atmosphere and energy in the room.

**Back-up:** Store all files in a shared folder, file sharing or chat platform, such as Dropbox or Google Drive (5.5.6 Workflow).

Tips for the designer

**Keep the team contract clearly visible when you are sitting and working. At regular intervals, you can review the contract and discuss whether the rules are being complied with and whether they help you to function as well as you want and need. If you see that adjustments are needed, you adapt the contract to the need (Aakre and Scharning 2016).**

14 A stand-up meeting (or a 'standing meeting') is a common term in agile projects. It is a short meeting between a team standing on their feet. (Kanbanize.com)

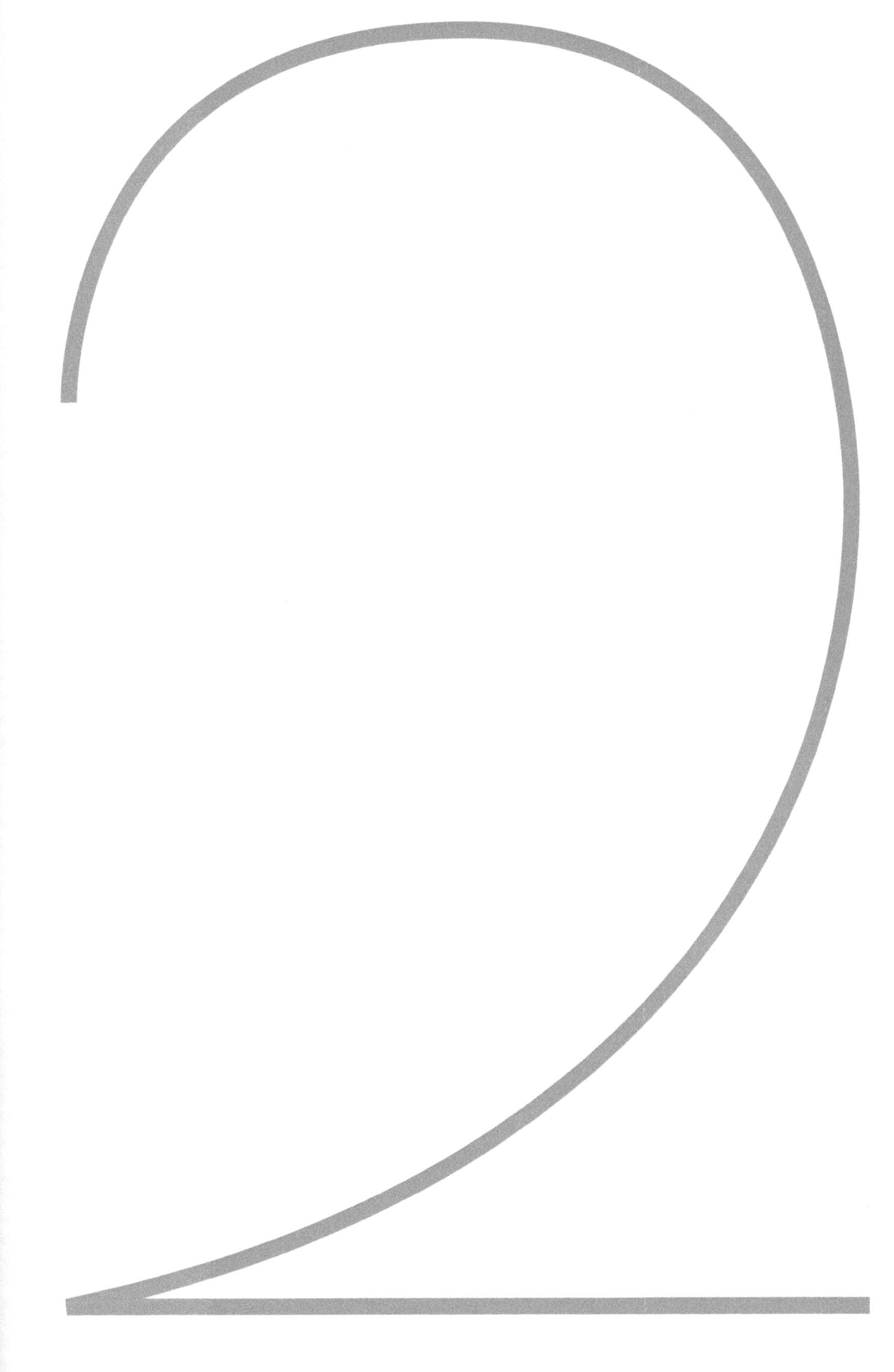

2.1 Understanding the company 50
2.1.1 Value creation 51
2.1.2 Decision making 51
2.1.3 Organisational culture 53
2.1.4 Organisational development 53
2.1.5 The company's universe 54

2.2 Situational study 55
2.2.1 Situational study process 56
2.2.2 PIPI workshop 56
2.2.3 Where are we – where will we? 57

2.3 Problem statement 58
2.3.1 Problem 60
2.3.2 Problem statement process 61
2.3.3 Problem definition 61
2.3.4 Problem statement formulation 62
2.3.5 Problem statement delimitation 63
2.3.6 Problem statement analysis 65
2.3.7 Problem statement requirements 67
2.3.8 A good problem statement 67
2.3.9 Wicked problems 68

2.4 Method selection 70
2.4.1 Qualitative method 70
2.4.2 Quantitative method 71
2.4.3 Method triangulation 73
2.4.4 Research question 73

2.5 Research process 74
2.5.1 Problem statement (Step 1) 76
2.5.2 Research design (Step 2) 76
2.5.3 Choice of method (Step 3) 78
2.5.4 Choice of units (Step 4) 79
2.5.5 Data collection (Step 5) 80
2.5.6 Data analysis and discussion (Step 6) 80
2.5.7 Data interpretation (Step 7) 81
2.5.8 Report preparation (Step 8) 82

2.6 Research 82
2.6.1 Survey 82
2.6.2 Interview 90
2.6.3 Observation 97
2.6.4 Focus group 102
2.6.5 UX Research 104
2.6.6 Experiment 106
2.6.7 Scientific research 108
2.6.8 Artistic research 112
2.6.9 Design research 113

2.7 Analyses 115
2.7.1 Situational analysis 117
2.7.2 Internal analysis 119
2.7.3 Value chain analysis 121
2.7.4 Competitor analysis 122
2.7.5 Positioning analysis 125
2.7.6 Target group analysis 129
2.7.7 Brand analysis 137
2.7.8 Visual analysis 142
2.7.9 PESTLE analysis 146
2.7.10 SWOT analysis 148
2.7.11 Gap analysis 153

2.8 Mapping 155
2.8.1 Mapping methods 156
2.8.2 Moodboard 156
2.8.3 Storyboard 159
2.8.4 Customer journey 160
2.8.5 GIGA mapping 160

2.9 Testing and measuring 164
2.9.1 User testing 165
2.9.2 A/B testing 166
2.9.3 Funnel 167
2.9.4 Zero-point measurement 167
2.9.5 Why do we measure? 167
2.9.6 KPIs and metrics 168
2.9.7 Qualitative indicators and metrics 169
2.9.8 Mental availability measurements 169
2.9.9 Category entry points 170

Insight is the second of six phases. It is about acquiring the knowledge and understanding necessary to carry out a design project. This may be done through studies, surveys, interviews, observations and analyses. Insight can also be gained through design, by exploration, experimentation and iteration in the design process. Insight is essential at an early stage of a project, but also necessary in the other phases. In the early phases, insight helps shed light on the current situation, identify needs, serve as a basis for formulating a problem statement and delineate the project. In subsequent phases, new insight is needed to solve the task. There is a variety of different research processes and methods, both simple and more advanced. Some provide data in the form of numbers and statistics, while others provide information through words and images.

Insight, also called research, helps gain deeper understanding and knowledge, and discover connections not seen before. The concept of insight can be applied to the entire scope of a project, from simple gathering of information to scientific research, depending on what insight is aimed at and what methods and processes are used (2.6 Research). We often associate insight with information and knowledge that we can acquire, convey or verbally share. Insight can also, and perhaps to a greater extent, be something unspoken or implied, known as 'tacit knowledge', a term taken from the philosopher Michael Polanyi (1966/2009). In such cases, we are talking about experience-based knowledge and know-how, which are often not immediately possible to convey to another person using words, but which can be explained or demonstrated, as when learning how to ride a bicycle or how to swim. Such knowledge transfer often occurs in traditional crafts, where knowledge is transferred by showing something to a student or apprentice, or by instructing them in something. Traditionally, part of this craft dimension is also included in the field of design, where much of the knowledge has more often been acquired by doing and by learning from experienced practitioners, than from reading a book. Common sense is also a form of insight that is often naturally present. According to Edmund Husserl (1986), 'common sense' refers to obvious things or central features in our lives about which we possess knowledge regardless of our religion and cultures. 'For example, if you see something as a table, you will expect it to appear to you in certain ways if you go around and observe it' (Husserl, 1986, Beyer, 2020).

Tips for the company
**Insight is important to get the project off to a good start. Through insight, you as a client will experience many aha-moments and will learn more about your own company, employees, competitors, customers, etc. It allows for greater understanding and awareness, and is important for developing goals and strategies. Insight can also lead to new opportunities, which may contribute to development and innovation (2.6 Research, 2.7 Analyses).**

#### How do we gain insight?

There are different ways to gain insight. The use of algorithms,[1] big data technology[2] and data analytics[3] have to a great extent revolutionised the way we can obtain and extract data. Traditional methods for research, which we will mainly talk about here, are still relevant to know and use and in some cases indispensable. They also serve as a basis for understanding the principles of data collection and information gathering. A combination of approaches can often be beneficial. One does not have to know all about every method for insight, but it can be helpful to know what they can be used for. However, there are a number of methods that one must really be familiar with. A design process can in itself be an insight process by virtue of the knowledge acquired through designing. One of the elements that design and the field of design, through strategic design and design thinking, have brought to marketing and business development is more qualitative insight. One gains cognitive, emotional and empathetic understanding of user needs and user-experiences, which is necessary for developing attractive and user-friendly products and services. Then, there is a whole bunch of methods that have been used for a hundred years to gain quantitative knowledge, and it is generally such methods that business consultants and researchers come up with. Quantitative research tends to confirm how things are and not why this is so, something achieved to a greater extent through qualitative research, which is more often used in design projects. In a design approach, one is not primarily concerned about verifying whether what one thinks is right, but one is more interested in insight in order to understand user needs

1 Generally, an algorithm is a series of instructions telling a computer how to transform a set of facts about the world into useful information. The facts are data, and the useful information is knowledge for people, instructions for machines or input for yet another algorithm (Denny, 2020).

2 Big data are extremely large data sets that may be analysed computationally to reveal patterns, trends, and associations, especially relating to human behaviour and interactions (Big Data, n.d.).

3 Data analytics refers to the process of examining datasets to draw conclusions about the information they contain. Data analytic techniques enable you to take raw data and uncover patterns to extract valuable insights from it (Lotame, 2019).

4 Postma et al., 2012. Challenges of Doing Empathic Design: Experiences from Industry. International Journal of Design 6 (1), p.59–70.

5 Market trends are changes in the market where the company operates that might affect the business, such as groundbreaking changes in technology, consumer preferences, industry-specific new regulations, etc. One generally talks about short-, intermediate- and long-term trends. (DJ Team, 2020).

1 Initiation
2 Insight
3 Strategy
4 Design
5 Production
6 Management

**Insight in all phases**

**Phase 1. Initiation:** Initial searches and studies in order to obtain information about the company, the product or service, the target group, the market and the competitors, problem areas and needs, etc. This insight is used in the initial sales meeting.
**Phase 2. Insight:** Studies, research and analysis in order to collect and process data about the company, the product or service, the target group, the market and the competitors, problem areas and needs, etc. The data is used to conduct a SWOT-analysis, as well as to decide the problem statement.
**Phase 3. Strategy:** Surveys such as reputation research, customer satisfaction research, internal analysis, etc. is conducted in order to facilitate strategy development.
**Phase 4. Design:** Design research, design methodology, experimentation, prototyping, user testing, focus groups, material studies, colour analysis, etc. is used in order to create solutions.
**Phase 5. Production:** Study of production techniques and publishing platforms for the production or programming of the solution, as well as final prototyping, testing, colour management, etc.
**Phase 6. Management:** Market surveys, opinion polls, etc. in order to measure and evaluate results.

and market demand or market challenges. In the area of service design, work is being done methodically to find user needs. Those who are really good at it are very clear that the design method and qualitative insight are about understanding the person or understanding the world from this person's perspective and standpoint (Postma et al., 2012).[4] And then both the cultural and empathetic dimensions are important to uncover and learn more about. Having said that, it might also be necessary to conduct quantitative studies in design projects, using surveys to gain statistic data, such as in connection with situational analyses. As far as any innovation is concerned, one has to know the current situation before one can start changing it. Knowledge of the future may also prove useful in foreseeing new technologies, materials and production methods, as well as market trends.[5] In the following paragraphs, we will have a look at both qualitative and quantitative methods (2.4 Method selection). Traditional research processes and methods derived from social science methodology are included in order to illustrate basic theories and principles (Figure 2.1 Data collection, 2.5 Research process, 2.6 Research methods). A number of methods in the field of design research, that can be used more intuitively and flexibly during the design project, are also presented (Figure 2.2 Design research, 4.3 Design methodology). How can we know what is necessary to know? All projects are different, and it is impossible to give a one-size-fits-all answer. Insight is simply about asking, digging, observing, doing and testing, and through a methodical approach, getting the work done systematically and purposefully. Asking the right questions requires some insight per se. The more insight there is, the easier it is to know what one should study further. A situational study will always be a good start (2.2 Situational study).

Research means
**To do/conduct/undertake research into/on something/somebody. 'A careful study of a subject, especially in order to discover new facts or information about it' (Research, n.d.).**

Methods of insight vary from simple intuitive to more advanced analytical ones. Some require more time and resources, others less, all depending on how much time goes into preparation, implementation and follow-up. Some insight can be gained by studying existing data online, while other forms require research. The time and effort put into studies and surveys must be in proportion to the project's size, time and budget. The least resource-intensive forms of information gathering are meetings, workshops and small-scale studies, utilising existing research and knowledge. Interviews, observations and field studies can be more time-consuming, while surveys can be effective but also costly, and might result in large volumes of information whose use should be carefully thought through.

Fig. 2.1 The figure shows a general data collection process in four steps. This is not necessarily a linear process. One may need to go back and forth between the steps. Information gathering and research follow the same process, but research involves a more thorough approach through method selection, data collection, analysis and interpretation as shown in step 3. Based on Jacobsen (2005).

Tips for the designer
It is easy to be fixated on certain methods of insight. Everyone has their favorite methods, for example user studies. When time and budget are tight you can apply the survey principles in a simpler way. You could just sit on the side of the road and observe people and their cars and take notes; you could call up the people that you know and try to get some insight, instead of setting up an elaborate user study. You could spend your time reading articles and books, and you could synthesise your answers from a lot of research that is already out there. (Baytas, 2021)

### When do we need insight?

The work on gaining insight already starts with the sales pitch process when the designer competes for the job, and it continues throughout the entire design project. The first thing the designer does is study and analyse the task in order to try to understand it and its purpose, the problem it should solve or the need it should meet. At the same time, it is necessary to find out more about the company. What are they doing, what is their standing, what challenges and needs do they have, and what opportunities and success criteria are there? How does the user perceive the products or services of the company in terms of usefulness, functionality and experience? What works and what does not work? Are they up-to-date, user-friendly and attractive? What trends and tendencies are typical of the time? How is the company's competitive situation, brand awareness and reputation in the market? What are the driving forces of the target group, their latent needs of which they are not necessarily aware of or which they do not necessarily express? What exactly are we offering them? What role can we play in their life? All this insight should help identify existing problems and challenges in order to formulate the problem statement (2.3 Problem statement) well and narrow down the task to be solved. One should strive to acquire insight throughout the entire design process. This is done by doing research and user tests, by studying sources and literature, by searching for and experimenting with materials, techniques and tools, by designing and learning what works and what does not work, and so on.

### Data collection

Data collection is a term widely used for acquiring insight. As a starting point, we can distinguish between two main groups of data collection; information gathering and research. In addition, there is a third main insight group, and that is one's own knowledge.

- Information gathering may take place, for example, through search and document study of existing information or of research materials.
- Research or methodological approach similar to that used in scientific research is used when it is necessary to do research, such as surveys, interviews and observations.
- One's own knowledge is always close at hand. The projects which do not require gathering brand new knowledge, such as small simple design projects, might be more a matter of systematising the knowledge one already has and bringing it into a more project-related context.

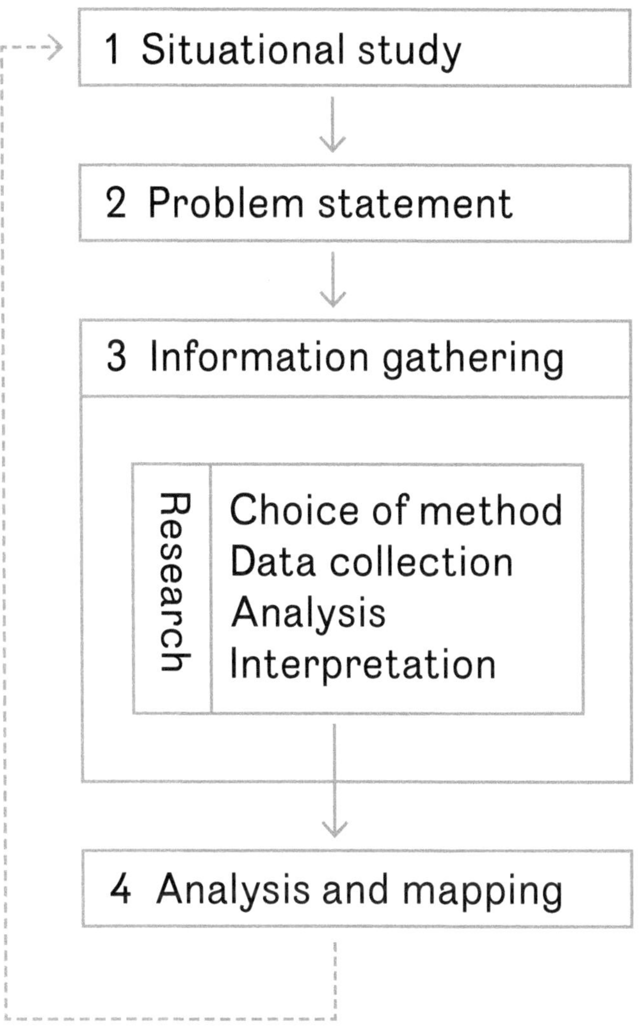


Fig. 2.1 Data collection

Explanation of Figure 2.1. What distinguishes the two forms of data collection, information gathering and research, is evident from step 3 of the process:

**1) Situational study**: The situation is determined by the assignment. The situational study clarifies current problem areas and provides a foundation for formulating the problem statement (2.2 Situational study).

**2) Problem statement**: The problem is determined by the assignment. The problem statement is what we seek to find answers to and what we use as delivery basis (2.3 Problem statement).

**3) Information gathering or research**: After steps 1 and 2, the question is: What kind of knowledge do we need in order to be able to solve the problem? If one sees a need to acquire more knowledge than what is already available, then there will be a need for information gathering or research. If research for a certain assignment is necessary, it will consist

> Research with big R vs. little r
> **Big R meaning work directed towards the innovation, and improvement of products or processes. Little r meaning the act of searching for or after a specified thing or person (Frayling, 1967).**

of several steps. The choice of method depends on the kind of knowledge one wishes to acquire, whether it is general knowledge or more situation-specific knowledge. This will in many ways determine whether qualitative or quantitative research is to be conducted. Then comes data collection, which is to conduct the research itself, the interviews, the observations, etc. Analysis and interpretation are necessary for assessing the relevance and validity of the findings and whether sufficient data have been generated. This research process, taken in isolation, is shown in Figure 2.1 and further explained in 2.5 Research process. See also 2.6.7 Scientific research.
**4) Analysis and mapping:** Summary and use of new knowledge. Once one has gathered the knowledge one needs, it forms the groundwork for a more situation-specific analysis, where the knowledge is used in the context of the assignment itself. An example of this could be a SWOT analysis, which assumes that data have been collected about the internal and external factors affecting the company and provides basis for analysing the situation (2.7.10 SWOT analysis).

The most relevant method of data collection depends on the nature, time and budget of the assignment. In larger design companies, gaining insight will often be distinguished as a specialised task. For example, the creative manager has direct contact with the client, while other design company employees or external consultants are engaged in information gathering or research, as stated in step 3. The product they deliver will be the research report, including results from research they have conducted, which they pass on to the creative managers in the design company. The creative managers will use results from this research report further in the context of the assignment. In small companies, designers will do all this on their own and choose research methods that are tailored to time and resources. Regardless of time and resources, it is an advantage that research results provide the most credible and valid data possible. This is important in strategic development of design, which should lead to targeted solutions for the company. Thus the research process and several of the research methods we discuss are explained using social sciences methods[6] (2.6.7 Scientific Research).

### Research through design

Research through design is an approach to data collection which to a great extent deals with gaining insight into the design process using design methodology. In a design-related context, acquiring knowledge through design is often just as important, and in some contexts crucial, to solving the problem statement. Research through design can be advantageously combined with more traditional research methods for data collection as presented in Figure 2.2. Research through design is one of three paradigms in the field of design research[7] namely research for design, research into design and research through design (Frayling 1993/Read 1974).[8]

- '*Research into design*' is research aimed at drawing valid conclusions about design practice, processes or methods from a theoretical and academically point of view.
- '*Research for design*' is data collection as explained in the previous chapter, the type of knowledge and analysis gathered for the purpose of designing a product or service with purpose.

Fig. 2.2 **Research through Design scheme (adapted from Findeli, 2010). The design question is a derivative of the research question (2.4.4 Research question). The design answer is then a partial answer to the research question (Findeli, 2010), derived from Eggik, 2019).**

6 Social science is a branch of science that deals with the institutions and functioning of human society and with the interpersonal relationships of individuals as members of society (Social science, n.d.). It is therefore the scientific method best suited in a design context. The Norwegian political and social scientist, Dag Einar Thorsen at the University of South-Eastern-Norway, has been an invaluable interlocutor and advisor throughout phase 2 to help explain the use of social science methods in a design process.

7 Design research is a systematic research method for acquiring knowledge related to general human ecology, which is concerned with the relationships humans have with each other, the nature and the surroundings, considered from a designerly way of thinking, i.e. a project-oriented perspective (Findeli, 2010, p. 294).

1 Initiation
2 Insight
3 Strategy
4 Design
5 Production
6 Management

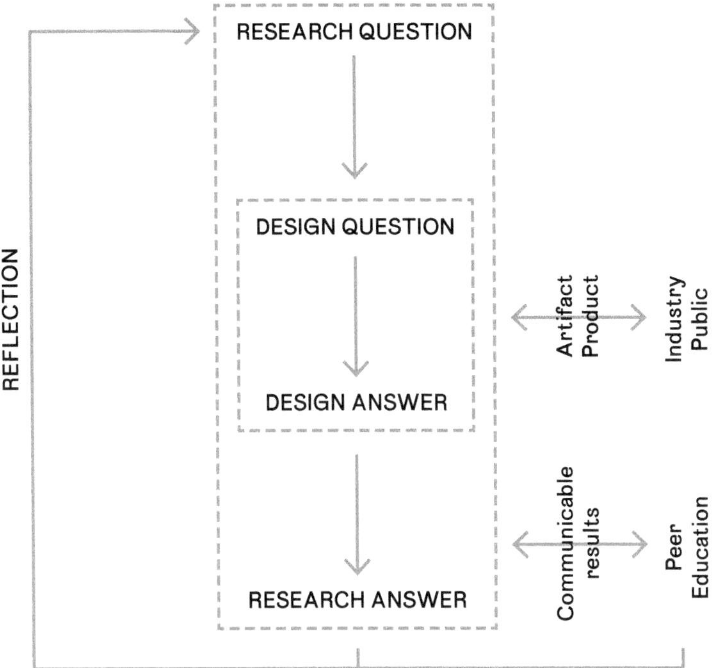


Fig. 2.2 Design research

- '*Research through design*' is the insight acquired through the process of designing, which Frayling describes as a category 'less straight forward, but still identifiable and visible'.

For *research through design* to have a research relevance it should include the use of design methodology such as iteration and exploration, as well as reflection and documentation of the process and findings, and thoughts on how the knowledge gained might fit into a project-related context. According to Frayling: 'materials research, development work and action research where a research diary tells, in a step-by-step way, of a practical experiment in the studios, and the resulting report aims to contextualise it. Both the diary and the report are there to communicate the results, which is what separates research from the gathering of reference materials' (Frayling, 1993). This way of doing design in practice can be a way of doing design research, see also Figure 2.18 Design research process. 'Research through design is the type of design research that differs the most from research in behavioural and natural sciences. In this type of research, the act of designing itself is the source of new knowledge' (Eggink, 2019).

Explanation of Figure 2.2: The figure shows how design practice, embedded in an academic context, is related to design research in 'research through design'. Research through design can thus be described as design activity that operates as research (Faste & Faste, 2012): a general research question is answered with a design project, which in turn can form a partial answer that reflects back on the research question (Findeli, 2010/ Dijk and Eggink 2019) (2.4.4 Research question, 2.6.9 Design research, 2.6.8 Artistic research, 4.3 Design methodology).

8 The categorisation is explained in different ways. This is based on Christopher Frayling (1993, p. 5), who derived it from Herbert Read (1944/1974). Originally the categories were described by Frayling as: Research into art and design, research through art and design and research for art and design. Frayling has been widely discussed, criticised and referenced by designers and academics since he wrote his paper 'Research in Art and Design' in 1993. Some of these were Nigel Cross (1999), Ken Friedman (2008), Fällman (2008), Frankel & Racine (2010), Wolfgang Jonas (2010), Faste & Faste (2012) and others who were engaged in the debate on Design research, as well as Henk Borgdorf (2012) among others who were active in the adjacent debate on artistic research. Frayling is still frequently referred to in recent academic and more popular online articles on design research, such as: 'The Three Faces of Design Research' by Mehmet Aydın Baytaş (2021). (2.6.9 Design research)

For the designer, understanding how a business works is a good starting point for a fruitful dialogue with the client.

A business is defined as an organisation or enterprising entity engaged in commercial, industrial, or professional activities (Hayes, 2021). Businesses vary in terms of size, branch, culture and the products and services they offer. Many designers run their own business and sell their services to other companies. In this book we talk about the designer's client as 'the company'.[9] One might define a company as 'related to or organised as a unified group of individuals. The term "company" covers organisations as a whole and also include businesses, schools, political entities, non-profit organisations, religious groups, sports clubs – any group of people who aim to participate in an activity that makes sense' (Brønn & Ihlen 2009: 35). In general, private and public companies are regarded as two main categories. We also distinguish between commercial, non-commercial and non-profit companies.[10] A private company is a business operation, most often run commercially by selling goods or services in the market in order to create value and achieve profitability. What characterises a commercial company is that it uses available resources, which it transforms into products, services and experiences that consumers or customers want[11] or looks for demands in the market and provides the resources necessary to develop products or services that meet these, see Figure 2.3.

Fig. 2.3 The figure shows one way to describe a company, by looking at resources that go into the company and what comes out in terms of products/services. The starting point is resources the company has or procures in order to develop products/services that the market needs (Lorentzen & Lund 1998).

All companies are run with the aim of creating some form of value creation.

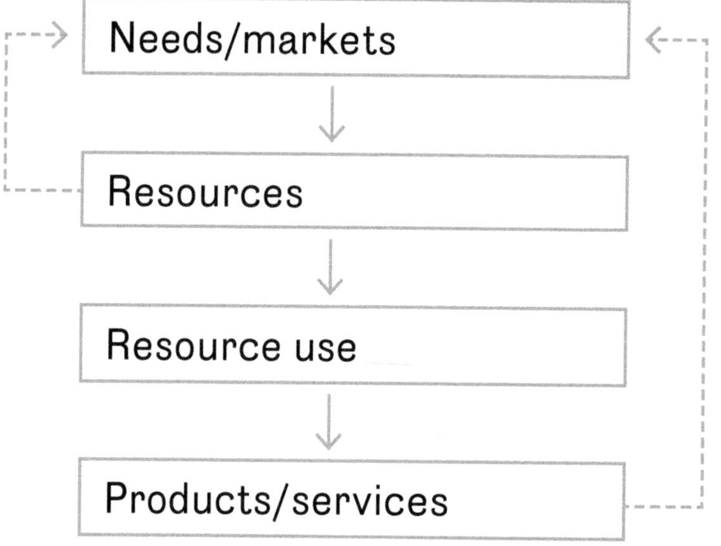

Fig. 2.3 The company

The resources of the company are a combination of a variety of factors such as management, employees, expertise, culture, technology, innovation, materials, raw materials, capacity, capabilities, capital, assets, portfolio, etc. Public or publicly owned companies are often non-commercial and financed through taxes, fees, charges or charity, but may also be operated commercially. Many of the same principles that apply to commercial companies, also apply to non-profit companies.

9 Company, enterprise or corporation refer to an organisation that produces and sells products or services. Companies or corporations are considered to be juridical persons in many countries, meaning that the business can own property, take on debt, and be sued in court (Hayes, 2021). The difference between company and corporation is that a company is a form of business that is suitable for small businesses and entities; whereas, corporation means a form of business that is suitable for bigger businesses and entities.
10 NGOs are non-profit organisations that operate independently of any government, typically one whose purpose is to address a social or political issue (NGO, n.d.).
11 Lorentzen and Lund (1998).
12 For example, more user-friendly and sustainable.

### 2.1.1 Value creation

1 Initiation
2 Insight
3 Strategy
4 Design
5 Production
6 Management

2.1 Understanding the company
2.2 Situational study
2.3 Problem statement
2.4 Method selection
2.5 Research process
2.6 Research
2.7 Analyses
2.8 Mapping
2.9 Testing and measuring

2.1.1 Value creation
2.1.2 Decision making
2.1.3 Organisational culture
2.1.4 Organisational development
2.1.5 The company's universe

All companies are run with some sort of value creation as a goal. For example, for non-profit companies, there may be values that help improve human and environmental conditions. For commercial companies, it can also be a driving force, but in general, value creation will essentially revolve around money. Capital is necessary to make the wheels turn in a company. Value creation is then created by transforming resources into products that can directly or indirectly meet needs, and that yield earnings and lead to profitability. The value of a product or service depends on the benefit it brings to the customer or user, and how much they are willing to pay. The ability of a company to create value can be used as a basis for its strategic choices and how it wishes to compete in the market. In order to create greater value than its competitors, a company must perform the same activities as its competitors, but better,[12] and more efficiently, or activities other than the competitors (Lien et al. 2016).

Design as a method can contribute to increasing the value creation and competitive power. According to studies conducted by the Danish Design Centre, companies that work systematically with design have higher earnings and greater exports than companies that do not use design (Danish Design Centre, 2018). The economic effects are greatest in companies where design is embedded in the company's business activities and where companies view design as a process or strategy (Grimsgaard & Farbrot 2020). This is also stated in 'The business value of design' report by McKinsey (2018). Businesses that score high on the design index[13] and use design strategically achieve significantly better financial results than competitors with a lower ranking on the design index (Sheppard et al. 2018). See also 4.3 Design methodology, 4.3.4 Innovation, 6.4 Design effect, 6.4.8 How to measure the design effect?

Design is a unique and powerful tool. A design approach can generally add greater awareness both when developing and marketing products and services. Using strategic problem solving in the processes, will help to carefully plan how to satisfy economic, technological and human needs, as well as to minimise the environmental footprint. This way, design can contribute to making products and services more useful, user-friendly, sustainable and thus more attractive for the user, who may be more willing to buy the product or service, and even pay more. For companies concerned with value creation, design is a key priority area, which requires decisions at both strategic, administrative and operational level. (4.4.2 Creative problem solving, 6.9 Sustainable management).

### 2.1.2 Decision making

Decision making is a series of decisions made by managers in the company to determine the planned path for business initiatives and initiate concrete actions. The decision areas can be divided into strategic, administrative and operational. They provide the framework for managing the various functional areas of the company. Functional areas can be such as production, technology, finance, accounting, human resources, organisation, design, marketing, research and development, see Figure 2.4. Each functional area uses strategic decisions as the basis, and then

13 McKinsey Design Index (MDI), based on a comprehensive study conducted in 2018 of 300 listed companies, rates companies by how strong they are at design and (for the first time) how that links up with the financial performance of each company:
*1) Analytical leadership*:
a) create a bold, user-centric strategy, b) embed design into senior management, c) employ design metrics.
*2) Cross-functional talent*:
a) nurture top design talent, b) convene cross-functional teams, c) invest in design tools and infrastructure.
*3) Continuous iterations*:
a) balance qualitative and quantitative user research, b) integrate user, business, competitor, and technological research, c) test, refine, repeat. Fast!
*4) User-experience*: a) start with the user, not the spec, b) design a seamless physical, service, and digital-user-experience, c) integrate with third-party products and services. (Source: McKinsey Value of Design survey of 300 global companies, July 2018, Sheppard et al., 2018).

Fig. 2.4 The figure shows a total management model for an industrial company. The example presents three decision areas that concern five functional areas. It provides fifteen different management areas. Row 1, strategic decisions, provides guidance for administrative and operational decisions (based on Lorentzen and Lund 1998).

| DECISION AREAS | FUNCTIONAL AREAS: Production/technology | Finance/accounting | Human resources/organisation | Design/marketing | Research/development |
|---|---|---|---|---|---|
| 1 Strategic decisions | | | | | |
| 2 Administrative decisions | | | | | |
| 3 Operational decisions | | | | | |

Fig. 2.4 Total management in a company

**The company's decision areas**

The decision areas of the company can be divided into three areas in order of priority based on Lorentzen and Lund (1998):

**1) Strategic decisions** to achieve competitiveness and value creation:

- What products or services should the company offer?
- Which markets should the products be offered to?
- How should the marketing be arranged?
- What resources should the company adopt?
- What should the company purchase and what should it refine?

**2) Administrative decisions on resource management:**

- How should resources be provided?
- How should resources be developed?
- How should resources be organised?

**3) Operational decisions** concerning implementation:

How to make the best use of available resources at all times in order to achieve the purpose of the activities?

**The company's functional areas**

The functional areas of the company vary from company to company. e.g., production/technology, finance/accounting, human resources/organisation, design/marketing, research/development.

14 'The companies in our sample that were most effective at decision making and execution generated average total shareholder returns nearly six percentage points higher than those of other firms' (Blenko et al., 2010).

15 Culture in this context can be explained as: 1) the customary beliefs, social forms, and material traits of a racial, religious, or social group. 2) the set of shared attitudes, values, goals, and practices that characterise an institution or organisation. 3) the set of values, conventions, or social practices associated with a particular field, activity, or societal characteristic. 4) the integrated pattern of human knowledge, belief, and behavior that depends upon the capacity for learning and transmitting knowledge to succeeding generations (Culture, n.d.).

16 An organisation is an organised group of people with a particular purpose, such as a business or government department (Organisation, n.d.).

17 'Organisational culture and corporate culture are usually used interchangeably. Both refer to the collective values, outlooks and approaches within an organization. Obviously, the term corporate culture focuses on for-profit corporations, while organizational culture extends to all forms of organizations including small business, privately held companies and nonprofit organizations' (Picincu 2018, bizfluent.com).

makes correct administrative and operational decisions (Lorentzen & Lund, 1998). The total management of a company is a combination of decision areas and functional areas. Research shows that decision effectiveness drives 95% of business performance[14] (Blenko et al., 2010).

### 2.1.3 Organisational culture

Organisational culture means the way people behave within the organisation, a collection of traits that make the company what it is. Culture[15] is the core of an organisation's DNA.[16] The organisational culture consists of shared beliefs and values that affect people's behaviours and actions and determines how the company's employees and management interact and handle external business operations. 'Corporate culture[17] is very often implied, not expressly defined, and develops organically over time from the cumulative traits of the people the company hires' (Tarver, 2021). Ideally the organisational culture is in line with the company's overall strategy and goal. Often it is established by leaders, and then communicated and reinforced through various efforts, ultimately shaping employee behaviours, perceptions and understanding on how to act on behalf of the company, as well as internally within the organisation. Idealistically a good organisational culture is best created through consistent and authentic behaviours, capturing culture and values that already exist in the company, and combining them with values top management believes the company should have (3.2.5 Core values). According to Alina Wheeler, 'long term success is directly influenced by the way employees share in their company's culture – its values, stories, symbols, and heroes. Building the company's values and brand assets from the inside out means inspiring employees to embrace the organisation's purpose' (Wheeler, 2018).

The effect of a consistent and strong culture which makes people happy at work can create increased job satisfaction and strengthen joint efforts to achieve the company's goals. This way the company's human resources[18] are used in a way that contributes to goal achievement and success for the company. 'The most successful brands have highly engaged employees who appear as their brand's biggest ambassadors' (Wheeler, 2018). A designers' role is important when understanding a brand. By using the designer as an interpreter for the brand you invite people from different departments and areas of responsibility to participate in creative workshops. In doing this the company will experience an engaging co-creation of core values and brand assets across organisational structure, thus strengthening the organisational culture and ensuring involvement towards common goals (3.3.1 Business goals). (3.2.5 Core values: Personality, corporate identity, value-driven culture).

### 2.1.4 Organisational development

Organisational development is the effort of aligning structural, cultural and strategic ambitions of work to respond to the needs of an ever-evolving business climate.[19] 'Organisational development is the practice of planned, systemic change in the beliefs, attitudes and values of employees for individual and company growth. The purpose of organisational


1 Initiation
2 Insight
3 Strategy
4 Design
5 Production
6 Management

2.1 Understanding the company
2.2 Situational study
2.3 Problem statement
2.4 Method selection
2.5 Research process
2.6 Research
2.7 Analyses
2.8 Mapping
2.9 Testing and measuring

2.1.1 Value creation
2.1.2 Decision making
2.1.3 Organisational culture
2.1.4 Organisational development
2.1.5 The company's universe


Diversity in decision making

'As many studies show, greater diversity brings greater collective wisdom and expertise, along with better performance. This is also true in decision making.' (De Smet et al., 2019)

Further reading

Decision making: The study 'Three keys to faster, better decisions' conducted by McKinsey, shows a strong correlation between quick decisions and good ones (De Smet et al., 2019).

18 Human resources (HR), is a term for 1) The personnel of a business or organisation, regarded as a significant asset in terms of skills and abilities. 2) The department of a business or organisation that deals with the hiring, administration, and training of staff (Human resources, n.d.).

19 The business climate is the economic and professional environment surrounding an industry, including governmental and political attitude, financial stability, etc (upcounsel.com).

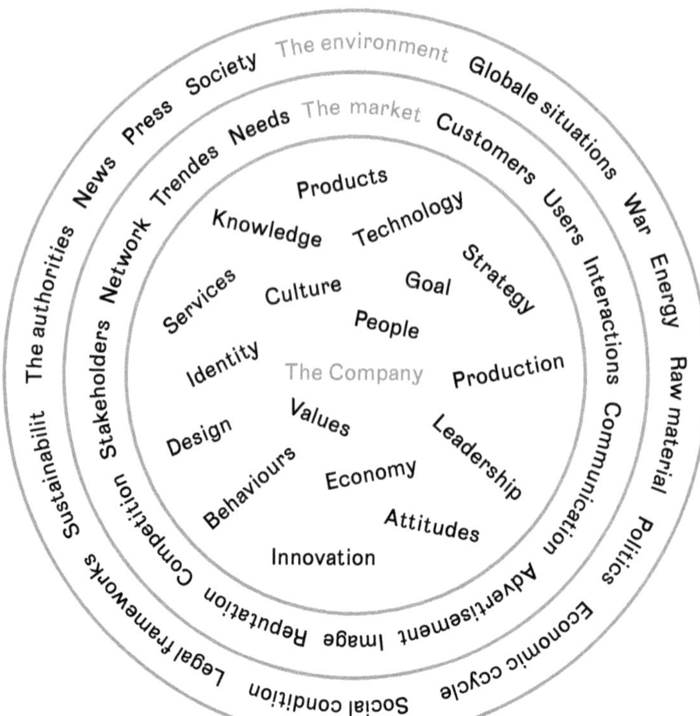


Fig. 2.5 The company's universe

Fig. 2.5 The figure shows which external and internal factors affect the company. © Grimsgaard, W. (2018)

Tips for the company
You have to know the current situation to be able to make a strategy to reach the goal.

Organisational development is about achieving higher efficiency and increased productivity by making better use of available resources.

development is to enable an organisation to better respond and adapt to industry/market changes and technological advances' (Sutherland, 2019), and transferring knowledge and skills to the organisation to improve their capacity for solving problems and managing future change. Organisational development involves a comprehensive process of organisational change through structuring, training and optimisation of work tasks. Professional qualifications in the field of organisational development, including research, theory, and practice are required. Internal analysis such as resource analysis, activity analysis and value chain analysis can serve as a good starting point (2.7.1 Situational analysis). The designer can contribute to the organisational development by introducing the use of design methodology, such as design thinking, in the innovation and development processes (4.3 Design methodology, 4.3.11 Design thinking).

## 2.1.5 The company's universe

The company is affected by a number of internal and external factors that it has to deal with in order to operate, develop and sell its products and services. These factors are found in the external circumstances of the company, such as the global situation, war, politics and the environment, which affect economic cycles, the supply of raw materials and the society as a whole. Among the external factors are also authorities, the public, the press and public opinion which act in ways that can be both restrictive and stimulating. External factors closer to the daily business of the company is the market in which the company stakeholders are located, all those who in one way or another have a direct or indirect relationship or contact with the company. In the centre of all these factors is the company itself, with its resources, values and culture, which influence how the world sees the company, which in turn affects the business in the form of reputation, brand awareness, sales, etc. These can be defined as the company's internal factors, see Figure 2.5.

The designer's task will be to try to see the company from the outside as well as from the inside: from the outside and in, and from the inside and out. In this way, the designer can contribute to the company being able to develop useful and attractive products and services that the target audience and the users want, while also being able to live in harmony with its surroundings, as a responsible and useful value creator in a larger context, for the benefit of both the company and its external environment (2.1 Understanding the company, 2.2 Situational study, 2.7.9 PESTLE analysis, 2.7.10 SWOT analysis, 2.7.11 Gap analysis, 3.1.4 Strategic workshop).



## 2.2 Situational study

Situational study examines the current situation of a company, and its products or services. It can be used as basis for formulating a problem statement and clarifying the task to be carried out in the design project. Situational studies also serve as a good starting point for developing goals and strategy.

Situational studies are carried out in the introductory stage of the project and are about describing the situation based on available information. This is information that employees and the management usually provide, which can be supplemented with information collected online, such as secondary data (previously performed surveys and the like) and by physical observations, simple studies and talking to people, etc. Whether it is a matter of a new logo, new website or a new product to be developed, a situational study will be a good starting point to identify the problem or the need, which the assignment is to help solve. A situational study is well suited for small and medium-sized projects with limited time and resources. A situational analysis may be more appropriate for larger projects. Such analysis requires new information through research, interviews and observations, the so-called primary data. This form of data collection requires a more methodological approach similar to what is used in research. The choice between situational study and situational analysis as method is determined by the amount of time and resources available for the project.

The situational study involves obtaining information about the background and history of the company, its products or services, target groups, organisation, economy and financial capability, competitive situation, etc. In addition, it is about studying their identity, products or services, strategy and goals, and clarifying visible needs or problems. The situational study is conducted through meetings, initial workshops, one-to-one conversations, internet searches and study of existing presentation materials, advertising, annual accounts, websites, social media presence and other things that may help clarify the situation.

Further reading
*The Global Business Environment: Towards Sustainability?* (2020) by Janet Morrison.

> Digital transformation
> 'Digitization and other trends are leading to a sharp increase in the pace of change. Businesses that master this handle emerging challenges better and create new value faster, and can leverage it to create business benefits and strengthen reputation and brand. Agile approach contributes to increased capacity for change.' (Sitre, 2022) (3.4.7 Agile strategy management).

A situational study will also provide good basis for assessing what one needs to know more about, and whether research and analyses should be conducted in order to obtain more information. The work carried out in a situational study can be extended with a situational analysis and swot analysis (2.7.1 Situational analysis).

Fig. 2.6 The figure illustrates the difference between identity and image. The organisational identity is how the company perceives itself. Image is how the outside world and the market perceives the company. Based on Figure 3.4 Corporate identity.

Tips for the designer
Your own knowledge and early ideas are part of the insight. Write down your own experiences, knowledge, thoughts, and ideas along the way. Make quick hand sketches if you will. Supplement with any other necessary information. Find photos of people, places, products, and other things that can visualise the insights you collect. Use moodboards and GIGA mapping. Make visual presentations. (2.8.2 Moodboard, 2.8.5 GIGA mapping).

Identity is who we are. Image is the perception others have of us.

## 2.2.1 Situational study process

What is today's situation/current situation of the company?
**Problems/challenges:** Challenges or problems the company faces, internally and externally?
**Background/history:** The company's development and history?
**Product/service:** The product or service, history, situation, relevance, recognition, position, brand assets, product environmental profile, etc.?
**Production/PD:** Product development (PD), product supply chain (from raw material to consumer, production process, material use, product value chain? Target group/segments: Who are they, where are they? Characteristics, wishes and needs? Social identity, affiliation, lifestyle?
**Market:** Segments, cycles and trends? Opportunities and threats?
**Competitors:** Who are they? Where are they? Product, position, trend?
**Organisation:** Organisational structure and culture, financial resources, ownership structure, management, decision making process, overall strategy and goal, corporate sustainability awareness and activities?
**Alliance partners:** Which ones? Where are they? Roles? Cooperation opportunities? Win-win potential?
**Report:** The study of existing data is compiled in a report with conclusions, summary and recommendations for further work. The situation description is an important tool in the further process of developing the problem statement, defining the task and preparing a plan.

## 2.2.2 PIPI workshop

In all contexts where the designer will work with a company, it is useful to clarify how the company sees itself, and especially in projects where a visual identity is to be developed. PIPI[20] are four simple primary questions that can help clarify how the company perceives itself. The questions may be included as part of a situational study to identify areas of concern and areas that should be studied further. This method is also well suited as introduction to a strategic workshop, or as basis for a simple strategic approach in projects with limited time and budget. Participants from the company can work on the questions in a joint brainstorming session or as individual tasks (1.4 Initial workshop):
P – Personality > Who are we?
I – Identity > Conscious of who we are?
P – Profile > Conscious of how we present ourselves?
I – Image > How do others see us? How are we perceived?

'P' stands for 'Personality', which can be largely unconscious. 'I' stands for 'Identity', the awareness of the company of who they are. 'P' stands for 'Profile', how the company presents itself to the outside world (consciously and unconsciously). 'I' stands for 'image', how the outside world perceives

20 The PIPI model was developed by the designer and professor Ken Friedman in collaboration with Anders Skoe and Frank Myrseth in the 90s.

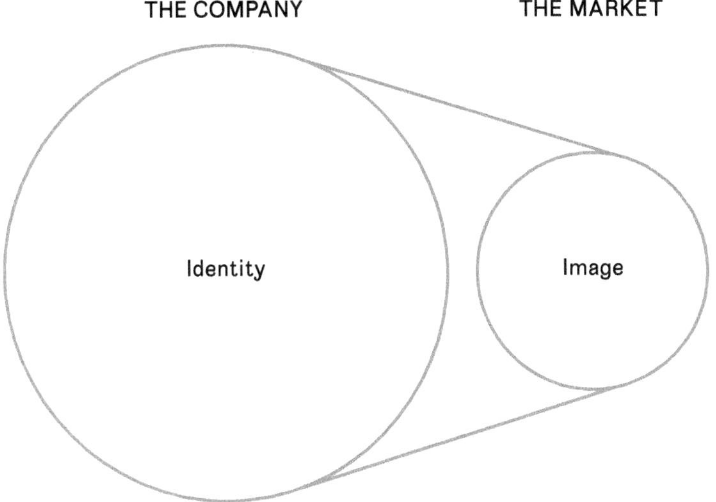


Fig. 2.6 How do others see us?

1 Initiation
2 Insight
3 Strategy
4 Design
5 Production
6 Management

2.1 Understanding the company
2.2 Situational study
2.3 Problem statement
2.4 Method selection
2.5 Research process
2.6 Research
2.7 Analyses
2.8 Mapping
2.9 Testing and measuring

2.2.1 Situational study process
2.2.2 PIPI workshop
2.2.3 Where are we – where will we?

the company. The first three questions (personality, identity and profile) are about how the company sees itself. The fourth question (image) urges the company to answer how they believe others see and perceive them.

How the company perceives itself is its organisational identity. How the company presents itself is its corporate identity (company identity). How others perceive the company is the 'image' people have of the company. Answers concerning how the company perceives itself (organisational identity) are best obtained by involving/asking the company's employees. A discrepancy between 'how' the organisation perceives itself and how it believes the outside world sees it, may have major consequences on how the members of the organisation act, and thus also on the implementation of changes (Colman, 2014, p. 98). Colman refers to research by Gioia and Thomas (1996), who found that image changes were the main driving force for changes in an organisational identity. This means that a company is willing to change in order to adjust its image so that it is perceived the way it wants it to be.

What the outside world thinks about the company is what we call 'reputation'. A company's reputation can be clarified to some extent through the use of qualitative or quantitative studies among the target audience and in the market. This way, it is possible to get a more accurate idea of how others actually perceive the company. If the answers to PIPI are ambiguous, it might be necessary to work strategically on how the company should present itself externally. Secondly, the question will be whether the company needs a redesign of its logo and visual identity, and clearer communication. A good start is to clarify problem areas and formulate a problem statement (2.3 Problem statement, 3.8.4 Desired reputation).

> Circular economy
> **Does the company aim for a circular economy, by designing and manufacturing products to be reusable, easier to repair, recycle, upcycle, or by reusing raw materials for new products?**

### 2.2.3 Where are we – where will we?

Clarifying the desired situation is just as important as clarifying the current situation. These are questions that can be included in a workshop as part of a situational study or as an introduction to a strategic workshop.

*The first questions asked are:*

- Who are we? Who do we think we are? How do others perceive us?[21] Does the company have a clear distinctive character and reputation?
- What do we do? Can the company describe in one sentence what they do?
- Where are we? Does the company have knowledge and an overview of the current situation?

*The next questions are about identifying the desired situation:*

- Who do we want to be? What do we want to do? Where do we want to go? How are we going to get there? These are strategic questions, which are about setting new goals and developing a plan to get there.

| SITUATION Current situation/ today's dituation | GOAL Desired situation/ future direction | STRATEGY A plan to achieve the desired situation |
|---|---|---|
| Who are we? | Who do we want to be? | How are we going to get there? Path selection? |
| What do we do? | What do we want to do? | |
| Where are we? | Where do we want to go? | |

Table 2.1 Situational study

Table 2.1 The matrix can be used as a tool in a strategic workshop to clarify the company's perception of their current situation, their desired situation and how to get there. The result can provide basis for defining goals and developing strategy.

Tips for the designer
'Designers who conduct research provide themselves several important advantages over those who don't. Not only are they apt to develop more insightful design solutions by aligning business goals and audience needs, they also provide their clients a competitive advantage. Lastly, research provides an imperative for moving forward. Research provides actionable information, business goals, audience need, competitive advantage, a rationale for design decisions, a basis for measurement' (Holston, 2011, p. 110).

Knowing the current situation, we have better foundation for setting real goals and developing solid strategies. The current situation is the starting line. We are here now, today. The desired situation is the goal itself. The path selection is the strategy. Such an approach assumes that the attention is also turned to the market in order to gain knowledge of and identify the opportunities and limitations that exist there. It provides a better starting point for determining whether one's own goals and ambitions are realistic, and for making the adjustments and adaptations necessary to succeed (2.7.1 Situational analysis, 2.7.10 SWOT analysis).

## 2.3 Problem statement

The problem statement is the starting point for defining the task and the guiding principles when choosing research and methods. It is developed based on the information provided during the initial workshop, in the situational study and through further research.

The problem statement is the focal point of a design project, the hub from which one works, what the project should be about, and which one should help to solve. It follows through all stages of the design

21 How others perceive us and what others think about us influence and shape our reputation.

project. The designer's first challenge in a design project is to listen to the obvious need and identify the problem behind it. What problems does the company have? What problem does the user have? What problem does the project have to solve? All planning and implementation of the design process depends on it, and the solution can often become apparent once the problem has been properly analysed and formulated. Design is largely problem-solving through mental effort, and not just graphic design, which non-designers often associate with the subject (Per Mollerup, 1998). Throughout the design process, the designer thinks back and forth between stages in order to explore, develop and make choices that lead to a solution to the task. A clearly expressed problem statement contributes to more targeted efforts and easier choice of work methodology. 'When we decide on a problem statement, we make an important choice: We define what to focus on' (Jacobsen, 2005). The problem statement however is never written in stone. It can be changed as you go. In some projects, the problem will be obvious and almost self-explanatory. In other projects, formulating it may be more challenging. Formulating a problem statement is a task per se, and can often continue throughout the entire project. However, it is an advantage to clarify and formulate a problem as early as possible in order to be able to define the task and get off to a good start. It is the problem statement we should use as a starting point, coordinate with along the way and answer to at the end (see 4.3 Design methodology). It is important to ensure that both the designer and the client have a common understanding of the problem to be solved, and that the client has approved the problem statement before the design project is started.

Often, what the client regards as a problem is not the actual problem. It might be just the tip of the iceberg. The designer's challenge is to study the causes and uncover the underlying problem. Once the actual problem has been identified, it should be used as a starting point for formulating the problem statement. Even after the problem statement has been formulated and the project is well underway, it may be necessary to adjust or redefine it, which in the worst-case scenario could involve taking a few steps back or starting all over again. However, it is better to adjust the problem statement along the way than to work with an unclear or incorrectly formulated problem statement, because it can push the project into a track that is completely wrong, leading to failure. At the same time, it is important to keep the momentum going so that the project does not stop (Larsen, 2007, p. 19). Sometimes, it might be necessary to develop several sub-problems. Then, it is a good idea to set priorities in order to make it clear what the primary problem statement is.

Developing a problem statement is a process that can be thorough, or more intuitive and simpler. In any case, the time spent should be proportionate to the size, complexity, timeframe and budget of the project. The work should be included in the price offer or in the project budget. The same applies to research and analyses that need to be carried out in advance, during the project and after its completion. It is the designer's task to inform the client about this since the client may not be aware of it (2.3.2 Problem statement process, 2.3.8 A good problem statement).



'Great research breeds great design. Design researchers carefully investigate human experience and behavior, dream up new ways to spark and distill insight, and inspire teams and clients to address people's needs through bold, optimistic design.'
– IDEO

## 2.3.1 Problem

In order to arrive at a problem statement, one should be clear about what a problem is. A problem is the distance between actual and desired condition, or a deviation from a norm or standard. The actual state is the perceived state, i.e. the current situation, while the desired state is the desired situation or goal. It is not possible to solve a problem without using this as a starting point. It is also important to consider the size of the problem. Is it a big problem or a small one? If you have trouble reaching a plane, the problem will be greater if the distance to the airport is long than if it is short. If a company aims to achieve a market share of 20% and its sales show 10%, this corresponds to an increase of 100% (double), meaning that the company faces a bigger problem than what would have faced had the sales been 18% (Sander, 2019) (2.7.11 Gap analysis).

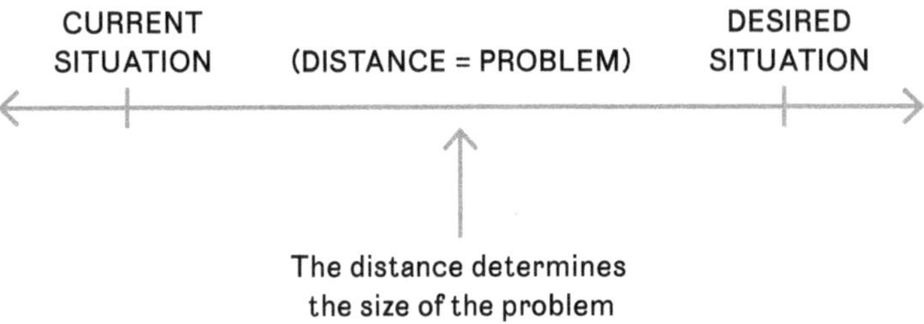


Fig. 2.7 The problem and goal

**Symptom vs. problem:** In order to be able to define the problem, it is necessary to know the difference between a problem and a symptom. The problem is the cause, while the symptom is the effect. The symptom is the external manifestation of a problem. It is easy to make a mistake. In many design projects; the problem may seem obvious, but the clear or obvious problem may actually turn out to be a symptom. Therefore, it is necessary to study and analyse the obvious problem. Let us look at an example. A company hires a designer to redesign its logo. The designer asks why they want a new logo. The answer is that they want to appear trendier. The pronounced problem is that the logo is outdated and out of style. In reality, this is a symptom. The designer's task is to find the cause of the symptom. It turns out that the problem goes deeper. After further research, it emerges that sales are declining, and that the company's strategy has not been updated for several years. The designer and the company sit down and review the problems in order to find the actual problem, the root cause itself, and decide how the designer can help solve it.

When the designer points out the client's problems it can be a harsh experience for the client, but through open communication about it during workshops or conversations, it is possible to achieve good dialogue, which can strengthen the collaboration and the outcome of the design project. Lack of understanding of the problem carries a risk of addressing only the symptom and not the problem. In the context of the example above, it may mean that the designer starts creating a new company logo without asking questions. Then, there is a risk that the result might be 'same shit, new wrapping', as the popular saying goes. Worse still, one might start solving the wrong problem. This will be a poor investment of resources for all parties.

Fig. 2.7 The figure shows that the size of the problem equals the distance (gap) between the current and the desired situation, between reality

Table 2.2 The table shows step 1. An easy way to find a problem statement. For small projects, this process may be sufficient.

Tips for the designer

It is easy to lose sight of design and the problem to solve, when you turn your focus to research. It is important to be oriented to insights that would help improve the service or product design. When you turn your attention to be very formal about your research, you turn your attention away from design. Good research for design is efficient; it gives you answers about what you should design. So, an error is to overinvest your time to very careful research at the expense of time doing the actual design. If you are doing research for design, it must be design happening in the end, which you are doing the research for. If no one is designing anything based on your research there is no point in it (Baytas, 2021).

## 2.3.2 Problem statement process

Insight is important both to arrive at a problem statement and to solve it. Both the formulation of the problem statement and the outcome of the project depend to a large extent on the kind of information which has been collected, how it has been understood and interpreted, and what reflections the designer has had. Using research methods that yield credible data will make the problem statement more real, while at the same time bringing more seriousness and professionalism into the project. Therefore, we use the social science method as a basis for formulating problem statements and research processes. We will look at the development of a problem statement in two steps. Step 1 is simple. Step 2 builds on step 1 and is more advanced.

### Step 1: Making a problem statement

Step 1 explains how to easily arrive at a problem statement formulation by defining the problem, analysing it, and formulating a problem statement. For most design tasks this will be sufficient. If studies, especially quantitative studies, are necessary, it may be a good idea to delimit the problem statement, see step 2, Table 2.3.

<table>
<tr><th colspan="3">STEP 1</th></tr>
<tr><td colspan="2">Problem definition</td><td>Problem statement</td></tr>
<tr><td>Problem</td><td>Need / Analysis</td><td rowspan="2">Formulation</td></tr>
<tr><td>Knowledge</td><td>Conclusion</td></tr>
</table>

Table 2.2 Step 1

**Defining the problem**

- Problem: Clarify the obvious or pronounced problem or symptom.
- Need: Identify needs and opportunities for change.
- Knowledge: Obtain information and knowledge to elucidate the problem.
- Analysis: Study the problem in order to identify its cause.
- Conclusion: The root cause (the underlying cause) has now been clarified, and the real problem has been identified.

**Problem statement formulation**

- Formulation: After the problem has been clarified, the problem statement can be formulated. It can be formulated as a question, a hypothesis, or a theme (2.3.5 Problem statement delimitation).

## 2.3.3 Problem definition

The problem can be defined in a 5-step process:
**Problem:** The first thing that needs to be done is to clarify the obvious or pronounced problem or symptom. Workshop with the client is a good method. Generally, more problems and questions arise, and some choices must be made by picking what is most important and what needs to be studied further.



It is necessary to know the difference between a problem and a symptom. The problem is the cause, while the symptom is the effect. It is the cause we want to solve.

**Need:** Once the problem has been clarified, it must be determined whether or not the problem triggers a need for change, whether it is desirable or necessary to make a change, and not least whether it is possible to do so. This can be assessed in relation to finances, time, resources, considering employees and the company's long-term strategy and aim.
**Knowledge:** In order to assess the need for change, knowledge of the company's situation is required. It might be necessary to do research such as interviews, observations, and surveys.
**Analysis:** Once sufficient knowledge of the situation has been acquired, it is time to analyse the problem by studying it and identifying the cause.
**Conclusion:** The original problem has now been analysed and the actual problem has been uncovered. This problem is the starting point for formulating the problem statement.

Table 2.3 The table shows steps 1 and 2. Step 1 is presented in Table 2.2. Step 2 builds on step 1 and involves defining the limits of the problem statement further and analyze it. Defining the limits of a problem statement provides a better starting point for research.

Tips for the designer
In smaller design projects, STEP 1 may be sufficient. If you feel that the problem statement is too general or unclear, it may be useful to read STEP 2 to find out how you can deliminate and analyse it, so that it becomes more useful as a starting point for doing research and solving the task.

### 2.3.4 Problem statement formulation

Based on the knowledge that has emerged, efforts to formulate the problem statement may begin. It involves describing or explaining the problem or phenomenon, which is to be examined or solved. Problem statement formulation is a combination of three factors:
- knowledge of the problem or phenomenon
- a creative formulation that is exciting and inspiring to work with
- a clearly expressed delimitation.

In addition, it should be possible to study a problem statement empirically (experience-based). In a design project, it is most common to formulate the problem as a question. Other options are to formulate it as a hypothesis or a topic.

The problem statement is 'the common thread' in the design project

**Question:** A question requires an answer. Questions are the most common starting point for empirical (experience-based) research, the aim of which is to elucidate or get answers to a problem or phenomenon. This approach provides imprecise delimitation as to what the problem statement should include or not include. However, it does have an implicit (indirect) delimitation, i.e. it is assumed that it is an implied delimitation, that is understood without being said. *Example 1:* How to increase the sales of the product X by redesigning the label? *Example 2:* How to increase the sales of X by adjusting the brand identity to approach a new potential target group? *Example 3:* A combination of 1 and 2.
**Hypothesis:** A hypothesis is a guess, assumption or explanation which seems reasonable based on the available knowledge and which one tries to either refute or confirm. Sometimes hypothesis means only a temporary and until now unsubstantiated explanation of known and observed but otherwise unexplained phenomena[22] (Tranøy, n.d.). The problem statement can be formulated as a hypothesis when there is a conviction or claim that one wishes to study further (2.6.7 Scientific research; Hypothesis). *Example:* There is a connection between a modern lifestyle and reduced use of the product X.
**Topic:** Most problem statements are usually defined within a topic, which is a good starting point for further defining the delimitation of research and work processes. In some cases, the problem statement is based on one topic alone, which is not recommended because such problems may become too open and imprecise. *Example:* Redesign of packaging.

22 A phenomenon is something (such as an interesting fact or event) that can be observed and studied and that typically is unusual or difficult to understand or explain fully (Phenomenon, n.d.).
23 'A research question is a question that provides an explicit statement of what it is the researcher wants to know about' (Bryman, 2008).

## Step 2: Delimitation of problem statement

Step 2 builds on step 1 and explains how the problem statement can be delimitated and analysed to provide a better starting point for conducting research, such as observations, interviews or surveys. This is a thorough process, which can be time-consuming, and is therefore best suited for larger complex projects and when quantitative studies are to be conducted, such as shown in Table 2.4 (2.3.6 Problem statement analysis).


1 Initiation
2 Insight
3 Strategy
4 Design
5 Production
6 Management

2.1 Understanding the company
2.2 Situational study
2.3 Problem statement
2.4 Method selection
2.5 Research process
2.6 Research
2.7 Analyses
2.8 Mapping
2.9 Testing and measuring

2.3.1 Problem
2.3.2 Problem statement process
2.3.3 Problem definition
2.3.4 Problem statement formulation
2.3.5 Problem statement delimitation
2.3.6 Problem statement analysis
2.3.7 Problem statement requirements
2.3.8 A good problem statement
2.3.9 Wicked problems

- Step 2: Delimitation of problem statement


| STEP 1 | | STEP 2 | |
|---|---|---|---|
| Problem definition | Problem statement | Delimitation | Analysis |
| | | Requirements | |

Table 2.3 Steps 1 and 2

After the problem statement has been formulated in step 1, it is assessed whether the focus of the task and research to be conducted is clear enough. This is done by delimitating, analysing and critically assessing the problem statement.

**Delimitation:** Define the delimitation of the problem statement to ensure that it is not too general and that it provides a clear basis for research and choice of work process. This is explained in chapter 2.3.5 Problem statement delimitation.

**Analysis:** Analyse the problem statement in order to determine which task is to be solved and what research is needed. This is explained in chapter 2.3.6 Problem statement analysis.

**Requirement:** Make a critical assessment of the problem statement. Assess how sensible it is and how suitable it is to work with. This is explained in chapter 2.3.7 Problem statement requirements. See also chapters 2.5 Research process and 2.4 Method selection.

### 2.3.5 Problem statement delimitation

Problem delimitation means that the problem is analysed and processed so that it is clearer and more precise (unambiguous). A delimited problem is generally easier to work with and saves more time compared to one that is broad and less specific. This is particularly important when planning and doing research. Whether the problem is too open or well-defined, a good approach to consider is to research the problem statement through one or more research questions[23] (2.4.4 Research question) or subordinate problem statements.

- *Implicit or explicit*: An implicit (indirect) delimitation of a problem statement means assuming that the meaning is implied, or that it is understood even if it is not expressed. This gives a broad, open and unclear problem statement, which may require more demanding than if the problem stement is more specific. An explicit (direct) delimitation of a problem statement, means that it has to be more directly, clearly and specifically worded. Ideally, a problem should be based on explicit delimitation, stating what is included, what has been discarded and why.

According to Jacobsen (2005), a problem statement is always based on a question, something we want to find answers to. It is also used as a starting point for a hypothesis or topic. Through the question, we define what we want to investigate, which is the topic. Furthermore, the content of the problem statement can be further delimited by sorting the contents of the four key parts: units, variables, values and context.

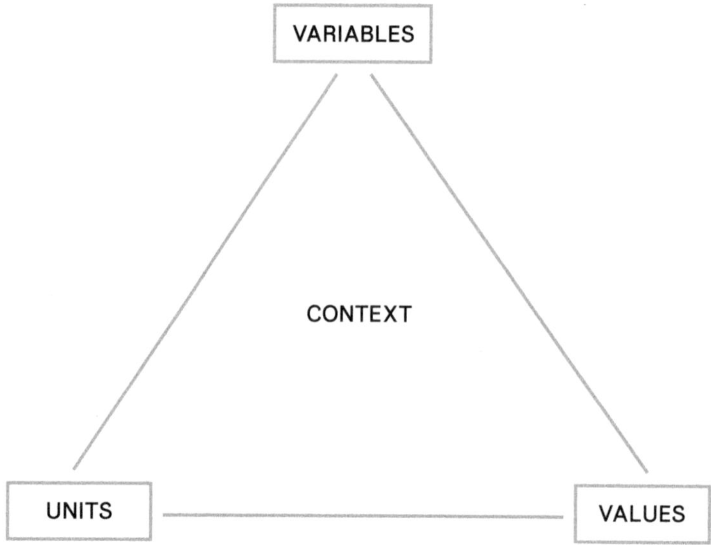

Fig. 2.8 Problem statement delimitation

- *What and who will be studied?* One way to define a problem statement is to decide which persons or groups (units) we want to study, which different characteristics (variables) of the units we want to know more about, which specific features (values) we want to measure in the units, and which frameworks or connections (context) the studies should be kept within (2.5.4 Choice of units).
  **Units** are the people or phenomena that we want to study further. They can be individuals or various collective groups such as companies, municipalities, countries. Selected units are the persons we actually study. Example: Students in a particular geographical area or university.
  **Variables** are what we want to study and compare in the units (individuals or groups) we research. It is the characteristics of the unit that vary from unit to unit (from person to person or from group to group). Example: gender, education, income.
  **Values** are a unit's specific characteristics for the variable. The value is our description of the variables (the characteristics covered by the variables) for each unit. If one of the variables is education, would we want to examine values concerning that particular type of education? Example: typical characteristics of education, completion rate, student loans, student environment.
- *Context* means defining the connections or framework within which the survey should be kept. It can be a delimited environment (company, organisation, etc.), a place (shop, park, arena), a group (based on interest, social identity, cultural background), etc. The context will thus also determine the scope of the study, i.e. the surroundings within which the study is to take place. Example: The context is a college in London.

  *Satisfaction survey*: A satisfaction survey is an example of a survey where problem delimination may be needed. In such a survey, it is possible to determine the impact of variables such as gender and income on product satisfaction. Survey example: Satisfaction with the design, answer on a scale of 1 to 10, see Figure 2.12 (2.6.1 Survey).

Fig. 2.8 The figure shows the elements of a problem delimination (Jacobsen, 2005). The three parts (units, variables and values) follow each other and merge. Finally, we decide what context to focus on.

Table 2.4 The table shows an example of a survey based on a problem delimitation problem. Satisfaction with the design: answer on a scale of 1 to 10. Gender: men and women. Income: income amount. Satisfaction with the product: answer on a scale of 1 to 10. I would buy it again! – Yes or No. Processed in a statistics program, the survey will resemble a spreadsheet, where variables appear in the columns, the units in the rows, and the value in each individual grid. The figure shows how measurement of the variable for each individual unit can be done, by displaying the value of the variable. Results may appear automatically in a spreadsheet.

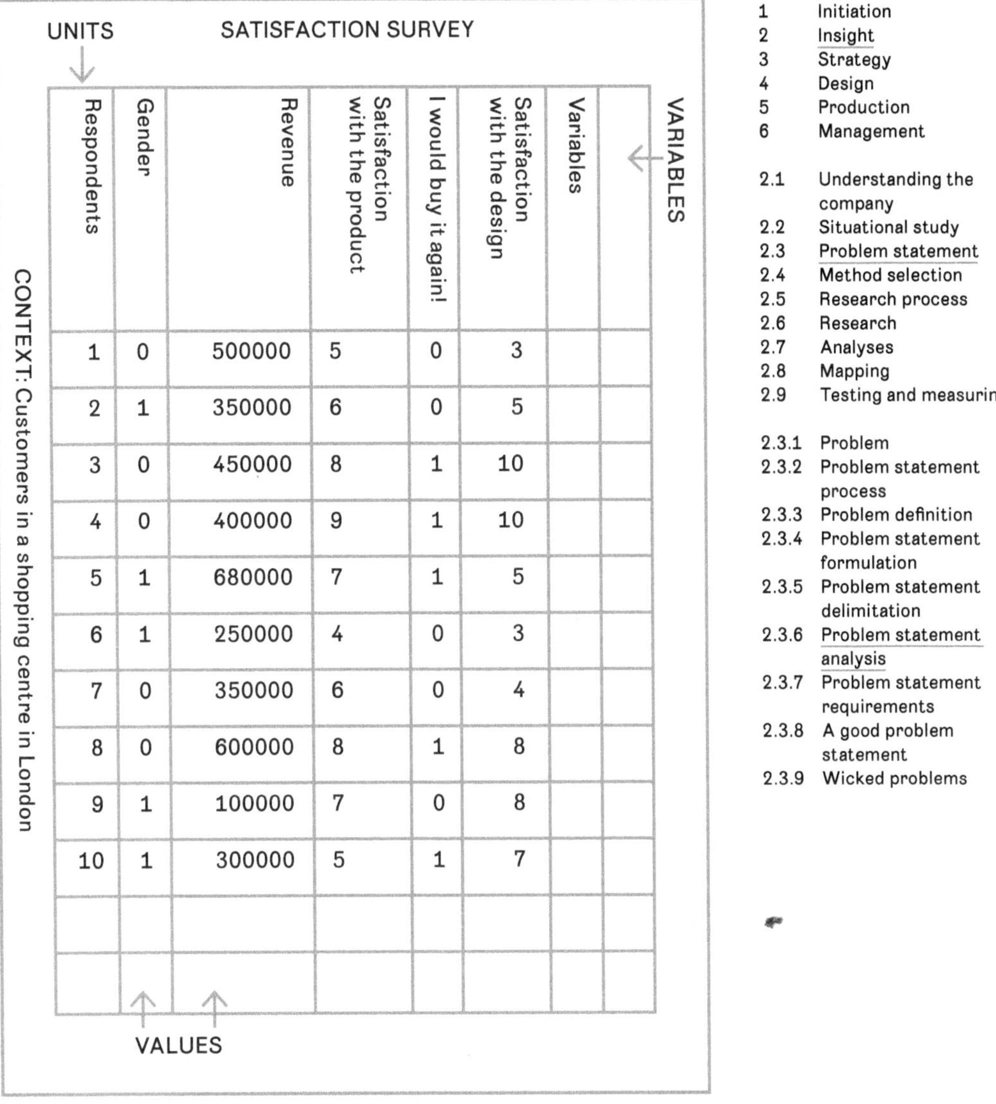


| Respondents | Gender | Revenue | Satisfaction with the product | I would buy it again! | Satisfaction with the design | Variables | |
|---|---|---|---|---|---|---|---|
| 1 | 0 | 500000 | 5 | 0 | 3 | | |
| 2 | 1 | 350000 | 6 | 0 | 5 | | |
| 3 | 0 | 450000 | 8 | 1 | 10 | | |
| 4 | 0 | 400000 | 9 | 1 | 10 | | |
| 5 | 1 | 680000 | 7 | 1 | 5 | | |
| 6 | 1 | 250000 | 4 | 0 | 3 | | |
| 7 | 0 | 350000 | 6 | 0 | 4 | | |
| 8 | 0 | 600000 | 8 | 1 | 8 | | |
| 9 | 1 | 100000 | 7 | 0 | 8 | | |
| 10 | 1 | 300000 | 5 | 1 | 7 | | |
| | | | | | | | |
| | | | | | | | |

Table 2.4 Satisfaction survey

1 Initiation
2 Insight
3 Strategy
4 Design
5 Production
6 Management

2.1 Understanding the company
2.2 Situational study
2.3 Problem statement
2.4 Method selection
2.5 Research process
2.6 Research
2.7 Analyses
2.8 Mapping
2.9 Testing and measuring

2.3.1 Problem
2.3.2 Problem statement process
2.3.3 Problem definition
2.3.4 Problem statement formulation
2.3.5 Problem statement delimitation
2.3.6 Problem statement analysis
2.3.7 Problem statement requirements
2.3.8 A good problem statement
2.3.9 Wicked problems

## 2.3.6 Problem statement analysis

Once the problem statement is defined, the time has come to clarify the nature of the issue, the purpose of the issue, and the expected outcome of working on the issue. Once a decision has been made, it is easier to assess what research should be conducted in order to answer or resolve the problem. This can be done through an analysis in relation to the following three dimensions (Jacobsen, 2005):

a) General/exploratory or specific/testing
b) Descriptive or explanatory/causal
c) Generalising or non-generalising

> Implicit vs. explicit
> **Implicit is indirect and explicit is direct. Explicit means clearly stated so there is no room for confusion or questions. Implicit means implied, not clearly stated, one assumes that the statement are understood without being said.**

Initially, the three dimensions can be treated as dichotomies (either... or), but usually there are smooth transitions, and often a problem statement arises as we are working on it, so that it can become clearer, more descriptive, or generalising after a while.

**Hypothesis vs. Theory**
**In science, a theory is a tested, well-substantiated, unifying explanation for a set of verified, proven factors. A theory is always backed by evidence; a hypothesis is only a suggested possible outcome, and is testable and falsifiable. (Diffen.com)**

**a) Unclear or clear problem statement:**
The relationship between an unclear and a clear problem statement is not 'either...or'. There may be smooth transitions, and the problem statement may become clearer while working on it.

- *Exploratory (unclear) problem statement:* This means that the problem statement is characterised by a topic or an open question, which also means that it is general and broad, and may be unclear, too. Such a problem statement is a good place to start open and free exploration. The result can be new and relatively unknown knowledge, which can lead to innovation. It may be necessary to adequately define the limits of the problem statement in order to be able to research in depth. Qualitative research, such as interviews and observations, are used when the problem statements are unclear. They provide data in the form of text or something visually descriptive. This type of problem statement is usually used in design projects.
- *Testing (clear) problem statement:* This means that the problem statement is relatively well-defined and less open, which also means that it is more specific or clear. Such a problem statement involves acquiring more and broader skills in order to strengthen a knowledge or theory, or refute a hypothesis. It is often a matter of examining a few nuances in many units (individuals) in order to compare and generalise. Quantitative research, such as questionnaires and market surveys, are used in case of a clear problem statement. This provides quantitative data in the form of numbers. Such a problem statement could be used, for example, to conduct quantitative research in a design project.

**b) Descriptive or explanatory problem statement:**
Descriptive or explanatory problem statements are often related to the purpose of the problem statement, what one hopes to gain from the research. Explanatory will always follow descriptive lines (Jacobsen, 2005):

- *Descriptive – how?* A descriptive problem statement will often be about describing differences and similarities at a particular moment in time, or an evolution over time. Possible questions could be: What does the situation look like? One can examine people's views or perceptions about a case, topic, or condition in order to be able to describe the situation. Qualitative research, such as situational studies, interviews and observations, is used for this purpose.
- *Explanatory (causal) – why?* Explanatory (causal) problem statements can be about finding the reason why an incident or situation has occurred. Possible questions could be: Why does the situation look like this? Why is the condition like this? What has caused the situation or condition? An explanatory problem statement will often be about explaining why there are differences. Quantitative research is used where one can make comparisons in order to get the facts.

**c) Generalising or non-generalising:**

- *Generalising*: If the problem statement is generalising, an example of research may be observing and comparing individuals in a larger group in order to arrive at an average response, which would apply as a general perception, rule, or law to the entire group. One has to gather quantitative data in order to be able to generalise. This is done by asking one person questions in order to find out what most people think.
- *Non-generalising*: One highlights differences rather than comparing similarities. For this purpose, qualitative research is used.

### 2.3.7 Problem statement requirements

Whether the problem statement is unclear or clear, descriptive or clarifying, generalising or non-generalising, it should be interesting and enjoyable to work with. A problem statement for a design project should meet three requirements (Sander, 2019):

- *Enjoyable:* It should be exciting to work with.
- *Easy-to-understand:* It should be simple and clear.
- *Fruitful:* It should be capable of yielding results.

### 2.3.8 A good problem statement

Good problem statements break down existing barriers, open up new dimensions and lead to new knowledge and innovative solutions. This requires both insight and creativity from those working on the problem statement. According to Sander (2016), what characterises a good problem statement is that it is identifiable, verifiable, realistic, hierarchical and consistent. At the same time, several options that can solve the problem should be available:

**Identifiable**: One must be able to identify the problem in order to be able to research it. For example, one cannot use statements of the type: 'The company's problem is too low profitability' as a starting point for a design project. We need to look beyond the problem and find its cause. Why is the profitability insufficient? Do they sell too little? Are the costs too high? The problem needs to be clarified further in order to make it possible to research it.

**Verifiable**: It should be possible to verify the problem. Is the problem based on intuition, assumptions, and subjective assessments or on objective facts? Are there source materials available for verification? Have reliable sources, relevant research methods and measurements been used? In order to verify the effectiveness of actions taken to resolve the problem statement, it must be possible to verify the extent to which the problem has been resolved and whether the objective has been achieved.

**Realistic**: The problem one is trying to solve must be realistic. The biggest constraint in any design project will be time and money. Therefore, it is important to select a problem statement for the design project, which is feasible within the current framework conditions for time and budget. Drug abuse and crime are two major problems in our society, but it would be unrealistic to think that a design project can be launched to address



Generalising = Universal.
Non-generalising = Highlights differences.

these two problems, not to mention that these problems are too big, complicated, complex, unclear and resource consuming.
**Hierarchical:** As a rule, our main problem needs to be broken down into different sub-problems in order to make it possible to research and solve the main problem. When there are several problem statements, they should be structured hierarchically. This way, solving the sub-problems will automatically lead to solving the main problem.
**Consistent:** The different problem statements included in the design project should not contradict each other. This means that solving one problem makes it impossible to solve the other problem.

Fig. 2.9 **The figure shows the 'seven wicked problems', based on (Sarkar & Kotler 2021).**

Tips for the company
**At best a wicked problem approach can be used as a tool to enlighten and respond to crises and intervene for a more sustainable future**

Wicked problems have virtuous solutions (Sarkar & Kotler 2021).

### 2.3.9 Wicked problems

A wicked problem is a social or cultural problem that is difficult or impossible to solve because of its complex, interconnected and contradictory nature, such as environmental crisis. By being concerned with the human aspect, designers are often confronted with the so-called wicked problems. Typical of wicked problems is that they are characterised by a high level of complexity, combined with a high degree of uncertainty and often attracting stakeholders with radically different world views. Such problems can have consequences that are hard to imagine and demanding to put an end to in the form of a single solution (DRLab).[24] According to Wikipedia classic examples of wicked problems include economic, environmental, and political issues. A problem whose solution requires a great number of people to change their mindsets and behaviour is likely to be a wicked problem. These include global climate change, natural hazards, healthcare, the AIDS epidemic, pandemic influenza, international drug trafficking, nuclear weapons, nuclear energy, waste and social injustice.

The concept of wicked problem was first introduced in 1967 in a seminar at the University of California Architecture Department in Berkeley, USA. In that seminar, design professor Horst Rittel suggested that 'the term "wicked problem" refers [*sic*] to that class of social system problems which are ill-formulated, where the information is confusing, where there are many clients and decision makers with conflicting values, and where the ramifications in the whole system are thoroughly confusing. The adjective "wicked" is supposed to describe the mischievous and even evil quality of these problems, where proposed "solutions" often turn out to be worse than the symptom' (Churchman, 1967, Lönngren and van Poeck, 2020). The concept of 'wicked problems' was more formally introduced by Horst W.J. Rittel and Melvin M. Webber (1973),[25] through 10 properties of a wicked problem:

1. There is no definitive formulation of a wicked problem.
2. Wicked problems have no stopping rule, i.e. there is no point in time at which the process of addressing a problem is completed.
3. Solutions to wicked problems are not true-or-false, but good-or-bad.
4. There is no immediate and no ultimate test of a solution to a wicked problem.
5. Every solution to a wicked problem is a 'one-shot' operation.

24 Design Research Lab, drlab.org
25 The concept of 'wicked problems' was introduced in the article 'Dilemmas in a General Theory of Planning', by Horst W.J. Rittel and Melvin M. Webber (1973).
26 'The wicked 7. Can we solve the world's most urgent problems?' (Christian Sarkar & Philip Kotler, 2021).

6. Wicked problems do not have an enumerable or exhaustively describable set of potential solutions, nor is there a well-described set of permissible operations for addressing wicked problems.
7. Every wicked problem is essentially unique.
8. Every wicked problem can be considered to be a symptom of another problem.
9. The analyst's world view is the strongest determining factor for explaining differences in descriptions of wicked problems and preferences for how they should be addressed.
10. The planner (those who present solutions to these problems) has no right to be wrong.


1 Initiation
2 Insight
3 Strategy
4 Design
5 Production
6 Management

2.1 Understanding the company
2.2 Situational study
2.3 Problem statement
2.4 Method selection
2.5 Research process
2.6 Research
2.7 Analyses
2.8 Mapping
2.9 Testing and measuring

2.3.1 Problem
2.3.2 Problem statement process
2.3.3 Problem definition
2.3.4 Problem statement formulation
2.3.5 Problem statement delimitation
2.3.6 Problem statement analysis
2.3.7 Problem statement requirements
2.3.8 A good problem statement
2.3.9 Wicked problems


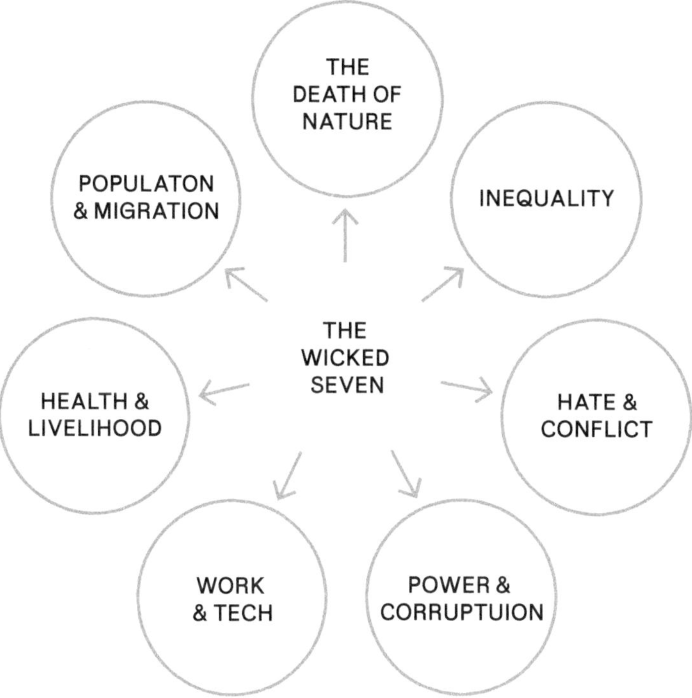


Fig. 2.9 The Wicked 7

Further reading
Check out wicked7.org. and wickedacceleration.org

Christian Sarkar & Philip Kotler (2021)[26] recently introduced new and updated characteristics and real life examples of wicked problems named 'seven wicked problems'. They argued that one of the main reasons that wicked problems aren't being addressed is because when we try to solve them individually, the boundaries we draw to frame the problem are reductive – they reduce and diminish the scope of the true underlying causes (Sarkar & Kotler, 2021). Sarkar and Kotler chose to include corruption, because they believe it is the primary reason *why* things don't change for the better: 1) The death of nature 2) Inequality 3) Hate & conflict 4) Power & corruption 5) Work & tech 6) Health & livelihood 7) Population & migration.

Rittel and Webber described natural science problems as 'tame problems' that are well-defined and that can be addressed through linear, reductionistic problem-solving approaches. Social science problems, on the other hand, were described as 'wicked' and were said to share the ten characteristics listed on pages 68 and 69 (Lönngren & van Poeck, 2020).

See also the chapters 2.8.5 GIGA mapping, 3.3.8 Sustainability goals, 3.5.2 Sustainable business model, 4.3.18 Systemic design, 5.3.5 Material life cycle, 5.4.7 Green packaging, 6.9 Sustainability managament.

## 2.4 Method selection

The choice of method depends on the research question, what one wants to investigate, what information can help elucidate or solve the problem, and what time and resources are available. Methods can be divided into two main categories: qualitative and quantitative.

The qualitative method is used when we want to do in-depth research, and this is the method most frequently used by designers.

The qualitative method provides greater understanding, which is documented with text.

In design projects, qualitative methods are most widely used and best suited for gaining the necessary insight into all phases of the process. The qualitative method provides greater understanding and in-depth knowledge. Examples of qualitative research methods are observations, interviews and focus groups (2.6 Research), and the use of iteration,[27] experimentation, prototyping and testing (4.3 Design methodology). Quantitative methods may also be needed in design projects to clarify the facts. Examples of these are surveys to get answers concerning brand awareness and opinion. Online surveys may be useful in a simple sense, and on a larger scale there may be broad market research, which requires extensive marketing resources. Both qualitative and quantitative methods provide data about reality (empirical knowledge). The qualitative method provides data in the form of words, while the quantitative method provides data in the form of numbers (Jacobsen). Qualitative research can be useful in all phases of a design project and is best conducted by the designers themselves, while quantitative research will usually require external expertise and should be outsourced to an analytical company. See also the chapters 2.3 Problem statement, 2.5 Research process, 3.3.5 Qual vs. quant goals.

### 2.4.1 Qualitative method

Qualitative method is used when we want to do in-depth research. It is a flexible and unstructured approach, meaning that the survey questions are not the same for all respondents. Therefore, data from qualitative research are not measurable and have low degree of generalisation.[28]

**Examples of qualitative research**

a) *Individual interview*: Interview with individual persons, open-ended questions.
b) *Group interview*: Interview with several people, as well as workshop, focus groups, role-playing, simulation.
c) *Observation*: Observation of human behaviour and interaction, ethnographic and anthropological studies, participant observation.
d) *Document research*: Text analysis, historical surveys. Use of secondary data/data collected by others.
e) *Studies of social context/social settings*: Network analysis and process tracking.

(Jacobsen, 2005)

27 Iteration = repetitions of processes that build on each other in order to get closer to a desired result (4.3.5 Iterative method).
28 Degree of generalisation: How general are the conclusions?

The objective of qualitative research is to establish greater understanding of a topic or phenomenon by exploring people's perceptions and experiences, social processes and social interactions. This can be done by interview, observation, focus group, discourse analysis, text analysis or the like with a relatively small sample of participants (respondents). For example, it may be an interview of selected employees, customers or users in order to hear their opinions, views or experience of the company, its products or services. The selection of individuals or groups (units) to be interviewed is discretionary or strategic, which means that they are selected based on what there is a need to understand or know more about. The devices being researched greatly affect the data or information we collect, and it is relatively easy to obtain additional information if necessary. Qualitative research can be made simple and intuitive or more thorough and analytical, depending on the purpose of the research, the nature of the project, time and resources. For example, in cases of simple qualitative research, these can be studies or observations made by the designer during a creative process, which are used immediately in the context of the assignment. In the same project, it may also be necessary to conduct more thorough research, which involve to a greater extent registering, interpreting, analysing and documenting the findings before the result can be used in the context of the project. The data collected in qualitative research is more time- and resource-consuming to process compared to quantitative method data because it provides text that must be rewritten. Qualitative data are not processed by computers, unlike quantitative data. For example, an interview with sound recording must be transcribed, processed and interpreted. Data and findings from qualitative research are presented in writing, with illustrations and photographs that make the content more visual and understandable.



## 2.4.2 Quantitative method

The quantitative method is used when we want to research something in breadth. This is a structured method, meaning that all survey questions are identical for each respondent. Data from quantitative research can therefore be measured and generalised, which means that what a few people think applies to many. The quantitative method can be used to produce facts and knowledge to elucidate a problem statement or phenomenon, or to test a hypothesis and determine whether the reality matches the assumption made. Examples of quantitative research are market surveys to measure customer satisfaction, brand awareness and purchasing habits. A large number of people (respondents) are asked some questions. The answer options may be, for example, yes, no, and I don't know. Data are generated by counting and measuring. Results are rendered as numbers presented in tables, graphs or statistics as opposed to qualitative data, which is rendered in words and visual descriptions. Quantitative data provide simple and superficial information, as opposed to qualitative data, which provide in-depth information. The investigator sets the terms for the answers/findings, and it is difficult to obtain additional information. It is important to ensure that the questions are as clear as possible to avoid misunderstandings. This can lead to misleading results, which weakens the outcome. Accuracy is

> Quantitative research is about generalising. What a few people think is true for many.
>
> The sample of respondents in quantitative research is not interesting per se, but because it represents the population the respondents are part of. They are interesting because they make it possible to arrive at results, which can be generated. The quantitative method provides facts that are documented with numbers.

essential. The selection of units to be studied should be representative; in other words, they have every prerequisite to mean something for the relationship in question, on which the survey is intended to shed light. This requires a clear problem statement and thoughtful planning of the variables, i.e. the characteristics of the units (people or groups) about whom we want to obtain information (2.5 Research process and 2.6.1 Survey).

**Examples of quantitative research**

a) *Personal interview*: Personal interviews are based on a questionnaire. The interviewer fills out the questionnaire on behalf of the respondent. The questions are the same for all respondents.

b) *Telephone interview*: A questionnaire is presented over the telephone. The interviewer fills out the questionnaire. The questions are the same for all respondents.

c) *Electronic questionnaire*: The questionnaire is presented on the Internet or by email. The respondent fills it out and returns it electronically.

d) *Mail questionnaire*: A questionnaire the respondent receives, fills out and returns by post.

e) *Experiments*: Use of experimental and control groups to research a hypothesis.

f) In addition, testing, laboratory experiments, numerical analysis and simulation can also be regarded as qualitative methods. (Jacobsen, 2005)

For example, in an opinion poll among Norwegian consumers, 1,000 respondents will be asked the same questions. These 1,000 respondents are not interesting per se; they are interesting insofar as they represent Norwegian consumers in general. Then, the data collected from the 1,000 members of the sample would be used to say something – not about the 1,000 members – but about 4 million Norwegian consumers (which makes up the consumers when one subtracts children and those who rarely buy anything, such as the elderly or others who leave all purchases to others). Such a statistical survey or sample survey involves looking at a sample of units in the population that the statistics should say something about. By examining a small part of the population, one can find information about large parts of the population, assuming that what applies to 1,000 randomly selected representatives in a population would also apply to the entire population. The fact that these 1,000 people are randomly drawn from the population is what makes them representative. In qualitative methods, one should have a discretionary selection of respondents. Here, the people are not randomly selected, precisely because one wants to find out exactly what this selection of consumers thinks about, for example, the redesign of a product. In quantitative sample research where many people are asked the same questions, one is not interested in what each of these people thinks about things, but what they can tell us about the opinions and perceptions of all Norwegian consumers.

29 'How to...write a good research question' (Mattick et al. 2018) *The Clinical Teacher*, April 2018, Vol.15 (2), p. 104–108 https://doi.org/10.1111/tct.12776

30 Alan Bryman (1947–2017) was Professor of Organisational and Social Research at the University of Leicester, known for the use of mixed methods and as the author of many books within social science research methods. *Business Research Methods* (2018) with Emma Bell and Bill Harley, 'Social research methods' (2005/2015), *Quantitative Data Analysis* with SPSS 12 and 13; *A Guide for Social Scientists* with Duncan Cramer (2004) and *Quantity and Quality In Social Research* (1988). (Alan Bryman, n.d)

### 2.4.3 Method triangulation

Method triangulation is the application/combination of two or more research and data collection methods. Triangulation refers to the use of multiple methods or data sources in qualitative research to develop a comprehensive understanding of phenomena (Patton, 1999). Triangulation also has been viewed as a qualitative research strategy to test validity through the convergence of information from different sources. (Carter et al., 2014). The use of several methods, such as observations, interviews, surveys and studies, can help determine the validity (verification) of the collected data. Collecting data from multiple sources provides an opportunity to assess one result against another, the so-called cross-verification, which may increase the validity and reliability of the collected data. By combining multiple units, theories, methods, and empirical materials, the investigator can overcome weaknesses or assumptions and problems that arise from the use of a single method, observation, or theory. (2.4 Method selection, 2.6.7 Scientific Research)



**Example of method triangulation**

Method triangulation can be a combination of quantitative and qualitative methods, for example:

1) Quantitative method: survey (e.g. questionnaires)
2) Qualitative method: user test (e.g. focus group)
3) Qualitative method: interview (e.g. face-to-face interview)

After a survey, one can perform a standard qualitative user test. Here, one can see the trends from the survey. Seemingly certain results can be completely shattered when put into a qualitative context. For example, a survey might say that users consider the site contains too much news. In a qualitative interview, members of the same target group respond that they want MORE news, but ANOTHER type of news. Triangulation gives a more detailed and balanced picture of the situation (Altrichter, 2008).

### 2.4.4 Research question

A research question is 'a question that a research project sets out to answer'.[29] To form a research question, one must determine what type of study one wants to conduct, and what methods to use, such as qualitative, quantitative, or mixed study.

It can be a challenge to use a problem statement as the starting point for a survey, if it is too broad or too general (2.3 Problem statement). In that case, one can research through one or more research questions based on the overall problem statement. According to Professor Alan Bryman[30] research questions are extremely important in the research process, because they force you to consider the issue of what you want to find out about much more precisely and rigorously. 'Developing research questions is a matter of narrowing down and focusing more precisely on what it is that

In a method triangulation, quantitative research will produce findings in the form of numbers and facts, while qualitative research will deepen the findings and provide greater understanding of the reasons behind them.

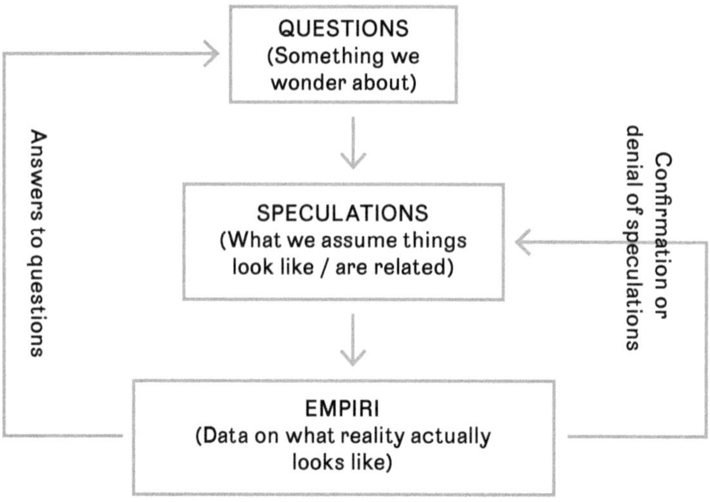


Fig. 2.10 Empirical research

Fig. 2.10 The figure shows the approach in empirical research (Jacobsen, 2005). We have a question and a few possible assumptions. We investigate what reality really looks like, and have our speculations confirmed or denied.

Fig. 2.11 The figure shows examples of a simple research process. Data collection is the phase in which the survey is carried out; the other phases are preliminary and follow-up work.

you want to know about' (Bryman, 2012). Lack of a research question or a poorly formulated research question will lead to poor research. It should be clearly specified. If not 'there is a great risk that your research will be unfocused and that you will be unsure about what your research is about and what you are collecting data for' (Bryman, 2012, p. 10).

## 2.5 Research process

A research process is the course of research for gathering information and collecting data. It most often involves the use of several different research methods. Here we look at the research process in order to identify, elucidate and respond to a problem statement.

Research is necessary in most design projects. Before we make changes and create anything new, it is important to study the actual conditions. For example, conducting user studies and observations of a sample of people in order to find out how a product is perceived and used. Alternatively, it may involve asking questions to a larger sample of people in order to find out what an entire population thinks about a case. Such research provides knowledge based on experience, or what we in other words call empirical knowledge. Any research or research process is based on a question, hypothesis, or topic, something we would like answers to in order to avoid speculation and assumptions, and to find real causes (2.3 Problem statement, 2.4.4 Research Question, 2.6 Research).

If we compare any study with a research process, the goal will always be to develop new knowledge. Different types of research generate different results:

- Exploratory research formulates new problems.
- Constructive research develops solutions to a problem.
- Empirical research tests a solution through empirical evidence.

31 Professor Dag Ingvar Jacobsen is the author of several books in the fields of organisation and management, political science and methodology. He has published articles in both national and international journals and lectures widely in Scandinavia. He is co-author of the book 'How Organizations Function', which is one of the most frequently read books in Scandinavia about organisation theory.

The design process is very similar to the research process. Much of the research done in a creative process is intuitive and open. There may be different types of experimentation, trial and error, and testing that occur through the design process which do not always need to be documented. In those contexts where there is a need to obtain concrete facts or shed light on a topic, situation, object or phenomenon, it will be necessary to have documentation and use credible and relevant sources and methods. For the result of a survey to appear reliable, it may be an advantage to choose generally accepted research methodology similar to that used in research. We will therefore look at the research process from a social science perspective. Explanation of the research process is based on Jacobsen (2005).[31] It can seem somewhat theoretical and formal, but it may be useful in order to gain a better understanding of the course of a qualitative and quantitative research process.

A research process starts by developing a problem statement. Once the problem statement has been formulated, the foundation is ready to select research methods. It is done based on what is most appropriate in order to gather the necessary information or data, and most often several different surveys are needed. After the research is completed and the data is collected, the information is analysed in order to identify data that are relevant to finding answers to the problem statement and solving the task. In simple intuitive research that is process-based, the findings will be immediately applied in the context of the task. For larger studies, it would be natural to create documentation by drawing up a report describing the process, highlighting the findings and reflecting on their significance for the task that needs to be solved.

The steps of a research process are closely linked. Incorrect assessment in one step could affect the results of the further process and impair the relevance and credibility of the research. The differences between the different steps may be fluid, and there may be a need to work on several steps at the same time as well as to go back to previous steps in order to make new assessments and changes. The size and complexity of the research design should be assessed in relation to the size of the project. In the further explanation of the research process, we will look at a simple approach and a more advanced approach.

Fig. 2.11 Data collection, simplified

**Simplified process:** A simplified research process can be used for a single survey or for multiple surveys combined. As shown in Figure 2.11, it involves less preparation and subsequent processing than a more advanced research process, as shown in Figure 2.12. The simplified process is well suited for smaller surveys such as visual analysis, user studies and document studies.



Qualitative research
In a design project, interviewing company employees and close business partners can help provide valuable information to shed light on the company's situation. Then it will be relevant to select people in the company who can provide nuanced and in-depth information. In this context, a small sample of units (respondents) is made.

Quantitative research
It might also be necessary to clarify how the customers perceive the company. This can be done through a survey. In that case, it would be appropriate to ask a larger group this question in order to get views that are representative of what the customers think. In this context, a larger sample of units (respondents) is made (2.4 Method selection).

Fig. 2.12 Data collection, advanced

Fig. 2.12 The figure shows an example of an advanced research process. Data collection is the phase in which the survey is performed, the other phases are preliminary and follow-up work. This process includes all phases for conducting thorough qualitative or quantitative research

Table 2.5 The table shows the progress of a research process based on social science method and research methodology. Qualitative and quantitative methods follow the same process, but have different implementation, as shown in steps 4 to 6. One key difference: In quantitative research (right side of the figure) the steps follow one after the other from step 1 to 8. In qualitative research (left side of the figure) one can make changes to the design without going all the way back to the start (based on Jacobsen, 2005).

**Advanced process:** An advanced research process, as shown in Figure 2.12, is more thorough and based on the social sciences research method. It is suitable for both qualitative and quantitative research. In the further explanation of the research process, we will elaborate on how such a process can be implemented.

**Research prosess**

**Steps 1 to 8:** Here follows an explanation of the different steps of a thorough research process based on Table.2.5. It may appear somewhat extensive as it is, but in theory it can be adapted to smaller surveys. In short: When planning research, it is necessary to decide which problem statement the research should be based on, how the research should be designed, what form of research should be used, whether a qualitative or a quantitative method should be applied, what or who should be studied, what kind of data it is necessary to obtain, how data should be processed, analysed and discussed, and finally how the final interpretation of data should take place and how the data should be compiled in a report highlighting these findings.

## 2.5.1 Problem statement (Step 1)

How the problem statement is formulated is crucial for the entire research, research form and content, what data one wishes to obtain, which units, variables and values are relevant to study (2.5.4 Choice of units, Step 4), how the collected data are to be analysed, what conclusions can be drawn, what the purpose of the research is, how the report is to be prepared, and how possible sources of error are to be traced. Each method used is a separate survey. This means that there may be a need to formulate different problem statements or research questions for each survey, but they should always relate to the overall problem statement and help clarify it (2.3 Problem statement, 2.4.4 Research question).

## 2.5.2 Research design (Step 2)

Developing research design is about creating a design for the surveys that is best suited to shed light on or find answers to the problem, also called survey design. It can also be used as basis for setting up a price or budget for the research. In order to create research design, we need to clarify the following first: 1) What is the purpose of the research? 2) What do we expect to get out of it? Once clarified, one can consider whether the research form should be deep (intensive) or broad (extensive), descriptive or causal.

| Qualitative | Quantitative |
|---|---|
| **1. Problem statement** Problem statement formulation. Question or hypothesis? | |
| **2. Research design** How should the survey(s) be set up? Choice of research design/survey design. | |
| **3. Method selection** | |
| Descriptive (word): One-to-one interview, observations, studies. | Statistics (numbers): Broad interview, structured questionnaire online, by post or telephone interview. |
| **4. Choice of units** | |
| Who and what should we research? Selection of units, variables, values and context. Selection of sources, informants, respondents for a smaller group. | Who and what should we research? Selection of units, variables, values and context. Selection of respondents for a larger group/population. |
| **5. Collection of data** | |
| The qualitative method provides data (information) that has been interpreted and analysed, referenced in text. | The quantitative method provides data (information) that is statistical and measurable, referenced in numbers. |
| **6. Analysis/discussion** | |
| Analysis and discussion of qualitative data. Systematisation of information. Assessment of the relevance and validity of the findings. | Analysis and discussion of quantitative data. Simple statistical analysis. Assessment of whether the findings and statistics produce enough data. |
| **7. Interpretation/validation** Interpretation of data. Assessment of interpretation errors. | |
| **8. Report preparation** Preparation of report. Highlighting findings and results, as well as consequences for further work. | |

Table 2.5 The research process


1 Initiation
2 Insight
3 Strategy
4 Design
5 Production
6 Management

2.1 Understanding the company
2.2 Situational study
2.3 Problem statement
2.4 Method selection
2.5 Research process
2.6 Research
2.7 Analyses
2.8 Mapping
2.9 Testing and measuring

2.5.1 Problem statement (Step 1)
2.5.2 Research design (Step 2)
2.5.3 Choice of method (Step 3)
2.5.4 Choice of units (Step 4)
2.5.5 Data collection (Step 5)
2.5.6 Data analysis and discussion (Step 6)
2.5.7 Data interpretation (Step 7)
2.5.8 Report preparation (Step 8)

### 2.5.3 Choice of method (Step 3)

The problem statement and the research form govern the choice of method for data collection, whether a qualitative or a quantitative method is necessary (2.4 Method selection). The method is selected based on what is to be researched, the purpose of the research, the desired effect, and the available time and resources.

Table 2.6 The tables show examples of different surveys, methods and purposes for selecting qualitative and quantitative methods, respectively (Based on Jacobsen (2005)).

| Qualitative methods | Procedure | Purpose |
|---|---|---|
| Individually open interview or in-depth interview | Interview with individuals. | Used to research individual, personal views concerning a phenomenon or relationship. |
| Group interview, focus group, user panel | Several people are interviewed at the same time. | Used to research group views, or agreement/disagreement within a group. |
| Observation, field study | Study and observation of human behaviour and interaction. | Used to study what users do in a certain context. The results can be compared to what they say that they do (interview). |
| Document study, Internet research | Use of data, which others have collected (secondary data). | Used to research relationships indirectly, where primary data have not been obtained, or as supplement to primary data to control, support and contrast the data. |
| Result: Interpretation of data (words). | | |

| Quantitative methods | Procedure | Purpose |
|---|---|---|
| Telephone interview | Telephone interviews, based on a questionnaire filled out by the interviewer. | Statistical measurement. Used when high response rate and fast response are needed. |
| Personal standardised interview | Interview based on a structured survey filled out by the interviewer. | Statistical measurement. Used to "capture" respondents who may have difficulty filling out surveys themselves. |
| Email or online form | The respondent fills out and returns the form electronically. | Statistical measurement. Used when fast response is required. Can be conducted at low cost. The risk is high drop-out rates. |
| Form sent by post | Survey by post. The respondent fills it out and returns it by post. | Statistical measurement. Used when no rapid response is required. |
| Result: Statistical data (numbers). | | |

Table 2.6 Method selection

32 A snowball effect: a situation in which something increases in size or importance at a faster and faster rate. A snowball effect in research: scheduled interviews lead to new unplanned interviews, or new new interviews with the same people (A snowball effect, n.d.).

In quantitative research, questions cannot be changed along the way, and the result is not obtained until one reaches step 8 (see Table 2.5). If one wants to make changes to the design, one must go back to step 1. In qualitative research, for example, one can go to step 6 and say: 'Okay, but maybe I should have heard what someone else thinks about the design', and decide to put together a focus group. It has a broad composition and those present are committed informants. Then one comes to the research analysis and sees in the video that one of the focus group participants influences the others to say certain things. Consequently, one decides to implement a new focus group with the same problem statement, but with new informants in order to find out whether it will yield the same results. This is done because we have no reason to believe blindly in the results of the first focus group. In that case, one will not jump back to step 1, but back to step 4 (Dag Einar Thorsen, 2016).



## 2.5.4 Choice of units (Step 4)

Selection of units is about selecting the people or groups we want to research. It is related to the studies that are relevant to gathering information that may shed light on the problem, what or whom we should study, what characteristics, what specifications and in what context.

*In qualitative research* (intensive, in-depth research), a unit is a person or a small sample of people. According to Jacobsen (2005), the most common sample forms are: random sample to get the most width, sample to get the most information, sample to capture the typical, sample to capture the extreme, or the snowball method, where one contact recruits' others.[32]

*In quantitative research* (extensive research, which runs in width), a unit is a representative sample of a group of people, a population, who should represent the opinions of the entire population. This means that we make a relatively large sample of units. In this context, units have been selected in order to be able to generalise the information. The challenge is to make a sample that is sufficiently representative to allow us to make generalisations. Here we distinguish between the entire target group (theoretical population) and the sample we make (actual population), who are the respondents (Jacobsen, 2005). Once units have been selected, the next step will be to consider which characteristics (variables) and conditions (values) we should study and which area the research should be limited to (2.3.5 Problem statement delimination).

### Respondent vs. informant

In qualitative research, the units are often called respondents or informants. A respondent is someone who has experienced what we want to research personally, while an informant is someone who has not experienced it personally but has good knowledge of what we want to study (Jacobsen, 2005).

Further reading
*The Process of Social Research* (2018) by Dixon, Singleton Jr. and Straits.

Research should shed light on or find answers to a problem statement!

**Units:** Who, which people or subjects are we going to study?
**Variables:** What different variations or characteristics, e.g., gender, age, place of residence, occupation, income, should we compare among the units?
**Values:** What values do the different units have on the variables? For example, the variable 'gender' has two possible values: male or female.
**Context:** In what context or defined (geographical) area, population or group is the research to take place?

Tips for the designer
**Primary data are new data collected directly from the source. Secondary data are data collected by others.**

Validity and reliability
**When collecting data to be used in a survey, first, the data should be relevant to the problem. Secondly, all measurements should be carried out correctly. They must be reliable. This is called validity and reliability (Dalland, 2000). Reliability can be verified by assessing strengths and weaknesses of the research structure and the reliability of the choices made in the research. For example, by the consistency and stability of the measurements carried out. Validity can be assessed by studying the relationship between one's own and others' research in the field and assessing the validity of one's own work in view of this.**

### 2.5.5 Data collection (Step 5)

- *Primary data*: Primary data are new data collected by going directly to the primary source, which is usually selected people or a group of people. Methods such as interview, observation or questionnaires are most appropriate. The disadvantage of collecting primary data is that it can be time-consuming and labour-intensive.
- *Secondary data*: Secondary data are information and research data not collected directly from the source but gathered by others, often for a different purpose and problem statement than the current one. The advantage of secondary data is that they are most often readily available, i.e. in surveys and statistics, reports, theses, books, research data and the like, and they are usually free of charge. It is important to examine the credibility of the source and to try to uncover possible factors allowing for error. The use of *qualitative* secondary data is about interpreting texts collected by others and making a critical assessment of whether the information is suitable for the problem statement at hand. It can be an advantage to use different types of data, both primary data and secondary data, because different data can be compared and used to verify each other, support each other and contrast different information and thereby help to strengthen the result.

### 2.5.6 Data analysis and discussion (Step 6)

After completing the surveys, the data should be processed in order to be nuanced and analysed. Data for qualitative and quantitative methods are analysed in very different ways. Qualitative data allow for subjective understanding and interpretation, while quantitative data are comparable figures, providing clear answers.

*Qualitative data:* Processing and analysis of qualitative data from, for example, individual interviews that have provided large amounts of text:

- Clarify the problem statement and purpose of the analysis.
- Sort and systematise data.
- Simplify and summarise large amounts of information/text (data reduction).
- Break down the whole into smaller parts. Examine the individual parts.
- Interpret impressions and information. Discuss results and reflect on them.
- Document findings. Describe possible consequences.
- Suggested use of findings.

*Quantitative data:* Processing and analysis of quantitative data from, for example, a large survey with many respondents who have received a few identical questions:

- Clarify the problem statement and purpose of the analysis.
- Sort and systematise data.
- Choice of technique to simplify and process large amounts of data material/numbers from many respondents.
- Convert survey responses to numbers.
- Data analysis/analysis of numbers. Use of statistical software.
- Document findings. Describe possible consequences.
- Suggested use of findings.

### 2.5.7 Data interpretation (Step 7)

Interpretation (validation) of results concerns the assessment of interpretation errors and tracking down error sources, critical discussion and assessment of the reliability, as well as internal and external validity of the data. Internal and external validity are concepts that reflect whether the results of a study are trustworthy and meaningful. 'While internal validity relates to how well a study is conducted (its structure), external validity relates to how applicable the findings are to the real world' (Cuncic, 2021). Interpretation is subjective, and people are clouded by their experience. We may therefore have different ways of interpreting data, which may affect the further application of the results. See also chapter 2.5.5 Data collection/ Validity and reliability and 2.6.7 Scientific research: The research process).

**Terminology**

**Problem statement:** Something we want to research, formulated as a question, hypothesis, or topic.

**Variables, units, values, context:** All problem statements have a set of variables (what we want to research), some units (who we want to research), some values (the specific features a unit has on a variable), and a context (the framework or scope of validity of the research) (Jacobsen, 2005).

**Qualitative vs. quantitative data:** Both are data on reality (empirical data), qualitative data are about words, while quantitative data are empirical in the form of numbers (Jacobsen, 2005).

**Intensive vs. extensive research:** Intensive research is in-depth qualitative research among a few units that provide many answers, such as interviews. Extensive research is broad research among many units that give a few answers, such as surveys.

**Generalisation:** A smaller sample is used as basis to find out what many people think, for example by asking 1,000 people in order to find out what an entire population thinks about a case.

**Falsification vs. verification:** Falsification (of Latin falsas = 'error') is an indication that a claim is incorrect. Falsification is done by rebuttal, not by verification (proof) of a hypothesis. According to Karl Popper, the more falsification attempts a hypothesis has survived, the stronger it stands (Jacobsen, 2005).

1 Initiation
2 Insight
3 Strategy
4 Design
5 Production
6 Management

2.1 Understanding the company
2.2 Situational study
2.3 Problem statement
2.4 Method selection
2.5 Research process
2.6 Research
2.7 Analyses
2.8 Mapping
2.9 Testing and measuring

2.5.1 Problem statement (Step 1)
2.5.2 Research design (Step 2)
2.5.3 Choice of method (Step 3)
2.5.4 Choice of units (Step 4)
2.5.5 Data collection (Step 5)
2.5.6 Data analysis and discussion (Step 6)
2.5.7 Data interpretation (Step 7)
2.5.8 Report preparation (Step 8)

Further reading
'Karl Popper', Standford Encyclopedia of Philosophy, Thornton (2021).

*Interpretation of results*:

- Qualitative data: Assessment of the relevance and validity of the findings. Consider the possibility of generalising.
- Quantitative data: Assessment of the relevance, credibility and quality of the findings. Whether the findings apply to others than those studied, so that they are representative of a larger group (population) and are generalisable. Assessment of whether the measurements provide sufficient data.

**The design process is a research process, where the solution to the task is the result of thorough studies, surveys, analyses, research, experimentation, trials, failures and tests.**

### 2.5.8 Report preparation (Step 8)

Structured and clear reporting and documentation of the research is essential for its further application. A report should provide a full description of the research process and design, including reasons for choices and reflections on findings. The most important thing is to document findings that can help elucidate or solve the problem statement and the task. The findings should be highlighted, and it should be evident how these contribute to illucidating the problem statement and how they can be applied and help solve the task. Designers have the advantage of being able to express their reports visually, for example using graphs and infographics (graphical visualisation), in order to provide a clearer common platform to use as a basis when interpreting the findings.

## 2.6 Research

Based on the previous chapters concerning the research process and choice of method, here, we will look at different research forms, such as surveys, interviews, observations, focus groups, experiments and research. In a design project, the whole process depends on employing different research to undertake the task.

Whether the research should have a generalising ambition (quantitative) or a non-generalising ambition (qualitative), depends on the purpose of the research and the availability of means to conduct it. We should start by looking at *surveys*, which usually has a generalising ambition.

### 2.6.1 Survey

Surveys are a much-used form of research at an early stage of a design project aimed at finding out what people think about a company, product or service, such as brand awareness and reputation. Different types of market research, customer research, employee research and opinion polls are often based on surveys. A survey is conducted in a relevant market or geographic area with the purpose of collecting data on people's attitudes, opinions, satisfaction and the like on some specific issues. The purpose of a survey may be to investigate brand awareness, customer satisfaction, identify target groups, or investigate user needs. A survey is usually based on a quantitative method, which involves obtaining as *much true* knowledge as possible about the conditions which the survey is to elucidate (2.4.2 Quantitative method). It involves asking the same question to a relatively large number of people, who are all part of a population or a market, in order to arrive at facts or truth through generalisation. What is true for someone is true for everyone.

Surveys may be conducted via email questionnaires, online, by telephone, on paper, by post, face-to-face or using a combination of these. Regardless of the selected approach, all respondents are asked the same questions. When the survey is conducted by telephone or face-to-face, the interviewer asks the questions and writes down the answers. A survey over the Internet or by post involves the respondent reading the questions and answering them personally. There should be a few easy-to-answer questions with a few answer options such as Yes, No, and I don't know. This way, it will be easy to process the answers afterwards. The results can be presented in the form of numbers in tables and statistics or in graphs. Visualisation using graphs and infographics can make data and information clearer and more understandable.



### Some survey categories

**Market**: Market surveys are used to map demographics (populations/market segments) and target groups, examine the needs and purchasing behaviour of target groups, identify new customer arenas to increase sales, acquire knowledge of one's own industry, identify strategic market opportunities, market developments and market trends, etc.

**Society**: Polling is a type of survey in which a representative sample of the population is asked about their stance on different social conditions.

**Customer**: Customer surveys are about examining customer satisfaction and gaining user insight by examining how the company, product or service is perceived by the customer, and what influences the customers' buying behaviour and perceptions. Connect with customers through their preferred devices and channels, compare competitive conditions and identify market trends. Gain insight for better follow-up of each customer.

**Internal**: Employee surveys and workplace health and safety surveys involve identifying problems and needs among employees, examining productivity, capturing negative trends early in order to reverse any negative developments, giving employees an opportunity to be heard, attracting and engaging the right people, and motivating them to do their best, which can give the company a competitive edge.

### Generalising ambition

When we talk about surveys that should have a generalising ambition, we talk about different approaches depending on the availability of funds, see Table 2.7. A small design start-up will not normally have assignments where large-scale quantitative research is relevant. In that case, they will use external expertise for this. That is probably what larger, more established design companies will do as well. They will call one of the many polling companies or analytical firms. If more resources are available, one

Further reading
*Social Research Methods* (2012) by Alan Bryman.

will be able to order one's own quantitative research from one of these companies. Another option is small-scale quantitative research, which could be carried out at a more affordable price for most people. This can be done by ordering a handful of questions as part of an omnibus survey, which the large polling companies or analytical firms regularly conduct. In omnibus surveys, 1,000 respondents are asked a battery of questions. Here, there will be different clients who have one or more questions. These questions are put together to make a large survey. Buying into an omnibus will be less costly than ordering one's own large-scale quantitative research. In general, it would normally be better to have one's own dedicated quantitative research for each assignment, but it is often cost considerations that make people choose omnibus surveys instead. On an even smaller scale, it will of course be possible for the designer to prepare and carry out quantitative research personally. It can be surveys via email, Facebook or other social media (Thorsen, 2017).

Table 2.7 The table shows an example of the correlation between availability of funds and choice of survey form.

| Access to substantial funds? / Generalising ambition? | YES | NO |
|---|---|---|
| YES | Quantitative sample research (large-scale) | Qualitative/quantitative* research |
| NO | Omnibus participation (small-scale) | Own qualitative research |

* For example, whether to interview everyone in a medium-sized enterprise

Table 2.7 Selection of survey form

Market surveys can in fact be done by anyone. Basically, a survey can be conducted by writing a few questions with a few answer options on paper, copying and distributing them in a classroom, at a workplace, or after a course. Other easy ways are to stand in front of a shop or pedestrian area and ask passers-by, or gather a user panel or test group of friends and acquaintances, or post a simple survey on Facebook. Many surveys can be done using online solutions. Here, there are a number of providers; some of which are free, while others are subscription-based. Such an online service gives access to templates to set up the survey and process the responses (data). The important thing is that respondents are representative of the population or group one wants to know something about, and that the number of respondents is large enough to allow generalisation.

### Respondents

A frequently asked question is how to get respondents. For workplace surveys, respondents will be the company employees, and for customer

33 There are several sampling techniques used by researchers and statisticians, each with its own benefits and drawbacks (Kenton, 2021).

satisfaction surveys, it will be the customer database. In cases of market surveys, where respondents are representatives of a larger group or population, it will be demanding both to select respondents and to get hold of them, unless one uses the option of purchasing access to large customer databases that can be segmented as needed. Such services are sold by analyst agencies and other professional service providers. If one does not have access to considerable funds, one can use whatever is available. It is possible to contact relevant organisations, clubs, associations or the like and ask to buy or use their databases. Other places where one might find respondents are one's own circle of friends, peers, colleagues, classmates, training companions, fellow club members or other community members. Personal and professional networks also have great potential, especially social media networks.

### Representative sample

Samples are used in surveys when population sizes are too large for the test to include all possible members. A sample refers to a smaller, manageable version of a larger group. It should represent the population as a whole and not reflect any bias toward a specific attribute (Kenton, 2021). In order to conduct a survey with a generalising ambition, there must be a known probability for the potential respondents (members of the population, e.g. a country's consumers in general) to be drawn to the survey and become one of the 1,000 people actually interviewed. This means that anyone from the population in question could be selected as one of the 1,000 respondents (units). This is the only way to obtain a representative sample[33] and valid and reliable statistical generalisations. The size of the population does not affect the size of the sample. You get the same margins of error in the US and China, as in a small

### Not valid and reliable

One example where a representative sample of respondents was not used was in the TV debate program Holmgang, where they had call-in questions. By paying 5 Norwegian kroner one could participate by answering Yes or No to a question. A typical question asked in 2006 was: Are you for or against tolls? And the answer was that about 95 percent were against tolls and about 5 percent were in favour of them. One political party's studio representative could gloat while the other representatives could go home in shame. After all, he had won in more than one way. The problem with this type of survey is that it is the respondents themselves who choose whether to be part of the sample, and then it is not possible to get generalisable results. Typical for those who choose to participate in such surveys is that they possess some special attributes, which make them systematically different from the normal population. In other words, those results cannot be used to say anything about Norwegians in general, Norwegian consumers or anything at all. (The example is from a talk with Dag Einar Thorsen in 2016). In this case, the outcome is likely to be known and thus triggers engagement in the target audience (Myhre, 2017).


1 Initiation
2 Insight
3 Strategy
4 Design
5 Production
6 Management

2.1 Understanding the company
2.2 Situational study
2.3 Problem statement
2.4 Method selection
2.5 Research process
2.6 Research
2.7 Analyses
2.8 Mapping
2.9 Testing and measuring

2.6.1 Survey
2.6.2 Interview
2.6.3 Observation
2.6.4 Focus group
2.6.5 UX Research
2.6.6 Experiment
2.6.7 Scientific research
2.6.8 Artistic research
2.6.9 Design research

- Generalising ambition
- Respondents
- Representative sample
- Margins of error
- Question formulation
- Survey questions writing tips
- Ethics
- Protection of personal data
- Survey process

country like Norway. Margins of error (confidence) are not affected by the size of the population (Thorsen, 2021). (2.5.5 Data collection/ Validity and reliability).

Fig. 2.13 The figure shows an example of a quantitative research in which all respondents are asked the same question for the answers to be generalised.

### Margins of error

The size of the population does not affect the size of the sample. You get the same margins of error whether you interview 1,000 in Norway with 5.5 million people or 1,000 in the US with 340 million people or China with 1.4 billion people. When you have a political opinion poll in Norway, it is often somewhere between 1.5% and 3% margin of error plus or minus. So, a party that gets e.g. 30% support will have a margin of error of around 3% points. If you say that a party has 30% support, then you assume that there is a 95% probability that the party is somewhere between 27% and 33% support. That is the margin of error. But the size of the margin of error is not affected by the size of the population. If you interview 1,000 voters in Norway (with about 3.5 million voters), you get a margin of error of 3%. If you interview 1,000 voters in the United States (with over 200 million voters), you also get a margin of error of 3% points, because the margins of error or the confidence of a sample survey are not affected by the size of the population (Thorsen, 2017).

### Question formulation

An important aspect of any survey is to ask the right questions in a good way in order to ensure the best possible data quality. It is an advantage to have more participants in the development of questions, in order to gather input, ideas and topics. Once input to questions has been gathered, a critical selection must be made of which questions are best suited for collecting data considering the objective of the survey. Questions and answer alternatives should be designed to produce the most valid information possible about the conditions in question, proofread and tested on a small sample of people. When formulating the questions, it is important to consider what needs to be taken into account in terms of language, concepts and other matters specific to the target group. If respondents differ largely by age (children, adolescents, seniors), interests or culture, further research should be considered.

### Survey questions writing tips

For example, question types may include questions concerning attitude, conduct, one's own situation, or knowledge.

- The questions must be answered with Yes, No, I don't know, or by putting a checkmark in one of several options. The answer alternatives may be: completely agree, partially agree, partially disagree, completely disagree, impossible to answer.
- Example of writing multiple choice questions. Use of hair shampoo: How often do you wash your hair? Options: Every day? Every other day? Twice a week? Once a week? Less often?
- Limit the number of questions to less than 10 or divide into multiple surveys.
- Think through the order of the questions. Simple questions first, then important questions, and finally any follow-up questions and comment fields.

34 CCPA: 'The California Consumer Privacy Act of 2018 (CCPA) gives consumers more control over the personal information that businesses collect about them' (oag.ca.gov/privacy/ccpa). A CCPA is a statement that outlines how you collect, share, and use California consumers' personal information, and what rights they have over their data (Dearie, 2020).

35 GDPR: 'The GDPR applies to the processing of European residents' data (technically, all residents of the EU plus residents of the other European countries that have adopted the GDPR), *no matter where in the world the data processing takes place*. If you want to sell to European residents, you need to be compliant with the GDPR, and what better way to be compliant than to adopt it' (Woodward, 2021).

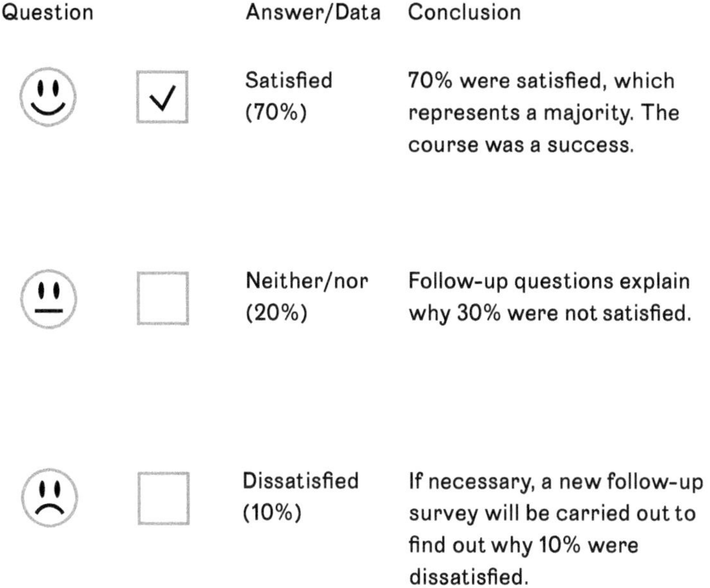

| Question | | Answer/Data | Conclusion |
|---|---|---|---|
| ☺ | ☑ | Satisfied (70%) | 70% were satisfied, which represents a majority. The course was a success. |
| 😐 | ☐ | Neither/nor (20%) | Follow-up questions explain why 30% were not satisfied. |
| ☹ | ☐ | Dissatisfied (10%) | If necessary, a new follow-up survey will be carried out to find out why 10% were dissatisfied. |

Fig. 2.13 Quantitative research

- Formulate the questions accurately so that they are relevant, easy to understand, and provide unambiguous answer options.
- Be neutral; avoid provocative or offensive formulations.
- Be consistent by following the same form of question and response scale throughout the entire survey.
- What questions are asked, leaves an impression. This can be used strategically to build a positive image. The client should approve the questions used in the survey.

### Ethics

In research ethics, requirements have been formulated to prevent respondents from getting hurt. Data should be stored and processed in such a way that unauthorised persons cannot become aware of what the individual respondent has answered. The results should be published in a manner that preserves the anonymity of the respondents (cf. privacy policy) and prevents individuals from being recognised, unless otherwise agreed. The respondents' consent to participate in the survey should be based on knowledge of the subject matter of the survey (informed consent). Some would argue that the researcher has a responsibility to offer the participants insight into the results of the survey in return for the time they have spent providing information to the researcher (Hellevik, 2015).

### Protection of personal data

If the survey is to collect and store personal data, measures should be taken to protect people's right to privacy. Laws like the California Consumer Privacy Act (CCPA)[34] and the General Data Protection Regulation (GDPR)[35] are instituted for this purpose. These laws seek to protect people's private information and prevent businesses from exploiting this information for monetary interests (Websitepolicies.com). GDPR coming



Further reading
*For the Common Good: Philosophical Foundations of Research Ethics* (2021) by Alex John London

into force on May 25th, 2018, has inspired new data privacy legislation worldwide. Many countries around the world have adopted a version of the GDPR or have similar laws to protect people's right to privacy although some countries are lagging behind[36] (Woodward, 2021). Examples of privacy protection in other countries: Qatar: Law No. 13, Turkey: Law on Protection of Personal Data No. 6698, Kenya: Data Protection Act, South Africa: Protection of Personal Information (POPI) Act (2020), Japan: Act on the Protection of Personal Information (APPI), South Korea: Personal Information Protection Act (PIPA) 2011, Canada: Personal Information Protection and Electronic Documents Act (PIPEDA), Brazil: General Data Protection Law LGPD (Woodward 2021/ securityscorecard.com).

Table 2.8 **The table shows examples of surveys, based on Surveymonkey.com**

Empathy
**The ability to empathise (empathy) with the participant's situation, needs and feelings are important in qualitative research forms such as interviews, observations and user surveys.**

**Survey process**

**Problem statement:** Which problem statement needs to be addressed or clarified?
**Purpose:** Clarify the purpose of the survey. What is the intention of the survey? What needs to be asked? How should the survey data be used? What benefit will they provide?
**Project framework:** Plan finances and time spent, survey time horizon, scope, etc. Estimate the use of own time, program licences, etc., to get an overview of the costs. For the designer, it is important to clarify the costs with the client.
**Demography/Target group (context):** Clarify the demographics. Which geographic area or context, population or group is interesting to research?
**Selection of respondents (units):** Clarify who will complete the survey. Which respondents (units) will produce results that can be generalised to the group or population one wishes to say something about? Consider the characteristics (variables) of the respondents, such as gender, nationality, occupation and interests, and make a selection of the specific choices (values) on the variable in which you are interested in, e.g. gender (variable): male or female (value on the variable).
**Method selection:** Consider which method works best in order to obtain the truest knowledge of the conditions the study should illuminate. Interview, online survey, telephone-based survey, paper survey, or other?
**Question design:** Design the questions and possible answers so that the answers can provide the most valid information about the conditions in question. Identify differences in age (children, adolescents, seniors), interests, cultures, languages, or other factors among respondents that may lead to special considerations or more surveys.
**Testing on questions:** Test the questions on a few people and make the necessary adjustments.
**Time selection:** Choose the right time. Timing can affect the quality of the responses as far as the share of respondents, the response decisions made, and the accuracy of responses are concerned. By collecting survey responses for at least one week, you ensure that you cover a wide range of people and opinions.
**Implementation:** Assess the duration of the survey and the follow up of informants who have not responded.
**Processing of data:** Consider how responses should be addressed, analysed and interpreted to provide the most accurate picture of the

Further reading
**Check out surveymonkey.com, surveyplanet.com, questback.com**

36 **The GDPR export rule is simple: data on European residents can only be exported to places with similar data protection rules (technically, the European Commission (EC) determines if your rules are adequate) (Woodward, 2021).**

| Surveys | | | | |
|---|---|---|---|---|
| Category | Research | Purpose | Questions | Effect |
| Market surveys | Needs and user survey | Gain user insight when developing new products or services. Map which designs and features the target group likes. Show customers that their opinions and needs matter. | "If you are not likely to use our new product, why not?"<br><br>"What would have made it more likely for you to want to use our new service?" | The result is used to identify market needs in the initial phase of product development, or during a design process to adjust the design, etc. |
| Market surveys | Segmentation surveys<br><br>It can be supplemented with such as psychographic studies of lifestyle, interests, opinions etc. | Map populations in order to find out who your customers are, understand their needs and make better business decisions, thereby developing goals and strategies. The age, gender, and income of the audience are examples of such characteristics. | "Which of the following categories best describes the job status of the typical customer?"<br><br>"How old is the typical customer?". | The result can contribute to the successful launching and marketing of the product or service. |
| Market surveys | Industry survey<br><br>Branch survey<br><br>Product survey | Get detailed information about own industry and industry-specific questions. Timeliness and relevance of the product or service. | "When choosing skin care products, which of the following factors are important to you?"<br><br>"Are you a first-time home buyer, or have you purchased a home before?". | The result provides data that can be used immediately to fine-tune the product or service offered. |
| Customer surveys | Customer satisfaction survey | Map the customers' experiences of a product or a service. Find out how satisfied the customers are and what can be done better. | "What did you like most about the new product?"<br>"How likely are you to recommend our product (name) to others?" | The result is used to make adjustments that can enhance customer satisfaction. |
| Internal/ work environment surveys | Employee survey | Identify problems among employees, study productivity, capture negative trends early to reverse any negative development. Give the employees a voice. | "How effective is the training you receive from your supervisor?"<br><br>"How much room did you have for professional growth in the company?"<br><br>"In a normal week, how often have you felt stressed at work?" | Identify problems and needs among co-workers. Measuring productivity, company culture, competitiveness and value creation. |

Table 2.8 Examples of different surveys

question (phenomenon) to be investigated, and how responses can help elucidate the phenomenon or respond to the problem statement at hand.

**Reliability assessment (reliability):** Consider reliability choices made in the survey. Record strengths and weaknesses of the plan and relevant issues that arose. What supports your assumptions, and what does not?

**Validity:** Assess the universality, overall value and significance of the results in the light of comparisons with other studies in this area.

**Ethics and privacy:** Consider whether all privacy and ethical considerations have been addressed and informed.

**Reporting:** Create a reporting form that presents the survey and results in a legible and easy-to-understand manner. Highlight findings. Reflect on findings and further application. Consider using illustrations, graphs, and infographics to make the survey more accessible and understandable (Survey Monkey, n.d., Questback, n.d.).

**Survey form structure**

**Form title:** Name of survey.

**Logo:** Sender, logo and contact details.

**Description:** Brief description of the survey, who is conducting it, what is its purpose, why the person in question is invited to participate, response deadline, user support information, signature requirements, etc.

**Response time:** Precise specification of the time the survey takes and a nice thank you for participating.

**The questions:** Formulation, answer options and explanatory text for each question.

**Form layout:** Simple, well-structured and clear; readable typography, with infographics and colours, if relevant to make the content more understandable and motivating to respond to.

**Time:** Start and end date of the survey.

**Other:** Option to select anonymous or not. Selection of the number of responses the respondent can submit.

**Motivation:** Incentive for those who complete the survey by participating in the drawing of a prize, for example.

**Online surveys:** Email with invitation to participate, brief description of the survey and link to the form. Follow-up email with reminder about the survey to those who have not responded.

(Based on Survey Monkey, n.d.)

### 2.6.2 Interview

A qualitative interview takes place through an open dialogue between interviewer and interviewee. This method is used when there is need to go into depth and gain more insight and understanding. In an interview, there are few or no predetermined questions, unlike a questionnaire, where all the questions are predetermined.

The information one is looking for is based on the interviewees' personal opinions, perceptions, and experiences. An interview is not

Tips for the designer

How to know what to ask and whom to ask? It is all about the goal of the survey, what task you have to solve, what questions you need answers to in order to solve it, and what capacity you have. It is not 100% certain that you need a survey. Maybe you need one or more personal interviews instead or first. Think carefully before you start spending time on a survey. Discuss it with the client and make sure that time and resources are put to good use. Here are some important questions to consider: 1) Why are you conducting a survey? 2) What is the scope of the survey? How many questions do you plan to ask, how many answers do you need, and how many people do you need to ask? 3) How are you going to implement it? Which distribution and analysis tools are you going to use? 4) How are you going to recruit respondents? Who would you like an answer from? Who is in the target group? 5) How will you process the data and use the findings?

37 Empathic design is a design research approach aimed at building 'creative understanding' for users and their everyday lives when developing new products and services. Creative understanding is the combination of a rich, cognitive and affective understanding of the other, and the ability to translate this understanding into user-centric products and services (Wright and McCarthy, 2005). This means obtaining information about the user and their everyday life, which gives inspiration for design and empathy or 'a feel' for the user (Postma et al., 2009).

38 'The term *rich data* describes the notion that qualitative data and their subsequent representation in text should reveal the complexities and the richness of what is being studied' (Given, 2008).

1 Initiation
2 Insight
3 Strategy
4 Design
5 Production
6 Management

2.1 Understanding the company
2.2 Situational study
2.3 Problem statement
2.4 Method selection
2.5 Research process
2.6 Research
2.7 Analyses
2.8 Mapping
2.9 Testing and measuring

2.6.1 Survey
2.6.2 Interview
2.6.3 Observation
2.6.4 Focus group
2.6.5 UX Research
2.6.6 Experiment
2.6.7 Scientific research
2.6.8 Artistic research
2.6.9 Design research

- Types of interviews
- Good questions
- Bad questions
- Types of questions
- What to avoid
- Processing of data
- Interview process

an arena for debate, but a conversation between interviewer and interviewees, where the interviewee is the protagonist and should talk as much as possible, while the interviewer should say as little as possible. Interviews can be used as a stand-alone research method or in combination with other methods. Interview and observation can be a good combination, for example, to find out if a product or service is sufficiently user-friendly and appealing (2.6.3 Observation, 4.3.1 Human-centred design). Listening to the user's views and observing the user's behaviours and attitudes can be used to compare the results against each other. It can increase the validity and reliability of collected data. Empathy with the user is important in an interview. It provides deeper understanding of how the interviewee perceives the situation or condition discussed.[37]

Qualitative interviews provide data in the form of text and are a relatively time-consuming method because of the time it takes to conduct the interviews and process the text. Long interviews of one hour or more require a lot of follow-up work. By limiting the time to, for example, 20 minutes, the interview will be more structured and condensed, and easier to process afterwards. It may be possible to give an extra five minutes at the end if there are any good points when closing. The advantage of long interviews is that they can reveal more complex and richer data[38] of what is being studied. (2.4.1 Qualitative method)

### Types of interviews

Interviews usually take place individually, between interviewer and interviewee (one-to-one conversation). Interviews can also be conducted in groups (one-to-many conversation), or by telephone or email. Group interviews are particularly useful if the goal is to obtain 'discussion information' (consensus, disagreement, opinion-forming, etc.), group dynamics (such as power relations), or relationships between group members. (See also 2.6.4 Focus group.) Qualitative interviews can be divided into three main types:

- Unstructured/informal interview (without planned questions)
- Semi-structured interview (some planned questions)
- Structured/formal interview (planned questions)

The advantages of the unstructured conversation are that there is better flow of the conversation and opportunities for new and unexpected information. The advantages of a structured conversation are that the interviewer gets the desired information and has the opportunity to compare the responses of several interviewees. The interviewees are called either respondents or informants. The respondent interview is an interview with people who have personal experiences with the phenomenon or topic. The informant interview is an interview with people who know a lot about the phenomenon or topic. Regardless of the form of the interview, one should think through what one wants answers to before the interview, should prepare questions, and get acquainted with the matter in order to be able to ask reasonable follow-up questions. Even if there is a plan, it should be flexible. There may be interesting information that the interviewer did not intend to ask about. At the same time, it is important not to be led too far away from the topic. It is important to ask open questions, let the interviewee speak, and not put

> 'If the exploration of the location of treasure is wrong in the beginning, even if we dig for hundreds years we still will not find the thing we want' (Qiany, 2020).

opinions in their mouth. The interviewer listens with a positive attitude and comes up with follow-up questions when the conversation is on an interesting topic (Nordby Lunde, 2008, Jacobsen, 2005).

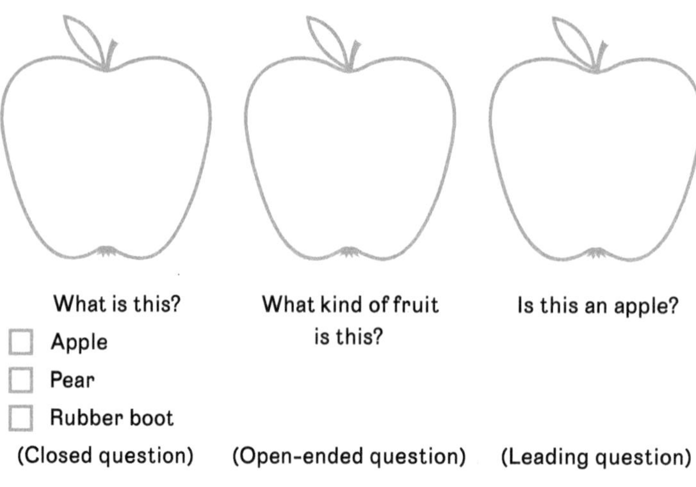

What is this?
Apple
Pear
Rubber boot
(Closed question)
What kind of fruit is this?
(Open-ended question)
Is this an apple?
(Leading question)

Fig. 2.14 Survey questions

Fig. 2.14 The figure shows three versions of a question that will influence the outcome of a survey; closed, open-ended and leading. A fourth version is the neutral question – 'Are you for or against?', which is neutral because both options are pre-centred. We also have closed questions, which can be half-open with an additional answer option: Is it an apple, a pear, a rubber boot (put a checkmark), or (fill in). In a qualitative interview, it is an advantage to ask open-ended questions to get as much information as possible, while in a quantitative survey it is advantageous to ask closed questions in order to generalise.

Table 2.9 The table shows a matrix in which the main groups of question forms, closed or open and leading or neutral, allow for different question variations.

### Good questions

Questions should trigger answers and inspire and motivate the interviewer to talk more. Good questions are simple, neutral, open, and focused, and asked in a sequence that creates meaning and flow. The most appropriate question form in an interview is open-ended questions because they result in individual answers, cause the other person to talk, and lead up to new questions. Open-ended questions begin with an interrogative pronoun: Who, what, where, when, how, etc. It is not possible to answer 'yes' or 'no'. For example: Which product do you use? What do you think? What is your experience with the product? The answer is subjective or personal and provides much information and insight into the life of the interviewee. The interviewer's job is to think of the other person and take them into account by avoiding leading, charged, or offensive questions. The interviewer should be cautious about the word 'why'. A question beginning with 'why' may sound like an accusation and lead the interviewee into a defensive position. Instead of 'Why do you think so?' you should say: 'What do you think is the reason for that?', 'What is it about this taste that you don't like?', 'Can you explain in more detail what you mean?'. The interviewer should always provide positive feedback on what the informant says. It is important to encourage the informant to say more if he or she touches on an interesting topic. 'Can you say more about this?' 'How did you perceive...?' 'Do I understand you right when I...?' 'Can you give me any examples of this?' (Blekesaune, s.a.). If the interview stops, it is up to the interviewer to improvise with new perspectives.

### Bad questions

The questions the interviewer asks, and the way they are asked, can negatively affect the outcome of the interview. If the interviewer talks too much, interrupts, asks leading questions or questions that are not relevant, it may harm the outcome of the interview. The result might also be deceptive if the interviewee takes control, if the interview becomes incoherent and without structure, and if it is not possible to go into the depths of the topic. A question can influence the outcome of a survey in several ways, according to Thorsen (2017): One can ask questions in a neutral way, for example: 'Are you for or against Norwegian membership in the EU?' This is neutral because both answer options are presented. If the question is asked differently: 'Are you for?' without asking 'Are you against?', it will give a completely different type of answer. The outcome will be more supporters because people tend to agree with the latest proposal. Then we get what is called 'yes' effect. It is easier to answer 'yes' than 'no' to such a question. The opposite will happen if only the question 'Are you against EU membership?' is asked. Then the outcome will be more 'no' answers. If a third option is presented 'Are you in doubt?' or 'I don't know?', the result will be distributed differently.

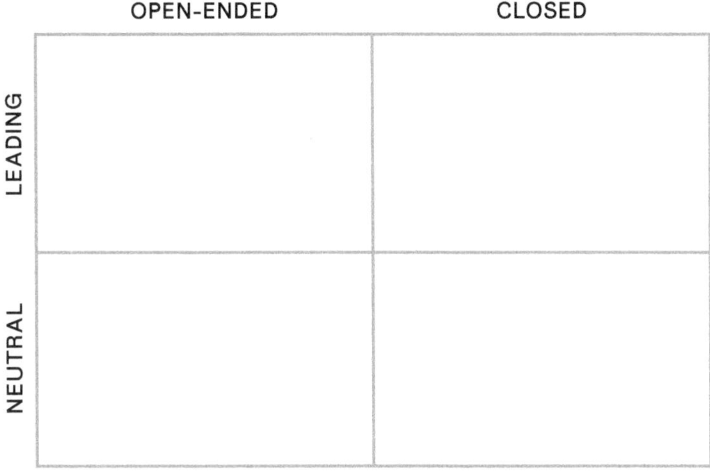


Table 2.9 Question form

**Types of questions**

There are many different question form variants between the extremes closed or open, and leading or neutral. A closed question may be leading or neutral, and the same applies to an open-ended question, see Table 2.9.

**Closed questions**: Answered with 'yes' or 'no'. They start with a verb. 'Do you agree with this?' 'Do you understand this?' They are suitable for quantitative research because they provide clarity; they are limited and targeted.

**Open-ended questions**: They make the other person talk. They provide personal answers and insights into each other's thoughts and opinions. They cannot be answered with 'yes' or 'no'. They start with an interrogative pronoun: Who, what, where, when. 'Which product do you use?' 'What do you think?' 'What is your experience of the product?' They are suitable for qualitative interviews.

**Leading questions**: The questions lead to the answers the interviewer wants to hear. They may give misleading or untrue answers because the question may be manipulative. 'We provide good service, don't

1 Initiation
2 Insight
3 Strategy
4 Design
5 Production
6 Management

2.1 Understanding the company
2.2 Situational study
2.3 Problem statement
2.4 Method selection
2.5 Research process
2.6 Research
2.7 Analyses
2.8 Mapping
2.9 Testing and measuring

2.6.1 Survey
2.6.2 Interview
2.6.3 Observation
2.6.4 Focus group
2.6.5 UX Research
2.6.6 Experiment
2.6.7 Scientific research
2.6.8 Artistic research
2.6.9 Design research

- Types of interviews
- Good questions
- Bad questions
- Types of questions
- What to avoid
- Processing of data
- Interview process

Further reading
Check out the chapters:
2.4.1 Qualitative method vs.
2.4.2 Quantitative method.

you think?' 'This product tastes fresh, don't you think?' Useful to get confirmation or persuade someone. Avoid asking leading questions.

### What to avoid

- Come up with own opinions/perceptions instead of asking questions: The interviewee will not be able to express their opinions.
- Leave out questions: The interviewee chooses what to talk about. The interviewer loses control during the interview.
- Ask double/multiple questions simultaneously: The interviewee chooses what to answer. The interviewer loses control during the interview.
- Overloading and long questions: It is unclear what is being asked. The interviewee may become confused.
- Be persistent/make allegations: The interviewee becomes defensive, gets annoyed, or chooses another topic for conversation.
- Charged words, such as strong words and phrases: The interviewee becomes defensive, gets annoyed, or chooses a more convenient topic for conversation.
- Exaggerations, such as use of reinforcing adjectives: The interviewee will try to maintain balance and dampen the effect.
- Leading questions: The interviewee may be influenced to give an answer that is not representative of their own opinion or perception.
- Closed questions: Often contain statements or value-laden words. They give answers containing little information.
- (Based on Jacobsen, 2005)

### Processing of data

It is an advantage to use an audio recorder during the interview. In addition, make notes to maintain structure and remember follow-up questions. After transcribing the interview, which can be a laborious process, make sure to structure the answers and highlight findings. When processing an interview, consider how the interview should be used. For example, if the interview is to be used in an article or newspaper, it will be important to think about the reading experience, how it is to be read, in what context. Style, tone of voice and structure should be consistent with the purpose. It may also be necessary to cut something out in order not to go too far, while at the same time it is important to preserve authenticity by bringing out the personality and voice of the interviewee. Documentation and presentation of the interview should state:

- Who conducted the interview?
- Who has participated?
- Why was the interview conducted?
- What questions were asked?
- What questions were not asked?
- In what order were the questions asked and in what way?
- For quantitative surveys:
- What response options were provided? How were they designed? (Based on Jacobsen 2005)

39 Tony Ulwick. Founder of the innovation consulting firm Strategyn, pioneer of Jobs-to-be-Done Theory, creator of Outcome-Driven Innovation.
40 jobs-to-be-done.com
41 The book *Contextual Design: Design for Life*, describes the core techniques needed to deliberately produce a compelling user-experience.
42 Contextual inquiry (CI): Contextual inquiry at UsabiliLyNet/ Contextual Interviews at Usability.gov/ Getting Started with Contextual Techniques.

1 Initiation
2 Insight
3 Strategy
4 Design
5 Production
6 Management

2.1 Understanding the company
2.2 Situational study
2.3 Problem statement
2.4 Method selection
2.5 Research process
2.6 Research
2.7 Analyses
2.8 Mapping
2.9 Testing and measuring

2.6.1 Survey
2.6.2 Interview
2.6.3 Observation
2.6.4 Focus group
2.6.5 UX Research
2.6.6 Experiment
2.6.7 Scientific research
2.6.8 Artistic research
2.6.9 Design research

- Types of interviews
- Good questions
- Bad questions
- Types of questions
- What to avoid
- Processing of data
- Interview process

### Example of different types of interviews

**Directed storytelling:** This type of interview is rooted in the social science method of narrative inquiry triggering detailed user behaviour. Participants share their past experiences in detail, while the interviewer understands people and documents their experiences from the personal stories they tell (Martin & Hanington, 2012).

**'Jobs to be done':**[39] This type of interview helps the company understand the efforts/'journey' the customer has to make in order to purchase the company's product. A timeline tool is used to capture the sensitive moments when the customer gets a small push (nudge) and goes on with the purchase. A friend's sudden purchase of a large TV can lead the customer to consider a similar purchase, or at least to pay more attention to TVs (Balaz, 2015).[40] (2.8.4 and 4.3.12 Customer journey).

**Artefacts interview:** Interviews can be made more productive by integrating objects, picture cards, or anything else that brings out personal experiences in the participant (Martin & Hanington 2012). Having a product to interact with can help a user think of more details, especially if the user is shy or has never had an interview before (Murray, 2017).

**Contextual inquiry (CI):** This type of interview is a user-centred method developed by Hugh Beyer and Karen Holtzblatt 1988.[41] It can e.g. be structured as a two-hour, one-on-one interaction in which the researcher aggregates data by watching the user in the course of the user's normal activities and discussing those activities with the user ('Contextual inquiry,' n.d.).[42]

**Touchstone tour:** A tour of the participant's familiar surroundings. A contextual, empathetic method that effectively puts the interviewer into the participant's world, to understand how he or she organises information and systems through the use of space and cognitive objects. Participants are usually calmer in their own surroundings and are often excited to share their space and objects with an interested researcher. The conversation can be guided carefully but should be flexible enough to allow the interviewee to speak openly (Martin and Hanington, 2012).

Further reading
Check out the book *Nudge: Improving Decisions About Health, Wealth, and Happiness* (2009) by Richard H. Thaler and Cass R. Sunstein.

Involve the user: User observations, user input, user involvement and user-centricity are all concepts of approaches that involve the user and put them at the heart of the use and experience of products and services (4.3.1 Human-centred).

## Interview process

**Problem statement**
Which problem statement should be addressed or clarified?

**Purpose**
Clarify the purpose of the interview. What is the goal of the interview? What is there a need to ask? How should the survey data be used? What good will they do?

**Preparations. Step 1**
- Get insights on the topic.
- Prepare an interview guide (individual questions and structure).

- Select the interview type (respondent or informant/ individual or group).
- Select interviewees – which ones and how many?

**Preparations. Step 2**

- Choose the format (e.g. face-to-face, telephone or email).
- Determine response registration (minutes, audio recording, both).
- Make interview appointments (what, where, when and for how long).
- Distribute interviewees (if there are multiple interviewers).
- Plan the duration of the interview. Short interviews give less follow-up work.

**Interview guide**

Start with simple (preferably fact-related) questions. Proceed with the questions of substance:

- The ones that are particularly relevant to your problem statement.
- Controversial or sensitive questions.
- Detailed question list or main theme with keywords.
- Finish by requesting a closing comment.
- Conduct a test interview.

**Selecting interviewees**

Many possible approaches:

- Strategic selection – the ones that are most interesting and relevant.
- Variation selection – capture different experiences, opinions, arguments, perceptions, perspectives.
- Type selection – capture the usual and normal.
- Convenience selection – the ones who are easiest to get in touch with.
- 'Snowball Selection' – tips from interviewees about other people who should be interviewed.
- Random selection – the lottery principle.
- Number of interviewees? As many as appropriate.

**Implementation**

*Step 1) Presentation of the purpose of the interview:*

- Topic/problem statement.
- How to use the material (anonymity, direct quotations, review).

*Step 2) Conducting the interview:*

- Ask questions – be quiet – listen.
- Do not get too tied up by the interview guide.
- Ask follow-up questions if applicable (it will often be).
- Positive feedback to the participant.

**Follow-up work**

- It should be done immediately after the completion of the interview (for example on the same or on the next day).
- It consists of: 1) Typing out notes. 2) Transcription of audio recording.
- Follow-up work usually takes 2–4 times longer than the interview itself.

**Analysis of the responses**

Reduce the amount of information – bring out the most interesting/relevant information. There is no standard recipe for this, but some options:

Subjective observation vs. objective observation

A situation can be interpreted in many different ways. It is important to distinguish between what we actually see and what we think we see. It is easy to believe that others know and think like us. Example: Mrs. Hansen is sitting quietly and looking out the window. She is not smiling. What do you do next? Subjective observation: You describe the situation based on your own interpretations. For example: 'Mrs. Hansen enjoys looking at the birds flying between the trees' or 'Mrs. Hansen seems sad and reserved and is not interested in social interaction.' Objective observation: You describe what you observe, without interpreting it. 'Today Kari Hansen sat in the chair by the window for over an hour' (Sørhøy & Heir, 2010/2017).

43 Read the interview with Kjell Reenskaug, available at designandstrategy.co.uk.

1) Review and highlight particularly interesting/relevant answers or partial answers.
2) Organise responses and highlight what provides the most relevant information.
3) Create a categorisation and comparison of responses.
4) Arrange the results for the clearest possible presentation.

*Structured analyses:* They pay little attention to the informant's interpretations.
*Unstructured analyses:* They emphasise the informants' own interpretations (based on Blekesaune n.d.).



### 2.6.3 Observation

Observation is a research method that involves observing, watching, following, studying, and recording behaviour, actions, and social situations. It involves understanding how the target audience of a product or service uses and perceives the product or service. This type of research is frequently used in user surveys and customer journey studies.

The ability to see and observe people and surroundings is among the designer's foremost strengths and essential to understanding the behaviour and needs of the target group, which is of key importance for developing user-friendly and attractive solutions. This method provides greater proximity to the subjects compared to an interview or survey. This is because one meets people in their own environment, or in a situation, activity or interaction with a product or service. The context or cultural framework of the survey is central to understanding the person's behaviour and reactions. The person's motivation, interest, cultural affiliation, and lifestyle will also have an impact. So will the person's level of knowledge and understanding and logic. The observer needs a great deal of empathy and sensitivity in order to get in the user's shoes and gain the necessary insights.[43]

Observation is about systematic observations mainly using the sense of sight (Larsen, 2007). It involves observing in its entirety and then recording, writing down, and concretising the impressions. An observational survey may include, for example, recording human behaviour in a public domain in order to identify problem areas and improvement potential in the urban space or a service offering.

Observations can be made without much preparation, but can be time-consuming in terms of implementation and follow-up work. A good observation is based on trust and mutual understanding between the observer and the person or persons to be observed. This applies both to what the observation is to be used for and what specifically to look for. Observation is more about recording what people are doing than examining what they think and believe. The result of an observation survey is often characterised by the observer's subjective experience and interpretation (Fangen, 2011), which may lead to misunderstandings or misinterpretations. In addition, phenomena that are not directly observable will be captured to a small extent (Jacobsen, 2005, p. 160), therefore it may be advantageous to repeat the observation process and follow up with some type of interview. Observations often provide hypotheses that are tested afterwards, either qualitatively or quantitatively.

**What are we looking for?**

During the observation phase, a significant amount of data is collected in a number of areas, such as field notes, interview transcripts, photographs, videos and audio recordings. According to Beckman and Barry (2007, p. 36), the recorded information should ideally include:

**Space:** the physical place or places
**Participants:** the people involved
**Activity:** a set of related things that people do
**Object:** the physical things that are present
**Action:** single actions that people do
**Event:** a set of related activities that people carry out
**Time:** the sequencing that takes place over time
**Target:** the things people are trying to accomplish
**Feeling:** the emotions felt and expressed[44]

The essence of good observation are activities that give the designer an opportunity to understand how a product or service is used and how its characteristics work in a user situation. It is about empathising with the user and understanding the user's state of mind and feelings in interaction with people, objects and surroundings.

Fig. 2.15 The figure shows the AEIOU Empathy Map, a mapping tool that is well suited for user studies, for analysing, planning and implementing projects. The purpose of the method is to be empathic with the user by, for example, finding out what problems the user has in interacting with his or her environment, technology, products or services he or she uses. This constitutes valuable insight for creating user-friendly products and services. (Based on Dave Gray/Beckman and Barry (2007). Available at canvasgeneration.com).

Tips for the designer
To observe, you should see, listen, feel, and smell. Try observing and writing down what you see. Imagine being observed in the role of designer. How would that feel?

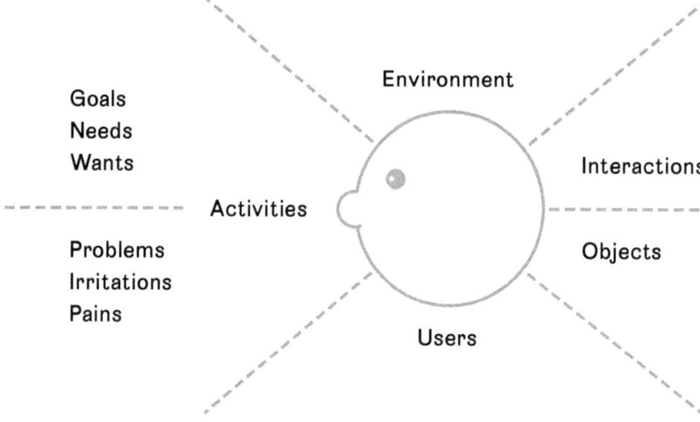


Fig. 2.15 AEIOU Empathy Map

**AEIOU Empathy Map**

When using observation as research method, the information is sometimes easier to capture using an 'AEIOU' diagram (Beckman and Barry, 2007). Empathy is the key word. An empathy map is a method of getting into the user's shoes, and being empathic with the user, a tool originally created by Dave Gray many years ago.[45] The tool should 'help cultivate a collaborative effort to understand and organise what we know about users' goals, pains and causes of their behavior' (canvasgeneration.com). That involves mapping and organising observations of activities that show different aspects of a person's life and interaction with the environment. The purpose is to use the data to map a person's problems and help solve them. Many UX practitioners use the AEIOU Empathy Map[46] because it is

44 'Participant observation', Spradley 1980
45 Gray (2017) 'Updated Empathy Map Canvas' (medium.com).
46 The AEIOU framework was developed in 1991 by Rick Robinson, Ilya Prokopoff, John Cain, and Julie Pokorny at the Doblin Group in Chicago (EthnoHub, n.d.).

### AEIOU Empathy Map

'What is important is not only understanding and describing each element of the framework, but also understanding the interactions between the elements' (Wasson, 2000).

**Activities** are goal directed sets of actions – things which people want to accomplish. What are the pathways that people take towards the things they want to accomplish, including specific actions and processes? How long do they spend doing something? Who are they doing it with?

**Environment** include the entire arena where activities take place- For example, what describes the atmosphere and function of the context, including individual and shared spaces?

**Interactions** are between a person and someone or something else, and are the building blocks of activities. What is the nature of routine and special interactions between people, between people and objects in their environment, and across distances?

**Objects** are building blocks of the environment, key elements sometimes put to complex or unintended uses, changing their function, meaning and context. For example, what are the objects and devices people have in their environments, and how do these relate to their activities?

**Users** are the consumers, the people providing the behaviours, preferences and needs. Who is present? What are their roles and relationships? What are their values and prejudices?

Retrieved from Christina Wasson (2000) and canvasgeneration.com.



well suited for describing a person's ecosystem (canvasgeneration.com, Wasson 2000). AEIOU is an acronym for Activities, Environment, Interaction, Objects, Users.

### Open or concealed observation

It is common to distinguish between open and concealed observation. Open observation means that the units (persons) know that they are being looked into. Concealed observation means that the persons do not know that they are being examined, the so called 'fly on the wall observations' which separates the researcher from any direct involvement. The advantage of concealed observation is that those being examined have no reason to behave abnormally, which is a drawback in open observation. Once people know they are being examined, they tend to change their behaviour, including by trying to satisfy the investigator or deliberately trying to avoid doing something that might be perceived as stupid (Jacobsen, 2005, p.160). Therefore, many assume that reliability is improved if the observation is concealed. In case of concealed observation, it is important to take privacy into account by making sure that the survey would not reveal details about a person's identity or behaviour. The general rule of observation is that those being examined should be informed. Another distinction is made between participant observation and non-participant observation.

Human ecosystem

A human ecosystem can be described as the interaction of humans, the environed units, with their interrelated environments. These are conceptualised as three interrelated environments: natural, human constructed and human behavioral. Using a human ecological framework for study, quality of life indicators can measure aspects of the environed units, environments, and their interaction (Bubolz et al., 1978).

### Participant observation

This method implies that the observer is visibly present along with the informants. It can also mean that the observer participates on an equal footing with those being examined (Jacobsen, 2005, p. 161). Participant observation is open observation, which means that those being examined know that they are being examined. It resembles the interview as far as form is concerned, because the observer can interact and converse with the subject, but here the focus is more on behaviour, actions, interaction, experience and empathy with the user. Participant observations may, for example, be useful in developing or testing a product in order to examine how the user perceives the functional and emotional characteristics of the product in terms of utility value, usability, shape, function, aesthetics, familiarity, product information and the like. This makes it possible to better adapt the product to the needs of the user. The result of participant observation provides qualitative data (descriptive).[47]

Tips for the designer
**Observations are often only part of a survey or mapping and can be performed both qualitatively and quantitatively.**

#### Tips for participant observations

- Plan how you would like to conduct the observation. Will you study people in their everyday activities, or will you recreate or simulate a particular event and ask them to complete tasks?
- Participate only if this does not distract or affect the user.
- Select or simulate areas that are as natural to the user as possible.
- Do not demonstrate how a product or a task is to be solved. It may cause the user to do so in the same way.
- Ask the user to put their thoughts into words during the task and process. This can help you to understand their perceptions and decision-making.
- Do not ask questions unless you plan to follow them up in combination with an interview.
- Take photos, preferably record a video, as it allows you to capture complex situations easily. Recordings can then be examined in more detail later.
- When videoing try to set up the camera in a location where it is obvious and will soon be forgotten by the users.

(Plumbe et al., 2010, p. 80).

### Non-participant observations

In non-participant observations, also called field research, the observer is usually not visible and looks at people's behaviour from a distance or without their realising the observer's presence. Such concealed observation should take place in a public, and not in a private area, to protect people's privacy. The goal is to get an idea of the problems the survey objects may have when moving in an environment, and gather information about their behaviour, actions, conduct, interactions, and context, on a general and not on an individual basis. To get enough data, one often needs to stay on site for a long time. This method can be useful in mapping a target group's movements and behaviour, in order to adapt and strengthen the service (2.8.4 and 4.3.12 Customer journey). Such an observation will provide qualitative data (in text form) that can be

47 Descriptive: 1) Presenting observations about the characteristics of someone or something: serving to describe 2a) Referring to, constituting, or grounded in matters of observation or experience. 2b) Factually grounded or informative rather than normative, prescriptive, or emotive. 3a) Expressing the quality, kind, or condition of what is denoted by the modified term 3b) Non-restrictive (Descriptive, n.d.). Non-restrictive means: 'A *restrictive clause* modifies the noun that precedes it in an essential way. Restrictive clauses limit or identify such nouns and cannot be removed from a sentence without changing the sentence's meaning. A nonrestrictive clause, on the other hand, describes a noun in a nonessential way' (Traffis, n.d.).

**Tips for non-participant observations**

- Choose a location that relates to your research topic and observe how people behave within that space.
- Be prepared to stay in one location for a long time. 1–2 hours are usually enough to gather information of significance or to indicate whether the location is suitable.
- Pay attention to the context, even information that may not seem immediately important. Try to record points of interest, time intervals, schedules, movements, and action patterns.
- Sketch layouts, floor plans, movements and dynamics.
- Use photo and video wherever possible and justifiable as far as privacy is concerned. You can capture complex situations in great details and examine them later. (Plumbe et al., 2010).


1 Initiation
2 Insight
3 Strategy
4 Design
5 Production
6 Management

2.1 Understanding the company
2.2 Situational study
2.3 Problem statement
2.4 Method selection
2.5 Research process
2.6 Research
2.7 Analyses
2.8 Mapping
2.9 Testing and measuring

2.6.1 Survey
2.6.2 Interview
2.6.3 Observation
2.6.4 Focus group
2.6.5 UX Research
2.6.6 Experiment
2.6.7 Scientific research
2.6.8 Artistic research
2.6.9 Design research

- What are we looking for?
- AEIOU Empathy Map
- Open or concealed observation
- Participant observation
- Non-participant observations
- Observation process
- Examples of different methods of observation


successfully visualised using photos, illustrations or infographics. For example, if the purpose of the survey is to keep statistics, the survey will provide quantitative data (numbers and statistics). Examples of this are when it is necessary to record the number of visitors on a day, when they come and go, how long they stay on site, what they do, how much they buy, and so on.

**Observation process**

Observing is watching, discovering, recording, and concretising.
**Problem statement:** Clarify which problem statement is to be answered, resolved, or clarified?
**Objective:** Clarify the purpose of the observation. What is the objective of the observation? What is to be observed? How should the observation data be used? What good will they do?
**Plan:** What does one need to look for in order to clarify the research question? Where/how will the research take place?
**Observation objects:** Which persons, locations and observation points should be sought out and observed?
**Observation protocol:** Create an observation protocol or registration form in advance. It should contain a plan for the observation, what to record as well as relevant questions. It should be short and simple so that it can be used if there are several observers.
**Photo/video/notes:** Use photos and videos (do not overdo it; remember it takes time to analyse afterwards).
**Notices:** Take quick notes that can be concretised afterwards. Collect and process notes as soon as possible after the observation. It is important not to trust one's memory!
**Research ethics:** Determine how the survey objects can be kept anonymous?
**Report:** Develop a report with concrete impressions and findings based on the observations.

**Examples of different methods of observation**

**Mystery shoppers:** A person is commissioned to visit a store or restaurant incognito in order to assess its service and the quality of the goods or other services.

Inductive vs. deductive
Inductive reasoning, or induction, moves from specific observations to broad generalisations. Deductive reasoning, or deduction, starts out with a general statement, or hypothesis, and examines the possibilities to reach a specific, logical conclusion (Bradford 2017). Read more: 2.6.7 Scientific research

**Heat mapping:** A graphical representation of data where the individual values in a matrix are represented as colours, which can show where customers are staying in the store. Web heat mapping, for example, can be used to display areas of a web page that are most often searched or observed by visitors. These tools are often used along with other analytical tools.
**Eye tracking:** A method of measuring eye positions and eye movement, where one's eyes pause or how the eyes move relative to the head. The method is used in visual system research, in psychology, marketing, digital user interaction, and in product and service development. There are various methods for measuring eye movement, such as video images in which the eye position is extracted ('Eye tracking', n.d.).

### 2.6.4 Focus group

A focus group[48] is a structured group interview with a limited number of participants, led by a moderator (group leader/interviewer). The aim of the survey is, for example, to find out what a relevant target group thinks about an existing or new product or service, where they themselves are among the users/customers.

The questions are planned in advance and are answered through an informal open dialogue between the participants, 'which are usually 6–8, and rarely more than 12' (Wilkinson, 1998). The feedback from interviewees can, for example, be used as a basis for decision-making in connection with the development of a new product concept, new product design or new logo design, based on what the target group thinks and feels about the product or design concept. A focus group only reveals the participants' views and not their behaviour, and should therefore not be confused with a user test, which involves participants physically testing a specific product or service. Focus groups are often conducted with a two-way mirror[49] on one of the walls, so that the client and designer can follow the group conversation without being present themselves (Vikøren & Phil, 2016). 'The focus group does not aim to agree on or present solutions to the problems being discussed, but to get different views on the matter' (Kvale & Brinkmann, 2009).

Focus group research can be purchased from analytics agencies that have the necessary equipment, professional moderators and access to databases of focus group participants from a wide range of different target groups. Those invited to participate in focus group research should preferably form a cross-section of the defined target group. It may be potential customers or users of the products or services to be tested. Participants usually receive a gift card with a symbolic amount of money for attendance. A moderator prepares and conducts the survey. During the focus group, the moderator starts by presenting the relevant topics and questions and encourages open-minded interactive conversation between participants. One important detail is that the moderator creates an atmosphere that makes participants express both personal and conflicting views.

Focus groups can also be arranged by the designer or company without the use of professional analytical agencies. Participants can then be obtained from the company's customers, employees or partners, or from the designer's professional or private network. Conference rooms

48 Sociologist Robert Merton, together with colleagues Patricia Kendall and Marjorie Fiske, is usually credited as the 'inventor' of focus groups-although social psychologists Emory Bogardus and Walter Thurstone had used group interviews to develop survey instruments in the 1920s (cf. Bogardus 1926). Merton and Paul Lazarsfeld initially used group interviews to develop propaganda during World War II (Wilkinson, 1998).
49 A two-way mirror (more accurately called a 'one-way glass') allows observers to see through one side of the mirror while participants on the other side see only their own reflections.
50 Origin: John Heywood 1546. 'Head' here means 'mind', as opposed to heart or spirit. (John Heywood, n.d.)

with audio systems, camcorders and one-way mirrors may be rented from operators providing such services. Alternatively, participants can gather in a regular conference room and use the equipment available.

The core idea of focus groups is that 'two heads think better than one'[50] and that group dynamics can produce interesting and relevant information about what is to be researched. When participants discuss their experiences, one can obtain more information than by interviewing each group member separately. According to Sue Wilkinson, the theory behind this presupposes that opinions are formed collectively, and within the scope of social interactions between individuals (Wilkinson, 1998). This means that opinions can form during the discussion. 'The social process of collective sense-making is open to the researcher's scrutiny' (Wilkinson, 1998). Following up with qualitative interviews after the focus group survey could provide answers as to whether respondents say the same thing when they are alone, as when they are in a focus group (2.6.2 Interview, 2.6.3 Observation).



### Focus group process

Explanation of the process is based on Geyti (2011).

**Focus group preparation:**

- Think carefully about who you would like to have as participants, and how many surveys you think would be necessary to conduct in order to get enough data.
- Consider which criteria should be applied to the target group in terms of gender, age, social standing, occupation, interests, etc.
- Assemble the group based on differences such as what they may have opinions about, attitudes to, or experience of.
- Join the group as an observer if appropriate or behind a two-way mirror.
- Think about how you want to process data.
- Should it be recorded with an audio recorder and transcribed, or is it enough to take notes along the way or summarise the findings?
- Can you get someone to transcribe for you?
- Inform the participants in detail about the use of data and the purpose of the interview.
- Provide food for the participants.

**Focus group implementation:**

- Welcome and presentation by the moderator and the observers.
- Presentation of the participants.
- Serving hot/cold drinks and simple food/snacks.
- Information on the use of the audio recorder, video camera or other technology.

**Presentation of rules for the focus group:**

- The role of the moderator (and possibly co-interviewer).
- Confidentiality in the group and anonymisation (data protection). Optionally, offer informants the option of withdrawing statements within a week, for example, if they regret anything they have said.
- Respect for other participants (not talking all at once, being brief).
- There are no right or wrong answers.

**Presentation of discussion topics in the form of questions:**

- Questions should be formulated openly, relate to the current topics and be suitable for an open discussion.

Further reading
*Reflective Journal for Research Interviews and Focus Groups: A guided journal and dairy for writing notes on your qualitative research interviews and focus groups Paperback* (2018) by Diyas Gogo Journal.

- Be sure to have a priority or a logical order of questions. It can provide richer and deeper answers than if the group were to rush to answer a lot of incoherent questions.
- Encourage open-minded thinking and exchange of views, attitudes, and feelings.
- Please note that dominant individuals, who speak a lot, should sometimes be politely interrupted, while silent and shy participants should be encouraged to share their views.

**Rounding off and concluding remarks:**

- Thank participants for their participation and talk briefly about the future course of the survey.

### 2.6.5 UX Research

UX research (User-experience research) is a human-centred approach to data collection. The purpose is to learn about the needs, pains, barriers, and frustrations people face when interacting with websites, products, services, or systems, in order to optimise their user-experience (4.3.2 User-experience). User researchers use various methods to expose problems and design opportunities, both before and during the design process, as well as an ongoing process afterwards to improve the solution. UX research is also referred to as a human-centred approach to problem solving (4.3.1 Human-centred design, 4.4.2 Creative problem solving). According to Peter Morvilles[51] each factor of experience design can be

Fig. 2.16 The figure shows a landscape of user research methods within a 3-dimensional framework with the axes Attitudinal vs. Behavioral, Qualitative vs. Quantitative and Context of Use. The framework can be used within a typical web or product-development process. Each dimension provides a way to distinguish among studies in terms of the questions they answer and the purposes they are most suited for. Figure and text based on Christian Rohrer (2014), Nielsen Norman Group, nngroup.com.

Tips for the designer
Ensure strategic anchoring. Take a look at 3.1.3 TOP 5 and 3.3 Goals and subgoals.

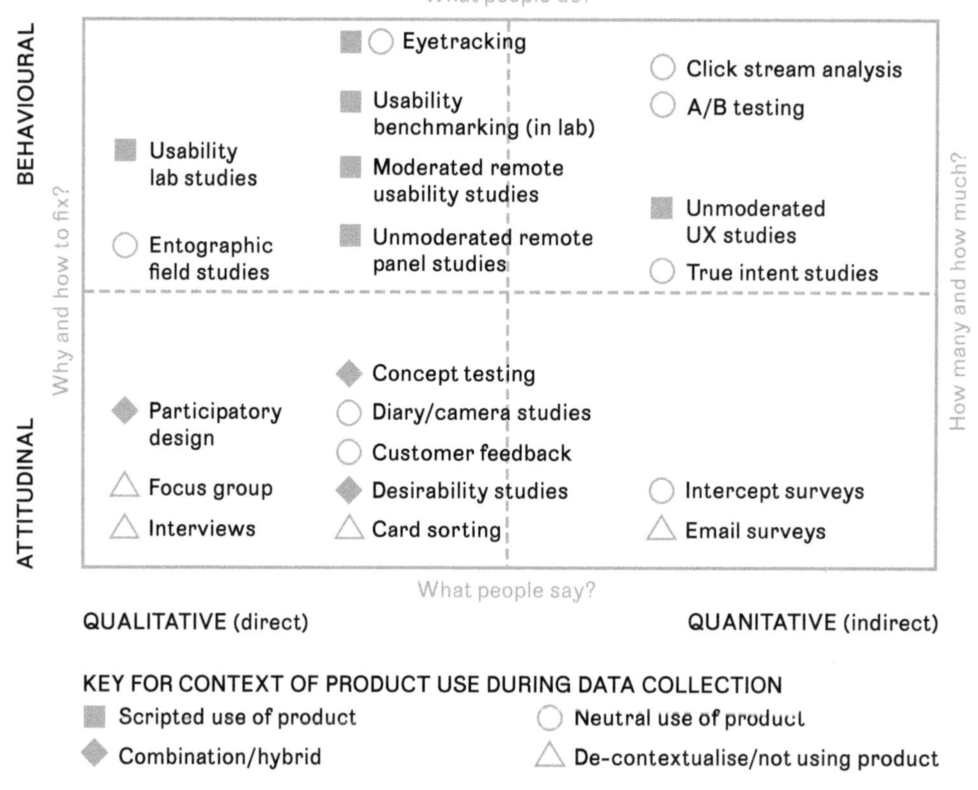


Fig. 2.16 A landscape of UX research methods

defined by focusing on balance of context, content and users, to create products, services, or systems that are useful, usable, findable, credible, accessible, desirable and valuable. The 7 facets can be grouped based on how the user interacts (uses, thinks, feels) with a product (Karagianni, 2018). Conducting UX research can help clarify which problem to be solved and redefine the goal and strategy of an assignment. The process and the result should be anchored in the company's overall strategy and goal and should help the company achieve its goals, or other value creation.

**20 UX methods in brief**, Figure 2.16 explained (based on Rohrer, 2014):

**Attitudinal vs. behavioural:** The distinction between 'what people say' versus 'what people do'. The purpose of attitudinal research is usually to understand or measure people's stated beliefs, while usability studies rely more on people's behaviour.

**Qualitative vs. quantitative:** Studies that are qualitative generate data about behaviours or attitudes based on observing people directly through field studies and usability studies. Quantitative studies generate data about the behaviour or attitudes in question indirectly, through measurement and statistics using survey or analytics tools (2.4 Method selection).

**Context of use:** The distinction of users and non-users of the product.

- *Natural use of the product*: The aim of the study is to understand behaviour or attitudes as close to reality as possible.
- *A scripted study of the product*: The aim is to focus on the insights on specific usage aspects, such as a newly redesigned flow.
- *Studies where the product is not used*: The aim is to examine issues that are broader than usage and usability, such as a study of the brand or larger cultural behaviours.
- *Hybrid methods*: The study uses creative form of product usage to meet goals, such as 'partici-patory-design methods that allows users to interact with and rearrange design elements that could be part of a product experience, in order discuss how their proposed solutions would better meet their needs and why they made certain choices' (Rohrer, 2014).

A short description of a selection of user research methods:[52]

**Usability-lab studies:** The participant is given a set of scenarios that lead to tasks and usage of specific interest within a product or service.

**Ethnographic field studies:** Researchers meet with and study participants in their natural environment, where they would most likely encounter the product or service in question.

**Participatory design:** Participants are given design elements or creative materials in order to construct their ideal experience in a concrete way that expresses what matters to them most and why.

**Focus groups:** Groups of 3–12 participants are led through a discussion about a set of topics, giving verbal and written feedback through discussion and exercises (2.6.4 Focus group).

**Interviews:** Conducted one-to-one to discuss in depth what the participant thinks about the topic in question.

**Eyetracking:** Conducted to precisely measure where participants look as they perform tasks or interact naturally with websites, applications, physical products, or environments.

**Usability benchmarking:** Tightly scripted usability studies are performed with several participants, using precise and predetermined measures of performance.



Further reading
*101 UX Principles: Actionable Solutions for Product Design Success* (2022) by Will Grant.

51 Peter Morville's UX Honeycomb depicts the 7 aspects of the user-experience. Peter Morville is a writer, speaker, and consultant best known for helping to create the discipline of information architecture. His bestselling books include *Information Architecture for the World Wide Web, Ambient Findability,* and *Search Patterns. (TUG, understanding-group.com/peter-morville)*

52 The studies can be done one-on-one or with larger numbers of participants, and either in person or online.

**Moderated remote usability studies:** Conducted remotely with the use of tools such as screen-sharing software and remote control capabilities.
**Unmoderated remote panel studies:** A panel of trained participants who have video recording and data collection software installed on their own personal devices uses a website or product while thinking aloud, having their experience recorded for immediate playback and analysis by the researcher or company.
**Concept testing:** The researcher shares an approximation of a new concept, product or service that captures the key essence (the value proposition) to determine if it meets the needs of the target audience.
**Diary/camera studies:** Participants are given a mechanism (diary or camera) to record and describe aspects of their lives that are relevant to a product or service.
**Customer feedback:** Open-ended and/or close-ended information provided by a self-selected sample of users, often through a feedback link, button, form, or email.
**Desirability studies:** Participants are offered different visual-design alternatives and are expected to associate each alternative with a set of attributes selected from a closed list (qual or quant).
**Card sorting:** Users are asked to organise items into groups and assign categories to each group. Useful to create or refine the information architecture of a site by exposing users' mental models (Qual or quant).
**Clickstream analysis:** Analysing the record of screens or pages that users click on and see, as they use a site or software product; it requires the site to be instrumented properly or the application to have telemetry data collection enabled.
**A/B testing:** Scientifically testing different designs on a site by randomly assigning groups of users to interact with each of the different designs and measuring the effect of these tasks on user behaviour: to multivariate testing, live testing and bucket testing (2.9.2 A/B testing).
**Unmoderated UX studies:** An automated method that uses a specialised research tool to capture participant behaviours (through software installed on participant computers/browsers) and attitudes (through embedded survey questions), usually by giving participants goals or scenarios to accomplish with a site or prototype (qual or quant).
**True-intent studies:** Asking random site visitors what their goal or intention is upon entering the site, measuring their subsequent behaviour, and asking whether they were successful in achieving their goal upon exiting the site.
**Intercept surveys:** Used to gather onsite feedback from a target audience by intercepting website visitors to ask them timely and relevant questions.
**Email surveys:** The survey, such as a questionnaire is sent to a respondent via email. (2.6.1 Survey)

Fig. 2.17 The figure shows example of planning and conducting an experiment. Based on Næss & Petersen (2017).

> 'A good UX research can lead designers and stakeholders to find the right question to work on, and it can also support them to find the real needs of users and markets. This is why UX research so valuable in all the stages of the products development' (Qiany, 2020).

## 2.6.6 Experiment

A scientific experiment investigates the causal relationship between two or more events, based on an assumption (hypothesis) to be tested in order to make a discovery or to test a known fact. Experimenting is something most designers do in the course of a design process. It can be, for example, to find out how a product works with other features,

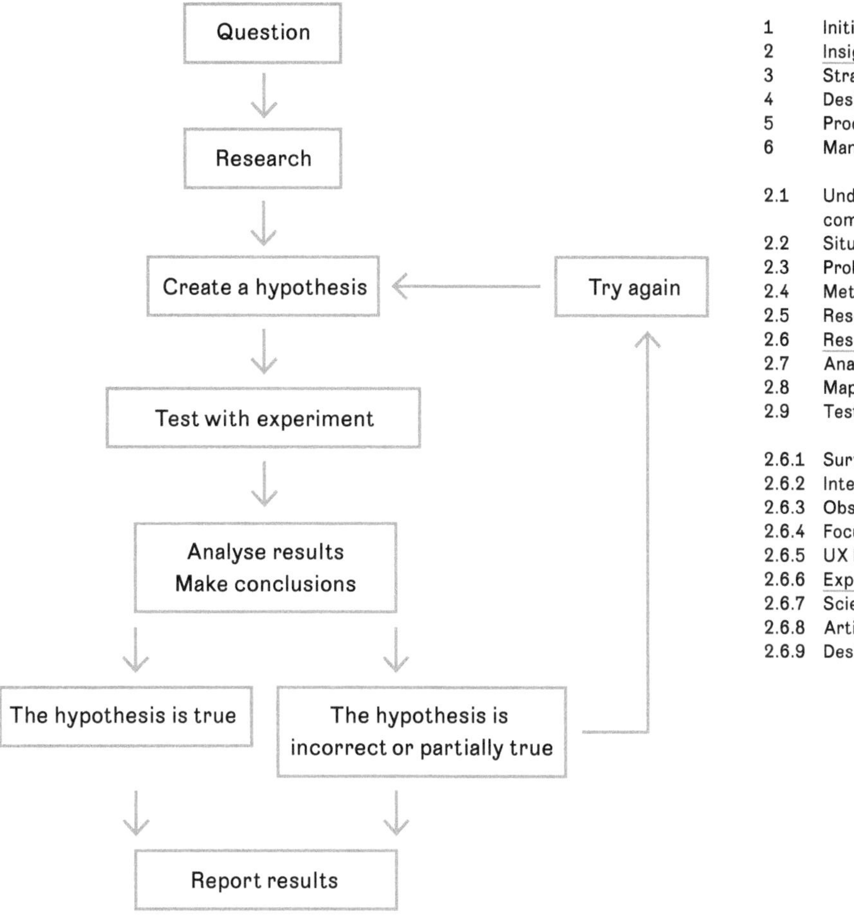


Fig. 2.17 Experiment design



how a shape appears with different colours, what a title looks like with other typefaces, how a room is perceived with different lighting and so on. Experimentation in design context can be made intuitive or systematic and scientific.

Experiment is an approach to research that involves the researcher's manipulating or influencing one of the given conditions in order to examine its effects. The purpose is to demonstrate how a factor affects a measured variable (Svartdal, 2015). A variable is a characteristic of a unit or phenomenon that one wishes to examine. It is a term used in science theory when examining in an experiment the causal relationship between two factors. The factor whose effect one is interested in is called an underlying or independent variable. The factor resulting from the effect is called a dependent variable. This means that one factor is varied and the others are kept constant so that the effect of the factor being examined can be assessed (see 2.9.2 A/B testing). The experiment is usually based on a justified expectation, i.e. a hypothesis. The experimental data are collected using good, accepted methods that produce reproducible results. A correct reference (control) must be selected to ensure that the data are verifiable (2.4.4 Research question, 2.5 Research process, 2.6.7 Scientific research).

How does the choice of motif, colours, typography, shape and materials affect the response of an ad? This can be measured through an experiment. A group gets to see an ad with one photo, while another group gets to see the same ad with a different photo. Do these groups respond differently? If the same experiment is done with two different typefaces, will it change one's perception of the ad differently?

Scientific experimentation forms the basis of the scientific method. Scientific method is in principle sequential, but an experiment is more circular than linear. This means that there may be a need to change the design after a set of results and do the experiment again.

**Experiment design**: Here are examples of steps in an experiment based on Næss & Petersen (2017):

1) Define a research question; based on an observation, problem, or assumption.
2) Formulate a hypothesis; it may be a statement that you wish to confirm or refute.
3) Select variables to be tested:
   - The dependent variable;[53] the one affected by something (A).
   - The independent variable (the cause variable); the one whose effect we want to study (B).
   - The experiment is to observe how the dependent variable (A) changes when changing the independent variable (B).
4) Controlled experiment:
   - Develop a standard for comparison.
   - Select basis for comparison.
   - The basis for comparison is used to check for other factors that may influence the experiment (causal variables).
   - The basis of comparison is treated in the same way as the dependent variable (A), but is not subjected to the independent variable (B).
   - After the experiment, the basis for comparison can be measured against the dependent variable (A), to see the outcome for the independent variable (B).
5) Data are collected and analysed;
   - The data can be entered in a chart with x axis (horizontal) and y axis (vertical).
   - On the y axis, results from the dependent variable are recorded.
   - On the x axis, results from the independent variable are recorded.
6) Analysis, discussion, interpretation and validation. Conclusions are prepared.
7) The process is repeated to confirm/verify the results.

### 2.6.7 Scientific research

Research is thorough and systematic examination to produce new and increased knowledge in the form of explanations or predictions about the universe, people, society, mathematics, health, etc.

A design process can in many ways be compared to research because it is based on a problem statement that people seek to solve through research and experimentation. Many of the same data collection and analysis methods that are used in research can also be used in different phases of a design project. Therefore, in this book, we have used the social sciences method to explain the problem statement, method, and survey process. For a design project to be considered equivalent to

Wizard of Oz experiment
**The Wizard of Oz experiment can be used to examine human interaction with data. The method is widely used in UX to improve user-experience. It takes place as an experiment in which the subject interacts with a computer system that he or she believes is anonymous but is actually controlled or partially controlled by an invisible person (see also 5.2.13 Wizard of Oz prototyping).**

53 The independent variable is the variable the experimenter manipulates or changes, and is assumed to have a direct effect on the dependent variable The independent variable is also called the cause variable, explanatory variable or predictor variable.

54 Available at: DOI:10.1086/341573

55 Frascati Manual: The internationally recognised methodology for collecting and using R&D statistics, the OECD's. It includes definitions of basic concepts, data collection guidelines, and classifications for compiling R&D statistics (OECD, n.d.).

56 Research and development (R&D) include activities that companies undertake to innovate and introduce new products and services. The goal is typically to take new products and services to market and add to the company's bottom line (Kenton, 2021).

**Example of experiment**

The research article 'When Web pages influence choice: Effects of visual primes on experts and novices' (Mandel and Johnson 2002), refer to experiments conducted on response, based on variation in the use of visual tools. The experiments showed that only by changing the background of the object on a web page it is possible to get the target group to focus on different things. If the background were money, the buyer focused on price, while if the background were clouds, the buyer focused on comfort. An experiment was conducted on a website for sofas. 'The screen showed a sofa web site contained either a blue background with fluffy clouds, designed to prime comfort, or a green background with embedded pennies, designed to prime price. The experiment was conducted with 47 respondents.

Subjects who saw the comfort prime were more likely than those who saw the price prime to cite comfort as an important feature when buying a sofa (90% vs. 78%), and those who saw price prime were more likely than those who saw comfort prime to cite price (94% vs. 66%). Other features that were frequently mentioned were appearance and durability, but these attributes were equally likely to be mentioned by both treatment groups.' (Mandel and Johnson 2002).[54]

scientific research, it must satisfy the requirements for research quality (2.6.8 Artistic research). According to the Frascati Manual 2015 (OECD n.d.),[55] research and development (R&D) covers three types of activity: *basic research, applied research* and *experimental development*: *Basic research* (pure research) 'is experimental or theoretical work undertaken primarily to acquire new knowledge of the underlying foundation of phenomena and observable facts, without any particular application or use in view' (Frascati Manual 2015). Basic research is mostly driven by the researcher's own interest and curiosity, with no practical objective or guaranteed results. Research most often occurs over time and can lead to something useful in the long term or result in new, unexpected discoveries, knowledge, advances and development. In general, it contributes to the advancement of human knowledge (Skoie, 2018). *Applied research* 'is original investigation undertaken in order to acquire new knowledge. It is, however, directed primarily towards a specific, practical aim or objective (Frascati Manual 2015). Applied research and basic research are often practised simultaneously in coordinated R&D,[56] as a set of innovative activities undertaken by corporations or governments in developing new services or products and improving existing ones (Kenton, 2021). *Experimental development* is systematic work, drawing on knowledge gained from research and practical experience and producing additional knowledge, which is directed to producing new products or processes or to improving existing products or processes (Frascati Manual 2015). Research activity carried out in a design project related to an assignment, might be similar to applied research or experimental development, where the findings will be put to use to solve a problem statement or task.

Basic research vs. applied research

**Basic research, also called pure, theoretical or fundamental research, tends to focus more on 'big picture' topics, such as increasing the scientific knowledge base around a particular topic. Applied research tends to drill down more toward solving specific problems that affect people in the here and now. (Cherry, 2020). 'Theoretical research aimed at discovering scientific principles and facts; opposed to applied research, which puts those principles to practical use' (UK Dictionary).**

### The research process

A research process is a self-correcting system[57] (Ioannidis, 2012)[58] in which results and methods should be verifiable and subject to critical review. The research process is usually cyclical. It starts with a problem, and ends with pointing out new problems that can be further researched. The research begins with mapping of the existing knowledge in the field to be researched, also named 'State of the art'[59] in order to see if the research question or problem has already been resolved by other researchers. This phase is about searching for literature or published materials. The researcher understands which questions have been resolved and what peers wish to research further. Based on this understanding, the problem statements in one's own project can be reformulated and fine-tuned to specific research problems. The problem statement is broken down into a set of sub-problems that are tentatively (unsettled) addressed when formulating assumptions or hypotheses. The problem statements/hypotheses should have theoretical basis with references to other researchers. Once this is in place, a research plan is drawn up for how the research is to be carried out. Then comes the implementation, conducting the research or trials, where data are collected, systematised and analysed. Finally, the project is to be discussed before conclusions are drawn and new research problems formulated (Refsum 2004, Lundequist 1992) (2.5 Research process).

### Hypothesis

A hypothesis is an idea or explanation of something that is based on a few known facts but that has not yet been proved to be true or correct (Hypothesis, n.d.). It is a suggested solution for an unexplained occurrence that doesn't fit into a currently accepted scientific theory (Bradford, 2017). In science, a hypothesis is tested through study and experimentation. Outside science, a theory or guess can also be called a hypothesis, e.g. a detective might have a hypothesis about a crime (hypothesis, n.d.). Scientific theory often starts as a hypothesis, making the hypothesis the core of the research. A hypothesis can never really be proven (verified), only disproved (falsified).[60] When a hypothesis has been the subject of repeated scientific tests, it may be adopted as 'true', but there will always be a possibility that it can be refuted in new experiments (2.6.6 Experiment). A hypothesis is an assertion or an uncertain theory, a preconceived notion that has not been further investigated. 'If enough evidence accumulates to support a hypothesis, it moves to the next step – known as a theory – in the scientific method and becomes accepted as a valid explanation of a phenomenon' (Bradford, 2017). The object of a hypothesis is often a phenomenon or occurrence that is possible to test empirically. Therefore, the 'degree of generalisation' is often essential to determine whether a hypothesis is true or not. Degree of generalisation refers to how general (common) a conclusion is. The degree of generalisation can be explored through both qualitative and quantitative methods. The choice of research method depends on whether the survey is based on a few or more assumptions. Here we come to induction and deduction, which are essential factors in the formulation of scientific research results. A research process is either inductive or deductive.[61] (2.3.4 Problem statement formulation; hypothesis).

57 The notion of a self-correcting science is based on the native model of science as an objective process that incorporates new information and updates beliefs about the world depending on the available evidence. When new information suggests that old beliefs are false, the old beliefs are replaced by new beliefs. (replicationindex.com 2019).

58 'The ability to self-correct is considered a hallmark of science. However, self-correction does not always happen to scientific evidence by default. The trajectory of scientific credibility can fluctuate over time, both for defined scientific fields and for science at-large' (Ioannidis, 2012).

59 In scientific writing, the state of the art describes the current knowledge about the studied matter through the analysis of similar or related published work (dos Santos 2019).

60 'The Falsification Principle, proposed by Karl Popper, is a way of demarcating science from non-science. It suggests that for a theory to be considered scientific it must be able to be tested and conceivably proven false. For example, the hypothesis that "all swans are white," can be falsified by observing a black swan' (McLeod, 2020).

61 There are two ways to think logically; induction and deduction. *Inductive approach*: we want to observe the problem in order to arrive at a theory of a phenomenon (e.g. why sales are declining). *Deductive approach* is basically the opposite: we have a theory about a phenomenon that we want to test the tenability and correctness of (e.g. the decline in sales is due to the increased competition in the market) (Sander, 2020).

62 David Hume (1711–1776), Scottish philosopher.

63 The term, '*A black swan* is an extremely rare event with severe consequences. It cannot be predicted beforehand, though after the fact, many falsely claim it should have been predictable' (Scott, 2021).

## Induction and deduction

*Inductive* (intensive) method means that there are a few assumptions underlying the study and that empirical (experience-based) knowledge arises through research or experimentation. Here, the qualitative method is best suited for obtaining data; however, this data is uncertain. The *deductive* (extensive) method is the opposite of inductive, which means that there are logical assumptions underlying the study/research. When using a deductive method, a hypothesis (an allegation or assumption) is assessed in relation to whether it is true or must be refuted. Here, the quantitative method is best suited and is something that provides secure data. The hypothetical deductive method is based on a (hypo) thesis (H), whose validity one wishes to examine. This is done by drawing (deducing) inferences (S) from the hypothesis: the reasoning is that if H is true, then S must also be true, because S follows logically from H. S should preferably be something that can be observed by way of sensory experience, usually using special instruments (for example binoculars or microscopes) or by doing an experiment (Alnes, 2015). A classic example is based on Hume and is further developed by Popper: Do crocodiles like caramels? Inductive: 1) Some crocodiles like caramels. 2) This is a crocodile. 3) Consequently, this crocodile likes caramels. Deductive: 1) All crocodiles like caramels. 2) This is a crocodile. 3) Consequently, this crocodile likes caramels. Falsification: If it turns out that there is a crocodile that does not like caramels, then the claim that all crocodiles like caramels can be refuted. The claim will then be falsified.[62]

## The problem of induction

In research, it will often be a matter of whether a theory or hypothesis (allegation) is true or not, whether it can be falsified (disproved) or verified (proven). The problem of induction concerns the problem of justifying validity and demonstrating the reasonable basis for drawing inductive conclusions, i.e. conclusions based on experienced knowledge (Holmen, n.d.), e.g. the inference that 'all swans we have seen are white, and, therefore, all swans are white', before the discovery of black swans[63] or e.g. that the laws of physics will hold as they have always been observed to hold, called 'the principle of uniformity of nature' by David Hume (Vickers, 2011). Philosopher Karl Popper[64] developed the 'problem of induction' based on David Hume's philosophy.[65] Hume's philosophy was that the typically metaphysical questions about whether there is a reality, whether things are real, and whether they have lasting existence and so on are meaningless.

## Scientific method

Science is often used synonymously with research, but research is usually used for the activity that produces insight or knowledge, while science is preferably used for the knowledge resulting from research. Science is the careful study of the structure and behaviour of the physical world, especially by watching, measuring, and doing experiments, and the development of theories to describe the results of these activities (scientific, n.d). There are several scientific fields with different methods and purposes such as formal sciences (mathematics and logic), natural sciences (physical and biological phenomena) and social sciences (human society and social relationships).



64 Karl Popper (1902–1994), Austrian-British philosopher and science theorist. Popper's fallibilism: man is erroneous, all knowledge is uncertain. Popper advocated a new philosophical fundamental position, critical rationalism, which takes into account the error of knowledge ('Karl Popper,' n.d.).

65 The original source of what has become known as the 'problem of induction' is in Book 1, part iii, section 6 of *A Treatise of Human Nature* by David Hume, published in 1739. In 1748, Hume gave a shorter version of the argument in Section iv of *An Enquiry Concerning Human Understanding*.

The social science method is the most common approach in design projects. Social science is a generic term for several disciplines, including sociology, anthropology, psychology, organisational science, political science and economics. This branch of science studies how people interact with each other, behave, develop as a culture, and influence the world (Liberto, 2021). Social sciences study social conditions with the aim of gaining a better understanding of society and the market. Since people act and think to a greater extent as members of a group rather than as individuals, social science tries to understand how individuals think and act by studying their behaviour in different social groups.

### 2.6.8 Artistic research

Artistic research (AR) is an artistic parallel to research. It includes artistic or design projects that produce results at high artistic levels and with national and international relevance.

Research in the context of arts (including design) can be understood from three different approaches according to Borgdorff 2006:[66]

- *Research on The Arts:* Research that has art practice in the broadest sense of the word as its object. It refers to investigations aimed at drawing valid conclusions about art practice from a theoretical distance, such as art history. Theoretical distance implies a fundamental separation, and a certain distance, between the researcher and the research object.
- *Research for The Arts:* Applied research for a specific purpose. The research provides insights and instruments that may find their way into concrete practices in some way or other. Examples are material investigations of particular alloys used in casting metal sculptures, investigation of the application of live electronics in the interaction between dance and lighting design, or the study of the 'extended techniques' of an electronically modifiable cello.
- *Research in The Arts:* Research with or through the art. It concerns research that does not assume the separation of subject and object, and does not observe a distance between the researcher and the practice of art. Instead, the artistic practice itself is an essential component of both the research process and the research results. The research is an important part of both the research process and the research results. 'Reflection in action' (Donald Schön, 1982).

While in different European and international design environments there are different perceptions and practices of artistic research, it is dedicated organisations that are continuously working to safeguard the research status of creative disciplines. One of these is the Society for Artistic Research (SAR),[67] publisher of the *Journal for Artistic Research* (JAR).[68] JAR is supported by the Research Catalogue (RC),[69] which is a searchable, documentary database of artistic research.

Central to the work process of artistic research is experimental exploration and critical testing. For the work to qualify for research, there should be reflection on the content, process and methods, as well as on what is the new insight into this project. Reflection can be expressed in various forms, such as speech, writing, film, illustration, photo, or other means of expressions. 'We can justifiably speak of artistic research ('research in the arts') when that artistic practice is not only

66 In leading design environments in Europe and internationally, there was ongoing debate on whether artistic research could be placed on a par with scientific research. The debate was initiated by Borgdorff, among others, with the article 'Debate on Research in The Arts' (2006) resulting in many countries today equating artistic research with scientific research.

67 SAR is an international non-profit, artistic and scientific society devoted to developing, connecting and disseminating artistic research.

68 JAR is an international, open-access and peer-reviewed journal for the identification, publication and dissemination of artistic research and its methodologies, from all arts disciplines. JAR is supported by the Research Catalogue (RC): jar-online.net.

69 The Research Catalogue (RC) is a searchable, documentary database of artistic research work, supported by JAR. Anyone can write a research paper and add it to RC online, and suitable reports can be sent to the editorial team for peer review and publication in JAR: researchcatalogue.net.

70 Henk Borgdorff: The Debate on Research in the Arts, Sensuous Knowledge no 02, Faculty of Fine Art, Music and Design, UiB 2006, p. 12. Borgdorff built on earlier input from Christopher Frayling, 1993/94.

71 Appelong, Birgitte completed a project in artistic research, 2016: 'Light in space: critical reflection'.

72 The first milestone was a conference on design methods at Imperial College London (1962). John Christopher Jones founded a postgraduate Design Research Laboratory programme at the University of Manchester. L. Bruce Archer supported by Misha Black founded the postgraduate Department of Design Research at the Royal College of Art, London, becoming the first Professor of Design Research ('Design Research,' n.d.).

the result of the research, but also its methodological vehicle, when the research unfolds in and through the acts of creating and performing. This is a distinguishing feature of this research type within the whole of academic research' (Borgdorff 2006/2010).[70]

It is possible to create insight, not just gather it. Methods used in artistic research may be individual or specific to the art field in question, such as composition, design or dance. 'Within traditional research, methods related to obtaining information are often divided into four main categories: observation, interview, surveys and document data. Artistic research stands out here in that research through creation is the overriding method. It involves such as concept development, sketching, prototyping, mock-ups, building and using 3D models, etc' (Appelong, 2016).[71]



### 2.6.9 Design research

Design research was originally founded primarily as research into the design process, and the use of design methods, but the concept stretched to include research integrated into the design process, including working in a design context and research-based design practices. Essentially, design research is about understanding and improving design processes in general and independently of profession. As in artistic research (2.6.8 Artistic research) the literature distinguishes between 'in', 'for', 'through', based on various theories, e.g. Research into design, Research for design, Research through design (Frayling 1993/Read 1974). The three different approaches are explained in the introduction of Phase 2 'Research through design' (page 41).

Design research developed as a concept between 1960 and 1980.[72] The Design Research Society (DRS), founded in 1966, was among the pioneers.[73] In the 1980s, design research became more established and continued to expand. A research base, including doctoral programmes, was developed within many design schools that were formerly art colleges, at the same time as new areas such as interaction design emerged. Several new journals turned up, such as *The Design Journal, Journal of Design Research, CoDesign and Design Science*, simultaneously with major growth in design conferences internationally – not only within design research, but also within Design thinking, PhDs in Design, Design computing and cognition, Design and emotion and more.

The development of design research led to the establishment of design as a discipline. Bruce Archer stated his belief that 'there exists a designerly way of thinking and communicating that is different from both scientific and scholarly ways of thinking and communicating, and as powerful as scientific and scholarly methods of enquiry when applied to their own type of problems.'[74] This view was developed further in a series of research articles by Nigel Cross and compiled in the article 'Designerly ways of knowing'.[75] Donald Schön[76] promoted this view further in his book *The Reflective Practitioner*, in which he attempted to establish a textbook that addresses the artistic, intuitive processes that designers and other practitioners create through uncertainty, instability, uniqueness, and value conflicts.

73 The Design Research Society affirmed the goal of design research: to promote 'the study of and research into the process of designing in all its many fields' (designresearchsociety.org).

74 Archer, Leonard Bruce (1979). 'Whatever Became of Design Methodology?'. *Design Studies*, 1 (1): 17–20.ISSN 0142-694X.

75 Cross, N. (2001). 'Designerly ways of knowing: Design discipline versus design science'. *Design Issues*, 17 (3): 49–55.

76 Schön, Donald Schön (1983). The reflective practitioner: How professionals think in action.

Design research now exists on an international scale, through the founding of the International Association of Societies of Design Research in 2005, in a recognised collaboration with Asian design research societies.

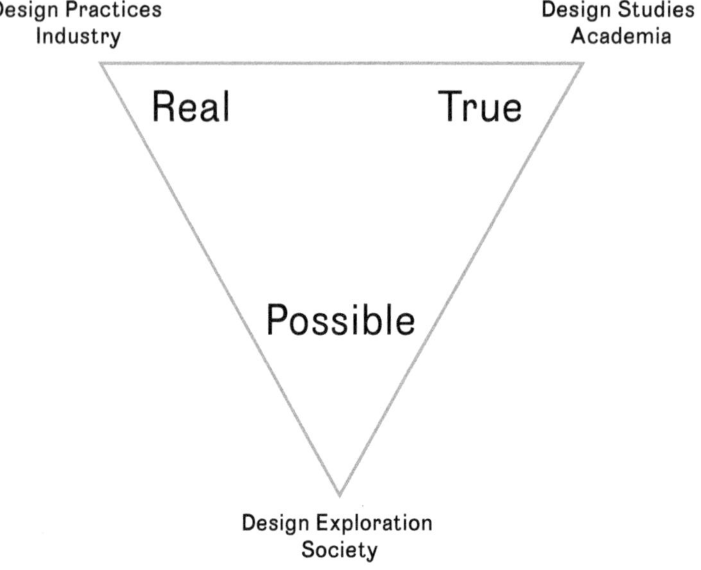


Fig. 2.18 Design research process

Design research is according to Nigel Cross[77]

- **Target-oriented:** Based on the identified problem, which is worth studying and feasible to study.
- **Curious:** Seeking to acquire new knowledge.
- **Informed:** Performance based on awareness of past, related research.
- **Methodical:** Planned and conducted in a disciplined manner.
- **Transferable:** Generates and reports results that are testable and available to others (See also Figure 2.2 Design research, on page 41).

**Research through design**

'One observe and discuss, experiment and iterate, and create something in the process that adds insight and knowledge; creates a product, a model, reflects, tests, goes back, explores and repeats.' Linda Lien emphasises that a distinction must be made between research through design and research for design. 'More and more people are developing new products, new software, or new instruments as part of their projects. Then, there is often a combination of research for and through design, but if you take away designing as part of the process (developing sketches, developing prototypes, conducting tests, etc.), then you stop researching through design with design. So it is about that confidence that something is actually happening in the design process that provides new insights, and that affects its outcome. Pluralistic (diverse) methods of creation are the most important' (Lien, conversation 2016).

Fig. 2.18 The figure shows how the design research process according to Fällman can be seen as a triangular process, defined in the three different areas of design, namely practice, design studies and design research (or in the sense 'exploring/investigating'), which also reflects what is 'real', 'true' and 'possible', respectively. The corners of this model led to the three external interfaces: industry, academia and society as a whole. During an ongoing design research project, the researcher can move across the different activity areas and gain new insight into the matter being studied, which is different compared to traditional research motivation and methods. (Figure and text are based on Fällman, D. (2008) and Design Research Lab, drlab.org.

Fig. 2.19 The figure illustrates research vs. analysis. Research at the forefront of analysis is about going wide, while analysing involves going deep. ©Grimsgaard, W (2018).

Tips for the designer

It is possible to create insight, not just gather it.

**Strict requirements**

In order for a piece of work to be given the status of artistic research, artistic essence should occupy a central position at a high artistic level, coupled with reflection on process, methods and context, as well as visibility of results.

77 In the 1960s Nigel Cross was one of the people who established theories and principles of design research as a method, undertook research and developed theories in computer-aided design and interaction, and was later one of the pioneers in establishing Design Thinking as a method. He wrote, among other things, the research article 'Designerly Ways of Knowing' (1982) and the book *Design Thinking* (2011).

1 Initiation
2 Insight
3 Strategy
4 Design
5 Production
6 Management

2.1 Understanding the company
2.2 Situational study
2.3 Problem statement
2.4 Method selection
2.5 Research process
2.6 Research
2.7 Analyses
2.8 Mapping
2.9 Testing and measuring

Analysis is about breaking down a whole into smaller parts in order to investigate and research the different parts and find information that is not immediately visible or available. Analysis is an essential part of a survey or experiment, but may also in itself be a form of research.

As surveys go wide, analyses go deep. In a design project, both an analytical and a creative approach are needed in order to arrive at new angles and solutions to tackle a problem or task. An analysis can open up for new views, questions, opinions and interpretations and provide greater understanding, knowledge and experience. Designers often make intuitive analyses in the course of the design process, and that is both necessary and positive. The advantage of more planned and structured analyses is that they provide basis for making conscious choices that can be justified, explained and verified by others. A structured analysis involves exploring different aspects of an object, a person or a phenomenon, and interpreting it using the problem statement as a starting point, and the objectives and criteria underlying the analysis, as well as describing it in the most professional and objective way possible.

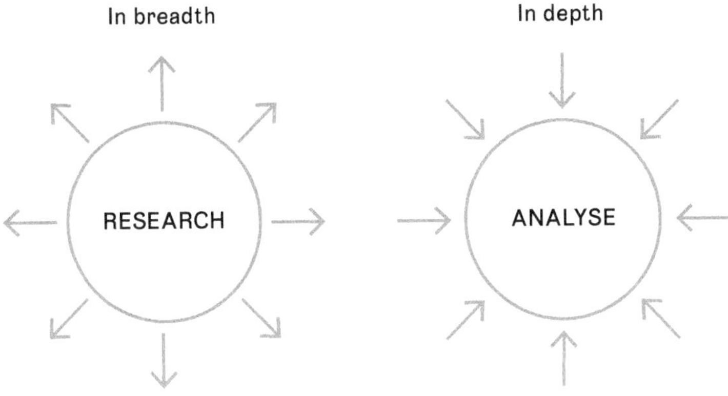


Fig. 2.19 First research – then analyse

Analysis means research where something complex (a matter, a thing, a concept) is broken down into its constituent parts. The opposite of synthesis (Tranøy and Tjønneland, 2012), which means that a multitude of different constituents are brought together into one whole, so that it appears as one entity. There are numerous analyses that can be used in different phases of a design project. Analyses are selected based on the information and insights needed to solve a problem or respond to an assignment. The scope should be seen in the context of the timeframe, financial framework and level of ambition of the project (2.3.3 Problem definition, 2.4.4 Research question, 2.5 Research process, 2.6 Research, 2.7 Analyses).

An analysis assumes that as much information as possible is gathered about what is to be analysed, and that there is a clear problem statement.

| Analyses that provide insight<br><br>The following analyses may be used in conjunction with a situational analysis. A SWOT analysis can be used to analyse key takeaways from all the different analyses used. | |
|---|---|
| Situational analysis: | Analysis of the current situation of a company and its products or services. The purpose is to clarify the actual circumstances of today's situation as basis for defining goals and strategies. The result can be included as internal or external factors in a SWOT analysis. All the insight gathered, and analysis conducted in Phase 2 Insight, can be included in a situational analysis report (2.7.1 Situational analysis). |
| Internal analysis: | Analysis of the company's internal environment, available resources and potential for improvement, through resource analysis, activity analysis and value chain analysis. The result can be included as internal factors in a SWOT analysis (2.7.2 Internal analysis). |
| PESTLE analysis: | Analysis of the external macroenvironmental factors to be taken into account by the company. They can be included as external factors in a SWOT analysis (2.7.9 PESTLE analysis). |
| Competitor analysis: | Analysis of competitors. Who are they? Where are they? Products or services, knowledge, position, market share (2.7.4 Competitor analysis, 3.6.5 The four Ps, 3.6.6 The four Cs). |
| Position analysis: | Analysis of the current position, desired position and gap (the distance between the current situation and the desired situation). Mapping of relevant and available position (2.7.5 Positioning analysis). |
| Target group analysis: | Analysis of the target group. Who are they? Where are they? Social identity, needs, desires? (2.7.6 Target group analysis). |
| Brand analysis: | Analysis of a company's logo or brand, product or service. Assessment of the qualities/variables of the brand, which are to be analysed (2.7.7 Brand analysis). |
| Visual analysis: | Analysis of the visual design of such as corporate identity, packaging, magazine, website, etc. in order to identify problem areas and potential for improvement (2.7.8 Visual analysis). |
| PIPI workshop: | Analysis of personality, identity, profile and image in order to clarify how the company perceives itself, and how it believes (or knows) it is perceived by the outside world (2.2.2 PIPI workshop). |
| Identity prism: | Analysis of the current identity of a company, product or service (3.7.5 Brand identity). |
| SWOT analysis: | Key factors from the analysis performed can be used in order to analyse the company's strengths and weaknesses, opportunities and threats (2.7.10 SWOT analysis). |
| Gap analysis: | Analysis of the distance between the current situation and the desired situation, and identification of the gulf (2.7.11 GAP analysis). |

Table 2.10 Analyses that provide insight

Table 2.10 The table shows examples of some analysis that can be helpful to use in a strategic design project.
© Grimsgaard, W. (2018).

Fig. 2.20 The figure shows a plain presentation of the progress of an analytical process.

Tips for the company
Sufficient insight is needed to have the necessary data to conduct an analysis of any value.

78 The situational analysis contains many of the same points as the situational study but involves more in-depth research and analyses to obtain more information about the facts.

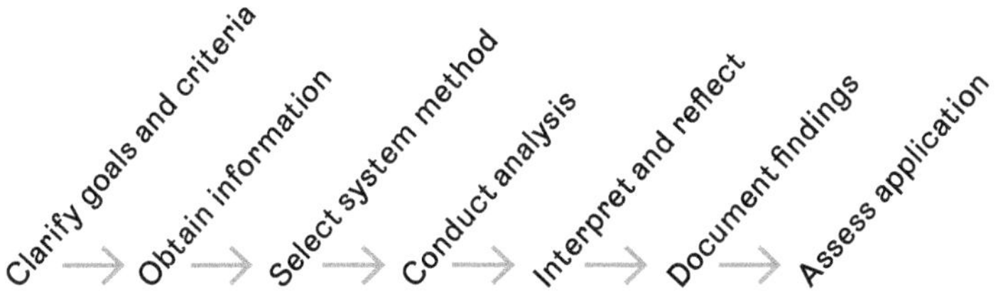


Fig. 2.20 Analysis process

1 Initiation
2 Insight
3 Strategy
4 Design
5 Production
6 Management

2.1 Understanding the company
2.2 Situational study
2.3 Problem statement
2.4 Method selection
2.5 Research process
2.6 Research
2.7 Analyses
2.8 Mapping
2.9 Testing and measuring

2.7.1 Situational analysis
2.7.2 Internal analysis
2.7.3 Value chain analysis
2.7.4 Competitor analysis
2.7.5 Positioning analysis
2.7.6 Target group analysis
2.7.7 Brand analysis
2.7.8 Visual analysis
2.7.9 PESTLE analysis
2.7.10 SWOT analysis
2.7.11 Gap analysis

**Analysis process**

**Clarify objectives and criteria:** Clarify the objective of the analysis, what should be analysed and what criteria should be used as basis?

**Obtain information:** Collect information in the form of text and/or numbers. The collected data may concern an object, person or phenomenon. It can also be a matter of creative or visual data, such as images, colours, shape, structure, materials, etc.

**Select system method:** Categorise and organise information. Use systems or methods to create an overview so that both the overall picture and the details materialise.

**Conduct analysis:** Divide an object, person, or phenomenon into its constituent components in order to bring out different aspects and details. Create an overview. Research all the aspects and details, bits and pieces of the object, person or phenomenon, ask questions, observe, find, test out, try out, etc.

**Interpret and reflect:** Clarify, explain, and reflect on findings and discoveries that have emerged from the analysis. Discuss and interpret the findings based on own subjective perception. Arrive at an interpretation that is as plausible and objective as possible.

**Document findings:** Assess how plausible the findings are and how they can be used further.

**Assess application:** Document the analysis and findings in the most objective and comprehensible manner possible. Visualisation of the result facilitates implementation in the later stages of the strategy and design process.

## 2.7.1 Situational analysis

A situational analysis is an analysis of the current situation of a company and its products or services in order to identify the actual situation and uncover real problems and needs. All insights gathered in phase 2 can be used in the situational analysis, to get a real impression and understanding of the current situation.

When initiating a design project, such an analysis will be a good starting point for clarifying the problem statement and objectives of the assignment. The situational analysis is performed instead of or in addition to a situational study (2.2 Situational study).[78] A situational analysis is about getting to know the company's perceived and real situation. It involves clarifying the company's products or services in terms of factors such as timeliness, competitiveness and brand awareness, and gaining an overview of the structure, financial resources and competencies of the organisation. It is also about understanding the company's culture, how employees perceive their workplace, tasks, role, the working environment

Situational analysis
**The data from all the studies and analyses conducted in Phase 2 are compiled in a situational analysis report and used as a basis for a SWOT workshop and a SWOT analysis.**

and common goals and strategies, and what internal strengths and weaknesses exist. Equally important is to have knowledge of the market situation and the opportunities or threats that exist. What potential is there in the market? Is there any unfulfilled need? Who are the competitors and how is the competitive situation perceived? Do customers and partners perceive the company the way it wants to be perceived? Do products and services meet expectations? To get answers to these questions, research and analyses are carried out to produce information and facts. For example, a situational analysis may include: market research, market surveys, interviews, focus groups, competitive situation survey, brand awareness, buying trends, etc. Visual analysis and brand analysis also help clarify the current situation. A situational analysis gathers all relevant information about the market and the company's own prerequisites for success. 'We need to know the target groups, competitors and the entire market development in order to make sensible decisions about both communication measures and the entire market mix in general' (Helgesen, 1998). To succeed in the market, the company must understand what factors exert impact on their development. Knowledge of positive and negative effects inside and outside the company is crucial when the company is to develop strategies and marketing plans. Based on knowledge of the situation, the internal and external factors[79] affecting the company are identified as basis for a further SWOT analysis, which can be initiated with a SWOT workshop (2.7.10 SWOT analysis: SWOT workshop).

Tips for the designer

**All the insights you gather in phase 2 are included in the situational analysis and should be compiled in the report. Findings from the analysis are important data that should be highlighted in the report. Based on the data from the situational analysis and the information that has emerged one considers what main internal and external factors are affecting the company. These factors are included in a further SWOT analysis (2.7.10 SWOT analysis: SWOT workshop).**

Situational analysis report

**The report should include all the studies and analysis that are conducted to clarify the current situation of the company. For each of the studies you should explain what type of study it is, why you conducted it, what you expected to get from it. Highlight your actual findings and explain how you will use them in the further process of your assignment.**

### Situational analysis process

Analysis of today's situation of the company. Outline example:
**The current situation:** Where are we? Challenges or problems the company faces? Clarify specific conditions. Conduct interviews, surveys and workshops internally within the company (2.2.2 PIPI workshop, 2.2.3 Where are we – where will we? 2.7.2 Internal analysis).
**Background/history:** Who are we? Describe the company, the company's development and history. Can its history be used in communication/marketing? (3.7.4 Brand story).
**Product/service:** What do we do? How do we meet customers'/users' needs? Product areas and product properties? Brand reputation, brand assets, customer awareness, mental availability? Perform visual analysis, value chain analysis, positioning analysis, and brand analysis (2.7.3 Value chain analysis, 2.7.5 Positioning analysis, 2.7.7 Brand analysis, 2.9.1 User testing, 3.7.9 Brand refresh, redesign, rebranding, 5.3.6 Product life cycle assessment).
**Production/product development:** Resource use? Product supply chain? Product life cycle? Product innovation? Conduct a product life cycle assessment (LCA) and examine the product environmental profile (5.3.5 Material life cycle, 5.3.6 Product life cycle, 4.3.4 Innovation).
**Target group/segments:** Who are they? Where are they? Characteristics, wishes and needs? Social identity, affiliation and lifestyle? Conduct target group analysis, observations, interviews and surveys (2.7.6 Target group analysis, 2.6.1 Survey, 2.6.2 Interview, 2.6.3 Observation).
**Market:** Which markets do we operate in? Segments, cycles and market trends? Opportunities? Threats? What external factors affect the company? Examine the existing market or conduct new market research. (3.6.1 Markets, 2.7.10 SWOT analysis: External factors).

79 **Internal factors and external factors that affect the business. *Internal factors*: Strengths and weaknesses internally in the company. *External factors*: Opportunities and threats in the market.**
80 **VRIO Jay B. Barney, *Looking Inside for Competitive Advantage* (1995).**

**Competitor**: Who are they? Where are they? Product, position, timeliness? The competitive situation? Conduct competitor analysis (2.7.4 Competitor analysis).
**Organisation**: Organisational structure, culture, ownership, management, decision-making, goals, objectives, and strategy? Sustainability targets and actions? Strengths? Weaknesses? What internal factors affect the company? Conduct internal studies, interviews, and surveys. (2.1.3 Organisational culture, 2.7.10 SWOT analysis: Internal factors).
**Finances**: Turnover, earnings trend, solvency, financial capacity, business fluctuations? Conduct studies and analysis of the finances (2.9.6 KPIs and metrics).
**Alliance partners**: Which ones? Where are they? Roles? Instances of win-win potential? Examine the situation of partners.
**Macro environment**: What external factors, political, economic, social, technological, legal and environmental affect the company? Perform a PESTLE analysis (2.7.9 PESTLE analysis).
**SWOT analysis**: Use insights gathered through the situational analysis as a basis for a SWOT analysis. Analyse the main strengths and weaknesses of the company against the opportunities and threats in the market. (2.7.10 SWOT analysis: SWOT workshop).
**Gap analysis**: Analyse the gap between the current situation and the desired situation and clarify the size of the problem/scope of the assignment or task (2.7.11 Gap analysis).
**Report**: The outcome of the situational analysis is compiled in a report with summary conclusions and recommendations for further work.



## 2.7.2 Internal analysis

Through an internal analysis, the company can get a clearer overview of its internal situation, such as available resources and potential for improvement. This way, it can clarify what should be done to meet the needs of potential customers in the market the company is targeting.

Resource analysis and activity analysis are the main components of an internal analysis, the aim of which is to identify the company's strengths and weaknesses. Knowing its strengths and weaknesses, the company has a greater chance of achieving its goals, which can be about strengthening its competitiveness and promoting growth and market leadership. An activity analysis aims to identify which activities are central to the company's value creation and how they contribute to the achievement of goals. A resource analysis aims to clarify which resources support the company's value creation and whether some of these resources are more important than others. Resources are the source of competitive edge. Resources means experience, knowledge, culture, technology, market relations, location, reputation, etc. (2.1 Understanding the company).

### Resource analysis

The VRIO model[80] is a resource analysis framework, 'for evaluating whether or not particular firm's resources can be sources of sustained competitive advantage' (Barney, 1991). According to Barney competitive analysis can not only be conducted through environmental analysis. He created VRIO to 'fill in the blanks' of Michael Porter's SWOT framework

> In general, when a firm's resources and capabilities are valuable, rare, and socially complex, those resources are likely to be sources of sustained competitive advantage (Barney, 1995).

and 'five forces model'. 'A complete understanding of sources of competitive advantage requires the analysis of a firm's internal strengths and weaknesses as well.' (Barney, 1995). VRIO is an abbreviation of the words: Value, Rarity, Imitability and Organisation:

- *Value (V)*: Do the firm's resources and capabilities add value by enabling it to exploit opportunities and/or neutralise threats? (Barney, 1995). 'The first question of the framework asks if a resource adds value by enabling a firm to exploit opportunities or defend against threats. If the answer is yes, then a resource is considered valuable. Resources are also valuable if they help organisations to increase the perceived customer value' (Jurevicius, 2021).
- *Rarity (R)*: How many competing firms already possess these valuable resources and capabilities? (Barney, 1995). 'Resources that can only be acquired by one or very few companies are considered rare. Rare and valuable resources grant temporary competitive advantage' (Jurevicius, 2021).
- *Imitability (I)*: Do firms without a resource or capability face a cost disadvantage in obtaining it compared to firms that already possess it? (Barney, 1995). 'A resource is costly to imitate if other organisations that don't have it can't imitate, buy or substitute it at a reasonable price. Imitation can occur in two ways: by directly imitating (duplicating) the resource or providing the comparable product/service (substituting)' (Jurevicius, 2021).
- *Organisation (O)*: Is the company organised to exploit the full competitive potential of its resources and capabilities? (Barney, 1995). 'The resources themselves do not confer any advantage for a company if they're not organised to capture the value from them. A firm must organise its management systems, processes, policies, organisational structure and culture to be able to fully realise the potential of its valuable, rare and costly to imitate resources and capabilities. Only then the companies can achieve sustained competitive advantage' (Jurevicius, 2021).[81]

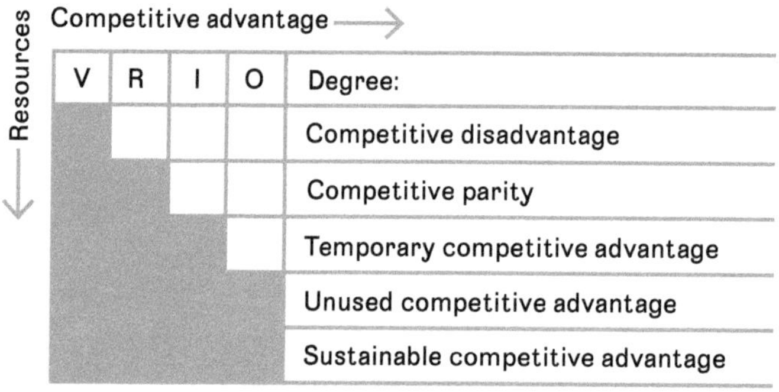

Competitive advantage →

Resources ↓

| V | R | I | O | Degree: |
|---|---|---|---|---|
| | | | | Competitive disadvantage |
| | | | | Competitive parity |
| | | | | Temporary competitive advantage |
| | | | | Unused competitive advantage |
| | | | | Sustainable competitive advantage |

Fig. 2.21 VRIO model

Using the VRIO analysis, the company's resources are first mapped, then it is examined whether the conditions are present for each of the resources. The analysis will provide an outcome that shows what type of advantage the company has. If the company has resources or capabilities that meet all of these requirements, they will have a realised and lasting competitive advantage. Owned resources such as patents, financial resources and brand names can create values for the company with greater certainty than leased resources such as employee expertise, relationships and reputation. The resource analysis can identify

Fig. 2.21 The figure shows the use of the VRIO resource analysis framework. VRIO stands for Value, Rarity, Imitability and Organisation. Adopted from Rothaermel's (2013) *Strategic Management*, p.91 Jurevicius 2021.

Tips for the company
It is an advantage to know the current situation internally in the company and externally in the market before using the VRIO model. See chapters 2.2 Situational study, 2.7.2 Internal analysis, 2.7.4 Competitor analysis, 2.9.8 Mental availability measurements.

Competitive positioning is a marketing strategy that refers to how a marketing team can differentiate a company from its competitors. The position of the company depends on how the value it provides with goods and services compares to the value of similar goods and services in the market (Indeed, 2021).

Further reading
2.1.3 Organisational culture, 2.1.4 Organisational development.

81 strategicmanagementinsight.com/tools/vrio/.
82 International Association for Impact Assessment, iaia.org.

strengths and weaknesses in the company's internal environment that can be used in a further SWOT analysis, where they are analysed in relation to opportunities and threats that exist in the company's external environment, such as the market, society and macro environment. (2.7.10 SWOT analysis, 2.7.4 Competitor analysis: Porter's Five forces).

#### Activity analysis

Activity analysis is the identification and description of the activities in an organisation and the assessment of their impact on the company. An activity analysis determines:

- what activities are carried out
- how many people perform the activities
- how much time they spend on them
- how much and which resources are consumed
- what operational data best reflects the performance of activities
- what value the activities give to the organisation

The activity analysis is conducted through observation, interviews, focus group discussions, questionnaires and review of the work tasks (2.6 Research). Other analyses that can be used is job analysis, impact assessment and project analysis (payrollheaven.com).

*Job analysis* is a procedure which involves determining the duties and responsibilities, nature of the jobs and finally to decide qualifications, skills and knowledge to be required for an employee to perform a particular job (Human Resource Management, n.d.).

*Impact assessment* (IA) is 'a structured process for considering the implications, for people and their environment, of proposed actions while there is still an opportunity to modify (or even, if appropriate, abandon) the proposals. It is applied at all levels of decision-making, from policies to specific projects' (Iaia, n.d.). [82]

*Project analysis* is used to define a clear scope and ensure that everyone understands the vision of the project (Jovaco, 2016), and ensure that the project purpose corresponds to the core objectives of the company. It can include process analysis, budgetary analysis, personnel analysis and risk analysis (2.1.3 Organisational culture).

### 2.7.3 Value chain analysis

Value chain analysis is an analysis of the value creation process and all the internal activities engaged in to producing goods and services in the company. Its purpose is to identify and further develop properties and characteristics that may give the company a competitive advantage, and 'to identify and/or develop the linkages and interrelationships between activities that create value' (Ensign, 2001). The goal is to recognise, which activities are the most valuable (i.e. are the source of cost or differentiation advantage) to the firm and which ones could be improved to provide competitive advantage (Jurevicius, 2021).

According to Michael Porter (1985) value chain analysis can be a useful approach in developing a competitive strategy. He introduced the generic value chain in 1985, which can be used as a basis for the analysis with necessary adaptations to the needs of the day. The analysis tool has



Further reading

Starbucks is an example of a company that understands and successfully implements the value-chain concept. There are numerous articles online about how Starbucks has incorporated its value chain into its business model. For example: 'Analyzing Starbucks' Value Chain' (Bajpai, 2021)

Risk analysis

Seeks to identify, measure, and mitigate various risk exposures or hazards facing a business, investment, or project. *What If* is a qualitative risk analysis method that uses structured brainstorming to identify risks (Card et al., 2012). FMEA, Failure mode and effects analysis is a quant or qual process of reviewing as many components, assemblies, and subsystems as possible to identify potential failure modes in a system and their causes and effects (FMEA, n.d.).

five links for primary activities: 1) procurement (inbound logistics), 2) processing and operation, 3) delivery (outbound logistics), 4) marketing and sales, 5) service and customer support. These points are assessed against four areas of analysis of supporting activities: a) company infrastructure/ownership/management; b) competence development/human resources management; c) technology development; and d) procurement.

Fig. 2.22 **The figure shows a value chain according to Michael Porter's classical approach.**

Fig. 2.22 Value chain

The analysis aims to identify strengths and weaknesses of each of the supporting activities in relation to each of the five primary activities and in relation to the total value creation. The purpose is to further develop the cost and/or other possible specific advantages of the product or service. If low costs appear as a clear and lasting advantage, it would be natural to choose cost management as a strategic option. If other unique characteristics are found (for example related to the company's core competence or brand characteristics) that can give lasting competitive advantages in specific segments or niches in the market, differentiation and focus will be current strategies (Vikøren, 2009). The result of the value chain analysis is seen in the context of the competitive situation and other external factors, and can be used as a basis for the company's choice of competition strategy (2.1.1 Value creation, 3.4.1 Competitive strategy).

### 2.7.4 Competitor analysis

Companies competing in a market should know their competitors, and navigate in relation to them. It is a prerequisite for being able to choose a strategy and position oneself in the market. Competitor analysis is about identifying and analysing the main competitors.

Even when a company comes up with a new innovative product or service that no one has ever seen before, they will be in a competitive position. Rarely or never is there a company without competitors. If there is no one selling the same product, there may be similar products, substitutes or other products that the buyer can choose instead. In the absence of direct competitors, there will usually be both indirect and potential competitors that the company should be aware of. If one is to compete in a market, one needs to know where one's competitors are and what threat they pose.

Competition analysis is an evaluation of the strengths and weaknesses of current and potential competitors in order to identify the threats they represent and the opportunities that exist in the market. These are important factors when making a SWOT analysis of the company (2.7.10 SWOT analysis) and an important starting point for choosing a competition strategy (3.4.1 Competitive strategy). A competitor analysis involves collecting and analysing all relevant sources and information about the competitors. It is argued that most companies do not conduct this type of analysis systematically enough, but base their knowledge of competitors on the impressions, assumptions and intuitions they have accumulated over time. The company may come a long way with such knowledge, but too little knowledge of competitors may also lead them into a dead end (Bergen, 2014). Blind spots can cause them to choose their competitive strategy under false pretences, which may mean wrong focus, misuse of time and resources, and not least it can negatively affect sales performance. Companies that will compete consciously in the market should continuously monitor the competitive situation in order to adjust their efforts and market activities.


1 Initiation
2 Insight
3 Strategy
4 Design
5 Production
6 Management

2.1 Understanding the company
2.2 Situational study
2.3 Problem statement
2.4 Method selection
2.5 Research process
2.6 Research
2.7 Analyses
2.8 Mapping
2.9 Testing and measuring

2.7.1 Situational analysis
2.7.2 Internal analysis
2.7.3 Value chain analysis
2.7.4 Competitor analysis
2.7.5 Positioning analysis
2.7.6 Target group analysis
2.7.7 Brand analysis
2.7.8 Visual analysis
2.7.9 PESTLE analysis
2.7.10 SWOT analysis
2.7.11 Gap analysis

- Competitors
- Porter's five forces analysis


### Competitors

A competitor is a person or organisation that another person or organisation competes with. The presence of competitors in an industry means that consumers have more options to choose from, which may force competitors to reduce the prices of their products or services in order to take maximum market share (Paditar, 2017). A market competition is rivalry between two or more companies aiming at the same target group, such as Coca-Cola and Pepsi, or McDonald's and Burger King.

**Identify the competitors:** In the process of developing a successful marketing strategy, the first step is to identify the main competitors in the market in order to achieve a competitive advantage by offering customers greater value than competitors. Not only do current competitors need to be identified, but so do future potential competitors too (Paditar, 2017). According to Ferrell et al. (1998) there are different types of competitors:

- *Brand competitors:* These types of competitors market exactly the same products, at the same price, and also to the same customers. For example, Pepsi and Coca-Cola.
- *Product competitors:* These types of competitors market similar products, but with different characteristics and advantages, and at different prices. For example Pepsi and Lipton Ice Tea (tea/fruit drink).
- *Generic competitors:* These types of competitors market different products but offer the same benefit or advantage. For example, Pepsi and Evian (water).
- *Total budget competitors:* These types of competitors market different products but compete for the same financial resources of their customers, like Pepsi and Lay's potato chips.

> It is said that if you know the enemy and know yourself, you need not fear the result of a hundred battles. If you know yourself but not the enemy, for every victory gained you will also suffer a defeat. If you know neither the enemy nor yourself, you will succumb in every battle (Art of War, Sun Zi).

**Analysis of competitors:** Conducting a competitor analysis requires sufficient data on competitors, such as who they are, what resources they have, what products or services they offer, and visible strengths

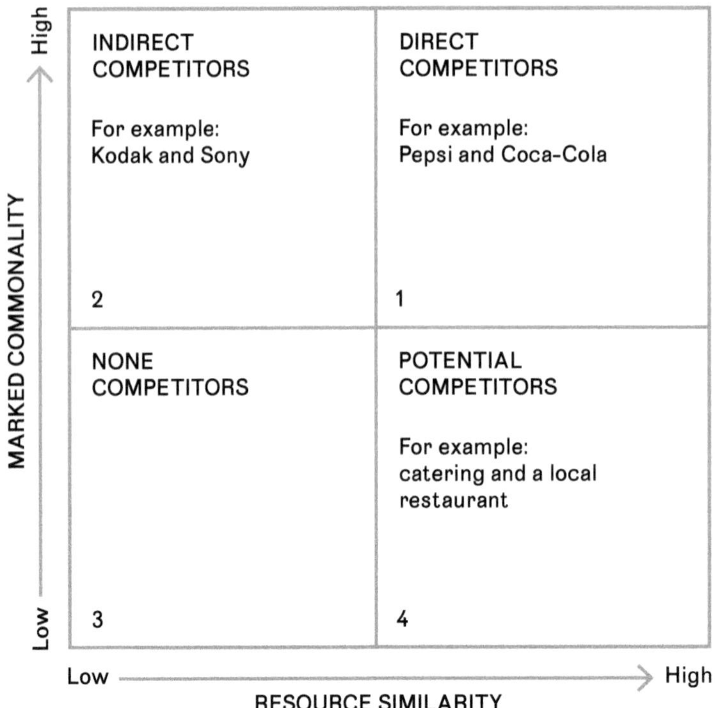


Fig. 2.23 Competitive analysis

and weaknesses of their strategies. One way of conducting a competitor analysis is to classify existing and potential competitors in the market based on the market demand they serve and their resource base. This could bring clarity as to whether, and to what extent, they constitute a competitive factor. In the analysis presented here, the focal firm (the company that makes the analysis) is referred to as the company, while the analysis objects are referred to as businesses. The analysis is based on Paditar (2017), see Figure 2.23:

*Direct competitors (Square 1):* High performance businesses in terms of both resource base and market commonalities serve the same market needs using the same type of resources as the company. Such a business is a direct competitor to the company. One example of a direct competitor is Coca-Cola, if Pepsi is the company we focus on.

*Indirect competitors (Square 2):* Businesses that score high in market commonalities and low in resource similarity serve the same market needs as the company but use different resources. These businesses are indirect competitors or substitutes. They meet similar needs using another resource or technology. For example, Kodak and Sony. The two companies offer similar products, but different technology.

*No competitors (Square 3):* Businesses that score low on both market commonalities and low in resource similarity serve a different market and use different resources. Such businesses are completely out of competition today, although this may change in the future as companies change positions. These businesses are not competitors to the company.

*Potential competitors (Square 4):* Businesses that score high in resource similarity and low in market commonality use the same resources

Fig. 2.23 The figure shows the identification and classification of competitors (based on Peteraf and Bergen, 2002). The analysis can be used to map the company's competitors. Under market commonality, we sort competitors according to the extent to which they serve the needs of the market similarly to the company. Under resource similarity, we sort competitors according to whether their competitiveness is equal to the company's in terms of company type, composition and resources, such as technological resources. High and low on each of the axes, represent high or low threat.

Fig. 2.24 The figure shows Michael Porter's five forces analysis. Based on Michael Porter 1979. Porter's 'Five forces of competitive position analysis' were developed by Michael Porter as a simple framework for assessing and evaluating the competitive strength and position of a business organisation.

Tips for the company
The company's distinctive brand assets are a competitive factor. Mental avilability can be measured. See chapters 2.9.8 Mental availability measurements, 3.4.6 Distinctive asset-building strategy.

83 *How Competitive Forces Shape Strategy* (Michael E. Porter 1979).
84 'A limitation of this study is its focus on the mining and IT industries, although the findings should be generalisable to other similar industries, given previous applications of P5F' (Isabelle et al. 2020).

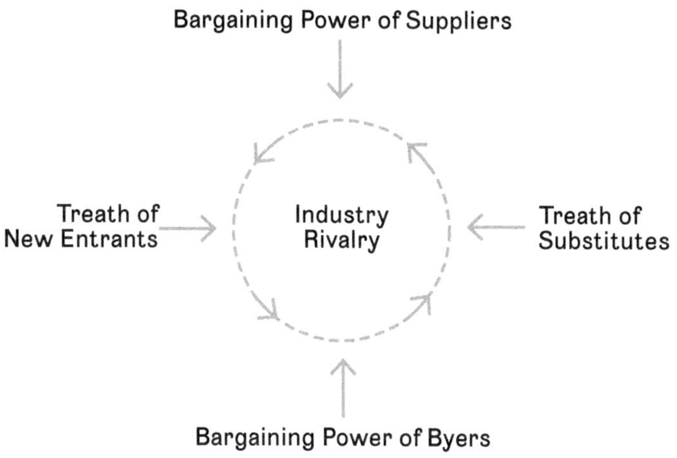

Fig. 2.24 Five forces

1 Initiation
2 Insight
3 Strategy
4 Design
5 Production
6 Management

2.1 Understanding the company
2.2 Situational study
2.3 Problem statement
2.4 Method selection
2.5 Research process
2.6 Research
2.7 Analyses
2.8 Mapping
2.9 Testing and measuring

2.7.1 Situational analysis
2.7.2 Internal analysis
2.7.3 Value chain analysis
2.7.4 Competitor analysis
2.7.5 Positioning analysis
2.7.6 Target group analysis
2.7.7 Brand analysis
2.7.8 Visual analysis
2.7.9 PESTLE analysis
2.7.10 SWOT analysis
2.7.11 Gap analysis

as the company, but address different market demands. These businesses are potential competitors to the company. An example of such a business could be a catering company as opposed to a local restaurant. Both use almost the same resources-like chefs, kitchenware, etc., but their market is different. Catering companies serve banquets and dinners for large gatherings, while restaurants serve individuals and small groups.

#### Porter's five forces analysis

According to Michael Porter, the state of competition in an industry depends on five basic forces: the threat of new entrants, the bargaining power of buyers, the bargaining power of suppliers, the threat of substitute products of services, and the rivalry among existing competitors. 'The collective strength of these forces determines the ultimate profit potential of an industry' (Porter, 1979).[83] In the paper 'Is Porter's Five Forces Framework Still Relevant?' (Isabelle et al., 2020), the authors propose to augment Porter's framework with four additional forces, 'to capture the increased interconnectivity and complexity of businesses operating in the 21st century' (Isabelle et al., 2020).[84] The additional forces: the competitor's level of innovativeness, exposure to globalisation, threat of digitalisation, and industry exposure to de/regulation activities.

### 2.7.5 Positioning analysis

Positioning analysis is about clarifying and analysing a brand's position in the market in relation to competing products. Analysis of today's position is useful when the company wants to strengthen its position or establish itself in new markets.

'Position' is the place occupied by a company, product or service in the market. This space is created first and foremost in customer awareness; a set of mental notions that govern the customers' choice in a buying situation. It may be something unique, distinctive, characteristic, or an experience that the customer associates with the product, service, brand, or name that makes them prefer one product or service to another. Creating a position is about building trust. There must be a connection between what the product promises and people's

Further reading
***Competitive Strategy: Techniques for Analyzing Industries and Competitors*** **(2019) by Michael E. Porter.**

experience of the product. The starting point for a positioning analysis should be real information about what people think about the product and whether it meets expectations. In addition, it is necessary to acquire good knowledge of the market and competitors. Preserving and strengthening a position requires regular monitoring of market needs and the competitors' position in the market. Such monitoring is done by following market trends and the competitive situation, and through regular studies, surveys and analyses of the target group(s) in order to know their needs and preferences (2.7.6 Target group analysis).

Positioning analysis is a natural part of a brand analysis (2.7.7 Brand analysis) and is important in all contexts where a product or service is to be positioned. A redesign of a product or corporate identity may provide an opportunity to adjust and strengthen the company's position vis-à-vis other actors in the same industry, or to reposition the brand. The positioning analysis can then be used as a basis for developing a positioning strategy, which defines how the company will compete and make its products stand out in the market (3.7 Brand strategy).

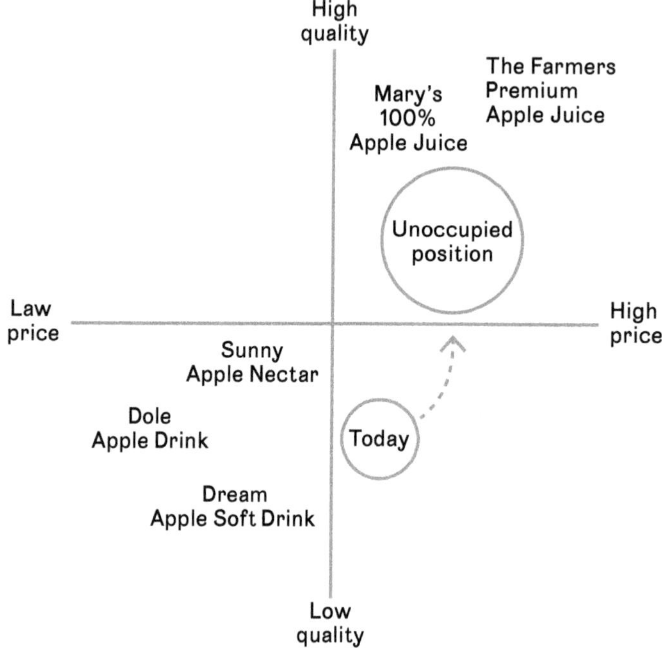


Fig. 2.25 Repositioning

Fig. 2.25 The figure shows the repositioning of a product. What appears in the figure as 'Today' is the current situation of the brand. What appears as 'Vacant position' is the target or desired position. The arrow between the two represents the strategy. How to achieve desired position? It is about a conscious branding strategy, conscious design and conscious marketing. Vacant position shows quality and price that are slightly above average. Price and quality are usually interconnected. It can therefore be contradictory to develop a high-quality product at a low price, or a low-quality product at a high price, but it can also be an ingenious combination if successful. Examples of products that can be perceived as high quality at low price are Toyota and Ikea. © Grimsgaard, W. (2018)

Fig. 2.26 The figure shows how the axis can be extended by several axes. This can provide a more accurate positioning of the product to be analysed and compared with competing products. Instead of points, product names or product photos may be used.

**Positioning axis:** The positioning axis is widely used because it is both visual and flexible in use. The aim of using a positioning axis is to identify where the company, its products or services are located in the market in relation to competitors. It can be a good starting point for assessing and analysing the current position and defining a new positioning strategy. A known positioning strategy is to position the product so that it fills a gap in the market, or to find a vacant (unoccupied) position, see Figure 2.25. Another strategy is to challenge the position of competitors by positioning oneself close by. There are many different positioning strategies (3.7.3 Brand position).

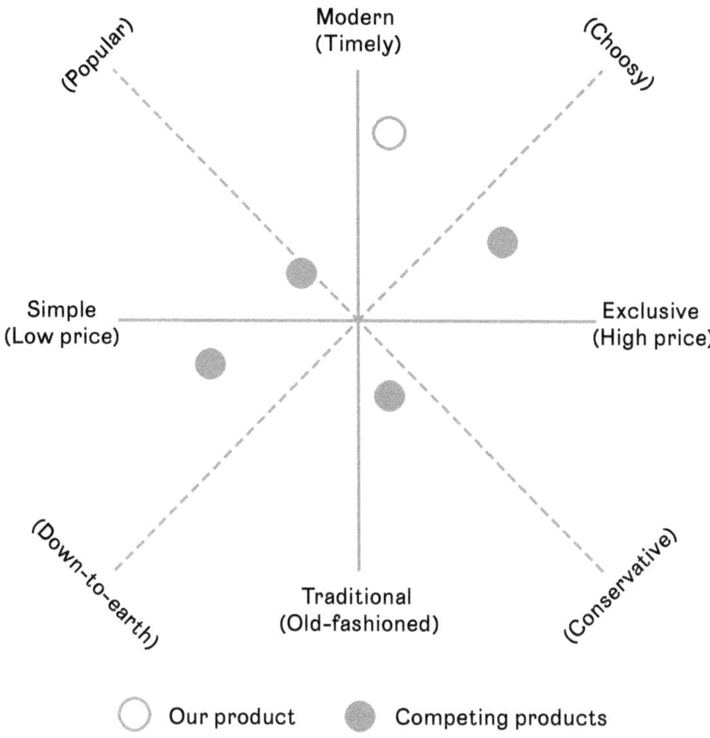


Fig. 2.26 Product positioning analysis

1 Initiation
2 Insight
3 Strategy
4 Design
5 Production
6 Management

2.1 Understanding the company
2.2 Situational study
2.3 Problem statement
2.4 Method selection
2.5 Research process
2.6 Research
2.7 Analyses
2.8 Mapping
2.9 Testing and measuring

2.7.1 Situational analysis
2.7.2 Internal analysis
2.7.3 Value chain analysis
2.7.4 Competitor analysis
2.7.5 Positioning analysis
2.7.6 Target group analysis
2.7.7 Brand analysis
2.7.8 Visual analysis
2.7.9 PESTLE analysis
2.7.10 SWOT analysis
2.7.11 Gap analysis

The basic structure of a positioning axis is two straight lines, an $x$ axis and a $y$ axis. The $x$ axis goes from left to right, and the $y$ axis goes from bottom to top. For a more thorough analysis, multiple axes may be used. The space between the axes' extremes represents the market or landscape in which the products compete. The final points on the axes are given a designation or criterion that forms the basis of assessment. The criteria are often contradictory. For example, high quality/low quality, high price/low price. The criteria used include, for example, product characteristics, features, style, experience, price, quality, reliability, etc. It is of great importance for the result that the criteria be relevant for the analysis in that they reflect, for example, existing or desired competitive strategy, or customer and user perceptions of the product or service. It may be that the product competes with price, in which case high/low price should be the criteria used. For example, if the strategy is innovation, the criteria could be innovative/traditional. When the axes are drawn and marked with criteria, the product to be analysed is placed together with competing products on the map, using product names or small product photos.

For smaller projects, it may be tempting to resort to subjective interpretations as a starting point for the choice of designation on the axes. If it becomes pure conjecture, this may give an incorrect picture of the product's existing position and possible future position. The risk may then be that the product does not deliver what it promises. In order to obtain the best possible result from the positioning analysis, the designations of the axes should be as realistic as possible. This is done by having enough knowledge of the product, the target group, the

Further reading
*Obviously Awesome: How to Nail Product Positioning so Customers Get It, Buy It, Love It* (2020) by Akash Karia.

market and the competitors. Quantitative surveying of a larger number of people is a good approach to revealing general perceptions of a product or business, in terms of familiarity, quality, satisfaction, price and other specific criteria that may need to be compared (2.6.1 Survey). It can be advantageous for the answers to be quantifiable and possible to convert into numbers. The downside of that is that the questions are then set, with a few answer options based on the fact that the product properties one wants a response to have been defined in advance. Qualitative research such as one-to-one interviews usually provides more information and understanding of how product characteristics are perceived, but processing the information may involve more work (2.6.2 Interview).

Fig. 2.27 The figure shows an example of analysis of today's identity in relation to the desired identity, in a complex coordinate system with different measurement parameters.

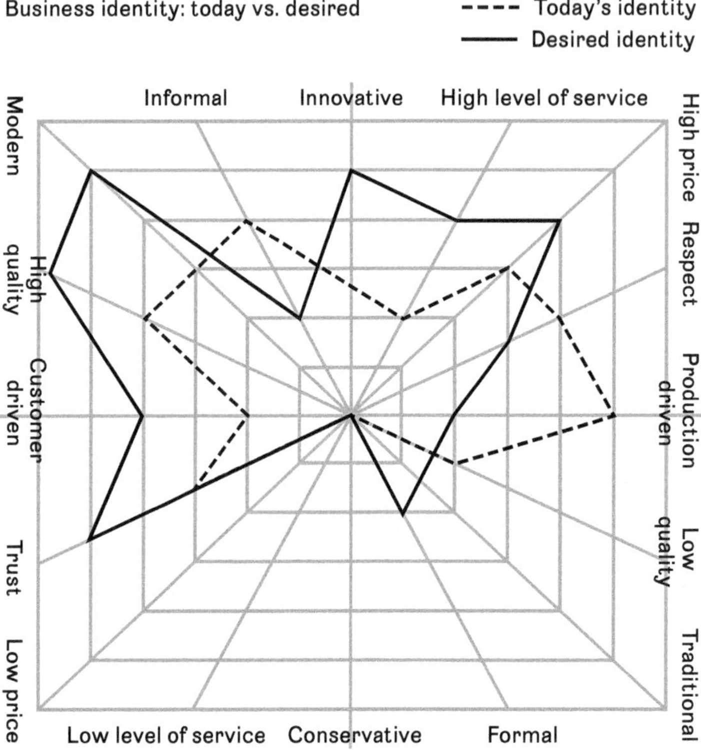


Fig. 2.27 Positioning analysis, business

**Product positioning analysis:** The positioning axis can be used to clarify the current position and the desired position, as well as to map the position of competing products. When planning a repositioning, the criteria displayed at the extremities of the positioning axis can represent both the current situation and the desired position; Figure 2.25 shows an example of this. It may be useful to create several positioning axes to analyse several aspects of existing or possible positions; Figure 2.26 shows an example of this.

**Positioning analysis of a company:** The positioning analysis may also be used internally in the company in conjunction with the redesign of their corporate identity, see Figure 2.27. The reference values are plotted into the coordinate system and a line is drawn between points. The lines may have different colour, thickness, dots, or anything else that distinguishes them from each other. This makes it easy to compare the reference values. Similarly, the characteristics of competing companies and their performance can be compared to one's own company.


1 Initiation
2 Insight
3 Strategy
4 Design
5 Production
6 Management

2.1 Understanding the company
2.2 Situational study
2.3 Problem statement
2.4 Method selection
2.5 Research process
2.6 Research
2.7 Analyses
2.8 Mapping
2.9 Testing and measuring

2.7.1 Situational analysis
2.7.2 Internal analysis
2.7.3 Value chain analysis
2.7.4 Competitor analysis
2.7.5 Positioning analysis
2.7.6 Target group analysis
2.7.7 Brand analysis
2.7.8 Visual analysis
2.7.9 PESTLE analysis
2.7.10 SWOT analysis
2.7.11 Gap analysis

- Market segmentation
- Automated segmentation
- Segmentation models
- Target group analysis process
- Maslow's hierarchy of needs


### 2.7.6 Target group analysis

Target group analysis is a systematic process of circling in a specific target group to whom one wants to sell one's products or services and to whom one will use resources through communication and market operations.One of the first things we think about when developing a new product or service is who needs it and who would want to buy it. Who is the user? Who is the buyer? Which target group will be most profitable and have the greatest potential for growth? We think about it when designing the product or service, when designing the packaging, when creating the communication, and when selecting the communication channel. Whom do we want to reach? What characterises the person in terms of lifestyle and phase of life, interests and attitudes, and how can we get our message across? It is about finding out what they like, what drives them, what is their problem or need that the market does not meet, and understanding that need.

Usually, one has a special target group in mind when developing a product or service, for example, when one wants to open a café that serves barista coffee. Then the target group will be those interested in good coffee. The target group has already been defined there. But who is really interested in good coffee? It can be costly to approach the entire market to reach the real coffee lovers. It is less resource-intensive to point market activities directly to those one wants to reach, at their location, and in a way that appeals to them. It is about finding out who they are, where they are, and what interests, needs, and desires they have. This way, efforts can be limited to a part of the market and communication can be adapted to this target group.

The extent of a target group analysis will depend on the time and resources available. Basically, one can study existing target group profiles and create a personality type, the so-called 'personas', and create an imagined image of the target group one wants to target. In a broad sense, systematic segmentation analyses can be carried out to circle in an exact target group, calculate the size of the market and determine which media should be used to reach the target group as effectively as possible. 'Identifying the complete personality of a user is a key feature in the marketing strategy of businesses today. That's because it's not good enough to only know who buys the product or service. Instead, companies need to know when, where and how consumers come into contact with their business, in order to devise strategies that play on competitive competencies to cater to customer needs' (Jalil, 2021).

Target group
A group towards which we direct the product, service, offer or message.

Buyer/customer
A person or group purchasing a product or service.

User
A person using a service or using a product.

#### Market segmentation

Market segmentation assumes that all products and services are developed for a specific target group with common characteristics, such as income, interests, background, educational level and other variables. Segmentation is about dividing a large market into smaller groups based on such common characteristics. In order to segment, each segment must be accessible and identifiable, and it should be profitable and in line with the company's objectives and strategy. Extensive segmentation processes and target group analyses require the use of both qualitative and quantitative market research to obtain information and facts about the user (2.4 Method selection). There are somewhat different approaches to business market segmentation (B2B)[85] and consumer market segmentation (B2C).

*The corporate market* is commonly segmented by 1) type of business/industry, 2) size, 3) geography, 4) importance and 5) system/technology use.

*The consumer market* is commonly segmented according to four main criteria: 1) geographical criteria, 2) demographic criteria, 3) psychographic criteria, and 4) behavioural criteria. One begins with the total market, which is the whole market. From there, one starts with rough segmentation based on demography, then dividing geographically. Eventually, one divides the market into even smaller parts based on psychography and behaviour. Finally, one is left with a small group, the target group itself, those who are most likely to buy the company's products and services. Segmentation is often done as part of the market strategy, through three steps: segmentation, target group selection and positioning (3.6.3 STP marketing strategy).

Fig. 2.28 **The figure shows the segregation principle as a funnel. At the top of the funnel is the entire market. The result of a segmentation process reduces the market until the target group is the only one left (Based on O'Neal, 2009).**

The Y&R 4Cs segmentation

**4Cs is short for Cross Cultural Consumer Characterisation. It is a values segmentation designed to explore priorities in brand choice. It divides people in to 7 groups depending on their motivation: Reformer. Explorer. Succeeder. Aspirer. Mainstream. Struggler. Resigned. *There Are Seven Kinds of People in the World* (Y&R, 2010): issuu.com/youngandrubicam/docs/4cs.**

**Demographic segmentation** involves dividing the market by variables such as age, family size, family life cycle, gender, income, occupation, education, religion, race, generation, nationality, and social class. These are variables that are useful in a marketing context because they are relatively easy to measure and they most often reveal consumers' needs and wants. In those contexts where one wants to describe the target group by personality type, it can provide a more realistic description of the target group. For quantitative research such as satisfaction surveys, such variables are necessary in order to obtain numerical data, which can be used to produce statistics (see Table 2.4 Satisfaction survey, and chapter 2.3.5 Problem statement delimitation. We will further look at a range of demographic variables such as age and life cycle, life phase, gender, income and generation based on Kotler and Keller (2016: 348):

*Age and life cycle:* People's needs and wants change with age and life cycle. The dividing lines between the age groups today are being erased, therefore a product intended for a younger target group might as well appeal to an older target group that is young at heart. It is easier to segment when it comes to products that are age-related, such as nappies:[86] It is also easier to segment when it comes to products that are age-related, such as nappies: new-borns (0–5 months), babies (6–12 months), toddlers (13–23 months) and children (24 months+).

*Life phase*: Life phases are the most important phases of a person's life, such as moving away from home, buying a house, moving in together, getting married, getting divorced, and so on. Some products and services target such life stages, such as home sales, weddings and funerals. Humans can be at the same stage in their life cycle, but in different phases of life. We are no longer talking about a particular age, but typical needs, wants, characteristics or other characteristics of the current life phase one wishes to reach with one's products and services.

85 **B2B: Business to business. B2C: Business to Consumer.**
86 **The example is from the Pampers brand.**

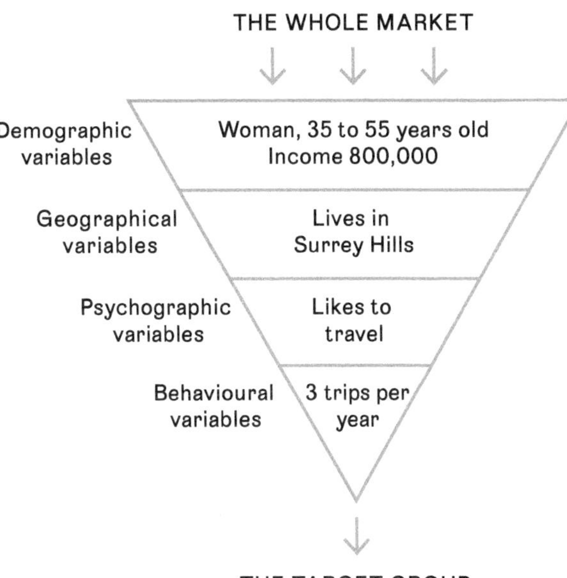

Fig. 2.28 Segmentation principle

*Gender:* Today's gender awareness is different from that of the past. We have not only he or she, but also they, which refers to a non-binary gender identity. Traditionally, gender is still male and female. Despite gender equality and gender balance in household tasks, occupation, and partially salary, there are still differences in physiology, attitudes, behaviour, needs, and wants. For example, women who watch TV, choose different channels from men. This is useful knowledge if one wants to reach out to the public using TV advertising.

*Income:* Income segmentation is a widely used method, especially in categories such as cars, clothing, cosmetics, financial services and tourism, and products that compete with price. A high-income person is more likely to buy expensive cosmetics and luxury cars than a low-income person.

*Generation:* Different generations have their specific characteristics, wants and needs. A generation is people born at roughly the same time. They are influenced by the times they grew up in music, films, politics, and important events of the period. Thus, they will also have some shared memories and values. This is something one can play on via communication and marketing, using icons, pictures, music, and stories from the period. Examples of generation groups are gen Alpha (2013–present), gen Z (1997–2012), gen Y 'the millennium generation' (1981–1996), gen X (1965–1980), baby boomers 'the '68' (1946–1964), and the pre-war generation (1928–1945) (Gosh, 2021).

**Geographical segmentation** involves dividing the market according to geographical variables, from the total market, which is nations, to provinces, counties, regions, cities, districts and down to local level. It is about analysing the market based on geographical criteria in order to customise marketing to population groups in a larger or smaller geographical area. Grassroots marketing is a concept of marketing at



Personalising the message

**'Marketers have always known that personalized messaging leads to better email stats, but adding a name and company to your message is no longer cutting it. Personalizing the message to fit the customers' distinct personality – i.e. communication styles and motivations – is the next step' (Skloot, 2022).**

micro-level, where the aim is to address the individual customer directly, in a personal and relevant way. Local marketing is about reaching the local population and leading marketing all the way down to postcode level. PRIZM[87] is such a method. It is an acronym for Potential Rating Index for Zip Markets.

**Psychographic segmentation** involves dividing buyers into different groups by psychological traits, personality traits, lifestyles, opinions, attitudes and values. Both psychology and demography are used to better understand the consumer. People in the same demographic group may have very different psychographic profiles. Examples of classification systems based on psychographic measurements are ROLL Framework, Minerva and Gallup's compass.

**Behavioural segmentation** is about dividing buyers into groups based on their knowledge of, attitude to, use of, and response to a product. Many marketing experts believe that this approach provides a better understanding of consumers compared to psychographic segmentation. These include needs and benefits, decision roles, and user-related variables.

*Decision roles*: It is not always the user who buys the product, and the buyer roles are constantly changing. A distinction is made between five roles in a purchase decision: initiator, influencer, decision-making authority, buyer, and user.

*User-related variables:* We distinguish between different variables for use and users:

- Occasions: Time of the day, week, month and so on.
- User status: Non-users, past users, potential users, first-time users, permanent users.
- Frequency of use: Small consumers, medium-sized consumers, large consumers.
- Purchase intention level: Don't know the product, know the product, are informed about the product, interested, want and intent to buy the product.
- Loyalty status: The hard core, the divided, the wobbly, the rootless.
- Attitude: Enthusiastic, positive, indifferent, negative and hostile.
- Multiple bases: Combining different variables can provide a better and more comprehensive overview of a market and its market segments.

### Automated segmentation

Artificial intelligence allows automated segmentation, monitoring the habits and behaviour of consumers which make customer segmentation much more valuable and insightful for businesses, because they give more value-driven characteristics. Instead of segmenting and targeting consumers on who they are, businesses now segment based on behaviour (Jalil, 2021), e.g. Hubspot.[88] Examples of automated segmentation models are Cohort analysis[89] and RFM modelling.[90]

### Segmentation models

A variety of segmentation methods and analysis tools are available for free online or available for purchase. One frequently used model for categorising personality archetypes, is the 16-Personality model[91] from

87 PRIZM has been developed by Nielsen Claritas.

88 Hubspot provides tools for social media marketing, content management, web analytics, landing pages, customer support, and search engine optimisation. The tools have integration features for salesforce.com, SugarCRM, NetSuite, Microsoft Dynamics CRM, and others. The software as a service product is free and integrates with gmail, G Suite, Microsoft Office for Windows, and other software. HubSpot is an American developer and marketer of software products for inbound marketing, sales, and customer service. Hubspot was founded by Brian Halligan and Dharmesh Shah in 2006. ('Hubspot,' n.d., hubspot.com)

89 'Cohort analysis is an analytical technique that focuses on analyzing the behavior of a group of users/customers over time, thereby uncovering insights about the experiences of those customers, and what companies can do to better those experiences' (Su, 2018).

90 RFM (recency, frequency, monetary) analysis is a marketing technique used to quantitatively rank and group customers based on the recency, frequency and monetary total of their recent transactions to identify the best customers and perform targeted marketing campaigns. RFM analysis is based on the marketing adage that '80% of your business comes from 20% of your customers' (Wright, 2021).

91 The 16-Personality test (the Myers-Briggs Type Indicator® MBTI® personality inventory), was developed by Katharine Cook Briggs and her daughter Isabel Briggs Myers. *Manual: A Guide to the Development and Use of the Myers-Briggs Type Indicator®* (myersbriggs.org, 16personalities.com).

92 VALS is an acronym for the words values and lifestyles. VALS (SBI, Strategic Business Insight): strategicbusiness-insights.com/vals/. Kotler and Keller p. 356.

**The 16-Personality Test**

Learning about the 16-personality types can help you better understand why people act and speak in certain ways, and, in turn, allow you to relate more to others and communicate more effectively with them. The tests draw on the method based on the types of Jung, Myers, & Briggs, sort people into 16 different types which are organised by four pairs of opposite traits.

- Extraversion (E) and Introversion (I)
- Sensing (S) and Intuition (N)
- Thinking (T) and Feeling (F)
- Judging (J) and Perceiving (P)

One of each pair is combined to create a 4-letter abbreviation for each personality type, such as:
ESFP: extraversion (E), sensing (S), feeling (F), perception (P)
INTJ: introversion (I), intuition (N), thinking (T), judgment (J)
(16personalities.com)

the 1940s which was built upon psychological research performed by Carl Jung in the 1920s (myersbriggs.org). This personality test available online describes the way in which a person interacts with the world. There are many segmentation models that have up-to-date data for specific countries and geographical areas, based on regularly conducted surveys. One example of this is VALS,[92] which divides adult Americans into eight primary groups based on answers to a survey with 4 demographic questions and 35 questions about attitudes. The measurements are based on new data from 80,000 surveys per year, which reveal different types of people and specify typical personal characteristics within the categories: Innovators, Thinkers, Believers, Achievers, Strivers, Experiencers, Makers, Survivors. One can find out which VALS type one is by going to the website of SBI. Similarly, Japan has its models, England has its models and so on, the Danes have the Minerva method (see Figure 2.29) and Gallup's compass, both of which are also considered Nordic models. And then there is Mosaic, which provides the opportunity to see the person behind the customer, to understand their drivers and needs (insightone.no/mosaic).

**The use of AI to understand the audience**

'Artificial Intelligence can analyze millions of data points at once to predict an outcome. It's the same way we make decisions – our brains weigh what we know (like our past experience and knowledge about how the world works) and use that information to help us choose. AI can store and process significantly more information than we can, and is often able to make more accurate conclusions. It gives marketers a chance to understand their audiences effectively and e.g. send better emails. Rather than viewing people based solely on their demographic information, you can understand their motivations, what gives them energy, how they like to communicate and more' (Skloot, 2022).

As AI technology is changing how companies communicate with their audiences, new software is being developed that can help marketers improve success rates by predicting their customers' personalities, such as Personality AI,[93] a technology that predicts personality by using AI and machine learning to analyse someone's LinkedIn profile.

Fig. 2.29 **The figure shows a target group analysis that segments based on people's lifestyle. Based on the segmentation model Minerva developed by Henrik Dahl.**

**Important insights can be gained by understanding personality type, such as optimal career choice, better romantic partnerships, and paths to personal growth (personalityperfect.com).**

**Target group analysis process**

**Identify the target market (customer segment):** If the company produces car parts, will those who want to own, who own or who work with cars be the target market? Use a variety of surveys and available resources. There is a wealth of data on the Internet from reliable and public sources. **Map the geographical market:** The market can be large areas such as countries, regions and counties, or smaller areas such as municipalities, cities, or neighbourhoods. Climate, population density and nature are

**The Minerva method**

The Minerva model, see Figure 2.29, is a Nordic segmentation model developed by the Danish sociologist and lifestyle researcher Henrik Dahl (1997),[94] It is based on a comprehensive lifestyle study associated with values of life, values that lie deep within the individual and form the basis of the personality. The model is based on a segmentation of Danes into uniform groups based on their lifestyle. It is built on the four primary lifestyles modern or traditional, combined with materialism or idealism. *Modern* refers to people who are keen on new technology and welcome everything that is new, while *traditional* people are opposed to new technologies and are often somewhat scared by all the new developments that take place. On the other hand, they appreciate tradition and good old-fashioned values. *Idealistic* people are concerned with values of proximity, such as the close values of family, and the well-being of all people on earth. *Materialistic* people appreciate things and possessions, expensive cars, houses and a great TV set. These divisions constitute four squares, blue, green, pink and violet, and some common values for people who in terms of values are placed in the same squares. *The grey area* in the middle was not included in Henrik Dahl's original model; it has been included later and represents the group of younger people who have not yet found their own place. The Minerva model is easy to use for segmentation, choice of media and choice of marketing activities. It is best used in combination with traditional demographic variables such as gender, income, education, place of residence, etc. Note that the characteristics in the four main segments are an expression of the extreme in the segments. Each segment also contains personalities, where the highlighted characteristics of the segment are less pronounced. A person might as well be somewhere between the blue and the green. For example, a person in the middle of the blue field will have a more traditional value set compared to one at the top of the field (Based on YouTube, Henrik Dahl, 2013).

93 'Personality AI takes multiple types of inputs – text samples, demographic data, real life observations, questionnaire responses – and outputs personality insights. It's a convergence of technology, psychology, and personality theory to help us understand how to communicate with anyone effectively' (Skloot, 2022).

94 Henrik Dahl developed the model when he was Chief of Research at the analytical company AC. Nielsen. He wrote the book 'If your neighbor was a car' (Original title: *Hvis din nabo var en bil*) (1997) a basic book on segmentation, lifestyle, and target groups.

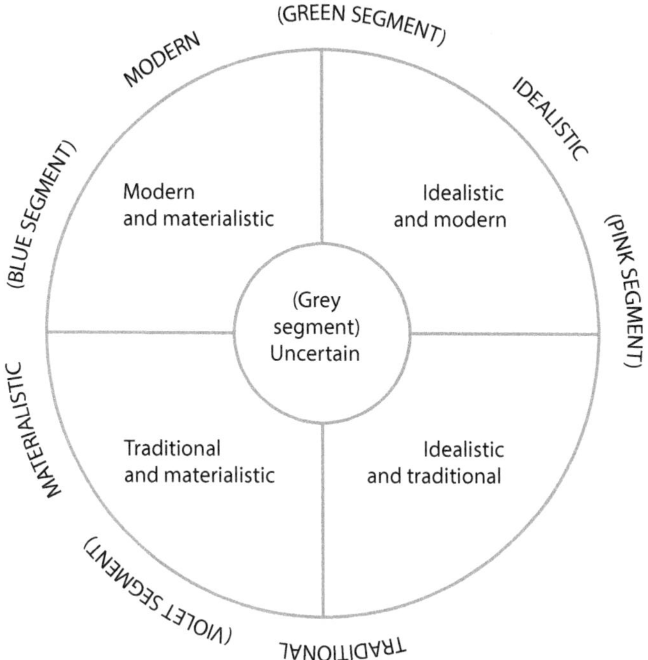


Fig. 2.29 Minerva target group analysis

also important factors. The aim is not to exclude any customers, but rather to identify the most likely ones.

**Examine the target market demographically**: Consumer market (B2C): Gender, nationality, ethnicity, race, age, generation, marital status, household size, family status, education, occupation, income, religion, social class. Such demographic information can often be found online. Businesses (B2B): Location, number of business areas, annual income, number of employees, sector or industry, how long the company has existed and so on. Such data can be obtained from annual accounts and the like, which are often officially available and online.

**Describe the target market psychographically**: It is about typical personality traits, values, attitudes, interests, lifestyle, group affiliation, social affiliation. This information can most easily be obtained through market research and focus groups. If approaching businesses, psychographic information can include the company's values or motto, how it wants to be seen by its own customers, and how formal or informal its work environment is. This information can be obtained most easily by observations, visits to the company's stores and through its websites and annual accounts.

**Understand the behaviour of the target group**: Behaviour concerns when, where, how and why customers act, and their attitudes towards use of and response to a product or service. Examining the behaviour of the target group makes it possible to understand why someone buys one product or service rather than another, how often they buy the product, how much or how many they buy, whether on a particular occasion, and how long it takes them to decide to buy the product. Such knowledge is particularly useful in individual marketing to potential

1 Initiation
2 Insight
3 Strategy
4 Design
5 Production
6 Management

2.1 Understanding the company
2.2 Situational study
2.3 Problem statement
2.4 Method selection
2.5 Research process
2.6 Research
2.7 Analyses
2.8 Mapping
2.9 Testing and measuring

2.7.1 Situational analysis
2.7.2 Internal analysis
2.7.3 Value chain analysis
2.7.4 Competitor analysis
2.7.5 Positioning analysis
2.7.6 Target group analysis
2.7.7 Brand analysis
2.7.8 Visual analysis
2.7.9 PESTLE analysis
2.7.10 SWOT analysis
2.7.11 Gap analysis

- Market segmentation
- Automated segmentation
- Segmentation models
- Target group analysis process
- Maslow's hierarchy of needs

Mosaic

Our Personality Tasks directly measure a MOSAIC of individual behaviours in order to assess the full picture of personality. The tasks identify the potential blind spots of personality using a combination of 7 digital tasks and a self-report questionnaire. Our direct measurement of personality offers a fake-resistant assessment. This means it offers a unique level of insight, objectivity and assurance to this nebulous and well-trodden science (mosaictasks.com).

customers in order to find out how important loyalty is to the brand or company, whether the potential customers are concerned with price or quality, whether they usually pay for the product or service, and whether they prefer to shop in a physical or on-line store. This type of data can be obtained through market research and data from various digital analytical tools.

**Presentation of target group analysis:** When preparing a report, it is important to consider the objective of the research and who should read and use it. Use graphs, charts, or other visual effects. For example, a pie chart can show 75 and 25 percent of the market much more vividly than just numbers and words. Here is an example of a report template:

- Introduction. Identification of the product or service, and definition of the target market.
- Description of the target market, including size and description of the general characteristics.
- Summary of the market research carried out in the analysis.
- Analysis of market trends and any expected changes in the purchasing habits of the target group.
- Risk and expected competition.
- Expected future growth or changes in the market.

(Based on Ramamoorthy, 2021).

Fig. 2.30 **The figure shows Maslow's hierarchy of needs. At the bottom of the pyramid are the basic and strongest needs, which, according to Maslow, must be satisfied before the needs of the next level become important (Mørch, n.d.).**

**Target market analysis**

This analysis is about measuring expected future growth. The fair value of a target market analysis is not only to describe the current state of the market, but also to anticipate or project the future, creating future scenarios. It is about assessing how certain changes in the market or in society can affect the company and be prepared if the changes actually occur. There is a lot of easily accessible information on the Internet about future forecasts and megatrends.

Add the following questions to the analysis:

- How many customers are coming back?
- How does the ageing of the target group affect their interest in your service or product?
- How do economic changes in your community affect your target market?
- How will the target market be affected by public changes, new rules etc.?

**Use of the analysis:** The target market analysis can operate separately, in a target group analysis or as part of a larger business plan for the company. Based on the analysis, is it possible to recommend which steps the company should take in the future? Should advertising in a particular area be increased or reduced? Should new target markets be added? A target market analysis is of little use if the company does not follow it up and continues to monitor the market (Ramamoorthy, 2021).

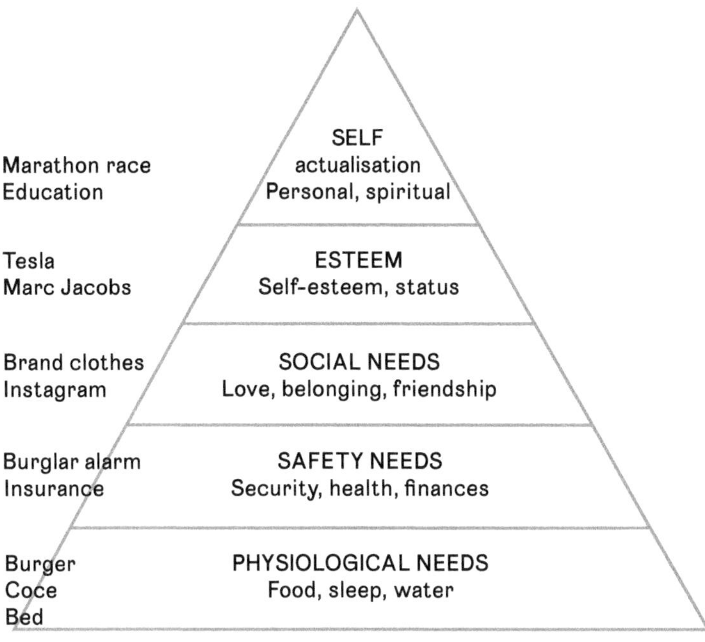


Fig. 2.30 Maslow's hierachy of needs

1 Initiation
2 Insight
3 Strategy
4 Design
5 Production
6 Management

2.1 Understanding the company
2.2 Situational study
2.3 Problem statement
2.4 Method selection
2.5 Research process
2.6 Research
2.7 Analyses
2.8 Mapping
2.9 Testing and measuring

2.7.1 Situational analysis
2.7.2 Internal analysis
2.7.3 Value chain analysis
2.7.4 Competitor analysis
2.7.5 Positioning analysis
2.7.6 Target group analysis
2.7.7 Brand analysis
2.7.8 Visual analysis
2.7.9 PESTLE analysis
2.7.10 SWOT analysis
2.7.11 Gap analysis

#### Maslow's hierarchy of needs

In all forms of product development and sales, knowing something about the customers' needs is of vital importance. This way, the product, design and communication can be adapted to influence the target group as effectively as possible. Maslow's hierarchy of needs was developed by American personality psychologist Abraham Maslow in 1943, and it is just as relevant today. Maslow regarded the evolution of personality as a balance between the need to secure one's existence materially and psychologically on the one hand, and the need for growth, self-actualisation and the quest for knowledge on the other (Mørch, n.d.). His theory was that people's motives are organised as levels: security and physiological needs, social needs (belonging and recognition), need for growth, and self-actualisation.

### 2.7.7 Brand analysis

Brand analysis is a form of situational analysis that involves clarifying the situation and change potential of an existing brand or branded item before developing a new brand strategy, a rebranding or redesign.

A brand is an asset that must be managed. Brand loyalty is the essence. The success of major brands such as Coca-Cola, Apple and Google is based on a long-term strategy for developing and managing the brand over time. A brand, which is not maintained and renewed, risks being perceived as traditional and outdated, and may lose competitiveness and position. There are many considerations to be taken into account. People would like the brands they identify with to be up-to-date and appealing. Yet changes can often feel uncertain. If the changes to a brand are too significant, the brand can become difficult to recognise and there is a risk that customers will not find the product. Major changes may also result

> A target market, or target audience, is the pool of customers to whom you want to potentially sell your products or services. Your target market is not everyone who is located in your business's area. It's only made up of the people who are good fits for your products (Kappel, 2017).

in brand associations that are different from the ones before, so that the customer no longer identifies with the brand. That way, one can lose loyal brand customers. High-status brands are regularly updated, often with only small adjustments, barely noticeable to most people. Examples are the redesigned logos of Coca Cola, Apple and Lacoste, which have been renewed over time with slight changes. That is how they have maintained their brands. Sometimes, there is also a need for major changes, completely new designs or expansion of the brand with new products. Brand analysis identifies changes it might be wise to make. It is about gaining insight into and knowledge about the current situation of the brand and clarifying the need and potential for change (3.7.8 Brand perspective).

Fig. 2.31 The figure shows a brand analysis with a division into the company's internal and external areas. How is the brand perceived internally in the company, among employees, and how is the brand perceived externally in the market, among the target groups and stakeholders? The model can be used as a basis for a SWOT analysis of the brand and is well suited for a workshop. Brand = company, product or service.

INTERNALLY
EXTERNALLY
Internal experience:
How is the brand perceived internally?
Pride, identity?
Brand target groups:
Is the target group homogeneous?
Today? In the future?
Brand history:
The history and evolution of the brand?
THE BRAND
Brand position:
How is the brand perceived?
How is the brand positioned?
What are the most distinctive assets?
Strategic direction:
Purpose of the brand?
How should the brand be developed and built?
Can the brand expand with new products?
Competing brands:
History, position and instruments?
GAP:
Define current vs. desired situation for the brand.
How can the desired situation be achieved?

Fig. 2.31 Brand analysis internally/externally

### Brand analysis process

The first step is to get acquainted with the current situation, the goal and strategy of the brand. A good approach is to conduct research and analyses in the company's internal and external environment in order to acquire a clear picture of the factors that affect the brand, how the brand is perceived internally in the company, how it is perceived externally in the market in which the brand operates and how it differs from its competitors in the market/industry in question, see Figure 2.31. Areas that may be useful to clarify can be brand position, brand recognition, brand awareness, distinctive brand assets, brand reputation, competitive situation, target groups/segments, market trends and tendencies within the relevant market, how people perceive the brand, what the problem with today's solution is, and what needs, opportunities and limitations may lie in a change of the brand. Both qualitative and quantitative research may be used. Qualitative research such as surveys, focus groups or interviews may be conducted among employees, stakeholders and target groups to clarify their perception, experience and views on the brand. Quantitative research such as market analyses and Gallup studies can produce clear numbers and facts about brand awareness, competitive situation and

95 AC2ID is based on several major tests and surveys conducted by J.M.T Balmer and S.A Greyser: *Trans-Atlantic Identity Study*, various multidisciplinary literature reviews, and *Harvard Case Studies*. The method is based on a previous method (ACID) launched by Balmer and Soenen (1999).

market shares. The next step is to clarify what the goal of changing the brand should be. There will, of course, be a gap between the current expression and the desired solution, between the current situation and the desired situation, which should be clarified or analysed to find out what to change as well as what resources to use and how much time to spend. Will there be a need for small or significant adjustments? The brand analysis can be used as basis for formulating a problem statement for redesigning of the brand, rebranding or developing a new brand. The brand objectives and strategy are defined in the brand strategy and anchored in the overall goals and strategy of the company. The brand analysis may be combined or supplemented with visual analysis (2.7.8 Visual analysis).


1 Initiation
2 Insight
3 Strategy
4 Design
5 Production
6 Management

2.1 Understanding the company
2.2 Situational study
2.3 Problem statement
2.4 Method selection
2.5 Research process
2.6 Research
2.7 Analyses
2.8 Mapping
2.9 Testing and measuring

2.7.1 Situational analysis
2.7.2 Internal analysis
2.7.3 Value chain analysis
2.7.4 Competitor analysis
2.7.5 Positioning analysis
2.7.6 Target group analysis
2.7.7 Brand analysis
2.7.8 Visual analysis
2.7.9 PESTLE analysis
2.7.10 SWOT analysis
2.7.11 Gap analysis

- Brand analysis process
- ACCID workshop
- Keller's Brand Equity Model


### Brand analysis process

**Brand history:** The brand's history, development, and narrative?
**Branding strategy:** Current objectives and strategy?
**Internal experience:** How is the brand perceived and experienced internally in the company?
**External position:** How is the brand perceived by the target group(s)? How is the brand positioned vs. its competitors?
**Competing brands:** Which ones? Where? History, position, instruments, reputation?
**Target groups/segments/users:** Who are they? Where are they? Characteristics? Social identity? Are they a homogeneous target group or grouping? Primary and secondary target groups?
**Relations:** Need, desire, usefulness, loyalty, identity and associations related to the brand?
**Problem:** What is the problem? Problem definition? Problems?
**Gap:** Current vs. desired situation for the brand? Gap analysis.
**Brand development:** What is the desired situation for the brand? How should the desired situation be achieved? Strategic direction and plan for brand developing?

### ACCID workshop

ACCID (AC2ID) is a workshop model that the designer can implement together with the company in order to clarify its brand identity. The questions asked are whether there is a connection between the brand's actual identity, how it is communicated, how it is perceived, how it is ideally designed and how one wants it to be. These are critical questions for identifying the situation of a brand, what is wrong and how to solve the problem. Uncovering correlations and cause/effect will be of key importance in the analysis.

The method developed by Balmer and Greyser[95] refers to the different relationships between the five identity types Actual, Communicated, Conceived, Ideal and Desired. The lack of coherence between any of these identity types is potentially risky for any company wishing to create a distinct brand. The aim is to reconcile the five identity types so that they are congruent (matching) with each other as well as with the environment (political, economic, ethical, social and technological). The five identity types are explained below:

**Actual identity:** It is shaped by corporate ownership, leadership style, organisational structure, business activities, market activities, quality of products and services, as well as values held by management and employees and the extent to which they identify with the actual identity or with the other identity types.
**Communicated identity:** Normally, corporate communications include advertising and PR, but may also include performance effects of products and services, as well as spin-off effect and publicity.
**Perceived identity:** Refers to the main perceptive (perceived) concepts that make up the company's image and reputation (a choice should be made about which groups and which concepts make up the perceived identity).
**Ideal identity:** This is a purely conceptual design that concerns articulation of strategic planners and others who drive the positioning of the organisation in the market. Normally, it is based on current knowledge of the organisation and how it is perceived by its surroundings.
**Desired identity:** It is created in the minds of business leaders, and is their vision for the organisation. It is not the same as the ideal identity since such an identity type may reflect the personality type and driving forces of the CEO or the Board of Directors, etc.

Fig. 2.32 The figure shows the ACCID model that can be used in a brand analysis to reveal errors or shortcomings, and plan how the problem can be resolved. (The figure is based on J.M.T. Balmer and S.A. Greyser.)

Fig. 2.33 The figure shows the Brand Equity Model (Keller, 2013). The pyramid explains how the customer relates to the brand. In a brand analysis, we examine the customers' relationship and loyalty to the brand.

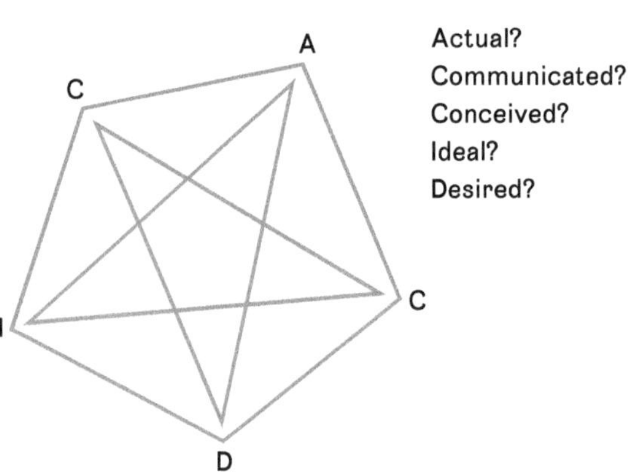


Fig. 2.32 ACCID

**Keller's Brand Equity Model**

This brand analysis is based on Keller's Brand Resonance Pyramid, also called Brand Equity Model, and Customer Based Brand Equity (CBBE) Model. The model focuses on the equity of the brand based on the relationship between the target group and the brand. In the brand analysis, we find out what experiences, thoughts, feelings, attitudes, opinions and perceptions the customer has about the brand. The model has all the factors needed to analyse a brand. It can also be used in the branding strategy to develop brand position and plan how the brand relationship can be established and built over time. Applying the model:

**1) Brand identity**

- *Salience*: Does the brand stand out? Is it recognisable? Is the target group aware of this? Is the perception of the brand 'correct'?
- *Target group/customer/user*: Who is the customer/user? How does the customer/user perceive the brand? Are there different market segments

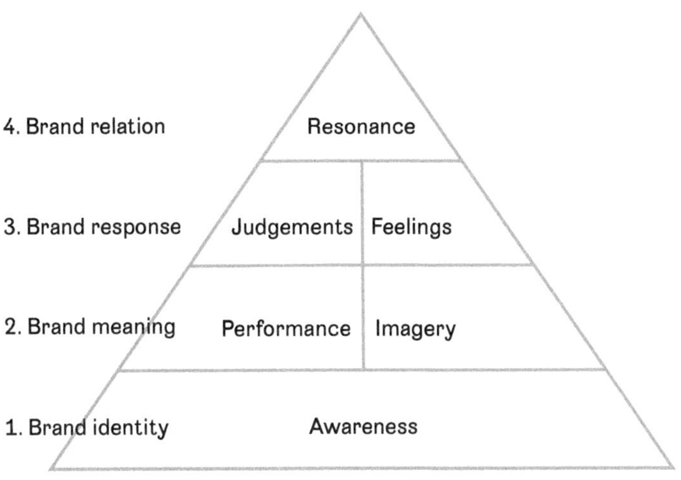


Fig. 2.33 Keller's Brand Equity Model

1 Initiation
2 Insight
3 Strategy
4 Design
5 Production
6 Management

2.1 Understanding the company
2.2 Situational study
2.3 Problem statement
2.4 Method selection
2.5 Research process
2.6 Research
2.7 Analyses
2.8 Mapping
2.9 Testing and measuring

2.7.1 Situational analysis
2.7.2 Internal analysis
2.7.3 Value chain analysis
2.7.4 Competitor analysis
2.7.5 Positioning analysis
2.7.6 Target group analysis
2.7.7 Brand analysis
2.7.8 Visual analysis
2.7.9 PESTLE analysis
2.7.10 SWOT analysis
2.7.11 Gap analysis

- Brand analysis process
- ACCID workshop
- Keller's Brand Equity Model

with different needs and different relationships to the brand? What assessments does the customer/user make when purchasing the brand? How strong is the brand at the moment of purchase? How does the customer/user choose between different brands? How do they classify the brand? How does the brand communicate the product benefits? Does the customer/user understand the communication when making his/her choice? Does the customer/user perceive the brand as intended by the company? Are there any visible or perceived problems that should be resolved, either by adjusting the product or service, or by adjusting the way it is communicated? What measures must be taken to know the customers/users and their needs, conduct and social identity? What needs should the product meet? Which category should the product belong to?

**2) Brand meaning**

- *Performance*: What significance does the brand have for the customer/user? How well does the product or service meet their needs, in terms of characteristic and distinctiveness; reliability, durability, service; efficiency; empathy (sensitivity); style, design and price. How does one find out the customers' or user's needs? How does one give them the idea that the product or service meets their needs?
- *Experience*: How does the customer/user perceive the brand? How does the brand meet them on a social and psychological level? How well does the brand hit directly, through its own experience with the product or service? How well does the brand hit indirectly, through targeted marketing or hearsay? Does the customer/user feel loyalty to the brand? What experience should the customer/user have of the product, in terms of performance and symbolic value? How should their needs be met in a way that exceeds their expectations?

**3) Brand response**

- *Assessment:* How does the customer/user assess or evaluate the brand in terms of: quality – actual or perceived? credibility – expertise, reliability?; relevance – trendiness?; priority – rank over other brands?

Further reading
***Branding: Brand Identity, Brand Strategy & Brand Development*** **(2018) by K. L. Hammond.**

- *Feeling:* How does the brand make the customer/user feel in terms of warmth, joy, excitement, security, social status and self-respect. How well does market communication work as in terms of appeal to people's needs? What can be done to strengthen the actual and perceived quality of the brand? How should brand credibility be improved? How does the brand stand out compared to competing brands?

**4) Brand relationship**

- *Resonance*: Identify the customer/user with the brand. Do they feel strong loyalty, attachment, belonging that triggers greater commitment? What is the customers' or the user's relationship to the brand like in terms of: *loyalty* - do customers have a loyalty of conduct that involves making regular and repeated purchases?; *attitude* - do they value the brand or product and see it as a special purchase?; *affiliation* - do they have a sense of affiliation with people associated with the brand, including other customers and representatives of the company?; *involvement* - are they actively involved in buying and using the product or service, but also in participating in a loyalty club of the brand, being active on the brand's social media websites etc.? How does one strengthen brand relationship so that the customer/user would feel loyalty and psychological attachment to the brand? For example, using a customer loyalty program or a reward program, which gives an opportunity to collect points or offers gifts with every purchase.

Fig. 2.34 **The figure shows an example of the position of communication and visual elements in an information hierarchy, on the various exposure surfaces of a product. © Grimsgaard, W. (2018)**

Tips for the designer
**Do a store test. Check out how the product looks on the shelf, compared to products in the same category. Which brand assets are most distinctive? Is it a special shape, colour or symbol? Can this be refined to become even more distinctive? See 3.4.6 Distinctive asset-building strategy.**

## 2.7.8 Visual analysis

Visual analysis is a form of situational analysis that involves analysing a design by identifying weaknesses and strengths in it before a redesign, or as a competitor analysis in connection with the development of a new design. The result can be used as basis for clarifying the problem and formulating an issue. Visual analysis is a qualitative method that involves assessing a visual design with critical professional eyes. The analysis does not require in-depth knowledge and can therefore be carried out early in the design project. For an experienced designer, it is natural to observe the surroundings with critical eyes and form one's own thoughts about the aesthetic, functional and possible improvement potential. For less experienced designers, it can take time to get used to using one's eyes in an active and professional way. Similarly, being able to explain and justify impressions using professional and technical terminology will require training and practice. A visual analysis requires precisely these characteristics and this approach (2.4.1 Qualitative method).

As a starting point, we use packaging design to explain how a visual analysis can be performed. The same principles can also be applied to a website, a company profile, a magazine etc. For example, the reason for redesigning a product may be greater competition from new products that look more tempting and appealing, loss of market share and downward sales performance. The design might be outdated and not perceived as trendy, or the product might not have been able to assume a clear position. It may also be that the information on the product does not deliver the message clearly, that the product is not visible enough on the shelf, appearance and taste do not match, or the product characteristics and benefits do not come out well enough. The

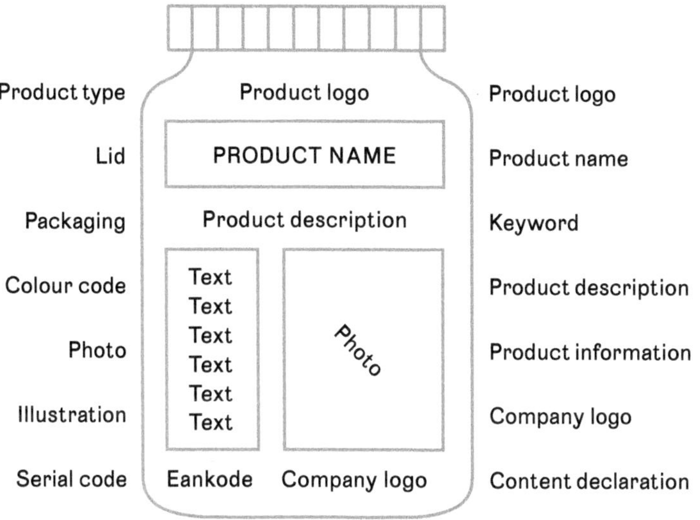


Fig. 2.34 Information hierarchy

1 Initiation
2 Insight
3 Strategy
4 Design
5 Production
6 Management

2.1 Understanding the company
2.2 Situational study
2.3 Problem statement
2.4 Method selection
2.5 Research process
2.6 Research
2.7 Analyses
2.8 Mapping
2.9 Testing and measuring

2.7.1 Situational analysis
2.7.2 Internal analysis
2.7.3 Value chain analysis
2.7.4 Competitor analysis
2.7.5 Positioning analysis
2.7.6 Target group analysis
2.7.7 Brand analysis
2.7.8 Visual analysis
2.7.9 PESTLE analysis
2.7.10 SWOT analysis
2.7.11 Gap analysis

- Preliminary studies
- Visual analysis process

reasons can be many. How a product is perceived is strongly linked to brand awareness, brand identity and brand relationship.

Before the analysis, it may be good to acquire knowledge of what is to be analysed by conducting the necessary research and studies of the product, target group, market, competitors, etc. A good starting point is to find out what users think about the product. Results are assessed, interpreted and described before making recommendations for the development of new designs. The aim is to arrive at an interpretation that is as likely and objective as possible. The result can be used to create a design brief with guides for the development of new designs. Visual analysis may also be part of a competitor analysis, positioning analysis or brand analysis as a part of the development of a brand strategy. The scope of the visual analysis should be seen in relation to the project time frame and budget.

### Preliminary studies

Prior to a visual analysis, it may be useful to conduct some simple studies or research in order to obtain a more complete picture of the situation. Here are some options:

*Situational study:* Examine all aspects of the product, including product characteristics, supplier, manufacturer, production, supply chain (from raw material to store), product exposure, history, strategy, target group, market and competitors. Clarify today's strategy and goals, history and developments. Examine which internal and external factors influence the product; it may be production, distribution, use of materials, availability, content, taste etc. (2.2 Situational study, 2.7.7 Brand analysis, 5.3.6 Product life cycle, 5.4.8 Packaging materials, 5.4.9 Ecolabelling and certification, etc.).

*User study:* Study customer behaviour when purchasing the product in a store, through concealed observation. Conduct interviews with users of the product to hear their views and opinions of the product. Conduct user studies where users are observed when opening the product packaging, reading the instructions for use and putting the product into service (2.9.1 User testing, 2.9.8 Mental availability measurements).

*Store study*: Study product exposure in stores, window displays, the internet, trade fairs, as well as other exposure arenas and advertising materials. Study exposure, communication, shelf placement, differentiation, and how the functional and emotional characteristics of the product appear.

*Competitor study*: Examine competing products that target the same segment. Which are they? What characterises them? Where are they sold? What do they communicate visually and verbally? Assess brand identity, awareness, position, function, strengths and weaknesses. Are there products that compete indirectly? In other words, not in the same segment but for the same target group, such as ice cream and chocolate. Compare the product in question with the competing products (2.7.4 Competitor analysis).

*Collect information*: Collect results from studies, observations and interpretations. Describe the process as well as possible consequences for the development of the new design. Use illustrative images and explanatory captions. Necessary excerpts from this work are used as a basis for or as part of the visual analysis.

Table 2.11 **The table shows an analysis form that can be used to compile the main strengths and weaknesses of the existing design, and the main opportunities in connection with a redesign. The form can be customised and expanded as needed.**
**© Grimsgaard, W. (2018)**

### Visual analysis process

Start by clarifying the background and purpose of the analysis. Describe the product and the company behind it. Clarify existing goals and strategies, including market position and brand awareness if available. Explain which causes or problems trigger the desire for redesign or new design, and what is the purpose of the change. It should also be specified where special limitations apply, and likewise whether the redesign of the product is part of a larger plan. Present a list of the studies and research that constitute the basis of the visual analysis and specify which findings are relevant. Conduct the analysis by looking at the whole first, and then examine the details.

| Details | Strength | Weaknesses | Opportunities |
|---|---|---|---|
| Logo | High knowledge | Complex | Simplify |
| Colours | Appealing | Not distinctive | Highlight |
| Photo | Personal | Outdated | Renew |
| Text | No strengths | Unreadable | Select new font |

Table 2.11 Visual analysis form

**1) Consider the overall impression:**

*a)* *General:* Eye-catcher, stop effect, brand recognition, shelf location, category affiliation, packaging, functionality, appeal, experience, narrative, expression, mood, style, trend, etc.

*b)* *Emotional characteristics:* Is it attractive? Does it appeal to the buyer's desire, needs, feelings, heart? How well is the packaging design perceived to match the product characteristics and product benefits?

*c)* *Functional characteristics:* Does the product have a distinctive identity that differs from its competitors (possibly similar to its competitors if this is the strategy)? Does it stand out on the shelf?

Is it easy to spot? Is it easy to grab or get hold of? Is the information clear, easy-to-read and understandable? Is the desired position communicated? Is the message communicated? Are the product properties visible? Is the logo visible and properly placed? Are illustrations or photographs clear and understandable?

**2) Consider the use of means:**

a) *Packaging:* Shape, distinctiveness, colour.

b) *Front:* Name, logo, pictogram/symbol, colours, shape, illustrations, graphic effects, photo, variant name, colour coding, marking, symbol use, product description, product information, etc.

c) *Back:* Information, table of contents, language, labelling, EAN code, etc. Assess the means individually and as a whole, as well as their placement and priority on the surface of the packaging, see Figure 2.34.

d) *Product exposure:* Location and shelf placement in store, shelf edge, lighting conditions, surrounding products, etc. Assess this considering how it affects the visual experience of the package design.

**3) Assess the details:** Study the details by looking at font, typography, colour use, image quality, material use, functionality, composition, layout, the components vs. the whole, tone of voice, whether there is consistent use of colours, shapes, line thickness, etc. Consider whether the use of instruments adequately expresses the brand identity, product identity and product characteristics.

**4) Analysis:** Perform an analysis of:

1) *Overall impression:* a) General, b) Emotional properties, c) Functional properties;

2) *Means:* a) Packaging, b) Front of product, c) Back of product, d) Product exposure;

3) *Details:* a) Typography, colours, photos, graphics, illustrations, layout, composition, etc.

4) *Distinctive brand assets:* Assess whether there are elements that are particularly characteristic, which give associations to the product and are important for the recognition, such as distinctive brand assets (3.4.6 Distinctive asset-building strategy, 4.2.4 Distinctive brand assets, 3.7.6 Brand assets). Those elements can be valuable to keep in the new design to preserve the recognition, and if necessary, revitalise gently.

   Focus on strengths, weaknesses, and opportunities. Describe the main observations and findings under each item. Show a good photo of the overall impression, front, back, and in-store exposure, explaining the photos. The result of the analysis can be compared to corresponding analysis of the competing products.

**5) Main conclusion and recommendations:** Prepare an overall summary with reflections and findings, as well as suggested applications. Recommendations are provided for the considerations that should be considered in connection with redesign or new design. The report is approved by the company before further work starts.

## 2.7.9 PESTLE analysis

PESTLE analysis is a way to identify which external factors influence the company at a macro environmental level.[96] It is about which political, economic, social, technological, legal and environmental factors affect the company or should be taken into account in its strategic planning. The analysis identifies the situation in the external environment in which the company operates or plans to operate, and the factor that may affect their activities and performance. This is a type of factors that is beyond the company's control and business operation, and that is necessary for the company to know about and have an overview of, when developing its goals and strategies. The company must plan how it should coexist with its surroundings and generate its profits despite eventual demanding situations at hand. PESTLE analysis is an effective tool to use in the context of a situational analysis and a SWOT analysis (2.7.1 Situational analysis, 2.7.10 SWOT analysis). The analysis includes both the collection and interpretation of information about external factors that have or may have an impact on the company. These forces can create both opportunities and threats for an organisation. The key factors to be included in the analysis will vary depending on the type of activity. Factors that are important to one company may not be equally important to another (Roos et al., 2014).

The purpose of a PESTLE analyses is to:

- find out which external key factors influence the company.
- find out how the company affects the environment around it.
- identify which of these factors are most important now and in the future.
- find out how the company can meet these challenges now and in the future.
- make better use of opportunities or defend against threats in a better way than competitors.

The result is an understanding of the big picture around the company. The analyses are also useful for assessing the potential of a new market. The general rule is that the more negative the forces affecting the company in the market in question, the more difficult it is to do business in it. The difficulties that need to be addressed, considerably reduce the profit potential and therefore the result if the company chooses not to engage in the relevant market (Jurevicius, 2013).

### Mega trends

One issue is the status quo. What is the situation like today? Another important matter is which changes and trends we see that cannot be revealed through PESTLE. If the situation is stable, this is something the company has been dealing with for a long time. If there are changes in progress, it is important to capture them. For example, it may be a matter of looking a few years ahead at society's technological development, which mega trends are crucial for the future and other future forecasts. A mega trend is defined as something that has been going on for the past 10 years and will continue for the next 10 years. Copenhagen Institute for Future Studies (CIFS) clarifies why mega trends are important in the issue of the magazine 'Future orientation 5/2006', named 'The megatrends matter issue'.[97]

Table 2.12 The table shows a PESTLE analysis set-up. Actual factors are inserted under each area.

Tips for the designer
The meaning of images, symbols and colours is always culturally dependent. What is acceptable in one culture can be offensive or even harmful in the next.

Macro environment
- The macro environment refers to the broader condition of an economy as opposed to specific markets.
- The macro environment can be affected by GDP, fiscal policy, monetary policy, inflation, employment rates, and consumer spending.
- The state of the macro environment affects business decisions on things such as spending, borrowing, and investing.

96 'A macro environment refers to the set of conditions that exist in the economy as a whole, rather than in a particular sector or region. In general, the macro environment includes trends in the gross domestic product (GDP), inflation, employment, spending, and monetary and fiscal policy' ('Macro Environment', *Investopedia* 2021).
97 Awailable at yumpu.com See also: Futureorientation.net: 'Trends, mega trends – and supertrends?' (Paludan, 2006). Soprasteria.no: 'Six Mega trends Deciding Our Future' (Lindgren, 2013).

**Explanation of PESTLE**

**P for political:** The political factors apply to all political activities that take place in a country and if an external power has influence in one way or another. It is about the political situation and the policy pursued by a government. Fiscal policy, trade tariffs and taxes are among the things that the government may impose on companies that have a significant impact on the companies' earned income.

**E for economic:** The economic factors concern the economic condition of the country and whether the global economic scenarios may or may not have an impact. These include inflation rates, exchange rates, interest rates etc. All these factors can affect the supply and demand cycle and can lead to major changes in the business environment.

**S for socio-cultural/social:** These factors have to do with the social thinking of the people living in a particular country. Factors such as culture, age, demography, gender and religion.

**T for technological:** Technological factors are about the pace of technological development and the challenges and needs these pose for the company.

**L for legal:** Legal factors have to do with all the regulatory and process components of an economy, and standards that the company should meet in order to be able to run production and marketing.

**E for ecological/environment:** These factors have to do with geographical location and environmental challenges, regulations and considerations that may affect the type of trade the company conducts.

(Frue, 2020).

| PESTLE-ANALYSIS | | | | | |
|---|---|---|---|---|---|
| External factors | | | | | |
| Political | Economic | Social | Technological | Legal | Environmental |
| | | | | | |

Table 2.12 PESTLE-analysis

**PESTLE analysis process:** The process of conducting PESTLE analysis should involve as many managers as possible in order to obtain the best results. It contains the following steps:

**Step 1.** Gather information on political, economic, social and technological, legal and environmental changes + all other factors.

**Step 2.** Identify which of the PESTLE factors represents opportunities or threats.


1 Initiation
2 Insight
3 Strategy
4 Design
5 Production
6 Management

2.1 Understanding the company
2.2 Situational study
2.3 Problem statement
2.4 Method selection
2.5 Research process
2.6 Research
2.7 Analyses
2.8 Mapping
2.9 Testing and measuring

2.7.1 Situational analysis
2.7.2 Internal analysis
2.7.3 Value chain analysis
2.7.4 Competitor analysis
2.7.5 Positioning analysis
2.7.6 Target group analysis
2.7.7 Brand analysis
2.7.8 Visual analysis
2.7.9 PESTLE analysis
2.7.10 SWOT analysis
2.7.11 Gap analysis

– Mega trends


Further reading

*The Politics of Design* by Ruben Pater (2016). BIS Publishers B.V.

Mega trends and future scenarios

In product development, it is necessary to look ahead in time to assess emerging needs and opportunities inherent in technological advances. Read about the product development process in the interview with Henning Rekdal. Available at designandstrategy.co.uk.

**Key factors of PESTLE analysis**

**Disposition:** Example of key factors as a starting point for a PESTLE analysis (pestleanalysis.com 2011). Priorities are necessary considering time and budget.

**Political factors:** Trade policy. The government is changing. Shareholders and their claims. Funding. Government management and restrictions. Lobbying. Foreign influence. Conflicts in the political arena.

**Economic factors:** Disposable income. Unemployment level. Exchange rates. Interest. Trade tariffs. Inflation rates. Foreign economic trends. General tax problems. Tax changes specific to product/services. Local economic situation and trends.

**Social factors:** Ethnic/religious factors. Advertising scenes. Ethical problem statements. Consumers' buying patterns. Big world events. Buying access. Changes in the population. Demographics. Heath. Consumer opinions and attitudes. Media photo. Legislative changes affecting social factors. Lifestyle change. Brand preferences. The work situation of people. Training. Trends. History.

**Technological factors:** Technological development. Research and development. Trends in global technological progress. Related technologies. Legislation in technological field. Patents. Licences. Access to the technological field. Consumer preferences. Consumer purchasing trends. Intellectual property and its laws. How mature a particular technology is. Information technology. Communication

**Environmental factors:** Environment. Natural environment. International. National. Stakeholder/investor values. Staff attitudes. Leadership style. Environmental regulations. Customer values. Market value.

**Legal conditions:** Employment law. Consumer protection. Industry-specific rules. Tender provisions. Current legislation, home market. Future legislation. Regulatory bodies and their processes. Environmental regulations.

Table 2.13 The table shows a matrix for sorting internal and external factors in a SWOT analysis. Internal factors: 'Strengths' are properties or assets of the company that give it an advantage over others (success factors); 'Weaknesses' are properties, shortcomings or potential weaknesses of the company that constitute a disadvantage in relation to others. External factors: 'Opportunities' are elements of the external environment (community, market, competition) that the company may exploit for its benefit in the future; 'Threats' are elements of the external environment (community, market, competition) that may lead to problems or obstacles for the company if it wishes to realise its opportunities.

### 2.7.10 SWOT analysis

SWOT analysis is a method for analysing strengths and weaknesses in the company's internal environment, and opportunities and threats in its external environment. The analysis is used in order to identify key factors that may lead to fulfilling goals or selecting a strategy. SWOT is an acronym for strengths, weaknesses, opportunities and threats. Time and resources devoted to a gap analysis should correspond to the scope and level of ambition of the project in question. A SWOT analysis may be performed for a company, project, product, geographic location, person, survey, etc. Here, we use company as an example. The analysis is based on a specified business goal and involves determining which internal and external factors are favourable and unfavourable to achieving this goal, see Table 2.13. The internal factors represent the strengths and weaknesses of the company (such as resources, production, profitability), while the external factors represent opportunities and threats in the market

98 The situational analysis contains many of the same factors as the situational study but involves more in-depth research and analyses to obtain more information about the facts.

(such as economic cycles, competitive situation and societal trends). The SWOT analysis involves selecting significant key factors and analysing them to determine their impact on goals achievement. In this context, an assessment is made of strengths and weaknesses, opportunities and threats in relation to each other in order to assess whether there is a potential for achieving the goal in question, see Figure 2.35. The same factors that represent strengths and opportunities for achieving a particular goal may, in another context, represent weaknesses and threats.

The purpose of the analysis is to arrive at a conclusion or a strategy formulation based on an assessment of the strengths and weaknesses of the company versus the opportunities and threats the market represents. For example, the purpose may be to identify the barriers that exist to the achievement of the company's goal, and identify available strengths and opportunities that can be activated or developed in order to counteract those barriers. The SWOT analysis can identify whether the company's internal resources and capabilities are proportionate to the opportunities present in the external environment. If the company's goal is unrealistic, a new goal may be set and a new analysis carried out. A SWOT analysis can reveal current steps in a plan to achieve the goal and is therefore very suitable as a basis for developing a strategy. If necessary, more SWOT analyses can be developed to compare these.



| SWOT-ANALYSIS | | | |
|---|---|---|---|
| INTERNAL | | EXTERNAL | |
| Strengths | Weaknesses | Opportunities | Threats |
| | | | |

Table 2.13 SWOT form

### Internal and external factors

A situational analysis is a good starting point for clarifying which internal and external factors affect the business (2.7.1 Situational analysis, 2.7.2 Internal analysis). 'The internal factors refer to anything within the company and under the control of the company no matter whether they are tangible or intangible' (Vanessa, 2021). The external factors are elements outside and under no control of the company. Study shows that 'external factors, in particular competitors' marketing mix elements,[98] have a greater

Further reading
Check out: *The SWOT Analysis: A key tool for developing your business strategy* (2015) by 50MINUTES.

influence on a company's business performance than internal (marketing and non-marketing) strategy variables' (Ibrahim & Harrison, 2019).

A SWOT form may be useful for sorting the main internal and external factors, but the SWOT analysis has little effect and usefulness if it only ends up as a matrix with many words based on assumptions. The SWOT analysis should be based on relevant information and clear facts if it is to be useful. If the quality of the information and facts is low or incorrect, it will propagate further in the SWOT analysis and the results will be inaccurate and useless. Internal factors in the company are best identified through a situational analysis and internal research, such as resource analysis, activity analysis and value chain analysis (2.7.1 Situational analysis, 2.7.2 Internal analysis). External factors of the company can be identified, inter alia, through PESTLE analysis, competitor analysis and/or visual analysis (2.7.9 PESTLE analysis, 2.7.4 Competitor analysis, 2.7.8 Visual analysis). An external competition factor is also the company's distinctive brand assets, and degree of uniqueness and awareness (4.2.4 Distinctive brand assets, 3.4.6 Distinctive asset-building strategy, 2.9.8 Mental availability measurements).

### SWOT Workshop

A workshop is a good approach to analyse the internal and external factors that affect the company and constitute basis for conducting a SWOT analysis. All necessary research and analyses to clarify the company's current situation should have been carried out in advance (2.7.1 Situational analysis). The workshop may take 3–4 hours or more, depending on the number of participants. Those invited to the workshop from the company are decision-making authorities, managers, the board and representatives of the marketing, production, engineering, manufacturing divisions, etc., in addition to the designer or the design agency. The participants are devided into groups of two to four. The designer (or someone from the company) presents questions and leads the process.

- Initially, the company's objectives and ambitions, any data from research carried out, and the purpose of the workshop are clarified.
- Questions to be answered are: a) What internal factors have a significant impact on the company/product/service? b) What external factors have a significant impact on the company/product/service?
- The chairperson writes down the answers on flipcharts or whiteboards.
- Responses are structured and prioritised to identify key points for each area.
- Key points are arranged in a matrix that shows division according to strength, weakness, opportunity or threat. These form the basis for a SWOT analysis.
- SWOT analysis is carried out at or after the workshop, based on the results obtained (2.7.10 SWOT analysis).

### Internal factors

What internal factors have a significant impact on the company/product/service? Clarification of internal factors can be based on internal analyses in the company. Factors that bring positive effects to the company can be considered as a strength. Factors preventing the development of the company can be considered as a weakness.

Further reading
Take a look at the chapters: 2.1.2 Decision making, 2.1.5 The company universe, and Figure 2.5 The company's universe.

99 E.g. The Irish news journal, thejournal.ie: 'New laws on alcohol advertising during sports and children's events come into force today' (Burke, 2021).

Focus on facts in the areas:
1) Functional resources: e.g., product supply chain, availability of raw materials, new technology.
2) Human resources: e.g., qualified competence, technology resources and dependencies, corporate culture.
3) Organisation, management: e.g., properties or changes in organisation and management, organisational structure, Code of conduct.
4) Corporate strategy: e.g., goals and strategy, policies, image/brand equity, value proposition, marketing mix elements.
5) Production, product development: e.g., production chain, task executions or operations, outsourced production, control and quality assurance, R&D.
6) Finance, profitability: e.g., profit, financial and marketing resources, liquidity, plant/machinery/equipment (physical assets).
7) Miscellaneous: What other internal factors influence the business area? e.g., board composition, financing, and investor composition.

What strengths and/or weaknesses do the internal factors represent? Extract one key point for each area. What is the impact on the company (one for each area)? What challenges or problems can be identified?

### External factors

What external factors have a significant impact on the company/product/service? Clarification of external factors may be based on market research, competitor analysis and PESTLE analysis.

Focus on facts in the areas:
1) Business area: e.g., strengths/weaknesses of imports or exports, lower/higher commodity prices, new taxes.
2) Competitors/competitive situation: e.g., competitors' marketing mix elements, multiple players, pressured prices.
3) Customers, consumer, market/media: e.g., customer purchasing power, economic cycles, interest rates, taxes, market trends, public policy.
4) Production, distributors, retailers, alliance partners: e.g., suppliers, distribution chain, distribution solutions, access to retailers.
5) The surroundings, society, government, the press: e.g., restrictions, laws and regulations, such as bans on advertising aimed at children or on alcohol.[99]
6) Macro factors: e.g., political, economic, social, technological, environmental, legal (2.7.9 PESTLE).
7) Miscellaneous: What other external factors affect the business area?

What opportunities and/or threats do the external factors represent? Extract one key point for each area. What is the impact on the company (one for each area)? What challenges or problems can be identified?

### SWOT analysis process

1) Specify what should be the subject of the analysis, such as a company.
2) Conduct a situational analysis and other research/analyses that clarify the company's current situation.
3) Specify the purpose of the assignment to be performed.

4) Clarify what strengths and weaknesses exist in the company's internal environment (internal factors) and what opportunities and threats lie in the company's external environment (external factors).
5) Identify key factors for each of the areas: strengths, weaknesses, opportunities, and threats.
6) The company can use strengths to take advantage of opportunities in the market or use strengths to eliminate threats. The company can do something about the strengths and weaknesses. There is nothing it can do about the opportunities and the threats. It just has to deal with them.
7) Insert the key factors into a matrix, see Figure 2.35.
8) Set the factors against each other and consider different strategies to achieve the goals.
9) Assess whether the goal is achievable with the opportunities and resources the company has or can provide.

Fig. 2.35 The figure shows an example SWOT analysis. Strengths and weaknesses are characteristics of the company's internal environment. Opportunities and threats are elements of the company's external environment. Weaknesses and threats represent obstacles to achieving the goal. Strengths and opportunities represent opportunities to achieve the goal. The four squares in the matrix represent four different strategies. The bottom right square is an uncertain strategy. Based on Porter (1985).

Fig. 2.36 The figure illustrates how the gap lies between the current situation and the desired situation. The current situation and the desired situation should be identified in order to clarify the gap.

| | OPPORTUNITIES<br>External/positive<br>1<br>2<br>3<br>4 | THREATS<br>External/negative<br>1<br>2<br>3<br>4 |
|---|---|---|
| STRENGTHS<br>Internal/positive<br>1<br>2<br>3<br>4 | Strengths/<br>Opportunities<br>Which of the strengths can optimise the possibilities?<br>1<br>2 | Strengths/Threats<br>How to use the strengths to minimise the threats?<br>1<br>2 |
| WEAKNESSES<br>Internal/negative<br>1<br>2<br>3<br>4 | Weaknesses/<br>Opportunities<br>How to use the opportunities to minimise the weaknesses?<br>1<br>2 | Weaknesses/Threats<br>How to minimise the weaknesses to avoiding the threats?<br>1<br>2 |

Fig. 2.35 SWOT analysis

### Choice of strategy

Set up the keywords in a 2 × 2 matrix. Insert the key factors that have been identified. Prepare an assessment of the key factors. Consider various strategic options:

- Strengths – opportunities – strategy: Which of the company's strengths can be used to maximise the identified opportunities?
- Strengths – threats – strategy: How to use the company's strengths to minimise the identified threats?

- Weaknesses – opportunities – strategy: What steps can the company take in order to minimise its weaknesses using the identified opportunities?
- Weaknesses – threats – strategy: How to minimise the company's weaknesses in order to avoid the identified threats?

Assess the responses against the goals that have been set in advance. Choose which of the four strategies offers the best chance of achieving the company's goals (3.3 Goals and subgoals, 3.4 Business strategy).

### 2.7.11 Gap analysis

A gap analysis is used when the company is not making the best use of its resources, capital, and technology, and therefore does not fully utilise their potential.

Fig. 2.36 Identifying the gap

Gap analysis involves identifying what the company is doing today (current situation) and where it wants to go in the future (desired situation), then identifying the gap (distance) and assessing what actions and resources are required to bridge the gap (strategy), and what areas can be improved or strengthened to accomplishing their goals. 'The "gap" in a gap analysis is the space between where an organisation is and where it wants to be in the future' (Kenton, 2020). To survive and grow, the company needs to fill this gap. The gap represents a problem or task that needs to be solved and can be used as a basis for formulating a problem statement (2.3 Problem statement). The size of the gap indicates the size of the problem or task (2.3.1 Problem). If the gap is large, it poses a greater challenge than if the gap is small. The gap between the current and the desired situation is analysed before a strategy is developed to achieve the desired situation. The company can use the gap analysis to re-examine their goals to figure out whether they are on the right track to accomplishing them.
**Current situation**: What is today's situation or current performance?
**Desired situation**: What is the desired situation or expected performance?
**GAP**: Current versus desired situation or performance.
**Problem**: The gap is the problem that needs to be solved. Define the problem. Formulate the problem statement.
**Strategy**: How should the desired situation be achieved? Strategic direction and plan.

#### Gap analysis process

*Step 1 – Desired situation*: Clarify the organisational goals and targets. At best these are specific, measurable, attainable, realistic, and timely.
*Step 2 – Current situation*: Find out how best to obtain information about the current situation. Historical data is used to measure the current performance of the organisation as it relates to its outlined goals (Kenton, 2020).

A situational study or analysis can be helpful to collect data (2.7.1 Situational analysis. Only the information relevant to the GAP analysis is extracted and presented in an as simple and easy-to-understand manner as possible. *Step 3 – Identify the gap*: Analyse collected data that seeks to understand why the measured performance is below the desired levels (Kenton, 2020). Describe the gap by means of numbers (quantitative evaluation) or verbally (qualitative evaluation).
*Step 4 – Build a bridge*: Compile a report based on the quantitative data collected and/or the qualitative reasons why the performance is below the benchmark. Make a list of action items that are needed to achieve the organisation's goals and bridge the gap between the current and the desired situation are identified in a report.

Fig. 2.37 The figure shows the current situation and the desired situation of a brand. Here, there are several gaps, which represent different milestones.

'Companies can re-examine their goals through a gap analysis to figure out whether they are on the right track to accomplishing them' (Kenton, 2020).

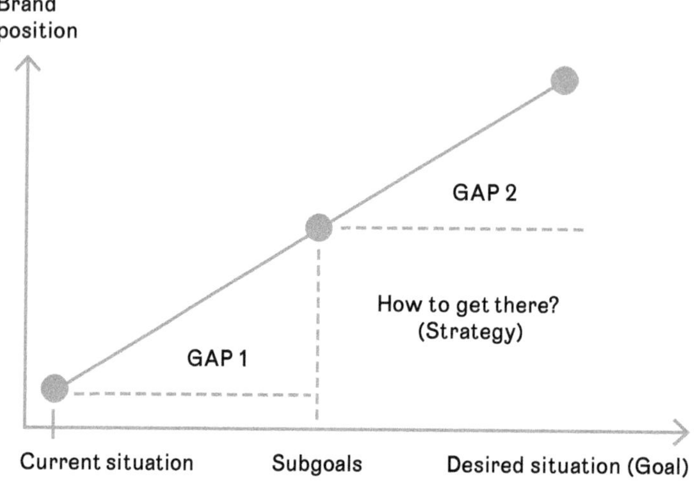


Fig. 2.37 GAP analysis

*Analysis of findings*: The gap analysis result can be made quantitatively using calculations if the information can be reproduced in numbers, or qualitatively using verbal formulations when numbers are not available.
*Example gap analysis*: A gap analysis can also be used to analyse gaps in processes and the gulf between the existing outcome and the desired outcome. This step process can be illustrated by the example below ('Gap analysis,' n.d.):

- Identify the existing process: fishing by using fishing rods.
- Identify the existing outcome: we can manage to catch 20 fish per day.
- Identify the desired outcome: we want to catch 100 fish per day.
- Identify and document the gap: it is a difference of 80 fish.
- Identify the process to achieve the desired outcome: we can use an alternative method such as using a fishing net.
- Develop means to fill the gap: acquire and use a fishing net.
- Develop and prioritise requirements to bridge the gap.[100]

### Needs analysis

Gap analysis is also called needs analysis.[101] Needs Analysis is a formal, systematic process of identifying and evaluating training that should be done, or specific needs of an individual or group of employees, customers,

100 One suggestion is to prioritise the requirements based on the results of the M.O.S.T. analysis (Clients. criticalimpact.com. 'Business Analyst | Do We Need a Mature GAP Analysis?'.)
101 Needs analysis has its origins in the 1960s. Jack McKillip's book *Need Analysis: Tools for the Human Service and Education* has often been referred to.
102 'Visual Thinking' (Arnheim, R. 1969/Ware, C. 2008).

suppliers, etc. Needs are often referred to as 'gaps,' or the difference between what is currently done and what should be performed (trainingindustri.com). A needs analysis can be used to classify how well a product or service satisfies a targeted need or requirement, and it can i.e. be used to find key explanations for changing needs in the organisation or in the market in order to understand how the need for a service is changing or may change in the future, so that the company is able to meet future needs.



#### Different gap analysis

There are many different gap analyses, both when it comes to application and methods used, for example:
**Gap analysis in the company:** A gap analysis can help identify areas in the company where improvements in efficiency and job performance can increase productivity and profit.
**Brand gap analysis:** A gap analysis can help identify the gap between the current position and the desired position of the brand to be used as a starting point for assessing what action can be taken to achieve the desired position.
**Gap analysis – user satisfaction:** A gap analysis can be prepared based on user satisfaction surveys, which reveal whether or not the product or service satisfies the user's needs for functionality, experience and attractiveness. Then a gap analysis can help identify the gap between today's solution/product/offer, as a starting point for assessing what actions can be taken to strengthen user needs and user-friendliness.
**Gap analysis – market share:** Consumer gap is a gap analysis that examines the difference between the existing turnover (market share) of a particular type of products and the total market turnover of the products as a whole. The difference is the competitors' share. Such gaps therefore concern competitive activity. Consumer gap = market potential or existing consumption. Such information is useful for setting market targets, which includes planning a future larger market share, a larger piece of the pie.

### 2.8 Mapping

Different methods of mapping can be used to visualise research and analyses. This makes data more accessible and easier to implement in the strategy and design process.

One of the main advantages for the designer is the ability to use visualisation as a tool in analysis, processes, and communication. This stems from the designer's unique ability to think in images[102] Mapping can be used in all stages of a design project, to plan, investigate, analyse, systematise, organise, and communicate. This way, data can be made more transparent and comprehensible, both for the designer and for the company. When data are presented visually, they also become easier to understand, making it easier to notice connections, new opportunities, and ideas (4.2.1 Mapping as a link).

Further reading
– The book: *The Brand Gap: How to Bridge the Distance Between Business Strategy and Design* (2005) by Marty Neumeier.
– Check out Miro 'System Mapping Toolkit': miro.com/miroverse/system-mapping-toolkit/.

### 2.8.1 Mapping methods

Numerous mapping methods exist. Mapping can take the form of maps, models, forms, timelines, movement patterns, or other visual structures. Established methods can be drawn and applied in an infinite number of ways, and one can develop one's own methods as needed; the only limits here are those set by one's imagination. Some mapping systems are small and limited, such as mind maps and moodboards, while others can be used to get an overview of more complex situations, such as GIGA mapping. Examples of mapping methods:

- Hierarchical maps: Mind maps
- Non-hierarchical maps: Concept maps
- Image maps: moodboard, photo, video and audio sequences
- Area and/or customer journey, way finding
- Flow charts
- Geographical maps
- Time-based maps: story boards, timelines, Gantt chart
- Key frame mapping
- Digital animated maps
- Intensity maps: gradations and interpolation of continuous strengths
- Infographics: graphic illustrations
- Mixed maps: GIGA maps

(Based on Sevaldsson, 2011)

### 2.8.2 Moodboard

A moodboard can be used in different stages of a design project, whether it is about visualising research, surveys and strategies, ideas or design concepts. Moodboard is a digital or physical poster or collage, composed of selected images and materials to promote a specific atmosphere. The moodboard is an easy and intuitive way to visualise thoughts, ideas and situations in different stages of a design project. In the insight stage, the use of moodboards can be useful to visualise studies and research, and in the strategic stage to visualise vision, values and target groups. Using a moodboard to visualise strategy can simplify the work of linking strategy to the idea and design development. When presenting ideas to the company, the moodboard can help express the designer's thoughts and ideas quickly and efficiently, making it easier to choose the direction for further work. This way, the moodboard can replace time-consuming sketching processes at an early stage of the design development. The use of the moodboard should be considered in the context of what one wants to achieve. The following are a few examples:

*Image moodboard*: Can be created digitally by putting together images on the screen, or physically by gluing images to a poster or hanging them on a wall. The advantage of putting up pictures and moodboards on the wall is that the information becomes more accessible and understandable. This makes it easier to see connections, new opportunities, and ideas. A moodboard is developed by selecting a photo that represents a desired expression. Some photos will be more important to express the mood than others and should be highlighted by size and location. Image sections that show motifs closely can be scaled

103 Photo credits: Provide information about the author, the person who took the photo. Photo by-line: Name of the photographer who took the photo. Often placed closely under the image or horizontally along the right edge of the image, in small font size, for example 5 to 7 pt.

down in size, while photos that have more complex motifs can be scaled up to get details. An image moodboard can consist of anything from one image to many images. The number of images, their size, the distance between them, and their placement next to each other may affect the mood, style, and expression. If the moodboards are to be published on-line or otherwise displayed officially, the images should be credited by applying a photo by-line. [103]

*Situation moodboard*: Used to visualise the current situation of the company, product or service which the task concerns. It can be a store, an interior, an exterior, architecture, a condition, a topic, genre, style epoch, trend, a place, a product, a use situation, etc. Visualising the situation can also be used to create an experience of the different contexts the new solution should enter, or of the situations in which the user encounters the product or service (user situations). The development of moodboards that show the situation is often done in the earlier stages of the project, as part of the work of gaining insight and developing strategies.

*Strategy moodboard*: Used in the strategy process to visualise e.g.:

- A situation: where and how the customer uses a service.
- An identity: core values, the logo, interior, exterior.
- A target group: the person, interests, style, typical features.
- A product: as is, in the store, in the environment, in use.
- A competitor: their logo, identity and products.
- A category: genre, style, expression, trend.

*Future image*: Moodboard is well suited to visualise a future image or vision. For example, it can be about the desired style, quality and user-experience of a product to be developed. By using images that represent these different attributes, one will be able to create an overall coherent image that provides a feel and description of the desired direction (Lerdahl, 2007, p. 105).

*Core values*: A moodboard is a widely used method for visualising words of value by developing one moodboard for each core value and one moodboard for all of them combined. These moodboards can be used further as inspiration to arrive at a choice for shape, colour, typography and image use in a further design process. In such a context, the moodboard becomes a link between strategy and design, by visualising the strategic definition of the core values as a basis for a further development of visual design (3.2.5 Core values).

*Persona*: Development of personas can be useful for visualising a target group. Based on gender, age, place of residence, education, occupation, economy, marital status, interests, etc., a description and an image of the personality of the typical user of a product or service can be developed. Visualising the persona in different contexts and situations can help create greater proximity to the user when working in an idea or design process (Lerdahl, 2007). The persona is often developed in the earlier stages of the project, as part of the work of gaining insight and developing strategies (2.7.6 Target group analysis, 3.8.2 Identifying the target group).

*Concept development*: A moodboard is well suited for visualising and presenting thoughts, ideas, storylines, and conceptual directions. Verbalisation as a supplement or as a combination could strengthen

**Moodboard development**

A moodboard can be created digitally using photos, fonts, patterns, and effects taken from the internet or from one's own archive. It can also be created physically by cutting out images from magazines, advertisements and newspapers or by using physical objects, substances and materials. Landscape orientation, format A4 or A3 is easiest to work with. Use photos, words, typography, colours, and materials that express the desired mood, atmosphere, style, idea, or narrative. It can be an advantage to create multiple moodboards on one and the same theme in order to visualise it in different ways. One version or a combination of two versions is selected for further work. This way, it may be easier to arrive at the desired expression.

**Image choice**: An image moodboard may consist of one or more images. The danger of displaying too many images is that it may cause you to see only a patchwork of images and not the theme in the images. A good tip is to ask yourself the following:

- If you can only select *one* photo - which one, will you choose?
- If you can select *one more* photo - which one, will you choose?
- If you can select a third photo - which one, will you choose?
- Supplement with other images to create the desired mood and expression. If relevant, you can do the opposite by deleting photos:
- What photo can I remove? Can I remove another one? And so on.

Consider which image is most important and if it is visible well enough in terms of size and location. Are there any other images you should enlarge or shrink? The same principles apply when using materials.

**Set-up**: How the images are composed in terms of placement relative to each other, and in considering format, distance between the images, contour, shape and background, influences the mood and expression. If the images are to speak for themselves, it may be a good idea to use a calm and neutral layout and background. In a scenario, the sequence of events influences the perception of the narrative.

**Verbalisation**: By giving the moodboard a name that indicates what it is to express, e.g., words of value or conceptual direction, you can enhance the experience.

**Typography**: Select a text font that matches the expression, style, mood, trend, or condition you wish to express. At the same time, you may feel inspired to select typography.

**Colour palette**: Feel free to create a colour palette on the moodboard, where it best fits in with the composition. Extract the colours from the images or materials on the moodboard. This way, you inspire colour selection at the same time.

one's presentation and facilitates understanding and choice of direction for one's further work (4.4 Concept development).

*Material moodboard*: A moodboard can be used to visualise materials, and to provide an experience of a visual, and tactile direction for the project.

*Customer workshop*: During a creative workshop, the company can participate physically in creating moodboards by selecting physical images or materials from a wide variety of images that are presented and that can be linked to the specific assignment. This is a good way to extract valuable information, views and ideas from the company as well as to ensure the company's feeling of involvement and ownership of the process and the result. A suitable premises and tools are needed for this purpose. Process:

- Include images with different motifs, genres, and expressions (images cut from magazines or printed from the internet).
- Bring material samples, objects, substances and other materials of different shapes, structures and textures.
- Divide participants into two or more groups.
- Ask the participants to put together pictures and/or materials based on a specific topic, such as: Who are we? Where do we want to go?
- The participants may also be given the opportunity to process or develop the materials.
- Discuss the results and choose the direction.

*Inspiration moodboard*: In the design process, the moodboard can be used to provide the necessary insights and inspiration and make it easier to determine shape, colours, typography, logo, illustration, patterns, design solutions etc. Examples of topics that can be visualised in the design process include:

- Product: example of product, applications and details.
- Service: examples of situations, activities, people, rooms.
- Environment: people, clothes, objects, places.
- Style directions: traditional, classic, modern, futuristic.
- Styles: retro, hipster, empire style, baroque.

*Scenario games*: In tasks where it is important to bring out a particular situation, it may be a good idea to try scenario games instead of or in addition to a visual moodboard. This involves creating an intended user scenario or user situation by creating the mood physically with body movements, sounds, and music (Lerdahl, 2007, p. 119).

*Storyline*: A moodboard can also be used to express or explain an intended storyline scenario, to express an action, situation or use of a product or service.

### 2.8.3 Storyboard

A storyboard is graphical mapping in the form of illustrations or images displayed in order to visualise a story or dialogue. Storyboard as a method was originally developed in Walt Disney Productions in the early 1930s. Originally, it was used to preview the action in a film, animated film, moving graphics, or interactive media sequences. The method can be used in the same way as the moodboard in all stages of a design project, and is particularly well suited to visualising a narrative, brand



Thumbnail Storyboards

A thumbnail storyboard is a way to quickly draft your ideas before drawing a more detailed version, like a traditional storyboard.
It involves making a series of small sketches on a few pieces of paper. Due to the small size, they are less detailed and take less time than traditional storyboards (Bedrina, n.d.).

narrative or any other form of storytelling or sequence. As design methodology, storyboarding can be connected to design sprint or any other iterative methods to quickly sketch out a conceived scenario or concept (4.3.7 Sprint). An example of another application is the visualisation of a customers' journey by visualising movement patterns or user situations.

### 2.8.4 Customer journey

Customer journey is both a metaphor and a method that is central to service design. It is about examining the customers' needs and adapting the services to the customer by 'Walking in the customers' shoes'.[104] Customer service is about implementing the entire value chain of the service in a way that makes the service more accessible and tailored to the individual customer. Customer journey is a mapping method and a design methodology that can be used to study the service from the customers' perspective, step by step and over time. The result is used to analyse the customers' experience of the service as a basis for a new customer journey strategy, and development of a new and better solution (4.3.12 Customer journey).

### 2.8.5 GIGA mapping

GIGA mapping is a technique and tool suitable for complex design projects, for creating visual structure and organisation, where the amount of information is large and confusing. The technique involves putting together different parts of information, insights, strategy and sketches and organising them to create overview and coherence between seemingly separate categories. By putting more structures together to build a new and larger structure, a clearer picture can emerge together with new contexts and opportunities that would not otherwise have been so easy to spot (Sevaldson, 2014). The GIGA map can be made up of established mapping methods, such as network diagrams,[105] concept maps,[106] customers' journeys and moodboards, or it can be based on structures and methods that the designer personally develops for the purpose. The information is presented or drawn in multiple layers and directions, and is processed and supplemented in the process run.

Birger Sevaldson[107] developed the technique to meet what he sees as a growing tendency for the design profession in general and design projects individually to become more complex. 'Very severe and crucial problems need to be solved in the future and designers are in a special position to make a difference to make design matter. Designers work with many levels of innovations and they are inherently trained to work with very complex problems in a holistic manner' (Sevaldson, 2011, p. 2).

Besides being a technique for organising and visualising large complex amounts of information, GIGA mapping is the ultimate tool for defining the framework of a design project. A problem is often defined and simplified prematurely and too quickly in a design project. Before a problem can be defined, it is necessary to fold it far beyond the horizon we consider relevant, and only when we know the landscape beyond the

104 Customerservice.com: 'Walk in your customers' shoes: Doing so will give you the information you need to grow your business.' (Tschohl, 2012). chieflisteningofficers.com: 'How did this company crush their trade show? By nailing their customers' Elevator Rant' (London, 2017). chieflisteningofficers.com: 'What is an Elevator Rant?' (London, 2017).

105 A project's network diagram is a visual representation developed to show of how activities interrelate with each other. It can be used digitally to map a network and all the elements it interacts with (Lucidchart.com).

106 A concept map or conceptual diagram is a diagram that depicts suggested relationships between concepts (Hager & Corbin 1997), such as ideas and information as boxes or circles, connected with labelled arrows (Lanzing, 1998).

107 Birger Sevaldson, Professor at AHO, has tested GIGA maps in several student projects at AHO (e.g. project for the care services company Attendo).

108 Problematiques is the complex of issues associated with a topic, considered collectively; specifically the totality of environmental and other problems affecting the world (Problematiques, n.d.).

109 Giga mapping as a dialogue tool used in workshops: 'Bridging Silos. A new workshop method for bridging silos' (Wettre et al. 2019).

horizon, can we consciously draw the boundaries. Small things far out at the outer edge of a chain of effects can be decisive for the course of the process. We need to find those crucial triggers that are not immediately visible. 'GIGA mapping ensures that all efforts are taken to track down what is relevant and to include it in the design' (Sevaldson, 2011, p. 6).

If complex problem statements are being addressed, GIGA mapping can be used in the early stages of the project. A GIGA map is developed by the designers in collaboration with relevant project stakeholders over several iterations (4.3.5 Iterative method). The map aims to establish a multidisciplinary overview of large amounts of information, allowing the designers and the project team to see the situation and form a common understanding of challenges and opportunities, as a starting point to critically discuss problem and situation understanding. The map will be further developed as a basis for testing out solutions and identifying which changes create the greatest possible positive change in the system with the least possible effort. During the further research and development process, a GIGA map can be adjusted, supplemented and in some cases simplified in order to be easy-to-understand for outsiders. Graphical tools and the designer's ability to visualise and systematise the information are central to creating a clear and functional GIGA map. The GIGA map is to be considered a design artefact (made by humans) per se. A good GIGA map can at best end up showing solutions to situations or problematiques,[108] which are networked problems (2.3.9 Wicked problems, 4.3.18 Systemic design, 4.4.2 Creative problem solving).

*The purpose of GIGA mapping is to:*

- Use it as a visual dialogue tool. Pointing and telling helps aligning differences in perspectives and views the actors are not necessarily aware of.[109]
- Gather and organise information and knowledge generated through studies, observations and research.
- Integrate early sketches and moodboards developed in the course of the research process.
- Visualise different fields of knowledge in a project to create a better overview.
- Draw and visualise the complexity of a situation, problem or problematiques.
- Produce structures in systems and processes schematically and graphically in diagrams.

*Advantages of GIGA mapping:*

- Organising and systematising large amounts of information.
- Separating process tasks and communication tasks.
- Establishing multiple layers with many different types of information and categories.
- Making it easier to see how different categories and channels of information can be related.
- Using the multi-scalable approach in GIGA mapping, ranging from global scale down to small details.
- Preventing failures in the design process, which are due to lack of clarity and the risk of overlooking important details.



GIGA map

Many mapping methods can be developed by a single person, but using GIGA maps provides the most synergy if developed in collaboration with multiple designers, or in workshops with the company. Working with GIGA maps is a process that requires time and resources to go back and forth in the system, to add and subtract, think about opportunities and contexts, adjust and expand – to identify the situation, see new links and generate new ideas that can help enlighten or solve the task or problem in question.

### GIGA mapping areas of application

Based on research on GIGA maps, Sevaldson has compiled a list of possible areas of use and benefits (Sevaldsson, 2011, p. 717):

- Learning: mapping and coordinating pre-existing knowledge
- Research: organisation of data from targeted research.
- Imagination: generative visualisation, iterative design.
- Management: working on involving the organisation as a complex social organism.
- Event mapping: working on orchestrating and systematising complex events.
- Planning: registering, describing and modifying complex processes
- Innovation: defining areas and points for intervention and innovation
- Implementation: involvement in all details of complex processes.

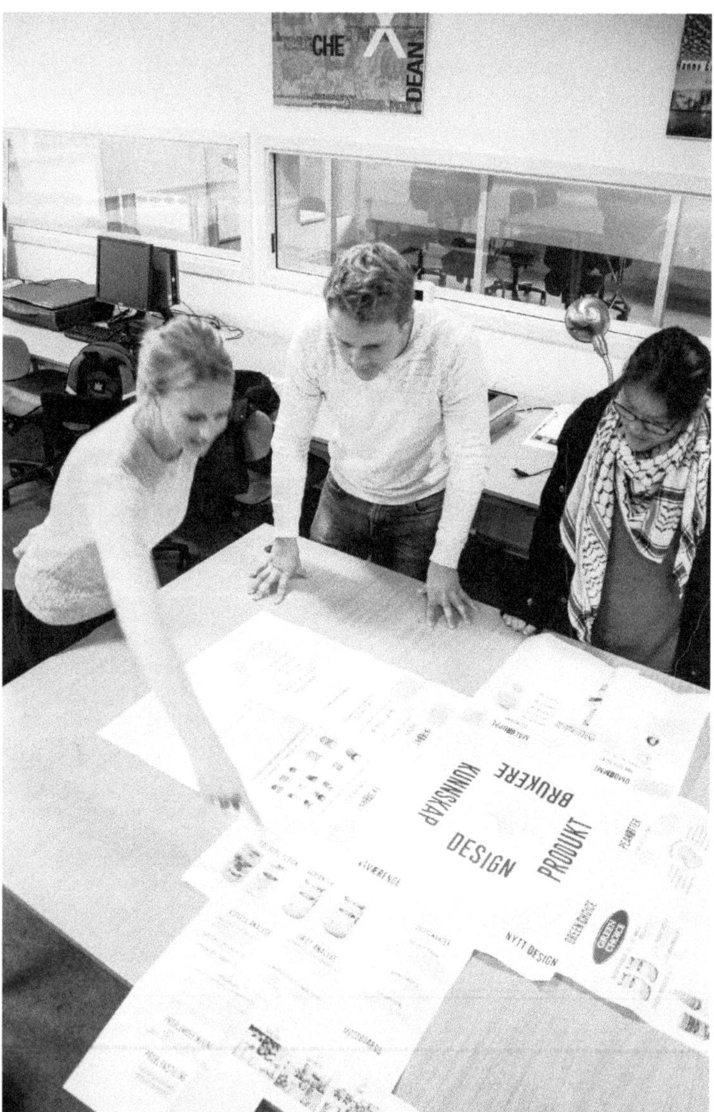


Fig. 2.38 Using GIGA mapping

Fig. 2.38 The design students Veronica, René and Sara at Visual Communications at the University of South-Eastern Norway, in dialogue over a GIGA map they prepared for a student project, the task of which was to develop redesign for the product Green Choice Peanut Butter. Photo: Anine Heitun 2015.

Fig. 2.39 The figure shows the principles of a GIGA map drawn by Halogen. 'The systematic approach has opened the doors for better involvement not only of our customers and their colleagues, but also of partners from other practices. It has opened up the design process and made it easier to share and therefore involve' (Romm & Paulsen, 2014).

> Much of the value of giga mapping lies in the ability to bridge ruptures through sense sharing (Wettre et al., 2019).

110 Halogen (halogen.no) is a Norwegian cross-disciplinary design and innovation consultancy specialising in solving problems in complex environments.

Fig. 2.39 Systematic use of GIGA maps


1 Initiation
2 Insight
3 Strategy
4 Design
5 Production
6 Management

2.1 Understanding the company
2.2 Situational study
2.3 Problem statement
2.4 Method selection
2.5 Research process
2.6 Research
2.7 Analyses
2.8 Mapping
2.9 Testing and measuring

2.8.1 Mapping methods
2.8.2 Moodboard
2.8.3 Storyboard
2.8.4 Customer journey
2.8.5 GIGA mapping

- GIGA mapping areas of application
- Development of GIGA maps
- Rupture in the design process


### Development of GIGA maps

Halogen[110] was an early adopter of GIGA mapping and System Oriented Design (SOD) (4.3.18 Systemic design). Based on their experience they developed four GIGA map template systems to be used in various projects and problem statements, see Figure 2.39 (Romm & Paulsen, 2014):

- *Contextual* structure is chosen when conversations with clients described their work in a special way, examples being a frontline service providers office, a car workshop or a hospital building.
- *Sequential* representation is used when customers describe chains of occurrences such as time-based processes, journeys and continual scenarios.
- *Exploratory* is used when conversations appear on a more strategic level, moving organisations or situations from A to B. For instance, where a shared understanding of the 'as is' state (A) and the desired state 'to be' (B) are more or less known, but the path in between the two is unknown.
- *Relational* structure is used on occasions where there are no descriptions of space or sequence, but rather a conversation about networks where understanding relations and connections are expressed.

'Our experience shows that during the process of mapping, the pre designed layout structures may very likely be changed iteratively or radically'(Romm & Paulsen, 2014).

'We argue and an increasing number of people start to see that early gigamapping saves a lot of time and risk. Spending more time in the early phases when changes are cheap is better than trying to change a wrongly framed process later when it is increasingly expensive' (Sevaldson, 2022).

### Rupture in the design process

The risk of design process failure is high and may have major consequences. Sevaldson, in his research report (2011, p. 4), highlights some critical aspects of the design process that may lead to rupture and negatively impact the outcome: A central aspect of working with very complex tasks is to keep as many aspects of a problem field in play for as long as possible throughout the process. A natural progression in the design process is to narrow down the number of perspectives and possible solutions towards the end of the process, after potential opportunities have been considered. Misjudgement in such a process can

'Systems oriented design (SOD) is a methodology for understanding relations and totalities in large and complex systems, enabling us to reveal the right problems and find better solutions' (Halogen, n.d.).

have serious consequences when investing time and resources. There are many opportunities to encounter problems and obstacles in such a process. One problem is that the amount of information is so large that not everything is properly taken into consideration. Small issues that seem unimportant can be crucial to the process in certain moments. If they are forgotten because of sheer information overload, the result can be a costly rupture in the process. Another typical rupture may be lack of understanding of how and when the project is to be anchored in the company's organisation. Early anchoring of the project in the relevant sections of the company can be crucial. Such sections would be marketing, economic, strategic management, technology and production.

Another example of ruptures is caused by problems occurring in the implementation phase when the product or service system is to be launched into the real world where it becomes a player in complex emergent systems like stock markets, trends, raw material markets etc. A careful early forecasting of the implementation phase and investigations into worst-case scenarios and risk evaluation might induce early interventions in the design that could prevent some of these problems.

To help avoid such ruptures, and to engage with as many issues as possible and keep them in play as long as possible, the author has developed the concept of the Rich Design Space (Sevaldson, 2008a). GIGA-maps are the central device in the Rich Research Space which includes social spaces, media spaces and physical spaces. All information throughout the process needs always to be highly accessible to remain active for a longer period in the process. This allows back tracking and rechecking information at any time to reduce risks of errors (4.3.8 Scrum, 4.3.18 Systemic design).

Fig. 2.40 **The figure shows a model from the book The user is always right: a practical guide to creating and using personas for the web (Mulder and Yaar 2007).**

**Using the GIGA map, designers can exploit their 'Visual Thinking' potential to develop new thoughts and solutions. 'The potential of real Visual Thinking is not evidenced only by documenting thoughts, but by visualizing and dynamically shaping analyses, and developing thoughts from the visualisation' (Sevaldson, 2011).**

## 2.9 Testing and measuring

Testing and measuring are two interrelated activities that are central to a strategic design process, in order to find out if the strategy, idea and solution are working as desired.

Testing and measuring are central to all phases of a design process, but the needs in the different phases will vary. Similarly, the use of testing methods may vary within different design disciplines and projects, although many can also be used universally.

*Testing* is about conducting experiments or research in order to find out, for example, what the target group thinks about a product, whether it is user-friendly, tastes good, whether it is attractive etc. The answers can be qualitative in the form of words, or quantitative in the form of numbers (2.4 Method selection). Testing is part of trial and error, and working iteratively, therefore testing is something one should repeat until the desired result has been achieved within the available time. For example, it may be more useful to user test an app function by developing a prototype during the development process than to user test it when it is fully programmed and thousands of hours have been spent

(4.3.5 Iterative method, Figure 4.18 Time vs. costs). The principles used for the choice of method, i.e. the qualitative and quantitative method, as well as the use of the research process and several of the research methods, are described in Phase 2.

*Measuring* is something often done to compare results from one measurement to another, such as to measure impacts, sales and return on investments. Measuring performance is a crucial part of monitoring the growth and progress of any business. It requires measuring the actual performance of a business against intended goals. Thus, defining precise and achievable goals will make it easier to measure results and evaluate them thoroughly afterwards. This way, one will know whether time and resources are well spent or not and use the experience to make necessary adjustments in goals, strategies and measures (3.3 Goals and subgoals). Modern advantages in data science, improved data access, data extraction, algorithms, and analytical tool sets constantly streamline and expand the way one can collect and retrieve different data for measurements. There are countless methods of testing and measuring. We will look at a small selection that may be relevant both for the company and the designer.



## 2.9.1 User testing

There is a wealth of user tests, many of which are naturally present in qualitative research such as interviews and observations of various kinds. What characterises conscious user focus is attention to the user's attitudes and behaviour, their needs and problems, their 'jobs-to-be-done', and attention to empathy in the research. Figure 2.40 shows examples of user testing for the web, which distinguishes between what people say and believe, and what they actually do. While an interview reveals what people believe to a greater extent, an observation and physical user tests will reveal what they are actually doing.

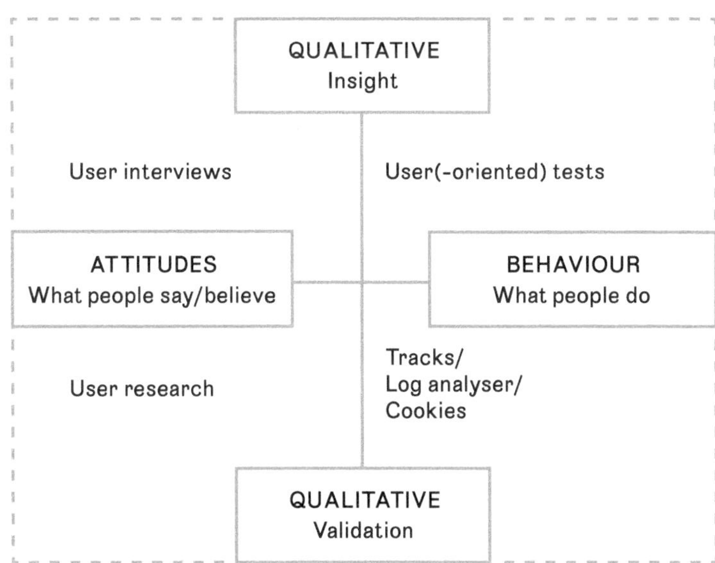


Fig. 2.40 User testing for the web

While quantitative metrics are important, I believe that qualitative metrics are more meaningful measures of success (Fallstrom 2021, Forbes).

## 2.9.2 A/B testing

In marketing and web analysis, A/B testing, also known as split testing, is a controlled experiment with two variants, A and B. Watkins (2014) explains the test as follows: 'When a web page is to be A/B tested, we start with the landing page as it is now (A). We then make one variant (B) of the page. In this variant, we replace the image on the original page with an image we think can yield better results. We define what is the goal of the pages, such as submitting a contact form or booking. Now the test can start. Half of the traffic is sent to variant A and the other half to variant B. During the test, the number of visitors to the different page variants and the number of goal completions, such as submitted contact forms, are measured. For example, variant A has 1,000 visitors and 10 form submissions, while variant B has 1,000 visitors and 15 form submissions. In other words, by replacing the image on the landing page, we can get 50% more contact forms submitted from traffic on the website. That means 50% more customers, with no increase in marketing costs.' A/B testing can also be used by product developers and designers to demonstrate the impact of new features or changes in a user-experience. Product development, user engagement, models and product experiences can all be optimised with A/B testing as long as the goals are clearly defined, and there is a clear hypothesis (optimizely.com).

**A/B testing process (based on optimizely.com):**
Collect data: Start with areas of the website or app that have high traffic. This way it is faster to collect data. Look for pages with low conversion rates or high settlement rates that can be improved.
**Identify goals:** The conversion targets are the estimates used to determine whether test variant (B) is more successful than the original version (A). Goals can range from clicking on a button or linking to a product purchase and emails.
**Generate hypothesis:** Once the goals have been identified, a list of ideas and hypotheses is created on how better results can be achieved. Prioritise hypotheses with respect to expected impact and implementation problems.
**Create variations:** Using an A/B testing software makes it easier to make the desired changes to an item on a website or mobile app. This can be changing the colour of a button, switching the order of the items on the page, or hiding navigation items.
**Run the experiment:** Start the experiment and wait for visitors to participate! At this time, visitors to the website or app will be randomly sent to either control (A) or variant (B). Users' interaction with the two versions of the page is measured, counted, and compared.
**Analyse the results:** When the experiment is completed, the result can be analysed. The A/B testing software will present the data from the sample and show the difference between how the two versions of your page were executed, and whether there is a statistically significant difference. If the experiment generates a negative result or no result at all, it can be used as a learning platform to generate new hypotheses that can be tested (see also 2.6.6 Experiment).

Fig. 2.41 The figure shows an example of a 'funnel'. There are many different variants for different purposes. The method can be used to plan and evaluate marketing and sales. Conversion refers to the conversion rate, which is the basis for measuring the effect. Please see the explanation of the figure in the framed text.

Tips for the company
It may be that the KPIs you are trying to measure are not the most important and that they are disturbing the qualitative indicators.

A/B testing
Alongside Optimizely, there are a number of tools to make A/B testing for valuable customer insights, for example: HubSpot's A/B Testing Kit, Google Optimise, Freshmarketer, VWO, Optimizely, Omniconvert, Crazy Egg, AB Tasty, Convert, Adobe Target, Leadformly (Chi, 2022).

111 For example, the conversion rate is the share of visitors to your site who complete a desired goal (a conversion) out of the total number of visitors. A high conversion rate is a sign of successful marketing and web design: It means that people want what you are offering and they are easily able to get it! (wordstream.com). (6.4 Design effect.)

## 2.9.3 Funnel

Funnel (marketing funnel/sales funnel) is a widely used method for measuring the impact of activities, sales and progress. It is especially used in content marketing and inbound marketing (3.6.8 Inbound marketing, 3.6.7 Content marketing). 'Funnel' is a journey one believes that customers should go through to make a purchase. One can imagine a purchase in three, four or more steps, depending on what should or can be measured. For example, one starts with an ad on Facebook to get customers to visit their website. Once customers go to the website, the goal is to get them to decide to buy something. Then the goal is to make them go through with the purchase. The question is how many people see the ad, how many clicks, how many purchases? *Conversion rate* is a way to measure and evaluate the impact.[111] If you have a thousand customers coming to your website and only 10% buy something, the conversion rate is 10 percent. If 10,000 people have seen an ad, the conversion rate from advertising to sale is 1%. The question then becomes how to increase the conversion rate? You can create better advertising, pay per click, improve the website, etc.

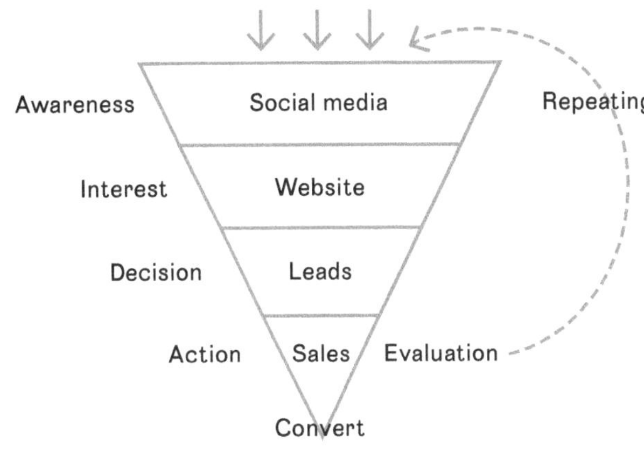


Fig. 2.41 Funnel

## 2.9.4 Zero-point measurement

Zero-point measurement is a method widely used in marketing. It involves measuring the condition before and after a project or measure is implemented in order to compare and assess what its effect has been. Such measurements are also used to isolate the data, actions, strategies etc. that affect the result as well as to evaluate change.

## 2.9.5 Why do we measure?

Measurement permeates every aspect of human life, and we are concerned with measuring different things in our free time compared to when we are at work. Consciously or unconsciously, we constantly make measurements. Measurements provide structure and remove the chaos that would result without them. It gives us rewards in the form of control, mastery and satisfaction when we reach our goals. Mostly we are making estimations, such as: How much time do I have to allow to reach the meeting? We are more



> Zero-point measurement
> The zero point sets a reference point from which all subsequent measurements are made. The zero point on the measurement scale is the point where nothing of the variable exists (e.g. no money, no behaviour, etc.) and, therefore, no scores less than zero exist (Donncha and Dempster, 2016).

concerned with accurate measurement when participating in sport. 'Time, size, distance, speed, direction, weight, volume, temperature, pressure, force, sound, light, energy, are among the physical properties for which humans have developed accurate mathematical measures, without which we could not live our normal daily lives' (MSL, 2020).

There are several answers to why businesses are making measurements. The most common answers are: 1) to answer questions, 2) to show results, 3) to demonstrate value, 4) to justify their budget (or existence), 5) to identify opportunities for improvement and 6) to manage results. (Vance, 2018). To measure business performance, one needs to track relevant business metrics, also known as key performance indicators, that display a measurable value and show the progress of business goals. Measuring performance is a vital part of monitoring the growth and progress of any business.

Tips for the designer
**Key Performance Indicators (KPIs) are the critical indicators of progress toward an intended result and metrics are quantifiable measures used to track progress and evaluate success.**

Tips for the company
**Identify the right KPIs, focus on a few key metrics, and use them to improve organisational or business performance according to the targets.**

Key KPIs to measure corporate sustainability
**Carbon footprint**
**Energy consumption**
**Product recycling rate**
**Supply chain miles**
**Water footprint**
**Waste reduction rate**
**Waste recycling rate**
**Social impact**
**ESG visibility**
**(6.9.2 Corporate sustainability: ESG criteria).**

**Social media sales funnel** (explanation of Figure 2.41): The method may vary for the different projects, depending on your buyers, your niche and the types of products and services you sell. You can design the funnel with as many stages as you like. In general, it is these four that you need to pay attention to.
**Awareness:** At this stage, your target group learns about your solution, product or service. They may also become aware of a need or problem that they need to resolve and possible ways to deal with it. This is when they visit your site for the first time, which they have found in an ad, Google search, social media post, or another source.
**Interest:** At this stage, your target group is actively searching for solutions and alternatives on Google. This is where you can appeal to them with relevant content. This is when they expresses their interest in your product or service. The people concerned will follow you on social media and subscribe to your mailing list.
**Decision:** At this point, your target group decides that they want to use your solution and pay more attention to what you offer, including different packages and options, so that they can make the final decision to go through with a purchase. This is when offers are made using sales pages, webinars, conversations, etc.
**Action:** At this stage, your target group becomes the customer by signing the agreement and clicking on the buy button. The money will then be transferred to your account.

### 2.9.6 KPIs and metrics

Used deliberately, KPIs and metrics can contribute to good performance management for the business. The concepts and process of using KPIs and metrics are based on FreshBooks (2019):
**Measurable goals:** Examples are lead generation, increasing sales, better customer service, increasing profit margins, increasing production efficiency and capturing bigger market share.
**Objectives and key results (OKRs):** OKRs can help to measure the right things and track measurable goals.

**Critical success factors (CSFs):** CSFs is established by clarifying which specific key activities the business should focus on in order to succeed.
**Key performance indicators (KPIs):** KPIs are standard ratios that provide insight about business performance, for example revenue generated per employee or financial statements. Such performance indicators help measure performance against the goals one has identified. KPIs are chosen based on key business goals, thus it is important to choose KPIs that can be measured and provide outcomes to achieve the goals.
**Define suitable metrics:** Metric is a system or standard of measurement that uses the metre, litre, and gram as base units of length (distance), capacity (volume), and weight (mass) respectively. To measure smaller or larger quantities, we use units derived from the metric units. Business metrics are quantifiable measures that track and assess the status of a specific business process. These metrics keep business owners, employees, investors and customers informed and aware of how a company is performing. Choice of metrics depends on the type of business and goals; examples are marketing metrics, sales metrics, accounting and financial metrics and online metrics.
**Track and measure:** One should narrow down on the information that is crucial to track, by choosing a few major business goals, developing related KPIs and focusing on tracking and collecting relevant data.
**What does KPI measure?** Businesses set KPIs to measure their success at reaching targets, for example:
*Measuring financial performance*: Conducting a financial review of the business, assessing the business cash flow, working capital, cost base and growth. Other key financial ratios are efficiency ratios, sales growth, liquidity ratios and financial leverage: measuring profitability, measuring customer loyalty and retention, employee performance measurement, benchmarking, competitor analysis, and regular monitoring.



## 2.9.7 Qualitative indicators and metrics

Some indicators are hard to measure, such as for example, employee engagement, commitment, motivation, passion, impact of initiatives on results, training effectiveness, happiness, creativity, culture, maturity, collaboration, employee morale, quality of life, value of life, sustainability, risk management, business reputation, direct impact of consulting, helpfulness to customers, reliability of customer relationships (Barr, 2017). Those are the the qualitative indicators. It may be more important for the business to keep up with the qualitative ones. Examples of a qualitative indicator that organisations regularly use would be an employee satisfaction survey. 'Qualitative indicators are not measured by numbers. Typically, a qualitative KPI is a characteristic of a process or business decision' (Perez, 2021).

Further reading
– Check out kpi.org/KPI-Basics.
– 8 KPIs to Drive Your Digital Marketing Strategy, Nigam (2019): blogs.perficient.com.

## 2.9.8 Mental availability measurements

Qualitative metrics can be used to measure *mental availability* measurements such as experienced brand uniqueness, mental market share and message resonance. Here are some recent approaches:
**Distinctive brand assets (DBAs):** Measuring uniqueness and fame (3.4.6 Distinctive asset-building strategy).

> 'By measuring marketing effectiveness you are able to track how the sum of all activities comes together to make or break a brand' Les Binet & Peter Field.

**Category entry points (CEPs):** The measurement of mental market share, such as brand awareness. Read more at 3.8.3 Communication goals: category entry points (CEPs), 2.9.9 Category entry points (CEPs).
**Share of voice (SOV):** SOV is measured by comparing the company's media placements to its competitor's placements. 'Share of voice demonstrates how much you dominate the conversation in your industry and how you disrupt your area of expertise compared to other companies' (Fallstrom, 2021).
**Share of market (SOM):** The correlation between *Share of voice* and *Share of market* is the relationship between the companies ad buying strategy and their market share growth. Read more at 3.8.9 Communication measurement: Share of voice/Share of market
Message resonance: This is a way to assess which of the company's communication activities are hitting the mark with your audiences. It is measured by assessing the percentage of placements in news articles and analyst reports focused on a chosen area that includes at least one of your company's key messages. 'This shows how you control the narrative framing of your brand' (Fallstrom, 2021).
**Average tonality:** This is a metric that shows the company's popularity in media coverage. The measurement assigns each media placement a numeric value –2 (very unfavourable) and 2 (very favourable), calculating the average by adding the placement totals and dividing by the total number of placements. 'Average tonality gives the insight into how positively your company is perceived in media coverage' (Fallstrom, 2021).

Tips for the company
**Management needs to clearly communicate the benefits and the value of the KPIs as they relate to the business, to ensure the use of KPIs, and that they are not completely ignored by employees.**

Tips for the designer
**The Ehrenberg-Bass Institute can identify the CEPs that your client's brand can develop to improve mental availability.**

**Strong mental availability (being easily thought of in buying situations) is essential for building a successful brand. Without it, the brand can't get bought (Ehrenberg-Bass Institute, 2022).**

### 2.9.9 Category entry points

Measuring category entry points (CEPs) is the measurement of mental market share.[112] CEPs represent the multiple mental cues and associations people get when they see a brand. The more CEPs a brand is attached to, the greater the number of mental retrieval pathways are attached to the brand. 'Category entry points (CEPs) are the building blocks of mental availability – they capture the thoughts that category buyers have as they transition into making a category purchase' (Ehrenberg-Bass Institute, n.d.). The key metrics to assess the mental availability are (Romaniuk and Sharp, 2022, p. 75):

- *Mental market share*: The brands percentage of CEP associations, of the total CEP associations for the brand and competitors. It reflects the brand's relative retrieval competitiveness in the whole category.
- *Mental penetration*: The percentage of category buyers who link the brand with at least one CEP. This measures brand awareness more in line with associative network theories of memory, as it calculates the possibility of retrieval across the multiple potential pathways to retrieve the brand. The higher the mental penetration, the more category buyers have the brand mentally available.
- *Network size*: How many CEPs the brand is linked to in the minds of those aware: the wider the network, the more potential pathways for brand retrieval. This metric is useful for assessing if advertising is maintaining or building the CEP network (3.4.6 Distinctive asset-building strategy, 3.8.3 Communication goals: category entry points (CEPs), 3.8.9 Communication measurement: Share of voice/Share of market).

Further reading
***How Brand Grows*, part 2 by Jenni Romaniuk and Byron Sharp (2022).**

112 **The CEPs approach is based on studies conducted by Byron Sharp, Jenni Romaniuk, and Ehrenberg-Bass Institute.**

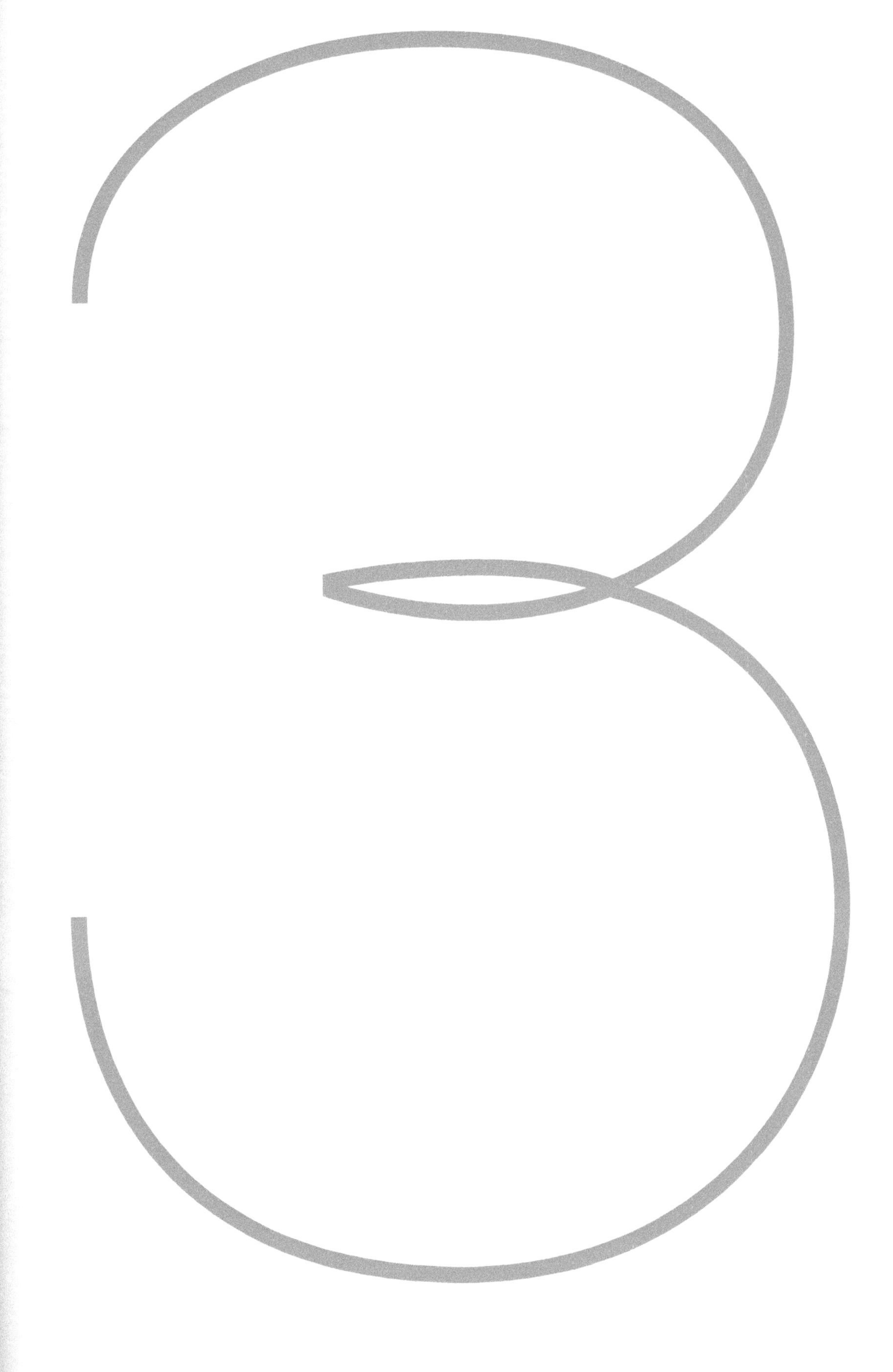

3.1 Strategy development 176
3.1.1 Different approaches 177
3.1.2 Strategic management tool 181
3.1.3 TOP 5 182
3.1.4 Strategic workshop 182
3.1.5 Workshop process 182
3.1.6 Strategic workshop report 184
3.1.7 Workshop template 185

3.2 Overall strategy 186
3.2.1 Purpose 187
3.2.2 Mission 187
3.2.3 Business idea 187
3.2.4 Vision 189
3.2.5 Core values 191
3.2.6 Value proposition 196
3.2.7 The value pyramid 198
3.2.9 Strategic narrative 201

3.3 Goals and subgoals 201
3.3.1 Business goals 202
3.3.2 Big hairy goals 203
3.3.3 Development of goals 204
3.3.4 Goal hierarchy 204
3.3.5 Qual vs. quant goals 207
3.3.6 Measurable goals 208
3.3.7 Goal achievement 208
3.3.8 Sustainability goals 209
3.3.9 Goals for design project 210

3.4 Business strategy 211
3.4.1 Competitive strategy 211
3.4.2 Porter's generic strategies 212
3.4.3 Sustainability strategy 215
3.4.4 Blue Ocean Strategy 215
3.4.5 Transient advantage 217
3.4.6 Distinctive asset-building strategy 219
3.4.7 Agile strategy management 222
3.4.8 Is the right strategy chosen? 223
3.4.9 Strategy implementation 224

3.5 Business model 225
3.5.1 Business model canvas 227
3.5.2 Sustainable business model 227
3.5.3 Business model innovation 228
3.5.4 Lean start-up 229

3.6 Market strategy 230
3.6.1 Markets 230
3.6.2 Marketing tasks 231
3.6.3 STP marketing strategy 232
3.6.4 Customers' needs 233
3.6.5 The four Ps 234
3.6.6 The four Cs 236
3.6.7 Content marketing 238
3.6.8 Inbound marketing 239
3.6.9 Digital strategy 241

3.7 Brand strategy 245
3.7.1 Brand platform 251
3.7.2 Brand architecture 251
3.7.3 Brand positioning 260
3.7.4 Brand story 271
3.7.5 Brand identity 276
3.7.6 Brand assets 280
3.7.7 Brand name 289
3.7.8 Brand perspective 296
3.7.9 Brand refresh, redesign, rebranding 299

3.8 Communication strategy 300
3.8.1 Communication audit 304
3.8.2 Identifying the target group 307
3.8.3 Communication goals 309
3.8.4 Desired reputation 311
3.8.5 Communication platform 315
3.8.6 Communication elements 318
3.8.7 Communication development 321
3.8.8 Channels and media 325
3.8.9 Communication measurement 329

3.9 Design strategy 332
3.9.1 Design strategy compass 333
3.9.2 Design strategy development 333
3.9.3 Design strategy content 334
3.9.4 Design goal 334
3.9.5 Operational strategy 335
3.9.6 Design platform 335
3.9.7 Visual assets 336
3.9.8 Elements and surfaces 336
3.9.9 Design strategy vs. design brief 336

Strategy is the third of six phases. It is about the strategic anchoring of a design project. It involves the development of the company's goals and strategies, and the use of strategy as a management tool for the design process. It requires sufficient insight into the company's situation and the problem the assignment is intended to help solve. Several sub-strategies may need to be developed in a project, such as brand strategy, communication strategy and design strategy. While goals are about what we want or where we want to be, strategy is about how to get there. 'Strategy' is the plan.

Strategy and goals are the cornerstones of the company, and the foundation for all design assignments that will be carried out for the company. Only by strategic anchoring can a design investment lead to goal achievement for the company. Therefore, at an early stage of the design project, designers must familiarise themselves with the company's overall goal and strategy and, where appropriate, contribute to adjusting or developing it. It might also be necessary to draw up sub-strategies such as brand strategy, communication strategy and web strategy. In addition, a design project might require the development of a design strategy to serve as a management tool for design development. The situational analysis conducted in phase two is an important starting point for strategy development, while new studies and analyses may be necessary along the way (2.6 Research, 2.7.1 Situational analysis). Strategy means a plan to achieve a certain goal. We need to know where we stand and where we are headed to be able to plan. Strategy means to decide what to do and how to do it to achieve the goal. The goal is the desired situation. The goal determines the direction. The strategy determines the path to follow.

Fig. 3.1 Strategy

In this phase of strategy, we move onto the home territory of business developers, marketers, brand builders, and communications consultants, with designer glasses on. This will affect the way we talk about strategy and what examples are shown. The goal is for the designer to gain a better understanding of strategy at different levels to be able to contribute to developing strategies and linking them to the design process. Strategy and design go hand in hand – always. A strategic designer who is asked to develop a website does not think solely about the visual design of the website, but also considers how the website should help the company achieve its business goals or other value creations, how to make it as user-friendly as possible, what should be communicated, how to make the company's identity visible and so on. These are questions that interlock with the company's goals and strategies.

The company often has strategies ready when the designer enters the project, but it may still be necessary to make some adjustments so that the basis the designer will work from, corresponds to the intentions and goals the company has for the design project. Where no strategies have been defined, or they have not been updated for some time, it might be necessary to start with that. Initiating a design project can often mean a crossroads for the company, an opportunity to think in a new and different way. To succeed, good processes are required to reveal the current situation, define new goals and develop new strategies. The designer makes a good partner in such processes. What characterises a strategic designer is precisely the ability to think creatively and analytically, which is a success factor in developing smart strategies and solving complex problems (2.3.1 Problem, 2.3.9 Wicked problems).

Fig. 3.1 The figure shows how strategy includes defined path choices and measures against a defined desired situation, based on a clarified current situation. Where are we? Where are we heading? How are we going to get there? The goal is the destination, while the strategy is the plan for how to reach it. See also chapter 2.2.3 Where are we – where will we? © Grimsgaard, W. (2018)

Fig. 3.2 The figure shows examples of a company's strategy hierarchy. The overall strategy comes first and is about WHAT the company should do. Then comes the competitive strategy, which is aligned with the overall strategy. It defines HOW the company will compete in the market to achieve its goals. In larger groups, more business strategies might be necessary for the different departments or business areas. Next comes several functional strategies that determine how the company should implement its business strategy, and which targeted operational measures should be implemented. What strategies the company has in its strategy hierarchy depends to a great extent on the type and size of the company. © Grimsgaard, W. (2018).

Tips for the company
Strategy development takes time. Not everything can be done at once. It is important to think things through – What strategies do we need?

Tips for the designer
In principle, the designer should relate to strategic paths relevant to the project, and have the solution reflect them.

Choosing what to do, and what not to do, is the definition of strategy (IDEO U, n.d.).

### Strategy on different levels

Many design assignments and tasks are interlinked with the company's identity and core values, such as when developing a logo. Then the designer should become familiar with the company's overall business strategy in order to understand what the company is doing, its characteristics, competitive advantage and goals. This should then be communicated through the logo and the overall visual identity. The designer often has to deal with strategy at several levels, and there are many different theories for the levels into which strategies can or should be divided, and what the different levels should contain, see Figure 3.2. Roos et al. (2014) distinguishes between three strategic levels: overall strategy, business strategy and functional strategies. Simply put, overall strategy is about WHAT the company should be doing, while business strategy is about HOW the company should compete in the market to achieve its goals. Functional strategies are about implementing targeted operational actions. Here we will take a closer look at the three levels.

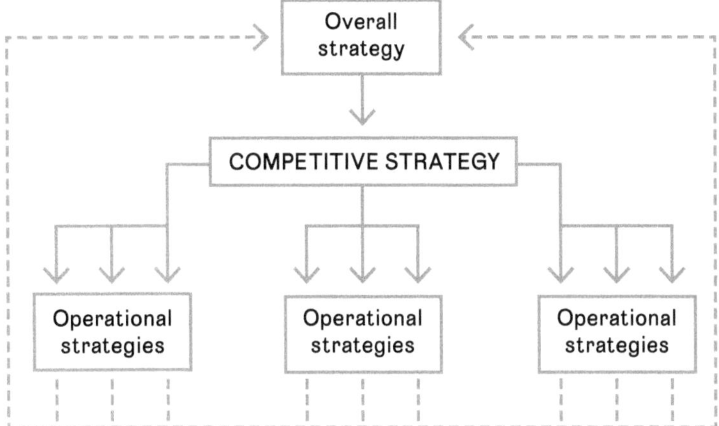


Fig. 3.2 Strategy hierarchy

*Overall strategy*: The top strategic level is often referred to as overall strategy or corporate strategy. Here, the company's business idea, vision, and values are defined. In reality, overall strategy is mostly to be regarded as a strategic intention, or a strategic platform, because it essentially defines *what* the company should do and why. Developing an overall strategy is generally about planning what the company should do, what values the company should follow, how the company should be structured and run financially, what overall goals the company should work towards, and what decisions should be made to achieve these goals. 'Some people include goals as part of the strategy, while others are careful to distinguish between goals and strategy' (Roos et al. 2014). Decisions at this level should be taken jointly by the senior management (3.2 Overall strategy, 3.1.4 Strategic workshop).

A design assignment should always be aligned with the strategies and goals of the company in question. It is therefore essential for the designer to understand strategy and be able to link strategy to design work.

*Competitive strategy*: The next strategic level is often called competitive strategy or business strategy. The business strategy is based on the business idea and determines how the company will compete in the market. It's about what strategy the company should choose to achieve its goals, what market the company should operate in, what products and services it should be developing and offering, and how they should meet customer or user needs and requirements. Business strategy is the starting point for how the products or services should be positioned, and which target group they should approach. In larger corporations, business strategies are often created for different departments or business units (3.4 Business strategy).

*Functional strategies*: The third strategic level is often called functional or operational strategies. They can also be referred to as sub-strategies. Functional strategies apply to various functions within the company, such as finance, HR, production, design, distribution, and marketing (Roos et al., 2014, p. 65). One important aspect of functional strategies is the planning of the actions that should be taken to accomplish the set goals and objectives. There is a need for operational strategy when one knows which objectives to work towards, and there is a decision on realisation (Lorentzen and Lund, 1998, p. 17). A design assignment is often at operational level and requires its own goals and strategies. Design can also be part of the overall strategy, the competitive strategy, or a subgoal. Examples of functional strategies that the designer often needs to use, or can help develop are brand strategy, communication strategy, web strategy, and design strategy (3.7 Brand strategy, 3.8 Communication strategy, 3.9 Design strategy).

Tips for the designer

**Everything you need to know about the company, absolutely everything, should be found in the strategy: what they do, why they are on the market, what target groups they have, how they see themselves and their surroundings, what values they have, etc. If it isn't they might need help sorting things out.**

Tips for the company

**Strategy is built from the inside out, and from the outside in. It's not just about knowing the competitors and the target groups. It is just as much about good insight and understanding of the major external economic, social and environmental factors that affect the business and the way the business affects them.**

Strategic anchoring ensures targeted design solutions.

## 3.1 Strategy development

Strategy has become a broad concept that encompasses intentions, strategies, and planning at different levels. There are countless models and planning tools that can be used to create strategies and make plans.

Strategy is practised and explained in various ways by professionals, in literature and in companies. 'Although several strategists have described how best to implement a strategy process for companies, it is also clear that there is no definitive answer' (Roos et al. 2014).[1] Moreover, all companies are different and have different needs as far as strategy goes. What matters is that the strategy developed for the company makes sense for what the company should be doing and how it can best help the company achieve its goals. In a competitive situation, achieving the goal may involve a battle for market shares and customer attention. Battle is also deeply rooted in the strategy concept, which originates from military warfare, where strategy is about deciding on the necessary measures to fight the enemy. Just as in warfare, where the responsibility for choosing an overall goal and strategy lies with the commander, in a company this task is the manager's responsibility. That said, it is a plus to also involve employees from different functional and responsibility areas within the company in strategy development processes, and not just the senior management, even if all responsibility lies with the management, the owners, and the board of directors. Knudsen and Flåten (2015) formulate this as follows: 'The person or persons primarily responsible for the strategy work in a company should firstly understand the interaction

1 The strategists referred to here are Hax and Majluf, Lant and Mezias, Mezias and Glynn.
2 Based on: Knudsen and Flåten (2015).

**From strategy to design brief**

**Situational analysis:** The company's current situation?
**Overall goal:** Long-term qualitative/quantitative objectives?
**Overall strategy:** Purpose, mission, vision, values?
**Competitive strategy:** How to compete in the market?
**Business model:** How to best create, deliver and increase values?
**Consequences:** Need for change and improvement?
**Action plan:** Tasks. Priorities. Planning. Progress.
**Sub strategies:** Market strategy, brand strategy, communication strategy, web strategy, SoMe strategy, etc.
**Design strategy:** What consequences should the strategy and objectives have for how the design should be developed and used?
**Design brief:** The design project's goal, tasks and deliverables?


1 Initiation
2 Insight
3 Strategy
4 Design
5 Production
6 Management

3.1 Strategy development
3.2 Overall strategy
3.3 Goals and subgoals
3.4 Business strategy
3.5 Business model
3.6 Market strategy
3.7 Brand strategy
3.8 Communication strategy
3.9 Design strategy

3.1.1 Different approaches
3.1.2 Strategic management tool
3.1.3 TOP 5
3.1.4 Strategic workshop
3.1.5 Workshop process
3.1.6 Strategic workshop report
3.1.7 Workshop template


between people, processes and methods, and second, they must take responsibility for involving the right people in the processes. They must take responsibility for the best possible processes, and they must see to it that methods and tools are utilised in the best possible sensible way, with as little distortion and political meddling as possible, with as much as possible room for creative improvement, and with the best possible anchoring of the chosen strategy among employees and stakeholders'.

Strategy development generally takes place through processes and methods, which lead to the formulation of a strategy. The starting point for a strategic process is usually a defined goal, but one often starts by defining a business idea and a vision, which says something about what one wishes to do. A strategic process can be divided into different steps. The first step is to conduct and clarify the company's internal and external situation by means of a situational analysis (2.7.1 Situational analysis). This could identify, among other things, what resources the company has at its disposal, and what opportunities exist in the market. This knowledge is necessary in order to set a realistic overall goal. Once the goal has been defined, a strategy is selected for how the company should achieve the goal. In some contexts, it might be necessary to go back and forth between goal and strategy in order to arrive at the ultimate definitions for these. Subgoals and operational plans are drawn up based on the overall goal and strategy. Then comes the implementation of goals and actions to achieve the goal. The results of the actions are checked against goals and strategy. If control shows that the goals are not met, the strategic process should or must be repeated.

### 3.1.1 Different approaches

Traditionally strategy development for companies can be understood from two different directions:[2]

*The linear process* originates from 'the design school', a school in the field of strategy in the mid-20th century, which meant strategy development carried out by the senior manager with the help of experts using an analytical process, including a SWOT analysis, which resulted in a strategy formulation with a top-down approach. Such an approach

Strategy and tactics

There is a distinction between strategy and tactics. Strategy involves understanding what needs to be done and how, while tactics refer to the execution plan. A strategic designer employs strategy for establishing direction and planning, while tactics are the actions employed to develop the appropriate solution.

| Strategy overview and definition of terms | | | |
|---|---|---|---|
| At corporate management level | Overall strategy and goal/Strategic intent | Purpose | The fundamental reason why the comapny should exist, beyond making money, such as a positive change one wants to see in the world. |
| | | Mission | The mission or business idea is the basic concept for why the company exists. What do we do, for whom and where? |
| | | Vision | The vision is the future come true and the guiding star that shows the path the company should follow. |
| | | Core values | The core values are the main characteristics of the company, expressed through a set of values or adjectives. They influence its behaviour and actions and are the starting point for developing visual identity, core messages, and tone of voice. |
| | | Value proposition | The value proposition is the unique and distinctive features of the company, something they can promise to deliver on. A starting point for choosing a position. |
| | | Overall goal | The overall goal of the company leads to various subgoals that should deliver results in order to make it possible to achieve the overall goal. |
| | Business plan/business strategy | Competitive strategy | The competitive strategy is the company's choice of strategy to achieve its overall objectives. These strategic choices are essential for all further strategies and actions. |
| | | Business model | The business model is an operational plan for how the company will make money, or other value creation, based on the strategy it has chosen. |
| | | Business plan | A business plan explains all aspects of the company and compiles them in a well-organised business document. |
| | | Market strategy | The market strategy is about how the business should compete in the market, whom it will sell its products and services to, what the company should achieve in different markets, and how it will do it. Target group segmentation and positioning are crucial here. |
| | | Digital strategy | A digital strategy establishes the overall direction that a business will follow digitally. It should help maximising the business benefits of data assets and technology-focused initiatives. A digital marketing strategy is a plan and a series of actions that use online marketing channels to achieve various marketing goals. |
| | | Action plan | The action plan is a structured overview of activities and actions to be undertaken by the company based on its business strategy and with a view to achieving its overall goal. An action plan may include a progress schedule, with a weighting and prioritisation of actions. |

Table 3.1 The table shows the definitions and order of some strategy concepts that we will discuss in more detail in the next sections. Goals and subgoals follow consistently in all phases. © Grimsgaard, W. (2018).

Tips for the company

Strategy development is creative work! The use of design methodology and visual devices in the strategy phase can facilitate the transition to the design phase.

| Strategy overview and definition of terms | | | |
|---|---|---|---|
| At product and service level | Functional/operational strategies | Brand strategy/ positioning | Brand strategy is a plan for the development and management of corporate and product brands, which should contribute to a targeted brand positioning and brand building. It includes brand analysis, brand platform, brand architecture, brand name, brand statement, brand perspective, and brand management. |
| | | Communication strategy | The communication strategy is a plan for the company's communication. It should contribute to targeted communication of the company's brands and positioning strategy towards stakeholders. It should also help ensure that communication of the company and its products or services is consistent and holistic in all contexts. |
| | | Media strategy | Media strategy is an operational plan for communication and impact in analogue media, audiovisual media, and digital media. It is based on the market and communication strategy. The media strategy includes choice of media, segmentation, frequency, continuity, and effect measurement. |
| | | Web strategy | Web strategy is an operational plan on how to develop and build the online visibility of the company adhering closely to the digital marketing strategy, the communication strategy and the brand strategy. A web strategy is based on the user's need to seek out the company's website and should aim to continuously respond to the user's actions and mood, to optimise the solution. |
| | | Social media strategy | Social media strategy is an operational plan to provide the best possible synergy of the company's presence and activities in social media. It is based on the digital strategy, communication and media strategies. |
| | | Product strategy | Product strategy is a plan for the development of a new product, customisation of an existing product, product line extension, or brand extension. |
| | | Service strategy | A customer service strategy is a plan and tool for handling customer interactions and customer experience throughout the customer journey. |
| | | Design strategy | Design strategy is a strategic management tool for development, implementation, and use of design to achieve the company's goals. It determines what consequences the company's strategies and goals shall have for the development of design. A company that uses design strategically when creating products or services, needs a design strategy. |
| | | Design brief | The design brief should describe which task the designer should solve based on a defined strategic platform and a formulated problem statement. |

Table 3.1 Strategy overview and definition of terms

is still frequently considered ideal by many,[3] and many contemporary strategy work models are based on similar processes. However, a bottom-up approach is likely to be more contemporary today, where everyone in the business is involved. In this way, emerging strategies can be captured.

*The emerging process* assumes that strategy can have the characteristics of a pattern, and not just a plan, and that the strategy is the result of emerging elements of the company that cannot be planned. Henry Mintzberg (1978, 1995) was critical of a purely linear process, arguing that much of the strategy, which is actually realised in a business, is based on emerging elements, and that much of what is planned is never implemented.[4]

**Five Ps for strategy** was developed by Mintzberg (1987), as five different definitions of or approaches to developing strategy, which is still useful to reflect on today. (Gordon, 2021):[5]

- *Plan* – Adopt brainstorming options and planning how to deliver them.
- *Ploy* – Get the better of competitors, by plotting to disrupt, dissuade, discourage, or otherwise influence them, can be part of a strategy.[6]
- *Pattern* – Sometimes, strategy emerges from past organisational behaviour. Rather than being an intentional choice, a consistent and successful way of doing business can develop into a strategy.
- *Position* – Deciding a position in the marketplace helps explore the fit between the company and its environment, and helps develop a sustainable competitive advantage.
- *Perspective* – The choices an organisation makes about its strategy rely heavily on its culture just as patterns of behaviour can emerge as strategy, patterns of thinking will shape an organisation's perspective and the things that it is able to do well.[7]

The advantage of knowing several approaches to strategy development provides the opportunity to look at them as a variety of viewpoints that can be considered while developing a strategy.

**Strategy innovation** Strategic work is largely a creative process and an arena for innovation. Today we aren't talking solely about the business idea; we also talk about the opportunities that lie in start-ups and business innovation. One success factor that is highlighted is the use of design methodology in strategy development, and greater emphasis on value creation for the end customer. Design thinking is a method that spreads across the business world and is used for both strategy development, problem solving and innovation. It involves thinking about the combination of desirability, feasibility, and viability. 'A desirable solution, one that your customer really needs. A feasible solution, building on the strengths of your current operational capabilities. A profitable solution, with a sustainable business model' (Orton, 2017). It is about asking the questions: What do people need or want? Is it technically possible to make? Is it sustainable and can we make money out of it? More and more companies are adopting lean and agile methodology and iterative methods. It is about involving the customer or user early on and quickly testing the idea of a product, service or similar. *Agile strategy management* is to enable the organisation to think ahead of the market, quickly mobilise itself, adapt to market changes, fill capacity gaps, capture new revenue ahead of competitors, and create new markets.

Tips for the company
**Developing strategy is a creative process. Involving designers and design methodology is a success factor for strategy innovation.**

Tips for the designer
**In principle, you should relate to strategic paths relevant to the project, and have the solution reflect them.**

**TOP 5 is the designer's most essential strategic management tool.**

Further reading
**Check out IDEO U's course on 'Designing strategy. Unite rigor and creativity to create a successful strategy': ideo.com.**

3 Many companies nowadays would prefer a flat structure with more employee involvement.
4 Mintzberg also claimed that the ideal strategic process did not necessarily show a complete view of the strategy of an organisation.
5 Mintzberg, H. (1987, Fall). 'The strategy concept I: five Ps for strategy'. *California Management Review*, 30(1), 11–24.
6 Here, techniques and tools such as the Futures Wheel, Impact Analysis, and Scenario Analysis can help explore the possible future scenarios in which competition will occur.
7 To get an insight into your organisation's perspective, use cultural analysis tools like the Cultural Web, Deal and Kennedy's Cultural Model, and the Congruence Model.
8 Clayton Christensen was an American academic and business consultant who developed the theory of 'disruptive innovation'. Forbes called him 'one of the most influential business theorists of the last 50 years' in a cover story by Whelan March 14, 2011.
9 We also see that leading companies to a greater extent employ designers to primarily contribute to business development, startups and innovation.

All is involved using live input: utilise others' best ideas; work together to coordinate, and implement. The process of agile strategy involves the use of design methodology, such as design thinking combined with an agile approach (Neumeier, 2018) (3.4.7 Agile strategy management).

*Disruptive strategy* is an executive-level strategy that organise for innovation. That includes articulating complex viewpoints and applying strategic frameworks to assess new opportunities and potential threats to discover big ideas that can lead to innovation. It is based on the theory of disruptive innovation, first coined by Harvard professor Clayton Christensen.[8] A disruptive innovation is a groundbreaking innovation that disrupts an existing market by making an existing business model irrelevant (Scott et al., 2008) (4.3.4 Innovation).

### 3.1.2 Strategic management tool

The designer's involvement in the company's strategy is usually primarily linked to the value of the strategy as a management tool in the context of the assignment.[9] It is important to decide which strategies the design project should be based on, and which strategies need to be developed. Strategic definitions relevant to the design project are implemented in a design strategy, with guides and plans for the development of design solutions. The challenge is to decide how strategy and goals should impact the design development (3.9 Design strategy). The design strategy will serve as a management tool for the design process ahead.

Strategy development may require extensive work, which to some designers might seem like a long hike in the desert before one can start developing visual solutions. Strategy work can also eat the time and budget allocated for the design project. If it is necessary for the designer to participate in strategy development beyond what is required to complete a specific design assignment, creating a separate project for this task should be considered. This way, the strategy will not affect the time and budget originally earmarked for the assignment.

The scope of the strategy work is assessed in relation to the framework of the project. For example, a communication strategy can be made very comprehensive, or it can be limited to simple communication guides, more like a communication platform. Strategic work is not necessarily done only before a design project, but during the project too, one has to navigate back and forth through strategic and analytical thinking and planning. In some contexts, there may be a new turn in the design project that makes it necessary to go back and adjust the strategy. This could mean going all the way back to the overall strategy and adjusting so that everything can fit together and become a coherent whole. It is absolutely crucial that strategies are clearly formulated. Errors in the strategy can guide the design project in a completely wrong direction and affect the final solution. For example, a product may end up looking exclusive and expensive, when it is supposed to compete on price and availability. Strategic work at overall level is something the designer never does alone but in collaboration with the company's management. In any case, all strategies are subject to the client's approval. Strategic anchoring of a design project presupposes that the strategy is actively used as a management tool throughout the entire project.



Strategic process

Start with an idea, a problem or a vision. Opportunities and threats of the current situation are analysed by means of a situational analysis. A clear overall goal for the desired situation is set. Or the goal is set first, and then the situation is examined. A strategy is chosen to achieve the goal. Using this as basis, operational plans are drawn up for the actions that should be taken. Control steps back to what has been accomplished, and whether it has contributed to the achievement of goals in line with the adopted strategy. Everything has to be seen in context. Is the result in line with the business idea, does it solve the problem, and does it contribute to the achievement of goals? If not, the process should start again.

### 3.1.3 TOP 5

TOP 5 is a strategic management tool. It includes the company's business idea, vision, core values, value proposition, and position, see Table 3.2. These strategic definitions are the designer's key points of reference in most design projects. Together, they can serve as a management tool and a bridge to the design work. Purpose, business idea, vision, core values and value proposition are defined in the overall strategy, while position is defined in the brand strategy,[10] and desired reputation is defined in the communication strategy. The position defines how the company and its products or services will compete in the market, which is the real strategy. Reputation is a consequence, something the company earns by delivering on its promises and demonstrating good practices. *Desired* reputation is also a goal of sorts, which is about how the company wants to be evaluated. One option is to turn the management tool upside-down and use desired reputation as a starting point when revitalising the strategy. Thus, one can decide what to do to deserve the desired reputation and use that ambition to define e.g. core values, value proposition and position. TOP 5 can be complemented by other strategies according to the needs of the individual project in order for the designer to have a management tool that is relevant. Design assignments are different; not every project is about positioning and corporate branding. It is therefore important that the designer has a conscious approach to what should be included in the strategic management tool and how to use it consciously in the development of solutions (3.2 Overall strategy, 3.4.1 Competitive strategy, 3.7.3 Brand position, 3.8.4 Desired reputation).

Table 3.2 **The table shows TOP 5 – a strategic management tool for designers, which covers the company's overall strategy and position. Position is about how the company wants to compete in the field. The desired reputation is the acid test of whether the company lives up to its promises. The different strategy concepts are clarified in the next chapters.**
**© Grimsgaard (2018).**

Tips for the designer
**Strategic workshops can be used to initiate a strategic process, as well as throughout strategy development.**

Tips for the company
**How to use the company's strengths and opportunities to create a winning strategy.**

> Strategy process map
> **1) Identify the problem**
> **2) Frame a question**
> **3) Generate possibilities**
> **4) What would have to be true?**
> **5) Barriers**
> **6) Test**
> **7) Choose**
> **... bring what you learned and start over again (Roger Martin: *Strategic Planning: How to get started by IDEO U*, ideo.com 2021)**

### 3.1.4 Strategic workshop

Strategic workshop is a creative collaboration where the designer and the client work together to develop goals and strategies through brainstorming, discussions, and analyses. The starting point is preliminary research, surveys and analyses carried out in phase 2.

Strategic workshop is a flying start to a strategy development process. The designer can play an significant role in a strategic workshop both as a facilitator, meeting leader and discussion partner, where the designer's ability to think both creatively and analytically can be beneficial. Strategy development is first and foremost a creative process in which one seeks to arrive at formulations and definitions that best express the plans and goals one envisages. The designer's ability to simplify and visualise the strategy, can help make it easier to communicate, both internally in the company and externally to collaborators, such as designers. This can also contribute to better link the strategy to the further design process. The next chapters shows examples of preparations, invitation, and management of a strategic workshop, see also 1.4 Initial workshop.

### 3.1.5 Workshop process

**Participants:** Who participates in the strategic workshop is decisive for the outcome. Overall goals and strategies for a company are decided by the owners, the board and the management. It is therefore crucial that

10 **The brand strategy is based on the choise of competitive strategy.**

| Goal | TOP 5 | | |
|---|---|---|---|
| | Purpose: | Why do we exist? | Defined in the overall strategy |
| | Mission: | What do we do, for whom and where? | |
| | Vision: | What is our future dream and guiding star? | |
| | Values: | Core values: Our three main emitional attributes? | |
| | | Value proposition: Our promise/rational attribute? | |
| | Position: | How should we differentiate ourselves? | Defined in the brand-strategy |
| | + | | |
| | Desired reputation: | How would we like people to think and talk about us? | Defined in the communication strategy |

Table 3.2 Top 5 – strategic management tool


1 Initiation
2 Insight
3 Strategy
4 Design
5 Production
6 Management

3.1 Strategy development
3.2 Overall strategy
3.3 Goals and subgoals
3.4 Business strategy
3.5 Business model
3.6 Market strategy
3.7 Brand strategy
3.8 Communication strategy
3.9 Design strategy

3.1.1 Different approaches
3.1.2 Strategic management tool
3.1.3 TOP 5
3.1.4 Strategic workshop
3.1.5 Workshop process
3.1.6 Strategic workshop report
3.1.7 Workshop template


some of these participate. There should always be decision-makers among the participants so that the process will not need to be approved at a later stage by someone who was not present. In addition, it is often an advantage to have employees from different parts of the company who can contribute knowledge and experience that is useful for the process, such as people in marketing, production, or IT. An important synergy is that employees gain ownership of the strategy process and can contribute to the result that is developed.

**Invitation:** The invitation to a workshop should not be too detailed but should briefly mention some of the areas that will be appropriate to work on. Here's an example of an invitation from the designer to the company: Through a strategic workshop, we would like to clarify some strategic aspects that are part of your overall strategy, and that will be relevant to the design assignment, which is to be solved, including business idea and core values. Together, we will also identify what the core message should be, as an introduction to getting the communication strategy started. The duration of the workshop is approximately three to four hours. We reserve the right to organise one or more follow-up workshops, if necessary. Budget and delivery: The price per workshop will be (...), which includes preparation, implementation, and a brief report. The report will include the strategic definitions we have arrived

'Purpose is the fundamental reason why the business should exist, beyond making money, such as a positive change one wants to see in the world.' Quote from the book: *Point of Purpose. How purposeful brands attract top employees, seduce customers, & fuel profit*, Annweiler, B. (2019).

at, recommendations for further work, and notes from the brainstorming session. The result of the strategic workshop can be included as part of the company's overall strategy and sub-strategies and will serve as a tool in the further work to solve the design assignment.

**Preparations:** Before the workshop, the designer should have read the company's existing strategies, to look for typical weaknesses, defects, needs and possible potential for improvement. If the company is newly established, more options are open, and it may be a good idea to have familiarised oneself with the preliminary plans for the new company, if any. It is also an advantage to have conducted a situational analysis, but this analysis is not a prerequisite for a workshop. The company's situation can also be clarified through the questions asked. Based on this insight, questions, and tasks are to be completed during the workshop (2.2 Situational study).

**Implementation:** A strategic workshop takes place through brainstorming, exercises, group work, debates, and discussions. The purpose is to obtain answers that can contribute to the development of strategic definitions. Answers are written concisely, in one to three lines, or as individual words. The questions it may be natural to ask, and their order, should be seen in the context of what is appropriate for the individual project. See examples of questions at the end of this chapter and in the various strategy explanations that follow. Read chapter 1.4 on how to conduct a workshop (1.4 Initial workshop).

**Confidentiality:** During a strategic workshop, it is important that participants feel safe and can speak openly. Confidential information about the company is not uncommon. Some may feel it is unsafe, and therefore wish to withhold such information. The designer can bring this up at the beginning and explain how the information will be used and stored, to establish a safe and open dialogue as early as possible. Some companies have their own rules and practices regarding confidential information, such as signing a non-disclosure agreement.

| The 5 Qs of Strategy | The Five Ps of Design Thinking: |
|---|---|
| 1. What is our purpose?<br>2. Who do we serve?<br>3. Where should we compete?<br>4. How will we win?<br>5. How will we grow? | 1. Problemising<br>2. Pinballing<br>3. Probing<br>4. Prototyping<br>5. Proofing |

Table 3.3 Principles of agile strategy

Table 3.3 **Principles of Agile strategy (Based on Marty Neumeier, 2018):**[11]

*The Five Qs of Strategy:*

1. What is our purpose, our raison d'être?
2. Who do we serve? How do we take great care of our people: our employees, our customers; our shareholders?
3. Where should we compete? What category should we choose to compete in, with our products and services?
4. How will we win? How will we be different in ways that customers find compelling?
5. How will we grow? How will we to continuously adapt to shifting circumstances and succeed in today's volatile marketplace?

*The Five Ps of Design Thinking*:

1. Problemising: Framing problems. What is the real problem? 'Is this the right problem to solve?'
2. Pinballing: Put options on the table that weren't there before, e.g: 'Why not a sunscreen lotion that repels mosquitoes?'
3. Probing: You view an idea through six symbolic modes of thinking: white for helpful information, red for evaluation based on emotions yellow for positivity, black for caution and disagreement, and green for creative thinking. Blue for the group leader who determines which mode of thinking will guide and direct the discussion.
4. Prototyping: The making step between knowing and doing. It's the difference between deciding the future and designing the future.
5. Proofing: Assumption is the enemy of strategic thinking. Make assumption about the way the world works, but assumptions can blind us to possibilities – and even reality itself...To get the most out of proofing, test two or more prototypes against each other."

### 3.1.6 Strategic workshop report

It is an advantage to have a structured, clear, and transparent report, so that it is easy to use in the design process, or in a further strategy process. Include an excerpt of the main strategy definitions on one page initially.

- The report should contain the project name, date, purpose of the workshop, representatives from the client in attendance, and the designer.
- Begin with a brief description of the company, product, or service, and the purpose of the strategy work.
- Describe what has been accomplished and concluded. Ensure that strategic definitions that have emerged during the workshop are presented

11 Based on Scramble (2018) by Marty Neumeier, an American author and speaker who writes on the topics of brand, design, innovation, and creativity (bobmorris.biz).

properly highlighted and clearly visible. Describe any outstanding questions and remaining work, as well as any surveys that should be conducted.
- Explain how the results can affect the project to be carried out. Come up with recommendations for further work based on the results. Changes to the assignment can be included in a design brief, which is prepared once the strategy work is complete (4.1 Design brief).
- Suggest further progress and, if relevant, a date for a new meeting or a follow-up workshop.
- Questions and notes from the brainstorming may follow as attachments.

### 3.1.7 Workshop template

Example of questions for a strategic workshop:
**Problems:** Identify strategic problems and brainstorm possibilities to solve them.
**Purpose:** What is our reason to exist?
**Mission:** What is our business idea?
**Vision:** What is our guiding star and dream for the future?
**Values:** What are our core values? The ones that shape our identity and distinctiveness, and govern our actions?
**Promises:** What can we promise our customers? Promises to communicate and deliver on? What should be our value proposition?
**Uniqueness:** How is our company unique and distinctive?
**Overall goal:** What do we want to achieve with what we do? Quantitative (e.g. market shares) and qualitative (e.g. focus on high quality and usability)?
**Strategic management:** How should we compete in the market? Should we compete on price, should we differentiate, should we concentrate on a small, limited target group?
**Competitors and competitive situation:** Who are our competitors? Where are they? What do we know about them? Identity, position, market share, etc.? What do they say about themselves? What will their strength ratio look like in a SWOT analysis?
**Position:** What position should we take in the market relative to our competitors? How are we supposed to stand out? What mental associations should we establish in the target group?
**Market:** Which market are we addressing? What characterises the market? What do we know about trends, business cycles, market leaders? Why do we choose this market?
**Target group/segment:** Who is the main target group (the customer, consumer, user)? Where are they? Special characteristics? Desire, needs, social identity, lifestyle?
**Desired reputation:** How will we be perceived by our customers and stakeholders?
**Core message:** What should our core message be? What is the most important, the very essence of what we want to convey? For example, it could be our position, our vision, our promise or value proposition.

The questions are set here in a logical order. Sometimes, it can be a good idea not to ask questions in a logical order. One can begin by mapping the desired reputation by asking: What do we want others to think about us? The next question will then be: What do we have to do for them to feel that way about us? (3.1.3 TOP 5, 1.4.7 Workshop report)



The workshop is an arena for new thoughts! The workshop should be set up outside the office in inspiring surroundings, where the mind can be given free rein.

## Overall strategy

Overall strategy is a strategic intent that defines what the company should do, its purpose and choice of direction. It includes the company's mission, vision and values, and is the company's most important management tool.

The overall strategy governs the company's way of thinking, and everything it plans and implements. It also represents the strategic guideline for how the company should appear and how it should present itself to the outside world, through its visual profile and its communication. All other strategies or sub-strategies are based on the company's overall strategy. Every design project should be anchored in the company's overall strategy.

The overall strategy is a strategic intention that defines WHAT the company should do in order to achieve its goals. In addition, the company needs a competitive strategy and one or more operational strategies describing HOW to do it. The responsibility for developing an overall strategy rests with the company's management, owners and board of directors, and cannot be changed without their participation and consent. Operational strategies, on the other hand, can be continuously adjusted and processed by middle managers, project managers, or others with operational responsibility in the company, but they should always be based on an overall strategy and should help the company achieve its overall goals. The needs of for-profit and non-profit companies will differ when it comes to what should be included in the overall strategy. Nonetheless, the trend is that non-profit and public enterprises are also in a competitive situation similar to commercial enterprises and are using several of the same strategic instruments.

**Overall strategy**

- Purpose: Why do we exist?
- Mission/business idea: What do we do, for whom and where?
- Vision: What is our dream for the future?
- Core values: What values should govern our behaviour and identity?
- Value proposition: What do we promise our customers?
- Culture: The company's culture is based on its core values.

Where there is no up-to-date and clear overall strategy, the designer may propose to develop such a strategy in collaboration with the company. A designer with a good understanding of strategy development will have good conditions to help the company do this. The advantage of designer participation in strategy development is the designer's ability to see both the big picture and the details, to come up with new opportunities and approaches, and to link the strategy to the design development ahead. The development of an overall strategy requires insight into the company's competitive situation, market situation, and other factors of the outside world, as well as what opportunities the market represents, and what success factors the company is in possession of. This insight is obtained through various

Tips for the company

**The overall strategy and goals should say little about profitability and more about the values and vision that will drive the company forward. Such as responsibility and commitment to social and environmental concerns and the concept of a triple bottom line: profit, people and planet. Read more in chapter 6.9 Sustainable management.**

Tips for the designer

**All design development for the company must be aligned with the company's overall strategy and objectives.**

**'A big idea functions as an organisational totem pole around which strategy, behaviour, actions, and communications are aligned' (Wheeler, 2013).**

Further reading

***Point of Purpose. How purposeful brands attract top employees, seduce customers, & fuel profit,*** **Annweiler, B. (2019).**

12 **The French term 'raison d'être' comes from the Latin *ratiō* (reason) and *esse* (to be), in English 'reason for being' meaning the most important reason or purpose for someone or something's existence. Examples: 'seeking to shock is the catwalk's raison d'être' (Raison d'être, n.d.). 'The main raison d'être for the "new police" was crime prevention by regular patrol.' (Butterfield, 2015)**

surveys and analyses (2.7.1 Situational analysis, 2.6.1 Survey, 2.7 Analyses). There are many different perceptions of what an overall strategy should contain and what terms should be used, and there are many different approaches. The chart below shows the business purpose, business idea/mission, vision, values and value proposition, as well as a brief explanation of these. These will be thoroughly presented in the following chapters.


1 Initiation
2 Insight
3 Strategy
4 Design
5 Production
6 Management

3.1 Strategy development
3.2 Overall strategy
3.3 Goals and subgoals
3.4 Business strategy
3.5 Business model
3.6 Market strategy
3.7 Brand strategy
3.8 Communication strategy
3.9 Design strategy

3.2.1 Purpose
3.2.2 Mission
3.2.3 Business idea
3.2.4 Vision
3.2.5 Core values
3.2.6 Value proposition
3.2.7 The value pyramid
3.2.8 Business innovation
3.2.9 Strategic narrative


### 3.2.1 Purpose

Purpose or business purpose is about the 'why'. Why do we exist? Why do we do what we do? Why another company? The purpose is the fundamental reason why the business should exist, beyond making money, its raison d'être.[12] Often based on a positive change one wants to see in the world. It is the source for the motivation, and a statement of intent that should inspire others to follow (Annweiler, 2017). 'Purpose is a way to express the company's impact on the lives of customers, clients, students, patients – whomever it's trying to serve' (Kenny, 2014).

**Purpose statement:** 'Purposes should not be created in isolation, but should involve colleagues from all over the company, in order to create something that everyone can relate to' (Annweiler, 2017, p. 14):

1) The objective should offer a deeper meaning than making money.
2) The objective should be inspiring for the company's employees.
3) The objective should be convincing.
4) The objective should be motivating for customers.
5) The objective should be relevant 10 years from now.

### 3.2.2 Mission

The mission is the very concept behind the company, the basic idea of what the company should deal with, achieve results on and make a profit from. 'The mission is developed when starting up the company and is the point of departure when defining goals and strategies. It governs the company's entire way of thinking, everything it plans and does' (Annweiler, 2019).

**Mission statement:** A mission statement defines what an organisation is, why it exists, its reason for being. For a non-profit company it means describing shortly the organisation's fundamental, unique purpose, the value the non-profit delivers, what groups it serves, and how. For a pro-profit company the mission statement should be a sentence describing the company's function, markets and competitive advantages, including eventually a short written statement of business goals and philosophies. The concept of business idea can be used instead of the concept of mission or as a basis for defining the mission statement.

> Purpose
> 'Refresh the world. Make a difference' (coca-colacompany.com 2022).
>
> Mission
> NIKE: 'Our mission is what drives us to do everything possible to expand human potential. We do that by creating groundbreaking sport innovations, by making our products more sustainably, by building a creative and diverse global team and by making a positive impact in communities where we live and work' (about.nike.com 2022)

### 3.2.3 Business idea

The business idea should provide a description of what the company should make or offer, whom to sell to, where to sell, and why. How is not a question defined in the business idea. It is defined in the business strategy, which states how the company will compete in the market

(3.4 Business strategy). When developing the business idea, it is important to ask: What is unique about this idea? What is the success factor? What is the unmet need in the market that leaves room for the product or service we want to sell? 'A business idea is not necessarily just a description of what you want to do, but equally why you want to do it' (Lorentzen and Lund 1998). Why is the purpose (3.2.1 Purpose).

A business idea is usually created when a new business is started. The problem companies face after a certain period of time is whether their business idea is still valid (Lorentzen and Lund 1998). Regardless of what the company uses as the basis for its operation, market cycles, technology, and competitive conditions will change over time, and so will the company. This means that, as the changes occur, the business idea should be constantly assessed, and modified, or redefined as needed in order to maintain competitiveness and profitability. This can be done by adjusting and refining the existing business idea or by pursuing different or new business concepts.

What do we do, for whom, where and why?

Fig. 3.3 Business idea

Fig. 3.3 The figure shows the content of a business idea. The business idea is formulated in one or two sentences, which explain what we do, for whom, where, and why.

Tips for the designer
If you are developing a new profile for your company, find out what it does or should do. The answer should be found in the company's business idea.

'Not all companies have a clear business idea, perhaps because they may have started on a more random basis, or because it has "evolved on its own". But with today's hectic development and fierce competition, all companies should try to become aware of "what they are really doing, or should be doing", that is, related to their present and future reason for being' (Helgesen, 1998).

An updated business idea is an absolutely necessary starting point for the designer regardless of the task to be solved. That is because it easily explains what the company does, for whom, where and why, providing the designer with the most important information about the company.

A business idea is *not* a selling text that speaks to the customer. A business idea is something the company makes for itself, to define what they should do. Therefore, phrases like us, our name, or the company's name are used. We should..., We offer ..., Our idea is ...

#### A good business idea

- It should mean a competitive advantage.
- It should be simple and clear enough for it to be understood by the company's employees.
- It should govern the company.
- It must be maintained, improved and renewed.

#### How to create a business idea?

The business idea can be developed through a strategic workshop. Facts, words and thoughts are discussed and filtered in several rounds, until an essence remains that makes clear, precise, and understandable sense. The business idea should answer the questions (in one sentence):

a) What do we do? (Product, service or experience)
b) For whom? (Target group/customer/user)
c) Where? (Market/geographic area/location)
d) Why? (What need do we meet? Why do we exist? What is our purpose?)

Answers are compiled into a brief and clear business idea consisting of one to two sentences. Every word should be carefully considered and coordinated. Examples of business idea statements of a lunch restaurant: a) We will offer tasty snacks prepared from clean, ecologically traceable

13 Ingebrigt Steen Jensen is a Norwegian advertiser and author.

ingredients, b) to young adults who are conscious of good taste and a healthy lifestyle, c) in a relaxed and stylish atmosphere centrally in London, d) a place where they can enjoy the food with a good conscience and know that we support fair trade and sustainable use of resources. Overall, it will be as follows: We will offer tasty snacks prepared from clean, ecologically traceable ingredients, to young adults who are conscious of good taste and a healthy lifestyle, in a relaxed and stylish atmosphere in Central London, a place where they can enjoy the food with a good conscience and know that we support fair trade and sustainable use of resources.

*Business concept:* The business idea may be further expanded to provide a more complete and detailed explanation, included a business model. It can be called business concept and should begin with the business idea itself (3.5 Business model).


1 Initiation
2 Insight
3 Strategy
4 Design
5 Production
6 Management

3.1 Strategy development
3.2 Overall strategy
3.3 Goals and subgoals
3.4 Business strategy
3.5 Business model
3.6 Market strategy
3.7 Brand strategy
3.8 Communication strategy
3.9 Design strategy

3.2.1 Purpose
3.2.2 Mission
3.2.3 Business idea
3.2.4 Vision
3.2.5 Core values
3.2.6 Value proposition
3.2.7 The value pyramid
3.2.8 Business innovation
3.2.9 Strategic narrative

- The purpose of vision
- How to formulate a vision?
- Changing the vision


## 3.2.4 Vision

The vision is the company's dream for the future. It is the guiding star the company should follow. It is defined as part of an overall strategy when starting a new business, or when the company needs a new initiative and wants to change course.

For many companies, the concept of vision can be both confusing and undefinable to relate to. Should it be a goal or not? Should it be a dream? If so: do we have a dream? 'Sometimes it is difficult to distinguish between visions and overall goals. Visions tend to be more of a wishful dream, while overall goals to a greater extent express concrete results one wishes to achieve' (Knudsen and Flåten 2015). According to Jensen (2002)[13] a vision can be compared to a lighthouse that blinks in the distance and helps us stay on course. That sends rays of light to us when it's dark and cold, and no one really knows what's going on until we see the light: There it is! That's where we are going! Not to the lighthouse but far past it. A vision should therefore not be measurable; it should not even be fulfilled. It should give us the power to always want to go a little further'. Developing a vision is about finding answers to the following crucial questions: Why do we exist? Why do we go to work? Why do we play a part? The vision should be the answer, in a short and energising sentence that creates commitment and motivation. A good example is Walt Disney's original vision for Disneyland: 'A place where parents and children could have fun together' (Schmidt, 2018). In other words 'To make people happy'. It means that each and every one of those who work at Disney should think: 'I want to make people happy'. A vision should be brief. It is supposed to give energy and give us direction. It should be a rallying cry, you should be able to – yes, more than that, you should want to – stand on the chair and shout out loud: I WANT TO MAKE PEOPLE HAPPY!!! (Jensen, 2002).

Further reading
***The Vision-Driven Leader: 10 Questions to Focus Your Efforts, Energize Your Team, and Scale Your Business*** **(2020) by Michael Hyatt.**

> The vision is our guiding star, our dream of the future! For an industry a good example of vision could be 'ZERO EMISSIONS'.

### The purpose of vision

The vision is a dream to contribute and do something meaningful, which does not necessarily have anything to do with profit but is linked to other values or philosophies. Dreams *can* come true if you work purposefully. That is what lies in the vision. This dream is the butterflies in the entrepreneur's stomach when they start their business, and it is important to convey this dream to all employees in order for them to feel the same commitment and understand the meaning of their work. All goals and milestones set by the company should be aimed at the vision (3.3 Goals and subgoals).

A vision should be visionary, a look into the future. It should guide the company like a beacon that shows the way. The company should be *driven* by the vision. The vision should provide a framework for the choices the company makes. It is intended to give meaning, direction, and power within the company for its employees, and to help everyone who works in and for the company join forces and move in the same direction. It should also be meaningful for customers, partners and others. Therefore, the vision is also an important starting point for developing slogans or core messages (3.8.6 Communication elements, 3.8.7 Communications development).

Tips for the company

**The vision gives direction, while it is not some achievable goal.**

Tips for the designer

**'Defining core values is mostly about elimination. The power of choosing core values lies in the fact that they must be few and weighed very carefully. The challenge is not to choose values we can live with, but values we cannot live without' (Jensen, 2002).**

**'Through it all, Walt Disney World in general, and the Magic Kingdom in particular, has remained true to Walt Disney's original vision for Disneyland: That it would be a place where parents and children could have fun' (Schmidt, 2018).**

### How to formulate a vision?

The vision can be developed during a strategic workshop. Employees, managers, and owners must ask themselves the question: What do we want and hope the company to become, achieve, or accomplish? What drives us forward, provides motivation and energy? What gives the feeling of doing something meaningful, profitable, innovative, or revolutionary? What should be our guiding star to show us the way? Words and thoughts are discussed and sifted time and time again until there remains an essence that serves as the basis for formulating the vision. In the process, there will be suggestions that should rather be regarded as goals. These can be useful in the development of goals for the company. Often, it can be an advantage to start with goals before working on the vision.

### Examples of vision

**IKEA**: 'To create a better everyday life for the many people' (ikea.com 2022).
**Nike**: 'To bring inspiration and innovation to every athlete in the world' (about.nike.com 2022).[14]
**Nasa**: 'To discover and expand knowledge for the benefit of humanity' (nasa.gov).

The vision is formulated in one short and precise sentence, which makes sense and is charged with power, motivation, and inspiration, a phrase that is easy to pronounce and easy to remember. Visionary messages are often too dry. Whether it is a matter of common goals and subgoals or vision, they are often focused on market share, growth and profit. Such goals can hardly inspire or motivate and are hardly easy to remember. In order for a vision to guide actions in everyday life, it should be formulated so that employees remember it. Just as our brain stores memories from way back in time, our brain can store memories that lie ahead of us in time. It uses the so-called representation systems. It is easier for the brain to store memories if they can represent or be associated with something visible, or audible, or something that tastes or smells, or something that touches us emotionally (Knudsen & Flåten 2015) and creates commitment. In order to create commitment and support for a vision, its message should be associated with something exciting and

14 'If you have a body, you are an athlete' (about.nike.com 2022).
15 The THRIVE Project is a UN affiliated research group. A not-for-profit research, education and advocacy group, based in Australia. THRIVE helps people and entities measure, analyse and improve their strategies, guiding society towards a thrivable future: strive2thrive.earth/about/.

truly challenging, and give the employees the feeling of building the company, being part of something significant of creating something of importance together, going to work every day having this feeling.

An important leadership task is thus to help co-workers experience what it is like to be involved in something significant. Therefore, all employees could benefit from participating in developing the vision. This way, they own it and the business can be built and developed from the inside out.


1 Initiation
2 Insight
3 Strategy
4 Design
5 Production
6 Management

3.1 Strategy development
3.2 Overall strategy
3.3 Goals and subgoals
3.4 Business strategy
3.5 Business model
3.6 Market strategy
3.7 Brand strategy
3.8 Communication strategy
3.9 Design strategy

3.2.1 Purpose
3.2.2 Mission
3.2.3 Business idea
3.2.4 Vision
3.2.5 Core values
3.2.6 Value proposition
3.2.7 The value pyramid
3.2.8 Business innovation
3.2.9 Strategic narrative

- Personality
- Corporate identity
- Value-driven culture
- Choice of values
- How to explain core values?
- How to develop core values?


#### Changing the vision

It is never too late for a company to change their vision. A new vision can help breathe life into and bring new commitment to a company that has been around for years and perhaps has forgotten why it exists. A new vision is particularly needed when a company wants to reorient itself, reverse a negative trend, or get something more out of existing resources. Having employees involved in the process of developing the vision is crucial for them to gain ownership to it. The developement of a new vision will have to be followed up internally in order for everyone in the company to focus on a new direction in mindset and work method.

### 3.2.5 Core values

Who are we? That is what we should communicate to our customers and stakeholders! It is defined in our core values. Value is a positively charged word, associated with characteristics and abilities that a company fully relies on in order to succeed. Choosing values for the company is a strategic choice that will help drive the company towards the vision. Companies that unite around clearly stated common core values have clear opinions about what should govern their choices and actions, and how these values should contribute to creating a positive impression of the company externally in the market and internally in the company (Jensen, 2002). Value means 'the quality of something; what is good about something. The value of a thing is said to determine its importance with regard to how we should form our judgements and decisions' (Sagdahl, n.d.).

#### Personality

Values are identity, and identity is values. Our values govern our choices and actions and make us the people we are and are perceived to be. Our inherent values are at the heart of our personality. To put it simply, a personality can be explained by the attributes that are characteristic of the individual: a sum of the individual's thoughts, actions, and feelings.

Personality is what sets a person apart: a result of nature and nurture. Identity is linked to personality but can also be perceived as something that emerges from an interaction between people within specific social and cultural systems. If a person has qualities that can be defined as *friendly*, *knowledgeable*, and *energetic*, they are likely to be reflected in this person's behaviour and identity. An *energetic* person is one who chooses to act when necessary, something which will be visible to those around them. So, although few people have a clear relationship to their core values, these values will still be reflected in their behaviour and actions. Those who are conscious of their values will also be able to use their attributes in a more targeted way.

THRIVE's vision:
Our vision is a world where all living forms live in harmony and solidarity with each other, in the pursuit of global shared value creation and collective collaborative peaceful partnerships for people, planet, profit with purpose and prosperity.[15]

THRIVE's slogan:
Measuring what matters most (strive2thrive.earth).

Just as a person has personality and identity, we can say that a company has special characteristics and values similar to personality traits. A company will never be a person, but by comparing the values of the company with typical personal traits, one can create real values. Personalising the company is a widely used method to arrive at real values, well suited as a starting point for brainstorming during a workshop, to arrive at the company's core values.

*Personality* is the backdrop of the identity. Personality is the characteristic traits that give a person their individual character. In psychology, personality can be explained by a person's characteristic pattern of thoughts, actions, and feelings. Personality includes a person's attributes, such as needs, temperament, abilities, habits, attitudes, values, interests, self-perception and typical behaviour. These attributes are often called personality traits. A personality can be described as the composite image of all personality traits of a person (Malt, 2016). Identity is other people's perception of one's personality. Personality can be expressed through core values.

Fig. 3.4 **The figure shows the four elements of a corporate identity: product, behaviour, symbol, and communication. They emerge from the core values of the company which are at the heart and govern all choices and actions of the company. A good correlation between the four factors gives a clear picture or image, in the market – a strong identity. It is important for building knowledge, position, and corporate branding. The core values (personality) are the heart. Based on Birkigt and Stadler (1986) and Cees van Riel (1996). Further developed by Karlsen, H. (1999), and Grimsgaard (2018).**

Tips for the designer

**The core values are defined in the overall strategy and are a key starting point for developing a visual identity (logo, symbol, and other identity elements).**

Tips for the company

**When successfully implemented, the company's core values guide the organisation's attitudes and behaviours and form the basis for a healthy organisational culture and a clear and strong corporate identity.**

### Corporate identity

A company is an interconnection of a multitude of individuals and personalities. The core values are important for clarifying the typical attributes that should emerge in visual and verbal communication, and for creating a corporate identity. When developing core values, the question is whether the values should represent the intrinsic values of the company, or whether they should be designed on the basis of how the company wishes to appear, or a combination of both. Brønn and Ihlen (2009) distinguish between organisational identity and corporate identity. The organisational identity are the inner values of the company, the ones that come from the people who work there and the conscious or unconscious culture that arises. The corporate identity is the constructed identity which the management develops and presents externally in order to make the company appear as attractive and up to date as possible. 'Organisational identity is "who and what we are", and corporate identity is "who and what we say we are"' (Brønn and Ihlen, 2009). Definition of what should be the corporate identity is the core of the company's overall strategy, and is most strongly expressed through its core values. The responsibility of defining the corporate identity lies with the company's managers, owners and board of directors, who prepare it in collaboration with their advisers, consultants, and employees, well anchored in the organisational identity. 'The company's profile - that is, the way the company is perceived by all stakeholders - is created through everything the company says and does in all contexts. A positive corporate profile is therefore not created through 'PR measures' alone. The company profile is formed as a result of the company's identity - that is, what the company *is* in a more actual and real sense. The company's identity appears as *a sum* of everything the company says and does' (Helgesen, 1998). A corporate identity can emerge as a result of unconscious actions and patterns, or it can be formed consciously; ideally, as a combination of the inherent

**'Values have no particular significance when viewed outside the context. It is when they are used to support the company's purpose that their meaning becomes clear and effective' (Annweiler, 2017).**

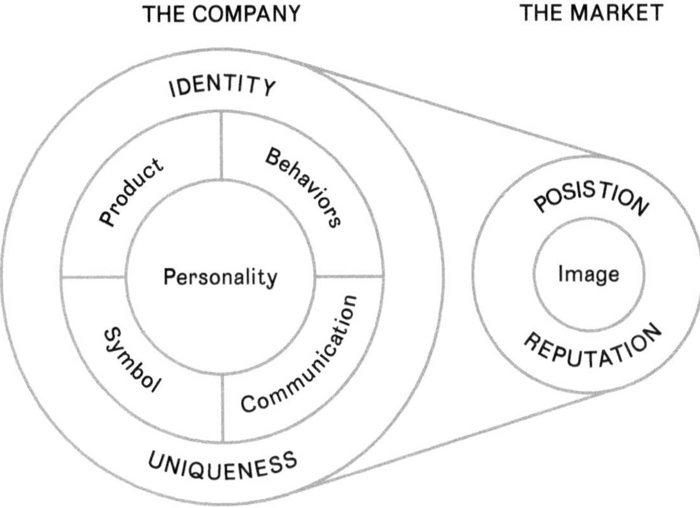


Fig. 3.4 Corporate identity


1 Initiation
2 Insight
3 Strategy
4 Design
5 Production
6 Management

3.1 Strategy development
3.2 Overall strategy
3.3 Goals and subgoals
3.4 Business strategy
3.5 Business model
3.6 Market strategy
3.7 Brand strategy
3.8 Communication strategy
3.9 Design strategy

3.2.1 Purpose
3.2.2 Mission
3.2.3 Business idea
3.2.4 Vision
3.2.5 Core values
3.2.6 Value proposition
3.2.7 The value pyramid
3.2.8 Business innovation
3.2.9 Strategic narrative

- Personality
- Corporate identity
- Value-driven culture
- Choice of values
- How to explain core values?
- How to develop core values?


values of the company and the values that the company wants to live by and stand with. Figure 3.4 shows an example of the elements that determine the company's identity, originally derived from Birkigt and Stadler (1986): 'The key element is *personality*, meaning a conscious, governing entity which determines what is to happen in the other four dimensions (behaviour, communication, symbolism and product). By *behaviour*, we understand all the physical dimensions of the company, such as buildings, products, employees, service and so on. By *communication*, we understand all the physical dimensions of the company, such as people, actions, attitudes, service, interactions, and so on. *The symbolism* that stands out through the name, logo and visual presentation of the company'. Finally, the forth element, *product*, was further implemented in the model by Karlsen (1999) meaning the company's deliveries in the form of products, services, experiences, etc.

A strong identity can be compared to a solid person which for a company means that it appears holistic and consistent in all contexts. It presupposes that the four elements shown in Figure 3.4, both individually and collectively, express the company's identity the way the company wishes to appear. A strong and clear identity is a competitive advantage and a success factor in standing out from competitors and creating a clear position in the market (2.1.3 Organisational culture, 2.1.4 Organisation development).

Brand consistency
To be consistent means acting or appearing in the same way every time and over time, so that one is easily recognised. For a company, consistency is crucial for building identity and brand awareness. It presupposes that the company is able to 'maintain communication and positioning in line with its values and the elements that make up its identity' (rockcontent.com 2020).

### Value-driven culture

Corporate culture (organisational culture) refers to the collective mindset and behaviours of the people in the company. Corporate culture is an organisation's values, ethics, behaviours and work environment. The success of a company depends to a large extent on a healthy culture. It affects how employees and management interact and handle outside business transactions, service, etc. The culture may be shaped intentionally, but often 'it is implied, not expressly defined, and develops organically over time from the cumulative traits of the people the company hires' (Tarver,

2021). It can also be influenced by external factors, such as economic conditions, the size of the company and national or global trends. Whether the culture is intended or emerged it affects all facets of a business, such as internal climate and working conditions, employees' external behaviour towards customers and ultimately it influences the company's image and reputation. Therefore, corporate culture is an essential issue for the management and employees of the companies. The first concept of corporate culture came on the agenda in the 1980s[16] and since then there are numerous examples and approaches to corporate cultures.

'Value-based organizational culture is a culture in which successful leaders' practice by modeling the behaviours that create that desired organizational culture' (Davidoff, 2019). According to Richard Barret "values-driven cultures are typically consciously created (...) the leader and the leadership team actively live the values of the organization (Barret, 2017). According to (Davidoff, 2019) 'experts speak to values as a fundamental component in understanding an organization's culture'. How to create a value-based organisational culture is ideally to observe practised values through measurement and/or observation of actual behaviours. 'Changing organizational culture then requires behavioural change demonstrating the practice of desired values' (Davidoff, 2019).

Tips for the designer
**The company's culture is based on its core values.**

Tips for the company
**Be sure to involve employees in the process when developing core values for the company.**

> **'Businesses that treat employees well during the toughest of times will attract talent, even when the war for talent heats up' (Fortune, 2021).[17]**

### Choice of values

The core values are the attributes describing the company's typical character traits and personality. These are *the emotional* attributes, the ones that govern the company's behaviour, actions, and choices. The core values are defined through a set of adjectives, usually three to five words or terms, which tell what the company is and wants to be. The value words chosen should complement each other so that they can represent the personality as a whole. For a company, it is important to define values that one can be proud of, and that are important for the way in which the company operates and is perceived. It can be tempting to choose value words that best reflect the customers' and the society's demands for good values. But most importantly, is that the values represent the company's actual values and attitudes. For example, one should not choose value words like innovative, customer-centric, and sustainable simply because they sound good and are words that sell. Values must be consistent with the overall ethical principles that both the company's employees and the management have.

A major European survey conducted in 2006 showed that many companies described themselves using fine words to present their core values, such as innovative, ethical, sustainable, reliable, and quality-conscious. 'Apparently, it looked like the values one was furthest away from often were the ones that ended up at the top of the poster' (Lydersen, 2006).[18] Of course, the company may choose values that say something about how they *want* to be perceived, but they have to commit to them if they want to be taken seriously. This also assumes that they live by their value choices which are reflected in their behaviour and actions. Consequences of value choices are about proving/showing who you are. If one of the core values is 'smart', it should be expressed through intelligent and innovative products or services. If one of the core values is 'caring', it should be expressed through good service, good working conditions and user-friendly products or services. If one of the core values is 'bold',

16 **'The term corporate culture developed in the early 1980s and became widely known by the 1990s. Corporate culture was used during those periods by managers, sociologists, and other academics to describe the character of a company. This included generalised beliefs and behaviours, company-wide value systems, management strategies, employee communication, and relations, work environment, and attitude' (Tarver, 2021).**

17 **From the *Fortune* magazine's list ranking of '100 Best Companies to Work For.'**

18 **5,000 companies had their values thoroughly examined in a major international survey in 11 countries (10 European and US) conducted by the ECCO International Communications Network, in the study 'First International Corporate Value Index 2006'. A recent study is 'Ecco Network Corporate Values Index 2013', available at issuu.**

it should be expressed through non-traditional solutions and efforts. The core values are a key factor in developing the visual identity of the company and its products or services (2.1.1 Value creation).


1 Initiation
2 Insight
3 Strategy
4 Design
5 Production
6 Management

3.1 Strategy development
3.2 Overall strategy
3.3 Goals and subgoals
3.4 Business strategy
3.5 Business model
3.6 Market strategy
3.7 Brand strategy
3.8 Communication strategy
3.9 Design strategy

3.2.1 Purpose
3.2.2 Mission
3.2.3 Business idea
3.2.4 Vision
3.2.5 Core values
3.2.6 Value proposition
3.2.7 The value pyramid
3.2.8 Business innovation
3.2.9 Strategic narrative

- Personality
- Corporate identity
- Value-driven culture
- Choice of values
- How to explain core values?
- How to develop core values?


### How to explain core values?

Here's a simple way to explain core values:

- What is in your passport? Answer: Your name, personal ID number, height, hair colour, etc.
- What is NOT in your passport? Answer: Your personal qualities and values.
- What are your main qualities (adjectives)? Answer: Caring, wise, creative.
- These qualities are your core values.

A company's identity can be compared to that of a person. A person's identity can be verified by a personal ID number, just as a company's identity can be verified by a company organisation number, a product can be verified by an EAN code and a book by its ISBN number. But the numbers say little about the qualities and distinctive features of 'the person' in question. These are found in the core values as a set of values that describe the attributes, characteristics and distinctive features of the person, company, product, or service.

Often, the company's products or services should reflect the company's values, while at the same time, these products or services should have values of their own that express their specific attributes. Here is an example of a) the core values of a company that makes jewellery; b) the core values of a jewellery brand that the company sells:

| a) **Company:** | b) **Product:** |
|---|---|
| Genuine | Quality-conscious |
| Conscious | Design-conscious |
| Experienced | Self-conscious |

### How to develop core values?

Value words are defined through a brainstorming process where the goal is to come up with as many values as possible that can be associated with or that can explain one's personality.

*Development*: The values chosen should express different aspects of one's personality and should be prioritised based on their importance. Start by listing a wide range of adjectives that describe the attributes and characteristics of the company. Write as many adjectives as you can think of that represent the attributes and distinctive features which are, or which you want to be typical of your company (the product or service):

- If you could only select one value word to describe the company's attributes which one would it be? Underline it.
- If you could select a second value word to describe the company's attributes which one would it be? Underline it.
- If you could only select a third value word to describe the company's attributes which one would it be? Underline it.

*Processing:* Pick three to five value words which together explain the identity with the greatest possible breath. List the selected value words in a priority order. Consider whether the value words complement each other and whether they cover the qualities and characteristics that emerge from the business idea and vision. Check out synonyms and consider if there are

Further reading
'Values-Driven Organization. Cultural Health and Employee Well-Being as a Pathway to Sustainable Performance' by Richard Barrett, 2017.

If you want to succeed in building a bridge between strategy and design, you have to create a culture for it in the business.

any other adjectives to explain the identity better. Explain each value word in one sentence or use words from the brainstorming that have not been used. Make the necessary adjustment to create as comprehensive and broad a picture of the personality as possible. Example of three value word:
Smart: Knowledgeable, curious, and innovative.
- Enthusiastic: Happy, dynamic, and energetic.
- Empathetic: Friendly, understanding, and helpful.
Note: The order of the value words affects the overall perception.

*Visualisation*: A good way to convey the core values of the design process is to develop a moodboard for each of the values. This way, the values are visualised through elements, shapes, typography and colours that can be used as inspiration when developing the logo and visual identity, bridging strategy and design (2.8.2 Moodboard, 4.2 Strategy><Design). Note: If the values are inconsistent with the company's attributes and characteristics, and not least in relation to their desired position, the visual identity created based on the values may take a completely wrong direction. It is like taking a personality test and and giving wrong answers to all the questions; you become another person (4.2.2 Visualise strategy: Visualise values).

*How to express the core values*? The core values' transformation from strategy to design is about asking questions such as: What shape does the word have, what font does it have, what colour, what sound, what smell, what feeling? Assume that 'sociable' is one of the values the company chooses. It will clearly have a lot to say for their behaviour and service. The question will be how it can be expressed visually and verbally. The visual shape is certainly not stiff and angular, but rather soft and round. The typeface is probably not a heavy Grotesk Bold, rather an Antikva with friendly shapes, rounded serifs, and a light, open expression. The colours are probably not dark and heavy, but rather cheerful and fresh. The tone of voice is not formal and cold, but merry and bright. The choice of words will be pleasant and jovial, perhaps in an informal tone. The smell is warm, and the feeling is safe and happy.

Fig. 3.5 The figure shows the Value Proposition Canvas. It consists of two main fields. The field on the right is the customers' (or user's) needs, benefits and profit from the company's products or services. The field on the left is what the company offers and promises the customer. Right side: *Customer needs* ('Jobs to be done'): What does the customer want to do, perform or buy? *Pain*: What does the customer find annoying and unfavourable? *Gain*: What is the positive result the customer envisions? Left side: *Pain reliever*: How to ease the customers' negative experience? *Gain creator*: How to meet the customers' needs? *Products and services*: What can the company promise to deliver that meets the customers' needs? The figure is by Osterwalder 2012, www. strategyzer.com.

A value proposition can be used as a basis for creating a positioning strategy. 'Strategy is based on a differentiated customer value proposition. Satisfying customers is the source of sustainable value creation' (Kaplan and Norton 2004).

### 3.2.6 Value proposition

What do we promise? That is what we should communicate to our customers and stakeholders! It is defined in our value proposition. The value proposition is what the company promises its customers, employees, and partners, what the company will deliver and will be measured by. Value proposition, also called customer promise, should be the company's seal of approval and is a central management tool within the company. Making a promise is a serious matter. In principle, the word 'promise' is a legal term related to laws and rules which implies both conditions and obligations. A promise is a declaration that binds and is to be honoured in accordance with the conditions that have been outlined. A breach of promise is a serious incident that creates distrust. For a company, the consequences of a breach of promise can result in a bad reputation. Promises kept can create trust, loyalty, and solid long-term customer relationships.

*Choice of promise*: The choice of promise is made based on the *rational attributes* of the company, in contrast to the core values, which are based on the *emotional attributes* of the company. They should tell the outside world what the company actually does and how competent

19 Unique can be understood to be delimited within a specific category, context or arena.

20 The Value Proposition Canvas is created by Alex Osterwalder (2012), inventor of the Business Model Canvas, and co-author of Business Model Generation with Yves Pigneur.

its people are. These are values that are important, measurable, and that give clear competitive advantage. The company may make promises for various purposes, but a main promise, which should be the most important one, should be chosen. The main promise should be something the company is best or unique at,[19] something the company does better than others, to meet market needs. The promise is therefore a good starting point for clarifying what the main competitive advantage and the basis for a positioning strategy should be (3.4.1 Competitive strategy, 3.7.3 Brand position). If the company wants to tell its customers what it promises, it can for example be expressed through a value propostion which can be included in their core message or through a slogan. An example is IKEA's value proposition 'Low prices'. 'In order to make it possible to keep prices low, the set-up should involve a high degree of self-service; customers should be able to do everything online. In the shop, they collect the parts in stock and assemble everything on their own. This lays the foundations for IKEA's customer relationship. Such a customer relationship is not negative because it is something customers expect and whose background they understand' (Innovation Norway).

The promise is not just about what a company promises its customers. It is just as much about what it promises to its employees, stakeholders, collaborators, the press, and community actors like the public sector, the government and society. If, for example, an activity involves some form of noise, environmental emissions, traffic, etc., it may be necessary to make a promise to the residents in the area that the activity will not have an impact on their living situation and quality of life. Thus, promises can also be linked to societal responsibility and sustainability goals. The promises are what we will deliver, and based on our delivery, we will be measured. Promises trigger expectations and instil trust and loyalty when fulfilled. It is a success factor. The question is: What can we promise that is unique and that sets us apart from our competitors? A unique promise can be used as a position.

### Value Proposition Canvas

Value Proposition Canvas (Osterwalder, 2012)[20] is a tool that can be used to arrive at the company's value proposition, by focusing on how the company can help meet its customers' needs and make their everyday life easier. It is about finding out why the customer needs a product or

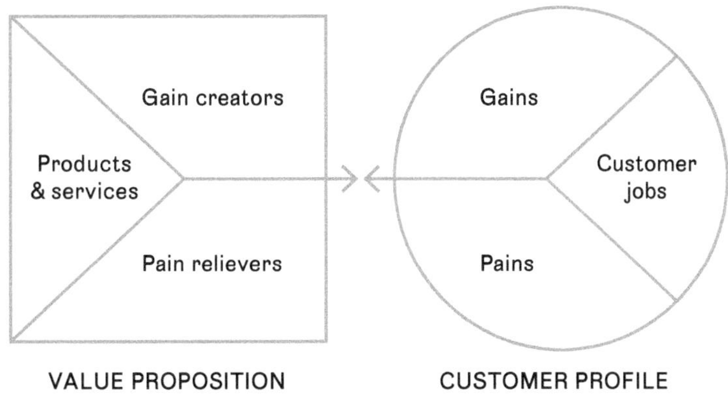


Fig. 3.5 Value Proposition Canvas


1 Initiation
2 Insight
3 Strategy
4 Design
5 Production
6 Management

3.1 Strategy development
3.2 Overall strategy
3.3 Goals and subgoals
3.4 Business strategy
3.5 Business model
3.6 Market strategy
3.7 Brand strategy
3.8 Communication strategy
3.9 Design strategy

3.2.1 Purpose
3.2.2 Mission
3.2.3 Business idea
3.2.4 Vision
3.2.5 Core values
3.2.6 Value proposition
3.2.7 The value pyramid
3.2.8 Business innovation
3.2.9 Strategic narrative

– Value Proposition Canvas


Further reading

– Value Proposition Design: How to Create Products and Services Customers Want (The Strategyzer Series) by Alexander Osterwalder, Yves Pigneur, et al. 2014.

– Check out: strategyzer.com/books/value-proposition-design.

a service (their jobs to be done),[21] what the customer finds annoying or unfavourable (pains) and what the customer can perceive as added value (gains). This approach uses elements from behavioural psychology and design thinking (4.3.11 Design thinking). According to Osterwalder, a company's *Value Proposition* is what sets it apart from its competitors. The value proposition brings value through various factors such as novelty, performance, design, brand, status, price, cost reduction, risk reduction, accessibility and convenience, and user-friendliness.[22]

Value propositions can include both quantitative and qualitative factors. Quantitative value propositions may, for example, be about price and efficiency, and qualitative value propositions may be about customer experience and benefit. The method is suitable for workshops, in that it can be drawn up on whiteboards and provides input with Post-it notes, see Figure 3.5. The starting point should be real information obtained through conversations with customers and by observing the market. By writing down the answers, categorising and prioritising using the canvas, one can get a clearer picture of how the business can best serve its customers. The result may form the basis for new products or services.

Fig. 3.6 a) The figure shows the value pyramid which is a method of arriving at a value proposition for the company or its products and services. The method is well suited for brainstorming sessions during a strategic workshop.

Tips for the designer
The company's emotional attributes can be used to define the core values. The rational attributes can be used to define its value promises. The rational attributes govern what the company does; the emotional attributes govern the way it does it. It is the combination that creates the distinctive features.

Unique
What do we mean by being unique? The business can be unique in different ways, through business idea, value proposition, brand identity or other. Although a value proposition or a visual element is generic, one can have ownership and be unique in a given context or category.
For example, Red Cross. A red cross is generic, but in the context it is used it is unique in the category; in addition, *they* own the symbol quite naturally through the name.

### 3.2.7 The value pyramid

The value pyramid is a method for arriving at rational values and unique characteristics the company can promise its customers to deliver on, see Figure 3.6 a). It is well suited for brainstorming sessions during a strategic workshop. The value pyramid is drawn on a whiteboard or flip chart. Participants attach Post-it notes with value words proposals on the pyramid. 'It goes without saying' are attributes that most companies in the same industry can offer. 'Best in class' are attributes the company is best at. 'Unique' are attributes only the company has. The unique can be used as a basis for choosing an overall customer promise and creating a value proposition. The choice of *rational values* and *emotional values* can be developed in a workshop, using the value cabal.

#### The value cabal

The choice of core values (emotional attributes) and value promises (rational attributes) can be made using the value cabal in a strategic workshop, see Figure 3.6 b). B and C are drawn separately one by one on a whiteboard or flip chart. All participants write value words on yellow Post-it notes and attach them to the board or write with markers directly on the board. The meeting leader directs the process and sorts the input in collaboration with the participants. One starts with a jumble of words in A, then one picks words from A and attaches them to B, then one selects words from A and B and attach to C.

**a) Personality (all attributes):** Here, we list our role models, heroes, and our best qualities/values. Complete one or more of the following exercises:

1) How can we describe the company as a person? By gender, age, occupation, family, friends, car, favourite colour, hobby, etc. What do friends and family say about the person?
2) Which celebrities do we compare ourselves to? What characterises them?

21 'Jobs to be done' (JTBD) is a theory based on the idea that people buy products and services to get jobs done.
22 Value proposition: A value proposition is a promise of value to be delivered, communicated, and acknowledged. It is also a belief from the customer about how value will be delivered, experienced and acquired. A value proposition can apply to an entire organisation, or parts thereof, or customer accounts, or products or services ('Value proposition,' n.d.).

3) What personal qualities do we have as a company, of which we are proud, and which characterise us and give us distinctiveness?

**b) The core values (the emotional attributes):** Here we collect words from a) and sort and prioritise in order to arrive at our three most essential values. Complete one or more of the following exercises:

1) What *emotional attributes* best characterise us, of which we are proud, and which should govern our behaviour, choices and actions?
2) Pick the three value words (adjectives) that describe us most fully and that should be our core values. Use the other value words to explain these.
3) How can the core values be anchored in the company so that everyone can identify with them and act according to them? How can the core values be used to create a visual identity? (Questions 2 and 3 may be dealt with at a later stage.)

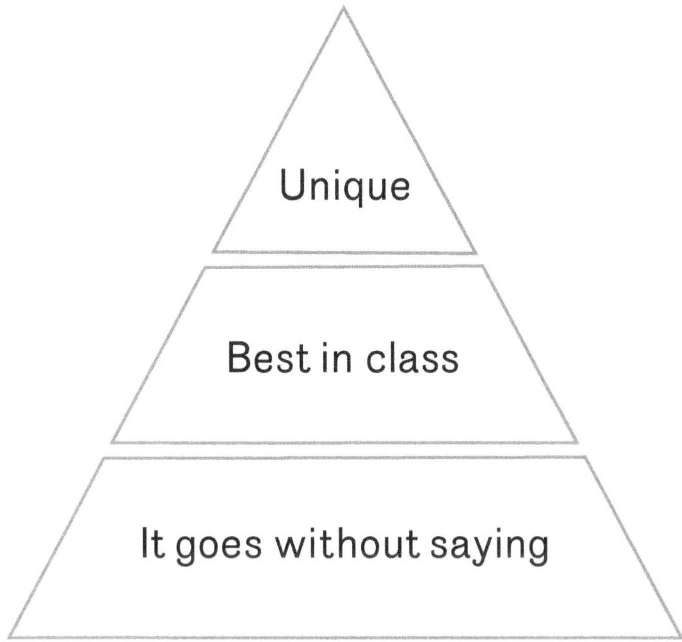


Fig. 3.6 a) The value pyramid

**c) The value promises (the rational attributes):** Pick words from a) and b) that describe our characteristics; the things we are good, best or unique at, and on which we can promise our customers to deliver.

1) Which *rational attributes* best characterise us? What are we good, best, and unique at? Which of these qualities can give us a competitive advantage?
2) What unique property can we promise our customers, employees, stakeholders, partners, the press, the public sector and society in general?
3) How can the value promise be communicated inward within the company as well as to the outside world in a clear and attractive way, as for example as a value proposition, core message or slogan? (Questions 3 may be dealt with at a later stage.)



Further reading
The book *Value Proposition Design* (Osterwalder, 2014) and the website strategyzer.com.

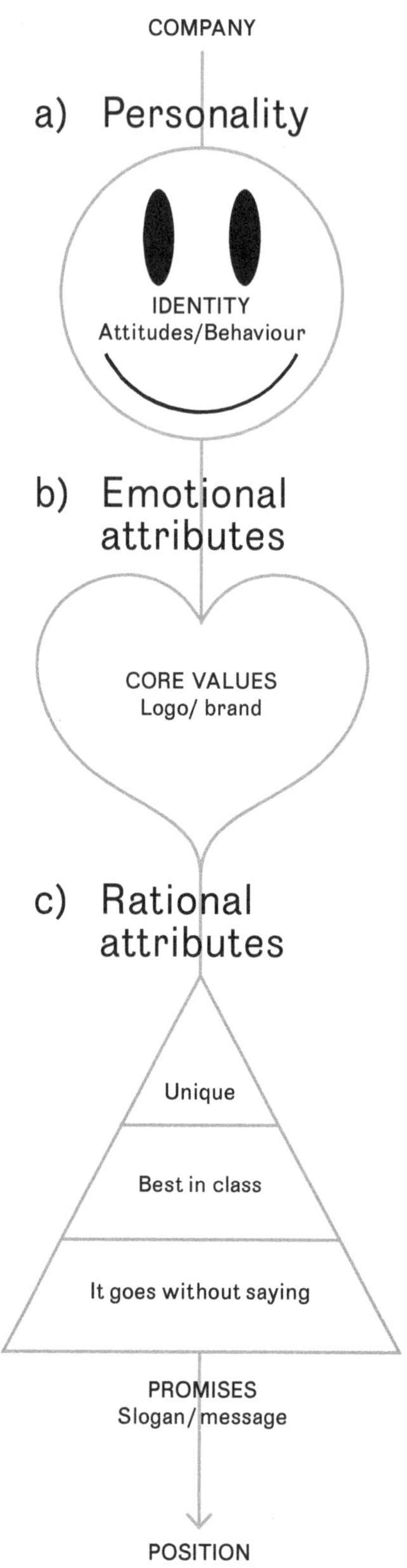

Fig. 3.6 b) The value cabal

Fig. 3.6 b) The figure shows the value cabal, a method for developing core values and value promises that can be implemented at a strategic workshop with participants from the company. The method assumes participation through brainstorming where value words are proposed, processed, and sorted in three steps; a) personality, b) core values and c) value promises. The three fields can be drawn in columns on a whiteboard. © Grimsgaard, W. (2018)

Fig. 3.7 The figure shows: 'Strategic narrative is a virtuous cycle' based on Chakhoyan (2020). Reflect on your story: How compelling and credible is it? What is the level of congruence (consistency or appropriateness) between the words and actions? Adjust how you act: There are two ways to address incongruence. Change what you say or change what you do to stay true to your narrative. Tell your story. In a boardroom or on a public stage. Hear yourself tell it. It is the best way to know if the story resonates. Accept feedback: How is your narrative received by your stakeholders? Embrace pushback and scepticism. That is how you can ensure authenticity and coherence.

Workshop
Use a), b) and c) separately in a physical or digital workshop. Have participants use Post-its to to show their input. The result is co-created.

23 Narrative: 1a): something that is narrated: story, account, b): a way of presenting or understanding a situation or series of events that reflects and promotes a particular point of view or set of values (Narrative, n.d.).
24 'We tend to become the story we tell. This is the starting point for the narrative method' (*Narrative Therapy*, Michael White 2006).
25 Based on the interview with Mathias Haddal Hovet. Read it at designandstrategy.co.uk.

### 3.2.9 Strategic narrative

A typical design approach is to present the strategy as a narrative to make it more accessible. Narrative means 'storytelling', that is, the course of action in a narrative, of Latin *narrare* 'to tell'.[23] 'We tend to become the story we tell' (White, 2006).[24] Most people will hardly think of a strategy as narrative, but herein lies the key to communicating the content in a more accessible way. A strategy dramatised as a narrative can be easier to implement internally in the company among employees and externally among stakeholders than dry facts and fragmented information. The purpose, business strategy and brand strategy, even for those involved from the company, can become comprehensive and difficult to follow, even when they appear as structured points in a strategy document. A good supplement is a narrative, which brings together the strategy key elements in a compelling and credible way. This way it can be easier to understand and use, and not least, it can provide easier access to further development of communication and visual solutions. The strategy can build the story and the story can build the strategy[25] (3.7.4 Brand story, 3.4.9 Strategy implementation).

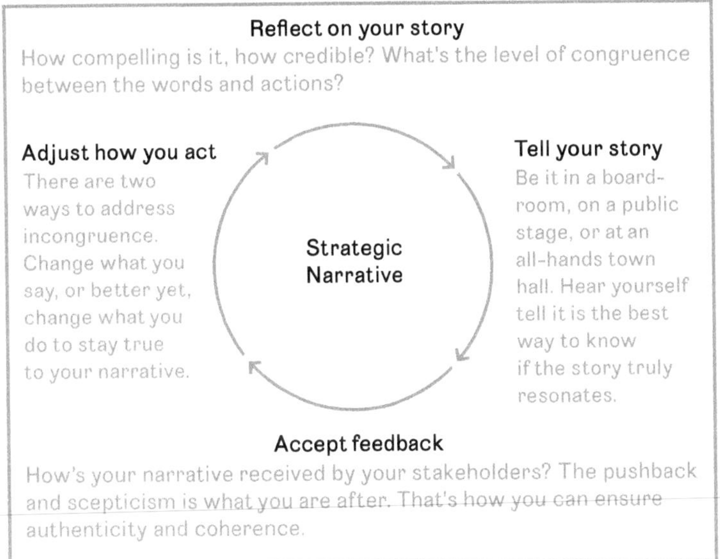
Reflect on your story
How compelling is it, how credible? What's the level of congruence between the words and actions?
Adjust how you act
There are two ways to address incongruence. Change what you say, or better yet, change what you do to stay true to your narrative.
Strategic Narrative
Tell your story
Be it in a board-room, on a public stage, or at an all-hands town hall. Hear yourself tell it is the best way to know if the story truly resonates.
Accept feedback
How's your narrative received by your stakeholders? The pushback and scepticism is what you are after. That's how you can ensure authenticity and coherence.

It's not what you say, it's what you do.

Fig. 3.7 Strategic narrative

### 3.3 Goals and subgoals

A goal is a desired situation which is based on a defined current situation. For the company, goals guide the choice of strategy and all measures they implement.

A design project should contribute to the achievement of goals for the company, while it is also necessary to define a goal for the design project. Goals indicate a future condition, a direction, and a desired situation, what results you want to achieve. It is a matter of where you want to be, based

Strategyic narrative
'It is not what you say, it's what you do' (Chakhoyan).

on where you are. That is why you should know the present situation. This can be done through a situational analysis (2.7.1 Situational analysis). The starting point is the current situation, the goal is the desired situation.

For the company, goals are a future ambition and direction for the choice of strategy. It can be a desire to take a particular position, take greater market shares, increase profits, increase the number of employees, become the greatest, become the best, become a leader, gain increased knowledge and attention, become recognised and famous, achieve honour and glory, save the world and contribute to a better future for all, or other things. Goals can be about market goals for usability, ideological goals, environmental goals, social responsibility, more diversity and so on. Goals can be quantitative and qualitative. Not all goals are measurable, but all represent a direction and require a choice of path. Goals are direction. Choice of path is strategy.

Some goals have no time limit, others are limited in time. Some goals are short-term, others are long-term. Short-term goals should be achieved within a period of time and are often related to long-term directional goals. Goals can be defined, pronounced, or implied. The company may have goals that they have not written down and have not expressed specifically, but which are nevertheless implicit for all employees. For example, it could be a matter of performing better than the neighbouring store. 'Goals can be both explicit (expressed) and implicit (not expressed). Implicit goals, such as when everyone knows what they are working to achieve, but without this being explicitly formulated anywhere, can be as important as explicit goals' (Knudsen & Flåten, 2015).

CURRENT SITUATION

DESIRED SITUATION

Clarify the current situation through situational studies

Decide what we want to accomplish

Fig. 3.8 Desired situation

For a design project, the goal will most often be derived from the company's goals and should help the company achieve these. The goal for a design project defines what the project will do for the company and what level of ambition the project will be at. A high level of ambition presupposes greater use of resources compared to a low level of ambition which determines time use, price and quality. The designer can have their own goals that implicitly govern choices and influence solutions, e.g. it may be related to such things as environmental considerations and sustainability.

### 3.3.1 Business goals

Most companies like to start with one idea, some ambitions, and some thoughts about a goal. Organisations or companies, regardless of kind, should ask themselves: What is the goal of what we do? Where do we want to go? In what direction should we move? To operate without goals and purpose can be both demanding and not very cost-effective. Without

Fig. 3.8 The current situation is: the starting line, the desired situation is the goal. Goals are about where you want to be, based on where you are. It is necessary to know the current situation in order to plan the path to your goal. We are here! We want to go there! How are we going to get there? It is the choice of strategy.

Fig. 3.9 The figure shows how power and effect multiply if everyone in the company is united in pursuing one and the same direction. The model is inspired by Ulf Winther (2017).

Tips for the company
Once insight and knowledge about our current situation are in place, we are able to draw the map and path for the future.

26 Newton's Second Law of motion: 'The acceleration of an object depends on the mass of the object and the amount of force applied' (Glenn Research Senter, nasa.gov). The effect of pulling in the same direction is explained in mechanical physics by Newton's Second Law of motion which states that when a body is affected by forces, it will accelerate in the direction in which the sum of the forces acts (Ormestad 2015, Glenn Research Senter, nasa.gov).
27 The term 'hairy goals' comes from 'Big Hairy Audacious Goal' (BHAG), launched by authors James Collins and Jerry Porras in 1994, in the book Built to Last: Successful Habits of Visionary Companies.

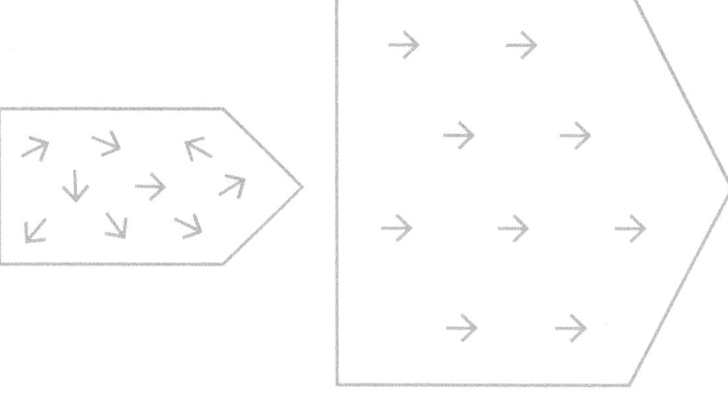

When everyone pulls in different directions, power or propulsion decreases.

The sum of all forces pulling in the same direction gives greater power and momentum.

Fig. 3.9 Pull in the same direction

a clear overarching goal, it becomes difficult to choose a strategy and measure results. It can also cause employees and partners to believe they know the goal or to create their own goals which can lead to going in different directions. If everyone in the company is united around a common goal and pulls in the same direction, they all join forces. It becomes more powerful, see Figure 3.9. Such a force is a success factor in creating targeted results and satisfied employees.[26]

Good results create major ripple effects, such as customer satisfaction, increased competitive power, increased attention and so on. A targeted and successful company stands with a clearer external image and can secure a stronger position (3.3.8 Sustainability goals).

## 3.3.2 Big hairy goals

Many *goals* aim to describe what one hopes to accomplish in the coming days, months, or years. These goals are important for everyone in the company to know what to aim for and to collaborate more effectively. Often, these goals are about growth in turnover and other measurable results, and, of course, this means a lot to those who are concerned with bottom-line results, but to many, it gives little meaning and motivation in their daily work. Goals can represent a sense of compulsion and duty, something to perform and be measured by, and it is not always a motivating factor. The vision should motivate and inspire by being a dream for the future and a guiding star. The problem is that visions can become very vague and not very concrete. What the company may need in addition to a vision is a goal that is big, exciting, and ambitious, almost like a vision, but more achievable and, if possible, measurable; a goal that is within reach but that requires extra work and effort to achieve, a goal that triggers the desire to work and gives job satisfaction. We are talking about hairy goals.[27] 'There are many companies that have big goals, but there are few that have big *hairy* goals; goals that are so big that hair grows on them, that we have to swallow before we dare say them out loud. The companies that change the world dare say it out loud. Henry Ford did it when he said every worker should be able to

> Jim Collins and Jerry Porras created the term BHAG, pronounced Bee-Hag, short for 'Big Hairy Audacious Goal', in their book entitled *Built to Last* (1994). 'BHAG is a powerful way to stimulate progress. A BHAG is clear and compelling, needing little explanation; people get it right away. Think of the NASA moon mission of the 1960s. When an expedition sets out to climb Mount Everest, it doesn't need a three-page, convoluted "mission statement" to explain what Mount Everest is. BHAGs are bold, falling in the grey area where reason and prudence might say "This is unreasonable," but the drive for progress says, "We believe we can do it nonetheless." Again, these aren't just "goals"; these are Big Hairy Audacious Goals' (Jim Collins, Excerpts from *Built to Last*, retrieved 2021 from: jimcollins.com).

afford a car. When he set the goal, there were about fifty cars on the road in America, but now every worker in the United States can afford a car. The American computer industry did it when they said there should be a PC on every desk. It was in the late 70s before most of us had even heard the word PC' (Jensen, 2002). Future settlement on Mars is said to be a hairy goal; SpaceX[28] has embraced it with its ambitious ambition: 'Enable human exploration and settlement of Mars'.

### 3.3.3 Development of goals

If the company has not clarified its goals, the designer can be a good partner in getting this done. It applies to new companies or to companies where the goals are implicitly present but not clearly defined and recorded. It can be a matter of overall goal, competitive goals, market goals, or other goals. A goal is about what you want to achieve, while a strategy is a plan for how to achieve the goal. Therefore, goal is usually defined before strategy, especially in terms of operational planning which requires taking the appropriate measures to achieve a goal. When developing a new business idea, on the other hand, it is more natural to clarify goals after defining the business idea. Therefore, overall goals are often developed in parallel with the overall strategy. According to Lorentzen & Lund (1998), the development of overall business goals is best achieved through strategic planning. This involves *first* clarifying assumptions for future operations, *then* carrying out impact assessments, *and finally* formulating goals. If the consequences are accepted, the goal can be formulated. If not, the process is repeated. In short, it means considering possible goals in terms of how they can be achieved.[29] One way to clarify this is by answering three questions: What do we want to do? What should we do? What can we do? The work on defining the company's overall goal can be done in a strategic workshop with senior management and other decision-makers present, as well as representatives from relevant areas of the organisation. Goals can be sorted hierarchically. For example, will subgoals and operational ones, naturally be defined after the competitive strategy has been defined. The designer, in collaboration with the client, clarifies which goals the design project should contribute to achieve.

### 3.3.4 Goal hierarchy

It may be helpful to create a hierarchy of goals to structure and prioritise the company's goals. An easy way to do this is to define an overall goal and subgoals. The company's overall goal is the very management goal. It is the starting point and the foundation of a strategy (Lien et al., 2016).

The overall goal should usually be developed by the company's management, owners, and board of directors. It can be qualitative or quantitative. The desire to take a larger market share or to become a market leader are typical quantitative measures. If the overall goal is qualitative, it can be attributed a deeper meaning than making money. A qualitative goal often bears the hallmark of a vision. The overall goal is often long term, transparent, and value-oriented, while subgoals are more precise and specify what is meant by the overall goal. Subgoals that are high up in the hierarchy are a form of main goals, such as, e.g.

Fig. 3.10 The figure shows an example of a hierarchy of goals with overall and subgoals. The different main and subgoals may have different market targets and segments. All goals should lead to the overall goal. The overall goal should lead to the vision. The subgoals should explain what the overall goal is, not how it is to be achieved. How the goals should be achieved is defined in the operational strategies. See figure 3.2 Strategy hierarchy.


Tips for the designer

Your own business also needs strategy and goals. Reflect on why your business exists, what you should pursue, what values should govern your behavior and actions, what should be your vision and goals? How can you as a designer use your voice and influence to argue for one more sustainable solutions?

'Goals should be meaningful and carefully thought through in order to represent the company as it is now and as it hopes to be in the years to come' (Mission, 2017).

28 Space Exploration Technologies Corporation, SpaceX, established in 2002 by PayPal and Tesla founder Elon Musk with the goal of creating technology that reduces space travel costs and makes settlement or colonisation on Mars possible ('Space X,' n.d.).

29 As described initially in Phase 3, we can distinguish between strategic planning and operational planning. Strategic planning is carried out in order to clarify or find the goal to work towards, which are the company's overall goal. Operational planning is carried out in order to achieve the overall goal, through development of subgoals and planning of actions.

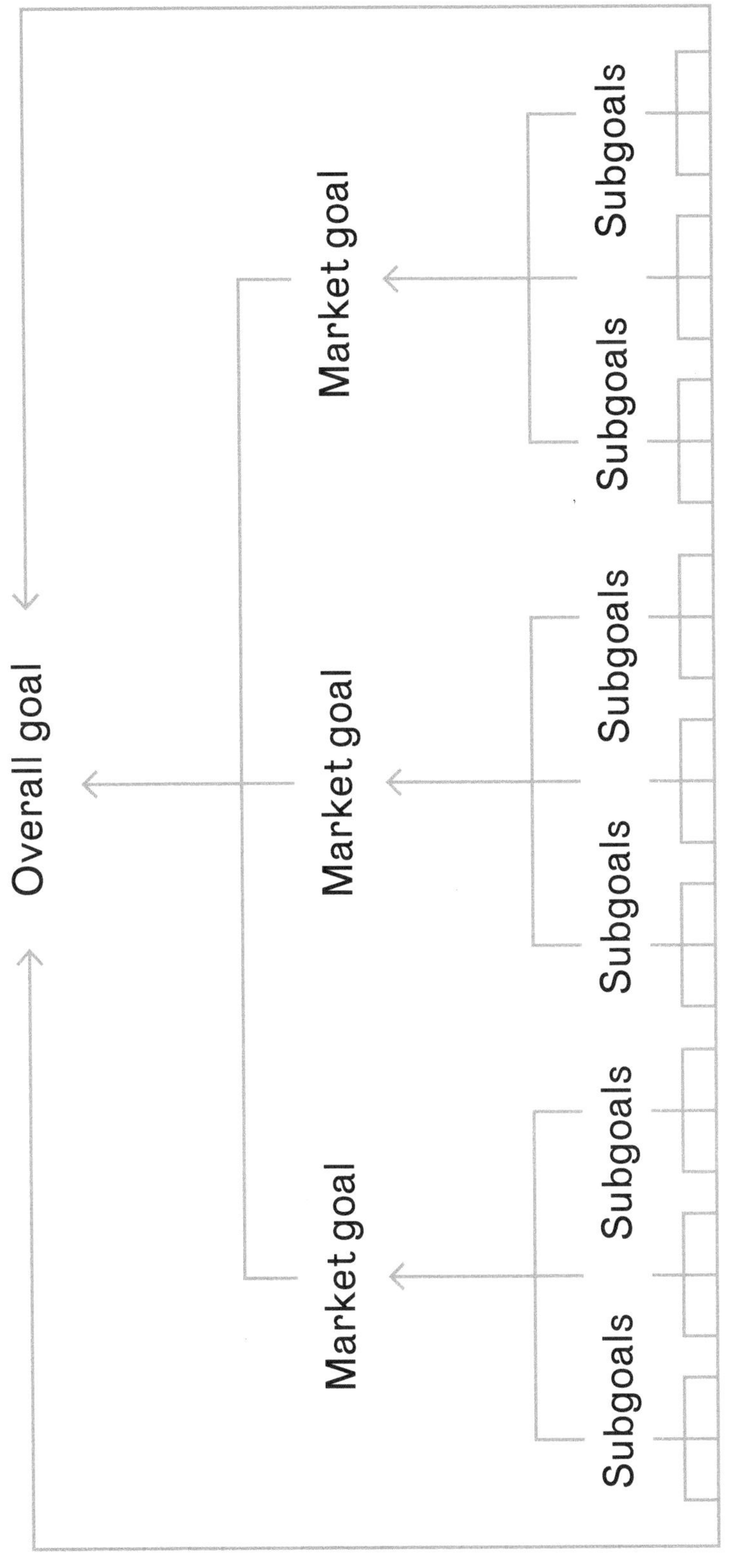


Fig. 3.10 Goal hierarchy

1 Initiation
2 Insight
3 Strategy
4 Design
5 Production
6 Management

3.1 Strategy development
3.2 Overall strategy
3.3 Goals and subgoals
3.4 Business strategy
3.5 Business model
3.6 Market strategy
3.7 Brand strategy
3.8 Communication strategy
3.9 Design strategy

3.3.1 Business goals
3.3.2 Big hairy goals
3.3.3 Development of goals
3.3.4 Goal hierarchy
3.3.5 Qual vs. quant goals
3.3.6 Measurable goals
3.3.7 Goal achievement
3.3.8 Sustainability goals
3.3.9 Goals for design project

If everyone agrees on the destination, it will be easier to agree on how to reach it.

business goals or market goals for different departments, or business areas that target different markets and segments. Market goals and business goals are performance goals, which involve setting goals for the desired results over a certain period of time. Typical performance goals are turnover, growth, profitability, and company value targets. Such goals are often quantitative, allowing for measurement of resource use and return on investment (ROI).[30] The target areas are followed up with several subgoals or operational goals for the activities and measures that should be implemented. All subgoals combined should lead to the achievement of the main goal, and all goals should lead towards the vision. The overall goal is what the company should work to achieve, while the vision is something the company should strive for (3.2.4 Vision).

Tips for the company
**Sustainability is a measure of something's ability to continue. The more sustainable something is, the longer it can go on for. We don't just measure sustainability, we focus on thrivability (strive2thrive.earth).**

**'Goals should be meaningful and carefully thought through in order to represent the company as it is now and as it hopes to be in the years to come' (Annweiler, 2017).**

**Different types of goals**

Here are some characteristics of different types of goals for a company, all of which are important in strategic management (Knudsen & Flåten 2015):

*An overall goal* should set the direction and should be a prerequisite for strategic action. The purpose of the overall goal is to provide market positioning, organisational strategies, and competence development with a long-term perspective. Overall goals should be generally formulated, but at the same time sufficiently precise to indicate what is important and what should be given priority. They should not say anything about who is responsible for what, beyond the management's overall responsibility for achieving the goal. In order for them to function as a whole, they should at the same time be properly anchored and accepted by everyone in the business. The overall goal is directed towards the vision, but an overall goal can also be a vision (3.3.4 Goal hierarchy).

*Goals as guideline* are about using specific goals and subgoals for task allocation and performance assessment, as tools for implementing the planned strategy. These goals need to be much more precise, both in terms of performance level and deadlines. Typically, the periods of the goals are short, and the goals should clearly state priority and responsibilities (who is responsible for the goals to be achieved). Such goals may be important at administrative and operational levels. At the strategic level they may be important for the implementation of plans, and for follow-up and control.

*Goals as search area* are often imprecise and stem from creative processes, brainstorming sessions and rapidly emerging strategic changes. We have clear ideas about direction and vision, but we lack the knowledge to refine our goals. In product development it can be about product properties that we know nothing about until we have researched it for some time. In strategy development, it can be something that one understands that needs to be done, something one needs to improve, for example within new technology, but one does not yet have enough knowledge to set concrete goals. The process here is about narrowing down the search area until you are left with a precise target.

*Stretch goals* Another goal type in the search area category is the *stretch goal*, that is, a goal one should stretch out for (Sitkin et al., 2011; Knudsen & Flåten, 2015). In that case, the goal is precisely defined, but what is unclear is how to achieve it, which may mean acquiring completely new knowledge and performing at a higher level than before. A good

30 'Return on investment (ROI) compares how much you paid for an investment to how much you earned to evaluate its efficiency, using a financial ratio to divide the net profit (or loss) from the investment by its cost (Birken & Curry 2021/ forbes.com).
31 Retrieved from: jfklibrary.org

**Balanced Scorecard:** Based on three articles in *Harvard Business Review* (1992, 1993 and 1996) and the book *The Balanced Scorecard: Translating Strategy into Action* (1996) by Robert Kaplan and David Norton. The model provides the company with a better understanding and insight into the driving forces of future financial performance. As a starting point, vision and strategies are concretised and communicated to all employees, so that each person knows what to do each day, in order to contribute to the achievement of the company's overall goal. The four focus areas of the original model are directly related to the company's vision and strategy: financial focus, customer focus, process focus and focus on learning and growth. A fifth focus area was later included by the Swedish insurance company Skandia: 'focus on human resources. Human resources are the "glue" that binds it all together'. According to The Balanced Scorecard Institute (BSI) the balanced scorecard is a strategic planning and management system used by organisations to communicate and align around strategy, prioritise, and measure performance. The name 'balanced scorecard' comes from the idea of combining strategic measures and financial measures to get a more 'balanced' view of performance. Business, government, and nonprofit organisations worldwide use the balanced scorecard system to (balancedscorecard.org):

- Break down intangible strategic vision into specific, actionable steps
- Get everyone focused on strategy
- Choose measures that help you achieve tangible results

example of a stretch goal is Kennedy's famous ambitious goal from 25 May 1961, of landing a man on the Moon and returning him safely to the Earth'.[31] Knudsen & Flåten characterise this as a goal and not a vision, because it indicated a concrete result. It was clear and measurable, explicit and sharp. You either land on the Moon, or you don't.

### 3.3.5 Qual vs. quant goals

We can distinguish between qualitative and quantitative goals. Quantitative goals are mostly numerical and specific and are used to set measurable targets. Goals that aim to increase sales figures and visitor count are typical quantitative goals. Quantitative goals can be measured because they generate specific, measurable data, such as numbers and statistics, e.g. currency, percentages, quantity, or the like. They are often used for business purposes to measure financial performance, survey response rates, conversion rates (i.e. number of clicks on web ads), etc. Qualitative goals are general and less specific and are often used to set goals that say something about the quality of what one wants to achieve. Qualitative goals are usually more difficult to measure than quantitative ones because they are not quantified. For example, a qualitative goal may be about customer satisfaction, while a quantitative goal may be about the number of customers per day. How many customers visit the shop in one day can be easily measured by counting them, but whether customers are

The G'SOT

Goals, Strategies, Objectives and Tactics (the G'SOT)
A *goal* is a broad primary outcome.
A *strategy* is the approach you take to achieve a goal.
An *objective* is a measurable step you take to achieve a strategy.
A *tactic* is a tool you use in pursuing an objective associated with a strategy (Belicove 2013, forbes.com).

satisfied is not so easily observable because it cannot be seen immediately. Nevertheless, it can also be measured through surveys and observations.

### 3.3.6 Measurable goals

In order to measure the impact of an action, measurable goals and objectives should be defined to make it possible to compare data from one measurement to the next. By measuring change as a consequence of the company's efforts, it is possible to assess whether the time and resources invested are proportionate to the achieved results (ROIs). It can, for example, be to measure sales performance and market share after increased investment on design and marketing. For the designer, being able to refer to measurable results and the impact of design can be an important reference when pitching new projects (2.9 Testing and measuring, 2.9.6 KPIs and metrics, 2.9.7 Qualitative indicators and metrics, 3.8.10 Measurement and evaluation, 6.4 Impact measurement).

#### SMART goals

SMART is a well-known method for setting clear and measurable goals, based on the requirement that they be specific, measurable, attainable, realistic and timely. SMART[32] was originally an acronym of the following five criteria (Haughey, 2014):

- *Specific*: Target a specific area for improvement.
- *Measurable*: Quantify, or at least suggest, an indicator of progress.
- *Attainable*: Specify who will do it; perform it.
- *Realistic*: State what results can realistically be achieved given available resources.
- *Timely*: Specify when the result can be achieved.

The acronym has also expanded to SMARTER, which includes two additional criteria:

- *Evaluated*: Appraisal of a goal to assess the extent to which it has been achieved.
- *Reviewed*: Reflection and adjustment of your approach or behaviour to reach a goal.

Among the key benefits of SMART is that it is easy to use and that it creates more awareness when it comes to being more precise when defining goals, something which reduces the risk of vague and unclear goals that are impossible to achieve. There are also people who criticise SMART and think it does not work for long-term goals, because it lacks flexibility and because it can be difficult to achieve a SMART goal if there are changes further down the line.

### 3.3.7 Goal achievement

Good *bottom line* results are something any manager who is engaged in business activities has at the back of their mind. The bottom line is the sum of all accounts which shows the company's turnover. When the bottom line is positive, it means profit when it is negative, it means loss. Profit is often the driving force and the unspoken highest goal. Liquidity (availability of liquid assets) provides capacity for action and opportunity for further development and growth and is proof that something is being

Table 3.4 The Oslo Manifesto is about energizing a movement of designers, architects and creative professionals to embrace the SDGs as design standards for a new sustainable world. Text and table based on Oslomanifesto, 2022.

Tips for the company
Measurable goals deliver measurable results.

Tips for the designer
Design should help the company achieve its goals. A design project also needs its own goals. To set goals for a design project, you should clarify which problem to solve, conduct a situational study, and do necessary research and analyses.

> 'How does one reach goals? Or more precisely, why do some people reach them, while others just have them all the time? Results are consequences and not driving forces. One cannot reach one's goals by nagging about them or having one's eyes firmly fixed on the bottom line. Goals are achieved when we do not nag about them. Nice bottom lines come when we are driven by values, think like visionaries, tell dream stories, and build culture' (Jensen, 2002).

32 The Origin of SMART is an article with the title 'There's a S.M.A.R.T. Way to Write Management's Goals and Objectives', written in 1981 by George T. Doran, Arthur Miller and James Cunningham. The meaning of SMART has changed over time and continues to vary depending on needs or how the words are understood. For example, achievable or assignable instead of attainable, and relevant instead of realistic are often used.

done right. Regardless it is important to remember that setting goals is not just about the bottom line, but also about values and ambitions for creating something important to people, society and the environment in one way or another. The concept of triple bottom line (TBL) maintains that companies should focus as much on social and environmental concerns as they do on profits. Instead of one bottom line, there should be three: profit, people, and the planet. 'A TBL seeks to gauge a corporation's level of commitment to corporate social responsibility and its impact on the environment over time' (Kenton, 2022).

### 3.3.8 Sustainability goals

The pressure on businesses to operate sustainably are escalating. UN climate report 2022 states that 'It's "now or never" to limit global warming to 1.5 degrees'. Customers are increasingly aware and make ever more sustainable choices, which puts businesses that do not make sustainable choices on the sideline. Sustainability is becoming a hygiene factor, a common practice. Companies that take sustainability seriously set clear sustainability goals and assess their efforts based on a triple bottom line, by measuring their social and environmental impact in addition to their financial performance. Circular economy is at the top of their agenda, which involves securing resources to remain in the economy as long as

/THE OSLO MANIFESTO

/01 How can this design contribute to the goal of ending poverty in all its forms, everywhere?
/02 How can this design contribute to ending hunger and encouraging the transition to sustainable agriculture?
/03 How can this design help ensure healthy lives and well-being for all at all ages?
/04 How can this design support quality education and lifelong learning?
/05 How can this design contribute to gender equality and the empowerment of women and girls?
/06 How can this design help ensure the sustainable management of water and universal access to sanitation?
/07 How can this design contribute to a sustainable energy transition?
/08 How can this design promote decent work for all?
/09 How can this design advance sustainable industrialisation and innovation, especially in those places that do not have access to modern industry?
/10 How can this design contribute to reduce inequality within and among countries?
/11 How can this design make our cities more inclusive, safe, resilient, and sustainable?
/12 How can this design transform production and consumption patterns, to make them more sustainable?
/13 How can this design be part of the urgent action that is needed to combat climate change and its impacts?
/14 How can this design be part of caring for our oceans and seas?
/15 How can this design help to protect and restore ecosystems and preserve biodiversity?
/16 How can this design contribute to the development of peaceful, inclusive, and just societies?
/17 How can this design advance the global partnership needed to achieve all of these goals? (oslomanifesto.com)

Table 3.4 The Oslo Manifesto



Further reading
IPCC Sixth Assessment Report. 'Climate Change 2022: Impacts, Adaptation and Vulnerability' The report warns that climate change is causing dangerous disruption in nature and is affecting billions of people, stressing the urgency to act (www.un.org/en/climatechange/reports).

possible, by reducing raw material use, waste, emissions, and energy consumption to a minimum. Net zero emissions is a goal, not a vision.

**UN Sustainable Development Goals**

For the company to be able to develop a circular economy and succeed in achieving results on a triple bottom line, sustainability goals must be included at an overall level, and actions must be taken to bring them to life in the company's various decision-making areas and functional areas. Deciding on some sustainability goals is important in determining a direction for the business's sustainability activities. A common template is the UN Sustainable goals (SDG), available online.[33] They are universal, apply to all nations, all sectors, all industries and all professions.
**/The Oslo Manifesto:** Design has an impact, both visually and verbally. The designer can, through choice of measures, materials, and message, influence the business and its customers to more sustainable attitudes and actions. 'The Oslo Manifesto embraces the SDGs as the ultimate design brief, and translates each goal into a simple design question that you can use to guide your work' (oslomanifesto.com). Oslo Manifesto was coined in 2015 by Design and Architecture Norway (DogA) (3.4.3 Sustainability strategy, 3.5.2 Sustainable business model, 6.9 Sustainable management).

Fig. 3.11 The figure shows how the choice of instruments is a consequence of the goal, with the aim of achieving the goal.

Tips for the company
We must think climate action in everything we do!
The UN Sustainable Goals are available online.
This is the official site: https://sdgs.un.org/goals.

Tips for the designer
Sign up for the Oslo Manifesto (2017) by the Norwegian Design and Architecture Centre (Doga), based on the UN Sustainable Development Goals (SDGs). Doga is an advocate for sustainability and value-creation through design and architecture (doga.no).

You have the key
'You as a designer hold the key. In close collaboration with the client, you design products for circularity. This means making products that will last a long time and be easy to repair and recycle.' – Kristensen, I.H., CEO of Vestre (Doga, 2022).

### 3.3.9 Goals for design project

A design project is often a subgoal, one of many actions the company takes to achieve its long-term goals. Therefore, it is necessary to anchor the design project in the company's overall goal and vision. A design project can also have its own hierarchy of goals, with overall goals and subgoals, but it is important to remember to distinguish between the goal of the design project and those of the company. Both must be clarified before the design process begins. The goals you set for the design project has consequences for the choice of means, methods and activities.

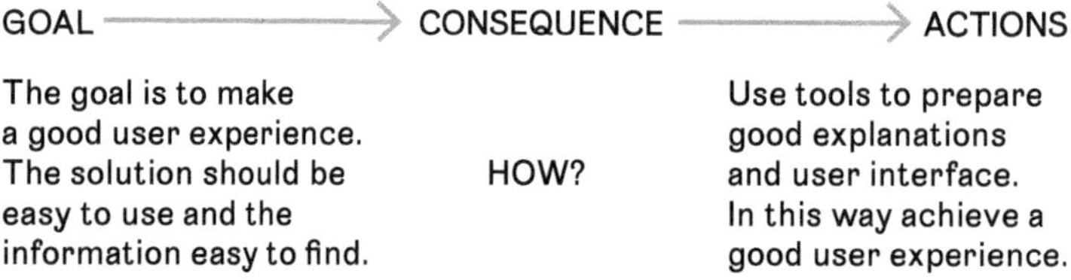
GOAL
CONSEQUENCE
ACTIONS
The goal is to make a good user experience. The solution should be easy to use and the information easy to find.
HOW?
Use tools to prepare good explanations and user interface. In this way achieve a good user experience.

Fig. 3.11 Goals > Consequence > Actions

The level of ambition says something about the expected quality and effort. A high level of ambition implies the use of more time and resources than a low level of ambition, implicitly entailing a higher price and larger budgets. When setting goals for a design project, it is crucial that the designer and the client agree on the level of ambition the goal represents. Some companies have high ambitions and low budgets. The level of ambition can therefore also be explained as scope, the extent of the project. If the client says: 'We envision a smaller scale project that does not require so many resources,' it might imply a lower level of ambition. In case, this should be reflected in, for example, fewer meetings, fewer idea processes, fewer design sketches, and so on.

33 The 2030 Agenda for Sustainable Development, adopted by all United Nations Member States in 2015: https://sdgs.un.org/goals.
34 Lafley, A. G. and Martin, R. L. (2013). *Playing to Win*. Harvard Business Review Press.

## 3.4 Business strategy

1 Initiation
2 Insight
3 Strategy
4 Design
5 Production
6 Management

3.1 Strategy development
3.2 Overall strategy
3.3 Goals and subgoals
3.4 Business strategy
3.5 Business model
3.6 Market strategy
3.7 Brand strategy
3.8 Communication strategy
3.9 Design strategy

3.4.1 Competitive strategy
3.4.2 Porter's generic strategies
3.4.3 Sustainability strategy
3.4.4 Blue Ocean Strategy
3.4.5 Transient advantage
3.4.6 Distinctive asset-building strategy
3.4.7 Agile strategy management
3.4.8 Is the right strategy chosen?
3.4.9 Strategy implementation

Business strategy defines how the company will compete in the market to achieve its overall goal. It will affect whom you approach and how the design and communication should be solved.

The business strategy is based on the business idea defined in the overall strategy. While the business idea says something about WHAT the company will do, the business strategy says HOW it should do it. In other words, *how* it should compete in the market to achieve its goals. This is determined based on the company's prerequisites and the opportunities available in the market. A key question is which products and services are to be developed and in which markets they should be offered, and to what extent these products and services can satisfy the needs and requirements of the customer or user, for the company to achieve its goals. Examples of such goals could be profitability, market growth, and efficiency (Roos et al., 2014). Choosing a competitive strategy *traditionally* implies that the company deliberately decides how best to compete and secure long-term competitive advantages. A company can have a competitive advantage when it is more profitable than the average for the market in which it competes (Porter, 1985). 'More value creation than competitors can be achieved by carrying out some activities or processes more efficiently than competitors, by carrying out the same activities in a different way, or by carrying out other activities' (Lien et al., 2016). 'Strategy is about making specific choices to win in the marketplace. It requires making explicit choices to do some things and not others.' (Lafley & Martin 2013).[34] In *Strategy Choice Cascade*, the two authors present five key choices when planning a competitive strategy:

1) What is our winning aspiration? (Purpose)
2) Where will we play? (Market)
3) How will we win where we have chosen to play? (Strategy)
4) What capabilities must be in place to win? (Value proposition)
5) What management systems are required to ensure the capabilities are in place? (Measures)

The competitive strategy chosen by the company will have an impact on how the company positions itself and its products or services in the market in relation to its competitors. It will affect the choice of the target group, and how products or services are designed and communicated in order for the company to reach its target group and achieve its competitive goals (2.1.1 Value creation).

### 3.4.1 Competitive strategy

Those who write about strategy often refer to Michael Porter's classic strategy theories, which we will also use here to highlight some general characteristics when choosing a competitive strategy. Developing a competitive strategy is about developing a general formula for how the company should compete, clarify the goals, and define the *policy* (guidelines and decisions) required to achieve the goals.

Target image
**As a whole, there can be many goals to deal with in a design project. Target image is occasionally used as a term for the overall image of the goal, audience, and assignment. It involves forming an overall picture of all goals, prioritising the goals to be pursued in the project and specifying what should be done to achieve the goals.**

The competitive strategy combines the company's goals and how to get there (Porter, 1980). According to Porter, his model 'The wheel of competitive strategy' shows the main areas of a competitive strategy as a whole, see Figure 3.12. The company's specific goals and policies about how it wants to compete are at the centre of the wheel, which is the strategy itself. The company's most important decision areas are at the outer edge of the wheel. By considering activities in these areas, the company may gain a good overview and context regarding goals, strategy and decision areas. The point here is that these decision areas should be considered when selecting and formulating a competitive strategy. The decision areas involved, and their importance, may vary for different companies.

Porter emphasises the importance of knowledge of the company's *internal and external* factors to succeed in choosing a strategy. He points out that critical factors are the company's internal strengths and weaknesses compared to those of its competitors, combined with the motivation and needs present in key individuals and other employees to have the chosen strategy carried out. In addition, he highlights the opportunities and threats that exist in the company's external environment and the risks and potential the competitive situation represents (2.7.1 Situational analysis, 2.7.9 PESTLE analysis, 2.7.10 SWOT analysis, 2.7.11 Gap analysis).

Fig. 3.12 **The figure shows The wheel of competitive strategy, which provides an overview of the company's most important decision areas, according to Porter. Activities in these areas will impact the achievement of the business goals (based on Michael Porter, 1980, *Competitive Strategy*. Figure 1.1. p. xvii).**

Tips for the designer
**The choice of competitive strategy will have a direct impact on the design work. Should it be an exclusive product or a low-priced product? This should be reflected in the design.**

Tips for the company
**How will the company compete in the market to achieve its goals? This is defined in the business strategy as a competitive strategy.**

## 3.4.2 Porter's generic strategies

There are many different theories and principles that companies may use to design a competitive strategy. According to Michael Porter choosing a competitive strategy involves deciding whether to become a market leader, market challenger or invest in a niche market. If you are a market leader, the question will be whether to grow by stealing customers from others or getting customers to buy more products. Should you take a more significant piece of the cake or make the cake bigger? For example, get people to drink more Coke. This is what competitive strategy is about. It depends on whether you are a market leader, market challenger, or niche in terms of how you approach your competitors. Porter's three generic strategies are a classic approach: cost leadership, differentiation, and focus. We will look at these three strategies based on Roos et al. (2014) and Porter (1980, p. 34).

Cost leadership strategy
**Increasing profits by reducing costs, while charging industry-average prices.**

Low-cost strategy
**Increasing market share by charging lower prices, while still making a reasonable profit on each sale because you've reduced costs (mindtools.com)**

### Cost leadership

*Cost leadership* strategy and *low-cost strategy* are not necessarily the same. A company may have cost leadership without having a low-cost strategy. It just means it has more capital on the bottom line. Cost leadership involves streamlining operations to reduce costs. A low-cost strategy implies a willingness to take a lower profit margin to win the market (3.7.3 Brand position; high or low price). A company that invests in *cost leadership* reduces operating and production costs and not necessarily the product's price. Such a strategy requires maximum effort by the company on cost-minimising measures, such as building rational production facilities, tight cost control, maximum reduction in areas such as research and development, service, sales, distribution, etc. Instead, it is essential to put resources into product design that simplifies production, thus reducing production costs. Efforts in branding and visual design, such

35 **Private lables (PL) are the retailer's own products, with retailer's name, but manufactured by another company. Also called private brands and store brands.**

36 **Using a differentiation strategy means that a firm is competing based on uniqueness rather than price and is seeking to attract a broad market (onestrategy.org).**

Fig. 3.12 The wheel of competitive strategy


1 Initiation
2 Insight
3 Strategy
4 Design
5 Production
6 Management

3.1 Strategy development
3.2 Overall strategy
3.3 Goals and subgoals
3.4 Business strategy
3.5 Business model
3.6 Market strategy
3.7 Brand strategy
3.8 Communication strategy
3.9 Design strategy

3.4.1 Competitive strategy
3.4.2 Porter's generic strategies
3.4.3 Sustainability strategy
3.4.4 Blue Ocean Strategy
3.4.5 Transient advantage
3.4.6 Distinctive asset-building strategy
3.4.7 Agile strategy management
3.4.8 Is the right strategy chosen?
3.4.9 Strategy implementation

- Cost leadership
- Differentiation
- Focus
- Is a combination possible?


as packaging design, may be given lower priority in such a strategy. By having lower costs than competitors, the company can charge the same price as they do while at the same time making greater profit. A *low-cost strategy* is more about the company wanting to increase its market shares or to enter a new market by offering lower prices than its competitors. It involves, for example, offering an almost identical product or service as competitors at a lower price. This affects the *design strategy* (3.9 Design strategy). For example, the design strategy may be to design the product to be perceived as cheap, as is often done for private labels.[35] A low-cost product should signal just that and that it is available to many instead of expensive, exclusive products that are available to few. Products at the same price level as competing products but have lower production costs can benefit from being visually similar to their competitors, thus taking advantage of their established customer trust. In this way reduce the costs of visual design. Although the company focuses on cost control, things like service, quality, and sales are still areas that cannot be ignored (3.7.3 Brand position; High price or low price).

### Differentiation

Choosing *differentiation* as a strategy[36] means that the company offers products or services that are different from those offered by competitors so that customers are willing to pay a higher price. Factors that can help make the product unique or somewhat special are, for example, brand name, product characteristics, distinctive brand assets, usability, technology and customer service. Differentiation does not necessarily imply

How should the company compete in the market?
*Cost leadership*: Should the company choose to compete on price and be concerned with taking market shares and becoming a market leader?
*Differentiation*: Should the company choose to sell products or services that are unique and different from those offered by competitors, and instead put all efforts in building a distinctive brand?
*Focus*: Should the company operate in a narrow market, reaching a particular group of buyers in a defined geographical area?

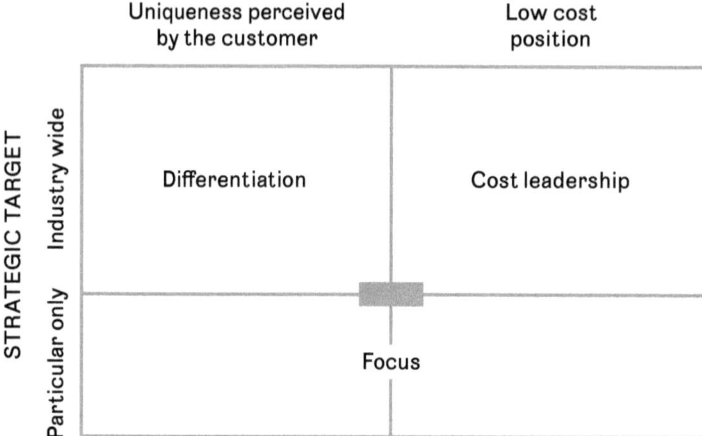


Fig. 3.13 Porter's generic strategies

Fig. 3.13 The figure is based on the classic model by Porter (1980, p. 39), which shows three generic competitive strategies: differentiation, cost leadership, and focus. *Differentiation* involves tailoring different products to different customer groups and investing in branding. *Cost leadership* involves producing at a lower cost than competitors, and often at a lower price. *Focus* can be 'differentiated focus' (new market/new technology/new products) or 'focus on cost' (niche market/cost leadership). Cost leadership is not implicitly only a low-cost position; it can also be streamlining of operations that provides higher profit margins. 'Industry wide' means broad target group/large market. 'Particular only' means narrow target group/niche market.

that only one instrument is used. A combination of different instruments often causes the product to stand out and contributes to successful differentiation. Roos et al. (2014) refer to two possible consequences when choosing a differentiation strategy. The product has less chance of achieving a high market share because it can be perceived as exclusive. The second is that the business cannot achieve cost leadership because differentiation in itself leads to higher costs in research and development, technology, manufacturing, design, branding, marketing, quality, service, etc. A *design strategy* in this context would be to provide some guidelines on how to differentiate the product to stand out as much as possible from competitors and appeal to the target group (3.7.3 Brand position, 3.4.6 Distinctive asset-building strategy, 2.9.8 Mental availability measurements).

Tips for the designer
The choice of competitive strategy will have a direct impact on the design work. Should it be an exclusive product or a low-priced product? This should be reflected in the design. Check out the chapter 3.1.4 Strategic workshop.

'Differentiate or die'
– Jack Trout

### Focus

The third of the three generic strategies is what Porter calls *focus*. It involves focusing on a particular buyer group, or narrow customer group, with a limited product range in a defined geographical area. This strategy can be combined with either cost leadership or differentiation. Rather than reaching out widely to many, this strategy aims to serve a narrow target group by either offering higher quality or lower prices than competitors investing in a larger market. Examples of a differentiated focus may be a store in a central shopping street that sells its exclusive brand in, for example, bags and shoes, and that is not part of a larger chain. Examples of focus on cost may be a local shop selling fruit and vegetables in bulk at a lower price than the supermarket chains. In marketing terminology, focus strategy is often referred to as *niche strategy*.

### Is a combination possible?

Porter stated that cost leadership and differentiation are two mutually exclusive strategies because companies trying to achieve both are 'stuck in the middle and experience low earnings. Others[37] believe that the two strategies can be reconciled. A combination strategy creates a

37 E.g. Miller and Dess 1993, Parnell 2000, Fjelstad and Haanes 2001, Lubatkin et al.
38 The book *Blue Ocean Strategy: How to Create Uncontested Market Space and Make Competition Irrelevant* by Kim and Mauborgne (2005), is based on studies of strategic choices in companies in more than 30 industries in the period from 1880 to 2000.

competitive advantage because modern technology and management practices, such as quality management and flexible production technologies, allow companies to simultaneously lower costs and differentiate their product range (Roos et al. 2014). Roos mentions furniture giant IKEA as an example of a company that does not fall under these generic strategies. IKEA has acquired a position as a cost leader while having a differentiated position in the market and a powerful brand name. Many people would probably think that IKEA initially had a cost strategy, but they gradually built up different added value for customers. IKEA is also a typical example of the Blue Ocean strategy (3.4.4 Blue Ocean strategy).

### 3.4.3 Sustainability strategy

As sustainability can largely be considered as a hygiene factor or a common practice, using sustainability as a differentiating factor, generating a competitive advantage, will be more demanding. According to Michael Porter and Mark Kramer (2011) sustainability is a shared value and not at the center of what the companies do and therefore not practices through which they can achieve economic success, but they can benefit by being recognised as legitimate. Nevertheless, studies show that companies with high research and development pace in the field of sustainability perform above average (i.e. 'doing well by doing good'), and obtain long-term competitive advantages, as well as higher performance on ESG measurements and other KPIs (2.9.6 KPIs and metrics, 6.9.2 Corporate sustainability). 'For example, companies that adopt innovative circular-economy-based business models, or adopt practices that enhance employee recruitment, engagement and retention do so to differentiate themselves and therefore, occupy an unexploited or underexploited position through developing a unique and difficult to imitate strategy' (Ioannis and Serafeim, 2019). The research article 'Corporate Sustainability: A Strategy?' (Ioannis and Serafeim, 2019), explore the conditions under which firms maintain their competitive advantage through sustainability-based differentiation when faced with imitation pressures by industry peers. 'The study finds that actions characterised by low regulatory uncertainty are more likely to be imitated whereas those characterised by high novelty are less likely to be imitated'(Ioannis and Serafeim, 2019). Read more in the chapter 6.9 Sustainable management and 6.9.3 Circular economy.

### 3.4.4 Blue Ocean Strategy

Blue Ocean Strategy challenges traditional strategies based on Porter, which is about competing to give one's own company a larger share of the cake. Contrary to traditional thinking, the Blue Ocean Strategy creates new paradigms, companies and markets that render competition insignificant. From this perspective, the markets are made up of red and blue seas. The red ocean represents the well-known market where all industries operate today, in the ongoing competition between companies. It is increasingly difficult for operators to achieve profit and growth as markets fill up. Blue ocean represents unexploited markets where needs are created and potential for profitable growth.[38]



Setting sustainability goals for the company also presupposes that the company creates a strategy for how to put them into action. A sustainability or corporate responsibility strategy is an agreed framework and a prioritised set of actions in order to:
1) Build faith and engagement amongst colleagues, management, investors, etc.
2) Determine resource allocation, investment and innovation into the areas that are most important.
3) Create a dialogue with external stakeholders (supply chain, customers, local residents, etc.)
4) Drive performance by stretching the company to achieve goals. (McIlhatton, 2021).

| Red Ocean Strategy: | Blue Ocean Strategy: |
|---|---|
| Compete in existing market space. | Create uncontested market space. |
| Beat the competition. | Make the competition irrelevant. |
| Concentrate on existing costumers. | Concentrate on non-costumers. |
| Exploit existing demand. | Create and capture new demand. |
| Make the value-cost trade-off. Find the balance between value and cost (create added value for the customer at a higher price or create good enough value at a lower price). | Break the value-cost trade-off. Break the link between value and cost (both seeking added value for the customer and low costs). |
| Align the whole system of a firm's activities with its strategic choice of differentiation *or* low cost. | Align the whole system of a firm's activities in pursuit of differentiation *and* low cost. |

Table 3.5 Red vs. Blue Ocean strategy

Table 3.5 The table shows red vs. blue ocean strategies based on Kim and Mauborgne (2005/2010) and Roos et al. (2014).

Fig. 3.14 The figure shows a Blue Ocean model based on Kim and Mauborgne, 2006. A Blue Ocean strategy is based on creating new markets instead of competing in established ones. The principles include identifying which established competitive factors can be eliminated, which price factors can be reduced, which buyer values can be increased and strengthened, and which new values can be created that are new to the buyer (buyer value).

This strategy creates a market without competition by breaking the link between value and cost, combining differentiation and low cost. This means keeping costs low while at the same time being able to give the customer added value. Blue Ocean strategies are based on a restructured strategy perspective where companies can increase productivity margins by expanding markets to make the economic cake bigger. One objection to the Blue Ocean strategy approach is that the new markets it represented were simply a redefinition of the composition of the existing marketplaces'. (Roos et al. 2014).

In 2005, Kim and Mauborgne conducted a study of 108 start-ups to quantify the impact of creating a blue ocean on a company's growth in sales and earnings. They found that 86% of all launches were line extensions, i.e., incremental (gradual) red ocean improvements in existing markets. These companies accounted for 62% of the total income and only 39% of the total profit. The remaining 14% of launches were aimed at creating a blue ocean. They generated 38% of the total income and 61% of the total profit. Although the study has not taken into account the total investments made to create a red ocean and a blue ocean, as well as the consequences in subsequent income and profits, including errors, the study shows that there are clear benefits to creating a blue ocean (Kim and Mauborgne (2005, p. 7), Harvard Business Review).[39]

### The Sequence of Blue Ocean strategy

Questions that may be included in a workshop when developing a Blue Ocean business strategy (Kim and Mauborgne, 2005, p. 118).
**Buyer utility:** Does your business idea have any utility value for the buyer?
**Price:** Is your price easily accessible to the mass of buyers?
**Cost:** Can you achieve your cost target while profiting from your pricing strategy?
**Adoption:** What decision issue prevents you from realising your business idea? Have you faced the problem, and are you doing something about it?
**Result:** If no to the questions, then rethink. If yes you have a commercially viable Blue Ocean idea.

39 An expanded edition of *Blue Ocean Strategy* was published in 2015. W. Chan Kim & Renée Mauborgne (2005/2010/2015).
40 This chapter is based on and sited from 'Transient Advantage' by Rita Gunther McGrath, *Harvard Business Review*, June 2013. Also published at Harvard Business School Publishing (2022).
41 Rita McGrath is an author, speaker, and professor at Columbia Business School. She is one of the world's top experts on innovation and growth and ranked among the top management thinkers in the world. Among her books are *The End of Competitive Advantage* (2013) and *How to Spot Inflection Points in Business Before They Happen* (2019) (ritamcgrath.com 2022). Harvard Business School Publishing 2022.

An example of a Blue Ocean strategy is for the company not to spend on assembling furniture but to save money and lower its prices by letting people assemble the furniture themselves. Like IKEA, for example.

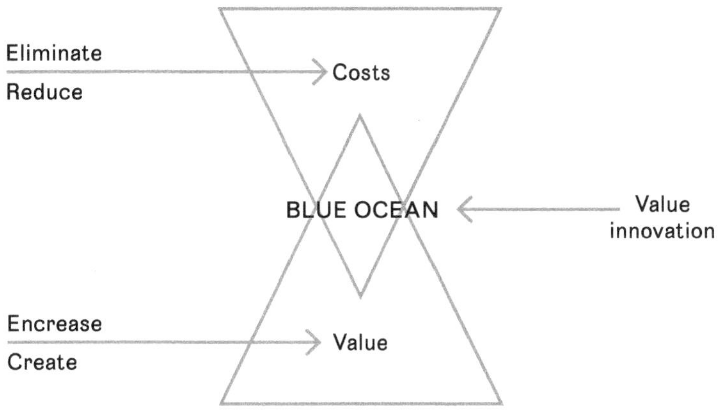


Fig. 3.14 Blue Ocean

**Blue Ocean strategy in practice**

Starbucks is an excellent example of a company that has successfully implemented a Blue Ocean strategy. Many coffee shops were better established when Starbucks came into the picture. Instead of focusing on the coffee alone, they branded Starbucks as something different, meeting an untapped demand among consumers. The most important thing they offered was variety. They offered coffee, but they also offered tea, smoothies, and Frappuccino. They also sold CDs and newspapers, encouraging coffee lovers to hang out and chat. This allowed Starbucks to become a social place too. Instead of hiring regular store employees, they hired professional baristas trained to make their specialty coffee drinks. This provided an experience of art and professionalism that helped Starbucks achieve 'brand awareness' (Jessica Porter 2016).

### 3.4.5 Transient advantage

Transient advantage[40] challenges the traditional perception of a competitive strategy. This strategy implies that companies move from one long-term competitive strategy to investing in several transient competitive strategies through continuous competitive advantage development. Developing a competitive strategy and securing a strong position is the traditional approach to succeed. Many large companies like IKEA, Unilever, GE, etc. have succeeded in establishing a strong position, competitive advantage and protecting it over an extended time. According to Rita Gunther McGrath (2013),[41] it is now rare for a company to maintain a truly lasting advantage over time: 'Competitors and customers have become too unpredictable, and industries too amorphous. The forces at work here are familiar: the digital revolution, a "flat" world, fewer barriers to entry, globalization'. In a world where a competitive advantage often evaporates in less than a year, companies cannot afford to spend months at a time creating a single long-term competitive strategy. To be at the forefront, they must continually launch new strategic initiatives,


1 Initiation
2 Insight
3 Strategy
4 Design
5 Production
6 Management

3.1 Strategy development
3.2 Overall strategy
3.3 Goals and subgoals
3.4 Business strategy
3.5 Business model
3.6 Market strategy
3.7 Brand strategy
3.8 Communication strategy
3.9 Design strategy

3.4.1 Competitive strategy
3.4.2 Porter's generic strategies
3.4.3 Sustainability strategy
3.4.4 Blue Ocean Strategy
3.4.5 Transient advantage
3.4.6 Distinctive asset-building strategy
3.4.7 Agile strategy management
3.4.8 Is the right strategy chosen?
3.4.9 Strategy implementation

- The Sequence of Blue Ocean strategy
- Blue Ocean strategy in practice


Further reading
– *Blue Ocean Strategy, Expanded Edition* by Kim and Mauborgne (2015).
– Check out blueoceanstrategy.com. Apply for newsletter: news@blueoceanstrategy.com

The six principles of Blue Ocean strategy
1. Reconstruct market boundaries
2. Focus on the big picture, not the numbers
3. Reach beyond existing demand
4. Get the strategic sequence right
5. Overcome key organisational hurdles
6. Build execution in the strategy
(Kim & Mauborgne, 2014).

simultaneously building and exploiting many short-term competitive advantages. Although individual and temporary, these advantages can keep companies at the forefront in the long run. Companies that have discovered this include Milliken & Company, Cognizant, and Brambles. They have ceased to believe that company stability is the norm. They do not even think it should be considered a goal. Instead, they work for continuous change and avoid dangerous rigidity. They see the strategy differently – more fluid, customer-centric, less industry-bound. Furthermore, the ways they articulate it – the approach they use to define competitive rules of the game, their methods of assessing new business opportunities, and their approach to innovation are also different. The use of iteration, design methodology and involvement of designers in strategy development is the new approach (4.3 Design methodology, 4.3.5 Iterative method).

Any competitive advantage, whether lasting two seasons or two decades, goes through the same life cycle, see Figure 3.15. When the advantages are temporary, the companies must go through the cycle much faster and more often. That means they need a deeper understanding of past and recent stages and insight into new opportunities, technological developments, and trends than maintaining a strong position for many years.

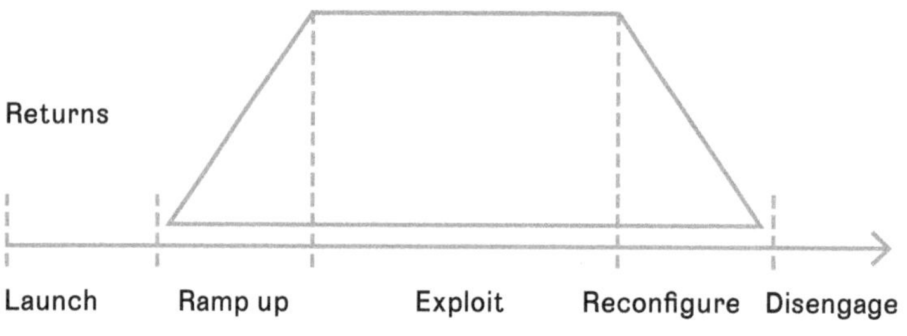


Fig. 3.15 The wave of transient advantage

Fig. 3.15 The figure shows an example of the course in a competitive strategy. *Launch*: The company identifies an opportunity and mobilises resources to exploit it. *Ramp up*: The business idea is developed and initiated. *Exploit*: If the company is lucky, this is a period of profit that forces competitors to react. *Reconfigure*: Success can weaken the advantage or benefit; therefore, the company must redefine what it does to preserve it. *Disengage*: In some cases, the advantage is completely eroded and forces the company to start a downsizing process in which resources are extracted and redistributed to a new generation of competitive advantages. In a high-speed company, the success factor will lie in using people with different skills to manage the tasks that lie in each phase of competitive advantage development (Caption/model: McGrath 2013).

'Transient-advantage firms seldom engage in restructuring, downsizing, or mass firings' (McGrath, 2013).

**Transient advantage strategy:** Companies that want to create a portfolio of transient advantages need to make eight major shifts in the way that they operate, based on McGrath (2013):[42]

**1) Think about arenas, not industries.** Today's business analytics think less about industry-level analysis, and more about 'arenas'; a combination of a customer segment, an offer, and a place in which that offer is delivered.[43] Think less about making more money than your industry peers and more about responding to customers' 'jobs to be done'.[44]

**2) Set broad themes, and then let people experiment.** Today's gifted strategists use advanced pattern recognition, direct observation, and the interpretation of weak signals in the environment to set broad themes. Within those themes, they free people to try different approaches and business models, and they use the input to rethink their models.

**3) Adopt metrics that support entrepreneurial growth:** Businesses concerned with innovation use the logic of 'real options' to evaluate new moves, and allow the organisation to learn through trial and error. They focus on the problem rather than on the solution, and iteration while working toward the answer.[45]

42 Rita McGrath (2013) *Strategy for Transient Advantage: The New Playbook.*

43 This is contrary to Michael Porter's classic competition model 'Five forces model', where one compares one's company with other players in the same industry.

44 *Jobs-To-Be-Done Theory and Methodology* by Tony Ulwick, 2020.

45 Brand equity is the commercial value that derives from consumer perception of the brand name of a particular product or service, rather than from the product or service itself (Brand equity, n.d.).

46 Contrary to the classic Net Present Value (NPV) principle, which assumes, for example, that one completes every project one starts and that the competitive advantages will last for a long time.

**Transient Advantage Workshop**

Ask which of these statements apply to the company:
- I don't purchase my own company's products or services.
- We invest at the same or higher levels and don't get better margins or growth in return.
- Customers finds cheaper or simpler solutions to be 'good enough'.
- Competition is emerging from places we didn't expect.
- Customers are no longer excited about what we have to offer.
- People we'd like to hire don't consider us a top place to work.
- Some of our very best people are leaving.
- Our stock is perpetually undervalued.

If you recognise a problem, it's time for a strategy reinvention.

**4) Focus on experiences and solutions to problems:** What customers crave, and few companies provide, are well-designed experiences and complete solutions to their problems. Companies, that exploit transient advantage put themselves in their customers' place and consider the outcome customers are trying to achieve.
**5) Build strong relationships and networks:** A strong relationship and interaction with customers are a profound source of competitive advantage. Companies that invest in communities and networks, deepen their ties with customers.
**6) Avoid brutal restructuring; learn healthy disengagement:** Companies operating in a transient advantage economy rarely downsize and fire people. Instead, they continually adjust and readjust their resources.
**7) Start with early-stage innovation:** Companies that set aside a separate budget and staff for innovation avoid having new initiatives compete with established resources. They hunt systematically for opportunities, usually searching beyond the given boundaries and instead figuring out what customers want and need and how they can help them with that.
**8) Experiment, iterate and learn:** Companies that focus on new approaches, experimentation and learing are preprared to make a shift or change focus as new discoveries happen. The discovery phase is followed by business model definition and incubation, in which a project takes the shape of an actual business and may begin pilot tests or serving customers. Only once the initiative is relatively stable and healthy can it escalate.
'Transient-advantage leaders recognise the need for speed. Fast decision making will replace deliberations that are precise but slow. (...) It still requires making tough choices about what to do and, even more important, what not to do. (...) Defining where you want to compete, how you intend to win, and how you are going to move from advantage to advantage is critical' (Rita McGrath 2013) (2.1.2 Decision making).

## 3.4.6 Distinctive asset-building strategy

The concept of distinctive brand assets emphasises how the most distinctive brand elements can constitute the most valuable assets of a brand. This strategic approach brings the visual design up front to build brand equity,[46] thus bridging strategy and design. It is about


1 Initiation
2 Insight
3 Strategy
4 Design
5 Production
6 Management

3.1 Strategy development
3.2 Overall strategy
3.3 Goals and subgoals
3.4 Business strategy
3.5 Business model
3.6 Market strategy
3.7 Brand strategy
3.8 Communication strategy
3.9 Design strategy

3.4.1 Competitive strategy
3.4.2 Porter's generic strategies
3.4.3 Sustainability strategy
3.4.4 Blue Ocean Strategy
3.4.5 Transient advantage
3.4.6 Distinctive asset-building strategy
3.4.7 Agile strategy management
3.4.8 Is the right strategy chosen?
3.4.9 Strategy implementation


Further reading
Read about transient advantage and business development in the interview with Torbjørn Sitre. Available at designandstrategy.co.uk.

'Today industry lines are quickly blurring.' ... 'As barriers to entry tumble, product features can be copied in an instant' ... 'Once a company has demonstrated that demand for something exists, competitors quickly move in. What customers crave – and few companies provide – are well-designed experiences and complete solutions to their problems' ... 'Speed is paramount. Fast and roughly right decision making must replace deliberations that are precise but slow' (Rita McGrath, 2013).

creating successful brands through developing, refining and monitoring distinctive brand assets, as the foremost resource. For designers and marketers who have felt that positioning is overestimated and that visual brand elements are underestimated, this is an approach that can create more balance. The concept of distinctive brand assets is based on research and books written by Jenni Romaniuk.[47]

A brand usually consists of one or more visual brand elements. Overall, the brand elements should help to express values, promises and position, through a unique visual expression, to build desired associations. But which of the brand elements, or fragments of a brand element, is what people really remember and which contributes to brand recognition? These are distinctive brand assets. Building distinctive brand assets means creating proxies for the brand. They can help replace the exposure of the brand name. So, when one sees the asset, one thinks of the name. The brand should also be regularly monitored to follow how external influences and trends affect people's views of the brand. It can also be a strategy in the development or redesign of a brand. The metrics in question are Fame and Uniqueness, see Figure 3.17. What is measured is the strength of the brand assets on their Fame (% of consumers that link the asset to your brand) and Uniqueness (the asset links to your brand, and not competitors). Based on an asset's performance combined on fame and uniqueness, one learns the most fruitful course of action for the brand to grow further (unravelresearch.com).

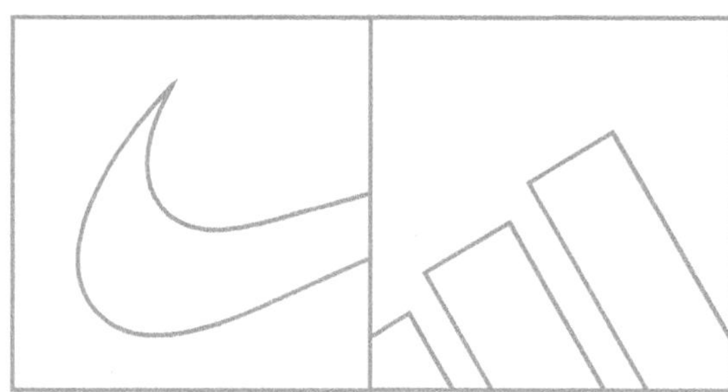

Fig. 3.16 Distinctive brand asset

Two metrics, Fame and Uniqueness provide strategic guidance for selecting distinctive assets to use and build. 'These two metrics integrate knowledge from how memory works, which is where distinctive asset associations are stored, and the role distinctive assets play in category buyer's lives, which influences how and when we want buyers to use these associations' (Romaniuk, 2016; Romaniuk & Nenycz-Thiel, 2014).[48] Romaniuk urges not to limit the distinctive asset-building potential, but to aim for 100% Fame and 100% Uniqueness, and aim to cultivate and refine an asset that can replace the brand name.

**Fame:** How well known is the asset amongst category buyers? A distinctive asset's Fame score dictates its value as a brand proxy:[49] the higher score, the greater the value of the asset; the lower score, the higher risk associated with using that asset as a stand-alone branding device. Fame, as a metric for distinctive asset strength, is quantified as how many of the people you are trying to influence link your brand to the asset (Romaniuk, 2018, p.81).

Fig. 3.16 The figure shows examples of typical distinctive brand assets, which means that we recognise the brand by only seeing part of the visual element or symbol. Based on Jenni Romaniuk (2018).

Fig. 3.17 *Use or lose*: Assets are close to 100% Fame and 100% Uniqueness. It can be used as replacement for the brand name. *Investment potential*: Assets gain high degree of response (greater than 50% Uniqueness), but only amongst a minority of category buyers (less than 50% Fame). It has an investment potential. *Avoid*: Category buyers link the asset to those of competitors. Should be concerned to be a copycat. *Ignore or test*: Assets fail to reach the majority of responses in both Fame and Uniqueness. New brands have a potential of testing yet-to-be-introduced assets. Taken from Jenni Romaniuk (2018).

Distinctive brand assets must be used on both packaging and in communication. Unique and famous distinctive brand assets help to increase the brand attention in communications and brand recognition in buying situations. DBA increases the effect of communications and increases the propensity to be chosen in buying situations (Bendixen, 2022).

47 *Building Distinctive Brand Assets* (Romaniuk, 2018). Jenni Romaniuk is author, research professor and associate director of the Ehrenberg-Bass Institute at the University of South Australia Business School.

48 'The real difference between consumers' perceptions of private labels and national brands'. Nenycz-Thiel and Romaniuk. *Journal of Consumer Behaviour*, 2014–7, Vol.13 (4), p.262–269.

49 Proxy: 1) The authority to represent someone else, especially in voting. 2) A figure that can be used to represent the value of something in a calculation (Proxy, n.d.).

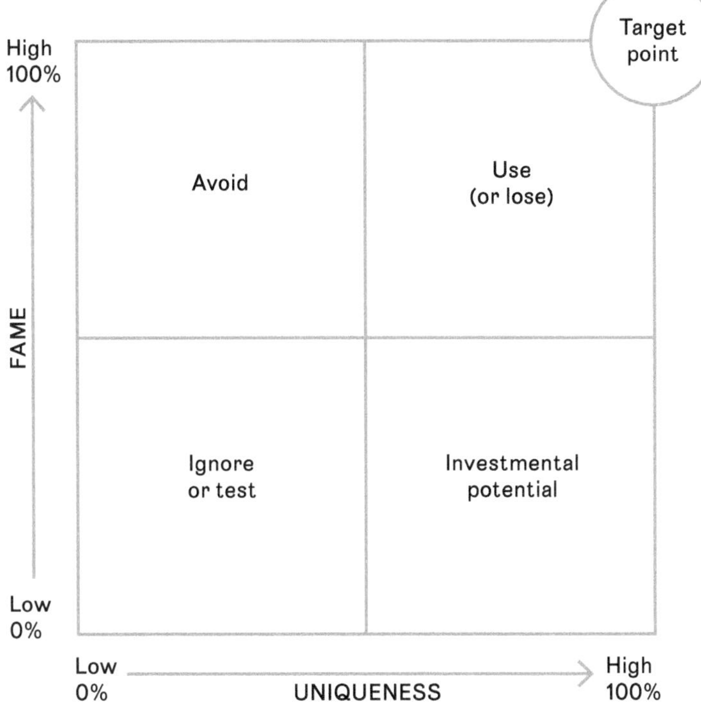

Fig. 3.17 The distinctive asset grid

1 Initiation
2 Insight
3 Strategy
4 Design
5 Production
6 Management

3.1 Strategy development
3.2 Overall strategy
3.3 Goals and subgoals
3.4 Business strategy
3.5 Business model
3.6 Market strategy
3.7 Brand strategy
3.8 Communication strategy
3.9 Design strategy

3.4.1 Competitive strategy
3.4.2 Porter's generic strategies
3.4.3 Sustainability strategy
3.4.4 Blue Ocean Strategy
3.4.5 Transient advantage
3.4.6 Distinctive asset-building strategy
3.4.7 Agile strategy management
3.4.8 Is the right strategy chosen?
3.4.9 Strategy implementation

– The distinctive asset grid

**Uniqueness:** What level of asset ownership does the brand have? A distinctive asset's uniqueness score dictates its mental uniqueness among category buyers or non-buyers. *Lower score*: If a brand's uniqueness is under 50% for a given asset, competitor brands dominate responses, making the asset risky to use. *Higher score*: The risk is lower as uniqueness moves closer to 100%. Measuring uniqueness provides an assessment of the level of mental competition the brand faces from other brands in the category, and the nature of this competition (Romaniuk, 2018, p., 87). See also 2.9.8 Mental availability measurements.

### The distinctive asset grid

The two metrics Fame and Uniqueness combined, create the distinctive asset grid (Romaniuk, 2016b) and set a distinctive asset-building strategy, see Figure 3.17. The distinctive asset grid can help identify which assets provide the best opportunity to develop, based on Romaniuk (2018):

The *use or lose* quadrant: Brands in this quadrant with close to 100% Fame and 100% Uniqueness, can be used as replacements for the brand name, while the asset needs to be used if you want to retain value, hence the name *use or lose*.

The *investment potential* quadrant: Brands in this quadrant have gained a high degree of response (greater than 50% Uniqueness), but only amongst a minority of category buyers (less than 50% Fame). These brands have an investment potential because high Uniqueness score gives a head start as Fame is easier to build than Uniqueness.

The *avoid* solo use quadrant: Brands in this quadrant should be concerned as it means category buyers link it to your brand and to

Further reading
– ***Building Distinctive Brand Assets***, Jenni Romaniuk (2018).
– ***How Brands Grow: What Marketers Don't Know***, Byron Sharp (2010/2019).
– ***How Brands Grow: Part 2: Emerging Markets, Services, Durables, New and Luxury Brands***, Jenni Romaniuk and Byron Sharp (2016/2022).

Fame and Uniqueness metrics
**'When a brand has over 5=% Fame, then a category buyer is more likely than not to think of the brand when exposed to the asset. If a brand has over 50% Uniqueness, then that brand dominates the responses for that asset' (Romaniuk, 2018, p. 97).**

those of your competitors. This might occur if an asset has become a category indicator, signals a functional variant or if a competitor mimics a category leader or copies successful elements from foreign brands.

The *ignore or test* quadrant: Brands in this quadrant fail to reach the majority of responses in both Fame and Uniqueness. This is where potential new assets might end up, but they can still have potential. The purpose of testing yet-to-be-introduced assets is to double check whether competitors already have existing traction on that asset, which will hamper efforts to build this new asset. (2.9.9 Category entry points (CEPs)).

### 3.4.7 Agile strategy management

An agile strategy framework, *Strategile*, enables the organisation to adjust and adapt more quickly towards the strategic impact of changing environments. Agile approach to strategy uses Agile workflow patterns, in contrast to traditional strategy development. 'Strategic opportunities are discussed, evaluated, broken down into sizable and manageable constituents, prioritized, executed, constantly monitored and revised by a strategy team or dedicated function. In doing so, the strategic direction is frequently checked towards strategic obstacles and reviewed in terms of changing needs' (Deloitte, n.d.).

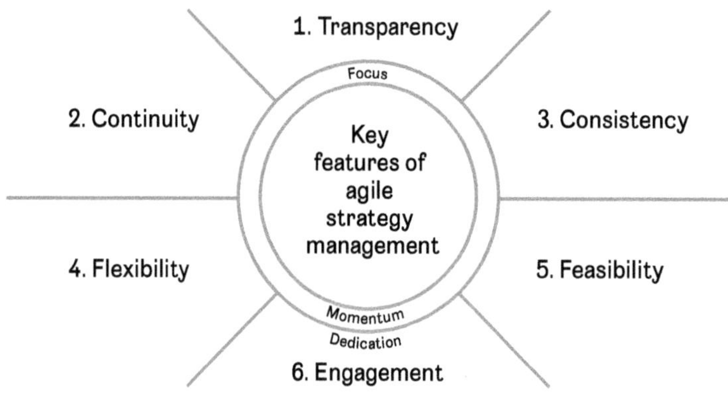


Fig. 3.18 Agile strategy framework

Fig. 3.18 Agile Strategy frameworks: *1) Transparency: Visibility and tangibility, 2) Continuity: Incremantal and interative, 3) Consistency: Continuation and optimisation, 4) Flexibility: Tackle critical matters, 5) Feasibility: Fail and learn fast', 6) Engagement: Team autonomy* (Based on Huque, 2022, Deloitte).
–*Momentum*: Using incremental approach, strategic initiatives are evaluated by iterations, which promotes a relentless optimisation of strategy planning and execution. This helps organisations to build strategies from different angles using these new insights and increases momentum on a frequent pace.
–*Focus*: The iterative proceeding defies the rigidity and flaws of traditional strategic management. It centres the view on business value and increases the focus on managing strategic initiatives in a predefined time.
–*Dedication*: The top management is promoting the team in its autonomy. This encourages a higher dedication by all involved parties. Fail and learn fast!

**Key features of agile strategy management:**
Deloitte proposes six coherent key features of agile strategy frameworks.[50]

*1. Transparency*: Constant visibility and tangibility enhance good decision-making. A collective view of the strategic progress will make organisations more aware of emerging events, risks and issues but also potential synergies between existing initiatives. Kanban boards, strategic backlogs and sprint plans are used as basic tools. Activities and feedback loops are monitored to find out whether the initiatives are aligned with the strategic vision (2.1.2 Decision making, 3.2.4 Vision, 4.3.8 Scrum, 4.3.9 Kanban, 4.3.7 Sprint, 4.3.5 Iterative method).

*2. Continuity*: Through an incremental approach, strategic initiatives are divided into different, manageable sizes that fit into one iteration. In doing that, each part builds on the previous one leveraging new attained insights and learnings. For instance, an initiative that usually takes one year can be divided into four to five pieces (each for one sprint).

Further reading
– 'A guide to agile strategy' by Marty Neumeier: martyneumeier.com/a-guide-to-agile-strategy.
– 'SCRAMBLE. How agile strategy can build epic brands in record time' by Marty Neumeier, 2018.

50 Based on Deloitte Germany. 'Agile strategy management – Part I. Why 'Strategile' is the new Strategy Management!' (David Huque n.d.): www2.deloitte.com/de
51 Experimentation-based 'trial and error' activities, piloting and data-driven automation procedures lead to alternative conclusions that can change a previously anticipated status quo immediately.
52 Congruence: agreement or harmony, compatibility (Congruence, n.d.).

At the end of each iteration, conclusions for identified improvements are evaluated.

*3. Consistency*: After each sprint, the outcomes can be verified, and measurements for the next steps investigated. By releasing a steady stream of strategic artifacts, short-term and long-term needs can be addressed more effectively. Strategic plans are treated as growing strategies that are continued and optimised. (Re)design > execution > monitoring > adaption.

*4. Flexibility*: After each iteration the value contribution of an achieved strategic artifact is evaluated against the present situation. It can be further developed or stopped to tackle more critical matters, any new risks or issues that have emerged in the meantime. Previous initiatives hereby will be set back to a strategy backlog until the next iteration.

*5. Feasibility*: Dynamic decision-making methods such as hypothesis-driven and scenario-based planning help to explore and test complex and uncertain problems. They lead to repetitively new assumptions or selective options until a fitting solution has been narrowed down. 'Fail and Learn fast' mentality is the key to increasing the success rate of strategic realisation.[51]

*6. Engagement*: A success factor is to use dedicate self-organised, interdisciplinary strategy teams to put these strategies into practice. The top management ensures that the strategic team adheres to the strategic direction while promoting the team in its autonomy.

Agile strategy management is another paradigm shift that requires organisations to come to terms with volatility (rapid adjustments) as the norm in the digital age, to deal with digital transformation and other complex questions (1.9.3 Agile process management, 4.3.10 Lean and agile).

### 3.4.8 Is the right strategy chosen?

According to Porter (1980, xix), the appropriateness of a competitive strategy can be determined by testing the proposed goals and policies for consistency:

**Internal consistency:** Are the goals mutually achievable? Will the key operating strategies meet the objectives? Will the key operating policies reinforce each other?

**Environmental fit:** Will the goals and strategies exploit industry opportunities? Will the goals and policies deal with industry threats to the degree possible with available resources? Will the timing of goals and strategies reflect the ability of the environment to absorb the actions? Are the goals and strategies responsive to broader societal concerns?

**Resource fit:** Will the goals and policies match the resources available to the company relative to competitors? Will the goals and strategies reflect the organisation's ability to change?

**Communication and implementation:** Are the goals well understood by the key implementers? Is there enough congruence[52] between the goals and strategies and the ability to commit among those who are to implement them? Is there sufficient managerial capability to allow for effective implementation? (3.1.2 Strategic management tool, 3.1.3 TOP 5).



Agile strategy phases

The four activities are based on the 'Agile Strategy Manifesto' (Kumar, 2011):
*Initiation*: Unique value creation (usually radical innovation) through perceived usefulness or desirability
*Realisation*: Establish brand equity through incremental adoption of perceived value
*Retention*: Value enhancement through iterative and adaptive value chains
*Transformation*: Incremental innovation through re-inventing value.

### 3.4.9 Strategy implementation

If strategies are to be of any use, they should be implemented consistently in the organisation so that all employees understand and use them to help the business achieve its goals. Strategy implementation is a large subject area and there are many different theories for how it can best be done. 'It has long been recognized that the majority of failed strategies break down in the implementation phase, researchers and practitioners have little concrete knowledge of this area' (Noble, 1999).[53] Research shows that there are many reasons why the implementation does not succeed.[54] These can be divided into four categories: the strategy (or system) is too complicated, the people are not skilled enough to implement, reality moves faster than the strategy, or the strategy is unrealistic to implement. Obed Madsen proposes a fifth reason: We do not know exactly what we mean when we say implementation. It creates ambiguity in organisations when implementing because the concept can have many meanings. Thus, there is a possibility that different actors in the same organisation implement in vastly different ways (Obed Madsen 2018). 'The current practice of implementation turns out to suffer from the fact that strategy is often made to be adopted, and not to be implemented. This means that strategies often end up being abstract in their wording because it is easier to agree on something abstract than on something concrete' (Obed Madsen).

A success factor is to involve employees in the strategy development process from the beginning. Strategy implementation is a matter of consensus (general agreement), communication and understanding. The choice of strategy language and the way strategies are presented affect the cognition and perception of the strategy. This applies both when strategy is communicated between management and employees, and between managers and middle managers towards suppliers. One question that is important to clarify is, for example, how strategy is understood differently among management and other employees, as well as among businesspeople and designers. When it comes to the designer working on behalf of the company, an essential question will be: How does the way the strategy is communicated affect the design? One success factor is to involve the designer, in the strategy development and implementation process. The designer can help make the process

**Seven strengths of *drawing* strategy:**

1) Enables greater memory retention
2) Promotes more effective decision-making and action orientation
3) Encourage grounded innovation
4) Promotes pre-building prototyping
5) Drawing helps *see* your thinking and uncovers new possibilities
6) Drawing aids collective engagement
7) Drawing is an alternative to conventional approaches to strategy presentation

'A strategy is only as good as its implementation'
(Cummings and Angwin 2015).

Table 3.6 The terms business strategy, business model, and business plan are confusing. There are many different views and no clear answers as to how best to use these concepts. The table shows a simple explanation to distinguish the different concepts. See also Table 3.7 Brand strategy process.
© Grimsgaard, W. (2018)

Tips for the designer
While the business idea and business strategy describe what the company should do and how it should compete in the market, the business model describes how the company should put this into practice, to create value.

'Within strategy, implementation is about the strategy going from idea over decisions to practice' (Madsen, 2022).

Further reading
'The future of work'. Cognizant (a global IT service company) helps companies to rethink their business models, reinvent their workforces, and rewire their operations (cognizant.com).

53 Noble, C.H. (1999) 'The Eclectic Roots of Strategy Implementation Research', *Journal of Business Research*, 45, 119-134. In this research article Noble proposes various conceptualisations and definitions of implementation, a broad range of literature fields of the study of strategy implementation and a framework that distinguishes between structural and interpersonal process views of implementation.

54 According to Verweir (2014), Wheelen & Hunger (2012) and Holst-Mikkelsen (2013).

| Business strategy vs. business model vs. business plan | | |
|---|---|---|
| Goals and objectives | Business strategy | The business strategy is the competitive strategy, the company's choice of strategy to achieve its overall goal. Should the company choose to compete on price, differentiation or a narrow customer segment? These strategic choices are essential for all further strategies and actions. |
| | Business model | A business model is an operational plan for developing values and earning money based on its chosen strategy. |
| | Business plan | A business plan, in many cases, comprises both business strategy, marketing strategy and business model. It explains and links together all aspects of the company and compiles them in a well-organised business document, a roadmap for the firm from marketing, financial, and operational standpoints. |
| | Market strategy | The market strategy is about how the company should compete in the market, to whom it will sell its products and services, what the company should achieve in different markets, and how it will do it. Target group segmentation and positioning are crucial here. |

Table 3.6 Clarification of concepts

more understandable, flexible and visual by using design methodologies, such as design thinking, iterations and co-creation. This is an approach that makes the process more people-oriented and translates strategic words into visual models and examples that make it easier to understand.

## 3.5 Business model

### The business model is the company's plan for the operation of the business in line with their purpose and business idea.

In the previous section, we talked about business strategy, which is mainly about choosing a strategy to achieve its goals. The business model takes this strategy further at a more operational level and describes what specific actions a company must take to create value and achieve its goals. As a whole, it can serve as a platform for managing the entire company. For new business ideas and start-ups, the business model is an important management tool for realising the idea and bringing it out to the market. As a whole, it can serve as a platform for managing the entire company. The content of the business model provides an overview of all the main factors involved in the business operations. 'A business model can best be described as a set of basic building blocks or dimensions that show the thinking behind how the company intends to make money. The building blocks cover the four main areas of a company: customers, products, infrastructure, and economic viability' (Roos et al. 2014). These areas are put in the business model's context and system.

When a company is to bring a new idea to the market for the first time, it is important to have thought through the entire business cycle. For this purpose, one needs a business model. A bank, potential investors

> Strategy implementation fails due to lack of skills, lack of resources, poor strategy, decoupling, hypocrisy, lack of agreement or power struggles and lack of perspective (Obed Madsen 2018).

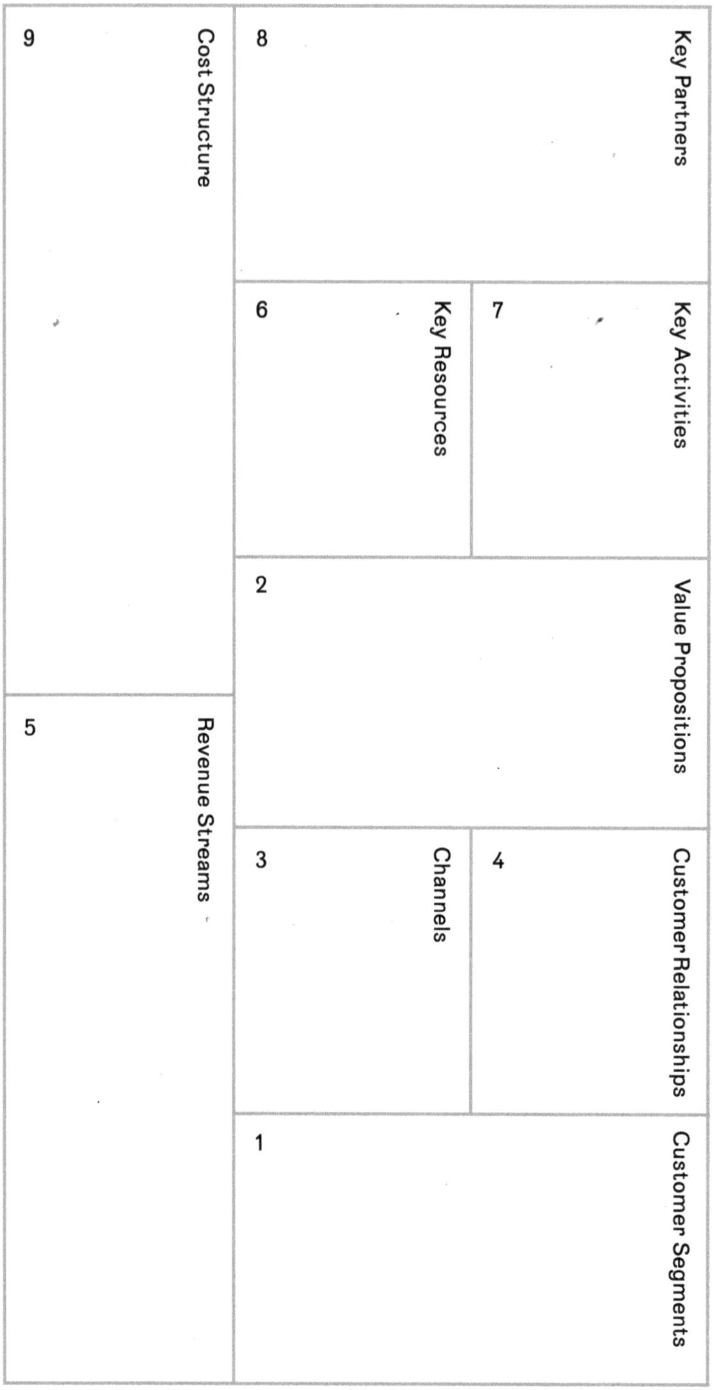

9 Cost Structure
8 Key Partners
6 Key Resources
7 Key Activities
2 Value Propositions
5 Revenue Streams
3 Channels
4 Customer Relationships
1 Customer Segments

Fig. 3.19 Business model canvas

and public supporters will require the company to have a well thought-out business model before receiving funding and other support. Therefore, starting early by developing a business model may be a plus. The employees and any external expertise in business development should be included in the planning (Innovasjonnorge.no).

Fig. 3.19 The figure shows the Business model canvas, based on Osterwalder (2012). It consists of nine building blocks which help the company map customer segments, value propositions, channels, customer relationships, revenue streams, key resources, key activities, key partners, and cost structure. The model can be devided into three areas: Desirability. Do customers want it?: Blocks 1, 2, 3, 4. Viability. What is it worth?: Blocks 5, 9. Feasibility. Can we deliver it?: Blocks 6, 7, 8 (strategyzer.com).

Tips for the company
'The business model is like a blueprint for a strategy to be implemented through organizational structures, processes, and systems' (Strategyzer, n.d.)

Further reading
– YouTube: Osterwalder explaining the Business Model Canvas (2012): youtube.com/watch?v=RzkdJiax6Tw
– *Business Model Generation: A Handbook for Visionaries, Game Changers, and Challengers* (The Strategyzer series) by Alexander Osterwalder and Yves Pigneur (2010).
– 'The Uber Business Model Canvas'. January 27, 2016. By Denis Oakley: denis-oakley.com/uber-business-model-canvas-success/

55 *'Why Sustainability is now the Key Driver of Innovation'.* Nidumolu et al., 2009-10-01 (4), p.10.

### 3.5.1 Business model canvas


1 Initiation
2 Insight
3 Strategy
4 Design
5 Production
6 Management

3.1 Strategy development
3.2 Overall strategy
3.3 Goals and subgoals
3.4 Business strategy
3.5 Business model
3.6 Market strategy
3.7 Brand strategy
3.8 Communication strategy
3.9 Design strategy

3.5.1 Business model canvas
3.5.2 Sustainable business model
3.5.3 Business model innovation
3.5.4 Lean start-up


There are many different definitions and understandings of the business model concept and many approaches to creating business models. One widely used business model is the Business Model Canvas (BMC), also called the Osterwalder model, initially developed by Alexander Osterwalder in 2005 (Strategyzer, n.d.). The model consists of nine modules that can help the company map and plan its activities: customer segments, value propositions, channels, customer relationships, revenue streams, key resources, key activities, key partners, and cost structure. BMC offers some key fundamental principles for developing a business model that can be designed to best suit the company. This way, it can also serve as a design method to iterate over concepts (4.3.5 Iterative method). Iteration as an approach to business model development is a creative approach that entrepreneurs and business people can benefit from using. The designer can be an excellent partner to discuss and visualise ideas and models. If the designer should contribute beyond the pure idea- and communication-related aspects, it is an advantage for the designer to have business and organisational knowledge, or involve a subcontractor. Designers who have expertise in this area can also view themselves as business designers or business developers.

**Building blocks of a business model canvas**

The Business Model Canvas consists of nine modules, see Figure 3.19:

**Customer segments:** For whom are we creating value? Who are our most important customers, clients, or users?

**Value propositions:** What value do we deliver to our customers? Which one of our customers' problems are we helping to solve?

**Channels:** Through which channels do our customer segments want to be reached?

**Customer relationships:** How should we deal with our customers?

**Revenue streams:** What are our customers willing to pay? How would they prefer to pay? Sales in percentages of the total revenue?

**Key resources:** What are our most important costs? Where do they come from?

**Key activities:** What do we need to do to deliver the value proposition?

**Key partners:** Who is going to help us with key activities we do not do ourselves? Who are our partners and suppliers?

**Cost structure:** What are our most important costs? Where do they come from? Based on Strategyzer (www.strategyzer.com/canvas/business-model-canvas).

Further reading
'Building Blocks of Business Model Canvas' by Strategyzer: www.strategyzer.com/canvas/business-model-canvas

### 3.5.2 Sustainable business model

Consumers are seeking out sustainable products, and that is how sustainability is transforming the competitive landscape that would force companies to change their products, processes, technologies, and business model (Shakeelab, et al., 2020).[55] What characterises a sustainable business model is that it includes in its calculations what effect the business has on the world, and conversely what impact the

> 'A business model for sustainability helps describing, analyzing, managing, and communicating (i) a company's sustainable value proposition to its customers, and all other stakeholders, (ii) how it creates and delivers this value, (iii) and how it captures economic value while maintaining or regenerating natural, social, and economic capital beyond its organizational boundaries' (Schaltegger et al., 2016, p. 6).

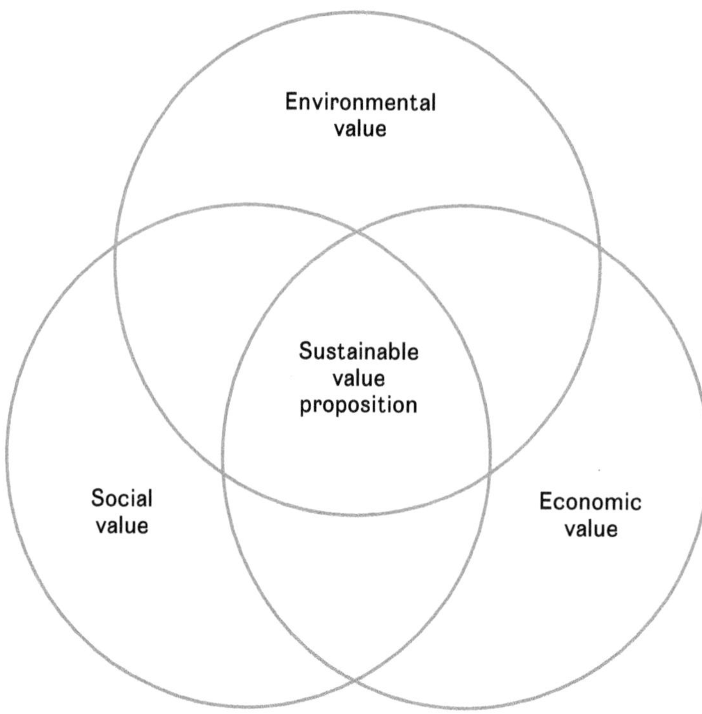


Fig. 3.20 Sustainable business model

Fig. 3.20 The figure shows example of a sustainable business model and with a sustainable value proposition: *Environmental value*: Renewable resource, low emissions, low waste, biodiversity, pollution prevention (air, water, land). *Social value*: Equality and diversity, well-being, community development, secure livelihood, labour standards, health and safety. *Economic value*: Profit, return on investments, financial resilience, long-term viability, business stability. (Based on Evans et al., 2017)

Fig. 3.21 The figure shows a Lean start-up process based on iterative methodology which involves testing along the way in the development process and using the experience to create more user-oriented products. The method minimises the total time it takes to develop a product and brings it more quickly to the market, while making the product more attractive to the user.

global effects have on the business itself. It involves looking beyond what is involved in creating value for the customer, the business owner, internal stakeholders and shareholders. Sustainable business models include external stakeholders, such as society and the environment. 'A sustainable business is one that takes a holistic approach. No business operates in isolation; it exists within an ecosystem' (Thrive Project n/d).[56] According to Thrive project,[57] this changes the calculation of any value creation model, as the company must include the full impact their business practices have on external stakeholders to determine the net value it produces. Based on their research, Patala et al. (2016) define a sustainable value proposition as the major element of a sustainable business model. 'We define sustainable value propositions as a promise on the economic, environmental and social benefits that a firm's offering delivers to customers and society at large, considering both short-term profits and long-term sustainability' (Patala et al., 2016) (3.3.8 Sustainability goals, 3.2.6 Value proposition, 6.9 Sustainable management, 3.3.7 Goal achievement: Triple bottom line).

### 3.5.3 Business model innovation

Business model development can also be a method of innovation and can contribute to faster product development, lower costs, and more innovative products. 'Business model innovation is about the company's ability to acquire added value and how it can make the most of the values it creates. Business model innovation can have a much greater effect on profitability than any other type of innovation. Examples are Apple's

56 Ecosystem is a biological community of interacting organisms and their physical environment (in general use) a complex network or interconnected system (Ecosystem, n.d.).

57 THRIVE is The Holistic Regenerative Innovative Value Entity. The THRIVE Project is a UN affiliated research group. A not-for-profit research, education and advocacy group, based in Australia. THRIVE consists of a framework, platform and a sustainability performance scorecard to help people and organisations measure, analyse and improve their sustainable strategies for a thriveable future: strive2thrive.earth/about/.

58 Casadesus-Masanell and Ricart (2007:6) have illustrated an example of business model innovation for Ryanair.

iPhone business model (which is about accumulating the largest share of the total profit – in a very short time), and Ryanair's low-cost airline model (which is about accumulating the most profitable airline in Europe in a very short time). 'Ryanair has realized that some passengers prefer separate services so that they can choose which services they want to pay for'(Roos et al. 2014).[58] 'Business model innovations for sustainability are defined as: Innovations that create significant positive and/or significantly reduced negative impacts for the environment and/or society, through changes in the way the organisation and its value-network create, deliver value and capture value (i.e. create economic value) or change their value propositions' (Bocken et al., 2014).

### 3.5.4 Lean start-up

Methods such as Lean start-up and the idea of Transient Advantage (3.4.5 Transient advantage) are changing the traditional perception and understanding of the business model and business strategy. There is a movement in the direction of lean in many areas and an increased need for an experimental approach, including design methodology (Sitre, 2017). Lean start-up is an example of a methodical business model innovation. Traditionally, a start-up begins with an idea for a product that you think people want (3.2.3 Business idea). With such a starting point, some companies need months and sometimes years to develop and perfect a product without showcasing or testing it on a potential customer. Many start-ups fail because those who developed the product never talked to potential customers to decide if the product was interesting (Adler, 2011). 'Most start-ups fail, not because they cannot build what they have decided to build, but because they waste time, money, and effort building the wrong product' (Maurya, 2012). The Lean start-up business model principles are about shortening the development time and costs of testing

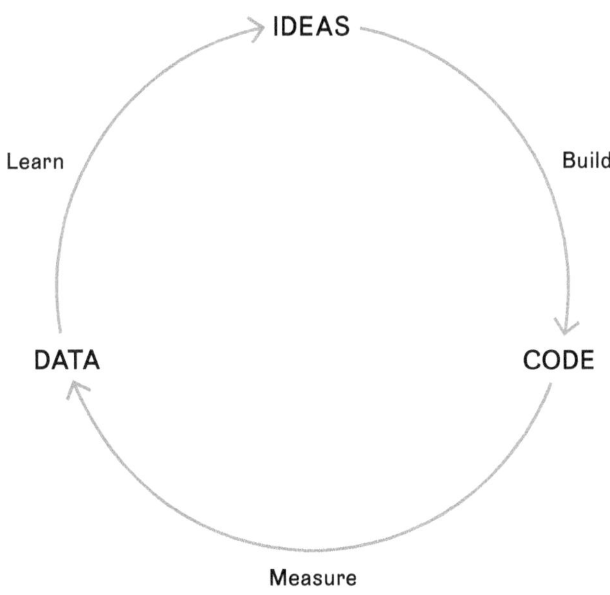


Fig. 3.21 Lean start-up



1 Initiation
2 Insight
3 Strategy
4 Design
5 Production
6 Management

3.1 Strategy development
3.2 Overall strategy
3.3 Goals and subgoals
3.4 Business strategy
3.5 Business model
3.6 Market strategy
3.7 Brand strategy
3.8 Communication strategy
3.9 Design strategy

3.5.1 Business model canvas
3.5.2 Sustainable business model
3.5.3 Business model innovation
3.5.4 Lean start-up

Further reading
– Sage Journals, Special Issue: *Business Models for Sustainability: Entrepreneurship, Innovation and Transformation*. Available at journals.sagepub.com/toc/oae/29/1
– Check out: sustainablebusinessmodel.org and strive2thrive.earth

> Lean start-up/Lean enterprise is a practice that focuses on value creation for the end customer first and foremost by involving the customer/user early on and testing and failing early. This approach makes it possible to determine whether the competitive strategy is sustainable at an early stage. If a strategy is tested early, it can save the company time and resources and minimise the risk of focusing on the wrong things.

the product or service along the way and learning what people want, and then using this knowledge in product development. Such an approach is about 'How can we learn more quickly what works, and reject what doesn't?' (O'Reilly, n.d.). Lean start-up is based on the use of iterative methods (4.3.5 Iterative method). This means that ideas are quickly tested and further developed to a solution that is attractive to the customer and the market. The procedure provides a scientific approach to creating and managing a start-up and getting a desired product to customers faster (4.3 Design methodology, 4.3.10 Lean and agile).

For any company that for one reason or another needs to turn to specific target groups. For specific target groups with a new business concept, product, or service, it is necessary to have a market strategy.

## 3.6 Market strategy

Market strategy is about choosing which markets the company should focus on, to whom the company should sell its products and services, what the business should achieve in different markets, and how it will do so.

All market strategies are based on segmentation, targeting, and positioning, as well as the use of communication as a key tool to break through with messages and offers. It usually starts with a company that discovers different needs in the market and focuses on what it can best satisfy, then positions its offers towards the relevant user group. By meeting customer needs, the company can deliver higher customer value and customer satisfaction, which in turn leads to repurchase and, ultimately, to higher profitability for the company (Kotler and Keller, 2016, p. 379).

Originally, a market was a place where buyers and sellers met to buy and sell goods, very similar to what economists associate with a market today; small or large sales arenas, or geographical areas, where sellers and buyers meet, digitally or physically. In marketing, the term 'market' is used to refer to different segments or all those likely to purchase the products or services offered by the company. In such a context, sellers are representatives of the industry, while buyers are representatives of the market. In the event of high demand, there is a sellers' market, in the event of high supply, there is a buyers' market (Vikøren, 2018).

### 3.6.1 Markets

The market can be divided into different categories, such as demand markets (the dieting market), product markets (the shoe market), demographic markets (the Chinese market), or other variants such as electoral markets, labour markets and donor markets (Kotler and Keller, 2016, p. 37). Both sector and market play a role, but what is actually the difference? The terms *sector* and *industry* tend to be used about very broad overviews and demarcations, such as the entertainment industry and the film industry. These will include, respectively, all entertainment products and almost all films being made. The term market is often used to refer to a slightly narrower definition, such as the cinema market or the market for high-quality TV series, while segments in turn tend to be used for even narrower definitions, such as the segment for romantic

59 Use of market and target group analyses.
60 Jena McGregor, Matthew Byle and Peter Burrows, 'Your New Customer: The State', Business Week, 23 and 30 March 2009, p. 66.
61 Differentiation help building strong brands, which is beneficial in promotion, value creation, image development, product positioning, brand loyalty and expansion of product lines.

comedies' (Lien et al., 2016). Often, the terms are used interchangeably but this should not be so important if the market definition is clear. Markets can be defined through knowledge of the market and competitors against which the company is compared to determine the profitability potential of its own products and services.[59]

Which market the company is to serve is important for how it communicates, both visually and verbally, to sell its products and services. The main customer markets are the consumer market, the business market, the global market, and non-commercial markets (based on Kotler and Keller, 2016, p. 37):

*The consumer market*: 'Business to consumer' (B2C) are companies that sell goods and services for mass consumption such as juice, cosmetics, trainers, and flights. They spend a lot of time and resources establishing a strong brand identity by offering an attractive product with appealing packaging, by making the product available and by providing good information and service.

*The business market*: 'Business to business' (B2B) comprises companies that sell goods and services to other companies. Corporate customers are often well-informed professional buyers with expertise in assessing competitive offers. Advertising, websites, and direct marketing can play a role, but the price and the seller's reputation and professionalism can be just as important.

*The global market*: There are companies operating in international markets. They often have to take into account cultural, linguistic, legal, and political differences when deciding which markets to enter. They should consider how to enter individual markets (consignor, licensor, joint venture partner, through representatives or as sole producer), how to adapt product and service functions to each country, how to set prices, and how to communicate within different cultures.

*The non-commercial market*: These are companies that sell to non-commercial organisations and that, depending on their business model, have higher or lower purchasing power. For example, universities, public bodies and churches often have higher purchasing power than charities. State actors are bound by frameworks and regulations when ordering services and setting prices. Many public procurements require tenders, and the buyers often focus on practical solutions and the lowest price.[60]

### 3.6.2 Marketing tasks

Traditionally, a company's marketing tasks are divided into the following disciplines, which are also part of the company's market strategy and marketing mix:

**Market analysis:** Understanding the customers' needs and ability to pay.

**Market segmentation:** Grouping customers into segments and target groups to which sales and marketing efforts should be directed.

**Innovation and product development:** Creating or further developing products that meet the customers' needs and differentiate the product from its competitors.[61]

**Pricing, cost accounting and payment arrangements:** Differentiating the product on price and meeting different customers' ability to pay.



Marketing management is 'the art and science of choosing target markets and getting, keeping, and growing customers through creating, delivering, and communicating superior customer value" (Kotler). Marketing management uses tools from economics as well as competitive strategy in order to analyse the industry context in which the company operates. These are, among others, Porter's Five Forces, the analysis of strategic groups of competitors as well as value chain analysis.

**Distribution:** Reaching out to customers with the products, deliver value and strengthening direct relationships.
**Advertising and branding:** Influencing customers' perception of the company's products or services and evoking purchase impulses.

### 3.6.3 STP marketing strategy

STP-model is a method for developing an effective and targeted market strategy. STP marketing focuses on commercial effectiveness, selecting the most valuable segments for a business and then developing a marketing mix and product positioning strategy for each segment (Hanlon, 2021).[62] A situational analysis (2.7.1 Situational analysis) forms the basis of this planning, which helps in detecting the arenas in which efforts or change is to be applied (Kalam, 2020). STP stands for segmentation, targeting, and positioning.

Fig. 3.22 The figure shows the STP model; market segmentation, targeting, and positioning (based on økonomiforlaget.no.).

A market segment is an identifiable group of individuals, groups of people, or population sharing one or more characteristics or needs within the same market. Market segments will typically respond predictably when presented with a marketing offer.

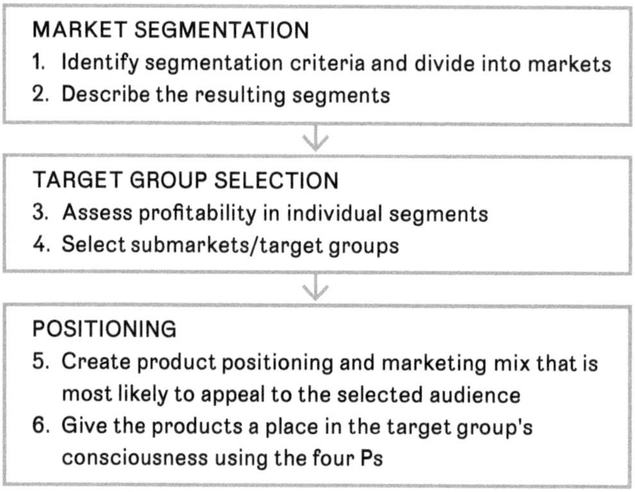

MARKET SEGMENTATION
1. Identify segmentation criteria and divide into markets
2. Describe the resulting segments

TARGET GROUP SELECTION
3. Assess profitability in individual segments
4. Select submarkets/target groups

POSITIONING
5. Create product positioning and marketing mix that is most likely to appeal to the selected audience
6. Give the products a place in the target group's consciousness using the four Ps

Fig. 3.22 STP model

**Segmentation:** Market segmentation is about dividing the market into smaller groups and finding out on which part of the market it is most profitable to focus. This means selecting the most interesting target groups based on who is most likely to buy the company's products or services. A market is divided into segments based on common customer and user characteristics. There are various segmentation variables or characteristics that can be used as a starting point. Within *the consumer market (B2C)*, it is common to use the four main criteria: geographical, demographic, psychographic, and behavioural (2.7.6 Target group analysis). Within the *corporate market (B2B)*,[63] it is common to start with type of industry, size, geography, importance, and systems and technology usage. For segmentation to be possible, the segment must be accessible and identifiable, while at the same time it must be profitable and adapted to the company's resources and goals.

Traditionally, there are three different segmentation strategies for selecting the most attractive target groups; *undifferentiated marketing*

62 SmartInsight: The segmentation, targeting, positioning (STP) marketing model (2021).
63 Salesessentials: The key differences between B2C & B2B Sales Market Segmentation (n/d).

involves treating the entire market as a single large segment; *differentiated marketing* involves dividing the market into several segments according to different needs, and offering products tailored to the individual segments; *concentrated marketing* involves picking out a single segment from the total market and processing it specifically, also called niche marketing. When segmentation is completed, one or more target groups are formed.
**Targeting:** 'Targeting' means that the company selects one or more segments to what it wishes to sell and direct its market initiatives. Target groups are those of (or in) the segments the company should reach or target. When talking about target groups, one can go into more depth and say who they are, where they are, what interests, desires, and needs they have, and so on. In selecting the target group, it is important to consider the size of the segment and the possible growth and competitive situation. If the goal is to take market shares and rapidly grow, it is important to select target groups that are large and profitable; if the goal is to compete in a smaller market and be a small and profitable player, it may be more appropriate to concentrate on a smaller target group. Whether the goal is to serve a large or small market, it is necessary to consider what resources the company must serve the market, and if the investment is profitable. If the company only has capacity to serve a small market, focusing on a large one could be considered improper use of resources. Small niche markets can be profitable if the target group is willing to pay (3.4.2 Porter's generic strategies). It is common to deepen the target group(s) further in connection with the development of a communication strategy. It involves going more specifically into personal characteristics, social identity, and what media they use and so on to select communication channels, communication activities and tone of voice, signal effect, etc. (3.8 Communication strategy, 3.8.2 Identify the target group).
**Positioning:** Positioning is a strategy to distinguish (differentiate) products from competitors and make them visible in the market. It involves giving the product a specific place in the consciousness of the target group by creating some desired associations that one wants them to make with the product. It is about the way the product is communicated visually and verbally to build its desired perception in the market. This involves, among other things, highlighting the unique advantage of the product and using it as a selling point (2.7.5 Positioning analysis, 3.7.3 Brand position).

### 3.6.4 Customers' needs

As part of the target group or segment selection, the market strategy focuses on how the company meets or should meet customer and user needs. Key criteria are:

- How should the product meet the customers' need for solutions?
- How should the price reflect the customers' valuation of the product?
- How should the distribution give the customer easy access to the product?
- How should the communication provide the customer with information about the product? 'The four Ps' and 'The four Cs' are methods that, with somewhat different approaches, cover these questions.



B2B, Business to business: In B2B sales we are still talking to people, however, they are now representing businesses, not necessarily their own interests (as in B2C, Business to consumer). We are now talking to a group of people that are looking at ways to improve performance or guard themselves against risks. The stakes are higher for B2B clients because more people are involved. In B2B sales we need to break down markets into specific segments, then into sub and micro segments, then into types of businesses and stakeholders in these businesses. Sales teams need to know the differences here as this can affect who and how they approach different types of clients and thus affect sales productivity and performance outcomes (Barrett, 2019).

### 3.6.5 The four Ps

Fig. 3.23 The figure shows 'the four Ps': product, price, place, promotion. This is a traditional method for developing a market strategy. The order of the four Ps may vary. In strategy development, it can be natural to think about place before promotion, while from the customers' perspective, promotion can come before the customer finds the product's place in the store.

Within traditional marketing, 'The Four P's, product, price, place and promotion,[64] are considered to be key elements in the company's marketing mix. Marketing mix is a concept coined by Neil Borden[65] in the late 1940s; a combination of all the key elements required to market a brand or a product's unique position which distinguishes it from its competitors. The idea behind Borden's model was further developed and reduced to four elements by E. Jerome McCarthy (1960). 'McCarthy's Four P's (4 Ps), product, price, place, promotion) were established to translate marketing planning into practice (Bennett, 1997, Goi, 2009). Phillip Kotler popularised the model and helped spread it (Kotler, 2000, Keelson, 2012). 4 Ps has been used as classification model by marketing, branding and web design companies around the world. It is based on the principles that the customer perceives the brand based on the product, the price, where it is sold or placed, and how it is communicated. In positioning work, these are the most important factors, because the way the four Ps are used influences how customers perceive the brand (3.4.1 Competitive strategy, 3.7.3 Brand position).

The four Ps often appear in a different order. (Gai, 2009, p. 4) refers to studies that reveal different opinions about which order is most relevant and whether the four Ps have the same degree of importance. 'The studies show that company leaders do not consider the four Ps to be as important but assess price and product components to be the most important' (Kellerman, Gordon and Hekmat 1995, Goi 2009: 4). Here, the four Ps are in the order product, price, promotion, place (based on purelybranded.com):

*Product*: Product means the goods to be sold. A product can be either a tangible object or an intangible service that meets a need or a desire of the consumers. It is important to have clarified what the product is and what makes it unique before one can start marketing it. The design and characteristics of the product, production conditions and production methods are factors that should be clarified (2.7.1 Situational analysis, 2.7.7 Brand analysis, 2.7.8 Visual analysis).

*Price*: Once the unique properties/values of the product are defined, one can start making some price decisions. Price decisions will affect profit margins, supply, demand, and marketing strategy. Price is a factor that is always present. Depending on the competitive strategy, one will

**Marketing mix**

The term 'marketing mix' has been defined as the set of marketing tools that the company uses to pursue its marketing objectives in the target market. According to Philip Kotler (1967) marketing mix can be described as the set of controllable variables a firm can use to influence buyer response, and 'a set of marketing tools that the firm uses to pursue its marketing objectives in the target market' (Kotler, 2001). The term 'marketing mix' is a term that is inextricably linked to product, price, place, and promotion, named 'The 4 Ps', and variations derived from it.

64 Promotion: 1) The publicising of a product, organisation, or venture so as to increase sales or public awareness. 2) Activity that supports or encourages a cause, venture, or aim (Promotion, n.d.).

65 Neil Borden's article 'The Concept of the Marketing Mix' (1964) demonstrated the ways that companies could engage their consumers, using tactics of advertising.

66 Price elasticity is a term for a mathematical calculation used to find the relationship between the price and demand for a specific product (Visma.no).

67 Search Engine Marketing (SEM) is 'a phrase often encompassing everything your business does to market or advertise its web pages on search engines like Google, Bing and more. Most commonly in 2020, the term 'SEM' tends to refer more to paid activities in search engine marketing' (digivizer .com).

68 Search Engine Optimisation (SEO) 'is the process of improving a website to increase its visibility, or rankings, on search engines. SEO work involves keyword research and targeting, on-page and mobile optimisation, and content marketing and link-building' (digivizer .com).

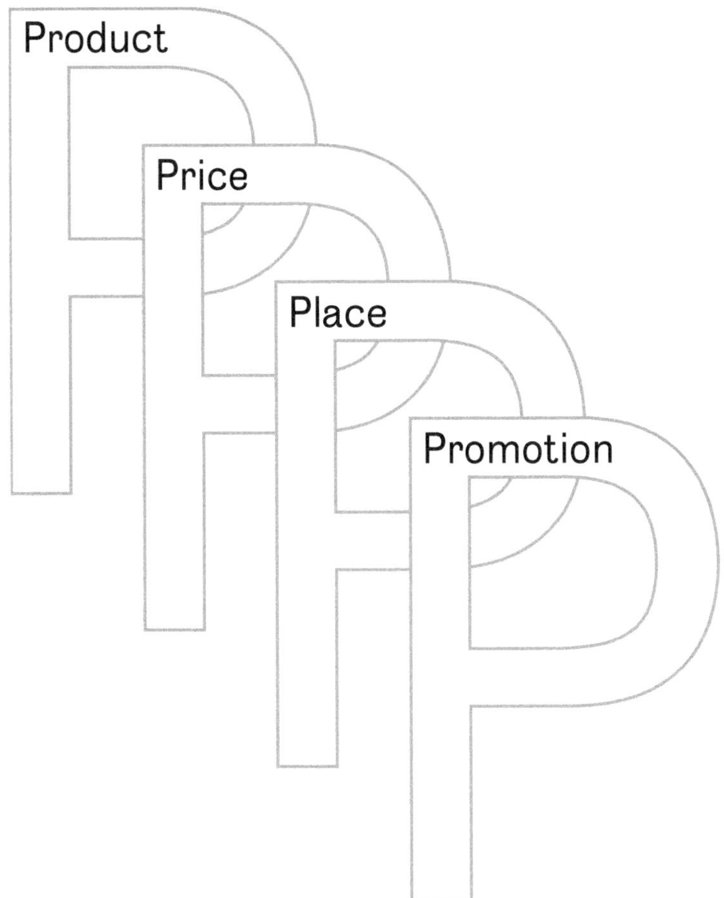




Fig. 3.23 The four Ps

generally choose a price strategy in the range between high price and low price. The selected price strategy will affect the next two Ps. Products should be positioned differently based on price variations. Price elasticity[66] consideration is also an important factor (3.4.1 Competitive strategy, 3.7.3 Brand position).

*Promotion*: Once product and price have been defined; marketing is the next step. Promotion means the communication measures or advertising aimed at consumers. It involves considering different ways of spreading product information which best distinguishes the product from its competitors in the market. A marketing campaign includes elements such as design, advertising, promotions, PR, social media marketing, email marketing, influencers, inbound marketing, search engine marketing,[67] search engine optimisation[68] video marketing,[69] etc. Each contact point should be supported by a good brand position to maximise return on investment.

*Place*: Place means distribution and visibility. Distribution refers to the geographic locations to which the goods are delivered, the outlets from which they are to be sold, and the placement of the goods in the store. It implies digital marketplaces, online stores, price comparison services, etc. Shipping and transport involve costs that may affect the

69 Video marketing means using videos for promoting and telling people about your product or service. It helps increase engagement on your digital and social channels, educates your audience, and allows you to reach them with a new medium. (Hookle.net) *Video Marketing Statistics* 2021: Renderforest has collected some data to show the clear benefits of using videos in marketing campaigns, such as explainer videos, promotional videos, branded intro videos, or animations. The study shows that 78% of users got more traffic to their website after using videos. 69% of users generated more leads with the help of video content, and 54% of users increased their sales. 'The style of your videos depends on your goals and your target audience' (Bojukyan, 2022).

price and profit from the goods, where co-distribution[70] might lower the costs. A phrase one often hears is that marketing is about offering the right product, at the right price, in the right place, at the right time. It is therefore extremely important to consider where the ideal locations are for converting potential to actual customers. Today, even in situations where the actual transaction does not take place online, the first touch point where potential customers are engaged and converted is online.

Fig. 3.24 The figure shows 'the four Cs': Consumer, Cost, Communications, Convenience. The four Cs are a method for developing market strategy that challenges the more traditional method, 'The four Ps', by putting the user, and not the product, at the centre. Consumer replaces Product. Cost replaces Price. Convenience replaces Place. Communication replaces Promotion.

#### Critique of the four Ps

Although the four Ps are widely used in marketing, the model is also criticised. The criticism is that the model applies primarily to the consumer market (Business to Consumer/B2C) and not sufficiently to the corporate market (Business to Business/B2B). In addition, the marketing model is criticised for investing too much in products, failing in terms of the provision of service. Another criticism is that it is based too much on the organisation's perspective and less on that of the consumer (Van Vliet, 2011). The four Cs are a model that addresses this criticism by putting the customer first (3.6.6 The four Cs).

'Content-first' vs. design-first approach
Content-first is determining the essential content of a website, packaging design or the like before developing the visual design. 'Designing a website before determining a firm's essential content is a misstep that can offset strategy and waste both time and money. Instead of forcing content into a beautiful design, the beautiful design should be created around the actual content to highlight the most important information in a meaningful and user-friendly way.' (Asimos, 2020).

#### Extended model

Over the years, McCarthy's four Ps have been adjusted and expanded several times. 'Personnel' is often referred to as the fifth 'P'. Personnel are the key players in an organisation, and without good personnel, Ps do not function optimally. 'Periphery' is also seen as an additional 'P'. Periphery refers to the external factors such as economic, technological, and political factors that can affect an organisation (Van Vliet, 2011).

'The four Ps were designed at a time when companies were selling products rather than services, and customer service as part of brand development was not as well known. Over time, Booms and Pitner expanded the model with three new Ps: 'service mix Ps', Participants (later People), Physical evidence and Processes. Today, it is recommended to consider all seven Ps when developing a market mix and selecting a competitive strategy'. (Hanlon, 2017). An eighth 'P' for Partners (Chaffey & Smith, 2016) is also proposed in this context.

### 3.6.6 The four Cs

The four Cs have a more customer-oriented approach to the marketing strategy than the four Ps, which are essentially product-oriented. The two methods can advantageously be combined. The four Cs stand for Customer, Cost, Convenience and Communication, introduced by Bob Lauterborn (1990).[71] It is an approach that focuses not only on the marketing and sales of a product, but also on the customers' wishes and needs. It is a marketing strategy that involves thinking about the customer first and communicating with them along the way, from the beginning to the end of the process. It is about satisfying your customers' needs better than your competitors (Warren, 2016):

*Consumer*: The first C in this market strategy is the 'Consumer wants and needs. Instead of focusing on the product itself, this strategy focuses on filling a void in the customers' life. This marketing strategy is important for companies interested in understanding their customers' needs.

70 Co-distribution: A distribution of two or more things at the same time or e.g. a company can join other companies' distribution channels for home delivery.

71 In the 1993 article in Advertising Age by Bob Lauterborn stated that 4Ps is dead and today's marketer needs to address the real issues. 'His model shifts the focus from the producer to the consumer and is a better blueprint to follow for smaller businesses that are marketing to a niche audience' (Wong, 2016).

Understanding the customer makes it much easier to create a product that will benefit them. The customer is responsible for the purchase decision and is therefore the most valuable resource in any marketing strategy.

*Cost*: The second C is 'Cost to satisfy'. It should not be confused with the price of the product. Cost in this context includes not only the price of the product but may also include what the customer needs to do to get to the place of purchase, and the costs it entails, such as petrol or other transportation. The costs may also include the product's perceived or actual value, and benefits or shortcomings.

*Convenience*: The third C is 'Convenience to buy'. Convenience is often compared to 'place' in the 4Ps marketing strategy. However, these two are very different. 'Place' refers only to where the product should be sold. 'Convenience' is a much more customer-oriented approach. It is about things such as usability and perceived comfort. This knowledge can be gained by studying or examining the customers' habits. You should know if they shop online or in physical shops, and what they are willing to do to buy the product. The total price of the product will partly determine its convenience for the target group. The principle is to make the product cost effective and easy enough for the customer to acquire without it being too complicated.

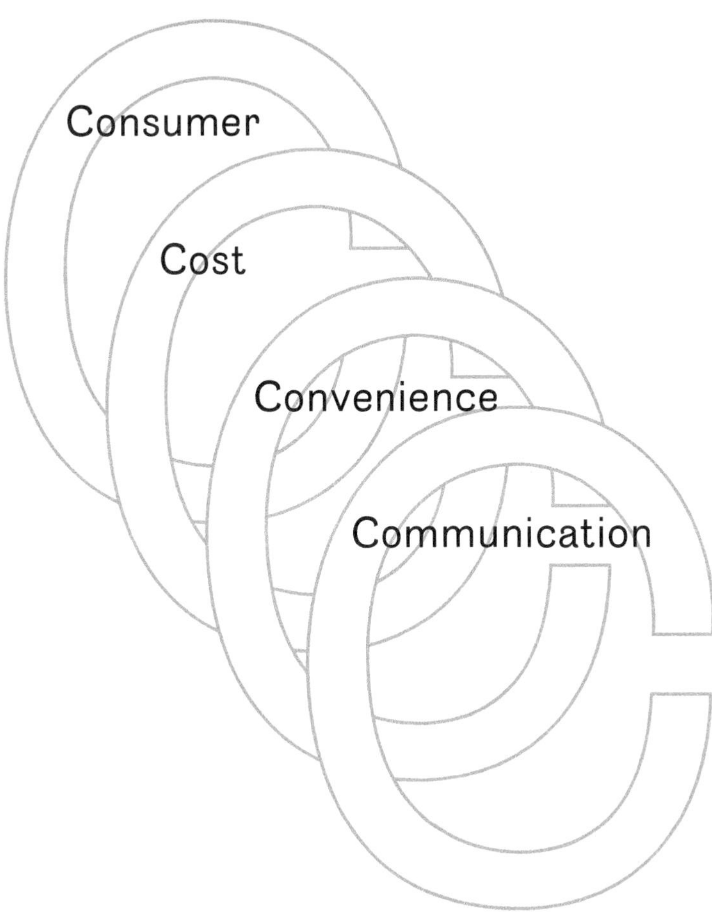


Fig. 3.24 The four Cs



Further reading
'How to Create a Global Content Marketing Strategy': rockcontent.com/blog/global-content-marketing/.

*Communication*: The fourth and final C is communication. Communication is often compared to the fourth P, promotion, but it is very different, however. Promotion of a product is used to convince customers and get them to buy a product. The campaign can often be manipulative and ineffective. In the four Cs, communication is a customer-oriented approach to selling products. Communication requires interaction between buyer and seller, which may very easily be implemented by using social media. Among other things, this allows them to interact with the brand on a personal level, which can lead to greater brand neutrality.

The four Cs can be very beneficial. A marketing strategy based on the four Cs forces marketing experts to truly understand their audience before developing and marketing a product. Such an approach requires communication with the user throughout the process, from start to finish (Warren, 2016).

Fig. 3.25 **The figure shows a content strategy process and workflow. The figure is based on Brenner (2021):** ***Five steps you can take to develop a practical and powerful content strategy for your nonprofit.***

Tips for the designer
**'Instead of pitching your products or services, you are providing truly relevant and useful content to your prospects and customers to help them solve their issues' (Content Marketing Institute, CMI, contentmarketinginstitute.com).**

### 3.6.7 Content marketing

Content marketing is a strategic marketing approach that involves engaging customers to build long-term relationships that have measurable business value. In principle, it means creating and distributing valuable, relevant, and consistent content to attract and retain a clearly defined audience, 'Content marketing is the process of consistently publishing relevant content that audiences want to consume, to reach, engage, and convert new customers. It involves brands acting more like publishers and creating content on a destination you own (your website) that attracts visitors' (Brenner, 2021). Content marketing takes place through multiple channels, such as YouTube, Instagram, podcasts, apps, social networks, influencers, blogging, etc. Content can be blog posts, video, photos, surveys, e-books, etc. Content marketing does not promote your products and services directly. Instead, resources are used to build a long-term relationship with customers by creating useful content at all stages of the purchase process. Content marketing is about owned attention as opposed to paid attention in media platforms (see Figure 3.25 Paid, owned, earned attention). This is done by continuously producing relevant, valuable, and engaging content that customers need and look for, and in the places they are looking, so that one actually gets their attention. If done correctly, potential customers will seek out the company instead of the other way around.

Conent marketing
**A marketing approach focused on creating and distributing content that drives customer action.**

Inbound marketing
**A business methodology focused on creating experiences designed to build and strengthen relationships between a business and buyers.**

**Five steps to develop a content strategy**

Content strategy is a way of describing the process of planning, developing, and managing useful and usable written or other forms of consumable interactive content. It is about deciding the who, what, where, when, how, and why (Martin, 2017):

1. *Align Your Content*: Align your content with the customer journey. Identify what topics, needs, and questions will be addressed in your content.
2. *Conduct a Content Audit*: Audit your existing content to determine what can be used as is, what must be updated, and what must be created from scratch.

3. *Create Your Content Production Plan*: Determine the genre and format of each content piece. Identify who will be the subject matter experts, authors, and other contributors.
4. *Define Your Key Performance Measures*: Determine the objective of each piece of content and how performance will be tracked and measured.
5. *Identify Your Content Distribution Channels*: Identify what online and offline channels will be used to get content in front of constituents, members, and donors.

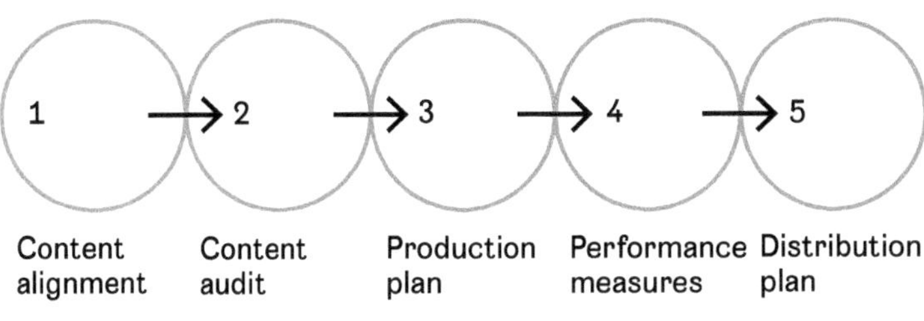


Fig. 3.25 Five steps to develop a content strategy

1 Initiation
2 Insight
3 Strategy
4 Design
5 Production
6 Management

3.1 Strategy development
3.2 Overall strategy
3.3 Goals and subgoals
3.4 Business strategy
3.5 Business model
3.6 Market strategy
3.7 Brand strategy
3.8 Communication strategy
3.9 Design strategy

3.6.1 Markets
3.6.2 Marketing tasks
3.6.3 STP marketing strategy
3.6.4 Customers' needs
3.6.5 The four Ps
3.6.6 The four Cs
3.6.7 Content marketing
3.6.8 Inbound marketing
3.6.9 Digital strategy

### 3.6.8 Inbound marketing

Inbound marketing is a variant of content marketing where you get the customer to come to you, instead of pestering the customer (Furu, 2015). The trend is towards buyers not looking at the company's marketing materials to make that decision. Instead, third-party review sites, peer-to-peer recommendations, and word-of-mouth play a bigger role in buying decisions than ever before (Hubspot, n.d.). Inbound marketing is more about loyalty-building activities aimed at individuals on the internet/social media than about traditional marketing (outbound marketing), which involves addressing many via TV and radio advertising, printed media, telemarketing, direct mail, and outdoor advertising. Inbound marketing is about attracting customers to products and services through content marketing, social media marketing, search engine optimisation, and through loyalty building activities targeting individuals, including through dialogue programs, and by giving people information and content that they value - to achieve *earned attention* (Prescott, 2012). The method is based on a cyclic three-step process of finding, converting and analysing:

*Be found*: Be found is the first step to starting a cycle. A company's content should be visible to the right audience at the right time. This is a very long process, which involves thorough insight and content planning (Rudello, 2017). Figures from HubSpot show that companies blogging one to two times a month generate 70 per cent more leads compared to companies that do not blog at all (Førsund, 2015).

*Convert*: The second step is the conversion of followers into prospects. This may seem like a very simple process, but it is not easy at all. This process is long and involves the use of time and energy for the business. The conversion rate is the percentage of visitors who take a desired action. It forms the basis for the analysis of the effort, for example based on measuring activities such as clicks, likes, and comments.

Further reading
– 'Replacing the Sales Funnel with the Sales Flywheel' by Brian Halligan. *Harvard Business Review*, November 20, 2018.
– 'The Flywheel. How the flywheel drives business growth and customer delight' (hubspot.com/flywheel).
– Check out the book: *Content Inc.* (2021) by Joe Pulizzi.

Content strategy
Describe the process of planning, developing, and managing useful and usable written or other forms of consumable interactive content (Martin, 2017).

*Analyse*: The third and final step is analysis. After the customer has become aware of the product/service, and after converting followers to a lead, the company should analyse and evaluate the data to understand what they need to change in the process in order to improve the results. Inbound marketing uses owned and earned media to engage potential customers in creative ways (3.8.8 Channels and media: paid, owned, earned attention).

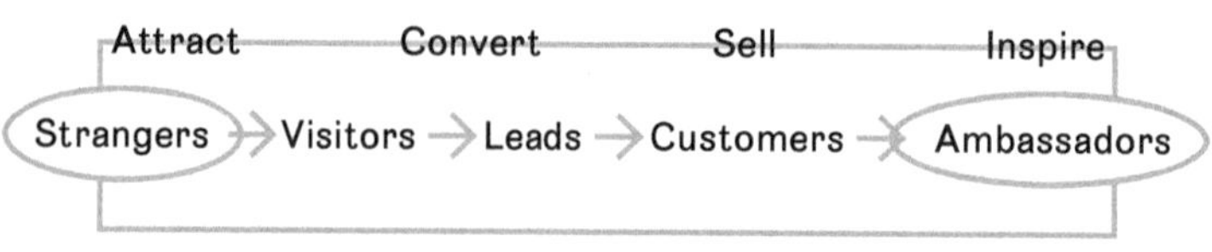


Fig. 3.26 Inbound marketing

Fig. 3.26 The figure shows an example of a model for an inbound marketing campaign. There are many, almost equal models online. Explanation of the model and the basis for the illustration are taken from Førsund (2015). 1) *Attract strangers*: They discover you on social media through their contacts' sharing of your content. They find you after a search (Google). 2) *Convert visitors to leads: Offer* visitors premium content (content that has a high perceived value), and for which the visitor is willing to pay by way of their contact details. 3) *Sell*: A lead usually needs 8–12 touchpoints before they are ready to buy or talk to a seller, so best practice is not to send these people directly to the sales department. Leads should be processed and 'warmed up' before making sales advances. This process is called lead nurturing and is a very important part of IM. 4) *Inspire*: You should continue to give value to your customers, as they are your best ambassadors. Conduct surveys to discover how satisfied they are with you and your content and 'monitor' what is said about you on social media.

### Inbound vs. Outbound

According to (Førsund, 2015), marketing can be broadly divided into two categories: inbound and outbound:

*Inbound* marketing and sales activities are aimed at people who have a need or a problem to solve. In nine out of ten cases, they will start their search on Google. The basic principle is to achieve visibility in searches and social media, direct traffic to the web, convert traffic to leads (concrete enquiries from potential customers), and convert leads to customers. It is the buyer who takes the initiative to establish contact with the company, and therefore this type of market communication is also referred to as buyer-initiated marketing. Inbound is essentially a form of digital marketing.

*Outbound* sales and marketing activities are aimed at persons without a recognised need. This category includes outreach sales, mail advertising, commercials, TV and radio advertising, events, sampling, etc. Here it is the seller who takes the initiative, and outbound is therefore also referred to as seller-initiated marketing. Outbound can be both digital and analogue. Tips for using the two strategies:

1) First, establish an inbound strategy that ensures that the company utilises the buyer initiative in the market.
2) If the inbound approach does not produce enough impact, outbound measures can be brought in.

### Content marketing vs. Inbound marketing

Content marketing and inbound marketing have a lot in common. 'For both types of marketing, content is a key element. The philosophy is to help one's potential customers instead of pestering them. This is done by offering them valuable content instead of pushing advertising on them' (Førsund, 2015). According to Førsund, the difference between content marketing and inbound marketing is as follows:

*Content marketing (CM)* can be both outbound and inbound, both analogue and digital. The measures in a CM strategy may include websites, customer magazines, and events. CM can support several marketing goals, but especially branding and customer loyalty.

72 Nina Furu is a Norwegian journalist, author, course leader and general manager of Webgruppen. She is at the forefront of building and managing a leading competence environment within digital marketing and web communication in Norway.

73 Conversions means user actions you want to announce, e.g. that the user orders products, fills out a contact form, finds a retailer, subscribes to newsletters and similar.

74 Conversion rate optimisation (CRO) 'is the process of increasing the percentage of conversions from a website or mobile app. CRO typically involves generating ideas for elements on your site or app that can be improved and then validating those hypotheses through A/B testing and multivariate testing' (optimizely.com)

1 Initiation
2 Insight
3 Strategy
4 Design
5 Production
6 Management

3.1 Strategy development
3.2 Overall strategy
3.3 Goals and subgoals
3.4 Business strategy
3.5 Business model
3.6 Market strategy
3.7 Brand strategy
3.8 Communication strategy
3.9 Design strategy

3.6.1 Markets
3.6.2 Marketing tasks
3.6.3 STP marketing strategy
3.6.4 Customers' needs
3.6.5 The four Ps
3.6.6 The four Cs
3.6.7 Content marketing
3.6.8 Inbound marketing
3.6.9 Digital strategy

– Digital market strategy

*Inbound marketing (IM)* is exclusively digital and narrower in its approach. Typical actions in an IM strategy are blogging, social media, search engine optimisation, search engine marketing, email marketing, and web. IM is a highly effective tool if the company generates leads (generating enquiries from potential customers, applicants, students, members) as its main marketing goal (3.8 Communication strategy).

### 3.6.9 Digital strategy

A digital strategy specifies how the business will use technology to improve business performance and create new competitive advantages with technology. This involves both internal process development, product development, marketing and more. The digital strategy should be anchored in the company's overall goal and strategy, and support their digital transformation. Digitisation is not a goal in itself, but is about finding ways to use technology that creates value. This value is always about meeting people's needs. The design approach provides many good tools to get to know the target group and their needs, and to develop, test and continuously improve concepts, solutions and initiatives (Sitre, 2021). The part of a digital strategy that involves digital marketing is also called digital market strategy or digital media strategy.

#### Digital market strategy

Digital and mobile channels are vital for acquiring and retaining customers. The company should have an integrated plan for how to engage their audiences effectively online. A digital marketing strategy is a plan and a series of actions that use online marketing channels to achieve various marketing goals. 'The digital strategy outlines the channels, assets, platforms and tools required to achieve these objectives and deliver the results' (incremental.com.au). When creating results in the digital field, there are many elements that must be in place. Figure 3.27 Digital strategy shows the most important needs and elements of digital marketing and how they belong together. The figure and further explanation is based on Nina Furu/Webgruppen (webgruppen.no, 2021):[72]

**The website:** The website is the hub of digital marketing, a digital point of sales of products and services, a place where the company presents its business, conducts conversions, promotions, etc.[73] For companies that run an online store, it is usually the online store that is the website, but also companies that do not sell anything directly online should have a website, as it is this that determines the company's visibility on Google. Website conversions are measured with web analytics, typically Google Analytics. It is important to examine which channels actually drive traffic and who the actual users are. In addition, one should have processes to optimise the percentage of visits that end with a conversion, i.e. operate with so-called CRO (conversion rate optimisation).[74] Web development and web design require careful consideration of user-experience (UX) and user interface (UI).

**a) Development drives the website:** Content management system (CMS), web design, functionality and content are the elements that affect the website and how to work with it, both to get it up and running on an ongoing basis.

Further reading
– *9 best social media and content marketing tips from buffer*: Widrich
– *How to build social media into your content marketing process*: Content Marketing Institute
– *100 killer ideas for your social media content*: Medium
– *How to choose the best digital marketing analytics software*: Forbes
– *How to measure the ROI of marketing programs*: MarketoBlog
– *How to integrate Email marketing with a social media strategy*: Campaign Monitor

- *CMS*: the publishing solution, i.e. the tool you use to manage the pages.[75]
- *Webdesign*: The appearance, layout, information structure, user-experience and, in some cases, content of the website.
- *Functionality*: The development of necessary features which should be possible to do on the web pages, such as buying tickets or booking an appointment.
- *Content*: The content on the website. It must be continuously updated and maintained, typically by a web editor or webmaster. This person uses the company's CMS to enter new texts, manage menu items, post new services or products, update prices etc. The larger the website, the more important the content management. The public sector often has a lot of content which needs continuous updating.

**b) Content includes text, image, video and sound.** All companies that are online need a lot of content – both for social media and newsletters, but also to disseminate information, update the website and sell products and services. This often requires separate processes to both create content and share content on social media. Ongoing access to texts, images, audio and video is necessary, wether this must be made in house, or it must be purchased externally. In any case, both marketers and webmasters must have access to these resources in order to manage both the website and other marketing channels in a good way. In addition, the company needs someone who can publish content in different channels, e.g. those who have market responsibility in the individual channels.

**Channels:** There are primarily three digital marketing channels that work to generate traffic: search, social media, and the 1:1 channels. In order to get traffic to the web pages, and thus get leads as to who can potentially be converted into customers, we use the marketing channels. We will say something about each of these:

**c) Search is pull marketing:** Google typically accounts for over 50% of all web traffic, and is therefore often the most important market channel. In addition, it is on Google that you will find the customers who are already actively asking for what you are selling by searching for it – which also means that these customers are happy to get a good conversion rate. This type of marketing is often called on-demand marketing, because you market towards the customers' active demand. Another word for this is pull marketing, because the customer himself retrieves (pull = pulls out) the information he needs. Becoming visible on Google can be done by one or a combination of these:

- SEO (Search Engine Optimisation): Work with the website and the content in such a way that it makes you come up with good rankings for free. This is what is called search engine optimisation or Search Engine Optimisation.
- Pay Per Click (PPC): Buy ads through Google Ads. These ads are priced according to the model called pay per click meaning you do not pay anything for your ad before someone clicks and thus visits your landing page.
- YouTube: Work with YouTube SEO, i.e. steps that give better visibility of videos on YouTube.[76] Hits from YouTube are fully integrated into the search engine results page on Google. Everything that is easier to watch being demonstrated, rather than being explained, is content that could be well-optimised videos on YouTube.

Fig. 3.27 The figure shows an example of some of the most important elements, skills, needs and actions needed to develop a digital marketing strategy. The website is the hub. The main areas surrounding the hub is customer, development, content and channels. The subareas of these are explained in the chapter. The figure is based on Nina Furu/Webgruppen 2021.

Tips for the designer
Social media resources: Feedly. Buzzsumo. TwelveSkip. RazorSocial. The Zero BS Guide. SproutSocial. Convince and Convert. Buffer.

Tips for the company
Tools to measure social media marketing results: Native analytics tools on Facebook, Twitter, etc.; Social media management platforms like HootSuite and Buffer; Web analytics such as Google Analytics; Dedicated social medi measurement platforms.

Further reading
– *How to Create Buyer Personas with Social Media Data – Hootsuite*; blog.hootsuite.com/buyer-persona/.
– 'How to set (and achieve) meaningful social media goals' by Brent Barnhart, January 2, 2020: sproutsocial.com/insights/social-media-goals/.
– PicMonkey and Canva are photo editing tools for visual social media posts.

75 CMS (Content Management System): The world's most widely used publishing solution is called WordPress, and is basically free. Other common publishing solutions are EpiServer (used mostly by larger companies and the public sector) and EZ Publish, just to name a few.
76 YouTube is the world's second largest search engine, and it's owned by Google.
77 Updated user numbers for each of the channels internationally can be found on statista.com.

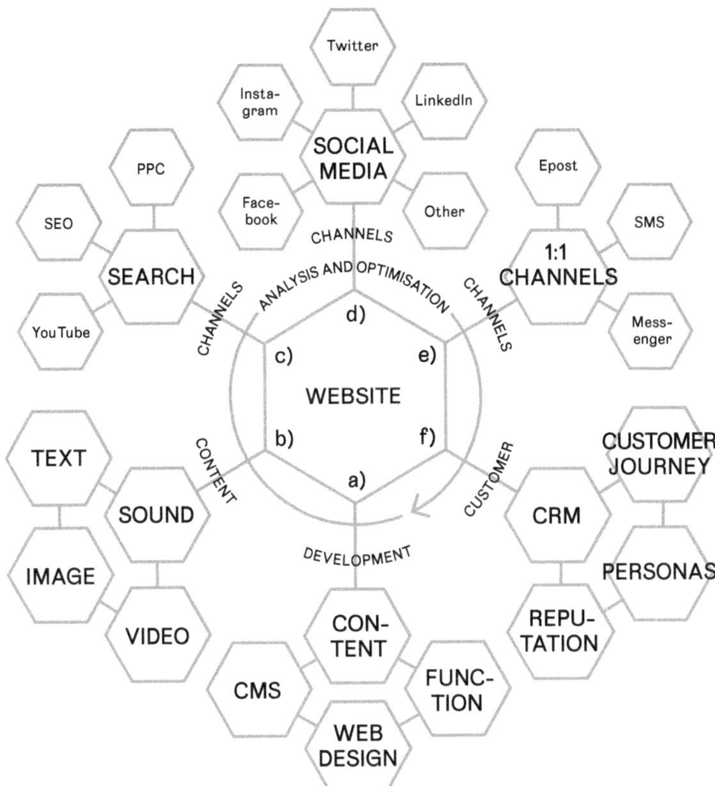


Fig. 3.27 Digital strategy



**d) Social media is push marketing:** These are channels that reach out to the potential customers who do not already actively demand the current goods or services that the company sells, but who may be interested in these if they are suggested. This is what is called push marketing. Which channels to choose depends on the individual company's needs.

- *Facebook*: They have marketing products that allow the customer to put an update in the news feed of any user around the world, segmented in detail on geography, demography and also psychography, i.e. what interests and inclinations the individual potential customer has.
- Instagram: If the purpose is to visually profile a brand, Instagram is a natural choice.
- Twitter: If the company has political influence and wants to participate in the public debate, Twitter can be a good place.
- Linkedin: This channel is a natural part of the mix for those who work business-to-business.
- YouTube: This is a central ad placement channel if the company are talking to younger target groups. YouTube is also a great channel for creating search visibility for your own videos.
- Snapchat: This channel has a number of challenges which means that it is often not chosen unless all other channels have already been optimised.[77]

**e) Channels for resale purposes:** These channels are; emails, SMS or Messenger. These channels are proven to be most suitable for resale to customers who already know you from previous encounters. For new

'Research consistently finds that good, clear, coherent digital strategy is critical to success when it comes to delivering complex digital projects. This suggests that a digital strategy is indeed something tangible, and quite valuable' (Hovey, 2020).

sales, search and social media are better. What characterises these channels is the fact that you need prior consent in order to be allowed to address a lead or prospect. There are specific legal regulations for EU which are important to know and follow.[78] The 1:1 channels are very sales-triggering, and often account for a high proportion of the company's overall conversion rate when used systematically.

**f) The customer is most important:** When working with SoMe (Social Media) it is as always important to communicate based on the specific channels standards.

- *Personas*: It is common to create personas. The company usually has 4–5 different personas and develops content and lead processes that are relevant to each of these.
- *Customer journey*: In this context, a costumer journey can be used to find out which channels customers choose to use. The customer journey describes the process the customer goes through from identifying a need to buy and perhaps also recommending the product further. It can be assessed in light of personas. It can be an advantage to create different customer journeys relevant for each persona, and define relevant points of contact with each individual customer in the different channels, based on where the individual potential customer is in their customer journey.
- *CRM*: To manage and automate the dialogue with the individual customers, you often use a Client Relationship Management system (CRM), such as SuperOffice or other tools. The most comprehensive of these tools, such as HubSpot, are also tools for marketing automation.[79]
- *Reputation*: Online the company are dependent on their reputation, whether it's star ratings on social media or dealing with customer service inquiries and feedback on various SoMe channels. The very best is when customers are so satisfied that they act as the company's ambassadors in their own networks (2.9.1 User testing, 2.9.2 A/B testing, 2.9.3 Funnel, 2.7.6 Target group analysis, 3.1.3 TOP 5, 3.8 Communication strategy, 4.3.2 User-experience, 5.6 Production for digital media).

Tips for the designer
**The benefits of blogging**
**1) It helps to drive traffic to your website**
**2) Gets you discovered on social media**
**3) Increases conversions**
**4) Establishes authority.**

Tips for the company
**Blogging can help generate more leads for your business, help establish authority and build trust, help drive traffic to your website, which increases the chance of being found in search results. (Shore, 2020)**

Mobile app
**The role of mobile apps in a digital strategy: Mobile's role should be considered in the end-to-end customer journey and in light of the customer expectations. The consumer does generally expect to be connected beyond the browser. A mobile app should be simple and plugged into the digital ecosystem, e.g. leveraging integration of GPS, maps, sensors and online payments (centric-consulting.com).**

### Influencer marketing

The term *influencer* is often used about people who have established a reputation for having an expert level of knowledge or social influence in their field and who make money by profiling various products in social media. *Influencer marketing* is a type of social media marketing that involves endorsements and product placements from influencers. One does not address the advertising message directly to buyer groups and the public, but instead uses influential individuals in marketing communication. 'Manufacturers, retailers and advertisers then try to drive brand building and increase sales by linking specific products to popular personalities who have an impact on potential buyers. By exploiting the trust and credibility of influencers as trendsetters and role models for their loyal followers and admirers, one can reach out and influence the target groups for the products more effectively' ('Influencer marketing', n.d.). There is also the phenomenon of 'micro-influencers'. Compared to ordinary influencers, micro-influencers reach a niche. They have fewer followers but often greater credibility with the target group they communicate with (3.6.7 Content marketing, 3.6.8 Inbound marketing, 3.8.8 Channels and media).

78 According to relevant laws, e.g. The Digital Markets Act: ensuring fair and open digital markets (https://ec.europa.eu/). See also: 2.6.1 Survey: protection of personal data.

79 Marketing automation: Automated sending of follow-ups, and pre-programming of races for lead nurturing and the like.

1 Initiation
2 Insight
3 Strategy
4 Design
5 Production
6 Management

3.1 Strategy development
3.2 Overall strategy
3.3 Goals and subgoals
3.4 Business strategy
3.5 Business model
3.6 Market strategy
3.7 Brand strategy
3.8 Communication strategy
3.9 Design strategy

Brand strategy is a planning and management tool for the development and building of one or more brands owned by the company. Development of a brand strategy involves working consciously on how a brand should be developed and managed over time to achieve maximum value and competitiveness. A brand strategy is based on a target group and market analysis that identifies which market segments and specific target groups the brand should be aimed at.

Brand strategy is about how a brand should be governed, managed, and developed over time. A brand strategy may be needed when developing a new brand, rebranding, or when there are plans to expand a product range and invest in new markets. For example, it can be a brand extension into new territories or markets or a line extension with new variants and flavours. A key question when developing a brand strategy will be whether to use one or more brand names. If the company is to have several brands, the question will be what should be the difference between these brands, what role they should play in the company's product portfolio, what the brands should stand for, and whom they should be aimed at. Secondly, the question will be how the brand(s) should be positioned and communicated in the market and what significance they should have for the target group(s) concerned. This will depend to a large extent on the competitive strategy the company has chosen, whether it will compete on price, differentiation, or focus on a narrow customer segment (3.4.1 Competitive strategy). In the case of redesign, rebrand or brand extension, it will be necessary to conduct a brand analysis to clarify the current situation of the brand to assess the potential and possibilities for change. The goals and plan for the development and building of the brand are determined based on the brand analysis (2.7.7 Brand analysis). There are many different opinions as to what a brand strategy should contain, which depends, among other things, on the nature of the product and the company. For example, it will provide different prerequisites to work with a private company, a public company and/or a non-profit organisation, as well as in terms of the products and services they provide, and the target groups they are aimed at. We would prefer to talk about brands from a competitive perspective here.

The brand strategy is compiled in a report with recommendations for further work and is followed up with a communication strategy, defining how and where the brand should be communicated, in which channels and platforms the brand should be exposed, and which brand activities should be carried out. The brand strategy can provide basis for a design strategy which should give guidance on the design tasks that should be solved (3.9 Design strategy). The scope of a brand strategy should be seen in relation to needs, time and budget. Before we go into the various factors of a brand strategy, we will clarify some of the most common concepts used.

Brand goal, brand strategy and brand monitoring

Brand goal: What is the desired situation for the brand? Overall goal?

Brand strategy: How should the desired situation be achieved? Path selection? How to ensure targeted brand development? With what measures and instruments?

Brand monitoring: How to ensure (continuous) monitoring of brand position, brand recognition, and reputation? How to establish good practices for measuring and evaluating the brand?

### Trademark vs. brand

*A trademark* is used as regards to the name, symbol or logo representing a company, product or service. A *registered trademark* means it has been registered with a national trademark office (6.2 Legal protection). The registered item is then legally protected against plagiarism or other improper use within defined geographical areas and product categories, giving rise to the use of the ® symbol associated with the service mark.[80] Such registration presupposes that the name (word) or the mark has a distinctive character. A mark which is not registered, but which is incorporated and established over time and has a sufficiently distinctive character, may enjoy the same legal protection as a registered trademark (6.2.2 Trademark). A trademark may develop into a brand.

*A brand* is something more than a trademark. A brand is a combination of all the associations that the consumer (buyer, user, or recipient) has with a name, logo, or symbol of a company, product, or service. Such associations can be constructed and built over time, and will together with the real experience of what the brand represents, create lasting relationships with the consumer. 'A brand is a set of mental associations in the customers' awareness which are added to the perceived value of a product or service (Keller, 1998). These associations should be unique (exclusivity), strong (saliency) and positive (desirable)' (Kapferer, 2012, 7). The brand is the totality - everything we associate with a business, product, or service - our overall perception, sympathies, and antipathies. Among the world's most famous brands are Coca-Cola, Nike, and Apple. Simply by hearing these names, we know what products they represent, images come to our minds, along with a variety of abstract and concrete memories (2.9.8 Mental availability measurements).

Table 3.7 The table shows an example of a brand strategy development process. © Grimsgaard, W. (2022).

> A trademark is a recognisable insignia, phrase or symbol that denotes a specific product or service and legally differentiates it from all other products.
> 'A brand is a mix of tangible and intangible unique attributes employed in creating the image and language that identifies a product and its brand purpose and differentiates it from its competitors' (IGERENT 2021, igerent.com).

### Brand

A *brand* is a name, term, design, symbol, or any other feature that identifies one seller's good or service as distinct from those of other sellers.[81] ISO brand standards add that a brand 'is an intangible asset' that is intended to create 'distinctive images and associations in the minds of stakeholders, thereby generating economic benefit/value.'[82] Brand originates from the Norse word *brandr*, which means fire or burning (Falcon and Torp 1991),[83] and which was used, among other things, for the branding of cows, or for burning a mark or symbol on the gable of a house or bow of a ship to mark the owner. Hence, there is a clear link to today's use of the word 'brand' for marking an item. Branding is the strategic and tactical development and establishment of a brand. Branding is used in design and advertising to establish and position a company, product, or service in the market and in the consumer's mind.

### Corporate brand vs. product brand

Product branding has been around for a long time, while corporate branding is a more recent construct. While a product is relatively concrete term, a company is a much more faceted and complex one. An important difference between branding of company and product is the goal of the brand. A product brand is mainly aimed at consumers, while a corporate brand is aimed at all stakeholders: from suppliers, partners, and business environments, to society, and the public. A fundamental responsibility for

80 In some countries it is against the law to use the registered trademark symbol for a mark that is not officially registered in any country ('Registered trademark', n.d.).
81 Cited: 'Brand', *Common Language Marketing Dictionary* (2020), American Marketing Association, AMA Dictionary.
82 Cited: 'Brand', *Common Language Marketing Dictionary* (2020), International Organisation for Standardization, Brand Evaluation – Principles and Fundamentals.
83 According to Wikipedia the origins of brand as a term may originate from ancient Egypt 'The practice of branding – in the original literal sense of marking by burning – is thought to have begun with the ancient Egyptians, who were known to have engaged in livestock branding as early as 2,700 BCE' ('Brand,' n.d.)
84 Alizadeh 2014: *The Comparison of Product and Corporate Branding Strategy* (2014).

| Brand strategy process | |
|---|---|
| Brand analysis/ brand audit | What state is the brand currently in, how is the brand meeting customers' needs and what are the competitors doing? When rebranding, redesigning, doing a brand maintenance or after a merger, one should start with a brand analysis prior to preparing a new brand strategy (2.7.7 Brand analysis). |
| Brand platform/ brand strategy and goals | What should the overall strategy and goal of the brand be? What strategic directions should be used as a basis for the development of brand name, brand identity, and communication? (3.7.1 Brand platform). |
| Brand architec-ture and brand structure | What role should the brand play? Is the brand monolithic, endorsed, or pluralistic? Should one have more brands? Where is the brand located in the brand hierarchy? (3.7.2 Brand architecture). |
| Brand position | How should the brand be differentiated from competing brands and express the right associations? How should it take a position in people's minds (3.7.3 Brand position). |
| Brand narrative and brand story | What story should the brand tell? Which narrative should bear the brand associations? (3.7.4 Brand story). |
| Brand identity | How to create a brand identity in line with the desired position? How to reinforce the brand's core and contributes to differentiation? How to create good brand relationships? (3.7.5 Brand identity). |
| Brand assets | Which brand asset types should contribute to create the right brand experience? How should the brand elements work together? How can the brand work on different exposure surfaces and profile carriers? (3.7.6 Brand assets). |
| Distinctive brand assets | Brand assets types: name, logo, symbol, character, slogan, audio logo (jingle), sense elements, packaging (3.4.6 Distinctive asset-building strategy, 4.9.7 Distinctive assets, 2.9.8 Mental availability measurements). |
| Brand perspective | How should the brand be developed and managed over time? Can the brand be expanded with new product areas? What should the strategic direction for developing the brand be? What should the guidelines for long-term branding, development and management of the brand be? (3.7.8 Brand perspective). |
| Brand management | How should the brand assets be managed? (6.2 Legal protection). |

Table 3.7 Brand strategy process

all companies is a healthy organisational culture, focusing on employees and organisational behaviour which indirectly or directly affects the company's brand identity. While branding work for products is often the responsibility of marketing departments in a company, corporate branding requires anchoring throughout the organisation (Alizadeh et al., 2014).[84]



Originally, branding stems from the need to offer products and services to the market in a way that sets them apart from competitors. Branding is the basic way to build consumer awareness by naming the offer, and by distinguishing the offer from other similar products or services within an established category. 'Branding is about differentiation' (Kay 2006/ Alizadeh et al., 2014).

Davies (2012) believes that there is a change in progress, where the focus is generally shifting from product to company. As a result, the need for a healthy organisational culture is becoming important. 'The study of branding has traditionally been dominated by emphasis on product brands. However, the rapid innovation, increased service levels, and reduced brand loyalty that characterises today's markets have made corporate branding a strategic marketing tool (Xie and Boggs, 2006). Ward and Lee (2000) found that there was a shift among companies from focusing on product brands to focusing on corporate and service brands. Companies should therefore decide whether to build the identity of the product or the identity of the company' (Alizadeh et al., 2014).

Fig. 3.28 **Brand strategy should be the core of the company for it to succeed in taking a clear and sustainable position in the competitive arena. Text and figure based on Karlsen (2009).**

Tips for the designer

**A corporate brand is rooted in the company's overall goals and strategy. A product brand should also be based on the company's goals and values, but depending on which brand architecture is chosen, a product brand can be more independent.**

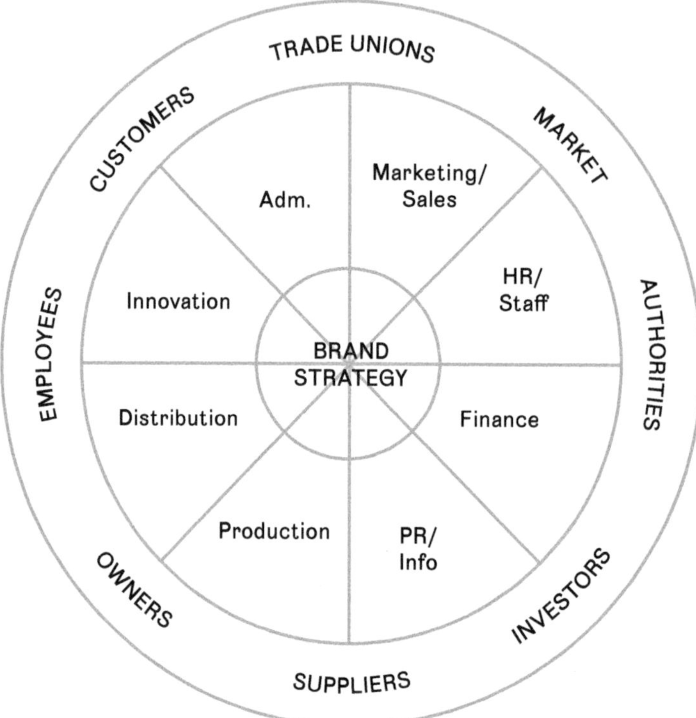


Fig. 3.28 The company's brand value chain

## Branding

A brand can come into existence on its own over time based on the consumer's own experience and relationship to the product, but conscious branding is the result of many factors, such as product development, price, distribution, and so on, and not least market communication, where it is crucial to position the brand in the consumer's mind. 'Branding is a disciplined process used to build awareness, attract new customers, and extend customer loyalty. Positioning a brand to be irreplaceable requires a daily desire to be the best. To be successful, brand builders need to stick to the basis, stay calm on the roller coaster of relentless change, and seize every opportunity to be the brand of choice' (Wheeler, 2018). It is essential for the company to live up to its values and deliver on its promises (3.2.5 Core values, 3.2.6 Value proposition). This requires the entire company to be united around a common brand strategy and value

85 Nielsen is a global leader in audience insights, data and analytics, shaping the future of media (global.nielsen.com/about-us/)

86 Karlsen, H. (18 June 2009). 'Ta kontroll over merkeleveransen' (Take Control of Brand Delivery), Metro Branding.

chain for how the brand should be developed, produced, distributed and presented in the market, see Figure 3.28. It can take years to build a brand; therefore, branding is about long-term planning and brand management to create competitive advantages that are attractive and profitable in the market in the long run.[85]


1 Initiation
2 Insight
3 Strategy
4 Design
5 Production
6 Management

3.1 Strategy development
3.2 Overall strategy
3.3 Goals and subgoals
3.4 Business strategy
3.5 Business model
3.6 Market strategy
3.7 Brand strategy
3.8 Communication strategy
3.9 Design strategy

- Trademark vs. brand
- Brand
- Corporate brand vs. product brand
- Branding
- Sustainable branding
- Brand management
- Creating a brand


### Sustainable branding

To create a sustainability strategy that is authentic, the company needs sustainability to be part of both short and long-term strategic planning. 'Authenticity comes through the end-to-end integration of sustainability into the processes and complete transparency with consumers along the way' (Wilson, 2018). The global sustainability report 'Sustainable shoppers buy the change they wish to see in the world' (Nielsen, 2018) underscores these five reasons for implementing sustainability in the brand strategy:

1. Sustainability encourages a culture of innovation, pushing you to embrace new methods, technologies and ideas.
2. Sustainability is a way to build authenticity, creating more transparency in your supply chain.
3. Sustainability is a consumer-centric strategy. It requires you to understand and empathise with the concerns your consumers have.
4. Sustainability drives greater efficiency, e.g. transition to manufacturing processes that reduce waste, requiring investment in research and development and sometimes the overhaul of supply chains. That upfront investment can pay off as your business benefits from a more efficient process and enhanced reputation.
5. The positive effects of sustainability are good for us, and they make us feel good too. That goodwill can cut across your employees, consumers, and other stakeholder groups.

(3.3.8 Sustainability goals, 3.4.3 Sustainability strategy, 3.5.2 Sustainable business model, 5.4.7 Green packaging, 6.9 Sustainable management).

### Brand management

Branding requires the business to conduct conscious brand management. 'In general, one can say that brand management is about aligning the company with a basic concept, which involves building the entire value chain around a clearly defined brand platform. A brand platform elucidates the vision, mission, and values of a brand and its position in the market' (Karlsen, 2009),[86] see Figure 3.28. Some companies have this expertise internally, others buy it from design, communication or strategy advisors. In any case, this responsibility lies with the company's top management and their board of directors and implies a willingness to invest in the future. Brand management means that a person has the responsibility and mandate for the development, management, handling, and operation of the brand, and uses brand strategy, design manual, and other management tools to ensure long-term and targeted brand use and development (3.9 Brand strategy, 6.5 Design Manual).

Further reading
The NielsenIQ report: 'Sustainable shoppers buy the change they wish to see in the world' (16 November 2018, nielseniq.com).

> 'When sustainability initiatives are integrated thoughtfully into the strategic plan, it can do everything from streamline the supply chain to unlock a new level of consumer love and loyalty' (Wilson, 2018).

### Creating a brand

Creating a brand is about linking associations to an identity in people's minds, so that it is perceived as a value that they want to acquire or identify with. It is about taking a position, creating an image, and being preferred to

| Brand platform (Brand strategy and goals) | | |
|---|---|---|
| The main idea, mission and core of the brand: | Brand purpose: | Why another brand? What is the brands' reason to exist? |
| | Brand mission: | Brand for what, for whom, where, why? What is the brand concept/business idea? What is the brand's basic task? |
| | Brand essence: | What is the fundamental core/main idea, 'Reason to live' of the brand? |
| The brand's vision, goals, and philosophy: | Vision: | What do we hope, dream that the brand will be? |
| | Goal: | What should the overall goal of the brand be? |
| | Philosophy: | What cause does the brand support, its culture, belief, or conviction? |
| Brand characteristics and values: | Uniqueness: | What makes the brand unique and distinctive? |
| | Core values: | What core values should the brand be based on? What emotional values should the brand express? |
| | Value proposition: | What rational values should the brand promise? Influence: brand personality, identity, message. |
| Brand position: | Brand position: | What position should the brand take in the market, in relation to its competitors, and in people's minds? How should the brand differ from its competitors? |
| Brand narrative: | Brand story: | Which story should the brand tell to help position itself and establish the right associations among the target group? |
| Market and target groups: | Market/ category/ industry: | In which market segment should the brand compete? Which category or industry should the brand identify with or belong to? Which competitors should the brand distinguish itself and take market shares from? |
| | Target group: | The consumer, the user, the buyer, the recipient? Who are they, where are they, characteristics, needs, social identity, lifestyle? |
| The brand seen from the target group's perspective: | Signal – effect: | Who am I, the user of this brand? What signals should the user send to those around him/her? |
| | Image: | What mental image should the buyer have of the brand? |
| | Reputation: | How do we want the brand's image to be perceived by the target audience and others? |
| | Distinctive assets: | What should be the distinctive brand assets? |

Table 3.8 Brand platform

Table 3.8 The table shows an example of what might be included in a brand platform. The brand platform should serve as a strategic foundation for the brand and a tool in the process of developing the brand and the brand identity, elements and message. When creating the strategy, each of the strategic definitions is written briefly and concisely in a clear structure. © Grimsgaard, W. (2022).

Tips for the designer

When creating a brand platform, the backdrop is the company's overall strategy and goals.

other players in the market. This is done through targeted work. It involves defining what the brand should be, what values and promises should be associated with it, and what story the brand should tell. Furthermore, it involves developing a clear brand structure, a brand name that gives the right associations, a logo, symbol, and other brand elements which visualise the identity, and a slogan that clearly positions the brand and signals its promises. It is equally important to consciously plan the market communication and the use of market channels, to reach the target group and influence their perception of the brand. Knowledge and credibility are key factors to creating a strong brand. It requires good control and brand management to ensure that it is always perceived consistently, and to ensure that the product or service keeps promises and meets expectations.

*Do we have a brand?* One could say that we have a brand when it has gained the power to influence the market. A strong brand conveys predictability, trust, and emotion (Kapferer, 2012). A brand should effectively reduce the consumer's risk. The perceived risk may concern economy (related to price), functional factors (related to performance and use), experience and perception (related to one's own self-image), or social (related to one's own social identity). Branding, trust, and emotional attachment are built over time. The keys to success are a good concept, a clear position, a good brand story, clear goals and a long-term perspective (3.7.3 Position, 3.7.4 Brand story, 3.7.5 Brand identity, 3.7.8 Brand perspective, 3.7.9 Brand refresh, redesign, rebranding).



### 3.7.1 Brand platform

The brand platform is the core of the brand strategy and should define the brand's purpose, mission, vision, values, position, and the brand promise, see Table 3.8 Brand platform. The brand platform should serve as an overall strategy for the brand and a platform for handling and managing the brand, to ensure that is perceived as authentic and consistent in all contexts. All the brand's contact points are defined, coordinated, and aligned with the help of the brand platform (Karlsen, 2009). The brand platform should act as a tool in the further work of developing brand names, branding elements and branding activities. There are many perceptions of how a brand platform should be designed and which concepts are best suited for use. The designer should assess the content and scope of the brand platform in relation to the goal and framework of the task to be solved. In some contexts, when time and budget are limited, it may be sufficient to define some of the key elements of the brand platform briefly or combine them. The Brand strategy is part of the further work on developing a communication strategy and design strategy.

### 3.7.2 Brand architecture

The brand architecture should provide a structured overview of the brands in the company's brand portfolio. It will show how the brands are related to each other and differentiated from each other and how they reflect or reinforce each other, see Figure 3.30 Brand architecture. Brand architecture is important in planning brand identity and how brands should appear on products and in marketing communication.

'The brand architecture is the organising structure of the brand portfolio that specifies brand roles and the nature of relationships between brands' (Rajagopal and Sanchez 2004). Brand architecture is a consequence of the company's competitive strategy, which defines, among other things, whether it will operate with one or more brands. A company that operates with one brand is called branded house. A company that operates with several brands is called house of brands.[87] In addition to these two groups, there are different in-between variants.

Fig. 3.29 The figure shows examples of brand exposure for monolithic, endorsed, and individual identity, respectively. © Grimsgaard, W. (2018).

### Brand architecture development

Brand architecture can appear in a variety of ways. To develop a solid brand architecture, one should think about how existing and new brands can best be related to each other or differentiated from each other, and how the brands should best reflect or reinforce the brand of the company to which they belong. Keller (2013) highlights two key goals for brand architecture: 1) Strengthen brand awareness by improving consumer understanding and communicating similarities and differences between different products and services. 2) Strengthen the brand by transferring values between the brands and the various products and services in order to improve sales and repeat purchases.

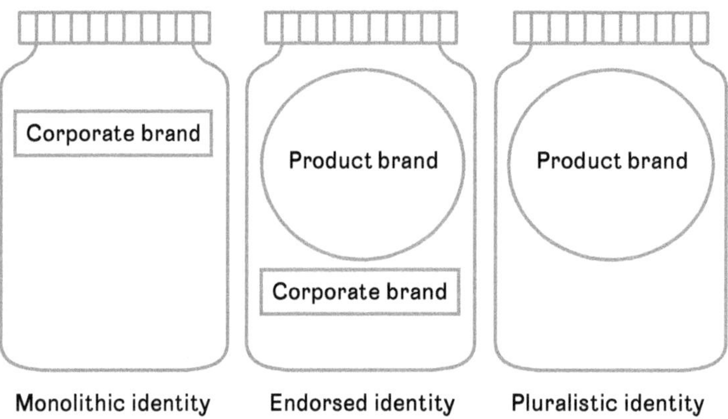


Fig. 3.29 Brand identities

Brand architecture development requires three steps:

1) *Define* the potential of the brand based on brand awareness, the brand's purpose, mission, vision and position (3.7.1 Brand platform).
2) *Clarify* which new products or services can help the brand realise its potential. Should a new product or service be established within an existing category (line extension) or outside existing categories (category extension) (3.7.8 Brand perspective).
3) *Specify* which brand elements should be associated with the brand's new and existing products or services, including name, logo, and visual elements (Keller, 2013, p. 386–392) (3.7.6 Brand assets).

Brand architecture can be divided into three main categories, monolithic, endorsed and pluralistic identity. There are smooth transitions between these categories, as shown in Figure 3.29 Brand architecture, among these are varieties such as sub-brands and hybrids.

87 A house of brands is also called a multi-brand company.

### Monolithic identity

The term *monolithic identity* is used for a brand in a branded house strategy, where the corporate brand is used both for the company and all its products, as a parent brand. It is this one brand that is used in all commercial contexts and that the consumer associates with both the company and the products. Other designations used are master brand, family brand or umbrella brand. Products with a monolithic identity often have generic (descriptive) product names, such as milk, cheese or sausages in addition to flavours, functional range or the like. Examples of monolithic identity are Heinz, Virgin, Fedex.

*Monolithic identity is selected when*:

- the corporate brand is well established or new products are easier to establish among consumers if they bear a known brand name.
- the corporate brand is unknown, or the company wants to put all its efforts into building a single corporate and product brand.
- the company's own brand will head a product range, product category or different products. In this case, the products will be positioned in line with the characteristics and core values of the overall brand.

### Endorsed identity

The term *endorsed identity* is used about product brands in a house of brands strategy when the company brand (parent brand) is used as an endorser brand (endorses a product brand). On a product package, an endorsed identity will show two brands, one for the product and one for the company. The size ratio of the brand depends on how much the product brand should be endorsed by the corporate brand. Typically, the product brand is larger than the parent brand. The size of the parent brand may be reduced as the product brand gets incorporated. Examples of endorsed identities are Nestlé, Kellogg and Apple.

*Endorsed identity is selected when*:

- a new product brand is to be introduced to the consumer and needs birth assistance and endorsement from the parent brand.
- sub-brands, product lines or product categories should be grouped under a common brand or endorsed by a parent brand.
- one wishes to fortify, build, and maintain the parent brand; synergy is created from the parent brand's endorsement of the product brand, or the product brand's endorsement of the parent brand, or the parent brand's and the product brand's endorsement of each other.
- the product name/brand should help give the product its own identity on the market.

### Pluralistic identity

*Pluralistic identity* is used about a brand architecture with series of unrelated brands (freestanding brands) with individual identity. The term is used about product brands in a house of brands strategy, where the company has several brands in its product portfolio, with individual identities. It means that only the product brand is exposed, and the company brand (parent brand) or name is absent or placed on the back of the product. It is an advantage that the parent company's name is included on the product so that those who want to know the manufacturer's name can find it. Examples of pluralistic identities are Gillette, Pampers and Swiffer.

*Individual identity is selected when:*

- it is appropriate to build an independent product brand.
- an endorsed identity is established and no longer needs support from the parent brand, but can function independently.
- a company has a large product portfolio of products within different product categories, with different identities, and core values.

Tips for the designer
**If neither the parent brand nor the product brand has been developed yet, it may be beneficial to start building one brand instead of presenting two unknown brands to the market.**

### Hybrids

Hybrid brand architecture is a mixture of two or more brand architectures, e.g. masterbrand, sub-brand, endorser brand and freestanding brand. It is typically used when a firm is changing brand architectures, or acquiring existing brands through mergers or acquisitions.

### Sub-brand

*Sub-brand* is a form of endorsed identity which is used in contexts where the company comes in with a new sub-brand that they wish to establish. The new brand will be closely linked to the parent brand, so that they always work together; it is not meant to work on its own. Coca-Cola Zero is a sub-brand because Coca-Cola is the main brand and Coca Zero is the sub-brand. It has probably never been the intention to remove Coca-Cola.

### Co-branding

*Co-branding* (dual branding) is when two brands from the same manufacturer or different manufacturers are exposed on the same product. The brands endorse each other and achieve mutual synergy from this. Examples of dual branding include Master Card and Apple Pay, and Milka and Oreo.

### Branded house strategy

This brand strategy means that the business and its products are profiled under the same brand. In such a brand strategy, the brand will have *a monolithic identity*. New products are launched as a brand extension, under an established corporate brand, as an alternative to developing a completely new product brand. Branded house is often a structure that is present in companies that have existed for many years, where strong leaders have left their mark on the company, and wants to maintain the history, traditions, values, and culture that have grown over time (Olsen, 2004).

According to Olsen (2004), a major advantage of choosing a branded house strategy is that this strategy reduces the risk of launching new brand extensions. According to research, customers rely more on brands supported by numerous products than on brands that are not, and this trust adds a higher brand value to the brands (if the brands expand with products that match the brand). These results contradict a notion that one can 'water down' a brand by adding more products (Ries and Trout 1986). The branded house strategy is the best organisation for companies with small product portfolios and limited financial resources, because it has the benefits of acquired knowledge, streamlined communication, and building customer loyalty. It means that a company communicates several products with a single brand, and over time appears clearer and easier to understand for customers than if they had had several different brands. Moreover, it is less costly to build one brand as opposed to several. Such a brand strategy poses great demands on the brand to have distinct core values and requires sound management of the company's product portfolio to ensure that all products can be associated with the brand's core values. Thus, the brand will help strengthen its position, not weaken it. According to Olsen, one disadvantage of branded house is that new products that are added to the portfolio may fail in the market, create negative associations, and damage the parent brand. See Figure 3.30 Brand architecture (3.7.8 Brand perspective).

### House of brands strategy

House of brands includes different product brands in the portfolio, as opposed to branded house which has one brand for all products (Kapferer, 2012). In such a brand strategy, with a pluralistic brand architecture, the product brands have individual identities. It opens the possibility of giving each product a unique brand name and positioning it in attractive niches in the market, regardless of the parent company or any other products it may have in its product portfolio. This may often be appropriate where the product is not suitable as a brand extension of the parent brand or other corporate brands. This may be because it does not fit, or because it may fail, thereby damaging the parent company's position and reputation. Examples of house of brands are Unilever and Proctor and Gamble.

According to Olsen (2004), one of the advantages of such a strategy is to avoid association with the corporate brand if it is not compatible with the product brand. Another advantage is that you can take ownership of a new category association using the brand name and avoid channel conflicts. A disadvantage is that you do not draw benefits or positive spillover effects from established brands, as in the case of brand expansion or endorsed identity. Another disadvantage is that it takes time to build a brand and that it is costly to both develop and establish a new brand in the market.

### Endorser brand

When a parent brand supports a sub-brand or a new brand it is given the role of an endorser brand. In such a brand strategy, the product brand will have an endorsed identity. According to Olsen (2004), the advantage of using an endorser brand is that the user is more likely to try a new product brand if it is presented together with an established and well-developed brand. It signals the credibility of the new brand in the eyes of the consumer. It is less time-consuming and less costly to establish the new brand and gain a market share when the parent brand has already been established in the market. Similarly, it is easier to get shelf space when the parent brand already has other products in the grocery shop. All communication can take place more easily and efficiently when the parent company already has an established communication apparatus in place. Such a brand strategy places great demands on the identity and properties of the new product, demands to be compatible and easily associated with the core values of the parent brand. This way, the brands will eventually help endorse each other. In the case of a start-up, it may be important to keep in mind that it is easier to establish one brand in people's minds than two, and it is cheaper too.



Masterbrand

**A Masterbrand is a single corporate trademark, an overarching brand name for a variety of products in a portfolio branding, such as Virgin and Procter & Gamble.**

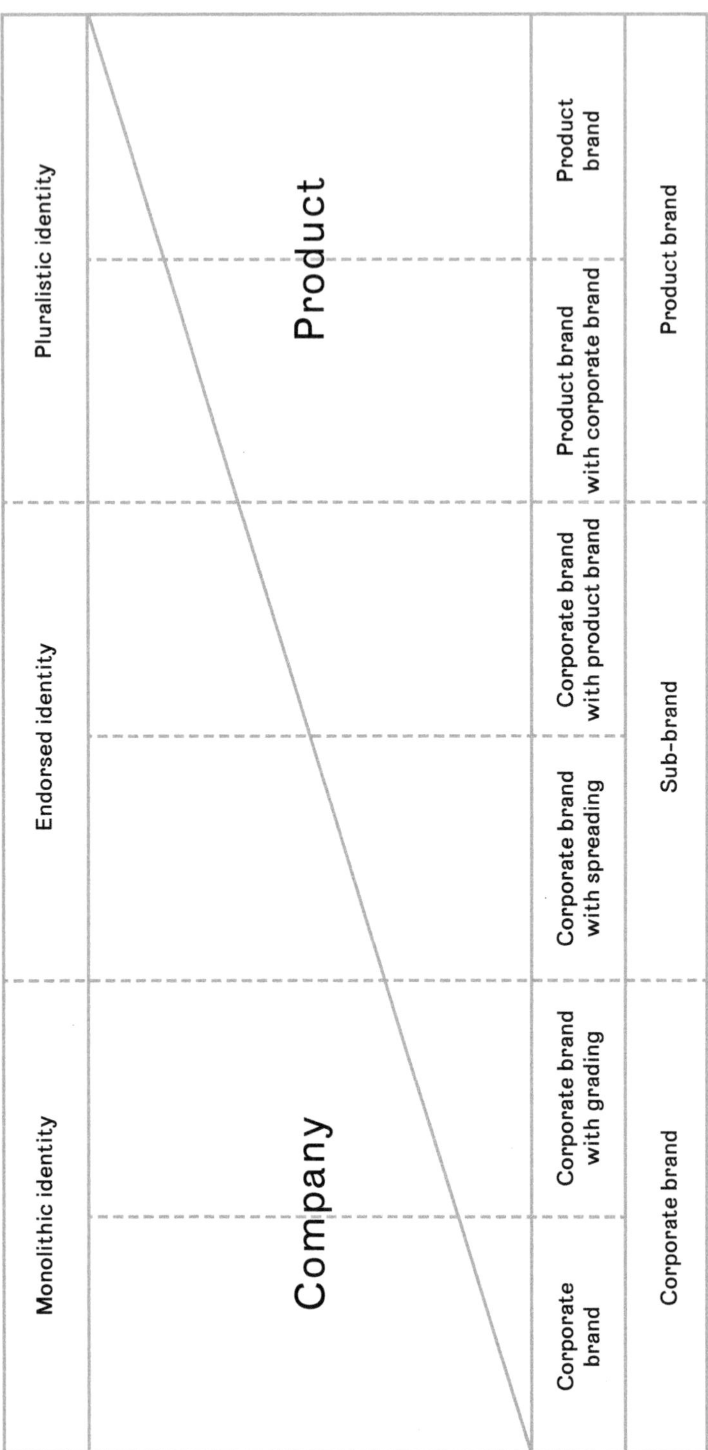


Fig. 3.30 Brand architecture

Fig. 3.30 The figure shows the principles of brand architecture broken down into different brand identities: monolithic, endorsed and individual identity. In the case of monolithic identity, only the corporate brand is exposed. In case of endorsed identity, both the corporate brand and the product brand are exposed, with possible variations in size ratios between the two brands. In the case of individual identity, only the product brand is exposed, possibly with a small-sized company name or brand placed in behind, under or on the side of the product (based on Kunde, 2002, p. 155).

Tips for the designer
When a product has an endorsed identity, the parent brand is an endorser brand.

88 Jesper Kunde: *Unik nå eller aldri,* 2002.

**Different brand strategies (based on Kunde, 2002)[88]**

**Corporate brand:** Heinz is an example of a company that has refined its corporate brand and mostly created new product brands rather than diluting the value of the Heinz brand.

**Corporate brand with grading:** Audi has a grading system whereby it names the cars with letters and numbers Audi A1, Audi A3, Audi A4, Audi A5, Audi A6, Audi A7, Audi A8, Q2, Q3, Q5 etc. 'Numbers say something about the size and the letter indicates the model. Effective branding, which helps build the corporate brand' (Kunde, 2002, p. 181).

**Corporate brand with spread (denomination):** Used when the company wants to stretch (exploit) its brand. An example of this is the airline SAS Cargo. 'The corporate brand of the airline is SAS, and in addition to flying passengers, it also flies cargo. By adding the word "Cargo", SAS provides a clear description of the company's scope, without interfering with its corporate brand'. (Kunde, 2002, p. 198).

**Corporate brand with differentiation:** Used when companies that have created a strong brand want to grow and spread into new segments. 'The original brand sets clear limits on what one can do on the product and price level, and one is locked into a particular segment. Italian garment giant Giorgio Armani solved this with the sub-brand Giorgio Emporio, which targets a younger segment' (Kunde, 2002, p. 217).

**Combined brands:** A new product brand (sub-brand) is placed in combination with the company's corporate brand for combined branding. This way, the company transfers the core values from its corporate brand to its sub-brand. One condition for this to succeed is for the corporate brand to have a strong position (Kunde, 2002, p. 228).

**Product brand with endorsement:** In case of endorsing (endorsed identity), one tries to transfer some of the positive value in one's corporate brand to another brand. Endorsement differs from combined brands in that the brand to be endorsed plays a subordinate role to the brand to be supported. This is done by displaying the corporate brand in a small size in relation to the product brand to be endorsed.

**One-product – one brand:** An independent product brand is the safest way to build a strong and focused brand without confusing your customers with different signals from other product areas (Kunde, 2002, p. 266). It is also effective in building a strong position and taking ownership of the position of one's product range.

According to Olsen, a disadvantage with the use of an endorser brand is that the new product brand may fail, thereby adding wrong associations to the parent brand, which may adversely affect the market position of the parent brand. A failed product may also result in a negative reputation for the parent company.

## Brand hierarchy

Brand hierarchy is also called brand levels. Brands can have different levels and roles. Brand hierarchy can summarise the different brand levels across the company's products, for each individual product line or for the individual product. Brand hierarchy is particularly useful for getting an explicit order of the different brand assets and how these should be prioritised and weighted on packaging and in marketing communications (Keller, 2013). As shown in Figure 3.31, some brand assets may be shared by many products (such as Toyota), while other brand assets may be unique to certain products (such as Corolla). The brand hierarchy goes from the top to bottom level and expands with multiple brands at each subsequent level.

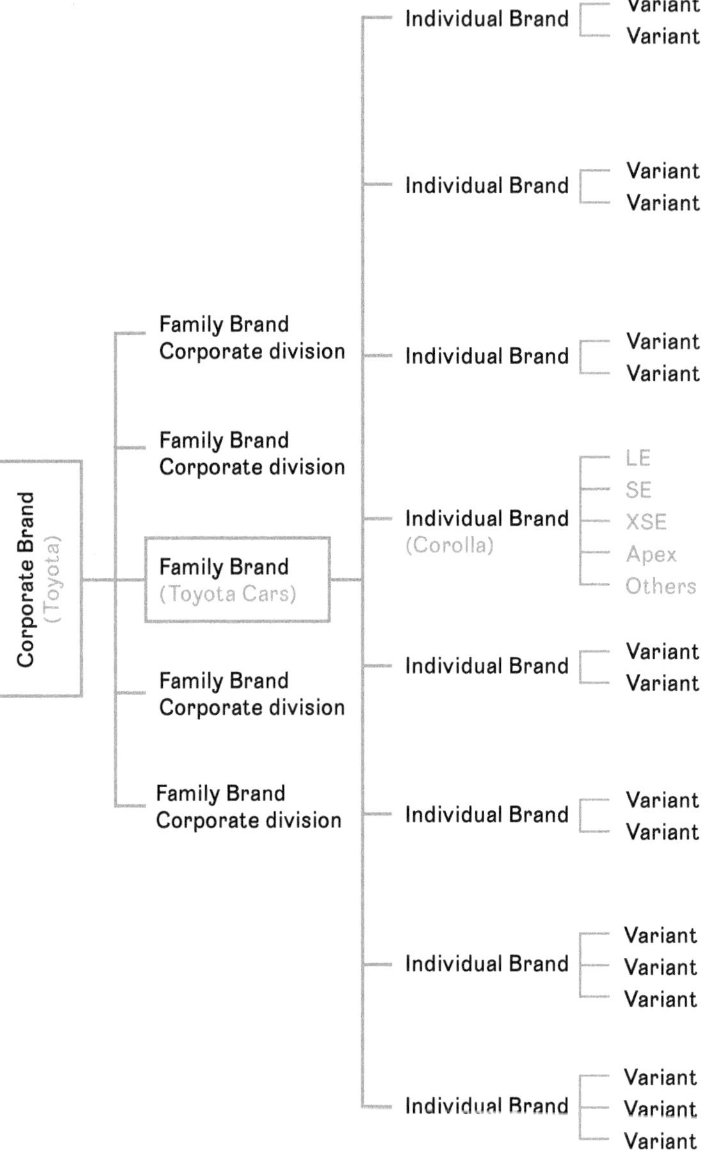


Fig. 3.31 Brand hierarchy

Fig. 3.31 The figure shows an example of a brand hierarchy model. Corolla from the car manufacturer Toyota is used as an example. (Inspired by Keller, 2013).

Fig. 3.32 The image shows a Scotch package that has as many as four brand levels displayed on one package: 3M, Scotch, Magic Tape, Matte Finish.
Level 1) Company's corporate brand: 3M
Level 2) Product brand and umbrella brand: Scotch
Level 3) Individual trademark product. Product line brand: Magic TM Tape
Level 4) Designating element or model (modifier). Product description/designation, specifying the variant and properties: Matte finish
(The example is based on Kapferer (2012, p. 311). Photo: Grimsgaard, 2022).

What aspect of the brand should be communicated? What does the customer actually buy? When it comes to sports equipment, Swix communicates something called Triac on ski poles. People ask for a Triac, which is the designation of the product properties of the pole. Triac is a Swix pole, and everyone in the field knows that Triac is the most expensive Swix pole. At the same time, it varies greatly what customers say they have bought. Some say they have bought a Swix pole, while others say they have bought Triac. Triac has developed as a brand name to include sports clothes as well (Opstad, 2022).

When planning a brand hierarchy, the question will be which brands or which brand to display on a product, a product line or across product lines. What is also important to consider is what aspect of the brand should be communicated, or what the customer buys. Those who buy the Japanese car brand Lexus don't say they've bought a Toyota. Even though it's Toyota that manufactures it, they say they have bought a Lexus. Those who have purchased a Nissan Leaf say that they have bought a Leaf, even though it says Nissan on the car. Those who buy Passat GTE, i.e., Volkswagen Passat GTE, often say that they have bought a GTE; they don't even say that they've bought a Passat, or that they've bought a Volkswagen. This is the hierarchy: different designations for one and the same brand. Within the same brand one has the brand name, producer name, product name, model name, variant, etc., i.e. the same brand communicates different sub-brands (Opstad, 2017).

**Which brand to highlight?**: What should be the main brand? Which brand name should be bigger, and which should be smaller? What is important when communicating and differentiating the product is what the customer asks for. What does the customer buy? At first people bought Toyota Prius and eventually they might start buying Prius. Therefore, it is necessary for the design to be changed gradually. In a redesign process, the question is which brand name will be bigger and which will be smaller and how should the design evolve in the long term? That is what brand hierarchy is used for.

Let's take Magic Tape as an example, Figure 3.32. What kind of tape do people ask for when they come to the shop to get that tape? Are they asking for Scotch tape, 3M or Magic? In fact, there is a good chance they will ask for 'the invisible tape'. People like to remember the feature of the product that is interesting, unique, or different, and that meets a need. Magic Tape is a concept, with a clear idea, which was innovative

Fig. 3.32 Brand levels

and new when it appeared in the market in 1961. It is invisible, one can write on it with a pen, and it comes in a removable variant. Brands with a simple and clear brand concept that meet a consumer or user need are more likely to succeed.

### 3.7.3 Brand positioning

Positioning is about standing out in the market in relation to competitors and working to get high up on the target group's mental ladder. Having a clear and strong position provides a competitive advantage and is a clear success factor. Taking a position means doing something different or better than competitors and being preferred by customers or users. It can mean a be or not be, for the company to be able to sell its products and services. Therefore, choosing a position is the company's most important strategic choice. The company first decides on its competitive strategy before choosing its position. Choosing a competitive strategy is generally a matter of whether to compete on price or differentiation (3.4.1 Competitive strategy). If the answer is differentiation, the next question will be which unique characteristics of the product or service can be highlighted to appeal to the market, and which should come to the consumer's mind as a set of associations when they see the brand.[89]

Fig. 3.33 The figure shows a combination of four key questions that can help clarify which position the brand should take, based on Kapferer (2012):
Brand WHY?: What is its purpose?
Brand for WHAT?: What is its promise?
Brand for WHOM?: Who is it for?
Brand against WHOM?: Who is it fighting againts?

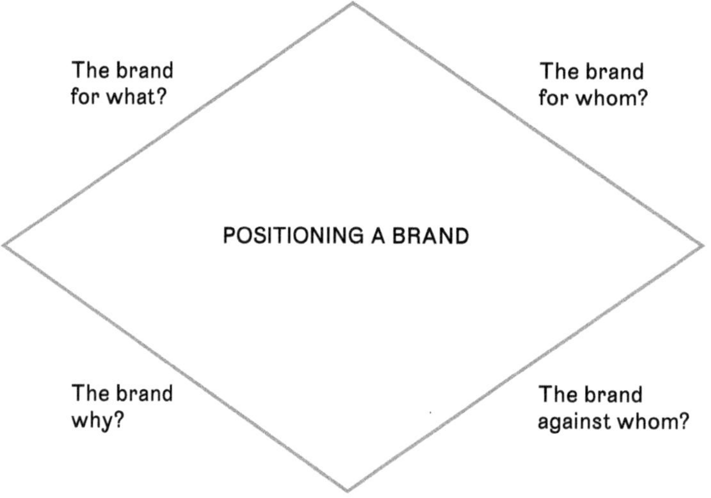


Fig. 3.33 Kapferer's positioning rhombus

Taking a position is about establishing a place in the mind of the target group so that they remember why they should choose one product over another. It is about saying out loud what one specialises in and taking ownership of those words, so no one else can come along and say the same thing. It is about being the first to take a position, find an unoccupied position, a hole in the market, challenge a position that has already been taken, or keep the position one already has. It is basically about finding an opening in the market, an unmet need, or some competitors one can steal customers from (2.7.5 Positioning analysis). A position is defined based on a unique characteristic that distinguishes the product from its competitors.

89 The term 'brand' is used for the overall brand experience of the company, product or service.
90 The brand is the business, product or service.
91 Brand purpose is the reason for the brand to exist beyond making money. If you want a really powerful brand purpose, it needs to relate to the product or service itself. ... A promise gives the customer an indication of what to expect e.g. low priced groceries whereas the brand purpose is the reason the brand exists. May 17, 2018 (www.burnthebook.co.uk).
92 Read more in 3.2.6 Value proposition. A brand promise is a value or experience a company's customers can expect to receive every single time they interact with that company. The more a company can deliver on that promise, the stronger the brand value in the minds of customers and employees, May 7, 2018.
93 The frame of reference (FOR) is the segment or category in which your company competes (Stayman, 2015).

## Kapferer's positioning rhombus

Kapferer presents brand positioning as a two-step process: 1) First indicate which product categories the brand should be associated with and compared to. 2) Then indicate what the brand's main differences and raison d'être are, compared to other products and brands in the same product category. Implicitly, it is a matter of whether the brand has a right to exist, whether there is an actual need for such a product, or another similar product. The positioning rhombus summarises the most important questions to consider when selecting brand position[90] (Kapferer, 2012, p. 152):

**Brand WHY?**: What is its purpose, its raison d'être?[91]
**Brand for WHAT?**: What is its use? What do the brand promise?[92]
**Brand for WHOM?**: Who is it for? Who will be the target group?
**Brand against WHOM?**: Who are its main competitors? Who can we take customers from?

*Positioning is basically about this*: What can you offer to the market, and what advantages and by which characteristics can you distinguish yourself from your competitors? According to Percy and Elliot (2005), it presupposes being able to answer two questions: What is the brand? What does the brand do?

By Using Chobani® Oatmilk Zero as a good example, this is what the food brand Chobani say on their websites (2021): 'Better food for more people. Making high-quality and nutritious food accessible to more people, while elevating our communities and making the world a healthier place.' Looking into Chobani Oat, the website says: 'Chobani® Oatmilk Zero Sugar. Our most delicious and creamy plant-based milk made with absolutely no sugar (not a low-calorie food). An unsweetened, absolutely no-sugar-added version of our rich creamy Chobani® Oatmilk, made with the goodness of gluten-free oats. A good source of calcium and vitamins A and D, without nuts, dairy, lactose, or sugar.

## Brand categorisation

Brand categorisation is an important starting point for gaining knowledge of how a product can compete within a category and which categories are relevant to consider. Defining category affiliation or 'frame of reference'[93] is also necessary for understanding and clarifying how the product or service, or brand, should stand out and create a position in the category. Category can be defined as pure categories or subcategories, for example, tea, coffee, and soft drinks are in the beverages category, while coffee and tea can be categorised into a hot beverage subcategory, soft drinks as part of cold beverages, and so on. Categorisation is largely about user insight, understanding the user's needs, and buying behaviour. Initially, it is the user or customer who defines the category, what they perceive as category. It can be based on how the product meets relevant needs: functional needs such as good parking, good items sales and good service or emotional needs such as good experience, social environment, nice atmosphere. It can also be based on when the product should be consumed or used, such as cereal in the morning and beer in the evening, or a particular sentiment, for example, if it is a matter of basic items or of goods one might want to experience or have. 'Sometimes, and especially for more symbolic

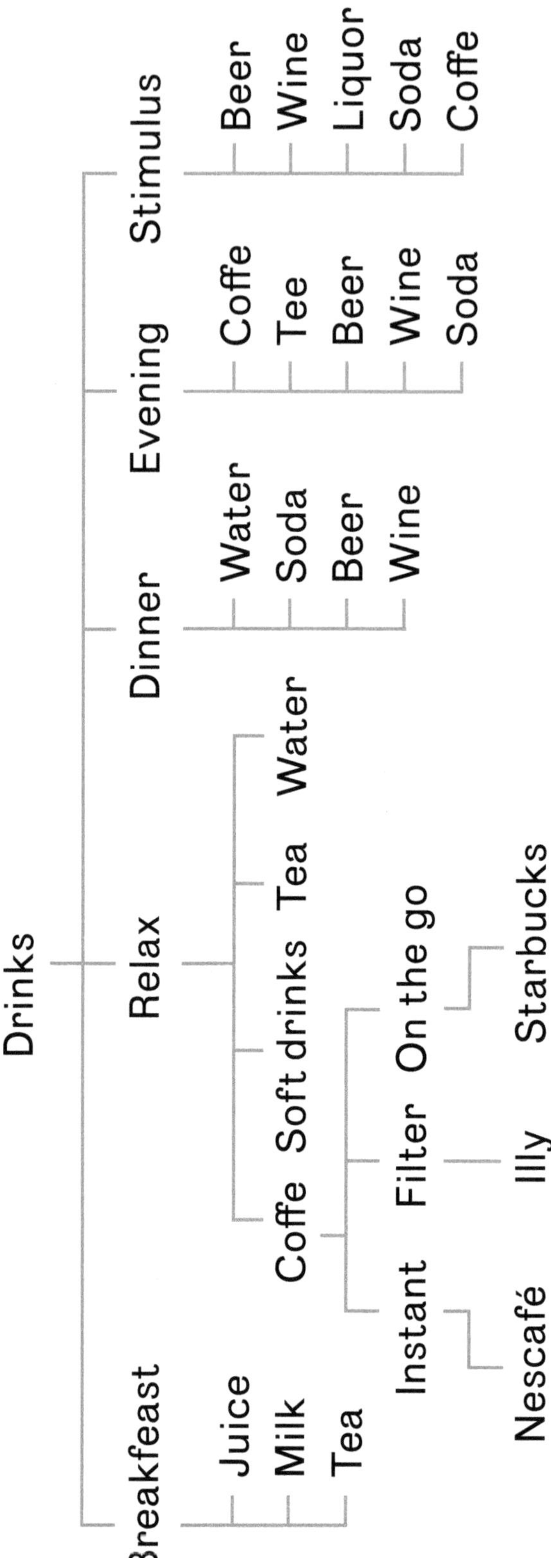


Fig. 3.34 Use situation for beverages

Fig. 3.34 The figure shows an example of a hierarchy category map, illustrating an approach to categorising beverages, based on use situations (taken from Olsen 2010; Percy and Elliot, 2005). The example is a rough simplification of reality.

Table 3.9 The table shows a constructed example of a categorisation of Yoplait. As an example Yoplait can organise its marketing in line with when the various products are consumed (breakfast, lunch, dinner) and not with the more traditional product-oriented approach (Based on Olsen, 2010).

brands, customers categorise the brands based on the typical users of the products or services. Who is the typical Ikea customer? What kind of people drive Mercedes? The different trademark products used by a particular type of customer can be defined as belonging to a separate cognitive category and thereby competing. It is essential to understand that a specific brand can potentially belong to many different cognitive categories' (Olsen, 2010). A central concept in positioning may therefore be to try to influence how customers mentally categorise the brand in question. Taking a position is about influencing customers to interpret the brand information the way we want, thus determining which other brands we want to define as competitors. This makes it possible to plan differentiation and thereby make the brand product more attractive.

| Yoplait categorisation | | |
|---|---|---|
| Question | Categorisation criteria | Answer |
| What is the product? | Product-oriented | Yoghurt can be eaten |
| Why do you want to eat yogurt? | Needs-based | Yoghurt is sweet<br>Yogurt is fresh<br>Yogurt is healthy |
| When do you eat yoghurt? | User situation | For breakfast<br>For lunch<br>For dessert<br>For supper |

Table 3.9 Yoplait categorisation

A good approach to brand categorisation is to design hierarchical category maps. This is done by identifying different needs, use situations, goals of consumption, and product characteristics. On the map, both one's own brand and competitors' brand can be included to map similarities and differentiations.

The example in Figure 3.34 shows a simplification of reality, where a central question for the coffee brand Illy will be whether they should define the competition arena to only be Lavazza and similar, whether they should also include coffee brands within another technical area (Nescafé), or whether they should broaden their scope and consider Illy as a potential competitor of alcohol, soft drinks, juice, and water brands. This is a difficult strategic matter that depends on several factors (Olsen, 2010):

- What resources are available (what can you 'bite over')?
- What is the competitive situation in potential new 'markets'?
- What is the customer potential in the defined categories?
- Can necessary similarities in selected categories be satisfied?
- What are the potential differentiation points to offer to achieve competitive advantage? (3.7.3 Brand position: Points of parity).

Starting to define the brand category, the next step is to find the points of parity (similarities/hygiene factors) – and the points of differentiation (the uniqueness), and compare this with the competitors.



Further reading

Check out the classic: *Positioning: The Battle for Your Mind* (2001) by Al Ries and Jack Trout.

### Points of parity

When talking about differentiation, which is the core of brand positioning, one must also talk about the competition because the brand's position is defined in relation to its competitors. As opposed to differences, there will be similarities, points of parity, which are some characteristics of the brand that are the same for all brands in the whole category. That is, a characteristic is present both in 'your' brand and in the competitors'. For example, for the category C vitamin tablets, a point of parity will be vitamin C. The question is then what is unique about 'your' vitamin C product which can differentiate it from the others. It can be the taste, shape, or design. The question therefore becomes: Who are our competitors? What are the points of parity? It is also important to examine competitors in other categories. If the consumer is generally looking for vitamin C, they will be able to buy it in oranges, orange juice or tablet form, i.e. three different categories (Opstad, 2017).

'Points of parity are the hygiene factors, attributes and properties on which a brand should deliver, to be perceived as an acceptable player in the category. It is the similarities that determine to which category a brand belongs. These attributes or benefits are not unique or differentiating for the individual brand but are shared with the other competitors. The most important thing for a brand is that the points of parity ensure that customers find no reason *not* to choose the brand (Samuelsen et al., 2010). Often, properties that once used to be differentiating, evolve over time to become similarities within the category, such as the spreading of Soft Margarine, seat belts for Volvo, etc.)' (Olsen, 2010). First, the company should define which points of parity they will provide, and in what category they will compete, before they can tell what characteristics and benefits, they should distinguish themselves by, see Figure 3.34.

Table 3.10 The table shows an example of points of parity vs. points of differentiation for hair shampoos (based on principles from Samuel 2007).

Fig. 3.35 The figure shows how we can distinguish between hygiene factors (goes without saying) and differentiation factors (what we can distinguish ourselves). 70% of positioning occurs through emotional differentiation factors. The X factor is the unique differentiation factor, the positioning basis itself. Based on Myhre, 2017.

The point of differentiation (POD) describes how your brand or product benefits customers in ways that set you apart from your competitors (Stayman, 2015).

### Points of differentiation

After the work on defining a category and identifying points of parity has been completed, the work on finding points of differentiation[94] will be much easier. By then one knows both competitors and users better, what competitors offer, what is important to customers, and what one's own brand offers. This is a good foundation for identifying the uniqueness that will distinguish the company's products from those of its competitors, and the values that will be promoted and communicated

**Points of parity vs. points of differentiation**

*Points of parity* are the 'must-haves' of any brand to be considered a legitimate competitor in its specific category. These attributes are not brand differentiators, and should not be used as the key message in your advertising.
*Points of differentiation* are the attributes that make your brand unique. It is your brand's value proposition, its competitive advantage. The points of differentiation are the reasons why consumers should choose your brand over competition. These attributes must be consistently reflected in your brand slogan, and advertising. (branduniq 2011, branduniq.com)

94 The point of differentiation (POD) describes how your brand or product benefits customers in ways that set you apart from your competitors (Stayman, 2015).
95 This also applies to Kotler and Keller (2016: 389, 405).

| Points of parity and points of differentiation for hair shampoos | |
|---|---|
| Points of parity | Points of differentiation |
| All hair shampoos have<br>– a detergent<br>– antistatic a substances<br>– preservatives<br>– fragrances | Some hair shampoos have<br>– detergent with better oils<br>– antistatic substances that soften the hair and make it easier to comb<br>– preservative stances that are paraben-free<br>– natural fragrances<br>– hair-strengthening additives<br>– additives that give more volume |

Table 3.10 Points of parity vs. points of differentiation

to customers. 'Points of differentiation are about associations in the customers' memory. Well-differentiated brands stand out by having strong, positive, and unique associations attached to them. The points of differentiation can be very specific (for example, contain extra fibre, always the lowest interest rate) or more abstract (best customer service, gives higher status among friends). It is the customers who ultimately decide which points of differentiation are important, and it is the brand owner's task to gain sufficient customer insight to be able to design the points of differentiation in a correct and profitable way (Olsen, 2010). Both Percy and Elliot (2005) and Keller (2002)[95] maintain the same basic principles in terms of positioning. First, the market and the competitive arena should be defined, together with associated key similarities, then work can be strategically started on designing a product, service, or communication that distinguishes the brand from its competitors in a positive, relevant, and unique way (Olsen, 2010) (3.4.2 Porter's generic strategies; Differenciation).

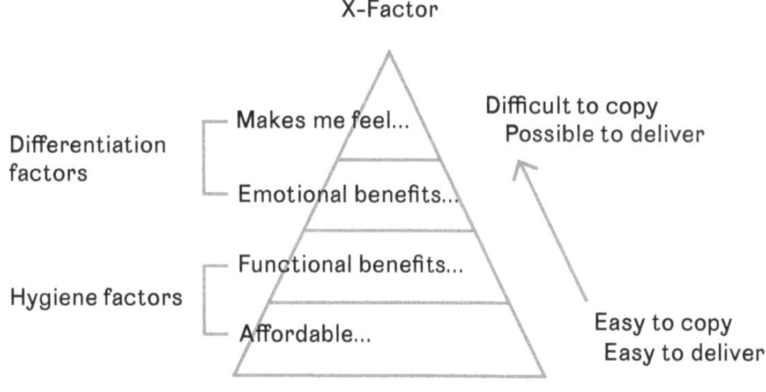


Fig. 3.35 The X factor

### The X factor

The hunt for the X factor is about finding the differentiation factor for the visual profile. It's about distinguishing between hygiene factors and differentiation factors. 'The greatest potential lies in the emotional landscape. We're looking for the emotional benefits that "make us feel something for the brand", that's the X factor' (Myhre 2017, Dinamo design).



'Brand hygiene factors are the basic set of values that the consumer expects to be in place for any business/service that they are considering purchasing. However, if a brand wishes to rise above competitors and stand for something that sets it apart – it needs to demonstrate that the hygiene factors are in place but communicate a positioning that exceeds these and provides a clear point of differentiation' (Hatched, 2012).

### Performance and experience

Brand performance and brand experience are two factors that should deliver on both points of parity and points of differentiation. Performance is about the brand's rational attributes, while experience is about its emotional ones. Rational brand attributes: What performance should the brand offer that is like other brands? What should lie in the brand performance that differentiates the brand from other brands? Emotional characteristics of the brand: What experience should the brand offer that is like other brands? What should lie in the brand experience that differentiates the brand from other brands? It is a matter of attention, performance, and experience. These are factors that are part of Keller's brand resonance pyramid. The brand pyramid shows how to build a brand (2.7.7 Brand analysis: Brand resonance pyramid).

A study performed by Deloitte 2020 revealed that 'Knowing how to sense and respond to not only the emotional but also the rational needs of customers at an individual level is no longer a nice-to-have for brands; it is becoming a vital bulwark against competition and a driver of value in today's increasingly crowded markets.' (Deloitte, 2020). From the research white paper 'Creating human connection at enterprise scale'.

### A unique mix of values

Taking a position means having a clear idea of why you should be the customers' preferred choice. According to Porter (1996), it is about being different from competitors and about carrying out conscious activities that make it possible to deliver a unique value mix. Success is all about matching the consumer's desire for an advantage and deliver on it. Value is created by companies carrying out various activities and processes to serve a position in the market. How they perform the activities determines how they will be perceived by the customers in the long run. If Ryanair is to be perceived as cheaper than its competitors, they must perform some key activities more cost-effectively than their competitors. If Apple is to be perceived as having the best user interface, it should be better at developing the relevant technology than its competitors. For a large airline to be the most punctual in the world, there are certain activities that they must do differently than less punctual airlines. A desired perception by customers should therefore be 'reflected' in the attributes of one or more activities (Lien et al., 2016).

### First position

Taking a position is a competition to come first and be the best. Because what do people remember? They like to remember the one that came first, the one that was the best, the one that is the greatest, the highest, the fastest, or the smartest. Most people remember that Neil Armstrong was the first man on the moon, that Mount Everest is the highest mountain in the world, and that the first book Gutenberg printed was the Bible, which is also the world's best-selling book. Few people remember who was second on the moon, what the world's second highest mountain is called, or which is the second best-selling book in the world. The very first person, the highest mountain, the first brand you became aware of, all occupy a place in your mind that is almost impossible to sway (Ries and Trout, 1986). The company that first launches a new product on the market can easily find its place in the mind of the target group. According to Rita Gunther McGrath (2013), it is now more difficult for a company to maintain a truly lasting advantage over time, than before, see 3.4.5 Transient advantage.

96 Doyle Dane Bernbach, DDB.
97 Adage.com (27 August 2012): 'After 50 Years, Avis Drops Iconic "We Try Harder" New Campaign Repositions Car-Rental Firm to Appeal to Busy Businessfolk'.
98 The famous Volkswagen ad was created at DDB in 1959 by lyricist Julian Koenig and art director Helmut Krone.
99 Mad Men is an American TV series created by Matthew Weiner and produced by Lionsgate Television (2007–2015). The series provides an insight into the advertising world of the 1960s.

### Second position

One of the most talked about positioning stunts of all time was developed by the American advertising agency DDB[96] for the car rental company Avis in 1962. Hertz car rental was by far the largest car rental company in the 1960s, at a time when being 'the biggest' and 'the best' was what mattered. The much younger and smaller Avis chose in its positioning strategy to take the position as number two by comparing itself with Hertz. Avis reached out with an ad campaign focusing on the consequence of being number two. Instead of highlighting the negative aspects of being number two, they figured out what their advantage of being number two was (to customers). When you are second best, you have to try harder. The ad campaign launched one of the most talked-about slogans of all time with the text: 'Avis is the second-largest car rental company. Why use us? We try harder!' They consolidated their position as the car rental company that tries a little extra to satisfy their customers. 'We try harder!' became a central element in the company's communication and visual identity.

It was a huge success for Avis. Within a year, Avis went from a loss of $3,200,000 to earning $1,200,000. It was the first time the company had made a profit in 13 years. From 1963 to 1966, the gap in market shares between the two brands narrowed from 61–29 to 49–36. 'If you are the first on the market, you have acquired a position that is difficult to sway once you have found your place in the consumer's mind. If you are not first, you must find your own position by comparing yourself to that product, that politician, that organisation, or that person who came first' (Ries and Trout, 1986). When Avis took its new market position in 1962, they also weakened the position of Hertz at the same time, in the sense that the biggest does not necessarily have to be synonymous with the *best* (Parekh, 2012).

After 50 years of 'We try harder', in 2012 Avis launched a new ad campaign and a new slogan: 'It's Your Space'. It can be argued whether it was the right choice. The campaign created by Leo Burnett USA in New York aimed to help better position the company with busy business travellers than with leisure travellers as it used to be. The new slogan should communicate that the interior space of rental cars is where business travellers can re-charge or be optimally productive while travelling. 'Customer-centric brands must always evolve to keep up with ever-changing customer needs and preferences. Avis evolves as a premium brand to better meet these needs. The new slogan reflects Avis's continuous goal of being a customer-oriented, service-driven company, and presents the brand in relation to customer experience and the benefits of renting a car from Avis' (Avis's Marketing Director Jeannine Haas, interviewed by Ad Age 2012).[97] The new position is a significant strategic choice that clearly states how Avis chooses to focus ahead.

### A gap in the market

A well-known classic example of positioning is the one developed for Volkswagen in 1959 by the US advertising agency DDB, the same ones that developed the Avis ad mentioned above. They created the most effective ad ever made for Volkswagen.[98] This was during the so-called 'creative revolution' in America, the time when *mad men* were living high on their customers' budgets[99] 'Let us prove to the world,' wrote William



> 'Brand experience is the sum of all the sensations, thoughts, feelings, and reactions that individuals have in response to a brand. Brand experience is not specific to a channel or media type. (...) To be competitive today, you need to create a consistent brand experience across every channel' (Schueller 2021).

Bernbach in his 1949 manifesto, *The creative revolution*, 'that good taste, good art, good writing can be good selling'. This was undoubtedly the case for Volkswagen when they were to launch the Volkswagen Beetle 'The Beetle' in the US market. Initially, it seemed like a hopeless task to sell a car that was small, clumsy, and ugly to the American population where 'long and low' were keywords, and where new models each year became slightly wider, slightly longer, even more streamlined, and even hotter. It was not a plus in a post-war period to have had the Volkswagen produced in Germany during the war. So what happened has gone down in advertising history as one of history's best advertising and positioning stunts. The ad creators found a gap in the market. 'How would you manage to sell such a car on the American market? The traditional method would be to get a creative photographer who could photograph the car looking a little better than in real life, arguing that it was cheap and reliable. But the gap or niche was about *size*. The ad made the position perfectly clear. 'Think small'. The headline consisted of these two simple words that did two things. First, they established Volkswagen's position. Second, they challenged the current perception which was 'the bigger, the better'. Naturally, this approach is effective only if there is an open gap in the consumer's mind, where one can accommodate the idea of a 'small car'. There were other small cars on the market when Volkswagen was launched, but none of them had claimed this position' (Ries and Trout, 1986, p. 81). It is about being the first to take a position.

Tips for designers
**The research article: 'Holistic Package Design and Consumer Brand Impressions', *Journal of Marketing* (Orth and Malkewitz 2008) mentions empirically based guidelines for selecting or modifying packaging designs for achieving desired consumer responses. Seven studies identify the key types of package designs, including the factors that differentiate those package designs, and determine how they are related to consumer brand impressions. Available at: doi.org/10.1509/jmkg.72.3.64.**

**The chain stores' own brands (private labels, PL/store brands) should initially be a low-cost alternative to established quality brands. Nevertheless, there are private brands that are positioned as 'premium products' to compete with existing trademark products. What happens when a PL gets the same design as big-name brand? What are the next-generation attributes of a premium product facing tougher competition from private labels and other copycats? (Hem, 2017).**

### High price or low price

While the best thing is to be the first one out there, finding an unoccupied position or a gap in the market, there are established positions against which to compete on price (3.4.2 Porter's generic strategies; Cost leadership).

A *low-pricing strategy* involves selling the same goods as the competitor at a lower price, so that the buyer feels that they have received greater value. Such a strategy often involves approaching a wide market and selling large quantities to lower the price. Choosing a low-cost strategy usually means that the leading competitive advantage is the price. At the same time, lower prices will automatically be perceived to have lower quality. If the customer nevertheless experiences the quality as good enough or better than expected, it can lead the customer to feel that they are getting greater value at a lower price. The opposite happens for a high-end product. Here, the product should automatically be perceived to be of high quality. In this context, it is important to make sure that the customer perceives the added value as so much higher that they are willing to pay that price. Many designers fail when their ambition to create a visually stunning design ends up communicating the same quality of low-quality products as those of high quality. This may lead the customer to believe that a low-priced product is of the same quality as a high-priced one, and that they have gained a higher value at a lower price. A dissatisfied customer will probably not buy the product again. Everything that is communicated about a product either verbally or visually, whether via the advertisement or the packaging, is part of a promise to the customer that should be fulfilled. Failure to deliver can lead to dissatisfied customers and poor reputation.

100 **A defined market position that targets a niche market is a great opening play for a new business, or a business breaking into a new market.**

A *high pricing strategy* involves approaching the same market as competitors, but with a higher price and added value that makes the buyer willing to pay more. It requires a clear differentiation and positioning. High price is often associated with high quality and reliability and is a strategy that is open to positioning all types of products. Such a high price postioning should be communicated and not come as a surprise in the shop. Moreover, there is an implicit promise of quality that should be fulfilled. A good example is L'Oréal which has chosen *a high pricing strategy* with the position 'Because you're worth it'.

**How to select a position that increases the customers' willingness to pay?**

Different positions a company may take to increase customers' willingness to pay (Lien, Knudsen and Baardsen 2016: 121):

**New product:** The company satisfies new demands that the customer previously did not perceive they had, and those others do not meet.

**Performance:** The company delivers better than others on services that customers highly value (and those others do not offer).

**Customisation:** The company can customise better or cheaper than its competitors and thus offer a better price-performance ratio than others.

**Gets the job done:** Customers can 'leave the job' to the company to a greater extent than to their competitors, so they don't need to think any further about the matter.

**Design:** The company has a superior design/aesthetics compared to its competitors.

**Status:** The company gives the customer status or the opportunity to express specific values.

**Cost reduction:** The company lowers the customers' total costs more than others.

**Risk reduction:** The company lowers the customers' risk more than its competitors do.

**Availability:** The company has better availability or product selection than others.

**User-friendliness.** The company's solutions are simpler and more practical to use than the competitors' solutions.

### Niche or upstream

Niche positioning[100] is marketing a very special product or service to just one niche segment within a chosen market based on the competitive strategy Porter calls *focus* (3.4.2 Porter's generic strategies). Such a niche may be *age segmentation*, where the product is clearly aimed at, for example, the elderly, adolescents, or children. It can be *unconventional distribution* like shop-in-shop or pop-up shop.

Moving against the flow has proven to be the key to success in establishing one's position, not doing what everyone else is doing or what is expected but doing something unexpected new or different. The perfume brand Revlon was successful in sales when (in 1973) they, unlike all their



One example of a high pricing strategy is the grocery chain Waitrose, which has higher prices than many of its competitors, but people like to go to Waitrose to buy the same products they can get cheaper at, say, Lidl, Aldi and Iceland. The reason for this could be, for example, accessibility, greater product range, better service and better quality of fresh produce.

competitors who thought *the more feminine and cuter, the better*, instead moved against the flow and named a new perfume Charlie. In product advertisements, there was a young girl wearing trousers and a jacket.

A positioning declaration contains four main elements:
1) Who is the target group?
2) Which category and market should the brand operate in?
3) What brand attributes (emotional, rational, and utility value) should the brand express?
4) What is the brand's promise (reason to believe)? (Robertson, 2013)

### Repositioning

A position can emerge entirely by itself. For example, a company regarded as the largest can automatically get the position as the largest. But a large business can also be cumbersome and inflexible, which does not make the largest an exclusive advantage, but rather a disadvantage. It can often be an advantage to be small. A small company is generally more flexible. It is easier to make decisions in a small administration, easier to make changes and develop, and it needs to make a little more effort. The biggest is not always the best, or the same as a good position.

If a product is not intentionally positioned, it is still not too late. A good start is to find out whether the product has some unique characteristic or advantage that is possible to deliver on, that the competitors do not have, something that has not been communicated yet. Such a unique property or value can be used as a position. It does not matter if competing products can deliver the same value, because taking a position is about being the first to communicate it. The company does not necessarily need to change the product, but it might need to adjust the communication and change the packaging design to signal the new position.

A position may eventually expire, as Avis experienced with its position. The deliberate change of position is called repositioning. Repositioning is not just a game of words for choosing a new slogan. Position is strategy. Therefore, the company should reconsider its competitive strategy and choose how best to compete in the market. A good start is to look out into the market to find a need that is not met, a gap in the market or to look at the possibility of creating new markets (3.4.1 Competitive strategy, 3.4.4 Blue Ocean Strategy, 3.2.6 Value proposition).

### Positioning statement

The basis for the choice of position should be defined in as a concise description of the target market as well as a compelling picture of how one wants that market to perceive the brand. 'Every product and marketing decision you make regarding your brand has to align with and support your positioning statement' (Stayman, 2015).

Template for Writing a Positioning Statement strategy (Stayman, 2015): For [insert Target Market], the [insert Brand] is the [insert Point of Differentiation] among all [insert Frame of Reference] because [insert Reason to Believe].[101]

Positioning is communication. Positioning is not only a strategy but also the company's most important message to the outside world. A positioning statement is expressed in one phrase or sentence, it clearly states where the brand or the company wants to be positioned in the market and towards the correct target groups. A positioning statement should mean something to the target group. 'The big challenge for a company or organisation is to acquire a "position" in the consumer's mind. A position that not only says something about the brand, but also tells the story about the brand in relation to its competitors' (Ries and Trout, 1986). A positioning

101 'The point of differentiation (POD) describes how your brand or product benefits customers in ways that set you apart from your competitors. The frame of reference (FOR) is the segment or category in which your company competes. The reason to believe is just what it says. This is a statement providing compelling evidence and reasons why customers in your target market can have confidence in your differentiation claims.' From: *How to Write Market Positioning Statements* (Stayman, 2015).

102 Many different terms are used to express the benefits, properties and values a brand has and should build in people's consciousness: brand personality, brand archetype, brand essence, brand benefits, brand attributes, primary brand benefit, brand associations, brand position, brand promise, unique value proposition, brand triggers, brand mantra, etc.

103 Petrány (2014).

statement may be expressed, in a slogan, or in a tagline with the logo. How the brand is perceived is very much about how the brand is expressed through tone-of-voice, and brand identity. A brands tone-of-voice is very important and often forgotten as an important positioning tool.[102]

What is being said is also promised and thus constitutes a promise. A promise triggers an expectation. This expectation should be met. Only when trust and credibility are established may the promise become a position and gain a place in people's consciousness. An example of this is Volvo with its slogan 'Volvo, for life'. That Volvo is a safe car is anchored in most people's minds. That is a strongly embedded position, which is perceived as credible. The reason for this is, among other things, that the company Volvo has demonstrated, through its choices and actions, that they live up to their position. They were the first to offer seat belts (three-point belts) in 1959 and they are continuously working on new safety and safety equipment technologies. Volvo believes they can eliminate all deaths in their cars by 2020[103] (3.8.6 Communication elements).

What makes a good positioning statement/slogan? Here are six keys to keep in mind (Stayman, 2015):

- It is simple, memorable, and tailored to the target market.
- It provides an unmistakable and easily understood picture of your brand that differentiates it from your competitors.
- It is credible, and your brand can deliver on its promise.
- Your brand can be the sole occupier of this particular position in the market. You can 'own' it.
- It helps you evaluate whether or not marketing decisions are consistent with and supportive of your brand.
- It leaves room for growth.


1 Initiation
2 Insight
3 Strategy
4 Design
5 Production
6 Management

3.1 Strategy development
3.2 Overall strategy
3.3 Goals and subgoals
3.4 Business strategy
3.5 Business model
3.6 Market strategy
3.7 Brand strategy
3.8 Communication strategy
3.9 Design strategy

3.7.1 Brand platform
3.7.2 Brand architecture
3.7.3 Brand positioninging
3.7.4 Brand story
3.7.5 Brand identity
3.7.6 Brand assets
3.7.7 Brand name
3.7.8 Brand perspective
3.7.9 Brand refresh, redesign, rebranding

- Brand narrative as positioning strategy
- The Concept Story
- Cultural anchoring
- Brand narrative process
- Dramaturgy
- The Hollywood models
- Three-course menu


## 3.7.4 Brand story

A narrative that is well written sneaks into the reader's metaphorical universe and appeals to mental notions through text and images. Therefore, the narrative is an important part of branding, where it is precisely the mental consciousness of the recipient one wants to reach. Kotler and Keller (2016, p. 402) refer to Randall Ringer and Michael Thibodeau, who explain narrative branding to appeal to deep metaphors that are anchored in people's memories, associations, and stories. They identify five elements that form part of a narrative branding:

1) The brand history in words and metaphors.
2) The consumer's behaviour in relation to the brand over time and their contact points with the brand.
3) Visual language or expression of the brand.
4) What experience-related expression the story gets, and how the brand engages the senses.
5) The role the brand plays, or the relationship the consumer has with it in their life.

Further reading
*Building a StoryBrand: Clarify Your Message So Customers Will Listen* (2017) by Donald Miller.

'We tend to become the story we tell. This is the starting point for the narrative method' (Michael White, 2006).

### Brand narrative as positioning strategy

Creating a brand story, or a narrative, has become the new gold both as a positioning strategy and in creating great brand concepts and distinctive unique brand identities. The only limits are those set by one's imagination, and the ability to formulate a good narrative that has distinctiveness, dramaturgy, and credibility. Positioning strategies that we have talked about so far are based on methods that involve thorough investigation of the target group, the company, and the competitive situation. Brand narrative as an alternative or in addition to traditional positioning is based on the creativity and imagination one can get out of a story, and how it can be expressed through visual brand elements and communication to create desired brand associations and distinctiveness. 'Strong brands, places of significance, and meaningful experiences share many of the same characteristics. They have many dimensions and a rich network of associations attached to them. They have attitude, clear symbols, evoke emotions, and respond to both functional and emotional needs. Using narratives as positioning tools makes it easier to operationalise and develop a distinct and significant brand expression' (nasjonalkolleksjon.com/riss).[104]

Fig. 3.36 **The figure is based on The Concept Story a strategy tool developed by Strømme Throndsen Design. The model includes nine main areas: product, value, origin, place, culture, person, experience, history, and nature. Any brand can find anchoring for its values within one or more of these nine areas. The model can be used as a basis for developing a brand concept, a brand narrative and eventually defining a brand positioning strategy. Ultimately this may be used in developing a brand name, logo etc.**

### The Concept Story

The design agency Strømme Throndsen Design[105] has developed The Concept Story as a strategy tool that can be used to create brand concepts and brand positions, based on the principles of brand narratives. The purpose of The Concept Story is to create unique brand identities and holistic product experiences, anchored in the cultural, functional, and emotional characteristics of the company. The Concept Story divides the product's possible characteristics into nine main areas: product, value, origin, place, culture, person, experience, history, and nature, see Figure 3.36. Within one or more of these areas, one can find the starting

### Black Tower Example

The design agency Strømme Throndsen Design (stdesign.no) carried out a revitalisation of Black Tower to make the brand relevant to a new generation of young consumers (20s) and at the same time retain existing customers. 'The brand has had an undercommunicated history. We added wine language by communicating Origin, Place, Person / Experience (winemaker), Culture and History' (Morten Throndsen 2022).

### Sales increase after redesign

Strømme Throndsen Design's collaboration with Reh Kendermann GMbH resulted in a revitalisation of identity and packaging design for Germany's largest export wine series, Black Tower wines. The revitalisation has yielded solid results; Retailtimes reports, among other things, a sales increase of 61% for Black Tower Rosé. Their goal of reaching a new generation of consumers without losing the brand's established buyers has given the brand an increase in sales beyond all expectations, on the entire redesigned range. 'Strømme Throndsen Design managed to give our wine a look which captures the attention of consumers without losing its personality. It just got a lot more style and sophistication!' – Esther Schumacher, Marketing & Brand Manager, Wienkellerei Reh Kendermann

104 **Riss (nasjonalkolleksjon.com/riss) has been developed by Innovation Norway to make Norwegian experiences and destinations more accessible to tourists. Read more about Riss in the interview with Kjell Reenskaug, former creative leader and partner at Bleed-Studio (bleed.com), now Head of Experience Strategy and Design Europe at Cognizant.**

105 **Strømme Throndsen Design is an award-winning design agency, recognised as one of the best in the fields of concept development and packaging design They are based in Oslo and work internationally.**

106 **Experts have described this as 'wikification of brands', because for comparison, wikis are written by contributors from all social strata and from all possible angles of approach (Kotler and Keller).**

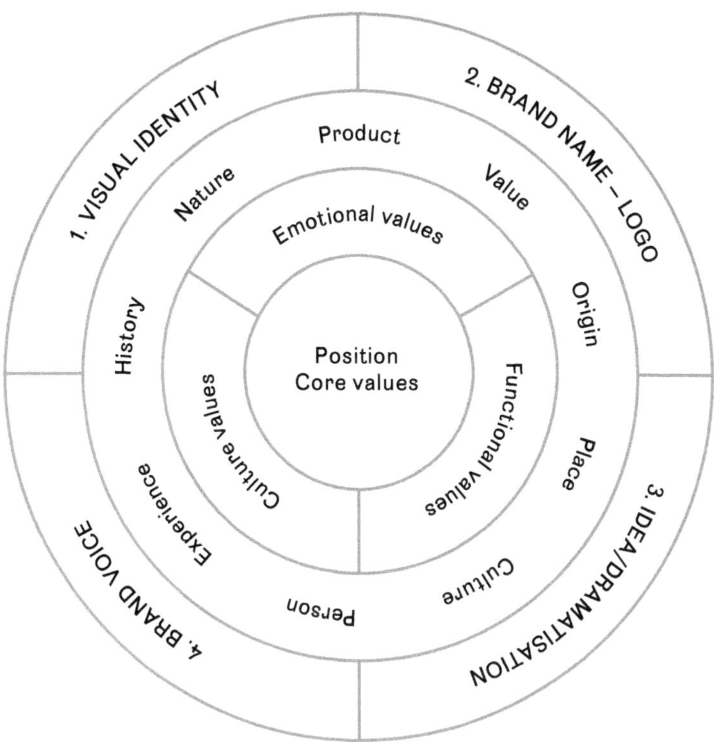


Fig. 3.36 The concept story

1 Initiation
2 Insight
3 Strategy
4 Design
5 Production
6 Management

3.1 Strategy development
3.2 Overall strategy
3.3 Goals and subgoals
3.4 Business strategy
3.5 Business model
3.6 Market strategy
3.7 Brand strategy
3.8 Communication strategy
3.9 Design strategy

3.7.1 Brand platform
3.7.2 Brand architecture
3.7.3 Brand positioninging
3.7.4 Brand story
3.7.5 Brand identity
3.7.6 Brand assets
3.7.7 Brand name
3.7.8 Brand perspective
3.7.9 Brand refresh, redesign, rebranding

- Brand narrative as positioning strategy
- The Concept Story
- Cultural anchoring
- Brand narrative process
- Dramaturgy
- The Hollywood models
- Three-course menu

point for the brand narrative and position of any brand. The brand concept and narrative developed through this method form the basis for the development of names, logos, and profile supports. 'We believe in telling honest and convincing brand narratives that establish long-term customer relationships. At the same time, we want the visuals to be great and engaging, we want them to be supported by a good concept and a credible strategy. This we create through proprietary processes that guarantee that each solution is unique and do their part to enhance the brand's credibility' (Morten Throndsen 2022).

### Cultural anchoring

The question is what story the brand should convey. Is it the attributes of the product, its qualities, origin, history, the person behind it, or is it the place and the culture? The narrative can have an authentic anchoring, a dramatisation of the product's origin, traditional production methods, distinctive cultural surroundings, attributes, and qualities of the raw materials, or it can be designed to create a similar experience. A brand narrative based on the cultural heritage and origin of the business, product, or service creates credibility and a relationship to the brand.

Craig Thomson, professor of marketing at the University of Wisconsin, regards brands as socio-cultural templates (Kotler and Keller 2016). He refers to research that studies brands as cultural resources. In this context, consumers are seen as active co-players in the process of creating meaning and position for brands.[106] For companies that want to build iconic leading brands, according to Professor Douglas Holt at

> 'Together with our clients, we develop effective, relevant and interesting design concepts, logos and identities that foster brand loyalty and evoke emotionsm' (Strømme Throndsen Design, stdesign.no).

Oxford University, it is necessary to acquire knowledge of culture and develop strategies based on cultural principles of branding, as well as hire and train cultural experts.

Fig. 3.37 The Hollywood model refers to the workplace methods movie studios and filmmakers use to make films, in order to effectively tell their story. Either way, it can be used dramaturgically to plan any narrative, story or content.

Tips for the designer
The brand narrative can be the underlying brand asset, from which the brand concept and the other brand assets types such as name, logo and slogan are derived. The brand narrative can also supplement and strengthen an existing brand concept by building a story around it.

An example of a narrative from the Super Bra website, selling products in the category muesli, rice and pizza sauce: 'What is better than good food made by people who care for the earth and who work on it? To us, it is important to know where our food comes from and how it comes into being. When we make a product, we sometimes must go where the pepper grows, if it is pepper that we want then' (superbra.no).

### Brand narrative process

Creating brand narratives requires insight into the current situation or theme on which the narrative should be based. For example, if the narrative is to be linked to a geographic location, it will be necessary to do research and get to know the history, traditions, and distinctive features of the location, to find out what it is relevant to elaborate on in the narrative in order to make it as authentic as possible. Randall Ringer and Michael Thibodeau have come up with the following brand narrative framework (Kotler and Keller, 2016, p. 403):

**Environment:** time, place, and context.

**Role design:** the brand as a character, including the role it plays in the life of the audience, the conditions, and responsibilities in which it is included, and its background or origin.

**Narrative structure:** how the inner logic of the narrative plays out over time and includes actions, desired experiences, defining events, and the defining moment.

**Language:** the voice that creates credibility, metaphors, symbols, themes, and review motifs.

An idea process is a good starting point for developing a brand narrative, for bringing out a wide range of approaches. Ideas are sorted and prioritised, and two to three ideas are selected, which are developed sufficiently to make a choice as to which idea should form the basis of the story. Storyboards and moodboards are well suited for visualising conceptual directions. Brand history can be communicated verbally and visually, by photography and illustration, and other perceptible effects. What tone of voice should carry the narrative, and which communication channels the narrative should function in, are anchored in the communication strategy (3.8 Communication strategy).

### Dramaturgy

By writing, speaking, and body language we can make our narratives and stories exciting, interesting, and compelling. The word 'dramaturgy' comes from Greek *dramatúrgein*, which means to create drama. The term is basically used to describe storytelling in the theatre and structure of play. In classical theatre, the choice of instruments, such as the use of breaks, contrast, and story-building, applies. It is based on traditions dating back to Aristotle's *Poetics* from ca. 330 BCE (Leinslie and Arntzen 2016). Today, dramaturgy is used in many areas, such as film, books, journalism, advertising, and design, to plan and create visual and verbal stories. We can also say that dramaturgy is strategy, if, through dramaturgic approaches, we can build brand associations and create customer experience. To put it simply, dramaturgy is about how a good story is put together (Jensen and Tørdal, 2017).

Aristotle divided drama into three main parts: beginning, middle and end, thereby creating a logical context and a plot. When assembling a narrative, you can use several different tools to drive the narrative forward. 'It may be how *the characters* are portrayed, how *conflict* is present in the narrative, and whether the story has one *or more elements of surprise*' (Jensen and Tørdal 2017):

**Characters:** The actors in a narrative are called characters. *Dynamic* characters evolve and change during the action. *Static* characters do not change. The protagonists of media narratives often appear with distinctive traits. They like to be either good, smart, bad, or stupid.

**Conflicts:** A good narrative depends on clear lines of conflict as a means of creating tension.

**Surprises:** A good story should surprise the recipient. In the media, this is called set-up and pay-off. You give the recipient a hint during the story. The recipient experiences deep satisfaction when what they have only suspected eventually turns out to be true.

'Dramaturgy has many faces. The classics are tragedy, love, and comedy. How we respond to dramaturgy constitutes part of evolutionary theory, something we can read about in brain research. The brain releases dopamine when we feel joy, look at art, images, and other things we experience as visually appealing. This does not happen when we look at things we perceive as neutral. In the context of design, we create visual tension and dynamics using visual instruments. When dopamine is released, it becomes easier to remember the message, and we remember it with greater accuracy. Therefore, when translating information into visual communication, it is important to know your target group, what they are responding to, and what triggers and releases dopamine. What is perceived as visually appealing to one is not perceived the same way by another. It again has to do with their experience and reference basis' (Sikkes, 2017).

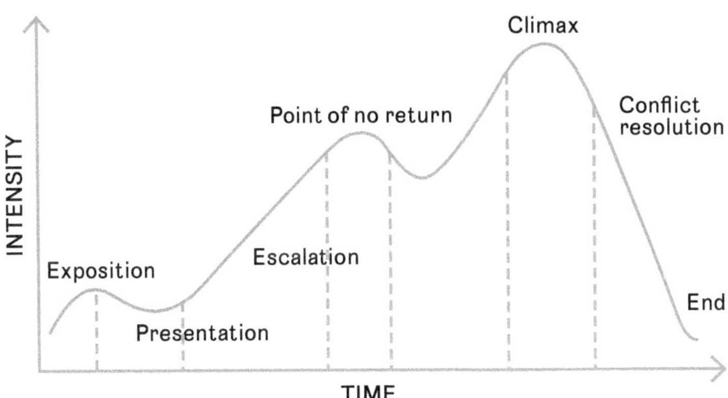


Fig. 3.37 The Hollywood model

### The Hollywood models

The linear dramaturgy model is based on Aristotle's thoughts on how history in a drama should be built up. There are a lot of different dramaturgy models for different purposes. The Hollywood model is named after its use in Hollywood movies. The course of events consists of seven steps, designed to help the viewer really get into the film, get interested, and stay interested ('Hollywood model', n.d.):

**Exposition:** One starts with a small tension curve to hold the viewer. The viewer should understand what genre the film belongs to. Already

1 Initiation
2 Insight
3 Strategy
4 Design
5 Production
6 Management

3.1 Strategy development
3.2 Overall strategy
3.3 Goals and subgoals
3.4 Business strategy
3.5 Business model
3.6 Market strategy
3.7 Brand strategy
3.8 Communication strategy
3.9 Design strategy

3.7.1 Brand platform
3.7.2 Brand architecture
3.7.3 Brand positioninging
3.7.4 Brand story
3.7.5 Brand identity
3.7.6 Brand assets
3.7.7 Brand name
3.7.8 Brand perspective
3.7.9 Brand refresh, redesign, rebranding

- Brand narrative as positioning strategy
- The Concept Story
- Cultural anchoring
- Brand narrative process
- Dramaturgy
- The Hollywood models
- Three-course menu

The purpose of using dramaturgy is to arouse the recipient's interest, keep it, and increase it.

here, a bond with the protagonist is created as well as expectations of what is to come.

**Presentation:** The surroundings and characters are presented in greater detail. One learns the connection between the protagonist and the consequences of the plot.

**Escalation:** The tension curve rises slowly, while small conflicts escalate, ending in solutions that can resolve the great conflict that awaits. There will be more obstacles and more resistance. The viewer identifies more and more with the protagonist.

**Point of no return:** At the 'point of no return', the action comes to a point where it is no longer possible for the protagonist to go back. The tension rises sharply and can suddenly take a surprising new turn.

**Climax:** The tension curve and intensity peak. The viewer will notice that things are happening fast as one approaches a resolution of the conflict.

**Conflict resolution:** The conflict is resolved, the tension curve slows down, and the plot is close to its end.

**End:** After the climax of the action comes a small part that rounds off the entire film. Hollywood films almost always end with a 'happy ending' where equilibrium has been restored (Jensen and Tørdal 2017).

**A successful brand identity reflects the user's self-image!**

#### Three-course menu

This is a simple method that can be used to create dramaturgy in verbal storytelling, or in a visual layout, presentation, portfolio, or anything else that has a visual and verbal flow. For example, if the task is a magazine, it will be necessary to consider dramaturgy in the text of individual articles, in the design of each article, and of the magazine as a whole. The method compares the progress with a three-course menu: The appetizer is small, it should awaken the taste buds, set the tone for the meal and create expectations for the main course. The article may involve displaying an image that arouses curiosity, along with a brief introduction of the content. The main course is big and should satisfy expectations and hunger, but not so big that one can't handle another bite. The main content of the article will explain the case, along with pictures and illustrations to hold the reader's attention. Dessert is the finishing touch. It is supposed to tickle one's belly and leave a smile on one's face. In the article, it will be a matter of keeping the reader's interest to the end.

### 3.7.5 Brand identity

Brand identity is a combination of the brand's intrinsic attributes and values and the outer visible part expressed through a set of visual brand assets, such as logo, symbol, and slogan. According to Kapferer (2012), the two main tools for developing a brand are brand identity, which defines the brand's values and distinctive features, as well as brand position, which outlines the brand's advantages in a specific market. The distinctive feature of the brand is the visual perception of the brand and the associations made with the brand. 'Brand identity is tangible and appeals to the senses. You can see it, touch it, hold it, hear it, watch it move. Brand identity fuels recognition, amplifies differentiation, and makes big ideas and meaning accessible. Brand identity takes disparate elements and unifies them into whole systems' (Wheeler, 2013, p. 4).

The success factor lies in the potential of the brand to appeal to a specific audience, create a sense of loyalty, and forge lasting relationships.

Brand identity is what the company says about who they are, about the product or service they deliver, the quality they provide to customers, and the company's advantages over competing brands. Brand image, on the other hand, is how the brand is perceived by the audience. One challenge that every company faces when trying to build a brand, is to make sure its brand identity matches the image the audience has of it. A negative gap between brand identity and brand image means that the company has lost contact with the market pulse. It is a strong signal to take action in order to prevent loss of revenue. Brand identity is greatly influenced by brand architecture (3.7.2 Brand architecture).

*A holistic brand identity*: According to Kapferer, brand identity is about the overall image the audience gets of the brand – the overall impression of what the brand is and stands for. The overall brand identity can be defined by answering the following questions (Kapferer, 2012):

- What is the brand's specific vision and goal?
- What makes the brand different? What is unique?
- What needs does the brand meet? What is the brand's task?
- What is the brand's unflagging battle? Philosophy?
- What are its values? Emotional, rational, cultural?
- What is its area of competence? Its reason to exist?
- What are the elements to make the brand recognisable?

### Identity prism

One good way to analyse and define the brand is by using the Brand identity prism (Kapferer, 2012, p. 158). The identity prism explains brand identity using six facets: physical characteristics, personality, relationship, culture, reflection, and self-image, Figure 3.8 (based on Kapferer 2012):

*Physical characteristics:* A brand has some physical characteristics and product benefits that immediately come to one's mind when the brand is mentioned, a combination of what the brand specifically delivers and its added value. An example of that is Coca-Cola. Everything we physically associate with the brand: product, quality, position, packaging, combined with the brand's perceived identity based on the logo, the drink, the bottle, the colour red.

*Personality*: A brand has a personality that emerges gradually through brand communication. The way we talk about the brand's products or services shows what kind of person the brand would be if it were a human being. Brand personality has been the focus of brand advertising since 1970. The easiest way to create a personality is to give the brand a familiar spokesperson, frontperson or mascot. An example of this is Kellogg's use of Tony the tiger on packaging and advertising.

*Relationship*: A brand is a relationship, a relationship between sender and recipient. The relationship to the brand often determines a purchase or how the brand is referred to between people. The relationship is often created because of the target group's identifying with what the brand stands for, its ideology, and culture. An example of this is Nike, which, with the slogan 'Just do it', joins forces with one's individual mastery and willpower.

*Culture*: A brand is a culture. The cultural facets of a brand help the target audience identify with the brand. The brand may be perceived

1 Initiation
2 Insight
3 Strategy
4 Design
5 Production
6 Management

3.1 Strategy development
3.2 Overall strategy
3.3 Goals and subgoals
3.4 Business strategy
3.5 Business model
3.6 Market strategy
3.7 Brand strategy
3.8 Communication strategy
3.9 Design strategy

3.7.1 Brand platform
3.7.2 Brand architecture
3.7.3 Brand positioninging
3.7.4 Brand story
3.7.5 Brand identity
3.7.6 Brand assets
3.7.7 Brand name
3.7.8 Brand perspective
3.7.9 Brand refresh, redesign, rebranding

- Identity prism
- Brand relationship

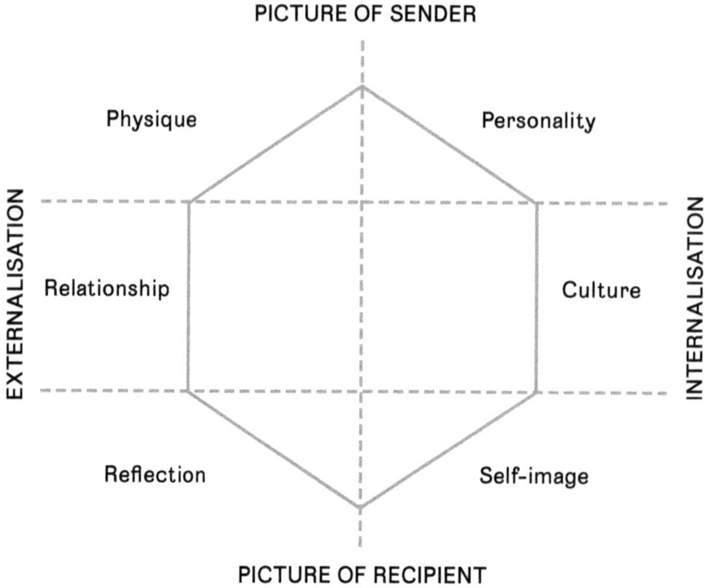


Fig. 3.38 a) Identity prism

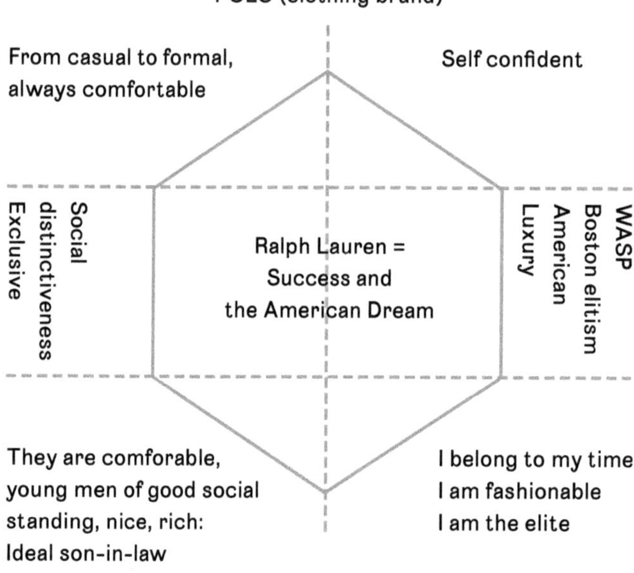


Fig. 3.38 b) Identity prism

Fig. 3.38 a) The figure shows The Kapferer Brand Identity Prism. The facets on the left (physical characteristic, relationship, reflection) are the social facets that give the brand its outer expression; all three facets are visible. The facets on the right (personality, culture, self-image) are the inner attributes, the soul and spirit of the brand. 'Physical properties' and 'personality' define the sender. 'Reflection' and 'self-image' define the recipient. 'Relationship' and 'culture' link sender and recipient.

Fig. 3.38 b) The figure shows an example on the use of identity prism to describe the brand identity for the clothing brand POLO (Kapferer, 2012, p. 163)

to fit one's own social identity, views, and beliefs. In a world where environmental concerns, sustainability, and human dignity are central to society, there is a cultural competition to meet the target group's own ideals. An example of this is the brand Innocent, which by virtue of its product name and product attributes, signals clean conscience.

*Reflection*: A brand reflects the customer. Over time, a trademark product can become a reflection of the user it addresses and vice versa. An example of that is when people are asked about their views on car brands. They immediately answer who they perceive as the brand's customer group; Volvo for families, Porsche for people who want to show off, BMW for young men who like speed, and so on. The user is reflected in the way they want to be seen because of using the brand. The signalling effect of the brand: Who am I, driving the Tesla? The success factor here is not to show the target group in advertising as they are, but as they want to be. Reflection should not be confused with the target group. Examples include Coca-Cola which has a much larger target group than the 15- to 18-year-olds shown in advertising campaigns. By showing their dreams in the ads, they also appeal to both younger and older target groups who can identify with the same dreams.

*Self-image*: The brand speaks to our self-image. The image others have of the target group is: 'they are ...' the self-image of the target group is: 'I feel, I am...' For example, many of those who buy a Porsche will want to prove to themselves and others that they can buy such a car. Through our attitude toward certain brands, we are clearly developing a special type of inner relationship with ourselves, and a self-image related to the brand. By swearing faithfulness to a brand, we also help promote the brand and signal a community that can, on certain occasions, both facilitate and stimulate conversation with others in the same community.

The identity prism conveys how the six facets are interrelated and interact. The starting point of the identity prism is the brand's ability to communicate. 'Brands can only exist if they communicate. Brands become obsolete if they remain quiet and unused for too long. A brand is communication because it communicates with the product that carries it. The brand communicates with both sender and recipient' (Kapferer, 2012, p. 163), see Figure 3.38.



### Brand relationship

Identity is how one's personality is perceived by the outside world or in relation to other people. Who are you, who am I, do we have anything in common? Having a clear brand identity, conscious relationship-building and follow-up of response are key factors in building a strong brand and achieving brand loyalty.

According to Keller (2013), the following four steps are central to all branding:

1) Establish identification between brand and customer, and an association to the brand in the customers' consciousness with a special product quality, product advantage, or customer needs.
2) Establish the overall brand structure in the customers' consciousness, by strategically linking several tangible and intangible associations.
3) Bring out the right customer response to the brand.
4) Convert brand responses to create brand resonance and an intense, active loyal relationship between the customers and the brand.

These steps raise a set of fundamental questions that customers always (at least implicitly) ask about brands. The questions follow one another hierarchically, so that one question forms the basis of the next (Keller, 2013):

1) Who are you? (Brand identity)
2) What are you? (Brand meaning)
3) What about you? How do I think and feel about you? (Brand response)
4) What about you and me? (Brand relationship)

Branding and brand association are the magic keywords. How can the different brand assets help establish or strengthen brand awareness and leave a set of positive brand associations in the consumer's consciousness?

These questions appear in Keller's brand resonance pyramid. The model is suitable both for analysing an existing brand and for defining a strategy for a new brand. See further explanation in 2.7.7 Brand analysis/Brand Resonance Pyramid. Response and relationship building are important communication tasks (3.8 Communication strategy).

**Performance and experience:** Once the brand has gained attention, questions about brand *performance* and *experience* will be two key factors that affect the impression. The impression can be crucial for possible response and further relationship. Therefore, performance and experience are two possible differentiation points which can be used to position the brand (3.7.3 Brand position; Points of parity/Points of differentiation). The brand position, brand narrative, and brand identity provide the basis for further development of brand assets.

Fig. 3.39 The figure shows the most central brand elements that a brand can consist of: name, domain name (URL), logo, symbol, character (figure or spokesperson), slogan, colour, shape, audio logo (or jingle), packaging, and sense effects.

Brand assets are elements that define the look of your brand, and together make up the brand experience.

### 3.7.6 Brand assets

A brand consists of a combination of brand assets (brand elements), both visual and verbal. The task of these elements is to help identify and differentiate the brand from other brands, make it easy to recognise, and establish correct brand associations. The purpose is to build brand awareness and brand relationships with the target group. The brand elements are the embodiment of the brand strategy. Performed consciously, they can be carriers of values and positioning strategies, and essential for building brand equity, see Figure 2.33 Keller's Brand Equity Model.

The more established a brand is, the fewer visual elements need to be present to achieve recognition. A symbol may be sufficient to evoke knowledge and associations of the brand name and product. Nike is a good example. You see the symbol and think about the name, the product and maybe the slogan: 'JUST DO IT.'

Brand assets are devices that can be registered as a trademark and that identify the brand and make it stand out, such as a brand name, logo or distinctiveness (Kotler and Keller, 2016). To register a brand asset as a trademark it must be unique, i.e. it must have distinctive character (6.2 Legal protection).[107] A colour can be an important element of identity that can help differentiate a brand, but colour alone is too generic to be trademarked. The most central brand assets types are name, domain name, logo, symbol, slogan, brand character, as well as packaging. It is also possible to supplement with other elements that have distinctive features and character, such as taste, smell, movement and sound. An example is the beverage brand Snapple's distinctive sound of the metal cap when it's removed off the bottle. Whether such effects can be registered as trademarks are uncertain. App icons and favicon are also important reference elements for the brand. The brand assets types mentioned here are also what we call identity elements involved in developing the visual identity of a company, product or service (4.9 Identity development).

All brand assets have one common task, to help identify and differentiate the brand and leave a memorable impression in the consumer's memory. The ideal is that all brand assets build up under the brand in a consistent way, so that the brand is experienced as similar as possible

107 'A trademark may only be registered if it is suitable to distinguish your goods and/or services from those of others' (Patentstyret, 2016).
108 Proxy can be explained as an authority given to someone to act for you. A figure that can be used to represent the value of something in a calculation (Proxy, n.d.).
109 URL: uniform resource locators.

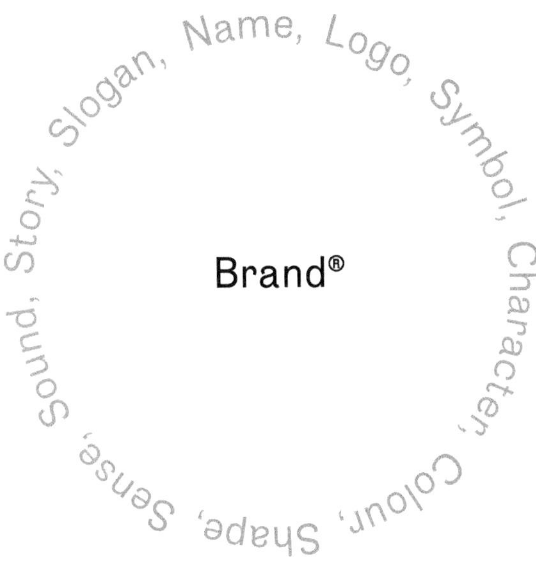


Fig. 3.39 Brand assets

1 Initiation
2 Insight
3 Strategy
4 Design
5 Production
6 Management

3.1 Strategy development
3.2 Overall strategy
3.3 Goals and subgoals
3.4 Business strategy
3.5 Business model
3.6 Market strategy
3.7 Brand strategy
3.8 Communication strategy
3.9 Design strategy

3.7.1 Brand platform
3.7.2 Brand architecture
3.7.3 Brand positioning
3.7.4 Brand story
3.7.5 Brand identity
3.7.6 Brand assets
3.7.7 Brand name
3.7.8 Brand perspective
3.7.9 Brand refresh, redesign, rebranding

- Name
- Domain name
- Logo
- Symbol
- App icon
- Favicon
- Brand colour
- Slogan
- Brand character
- Packaging
- Sense elements
- Audio Logo
- Brand identity

in all contexts. Romaniuk (2018) draws three primary reasons for how and why we need a brand, as well as branding: 1) Proclaiming ownership: The presence of a brand proclaims that item's ownership. 2) Anchoring knowledge in memory: The brand can act as an anchor for messages in memory. 3) Bridging activities with a common origin: The brand act as a bridge for otherwise seemly disparate items (place, time, content, message). 'The power of a distinctive asset is that it can act as a proxy[108] for the brand, and so, if sufficiently strong, can achieve the same ownership, anchor and bridge roles' (Romaniuk, 2018). Romaniuk emphasises the importance of having an overall long-term goal for the brand's asset building activities. When deciding among assets Romaniuk suggests asking category buyers to rate their liking of different assets, and select the most read, more in chapter 3.4.6 Distinctive asset-building strategy.

Here is an overview of brand assets based on Keller (2013) and more recent approach of Romaniuk (2018).

**Name:** The name is the most important brand asset. It is always present. It is what the business, product or service is known by, which one remembers, associates with, refers to, and which is present without it having to be visible. A brand name can be a very effective means of communication. A customer can perceive a name, record its meaning and activate it in memory in a matter of seconds. Because the brand name is so tightly linked to the product in the customers' memory, the brand name is also the most difficult element to change. Coming up with a satisfactory new brand name for a product can also be difficult and time-consuming, because so many attractive brand names have already been taken (3.7.7 Brand name).

**Domain name:** Today, securing ownership of a domain name or URL[109] is a must when developing the brand name. An URL representing the brand name increases the possibility that consumers will remember the URL to access the website. Ideally, the domain should be identical to the brand name, which is more and more difficult because many are

'Names need to be judged against positioning goals, performance criteria, and availability within a sector' (Wheeler, 2018)

already in use and taken. Therefore, in a naming process, there may be good suggestions that must be eliminated. Many companies end up choosing a constructed name to secure a matching internet address. If a desired domain name is taken, it is in some cases possible to buy the domain, or bypass it by combining the name with category, geography, etc. For example, the Gael restaurant chain was registered as gaelpitstop.no, gaelkitchen.no, and so on. Other suffixes, such as .com, may also be considered if the country code has been taken. One should register a domain quickly to avoid *name snatching* (6.2.3 Domain name).

**Logo:** The logo is a wordmark, a visual representation of the name. Next to the name, it is the logo that is the most important brand asset type, because it shows the name. Therefore, it plays a key role in creating brand awareness and value. Unlike brand names, logos can be customised over time to achieve a trendier look through a redesign. When redesigning a logo, it will always be an important question whether to preserve familiarity. If the brand name is distinctive, strong, and well established, the logo can withstand major upgrades. A logo can range from word pictures that are clearly legible (text-only logos) written in a distinctive way, to completely abstract designs with no relation to the name (4.9.3 Logo).

**Symbol:** The use of a pictogram[110] or a symbol in the logo can bring in pictorial associations that help support and reinforce the meaning. Like names, symbols or abstract logos can become very distinctive and recognisable. A new symbol will need to be accompanied by the name, a slogan, a brand story, or anything desired associated with the symbol. Otherwise, there is a risk that the consumer will not understand what the symbol is intended to represent. Symbols that have been established together with the name over time may eventually represent the name alone. For brands that are well established, it may be sufficient to see a symbol to remember the name. Examples include the Nike Swoosh, the Mercedes star, and the Olympic rings. These are symbols that are initially relatively abstract. Other symbols provide a more literal representation of the brand name, such as Shell, the Red Cross symbol, and the Apple logo. Such symbols can contribute to strengthening the brand meaning (4.9.4 Symbol).

**App icon:** App is short for application, which refers to a software program for any hardware platform. App icons[111] are used to depict an application in a phone or computer. By tapping or clicking the icon, it would open up the corresponding program or website. An app icon is basically a pictogram, which is a part of graphical user interface, linked to an application to help a user navigate through their mobile devices, such as smartphones (Iconion n.d). The app icon might be the users first impression of the brand. Therefore, when developing an app icon one of the prime factors is to bring out the most distinctive from the brand assets it should represent, so that the app is easy to recognise and helps build brand awareness; it could be an abbreviation or first letter of the brand name, a simplified and stylised illustration derived from the logo, symbol or another identity element. Development of the icon is best done through an iterative process to arrive at a simple shape that best represent the brand. The icon should be tested against different wallpapers, and by the use of A/B testing (2.9.2 A/B testing). For the design process a vector-based drawing program, such as Adobe Illustrator, is most suitable, while for the final output, using a raster graphics editor program,

Fig. 3.40 The figure shows a survey that can be done among category buyers to find out if a brand colour has potential as a distinctive brand asset. Questions are: Does the color signal a category? Does the color signal a subcategory? Does the color signal a competitor brand? If the answer is no to the questions, then the color is a contender! (Based on Romaniuk 2018, p. 115).

Tips for the designer
In the development of brand elements lies the opportunity to create distinctive brand assets, build brand awareness and brand equity.

110 'A pictogram, also called a pictogramme, pictograph, or simply picto, and in computer usage an icon, is a graphic symbol that conveys its meaning through its pictorial resemblance to a physical object' ('Pictogram,' n.d.). A pictogram cannot be called a symbol until it is loaded with meaning and symbolises something.

111 'Apps emerged from early PDAs, through the addictively simple game Snake on the Nokia 6110 phone, to the first 500 apps in the Apple App Store when it made its debut in July 2008' (Strain 2015, theguardian.com).

112 Read more: 'App Icon. How to create an app icon: Essential insights and best practices' at developer.apple.com and App icon Generator: appicon.co.

113 Favicon came in 1999 with Microsoft's release of Internet Explorer 5, used on bookmarked pages, next to the URL in the address bar ('Favicon,' n.d.).

114 Should consumer preferences matter when selecting colour assets? An online survey of 880 Australian consumers conducted in October 2009, tested the hypothesis: If liking a colour helps build distinctive assets, there should be a relationship between how much a colour is liked and the level of colour-liked linkage. The study showed that more liked colours were not stronger distinctive assets (Romaniuk, 2018).

such as Adobe Photoshop is needed. Choosing the right resolution is crucial since that would impact the display quality of the icon. Redesign of known app icons shows a tendency towards constant simplification (Wetzler, 2021): Google (2020), Instagram (2016), and Amazone (2021).[112]
**Favicon:** The smallest exposure of a brand identity is the little icon typically displayed in the address bar at the top of various tabs in the browser, the favicon (short for favorite icon)[113] with the size of 16x16 px (or 32x32). Creating a favicon is a perfect way to test and bring forward the distinctive brand assets of the logo, symbol and assets types, which represents the brand. Then it is crucial to choose the one subtle shape, the most recognisable letter or the most distinctive colour from the brand universe, that best represents the brand. Thus to help create brand awareness. In a usability perspective, it is more about leaving a signature and helping users navigate the address bars of the browser. The development of the favicon can mostly follow the same process as an app icon development.

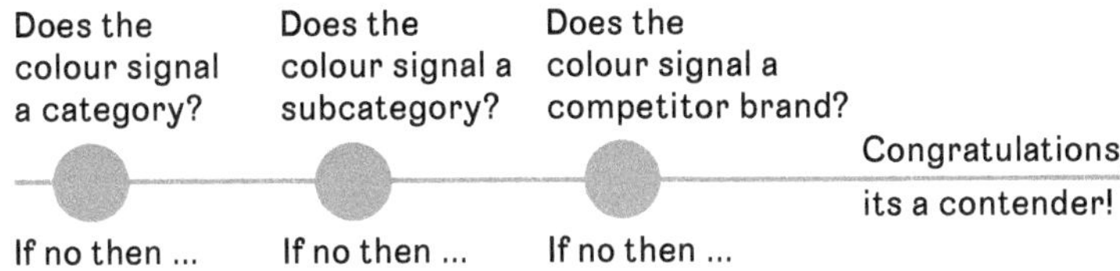


Fig. 3.40 Colour assets

**Brand colour:** Conscious use of color can make brands stand out and capture attention, but a colour based asset can be hard to build. First and foremost, colours may be associated with other identities, moreover colours have the tendency of blending into backgrounds. Some succeed in taking ownership of a colour, such as Coca-Cola (red), Facebook (blue), Starbucks (green). According to Romaniuk, if one manages to take ownership of a colour, one should take good care of it and not be tempted to change it by a redesign. 'Color is one of the most valuable assets your brand can develop – so protect it' (Romaniuk, 2018).[114] Romaniuk proposes three types of colour assets: single-colour asset, colour combinations and colour-and-design combinations.

- *Single-colour asset*: An individual colour is linked to the brand, such as Coca-Cola (red). For the colour to be a contender for a brand's distinctive assets, it needs to pass through three filters: 1) It should not signal a category. 2) It should not signal a subcategory. 3) It should not signal a brand.
- *Colour combinations*: A colour combination. They need to be used simultaneously, such as Mastercard (red and yellow). The color combination can be tested, by gathering appropriate metrics, to find out if one of the colours has the strength to be used in isolation and develop to a distinctive asset.
- *Colour-and-design combinations*: Colours combined with design elements, such as a shape, to create a distinctive asset. One example is the Red Bull can, with the red logotype and the slanted blue and silver rectangels. 'This combination of design and colour can create greater uniqueness than a solo colour, and become a valuable distinctive asset' (Romaniuk, 2018) (4.6.2 Colour, 3.4.6 Distinctive asset-building strategy).



The sequence of cognition

'The brain acknowledges and remembers shapes first. Visual images can be remembered and recognized directly, while words must be decoded into meaning' (Wheeler, 2018, p. 24).

**Slogan:** A slogan is a brief memorable phrase or motto that communicates descriptive or compelling information about the brand, expressing an idea or purpose of the brand to a specific audience or target group. The slogan can be based on the core values, the promise, or the position of the company, product or service. In this way, the slogan can help build identity and position. A strong slogan has qualities that make it concise, memorable, and attractive. It is common to use slogans in advertising, but they can be equally effective on packaging and in other contexts where the brand is to be exposed. A slogan can act as a kind of cue or clue that helps the consumer understand the meaning of the brand – what it is and what makes it special. It thus helps to build valuable mental associations to the brand. Therefore, the slogan should be used consistently in all contexts and over time, as a tagline or accompanying the logo. Some slogans can be used to create brand awareness by playing with the brand name in one way or another. Other slogans can build brand awareness by linking the brand to the relevant product category. A slogan can also be useful for other purposes, such as communicating the core message of a marketing campaign. But above all, slogans can help consolidate and reinforce the brand position (3.7.3 Brand position, 3.8.6 Communication elements).

**Brand character:** A brand character or mascot is a kind of brand symbol, a type of cartoon, animated, or real-life character that can have human characteristics or that can be a real person. Such characters are often introduced through advertising, promotions, and packaging design. Because they are often colourful and full of symbolism, they can get a lot of attention and therefore be useful for acquiring brand awareness. A consumer may be more likely to relate to a brand when the brand literally looks like a human or other lifelike creature. The mascot brings the brand personality to life and lowers the threshold for the customer to feel rapport and loyalty to the brand (Figure 2.33 Keller's Brand Equity Model). A positive aspect of such constructed characters is that they do not get older or need to be paid, as opposed to human spokespersons. The brand character can occur in very many different forms, distinguishing most often between cartoons. Examples are *Tony the Tiger*, the advertising mascot for Kellogg's Frosted Flakes (Frosties), the *M&M's characters* of the multi-colored button-shaped chocolates,[115] and actual people characters as *The Marlboro man* known from tobacco advertising campaigns for Marlboro cigarettes. The purpose of the brand character is: 1) to make it easier for the consumer to recognise the product, 2) to help differentiate the brand from its competitors, 3) to be able to communicate a unique characteristic, 4) to increase the personification of the brand and 5) ideally, to create ties between brand and consumer' (Hem and Grønnhaug 2002).

**Packaging:** One of the strongest associations the consumer has with the brand is often related to the appearance of its packaging. The packaging is itself a brand asset if it has a distinctive form, physical structure, shape, unique size, or material. One of the oldest examples is the traditional shape of the Coca-Cola bottle. In addition to the shape of the bottle, the product label is used to create brand identity, differentiation, and awareness, by adding product name, logo, symbol, color and slogan, as well as product information, graphic illustrations, photos, colour code, etc. (4.9.1 The identity principles, 4.9.2 The identity elements).

Tips for the designer
**If the product has a lot of shelf space with many products and product variations in width and height, it can create a powerful poster effect.**

Tips for the company
**The package itself is a poster consisting of some or all brand assets.**

**Shape, colourful graphics, custom presentations, unique messaging and technological assistants are a few of the tools experienced packagers use to stay ahead of consumers (Shaw, 2015).**

Further reading
***Packaging and the Metaverse: AR, VR and Beyond,* by Dube 2021: https://www.industrialpackaging.com/blog/packaging-and-the-metaverse.**

115 **Reading: 'The Making of the M&M's Characters, Advertising's Classic Comedic Ensemble How a seemingly bum assignment turned legendary' (Susan Credle 2019).**

**The Michelin Man**

One of the world's oldest brand mascot trademarks from 1898 still in active use is Bibendum (French), commonly referred to in English as the Michelin Man or Michelin Tyre Man, the official mascot of the Michelin tyre company. Created by the Michelin brothers and cartoonist 'O'Galop' and designed from a stack of tyres. The Michelin man was white because rubber tyres were naturally white, until carbon chemicals were mixed in from 1912 and turned them black. The Michelin company began reviewing restaurants so that people would travel further distances in their cars to eat at these restaurants. This in turn would wear down their tyres faster, and force them to buy more (it says). The Michelin Guides (since 1904) awards up to three Michelin stars for excellence: A very good restaurant in its category, excellent cooking, worth a detour. Exceptional cuisine, worth a special journey (Michelin.com, 'Michelin Guide,' n.d.).

The slogan, like brand name, is an extremely effective tool for building brand associations.



Packaging design is a battle for the customers' attention. 'The shelf is probably the most competitive marketing environment that exists, and we make our decisions about what to pur-chase in seconds' (Wheeler, 2018, p. 180). The expression in many product categories is relatively unified, which makes this an arena with a potential to stand out. A question then becomes which design element should be dominant and stand out. Dominance can be created in size, colour, font selection, contrast or other. One of the most important eye-catchers of packaging design is the colour. But breaking through with a new colour that differs from the category colour may be a challenge, as customers may associate colours with category. Colours can also be 'taken' because they are associated to a great extent with a well-established brand in the same category. Examples are Ritz crackers, Colgate toothpaste and Coca-Cola, all of which have taken ownership of the colour red in different product categories. Bigger and more glaring is not always the solution, especially when competitors follow suit.

For the packaging to have a strong brand impact, a key task for the designer is to assess which distinctive brand assets should dominate the packaging. Metrics can be used to test and evaluate which brand asset is the strongest, using 'The distinctive asset grid' (Romaniuk, 2018) (see 3.4.6 Distinctive asset-building strategy).

Packaging design is in a shift where new technology and requirements for more environmentally friendly materials are escalating. New, innovative, functional, or user-friendly packaging can increase the demand of a product. In addition, packaging innovation can help lower costs by developing smart solutions that reduce the amount of material, reduce the packaging size, make use of more affordable and eco-friendly materials, etc. Appearing environmental friendly and sustainable is also a good way of creating brand value. When working with packaging design, consider the entire life cycle of the package and its relationship

'Packaging design is a unique discipline, and it routinely involves collaboration with industrial designer, packaging engineers, and manufacturers' (...) For the company it includes different facets, such as supply chain management, manufacturing, distribution or shipping, sales force meetings, marketing, advertising, and promotion' (Wheeler, 2018).

to the product: source, print, assemble, pack, preserve, ship, display, purchase, use, recycle/dispose (Wheeler, 2018).

The internet and launch of digital payment tools have contributed to the increase in online shopping and changed the packaging industry for companies worldwide. New technologies will continue to evolve in the realm of packaging. The next step is how the future relationship between packaging and the metaverse, AR og VR teknologi,[116] will affect product packaging and branding for companies all over the world (Dube, 2021).

**Sense elements:** Brand assets are not always visible. They can be present in our senses, in our associations, in a positive experience, in a sense of happiness, in a captivating sound, in a characteristic taste, or in a delicious smell. A brand experience is a composite sensory experience that involves one or more of the senses, linking the impression to the memory. Martin Lindstrøm brings up all five senses (sight, sound, taste, touch and smell) in his 5-D Brand Sensogram,[117] which is based on a comprehensive survey of brands and the five senses of humans, carried out in 13 countries, the Brand Sense Survey. It concluded that the sense of smell comes second after sight. The sensogram provides a way to measure how a brand performs, by including all five senses. The fact that brands can appeal to more of our senses than just sight and hearing is not in itself new. Naturally, we associate emotion, smell, and taste with many products without this necessarily being intended as part of the branding. But deliberately used, appealing to more of our senses can have an amplifying effect. Emotions and senses are strongly linked to brands. Conscious use of sensory experiences can provide strong brand associations and represents an important brand identity and brand value. 'The more senses are activated in the development of the brand, the higher the number of sensory memories will be triggered about the brand' (Lindström, 2005).

Fig. 3.41 The Brand Sense Survey conducted internationally in 2005 by Martin Lindström, showes a clear correlation between the number of senses a brand appeals to and the price of the product. The figure is based on Lindstrøm (2005, p. 84).

Fig. 3.42 Results of Lindström's 2005 survey showed that McDonald's was the brand on the Fortune 100 list which represented the greatest sensory conflict. The graph shows the results compared to possible future potential. The figure is based on Lindström (2005, p. 85).

We taste with the nose. We see with our fingers and hear with our eyes (Lindström, 2005).

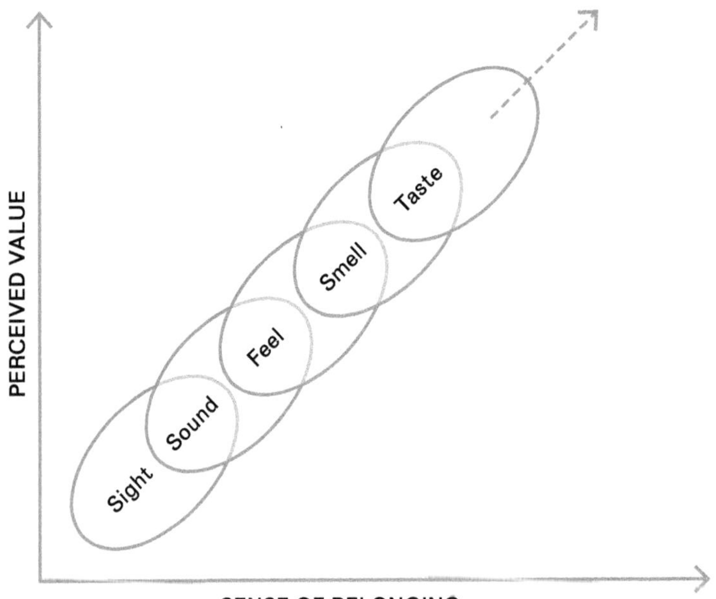


Fig. 3.41 The Brand Sense Survey

116 Metaverse is a virtual-reality space in which users can interact with a computer-generated environment and other users (Metaverse, n.d.). Augmented reality (AR) is an utvidet version of the real physical world that is achieved through the use of digital visual elements, sound, or other sensory stimuli delivered via technology (Hayes, 2020). Vitual reality (VR) is a computer-generated simulation of a three-dimensional image or environment that can be interacted with in a seemingly real or physical way by a person using special electronic equipment, such as a helmet with a screen inside or gloves fitted with sensors (Virtual reality, n.d.).

117 Martin Lindstrom's 5-D Brand Sensogram presented by the American Institute of Healthcare Management amihm.org/martin-lindstroms-5-d-brand-sensogram/

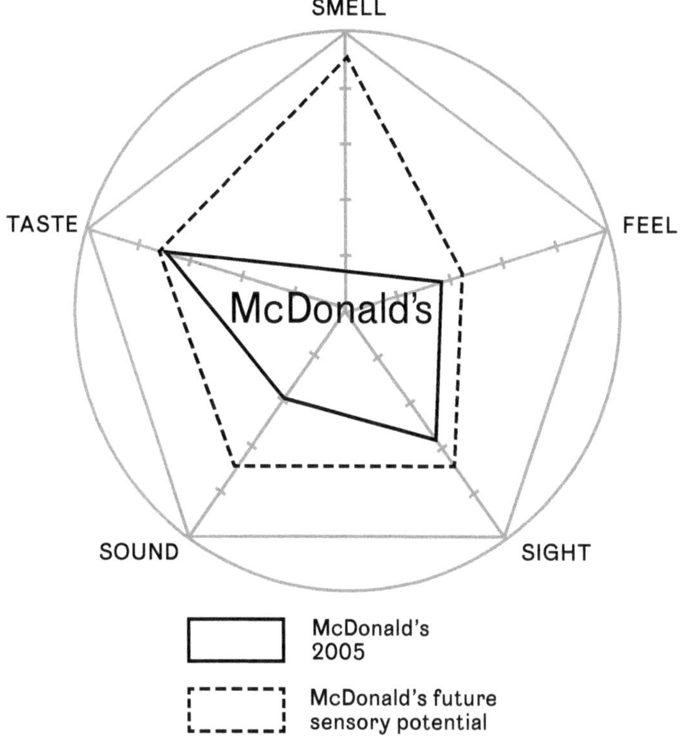


Fig. 3.42 McDonald's

1 Initiation
2 Insight
3 Strategy
4 Design
5 Production
6 Management

3.1 Strategy development
3.2 Overall strategy
3.3 Goals and subgoals
3.4 Business strategy
3.5 Business model
3.6 Market strategy
3.7 Brand strategy
3.8 Communication strategy
3.9 Design strategy

3.7.1 Brand platform
3.7.2 Brand architecture
3.7.3 Brand positioning
3.7.4 Brand story
3.7.5 Brand identity
3.7.6 Brand assets
3.7.7 Brand name
3.7.8 Brand perspective
3.7.9 Brand refresh, redesign, rebranding

- Name
- Domain name
- Logo
- Symbol
- App icon
- Favicon
- Brand colour
- Slogan
- Brand character
- Packaging
- Sense elements
- Audio Logo
- Brand identity

Lindstrøm conducted an international survey in 2005, which examined, among other things, the cause of the decline in sales for McDonald's in the second half of 2003 (2005, p. 81). Through the survey he was able to document that a change in the world's eating habits and a lack of service were some of the reasons, as well as the fact that many people thought the place smelled like deep-frying oil. A third of the consumers interviewed in the USA said their aversion to the smell of deep frying made them negative towards the food and the brand, which 42% of those in the United Kingdom agreed with. But paradoxically enough, half of all consumers participating in the survey said they loved the smell of the cooked food and that a visit to McDonald's made their mouths start watering. A similar survey of Burger King showed that 70% of the same consumers declared that they had a similar sensory experience with Burger King. The smell is not the only sense that triggers brand associations. The survey also found that 14% of all respondents said the food looked unappealing, 15% were dissatisfied with the appearance of the restaurant, and about 24% of those affected by the noise in restaurants said the sound in McDonald's restaurants gives them 'negative' feelings (partly caused by the sound of screaming kids and the beeping from the fryer). One might ask why restaurants like McDonald's had not put more conscious effort into the use of sensory experiences. The survey by Lindström also showed that there is generally a correlation between the number of senses a brand appeals to and the price. Multiple sensory brands may charge a higher price than similar brands with fewer sensory experiences.

Further reading
– Timeline: Key Events in the History of Online Shopping by Ang 2021: https://www.visualcapitalist.com/history-of-online-shopping/.
– Check out: packagingdigest.com

**Audio Logo:** Audio logo (sound logo) is a branded item in line with a visual logo. It is a short, characteristically captivating audio sequence or melody, which is most often heard at the beginning or end of an advertisement, usually on the web, radio or TV, and whose task is to repeatedly create recognition and associations with the brand. Large brands such as Audi, Mercedes, McDonald's, LG use the audio logo in their advertising.[118] The combination of an audio logo and a visual logo can strengthen brand awareness and is an important part of a company's audio identity. The human brain often best remembers sequences from the beginning or end of a song, which also makes it easier to remember an audio logo that is played before or after an ad. To get the best effect from an audio logo, it needs to be unique, flexible, and easy to remember. 'Because the audio logo tends to be stored easily in memory, in many cases consumers can be heard humming the audio logo even after the commercial has ended. This is, of course, a very favourable situation for a brand. Another form of sound branding is the *jingle*, a short song or tone that is used in radio and television advertising, among other things. Jingles can be characterised as a form of musical slogans.

**Brand identity**

The task of the brand assets is to support each other. What you do not get to say through the name can be amplified in the logo and slogan, in a symbol or sound. One prerequisite is always that brand assets can be easily used in different contexts where the brand is to have exposure. Each asset type plays a role in creating brand value and brand awareness. For example, a brand name visually presented through a logo will be easier to remember. The combination of all brand assets makes up the brand identity. Success in creating brand identity depends on the degree to which the elements are consistently presented. It concerns the placement of each element relative to each other (e.g. logo, symbol, and slogan) and how they appear together on different exposure surfaces. A success factor is to cultivate the unique and create a distinctive brand asset that can represent the brand. It does not have to be a logo or symbol, it can just as easily be a shape or pattern (4.9 Identity development).
*Brand elements choice criteria* (Kotler & Keller, 2016, p. 331):
**Memorable:** How easy do consumers recall and recognise the brand asset, and when - at both purchase and consumption?
**Meaningful:** Is the brand asset credible? Does it suggest the corresponding category and a product ingredient or the type of person who might use the brand?
**Likeable:** How aesthetically appealing is the brand asset?
**Transferable:** Can the brand asset introduce new products in the same or different categories? Does it add to brand equity across geographical boundaries and market segments?
**Adaptable:** How adaptable and updatable is the brand asset?
**Protectable:** How legally protectable is the brand asset?

*Development of a brand identity* is based on a brand analysis and a brand strategy with clearly defined values, promises, and position, which are among the most central strategic benchmarks. It is also an advantage to have a communication strategy at the bottom, but it can also be

Fig. 3.43 **The figure shows examples of checkpoints. Insert the brand name in the middle, and the appropriate checkpoints for brand name requirements on the left and right, respectively. Assess whether the name meets the requirements. The analysis can advantageously be conducted in a test group/ focus group.**

Tips for the designer
**The composition, including the placement of the brand elements on the packaging have an impact on the brand experience, differentiation and awareness.**

Tips for the company
**'By associating unique characteristics with their products, brand owners create instant recognition and authority within their niches, leading to higher sales as visibility and credibility rise' (Shaw, 2015).**

**Brand elements facilitate the process of consumer brain mapping and play a key role in building brand equity (Farhana, 2012). Consumers over a period are able to identify the brand through brand elements. The idea is to develop brand elements, which can properly communicate about brand and its point of difference from competing brands (MSG n.d.).[119]**

118 Sound Branding: www.youtube.com
119 MSG is a leading global provider of management & skill based education addressing the needs 3,000,000+ members across 198+ countries (managementstudyguide.com).

developed in tandem or as a consequence of the brand strategy. The development of a brand should be anchored in the company's overall strategy and goals, when it comes to a branded house strategy. If it's a house of brands strategy, one is freer. The brand strategy constitutes the basis for a design brief, which clarifies the basis for the development of the design elements. Name as brand asset is a strategic choice, which belongs in the strategy process (3.1.3 TOP 5, 3.2 Overall strategy, 3.3 Goals and subgoals, 3.7.3 Brand position).


1 Initiation
2 Insight
3 Strategy
4 Design
5 Production
6 Management

3.1 Strategy development
3.2 Overall strategy
3.3 Goals and subgoals
3.4 Business strategy
3.5 Business model
3.6 Market strategy
3.7 Brand strategy
3.8 Communication strategy
3.9 Design strategy

3.7.1 Brand platform
3.7.2 Brand architecture
3.7.3 Brand positioning
3.7.4 Brand story
3.7.5 Brand identity
3.7.6 Brand assets
3.7.7 Brand name
3.7.8 Brand perspective
3.7.9 Brand refresh, redesign, rebranding

- Name
- Domain name
- Logo
- Symbol
- App icon
- Favicon
- Brand colour
- Slogan
- Brand character
- Packaging
- Sense elements
- Audio Logo
- Brand identity


### 3.7.7 Brand name

The name is what you know, to what references are being made; it is always present, both in written and oral presentation, the only thing you do not need to see. Therefore, the name is perhaps the most important brand asset. The choice of brand name is an important strategic decision, developed based on the brand strategy, and anchored in the company's overall strategy and goal. The brand position defines how the brand name should be differentiated in the market. The brand identity defines which attributes, culture, and relationship the brand name should reflect. The brand narrative links the brand name to the story it should help tell. The selection or development of brand names also depends on what one comes up with in brand architecture. If a product is to have a monolithic identity (the same name as the manufacturer), there will normally be no need to develop a brand name. It is different when it comes to endorsed or individual identity (different names of company and product). When redesigning a logo, it is important to examine whether the existing name meets the requirements for a good brand name, whether it should be changed, or a new name should be developed.

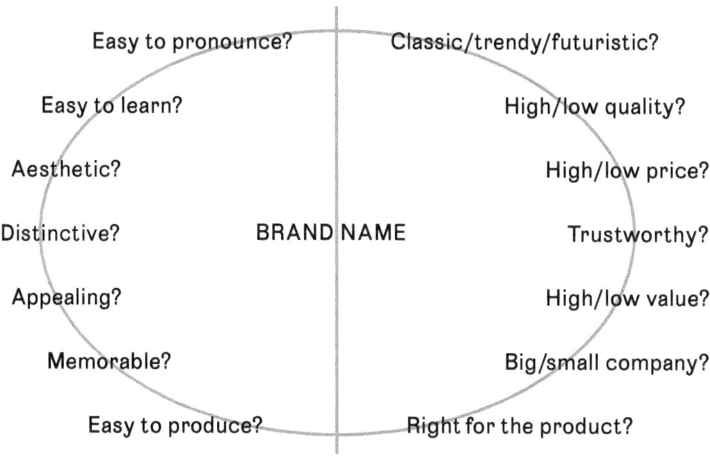


Fig. 3.43 Name test

**Key questions when developing a brand name are:** What is the purpose of the name? What should the name be used for? Should the name be a brand name and form the basis for a logo/brand? Where should the brand be used? On what surfaces? What kind of logo/brand? What kind of trademark products: goods, services, organisations, companies, people,

> The use of audio logos is a form of sound branding or sound design, which can help to strengthen the users' memory and perception of the specific business or product.

groups, events, geographic locations, media, trademark products, e-brands, etc.? Different brands have different possibilities for brand exposure. What role should the brand play in the brand hierarchy? How should the brand be organised and exposed in relation to other brands? (3.7.2 Brand architecture).

### Name development

One of the brand name's most important tasks is to achieve brand awareness. Brand names that are easy to pronounce or spell, familiar and meaningful, differentiating, distinctive, and unique can obviously improve *brand awareness* (Keller, 2013). Here, we will discuss some factors that may be useful to know when developing names based on Keller, 2013, p. 148–149):

**Easy to pronounce and spell:** Simplicity reduces the effort consumers need to invest to understand and process the brand name. Short names are easier to remember because they are easier to encode and store in one's memory. It is also possible to shorten established names to make them easier to remember, for example the car brand Chevrolet has over

**A good brand name should:**

- Express and support the brand's core, position, identity, and image.
- Be short, preferably under six letters, see Figure 4.78. Long names can have distinctive features that outweigh the fact that they are long.
- The names should be possible to render in letters. Numbers may mean an unclear pronunciation.
- Avoid letters that may pose challenges internationally and when rendered in different typefaces, eg. Ђ, ђ, δ, ξ ж, ф, æ, ä, ø, ö, å .
- The names should be unambiguous, distinct, easy to pronounce, without several pronunciation options.
- Easy to remember. Easier to establish into the market, easier to achieve recognition and easier to refer to.
- They should trigger the right associations. The associations will build the brand.
- They should provide basis for an interesting graphic form, such as a word-picture or figure.
- They should be appealing and have a positive ring to them. Names that easily roll off the tongue, which are easy and pleasurable to say, are also easier to remember and identify with.
- Provide opportunities for development and brand extension. This applies if the product has a long-term perspective.
- Names should be unique and stand out from competitors.[120]
- They should maintain a balance between the functional and the emotional. The emotional is about the name being appealing and attractive, and the functional is about being accessible, clear, and easy to read.[121]
- Other criteria, which are important to examine, are whether the name is available as a domain name, and whether it can be registered as a trademark.

120 In case of a differentiation strategy, it is important to come up with something unique and distinctive, but if it is a copying strategy, such as when it comes to competing on price with the same type of product, it may be more relevant for the name to be like that of competitors.

121 Balance between aesthetic and functional is often ideal, but not always. A product for cleaning drains should not be too aesthetic and appealing in design, to minimise the risk of someone confusing it with something drinkable.

the years become known as 'Chevy'; the beer Budweiser has become 'Bud', and Coca-Cola is also 'Coke'. Brand names that have a difficult pronunciation, as is often the case with international brand names such as Hyundai, can cause people to be reluctant to say the name. To improve spelling and pronunciation, thereby the ability to remember, one should try to create a special frequency or pleasant tone in the brand name, which is a widely used method. For example:

- *Alliteration (letter rhyme)*: Repetition and sound similarity between consonants in heavily stressed syllables (as in Coleco, where the consonant 'c' is repeated).
- *Assonance*: Repetition of vocal sound (as in Ramada Inn, where the vowel 'a' is repeated).
- *Consonance*: Repetition of consonants combined with various vowels (as in Hamburger Helper, where repetition of H provides a stabilising and rhythmic effect).
- *Rhythm*: Repeated pattern or syllable emphasis (as in Better Business Bureau).
- *Onomatopoeia*: Imitative or muffled words with meaning that coincide with the physical impression the language sound evokes, such as zoom, moo, beep, splash, bam, bang, click and crunch as in Cap'n Crunch cereal and ping as in Ping golf clubs.

**Familiar and meaningful:** A brand name that is familiar and has a known meaning can be more easily included in the existing memory apparatus. Since familiar names of people, objects, birds, or animals that already exist in the consumer's memory make it easier to understand the meaning and remember the brand name. To create strong category affiliation and enhance brand awareness, the brand name may also refer to product or service category (for example, Costa Coffee and *The Daily News*). A disadvantage of brand names describing the category is that they may constitute a limitation when it comes to expanding the product to new categories, where the name does not give the same associations, or to changing the concept, for example if *The Daily News* should become a weekend publication or weekly magazine.

**Differentiating, distinctive and unique:** Recognition of a brand name depends on the consumer's ability to distinguish between brands. A brand can be distinctive because it is unique, or because it is unique compared to other brands in the category. Distinctive words can be those that are rare or atypical words for the category (like Apple), unusual combinations of real words (like Toys'R's), or fantasy words (like Kodak). Complex, distinct, and unique names, unlike generic names, are easier for the consumer to differentiate.

**Creating association:** In addition to contributing to the identification of the sender, the main purpose of the brand is to make it possible to establish positive associations in the consumer, associations pointing to the characteristics and position of the product compared to other brands. Keller suggests a means that can help the brand name provide the right associations (Keller, 2013, p. 150): Precisely because a brand name is a compact form of communication, the explicit and implicit meaning as interpreted by the consumer is essential. A descriptive brand name can make it easier to connect to an amplifying feature or advantage. For example, it will be easier to connect 'gives fresh fragrance'



Further reading

- *The Naming Book: 5 Steps to Creating Brand and Product Names that Sell* (2020) by Brad Flowers.
- *Brand New Name: A Proven, Step-by-Step Process to Create an Unforgettable Brand Name* (2019) by Jeremy Miller.

to a detergent called 'Blossom' than one called 'Circle'. Even a fantasy name can make sense if it can trigger experienced product associations, but it requires that the consumer be sufficiently motivated.

**Morphemes:** A widely used way of creating fantasy names is to use morphemes. A morpheme is the smallest grammatically meaningful unit in a language. A morpheme is the same as a word, it can stand alone or be linked to a word. When linked to a word, it is either in the front (prefix) or back (suffix). By linking together two morphemes, words can be constructed that have relatively simple general or implied meanings. Norema – the Norwegian kitchen manufacturer is an example of constructed names, where Nor is used as a prefix, giving associations to the north, and Ma as a suffix, giving associations with food ('mat' in Norwegian).[122] Even some letters can make sense that can be useful in developing a new brand name, for example X, which to many means extreme, an extra factor or an unknown factor.

It also applies to the sound of certain letters or their phonetic attributes. Some words begin with phonetic attributes called *plosives* (such as in English: t, k, and p (voiceless) and d, g, and b (voiced). There are consonants that are produced by stopping the airflow by lips, teeth, or palate, followed by a sudden release of air. In other words, it can begin with so-called *sibilants* (sounds like s, z, sh and zh), which are made or characterised by a hissing sound. Plosives disappear from the mouth faster than sibilants, and are harder and more direct, which is positive for a name to become more specific and less abstract and more easily recognised and remembered. But because sibilants have a soft tone, they are well suited to products such as perfume (e.g. Chanel, Shalimar, and Samsara). The font, logo or word picture used to express the brand name in question can also influence the consumer's perception, experience and understanding of the name as well as contribute to the creation of desired brand associations and distinctiveness.

The name 'Sony' was chosen for the brand as a mix of two words: one was the Latin word 'sonus', which is the root of sonic and sound, and the other was 'sonny', a common slang term used in 1950s America to call a young boy' (Sony.co.jp).[123]

### Different name types

It is important to look at the possibilities used as a basis for the development of the brand name when it comes to the expression and associations the name should signal:

**Association-triggering name:** Powerful, affecting both intellect and sensory apparatus, e.g. Nike, associated with the Greek goddess of victory.

**Descriptive name:** Describes actual conditions, e.g. Fazer Pure Dark 70% Cocoa.

**Category name:** Descriptive name, explaining what you are doing, e.g. EAT, Playmobil.

**Family/personal name:** Creates credibility/proximity, e.g. Giorgio Armani, Ralph Lauren.

**Geographical:** Natural origin/commercial area, e.g. Voss Water, Lofoten seafood.[124]

**Fantasy name:** Unique name. One may incorporate the desired associations, e.g. Kodak.[125]

**Abbreviations:** Short, but complicated. Abbreviations often emerge over time when names are established, such as the CIA (Central Intelligence Agency) and CNN (The Cable News Network). A new name in the form of an abbreviation is often difficult to understand and takes longer to establish.

122 Whether this is the original intent of the name choice Norema has not been revealed.

123 Sony Corporate History (Japanese), (Sony.co.jp, 'Sony', n.d.).

124 'Throughout the twentieth century, most of the really successful international brands have come from countries that are successful brands in their own right, and substantial transfer of imagery and brand equity can often be seen to occur between the two' (Anholt, 1998).

125 fantasynamegenerators.com.

126 Eponym: a word that is named after a person, preferably one who is behind an invention, such as Celsius after Anders Celsius, and fahrenheit after Gabriel Daniel Fahrenheit.

127 If a trademark loses its intellectual property rights of the trademark, it gives competitors the opportunity 'to use the genericised trademark to describe their similar products, unless the owner of an affected trademark works sufficiently to correct and prevent such broad use' (Fisher, W. (n.d), Hyra 2010, 'Trademark,' n.d.).

**Number-based names:** International, e.g. 7-Eleven, Chanel No. 5.
**Composite names:** Long and hard to remember, e.g. Dun & Bradstreet, Abercrombie & Fitch.
**Metaphors:** Animals, places, people, objects, or mythological names may be used to depict or allude to the attributes of the mark, e.g. Jaguar, Nike, Puma.
**Word games/syllables:** Changing the syllable of the name to create a distinctive and unique name. Easier to register, e.g. Flickr, Tumblr, Timly.
**Combined names:** Composed of two words that make sense individually and together. This creates several associations, e.g. Citibank, Pinterest of pin and interest.

### Registration of names

**The name** may be registered as a trademark if the name is not generic, misleading or may be confused with other names, word pictures, or figurative marks (6.2.2 Trademark).
**Generic names** are descriptive, general, or common, e.g. barbecue sausage, milk, cheese. A generic name cannot be registered as a name in the trademark register, but it might be registered as *a word mark* if it has a distinctive design. A brand name can because of its popularity or significance evolve into a generic name and become the generic term for, or synonymous with, a general category of products or services. It has then become a *genericised trademark*, a *generic trademark* or *proprietary eponym*,[126] and can lose its intellectual property rights of the trademark.[127] Examples of protected trademarks frequently used as generic terms are Kleenex (Facial tissues; Kimberly-Clark), Post-it (sticky notes; 3M), PowerPoint (slide show presentation program; Microsoft). Examples of former trademarks that have been genericised are Escalator (originally trademark of Otis Elevator Company until 1950), Cellophane (originally trademark of DuPoint), Linoleum (originally coined by Frederick Walton in 1864), ('Trademark,' n.d.).
**Word mark (word picture)** in this context is the name used for the visual image of the name, the logo. If the logo has a distinctive design with a distinctive character, the word picture may be patented as a registered trademark. *Figurative mark* in this context is a logo that is shaped like a figure, possibly in combination with a symbol.

### Naming process

There are many different practices and methods for developing brand names. Examples of a name process are shown here. Content and scope should be assessed in relation to the goals and framework of the project.
**Criteria:** Set up the relevant criteria, guides, and assumptions that will form the basis for developing the name. Example of criteria for the name where the purpose is to develop a new name for a new juice series:

- The purpose of the name? For example, to differentiate the juice series from competing products.
- Purpose of developing a new name. For example: The name should provide a basis for a product logo with endorsed identity.
- Strategic anchoring for the new name? For example: Brand position, brand identity, and brand architecture.

| Keywords from brainstorming | Synonyms / variants | Associations (feeling, taste, utility) | Spanish (or any other language) | Latin (or any other language) | Imagination (combinations) | Name suggestions |
|---|---|---|---|---|---|---|
| Juice | Drink, liquid, juice, cider, nectar, ... | Fruit, smoothie, juicer, colour, thirst, ... | Zumo (juice)<br>Fresco (chilled)<br>Refresco (cold drink) | Sucus<br>Sitis (thirst)<br>Bibere (drink) | Fresco<br>Crema<br>Siccus | Fresco |
| Fruit/vegetables | Orange, apple, mango, cucumber, ... | Healthy life, health, five per day, ... | Fruta (fruit)<br>Manzana (apple) | Fructus (fruit)<br>Malus (apple) | Frutti<br>Manzo | Frutti |
| Exotic | Unknown, peculiar, alien, different, ... | Travel, heat, south, palm trees, | Exótico (exotic)<br>Yuca | Meridies (south)<br>Oceanus (ocean) | Xotic<br>Yucos | Xotic |
| Healthy lifestyle | Health, exercise, common sense, nutrition, ... | Long life, joy, excess, ... | Júbilo (joy)<br>Salud (health) | Laetus (happy)<br>Salus (health) | Jubilus<br>Salud | Salud |
| Etc. | Etc. | Etc. | Etc. | Etc. | Etc. | Etc. |

Table 3.11 a) Name development

Table 3.11 a) The table shows examples of sorting and processing of name suggestions for a new fruit drink, based on brainstorming. The name suggestions are systematically tested in different languages, fruit names, associations, combinations, etc.
© Grimsgaard, W. (2018).

Table 3.11 b) The table is based on Table 3.11 a). The best name suggestions are selected and tested in different typefaces, degrees, as well as in upper and lowercase, to get an idea of how the letters of the different name suggestions are perceived when placed together. It is essential that a logo should have a good word picture. Different typefaces may vary in size, even if the dot size is the same, as shown in the illustration.
© Grimsgaard, W. (2018).

| fresco | Fresco | FRESCO |
|---|---|---|
| fresco | Fresco | FRESCO |
| fresco | Fresco | FRESCO |
| xotic | Xotic | XOTIC |
| xotic | Xotic | XOTIC |
| xotic | Xotic | XOTIC |
| salud | Salud | SALUD |
| salud | Salud | SALUD |
| salud | Salud | SALUD |

Table 3.11 b) Name development



- The main criteria for the name? For example: The name should be short, give a good word picture, and legible on juice cartons and bottles.
- Specific guides and assumptions? For example: The name should be associated with fruit, soundness, and health. The name could be a fantasy name. The name may have a local or geographical affiliation or anchoring.
- Anything else? The name should be possible to use internationally.

**Insight:** If the product is a fruit drink and the name should trigger associations of fruit, soundness, and health, it may be useful to obtain more information and knowledge about all aspects of the theme, as well as products within these categories. For example, if the name is to indicate geographic affiliation, it may involve examining the location in question in terms of geographical location, identity, and social environment.

**Brainstorming 1:** Conduct a broad and in-depth brainstorming session based on words that appear in the criteria and policies for the name, product attributes, ingredients, position, etc. Brainstorming can be done at workshops with the design team using flip charts, whiteboards, Post-it notes, etc. If you work alone, you can create mind maps and use the Internet, dictionaries, etc.

**Preparation 1:** Take a wide range of words from all or part of the brainstorming session and then screen and prioritise. Work with the words to create names by finding synonyms, new associations, translation into other languages. Try out combinations and fantasy variants. Divide into different categories, directions, languages, and associations. Try the names in capitals, lowercase, and various typefaces to get an impression of the word picture. Figure 3.40 shows an example of how results from brainstorming can be sorted and processed.

**Brainstorming 2:** Work further on the results of the processing. Associate broadly, find synonyms and different combinations. Screen and prioritise.

**Preparation 2:** Select 3–10 alternative names, and try them considering:

- Phonetic pronunciation: Does the name roll well off the tongue? Is it easy to say?
- Letter composition: Does the combination of letters provide a good starting point for a word picture that is both aesthetic and up to standard? How does the name work in different typefaces, using capitals and lowercase?
- Identity: Does the name express the desired identity?
- Associations: Does the name trigger good and correct associations?
- Criteria: Does the name meet the specified criteria?
- Domains: Are domain names/URLs available for each of the suggested names?
- Trademark protection: Are there possibilities for legal protection of the name?
- Testing: Implement selected names on surfaces or moodboards that show the names in the right environment.
- Font choice: Try alternative typefaces to examine the word picture.
- Logo sketches: Make rough sketches for logos of the different name suggestions.

Brand extension vs. Line extension

**Brand extension: An extension of an existing and well-established brand or brand name to new product categories and new markets.**

**Line extension: An extension or expansion of a product line is the use of an established brand for a new item in the same product category, adding new product variants to the product line, targeting the same segment/ target group.**

**Presentation:**

- Select names for the presentation.
- Draw the client's attention to the fact that the name suggestions can trigger associations with new alternatives.
- Clarify the criteria and policies for the name
- Present each name in large print on separate sheets.
- Hang the sheets on the wall so they can be compared and discussed.
- Provide a verbal explanation/elaboration for each of the names.
- 1–3 names are selected for further examination and processing.
- The whole or part of the naming process is repeated, if necessary, until the final name is selected.

### 3.7.8 Brand perspective

All branding is about perspective because a brand is built and developed over time. Creating a brand can take many years. Once the brand is created, work begins on managing the brand value, *the brand equity*, and ensuring that the brand is perceived as trendy and that it yields the maximum return. For both new and existing brands, it is a matter of planning a long-term targeted brand development, which safeguards the brand's core values and helps strengthen its position.

When developing a new brand, it is difficult to predict how the market will respond to it. Therefore, it is not an easy task to plan the brand development from the very beginning. There must be room to develop the brand continuously as one sees how the product is selling. It requires continuous monitoring of the brand. Over a longer period, the brand will undergo cyclical market fluctuations, changing trends, and varying purchasing power. It is therefore important to develop the brand continuously to exploit its potential. If brand development is based on solid research and a targeted perspective, the brand is most likely to succeed. Not everything can be planned, but it is essential to be true to the brand's core and values. One must stand firm on the ground to build and safeguard solid and stable brand associations for the consumer. Conscious brand development involves, among other things, finding out what the brand's potential is for growth, development, and extension. How can the brand be developed and strengthened in the short and long term? Can any new areas be easily and logically implemented to utilise and profit from the brand's position and recognition? Can the brand expand with new products or product categories? Do we see any clear pros and cons?

If a new product does not become popular in the market, or if an established brand eventually loses its timeliness, a new strategy for developing the brand may be considered. This may include, for example, adjusting the product, changing the name, or redesigning the packaging. A well-known tactic for increasing sales and drawing more attention is to expand the product portfolio with a new variant (line extension) or to focus on another category with an entirely new product (brand extension). A brand is a value that can be measured in money. Developed and managed strategically, a brand can grow and yield increased returns. One can easily become greedy and think that a brand can be used on new products once it is known and well-established. But here, it is easy to make mistakes. Care must be taken so that new launches do not weaken the brand's reputation or create the wrong associations. The management and development of the brand should be seen in the context of the company's overall competitive strategy and how the development of the brand can contribute to the company's achieving its goals (3.4.1 Competitive strategy).



### Brand extension

Brand extension is a term for the extension of an existing brand to new product categories and new markets. A brand extension can be defined as: '... use of an established brand name to enter a new product category' (Aaker & Keller, 1990, p. 27). If the brand or company are well-established names, the name or brand alone can attract new customers and tempt them to try new products completely unrelated to the established products for which the brand is known. The consumer's perception of the new product is reinforced and perceived as safer because of their knowledge of the brand name. Developing and establishing a new product is costly and time-consuming, while at the same time it requires a marketing budget to build brand awareness and promote product benefits. Extension of the existing brand when launching a new product in an existing or new product category involves less effort and risk because the brand is already established. Whether a brand is 'extendible' depends on how strong the consumers' trust in and associations are with the brand's values and goals, and whether the new product category represents the same values and goals as the core product. An example of this is when the Norwegian milk producer Tine launched juice and iced tea. These products are both within the category of beverages, but different product categories. As Tine makes such steps, it expands its brand to new areas. It then takes advantage of both the trust and popularity that the consumer has in the Tine brand, while making the brand even more visible and well established.

Strategies for an extension can be:
- New flavours
- Different forms of product
- New colours
- Different ingredients
- Different sizes
- New types of packaging

Start by:
- Figuring out your mission
- Leveraging no-inventory-required options
- Gathering audience feedback
- Test new product line extensions
(Odjick, 2021)

### Line extension

The most common brand development strategy is the extension of the product line of an established brand, *Line extension*, *Product line extension* or *Product line stretching*. This is done by adding new product variants to the product line. It is basically about utilising existing consumers' brand loyalty and brand awareness by making them more likely to buy a new product that has a brand they like and accept, for example, it may be a new flavour of a known soft drink or chocolate brand. The consumer will be more willing to try a product from a brand they trust, and the manufacturer can increase its product portfolio, gain a greater grip on the market in which they operate and increase revenue. A line extension may also be a strategy to appeal to a new or broader customer base by entering a new market segment or revitalising brands that have stagnated. See also 5.3.7 Product life extension and 5.3.6 Product life cycle.

Coca-Cola is a good example of line expansion. Over the years, they have tried, failed and succeeded with several line extensions, such as Coca-Cola Life, Coca-Cola Zero Sugar, Coca-Cola Vanilla, and so on. The release of Diet Coke in 1982 was used to target the growing weight- and calorie-conscious market. Since then it has expanded with new flavors such as Ginger Lime and Feisty Cherry to appeal to millennial consumers. 'Coca-Cola's products are similar, but different in that they pursue different audiences. This gives the global brand a chance to take up more market share and grow sales for the corporation' (Odjick, 2021).

### Advantages

An extension or expansion of a brand can increase profits by broadening the product portfolio range or opening for sales in new markets. At the same time, it allows the company to promote new products at lower promotional costs because the new product or brand benefits from being part of an established name. The company may use such product development strategies to breathe life into an existing product line and attract public attention, thereby strengthening and utilising the established and recognised brand equity. The new product becomes a side effect of the brand, a 'spin-off', which is a way to exploit the popularity of the original product by using the same brand name for new products. It can help increase the profitability of more than one product category, while increasing the visibility and awareness of the brand name. Thus, a spin-off can result in a kind of self-reinforcing promotion of the brand. It is important that a brand extension merge with the core values of the main brand, and that a communication strategy provides the right directions for the communication of the new products (3.8 Communication strategy). 'Limited edition' is an established method for testing a line extension. Launching a new product into an already established product line allows for a change in price level, by stretching the price up or down, because the consumer is happy to accept a rise in price, or an offer related to a new product.

*Downward stretching* means that the new product is offered at a lower price range than the other products in the same product line and can be used to increase sales of several units.

*Upward stretching* means that the new product is offered at a higher price range than the other products in the same product line.

Tips for the designer

**If you chooses to make major changes, you should set aside a good budget for a launch campaign to make the loyal target group aware of the changes. If the brand has a high awareness and enjoys good attention and publicity in prominent media, name and brand changes are more likely to spread rapidly to relevant target groups and other stakeholders. Yet, when major well-known brands get a new name or a new logo, this often generates reactions in the audience, including newspaper headlines and social media debates. Some like the new name or logo; others do not. The debate tends to calm down gradually and after some time people get used to the new brand and forget the old one.**

Brand extension vs. line extension

**Line extension refers to the expansion of an existing product line. For instance, a soft drink manufacturer might introduce a 'Diet' or 'Cherry' variety to its cola line Brand extension refers to the expansion of the brand itself into new territories or markets. For instance, if the soft drink manufacturer unveils a line of juices or bottled water products under its company name (Chron, 2020).**

### Risk

Extending or expanding a brand can be a good way to strengthen the brand and increase returns, but this type of product development strategy can go the other way and weaken or damage the brand and the brand's equity. Brand extension makes sense when new products serve to enhance brand awareness and what makes the brand special and different. If spin-off products create unclear or incorrect associations with the brand, there is a risk that the main brand may be diluted by lowering the brand's original core values. This can damage not only the parent brand, but also the entire brand family. Brand extension makes less sense if it is based on a desire for a quick profit with no long-term focus. A new product can work like a charm for a short period while undermining the brand position in the long term (Neumeier, 2006, p. 48). Any new extension of an established brand may blow back on the reputation of the parent brand (3.8.4 Desired reputation).

### Long-term focus

Managing and handling a brand over time requires long-term focus, fidelity, courage, and determination. When the company faces heavy pressure from the owners' expectations, unexpected competition, change in management, political interference, or other factors, it may be tempting to extend the product line for short-term profit, for example, by following new trends and tendencies in the market, even at the expense of the brand's market position and reputation (Neumeier, 2006, p. 48). In such situations, the designer has an important role as an advisor. Here, it is important for the designer not to succumb to the temptation to think of short-term profit for themselves, but to act as the advisor they are meant to be, by first examining the situation and assessing the consequences, and then being strict enough to discourage the client from the planned investment if it turns out that the new product may weaken the brand's position.

## 3.7.9 Brand refresh, redesign, rebranding

A brand represents an intangible value, a brand equity. To maintain and at best increase its value, it needs to be continuously updated. Over time the company may have grown, their goals and values changed, as well as their customers, the competition, trends, etc. Usually the audience hardly notices when companies upgrade their brand. They may find the product more up-to-date and attractive. Regular upgrading of the brand design is an important task for the brand to retain its trendiness and appeal. If the brand is perceived as outdated, a competing brand may suddenly appear more tempting. When planning any changes of a brand one should decide what the purpose is, the need, the goal, and what consequences a change may cause. As a minimum a brand analysis should be conducted, including examining whether brand attention is mainly related to the visual brand or the brand name. If it is primarily the brand name, this may provide greater scope for visual changes. If awareness is mainly related to the visuals, care should be taken to analyse what distinctive features of the brand assets people remember, which should be retained and strengthened (3.4.6 Distinctive asset-building strategy). One can distinguish between brand refresh (facelift), brand redesign (evolution) and rebranding (revolution).



Further reading
- 'Evolutionary or revolutionary packaging redesign?' by Caroline Hagen (n/d).
- www.reachbrands.co.uk/blog/evolutionary-or-revolutionary-packaging-redesign/.

*Redesign*: Examples of a brand refresh and redesign are Starbucks, Microsoft, Google, Burger King, Neflix. *Rebrand*: In a merger or acquisition, it is not uncommon that both names or a combination of the names are used in a transition period. After a while the name of the initiator or acquirer are often retained, usually with a completely new logo design. In 2010 Chile's Lan airlines merged with Brazil's Tam group and became the global airline group Latam. A combination of both names was used.

Here the transitions are smooth. What mainly characterises the various directions is to what degree only visual adjustments are needed or if also minor or major strategic changes are necessary.

Fig. 3.44 The FER model

Fig. 3.44 The figure shows the F-E-R model (facelift, evolution, revolution), a tool for strategic brand development. The model represents different degrees of change in a design and is used to assess how and why a product needs to be adapted, developed, renewed, or reconfigured for the future. How drastically should one act? Does the profile need a simple facelift, a genetic evolution, or a revolution where you see the brand in a whole new light? One tests the consequences by gradually adjusting and changing the design. Based on Myhre, 2017.

Tips for the designer
The communication strategy should be rooted in the company's overall strategy and goal.

> For a brand to survive in the long run, one should hold one's course and develop the brand over time.

*Facelift*: A brand refresh focuses on the appearance of the logo and some minor details. The aim is to preserve the brand integrity and awareness, adjusting them according to the current trends. That might include shape simplification, careful adjustments of colours and fonts, and subtle detail changes.

- *Evolution*: A brand redesign involves more serious revitalisation and sometimes creating a new logo and visuals. The aim may for example be to create a more distinctive, cohesive, and recognisable brand across all online and offline channels. This might involve restating the brand values and promise with more clarity.
- *Revolution*: A rebrand involves major changes, such as reassessment of brand name, logo, slogan and other brand assets based on strategic changes in the business, product, or service. It can also be a repositioning based on the same product strategy. Often the need for a rebrand is a result of a fundamental change of the business, as when companies merge[128] or when planning to conquer in a new market. The aim is to change the brand concept and message of the brand. This might include a complete change of the business strategy, brand strategy, brand identity, brand story, marketing strategy, and marketing materials.

## 3.8 Communication strategy

Communication strategy is a plan for what is to be communicated, to whom, when, where, why, and how, whether it is information, marketing, or PR. The purpose is to facilitate targeted communication of implemented activities.

For a company, communicating to the market is essential for conveying its products or services; a task that may be both demanding and costly. To be noticed in a society where all channels are at full volume, and we are exposed to multiple messages at the same time more than ever before, is the biggest communication challenge companies face today. Advertising and PR that a few decades ago used to take place via traditional media such as newspaper ads, radio and TV advertising, take place mostly via the Internet and social media now. This provides the opportunity for dialogue, and thus the situation becomes more like that between people. The form of communication and its staging have changed as a result. Sending out the right codes is becoming more and

128 A merger is when two separate companies combine forces to create a new, joint organisation. An acquisition is when one company take over another. 'Mergers and acquisitions may be completed to expand a company's reach or gain market share in an attempt to create shareholder value' (Majaski, 2021).
129 Based on a conversation with communications consultant Ulf Winther, 2017.

more important, as is follow-up of responses to utilise the dialogue. This means that the company also has to make plans to manage response, develop relationships with key groups, and use feedback for further development, adaptation, and marketing of its own operations. Here, a significant part of the value creation occurs through communication. A prerequisite for being able to establish a good dialogue with the target group is to be familiar with it, to know who it consists of, where they are, what needs they have, what they are concerned about, and how best to communicate with them one-on-one. Timing and timeliness are crucial components for drawing attention to a message (Winther, 2017).[129]

Communicating clearly and consistently is a challenge for most companies. What should we write on our websites, what should be in our ads, what should be posted on our Facebook page, where in social media should we be present? If there are no clear policies or plan as a basis for communication, there is a big risk that the communication will be random, unclear, and inconsistent. What the company says about itself, and its products or services should be in line with how the company wishes to



**Communication strategy development**

Communication strategy is a sub-strategy based on the company's overall goal and strategy and shall contribute to the company achieving its goals. Briefly, this means to:

- 1) clarify the current situation, define communication goals and desired reputation,
- 2) identify target groups and stakeholders,
- 3) determine how communication should take place,
- 4) clarify what should be communicated, in which channels and media, and how response should be followed up,
- 5) plan implementation, prepare an action plan and ensure internal anchoring,
- 6) facilitate measurement and evaluation,
- 7) compile the communication strategy in a report. The report serves as a tool for the company and the players contributing to the development of the company's communication measures. Initially in the communication strategy report, the overall goal and strategy can be presented on one or two pages. Such as market and target group analyses that have been performed, and sub-strategies such as market strategy, business strategy, and brand strategy, are also important and useful data, in addition to the design manual, which provides visual guidance. The market is continuously monitored, and the communication strategy is regularly updated to keep up with market developments.

There are many different opinions about what a communication strategy should contain. In addition, working with a government agency, large group, small company or NGO will pose different requirements. The scope of the work should be assessed in relation to communication needs, level of ambition, goal, time, and budget. Contribution by managers and other employees is essential for good process and internal anchoring.

What to communicate, to whom, when, where, why, and how? This is defined in the communication strategy.

| Communication strategy | |
|---|---|
| Strategic anchoring: (What is the company's strategy?) | – Purpose, vision, business idea, core values, value proposition<br>– Competitive strategy, positioning statement |
| Distinctive brand assets (Brand equity management) | – What distinctive brand assets types should be used above all? |
| Communication audit: (What is the current situation?) | – Situational study<br>– Communication audit<br>– Stakeholder mapping<br>– Analysis of relationships, situation, and development trends<br>– Defining challenges and potentials |
| Communication target group: (Whom should we reach?) | – Priority target groups<br>– Stakeholders |
| Communication goals: (Desired situation?) | – Desired effect<br>– Desired acceptance<br>– Desired reputation |
| Desired reputation: (How will people talk about us?) | – What expectations do we create?<br>– What promises should we fulfil?<br>– What do we want people to say/think about us? |
| Communication platform: (How should we communicate?) | – Strategy and target areas<br>– Resources and level of ambition<br>– Image (taken from brand strategy)<br>– Tone of voice<br>– Signal effect<br>– Internal implementation of the strategy |
| Communication content: (What should be communicated?) | – Communication elements<br>– Distinctive brand assets<br>– Core message<br>– Storytelling<br>– Information<br>– Standard text/boiler plate |
| Communication plan: (How to implement?) | – Communication arenas/channels<br>– Communication mix/actions<br>– Action plan with prioritisation and weighting<br>– Time and response planning |
| Communication measurement (How to measure effect?) | – Measurement, impact, and evaluation |
| Communication budget: | – Marketing and media investment planning<br>– Effect measurement<br>– Budget calculation based on: Share of Voice/Share of market |
| Follow-up: (How to follow up response?) | – Facilitate response/dialogue/follow-up<br>– Operation, maintenance, and updating of communication |

Table 3.12 Communication strategy

Table 3.12 The table shows a process for developing a communication strategy. The content and order of the communication strategy can be customised according to needs, time, and resources. Important approaches that have not been mentioned may be crisis communication, reputation communication, digital communication, community communication (public topics, press, media, politicians), language and rhetoric, campaigns, etc. © Grimsgaard, W. (2018).

appear and be perceived as well as in line with the company's visual profile. How the company communicates on the website should be compatible with its communication in advertisements, at trade fairs, or on social media. This applies regardless of whether it is a matter of communication with a large audience or one-on-one communication. It is not enough that the management has decided what the company should communicate to the market; it should also be rooted in the company's employees, salespeople, distributors, and collaborators, so that everyone contributes as good ambassadors and conveys the same message clearly and unequivocally in the arenas assigned to them. This way, the company can get everyone involved, pull in the same direction and join forces to achieve common goals. Clear and consistent communication is cost-effective because the message is impressed on the mind of the recipient. This way, communication helps build awareness and identity. A clear voice and a clear attractive identity are an essential competitive factor, key to branding.



### What is communication?

Communication comes from the Latin word *communicare* which means 'to make common' and is a term for the transfer or exchange of information or knowledge, related to reporting, communicating, notifying about something. Although human communication often involves the use of linguistic units such as words and phrases, this is not a prerequisite. Communication is also largely about the non-verbal communication, such as body language (gestures, facial expressions, posture), voice use (tone, volume, pace), appearance (clothing, hair, make-up), touch (for example, putting your hand on someone's shoulder or arm), location (space, place, condition), time use (punctuality, waiting time, visiting time), or symbolic elements that convey messages (Burgoon et al., 1999, p. 169–171). The non-verbal part of communication plays a crucial role when people communicate with each other. Information, associations, attitudes, and emotions all play a part and influence how it is perceived and interpreted by those who communicate (Jacobsen and Thorsvik, 2007, Pfeffer 1977). At the same time, factors such as situation, social identity, culture, religion, and nationality will also play a role. Even within a homogeneous group of people with strong common traits, there may be major differences based on various factors such as life experience, environment, individual attributes, and so on. Therefore, communicating will be about the conscious use of the codes one sends out in the right channel, and about the recipient's ability to decode the message. The complexity of communication is one of the things that contributes to making communication a challenging task.

While communication is largely about the way we produce, provide, or share information, *information* is more about the content. In everyday life, *information* has to do with data, proclamation, notification, message, feedback, training, teaching, and knowledge (Rossen, 2009). When we talk about a message, it is more of an announcement, something the sender conveys or sends to the recipient. It is usually brief information that is easy to perceive, such as a piece of news, an advertising message, or a slogan. There is a difference between the way information or messages are conveyed. For example, *propaganda* is a communication method that is about deliberately manipulating people's feelings and thoughts

> Ethos, logos, pathos
>
> Rhetoric is traditionally defined as the art of speaking to convince. Ethos, logos, and pathos are rhetorical devices (Grue, 2018): Ethos is a way of persuading someone. It relies on the character of the person who says or writes something, i.e. the sender's credibility and the likelihood that what is said is true. Logos is based on reason and argument, i.e. the sender's ability to use reasoning that is true or probable. Pathos uses the listeners' feelings to convince, i.e. the sender's ability to convince by arousing certain feelings in the recipient.

using powerful tools to promote specific perceptions and patterns of action. 'Recipients of communication today have had to become more critical of what to trust. Being believed is central to all communication. Therefore, it goes without saying that the company should ensure that the message being formulated has genuine and true content. Semitruths, double communication, or manipulation can ultimately weaken trust and thus damage the reputation' (Winther, 2017) (3.8.4 Desired reputation).

### 3.8.1 Communication audit

A necessary starting point for planning a targeted communication strategy is to know today's situation. A communication audit is about evaluating the impact of today's communication. See also 2.7.1 Situational analysis. A communication audit is about evaluating and assessing the impact of today's communication. Key questions are: What is the current state of communication in relation to the desired situation? Where have our stakeholders received information to date? How do we communicate, to whom and where? What did we want to achieve with communication, what communication goals did we have? How did this work in relation to our intention? Has our marketing communication contributed to creating brand awareness, shaping a brand image, creating positive brand associations and influencing customer choice in the purchase process? Has our business communication contributed to building alliances and creating good ambassadors? Has our communication contributed to profiling the company in a clear and consistent way?

First, it is clarified which messages and information have been communicated, which channels and exposure surfaces have been used, and

**A stakeholder** is a person or organisation that may influence or be affected by company matters, activities, and communication. The term is often used in the business world for the shareholders of a limited liability company. There are both direct and indirect stakeholders.

**Direct stakeholders**

- Corporate management, owners, decision makers.
- Users, the actual target group, the buyer, the consumer.
- The suppliers, internal or external, who provide the necessary expertise and resources.

**Indirect stakeholders** may, for example, be those who might otherwise influence or be affected by the company and communication. It may be the premise setters who manage internal or external regulations, standards, guidelines, or other provisions which the project should take into account.

**Other stakeholders** are those who have their own interest from private, commercial or any other perspective. They may be other companies, organisations and citizens, as well as media and various interest organisations. These stakeholders will often be less visible to the company than the other stakeholders but will still be able to have impact, for example by influencing the direct stakeholders (Difi, 2016).

Fig. 3.45 **The figure shows an example of a single stakeholder map. The question is: How does our dissemination of communication and information take place today and to which stakeholders? (Simonsen 2007/2012). There are more customised stakeholder maps for private and public companies respectively. NGO (non-governmental organisation) is used for voluntary or non-profit organisations that work in tandem with government agencies but do not answer to any government authority.**

Tips for the designer

**In which channels, media and arenas does the company communicate today? What is communicated on which surfaces? What works satisfactorily? Check the current situation, before deciding on new communication goals and creating a new communication strategy.**

Fig. 3.45 Stakeholder map

1 Initiation
2 Insight
3 Strategy
4 Design
5 Production
6 Management

3.1 Strategy development
3.2 Overall strategy
3.3 Goals and subgoals
3.4 Business strategy
3.5 Business model
3.6 Market strategy
3.7 Brand strategy
3.8 Communication strategy
3.9 Design strategy

3.8.1 Communication audit
3.8.2 Identifying the target group
3.8.3 Communication goals
3.8.4 Desired reputation
3.8.5 Communication platform
3.8.6 Communication elements
3.8.7 Communication development
3.8.8 Channels and media
3.8.9 Communication measurement

- Stakeholder mapping
- Analysis of the situation and development trends

what kind of materials have been developed. Next, an assessment or analysis is made of whether the content, channels, and instruments have been appropriate in relation to the desired impact on the relevant stakeholder groups. Have qualitative or quantitative measurements been carried out to detect the impact of implemented measures? Can these be used to assess whether the communication worked as intended? The communication audit may be supplemented with *a visual analysis* of communication materials, product packaging, and other visual communication (2.7.8 Visual analysis). The result of the communication audit may be used in the further planning of communication content, channels, and activities.

### Stakeholder mapping

The company does not stand still, nor do those with whom the company interacts or wishes to interact: customers, users, employees, partners, competitors, and other relevant groups. These stakeholders are also evolving and changing over the same period. Clarification of the current situation therefore also involves describing the current situation and expected development of the main stakeholders, for example over a period of 3–5 years (Samuelsen, 2016). Stakeholder or relationship analysis are methods that can be used to map this.

Essential to such mapping is to clarify the stakeholders' knowledge and perception of the company, its products and services, and to identify which stakeholders are *directly* or *indirectly* associated with the company (see framework text). By examining and analysing the company's relationships with internal and external groups, the company will have a broader basis for further identifying which target groups the company should focus on. This information is also necessary in order to define communication goals and select strategies for the different target groups.

How does our information circulation and communication work today and to which stakeholders? What is our relationship with our stakeholders? What characterises them? What communication needs do we see?

The organisation's own employees are also an important stakeholder group, given their perception of the company. Therefore, it is also important to find out how the internal communication and information flow in the organisation work. What is communicated, how and why? Is it bi-directional communication? Is the flow of information predominantly top-down or bottom-up? How can internal communication be assessed in light of possible developments in the outside world (Simonsen, 2007/2012)?

**Analysis of the situation and development trends**

Based on the stakeholder mapping and communication audit, an analysis of the company's situation, relationships, and developments can be conducted (based on Simonsen, 2007/2012):

*Stakeholder and relationships analysis:* How important are the different stakeholders for the organisation's strategic goals, and how good or bad are our relationships with stakeholders? How coordinated are we and our stakeholders on matters and conditions that are important to us?

*Analyse the situation*: What internal and external factors can influence our choices when planning our communication? Internal factors include different types of internal policies, formal governing principles. Strengths and weaknesses can manifest themselves in areas such as personnel, experience, expertise, attitudes, organisation, etc. External factors include, among other things, forces and conditions in the outside world that affect how the communication task can be solved (2.7.9 PESTLE analysis, 2.7.10 SWOT).

Tips for the designer

**In order to clarify the communication target group, it is necessary to identify who they are: What characterises them, their social identity, interests, and lifestyle? Are they direct or indirect users of the product or service? What are their needs, motives, goals and involvement in the product or service category? How do we reach them with our communication? In what channels and media? What tone of voice should characterise the communication in order to appeal to them? Feel free to create a persona, and describe them visually and verbally.**

Tips for the company

**Sometimes the target group is a smaller part of the recipient group. The strategy is that the communication should go out to far more people than the target group itself, because we believe someone outside the target group can reinforce the message (Simonsen, 2012).**

**Checklist: What do you know about the target group?**

- Do you know the target group well, its special information needs?
- What about the target group's use of media, channel preferences, language usage, etc.?
- What do they consider important values? What do they emphasise?
- What are our own value perceptions like in relation to those of the target group?
- Do you have any foundation for designing messages that will not be rejected by the target group?
- Are there any surveys? Are new surveys necessary?
- Are there any internal or external sources that can give you knowledge about the target group?

Once you have learned more about your target group, clarify these questions:

- Who is directly affected by the company's communication?
- How do they relate to what they are informed about?
- How aware are they of what they are being informed about?
- Are they active in relation to the company or its operation?
- How involved are they in the company or its operation?
- Who is more indirectly affected? (These include messengers.)
- Who else might need information?

(Simonsen, 2007/2013)

*What is the company's reputation* among *key stakeholders*: What is the company's reputation in general and among the most important stakeholders? What requirements does this impose on the organisation's communication activities?

*Analysis of developments in one's surroundings:* It has to do with identifying and analysing trends, problems, themes, debates, technology development, etc., which can have an impact on the organisation and thus focus on communication work both externally and internally.

The analysis can reveal developments and important communication challenges the company is facing, both in terms of internal information flow and weaknesses in communication activities in the market. The communication challenges can be used as a basis for defining areas of action and communication goals.

Based on the situational analysis and stakeholder mapping, the next step is to identify the target group.



## 3.8.2 Identifying the target group

Using the communication audit and the stakeholder survey as a basis, it is time to identify the target group that we want to reach with our communication. Knowing the target group is crucial to developing communication that reaches it. 'The target group largely controls the communicator's decisions about *what* to say, how, when, where and to whom' (Kotler and Keller 2016). When we talk about identifying target groups, we primarily refer to the segment or parts of segments to which the company wishes to sell its products or services. Target groups are the people the company should reach with its message through marketing communications. Other stakeholders such as the company's management, owners, employees, suppliers, shareholders, the government, society, the press, and others are also important target groups, but communication needs may be different there. The company wishes to reach those in a different way than through marketing communications. These are also groups that should be identified and assessed in relation to their role and importance, and when and how communication with these groups should take place. Identifying the target group involves finding out how they can be reached as a group or individually, specific characteristics, whether they are direct or indirect users of the company's offerings etc. 'The target groups we prioritise are based on analysis of who they are, what characterises them, and what level of ambition we can use when reaching them' (Simonsen, 2007/2012). Traditional segmentation criteria such as gender, age, education, place of residence, interests, and so on can also be used (2.7.6 Target group analysis, 3.6 Market strategy).

### Who is the recipient?

The target group is not necessarily a homogeneous group. Its members may also be different from each other, which should be taken into account in the communication in order to reach the different target groups. Because when one thinks about the main target group, one often thinks about who should buy or use the product or service, but it is not certain that they are the ones you should communicate with. We can divide

Further reading
***Raise Your Game, Not Your Voice: How Listening, Communicating, and Storytelling Shape Compliance Program*** Influence (2021) by Lisa Beth Lentini Walker & Stef Tschida.

them into recipient groups and target groups. The recipient is the one to whom you convey the information. The target group is the one you want to achieve results with. Sometimes they are one and the same, and then everyone receives the message directly, such as, for example, in environmental campaigns, where it is about trying to reach everyone with the same message.

A starting point for identifying target groups is often a goal to influence them to change their lifestyles or behaviours, attitudes, or dispositions. Simonsen (2007/2012) highlights examples such as anti-smoking campaigns or 'eat five a day' campaigns and stresses that the more the target group is required or encouraged to do, the more important it is to create a good relationship with it. This can be done by choosing messengers who are individuals with great credibility and trust among the target group.

High or low engagement is also a factor to consider. A group of partners may consist of highly engaged persons who share the company's view, who are very loyal, and are faithful buyers or users. These may also represent potential opponents if they have the opposite opinion. 'People affect people' is a possible strategy in such a context, as in an EU campaign, if someone, who is in opposition, is influenced by someone, who is in favour. People with low engagement may also agree or disagree with what the company stands for or with its message. If they disagree, one strategy would be not to provoke them. If they agree, the purpose could be to increase their engagement.

**Identify the target group:** Who are they, where are they? Typical characteristics, desires and needs? Social identity and affiliation? Needs, desires and benefits related to the purchase and use of the product or service? Behaviour and user attributes. Relationship and loyalty? 'Is the audience unfamiliar with the category or is it a current user? Is the target group loyal to the brand, loyal to a competitor, or does it usually switch between different brands? If the target group uses the brand, does it use it to a greater or lesser extent? The communication strategy will depend on the answers given' (Kotler and Keller, 2016, p. 751). Identifying the target group's level of knowledge and understanding is also essential for making it possible to customise the communication so that they understand the message.

**Identify the market segment:** Segmentation is based on geography, demography, psychography and behaviour (2.7.6 Target group analysis). Actions and activities are assessed based on where and how the target groups are reached. Who wants to receive a brochure? Who reads newspaper ads? Who listens to the radio? Who checks websites and who uses Google? Who uses social media, how active are they and where are they active? (Kotler & Keller, 2016, p. 343).

**Target group/segment ranking:** The ranking can be hierarchical with the most important at the top:

- Primary target group: e.g. the consumer/buyer/user?
- Secondary target group: e.g. company, dealer, etc.
- Others: for example, owners and employees in the company, business partners, government, society, etc. Although the consumer is ranked at the top, the dealer can be essential to getting the product on the shop shelf, for example when introducing a new product in the grocery shop.

130 According to Cees van Riel (1992), who uses the term business communication for market communication, management organisation communication.

## 3.8.3 Communication goals

Communication goals are subgoals to help the company achieve its overall goals. They are determined by the company's communication needs, communication tasks, and what they want to achieve with the communication. It provides a basis for prioritising activities, selecting channels and developing budgets. Important questions to consider are: Do we have enough time and money to do what we want to do? Do we have to re-evaluate our goals? Should we think differently? How ambitious should we be about what we want to achieve? The level of ambition is the starting point for formulating precise performance goals for each target area and target group. One problem is that unrealistic goals are often set for the communication strategy. The vital question is: *What kind of action do we want from the target group*? For example, it could be to get the customer to buy the product. Goals should be realistic if the desired impact of the communication actions is to be measurable (3.3 Goals and subgoals).

When developing communication goals, it may be appropriate to distinguish between *marketing communication*, where efforts are linked to the marketing of products and services, and *corporate communication*, where efforts are linked to the internal communication and profiling of the organisation. Corporate communication then includes both management and organisation communication[130] (Brønn and Ihlen, 2009):

### Corporate communication goals

*Corporate communication* is usually about explaining the company's mission, values, purpose and views in a coherent message to the company's stakeholders and integrating stakeholders into the company. Corporate communication is based on the company/group/enterprise itself and its positioning towards professional actors such as investors, partners, and authorities, but also employees, stakeholder groups and the public. The intention is to create positive views about the company and to establish the desired position and reputation among stakeholders on whom the company relies. Corporate communication is based on the company's identity, culture, and strategy, as a starting point for planning, implementing, and following up internal and external communication activities. Companies should aim to convey the same message to all their

> **Communication tasks**
>
> A company has various communication tasks, both internal and external, which according to Brønn and Ihlen (2009) are:
>
> **Marketing communication:** Sales of goods and services to customers through advertising activities, and communication of position and value propositions.
>
> **Management communication:** Internal communication from management to employees in the context of establishing good processes, strategies, and motivation measures.
>
> **Organisation communication:** Communication aimed primarily at target groups such as stakeholders, government, public affairs, and press contacts.

stakeholders, signalling coherence, credibility, and ethics (3.2 Overall strategy, 3.2.5 Core values: Corporate identity).

*Corporate communication goals*: Corporate communication aims to profile and position the company vis-à-vis *all* stakeholders. Examples of corporate communication goals:

- The communication should be clear and informative, and express the company's identity, core, and desired position.
- Creating positive views about the company and establishing the desired position and reputation among those whom the company relies on.
- Creating and developing intangible values[131] such as a positive reputation, a clear message, a consistent dissemination, better collaboration, a good atmosphere, stronger relationships, and goodwill.[132]
- Create and develop material values such as increased orders, additional sales, better paid services, more cost-effective transaction management, improved internal communication and procedures, and conscious behaviour.

### Marketing communication goals

*Marketing communication* usually involves communicating the company's products and services to a market. The intention is to influence the purchasing decisions of the target group in the desired direction as well as to build brands. It involves planning, developing, and presenting target group-oriented and consistent messages through appropriate channels and media in order to communicate with current and potential customers. The most common main activities are advertising, direct marketing, internet marketing, sales promotion and public relations. The most up-to-date form of marketing communication is inbound marketing, which is to a great extent about loyalty-building activities aimed at each person, including dialogue programmes (3.6.8 Inbound marketing). Marketing communication includes both one-way and two-way advertising. Just as important as the company presenting with their sales message, is that customers can reach the company with their wishes and needs. Marketing communication is also the 'promotion part' of a marketing mix or the four Ps (3.6.5 The four Ps). The communication strategy as presented here is essentially about marketing communication.

*Marketing communication goals*: Marketing communication is commercially motivated and aims to influence the *target group*'s brand awareness, brand attitude, and purchasing decisions, through brand positioning and communication in relevant channels and media. According to Percy and Elliot (2012), communication goals can be divided into four categories: 1) Category need: Create needs, 2) Brand awareness: Build brand awareness, 3) Brand attitude: Create a brand attitude, and 4) Brand purchase incentive: Get the customer to buy the product. These four categories build upon one another and must be seen in context.

*Mass communication* is a form of marketing communication. The most important thing about mass communication is that it reaches all potential buyers in the category and not targeted at a few segments. The task of mass communication is to build and refresh the memory of customers in the category of the brand. In the old days, it was believed

131 Intangible assets are company assets that are not tangible physical things such as buildings and money. Examples of an intangible value are ownership of a strong brand or 'brand' that brings added value to the company (6.1 Intangible assets).

132 Goodwill (goodwill, good reputation): The value a company has in addition to the sum of its individual assets, that is, the value of the established company name, regular clients, good connections, etc. Calculation of goodwill value is applicable, for example, in case of company sale or inheritance (Percy and Elliot, 2012).

that customers made careful assessments about which brand to choose. Recent research shows that most decisions are made very quickly. And little or no evaluation of the alternatives is done. Customers have a strong tendency to choose the brand they first come up with when a need or a situation arises. The task of mass communication/market communication is therefore to build mental accessibility (Bendixen, 2022).

#### Category entry points (CEPs)

A more recent approach to setting market communication goals is built on the principles of Distinctive brand assets and Category entry points (CEPs):

1) Build mental availability
2) Use distinctive brand assets to enhance the advertised brand and connect the category entry points (CEPs), i.e. needs, drivers and usage situations, to the advertised brand
3) Brand awareness will increase as a result
4) Brand purchase incentive will increase as a result

Distinctive brand assets are brand elements like colours, shapes, slogans, characters, jingles and music that can trigger a brand in the minds of customers when they are exposed to them in advertising and in buying situations (3.4.6 Distinctive asset-building strategy). CEPs represent thoughts and associations that can become cues to access options from memory. A brand attached to these cues has the chance to become mentally available (2.9.8 Mental availability measurement). 'Every brand must compete to be associated with the main category entry points. Size of the brand and budget set limits on how many CEPs a brand should communicate. The bigger the brand the more CEPs' (Bendixen, 2022). Goals and effects are related to budget, read more in chapter 3.8.9 Communication measurement.

### 3.8.4 Desired reputation

Desired reputation is a form of goal, which can steer the business in the right direction in terms of how it wishes to be perceived by the outside world. A company can influence how customers will perceive it by deciding what impression it wishes to leave behind and using this consciously in its behaviour and communication. It is a matter of defining a desired reputation as a goal and trying to live up to it. A good reputation cannot be created. It is something the company should earn through the products and services it offers, and through its behaviour and actions. 'It is important to understand that a company has an identity, that it may be able to construct an image, but that reputation is something it earns' (Brønn and Ihlen 2009).

Having a good reputation is a clear competitive advantage for any company. Most companies occasionally have their reputation tainted; they may have experienced defects in a batch, etc. and received negative publicity. If it is a well-established company that enjoys great trust among its customers, this can be quickly forgotten. However, if a new product is launched in the market and its taste does not meet expectations or its packaging is difficult to open, this may cause loss of revenue,


1 Initiation
2 Insight
3 Strategy
4 Design
5 Production
6 Management

3.1 Strategy development
3.2 Overall strategy
3.3 Goals and subgoals
3.4 Business strategy
3.5 Business model
3.6 Market strategy
3.7 Brand strategy
3.8 Communication strategy
3.9 Design strategy

3.8.1 Communication audit
3.8.2 Identifying the target group
3.8.3 Communication goals
3.8.4 Desired reputation
3.8.5 Communication platform
3.8.6 Communication elements
3.8.7 Communication development
3.8.8 Channels and media
3.8.9 Communication measurement

- Corporate communication goals
- Marketing communication goals
- Category entry points (CEPs)


The desired reputation should express how the company wants to appear and be perceived.

loss of reputation, or the product being played out of the market. It is precisely through what the company's customers and the outside world choose to think about it that reputation comes about, and so it is partly beyond the company's control to do anything about it. 'The company can hardly manipulate or control its reputation, but it is possible to influence its reputation by getting hold of its own values and behaviour. (...) Reputation is about whether a company meets the expectations of the outside world with regard to its behaviour or product quality. A company may have strong brands, but a poor reputation' (Brønn and Ihlen 2009). An example of this is the clothing chain H&M, which on some occasions has been accused of child labour being linked to their clothing production.[133]

We will also look at different definitions for reputation, and what we mean by image in relation to reputation, as well as how a company can develop and define a desired reputation.

Fig. 3.46 Identity is what the company sends out, image is what the audience perceives (Rybakken, 2004), while reputation is the audience's perception over time.
A company's identity may change without changing its reputation, and vice versa (Brønn and Ihlen, 2009, p. 83). The figure is based on Brønn and Ihlen (2009).

Fig. 3.47 The company's identity is the sum of its overall presentation of product, communication, symbol and behaviour. This is reflected in the market as the company's image: the impression the outside world has of the company, which in turn forms the basis for its opinion of the company, which is called reputation. Based on Birkigt and Stadler (1986) and Cees van Riel (1996). Further developed by Karlsen, H. (1999) and Grimsgaard (2018). See also Figure 3.4 Corporate identity.

### What is reputation?

There are a number of different definitions of reputation related to a company and its products, services, and activities. Brønn and Ihlen (2009) present various explanations: 'A stakeholder's general assessment of a company over time' (Gotsi & Wilson, 2001, p. 29) and 'Observers' collective assessment of a company based on the perception of its economic, social, and environmental consequences over time' (Barnett et al., 2006). It can also mean assessment, or opinion about something or someone.[134] The definitions emphasise that reputation is determined by people's opinions of the company over time, based on the experience they have had with the company's products, services, behaviours, etc., in addition to what they have conveyed. These experiences and the way they are passed on are often subjective, but over time a common perception emerges, reputation equity, which, if positive, can be a competitive advantage for the company. Whether or not the expectations the company creates through its communicated promises are met is crucial to how it affects its reputation. 'Reputation arises in the intersection of expectations and experiences created by the company's or the organisation's promise and delivery. It is not only what is delivered (the experience) that determines the reputation, but perhaps what is delivered in relation to what was promised (the expectations). ('Reputation,' n.d.).' Below is a more general definition that is clear and easy to work by when defining one's desired reputation: 'Reputation is the sum of all opinions expressed about an organisation' (Based on Bromley 1993; Brønn and Ihlen 2009, p. 81) (3.2.6 Value proposition, 3.1.3 TOP 5).

### Image vs. reputation?

Image is often used synonymously with reputation. Brønn and Ihlen attribute different meanings to the two concepts 'image' and 'reputation'. They explain 'image' with the immediate impression the company leaves on the outside world, which in turn forms the basis for its reputation, while 'reputation' is the perception of the company by the outside world over time. Brønn and Ihlen argue that the first step necessary to build a good reputation is to focus on identity and image. They explain this symbiosis with some brief definitions (Brønn & Ihlen, 2009, p. 14):

Further reading
*Brand New Brand You: How to build and maintain reputation and relevance* (2020) by Garry Browne.

133 H&M experienced reputation failure: 'Children in Cambodia Produce Clothing for H&M', Harbo/Ntb (2015).
134 Based on Bokmålsordboka.

**Identity:** An internally oriented core concept that says something about the profile and values communicated by an organisation, and the employees' views on this.
**Image:** The immediate impression the outside world has of the organisation, which in turn forms the basis of the organisation's reputation.
**Reputation:** The perception of the organisation by the outside world over time.

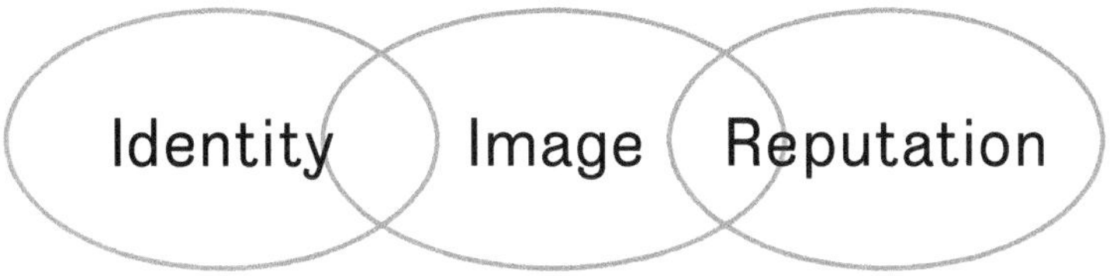


Fig. 3.46 Identity, image, reputation

A strong, holistic and consistent identity presupposes a good connection between what the company offers (the product/service), how it is visually presented in the form of logo, symbol, and visual devices (symbol), how this is communicated in different media and communication arenas (communication), and how the company's service, actions, and behaviour are experienced (behaviour). When these four areas are united, we are talking about a strong identity, see Figure 3.4 Corporate identity.

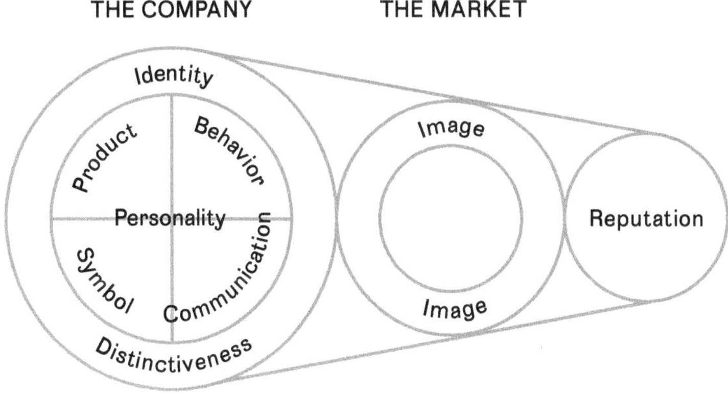


Fig. 3.47 Reputation

**Desired reputation**

By defining the desired reputation, the company may become more aware of what it needs to do in order to gain the audience's favour. But it is not enough to define the desired reputation; the company must consciously communicate who they are, the way they want to appear, and prove/demonstrate through their products/services, their behaviour, and their actions, that they live up to their promises and meet the expectations of the audience. The desired reputation should be a reflection of the company's core values, value propostion, and position (3.1.3 Top 5). The question the company should ask itself is: How can we, through our identity, communication, behaviour, and products, achieve to be perceived as we want? The

1 Initiation
2 Insight
3 Strategy
4 Design
5 Production
6 Management

3.1 Strategy development
3.2 Overall strategy
3.3 Goals and subgoals
3.4 Business strategy
3.5 Business model
3.6 Market strategy
3.7 Brand strategy
3.8 Communication strategy
3.9 Design strategy

3.8.1 Communication audit
3.8.2 Identifying the target group
3.8.3 Communication goals
3.8.4 Desired reputation
3.8.5 Communication platform
3.8.6 Communication elements
3.8.7 Communication development
3.8.8 Channels and media
3.8.9 Communication measurement

– What is reputation?
– Image vs. reputation?
– Desired reputation

company cannot just decide that: Our reputation is good service. Others have to say it. The company should live by it through its behaviour and actions. This way, they leave behind the impression of good service, which can affect their reputation: 'They are the ones with good service.'

Once a company has decided on a desired reputation, what they want customers and other stakeholders to say about them, it will be a good basis to consider: What should we do then in order to achieve the desired reputation?

**Formulating the desired reputation**

What do we want people to say about us? For example:
*When customer care is important*: At (company name) you feel taken care of from the moment you arrive to the moment you leave.
*When quality is important*: (Company name) are those with top quality.
*When sustainability is important*: (Company name) are conscious of fair trade at a competitive price.

**Reputation workshop**

Determining the desired reputation is a strategic issue. Ensure the involvement of decision-makers, owners and employees, so that everyone in the company delivers under the same conditions is a success factor in achieving the desired reputation.

**Clarification of desired reputation:**

- How do we think we are perceived?
- How are we actually perceived?
- How do we wish to be perceived?
- What do we want others to say about us?[135]

The main question is: What do we want others to say about us? To answer this question and formulate a 'desired reputation', the company must clarify:

- Who are we?
- What do we communicate about ourselves?
- What do we promise? How do we live up to our promise?
- What are our actions/behaviours like?
- What do our target group and other stakeholders say about us?

**Formulating the desired reputation:**

Words and thoughts are discussed and sifted time and time again until there remains an essence that answers the following questions: How do we (the company) prefer to be perceived? Examples of such a statement could be: (The company) *are the ones with a wide product range and low furniture prices*. In short, it is a matter of making some clear promises to the market and keeping one's promises, about doing things right and talking about it. 'Such behaviour leads to more people choosing to buy from our company, they recommend us to others, they trust us, talk positively about us, and apply for a job with us' (Ikea, 2012). For more workshops, see 2.2.2 PIPI, 2.2.3 Where are we – where will we?.

Fig. 3.48 The figure shows that 'image' is the perception the recipient has of the company. Brand image is the customers' perception of a brand based on their interaction with the company

Tips for the designer
In the communication platform, the policies on how communication should be brought about both verbally and visually are laid. TOP 3 are: Image, tone of voice and signal effect.

Tips for the company
The communication platform is a management tool for everyone in the company who works with communications internally in the organisation or externally to the market, as well as for designers and other subcontractors carrying out communications on behalf of the company.

135 Answers can be pure guesswork if surveys are not conducted in the market and among the target groups External surveys: The perception that the target audience, audience, market, and outside world have of the company can be clarified through a reputation survey. The survey can be conducted qualitatively, among a small group of respondents, for example through an online survey, or quantitatively through a market survey among a large number of respondents.Internal surveys: To clarify what perception the management, employees, and owners have of their own company, a strategic workshop, internal surveys, or personal interviews may be conducted.

## 3.8.5 Communication platform

The communication platform should provide visual and verbal strategic guidelines for the company's communication. It should say something about *HOW* the company should communicate in order to achieve its communication goals and deliver on the company's overall goals.

It is not just *about what* is communicated; it is *about* how the communication is set up. First, the communication should be loaded with the associations we want the recipient to make. Second, the language should have the right temperament, style, dramatic effect, and rhetoric. Even small nuances in the voice and tone, and subtle details in the language, could have an impact on how the recipient perceives the message. Such nuances can be planned by putting in place clear policies for tone of voice, signal effect and image, and by consciously choosing typeface, typography, layout and use of photos and illustrations (4.9 Identity development).

1 Initiation
2 Insight
3 Strategy
4 Design
5 Production
6 Management

3.1 Strategy development
3.2 Overall strategy
3.3 Goals and subgoals
3.4 Business strategy
3.5 Business model
3.6 Market strategy
3.7 Brand strategy
3.8 Communication strategy
3.9 Design strategy

3.8.1 Communication audit
3.8.2 Identifying the target group
3.8.3 Communication goals
3.8.4 Desired reputation
3.8.5 Communication platform
3.8.6 Communication elements
3.8.7 Communication development
3.8.8 Channels and media
3.8.9 Communication measurement

- Image
- Tone of voice
- Signal effect

### Image

*What immediate impression do we want the environment to have of the company through the way we communicate visually and verbally?* 'Image' is an English word also used for the typical traits of a person or the mental image the surroundings have of the person. We are talking about a person's image. Identity is what you send out and image is what the recipient sees. Image is the personality's reflection and can be perceived differently depending on who is looking (Rybakken, 2004). As a result, we can perceive one and the same thing differently based on background of different gender, age, nationality, culture, social identity, and interest.

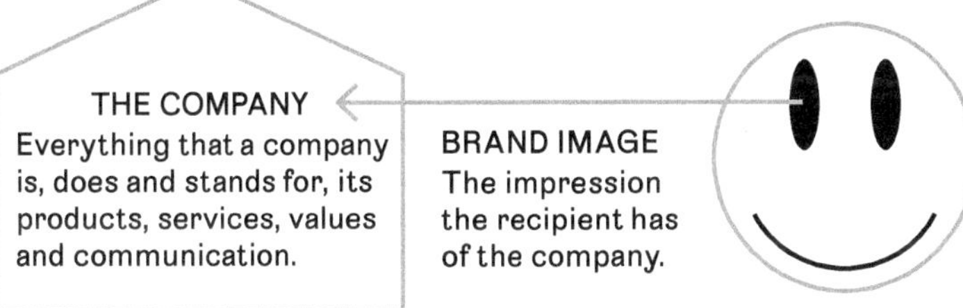

THE COMPANY
Everything that a company is, does and stands for, its products, services, values and communication.
BRAND IMAGE
The impression the recipient has of the company.

Fig. 3.48 Brand image

Within branding, a person's image is used metaphorically for a company's or a brand's face to the world. An image can be formed naturally by itself, or it can be designed in order to create the associations with the company that the company wants the audience or the target group to make. Image is the immediate impression the outside world has of the company (Brønn & Ihlen, 2009). Everything a company, product or service is and stands for is reflected in the market as an image. The image is a mental picture that exists in a person's mind, as something one remembers or imagines. The starting point for the mental picture does not have to be real. It could be something abstract or imaginary, some kind of notion.

Communication platform

For a company, the way it communicates will affect how the world perceives it and its products and services. How communication is to be conveyed verbally and visually is a strategic question, which is about building position, awareness, and reputation.

In order to define the desired image, the company should clarify what immediate impression it wants the outside world and stakeholder groups to have/get of it. Like 'the trendy super cool coffee shop'. Creating an image is about establishing this notion. Image is formulated in a short sentence, based on the question: What image do we want the world to have of us? The next question will be: How to create communication that supports the image we want the world to have of us?

Table 3.13 The table shows a tone of voice form. Include three rows for each of the primary attributes, accompanied by three columns – a brief description, what to do, and what not to do. If necessary, add a row for some secondary characteristics that need some extra explanation (Heald, 2015).

Fig. 3.49 The figure shows the thoughts of a Tesla owner. The signal effect is the signals the user thinks they send to their surroundings when driving around in a Tesla.

### Tone of voice

*What atmosphere, mood, temperament, and style should surround the way we communicate*? Tone of voice is often used to describe the 'tone' or 'voice' of the text. For example, prose, crime, or fact will have a different sentence, vocabulary, and tone of voice structure. The 'voice' will also be different if you speak to children, adolescents, adults, or the elderly, whether it is everyday or professional language, and so on. Tone of voice is a central part of the identity, comparable to the voice of a person. Defining the tone of voice makes it easier to create consistent language, which is in line with the company as it wants to appear. Similarly, tone of voice can provide guidance for the design to create the right tone, temperament, and style for the visual solutions, thereby also achieving holistic expression and clear identity in both design and communication.

By choosing the correct language when speaking to different target groups, one will be able to get the message across more easily and establish the desired associations. This way, the communication can express the desired identity and position, product category, industry, etc. The voice and tone of a brokerage firm or bank will necessarily differ from that of a nursing home or kindergarten. A product's brand voice versus the company's tone of voice may have some important differences. A company may have several brands, each with its own voice. The tone of voice for one brand can be completely different from that of other brands in the same company, as well as from the company's own. A trademark product's tone of voice needs to be updated to keep up with changes in customer expectations, while a company's tone of

| Voice characteristics | Description | Do | Do not |
|---|---|---|---|
| Passionate | We are passionate about changing the way the world works. | Use strong verbs.<br>Be a champion.<br>Be a cheerleader. | Be indifferent.<br>Be unclear.<br>Use passive voice. |
| Eccentric | We are not afraid to challenge the status quo and be ourselves. | Use unexpected examples.<br>Take the opposite position.<br>Express ourselves. | Use too much slang or obscure references.<br>Use jargon or exaggerated examples.<br>Lose sight of the audience and the core message. |
| Free speech | We take our product seriously, but we are not self-righteous. | Be playful.<br>Use colourful illustrations or examples. | Get too casual.<br>Use too many obscure pop-culture references. |
| Authentic | We will provide you with the tools and insights you need to do your job better. It may not always be through our product. | Be honest and sincere.<br>Meet any complaint or error and show how to present them.<br>We do what we promise to do. | Use marketing jargon and superlatives.<br>Promise more than we can keep. Oversell the product's properties. |

Table 3.13 Tone of voice

voice should be consistent and express the values and corporate culture of the organisation (Albrighton, 2010). At the same time, tone of voice can be used for dramatic effect and to amplify the message. Not only the sound, but the font, shape, colour, and other visual devices help create the desired tone of voice.

Tone of voice is a strategic definition, which is anchored in the core values for expressing the desired identity (3.2.5 Core values). In addition, it can be customised to the target group to which the communication is to be directed and to the message one wishes to communicate. Tone of voice can be formulated in a short sentence or in individual words based on different traits that characterise the voice. Example of tone of voice based on core value:

| Core values | Tone of voice |
|---|---|
| (Identity) | (What should characterise the voice?) |
| Passionate: | Expressive, enthusiastic, engaging |
| Special: | Cheeky, unexpected, different |
| Genuine: | Real, reliable, factual |

A tone of voice form is a method of clarifying what should characterise the language used in the communication (based on Heald 2015), see Figure 3.45.

### Signal effect

*Who am I using this product? How will I be perceived by those around me?* Who am I who works in this company, shops in this company, buys this product, buys this service? Signal effect is about which signals the user should send to others. The signal effect can be positive and negative; it can be conscious or unconscious. The signal effect used in branding should be positive and have a clear relationship to the company's identity and desired reputation. Developing signal effect is about deciding how we can verbalise and express what we want the target audience to think about themselves and signal to those around us.

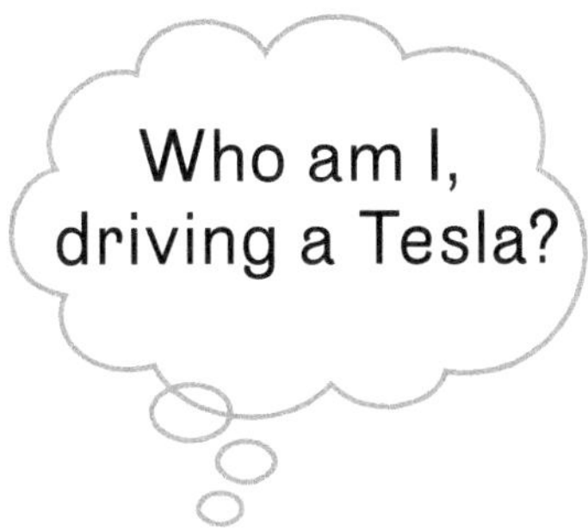


Fig. 3.49 Signal effect

Who am I driving a Tesla? The article 'What Sets Tesla Owners Apart from Other Car Owners?' refers to a survey of 120 owners of Tesla Model S conducted by TNS Gallup in 2015. The answers that emerged showed that the average Tesla owner is male, well educated, seven out of ten hold advanced degrees and are employed. Only 4% are retired, compared to 23% for new

1 Initiation
2 Insight
3 Strategy
4 Design
5 Production
6 Management

3.1 Strategy development
3.2 Overall strategy
3.3 Goals and subgoals
3.4 Business strategy
3.5 Business model
3.6 Market strategy
3.7 Brand strategy
3.8 Communication strategy
3.9 Design strategy

3.8.1 Communication audit
3.8.2 Identifying the target group
3.8.3 Communication goals
3.8.4 Desired reputation
3.8.5 Communication platform
3.8.6 Communication elements
3.8.7 Communication development
3.8.8 Channels and media
3.8.9 Communication measurement

- Image
- Tone of voice
- Signal effect

car buyers in general. 'In this picture, it is important to remember that those who buy a new car earn significantly more than the general population', says Anders Hovde, expert in the new car market at TNS Gallup. According to Tesla owners, the strongest positives are: driving comfort, low power cost, motor power, and a design score far above those of comparable cars (Hoem, 2015). For example, if we are going to create a signal effect based on this survey, it could read as follows: I drive a Tesla, I am well educated, I appreciate good design, and I care for the environment.

### 3.8.6 Communication elements

Consistent use of communication elements is an effective strategic instrument for building position, awareness, and reputation. The communication elements are also included as key factors in the visual communication of a company and its products or services. Examples of key communication elements include a concise selling message, a catchy slogan, or an inviting narrative. It is equally important to have clear product information and consistent company information (3.8.7 Communication development).

**Message**: A message is a compressed form of communication that conveys the essence of something a sender wants to communicate to individuals or groups. Messages can be in the form of advertising in the mass media, slogans for a brand, personal messages, etc. The challenge is to create a concise and clear message that is easily and quickly perceived. The message is to serve two basic functions (Samuel et al., 2007/2012):

- 1) Establish the desired brand awareness.
- 2) Contribute to establishing the desired position in the market through brand awareness.

It is essential to think carefully about what is to be communicated and what is the very core of the communication, the very essence of what we want to say, and to ensure that it comes out the way we intended. If you peel away all the decoration of impressive words and phrases and think that there is one thing, only one thing you can say, what is it that you want the recipient to know? What is the core? The essence of communication should be clearly displayed on the relevant communication surfaces and should help establish the desired associations in the recipients. The core of communication may appear in the slogan or tagline below the logo, in a standard text (*boilerplate*), in the history of the brand, or otherwise in relation to the brand and the visual identity.

**Slogan/tagline**: The slogan is a short convincing phrase, which in compressed form summarises the most important thing the company wants to say about the organisation or the products and services it offers. The slogan is a central tag element. It summarises vision, promise and/or position in one sentence. The slogan is central to the work of building position and establishing mental associations with the brand in the recipient (3.7.3 Brand position: Position is communication, 3.7.6 Brand assets: Slogan).

**Narrative/story**: A great brand narrative, rooted in culture, tradition, and origin, can carry or enrich communication, create an experience, and confidence. Do we have a story that might be interesting to tell? Or do we have a story we want to create that can express the experience, quality, sustainability, etc. that we want to convey to the outside world? *The question is*: How can we create a story that conveys the company, product, or service in an interesting way, that strengthens our identity and credibility, while at the same time creating an experience and commitment? (3.7.4 Brand story, 2.8.3 Storyboard).

**Standard text:** It is not always as easy to come up with a text about what the company is, what it does or offers. Nevertheless, this information should be present in all contexts where the company presents itself, whether at a trade fair or in a job advertisement. The standard text is short, clear and consistent communication of the company, product and/or service, which will help build the company's identity, position and the impressions it leaves. The standard text should say something about:

- Who are we? (Company)
- What are we selling? (Concept)
- What do we promise? (Promises)
- What is our story? (Anchoring)

**Elevator pitch**

An elevator pitch is a short sales pitch, a summary used to define a process quickly and easily, a product, a service, an organisation, or an event and its value proposition. The name reflects the idea that it should be possible to deliver the summary for the time of one elevator ride or from about thirty seconds to two minutes ('Elevator pitch', n.d.). The elevator pitch is an effective method many managers will benefit from using in order to communicate a quick, concise summary of what the company does or offers. Examples of other similar models are high-concept, mission statement, vision statement.

*'Boilerplate'* is a term for a standard text, a short text describing the company and/or its products, the purpose of which is to appear identical and consistent in all contexts, whether in a press release, advertisement, or other publication. The origin of the boilerplate concept dates back to the early 1900s in England, when it was not uncommon for iron or steel plates from old boilers to be used as sheet cladding to cover holes in ships' hulls. Such steel plates or boilerplates were also used to imprint text on. The advantage was that they could be sent directly to a newspaper printing plant for mass production and the so-called syndication. The fact that the text was embossed into the steel prevented any spelling mistakes or rewriting that might otherwise occur when typesetting text, which was common at the time ('Bolier plate,' n.d.).

**Product information:** Can our products and/or services be conveyed in a consistent manner, which highlights, reinforces, and anchors our concept and identity, and ensures clear and targeted communication? How can the information be communicated in a short and selling manner with the tone and mood we want to express and the associations we want to create?

**Other communication elements:** Communication links strategy, message, and visual identity. Communication elements therefore also include brand assets and identity elements (3.7.6 Brand assets, 4.9.2 Identity elements).

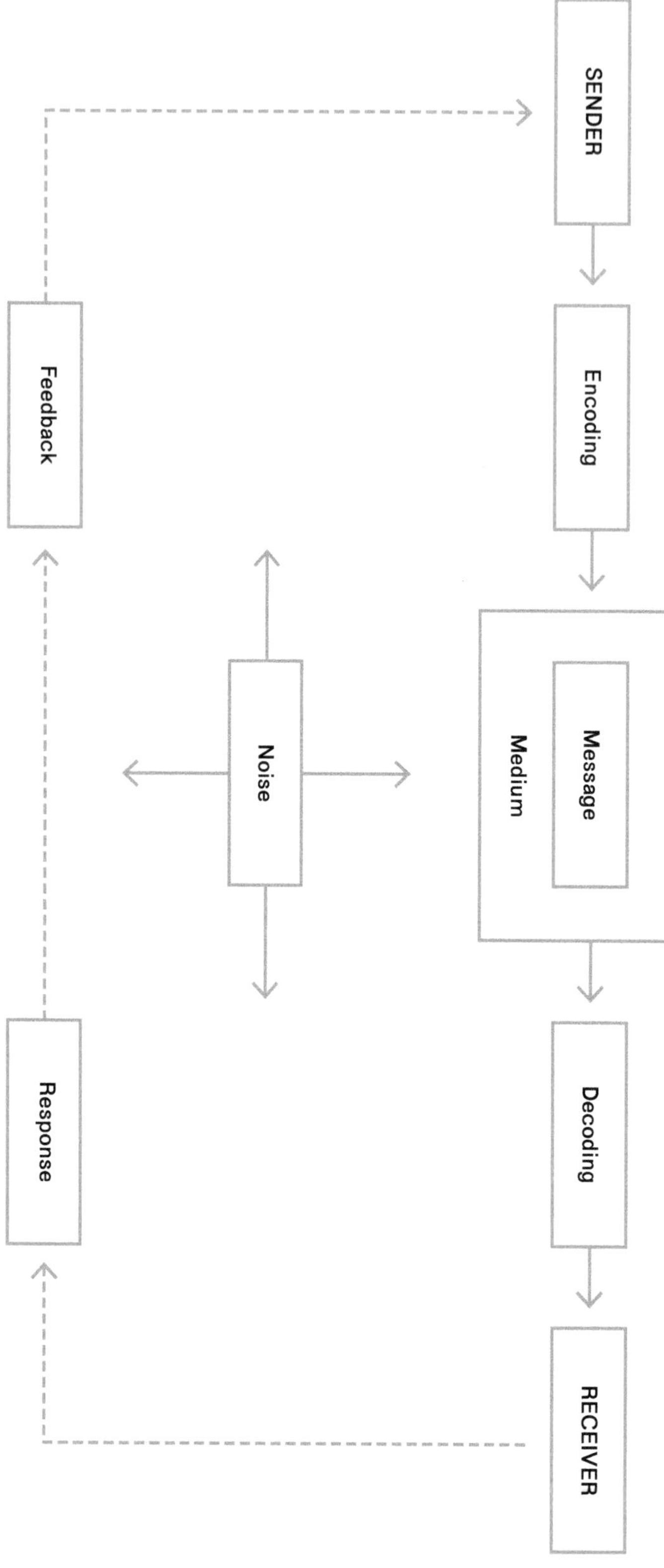


Fig. 3.50 Communication process

Fig. 3.50 The figure shows a communication process with nine key factors for effective communication. Two of them represent the main players *sender* and *recipient* Two factors represent the most important tools – *message* and *medium*. Four factors represent the main communicative functions *encoding, decoding, response*, and *feedback*. The last element is noise, i.e. arbitrary and competing messages that can interfere with the intended communication (model and caption based on Kotler & Keller, 2016, p. 748).

136 Explanation and examples in the chapter on message strategy, creative strategy, and message source are taken and partially quoted from Kotler and Keller (2016,p. 588), where many of the examples are research-based.
137 John Clement Maloney, American marketing consultant. American Association of University Professors (president Northwestern University, 1970), American Psychological Association (director consumer psychology division, 1964–1965).
138 Crossing this four types of reward with three types of experience generates 12 types of messages. For example, the appeal 'gets clothes cleaner' is *a rational-reward* promise following results-of-use experience.
139 Jeremy Bullmore is a former chairman of J Walter Thompson UK and the Advertising Association, and a current director of the Guardian Media Group and WPP Group PLC. He is the author of *Behind the Scenes in Advertising*.

### 3.8.7 Communication development


1 Initiation
2 Insight
3 Strategy
4 Design
5 Production
6 Management

3.1 Strategy development
3.2 Overall strategy
3.3 Goals and subgoals
3.4 Business strategy
3.5 Business model
3.6 Market strategy
3.7 Brand strategy
3.8 Communication strategy
3.9 Design strategy

3.8.1 Communication audit
3.8.2 Identifying the target group
3.8.3 Communication goals
3.8.4 Desired reputation
3.8.5 Communication platform
3.8.6 Communication elements
3.8.7 Communication development
3.8.8 Channels and media
3.8.9 Communication measurement


It is a challenge to create and convey the communication so that the recipient perceives the message as intended. The message can take different directions: what you mean to say; what you actually say; what others hear; what the other person thinks they hear; what the other person answers; what you think the other person would answer.

What to say, how to say it, and whom to say it to? Here are three strategies for developing sales-oriented messages in order to achieve the desired response (based on Kotler & Keller, 2016):[136]

1) Message strategy: What should be said?
2) Creative strategy: How should it be said?
3) Message source: Who should say it?

**1) Message strategy:** Creating the message strategy involves identifying messages, themes, or ideas that are consistent with the brand positioning and help establish points-of-difference, which also signal some kind of *benefit or reward*.

*Points-of-difference* may be directly related to the product or service performance, such as the quality, economy, uses features, or brand value, and/or they may be related to external factors, such as that the brand is timely, popular, or traditional (3.7.3 Brand position).

*Reward* may be related to the use or to the experience of the product or service. Kotler and Keller refer to researcher John C. Maloney,[137] who proposed one framework in which he argued that buyers expect one of four types of *reward* from a product: rational, sensory, social or ego-satisfaction. The feeling of reward may come from results-of-use experience, product-in-use experience, or incidental-to-use experience.[138] The phrase 'real beer taste in great light beer' is *a sensory-reward* promise connected with product-in-use experience' (Kotler & Keller, 2016).

**2) Creative strategy:** The impact of communication depends on both the content and design of the message. If communication does not lead forward, this may be because the message is wrong, or the message is right, but the presentation is wrong. Kotler and Keller refer to different methods of creating appeal:

*Informative appeal*: This approach highlights the attributes and benefits of the product or service. Examples are advertisements that promise to solve problems, that show the product in use, that compare products, that have recommendations from specialists or celebrities. Informative communication appeals to logic and reason.

*Transformative appeal*: This approach focuses on an advantage or image that is not product-related, which is often about arousing feelings that motivate purchase. One way to do that is to show the people who use a brand, or the kind of experiences that come from using it. The devices used may have emotional appeal such as humour, love, pride, and joy, or evocations such as cute little children or catchy music and similar.

*Negative appeal*: Another way to do that is to use *negative appeal* such as fear, guilt, and shame in order to get people to do things (brush their teeth, get an annual health check) or stop doing things (smoking, heavy drinking, overeating). It is important to ensure that appeals do

Message strategy:
The message is the impression the communications shall make. The idea is how to make this impression. The best way to explain this is by an example made by the advertising guru of UK advertising Jeremy Bullmore.[139]
Goal: I want people to perceive me as a fun person.
What should my message be?: I am funny (the strategy on print). Tell a very funny joke (creativity). (Bendixen, 2022).

not become too harsh, that the source has sufficient credibility, and that the communication convincingly promises to end the fears it evokes.

**3) Message source:** When using people in advertising, research has shown that the credibility of the communicator (person/source) is crucial for whether a message will be accepted. Examples of three sources of credibility are:

- *Expertise*: The specialised knowledge that a person has to support the claim.
- *Trustworthiness*: The extent to which the person is perceived as objective and honest. We trust friends more than sellers, and we would trust someone who does not get paid over someone who does.
- *Likability*: How attractive the person is and how easy it is to like them. Openness, humour, and naturalness are qualities that make a person easier to like. For example, medicine will become more credible when recommended by a doctor, because doctors have high credibility. Celebrity recommendations or messages delivered by attractive or popular sources can also add credibility.

Fig. 3.51 **Kotler and Keller refer to four classic response hierarchy models, all of which assume that the buyer goes through cognitive, emotional, and behavioural phases: the AIDA Model, the Effect Hierarchy Model, the Innovation and Adoption Model and the Communication Model. The order of the phases in the different models may vary depending on which product is the subject of the buyer's attention (the model is based on Kotler and Keller 2016, p. 748).**

**Communication is the exchange of information (disclosures, opinions, needs, desires) between individuals and groups.**

### Communication process

Communication is basically an interaction between sender and recipient, a mutual intention to make oneself understood and achieve some kind of response. In marketing communication, the aim is usually to achieve a desired effect in terms of attention, interest, awareness, attitude, response, or action by the consumer. 'The sender needs to know which audience they want to reach and what kind of response they want to achieve. They should encode the message in a way that allows the target group to decode it. They need to convey the message through media reaching the recipients and develop feedback channels to follow the response (see Figure 3.47). The more a sender's field of experience overlaps with that of the recipient, the more impact the message is likely to have' (Kotler & Keller, 2016, p. 748). Creating a response follow-up plan is a key and crucial factor. Surveys can be conducted to see whether the communication creates the desired effect (3.8.9 Communication measurement).

**Response hierarchy:** When designing the communication content and planning communication activities, it is necessary to familiarise oneself with the relevant purchasing process and assess which experiences and impressions will have the greatest impact at each stage of the purchasing process in order to achieve the desired response. According to Kotler and Keller, in a purchase process, the buyer will go through cognitive, emotional, and behavioural phases (by choosing the correct order, communication can be better planned):

1) The order 'learn-feel-do' applies when the audience is actively engaged in a product category that is perceived to have a high degree of differentiation, such as cars or houses.
2) The order 'do-feel-learn' is relevant when the audience has a high level of engagement but perceives little or no differentiation in the product category, such as plane tickets or personal computers.
3) The order 'learn-do-feel' is relevant when the audience is little engaged and perceives little differentiation, for example when purchasing salt or batteries.

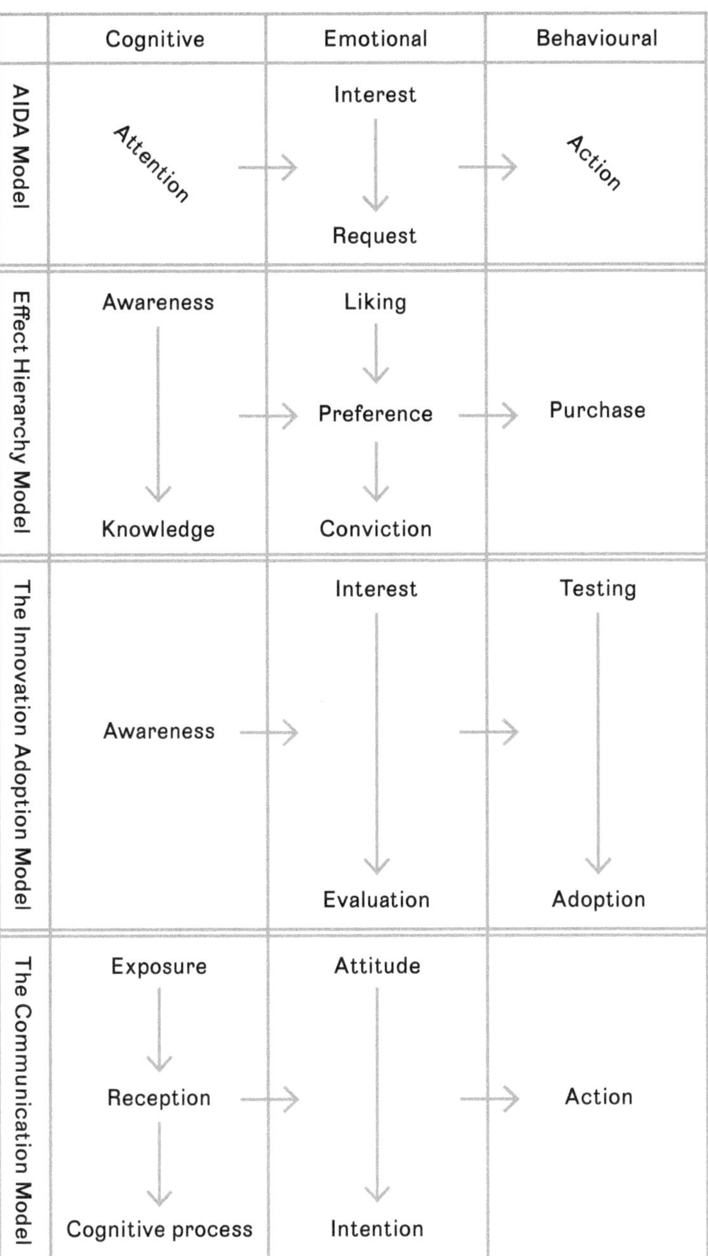


Fig. 3.51 Response hierarchy


1 Initiation
2 Insight
3 Strategy
4 Design
5 Production
6 Management

3.1 Strategy development
3.2 Overall strategy
3.3 Goals and subgoals
3.4 Business strategy
3.5 Business model
3.6 Market strategy
3.7 Brand strategy
3.8 Communication strategy
3.9 Design strategy

3.8.1 Communication audit
3.8.2 Identifying the target group
3.8.3 Communication goals
3.8.4 Desired reputation
3.8.5 Communication platform
3.8.6 Communication elements
3.8.7 Communication development
3.8.8 Channels and media
3.8.9 Communication measurement

– Communication process


**Effect Hierarchy Model:** Explanation of the Effect Hierarchy Model, see Figure 3.48, second column from the left (Kotler & Keller, 2016, p. 749);

- *Awareness*: If most of the target group does not know the product, the communicator's task is to create awareness.
- *Knowledge*: If the target audience knows the brand but does not know much more, the task will be to convey knowledge about the product.
- *Liking*: If members of the target audience are familiar with the brand, how do they feel about it? If there are negative feelings or problems, the task will be to find the cause, solve the problems, and convey the good quality.

Interaction and communication

Read about design and visual communication interaction in the interview with Nina Lysbakken. Available at designandstrategi.co.uk.

- *Preference*: The target group may like the product, but not so much that they would prefer it to other products. The communicator should then try to achieve consumer preference by comparing quality, value, performance, and other features with what is offered by relevant competitors. Example: Slogan of One Call: '*Just as good, only cheap.*'
- *Conviction*: A target group may have a certain preference for a particular product but is not convinced that they should buy it. The communicator's task is to strengthen this conviction and the intention of the members of the target group so that they decide to purchase the product.
- *Purchase*: Some members of the target group may also be convinced, but still do not come to act. The communicator should guide these consumers to the final step, possibly by offering the product at a lower price, offering an additional bonus or letting them try it.

Table 3.14 8 models of communication: According to Drew (2021) the main models of communication can be split into three categories:
*Linear models* – only looks at one-way communication.
*Interactive models* – looks at two-way communication.
*Transactional models* – looks at two-way communication where the message gets more complex as the communication event (e.g. conversation) progresses (based on Drew, 2021).

Tips for the designer
Position is communication: How should the message be formulated to differentiate the product or service from competitors?

| | | | |
|---|---|---|---|
| 1. | Aristotle's Model | Linear | Aristotle argues that we should look at five elements of a communication event to analyse how best to communicate: speaker, speech, occasion, target audience and effect. |
| 2. | Lasswell's Model | Linear | Lasswell's model is a basic framework for analysing one-way communication by asking five questions: Who, said what, through which channel, to whom, with what effects? |
| 3. | Shannon-Weaver Model | Linear | The Shannon-Weaver model is the first to highlight the role of 'noise' in communication, which can disrupt or alter a message between sender and receiver. |
| 4. | Berlo's S-M-C-R Model | Linear | Berlo's S-M-C-R model explains communication in four steps: Source, Message, Channel, and Receiver. |
| 5. | Osgood-Schramm Model | Interactive | The Osgood-Schramm model looks at reciprocal communication, showing how we have to encode, decode, and interpret information in real-time during a conversation. |
| 6. | Westley and Maclean Model | Interactive | The Westley and Maclean model shows that our communication is influenced by environmental, cultural and personal factors. |
| 7. | Barnlund's Transactional Model | Transactional | Barnlund's Transactional Model of Communication highlights the role of private and public cues that impact our messages. |
| 8. | Dance's Helical Model | Transactional | Dance's Helical Model sees communication as a circular process that gets more and more complex as communication occurs, which can be represented by a helical spiral. |

Table 3.14 8 models of communication

**Further prosess:** When the verbal content is in place, the job is far from done. A message has little value if it does not reach the recipient. Wrapping the message up is as important as its verbal content to convey the message in a clear and attractive way. The way the message is conveyed may also help reinforce its meaning. The presentation of the message will vary depending on channel and medium. 'In a printed ad, the communicator must decide on the title, text, illustrations, and colours. If it is to be communicated by radio, the communicator should select words, voice quality, and pronunciation. (...) If the message is to be broadcast via TV or directly, the body language should also be planned. If the message is to be posted online, the design, fonts, graphics, videos, music, and other visual and verbal elements should all be in place' (Kotler & Keller, 2016, p. 756).

### 3.8.8 Channels and media

Communication channels are different communication paths between sender and recipient (Kaufmann and Kaufmann, 2003, p. 288). Channels may include internet, social media, websites, blogs, chat rooms, text messages, TV, radio, email, direct mail, newspapers, magazines, meetings, conferences, exhibitions, information posters in shops and public offices, the service centres in municipalities, and outreach measures, to name a few. The appropriate channels depend on the goals, strategy, target groups, and situation, as well as the message we want to convey. Some crucial questions will then be: Who can we reach with this channel? Who can we not reach; who is excluded? What are the short-term and long-term consequences? What unintended effects could it have? Does the message change its nature because of the channel?

In addition to channels, the use of information intermediaries can be one way to get there. These may be resources and other people who carry the message to the target group or may pass on information to someone directly affected by a case or incident. The question will then be: Who can be information intermediaries? Who should you work with? Who has the background, expertise, and networks that can be valuable here in order to achieve the goals? What experiences do you have with them from earlier? For example, there may be people who often act as consultants, client managers, outreach personnel or influencers, but also journalists in the mass media who will often act as additional sources of information. These may convey the message further, but on their own terms (Simonsen, 2007/2012).

#### Media channels

Media channels are communication channels or means of mass communication, one-to-one communication and interaction. They can be divided into different categories:

**Mass media:** These are means/channels of communication that make it possible to distribute information or spread a message to many people over a larger area in a short period of time. Traditional mass media are newspapers, radio and TV, which reach a large audience daily, and periodicals, magazines, comics, books, and films. The Internet is also considered a mass medium and can be divided into different areas, such as the web, social media, and email.


1 Initiation
2 Insight
3 Strategy
4 Design
5 Production
6 Management

3.1 Strategy development
3.2 Overall strategy
3.3 Goals and subgoals
3.4 Business strategy
3.5 Business model
3.6 Market strategy
3.7 Brand strategy
3.8 Communication strategy
3.9 Design strategy

3.8.1 Communication audit
3.8.2 Identifying the target group
3.8.3 Communication goals
3.8.4 Desired reputation
3.8.5 Communication platform
3.8.6 Communication elements
3.8.7 Communication development
3.8.8 Channels and media
3.8.9 Communication measurement

- Media channels
- Paid, owned, earned attention
- Communication mix


Further reading
*All 8 Models Of Communication, Explained!* by Chris Drew, October 24, 2021

| Communication Mix – Explanation of Figure 3.52 | |
|---|---|
| Areas | Communication measures/materials |
| 1)<br>Corporate: | Identity/profile: Logo, symbol, visual identity<br>Corporate materials: Website, stationary, uniforms<br>Exterior/interior: Facade signs, door signs, decor<br>Promotion materials: Give aways, advertisements |
| 2)<br>Assortment.<br>Sales items: | Name/logo: Logo, symbol, visual identity<br>Product design and product range: Wrapping, packaging, retail, shop supplies, branding<br>Service design: Mapping, signage, uniform |
| 3)<br>Advertising, PR: | Advertisements: Paid ads, sponsored pages, campaigns<br>Display advertising: Banners, animations<br>Video advertising: Online display videos<br>Mobile advertising: Text ads via SMS or display<br>Native advertising: Campaigns in online publications<br>Content marketing: Buzz feed, live advertising<br>Inbound marketing: Loyalty-building activities on social media<br>Cinema/TV/radio: Videos, animations, jingles<br>Arena/campaigns: Placards/posters, ads<br>Direct marketing: Personal sales, telephone sales, direct mail<br>Dialogue marketing: Direct advertising with response option<br>Sales promotion: Gifts, discounts, and free coupons |
| 4)<br>Point-of sale, retail (Analogue): | Products: Packaging, labelling<br>Floor-space-concept, shop-in-shop: Location, equipment<br>POS materials: Digital screens, AR and VR exposure, posters, flyers, tags, brochures<br>Personal sales: Service, tastings, give-aways<br>Word of mouth: Sales talk, events, experience<br>Trade fairs: Stands, walls, materials |
| 5)<br>Point-of sale, e-commerce (digital): | Websites: Online corporate/product presentation<br>Online shops: Online sales/marketing<br>Social media: Advertising, sponsored posts. One-to-one connect, engage, create leads<br>Email campaigns: Newsletters, offers, information<br>Mobile telephone, smartphone: Telephone sales, SMSs, ads<br>Direct marketing: Personal inquiry, sales/offers<br>Content marketing: Personalised advertising, incentives<br>Search optimisation: Visibility, search engine ranking |
| 6)<br>Events: | Events internally and externally: Product launch, sponsorship, indirect commercials:<br>Festivals, happenings, parties, seminars and courses: Supported sports events, charity |
| 7)<br>Organisation value/ culture: | Management: Strategy seminars, management seminars<br>Logistics: Product and information flow<br>Internal/external behaviour: Attitude, ethics, service<br>Working environment: inclusive culture, diversity, security |
| 8)<br>Distribution: | Agreements: Distribution networks, alliances, partnerships<br>Training: Service, communication, sales<br>Channel selection: Distribution channel plan<br>Retailing: Sales promotion measures<br>Marketing: Marketing communication, advertising, PR |

Table 3.15 Communication mix

Table 3.15 Here Figure 3.52 is explained.

Fig. 3.52 The figure shows examples of communication areas, communication devices, and communication measures that can be included in a communication mix. The communication mix is anchored in the company's identity and strategies. (The figure is based on the brand mix, developed by Skule Storheill for Brand House 2004.)

140 'Influencer marketing involves a brand collaborating with an online influencer to market one of its products or services' (Geyser, 2021, influencermarketinghub.com).

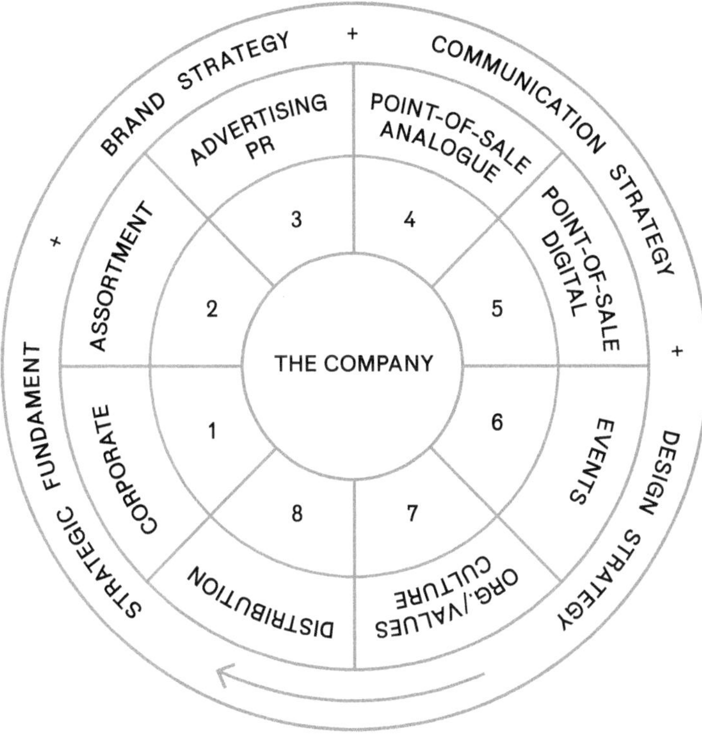


Fig. 3.52 Communication mix

**Interactive media:** Unlike traditional media, which are usually one-way channels of communication, the internet and web-based technology enable interaction between two or more people (users) and allow the intermediary to enter into two-way interactive dialogues with the recipient or target group. Interaction between users on the Internet allows for sharing, rating and tagging, and the ability to like and post comments about information, articles, photos, etc.

**Social media:** Social media includes a huge range of social networking communities, each representing different communication channels and arenas, where it is possible to meet different segments and target groups. Social media and app technology make it possible to reach a wider audience with a message or tailor it to individuals and create dialogue and interaction. Among the most used social networks are Instagram, YouTube, Facebook, Twitter, Linkedin and more, as well as blogs, influencers marketing,[140] forums, and web-based gaming platforms and channels.

**Personal media:** Personal media such as telephone, post, and email are also considered channels of communication. In addition, personal conversation may also be considered a channel, and then the non-verbal part of the communication plays a crucial role. Voice, body language, associations, thoughts and feelings influence how the information is perceived and interpreted.

Different media and channels represent different communication carriers, exposure surfaces, and communication capabilities. Communication media is chosen based on the knowledge of the different media and the media in which the target groups are active, and this requires good planning and anchoring in the company's communication strategy and overall strategy and goals. If we go back a few decades before the Internet, newspaper advertising and brochures were among the most common media used to present the company. Back then, it was crucial to examine which newspapers the target group read and how brochures should be distributed. In the 1990s, when it became common to use the Internet, web ads began to replace newspaper ads, and websites began to take over brochures. Today, a lot of marketing takes place on the Internet, web, and social media. These media represent an entirely separate world of opportunities to tailor communication to the target groups as well as of opportunities for dialogue and interaction. Content marketing and inbound marketing represent modern ways of planning, evaluating, and developing measures to follow up the target group and adapt marketing directly to the individual (3.6.7 Content marketing, 3.6.8 Inbound marketing). Whichever channels or media one chooses, one should decide which media, devices, and actions require separate budgets and strategies, such as advertising campaigns, web solutions, or social media communication.

Fig. 3.53 **The figure shows various ways a business can attract attention around its products and services, also referred to as paid, owned or earned attention. Paid attention is created through advertising in TV, radio, magazines, cinemas, posters, banners, search engine marketing, digital displays, outdoor advertising, and so on. Owned attention occurs through one's own website, company blog, Facebook page, Twitter, YouTube, Instagram, podcast, mobile apps, brochures, handouts, etc. Earned attention is created through commodity talk, editorial publicity, social media, blogs, debate forums, etc. (based on Moe Fredriksen, 2013).**

**Paid, owned, earned attention**

Not all media attention costs money. One example is attention created through *earned media* (free media), which refers to the publicity a company achieves through communication measures other than paid media advertising. Traditionally, this is called Public Relations (PR). Publicity obtained through advertising and other forms of advertising in purchased channels (mass communication) is referred to as *paid media*. Own channels controlled by the company, such as a website, social network, and own venues, are designated as *owned media*.

Bought, owned, earned is one way to divide media attention. Many consider earned media to be the most cost-effective method of

**International considerations: What considerations should be emphasised regarding geographical/ regional differences in the implementation of planned communication measures?**

**Example of media**

Digital media (modern technology):
- Internet, web, social media, blogs
- Digital TV, film, video, radio, mobile
- E-commerce, marketplace
- Web portals, web posters, search engine advertising
- Email, mobile telephone, smartphone
- Content marketing and Inbound marketing
- Direct Marketing (DM)
- Digital communication platforms/displays

Analogue media (traditional):
- Newspapers, magazines, radio, TV, film
- Magazines, periodicals, comics, books
- Retail, marketplace, square, shopping centre
- Poster walls, display windows, ads
- Personal sale, direct marketing (DM)
- Communication venues: events, launches, gatherings, banners

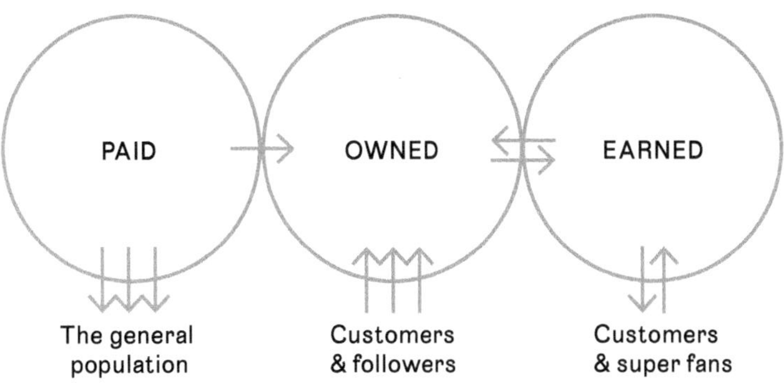


Fig. 3.53 Paid, owned, earned attention

1 Initiation
2 Insight
3 Strategy
4 Design
5 Production
6 Management

3.1 Strategy development
3.2 Overall strategy
3.3 Goals and subgoals
3.4 Business strategy
3.5 Business model
3.6 Market strategy
3.7 Brand strategy
3.8 Communication strategy
3.9 Design strategy

3.8.1 Communication audit
3.8.2 Identifying the target group
3.8.3 Communication goals
3.8.4 Desired reputation
3.8.5 Communication platform
3.8.6 Communication elements
3.8.7 Communication development
3.8.8 Channels and media
3.8.9 Communication measurement

- Media channels
- Paid, owned, earned attention
- Communication mix

marketing. As a result, many companies invest in earned media. The increased use of earned media reduces the use of traditional owned and bought marketing methods ('Yu, Jim,' 2014) (3.6.7 Content marketing and 3.6.8 Inbound marketing).

#### Communication mix

Communication mix is the combination of channels, media, and devices chosen to reach the desired target group, such as newspaper ads, commercials and radio advertising (see Figure 3.52). Deliberate choice of channels is essential for ROI (return on investment). Incorrect selection of channels may result in communication not hitting the target group as planned, which may mean spending money for little value. The choice of channels should be carefully thought out and based on extensive surveys of the target group's buying patterns, Internet habits, etc. Many communication measures will therefore require separate strategies, based on the communication strategy, in order to achieve the best possible impact, such as a media strategy or a social media strategy.

### 3.8.9 Communication measurement

Running marketing communications costs money. The costs stand in proportion to strategies, goals and budgets. There is a connection between effort and result. Results can be measured and used as a basis for strategy and budget to achieve the desired effect. Modern advantages in marketing, such as data science, improved data access, data extraction and analytical tool sets facilitate the rapid creation of data sets that gather different data points for unique insight and measurement. One can easily keep an eye on the effect of the market communication measures. But ... only when a clear line can be drawn from the activity that creates the data, the mathematics that creates the datasets and the insights gathered, can brands become confident in improved decision-making. 'Today's marketers have tremendous data access. Brands can compare competitors across domains and dimensions, measuring specific shares of voice across channels, customer segments, and precursors and drivers of voice and market dominance. Even marketers who are unable to aggregate and assess the voluminous data - from resource constraints, lack of data science skills, etc. - are mostly aware that these practices are foundational to the brand's strategic and tactical planning' (Arcalea, 2022).

Further reading
The 5 Principles of Growth in B2B Marketing: Empirical Observations on B2B Effectiveness (2020). Field, Peter, & Binet, Les. The B2B Institute.

Influencer marketing is a form of social media marketing involving endorsements and product placement from influencers, people and organisations who have a purported expert level of knowledge or social influence in their field (Geyser, 2022).

Brands compete more than ever to influence consumers in countless ways, across a crowded and versatile communication spectrum. They compete against brands within and outside their competitive categories and brands across different industries. A strong *Share of Voice* (SOV) is required to penetrate through an increasingly competitive market. Targeted SOV can help challenger brands break through the competitive noise.

Fig. 3.54 **The figure shows how eSOV works. For example, if you have a 10% share of market (SOM=market share) and a 12% share of voice (SOV=share of category adspend) then your eSOV is +2. Taken from Arcaléa.com (2022): *Share of Voice as a Strategic Accelerator*.**

**Share of voice/Share of market**

One of the most important elements in communication strategy, and marketing and media investment planning, is communication budget. A way to calculate it is to use the SOV and SOM-approach. SOV (share of voice) is defined as your organisation's percentage of the total media buying in your industry for a specific time period. SOM (share of market) is your percentage of the total revenue for that same time period. The correlation between SOV and SOM is the relationship between your ad buying strategy and your market share growth (Amor, 2016). Excessive SOV or ESOV (excess share of voice) is high communication budget compared with market share. The 'excess' represents the degree to which the brand's share of voice exceeds its share of market (Foster, 2021).[141]

As a rule of thumb:
SOV< SOM means the brand will decline
SOV=SOM means the brand will maintain its market share
SOV>SOM means the brand will grow in the future

According to Bendixen (2022) 'Brands that over invest in market communication have a tendency to grow faster than their competitors if they build mental availability and with consistent use off DBAs (distinctive brand assets). There are many cases where brands have succeeded in this. One good case is Lidl UK. Lidl had a SOM 3%, They over invested in communications over a five-year period of time and doubled its market share up to 6% in one of the most competitive markets in the world' (Bendixen, 2022).

**Effectiveness measurements**

If communication is to be evaluated, measurable targets must be defined. Measurement and evaluation are essential to adjust and strengthen the effect of the marketing communication activities. Sales -and marketshare growth will always be the most important. One approach is to measure *mental market share*, which is the number of Category entry points (CEPs)

> OTS (opportunity to see) is a traditional marketing metric meaning the ratio between the number of times an ad was seen, and the number of people who saw an ad. OTS is impact measurement (used in advertising and PR) that indicates the number of times the viewer is most likely to have seen/wanted to see an ad/media item. If 100 people buy a magazine which contains an ad for the company, then the reach can be said to be 100, but the number of times each one of them has seen or read the ad is denoted as OTS (OTS/mbaskool.com).

141 ESOV and 'The share of voice rule' was first launched by Professor John Philip Jones (Syracuse University), mid 1980s. He looked at a number of relationships between marketing and media investment and sales responses. In recent years the marketing effectiveness specialists Les Binet and Peter Field have re-examined this relationship and added some interesting findings about how the eSOV concept is impacted by creativity.

142 The IPA is recognised as the world's most influential professional body for advertising and marketing communication practitioners. The role of the IPA is to promote the value of media, marketing and advertising agencies, and is an advocate for the industry. It also runs a number of programmes to define, assist and maintain the highest possible standards of professional practice. These include reward systems such as IPA Effectiveness Awards (ipa.co.uk).

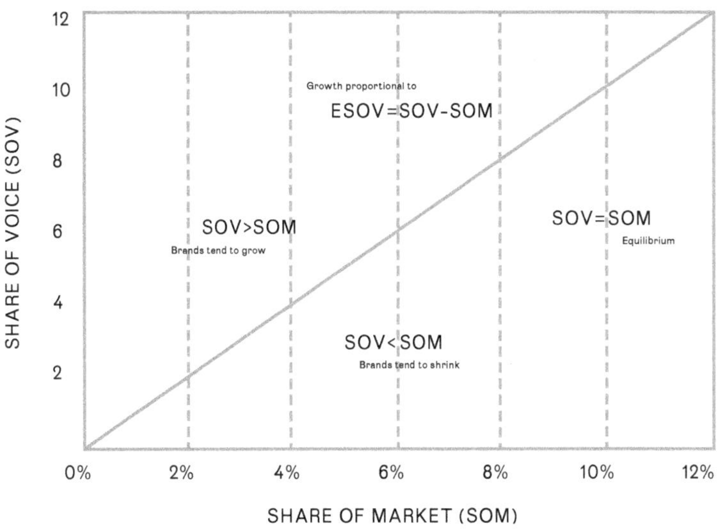


Fig. 3.54 The share of voice rule

1 Initiation
2 Insight
3 Strategy
4 Design
5 Production
6 Management

3.1 Strategy development
3.2 Overall strategy
3.3 Goals and subgoals
3.4 Business strategy
3.5 Business model
3.6 Market strategy
3.7 Brand strategy
3.8 Communication strategy
3.9 Design strategy

3.8.1 Communication audit
3.8.2 Identifying the target group
3.8.3 Communication goals
3.8.4 Desired reputation
3.8.5 Communication platform
3.8.6 Communication elements
3.8.7 Communication development
3.8.8 Channels and media
3.8.9 Communication measurement

– Action plan

associated with the brand and the number of people in the category that associate these with the brand. How many are there who associate *distinctive brand assets* (DBAs) with the brand and how unique these DBAs are? Top of mind and other awareness metrics can be used. The main question is, depending on the category: How well the brand delivers upon the CEPs compared with competitors. Most other metrics are soft metrics and less important (Bendixen, 2022) (2.9.8 Mental availability measurement).

Traditionally, advertisers and their consultants have given higher priority to communication goals such as awareness, attention, and liking than to key business goals. We then mean commercial goals such as sales growth or volume, increase in market shares, ability to retain market shares, or increased willingness to pay for products. Research related to the IPA Effectiveness Award[142] in England argues that communication goals should be better integrated into commercial goals that can verify the effectiveness of advertising. For any effectiveness measurement, it is essential to establish key figures for awareness, sales, etc. prior to an advertising campaign, in order to compare with results after activities to see the effectiveness of the measures (Ottesen, 2005) (2.9 Testing and measuring).

### Action plan

Once the communication strategy is in place, tactical and operational planning is required to implement it in practice. There may then be a need to outline the most important communication tasks in an action plan. This means determining short-term and long-term prioritisation and weighting of activities and actions, as well as the initiative for action and resource use over time. When implementing the action plan, it is important to consider how it should be organised and quality assured. Similarly, what can be done with internal resources and what needs to be purchased from external suppliers? The action plan is inserted into a single form! Good structure and overview are success factors needed to achieve the desired results. In addition to one main action plan, it may be necessary to create separate project plans for each of the projects (Simonsen 2007/2013).

Design strategy is a management tool for development, implementation and use of design as a tool for achieving the company's goals and other forms of value creation.

A design strategy is developed on the basis of previous work on gathering insight, conducting analyses, and developing strategies, as well as of anchoring in the company's overall strategy and goal. For a company that uses design as a strategic instrument at an overall level, a design strategy will be an important tool to ensure targeted design processes and will provide guidance on how the company should manage its design investments over time.[143] Strategic development and use of design can thus be an important success factor for innovation in the company. A design strategy shall ensure alignment and guidance for all parts, through the process and decision making, and must therefore be anchored in the decision-making bodies in the company and aligned with management.

A design strategy can also be developed in order to solve individual design assignments. Often, it is then the designer who develops it in collaboration with the client. In such contexts, the design strategy may be used for coordination between the designer and the client in order to

Fig. 3.55 The figure shows insight, strategy and other foundations unfolded in a GIGA map. Insight and strategy stored digitally or in a drawer become inaccessible and difficult to use. Creating a visual overview makes it easier for those involved in the project to see new contexts and opportunities that may be important for the development of a design strategy.


Tips for the designer
The development of a design strategy is about drawing up a plan on how the design task is to be completed based on insight and strategy from the previous phases.

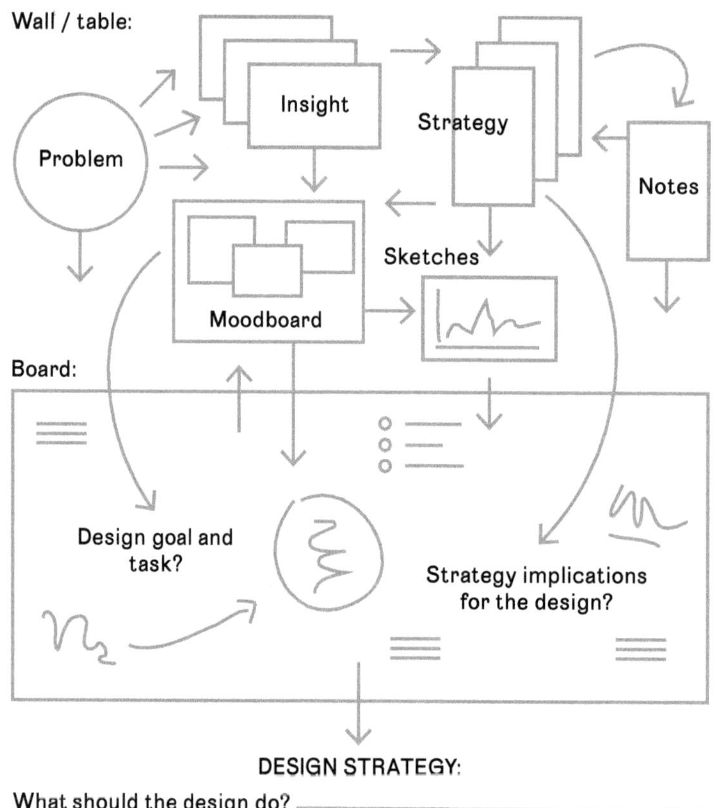


Fig. 3.55 Design strategy

143 The definition of design strategy is based on Design Forum, which was established by the Norwegian Design Council (to day named Design and Architecture Norway, Doga) in 2009 to discuss and clarify design-related concepts. Wanda Grimsgaard had the task of preparing the explanation of design strategy in 2011.
144 Grow – Tomorrow's design leaders: grow.empdl.com/#Education.
145 Grow – Design Strategy Summary.pdf

ensure common understanding of how the design is to be developed. It also provides a good starting point for the development of a design brief (2.1.2 Decision making, 3.9.9 Design strategy vs. design brief, 4.1 Design brief).

### 3.9.1 Design strategy compass

According to Grow[144] a design strategy is a high-level plan to achieve design objectives and goals within a certain business context. 'It helps to achieve overarching business objectives, to align peer strategies and to make the right choices in terms of design resources and capabilities' (Grow, n.d.).

The Design Strategy Compass[145] is a tool to link the corporate mission and vision with the design strategy. According to Grow, questions that should be answered are:

- Why do organisations develop and manage strategies and how are they linked to the purpose and vision of an organisation?
- What should a design manager do when managing design strategies?
- What are the key components of a solid design strategy?
- How are these components linked to the bigger picture of an organisation?
- What are the competencies and skills needed to manage design strategies?

This requires:

- Know how to apply the different components of a design strategy in order to be effective and efficient.
- Explain the business why you need a design strategy and what the relation between overarching business strategy and design strategy is.
- Demonstrate clarity and structure when discussing design strategy, even if its components are scattered.
- Show a clear and balanced picture, and how the design strategy can contribute to achieving the business objectives and goals.
- Gain understanding of how design can influence and direct the business strategy.

### 3.9.2 Design strategy development

When developing a design strategy, it is necessary to take a step back and get an overview of the insight, analyses and defined strategies that will be used as a basis for the assignment to be completed successfully. For example, there may be positioning and target group analysis, as well as competitive strategy, positioning and communication strategy. The challenge then is to be selective and pick out only what is necessary for creating a good management tool for the design work. A good approach is to create a visual overview of what data has been collected and what goals and strategies have been defined. The principles of GIGA mapping can be a good approach (2.8.5 GIGA maps). It involves displaying all the data on a table or hanging it on a wall. Surveys, analyses and strategy reports are printed and hung, preferably split up so that the content becomes more easily accessible as well as moodboards, graphs, sketches, and notes. This way, it is easier to get an overview and see contexts and opportunities. It may be necessary to do more research and get some inspiration to be able to write a good design strategy. One way to get inspiration is by looking at



Emotional attributes
What emotional values should the design express? Emotional values appeal to the senses, the heart, and allow one to be tempted. They can be aesthetic qualities such as beautiful, natural, fresh, or attributes that are consistent with the target group's value system, such as environmentally friendly and fair trade.

Functional attributes
What functional values should the design express? Functional values appeal to the rational, such as what the product promises, price, visibility, easy to understand, easy to read, good contrasts and so on.

brands and designs in the same category or similar. Involve the customer in assessing who responds to the strategy of their product or company. Has anyone come up with some nice and clever thoughts already? And why does it work? This is certainly not about copying, but rather about inspiring and showing the customer how far one can go. How far can one stretch a brief, which often says banal words like innovative, inspiring, and modern. Once one has established a kind of scale from expected to challenging visual expression, the designer together with the customer assess where on the scale one is. The question then is how challenging the company is willing to be and why? And is it in line with their strategy? (Brantenberg, 2022).

The designer or the design team studies the overview, extracts information that can be useful to highlight, as well as debates, discusses, writes and draws down thoughts and ideas. Such visualisation of the strategy process facilitates teamwork in thinking. At the same time, it opens up the possibility of clarifying what impact the collected data and defined strategies have on the project solution. The main question is: What consequences should strategy and goals have for the design development in phase 4? The answer lies at the heart of the design strategy, which will serve as a plan for further work on developing ideas, design sketches and a final solution, as well as on responding to the problem statement. The process leads to the development of a design strategy, but it may also lead to the need for further research or adjustments to the strategic foundation on which the design strategy is based. In the process, ideas and thoughts may also emerge that may be useful in the resolution process.

**'A design strategy should contribute to targeted design processes and should provide guidance on how the company should manage its design investments over time. The design strategy can also affect the company's overall strategy and other strategies' (Designfaglig forum, DoGA 2012).**

### 3.9.3 Design strategy content

A design strategy should reflect aspects of the design form, function and aestethics, as well as matters of priorities of these aspects (Kaspartu, 2022). The scope of the design strategy may vary depending on the assumptions underlying the design effort. But essential elements as presented here should always be clear to all involved parties.

### 3.9.4 Design goal

*What* do we want to achieve with the design? What is the task of the design? What should the design do? What problem should the design solve? What should the design communicate? There are questions that can be asked to define the task and the goal of the design. The goal should be derived from the overall goals and vision of the company and should contribute to achieving these goals. The goal of the design may be a subgoal for the company's overall design effort and may be governing and normative for any development or use of design for the company. The goal may also be more limited for a single design project or task. The problem statement for the project is then a good starting point for determining goals. For example, if the project is to develop packaging design, the question will be which task the design of the packaging should solve. If the company's competitive strategy determines that the product should compete on price, a possible goal will be for the packaging design to communicate low price.

### 3.9.5 Operational strategy

*How* should the design be developed and used? For example, if the goal is to develop a packaging design that communicates low price, the operational strategy will deal with which instruments to use in order to signal low prices. One possible strategy could be to emulate the visual expression of competitors while using devices that signal that the product is cheaper. It is to do with how the packaging should be designed in terms of material selection, shape, size, logo, colours, and so on in order to create the desired expression. The overall design strategy defined in the *design platform* will serve as a foundation.

If the product is to be differentiated on quality and high price instead, there will be other policies for the design. Examples of goals can then be: The design should signal high quality and help build awareness. An example of an operational strategy may then be to develop designs that differentiate the product from competitors and express the desired position.

### 3.9.6 Design platform

*What* identity, mood, style, and tone should the design express and communicate? The main strategic policies for developing the design may be compiled into a design platform. Examples of such policies are core values, image, position, reputation, signal effect, and tone of voice. These are strategy definitions that can be used for both visual and verbal solutions. The strategy definitions are taken from overall strategies and sub-strategies. The relevant strategy definitions are reproduced briefly and precisely with an explanation of how they are to be implemented in the design. For example:

**Core values:** What values/identity should the design express? The values the design should be based on are derived from the core values defined in the overall strategy for the company or in the brand strategy for the product or service (3.2.5 Core values, 3.7.5 Brand identity).

**Value proposition:** What should the design promise? The value proposition the design should communicate are defined in the overall strategy for the company or the positioning strategy for the brand (3.2.6 Value proposition, 3.7.3 Brand position).

**Tone of voice:** What atmosphere, mood, temperament, and style should surround the design and communication? Tone of voice is defined in the communication strategy. There should be a connection between the tone of the verbal and visual communication (3.8.5 Communication platform: tone of voice).

**Signal effect:** What should the user of the design signal to others? (3.8.5 Communication platform: signal effect).

**Image:** What image should the design create in the recipient's consciousness? (3.8.5 Communication platform: image).

**Miscellaneous:** Add any other strategic reference points.

The design platform includes the strategic points of reference that should provide policies for the development of the design solution.



Design strategy

**Design objectives: What is the task of the design?**

**Operational plan: How should the design be developed?**

**Design platform: What values should the design express?**

### 3.9.7 Visual assets

What should be the visual assets, the visual characteristics, the distinctive brand assets? It is important to have a visual understanding of the industry and the distinctive assets of the product or service category. A good start is to conduct a visual analysis of the category: Gather the most important competitors at home and abroad and analyse the visual drivers. Often an industry has quite similar drivers. Is there a colour, typography choice, composition, expression, illustrations, tone-of-voice that recur (like the category for ketchup is red)? In case why? Here, the designer's knowledge of colour psychology, typography history and similar, will benefit. If it points in many different directions, a good approach is to sort it in silos: The serious, the fun, the traditional, etc. It is important to see who runs the category and analyse the tools and point to the challenger. Then assess. Should we follow the industry norm or challenge it? (Brantenberg, 2022)

### 3.9.8 Elements and surfaces

Choice of elements and exposure surfaces is also a strategic issue, for example:
**Elements:** *What should the main elements of the design be? How should the basic elements be made visible in the design*? The main elements of the design are central to the perception of identity, communication and overall experience of the design. Elements may include, for example, logo, colours, graphic elements, slogans, typography, patterns, etc. One should decide what should be the distinctive brand assets (3.4.6 Distinctive asset-building strategy, 3.7.6 Brand assets, 4.9.2 Identity elements).
**Exposure surfaces:** *Which exposure surfaces or profile carriers are relevant*? Which current surfaces is it appropriate to implement the design on, or what kind of space should the design be placed in? For example: The car is a natural exposure surface for a courier car company, then the distinctive brand assets needs to work in motion. The aircraft body is a natural exposure surface for an airline, then the distinctive brand assets should be visible from the air. The bottle for a drink is a natural exposure surface for the product brand, then the distinctive brand assets should be visible from the shop shelf. The sign for a café, should be visible in passing, etc.

### 3.9.9 Design strategy vs. design brief

It may be somewhat unclear what the difference is between a design strategy and a design brief. A *design strategy* is a plan for what the design should do, how it is to be developed and used, all in line with what it is determined in the company's goals and strategies. *A design brief* is a description of the assignment or task to be carried out. It clarifies the details of the project, such as project goals, the tasks and deliverables involved, scope, timeframe, requirements and assumptions. It also includes areas of responsibility and persons responsible. The design brief serves as a basis for developing a budget or quote (4.1 Design brief). The design strategy is used as the basis for the design brief. It is fine to combine these.

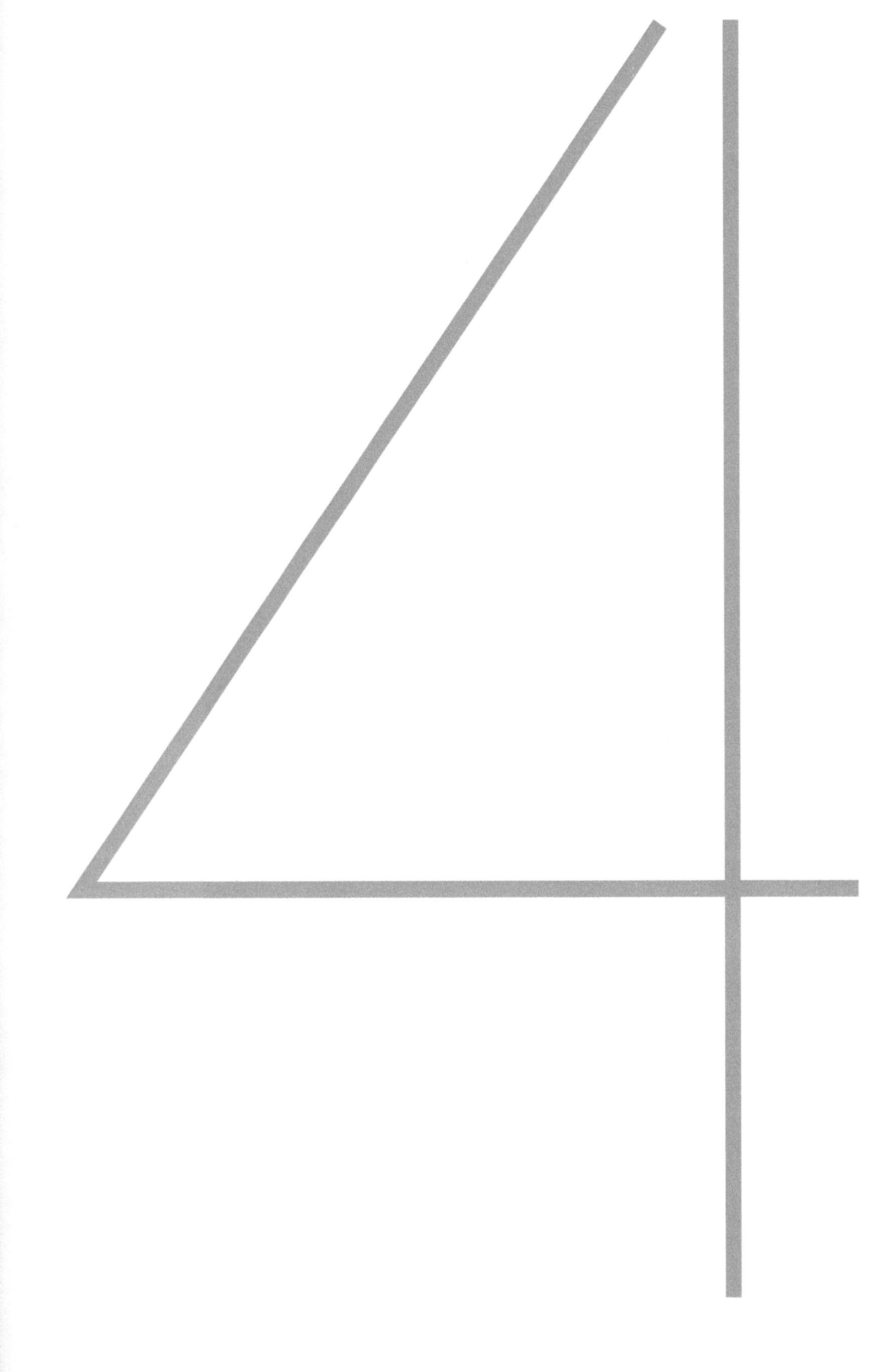

4.1 Design brief 345

4.2 Strategy><Design 348
4.2.1 Mapping as a link 349
4.2.2 Visualise strategy 350
4.2.3 Visualise name 352
4.2.4 Distinctive brand assets 352
4.2.5 Idea as a bridge 353
4.2.6 The fifth element 353

4.3 Design methodology 354
4.3.1 Human-centred design 355
4.3.2 User-experience 358
4.3.3 Emotional design 359
4.3.4 Innovation 360
4.3.5 Iterative method 363
4.3.6 Divergence and convergence 366
4.3.7 Sprint 368
4.3.8 Scrum 370
4.3.9 Kanban 371
4.3.10 Lean and agile 371
4.3.11 Design thinking 374
4.3.12 Customer journey 376
4.3.13 Need-finding 378
4.3.14 Service blueprint 380
4.3.15 Co-design 381
4.3.16 Business design 383
4.3.17 Strategic design thinking 385
4.3.18 Systemic design 386
4.3.19 In retrospect 389

4.4 Concept development 390
4.4.1 Foundation and framework 390
4.4.2 Creative problem solving 392
4.4.3 Brainstorming 396
4.4.4 Idea development 398
4.4.5 Conceptual directions 409
4.4.6 Verbalisation and visualisation 410
4.4.7 Prototyping of ideas 410
4.4.8 Testing of ideas 410
4.4.9 Presentation of ideas 411

4.5 Design development 412
4.5.1 The three-direction principle 412
4.5.2 Design sketches 413
4.5.3 Concrete design 417

4.6 Design elements 421
4.6.1 Shape 421
4.6.2 Colour 426
4.6.3 Texture 430
4.6.4 Space 430

4.7 Composition 433
4.7.1 Perception 433
4.7.2 Principles of composition 434
4.7.3 Unity/whole 436
4.7.4 Focal point 440
4.7.5 Proportions 441
4.7.6 Balance 442
4.7.7 Rhythm 445

4.8 Surface and format 448
4.8.1 Surface 449
4.8.2 Format 451
4.8.3 Aspect ratios 455
4.8.4 The A series 459
4.8.5 The golden ratio 463
4.8.6 Golden rectangle 464
4.8.7 The golden spiral 466
4.8.8 Fibonacci 467
4.8.9 The rule of thirds 469

4.9 Identity development 470
4.9.1 The identity principles 471
4.9.2 The identity elements 474
4.9.3 Logo 476
4.9.4 Symbol 489
4.9.5 Identity colours 494
4.9.6 Typography 498
4.9.7 Distinctive assets 515
4.9.8 Identity management 516
4.9.9 Grid system 517

Design is the fourth of six phases. It is about developing design solutions based on the previous phases of initiating the project, gathering insight and developing strategy. The challenge lies in linking the verbal to the visual, bridging the gap between strategy and design. It is at this point of intersection that the designer benefits from the knowledge acquired to develop good ideas and targeted solutions. A design project does not necessarily have to lead to visual design, the solution may as well be a plan or a concept. Design development can follow different principles, methods and models, and many of these work across different design disciplines and fields. Insight, idea development, prototyping, testing and evaluation are necessary factors and so are knowledge of technology, interaction and use of visual elements. Feasibility is important. Is the idea possible to realise? Is it viable? Does it solve the problem? The interaction between client, designer and user is a key factor. The main ambition should be to solve to the problem, meet client and user needs and help the company achieve its goals.

It is tempting to begin this design phase by explaining what design is, as in the previous phases, that start with a definition of initiation, insight and strategy. Unfortunately, there is no clear definition of design. This matter keeps popping up in the work of everyone who writes, does research on or is interested in design. The challenge lies in the very word, which in strictly grammatical terms contributes to the confusion. Design is a noun in that it denotes a product, object, sketch, pattern or composition. It is a verb in that it describes an act, like creating or constructing a product. Products can also be considered as a design activity in the way they are designed, through actions and interactions (Leerberg, 2009). 'Design acts as a verb, noun and adjective. You can perfectly well design a design of a designer chair, without damaging the sentence grammatically' (Skomsøy, 2017). Back to the question of what design is. A 'what' may provide the final answer to what it is and what it is not. But there is no consensus on the definition. In the research article *Rethinking contemporary design*, Leerberg suggests dislocating the question by changing 'what' to a 'how' and instead asking how design works. Asking the question this way puts an emphasis on the activity, that is, the verb. Verbs signify action which gives dynamism to the design concept. We see this development in the design environment, where one no longer focuses on design as traditional shape and colour, but as a way of thinking and problem-solving.

Design *how* is about how design can help solve problems and lead to the achievement of goals. This means working purposefully on the problem at hand from project start to project end. It requires strategic anchoring, sufficient insight, conscious user focus, and frequent testing and evaluation. Not least, it involves continuous attention to realisation and implementation. In their book *The Other Side of Innovation: Solving the Execution Challenge* (2010), Govindarajan and Trimble have introduced the concept of 'disciplined experiment'. It underscores the learning aspect of design, how to move towards better and better solutions – not by chance, but by targeted experimentation. In it lies a focus on the realisation and implementation of the ideas early in the innovation process (4.3.5 Iterative method); '... most companies, in their efforts to improve innovation, focus entirely on *the Big Idea Hunt*. Focusing on ideas may unleash more immediate energy, but focusing on execution is far more powerful' (Govindarajan and Trible 2010).

For the company, the designer is an important partner in rethinking, creating growth, innovation and competitiveness. 'Designers can address the entire problem of the company, and the system around it, and systematically analyse and come up with new solutions for the needs of both consumers and users in a fast and efficient way and thus act as a good partner and money-saving agent for the client. Revolutionary innovations and incremental innovations, changes that make the product, service or system better than before give a better user-experience, added value to the user and the client and ultimately create value for the community' (Rabben, 2017). The designer as partner and problem solver is gaining an increasingly important role in companies that consciously use design as part of their strategy. There have been significant developments over the past decade in

Fig. 4.1 **The figure and caption are based on *The Four Orders of Design* (Buchanan, 2001). Graphic design and industrial design as subjects were established/introduced in the early 1900s. Graphic design focused on identity, form and symbols, with four distinct activities, namely typography, illustration, photography and printing (Harland, 2011). Industrial design focused on working with material, physical objects, i.e. with things. Later, designers started solving problems with a broader scope and thus expanded the concept of design. In interaction design, the design focus is linked to action: designing experiences rather than physical objects. Since design veered towards interaction design from the mid-1990s,[1] in response to the growing need to design IT systems for and with the users, after a while the attention on the user-experience increased.[2] Environment design is concerned with 'the idea or thought that organises a system or environment' (Buchanan, 2001), focusing on human systems, the integration of information, physical artefacts, and interactions in environments of living, working, playing, and learning (Buchanan, 2001).**

1 ***Encyclopedia of Human-Computer Interaction*. Mads Soegaard and Rikke Friis Dam, The Interaction-Design.org Foundation (2008).**
2 **Daniel Fällman, 'The Interaction Design Research Triangle of Design Practice, Design Studies, and Design Exploration', *Design Issues* 24.**
3 **VanPatter and Pastor 2011: *Next Design Geographies: Understanding Design Thinking 1,2,3,4*.**

the direction of leading companies adopting design thinking to solve their organisational, strategic and creative challenges. *Design thinking* as a method is an approach to design, which is seen as a competitive factor in solving complex problems and a driving force for innovation development. It is one of the many new concepts and methodological approaches to design, which constantly emerge and cause the concept of design to expand.

The design field is evolving more and more in breadth and in more and more new areas, and it is as much about systems, technology, economics and interaction as it is about colour, form and composition. At the same time, design as problem solver is increasingly linked to the major complex issues: those that deal with infrastructure, housing problems, environmental crises and social responsibility. A design approach offers unlimited possibilities and the designer has a strong influence as a role model when it comes to important societal issues such as environmental considerations, equality, diversity, ethics and other sustainability matters (6.9 Sustainable management). Design is both about the big picture (macro) and about the details (micro). Even for small, isolated projects, such as the development of a single element or object within a defined context, the design ambition is often part of a larger whole. This is so because a design assignment is often more complex than what it might initially seem. The model 'The Four Orders of Design', developed by Buchanan in 2001, illustrates design from a micro and macro perspective, see Figure 4.1. Although this portrayal is a few years old and the design field is constantly changing, it still provides an interesting picture of the scope of different design challenges; from a simple graphic symbol to large complex societal problems.

| | SYMBOLS | THINGS | ACTION | THOUGHT |
|---|---|---|---|---|
| SYMBOLS | Graphic Design | | | |
| THINGS | | Industrial Design | | |
| ACTION | | | Interaction Design | |
| THOUGHT | | | | Environmental Design |

Fig. 4.1 The four orders of design

The design field is changing. According to VanPatter and Pastor (2011),[3] the changes are LARGE. The claim is based on studies showing that designers need to solve increasingly large and complex problems and navigate across multiple disciplines more and more often. Unlike in the past, when designers worked mostly alone within their discipline, designers nowadays work in teams, often cross-disciplinary. VanPatter and Pastor divide design challenges into four categories:

*1.0 Traditional design*: Communication perspective is about the communication challenge: What things look like; how people experience or perceive a message, small challenges, low complexity.

Further reading
Check out the introduction to this book: 'What is design?' on page X

*2.0 Product, service, experience design*: Product and service design perspective is about product, service, and experience challenges; creating a slightly larger design-oriented whole; higher complexity.

*3.0 System, organisation, industry*: Company perspective is more about organisational challenges, operations, systems; designing the entire ecosystem; high complexity.

*4.0 Country, society, the Earth*: The overall perspective is about social challenges, the state, the society, the entire world; designing the whole of reality; enormous complexity.

'Somewhere on this scale are all design challenges' (Sitre, 2016). Synchronisation across the four categories is, according to VanPatter and Pastor, an ongoing process that is currently observed around the world. The direction a design assignment takes is largely determined by the type of assignment, but also by the designer's capacity to see the potential of a design project. A communication assignment can develop into a much larger project where consideration for the user and the environment creates a completely new framework for the project.

Fig. 4.2 **The figure shows the main phases of a strategic design process. These are the phases the book is divided into. The phases are presented linearly, but in the process, one move back and forth as well as in circles. Initiation of the design project can start right with 'Design' in Phase 4 if the previous phases have been clarified and passed on in a design brief. © Grimsgaard, W. (2018).**

### The design process

The design process will vary depending on the problem the designer has to solve in each project and which design disciplines are required. At the same time, there are many similarities in the designers' working methods across design fields, and we are increasingly experiencing a kind of flattening as fields and disciplines blend together and almost merge. For example, it may be natural for a product designer to include brand building in their product development, while a graphic designer may find it natural to consider the development of the entire product and not just of the packaging design. Interaction design, service design and experience design are examples of disciplines that flow across other disciplines. This development in the design field leads to increased use of common processes and methods. In Phase 4, we will look at a variety of design methodology that can be used across disciplines. Some methods can be used for the entire design process while others are linked to specific needs and problems. We will also talk about design development and visual identity, as well as how strategic guidelines can be translated into shape and colours. Furthermore, we will address some general design field principles for composition, surfaces, grid and typography from identity and brand perspective.

### Planning the design process

The navigation plan on each right-hand page in this book is part of a phase structure that represents the entire design process from start to finish. The phase structure can be used as a starting point when planning and executing a design process regardless of the design discipline. The intention is to pick out the phases that are relevant to each project. See the explanation in the introduction to the book: Figure 0.1 Phase structure, Table 0.1 First and second levels, Table 0.2 Example of use of phases, and the Planning tool at page 648.

| | |
|---|---|
| 1 | Initiation |
| 2 | Insight |
| 3 | Strategy |
| 4 | Design |
| 5 | Production |
| 6 | Management |

**From understanding the problem to final outcome**

The design process is an in-depth exercise, where designers with their design expertise start with thorough research, understanding the problem, user insight at all stages, functional analyses, visualisation, prototyping, testing and improving iteration processes, production methods and sustainable resource use. All of this helps define what the final outcome should be. The design presented is the final product of a design process. The end product should be better than what existed before, or be something new that did not exist before, and preferably an innovation (Rabben 2017).

**Initiation:** A design project as shown in Figure 4.2 can start in Phase 1 Initiation or in Phase 4 Design. Phase 4 starts with choice of design methodology and development of ideas, assuming that all necessary insights and strategy have been prepared in advance. Regardless, the designer goes back in order to get to know the previous phases and link insight and strategy to the design work. If there are any discrepancies between the design ambition and the strategy, adjustments and changes might have to be made to the strategy basis. In this case, the project will start in Phase 1.

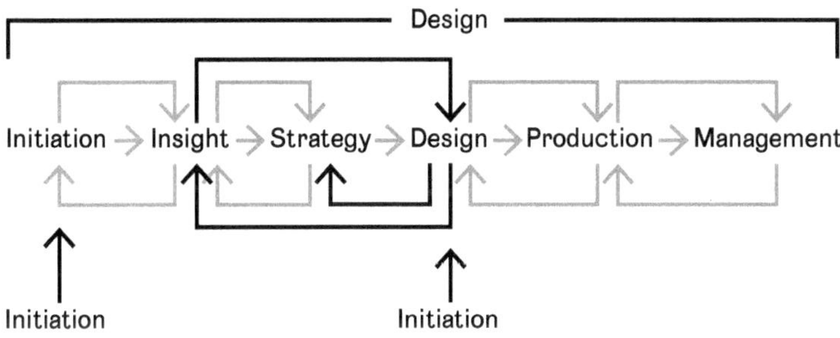


Fig. 4.2 The phases of a design process

**Division into phases:** The navigation structure in this book presents a total process, as shown in Figure 0.1 Phase structure and Table 0.1 First and second levels. Such a comprehensive process is rarely or never needed in a design project. The choice and emphasis of methods within the six phases will vary from project to project, see the example in Table 0.2 Example of use of phases. The design process as shown in Table 4.1 focuses mainly on phase 4.

The overview is divided into phases to serve as the basis for the development of project description, budget and work schedule or as a work platform. The division into phases and the names of the phases can be customised based on the nature and scope of each project. Phase 4 of the overview is what we will be looking at in more detail in the next chapters. Read the interviews with eight designers from different disciplines about their processes and methods. Available at designandstrategy.co.uk.

Increasing complexity cutting-edge expertise and multidisciplinary collaboration are needed to solve increasingly complex design tasks.

| The design process | |
|---|---|
| Basis (Phases 1 to 3): | |
| Initiation | Initial meeting, initial workshop, project description, progress schedule, price quotation and contract signing (Phase 1 Initiation). |
| Problem statement | Identifying the problem and the task to be solved, formulated through a clear problem statement (2.3 Problem statement). |
| Insight | Insight through studies, research and analyses (Phase 2 Insight). Insight is also necessary in the course of design development. |
| Strategy | Clarification and definition of goals and strategy. Project alignment with the overall goals and strategy of the company, and relevant sub-strategies (Phase 3 Strategy). |
| Design strategy | Definition of what consequences goals and strategy will have for the development of design? (3.9 Design strategy). |
| Design process (Phase 4): | |
| Design brief | Description of the design project, the problem statement, goal and strategy of the design assignment, desired results and deliveries, as well as strategic anchoring (4.1 Design brief). |
| Design methodology | Choice of methods, principles and processes for idea development, problem solving and design development (4.3 Design methodology). |
| Visual research | Collection of insight, knowledge and inspiration. Search (with critical eyes) in visual databases online and in libraries for case studies, specialised literature, art, design history etc. |
| Concept development | Idea generation through iteration, brainstorming, workshops and various idea development methods. Further development of ideas through visualisation and verbalisation, use of moodboards, GIGA maps, sketching, prototyping, testing and evaluation. Identifying conceptual directions. Presentation and selection of conceptual direction (4.4 Concept development). |
| Design sketches | Further development of the selected ideas and concepts. Iterations using freehand sketches, digital sketches, illustration, photography, infographics, materials, technology etc. Frequent implementation, exemplification, prototyping, testing and evaluation in real contexts. Sorting sketches in specific design directions. Processing and fine-tuning the design directions for presentation and choice of direction (4.5.2 Design sketches). |
| Concrete design | Further development and concretisation of the chosen design direction up to the final solution. Adjustment, concretisation, refinement and detailing of the design. Defragmentation of the whole and processing the various parts and details. Zoom out, zoom in. Fast implementations, exemplifications and prototypes to learn what works and what doesn't. Choice of final solution for completion (4.5.3 Concrete design). |

Table 4.1 The table shows the strategic design process as a whole, with emphasis on Phase 4. Strategic anchoring is a must. The common thread in the design process is the problem statement. An answer to this problem should be given in the final solution. © Grimsgaard, W. (2018).

Tips for the company
You can develop the design brief yourself before contacting the designer. It should give the designer the necessary information about the project and serve as basis for a price estimate.

Tips for the designer
The design brief applies to the part of a design project that deals with idea and design development, presented here in Phase 4, as well as the further process leading up to production and delivery in phase 5 and 6. Start with phase 6.9 Sustainable management.

| Design process (Phase 4) continuing: | |
|---|---|
| Testing, evaluation and adjustment | Development of digital or physical test models (dummy, mockup or prototype) to simulate, test out and present the final solution. Testing the design solutions through implementation of design elements on relevant digital and analogue platforms and surfaces, such as print, screen, physical model, as well as in relevant contexts. Testing the design in relevant customer and user groups, focus groups and surveys online. Evaluation and improvement of the solution based on the testing (2.9 Testing and measuring, 5.2 Model). |
| Completion and quality assurance | Proofreading, adjustments and quality assurance of the design based on the results of the testing. Completion of the design for implementation, production, programming, construction, assembly etc. Final approval by the client (5.9 Quality assurance). |
| Production and management (Phases 5 and 6): | |
| Implementation | Customisation and placement of the design solution on current digital and analogue surfaces, for display, printing, products, interior/room and exterior/surroundings (5.1 Implementation). |
| Design handbook, design templates | Development of design templates for digital and analogue surfaces, products, rooms and surroundings. Development of design manual with guides for implementation of visual identity on profile elements, as well as guidelines for further development and use of the design (6.5 Design manual/profile guide, 6.6 Design templates). |
| Production | Production, press, printing, programming, construction and assembly. Quality assurance (Phase 5 – Production). |
| Distribution | Distribution, dissemination and use of the finished design product or design material, analogue or digital. |
| Management | Design management, sustainable management, legal protection and long-term management of intangible assets (Phase 6 – Management). |

Table 4.1 The design process



## 4.1 Design brief

A design brief should describe the design project, the task to be solved and its goal. It involves identifying the scope, level of ambition, and strategic anchoring of the assignment.

In many cases, the designer is contacted after the completion of the previous phases of initiation, insight, and strategy. Initiation of the design project then takes place in Phase 4 once the basis for the assignment has been identified. In such cases, the client may prepare a design brief as basis for obtaining price offers, selecting a designer, and initiating

> Anchoring
> **A flying start to the design process is a good problem statement, a clear goal and strategic anchoring.**

the design project. The prerequisite is that the overall goal and strategy of the company, product, or service is defined, and that a decision has been made as to which task the design should help solve. A good design brief provides a clear and simple description of the design project, what is desired to be accomplished, the background of this, desired results and goal achievement. It presents the company's goals and business strategy and clearly states the strategic anchoring of the design project. Information about limitations, frameworks, scope, and level of ambition is also included, without prejudice to professional design assessments and choices. According to Peter Phillips[4] (2012) a design brief is 'a written document that thoroughly explains the problem that needs to be solved by a designer or a design team. It should primarily focus on results of design, outcomes of design, and the business objectives of the design project. It should not attempt to deal with the aesthetics of design. That is the responsibility of the designer' (Holston, 2011, p. 30).

Fig. 4.3 The figure illustrates how the design project can start in Phase 1 or Phase 4. The work carried out in Phases 1 to 3 forms the basis for what is to be carried out in Phase 4. Phase 4 is initiated with a design brief that clarifies the design task based on the work that is carried out in the previous phases, including the goal of the task and anchoring in the company's overall strategy and goal. © Grimsgaard, W. (2018).

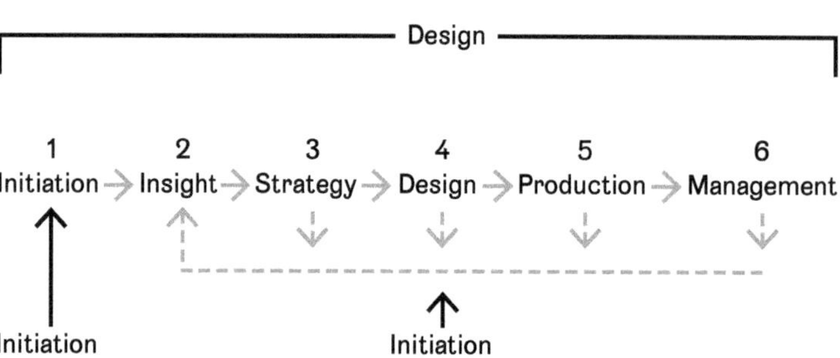


Fig. 4.3 Initiation of the project

If there is a lack of sufficient basis to prepare a design brief, the client may instead create a project brief (1.2 Project brief). In this case, the project will be initiated in Phase 1, as shown in Figure 4.3. In projects where the designer is involved from Phase 1, the designer will participate in the initial phases, which concern problem definition, research and strategy development. This is undoubtedly an advantage for the client because in these phases the designer will be able to help prepare the foundation for the assignment better than would have been the case if the designer stepped in at a later time. In those cases where the designer has been involved in the project from the beginning and has worked with the client to obtain the necessary insight and develop strategies, it is natural for the design brief to be prepared by the designer in collaboration with the client. The design brief will then be a confirmation that the designer and the client are in agreement and have a common understanding of the design task to be carried out, and the assumptions used as the basis. Based on the design brief, the designer can prepare a price quotation and progress schedule for the design work to be developed in Phase 4, as well as a price estimate[5] on completion and production (1.7 Price quotation).

In projects where the designer joins the team in Phase 4, the designer will have to go back to the previous phases to become familiar with the surveys, goals and strategy that constitute the basis for the assignment, and tie this to the work. If there are shortcomings in the basis, a strategic process may be needed. If relevant, it may be offered as a preliminary project or as part of the design project. After a strategy

4 Peter Philips, former corporate director for Gillette and consultant for Fortune 500 companies, considered by many as the guru of design briefs (Holston, 2011).

5 It can be difficult to estimate the price of production (programming, printing, press) before the design solution is developed and a decision is made on production technique, choice of material, and scope. A price estimate or budget is approximate.

6 Requirement specification is a list of desired attributes of something that should be procured, such as service or function specifications or a combination of thereof (Liseter and Rolstadås 2018). These requirements are the starting point for attributes to be included in the product or service that should be developed.

7 Delivery can, for example, be a logo, visual profile, website, car decoration, exhibition booth, etc.

8 A risk-benefit analysis is a comparison between the risks of a situation and its benefits. The goal is to figure out whether the risk or benefit is most significant (Study.com, n.d.).

process, it is not uncommon for the project to have changed in nature, in which case it will be necessary to prepare a new or adjusted design brief (1.2 Project brief: project brief vs. design brief).



### Design brief template

Example of a design brief template. Content and scope should be seen in the context of the type and size of the project.
**Title page:** Company name, project title and date.
**Contact information:** Project groups and project managers.
**Table of contents:** Simple content overview.
**Introduction:** Short introduction of the assignment that should be completed and background for designer involvement.
**The company:** Description of the company, its history and past accomplishments, their specialisations and current situation.
**The product/service:** Description of the product or service in question, history, brand assets and current situation.
**Current profile:** Any guidelines for design and communication (cf. design manual/profile guide). Previously performed assignments/materials.
**Problem statement:** Major challenges, problem definition or problem statement. Problem-based needs.
**Assignment:** Background for initiating the assignment. Description of the project that should be carried out and the design deliverables included. Project scope, due dates, framework, limitations and/or requirement specifications.[6]
**Goals and strategy:** Project goal, target groups, strategic directions and level of ambition for the assignment. Strategic anchoring to the overall goals and strategies. Business objectives of the project,
**Qualifications requirements:** Requirements for the designer and the production apparatus.
**Delivery and procurement:** Specification of the procurement, what is to be developed, produced and delivered.[7]
**Price or budget:** Budget framework, price estimation or price quotation.
**Progress schedule:** Plan for progress and delivery.
**Solution analysis:** Risk vs. benefits[8] of the planned solution.

### Why do we need a brief?

**Agreement:** The client and the design team should have the same understanding of the job and its framework.
**Direction:** After agreeing on the brief, we should know which direction to proceed with the job.
**Structure:** It should be clear where the responsibility lies, and we should agree on who does what and what tasks should be solved.
**Content:** The content of the brief should be an extract of the information we need regarding the company and assignment.
**Insight:** The brief will initially provide us with all the necessary information and strategic understanding.
**Clear choices:** A brief should not be filled in; it should be written. Clear choices should be made. Both problem statements and opportunities should be highlighted, depending on the underlying assumptions. A good brief will help us find a solution more quickly. There will be less ambiguity about tasks and responsibilities. An advantage for all parties (Myhre, 2017).

The brief works as both a project management tool and a design directive (David Holston, 2011).

## At the intersection of strategy and design, between the verbal and the visual, lies the answer to the problem statement and the key to the solution of the assignment.

With the approval of the strategy work, the designer's biggest challenge begins: transforming verbal strategic definitions into visual solutions, shape, colour, and font. The strategy work is now a completed chapter, approved by the client, compiled between two binders and summarised in a strategy narrative. The designer can now breathe a sigh of relief, because the design development can finally begin and all possibilities are open. A designer who has participated in the strategy process at this point will never start from scratch, but will have a backdrop of knowledge and understanding that will naturally flow into the design process. It is nevertheless necessary to compile all guides for the design work into a design brief that is approved by the client, so that both agree on the road ahead. This is how the design brief serves as an important link between strategy and design (4.1 Design brief). However, the question will be how design solutions can be created within the given framework and guides. How does one link strategy and design? The success factor lies in moving back and forth between strategy and design and translating strategy into good design solutions – or vice versa by moving from visual ideas to strategic innovation. Because even when the client thinks that there is a strategy in place, the design solutions may require new adjustments. It is all connected – always. Strategic design development is about developing design solutions that are aligned with the company's overall goal and strategy. That is always the starting point.

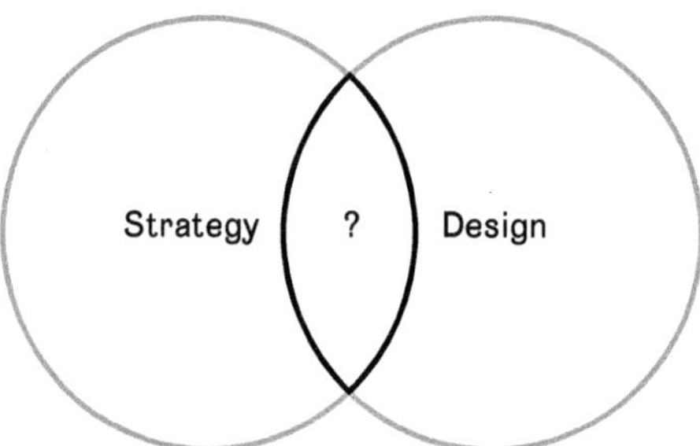


Fig. 4.4 The big challenge

At the intersection of strategy and design lies the key to creating unique and targeted design solutions. 'This is where the gold lies' (Bergan, 2017).[9] In this gap between the verbal and the visual lies the designer's greatest challenge and potential linking strategy and design, transforming insight, goals, and strategy into visual images, identities, and experiences. Basically, it is about moving from problem statement to idea development in order to come up with a solution. There is not just one way to do it, and there is no key to the answer. For some designers the process is intuitive, while others need to use certain methods. If the designer has used visual tools to describe insight and strategy, the transition to visual solutions could be more natural. It is about using

Fig. 4.4 The challenge is to transform verbal strategy into visual solutions. © Grimsgaard, W. (2018).

Fig. 4.5 The figure is based on Michael Johnson's *Branding in Five and a Half Steps* (2016: 137). The half-step 'translate' is between 'define' and 'create'.

Fig. 4.6 Moodboards can be an excellent bridge between strategy and design by translating verbal thoughts and strategies into visual images, fonts, patterns, and materials. © Grimsgaard, W. (2018).

9 From a conversation with Tone Bergan, when she was Director Design, Creuna (2017). Now she is Senior Advisor Design Innovation at Design and Architecture Norway – DOGA.

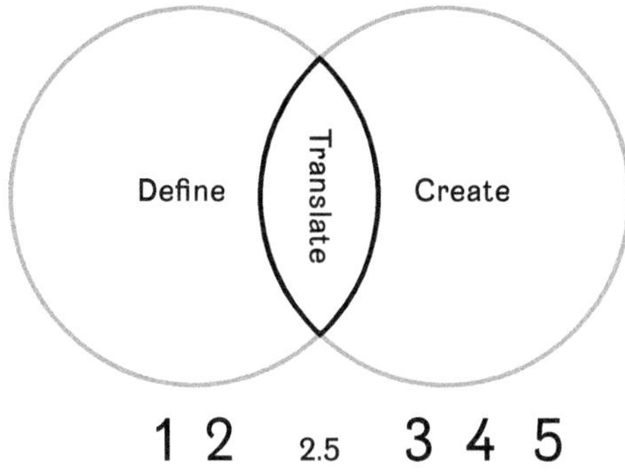


Fig. 4.5 Branding in five and a half steps

1 Initiation
2 Insight
3 Strategy
4 Design
5 Production
6 Management

4.1 Design brief
4.2 Strategy><Design
4.3 Design methodology
4.4 Concept development
4.5 Design development
4.6 Design elements
4.7 Composition
4.8 Surface and format
4.9 Identity development

4.2.1 Mapping as a link
4.2.2 Visualise strategy
4.2.3 Visualise name
4.2.4 Distinctive brand assets
4.2.5 Idea as a bridge
4.2.6 The fifth element

illustrations, graphs, infographics, moodboards, GIGA maps, early hand sketches, etc. as early as possible, whether it is a matter of reporting from a workshop, survey results or presentation of strategy definitions. On the one hand, it can provide a more precise description of surveys and strategies than using verbal descriptions alone; on the other hand, it could lead to a smoother transition between strategy and design. It is about bridging the gap between the verbal and the visual. In his book *Branding in five and a half steps*, Michael Johnson has highlighted the gap between strategy and design in what he describes as the 'half step' between the narrative and the creative. 'In the crossover between the verbal ideas in the last step and the visual creativity in the next, there are often decisions to be made that involve both sides. This half-step is concerned with the translation of one idea into another' (Johnson, 2016, p. 136), for example from a business idea to a visual idea. In the next subsections we will look at different ways of linking strategy and design.

### 4.2.1 Mapping as a link

Using systematisation and mapping can help visualise and explain insight, analysis and strategy. At the same time, it can simplify the work of incorporating the strategy into to the design process. Here, we will look at some mapping methods that are well suited for linking together strategy and design (2.8 Mapping).

**Moodboard:** Perhaps the easiest way to link strategy and design is to use moodboards. This method can be used in all phases of a design project to transform words, thoughts and ideas into visual images and expressions. Used in the insight and strategy phase, moodboards can

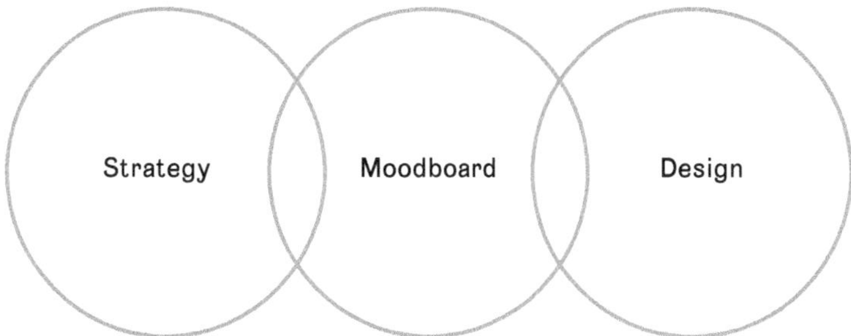


Fig. 4.6 Transfer by moodboard

help make surveys and strategic definitions more accessible and easier to present, while simplifying their use further in the design process. Visual expressions appearing in the moodboard can provide guidance and inspiration for shape, colours, typography, pattern, materials, and composition (2.8.2 Moodboard).

**Storyboard:** The use of storyboards and dramaturgical grips can simplify the path from verbal strategies to visual design, or vice versa. Words and images in symbiosis build and strengthen each other and create a bridge between the verbal and the visual, between strategy and design. Some examples of insights and strategy that can be visualised in a storyboard: a) a customer experience in a shop, b) a user-experience of a product, c) the product supply chain from raw material to production, d) the product life cycle and life cycle extension towards recycling and upcycling, e) an interview on the street, f) a target-oriented strategy plan from current to the desired situation. Insight and strategy can inspire a storyboard, and a storyboard can inspire new ideas (2.8.3 Storyboard).

**Customer journey:** Customer journey or user journey is a mapping tool that includes insight, analysis, strategy and visualisation in one and the same process. The purpose is to map and analyse how a service works for the user, by examining all the touchpoints in which a customer will come in contact, interact or engage with a company, product or service. The insight is used as the basis for developing new strategies and solutions. The method represents smooth transitions between visual studies, strategies and solution proposals (2.8.4 and 4.3.12 Customer journey).

Fig. 4.7 Customer journey

**GIGA map:** Moodboards, storyboards, customer journeys, systems and other mapping tools can be combined into a GIGA map and can be supplemented with insights, strategies, sketches, notes, graphs, and infographics. It provides a holistic overview and a solid basis for further design development and the problem-solving process. The use of GIGA maps is particularly suitable for solving complex problems, where it is necessary to see entire contexts in order to create solutions (2.8.5 GIGA maps, 2.3.9 Wicked problems).

### 4.2.2 Visualise strategy

Strategy visualisation is an important tool for making the strategy accessible and understandable to everyone who is going to use it. At the same time, it is also an effective instrument for linking strategy and design, and thus ensuring strategic anchoring of the design solution.

**Visualise values:** The core values are defined in the overall strategy and are an important platform for developing a visual identity. Translating value words into images, colours, fonts, patterns, and other expressions of the value words can create visual expressions and moods that can inspire logo and other elements of visual identity, see Table 4.2. Moodboards are well suited for this. The same applies to prints of images, physical objects, and various materials. Value words can also

Fig. 4.7 The figure shows a linear customer journey, with different touch points of the journey, from beginning to end.

Table 4.2 The table shows how the core values, referred to here as special features of the brand, can provide the basis for the development of logo and other brand elements, in that way bridging strategy and design. Using moodboards that translate the value words into images, fonts and colours, makes it easier to visualise the values. The result may be more or less subjective, depending on how many people participate in the process. Associations to the value words shown in the figure here are only examples. There is no answer key. The method can advantageously be based on user surveys, colour psychology, and other information providing concrete insights. © Grimsgaard, W. 2018.

Table 4.3 The table shows how values can be explained through abstract properties such as sound, smell, taste, and emotion. What sound does the value word 'supersmart' have, what odour, what flavour. It can be used as inspiration for visual instruments. For example, what colour is the sound, what shape is it, what typeface, and so on. The illustration is just an example. There is no answer key. © Grimsgaard, W. 2018

Fig. 4.8 The figure shows an example of how brand architecture can provide strong guides for the visual solution. A monolithic identity means that the same logo/brand is used for both the company and its products and services. © Grimsgaard, W. 2018

1 Initiation
2 Insight
3 Strategy
4 Design
5 Production
6 Management

4.1 Design brief
4.2 Strategy><Design
4.3 Design methodology
4.4 Concept development
4.5 Design development
4.6 Design elements
4.7 Composition
4.8 Surface and format
4.9 Identity development

4.2.1 Mapping as a link
4.2.2 Visualise strategy
4.2.3 Visualise name
4.2.4 Distinctive brand assets
4.2.5 Idea as a bridge
4.2.6 The fifth element

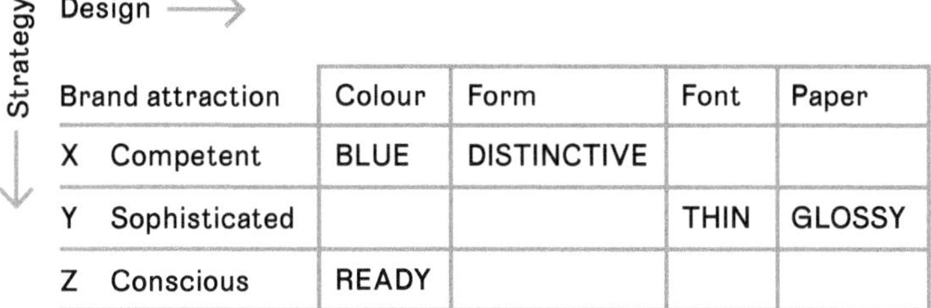

Strategy ↓ / Design →

| Brand attraction | Colour | Form | Font | Paper |
|---|---|---|---|---|
| X Competent | BLUE | DISTINCTIVE | | |
| Y Sophisticated | | | THIN | GLOSSY |
| Z Conscious | READY | | | |

Table 4.2 Visualise values

Strategy ↓ / Design →

| Brand attraction | Sound | Odour | Flavour | Feel |
|---|---|---|---|---|
| X Super smart | Ping | Mint | Cool | Ready |
| Y Super fast | Swoosh | Hasty | Hint | Wind |
| Z Super kind | Happy | Tempting | Sweet | Warm |

Table 4.3 Visualise sound, smell, taste, and emotion

be associated with sound, smell, taste, emotion, which in turn can be translated into shape, colour, font, and material, see Table 4.3. Thus, values that are strategic choices can help form the basis for the development of visual elements, sound elements, odour and taste-promotions, etc. (3.2.5 Core values, 4.9.5 Identity colours).

**Visualise brand architecture:** Brand architecture is a strategic choice that provides clear directions for the visual solution. For example, choosing a monolithic brand identity means using the same logo for both the company and its products, as shown in Figure 4.8 (3.7.2 Brand architecture).

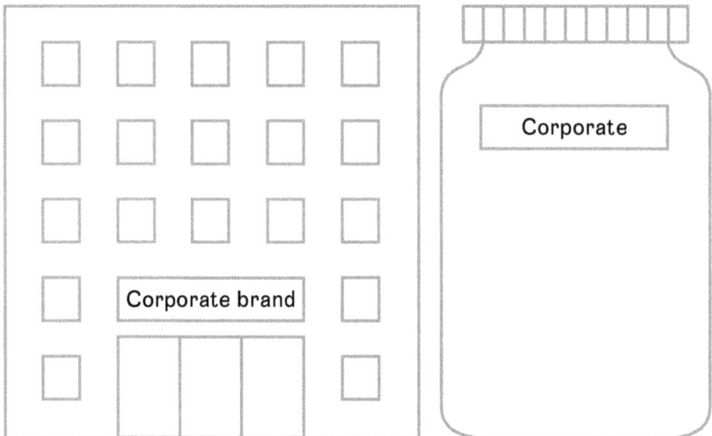


Fig. 4.8 Monolithic identity

**Visualise brand position:** The brand position defines how the product or service will compete in the market, which is at the heart of strategy. The position can be expressed in the slogan and/or through a brand narrative. Figure 4.9 shows how brand position and other strategic definitions such as core values and value proposition, can be used as a

Further reading
– *Shoe Dog* by Phil Knight 2016.
– *Something's off* by Virgil Abloh 2020.

starting point for the development of brand assets and communication on a product (3.7.3 Brand position, 3.7.4 Brand statement, 3.2.3 Core values, 3.2.6 Value proposition).

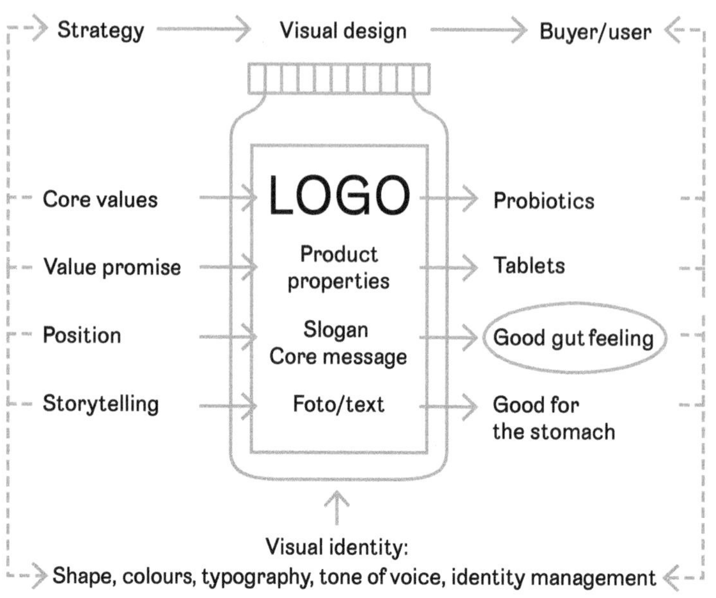


Fig. 4.9 Visualise position

Fig. 4.9 The figure shows an example of a link between strategy and design. Core values are linked to logo, value promise to product properties, position to slogan, narrative to photo and text. The position is good gut feeling. Position is visual communication. That is what we want the user/buyer to see, read, associate and think when they see the product. © Grimsgaard, W. 2018

Fig. 4.10 A distinctive brand asset is at the intersection of strategy and design. One starts with the visual design element, tests it among the target audience, makes a strategic assessment and uses the visual properties as the foremost brand building factor.

Fig. 4.11 The figure shows the fifth element as a bridge between strategy and design; a main idea, experience or element that can bring brand strategy and visual identity closer together. © Grimsgaard, W. (2018).

### 4.2.3 Visualise name

The path from name to visual associations can often be a short one. This particularly applies to names that are pictorial or metaphorical, such as the brand names Apple, Shell, Jaguar, and Nike. The sports brand Nike named after the goddess of victory of the same name symbolises the characteristics of the products, such as victory, fight and speed, visualised in the symbol 'the swoosh' – an abstraction of the goddess's wing.[10] Jaguar, named after one of our fastest mammals, symbolises the car's superior power and driving characteristics, expressed through a stylised jaguar in a dynamic leap. Associations implicitly or explicitly linked to the name, combined with letter combination and phonetic pronunciation, can be translated into visual images, shapes, colours, typography and other visual or sensory concepts, thus providing inspiration for the development of logo, identity elements, visual storytelling, etc. The physical attributes of the name are also important. Some names are calm and friendly, some are energetic and dramatic, while others can be charismatic and elegant. Some names roll easily off the tongue and inspire round shapes and cheerful colours; others have force and power, and inspire powerful and distinctive shapes (3.7.7 Brand name).

### 4.2.4 Distinctive brand assets

Owning or cultivating the most distinctive feature of the brand's assets is strategic use of visual tools, through analysis of existing brand identity, using metrics to measure which of the brand elements people remember,

10 Further reading: *Shoe Dog*. A memoir by the creator of Nike. Phil Knight (2018).
11 The fifth element name *aether*, was in ancient science added to the four elements of western culture: earth, air, fire and water. Aether was in Greek mythology thought to be the pure essence that the gods breathed, filling the space where they lived, analogous to the air breathed by mortals ('The fifth element,' n.d.). The fifth element is also known as quintessence. Quintessence can today be understood as 1) the most perfect or typical example of a quality or class, 2) a refined essence or extract of a substance (Quintessence, n.d.).

using this strategically and consistently in all contexts to create a unique and well-known brand. Or start from scratch – finding a colour, shape or sound, which is available in the product category, test it and cultivate it so that it stands out among the competitors and turn into a distinctive brand asset (3.4.6 Distinctive asset-building strategy, 4.9.7 Distinctive assets).


1 Initiation
2 Insight
3 Strategy
4 Design
5 Production
6 Management

4.1 Design brief
4.2 Strategy><Design
4.3 Design methodology
4.4 Concept development
4.5 Design development
4.6 Design elements
4.7 Composition
4.8 Surface and format
4.9 Identity development

4.2.1 Mapping as a link
4.2.2 Visualise strategy
4.2.3 Visualise name
4.2.4 Distinctive brand assets
4.2.5 Idea as a bridge
4.2.6 The fifth element

Fig. 4.10 Distinctive brand asset

### 4.2.5 Idea as a bridge

The idea is the real bridge between strategy and design, the one that will conceive and bring the solution forward. The idea can be a platform, a superstructure, or a subtle detail. The idea is unpredictable; it can wait to appear and come unexpectedly. It often comes as a result of enough insight, understanding and good processes. Then all of a sudden it is there, as visual as it is verbal, often just in the form of a thought. The challenge lies in concretising the idea and developing a clear concept using visual sketches, images and moodboards. Then it's about further developing, testing, further developing, and testing again. Does it solve the problem? Does it respond to the task? Is it in line with the strategy? Really good design solutions are often based on a clear idea (4.4 Concept development, 4.4.4 Idea development).

### 4.2.6 The fifth element

The quest for the fifth element in branding[11] can literally mean the pursuit of the essence; a main idea, experience or element that can bring brand strategy and visual identity closer together. It is something that represents the essence of the brand and simultaneously has visual potential. Finding the fifth element helps link strategy and design more closely so that they support each other. The best place to look for this fifth element is in the zone between brand strategy and visual design, an experience or feature that cuts across digital and analogue surfaces (4.9 Identity development, 4.9.7 Distinctive assets).

Fig. 4.11 The fifth element

> **Choice of design methodology**
> Conscious choice of design methodology can be useful in small simple tasks, as well as in large complex projects involving many people. When more people collaborate, choosing common processes and methods can contribute to better project progress, structure, and flow.

Tips for the company
Companies are no longer just buyers of design services, they use design methodology to a greater extent when solving internal tasks and developing their products and services.

Design methodology can be used in a broad sense for strategy development, innovation and problem solving.

There are endless approaches to developing design. Design methodology refers to different procedures of design development, which can be useful in either solving smaller design tasks or large complex projects. Design and design methodology are also linked to changes that are not about visual design and aesthetics. Today, design methodology is regarded just as much as a way of thinking and working which is equally relevant in the development of strategies and business models as it is in the development of products and services. Some design methods can be used for the entire project, while others can be included in different project phases.

Procedures used to complete a design project can be intuitive and unstructured, or planned and structured. The best is usually a combination. In a design project, one often works on the basis of an overall process and include different processes and methods as needed. Some processes are in-depth, while others have a broader approach. Some are linear, others circular. Some are confined to idea development, while others include analysis and strategy. In general, we can say that a *process* is about a variety of operations or activities that are done over time to produce a result through a variety of methodological actions, events, mechanisms, phases, or steps. *The method* is the procedure, a planned and orderly way of doing something using a specific technique or systematics. First and foremost, methods are useful tools, but they can also serve as comprehensive processes. Processes have methods, and each method has a process. There are smooth transitions, and we can often perceive a method as a process and a process as a method. We will discuss both as part of design methodology. Some design methods are associated with specific design fields or design disciplines, while other methods are more universal and can be used regardless of the nature of the project. Knowledge of different methods can be a good learning platform, both for the designer and for the client, to understand how design development takes place, and what procedures are suitable. Experienced designers often prefer developing their own methods and models.

Several of the design methods we will look at here are not only used by designers, but are methods also non-designers use and hail as their own. An increasing number of companies have discovered how the use of design methodology is a success factor in planning and developing new business areas, products or services. This is related to new ways of thinking and working. Design methodology has become the companies' new key to value creation and innovation. We refer here to methods that anyone can learn, such as *design thinking* (4.3.11 Design thinking). Thus, a new situation arises in which it may be difficult to distinguish between how design thinking should be used when developing visual design, compared to, for example, strategy development. It is not easy

12 For companies that produce goods, a value chain comprises the steps that involve bringing a product from conception to distribution, and everything in between – such as procuring raw materials, manufacturing functions, and marketing activities' (Tardi, 2020). (2.7.3 Value chain analysis)

to come up with an unambiguous solution to that. *Co-creation* might be a good approach, to fetch the best from the company, the designer, and the user/customer in the process (4.3.15 Co-design).

In a design project, the key to problem solving may lie in a conscious process and method selection. The starting point is often a design brief that clarifies the project's goals, problem statement, and strategic anchorage (4.1 Design brief), but the starting point may also be defining these through a design process. Alongside selecting overall processes and methods for the entire project, it will often be necessary to select subordinate processes and methods to solve some parts of the project. For example, in product development, it would be natural to think of an overall solution for the product, while at the same time solving problems that arise during the development process. There may be issues related to physical parts of the product, such as handles, buttons, and closing mechanisms, as well as technical issues concerning automation and digitisation that require separate processes.

No design projects are absolutely the same, and there is no definitive answer on how to proceed. A good start is to familiarise oneself with different methods and understand how they work. The challenge will be to choose which method works best at all times and adapt it to the problem that should be solved in the process, regardless of whether it is about the development of strategy or visual solution. There is also the potential to use and further develop methods so that they work best for the specific purpose at any given time. Common to many of the design methods we are going to look at, is that one should start by identifying the problem and solve it using insight, analysis, idea development, prototyping, and testing, often through an iterative method and strong user focus (2.3.3 Problem definition, 2.5 Research process, 2.7 Analyses, 3.4.6 Agile strategy management, 2.9.1 User testing, 4.4.2 Creative problem solving, 4.3.5 Iterative method, 5.2.5 Prototype).

1 Initiation
2 Insight
3 Strategy
4 Design
5 Production
6 Management

4.1 Design brief
4.2 Strategy><Design
4.3 Design methodology
4.4 Concept development
4.5 Design development
4.6 Design elements
4.7 Composition
4.8 Surface and format
4.9 Identity development

4.3.1 Human-centred design
4.3.2 User-experience
4.3.3 Emotional design
4.3.4 Innovation
4.3.5 Iterative method
4.3.6 Divergence and convergence
4.3.7 Sprint
4.3.8 Scrum
4.3.9 Kanban
4.3.10 Lean and agile
4.3.11 Design thinking
4.3.12 Customer journey
4.3.13 Need-finding
4.3.14 Service blueprint
4.3.15 Co-creation
4.3.16 Business design
4.3.17 Strategic design thinking
4.3.18 Systemic design
4.3.19 In retrospect

### 4.3.1 Human-centred design

Human-centred design is a design approach that involves designing products, services, systems and experiences that meet the core needs of those who experience a problem. The designer and the client often focus on different extremes of the value chain[12] of a product or service. While the client is concerned with profit at the end of the value chain, the designer focuses their attention on the start of the value chain in order to find out which need or problem the project should solve. Similarly, a technical developer and a designer may also have a different focus during the design process. While the developer may be most concerned with what is technically feasible, the designer will pay more attention to what serves the user best, what is user-friendly and functional. This should ideally be the designer's focus.

In a design-driven project, the human-centred approach is usually an overarching intention, either explicitly or implicitly, in how the company, the designer and the developer naturally work and think. *User-centricity* is about developing solutions to problems by involving the human perspective in all stages of the problem-solving process. It is a process that starts with studying the people one will be designing for and ends with

Further reading
***Designing for Growth: A Design Thinking Tool Kit for Managers*** **(Columbia University Press) by Jeanne Liedtka and Tim Ogilvie (2016).**

People at the centre
**User-centric design is a creative approach to problem-solving with people at the centre (IDEO).**

new solutions tailored to meet their needs. *Empathy* is a key word which means establishing deep insight, understanding, and sympathy for and with the users. It involves talking to the relevant people, making participatory observations and focusing on producing solutions to problems rather than just documenting them. Here also lies the potential to 'reach a higher level of empathy and emotional intelligence in order to see the real bigger picture, one that takes into consideration the environmental aspect[13] and non-human players too' (Bencini, 2021).

The human-centred approach is central to modern design methodology. During the last decades, it has been seen almost as a magic formula for innovation when it comes to developing profitable and attractive products and services. However, the trend has moved from thinking only of the user's needs, to also paying attention to the needs of the environment, as well as the possibilities of extending the product's life cycle.[14] There is no universal explanation as to how one should work with the human-centric approach, although many of the same principles are repeated. Large design firms, profiled design programmes, and design councils have become leaders as trendsetters, with good examples, case studies and human-centric courses, including IDEO, Stanford and the British Design Council.

Fig. 4.12 The figure is based on the IDEO HCD model (2009). It illustrates three phases of a human-centred design process: inspiration, idea development, and implementation. The method involves use of iteration in the overall process as well in each of the phases, which involves repeating rounds of diverging and converging (4.3.6 Divergence and convergence).

Fig. 4.13 The figure is based on The Hasso Plattner Institute of Design at Stanford, *An Introduction to Design Thinking* exercise. It proposes a user-centred prototype-driven design process.

### Using the IDEO HCD model

**Inspiration:** At this stage, you will find the problem or opportunity that motivates you to look for a solution. You will learn to understand people better, observe their lives, to put yourself in their shoes, hear their hopes and desires, and gather knowledge to meet their challenges. It is about learning along the way and being open to new creative opportunities and trusting that as long as ideas are based on what people really want, they will evolve into the right solution.

**Idea development:** Here you start the process of idea development: apply everything you have heard; create a multitude of ideas through iterations; identify design opportunities, and test and refine your solutions (4.3.5 Iterative method). In the course of this process, you come up with a lot of ideas, some of which are too crazy to work, and others which would be wrong not to try out. Then you get rid of the bad ones and improve the good ones. Creating things helps you learn and progress. Test your ideas. By building simple prototypes, you test your ideas on the people you design for. Without their feedback, you will not know whether your solutions hit the target or not. Have the user evaluate your ideas, continue to develop ideas, integrate, test, and get feedback until you have everything in place.

**Implementation:** Ultimately comes the phase leading from process to market; your opportunity to realise your solution. In this phase, you build collaboration, refine your product, service, or business model, and figure out how to bring your idea to market and maximise its impact in the world. Anyone can practise user-centric design, and everyone benefits because it means that all solutions are customised and approved by the user (IDEO designkit.org).

13 'Environment-centered design is an approach to product or service development that aims to make products or services environmentally, socially and economically sustainable by focusing on the needs, limitations and preferences of target human audience *and* non-human strategic stakeholders' (Sznel, 2020).

14 When a product reaches the decline stage, a business can act to extend its life cycle (5.3.7 Product life extension).

15 IDEO published the *Human-centred design Toolkit* (2009). IDEO is one of the world's largest design companies, founded in 1991, with offices around the world. The company uses design thinking as methodology for designing products, services, environments, digital experiences, and organisational design.

16 Also referred to as '5 Stages in the Design Thinking Process' and 'Design thinking process diagram'.

17 d.school introduces itself as a place for explorers and experimenters at Stanford University, and state that: 'We believe everyone has the capacity to be creative' (d.school.stanford.edu)

18 Action-oriented behaviour can involve going out, observing and engaging the users, and doing prototyping and testing.

1 Initiation
2 Insight
3 Strategy
4 Design
5 Production
6 Management

4.1 Design brief
4.2 Strategy><Design
4.3 Design methodology
4.4 Concept development
4.5 Design development
4.6 Design elements
4.7 Composition
4.8 Surface and format
4.9 Identity development

4.3.1 Human-centred design
4.3.2 User-experience
4.3.3 Emotional design
4.3.4 Innovation
4.3.5 Iterative method
4.3.6 Divergence and convergence
4.3.7 Sprint
4.3.8 Scrum
4.3.9 Kanban
4.3.10 Lean and agile
4.3.11 Design thinking
4.3.12 Customer journey
4.3.13 Need-finding
4.3.14 Service blueprint
4.3.15 Co-design
4.3.16 Business design
4.3.17 Strategic design thinking
4.3.18 Systemic design
4.3.19 In retrospect

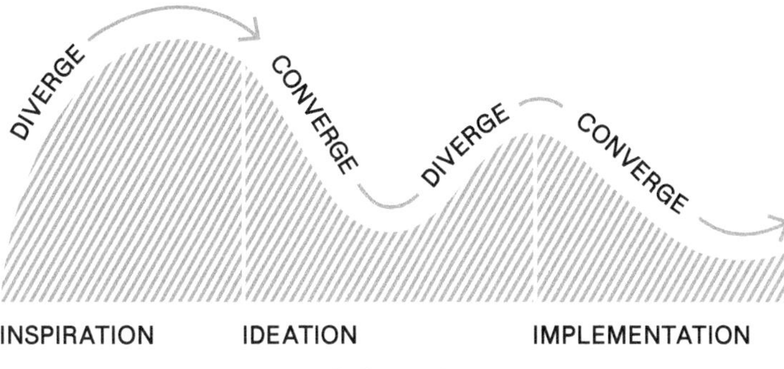


Fig. 4.12 IDEO HCD model

**IDEO HCD Model**

This model is one of many examples of the human-centric design process, proposed by IDEO[15] (2009). It explains the design process through the three phases: inspiration, idea development and implementation. In the inspiration phase, you learn directly from the people you design for as you immerse yourself in their lives and gain in-depth understanding of their needs. In the ideation phase, you will use what you have learned, identify design opportunities and prototype possible solutions. And in the implementation phase, you will realise the solution and eventually promote it. When you have the solution at hand, you will know that it will be a success because you have involved the users in the process (IDEO, HCD Toolkit 2015).

*Application*: The method focuses on user-centric idea development and is particularly well suited for developing a new business model or a start-up for a product or service.

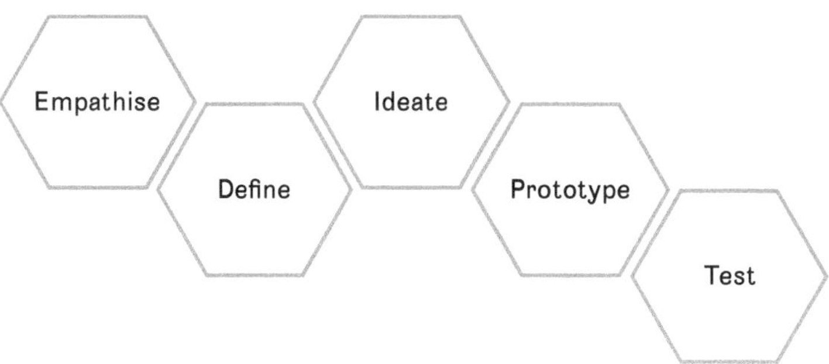


Fig. 4.13 Five-stage design thinking model

**Five-stage design thinking model**

This model[16] is developed by the Hasso Plattner Institute of Design at Stanford, known as the d.school.[17] The purpose of the method is to create innovative solutions to a problem through a human-centred prototype driven process. The method should inspire a mindset which involves: Show, don't tell; Focus on human values; Create clarity; Do experiments; Be present and aware in the process (mindfulness); Be action-oriented rather than discussion-based (Bias toward Action);[18] Encourage collaboration and co-creation (1.9 Team collaboration).

*Application*: The method focuses on user-centric problem definition and idea development and is well suited for both start-up and redesign of a product or service.

Further reading

HCD Toolkit: 'The Field Guide to Human-centred design. Design Kit' (IDEO, 2015). Available at designkit.org/resources/1

IDEO describes Human-Centred Design (HCD) as a design and management framework with the main focus on the user's needs and interests which emphasises making products and services more usable and understandable.

**Five-stage design thinking model**

**1) Empathise:** Empathy is the heart of user-oriented design. The user should provide inspiration and guidance for ideas. Responding to human needs makes it possible to create designs that are both useful and meaningful to people.

**2) Define:** Collect large amounts of information, extract what is important. Define which user or user group to focus on, what needs and problems have been identified. Develop an inspiring problem statement that can be used as basis for creating new solutions.

**3) Ideate:** Cut off obvious solutions. Work to create flow (volume) and flexibility (variety) in the idea process. Be inventive, wild and visual!

**4) Prototype:** Explore options, test ideas, achieve empathy, and follow the vision. 'If a picture is worth a thousand words, a prototype is worth a thousand meetings' (IDEO).

**5) Test:** Learn which aspects of the solution work for users and which do not. Such feedback is valuable throughout the development process. Test, adjust, test, adjust, test, adjust until the solution is consistent with the problem statement and user needs (Stanford (d.school)).

Fig. 4.14 A UX method may look relatively complex, like this one. Initially, it is based on three main principles: The product/service should fill a need (Look and Feel); it should be functional (Functionality) and profitable (Business Case) (Merryweather, 2014).

Tips for the company
UX is a human-centred holistic mindset.

## 4.3.2 User-experience

User-experience (UX) is a person's experience when using a digital product, such as a website or a computer application, especially considering how easy or comfortable it is to use. It was in the 1990s when computers became more and more widespread that greater attention was paid to the user's experience. Today, there is a separate ISO standard for user-centring within computer systems and system development named 'Human-centred design for interactive systems', and it explains *human-centred design* as: 'approach to systems design and development that aims to make interactive systems more usable by focusing on the use of the system and applying human factors/ergonomics and usability knowledge and techniques. The term "human-centred design" is used rather than "user-centred design" in order to emphasise that this document also addresses impacts on a number of stakeholders, not just those typically considered as users. However, in practice, these terms are often used synonymously. *Usable systems* can provide a number of benefits, including improved productivity, enhanced user well-being, avoidance of stress, increased accessibility and reduced risk of harm' (ISO 9241-210:2019, 3.7).[19]

While *user centring* is used more generally with regard to user focus, *user-experience* has evolved as a concept for the user's experience specifically related to the development of interactive digital products and services. To many, the two concepts are one and the same thing. UX has grown to become a separate design discipline, while also being referred to as a method.

Donald Norman,[20] who is known as the person who introduced the concept of user-experience in the 1990s, later criticised the extent to which the user-centric approach is used. In his research article

Further reading
– Check out Peter Morville's 'Honeycumb'.
– Read the interview with Nina Lysbakken (2017). Available at designandstrategy.co.uk.

19 ISO (the International Organisation for Standardisation) is a worldwide federation of national standards bodies (ISO member bodies). The work of preparing International Standards is normally carried out through ISO technical committees (ISO 9241-210:2019, iso.org).

20 Donald Norman is one of the great names in user-centring. He is the founder of the Nielsen Norman Group and a former professor of cognitive science.

21 Donald A. Norman is the author of *The design of everyday things*, released 1990, 2002 and 2013. It is about how design is communication between object and user, and how to make the experience of using the object more pleasurable. He also wrote *Emotional design. Why we love (or hate) every day things*, 2003, among others.

*Human-centred design Considered Harmful* (2005), he stated that unilateral focus on user centring can have negative consequences: 'What adapts? Technology or people? First, the focus upon humans detracts from support for the activities themselves; second, too much attention to the needs of the users can lead to a lack of cohesion and added complexity in the design' (Norman, 2005). [21] One possible solution to that problem could be to develop technology and user testing as two parallel paths to a common goal (Sitre, 2016).

*Application*: UX focuses on needs and interaction, functionality and profitability. The method is used especially in system development, web design and app technology.


1 Initiation
2 Insight
3 Strategy
4 Design
5 Production
6 Management

4.1 Design brief
4.2 Strategy><Design
4.3 Design methodology
4.4 Concept development
4.5 Design development
4.6 Design elements
4.7 Composition
4.8 Surface and format
4.9 Identity development

4.3.1 Human-centred design
4.3.2 User-experience
4.3.3 Emotional design
4.3.4 Innovation
4.3.5 Iterative method
4.3.6 Divergence and convergence
4.3.7 Sprint
4.3.8 Scrum
4.3.9 Kanban
4.3.10 Lean and agile
4.3.11 Design thinking
4.3.12 Customer journey
4.3.13 Need-finding
4.3.14 Service blueprint
4.3.15 Co-design
4.3.16 Business design
4.3.17 Strategic design thinking
4.3.18 Systemic design
4.3.19 In retrospect


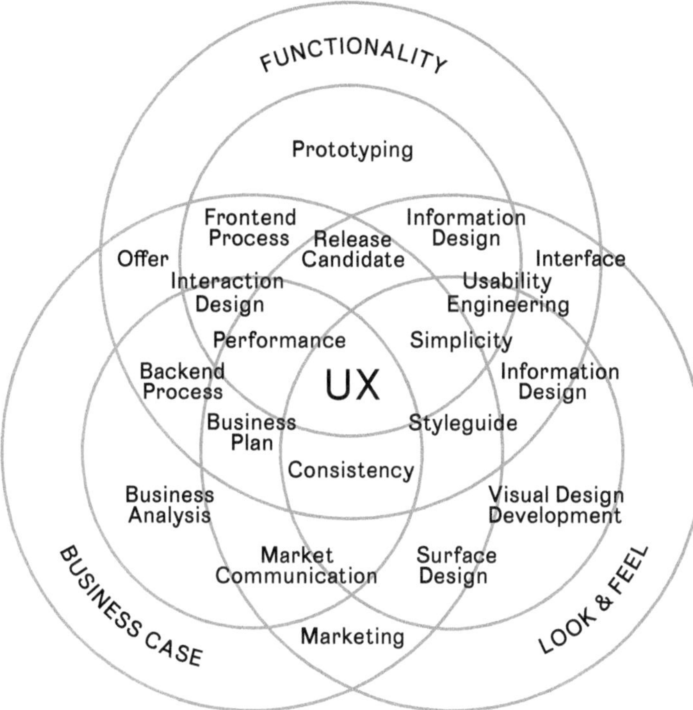


Fig. 4.14 UX model

## 4.3.3 Emotional design

Emotional design is about how to create design that evokes emotions and results in positive user-experiences. Experience is tied to emotions, to feelings.[22] Many products create feelings. They can be pretty, ugly, exciting, or vulgar. Some may also be neutral (brukertest.com). 'Beautiful Things Work Better,' according to Donald Norman, whose book *The Design of Everyday Things* (1988), presents three cognitive levels that together can influence people when they decide why they like or dislike a product:

- *'Visceral design'* refers to the emotions triggered at the first encounter with the product. It is a subconscious reaction based on appearance and experience. Emotions are immediate and often beyond our control. We have to go through this level to get to the next level.

Further reading
***Emotional Design: Why We Love (or Hate) Everyday Things*** **(2005) by Don A. Norman.**

22 Experience is a person's subjective experience, whether related to external stimulation of the senses (perception), emotional state (feeling), or thought processes and motivation (Snl, 2016).

- *'Behavioural design'* refers to what it feels like to use the product. How easy is it to use the product? Do we still like what we see after we have tried it? Do we want to share it with our friends and family? Here, we perceive what the product is, and not what it can be. After we have tried the product comes the reflection.
- *'Reflective design'* refers to self-image, experience and memories after the product has been tested and experienced. If we go through the whole process of coming across the product and putting it to use, does it change how we feel or think how we feel about it afterwards? What values do we associate with the product afterwards? Is it an experience of bonding and intimacy?

Fig. 4.15 The figure shows four classical types of innovation, based on Ottinger (2021). 'Technology newness describes whether an innovation is based on emerging or well-proven technologies. Low-market impact ideas are easier to implement, with compounding effects over time. High-market impact ideas tend to be difficult, costly, and risky to develop but arrive with high potential value.' (Ottinger, 2021).

> *Empathise*: 'To create meaningful innovations, you need to know your users and care about their lives.'
> *Define*: 'Framing the right problem is the only way to create the right solution.'
> *Ideate*: 'It's not about coming up with the 'right' idea, it's about generating the broadest range of possibilities.'
> *Prototype*: 'Build to think and test to learn.'
> *Test*: 'Testing is an opportunity to learn about your solution and your user.' (Michael Shanks, 'An Introduction to Design Thinking Process Guide', Hasso Plattner Institute of Design at Stanford).

> The Norwegian innovation lab for public sector StimuLab is a learning platform for public sector innovation that supports and encourages user-oriented experimentation and innovation, using a design methodology. It was initiated by the Norwegian government in 2016 and is run as a collaboration between Design and Architecture Norway (DOGA) and the Norwegian Digitalisation Agency, which represents a unique cooperation (Wildhagen and Strålberg, 2021).

### 4.3.4 Innovation

By involving designers in an early phase of an innovation project there is a greater chance of developing a product or service adapted to the actual needs of the user. There are different approaches to innovation, from the classic technology-driven, to the user- and design-driven, and future artificial-driven innovation.

Innovation is a concept widely used to talk about original thoughts, ideas and inventions. Innovation can be explained as 'the management of all the activities involved in the process of idea generation, technology development, manufacturing and marketing of a new (or improved) product or manufacturing process or equipment' (Trott, 2017, Silva & Marques, 2020). As an essence, innovation can be defined as creating something new that creates value. There are a variety of innovation approaches, and some provide more value than others. Ottinger (2021) points out four different ways innovation can take shape, which can lead to different outcomes, some more effective than others.

- *1) Disruptive innovation*: Disruptive innovation comes with effective uses of new technology and high-impact results. The most common organisations exhibiting the characteristics of disruptive innovation are startups targeting overlooked segments in the market to deliver an offering that is more affordable, convenient, or simpler than the established players can.
- *2) Incremental innovation*: Incremental innovation constitutes a gradual, continuous improvement of existing products and services. By continuously improving products, services, and business operations, organisations can reduce stagnation and consistently grow market share.

Further reading
*101 Design Methods: A Structured Approach for Driving Innovation in Your Organization* by Vijay Kumar (2012).

23 *User-Driven Innovation – the Concept and Research Results*. Elżbieta Szymańska / Procedia Engineering 182 (2017 ) 694–700

- *3) Sustaining innovation*: Sustaining innovation is the best way to protect an organisation's position in a market. Sustaining innovation focuses on larger changes to gain or maintain a market-leader position. This category is focused on creating new features or services that differentiate a product from all of its competitors.
- *4) Radical innovation*: Radical innovation typically utilises a technological breakthrough that transforms industries and creates new markets. It completely changes the organisational behaviours towards creating the right conditions for new ideas to be successfully commercialised.

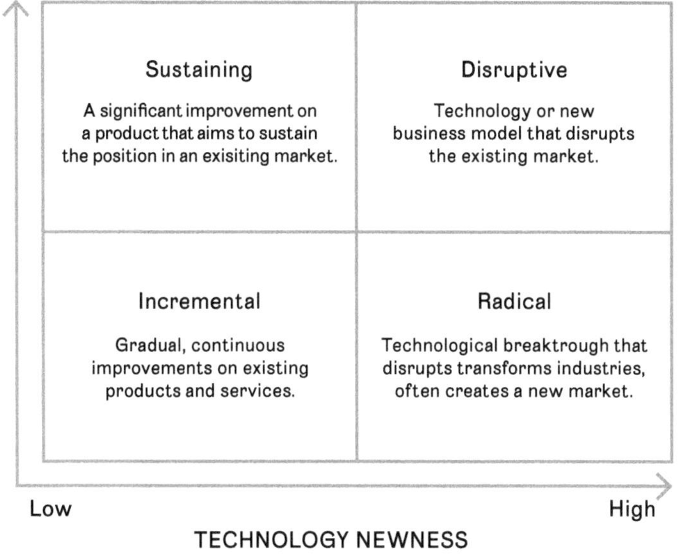


Fig. 4.15 Innovation for marketing impact

By implementing all four, a company ensures short-term success by optimising its current products and differentiating them from competitors while also protecting long-term sustainability. Innovation applied properly can be a strategy for both present and future success (Ottinger, 2021).

### User-driven innovation

User-driven innovation (UDI) can be defined as the 'process of drawing on users' knowledge to develop new products, services and concepts', which are based on a genuine understanding of users' needs and systematically engage users in the process of the development of an enterprise (Szymańska, 2017).[23] User driven innovation is more than user participation and user tests in the research process of a project. 'UDI is a business model and requires a business system and a company culture that under-pins it' (Venge, 2009). Studies shows that companies introducing *user-driven innovation* (UDI) systems represent a higher level of innovativeness than companies introducing the linear process (Szymańska, 2017).

### Design-driven innovation

In design-driven innovation the focus is on understanding why people attach meaning to things. 'Believing that people are not just looking for functional and technological features of products, it seeks to understand


1 Initiation
2 Insight
3 Strategy
4 Design
5 Production
6 Management

4.1 Design brief
4.2 Strategy><Design
4.3 Design methodology
4.4 Concept development
4.5 Design development
4.6 Design elements
4.7 Composition
4.8 Surface and format
4.9 Identity development

4.3.1 Human-centred design
4.3.2 User-experience
4.3.3 Emotional design
4.3.4 Innovation
4.3.5 Iterative method
4.3.6 Divergence and convergence
4.3.7 Sprint
4.3.8 Scrum
4.3.9 Kanban
4.3.10 Lean and agile
4.3.11 Design thinking
4.3.12 Customer journey
4.3.13 Need-finding
4.3.14 Service blueprint
4.3.15 Co-design
4.3.16 Business design
4.3.17 Strategic design thinking
4.3.18 Systemic design
4.3.19 In retrospect

- User-driven innovation
- Design-driven innovation
- AI-driven Innovation


> 'Products developed through design-driven innovation processes tend to have *higher margins* because they are clearly differentiated from the competition. Executed at the corporate level, this can lead to a sustainable competitive advantage and long-term profits.' (Duczek, 2021).

people's underlying desires and how to give meaning to things' (Duczek, 2021). According to Duczek the goal is to design a product that gives customers a new meaning that they have never seen before, thus create new markets by pushing users to create new habits and desires. Duczek points out Nintendo as one of many examples of design-driven innovation. Nintendo Wii was technologically inferior to competitors like Playstation and Xbox but offered a radical change in meaning by comparison. 'It was a physical experience to be played not with the thumbs, but with the whole body, using natural movements common to sports and vigorous games. The Wii changed the meaning of a console from immersion in a virtual world accessible only to niche experts to an active workout in the real world for everyone.' (Duczek, 2021). Design-driven innovation process can be divided into three distinct steps (based on Duczek, 2021).

1) *Absorption and listening*: Designers try to access knowledge about how people give meaning to things.
2) *Interpretation*: The knowledge gathered is combined with the knowledge of oneselves to create a unique proposal.
3) *Address*: The proposal is addressed to make it accessible to a broader context. The goal here is to establish a shift in the socio-cultural paradigm.

Verganti (2003) introduced the concept of design-driven innovation, which unlike previous frameworks explicitly concentrates on the innovation of product meanings (De Goey et al., 2018). The idea of design-driven innovation is rooted in the interpretation of Krippendorff (1989) which explains design as a meaning-making activity (De Goey et al., 2018).[24] The concept of *product meaning* refers to what values a product creates for a consumer, including utilitarian, emotional, psychological and socio-cultural values (Verganti, 2009, De Goey et al., 2018). In his research article (2008) Vergani states that 'No one questions the importance of user-centered design. Yet this is only one piece of the puzzle' (Verganti, 2008). According to Verganti, there are firms that have developed a different approach to rely on design that does not fit the user-centred model and, which to a large extent is independent of it. An approach he denotes as *design-driven innovation*. He points out that design-driven innovation 'is practiced at its most sophisticated and advanced level by successful Italian manufacturers, such as Alessi, Artemide, and Kartell, and allows them to be worldwide leaders in their industry, notwithstanding their small size and limited resources' (Verganti, 2008). He further claims that 'The innovation process of these Italian companies in furniture, kitchenware, lighting, and small appliance industries (as well as other worldwide leaders in different industries such as Apple or Bang & Olufsen), is definitely not user centered. Rather, these companies have developed superior capability to propose innovations that radically redefine what a product means for a customer. For them, design-driven innovation is the radical innovation of a product's meaning' (Verganti, 2008). Design driven innovation focuses on *why* consumers use a product, rather than what the product is or how it is used (Verganti and Öberg 2013, De Goey 2018).

Fig. 4.16 **The figure shows the 'Iterative development model' (according to Aflafla1, 2014), a classic example of an iterative process, which provides a good description of the different phases of the process.**

**According to Roberto Verganti design-driven innovation can be defined as 'an innovation in which the novelty of a message and of a design language prevails over the novelty of functionality and technology.' Companies see design-driven innovation as 'the radical innovation of a product's meaning' (Veganti, 2008, p. 437).**

Further reading
– ***Design Driven Innovation: Changing the Rules of Competition by Radically Innovating What Things Mean*** by Roberto Verganti, 2009.
– ***Overcrowded: Designing Meaningful Products in a World Awash with Ideas*** by Roberto Verganti, 2017.
– ***Innovation and Design in the Age of Artificial Intelligence*** by Roberto Verganti, Luca Vendraminelli, and Marco Iansiti, 2020. DOI: 10.1111/jpim.12523

24 'Design is making sense (of things) (...) the products of design are to be understandable or meaningful to someone' (Krippendorff, 1989, p. 9).
25 Iterative method is taken from mathematics. Newton's method is an iterative method used in numerical analysis to find the roots (zero points) of a function 'f(x)' (Hervik, 2015). See also revisionmaths.com/iteration.

### AI-driven Innovation

AI-driven innovation refers to the use of artificial intelligence technologies in the process of innovation (Gartner, 2021). Gartner predicts that AI-driven innovation will become mainstream in more than ten years. 'With the potential to significantly improve the innovation process, AI will reshape every aspect of the operational organisation, including how innovation is managed and supported' (Beale, 2022). In their research article Verganti et al. (2020) discuss the future of AI powered innovation, pointing out that there are many unanswered questions. Using Netflix and Airbnb as examples in their research they conclude that 'by removing the typical limitations (in scale, scope, and learning) of human-intensive design, AI can offer better performance in terms of customer centricity, creativity, and rate of innovation' (Verganti et al., 2020). They further reflect that 'to capture this potential, managers need to fundamentally rethink the way their organisation innovates. Design practice, in the age of AI, is completely different from the human-intensive innovation processes many organisations have in place today. For example, in AI-powered organisations, the role of humans is not to develop full solutions (which evolve in real time by AI), but to understand which innovation problems are meaningful, framing the innovation effort, and set up the software, data infrastructure, and problem-solving loops that will solve them' (Verganti et al., 2020).

## 4.3.5 Iterative method

The iterative method is a way of developing design that includes the user throughout the process. Iteration is a term for a circular way of working that has been used in technology and software development for a long time and that originates from mathematics.[25]

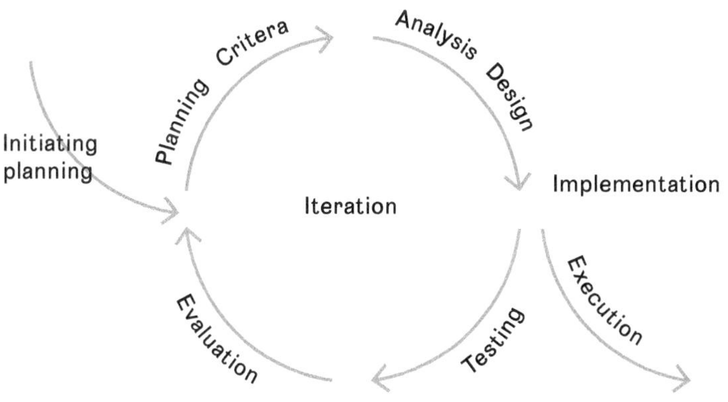


Fig. 4.16 Iterative process

W. Edwards Deming is recognised as the first to adopt something resembling a scientific method to ensure quality through iterations. In the 1950s, he suggested that business processes should be analysed and measured to identify links in the process that lead to product deviations from customer needs. He recommended that development processes take place in a continuous feedback loop so leaders can identify and change the parts of the process that need improvement. Deming

1 Initiation
2 Insight
3 Strategy
4 Design
5 Production
6 Management

4.1 Design brief
4.2 Strategy><Design
4.3 Design methodology
4.4 Concept development
4.5 Design development
4.6 Design elements
4.7 Composition
4.8 Surface and format
4.9 Identity development

4.3.1 Human-centred design
4.3.2 User-experience
4.3.3 Emotional design
4.3.4 Innovation
4.3.5 Iterative method
4.3.6 Divergence and convergence
4.3.7 Sprint
4.3.8 Scrum
4.3.9 Kanban
4.3.10 Lean and agile
4.3.11 Design thinking
4.3.12 Customer journey
4.3.13 Need-finding
4.3.14 Service blueprint
4.3.15 Co-design
4.3.16 Business design
4.3.17 Strategic design thinking
4.3.18 Systemic design
4.3.19 In retrospect

- User-driven innovation
- Design-driven innovation
- AI-driven Innovation

> We have seen that in AI factories solutions are created, improved, and personalised by machines, which operate through loops that scale up rapidly, with the potential of creating unintended outcomes, including the amplification of biases. Are existing theoretical frameworks that connect decisions to outcome in innovation still valid, when decisions are made by machines? (Verganti et al., 2020).

developed an iterative four-step management method, visualised as a simple diagram to illustrate this continuous process, known as *Deming's Cycle*[26] or *PDCA cycle* for Plan, Do, Check, Act:[27]

**Plan:** Design or revise business process components to improve performance.

**Do:** Implement the plan and measure performance.

**Check:** Assess the measurements and report the results to the appropriate decision makers.

**Act:** Decide what changes are needed to improve the process.

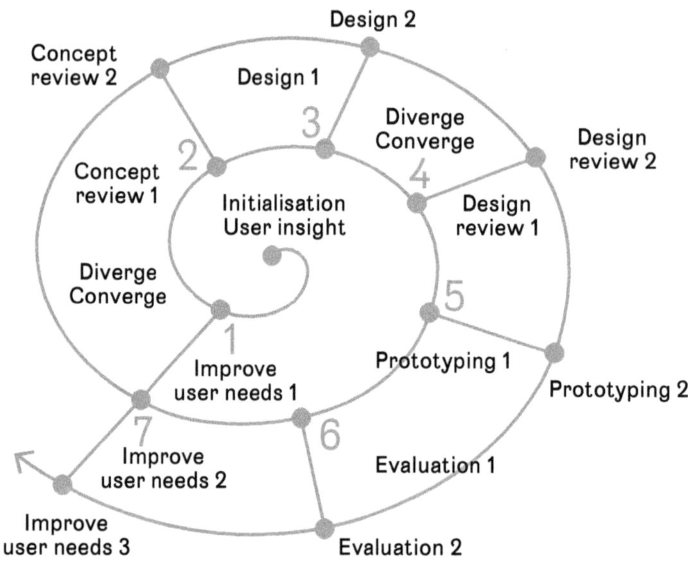


Fig. 4.17 Spiral UX model

Fig. 4.17 The figure shows the 'Spiral UX Model', an iterative model for a UX project, emphasising user insight, user needs and user-experience (based on Hang Guo, 2015).

Fig. 4.18 The figure shows the difference between invested time and costs when using a linear process vs. an iterative process. As shown by the model to the left, time use and cost increase steadily. In the model to the right we see that there are many small intervals of product development, based on rapid prototyping and testing, which for each process are carried forward in a new process and lead to a product that is well tested and ready for the market (the model is based on Sitre, 2016).

Today, the iterative method is linked to design thinking and innovation and is used across different design methods and processes. Iteration means that a process is repeated by a new process based on experience from the previous one until the desired solution to the problem emerges. Each iteration is a process. At each new iteration, a divergence occurs when the process opens up and a convergence takes place by closing it after the iteration is complete (4.3.6 Divergence and convergence). Perhaps the most important benefit of the iterative approach is the incremental learning that occurs through the iterations, which is a prerequisite for lowering the risk in product development, see Figure 4.18.

The starting point for an iteration is generally a problem to be solved and an idea to be developed for a solution, usually with a user-centric approach. The main activities in an iterative process are user insight, idea development, prototyping, testing and evaluation (4.3.1 Human-centred design). The process requires sufficient time and resources, combined with perseverance and patience, as well as room for *trial and error*.[28] 'Like the wheels on a bus, the wheels in iterative design go round and round ... round and round ... round and round ... until you have arrived at your destination. Iteration is a systematic, cyclical design loop. Products are prototyped, tested, analysed, refined and

26 The Deming Institute: demin.org
27 Another version of this PDCA cycle is OPDCA. The extra O stands for observation ('PDCA,' n.d., Rother, 2010: 129–158). 'Pay attention to the current condition'. A phrase from the literature on lean manufacturing and Toyota production system.
28 Trial and error: A phrase used for finding out of the best way to reach a desired result or a correct solution by trying out one or more ways or means and by noting and eliminating errors or causes of failure also: the trying of one thing or another until something succeeds (Trial and error, n.d.).
29 Based on Creuna 2017 (now a part of knowit.no).
30 ROI, 3 Incredible UX Case Studies! (Starley, 2017). See also: mashable.com: What's the ROI for This Article?

prototyped again. Then the process starts again. And it does not stop once we have a finished product. We iterate long after we launch, improve functionality, and complement complexity. We need to go through many different variations of the product, emphasise opportunities that exist in each of them and eliminate blind spots and obstacles' (zurb.com). The iterative method principle is easy to visualise; there is thus a multitude of different models. Figure 4.14 shows an example of a classic model. Newer models are often very simplified and require knowing the purpose of the method, for example: *Initiate: Shape - Do - Learn - Check (repeating loop): Deliver.*[29] An iterative process can also be explained as a spiral, where each loop is a new process based on the previous one, see Figure 4.16. Common to most iterative processes are:

- strong user orientation and user insight
- combination of fast and slow processes
- room for trial and error
- diverging and converging (open-close processes)
- fast-repeating prototyping (physical, digital, virtual, or a combination)
- testing and evaluation
- perseverance and determination

*Application*: The iterative method can take place over an extended period of time or as short 'sprints' over a few days, often based on one idea. The method is well suited for concept development, problem solving, and design development, in connection with start-ups and redesign.


1 Initiation
2 Insight
3 Strategy
4 Design
5 Production
6 Management

4.1 Design brief
4.2 Strategy><Design
4.3 Design methodology
4.4 Concept development
4.5 Design development
4.6 Design elements
4.7 Composition
4.8 Surface and format
4.9 Identity development

4.3.1 Human-centred design
4.3.2 User-experience
4.3.3 Emotional design
4.3.4 Innovation
4.3.5 Iterative method
4.3.6 Divergence and convergence
4.3.7 Sprint
4.3.8 Scrum
4.3.9 Kanban
4.3.10 Lean and agile
4.3.11 Design thinking
4.3.12 Customer journey
4.3.13 Need-finding
4.3.14 Service blueprint
4.3.15 Co-design
4.3.16 Business design
4.3.17 Strategic design thinking
4.3.18 Systemic design
4.3.19 In retrospect

– Allow errors and minimise risk


### Allow errors and minimise risk

Despite all the good benefits, the use of iterative methods can be a time-consuming and costly way of developing products or services. That is because the method involves many repeated rounds of prototyping and testing, and because it allows for more trial and error. In case of failure, there is a risk of having to go back many steps in the process and implement new processes. This can be time-consuming and costly. Nevertheless, the key to minimising risks lies in trial and error.

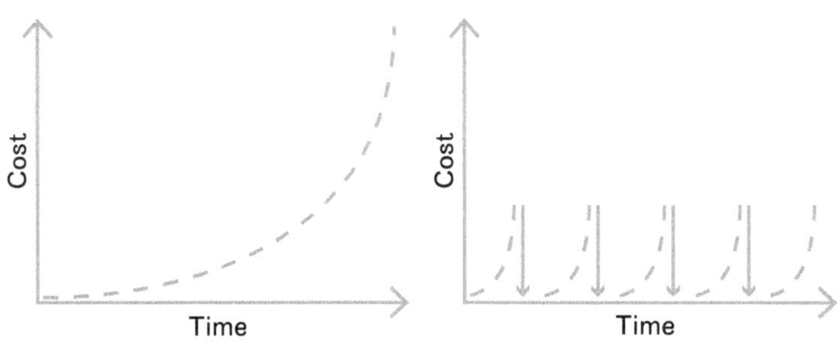


Fig. 4.18 Time vs. costs

The use of time and resources will generally be a matter of cost. A client will usually be concerned with cost/benefit and ROI (Return on investment),[30] which means that time and resources spent on a project lead to a profitable result. Linear processes based on analysis and step-by-step product development and eventually testing according to traditional principles may initially seem less time-consuming and costly than going

Iterative vs. linear process

Iterative processes are recurring and circular as opposed to linear processes that go straight from start to finish. A good combination is to base a linear process on one or more iterative processes.

back and forth with repeated user testing. The problem with traditional linear processes is that one does not get an answer to whether the solution works until the product is in its final phase and ready for the market. It may be very expensive to find out late in the process that the product does not capture the user's interest and needs as one would have imagined. One risks being left with a finished product that one has spent years developing and cannot sell. Considering that a large percentage of the products developed never enter the market, involving the user early on in the process and testing out the solution in the development phase can help reduce such a risk. It is about working in short intervals rather than long ones, making adjustments and improvements in the course of the process.

In an iterative process, rapid prototypes are made at an early stage. They are tested on selected user groups and evaluated. First, one finds out if it is user-friendly; second, if it is a product the user will be interested in buying. Such an approach would reduce the risk of unnecessary use of time and resources for developing a product that no one is interested in buying, see Figure 4.18. By testing early, you can learn something about the user's needs and desires and take this further into the process. This will increase the chance of ending up with a solution that is both user-friendly and attractive to the user.

### 4.3.6 Divergence and convergence

The iterative method involves repeated diverging and converging, which is a form of opening and closing processes, or a repeated opening and narrowing of a process. Divergence opens the process and explores different directions. In convergence, priorities and choices are made and the process is closed. Then new divergence and convergence follow based on the previous process. This is repeated until the desired result is achieved. One example of the use of divergence and convergence is a brainstorming process. The process opens wide as many ideas are thrown in, then the process is narrowed down by eliminating some ideas that one wants to work on further, then the process reopens with new brainstorming, some ideas are prioritised and carried forward into a new process, and so on. Divergence in reality means that different directions come from the same point. This can be opinions, representations or ideas with the same starting point, which are different or diverging. Convergence means that different directions come closer to each other

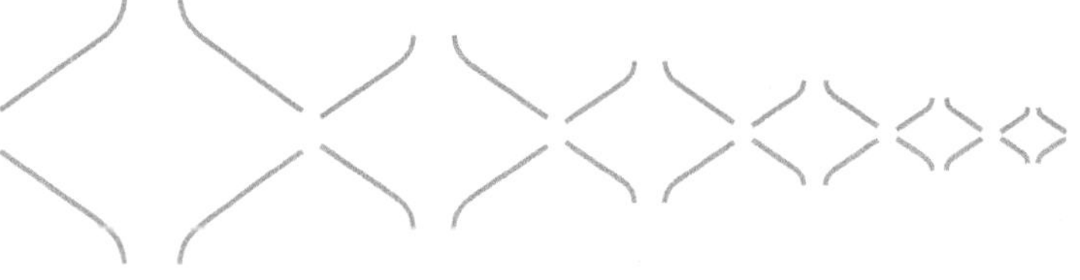


Fig. 4.19 Divergence and convergence

Fig. 4.19 The figure shows an example of what divergence and convergence look like in principle, with open and closed processes narrowing into a solution towards the end (based on Spoelstra and IDEO's Toolkit, 2009).

Fig. 4.20 The figure shows the section of divergence and convergence from Fig. 4.19. One could imagine divergence and convergence here being used at an overall level for the design process. The project opens up with insight, analysis, and idea development, and narrows down with implementation and assessment (based on Spoelstra and IDEO's Toolkit, 2009).

Fig. 4.21 The figure is based on The Double Diamond Design Process Model, developed by British Design Council. The model illustrates the design process as a diverging and converging process.

Further reading
Mashable.com: Five Dead Simple Ways to Track Social Media ROI, and What is ROI? redper- formance.no/definisjon/roi/.

Diverge
Develop in many directions. Diverge means to run apart (about lines); be different, deviate, be characterised by divergence (about meaning, presentation, or the like).

Converge
Collect different directions. Converge means running together, approaching each other; especially about light rays running together towards a specific point when they have passed through a lens ('Konvergere,' n.d.)

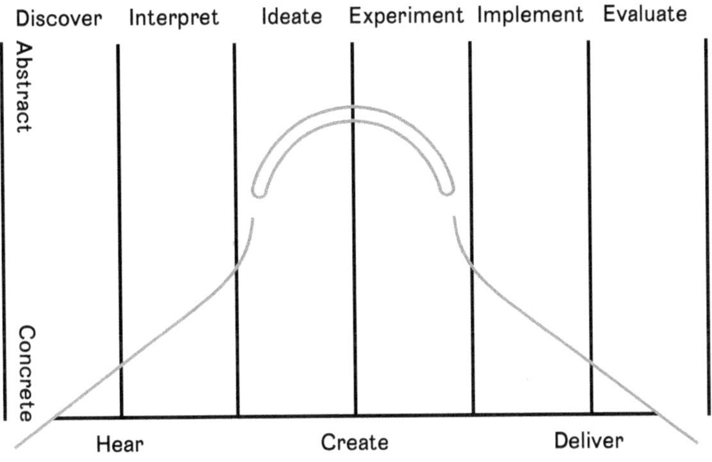


Fig. 4.20 Sections of divergence and convergence

as priorities are set and the number of directions is reduced, or threads gather (snl, n.d.).

*Application*: Divergence and convergence can be used in all phases of a design project, also as an overall method. It is particularly well suited to idea and design development.

### The Double Diamond

This method is a widely used and frequently referenced iterative method model, developed by British Design Council in 2005. Divergence and convergence are illustrated in the model's graphical open-closed form, which is divided into the four phases:

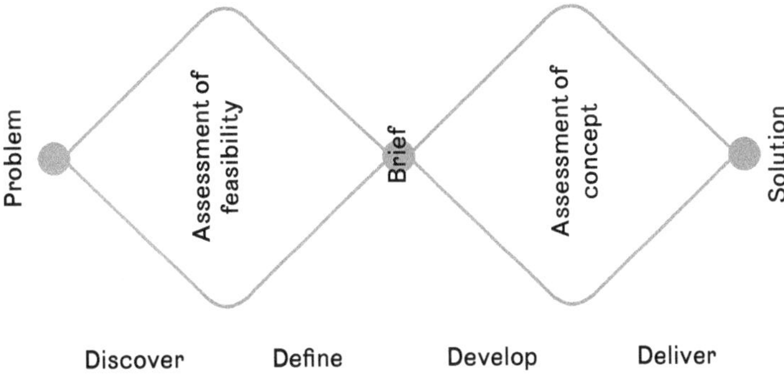


Fig. 4.21 The Double Diamond

**Discover**: The first quarter of the Double Diamond model marks the start of the project with an initial idea or inspiration, often starting from an insight phase where users' needs are identified. The stage includes market research, user insight, information management, and design research.

**Define:** The second quarter involves interpreting and anchoring these needs in the company's strategy. The stage includes project development, project management, and project duration.

1 Initiation
2 Insight
3 Strategy
4 Design
5 Production
6 Management

4.1 Design brief
4.2 Strategy><Design
4.3 Design methodology
4.4 Concept development
4.5 Design development
4.6 Design elements
4.7 Composition
4.8 Surface and format
4.9 Identity development

4.3.1 Human-centred design
4.3.2 User-experience
4.3.3 Emotional design
4.3.4 Innovation
4.3.5 Iterative method
4.3.6 Divergence and convergence
4.3.7 Sprint
4.3.8 Scrum
4.3.9 Kanban
4.3.10 Lean and agile
4.3.11 Design thinking
4.3.12 Customer journey
4.3.13 Need-finding
4.3.14 Service blueprint
4.3.15 Co-design
4.3.16 Business design
4.3.17 Strategic design thinking
4.3.18 Systemic design
4.3.19 In retrospect

– The Double Diamond

**The triple diamond**

A new diamond is suggested to be added to the double diamond. Wildhagen and Strålberg (2021) suggests a new diamond to be a diagnostic phase that emphasises how important it is to truly explore and understand root causes hidden in complex public issues. Charak (2020) suggests a third diamond to be strategy: One should define the strategy to tap into the opportunity and state problems that need solutions via a product.

**Develop:** The third quarter marks a phase in which solutions are developed, iterated and tested within the company. The stage includes a multidisciplinary work environment, design management, development methods, and testing.
**Deliver:** The last quarter represents the delivery stage, where the solution of the product or service is finalised and launched in the relevant market. The stage includes final testing, approval and launch, and ultimately measurement, assessment and feedback on the solution.

Fig. 4.22 The figure shows an illustration of a designsprint, based on Jake Knapp: 'The big idea with the Design Sprint is to build and test a prototype in just five days. You'll take a small team, clear the schedule for a week, and rapidly progress from problem to tested solution using a proven step-by-step checklist.' (thesprintbook.com). Check out: 'GV's Sprint Process in 90 Seconds' (YouTube).

### 4.3.7 Sprint

Sprint or design sprint is a method involving active user-centricity, iteration, diverging and converging, as described in the preceding sections. The method can be used in different phases of the design process, e.g. for start-ups, strategy development, ideas development, design development or to solve complex problems for the organisation. Daily questions businesses ask themselves are: Where should we focus? How should we get started? How will our ideas work in real life? How many meetings and discussions do we need to have before we reach a solution? How do we know that this is the right solution? These questions are crucial to whether a company will succeed with its efforts. Sprint is an intensive method that provides quick and correct answers, thus shortening the time from idea to market. For example, a sprint can take place through a five-day process where a group of people from the company (managers, engineers, IT people, designers, etc.) work together to come up with answers to critical questions and problem statements through design, prototyping, and testing ideas with customers or users.

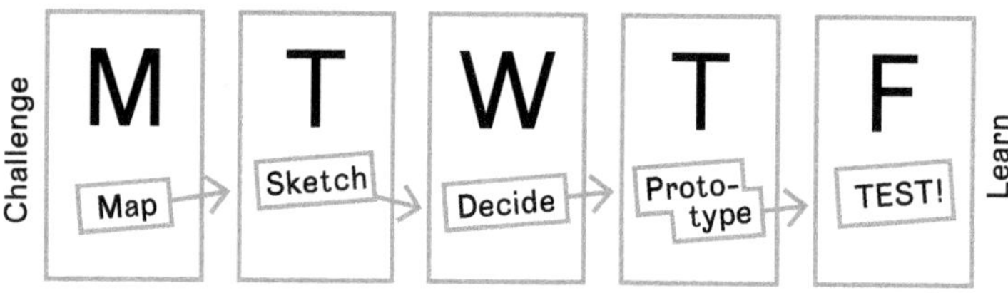


Fig. 4.22 GV's design sprint

The method was developed by Google Venture (GV),[31] and combines business strategy, innovation, behavioural science, design thinking, and more, wrapped in a compressed time-saving process that any team can use. Although GV developed the method for conducting effective start-up development, it is well suited for product and service development or other areas related to business development. Using design sprint can reduce the risk of bringing new products, services, or experiences to the market by quickly processing and testing critical questions on users. It avoids unnecessary use of time and resources on product development, which does not lead to anywhere, see Figure 4.18, and helps make new products more attractive to the market. 'Working together in a sprint, you can shortcut the endless-debate cycle and compress months of time into a single week. Instead of waiting to launch a minimal product to understand if an idea is any good, you'll get clear data from a realistic

31 Design sprint was developed by Google employee Jake Knapp and was used for everything from Google Search to Google X. He teamed up with Braden Kowitz and John Zeratsky in Google Ventures, and together they have run over a hundred sprints with companies in mobile telephony, e-commerce, health, finance, and written the book: *Sprint: How to Solve Big Problems and Test New Ideas in Just Five Days* (2016). GV collects sprint stories from around the world in SprintStories.com.

1 Initiation
2 Insight
3 Strategy
4 Design
5 Production
6 Management

4.1 Design brief
4.2 Strategy><Design
4.3 Design methodology
4.4 Concept development
4.5 Design development
4.6 Design elements
4.7 Composition
4.8 Surface and format
4.9 Identity development

4.3.1 Human-centred design
4.3.2 User-experience
4.3.3 Emotional design
4.3.4 Innovation
4.3.5 Iterative method
4.3.6 Divergence and convergence
4.3.7 Sprint
4.3.8 Scrum
4.3.9 Kanban
4.3.10 Lean and agile
4.3.11 Design thinking
4.3.12 Customer journey
4.3.13 Need-finding
4.3.14 Service blueprint
4.3.15 Co-design
4.3.16 Business design
4.3.17 Strategic design thinking
4.3.18 Systemic design
4.3.19 In retrospect

**Design sprint process**

**Before a sprint:** *Prepare* – get the right people, location, and things you need.

**Monday:** *Understand* – the problem and the focus area. Dive into the issue through surveys, competitor analysis, and strategy exercises. Start the day by creating a progress plan for the week, start with day five, and plan backwards. Identify the challenges. Throughout the day, examine what the experts in the company know. End the day by choosing a goal for an ambitious but affordable part of the problem, which you can solve within five days.

**Tuesday:** *Diverge* – focus on a solution. Quickly develop and sketch out as many different solutions as possible. Start the day with inspiration, a review of existing ideas that can be remixed and improved. Throughout the day, everyone will prepare sketches with an emphasis on critical thinking and creativity. At the end of the day, you schedule Friday's user test by recruiting customers that fit your target profile.

**Wednesday:** *Decide* – select the best ideas and turn them into hypotheses ready for testing. Put in place a user story, an informal description of the user function. Start the morning with critical analysis of each of the solutions and determine which one offers the best potential for achieving your long-term goal. Throughout the day, take the best sketches and implement them into a storyboard, showing a step-by-step plan for the prototype.

**Thursday:** *Prototype* – Build fast – a prototype that can be displayed to users. Start the day by turning the storyboard into a prototype, with a 'fake it' attitude. Focus on creating as realistic a visual 'wrapping' of the solution as possible within one day. Prepare everything for Friday's user test by reviewing the schedule, prototype, and writing an interview note.

**Friday:** *Confirm* – test out the prototype on real people (in other words: people outside your company) and learn what works and what does not. Start the day with user testing and learn how to take the solution one step further by observing and interviewing the user and learning how they respond to the prototype. The user test is what makes sense to the entire design sprint. After the user test, you will know what to do next (Based on gv.com).

prototype. The sprint gives you a super power: You can fast-forward into the future to see your finished product and customer reactions, before making any expensive commitments (Knapp, 2016).

The method may also have its limitations. 'My experience with Google Sprint (and similar initiatives) is that it takes some time for it to lead to actual results, even though the week is fruitful per se. Part of the challenge is that prototype testing is often not experienced very realistically, and that everything should go so fast that one often does not take the time to develop testable hypotheses.

Further reading
– *Sprint: How to Solve Big Problems and Test New Ideas in Just Five Days* by Jake Knapp, 2016.
– Check out: www.gv.com/sprint/ and
– 'GV's Sprint Process in 90 Seconds' YouTube.

## 4.3.8 Scrum

Scrum[32] is an iterative and incremental[33] methodology in an agile framework, where a task is solved jointly or co-created (4.3.10 Lean and agile). Incremental means adding units or small improvements that are needed to create a whole.[34] Such an approach is necessary when developing solutions consisting of several components, as is usually the case in software development. Scrum is suitable for managing projects where it is difficult to plan ahead of time, such as development of complex application and information systems. Functionality is key.

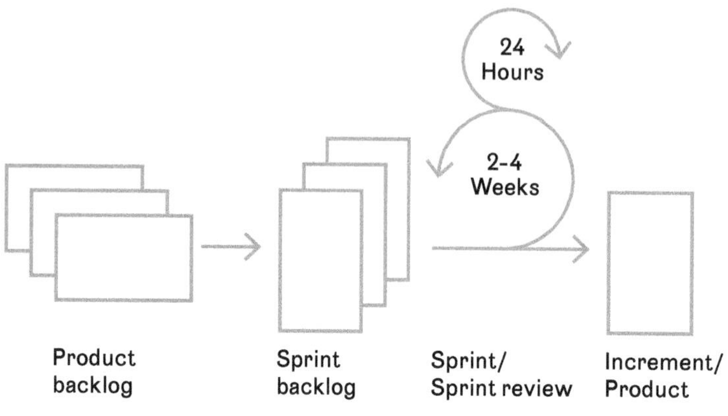


Fig. 4.23 Scrum

Fig. 4.23 The figure shows a Scrum process. Scrum requires a Scrum master to foster an environment where: 1) A Product owner orders the work for a complex problem into a product backlog, 2) The Scrum team turns a selection of functions into a sprint backlog, defining the why (sprint goal), the what (the items) and the how (delivering the increments). 3) The Scrum team turns selected items into an increment of value during a sprint. 4) The Scrum team and its stakeholders inspect the results and adjust for the next Sprint. 5) Repeat (Based on The 2020 Scrum GuideTM, scrumguides.org).

The iterations in Scrum are called sprints. The method is carried out by a multidisciplinary, self-managed team of product owner, developers and a Scrum master. The Scrum team is empowered to define goals for the development process. The goals are achieved by developing concrete, small product increments of 1–4 weeks in sprint. The various functions one wishes to develop are placed in a *product backlog*[35] in order of priority. The first thing to do in the sprint is to pick out a set of functions from the top of the product queue. For each of the functions one creates a list of tasks and ends up with a *sprint backlog*. The Scrum team seeks to refine tasks items during the *sprint process* to increase understanding and confidence. The increments resulting from the process are subject to evaluation and learning. During the sprint, daily meetings are held where team members coordinate their work with each other. The meeting is usually conducted as a stand-up meeting and should last a maximum of 15 minutes. During this period, all members of the team should keep the following three conditions in mind:

1) What has been done since the last Scrum meeting?
2) What do I have to do before the next meeting?
3) What has (possibly) prevented the group member from being effective in implementing this functionality?

The last thing one does in the sprint is demonstrate the increment that was created for some selected user groups. This is called *sprint review*. The purpose of this is to get feedback from those who have the needs and get valuable input for improvements based on what has been demonstrated. After this, the entire Scrum team conducts a *sprint*

32 The term originates from from rugby. A scrum is a formation of players.

33 Incremental generally refers to a series of small improvements.

34 In an agile context incremental development means that 'each successive version of the product is usable, and each builds upon the previous version by adding user-visible functionality' (agilealliance.org).

35 Backlog generally refers to the accumulation of work waiting to be done or orders to be fulfilled. Backlog can also refer to the product's recall, a list of requirements maintained for a product developed using methods such as Scrum ('Backlog,' n.d.).

36 The Japanese word 'kanban', meaning 'visual board' or a 'sign' (kanbanize.com).

37 The term Kanban orginates from the Toyota Production System (TPS). 'In the late 1940s, Toyota introduced "just in time" manufacturing to its production. The approach represents a pull system. This means that production is based on customer demand rather than the standard push practice to produce goods and push them to the market' (kanbanize.com).

*retrospective*. It is a flashback meeting where experiences from the last sprint are gathered and ways are found for the next sprint to increase quality and effectiveness ('Scrum,' n.d.).

*Application*: The method is suitable for the development of complex projects, software developments and advanced technologies.

### 4.3.9 Kanban

Kanban is a workflow management method that helps teams better define, manage, and improve processes. Like Scrum, Kanban[36] aims to help self-organising teams achieve the same goals of more productive work, greater team collaboration, and quicker product delivery (Rosin, 2021). Kanban was originally a logistic control system, developed and applied by Toyota as a scheduling system for just-in-time manufacturing[37] in the automotive industry. Here, the point was not to produce anything unless there was a demand for that particular item. Toyota's unique production system laid the foundation of Lean manufacturing or Lean methodology, as we know it today. The principle of Kanban has later become a territory claimed by Agile software development teams, as well as business units across various industries.[38] David J. Anderson[39] formulated the Kanban method as an approach to incremental, evolutionary process and systems change for knowledge work organisations (kanbanize.com).

The main principles of Kanban are to 1) Start with what you do now. 2) Pursue incremental change (denoting small positive or negative changes) and evolutionary change (relating to the gradual development). 3) Encourage acts of leadership at all levels to benefit from people's everyday insights and acts to improve their way of working. 4) Focus on customers' needs and expectations. 5) Managing the work by empowering people's abilities to self-organise around the work. 6) Regularly review the network of services and assess the applied work policies, to encourage the improvement of the delivered results. One can start building a Kanban system by setting up the most straightforward Kanban board with three basic columns, named: 'Requested', 'In Progress' and 'Done'. Use the Kanban board to 1) Visualise the workflow 2) Limit work in progress (WIP) 3) Manage flow 4) Make process policies explicit 5) Implement feedback Loops 6) Improve collaboratively (based on kanbanize.com).

When constructed, managed, and functioning correctly, it serves as a real-time information repository, highlighting bottlenecks within the system and anything else that might interrupt smooth working practices. It is focused on getting things done, and its fundamentals can be broken down into two types of principles and six practices (kanbanize.com).

*Application*: Suitable for Agile software development, R&D and other complex commercial sectors (1.9.3 Agile process management).

### 4.3.10 Lean and agile

User centring, interaction, iterative and incremental processes, and multidisciplinary teamwork are at the core of Lean and agile methods.[40] The two methods have many similarities, but different approaches and often different problem statements. Lean is typically applied to a repetitive, predictable process, and aims to improve *the process* in order to make a


1 Initiation
2 Insight
3 Strategy
4 Design
5 Production
6 Management

4.1 Design brief
4.2 Strategy><Design
4.3 Design methodology
4.4 Concept development
4.5 Design development
4.6 Design elements
4.7 Composition
4.8 Surface and format
4.9 Identity development

4.3.1 Human-centred design
4.3.2 User-experience
4.3.3 Emotional design
4.3.4 Innovation
4.3.5 Iterative method
4.3.6 Divergence and convergence
4.3.7 Sprint
4.3.8 Scrum
4.3.9 Kanban
4.3.10 Lean and agile
4.3.11 Design thinking
4.3.12 Customer journey
4.3.13 Need-finding
4.3.14 Service blueprint
4.3.15 Co-design
4.3.16 Business design
4.3.17 Strategic design thinking
4.3.18 Systemic design
4.3.19 In retrospect


38 Historically based on 'Kanban Method,' (2007) and leading figures in the Lean and agile community such as David Aderson, Dan Vacanti, Darren Davis, Corey Ladas, Dominica DeGrandis, Rick Garber, and others (kanbanize.com).

39 David J. Anderson is the author of ***KANBAN: Successful Evolutionary Change for Your Technology Business*** and the founder of David J Anderson School of Management (djaa.com).

40 Lean thinking, teams increase speed by managing flow (usually by limiting work-in-process), whereas in Agile, teams emphasise small batch sizes to deliver quickly (often in sprints) (Lynn 2022, planview.com).

better product. Agile applies to repetitive processes where we iterate on improving *one product* (Sigberg, 2019). The two methods also originate in completely different cultures. Agile comes from the United States, Lean from Asia. In Asian culture, the team and the process itself are key, while in the United States the individual is highlighted above all else (Eriksen, 2010).

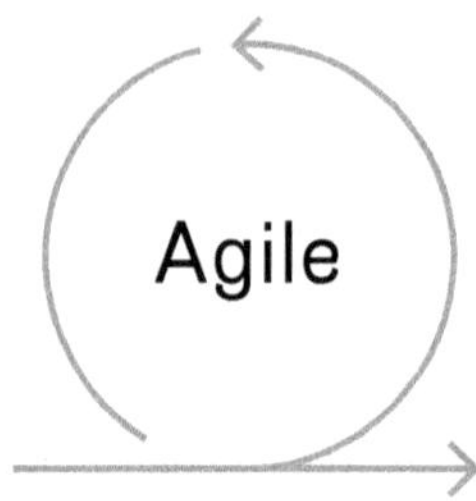


Fig. 4.24 Agile

**Agile**: Agile describes a set of values and principles for software development where requirements and solutions evolve through collaboration between self-organising, multidisciplinary teams (Collier, 2011).[41] Agile principles (Denning, 2020):

- Work is focused directly on meeting customers' needs and interaction with the customer is central.
- Work is done by self-organising teams, networks and ecosystems that mobilise the full talents of those doing the work.
- Work proceeds in an iterative fashion and progresses towards fulfilling the needs of customers is assessed at every stage.

Agile software development is an umbrella term for a set of frameworks and practices initially based on the values and principles expressed in the Manifesto for Agile Software Development[42] (agilealliance.org). It was written in 2001 by seventeen independent-minded software practitioners. They didn't agree on all the principles, but managed to gather around four core values: 1) Individuals and interactions *over* processes and tools, 2) Working software *over* comprehensive documentation 3) Customer collaboration *over* contract negotiation, 4) Responding to change *over* following a plan (agilemanifesto.org). There are a number of software development frameworks based on Agile, of which Scrum and Kanban are two of the most widely used ones (4.3.8 Scrum, 4.3.9 Kanban).

*Application*: When there is a need to streamline a process or solve a known task.

Here are examples of key Agile concepts, based on agilealliance.org:

- *User stories*: Each user story is expected to yield a contribution to the value of the overall product.
- *Daily meeting*: Each team member briefly describes any 'completed' contributions and any obstacles that stand in their way.
- *Personas*: When user-experience is a major factor in project outcomes - the team crafts detailed, synthetic biographies of fictitious users of the future product.
- *Team*: A small group of people, assigned to the same project or effort, nearly all of them on a full-time basis.
- *Incremental development*: Nearly all Agile teams favour an incremental development strategy; in an Agile context, this means that each

Fig. 4.24 The figure illustrates the smooth Agile process (based on Powel-Morse, 2017).

Fig. 4.25 The figure shows an example of how *design thinking*, Lean and agile can complement each other as methodologies. *Design thinking* can make it possible to see the product or service with new eyes, based on how users experience it. Lean can be used to optimise and streamline a product or service. Agile can be used to streamline the process and delivery towards the customer.

Table 4.4 The table shows Design thinking vs. Lean mindset. *Design thinking* is more user-oriented and innovative in its approach to problem solving. *Lean thinking* is more incremental, which implies continuous improvement and optimisation of the process to make a better product or service.

41 Stephen Denning is the author of *Doing Agile Right: Transformation Without Chaos* (Harvard Business Review Press, 2020). The book focuses narrowly on particular Agile methods and practices and addresses the broader topic of becoming an agile enterprise.

42 The Agile Manifesto of 2001 (agile101) includes four values and 12 principles. It is available at agilemanifesto.org/principles.html.

43 Toyota Production System – TPS.

successive version of the product is usable, and each builds upon the previous version by adding user-visible functionality.

- *Iterative development*: Allowing for 'repeating' software development activities, and for potentially 'revisiting' the same work products.
- *Milestone retrospective*: During or at the end of the project, the team invests from one to three days in a detailed analysis of the project's significant events (1.9.3 Agile process management, 3.4.7 Agile strategy management).

**Lean**: Lean is a process philosophy found in many different variants and used in many industries: Lean Production, Lean Management, Lean Healthcare, Lean Banking, Lean Software Development, etc. According to Lindblad (2008), Lean Philosophy is to eliminate waste in a production process, thereby reducing production time, resource effort, costs and so on. This is done by starting from the final product and defining the process flow accordingly in order to get the simplest possible process. In his article 'Lean – a philosophy', Lindblad describes the origins and thinking behind Lean. Lean was developed by the Japanese car manufacturer, Toyota,[43] as a tool to reduce waste. The Japanese considered

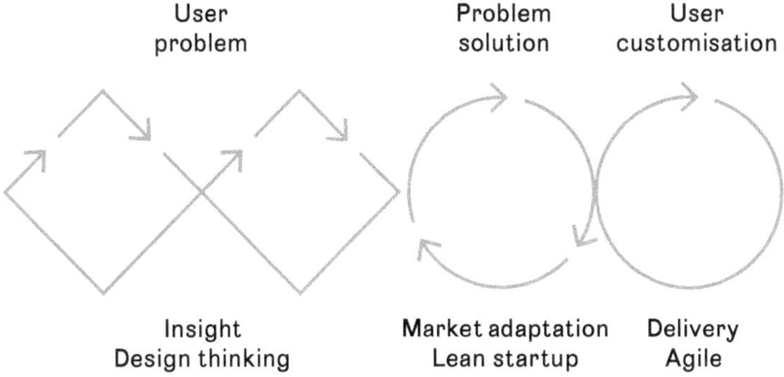


Fig. 4.25 Complementation

| Lean: | Design thinking: |
|---|---|
| Continual improvement. | Radical rethinking. |
| Based on the company's vision. | Based on observing and discovering unfulfilled needs. |
| Use of analytical processes and identification of improvement points. | Experimental approach, testing and prototyping, trial and error. |
| The goal is related to the business plan. | The goal is to solve a problem. |
| The target group is consumers/customers. | The target audience is users or people. |
| Look at an existing solution, improve, reduce waste, profitability/streamlining. | Develop or improve product or service from a user perspective, and what is technologically feasible and economically sound. |
| Focus on internal improvement, from the inside out. | Focus on the user, from the outside-in. |

Table 4.4 Design thinking vs. Lean mindset



Lean vs. agile

Lean applies to repetitive processes aiming to produce a new (and identical) product each time, improving process with better product quality as the intended outcome. Agile applies to repetitive processes where we iterate on improving one product. Agile focuses less on the process, and more on how can we make a better product (Sigberg, 2019).

wastefulness the ultimate consequence of all activities that do not create value for the customer. They defined seven types of wastefulness: overproduction, waiting, transportation, document processing, storage, unnecessary movements, defects. Five principles used in recent Lean thinking (Womack & Jones, 1996):

- Specify what the value is to the customer for each product.
- Identify the steps in the value flow for each product.
- Ensure that all value-creating activities are streamlined so that the product 'flows' towards the customer.
- Let the customers' demand drive the production.
- Strive for perfection.

Lindblad refers to Nordea as a successful example of using Lean: They started with Lean Banking as early as 2005. The intention was to streamline the bank's processes, thereby reducing costs. Nordea's CEO Lars G. Nordström illustrated the motive for using Lean as follows: 'There is no reason why granting a large loan should take two weeks if the process itself actually takes two hours. If it really takes two hours, the customer will get a response after two hours'. Nordea experienced very good results from its Lean venture, and today the bank has its own 'Lean Team', which continuously works to improve the bank's processes.

*Application*: Using multidisciplinary teamwork when we are not very familiar with the scope and content of the task, such as when starting a new business concept or start-up (3.5.4 Lean start-up).

**Design thinking vs. Lean and Agile:** *Design thinking*, *Lean* and *Agile* focus on various aspects of service and product development, but can also complement each other; it is not a matter of 'either or' (see Figure 4.25 and Table 4.4).

### 4.3.11 Design thinking

Positioning led by Jack Trout[44] in the 1980s and branding led by companies like Colgate, Unilever and Coca-Cola in the 1990s were new ways of thinking about business strategy. Similarly, *design thinking* led by Nigel Cross and Tim Brown from around 2008, created new ways of thinking by bringing design methodology into the business world. There is ever increasing interest in *design thinking*, and more and more businesses are putting the method into use. The industrial giants IBM and GE are examples of major international companies being at the forefront of implementing design thinking at an early stage. They are not alone in experiencing that increasingly advanced technology poses a greater challenge when products and services are to be user optimised. 'There's no longer any real distinction between business strategy and the design of the user-experience' (Bridget van Kralingen, IBM). In the article *Design Thinking Comes of Age*, Harvard Business Review (2015), Jon Kolko explains: 'There's a shift under way in large organisations, one that puts design much closer to the center of the enterprise. But the shift isn't about aesthetics; it's about applying the principles of design to the way people work'.

According to Tim Brown, *design thinking* is a collaboration between three different people with three different goals. It is the business that aims to make money or achieve other goals; it is the technology that

Fig. 4.26 **The figure is based on a model by Tim Brown (2009), which is widely used to explain the concept of innovation through design thinking. *Desirable*: What does the user want or need? *Feasible*: Is it technically possible to develop and implement? *Viable*: Is it profitable? Can we make money from it? The outermost circle, added by Grimsgaard, W. (2022), adds a new dimension to the model, which takes into account the environment and sustainability as a natural context.**

Tips for the designer

**Three key questions in design thinking are: What do people want? What can we actually do? Can we make money out of it?**

> **'Design thinking is a human-centred approach to innovation that draws from the designer's toolkit to integrate the needs of people, the possibilities of technology, and the requirements for business success.'**
> **— Tim Brown, CEO of IDEO**

Further reading

***Innovation as a Learning Process: Embedding Design Thinking*** **(Beckman and Barry 2007: 42 and 30). Available online as pdf.**

44 **Jack Trout and Al Ries, *Positioning – The battle for your mind* (1986). *Differentiate or Die* (2000/2008).**

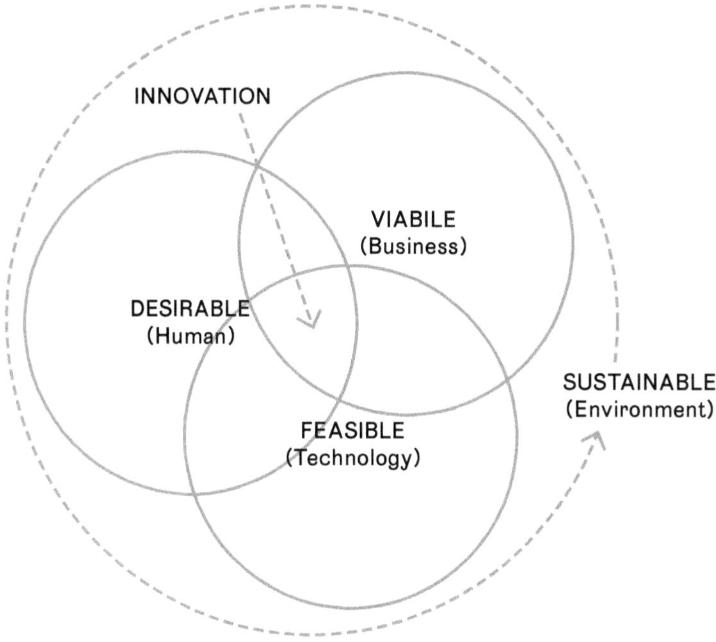


Fig. 4.26 Design thinking

aims to make things work, and it is the designer that aims to make the solution attractive and user-friendly. 'It must not be three people, but depth expertise in the three areas is necessary. It can also be people who have both business and design, or design and technology knowledge' (Wildhagen, 2017). The principles of design thinking are the combination of business, technology and people. This is a success criterion when the ambition is to create products that are usable for people, that are technologically feasible, and from which the company can make money. Three key questions in *design thinking* are: What do people want? What can we actually manage? Can we make money out of it? If we create something people want, the product will become attractive. If it is technically feasible and we make money out of it, it is viable and sustainable. Everything is connected, always. Which is also the reason why various extensions of Tim Brown's original model have emerged, based on the need to put it in an environmental context, to meet sustainability goals.

Many designers might think: Finally the business world has gained greater understanding of the value of design. Tim Brown puts it this way: 'Design is no longer just about creating elegant products and beautiful surroundings, and design thinking is not only valuable in creative industries or for designers who design products. Instead, design is often more effective when used in more multifaceted abstract problem statements, such as improving the guest experience in a hotel, encouraging bank customers to save more, or creating a compelling narrative for a public service campaign. The best designers turn necessity into utility, limitations into opportunities, and need into demand. These designers make thorough observations of how we use environments, products, and services; they discover patterns where others see complexity and confusion; they put together new ideas from seemingly incompatible fragments; and they turn problems into opportunities. Design thinking

1 Initiation
2 Insight
3 Strategy
4 Design
5 Production
6 Management

4.1 Design brief
4.2 Strategy><Design
4.3 Design methodology
4.4 Concept development
4.5 Design development
4.6 Design elements
4.7 Composition
4.8 Surface and format
4.9 Identity development

4.3.1 Human-centred design
4.3.2 User-experience
4.3.3 Emotional design
4.3.4 Innovation
4.3.5 Iterative method
4.3.6 Divergence and convergence
4.3.7 Sprint
4.3.8 Scrum
4.3.9 Kanban
4.3.10 Lean and agile
4.3.11 Design thinking
4.3.12 Customer journey
4.3.13 Need-finding
4.3.14 Service blueprint
4.3.15 Co-design
4.3.16 Business design
4.3.17 Strategic design thinking
4.3.18 Systemic design
4.3.19 In retrospect

Design thinking meets criticism

The concept of design thinking was introduced in 1987 with the book *Design Thinking* by Peter G. Rowe. After the concept was popularised two decades later, the term has been explained in many different ways, which has contributed to confusion and ambiguity about its meaning. Pentagram's Natasha Jen is among the critical voices with her article: 'Design is not a monster you "unleash" to fix the world' (Dawood, 2018). Further reading: *A Designer Addresses Criticism of Design Thinking* (Malamed, 2018).

is a method where there is no need for geniuses' (Change by design 2009). Designer John Maeda puts it this way: 'My role isn't to fix pixels. My role is to find strategic insights as to where design can have the most business impact' (co.design 2014, Ward, 2017).

With design thinking, greater awareness has emerged among major international companies in terms of hiring designers, not preferably to create visual solutions, but to help develop strategy and business concepts. Behind successful start-ups like Uber and Airbnb, funded and supported by major US investment companies, lies the use of design thinking at all stages, with the involvement of designers in planning, business development and visual design. 'Design Didn't Make Uber Good, But It Made Uber Great' (Mark Wilson, 2017/2014). This is just one of many examples of areas where the use of design thinking has contributed to innovation. Design thinking takes place through a circular iterative process by empathising > defining > idea developing > prototyping > testing.

*Application*: Design thinking can be used as an overall approach and a way of thinking in any project, whether about strategy development, business development, start-ups or design projects. The design mindset helps create better processes, solutions, and collaboration.

### 4.3.12 Customer journey

'Customer journey is a tool for logging a user's interaction or relationship with a service' (Bergan, T., 2018). Instead of looking at just part of a transaction or experience, the *customer journey* documents the entire experience of being a customer: before, during and after the 'journey'. The term *customer journey* is strongly linked to the method used in the subject area of service design to map and improve the user's experience of a service; how the customer or user perceives a service from beginning to end. For example, a journey may be a matter of the experience from booking a flight ticket to arrival at the destination, or it may be the use of an online banking service, or it may be user situations such as buying an item in the store; what the customer should do to get to and from the store, find the right item, as well as get the necessary service and follow up in case of complaint or item replacement.

When using journey mapping as a method, the company is more involved in the process than in traditional assignment processes and helps create a solution with the designer. The entire process takes place visually, which simplifies the collaboration between the parties involved, namely the company, the user and the designer. Visual mapping is important for the designer and the client to gain a common understanding and see the possibility of new solutions (2.8.4 Customer journey). 'Customer Journey Map is a graphical illustration that describes the journey to a user by displaying the different touch points that characterize the user's interaction with the service' (Roberta Tassi/servicedesigntools.org). Analysing a customer journey involves observing the user-experience and mapping the user through their various touch points with the company, service or product.

In addition, the various customer segments can be interviewed to gain insight into their experience with the service. The collected information is used to build customer journey maps, possibly one map for each customer segment, and one that reflects the experiences gathered and

Fig. 4.27 The figure shows an example of a customer journey, in this case a simplified graphical representation of a journey. The points on the map are touch points where the customer has an experience of the service. Each of the points can be examined using, among other things, observation and user interviews. The result can be further analysed and be used as a basis for adjusting the strategy and creating new ideas to strengthen the customer journey, and increase customer satisfaction. In this process, there is a smooth transition between the different phases of insight, analysis, strategy, and idea development. The designer is free to illustrate the customer journey as it best illuminates the customers' points of contact with the service before, during, and after, for example a flight, or purchase of goods in store or on the internet. One starts with rough sketches in the analysis phase and develops more concrete graphic illustrations in the solution phase.

Tips for the designer

'Beyond capturing the current experience your customers are going through, journey mapping can also be used to imagine and ideate on the future, using the format as a tool to speculate on what a customer might see and do in a future experience' (Miller and Flowers 2016).

Mapping the customers' user-experiences is a key part of being a human-centred business, and it is important to look at both what the person experiences, and what went on outside of their view to make it happen. Customer journey mapping and service blueprinting are two complementary methods that can help us see both sides of our services. Miller and Flowers (2016).

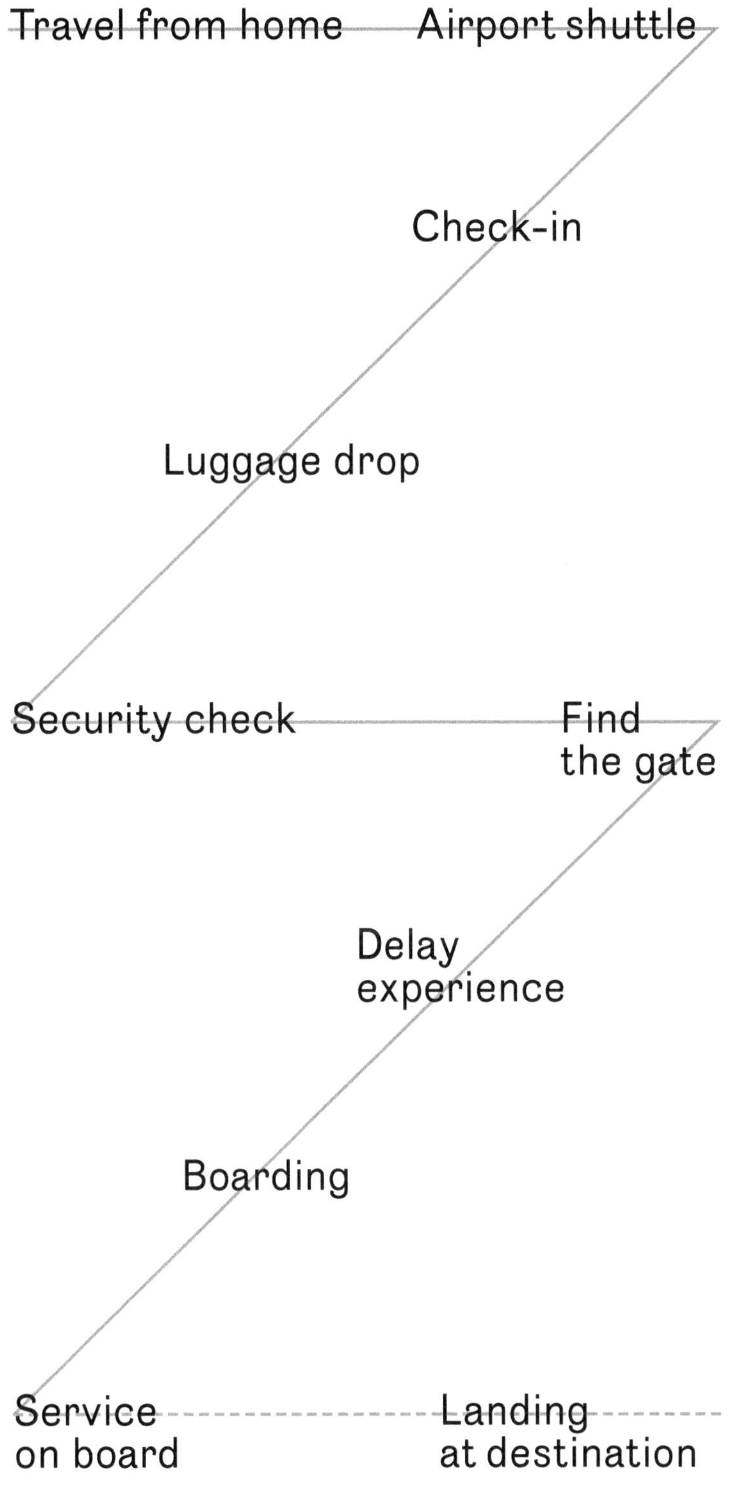


Fig. 4.27 Customer journey


1 Initiation
2 Insight
3 Strategy
4 Design
5 Production
6 Management

4.1 Design brief
4.2 Strategy><Design
4.3 Design methodology
4.4 Concept development
4.5 Design development
4.6 Design elements
4.7 Composition
4.8 Surface and format
4.9 Identity development

4.3.1 Human-centred design
4.3.2 User-experience
4.3.3 Emotional design
4.3.4 Innovation
4.3.5 Iterative method
4.3.6 Divergence and convergence
4.3.7 Sprint
4.3.8 Scrum
4.3.9 Kanban
4.3.10 Lean and agile
4.3.11 Design thinking
4.3.12 Customer journey
4.3.13 Need-finding
4.3.14 Service blueprint
4.3.15 Co-design
4.3.16 Business design
4.3.17 Strategic design thinking
4.3.18 Systemic design
4.3.19 In retrospect


Further reading

*The Design Thinking Playbook: Mindful Digital Transformation of Teams, Products, Services, Businesses and Ecosystems* by Michael Lewrick, Patrick Link and Larry Leifer (2018).

Customer journey process

Log customers' experience before, during and after 'the journey'. Identify and examine the main points of contact. Map problem areas and improvement potential. Develop suggestions for action that can be taken to resolve the problems and improve the service.

**Customer journey process**

There are many ways to create a successful customer journey map. Here are examples of nine steps (based on Martinuzzi 2015):
**Step 1:** Identify 'personas', types of customers or those for whom you want to design maps.
**Step 2:** Identify the different stages when a customer interacts with your company. What are the different points of contact, from beginning to end? What different channels do they use and what physical activities do they do at each point of contact? Plot each of these across the journey.
**Step 3:** Set the expectations customers have of your company, service or product at each of the points of contact on the map.
**Step 4:** Identify whether your service or product meets these expectations. Is there any gap?
**Step 5:** Identify points in the customer interaction where things sometimes or often go wrong. Describe these obstacles or blockages the customer experiences along the way.
**Step 6:** Document the customers' emotional response to each step of the journey.
**Step 7:** Identify 'the moment of truth.' These are important moments in your customers' journey when they can make a decision about your company, product or service: good or bad.
**Step 8:** Analyse potential opportunities for improvement of customer service and customer experience.
**Step 9:** Use the insights you get to list specific actions you could take to make these improvements and innovations.

Fig. 4.28 The figure is taken from the Stanford Design Innovation Process (2018), a circular process, which is based on user orientation and iteration.

Tips for the designer
There are two basic need-finding tools: observations and interviews.

Tips for the company
Today's designer not only works with design and visual solutions, but uses design as a tool to solve strategic tasks for the business.

shows the different problem areas. The goal is to identify the points of contact in, for example, a service interface, where interaction between the user and the company is established. The points of contact can be physical, virtual, or human. The user-experience is visualised by linking the different points of contact together in a whole sequence, using rough sketches, to get an overview. The overview is used as a starting point for an analysis of the service. The analysis is part of a further strategy and idea phase for adjusting and improving the service through more concrete and systematic use of graphic illustrations. By mapping competing services in tandem, it is possible to compare problem areas. It is advantageous to develop structures with uniform graphical language and criteria for comparison. This simplifies the description of different customer experiences and the work on comparing them. Customer journey is a typical example of a design assignment that does not necessarily end up with a solution to the problem, but results in a visual system and suggestions for action that can be implemented to resolve the problem(s).

### 4.3.13 Need-finding

*Need-finding* is a concept linked to customer journey, user-centric approach and *design thinking*, but may fit in any context where the company or the designer is looking for the potential to create something new

Further reading
See servicedesigntools.org for service blueprint tools.

45 d.design, Hasso Plattner Institute of Design at Stanford University
46 Stanford ME310 Design Innovation is a global network of designers, engineers and innovators who challenge complex real-world problems.

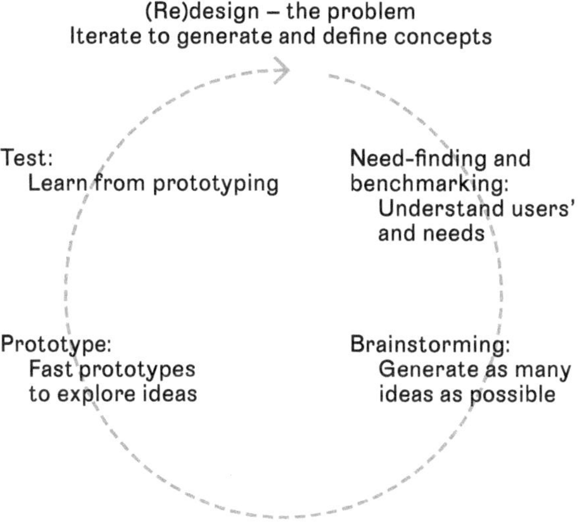


Fig. 4.28 Need-finding


1 Initiation
2 Insight
3 Strategy
4 Design
5 Production
6 Management

4.1 Design brief
4.2 Strategy><Design
4.3 Design methodology
4.4 Concept development
4.5 Design development
4.6 Design elements
4.7 Composition
4.8 Surface and format
4.9 Identity development

4.3.1 Human-centred design
4.3.2 User-experience
4.3.3 Emotional design
4.3.4 Innovation
4.3.5 Iterative method
4.3.6 Divergence and convergence
4.3.7 Sprint
4.3.8 Scrum
4.3.9 Kanban
4.3.10 Lean and agile
4.3.11 Design thinking
4.3.12 Customer journey
4.3.13 Need-finding
4.3.14 Service blueprint
4.3.15 Co-design
4.3.16 Business design
4.3.17 Strategic design thinking
4.3.18 Systemic design
4.3.19 In retrospect


that people may need. The most important thing about *need-finding* is that we *look* without knowing what we are looking for. We trust that with our ability to define the problem, it will emerge during *the need-finding* process (d.design, Stanford).[45] The two basic tools to gain insight into people's needs are observations and interviews (2.6.3 Observation, 2.6.2 Interview).

*The model of the Stanford Design Innovation Process* (2018) includes need-finding and is designed as a circle to emphasise that the design process is iterative. The principle is to experiment by trial and error: 'Fail early and fail often so you can succeed faster' (Stanford ME310).[46] The process has four steps:

- *(Re)design the problem*: Observe and interview users to better understand their needs. Iterate to generate and define concepts.
- *Need-finding and benchmarking*: Test and evaluate existing technologies and products to identify design opportunities. Understand the user's needs.
- *Brainstorming*: Conduct extensive brainstorming to produce obvious, crazy, and novel ideas.
- *Prototype and testing*: Quickly test ideas through repetitive iteratively prototyping to find out how they work.

Need-finding key points based on d.design, Stanford:

**1) Principle**

Human-centred design: Look to users for design inspiration.

**2) Purpose**

*Uncover latent needs*: Look for 'gaps' in use (what does not work), usability and meaning (look for surprises, differences between what people say they do and what they actually do).

*Gain empathy for users*: Discover the emotions that govern behaviour.

*Look for extreme users*: Users who are pushing the system may reveal needs before the mainstream (before most people jump on a trend).

Typically, a journey map is not a depiction of an actual real-world, single customers' experience. A journey map is an aggregate of experiences compiled from customer research and the knowledge of subject-matter experts in your organisation (Miller and Flowers 2016).

**3) Process**
*Insight*: Identify specific stories and artefacts (pictures, drawings, quotes, etc.) that communicate your insights.
*Observations*: Make observations and gather your team to share findings and insights. Try to capture observations in ways that are visual, divisible, and evocative.
*Photographs*: Photography is well suited to capture specific situations and serve as a basis for discussion. 20 per hour is a good pace.
*Quotes*: Short quotes can be a great way to communicate the essence of conversation with a user. Transfer to Post-it.
*Stories*: Write down notes while talking to users in the field. Good stories are a tool for building empathy that gives meaning.
*Audio recording*: Recordings of users expressing their needs are compelling. These recordings can be a good storytelling media in the long run.
*Artefacts*: Anything you can take with you from the location can be a good illustration of the culture detail.
**4) Anatomy of a good need-finding tool**
A good *need-finding* tool for interviews and interactions requires:
- Good theme/topic (interesting, open, professional, unusual, observant).
- Good surroundings (known, friendly, 'safe').
- Structure and flexibility (have a plan and goals, but pursue new opportunities).
- Great stories (capture images, quotes, etc. that bring your interview to life).
- Iterative design (iterate interview structure and goals based on results).
- Ways to drive past the explicit insight to implicit drivers.
- Ways to avoid the Hawthorne effect.[47]
- Allow silence – if you listen, they will speak.
- Respect your subjects.

**5) How do you know that you are having an aha-moment?**
- You will have implicit insight.
- You will have uncovered a surprise or found what is missing.
- You will be able to explain why people do unusual things.
- You will be able to explain a contradiction.
- In interviews, you will know what the subject will say next.
- You will be able to tell a good story.
- You will want to tell friends what you have learned.

### 4.3.14 Service blueprint

While the customer journey focuses on mapping the customers' experience of a service, *service blueprint* includes what happens behind the scenes. The service blueprint is a mapping method that visualises a service offering accurately. 'Its purpose is to help understand the service delivery process from the customers' perspective in order to assist the service design and improvement processes' (Athuraliya, 2021). *Service blueprint* involves mapping the entire service from the customers' front stage experience to what is at the core of the business at the backstage and behind the scenes of the service. That implies making visible how the company operates and delivers, and linking it to the customer experience (Miller and Flowers 2016). The very expression 'blueprint' is borrowed from old print houses[48] and is often used by architects and

Fig. 4.29 The figure shows how a service blueprint includes the entire organisation and also the process behind the service, which the customer cannot see. 'Stage' is used here as a metaphor. It consists of three perspectives: front stage, backstage and 'behind the scenes'. The stage is where the action happens and what the audience can see. Here the customers' experience of the service takes place. Back stage is where all the support processes are located: the lights, kits, the crew, all of which should be invisible to the customer, but often are not. Behind the scenes are also the company and all those who contribute to what is going to happen on stage. Then, behind the scenes is what the company should do to make both the stage and the backstage possible. Rules, regulations, guidelines, budgets: all those things that are not really part of either the front stage or the backstage. All the 'backstage' and support processes are documented and linked to the user-experience (Miller and Flowers, 2016).

47 The Hawthorne effect concept, originates from the Hawthorne studies in the United States in the 1920s, which showed that being examined in itself produces behavioural changes (distortion of behaviour due to observation).
48 Blueprint was a term used in offset printing from the late 19th century. It was a print made for the final proofreading or quality check of a publication before it went into the printing process. The blue print was printed in the original printing process in blue (cyan) print on a thin (kalk) paper.
49 Co-design has its roots in participatory design techniques developed in Scandinavia in the 1970s (Chrisholm; Steen, Manschot and De Koning, N., 2011).

engineers. If you have a blueprint, you should have an exact description, drawing or print of how something should be produced. That is part of the point here, too. With *a service design blueprint*, you have detailed documentation so the service can be put into action. Whether it is a recurring service, like an event or a festival, where a change of service providers take place, all agents involved will know what tasks need to be done (Bergem, 2013).


1 Initiation
2 Insight
3 Strategy
4 Design
5 Production
6 Management

4.1 Design brief
4.2 Strategy><Design
4.3 Design methodology
4.4 Concept development
4.5 Design development
4.6 Design elements
4.7 Composition
4.8 Surface and format
4.9 Identity development

4.3.1 Human-centred design
4.3.2 User-experience
4.3.3 Emotional design
4.3.4 Innovation
4.3.5 Iterative method
4.3.6 Divergence and convergence
4.3.7 Sprint
4.3.8 Scrum
4.3.9 Kanban
4.3.10 Lean and agile
4.3.11 Design thinking
4.3.12 Customer journey
4.3.13 Need-finding
4.3.14 Service blueprint
4.3.15 Co-design
4.3.16 Business design
4.3.17 Strategic design thinking
4.3.18 Systemic design
4.3.19 In retrospect


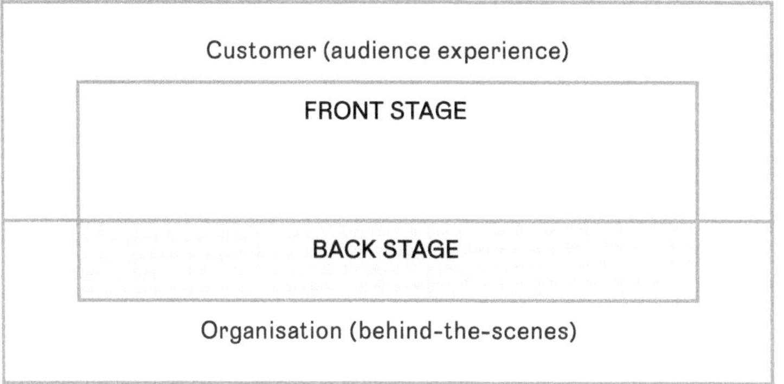


Fig. 4.29 Service blueprint

*Service blueprint* is an operational tool that describes the typical properties of a service interaction in sufficient detail to verify, implement, and maintain it. All points of contact where the customer is in contact with the service, and all process features behind what the customer can see, are documented and adjusted with respect to the user-experience (servicedesigntools.org). Service blueprint process (Bergem, 2013):

1) Identify the service to be blueprinted.
2) Identify the customer segment to receive the service.
3) Map the service from the customers'/user's perspective.
4) Add physical evidence. What is done, offered, and perceived.
5) Draw the line of interaction, and the line of visibility.
6) Map the service from the perspective of the customers' contact person, and draw the line of internal interaction.
7) Link the customers' and the contact person's activities with support functions needed backstage.
8) Check the physical evidence, and if necessary, add more.

### 4.3.15 Co-design

Alongside greater attention to the increased use of design and the hiring of designers in large leading companies, *co-design* has also become a concept or method of creation and innovation. Co-design[49] (co-creation) is often used as an umbrella term for participatory, co-creative and open design processes, whether in-house or under the direction of a design agency. This approach allows *many* people to make a creative contribution to the formulation and resolution of a problem. This can be done, for example, by the designer inviting the company and the company's customer into an idea and design process together with other parties with relevant interdisciplinary expertise. Co-design is also at the heart

Co-creation refers to a collaborative product or service development activity in which customers actively contribute (Auh, S., et al., 2007).

of *design thinking* where the trio: the company, the system developer and the designer work together to achieve results that are profitable, functional, and user-friendly.

An important part of co-creation is that users, such as 'experts', based on their own experience, become central to the design process. Typically, the process is conducted or coordinated by the designer, who has the role of facilitator. The task of the facilitator is to convince people to engage with each other, including offering ways to communicate and act, and ways to share insight and test new ideas. In addition, different methods of creating personas, storyboards and customer journeys can

Trial and error
**According to Thorndike's theory of trial and error (1913), learning takes place by trial and error.**

**Idea work process**

The book Idea-Work (Carlsen et al., 2013) presents ten items for co-creation, brainstorming, and innovation in organisations. The list can serve as a management tool for the entire design process.
**Prepping:** Practice where one carefully prepares, builds, revitalises, and shares knowledge in a way that maximises the potential for effective use in the creative moment.
**Zoom out:** Moving from details and analysis of individual parts to seeing the big picture, thinking about the whole, and seeing broad contexts, explanations, and strategies.
**Wonder:** The sensory experience of being in a mystery, a combination of feeling amazement or admiration, and being engaged in passionate searches. Wonder underpins all imagination, empathy, and deep interest in something beyond oneself.
**Drama:** Calling people to action – to battles, mysteries, missions, cathedral building, treasure hunting, or making a difference to other individuals – in ways that activate the very best of what one can be and aspires to. Why are we coming to work here? What is at stake here?
**Guidance:** The practice of leading the way into unknown territory, by creating common barrier-breaking notions, cultivating an opportunistic language, dealing with mistakes, and inspiring courage in others.
**Do it physically:** Forms of work that involve distancing oneself from one-sided dependence on electronic media and *touching* on ideas, *sketching* and *materialising* ideas in artefacts, *gesticulating* around ideas, and *moving* alone or together during idea work.
**Prototyping:** A way of working that quickly produces, tests and improves semi-finished ideas and challenges the solution space, so that ideas are shared and strengthened at an early stage.
**Liberating laughter:** Processes of energising co-creation through everyday jokes, unpretentious competition, small forms of play and humour that build social bonds, lifting limitations in thinking and encouraging original knowledge combinations.
**Creative resistance:** To actively treat doubt, friction, contradictions and criticism as tools for questioning agreed truths and creating better ideas, and not as noise that one is trying to avoid.
**Punk:** Use of reckless and direct, self-initiated action to mobilise against the established (truths, practices, authorities) and allow for realising ideas of high originality and value.

50 'The scenario technique is a strategic planning procedure and is used to project an existing condition into the future. The core of the scenario technique is the creation of different future scenarios that take several influences into account' (Scenario technique, n.d.).

51 Claudia Kotchka worked in PG (Procter & Gamble) as Vice President of Design Innovation and Strategy from 2001 to 2009. Roger Martin was Dean of Rotman School of Management, University of Toronto, from 1998 to 2013 and is the author of a number of business books, including *The Design of Business: Why Design Thinking is the Next Competitive Advantage*, 2009. David Kelley is founder of d.school at Stanford University and founder of IDEO. Patrick Whitney is Dean of the Institute of Design at the Illinois Institute of Technology.

be useful in the process of visualising the data and ideas that come up. Potential solutions can be tested through prototyping and scenario techniques.[50]

*The advantages of co-design are:*

- Generation of better ideas with high originality and user value.
- Improved knowledge of customer or user needs.
- Immediate validation of ideas or concepts.
- Higher quality, better differentiated products or services.
- More efficient decision-making.
- Lower development costs and reduced development time.
- Better cooperation between different people or organisations, and across disciplines.

*The long-term benefits include:*

- Higher level of satisfaction and loyalty from customers, employees and users.
- Increased level of support and enthusiasm for innovation and change.
- Better relations between product or service provider and customers.

A good example of co-design in action is the work done by the design agency TILT with Whittington Hospital in London. By bringing together a team of patients, employees, doctors and senior staff, they co-designed the hospital's pharmacy service. The newly developed service reduced waiting times, improved patient experience and increased staff morale (Chrisholm, n.d.). See the selection on co-design tools by Roberta Tassi (2009) on the website servicedesigntools.org.

### 4.3.16 Business design

A business design approach to innovation is largely *design thinking* and is based on the same principles. According to Rotman School, business design is a human-centred approach to innovation, applying design principles and design methodology to help organisations create new values and new forms of competitive advantage. Business design helps companies explore new opportunities in more robust or concrete ways, and to make better decisions that are customer-oriented, holistic, collaborative and innovative. In the centre are customer empathy, experience design, and business strategy. 'As the business world continues to evolve and accelerate, it has become clear that the company manager's traditional toolbox is incomplete. Data alone are insufficient to solve our most complex business problems. We believe that the success of our future business leaders will depend on their ability to integrate intuitive and analytical thinking. Empathy, creativity, and collaboration are the keys to driving innovation and discovering new opportunities for growth and creativity' (Rotman's DesignWorks, n.d.) (1.9 Team collaboration).

In the 21st century, Claudia Kotchka and Roger Martin, in collaboration with David Kelley and Patrick Whitney, developed a structured approach to innovation that could be used by both business people and designers.[51] This was a job that was initially started by Procter & Gamble (PG) in collaboration with Rotman School, and that had

1 Initiation
2 Insight
3 Strategy
4 Design
5 Production
6 Management

4.1 Design brief
4.2 Strategy><Design
4.3 Design methodology
4.4 Concept development
4.5 Design development
4.6 Design elements
4.7 Composition
4.8 Surface and format
4.9 Identity development

4.3.1 Human-centred design
4.3.2 User-experience
4.3.3 Emotional design
4.3.4 Innovation
4.3.5 Iterative method
4.3.6 Divergence and convergence
4.3.7 Sprint
4.3.8 Scrum
4.3.9 Kanban
4.3.10 Lean and agile
4.3.11 Design thinking
4.3.12 Customer journey
4.3.13 Need-finding
4.3.14 Service blueprint
4.3.15 Co-design
4.3.16 Business design
4.3.17 Strategic design thinking
4.3.18 Systemic design
4.3.19 In retrospect

Further reading
***Design: A Business Case: Thinking, Leading, and Managing*** **(Brigitte Borja de Mozota, Steinar Valade-Amland 2020).**

Fig. 4.30 3 Gears of business design

Fig. 4.30 The figure is based on Rotman's Three Gears of Business Design model.

Fig. 4.31 The figure shows UBC's Strategic Design Method (SDM) developed by Moura Quayle and Angèle Beausoleil. SDM practice focuses on multidisciplinary teams and enterprise units working along together, combining Design Thinking techniques, critical thinking, and data analysis to co-create, as well as test and deliver resilient solutions to systemic challenges to customers.

an impact on how PG today practises innovation. It combines three core elements:

- Empathy: What are the customers' unfulfilled needs?
- Prototyping: How can we better respond to these needs?
- Strategy: How can we create competitive advantage?

**3 Gears of Business Design**: This is an example of a framework and methodological approach to understanding customers, generating and testing ideas, and linking them to strategy.

**Gear 1**: Understanding customers (empathy and deep user understanding): Business design innovation begins with an unfulfilled customer need. Customers often lack the tools to formulate their own needs, and standard market research methods only scratch the surface. Empathy and 'need-finding' mean to become deeply engaged with customers and understand them in new and meaningful ways. In-depth and holistic understanding of human factors helps redefine challenges, define innovation criteria, and open new opportunities to create value for users.

**Gear 2**: Generate and test ideas (concept visualisation): Transform unmet needs into innovation. This is about creating new ideas, getting customer feedback and doing rapid testing to get a better solution. It involves using tools and techniques for ideation (idea development) and prototyping. Developing concrete solutions through rapid prototyping and iteration is a creative, energising, and risk-free approach, because it provides the opportunity to test ideas and complex solutions through trial and error.

**Gear 3**: Link to Strategy (Strategic Business Design): New ideas will fail if they are not backed by a solid strategy, including a clear set of opportunities for the success of the organisation. Mapping the company's various

52 UBC: University of British Columbia, UBC's Sauder School of Business.

strategies and tactics is a good aid in visualising where the development potential lies, prioritising what activities the company should undertake, and clarifying how it will affect the company's value and competitiveness. Ideas are tied to a strategy. Rotman School uses the strategy methods developed by Roger Martin and A.G. Lafley, presented in the book *Playing to Win: How Strategy Really Works*. Who is in charge? Examples of companies that use such an approach today are Procter & Gamble, SAP, GE and AirBnb. World-class innovation and design companies include: IDEO, SYPartners, MAYA Design and Ziba Design.


1 Initiation
2 Insight
3 Strategy
4 Design
5 Production
6 Management

4.1 Design brief
4.2 Strategy><Design
4.3 Design methodology
4.4 Concept development
4.5 Design development
4.6 Design elements
4.7 Composition
4.8 Surface and format
4.9 Identity development

4.3.1 Human-centred design
4.3.2 User-experience
4.3.3 Emotional design
4.3.4 Innovation
4.3.5 Iterative method
4.3.6 Divergence and convergence
4.3.7 Sprint
4.3.8 Scrum
4.3.9 Kanban
4.3.10 Lean and agile
4.3.11 Design thinking
4.3.12 Customer journey
4.3.13 Need-finding
4.3.14 Service blueprint
4.3.15 Co-design
4.3.16 Business design
4.3.17 Strategic design thinking
4.3.18 Systemic design
4.3.19 In retrospect

– UBC's Strategic Design Method


### 4.3.17 Strategic design thinking

Strategic design thinking should be a natural approach regardless of the design methodology chosen. Initially it means to identify the problem, the potential business opportunity and goal, and defining its coherence with the company identity and strategy. Thus, to ensure the problem solution will help the company reach its goals. The process, 5 easy steps towards a successful idea based on design thinking (Stratego.coach n/d):

1) Identify problem. Align it to the company strategy.
2) Explore. Empathise. Define strategic purpose.
3) Ideate. Creative process. Explore alternatives. Prototype. Test.
4) Evaluate alternatives. Choose the best alternative. Evaluate using analytic process.
5) Implement.

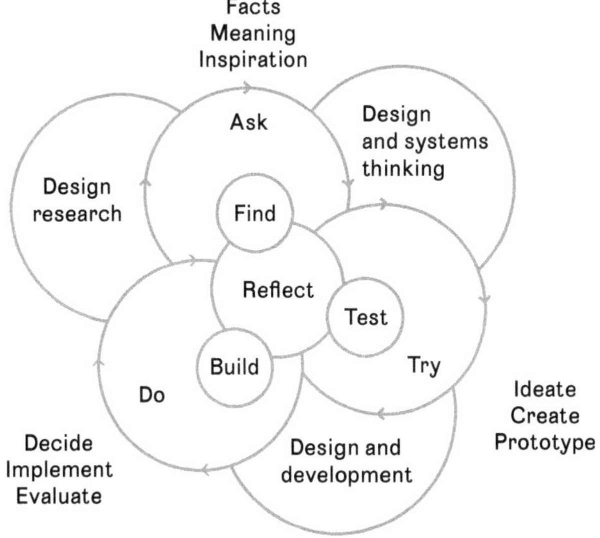


Fig. 4.31 UBC's Strategic Design Method (SDM)

**UBC's Strategic Design Method**

UBC's Strategic Design Method (SDM)[52] is one example of design methodology that ensures strategic anchoring and combines design with *systems thinking*. SDM is about problem identification by asking why (ASK), problem statement by trying and testing (TRY) and problem solving by realisation and evaluation (DO). The method is well suited for creating constructive dialogues, identifying problems, and arriving

> 'Businesspeople don't just need to understand designers, they need to become designers'
> – Roger L. Martin.

at solutions. The intention is to identify and integrate the company's internally oriented and organisational practices (communication and knowledge production), as well as the externally oriented practices (societal value, market needs, and competitive positioning). The purpose of the model is to allow for and explore new problem statements, before seeking to understand or solve them, using only available resources (Quayle, 2014). The model shows a structure that not only supports thinking and doing, but what it is important to think about and how to *do* or act. SDM is designed, taught, and practised at UBC's Sauder School of Business and Liu Institute.[53]

Fig. 4.32 **The figure is based on the Service System Design Process Model by Jones, P. (2015, p. 14), partly based on Dubberly and Evenson (2010).**

> 'If you do not understand the tone of voice of an organisation, and the way it functions, you cannot engage people in your project. If you don't - and sit there in a corner with all your fancy tools and your buzzwords and your multicoloured Post-its, it's like being the captain of a ship where no one wants to be passengers. So, learning the language, the processes, and the name of the game - including financial and orgaisational factors' - is one of the most important preconditions for working and understanding the context that one wants to change (Borja de Mozota and Valade-Amland, 2020, p. 153).

### 4.3.18 Systemic design

In those contexts where one faces more complex issues, a more system-oriented approach may be needed. Systemic design integrates systems thinking, people-centered design, design-led research, and advanced design methodology to tackle complex design challenges.

Systemic design is an approach to design that makes it possible to solve design tasks in a sustainable way at advanced environmental, social and economic levels. The designer must solve increasingly complex tasks. To help address current complex challenges and create solution for a broader change, the use of systemic design is at the core. The report Beyond Net zero: A Systemic Approach, launched by Design Council (2021),[54] is an example of that. 'The systemic design framework has been developed to help designers working on major complex challenges that involve people across different disciplines and sectors. It places our people and our planet at the heart of design' (Design Council 2021).

In the research article 'Systemic Design Principles for Complex Social Systems' (2014) Peter H. Jones argues that combining systems theory with practical design methods could be of great importance in resolving more complex problems. Typical examples of such problems are complex service systems, of a national, organisational and societal nature, which cannot be solved based on limited individual knowledge and traditional methods. These include services and systems such as health care, disease management, metropolitan planning, natural resource management, and large enterprise strategies and operations. None of these are isolated areas, because each is affected by unknown forces in society, climatic and ecological conditions, political and public

Further reading

- Combining service and systemic design in Norway's public sector (2021) by Wildhagen and Strålberg.
- Critical systems thinking and the management of complexity (2019) by Michael C. Jackson.
- Thinking in systems (2008) by Donella H. Meadows.

53 The idea behind the model came from landscape architect and professor Moura Quayle, who further developed it in collaboration with research fellow Angèle Beausoleil.

54 The framework is available online: Beyond Net Zero: A Systemic Approach (pp. 42–53), 22/04/2021, British design council, designcouncil.org.uk.

55 Systems thinking in design has a long history with people like Christopher Alexander, Horst Rittel, Russl Ackoff, Bela Banathy, Ranulph Glanville, M.P.Ranjan, Harold Nelson and others ('Systemic design,' n.d.). The systemic design dialogue is driven by the Relating Systems Thinking and Design (RSD) symposium series resulting in published proceedings and several special issues on systemic design in the scientific design research journal FORMakademisk.

1 Initiation
2 Insight
3 Strategy
4 Design
5 Production
6 Management

4.1 Design brief
4.2 Strategy><Design
4.3 Design methodology
4.4 Concept development
4.5 Design development
4.6 Design elements
4.7 Composition
4.8 Surface and format
4.9 Identity development

4.3.1 Human-centred design
4.3.2 User-experience
4.3.3 Emotional design
4.3.4 Innovation
4.3.5 Iterative method
4.3.6 Divergence and convergence
4.3.7 Sprint
4.3.8 Scrum
4.3.9 Kanban
4.3.10 Lean and agile
4.3.11 Design thinking
4.3.12 Customer journey
4.3.13 Need-finding
4.3.14 Service blueprint
4.3.15 Co-design
4.3.16 Business design
4.3.17 Strategic design thinking
4.3.18 Systemic design
4.3.19 In retrospect

- Systems thinking
- Systems theory
- System oriented design (SOD)


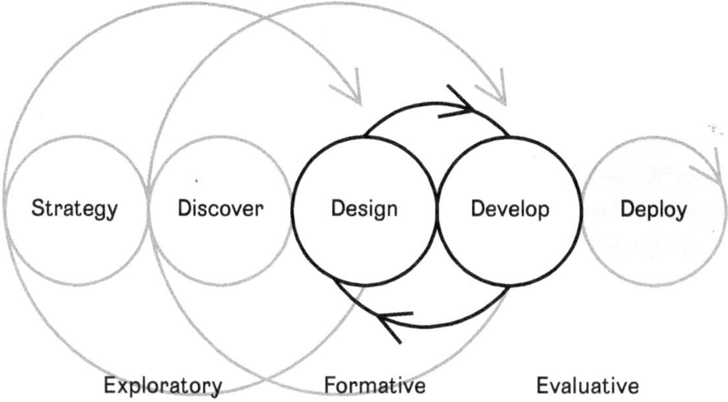


Fig. 4.32 Service system design process

regulations and technological development. Jones believes the ultimate goal is to co-design better rules, structures and service systems through system-oriented methods and user-oriented design. He argues that his model shown in Figure 4.32 provides a better process basis than IDEO's HCD three-phase model shown in Figure 4.12, because it includes strategy as a visible part of the process (Jones, 2014).

A universal pattern: In the same research report, Jones highlights four universal patterns, based on Van Patter and Pastor (2013), that can be used interdisciplinarily and across different frameworks: 1) Discovery and orientation, 2) Definition and concept formation, 3) Optimisation and planning, 4) Evaluation and measurement. These four universal patterns are implicitly integrated into the five-step process shown in Figure 4.32. A driving force for the contemporary attention on systemic design was Birger Sevaldson at the Oslo School of Architecture and Design and his intitative of the *Relating Systems Thinking and Design Symposia series* 2012 (RSD, rsdsymposium.org/).[55]

### Systems thinking

Systems thinking is a holistic approach of understanding the complexity of the world, a way to investigate factors and interactions and analyse the way that a system's constituent parts interrelate and how systems work over time and within the context of larger systems (Goodman n/d). It is a powerful tool for successful delivery of complex projects where there are many stakeholders and many possible solutions (Government office for science 2012). Systems thinking draws on and contributes to systems theory and systems science.

*Systems thinking* involves observing events or data for identifying patterns over time, to surfacing the underlying structures that drive those events and patterns, to see a situation more fully, acknowledge multiple interventions to a problem, expanding the range of choices available for solving a problem by broadening our thinking and helping us articulate problems in new and different ways. The purpose is understanding and changing complex structures and expanding the choices available to create more satisfying, long-term solutions to chronic problems (Michael Goodman n/d). Systems thinking is a mindset of how individuals can work together in different types of teams and

Further reading
Check out: Systemic design toolkit guide: systemicdesign-toolkit.org

*Systems thinking* is a diagnostic tool for examining problems more completely and accurately before acting. 'It allows us to ask better questions before jumping to conclusions' (Michael Goodman n/d).

through that understanding, 'create the best possible processes to accomplish just about anything' (Morganelli, 2020).

*Systems thinking* philosophy (Goodman, n/d, thesystemsthinker.com):

- is a sensitivity to the circular nature of the world we live in
- an awareness of the role of structure in creating the conditions we face
- a recognition that there are powerful laws of systems operating that we are unaware of
- a realis ation that there are consequences to our actions that we are oblivious to

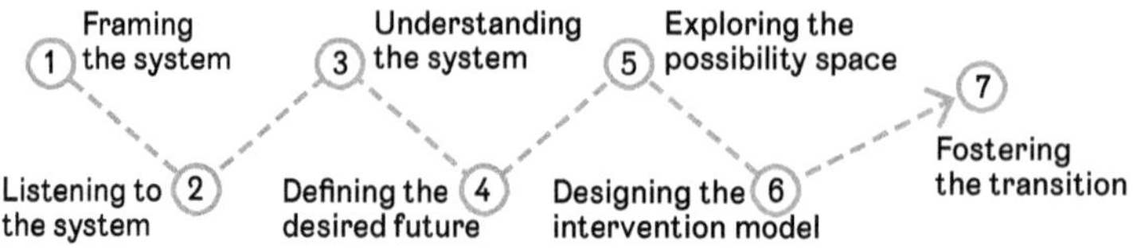


Fig. 4.33 Systems thinking

Fig. 4.33 The figure shows a 7-step sequence of interactions/journey for use in a full cycle of analysis and proposal building for a complex social system. The top 3 steps are systems oriented, the bottom 3 steps are design and design research oriented. The systems steps promote systems thinking with design ideation, multi-level system maps and causal loop diagrams, and the design steps infuse systemic principles with design methods and human-centred design approaches. The final step 7, Fostering the transition, draws on Geels' transition model and Three Horizons. Caption and figure are based on Peter Jones (2019).

Problems that are ideal for a systems thinking intervention have the following characteristics (Goodman, n/d, thesystem-sthinker.com):

- The issue is important.
- The problem is chronic, not a one-time event.
- The problem is familiar and has a known history.
- People have unsuccessfully tried to solve the problem before.

'Systems thinking uses computer simulation and a variety of diagrams and graphs to model, illustrate, and predict system behaviour. Among the systems thinking tools are:

- the *behaviour over time (BOT) graph*, which indicates the actions of one or more variables over a period of time;
- the *causal loop diagram (CLD)*, which illustrates the relationships between system elements;
- the *management flight simulator*, which uses an interactive program to simulate the effects of management decisions;
- and the *simulation model*, which simulates the interaction of system elements over time' (Lutkevich n/d, www.techtarget.com).

Systemic design is suitable if you are operating in a *complex environment* and if you *have the resources to take a step back* to analyse the problem' (Zhiang, 2021).

### Systems theory

Systems thinking originates from Ludwig von Bertalanffy and the General systems theory in 1968. The most typical components of the systems theory include: basic definitions, system thinking, system topologies, life cycles, system performance, conceptual design, current state evaluations, related sciences, solving methods, creative solutions, system synthesis, system analysis, optimisation, solution assessment, virtual optimising, system engineering, and evaluation of knowledge in the economy and society (Sieniutycz, 2020). General systems theory (GST), linked with cybernetics and information theory, is a science investigating general laws for arbitrarily complex arrangements, 'systems' which constitute functional integrities. Important contributions to developments of systems theory were made by G.J. Klir in the field of computer methods of solving various systemic problems (1969–1987) and J.G. Miller in the field of living systems theory (Miller, 1978) (Sieniutycz, 2020).

Further reading
- *Systemic Design, Theory, Methods, and Practice* (2018) by Peter Jones and Kyoichi Kijima.
- *Systems Thinking, Systems Practice* (1999) by Peter Checkland.

56 System Oriented Design: systemsorienteddesign.net Systemic Design Association: systemic-design.net

57 Archer, L.B. (1965) *Systematic Method for Designers*. London: Council of Industrial Design.

### System oriented design (SOD)

*System oriented design* (SOD) is a type of *system thinking* that combines *design thinking* and design in practice. It is tailored by and for designers who manage design practices at the highest level. SOD is based on a designer's approach to super complexity and refers to established approaches in modern system thinking, in particular *soft system methodology*, *critical systems thinking* and *systems architecting* (Sevaldson, 2011). Furthermore, it is based on supporting the designer's special ability to think visually and visualise processes for communication purposes. The term *System oriented design* (SOD) was initiated by Professor Birger Sevaldsson based on many years of research on methods and techniques used to solve the challenges and complexities that designers face in working with products, services, information, media, and various complex systems, and design processes. SOD refers to three conceptual frameworks (Sevaldson, 2011):

- Design thinking and design practice
- Visual thinking and visual practice
- System thinking and system practice

SOD is part of the growing field of Systemic Design.[56]

> **Clock and cloud problem**
>
> 'Systemic design is a *mindset*, a tool, and a *process* that enables you to solve cloud-like problems with the aim of making a sustainable impact at scale' (Zhiang, 2021).
>
> - *Clock-like problems* are like clocks, predictable, finite, and controllable. These problems usually have the right answer, for example, fixing a bike, albeit not obvious.
> - *Cloud-like problems* are like cloud, they are ever-changing, complex, and unpredictable. They are also known as wicked problems. Homelessness, reducing divorce rate, preventing suicide among adolescents are examples of cloud-like problems.

### 4.3.19 In retrospect

*Design methodology retrospective*: At the end of the 19th century and in the first half of the 20th century there were many industrial and technological breakthroughs that led to a more modern lifestyle but also created social and economic difficulties for people and their environment. In the 1960s, disciplines such as architecture, urban planning, engineering, and product development began to address new types of problems, addressed by Horst Rittel, John Chris Jones, Peter Slann, Henry Sanoff, Herbert A. Simon, Bruce Archer, among others. This led to more informed and methodological approaches to design, which further led to a greater interest in design processes and to more research in design. 'The most fundamental challenge to the conventional approach to design has been the growing recognition of systematic problem-solving methods borrowed from information technology and management theory for assessing design problems and developing design solutions' (Archer, 1965).[57]


1 Initiation
2 Insight
3 Strategy
4 Design
5 Production
6 Management

4.1 Design brief
4.2 Strategy><Design
4.3 Design methodology
4.4 Concept development
4.5 Design development
4.6 Design elements
4.7 Composition
4.8 Surface and format
4.9 Identity development

4.3.1 Human-centred design
4.3.2 User-experience
4.3.3 Emotional design
4.3.4 Innovation
4.3.5 Iterative method
4.3.6 Divergence and convergence
4.3.7 Sprint
4.3.8 Scrum
4.3.9 Kanban
4.3.10 Lean and agile
4.3.11 Design thinking
4.3.12 Customer journey
4.3.13 Need-finding
4.3.14 Service blueprint
4.3.15 Co-design
4.3.16 Business design
4.3.17 Strategic design thinking
4.3.18 Systemic design
4.3.19 In retrospect

- Systems thinking
- Systems theory
- System oriented design (SOD)


Further reading

- Check out www.systemicdesigntoolkit.org/methodology
- Systemic design association: systemic-design.org/
- Systemic Design Toolkit: Design for Services in Complex System Contexts: Introducing the Systemic Design Toolkit: www.service-designnetwork.org/

> Systems thinking ('fifth discipline') is a way for teams and individuals to look for changes that will provide long-term improvements (Peter Senge, 2006).

## 4.4 Concept development

At the heart of any design process is concept development, whether it is a matter of the development of a new product, service, business concept or other value creation. Concept development is the entire idea process, from the development to the concretisation of one or more ideas.

The term *concept* can be used when an idea or plan is so concrete that it can be understood and logically assessed in terms of how it can produce new solutions to a problem or task. 'A concept is an overarching idea that inspires, gives guidelines, and leads to the project's completion and realising its potential. A good concept should be the starting point of the design process and should act as a link between analysis and solution. Concept development is the process by which new thoughts and ideas are refined into strong and holistic user-experiences. Good concepts are developed through an analytical, holistic approach, not just through creativity and chance. The concept must deliver on goals and needs and inspire a solution' (Halogen.no) (3.3.8 Sustainability goals, 2.6.5 UX Research).

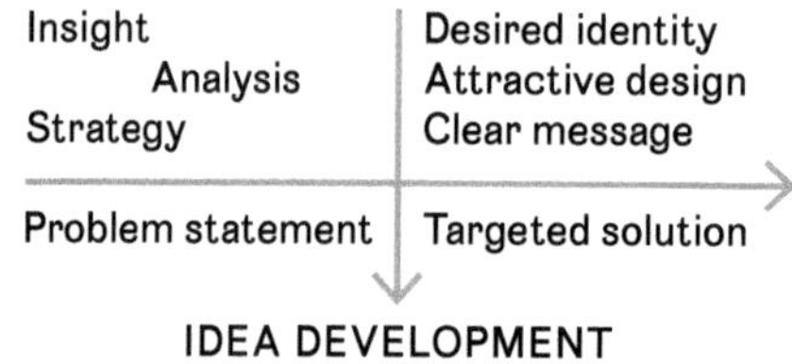


Fig. 4.34 The big challenge

Fig. 4.34 The figure illustrates the major challenge in strategic design development. How to use insight, analysis, and strategy as foundations for idea development in order to create targeted and strategically aligned solutions.

Tips for the company
A groundbreaking idea has little value for your company if it is not strategically anchored and contributes to goal achievement. Read more in the chapters 3.2 Overall strategy, 3.3 Goals and subgoals.

> What does 'concept' mean?
> The term 'concept' is used in many different contexts to refer to an idea, a plan or an intention, e.g. business, production, design, or communication concept. When we talk about a business concept or a product concept, we usually talk about the specific idea behind it which describes what the company or the product should do or lead to.

Successful concept development depends on clear goals, a good strategic management tool (3.1.3 Top 5), a clearly defined problem statement, good insight and user understanding, and a clear design brief. The solution must respond to the problem (2.3 Problem statement, 4.1 Design brief). A well-defined framework and a broad idea development process is the best starting point for the concept development.

### 4.4.1 Foundation and framework

Framework is essential in a creative process in order to focus, create, and later, make decisions. Therefore, before starting an idea process, one should clarify the foundation, criteria, and framework for the project. The problem statement, the insight, the goal and the strategic directions of the task serve as a point of departure. This is used as a management tool in the process and as the basis for evaluating ideas and solutions. The framework of an idea process is also about clarifying what expectations and requirements are set for the solution. Lerdahl (2007) suggests three general requirements:[58] 1) what the solution must satisfy, 2) what the solution should satisfy, 3) what the solution can satisfy. In addition, Lerdahl highlights vision, core values, and product specification as central frameworks for idea development. *The vision* provides a description and

58 Based on the book *Slagkraft* by Erik Lerdahl (2007). Erik Lerdahl is a professor of creativity, as well as an author, singer, innovation leader and speaker. Born in Brussels, Belgium with Norwegian father and American mother.

**Concept development process**

Concept development is part of the overall design process (Table 4.1 The design process, 4.5.1 The three-direction principle).

| | |
|---|---|
| **Problem statement:** | The starting point for idea development is a problem or a problem statement (2.3 Problem statement). |
| **Strategic management tool:** | Define a design strategy, including strategic anchoring, guides, and frameworks for the task (3.9 Design strategy, 3.1.3 Top 5, 4.4.1 Foundation and framework). |
| **Inspiration:** | Get inspiration, e.g. from Pinterest and Behance, or search in old literature, art and design history, photo archives, etc. Combine with data based on research, surveys, analysis (2.8.2 Moodboard). |
| **Idea generation:** | Conduct workshops with brainstorming, mind mapping, prototyping, testing, analysis, iteration, assessment, processing, prioritisation, and evaluation of results. Work in several different directions that both satisfy and challenge the client's stated needs and wishes (4.4.4 Idea development). |
| **Concept development:** | Develop several different (preferably three) conceptual directions through iteration. Visualise and verbalise the different conceptual directions using sketches, oral and written description, moodboards, storyboards, video, etc. The conceptual directions represent different solution suggestions or solutions to the problem (4.4.5 Conceptual directions). |
| **Evaluation and choice of concept:** | The choice of direction must be considered in relation to the project's problems and objectives. Consider whether the idea is consistent with the overall objective and strategy of the company, product or service. Conduct a critical assessment of functionality, finances, production, implementation, etc. (4.4.7 Prototyping, 4.4.8 Testing of ideas). |
| **Presentation and sales pitch:** | Conceptual directions (pitches) are presented to the person who, in consultation with the designer, chooses one direction or a combination of two directions for the continued work (4.4.9 Presentation of ideas). |
| **Operational plan:** | Prepare a plan for the development of the design solution based on the selected concept. Adjust goals and problem statement if necessary. |
| **Budget:** | Make the necessary adjustments to the budget as a sequence of the concept selection. The concept is used as a basis in the further design process (1.7 Price quotation). |


1 Initiation
2 Insight
3 Strategy
4 Design
5 Production
6 Management

4.1 Design brief
4.2 Strategy><Design
4.3 Design methodology
4.4 Concept development
4.5 Design development
4.6 Design elements
4.7 Composition
4.8 Surface and format
4.9 Identity development

4.4.1 Foundation and framework
4.4.2 Creative problem solving
4.4.3 Brainstorming
4.4.4 Idea development
4.4.5 Conceptual directions
4.4.6 Verbalisation and visualisation
4.4.7 Prototyping of ideas
4.4.8 Testing of ideas
4.4.9 Presentation of ideas


Idea vs. Concept
Idea: A wheeled mode of transportation
Concept: What form does the idea take? What kind of wheeled mode of transportation? (B. Opstad 2017)

feel of the desired direction, linked to context, expression, desired quality, and user-experience. *The core values* are the basis for the identity to be reflected in the solution. *The product specification* refers to measurable and robust solution requirements in terms of function, ergonomics, market, market segment, costs, production, distribution, environment, resource efficiency, etc. (3.2.4 Vision, 3.2.5 Core values, 4.1 Design brief).

A good way to use such a framework in an idea process is to visualise and materialise them using images, moodboards, Giga maps, storyboards, materials and scenarios, which are hung on walls and laid out on tables during the idea process (2.8 Mapping). For example, a persona moodboard can provide better understanding of whom the solution should be aimed at and how it should be used. Likewise, a situational moodboard of an actual user situation may give an idea of the different contexts in which the new solution should be used or of the situations in which the user encounters the product or service. Similarly, visualisation of the vision or idea of the future can help create direction in the idea process through images, materials, scenarios and other things that indicate future expression, shape, colours and material use. Such moodboards can give insight and inspiration throughout the idea development process (Lerdahl, 2007). See also 4.4.2 Idea development: thinking outside the box.

### 4.4.2 Creative problem solving

Most idea processes are based on a problem that needs to be solved. Many of today's idea development methods can be traced back to the CPS method, the Creative Problem-Solving Process from 1950, developed by advertiser Alex Osborn[59] in collaboration with Sid Parnes. The method consists of four phases, with a total of six process steps. Each step uses divergent and convergent thinking (based on creativeeducationfoundation.org):

| The Creative Problem-Solving Process | | |
|---|---|---|
| Stage | Step | Purpose |
| Clarify | Explore the vision | Identify the goal, wish, or challenge. |
| | Gather data | Describe and generate data to enable a clear understanding of the challenge. |
| | Formulate challenges | Sharpen awareness of the challenge and create challenge questions that invite solutions. |
| Ideate | Explore ideas | Generate ideas that answer the challenge questions. |
| Develop | Formulate solutions | To move from ideas to solutions. Evaluate, strengthen, and select solutions for the best 'fit'. |
| Imple-ment | Formulate a plan | Explore acceptance and identify resources and actions that will support implementation of the selected solution(s). |

Table 4.5 Creative problem solving

Table 4.5 The table shows the Creative Problem-Solving Process, based on Alex Osborn (1950).

Fig. 4.35 The figure is based on the Creative Education Foundation's version of the CPS method. The method is iterative and uses diverging and converging in each step of the process.

Tips for the designer
Idea and concept development can serve as an important bridge builder between strategy and design. Strategic anchoring is the key word. (4.2 Strategy><Design).

Tips for the designer
When making minor changes to an existing solution, the framework should be quite tight, linked to clear task and goals formulation. If we are talking about a conceptual project, where we want to completely rethink things, we need a more open framework. The framework of an assignment is something we can challenge and exceed (Lerdahl, 2007).

Creativity
The word 'creativity' comes from the Latin word 'creare', which means 'to make' or 'to create'.

59 Alex Osborn was the founder of the Creative Education Foundation and co-founder of the advertising agency BBDO. In 1954, Osborn created Creative Education Foundation, based on royalty income from his books. He co-founded Creative Education Foundation's Creative Problem-Solving Institute, the world's oldest international creative conference.

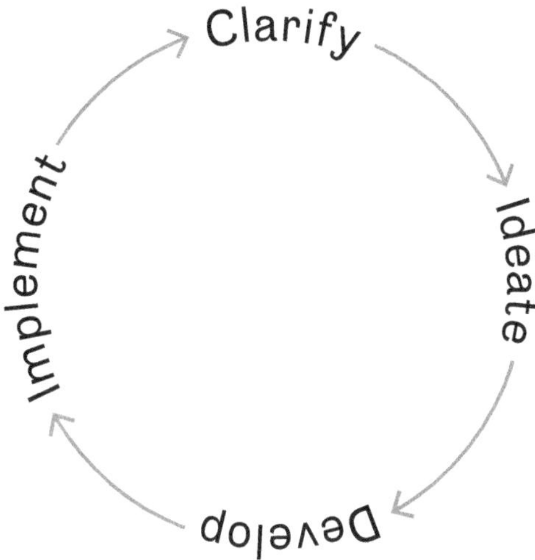


Fig. 4.35 The Creative Problem-Solving Process

**Core principles for creative problem solving:** The Creative Problem-Solving Process, starts with two assumptions (based on Creativeeducationfoundation.org): 1) Everybody is creative in one way or another, 2) Creative skills can be learned and enhanced.

**The main principles are:**

- Divergent and convergent thinking must be balanced: The keys to creativity include learning to identify and balance expanding (opening up) and contracting (pulling together) thinking (done separately), and knowing when to practise these (4.3.6 Diverge and converge).
- Formulate problems as questions: Solutions are more easily initiated and developed when challenges and problems are turned into open questions with more opportunities. Such questions generate a wealth of information, while closed questions tend to elicit confirmation or denial. Claims tend to generate limited or no response at all (2.3 Problem statement).
- Postpone or suspend the verdict: The instantaneous judgment in response to an idea will end the idea generation. The correct and appropriate time to apply discretion is only when the process is convergent.
- Focus on 'Yes, and ...' rather than 'No, but ...': When information and ideas are generated, language is important. 'Yes, and ...' makes continuation and expansion possible. The use of the word 'but' – preceded by 'yes' or 'no' – closes the conversation and negates everything previously said.

### What is creativity?

Creativity can be explained as ingenuity or the ability to think differently and in new ways, create something original, or put together familiar elements in a new way. Imagination is an important factor in creative thinking. It is about being able to imagine something that is not physically or sensually present, and having the ability to associate, give thoughts free reign, spin on words and impressions, and open up for new words, whim, and ideas. Ideas come to us many times during a day, ranging from how to solve everyday problems at work and at home, to how to resolve big crucial questions in our lives. In addition,

Further reading
Check out the audiobook *Unleash Your Mind* (2022) by Nic Saluppo.

we develop ideas and solutions for specific tasks we need to solve. Idea development is necessary in most disciplines and professions, and is not something only designers do, although some people may be more imaginative than others. Either way, an idea is just a casual thought until concretised, assessed, and translated into a real solution to a problem.

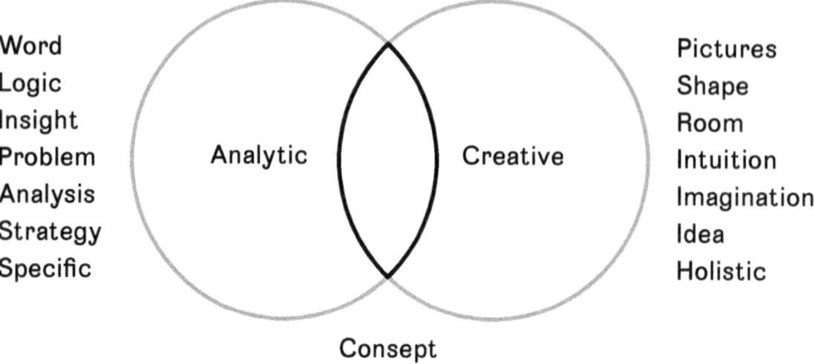


Fig. 4.36 Analytical vs. Creative

Fig. 4.36 At the point of intersection between the creative and the analytical lies the opportunity to translate an idea into a concept, by logically explaining and visualising the idea so that it can be understood by others. © Grimsgaard, W. (2018).

Tips for the designer
Creative mode is about (practising) disconnecting logic when being creative.

Right vs. Left
'The right hemisphere of the brain helps us find many different solutions to a problem, while the left hemisphere helps us choose the best one' (Per Edvardsen 2000).

Being creative is not just about getting ideas, but about being able to further develop, concretise, and realise them. The key lies in the link between idea and logic, in translating thoughts and ideas into words and images, making the idea accessible and understandable. The right hemisphere of our brain often gets credit for our intuitive and creative thoughts, while the left is credited for the logical and analytical. There are many explanations on how this is related, and much is attributed to popular science. A retrospect shows that in 1861, a researcher named Paul Brocas found the language centre to be in the left hemisphere, and later research localised our ability to imagine form and spatial orientation in the right hemisphere. New discoveries are continually being made that disprove previous claims, but we know for certain that we physically have two brain hemispheres and that they are connected by a thick bundle of thousands of nerve fibres called *Corpus callosum* (Holck, 2009). It acts as a bridge between the cerebral hemispheres and makes communication between them possible. This connection between the logical left and the creative right hemisphere is a useful metaphor to use when talking about idea and concept development.

It is precisely the interaction between the creative (intuitive) thoughts and the ability to think logically (analytically) which is the very success factor for being able to further develop a loose idea into a concrete concept, see Figure 4.36. At the same time, it is a plus not to make this connection prematurely. Logic can inhibit the idea processes by thinking about the solution too early; hence, it is an advantage to park our logical assessments until we have enough ideas. Good open idea processes require free thought flow and exhaustive idea generation before logical and analytical assessments are allowed to shine in. It is only when we reach the point of exhaustion in our brainstorming, and after resting and maturing, that logical choices and the realisation of ideas can begin. If we continue to use the brain as a metaphor, we can consider the following example: The left hemisphere defines a problem. The right

60 Eureka is Greek for 'I found it' or 'I have found it', and it is said to come from Archimedes. He had been commissioned to find out if a gold object was real, or if it was just coated with gold. The specific weight of pure gold was found after weighing accurately measured objects. The object in question could not be measured since it was a goldsmith's work. The problem of finding the volume of the object is said to have occurred to him while he observed buoyancy in his bathtub. He then shouted 'Eureka', jumped out of the bathtub and ran to the client with the solution. The principle born that day is known today as Archimedes' principle, which begins like this: 'When a body is immersed in water...'. ('Eureka,' n.d.)
61 'Creative person profile' consists of seven personality traits that are measured by a test of 216 questions divided into 27 sub-traits such as tolerance for ambiguity, preference for complexity, imagination, mood swings, tendency to get absorbed, cross boundaries between mental, conceptual systems, etc. The theory was published in *BI Leadership Magazine* 2012/13.

one comes up with a multitude of ideas to solve it. The left hemisphere evaluates the ideas, chooses the one that best solves the problem, and formulates it in words. The right hemisphere continues to spin on the idea and magnifies it. The left hemisphere materialises and realises it, and after some ripening time; a walk out in the park, a round on the football field, a nice hot bath, suddenly the really big ground-breaking idea is there! – EUREKA![60]

**Creative person profile:** What is creativity and what characterises creative people? Professor of organisational psychology Øyvind Martinsen (2011) has presented a theory that describes a creative personality[61] through seven different dimensions:

1) *Associative orientation*: Described by imagination, playfulness, ingenuity, ability to become absorbed, smooth transitions between dream and reality.
2) *Need for originality*: Resistance to rules and conventions. Rebellious attitude through a need to do something no one else does.
3) *Motivation*: Performance needs, determination, news-seeking attitude, persistence with difficult issues.
4) *Ambition*: Described by a need to have influence, to get attention and recognition.
5) *Flexibility*: An attitude characterised by being able to see different aspects in problem statements and being able to keep solutions open.
6) *Emotional instability*: Tendency to experience negative emotions, greater mood fluctuations and mood swings, and loss of confidence.
7) *Agreeableness*: Tendency to be inconsiderate, reckless, and to find faults and shortcomings in things and people.

According to the study associative orientation and flexibility have the greatest impact on creative thinking. Associative orientation is tied to ingenuity, while flexibility is associated with insight (aha! experiences). The other five characteristics describe more emotional propensities and motivational conditions that have implications for creativity or interest in creativity. The seven personality traits also have an impact on creative achievements in interaction with each other.

**A creative person**

'The truly creative mind in any field is no more than this: A human creature born abnormally, inhumanly sensitive. To him... a touch is a blow, a sound is a noise, a misfortune is a tragedy, a joy is an ecstasy, a friend is a lover, a lover is a god, and failure is death. Add to this cruelly delicate organism – the overpowering necessity to create, create, create – so that without the creating of music or poetry or books or buildings or something of meaning, his very breath is cut off from him. He must create, must pour out creation. By some strange, unknown, inward urgency he is not really alive unless he is creating'. – Pearl S. Buck (Belludi, 2016).



Further reading

Øyvind L. Martinsen (2011) 'The Creative Personality: A Synthesis and Development of the Creative Person Profile', *Creativity Research Journal*, 23:3, 185–202, DOI: 10.1080/10400419.2011.595656

### 4.4.3 Brainstorming

Brainstorming is an effective method for creative problem solving in groups and workshops. Brainstorming is well suited to getting started with an idea process or at any time during a project, regardless of phase. Brainstorming is a traditional technique of creative problem solving or idea development in which an unprepared group of participants meets and contributes the ideas they are currently getting. One goal of brainstorming is for the participants to be inspired by each other's thoughts and ideas, thereby generating even more ideas.
**Traditional brainstorming:** Brainstorming is best suited to a group of four to twelve participants. The participants contribute by impulsively making associations and expressing the ideas and thoughts they come up with, without allowing negative thoughts and prejudices to influence others' or their own input, or lack thereof. One prerequisite for good brainstorming is for the participants to feel safe and free to let loose, as well as that both *success factors* and *critical factors* are carefully reviewed. Brainstorming as a method originally introduced by Alex Osborn[62] is today among the most widely used methods of creative thinking. Osborn's method (1963) was based on four basic rules:
**1) Go for quantity:** This rule is about reinforcing idea production and facilitating problem solving through the principle that quantity yields quality. The idea is that the greater the number of ideas being

Tips for the designer
**LET GO OF CONTROL! This exercise fits well before the brainstorming: In teams of two. One with their back to the other falls backwards into the arms of the person behind. Then they switch places.**

100 ideas
**'One can decide in advance how many ideas should be generated in brainstorming. "Let's try to come up with a hundred ideas before we leave the room." It can be motivating – and numbering the ideas may help move back and forth between them without losing track' (Kelley, 2001/ Lerdahl, 2007).**

**Brainstorming process**

1) The starting point should be a well-defined and clear problem.
2) Create a group of four to twelve people.
3) Before getting started, clarify the problem to be solved, the goals for the idea process and the brainstorming rules.
4) Pick a referee. The referees write down all ideas, quickly and accurately, as these are told, without rewriting them.
5) Pick a leader. The leader should encourage the group to come up with ideas and write these on flip charts so everyone can see. Write the title and number on the flip charts and tape them to the wall.
6) Participants toss out ideas at a fast pace, in sessions of 15–20 minutes.
7) The participants choose one or more words from the brainstorming session that they think may be the starting point for an idea or that may otherwise be beneficial to explore further.
8) Selected words from the brainstorming session are highlighted and used as the basis for new brainstorming, in new sessions of 15–20 minutes. Brainstorm in multiple rounds using the selected words in order to get as deep as possible.
9) A good rule is to set a goal of coming up with 20–50 ideas and selecting three of them that are sharp enough to be presented as concepts.
10) Repeat the process until the desired result is achieved.

62 Alex Osborn (1963). *Applied imagination: principles and procedures of creative problem-solving*.

generated, the greater the chance of producing a radical, effective and innovative solution.

**2) Hold back criticism:** In brainstorming, criticising ideas should be put on hold. Instead, participants should focus on expanding or adding ideas. By deferring assessment, participants will feel free to generate unusual ideas.

**3) Welcome wild ideas:** To get a good long list of ideas, wild ideas are encouraged. They can be generated by thinking and making associations from new angles. These new ways of thinking can produce better solutions.

**4) Combining and improving ideas:** It is assumed that a process of making associations stimulates the development of new ideas. Expressed through the slogan '1+1=3'.

The four basic rules are intended to help reduce social inhibitions among the group members, stimulate the generation of ideas, and increase the overall creativity of the group.

**How to start a brainstorming session:** Brainstorming is, of course, a problem-solving method. It is therefore common to use the problem as a starting point. The problem can be clarified through brainstorming and possibly delimited so it is easier to work with (2.3 Problem statement). Another starting point for brainstorming may be a product that is to be redesigned. Questions for brainstorming can for example then be: a) What associations do we have with the product? b) How does the product meet the user's needs – or not? This can also be a good way to find out what the problem is. Instead of the product we can use the service, the company or something else that is essential for the project to be completed.

**Mind map:** If a person is to brainstorm alone, it is a good idea to use mind maps. Mind maps as a method date back hundreds of years, but were popularised by psychologist and writer Tony Buzan in 1977 (Lerdahl, 2007, p. 124). A mind map can be drawn by hand by putting a word or image in the centre, which should serve as a starting point for new associations and ideas. Here is one example of a mind mapping process:

1) Take a big sheet of paper.
2) Choose a word to elaborate on.
3) Put the word in the middle of the sheet.
4) Make associations based on the current word.
5) Write the new words on the sheet and then link them with a connecting line to the middle.
6) Make associations using the new words and draw new lines from them.
7) Use well-defined letters so that the text is legible.
8) Simple drawings are suitable for activating more of the senses.
9) Colours can be used to encode different parts of the information.

A good way to utilise a mind map is to make priorities and choices based on the idea process, and move a new word to a new mind map for a new idea process, which is repeated until you arrive at enough ideas or solutions.


1 Initiation
2 Insight
3 Strategy
4 Design
5 Production
6 Management

4.1 Design brief
4.2 Strategy><Design
4.3 Design methodology
4.4 Concept development
4.5 Design development
4.6 Design elements
4.7 Composition
4.8 Surface and format
4.9 Identity development

4.4.1 Foundation and framework
4.4.2 Creative problem solving
4.4.3 Brainstorming
4.4.4 Idea development
4.4.5 Conceptual directions
4.4.6 Verbalisation and visualisation
4.4.7 Prototyping of ideas
4.4.8 Testing of ideas
4.4.9 Presentation of ideas


'Brainstorming involves a group immersing themselves in a problem by tossing out a crossfire of ideas. The rules are that this happens over short intervals, preferably for a limited time, and that all ideas are written down on a board or flip chart so that everyone can see them, and most importantly, there should be no censorship or attack on the ideas that emerge. No ideas, however absurd, expensive, irresponsible, or even stupid as they might seem, should be rejected when presented. All the ideas are written down for later consideration' (Fletcher, 2001, p. 76).

Brainstorming rules

| Critical factors | Success factors |
|---|---|
| Sufficient time | Clarify the problem |
| Sufficient focus | Clarify the task |
| Sufficient insight | Set goals |
| Sufficient basis | Clarify the level of ambition |
| Sufficient sources | Plan the process |
| Sufficient debate | Plan the time |
| Sufficient number of participants | Clarify critical factors |

| Not allowed | Allowed |
|---|---|
| Criticism, no, ugh, sigh, groan | Spontaneity, quantity, combination, association, humour |

| Creative barriers | Creative atmosphere |
|---|---|
| Prevent creativity: Rules, standards, negativity, not daring to let go of control, choosing the first and best solution, limitations and prejudices. | Promote creativity: Safety, interaction, knowledge, spontaneity, association, humour, playfulness and openness. |

**YES to**

- Looking at the possibilities, not the limitations
- Being open, curious, intuitive, and spontaneous
- Yes (not but or no)
- Stupid ideas (personal, ridiculous, imaginative)
- Crazy notions, wild and extreme ideas
- Doodling with no restraints and no boundaries
- Asking a lot of 'why' questions
- Using a lot of 'what if' and 'imagine if'
- Building on each other's ideas, associate, combine and improve
- Being playful. HUMOUR, lots of humour

Tips for the designer
**Make it a habit to check the brainstorming rules before a brainstorming as well as read out the rules to all participants.**

### 4.4.4 Idea development

Idea development is the core of concept development. At the same time idea development is something that takes place in all phases of a design process. It is through the development of ideas that the problem solving and the opportunity for innovation and value development happens. Good idea processes require us to be able to let ourselves go and not be afraid to make a fool of ourselves or fail. Equally important is that we are able to zoom in and out, diverge and converge, see the details and the big picture and see opportunities and connections. The bottom line here is that the ideas we come up with actually solve the problem or task and answer the problem (2.3 Problem statement). There are countless methods of idea development. In this chapter we will look at a small selection. Many of these can be combined with design methodology such as iterative method and design sprint (4.3 Design methodology, 4.3.5 Iterative method, 4.3.7 Sprint).

### Success or failure

Every time we fail with a new idea, someone always says: Didn't I tell you? You should have listened to me [...] Every time we succeed with an idea, someone always says that we have been lucky [...]. If you want to succeed with completely new ideas, you must dare to fail. Whether you succeed or fail, you should still be praised for having the courage to try (Stig Hjerkinn Haug, stigogstein.no).


1 Initiation
2 Insight
3 Strategy
4 Design
5 Production
6 Management

4.1 Design brief
4.2 Strategy><Design
4.3 Design methodology
4.4 Concept development
4.5 Design development
4.6 Design elements
4.7 Composition
4.8 Surface and format
4.9 Identity development

4.4.1 Foundation and framework
4.4.2 Creative problem solving
4.4.3 Brainstorming
4.4.4 Idea development
4.4.5 Conceptual directions
4.4.6 Verbalisation and visualisation
4.4.7 Prototyping of ideas
4.4.8 Testing of ideas
4.4.9 Presentation of ideas

- Warm-up exercises
- Thinking outside the box
- Brainstorming methods
- Distortion methods
- Connection and analogy methods
- Scamper


### Warm-up exercises

Idea development is creative work that requires letting go and offering your wildest associations and ideas. It can be difficult to come straight out of everyday tasks or situations right into a group where everyone should go crazy and hatch new ideas. Therefore, it may be useful to start a creative process with some warm-up exercises. The goal of the warm-up exercises is to start association processes, arouse humour and engagement, release energy, and put the participants in a positive and open mood before the real idea process begins. In addition, it can be a great way to break the ice and loosen the mood if the group members do not already know each other. Being able to laugh and fool around a little lightens the mood and makes participants trust each other more, while increasing the tolerance limit for doing and saying something 'wrong'. 'Creative interaction in a group works best when there is room for play, madness, error and exploration. It is about creating an atmosphere where people lift each other up and leave their comfort zone. Urhamar (2014) presents four warm-up exercises before an idea development process:

**Scenarios:** Someone in the group starts an activity and the others should, quickly and without thinking too much, join the activity to make a complete scenario together. For example, if someone pretends that they are at the checkout in a shop, the other group members should join, taking up the roles of customers, children waiting in line, shopping trolleys, food, etc. The exercise may be linked to the task that should be completed.

**Throw-the-ball-stories:** Participants take turns telling stories. One goes after the other depending on whom the ball is thrown to. The story can be linked to the task. For example, if you are going to provide a new service, you can tell stories about this.

**The machine:** One participant in the group makes a movement and a sound to suggest a part of a machine. The others in the group do the same for other parts of a machine, so that together they create a whole machine with movements and sounds.

**Wild ideas:** Each participant should prepare ten wild and ill-conceived ideas in ten minutes, with no time for evaluation. The ideas are presented to the group.

In order for the brain to enter a creative mode, it should be occupied by problems that are not too easy to solve. If they are, the brain sees no need to work and resorts more often to familiar standard solutions. The downstream consequences of problem solving mindsets: How playing with LEGO influences creativity (Moreau and Engeseth 2016) highlights problem solving based on well-defined problems

Further reading
*Brainstorming* (2017) Alex F. Osborn

Crazy 8's is a fast sketching exercise that challenges people to sketch eight distinct ideas in eight minutes. The goal is to push beyond your first idea, frequently the least innovative, and to generate a wide variety of solutions to your challenge (Chung, 2020).

vs. poorly defined problems: 'Business leaders, governments and researchers are increasingly recognizing the importance of creativity. Recent trends in technology and education, however, suggest that many people face fewer opportunities to engage in creative thinking as they solve well-defined (versus poorly defined) problems more and more often'. In the experiment, a children's Lego building kit with the solution depicted on the package is a well-defined problem, while a poorly defined problem is a Lego set with few or no instructions on how to come up with the right solution (2.3.3 Problem definition, 4.4.2 Creative problem solving).

Fig. 4.37 The figure shows an exercise of connecting all the dots using four straight lines, without lifting the pen. Based on Micael Dahlén (2008). The solution can be found on page 528, Figure 4.121.

Tips for the designer
Explore the opportunity space.

| Idea process | |
|---|---|
| **1) Discover:**<br>I have a challenge. How can I approach it? | Define the problem. Define the goal and/or vision. Compile materials. |
| **2) Interpret:**<br>I have learned something new. How do I interpret it? | Examine and analyse. Organise materials. Incubation period. |
| **3) Develop:**<br>I see an opportunity. What do I want to create? | Brainstorming. Make associations. See new contexts and opportunities. Diverge and converge. Make more brainstorming rounds. The timely idea. Excitement about the solution. Joy rush. |
| **4) Experiment:**<br>I have an idea. How do I develop it further? | Develop the idea further through iteration and experimentation. Assess (critical, practical, logical, functional, financial). |
| **5) Implement:**<br>I have a concept. How can I present it? | Concretise the idea. Place on relevant digital or physical surfaces and in current contexts. Develop a model (dummy, mock-up, or prototype). |
| **6) Evaluate:**<br>I have tried something. How can I evaluate and test it? | Testing the idea among the target audience/user, in the relevant context, the environment. Evaluate and adjust. |
| **7) Present:**<br>I have a brilliant idea. How should I present it? | Think the idea through. Consider the number of suggestions to be presented. Select the correct time for the presentation. Clarify the problem statement and the task. Do not kill the idea by talking too much. Listen to the views of others. Do not try to convince others that the idea is good. Trust your idea and its value. |

63 In the 1920s Bluma Wulfovna Zeigarnik (1901–1988) conducted a study on memory, in which she compared memory in relation to incomplete and complete tasks. She had found that incomplete tasks are easier to remember than successful ones; this is now known as the Zeigarnik effect. In 1983 she received the Lewin Memorial Award for her psychological research ('Zeigarnik,' n.d.).

64 Gestalt psychology is a school of thought that looks at the human mind and behaviour as a whole. When trying to make sense of the world around us, gestalt psychology suggests that we do not simply focus on every small component. Instead, our minds tend to perceive objects as part of a greater whole and as elements of more complex systems (gestaltcleveland.org).

### Thinking outside the box

Thinking outside the box is something we like to associate with the ability to come up with amazing innovative ideas. The task shown in Figure 4.37 involves being able to think outside the box. According to Micael Dahlén (2008), most people, who try to solve the problem, fail the first time, and the bizarre thing is that most of us will have forgotten exactly how it is done the next time we are given the task. We usually devote more energy to trying to remember the solution than to come up with a creative solution to the problem. The right solution is perhaps so difficult to remember because it is so simple and obvious once we see it. This is exactly what the Zeigarnik effect is. It is named after the Soviet psychologist Bluma Zeigarnik[63] who discovered that people find it harder to remember easily recognisable images, because the brain does not need to create new memory lanes to remember these. It may be easier for us to remember the original task than the solution itself.

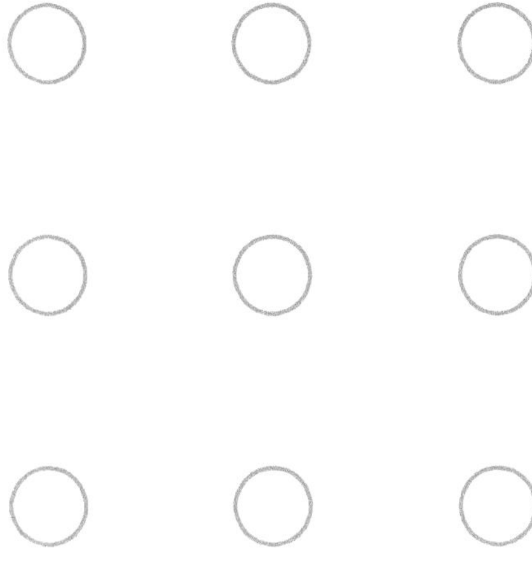

Fig. 4.37 Zeigarnik effect

The creative part where most people fail is to include the area outside the dots, see Figure 4.37. Here, gestalt psychology[64] comes into the picture. It describes the fact that we look for patterns and the big picture in the different impressions we encounter. The brain wants order; therefore, the nine dots will usually form a framed area, a frame, or a box in our heads. Without realising it, the walls of this box are so strong that we have great difficulty getting past them, which prevents us from solving the problem. The solution lies in working one's way through the wall of the box and thinking outside it. Many see this exercise as a metaphor for creativity: *Think outside the box*. But in theory, this solution is also a paradox. Firstly, because there is only one solution. Creativity is about coming up with many solutions. Secondly, it hinders creativity because it blocks other solutions since people *think* that there is only one right solution, and partly because people become too concerned with remembering the solution instead of trying to find it (if they have done the exercise before). Third, the metaphor is inappropriate because creativity, according to Dahlén, is not actually about thinking outside the box.

Dahlén is more concerned with what happens when we think inside the box than when we think outside the box, which he supports through the



'Creativity requires courage' (Henri Matisse). 'The true sign of intelligence is not knowledge, but imagination' (Albert Einstein). 'There are painters who turn the sun into a yellow spot, but there are others who, with the help of their art and intelligible gene, turn a yellow spot into sun' (Pablo Picasso).

following explanation: Contrary to what you might think, creative people have very concrete and limited boxes in their heads, and to many these walls are criteria for achieving creative results. Psychological research shows that creative people are fully aware of the frameworks that limit their thinking. At an abstract level, one can say that the box is made up of all the knowledge and experience in the field; for example, how to make cars, which means being perfectly familiar with what marks the limitations of the category 'car'. On a more concrete level, we can regard our own thoughts as a box. A box that gladly guides our thoughts along fixed roads and tunnels. Thinking creatively inside the box is about finding new paths that we can take in order to change direction. Without the box, there is a chance that the creative work will spread out and will be unproductive. Typical for creative people is that it is easier for them to produce new solutions when they are aware of the limitations (Dahlén, 2008, p. 105) (4.4.1 Foundation and frameworks).

Table 4.6 The table shows a form that can be used for the method Brainwriting 6-3-5, which can produce 108 ideas in 30 minutes. Based on Schr.er et al. (2010).

'Creativity is inventing, experimenting, growing, taking chances, breaking rules, making mistakes, and having fun' (Mary Lou Cook).

### Brainstorming methods

There are many different types of brainstorming. Here we will look into some variants.

**Rawlinson brainstorming:** This technique, developed in 1970, is named after author J. G. Rawlinson. There is no interaction between the group members, and all ideas are directed to the facilitator and chairperson. The procedure follows four steps, based on Markov (2018):

1) The chairperson presents the problem and goals.
2) Next, the chairperson provides background information, describes what options they have tried and failed with, and what would represent an ideal solution.
3) Group members present their solutions directly to the chairperson in words or short sentences.
4) The chairperson focuses on the ideas they find most helpful and comes up with new perspectives.

**Imaginary brainstorming:** This variant is like traditional brainstorming, but with a slight twist. The basic rules are the same. The differences are:

1) When defining the problem, make sure it has: A subject (that acts), a verb (which is the action), an object (whom/what the action is about).
2) Perform a traditional brainstorming process.
3) Define the essential parts of the problem and identify which of the above parts are most directly related to a successful solution. Suggest imaginary (hypothetic) replacements of the other elements. For example:

*The problem (the actual problem)*: How can we prepare a quotation in half the time?

*Suggested replacements (imaginary problems)*: How can children, Donald Duck, teachers build a house, make a million in half the time (this is the essence):

- Formulate a new problem by replacing one of the imaginary elements.
- Brainstorm ideas for the imaginary problem.
- Apply ideas from the imaginary brainstorming back to the actual problem.
- Analyse all the ideas (real, imaginary, and a combination of both) and highlight the most interesting ones.

65 Bernd Rohrbacj, a German marketing professional who published 6-3-5 Brainwriting in a sales magazine called *Absatzwirtschaft* in 1968.

66 The method at first included only writing down ideas. It was later extended by also drawing down ideas by Schröer et al. (2010) *Method 6-3-5-Extended*.

**Brainwriting 6-3-5:** The method was first published by Bernd Rohrbach[65] in the German magazine the *Absatzwirtschaft* in 1968 and later extended by Schröer et al. (2010).[66] The technique should be able to generate 108 ideas in 30 minutes. The process takes place with a chairperson and six participants. Each person has a blank 6-3-5 spreadsheet or form, see Table 4.6. Everyone writes down the problem statement at the top of their form (word for word from an agreed problem definition). Then each participant has five minutes to write down three ideas on the top row of the form in a complete and concise sentence (six to ten words). At the end of the five minutes (or when everyone has finished writing), each participant passes their form to the person on the right. Each participant can then add three more ideas. The process continues until the form is completed. When the process is complete, all 108 ideas can be assessed (mycoted.com, (Brainwriting, n.d.).

| | Problem statement: How can... | | |
|---|---|---|---|
| | Idea 1 | Idea 2 | Idea 3 |
| 1 | | | |
| 2 | | | |
| 3 | | | |
| 4 | | | |
| 5 | | | |
| 6 | | | |

Table 4.6 Brainwriting

**Brain modelling:** The idea behind brain modelling is that participants model different ideas and associations in clay, cardboard, or other materials. The method works well when the goal is to explore different modes of expression and to see how they manifest themselves in a three-dimensional form. The shapes created in the process are placed in the middle of the table so the others can work on them. Another option is for the shapes to be circulated to give others in the group ownership of the shapes being developed. Everyone is free to take pictures of their own forms during the process before others are set free and allowed to change them. As in any brainstorming session, here, too, everyone in the group should have a common understanding of the theme or problem about which they should make associations. The method is only an idea process, where the goal is not necessarily ending up with a physical product. This method works best if one already has some ideas in one's head that one wants to test and can therefore advantageously pursue a traditional brainstorming process (Lerdahl, 2008).

**Bodystorming:** Bodystorming is about using one's own body as a medium in a brainstorming situation to generate new ideas or to test ideas that are already in one's head. The method is to play out different use situations and patterns of action using one's body, thereby creating situations


1 Initiation
2 Insight
3 Strategy
4 Design
5 Production
6 Management

4.1 Design brief
4.2 Strategy><Design
4.3 Design methodology
4.4 Concept development
4.5 Design development
4.6 Design elements
4.7 Composition
4.8 Surface and format
4.9 Identity development

4.4.1 Foundation and framework
4.4.2 Creative problem solving
4.4.3 Brainstorming
4.4.4 Idea development
4.4.5 Conceptual directions
4.4.6 Verbalisation and visualisation
4.4.7 Prototyping of ideas
4.4.8 Testing of ideas
4.4.9 Presentation of ideas

- Warm-up exercises
- Thinking outside the box
- Brainstorming methods
- Distortion methods
- Connection and analogy methods
- Scamper


The COCD box
An idea selection tool helping to find out the most promising ideas after an idea generation session: tuzzit.com/en/canvas/COCD_box

that lead to new thoughts and associations. A good approach is to create scenarios for existing solutions and then new solutions to quickly test ideas in practice. The challenge of the method is that it requires to an even greater extent than traditional brainstorming that the participants cut themselves loose and dare to put themselves out there a little. It takes a great deal of courage and playfulness. Bodystorming can be advantageously supplemented with other idea development methods that bring thoughts into new tracks and create new connections, such as forced connection and rotation methods (Lerdahl, 2008).

**Imagine you are in a dream**
**Develop ideas based on a dream situation. For example: 'The pen writes on its own', 'Clothes wash and iron themselves', 'The knife cuts for me', 'The lamp is brighter when my eyes get tired'. This way of thinking can be used to get past some limitations and help bring up some crazy ideas that can unleash playfulness and laughter and create good social impact.**

**Trigger sessions:** Trigger sessions are a great way to register a lot of ideas from untrained participants.

- The problem owner defines the problem.
- Each member of the group writes down their ideas in brief form (only two minutes).
- One member quietly reads their lists; others quietly cross out ideas that are being read out and write down new ideas that are triggered by the ideas being read out.
- The next member reads out from their list any ideas which have not been covered yet, followed again by other members.
- The last member reads the original list and additional list, and the procedure is repeated upstream (i.e. if there are six people, the order goes 1, 2, 3, 4, 5, 6, 5, 4, 3, 2, 1, 2, 3, 4, 5, 6 ...).
- A good team will be able to handle seven rounds.

All papers are then gathered and can be used to make a single list of ideas. Duplicates should have been checked out during the session (mycoted.com).

**Brainstorming checklist**

Osborn's checklist is used for transforming an existing idea into a new one, through a trial-and-error approach:

- Put to other uses: As it is? If modified?
- Adapt: Is there anything else like this? What does this tell you? Is it comparable?
- Modify: Give it a new angle? Alter colour, sound, odour, meaning, motion, and shape?
- Refine: Can anything be added: time, frequency, height, length, strength? Can it be duplicated, multiplied or exaggerated?
- Minimise: Can anything be taken away? Made smaller? Lowered? Shortened? Lightened? Omitted? Broken up?
- Substitute: Different ingredients used? Other materials? Other processes? Other places? Another approach? Another tone of voice? Someone else?
- Rearrange: Swap components? Alter the pattern, sequence, or layout? Change the pace or schedule? Transpose cause and effect?
- Reverse: Opposites? Backwards? Reverse roles? Change shoes? Turn tables? Turn the other cheek? Transpose +/-?
- Combine: Combine units, purposes, appeals, or ideas? A blend, alloy, or grouping? (Based on Mycoted.com/Osborns Checklist)

67 The method is inspired by the Synectics theory, developed by George M. Prince and William J.J. Gordon, Arthur D. Little in the 1950s. ('Synectics,' n.d.)

## Distortion methods

Distortion or twisting methods can complement brainstorming methods, especially in the early stages of the idea process, as a way of exploring the task and are particularly well suited when the challenge is to come up with new ground-breaking and innovative ideas. It involves taking *an existing* idea or solution further by looking at it from a different perspective, twisting and flipping it, removing or adding assumptions, exaggerating and changing proportions, amplifying problems, and exploring new scenarios. The aim is to take ideas to the extreme in order to thus see new opportunities and come up with new ideas. 'When things are taken to the extreme, nuances emerge more clearly' (Lerdahl, 2007). It is easier to hold back too much than to get too extreme. Therefore, twisting methods is a good way of becoming more daring. We will look at a selection of distortion methods (based on Lerdahl 2007):

**With a different perspective:** One way to look at the problem from a different perspective is to look at it with the eyes of others. It could be fictional characters or celebrities. What would the product look like if Philippe Starck had made it? Another twist may be to complete the task for a different target group than the one relevant to the task. How would we design the solutions if they were intended for pensioners, children, youths, for men instead of women, or vice versa? Or what happens if the product should be twice as expensive, half as expensive or free? What if one changes industry? What would a garment look like if it were to be designed by automotive industry designers? How would they have thought about the shape and function of the clothes? Or, how can we use products made of metal, plastic, glass, mirror, etc. as inspiration? What about sound? What about driving experience? It is also possible to imagine oneself as a concrete solution or a product. If I were the product, what would I need? What do I lack? If I were an item in the shop, how could I attract more attention, seem interesting? What shape and colour would I have? What would I look like as a chair if I were to feel comfortable when others sat on me? This method[67] is well suited to playing out different scenarios with others.

**Remove or add prerequisites:** This method is based on removing or adding natural prerequisites to a product or service. One starts by listing all prerequisites, for example, for a knife; then, one removes the prerequisites one by one. What is a knife without a handle? What is a car without wheels? And the other way round: one can add prerequisites. They may be a little absurd, such as: Only guests who have dogs are allowed into the restaurant. What ideas does this inspire?

**Exaggerate or understate:** A common creative approach is to exaggerate or understate, to the extreme and absurd. The challenge is to find out what is interesting to exaggerate in order to get more exciting ideas. If the user is on the young side, what happens when you imagine they are five years old? Or, what happens if we change proportions by enlarging or decreasing? Or change the shape from square to round, long or narrow? What if we change the expression or mood to romantic, sexy, humorous, or sad? All different parts of the composition can be twisted and turned. Both drawing and sketching by hand and on a computer work well for this idea method.

What if ...?

**What if people, instead of hands, had pincers like lobsters do?**

**Release opposites:** This method is based on finding key opposites in a task, by working with the extremes of the solution space and thinking about both the optimal and the unimaginable. For example, a table should be extremely lightweight and extremely sturdy. The method then consists in reinforcing the optimal solution based on one condition at a time. How do we make the table as lightweight as possible? Similarly, other conditions should be met. What does an extremely sturdy table look like? In the end, one takes the best out of all draft solutions.
**Ideas that amplify the problems:** The method is to find solutions that amplify the problems we want to solve. How can we be destructive and make the most hopeless product possible? If a bottle has a dull and solid design, how can we make it even more boring and traditional? Can we make a list of everything that makes the product or service worse? The goal of amplifying the problem is that it can help us see the heart of the problem more clearly and identify the factors that are important for a further idea process. Moreover, it can be a liberating and fun approach to the task, which can contribute to a freer process.
**'What if' scenarios:** This is a method of exploring possibilities and ideas other than the more obvious ones, which challenge conformist attitudes and established truths. For example, one scenario could be: What if people, instead of hands, had pincers like lobsters do? How would a computer be set up then? How would we prepare and eat food? In order for the 'what if' scenarios to work well, it is important to envision the situation and take it seriously. It is important to analyse the scenario step by step, thus gaining an overview of the situation.
**Fantasy world and future scenarios:** This method is about looking at the problem in a different context, culture and social setting, or to create a new context or framework, which can provide new ideas. It can be in the real world, a fantasy world, or an imaginary scenario for the future.[68] It is a good method for creating more future solutions. The method requires an ability to abstract and inspire imaginative solutions and to transfer elements and ideas from an extreme alien world back to the familiar and real one. 'Make the familiar strange, make the strange familiar' (William Gordon, 1961) is a fundamental mindset in creativity. A new product should have something familiar in addition to something new (Lerdahl, 2007). The group works from an external context inwards, with each person in the group writing stories about, for example, how society works. The group rotates regularly so that everyone writes on the others' stories, as in the brainwriting pool method.

### Connection and analogy methods

Connecting solutions and elements that are not usually connected can lead to associations to new ideas and completely unexpected solutions, and can be useful when one is slightly stuck in the idea process. The aim is to drive one's thought away from familiar thought patterns by connecting elements that do not usually belong together.[69] We will look at some different connection and analogy methods (based on Lerdahl, 2007, p. 151–161).
**Forced-Relationship:** This is an intuitive idea-finding technique proposed by Charles Whiting (1958)[70] that focuses in particular on the areas of product and service innovations. The method involves taking a specific

Tips for the designer
**Embrace quantity: An idea process should be exhaustive. If you start putting ideas into practice too soon, this can limit the flow of ideas.**

An underlying idea is a springboard for responsible creative work (Wheeler, 2013).

68 Speculative Design is a methodical approach to the development of future scenarios: 'The speculative design framework focuses on possible, probable, and preferred future situations (Dunne and Raby, 2013), and provides designers with a tool to criticise their own time by creating fictional scenarios about possible societal, political, technological, or cultural circumstances' (Fuller, 2016; Bardzell et al., 2012; Rynning and Skjulstad, 2017). Read more about the research article 'Speculative graphic design: Visual identity branding as a catalyst for change', written by Rynning (2017).
69 Connections can be made to specific objects or to analogies or metaphors, and require good imagination while keeping focus on the task. Unrelated elements can provide more original ideas, but can be difficult to realise, while related elements, with a natural connection, can lead to more down-to-earth solutions.
70 Charles Whiting, British author. Similar to the Force-Fit game, Forced-Relationship works with so-called stimulus words and stimulates the imagination with unusual combinations of terms (ask-flip.com).
71 'Analogies in creative processes' (kreativtnorge.no).

element, which belongs to the task, and a randomly selected element, and connect these in different ways. The process can be accomplished by thinking and writing down, drawing, or by having the objects physically promoted, or by a combination of both. You start by making associations on the object in question and then switch to associating around other objects. In a group, you can use the brainwriting pool method to build on each other's ideas. You can also use a series of random images as inspiration instead of objects. Associations and feelings from the images can be linked to the problem or the specific product or service as inspiration for idea development.

**Random input:** Another twist method is 'random input' (Edward de Bono 1996), which entails using a random word, picture, or even sound, to open new lines and directions of thinking.

**Random word method:** It has been said that, when Campbell's Soup was brainstorming new ideas for soup products they used the random word tool and started with the word 'apartment.' Then they brainstormed around that word. No logic, they just let the ideas flow – apartment led to building, build, tools, hammer, saw, drill, knife, which eventually led to fork. Someone on team said, 'You can't eat soup with a fork. It would have to be in chunks to do that.' So Chunky Soup was born.

**Property connection:** In this method, attributes from other products are linked to the product in question, which has similar attributes. First, various product attributes that should be worked on are listed. Then you will find other products that have similar properties and words that describe these properties. For example, the attributes of a pocketknife could be solid, flexible, and lightweight. What do we associate with the word *solid*? Stone, sturdy, stable, Volvo etc. What do we associate Volvo with, and how can these new associations be connected to the knife?

**Metaphors and analogies:** Metaphors are words, expressions, or imagery used in the translated sense, such as 'hard as steel'. Analogy is a form of comparison such as 'A bird in the hand is worth two in the bush'[71] When we think metaphorically, we look for parallels, similarities, and analogies. It can be a good approach in creative processes to start from an existing solution and ask ourselves what metaphors we can associate with it. What kind of animal best describes the product or service? What kind of car? What if the car is a Lada and we want a Mercedes? By finding metaphors for the solution we want to make, we can become

**Association sequence:** This is a method that can be nice to warm up with if you do not know how to start the idea process. It is about linking words in an association row or a web of association rows, and then selecting words in the row that can further stimulate forced connections. The further out in the association sequence one gets, the more distant the connection becomes. For example: knife – food – kitchen – shelves – lighting. How can linking a knife and lighting lead to new ideas? For each of the words, one can draw new associations in a vertical line downwards and create an association matrix.

1 Initiation
2 Insight
3 Strategy
4 Design
5 Production
6 Management

4.1 Design brief
4.2 Strategy><Design
4.3 Design methodology
4.4 Concept development
4.5 Design development
4.6 Design elements
4.7 Composition
4.8 Surface and format
4.9 Identity development

4.4.1 Foundation and framework
4.4.2 Creative problem solving
4.4.3 Brainstorming
4.4.4 Idea development
4.4.5 Conceptual directions
4.4.6 Verbalisation and visualisation
4.4.7 Prototyping of ideas
4.4.8 Testing of ideas
4.4.9 Presentation of ideas

- Warm-up exercises
- Thinking outside the box
- Brainstorming methods
- Distortion methods
- Connection and analogy methods
- Scamper

Further reading

Check out the book *The Worst-Case Scenario Survival Handbook* (2019) by Joshua Piven and David Borgenicht.

clearer on the goal and desired change. Furthermore, we can analyse the attributes of the 'Mercedes' metaphor and see what kind of ideas we can come up with from these. Then we can continue to find new metaphors and repeat the process.

Idea vs. Concept
**An idea is but one inventive thought, until it is evaluated and concretised visually and verbally so that it can be presented to others, only then can it be called a concept.**

**SCAMPER questions**

Example of questions (based on mindtools.com):
**Replacement:** What materials or resources can you replace or change in order to improve the product? What other products or processes can you use? What rules can you replace? Can you use this product elsewhere, or as a replacement for something else? What will happen if you change your feelings or attitude about this product?
**Combine:** What would happen if you combined this product with another to create something new? What if you combined purpose or goal? What can you combine to maximise the use of this product? How could you combine talent and resources to create a new approach to this product?
**Adapt:** How can you adapt or adjust this product for a different purpose or use? What else is the product similar to? Who or what can you emulate to adjust this product? What else is like such a product? What other contexts can you insert the product into? What other products or ideas can you use for inspiration?
**Edit:** How can you change the shape, appearance or experience of the product? What can you add to modify this product? What can you highlight or mark to create added value? Which element of this product can you strengthen to create something new?
**Use in a different way:** Can you use this product elsewhere, in another industry? Who else could use this product? How would this product behave differently in another setting? Can you recycle waste from this product in order to make something new?
**Eliminate:** How can you streamline or simplify this product? What features, parts, or rules can you eliminate? What can you either underline or tone down? How could you make it smaller, faster, easier, or funnier? What would happen if you removed a part of this product? What would you get instead?
**Reverse:** What would happen if you reversed this process or sequenced things differently? What if you are trying to do the opposite of what you are trying to do now? Which components can you replace in order to reorder this product? Which roles can you reverse or swap? How can you rearrange this product?

The goal is to generate as many ideas as possible without thinking about whether any of them may be impractical or inappropriate. When evaluating ideas, it is time to consider which ones are not viable and which can be further explored. To get the best out of SCAMPER, it is a good idea to combine this method with other idea development techniques.

72 **Bob Eberle developed SCAMPER in 1971, based on Alex Osborne's ideas from the 1950s, and presented it in his book; SCAMPER: Games for Imagination Development. The method is also central in Michael Michalko's book *Thinkertoys*.**

### Scamper

Scamper is a technique for idea development that is particularly useful for generating ideas when the goal is to improve a product or service. SCAMPER is considered one of the simplest and most direct methods of idea development. The technique is based on the notion that all new things are actually a modification of existing old things around us, developed by Bob Eberle (1971).[72] SCAMPER stands for: Substitute, Combine, Adapt, Modify, Put to another use, Eliminate, Reverse. The method is to conduct a brainstorming session by asking questions about an existing product. It may be a product that should be improved, a product that is problematic, or a product that may have potential to serve as a starting point for future development. All answers that emerge are recorded and finally assessed. Does anything stand out as a good solution? Can any of them be used to create a new product or to develop an existing one? If any of the ideas seem viable, they can be explored further. The results may lead to creative ideas for developing new products or improving those of today.

## 4.4.5 Conceptual directions

After a broad idea process, the next step is to concretise ideas and develop conceptual directions. At an early stage of the design process, it is a good rule to come up with more than one idea direction. Getting attached too quickly to a single idea, or choosing the first and 'best' solution can penalise you later in the process and cause you to lock yourself in. There is not always enough time and resources in a project to go back and start over. Designers who have gained experience over the years will often have a stronger gut feeling and be more accurate in knowing which ideas are working or not, and will therefore be quicker in picking good ideas.

The textbook example is to draw up three conceptual directions (it might as well be two or five). This can be developing different directions based on completely different ideas or starting from one idea and letting it run in different directions. The three directions should be so different that they can be clearly distinguished from each other; for example, by representing extremes between the classical and the modern, the conventional and the extreme, the predictable and the unpredictable. That, of course, depends entirely on the task. For example, in cases where the client has strong wishes, the designer can deliver one direction that meets the client's request, one direction that does so partially, and one direction that shows something quite different from what the client has in mind. The latter direction may bring forth completely new thoughts and solutions. For example, when redesigning a logo, one direction may be as similar as possible to an existing design; the other may have elements of similarity, and the third may come up with something completely new. A good habit is to name the different directions, in order to be able to distinguish them from each other more easily, talk about them, and present them, for example:

- *Concept 1*: 'Tradition' Predictable, safe and conventional.
- *Concept 2*: 'Dynamic' Something new and challenging, but within the familiar.
- *Concept 3*: 'Futuristic' Something completely new, innovative and limitless.


1 Initiation
2 Insight
3 Strategy
4 Design
5 Production
6 Management

4.1 Design brief
4.2 Strategy><Design
4.3 Design methodology
4.4 Concept development
4.5 Design development
4.6 Design elements
4.7 Composition
4.8 Surface and format
4.9 Identity development

4.4.1 Foundation and framework
4.4.2 Creative problem solving
4.4.3 Brainstorming
4.4.4 Idea development
4.4.5 Conceptual directions
4.4.6 Verbalisation and visualisation
4.4.7 Prototyping of ideas
4.4.8 Testing of ideas
4.4.9 Presentation of ideas

- Warm-up exercises
- Thinking outside the box
- Brainstorming methods
- Distortion methods
- Connection and analogy methods
- Scamper


Innovation

**What is innovation, and when is an idea innovative? Innovation is a term for man-made change of value-creating activities. Innovation is used on innovation, new creation, change, new products, services, or production processes, to bring out changes in the way economic goods or other values are produced. Usually innovation is seen as an economic phenomenon and is defined as an intended change in the production of goods and services (Ørstavik, n.d.).**

The driving force can often be a combination of several ideas. The key here is that the ideas actually solve the problem or respond to the problem statement. Not to mention the objective and strategic anchorage. Is this us? Is this how we want to appear, be perceived? Is this what we promise? Can we deliver on that? The choice of direction will form the basis for further design work (2.3 Problem statement, 3.2.5 Core values, 3.2.6 Value proposition, Table 3.2 Top 5 – strategic management tools, 4.5.1 The three-direction principle).

Tips for the designer
**Carefully choose what ideas you present to your client. Pitch the two or three ideas you believe in, and which will be inspiring to work on further in the process. Make sure they are in line with the design strategy.**

Tips for the company
**When choosing from the ideas presented by the designer, it is important to ask yourself: Does it solve the problem defined, is it in line with the chosen strategy, does it meet business goals and sustainability goals, is the solution functional and attractive to potential users, customers and consumers?**

**Deciding on an idea or conceptual direction is primarily about assessing whether it solves the problem or task.**

### 4.4.6 Verbalisation and visualisation

The key to developing ideas for conceptual directions lies in verbalising and visualising the ideas. They need to be sufficiently concretised to present them, argue for them, compare them and choose the direction of ideas for further work. Verbalisation and visualisation of ideas also make it easier to develop them further. Visualisation can be done by creating moodboards, rough sketches, storyboards, video, prototypes, displaying material samples of plastic, wood paper or other materials, displaying examples of design cases, taking photos of situations, objects, or other things. Verbalisation can be done using simple explanations, narratives, or storylines. For the designer, it is necessary to concretise ideas in order to be able to assess which best solves the problem and in order to be able to present the best idea(s) to the client. Ideas to be sold to the client should be so concrete that the client can decide on them and make their choices. The very process of concretising an idea is in itself awareness-raising and can lead to improvement and further development of the idea (2.8.2 Moodboard, 4.6 Design elements).

### 4.4.7 Prototyping of ideas

During the idea process, the development of prototypes is useful for materialising the idea and testing it in relevant contexts and user situations. That way, it is easier to find out whether or not the idea solves the problem well. It can also be easier to sell ideas as digital or physical prototypes than as data presentations or drafts on sheets. A prototype can be created in infinite ways, from simple paper dummies to advanced 3D prints. Rapid prototyping is a term for a way to develop models fast at project level, which are well suited to the idea phase. This involves repeatedly developing prototypes during an idea process and testing them. That way, one finds out early what does and does not work, thus avoids pursuing ideas that do not lead anywhere. Instead, one can learn what adjustments can be made in the next round of the idea process in order to get closer to a solution to the problem or task. The development of prototypes is something one starts with early in the idea process and continues with until the final prototype is ready before production (5.2.1 Dummy, 5.2.3 Wireframe, 5.2.4 Mockup, 5.2.5 Prototype).

### 4.4.8 Testing of ideas

Testing and evaluation take place in all phases of a design process, but the need for them and the approaches vary in the different phases. The choice of testing method will also depend on time and budget. In an idea phase, it is natural to run tests based on simple examples, implementations and dummies, until the solution becomes more concrete and it is possible to create more elaborate prototypes. In general, testing can be done using simple qualitative methods such as user tests, observations, interviews and focus groups among a smaller selection of people, or using more extensive quantitative methods such as surveys among a larger group. During the idea phase, testing ideas for a product or service will be useful to see if the idea works and what can be done to reinforce it. For example, early ideas for an online shop can be tested on typical users in order to find out if they are navigating and interacting as intended. What you learn from testing is carried forward into the idea development process to reinforce the idea. Another example could be testing food packaging mockups on the shop shelf in a grocery store in order to find out what the packaging looks like compared to competing products and whether the solution meets the requirements and the problem statement. In such a test, both the user and the client can easily be involved (2.6.1 Survey, 2.6.2 Interview, 2.6.3 Observation, 2.9 Testing and measuring, 2.9.2 A/B testing).


1 Initiation
2 Insight
3 Strategy
4 Design
5 Production
6 Management

4.1 Design brief
4.2 Strategy><Design
4.3 Design methodology
4.4 Concept development
4.5 Design development
4.6 Design elements
4.7 Composition
4.8 Surface and format
4.9 Identity development

4.4.1 Foundation and framework
4.4.2 Creative problem solving
4.4.3 Brainstorming
4.4.4 Idea development
4.4.5 Conceptual directions
4.4.6 Verbalisation and visualisation
4.4.7 Prototyping of ideas
4.4.8 Testing of ideas
4.4.9 Presentation of ideas


## 4.4.9 Presentation of ideas

A idea development process may result in several conceptual directions, but this is not equivalent to the number of directions the designer presents to the client. The designer should assess, from a professional and strategic perspective, which of the ideas best solves the problem statement. In such an assessment, there are many things to take into account, which are not only aesthetic and visual, but have to do with technical issues, function, production, resource use and costs. The designer should be careful about pitching ideas that they initially have doubts about or do not believe in. In a worst-case scenario the client might choose this type of solution. It is the designer's task to advise and give professional reasons, reflections and arguments when choosing a concept. A good approach is to highlight the problem statement and strategy that underlies the work and to connect the conceptual directions with these to justify and argue which solution is best suited to proceed with. In general, only one direction is chosen, but it can often be beneficial to consider whether there is something useful in the other concepts that may add something to the selected concept. In some contexts, new rounds of conceptual processes and further development of conceptual directions may be necessary before choosing a final direction.

The number of conceptual directions developed in a project is related to time and budget. In large, ambitious projects, it is often necessary to develop many directions, and in some contexts almost finished solutions, before finally choosing a direction. Some clients are trained to understand rough concept sketches, while others will need more detailed design sketches in order to be able to decide on an idea direction. Once the client has chosen the conceptual direction of the design, the *design development* work can begin (1.1 Initial preparations: Pitch perfect, 2.3 Problem statement, 3.3 Goals and subgoals, 3.4 Business strategy, 3.9 Design strategy, 4.5.1 The three-direction principle).

Further reading
*Now Try Something Weirder: How to keep having great ideas and survive in the creative business* (2019) by Michael Johnson

> The conceptual directions developed represent different solutions to the problem and the choice of direction will form the basis for further design work.

## 4.5 Design development

Design development in this context is about further developing and refining one or more conceptual directions towards final solutions.

After the idea process has been completed and a conceptual direction has been chosen, we start working on design development. It is part of the total design process shown in Table 4.1 The design process. Design development here is divided into two main areas, which is design sketch and concrete design. *Design sketch* are covered by the sketch stage from rough to detailed sketches. *Concrete design* is furter development and refinement of the sketches toward completion of the design solution. Such a division can make it easier to plan the work in terms of time, progress and budgeting. In large projects, it may be advantageous to divide these two phases into more phases reflected in the price given. Various principles and methods that can be used for design development are presented throughout phase 4 of this book.

Fig. 4.38 The figure shows a design development process based on a three-way principle which consists of working with three directions in each step of the design process. For each step, a direction is selected, which will be developed further in the next step. Of course, the same principle can be applied if one works with more or fewer directions in the process. By working broadly with multiple directions in each phase of the design development process, one can avoid being stuck with 'first and best idea'. This method is funnel-based since one starts broadly and narrows down the process towards a desired result. © Grimsgaard, W. 2018.

Tips for the designer
Design sketches involve reopening the process and exploring different solutions by working with design sketches, design of visual elements and typography, and experimenting with shape, format, and composition.

> 'Identity designers are in the business of managing perception through the integration of meaning and distinctive visual form' (Wheeler, 2018, p. 24)

### 4.5.1 The three-direction principle

A classic textbook example of a design and development process is explained in the three-direction principle, shown in Figure 4.38.

- The basis is enough insight, a clear problem statement and strategic anchorage.
- The first step is concept development: Here, ideas are developed broadly. A selection of three different ideas are chosen and further concretised in three conceptual directions. One or (a combination of) two conceptual directions are selected for further development (4.4.4 Idea development, 4.4.5 Conceptual directions).
- The second step is design sketch: Here, broad work on design sketches takes place in order to further develop the concept chosen. The sketches are sorted into three directions, each representing different solutions to the task. One of the sketch directions is selected for concretisation (4.5.2 Design sketches).
- The third step is concrete design: Here, work is done on refining and detailing the design solution. Here too, work is carried out in three directions, but is limited to variations in the detailing work that can reinforce the final result. So it is not a matter of developing new directions, just looking at different ways of improving the design (4.5.3 Concrete design).
- The completion: Here, work continues on final prototyping, testing and completion of the solution, towards implementation, production, programming, or other output.

In the process as a whole and in each individual step, one works iteratively. One diverges (opens up the process) when developing the design and converges (narrows down the process) as one makes choices in the process, again and again, repeating until desired solution is achieved. The design process involves the use of design methodologies presented in 4.3 Design methodology, such as iteration, sprint, co-design. Throughout the design development process, attention is constantly directed towards the problem statement. It is in the problem statement the final solution

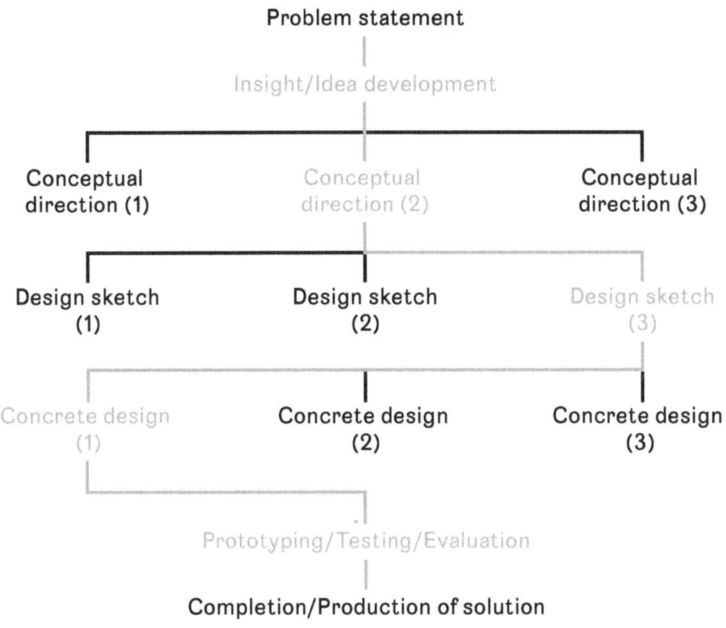


Fig. 4.38 Three-direction principle


1 Initiation
2 Insight
3 Strategy
4 Design
5 Production
6 Management

4.1 Design brief
4.2 Strategy><Design
4.3 Design methodology
4.4 Concept development
4.5 Design development
4.6 Design elements
4.7 Composition
4.8 Surface and format
4.9 Identity development

4.5.1 The three-direction principle
4.5.2 Design sketches
4.5.3 Concrete design


should resolve, based on strategic guidelines defined in the design strategy (2.3 Problem statement, 3.9 Design strategy).

### 4.5.2 Design sketches

Design sketch is a step in the design process, which is about further developing conceptual direction(s) towards a design solution that answers to the problem statement and solves the task. The client has approved the work so far and now comes the time to further develop the ideas and prove that they are feasible. At this stage in the design development process, it is natural for the designer to think: What now? How do I proceed from here?

- Strategic anchoring: Have the project goal, design strategy and the problem statement at the front of your mind.
- Make a plan: Stop, spend some time reflecting, and make a plan for the further process. This means thinking logically through what has emerged in the idea process and how this should be included and used in the further sketching process. Prepare lists, set priorities, allocate work, and ensure good overview and team dialogue in the process. Check the progress schedule to find out the amount of time available.
- Get an overview: Lay out your idea sketches, moodboards, storyboards, etc. from the idea process in order to get the overall picture. After some time in an open and free creative process, it is now important to think in a systematic and structured way.
- Clarify the task: Clarify which elements should actually be developed. If the task is to develop a visual identity, it may be, for example, logo, symbol and identity elements (3.9 Design strategy, 3.7.6 Brand assets, 4.6 Design elements, 4.9 Identity development, 4.9.1 The identity principles, 4.9.2 The identity elements, 2.9.8 Mental availability measurements).

> Design development
> It is in the basic design elements, composition principles and typographical grasps that the very key to the conscious development of design lies. The backdrop is a targeted strategy and a clear problem statement.

- Clarify what elements: Clarify what should be communicated, illustrated, and photographed? What is the theme and content? What slogan and core message should be used? What elements should be designed and in which contexts should the design work?
- Explore options: Then the question is: Which typeface, drawing style, and photo fashion fits the selected concept? How can they be aligned with the strategic directions of identity, brand and communication?[73] How can they be reflected in composition, grid and information structure?
- Work broadly: A broad sketching process is needed in order to come up with different ways to develop the concept. The work often starts with developing many rough sketches by hand and digitally.
- Make choices: The directions one believes in the most are chosen for further development up to a level that makes it possible to assess them against each other and determine which one works best.
- Present to the client: The selected design sketch(s) are presented to the client, who, together with the designer, chooses which direction to refine and concretise to a final design solution (4.5.3 Concrete design).

Tips for the designer
**Level of details: You should avoid getting lost in detail early in the sketching process. Fiddling with the Bézier curves in Illustrator can be time-consuming and should be postponed until the concretisation of the design. If the product looks too finished, the client may say OK and stop, which may deprive the designer of the opportunity to further develop it and arrive at an even better solution. Nevertheless, the various design sketches should be sufficiently detailed so that the solutions come out right and be understandable to the designer and others who will decide on them. Especially as this is necessary in order to create prototypes and test the solutions in the current context and on the current users.**

### Sketch process

**Framework:** A sketching process always starts with a look back at the problem statement, the goal, the strategic guidelines, the requirements specification and other project frameworks, which are clarified in the design brief. Equally important is the planning of process, time and resources, as well as ensuring that the necessary equipment is available (2.3 Problem statement, 4.1 Design brief).

**Insight:** In the design development process, new insights may be needed in addition to the ones that have emerged during the analysis and strategy phase of the project. A good start is to get an overview of collected data by mapping up results from customer journeys, personas, graphs, moodboards, early idea sketches, etc. on the wall, on a table or on a digital board. New insight can be obtained from online sites that show design cases by other designers, or relevant literature, magazines, materials, papers and other physical material that can be useful in the sketch process. This gives inspiration and insight into styles, trends, font use, visual instruments, photography, illustration, techniques, and methods. It is also important to seek out your own considerations and experiences, make observations, observe people, talk to people, do user tests, focus group surveys, etc.

What insight is needed for the sketching process? For example, if the task is to develop a new packaging design, it may be useful to visit retailers to study competitive products and look at typical features of relevant category language and genre. Should the category affiliation be followed or broken? Which products are attractive and stand out as good examples and inspiration? What characterises them? What are the brand exposure, font selection, choice of colour, use of contrasts, and packaging material like? What is the shelf placement like? How big is the shelf edge? Can it hide some of the packaging? What about the lighting? Do parts of the packaging become more illuminated? Is anything in the shade? How does this vary in different parts of the shop and in different shops? What is the product exposure like? What is the availability like for customers?

73 **Such guidelines are, for example, defined in the core values, brand platform and tone of voice (3.1.3 Top 5, 3.9 Design strategy).**

What is the customers' behaviour like in the shop? How do they move and what do they look at? And so on. What impact will these observations have on the sketching process? Contact printers to explore various production possibilities for labels, prices, materials, colours, etc. How do the different choices affect production time and price? Should we print on paper, metal or plastic. What is more functional? What is more sustainable? Which alternative printing techniques are appropriate? Can one print metallic on this material? How much more expensive is it? The sketching process is in itself an insight process, bringing about new understanding through exploration and experimentation, design research processes and the use of design methodology (2 Insight, 2.6.6 Experiment, 2.6.9 Design research).

**Hand sketches**; It is always good to start with rough hand sketches on paper, because it is a quick way to work and makes it easy to visualise thoughts and ideas. It can be used regardless of whether the end product is digital or physical. Whether or not you can draw is not important as long as you understand your own sketches. If you start right away with digital sketches, there is a risk of getting hung up on the details too early in the process. Of course, it depends a lot on how effortless you work digitally. If you know the program well and can work freely with it, it might be fine to start directly on a computer. Digital drawing boards and programs that allow using a finger or a pen to draw can be beneficial for easy digital sketching. Either way, it is always an advantage to have paper and pencil next to your computer to write down ideas and make quick sketch notes. Generally, it is about working as effortlessly as possible in the sketching process and as quickly as possible visualising thoughts and ideas flowing through your head.

> Systematic work begins by looking at typefaces in order to find the ones that fit the concept best; experiment with colours and colour maps to find colours that work; look at different illustration techniques to develop symbols, graphs, infographics and other things to illustrate; look at formats and aspect ratios; look at material choices such as paper, metal, textiles or other things that can help express and reinforce the idea; look into technologies that can be applied, and so on.

There may be a risk associated with overprocessing the sketches or starting with detailing work at this stage. If the drafts are perceived as almost finished solutions, the process may lock up prematurely, which may mean that the potential for further development and improvement of the draft solution is not tested. One can get the feeling of being stuck and not moving on. When that is the case, it may be necessary to take a few steps back and work out more sketch directions. It may also be useful to retrieve the design brief, take a look at the problem statement and the task goal, and assess whether one is on track. One may have to go back to the beginning and start over. If one gets too hung up on a sketch that does not really lead forward, the term 'kill your darlings' may be useful; reject and move on. Working iteratively in the sketching process,



Further reading
***UX/UI Design 2022: A Comprehensive UI & UX Guide to Master Web Design and Mobile App Sketches for Beginners and Pros*** (2022) by Carl Jones.

testing the sketches often, learning what works and not, will help make the process agile (4.6.1 Shape, 4.6.2 Colour, 4.6.3 Texture, 4.6.4 Space).

**Computer sketches**: When ready to start sketching on a computer a good way to begin is to scan hand sketches and use them as a starting point. If there are specific physical or digital requirements for draft, format, object, or space as a starting point for the task, it may be a good idea to take these into account from the very beginning. You may also want to challenge these requirements if you think it could help improve the solution. It is always an advantage to experience aspect ratio and shape as early as possible in the process, which can often be difficult on a screen. This can be done by implementing the sketches in the right digital and analogue interfaces, printing if necessary, and creating simple dummies for a physical experience of size and shape.

- *Digital*: If the end product is a mobile app, it will be important to test sketches for the app as early as possible on a smartphone, pad and computer screen. Also involve potential users early and often, to test along the way (4.8 Surface and format).
- *Analogue*: If the final product is to be printed matter, it may be useful to print rough sketches in different alternative formats. Holding a format physically in your hand offers a more realistic experience of the product you create compared to just watching it on screen. Last but not least, it provides opportunities to quickly find out what works and what does not, discover new ideas and opportunities, and make changes and improvements along the way.

When working with design sketches, exciting things could happen in the process, which may be helpful to keep. This can easily be done by storing numbered copies of the sketches. Creating an archive system for the various stages of the process and archiving frequently makes it easier to retrieve previous solutions and compare new and old sketches.

**Sketch prototyping**: The sketching process works towards a prototype that allows for a realistic impression of the solution, in order to be presented to the client, without the design being too concrete.

- *Digital*: If the final solution is to work digitally on different screens, prototype development may involve creating test models in the right formats, with some selected navigation and interaction features. The prototype is implemented on the devices in question and tested on selected users to determine whether the solution works as intended: functionally, emotionally, and visually.
- *Analogue*: If the task is to develop a packaging design, a dummy or mock-up in the sketch phase may involve visualising the outer shape (box, bottle, bag), the main design elements (logo, symbol, colours, illustration, photo, graphic elements), and the main communication (product name, slogan, and product attributes). Things like product information, product data, contents, gram weight, quality marks, EAN code (bar code), and QR code, or the like can wait until the design is concretised. However, it is important to set aside space for this early in the process. One can be surprised by how much space this takes on some sketches, and how this can limit the space for design elements, photos and the like (Brekke-Bjørkedal, 2017). On an early dummy, it may be a good idea to include some of these details, such as gram weight, if the role of the element affects how the solution is perceived. The text on the

Unit and whole

**In the sketching process, it is necessary to work with the individual elements separately while being aware of the role and task of the elements as part of the whole.**

back of the product can be displayed as blank text (Lorem Ipsum) and sketch photos can be used to illustrate motifs to be photographed later.

When working with design sketches, it is too early to make complex illustrations, grids or product features for each of the alternative design solutions. The solutions should, nonetheless, be presented as realistically as possible so that they can be tested in the store and on the user, and so that the designer and the client could gather sufficient impressions that would allow them to choose a solution. Final material selection, choice of fonts and detailing of the design can wait until the design direction is selected and the final prototype is to be developed, but here too it is important to start planning early in the sketching process (5.2 Model).
**Testing and evaluation:** In all phases of a design project, testing and evaluation are necessary in order to find out what works and what does not, and make choices that push the project forward. When testing the design solutions, it should be clear based on which criteria the tests should be assessed, and what need or problem the design should address. The purpose of testing is to find out whether or not the design solves the task well based on a given problem statement, and whether there are opportunities for further development and improvement of the solution.
**Adjustment:** Based on the test results, one makes the necessary adjustments, or goes back a few steps and makes new sketches and new dummies. In some contexts, it may be advantageous for the designer to include the client when testing the various solution options. This way, it may be easier for the client to choose a solution or provide input for adjustments.
**Choice of direction:** When several different design directions have been developed, it is time to present the solution to the client for the choice of solution or for further concretisation and completion of the design. On professional basis, the designer chooses the most suitable solution(s) in advance and presents them or it to the client. The designer's role in choosing direction is to act as a professional and as a consultant. It involves referring to the problem statement, strategy, and objectives that are used as the basis for the assignment and argue how the solution meets these requirements and directions. One or a combination of two design directions is selected for concretisation in the next phase (3.9 Design strategy, 4.1 Design brief).

## 4.5.3 Concrete design

Concrete design is a step in the design process, which is about concretisation of the design based on the sketches, as well as further refining, detailing and completing the design for production, printing or press. Only when the client, in collaboation with the designer, has reviewed the design sketches and chosen which direction should be used as basis for the final design, may work begin on concretising the selected direction. At this stage, the design proposals may appear almost finished when drawn out on a computer. One may be easily fooled by nice computer sketches, but it is important that the client is aware of how much work is needed from having a good design sketch approved to seeing the final design solution completed. The quality of the final result lies in the work on further developing, refining, and detailing the solution, both as a whole and down to the individual elements and the smallest of details. Not one

Concrete design
In the concretisation of the design lies the zealous detailed work that is the hallmark of quality. It is about further developing, refining, detailing.

| Detail checklist | |
|---|---|
| **Problem statement:** | Does the solution answer the problem statement? Does it solve the task? |
| **Strategy:** | Is the solution consistent with the objective and strategy of the task? |
| **User needs:** | Does the solution meet user friendliness and user-experience requirements? |
| **Whole and unit:** | Is it perceived as a whole? Can elements be gathered in units? What is the most important element? Are any items or objects redundant? |
| **Style:** | Have you designed a trendy or timeless expression? What serves the purpose best? |
| **Consistency:** | Is there consistent use of devices in the design? Is the location, sizes and shape of the elements used consistently and in accordance with the identity? |
| **Aspect ratio:** | Is the aspect ratio functional and consistent? Can the aspect ratio be part of a modular grid system? |
| **Form and expression:** | Is there any similarity between outer/external shape and the shape of the elements, and between elements and fonts? If not, has this been deliberately and consistently implemented? Does the shape express the right identity and tone of voice? |
| **Composition:** | Is there a deliberate placement of elements? Is there balance in the composition? Is it symmetric or asymmetric, or is it pure? Is there any clear focal point or eye-catcher? Is there sufficient contrast? Is the message or story evident? Is there dramatic effect and dynamism? |
| **Colour:** | Do the colours help reinforce the solution and highlight the message? Do the colours support the identity? Are there sufficient contrasts between the colours? Have other colour combinations, tones and shades been tested? Does colour help emphasise surface, shape, and space? |
| **Texture:** | Is it texture or an experience of texture? Can pattern or texture be added to surfaces to create a more tactile feel or experience? |
| **Typography:** | Does the typeface support the identity? Are text and message in agreement? Is there any similarity between the details of the text and the shape of the design elements? Is there deliberate choice of fonts, font sizes, line spacing, location, etc? Has a functional grid system been developed for baseline, gaps, margins, and so on? |
| **Sustainability:** | Is it possible to use more environmentally friendly materials? Can anything be done to minimise the consumption of materials and avoid waste? |
| **Aesthetics:** | Does the design give an aesthetic experience? Is it nice to look at? Is it appealing? Does it inspire pride? |

Table 4.7 Detail checklist

millimetre or dot should be randomly performed and positioned, and every detail should be deliberately and accurately executed. The end result should solve the task, address the problem statement, and be anchored in defined goals and strategies used as basis for it, including guidelines for the visual identity, user-experience, and communication (3.9 Design strategy, 4.1 Design brief).

Again, it is about opening up the process, but in a narrower manner compared to the iterations in the sketching process. This time it is about considering different ways in which the chosen design sketch and design direction can be refined and nuanced. Here too, there may be room to work in several directions (preferably three), which are relatively similar, but still executed in different ways. It is not a matter of developing entirely new ideas or directions, but about exploring the direction chosen in order to further develop and improve it. Often, there are no major changes at this stage, provided that the previous processes have been well-thought out, thorough and targeted, with adequate testing at the various stages. However, the further progress made at this stage can be time-consuming and, last but not least, very important for the final outcome. The work being done here can lead to a much better, more aesthetic and higher-quality result.

To make a design tangible involves exploring the overall parts of the design. And at the same time fragmenting, breaking and splitting up, picking elements apart, assessing, adjusting, and processing them individually. Putting them together in the same way or new ways, removing, adding, studying, and analysing the individual parts, looking at different ways for how they can be processed and reinforced, what role they should have and how they can best contribute to the whole. It is about zooming in and zooming out. Zoom in to look at the details and zoom out to see the big picture. Zooming in is about working on fine-tuning things like the outermost millimetre of a serif, changing a colour shade by five percent and increasing a line spacing by half a point. As for the overall impression, it is about trying a different shape, a different colour, a different typeface, a different image, a different element composition, a different grid system, and so on. Any changes made to the design may affect the other elements and the whole. Changes made, for example, to a grid system may require redefining and readjusting all elements, which should be included in the grid system. It is all connected – always. Not a tiny dot in the design should be randomly developed or placed, everything should be conscious – always. 'The devil is in the detail.'[74] (4.6 Design elements, 4.7 Composition, 4.9 Identity development, 4.9.6 Typography).

**The right solution?**

Does the design solve the task, does it answer the problem statement? No? There is no shame in turning around. It is better to turn around in time than to implement a solution you do not believe in. You may not have worked broadly enough with concept development and design sketches. You may have locked yourself in too soon. Better to take a few steps back, develop more directions, go deeper and wider and make new choices, before going back to making the design more concrete.



Table 4.7 The table shows a checklist that can be useful in the final phase of the designing process. © Grimsgaard, W. (2018).

Working with details is about zooming in and zooming out. Zoom in to look at the details and zoom out to see the big picture.

74 'The devil is in the detail' is an idiom alluding to a catch or a mysterious element hidden in the details (Titleman, 1996), meaning that the details can be complicated and likely to cause problems (macmillandictionary.com), or that something might seem simple at a first glance, but will take more time to interpret than expected. The phrase is said to originate from the earlier phrase, 'God is in the details', expressing the idea that whatever one does should be done thoroughly.

It is an advantage to to try to concretise as much as possible, archive frequently and go back and forth in the process. Create digital test versions, printouts and models and run tests along the way in the relevant context or on the relevant target group, preferably using focus groups (2.6.4 Focus group). It is about gathering experiences during the process, adjusting, nuance, further develop, and not give up to soon, but stay in the process long enough – be persistent. When you think it is good enough, check again. What can be improved and reinforced? Then make another (or several) additional versions. 'At the same time, it is important to meet the delivery deadline and weigh the time wisely when it comes to testing and adjustments. If too little time has been spent in the concept development phase and the concept has not been sufficiently thought-out and re-examined, the concretisation may be more time-consuming. Or maybe the solution will never be good enough. Therefore, it is very important to allocate time properly within the individual phases of the design process' (Brekke-Bjørkedal 2017).

After detailing the design solution, final prototyping and testing can be done before implementation to different surfaces, objects or spaces can begin. The necessary adjustments are made based on the testing. Originals for production are prepared according to the requirements specifications or settings applicable to the chosen publishing system or production method (4.8 Surface and format, 5.1 Implementation, 5.5 Colour management, 5.6 Production for digital media, 5.7 Production for printed media, 6.6 Design templates, 6.5 Design manual, 6.6 Design templates).

Tips for the designer
**Be aware of how changing a detail in the design can affect the whole and necessitate changes to other design details as a result.**

**Detailing is about millimetre precision.**

**Seven design elements**

Here are a selection of design elements (based on Lovett 1998):

**Line:** The line can be assessed in two ways. The linear marks made with a pen or brush or the edge created when two shapes meet.

**Shape:** A shape is a self contained defined area of geometric or organic form. A positive shape in a painting automatically creates a negative shape. Negative or white space may form between two shapes.

**Direction:** All lines have direction – horizontal, vertical or oblique. Horizontal suggests calmness, stability and tranquillity. Vertical gives a feeling of balance, formality and alertness. Oblique suggests movement, action, and dynamics.

**Size:** Size is simply the relationship of the area occupied by one shape to that of another.

**Texture:** Texture is the surface quality of a shape – rough, smooth, soft hard glossy etc. Texture can be physical (tactile) or visual.

**Colour:** All colours can be mixed using the basic colours blue, yellow, and red. Colour is also called hue.

**Tone:** Tone is the brightness or darkness of a colour. Tone is also called value. In the transition between light and dark tones, there are different degrees of contrast.

'Good or bad – all paintings will contain most, if not all, of the seven design elements, line, shape, direction, size, texture, colour, tone' (Lovett).

Further reading
**Check out 'Difference Between Shape and Form' (differencebetween.net).**

1 Initiation
2 Insight
3 Strategy
4 Design
5 Production
6 Management

4.1 Design brief
4.2 Strategy><Design
4.3 Design methodology
4.4 Concept development
4.5 Design development
4.6 Design elements
4.7 Composition
4.8 Surface and format
4.9 Identity development

4.6.1 Shape
4.6.2 Colour
4.6.3 Texture
4.6.4 Space

Conscious and purposeful use of shape, colour and texture is central to the strategic development of design, to create the desired identity and expression. The basic design elements shape, colour and texture are the building blocks in all visual design. It is the isolated individual parts or the aspects that make up a design.

Design elements in this context are the basic visual elements, namely the original geometric shapes square, circle and triangle, the basic colours blue, yellow, and red, as well as the visual or tactile texture that defines the surfaces of shapes and forms. Furthermore, basic phenomena such as space, time, direction, and size are considered design elements. Regardless of the problem and design discipline, when in a design project one is working on surface, object, or space, or a combination of these, the same design elements are used, either to dimensionally or three-dimensionally. This applies regardless of whether it is a matter of developing graphic elements such as logos and symbols, the shape of a product, the décor of a room, or its layout. The basic design elements are present in all visual design, either explicitly or implicitly, often used intuitively by designers and artists, because they are all around us and constitute a natural part of our lives. We often move away from the complexity of the idea phase and remove the redundant as we process the idea, until we are left with simple, pure shapes and functions, and distinct visual characteristics. In a strategic context, we bring in the project goal, the underlying strategy, the values to be expressed, the experience and message to be conveyed, the current idea and context, and the problem the task is to solve. *What we do with the design elements, how we use them, and consciously compose them, determines how good we are at creating a design or a piece of art* (Lovett, 1998). Using the design elements is part of the design development process. Some of the most essential design elements are:

- **Shape:** form, figure, design, line, dot.
- **Colour:** hue and nuance.
- **Texture:** structure, pattern.
- **Space:** physical room and illusion of room ('negative space').
- **Time:** progress; first, second, third, last. Past, future, present.

### 4.6.1 Shape

All the things we surround ourselves with are formally related to the three basic shapes, square, circle and triangle. These are the most central in any development of visual design, such as a symbol, format, space, object, and other. Conscious use of shapes is necessary to create solutions that communicate the desired expression, as well as functional and emotional attributes.

There are no limitations as to what a shape can be or what it can express. Simple shapes are remembered and understood more easily than complex ones. This is important to remember when developing design

> Shapes are often categorised according to their dimensions, their number of sides, and whether they are constructed out of straight or curved lines. Polygons are 2D shapes composed of straight lines. Polygons can be further divided by their number of sides.
> Polyhedra are 3D shapes composed out of straight lines and flat 2D surfaces. Polyhedra can be further divided by the number of faces. Ellipsoids are convex shapes made out of curved lines (Bolano, 2018).

elements, pictograms or symbols that should have a memorable shape, e.g. such as when developing a visual identity. One often goes from the simple to the complicated, and then goes back to the simple. Creating the simple pure expression is often the hardest part. 'Everything should be made as simple as possible, but no simpler' (Albert Einstein).[75] Shape is a broad concept and can have different meanings when used in philosophy, mathematics, art, design, music, linguistics, and technology to name a few.The word 'shape' in pictorial context can be used to describe a visually perceived area created with a defined or perceived contour. It can be an outline, colour, nuance, texture, or other that defines the outer edge, so that an image, object or element arises. Shapes can be varied endlessly and can assume a physical shape or the illusion of shape.

Shapes are two-dimensional areas with a recognisable boundary. They can be open or closed, angular or round, big or small. Shapes can be organic or inorganic, geometric and ordered. Shapes can be defined by their colour or by the combination of lines that make up their edges. Simple shapes can be combined to form complex shapes. Complex shapes can be abstracted to make simple shapes. The different characteristics of a shape convey different moods and meanings. Changing the characteristics of a shape alters how we perceive that shape and makes us feel differently about a design (Bradley, 2010). Shape as a term may also be used to describe an image or an object as a whole, including colour, texture, and composition. Conscious use of the basic shapes is about being aware of their inherent qualities, so that they support desired values, identity and user functions in the design and within the relevant context.

**Shape vs. Form**

The English language distinguishes between shape and form in visual arts. Shape is a flat, enclosed area of an artwork created through lines, textures, colours or an area enclosed by other shapes such as triangles, circles, and squares (Gatto et al., 2000). Likewise, a form can refer to a three-dimensional composition or object within a three-dimensional composition (Stewart 2006, 'Form,' n.d.). Forms are the 3D equivalents of shapes. It can easily be explained by saying that 'sphere' is to 'form' while 'circle' is to 'shape.' 'Form' and 'shape' define objects situated in space. The basic difference, though, between 'shape' and 'form' is that 'form' is in 3D while 'shape' is plain 2D. The latter is simply defined by lines (Julita 2018, differencebetween.net).

### Geometric shapes

Geometric shapes can be constructed with a compass and straightedge, and are based on the basic shapes square, circle and triangle.[76] In geometry a shape can be explained as a set of lines that enclose a space. According to this, 'the shape of an object is the external form or appearance of an object in space that can be represented by a set of lines oriented in some way' (Bolano, 2018). Strategic use of basic shapes is about knowing what they express, or what can be associated with them, for example:

Fig. 4.39 The figure shows the two-dimensional basic shapes square, triangle and circle.

Fig. 4.40 The figure shows an example of how the circle as an original shape is used to create identity. The number of circles and their position in relation to each other is what creates a distinctive character. The Olympics and Audi are both known by their symbols, which are made up of rings, but which are perceived differently due to their combination and colours.

The circle
'The circle has always represented and still represents eternity, with no beginning and no end' (Bruno Munari, 1971, p. 198).

75 This might be a paraphrased (compressed) version from a 1933 lecture by Einstein: 'It can scarcely be denied that the supreme goal of all theory is to make the irreducible basic elements as simple and as few as possible without having to surrender the adequate representation of a single datum of experience' (Robinson, 2018).

76 Bauhaus: These basic geometric shapes were essential to Bauhaus school in Germany from 1919 to 1933, founded by Walter Gropius. Bauhaus' philosophy was to create new, affordable, clean and ethical design that could be used by all kinds of people and in all areas (bauhaus.chrissnider.com). The Bauhaus school was made up of several departments, such as industrial design, art, typography, graphic design, photography and architecture. Influential names were, for example: Johannes Itten, Herbert Bayer, Vassily Kandinsky, László Moholy-Nagy. Bauhaus became a movement that fronted many significant controversial principles in design such as: 'Shape follows function' (Louis Sullivan), 'Typography matters' and 'Geometry is king' (sitepoint.com/nailing-detail- bauhaus-design/, bauhaus- movement.com).

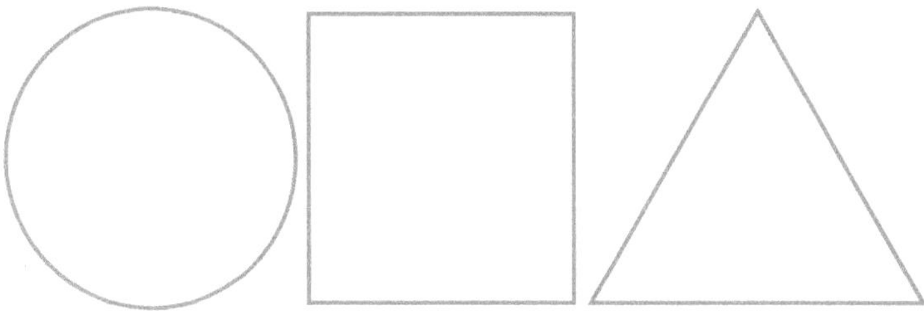

Fig. 4.39 Two-dimensional basic shapes

- The square can express stability and firmness.
- The circle has motion in it and can express something repetitive, organic and inclusive.
- The triangle has a more dynamic expression, and can be both stable and unstable depending on the rotation or perspective.

**Two-dimensional geometric shapes:** Two-dimensional (2D) shapes indicate flat shapes or images, which are displayed on, for example, paper or a computer screen. Such shapes may be designed, drawn, painted, trimmed, torn or cut. The basic two-dimensional geometric shapes are square, circle, triangle and rectangle, Figure 4.39.

Most logos and symbols are built on or include geometric two-dimensional shapes within them, whether intended or not. The circle is perhaps the most common shape and is found in a variety of combinations, which, despite small variations, can be perceived as having their own identity and symbolism. The perceived identity or symbolism stems from the context in which it is displayed, combined with colours and other visual devices and communication. Examples of logos that use the basic circle shape are the symbol of Audi (four rings) and Olympic Games (five rings), which due to their composition and the colour of their rings are perceived differently. Perceived relationships and associations with these brands are the result of conscious branding over time (3.7 Brand strategy).

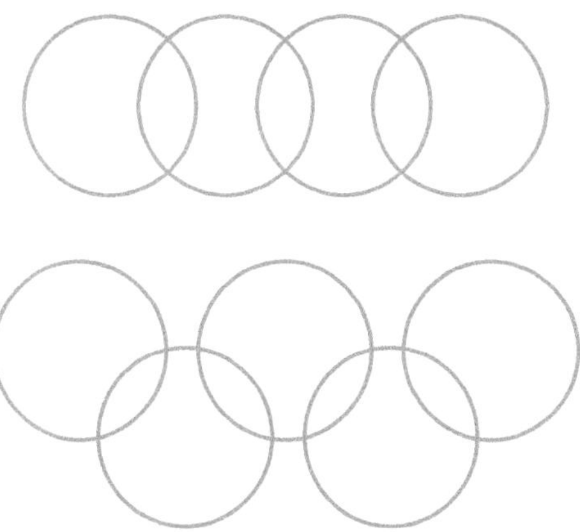

Fig. 4.40 Use of basic shapes

**Three-dimensional geometric shapes:** Although design often appears on surfaces like paper, screens, and fabric, the reality we find ourselves in is not flat. The room we are in has perspective and depth; it is

'All design, even the most advanced design solutions, have elements based on the basic elements shape, colour, texture, space, and time. There is only one way to follow: the one that includes analysis of the basic elements to arrive at a satisfying graphic expression' (Vassily Kandinsky).


1 Initiation
2 Insight
3 Strategy
4 Design
5 Production
6 Management

4.1 Design brief
4.2 Strategy><Design
4.3 Design methodology
4.4 Concept development
4.5 Design development
4.6 Design elements
4.7 Composition
4.8 Surface and format
4.9 Identity development

4.6.1 Shape
4.6.2 Colour
4.6.3 Texture
4.6.4 Space

- Geometric shapes
- Abstract shapes
- Organic shapes
- Lines and dashes
- Points

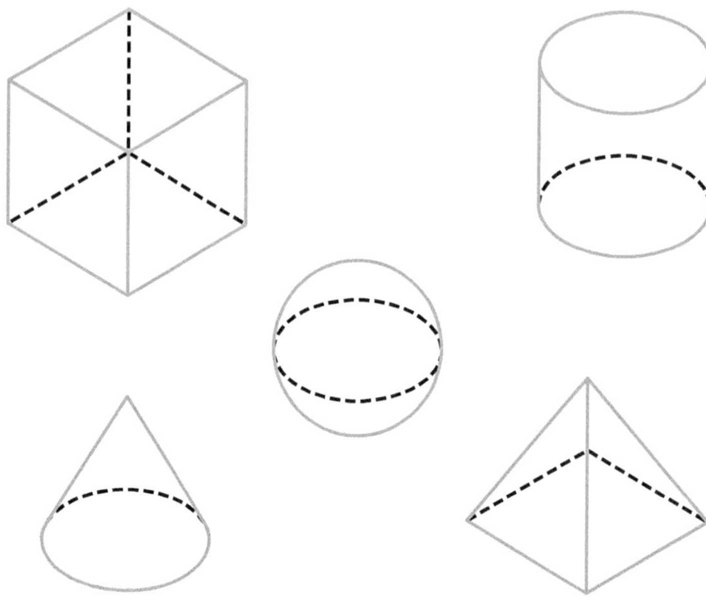

Fig. 4.41 Three-dimensional basic shapes

three-dimensional (3D). The basic three-dimensional geometric shapes are cube, prism, cylinder, sphere, pyramid, and cone. Most objects we surround ourselves with are three-dimensional in nature and include these shapes. Even most man-made things have three-dimensional shapes. A brick has the form of a straight, rectangular prism and a paint bucket has the form of a cylinder (Myklebust, 2017).

Fig. 4.42 Abstraction

### Abstract shapes

Abstract or stylised shapes are elements with recognisable shape, which are not 'genuine' the way natural forms are. Shapes can be stylised by simplifying or abstracting a natural shape, as we see in pictograms and symbols. Alphabetical characters or graphic patterns are also examples of stylised shapes (4.9.4 Symbol).

### Organic shapes

Shapes created by nature are natural, living and not built. Drawn elements may also have organic shapes. They would have a more inaccurate, natural and handcrafted expression, which can be more easily associated with something that is natural or living, that grows or is in motion. For example, it could be a cloud, a lake, a rock, or a leaf.

Fig. 4.41 **The illustration show three-dimensional basic geometrical shapes, cube, cylinder, prism, pyramid, cone, and sphere.**

Fig. 4.42 **The figure shows the stylisation and abstraction of shape. To the left is the Post's old symbol and to the right is the new one, developed in 2008. The symbol on the left is a stylisation of a post horn. The symbol on the right is an extreme abstraction of a post horn or a stylised ram's horn. (The figures are outlined examples and not original versions.)**

Fig. 4.43 **The illustration shows an example of an organic shape.**

Tips for the designer
**Some simple geometric shapes include: squares, circles, cubes, cones, hexagons, decahedrons.**

Tips for the designer
**Study different geometric shapes and their potential, such as squares, circles, cubes, cones, hexagons, dodecahedrons.**

Fig. 4.43 Organic shapes

### Lines and dashes

Lines drawn using a ruler or a computer tend to get a mechanical expression, while lines drawn freehand become more vibrant and organic (Sander, 2014). Lines can also be implicitly perceived between shape elements or in an organised grid system, where they do not exist physically. A line or dash may have many forms of expression. It can be straight, curved, or irregular. It can be calm, intense, vibrant, geometric, soft, hard, thick, thin, fully drawn, divided, rhythmic, unrhythmic, and so on. It can also create an illusion of direction and movement. Horizontal lines can *guide* eye movement. Vertical lines can *stop* eye movement. Here are examples of some effects or expressions that can be created using lines or dashes:

- Horizontal lines can express harmony and tranquillity, while diagonal lines can express dynamics and power.
- Thin lines can seem elegant and distinct, while thick lines can express power and strength.
- A line can direct attention to important information.
- Lines can be used to separate information, for example in forms.
- A line can consist of many points located so close to each other that they form a line.
- An illusion of line can occur between two points.
- A grid system can be perceived as lines in a composition.
- Lines are suitable for line drawings and quick sketches, or as a contour in a drawing.

Further reading
**Check out: John Lovett: www.johnlovett.com/painting-lessonsinstructions.**

### Points

In geometry the point is usually perceived as the smallest part or unit. 'Euclid[77] defined a point as "something which cannot be subdivided". It is implied that geometric objects like lines, surfaces, and so on, are made up of points. A point defined this way does not extend in any direction, and thus it can be said that it is a geometric object of dimension 0.' (Aubert, n.d.).

- A point can stand alone or in a group of several points, forming a shape.
- A point can serve as focal point to visually highlight or draw attention to important information.
- When multiple points are put in a row, they form a line. For example, we can perceive points in the starry sky as lines, contours, and shapes. Examples of this are the Big Dipper and Orion's belt (Figures 4.52. 4.53, 4.54).

## 4.6.2 Colour

Colour, like shape, is among the most important design elements. We are talking about the primary colours blue, red, and yellow, and the basic principles of how they can be mixed to get any colour. We are also talking about the light based colours red, green, and blue and how they can go from white to black. Colour plays an essential role in visual design as a graphic element, as a background, on a line, in texture, in typography, to create identity, mood, or a particular expression, used in a room, in illumination, on a figure or an object. However, colour is something that does not physically exist and is not an attribute or element in itself. Physical objects do not really have their own colour, but rather an ability to reflect certain wavelengths of light that can be perceived by the eye and interpreted by the brain as colour.

Colour is the perceptual experience of light falling into the retina, which is the nerve layer that lines the back of the eye, senses light, and creates impulses that travel through the optic nerve to the brain (Stöppler, 2021), where a visual image is formed. The retina is covered by millions of cells, called rods and cones. There are three different types of cone cells in the retina that are responsible for the perception of color (Lee BB, 2008). 'One cone receptor is sensitive to the colour green, another to the colour blue, and a third to the colour red. The combinations of these three colours produce all of the colours that we are capable of perceiving. Researchers suggest that people are able to distinguish between as many as seven million different colours' (Cherry, 2021). The cone receptors have sensitivity to different types of wavelengths. The brain interprets or guesses what colours the eye sees based on signals from the cones. Blue objects absorb all wavelengths except blue ones, and these are reflected back to our eye. Black absorbs all wavelengths, while white reflects all (5.5.1 Colour models).

In all areas of design, colour use and colour knowledge are essential, whether it is a matter of graphic design, interior design, industrial design, architecture, interaction design or any other design fields. However, the application of colours and the use of colour systems can be quite different (5.5 Colour management). In reality, all colour systems are based on some primary colours.

Geometric shapes and names

Polygons
A plane figure with at least three straight sides and angles:
Triangle: 3 sides
Rectangle: 4 sides, 4 right angles
Square: 4 equal sides
Trapezoid: 4 sides, two parallel sides
Rhombus: 4 sides
Pentagon: 5 sides
Hexagon: 6 sides
Heptagon: 7 sides
Octagon: 8 sides
Nonagon: 9 sides
Decagon: 10 sides
Dodecagon: 12 sides
Icosagon: 20 sides

Star-shaped polygons
Pentagram: 5 points
Hexagram: 6 sides
Star of David
Heptagram: 7 points

Polyhedrons
A solid figure with many plane faces, typically more than six:
Regular Polyhedra: 3D polygon
Tetrahedron: 4 faces
Cube: 6 faces
Octohedron: 8 faces
Dodecahedron: 12 faces
Icosahedron: 20 faces

Uniform polyhedra
3D figure made by some combination of at least two different regular polygons:
Triangular prism
Cuboctahedron
Rhombicosidodecahedron
Octogrammic antiprism
Great disnubdirhombidodecahedron

Curved shapes
2D curved shapes
Circle, ellipse, parabola, annulus, lone, reuleaux polygons.
(Bolano 2018, sciencetrends.com)

## Primary colours

In theory, there are infinitely many sets of primary colours which, through additive colour mixing, can produce all other colour shades. The theory[78] about the three additive primary colours red, green, and blue, is that none of them can be produced by mixing the other two.[79] We distinguish between additive and subtractive colour mixing, which are not attributes of light, but a result of how our eyes perceive colours.

*Additive* colour mixing has the primary colours red, green, and blue (RGB), which are generated from light colours. When the three primary colours are mixed in equal proportions, the eye perceives this as white. Additive colour mixing begins with the absence of light (black). When light in different colours hits a surface, several colours are placed on top of each other (added). The light is emitted with different wavelengths and different degrees of intensity, which is perceived by our eyes as colours, like when we are looking at a computer screen. Colours we see on a computer screen, TV screen or an image produced by a projector occur as a result of additive colour mixing.

*Subtractive* colour mixing has the primary colours red, yellow, and blue (magenta, yellow, and cyan). Different mixing ratios of cyan, magenta, and yellow give an infinity of colour nuances. When the three primary colours are mixed in equal proportions, the eye perceives this as black (or dark brown), i.e. the opposite of additive mixing which is then perceived as white. Subtractive colour systems begin with white light. When the light hits surfaces with pigments, such as paint or crayons, some of the light's wavelengths will be subtracted (absorbed into the surface), while others will be reflected, thereby becoming visible to the eye. In offset printing, CMYK represents the primary colours cyan, yellow, and magenta, in addition to the key colour, which is black. Black is used to add contrast and depth to images. Black is also used for text that should be pitch black, instead of mixing red, yellow, and blue to get a dark shade. It gives a cleaner black and less saturation.

## Primary, secondary and tertiary colours

Colour mixtures occur when the primary colours are mixed. Secondary colours are obtained by mixing primary colours. For example, in additive colour mixtures, equal parts of red and green produce the secondary colour yellow, while equal parts of blue and green produce turquoise (cyan), and equal parts of blue and red produce violet red (magenta). In subtractive colour mixtures, a mixture of blue and yellow will turn green, red and yellow will turn orange, and red and blue will turn purple. Tertiary colours are obtained by mixing primary and secondary colours, or by mixing secondary colours with each other.

## Complementary colours

Colours that are directly opposite each other on the colour wheel and are strongly contrasting with each other are called complementary colours. For example, the complementary colour of green is red. If you stare at a red field for a long time and move your eyes away from it, you will see the complementary colour green. This phenomenon is called afterimage. The deliberate use of complementary colours on elements and typography can be effective in some contexts, for example to achieve



77 Euclid was a Greek mathematician who around 300 BCE wrote *Elements*, a book collection of 13 volumes, which summarises and presents all knowledge in geometry and arithmetic in Euclid's time. This work has been a textbook in geometry for nearly 2,000 (Kline 1972, 'Euclid's Elements,' n.d.).

78 Trichromatic theory of colour vision is the possessing of three independent channels for conveying color information, derived from the three different types of cone cells in the eye. ('Trichromacy,' n.d.)

79 According to trichromacy theory, with certain lighting any object colour may be determined by comparison with additive mixing of three primary light colours on a white surface. It is assumed that the three primary colours are linearly independent, i.e. that none of them can be imitated by additive mixing of the other two (Holtsmark, 2009).

strong contrasts, but it can easily lead to problems. One example of this is red on blue or red on green. Red text on blue background will produce perception of vibration between the colours, which can impair readability. If printed in black and white, both colours will have equal greyscale, and it can be difficult to distinguish the text from the background.

Fig. 4.44 The figure shows how the same colours appear brighter when against a dark background compared to a light background where they seem darker. In addition, there is a change in the perception of foreground and background. Against the light background, the light colour fades into the background, while the dark colour stands out. On dark background, the opposite happens (Zwimpfer, 2001).

### Colour theories and systems

There are many colour systems with different primary colours, colour shades, and mixtures of black and white. Among these are the classic colour theories of Goethe, Itten, and Albers, which were developed one to two hundred years ago. Based on these colour theories, a variety of colour reference systems have been designed, with different colour codes adapted to different practical needs. Examples include CMYK and Pantone, which are used for offset and digital printing; RGB, which is used for screen-based presentations, and web. NCS, which is used for painting surfaces, and RAL, which is most commonly used for metal surfaces in industry. These colour reference systems should be assessed by colour samples in order to find the correct colour shade. One cannot trust that the colour that appears on the computer screen is correct. Therefore, colour management is a key factor in achieving the desired result (5.5 Colour management, 5.5.9 Colour reference systems, 5.7.5 Printing inks).

### Consistent colour

The fact that a colour can be perceived differently is a well-known challenge for designers where the task is to create consistent colour reproduction, i.e. it is perceived as similar as possible in all contexts. This is important, for example, when developing a visual identity, where the same identity colours will be used for the logo, materials, interior and exterior (4.9.5 Identity colours). Consistent colour perception is an important factor in acquiring knowledge and building a brand. In this context, it is common to prepare clear guidelines on how colours should be used on different surfaces and in different contexts. Working with colours requires knowledge of colour systems and colour- profiles. It is about understanding how colour is affected by its surroundings, the light and the surfaces on which it appears. A colour can appear very differently against different colour backgrounds, which governs whether we perceive the colour as foreground or background. In some contexts, one and the same colour may stand out clearly, while in other contexts it may merge with the background. In general, a colour will be brighter against a dark background than against a light background, see Figure 4.44.

A colour can be perceived quite differently in daylight as opposed to artificial lighting indoors. Similarly, it can behave very differently in flooding sunlight compared to in a dark shadow. In the sunlight it becomes more brilliant and absorbs yellow light from the sun, while in the shadow it becomes darker and can absorb blues or greys that are found in the shadow. In the contexts where colour is to be applied to a surface or printed on paper, it is important to note that the shade of the substrate or paper may affect the colour. Even white paper can affect the colour, especially bright nuances, because white paper can range from chalk white and almost bluish to warmer white with a yellowish shade. Colours are influenced by other colours and by light. As the light changes, so does

80 See the text in the box; #theddress. Read the full story: en.wikipedia.org/wiki/The_dress.

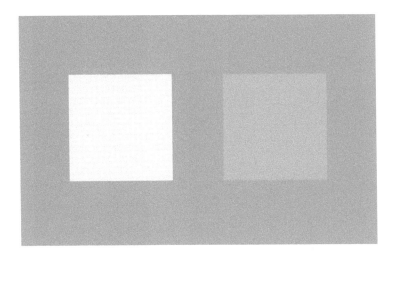

Fig. 4.44 Colour is influenced by surroundings

1 Initiation
2 Insight
3 Strategy
4 Design
5 Production
6 Management

4.1 Design brief
4.2 Strategy><Design
4.3 Design methodology
4.4 Concept development
4.5 Design development
4.6 Design elements
4.7 Composition
4.8 Surface and format
4.9 Identity development

4.6.1 Shape
4.6.2 Colour
4.6.3 Texture
4.6.4 Space

- Primary colours
- Primary, secondary and tertiary colours
- Complementary colours
- Colour theories and systems
- Consistent colour

the colour we see. However, our brain can usually interpret or guess the right colour even if it is in the shade or twilight. We have a perceptual experience that snow is white, even if it is in the shade or at night and the eye in reality perceives it as grey or blue. However, the brain does not always manage to guess correctly, see the example of 'The dress'.[80]

**#thedress**

The Dress or Dressgate, a phenomenon that went viral on social media in 2015, is a photo of a dress that was perceived to be white and golden by some, and blue and black by others. The phenomenon revealed differences in human colour perception and was the subject of several scientific studies, published articles and reviews from, among others, *Wired*, *Forbes*, *Business Insider* and *The Telegraph*. A simple explanation of the phenomenon: The image is overexposed. The dress has got bluish tint with a bright light from behind. As a result, those who see the dress as white read the dress as a shadow and compensate with white to make it lighter. The correct colour of the dress is blue (*Forbes*: Matthew Herper 2015/*Wired*: Adam Rogers 2015).

Further reading
*Color Theory: A Critical Introduction* (2021) by Aaron Fine.

## 4.6.3 Texture

Texture is included as one of the basic design elements, because it is always present on a shape or surface. It can be coarse, smooth, soft, hard, glossy, etc. It can be physical or visual. When it is perceptible by touch, we say that it is tactile or tangible.

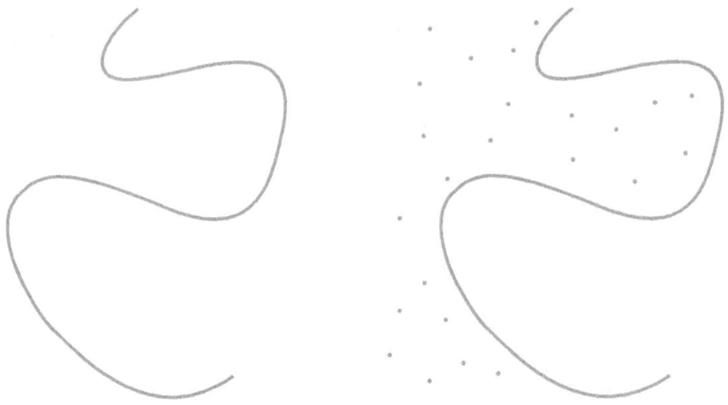

Fig. 4.45 Texture

Fig. 4.45 The figure on the left appears as a line, while the figure on the right is easier to perceive as two surfaces. The reason for this is the dots in the figure on the right, which leave an impression of structure and set apart the area surrounding the line better. The dots affect the entire surface and the effect can be compared with the use of a colour. Because the line does not constitute a closed shape, the relation of the figure to the background becomes ambiguous. What is figure, what is background? (Zwimper, 2001).

Fig. 4.46 Figures show examples of spaces around and inside elements, creating balance, highlighting shape, or creating shape.

Texture is the appearance or structure of a surface, material, fabric, paper, etc. Texture can be perceived physically. A non-physical perception of structure can also be created by giving an illusion of material, materiality, or pattern. When we talk about texture, we like to think of something that is interwoven with threads or fibres, which feels like fabric. It can also be a surface of an element, floor, or wall; for example, cement, which is rough to touch and has a visually recognisable rugged structure. Texture can be used to create contrasts between surfaces in a composition or on an object, to create a tactile expression or as an alternative to colour (4.7 Composition).

## 4.6.4 Space

In three-dimensional design, space is real and physical. We are talking about space in or around an object. In two-dimensional design, we can also experience three-dimensional space. In this case, it is drawn on a surface and is not a physical space, only an illusion! Even the most realistic 3D illustrations are illusions. Space is an abstract concept. Everything is space. For example, if you take a pen, there is a space inside the pen, but the pen also fills a space – because the pen occupies space, and is in the space. Everyone can find space wherever they look, whether outside or inside. Everyone decides personally whether or not to define something as space. Everyone can create visual spaces that one might not want to see right away. Everyone can learn to think and see a space. An object in space may have different amounts of spaces around it, depending on its location in the space. If a bottle is standing next to a lamp, there is space between the bottle and the lamp, this will not be the case if the bottle is further away from the lamp. Space is very abstract (Loe, M.G., 2017).

In the contexts where we talk about space as a design element, we often mean the space that occurs around, above, below, between or within an object or objects in a two-dimensional design on a page or screen, a kind of breathing room; what we also call white space, negative space or negative shapes. As Bradley puts it, by referring to Zappa: '...there's gotta be enough space in there (between notes) so that the sound will work in an air space. That's what makes the music work.' (Frank Zappa). No space, no music. Try to imagine that all notes are playing at the same time or that they are being played so fast that there is no distinction between one note and the next one. It would not be music. It would be massive noise. Like Zappa said:

'There's gotta be enough space in there (between the notes).' Without space there is no music. Try to imagine every note playing at the same time or being played so quickly that there's no distinction between one note and the next. You have to leave room for the sounds to be distinguished from each other, to be heard for what they are. A few notes played together form a chord. All notes played together form noise. To create rhythm and melody requires a measured and planned space. Music isn't sound. It's a balance between sound and space. Without both there is no music. The same is true visually. There's gotta be enough space. Without whitespace none of your elements gets seen. They become noise' (Bradley, 2010).

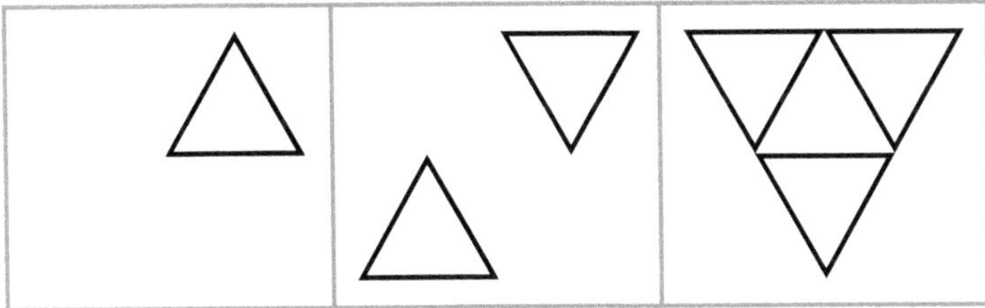

Fig. 4.46 Whitespace

A composition is essentially an arrangement of elements into a whole. In a two-dimensional composition our visual perception of the whole depends on our ability to recognise the borderline between foreground and background. The elements we see in a composition are either in the foreground or in the background. For example, the distance between two elements is part of the background, but we can perceive this distance as a shape, which has got to do with perception. The classic example of this is Rubin's vase, Figure 4.47.

Imagine letters without space, they will be illegible. In typography, the deliberate use of space between letters and lines is necessary to create legible text. Spaces are found inside the letter shapes, between and around them. In typography, spaces can be used or created to achieve the desired effects. For example, by using the space inside and between letters deliberately to create distinctive features and legibility (4.9.6 Typography: Optical adjustment).

In a composition, deliberate use of space is all about how the physical elements should be composed against the background and in the space that occurs behind, around, above, below, between, or inside. While a background may be 'invisible,' it may implicitly constitute an element (space) that creates balance, or imbalance, depending on what the intention is.

'Indeed rays, properly expressed, are not coloured,' said Isaac Newton, who in the 18th century studied how light breaks down through a prism to create a whole spectre.

## Time and motion

First, second, third, last ... page in the book, picture in the film. Time is change and motion. Motion means the course of time. Time and motion are elements that belong in all forms of design work, whether it is a book with many pages, where each page follows after the other in time, or animations for film and TV, which have a certain duration. Time is an element closely related to motion. Every word or image moves both in time and space. Motion is a kind of change, and changes occurs in time. Motion and time are key elements of design. Motion can be created physically or as an illusion. In a composition, diagonal positioning of elements will indicate movement, while perpendicular positioning will appear static. Time and motion can be created in various ways, for example, cutting elements may express a form of motion. The same applies to using a wavy line (sine line) or a pointed triangular shape. An animation includes image sequences, visual elements, colours, fonts, illustrative components, etc. that change and interact with each other over time.

A work of art may contain a specific motion or illusion of motion. Every time we look at it, we see a new work of art (Lucy Lamp). When we look at time in traditional art, it is also natural to think of timelessness. At the same time, traditional art often captures a moment in time. Some modern artists also challenge time as a static concept and explore what effect time can have on their work. Monet's paintings, e.g. The Rouen Cathedral series, captured light at different times of day.[81] Another example is *Nude Descending a Staircase, No. 2*,[82] a painting by Marcel Duchamp, known for its illusion of abstract movement (Ian Sands).

Fig. 4.47 Rubin's vase

Fig. 4.47 The figure shows an example of Rubin's vase, a classic example from perception theory of the foreground/background phenomenon. Originally developed around 1915 by the Danish psychologist Edgar Rubin. Do you see a vase or two faces? What is foreground and what is background?

81 Rouen Cathedral is a Roman Catholic church in Rouen, Normandy, France. The *Rouen Cathedral* series was painted in the 1890s by French impressionist Claude Monet. The paintings in the series each capture the façade of the Rouen Cathedral at different times of the day and year and reflect changes in its appearance under different lighting conditions. ('Rouen Cathedral,' n.d.)

82 *Nude Descending a Staircase, No. 2* (French: *Nu descendant un escalier n° 2*) is a 1912 modernist painting by Marcel Duchamp. The painting depicts a figure demonstrating an abstract movement in its ochres and browns. The discernible 'body parts' of the figure are composed of nested, conical and cylindrical abstract elements, assembled together in such a way as to suggest rhythm and convey the movement of the figure merging into itself. ('Nude Descending a Staircase, No. 2,' n.d.).

83 'Gestalt psychology is a psychological school founded in 1912 by the Germans Max Wertheimer, Wolfgang Köhler and Kurt Koffka. Based on studies of perception (sensory perception), gestalt psychologists emphasise that mental phenomena cannot be understood as a sum of simple, elementary units. According to gestalt psychology, psychological phenomena are organised entities with their own structure and form. For example, a melody is not just a series of single tones, it is perceived as one whole, even if single tones change value when transposed to another key' (Teigen, 2015). New research concludes that the principles of visual perception are still valid, 100 years after their origin, but is still unable to explain all aspects of the perception phenomenon (Wagemans et al., 2012).

1 Initiation
2 Insight
3 Strategy
4 Design
5 Production
6 Management

4.1 Design brief
4.2 Strategy><Design
4.3 Design methodology
4.4 Concept development
4.5 Design development
4.6 Design elements
4.7 Composition
4.8 Surface and format
4.9 Identity development

4.7.1 Perception
4.7.2 Principles of composition
4.7.3 Unity/whole
4.7.4 Focal point
4.7.5 Proportions
4.7.6 Balance
4.7.7 Rhythm

## 4.7 Composition

Composition is central to any design development. Conscious composition is the art of arranging visual elements to bring out the desired experience, message, and identity.

The principles of composition are among the methods designers have adopted from art. By purposefully applying the principles of composition, designers have more control over the tools needed to get the message across, create interesting visual compositions, and stop effects. Strategically used, this may be the key to creating awareness and differentiation, which are central to developing identities, building brands and promoting communication.

### 4.7.1 Perception

Composition is largely about understanding how people perceive and interpret what they sense and see. This was also recorded by gestalt psychologists in the early 20th century who used their own perception theories to understand human beings. The principles of composition presented this chapter are based on perception theories from the gestalt psychology.[83] Perception is largely about how the brain works to interpret what we sense and see so that we can understand it. The images we get into the retina must be analysed, selected, and organised. It is this interpretation that is called perception.[84] Perception is a process that goes on constantly when humans and animals are awake, and our experiences are crucial to how we perceive and interpret what we see. It turns out, for example, that ambiguous images that can be interpreted in different ways at perceptual level can be perceived differently by different people, as exemplified by the classic foreground-background figure (Ytterdal, 2012), see Figure 4.47.

**Gestalt theory**: The theory of perception (gestalt theory) is about how we unconsciously seek to see connections in what we see, through mentally grouping individual parts and putting them together into a whole. The word *gestalt*[85] comes from German and originally means *form, shape, pattern*, which in gestalt theory is tied to the concepts of unity and whole.

**Explanation of Rubin's vase**

The shape of elements in a composition helps influence whether we see the shape as foreground or background. A general rule of perception states that (all other things being equal) our eye tends to read convex shapes as figure (foreground) and concave shapes as ground (background). Concave means curved inward, like a cave. Convex is the opposite, a form that stands out. The colours of elements or objects in an image can affect whether we see them as foreground or background. The use of black foreground on a white background in a composition, as in typography, with limited colour use or other interferences, provide the simplest basis for interpretation (Pentak and Lauer, 2014, p. 153).

84 Perception: Borrowed from French *perception*, from Latin *perceptiō* ('a receiving or collecting, perception, comprehension'), from *perceptus* ('perceived, observed'), perfect participle of *percipiō* ('I perceive, observe') (en.wiktionary.org)

85 Gestalt: 1920s: from German *Gestalt*, literally 'form, shape'. An organised whole that is perceived as more than the sum of its parts. (Gestalt, n.d.). The word Gestalt is used in modern German to mean the way a thing has been 'placed,' or 'put together.' There is no exact equivalent in English. 'Form' and 'shape' are the usual translations; in psychology the word is often interpreted as 'pattern' or 'configuration' (Gestalt psychology, n.d.).

### Perception theory

Perspective theory is about how we, humans, perceive and interpret what we sense and see. Impressions from the surroundings we take in through our senses (sight, hearing, touch, smell, and taste). How we perceive unity and whole. The principles of composition are based on perception theories. Through conscious composition, we can organise the information so that it is perceived and interpreted as we wish.

Fundamental principles based on gestalt theory or 'laws of perception' are about what governs human perception and understanding. Gestalt theory is essentially about that the moment we see or recognise something, we sort the information and try to find a connection, by looking for: *grouping* and *proximity*, *similarity* in shape and colour, *closedness* or *mental completion*, *continuity* and *symmetry*. In principle, it is about building and interpreting the impressions we have based on the knowledge we already possess and trying to understand what we are seeing based on contexts and similarities in shapes, forms and colors. When we see multiple elements, we will automatically group them by how *close* they visually are to each other in order to find a connection and understand the whole. If a piece of the whole is missing, our brain will fill the gaps, see Figure 4.48.

Fig. 4.48 The figure shows how we apply the principles of grouping, unity and mental completion, perceiving that a shape emerges between the orange circles. In reality, we are exposed to an optical illusion

The principles of composition involve a number of devices that can be used to create deliberate composition. For example, it can be a matter of creating an experience where the elements in the composition belong together, make sense, convey a message, a shape and a whole, whether they are objects in a room, elements in a layout, a photo, an illustration or text, sound, or a live image.

In general, our brain connects perception and memory together, so that we recognise what we see, making sure that it matches the reality. Yet sometimes the brain is fooled in its attempt to interpret what the eye sees, and we are exposed to an optical illusion. This may mean that we perceive an image as something other than what it actually is, or as something that in our opinion is impossible. The reason is usually that the information our eyes send to the brain challenges our perception of reality, or that we evaluate a visual image based on certain embedded image codes (Van der Weel/Fugelsnes 2003).

## 4.7.2 Principles of composition

The term 'composition' is used in all artistic activities such as visual arts, design, drawing, photography, music, theatre, film, and literature. Composition comes from the Latin 'compositio', which means the act of putting together or developing individual elements into an aesthetic whole'.[86] Balance, rhythm, contrast, motion, and progression are among the composition principles that are just as essential in a musical composition as in a design composition. Conscious use of principles of composition can help us succeed in creating a harmonious and aesthetic expression, or the opposite, if so desired. The principles of composition constitute an integral part of the design process, and follow goals, strategy and guidelines defined in the design brief.

Many of the principles of composition, seen in isolation, are inherent in us as humans, such as sense of balance, need for contrast, and perception of good proportions. People with artistic expressions, such as artists, writers, and designers, have a special built-in touch or talent for seeing what is harmonious and aesthetic, as a kind of natural understanding of the principles of composition. Even for those with such intuitive abilities, studying different compositional principles will be useful and will allow them to use them in a more targeted and conscious way. For

86 Composition: Origin: Late Middle English: via Old French from Latin *compositio(n- )*, from *componere* 'put together'. Meaning; 1) The nature of something's ingredients or constituents; the way in which a whole or mixture is made up. 2) A creative work, especially a poem or piece of music. (Composition, n.d.).

1 Initiation
2 Insight
3 Strategy
4 Design
5 Production
6 Management

4.1 Design brief
4.2 Strategy><Design
4.3 Design methodology
4.4 Concept development
4.5 Design development
4.6 Design elements
4.7 Composition
4.8 Surface and format
4.9 Identity development

4.7.1 Perception
4.7.2 Principles of composition
4.7.3 Unity/whole
4.7.4 Focal point
4.7.5 Proportions
4.7.6 Balance
4.7.7 Rhythm

– Perception theory


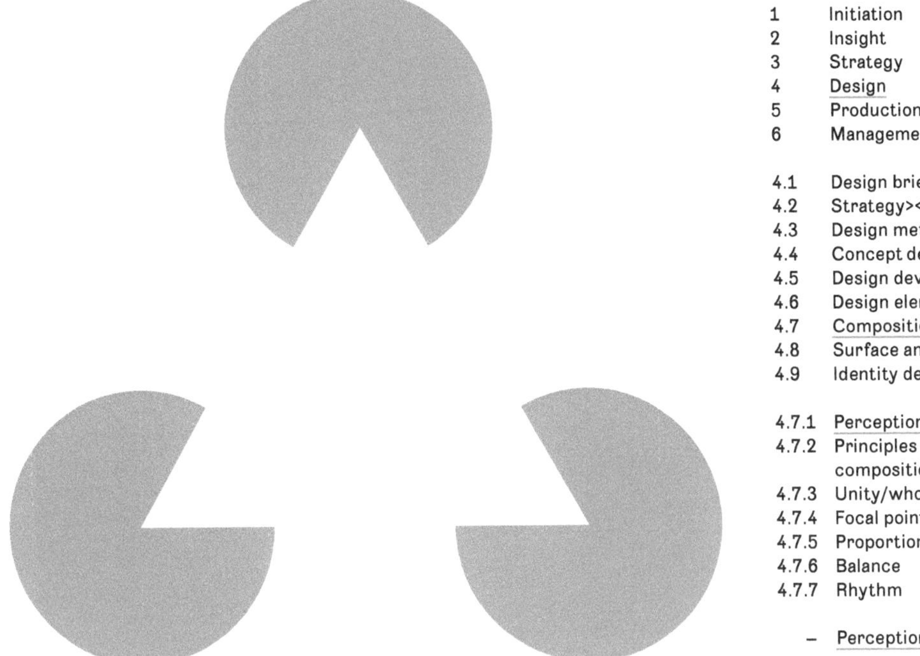

Fig. 4.48 Illusion

example, graphic design can be about creating a successful focal point or eye-catcher that guides the attention to a message, while interior design can be about organising elements in a room to create balance and harmony.

Strategic use of the composition principles is about the designer's using these principles consciously to achieve the desired expression, style and identity, based on the overall strategy, communication strategy and design strategy (3.2 Overall strategy, 3.8 Communication strategy, 3.9 Design strategy, 3.7.5 Brand identity, 4.9.1 The identity principles).

One should be familiar with the different perception theories, how the viewer perceives and interprets visual impressions, and consciously use this to appeal to the relevant target group. Generally, several principles of composition are used in the same composition, but it is important to remember that what is central to one composition may be less important in another. The next chapters present a selection of composition principles, mainly based on Pentak and Lauer (2014). Many of these composition principles can be applied to both surface (two-dimensional composition/layout) and space (three-dimensional composition/interior).

**Some of the most important principles of composition:**

- Unity/whole
- Focal point
- Proportions
- Balance
- Rhythm
- Symmetry/asymmetry
- Motion
- Contrast
- Progress
- Related elements
- Repetition
- Line/grid
- Dominance
- Shape

Perception is how we see the outside from the inside (Fletcher, 2001).

Perhaps I am dreaming right now and all my perceptions are false. René Descartes (1596–1650).

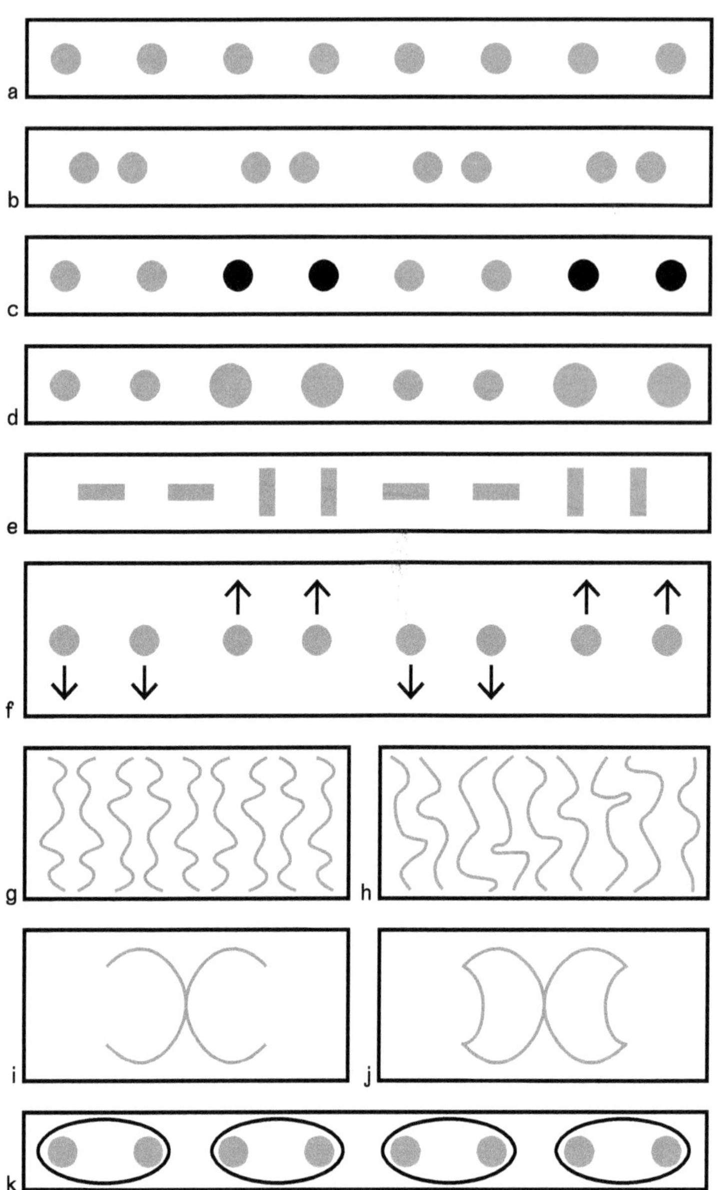

Fig. 4.49 Gestalt theory

Fig. 4.49 The figure is based on Wagemans et al. (2012). It shows different principles for grouping. The visual phenomenon which is most closely associated with perception is grouping, as people are for proximity in order to find a connection. Explanation to the figure: a) No grouping b) Proximity c) Same colour d) Similar size e) Similar orientation f) Common direction g) Symmetry h) Parallels i) Continuity j) Closure k) Common area.[87] See explanation of figure, next page.

Fig. 4.50 The figure shows a logo consisting of three elements; a name, a symbol, and a slogan. Together, the three elements are perceived as one group or a unity.

> Unity and whole are absolutely central among the principles of composition. When the elements are consistently used, we talk about a holistic identity.

### 4.7.3 Unity/whole

A composition may consist of different unities forming one integral whole. We also talk about uniform design language when related colours, shapes, and patterns are repeated. A whole is best achieved by perceiving a connection between the most prominent elements of the composition. The viewer will always try to find meaning or context in what they are looking at. If it does not exist, the viewer may quickly lose interest, and the meaning or message may be lost. 'An important aspect of visual unity is that the whole must predominate over the parts: You must first see the whole pattern before you notice the individual elements. Each item may have a meaning and certainly add to the total effect, but if the viewer sees

87 The figure and the explanation are based on: Palmer (2002a)/Wagemans, J. et al. (2012). 'A Century of Gestalt Psychology in Visual Perception: I. Perceptual Grouping and Figure–Ground Organization', *Psychological Bulletin*. Advance online publication. doi: 10.1037/a0029333

88 Notice that both common fate and proximity can actually be considered special cases of similarity grouping, with velocity and position as the relevant properties, respectively.

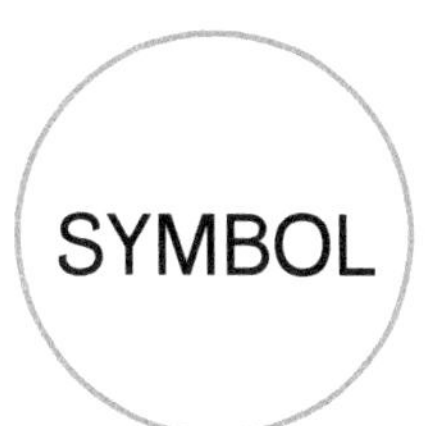


Fig. 4.50 Unity

1 Initiation
2 Insight
3 Strategy
4 Design
5 Production
6 Management

4.1 Design brief
4.2 Strategy><Design
4.3 Design methodology
4.4 Concept development
4.5 Design development
4.6 Design elements
4.7 Composition
4.8 Surface and format
4.9 Identity development

4.7.1 Perception
4.7.2 Principles of composition
4.7.3 Unity/whole
4.7.4 Focal point
4.7.5 Proportions
4.7.6 Balance
4.7.7 Rhythm

merely a collection of bits and pieces, then visual unity doesn't exist' (...) 'Visual unity denotes some harmony or agreement between the items that is apparent to the eye' (Pentak and Lauer, 2014, p. 30).

In a visual identity, creating unity can be about combining several elements such as logo, symbol and slogan, so that they are perceived as a unified whole, see Figure 4.50. When developing visual identity, we also talk about creating a holistic representation. This means, among other things, that all identity elements (logo, symbol, graphic elements, colour, typography, photo style, pattern, etc.) are consistently used on all surfaces/profile carriers in order to create a perception of similarity and

**Explanation of Figure 4.49:** In 1923, Max Wertheimer addressed the problem of perceptual grouping. He demonstrated that equally spaced dots do not group together into larger perceptual units, except as a uniform line (A). When he altered the spacing between adjacent dots so that some dots were closer than others, the closer ones grouped together strongly into pairs (B). This factor of relative distance, which Wertheimer called proximity, was the first of his famous laws or principles of grouping. Parts (C), (D), and (E) demonstrate different versions of the general principle of similarity: all else being equal, the most similar elements (in colour, size, and orientation) tend to be grouped together. Another grouping factor is common fate: all else being equal, elements that move in the same way tend to be grouped together (F).[88] Further factors influencing perceptual grouping of more complex elements, such as lines and curves, include symmetry (G), parallelism (H), and continuity or good continuation (I). Continuity is important in example (I) because observers perceive it as two continuous intersecting lines rather than as two angles whose vertices meet at a point. (J) illustrates the effect of closure: all else being equal, elements that form a closed figure tend to be grouped together. This display also shows that closure can dominate continuity, since the very same elements that were organised as two intersecting lines in Figure (I) are now organised as two angles meeting at a point in (J). Common region is the tendency for elements that lie within the same bounded area (or region) to be grouped together (Palmer, 1992), as (K) where the dots that lie within the same ovals are likely to be grouped into pairs.

identity. This implies that the elements have a uniform form language, or similarity, congruency and congeniality, see Figure 4.51, which expresses the same core values, tone of voice and style. In the context of interior design, creating a holistic expression can be about how unities such as sofa groups, dining sets and various objects are placed in relation to each other in the room, all through the conscious use of colours, patterns and materials that create coherence. To create a holistic expression, a combination of several composition principles is usually used. 'A whole is an act of balance. Too much wholeness quickly becomes stiff and boring. Too little is perceived as messy and unpredictable' (Sander, 2014) (3.2.5 Core values, 3.7 Brand strategy, 4.9 Identity development).

Fig. 4.51 **The left side of the figure shows elements with similarity. In two figures of similar shape, the ratio of two corresponding lengths is constant. The right side of the figure shows items with congruency. If we have two similar figures that are also equal in size, we say that the figures are congruent. Congruent figures cover each other completely, they coincide (Vedeld and Venheim 2012).**

Fig. 4.52 **a) Most people will group the two points and see a line.**

Fig. 4.53 **b) Most people will see two groups or two lines.**

### Tips for creating unity/whole

**1) Grouping:** *Unity* occurs when there is proximity between the elements of a composition, so that they are perceived as a group. According to perception theories, the viewer tends to group or organise the objects, which are closest to each other, looking for similarities between them. The viewer will also interpret empty surfaces, 'air' between elements and groups, as shape, and seek to find logic, context, or pattern.
**2) Repetition:** *Unity* can be created through repetition of shape, colour, pattern, and objects in the composition, like rhythm in music.
**Similarity:** In geometry, two figures are similar if they have exactly the same shape, but not necessarily the same size (Vedeld and Venheim, 2012). The term 'similarity' is often used more freely in visual design subjects, where one talks about a perception of similarity or common design language.
**Congruency:** In geometry, the term 'congruency' is used for shapes that are similar in that they have exactly the same size and shape, but may be different in orientation, both in position and rotation. Congruency means agreement or compliance (Aubert, n.d.).

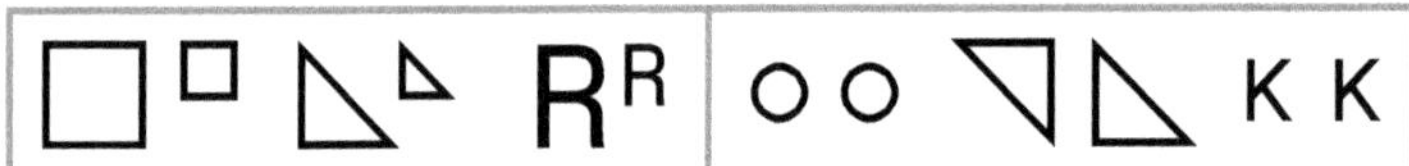


Fig. 4.51 Similarity and congruency

**3) Related elements:** *Device* can be created using related elements and a uniform design language.
**Uniform design language:** What does creating a unified design language mean?

- In a logo, uniform design language can be created by the details of the font, such as the serifs and arches, which have something in common with the corresponding details of the symbol.
- In an illustration, uniform design language can be created using a drawing tool (pencil, pen, marker) that provides the same structure continually throughout the drawing.
- In a layout, uniform design language can be created through the conscious use of design language, colour combinations, and style expressions.

**Congeniality:** Øivin Rannem (2012) uses the term 'congeniality' or 'kinship' as a typographical term for the associative, emotional connection between content and shape. The fact that the shape of the font instinctively feels consistent with the content conveyed by the text.

Fig. 4.52 Line a)

Other concepts that explain similar considerations are theme emphasis, theme character, and identity (Rannem, 2008). Congeniality is important not only in typography, but in all shapes, colours, and elements of visual communication and other forms of visual expression.

**4) Line/grid:** *Unity* can be perceived in the continuation of a line, edge, or direction from one element to another, as a result of which it is perceived as context, group, or whole.
**Line:** The line, edge or direction is not necessarily visible as a line or an arrow; it can be *a perception* of a line or context. The eye sees various

Fig. 4.53 Lines b)

objects and the brain optically seeks to connect the objects, creating lines or directions that do not physically exist, see Figures 4.52, 4.53, 4.54. What happens is that through perception, we interpret and organise what we see, and seek to create a context and meaning (4.6 Design elements: Seven design elements, 4.6.1 Shape: Lines and dashes).

Fig. 4.54 **c) Most people will group the dots and interpret the whole, as one object illustrating the Big Dipper constellation, the way people interpreted it in the sky all the way back to the Middle Ages.**

Fig. 4.54 Shape c)

**Grid:** People's desire to group things and see contexts and lines where they are not physically present shows our inherent search for meaning in what we see. This can be deliberately exploited in grid systems. A grid is a structure of horizontal and vertical lines, used as an invisible network in a composition to create coherence and system. Using a grid makes it easier to organise and position objects and text to create a unified and holistic expression (4.9.9 Grid system).

### 4.7.4 Focal point

The focal point is what first captivates the viewer's attention, for example, on a poster, a magazine cover or a product. This is also called eye-catcher or stop effect. Creating a focal point is about deliberately emphasising a central element of a composition to get the attention of the audience.

In today's information society with an abundance of communication from social media, the internet, newspapers, magazines, books, TV, signs and posters, capturing people's attention is a major challenge, not least keeping their attention long enough for them to perceive the message. 'Without an audience's attention, any messages, any artistic or aesthetic values, are lost.' (Pentak and Lauer, 2014, p. 56). In art paintings, the focal point is often well planned and safeguarded, especially in simple compositions like portraits. Layouts are often more complex, which is why it is important to decide what should capture the viewer's attention.

## Tips for creating a focal point

**1) Centring:** Positioning an optical element centrally in the composition provides a natural focal point. One example of the optimal focal point is *Bull's eye* in a darts game or a perspective point in a landscape, where all lines lead towards the point. An object located in the centre of a composition can be perceived as obvious and boring. A focal point can also be created without placing the element in the centre using instruments such as contrast, foreground, and direction. For example, the image of a face with a direct glance will create an eye-catcher without being centred.
**2) Contrast:** To highlight an item, contrast is absolutely essential. Contrast can be created by variation in size, colour, and shape. To achieve contrast, the difference should be so large that it is perceived as contrast. Contrast is important in any composition. Lack of contrast can be perceived as dull, and the meaning can be lost. When one element differs from the others in a composition, it can be perceived as a focal point. Whatever interrupts a regular pattern will attract attention (Pentak and Lauer, 2014, p. 58). There are different ways to achieve such an effect:

- When most elements are dark, a light shape will break the pattern and become a focal point.
- When most elements are muted or subdued, a hard contrasting shape becomes a focal point.
- When the focus of the items is black and white, items in colour will stand out.

**3) Isolation:** By isolating an element from the others, optionally combined with placing the element in the foreground, the element will stand out. When using magnification and colour contrast, the effect will be stronger.
**4) Direction:** Directions leading in towards the focal point will enhance and highlight the focal point, for example when people in an image look at the focal point, or when lines point in towards it. It is important that the eyes of the audience are not locked in the focal point, but are directed further in order to get the overall experience and understand the message.
**5) Dominance:** Using a visually strong object, enlarging an element (greater than) can be effective in achieving dominance and attracting attention. No matter how dominant and strong the focal point is, it should relate to other parts of the design in order to ensure coherence and integrity.
**6) Absence of focal point:** It is not always necessary to create a focal point; it depends entirely on the goals and guidelines in the project. When there is no focal point but instead an interesting whole, the viewer's attention will gradually be directed towards the individual details of the composition.



### 4.7.5 Proportions

Proportions are often used to describe the comparable size ratio between different parts of a unity or between things. In a composition, one can play with the opportunities that proportions can offer by creating contrasts in size, playing with good proportions, or putting things out of proportion. By proportion we mean the ratio or relationship between sizes, often used in the context of dimensions and aspect ratios. Dimensions

> Holistic or holism
> Comprehensive thinking, from the Greek word ὅλος (holos), whole, complete. 'The whole is greater than the sum of its parts' – Aristotle.

can be measurable, such as height and width, quantity and number, or volume and distribution. We like to talk about 'good proportions' when the aspect ratio between different parts of a unity, and the interaction between them, is perceived as harmonious in relation to each other and as aesthetically pleasing (4.8 Surface and format, 4.8.3 Aspect ratios).

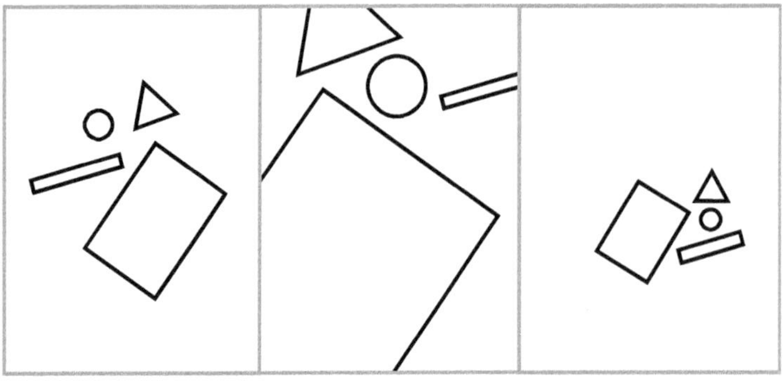

Fig. 4.55 Proportions

Fig. 4.55 The figure shows how, by exaggerating or understating the size and location of elements with equal proportions, different expressions can be created on a surface.

Tips for the designer
Symmetry can be created around any line (axis) depending on the effect one wishes to achieve.

**Tips for creating proportions**

**1) Aspect ratio:** An object in a composition is rarely of natural size, as it is usually scaled down to fit into a format. Placing an object of a known size, such as a matchbox, an apple, or a chair, next to another object will make it easier for the viewer to assess the actual size.
**2) Large and small:** large objects in the foreground and smaller ones in the background can serve as a focal point and provide a perception of perspective. If these objects are not usually seen in the same context, this can have a special effect.
**3) Out of proportion:** Sizes per se can be impressive and conspicuous when taken out of proportion, so they are much smaller or much larger than in reality.
**4) Internal proportions:** The relative size of the elements should be considered in the context of the goal of the design and the expression one aims to create. In an idea process, it can be inspiring to test aspect ratios by exaggerating or understating the size of the elements, see Figure 4.55.
**5) Ideal proportions:** The notions of the ideal proportions are probably inherent in us as humans, in relation to what we perceive as harmonious and aesthetic. An example of that is *the golden ratio* (4.8.3 Aspect ratios, 4.8.5 The golden ratio, 4.8.6 The golden rectangle, 4.8.7 The golden spiral).

### 4.7.6 Balance

Balance is a perception or state of equilibrium. The most perfect form of balance in a composition we create through symmetry. A more challenging task is balancing asymmetry, but the result can be more dynamic and exciting. One can also seek to break the balance in order to achieve a desired effect. The sense of balance is inherent in us as humans, and we seek to find balance from the day we learn to walk. Balance creates a sense of harmony and tranquillity. Imbalance or lack of balance is something we immediately feel and try to counteract. This is something

89 Further reading on symmetric composition: *The New Typography* (Jan Tschichold, 2006).
90 *Text Alignment in Web Design* (Karen, 2017): guppyfishweb.com

that unconsciously affects our visual perception of our surroundings, where feeling balance makes us more comfortable. The same happens when we look at a work of art or design, an advertisement, or a poster. Intuitively, we also seek to balance an image or composition.



### Tips for creating balance

**1) Symmetry:** Balance through symmetry can be created by mirroring objects around an axis, or by distributing objects evenly on either side of an axis so that they are perceived as balanced. An axis can be horizontal, vertical or at any angle, visible or invisible. A sphere or cube is symmetric around both the vertical and horizontal axis. Different objects can have anything from one to infinitely many planes of symmetry. For example, an equilateral triangle has three planes of symmetry, while a circle can have an infinite number. If one wants to create symmetry in a composition with portrait layout on a defined surface (a layout, an image, a wall), the most effective approach is to create balance around a centred vertical axis.[89] A center vertical axis acts as a kind of fulcrum or line of symmetry, and the two sides should achieve some kind of equilibrium or balance, like a horizontal see-saw. 'When this equilibrium is not present in a composition, a certain vague uneasiness or dissatisfaction results. We feel a need to rearrange the elements in the same way that we automatically straighten a tilted picture on the wall' (Pentak and Lauer, 2014, p. 88).

**Mirror symmetry and bilateral symmetry:** As humans, we have an inherent acceptance of symmetry, regardless of culture and geography. Symmetry is perceived as nice and often beautiful and aesthetically pleasing, like a symmetrically perfect face. This may stem from the original symmetry that lies in nature and in our anatomy. The easiest way to create symmetry is by mirroring objects around an axis. Mirror symmetry tends to provide an experience of harmony, tranquillity and equilibrium, and is often associated with a classic and formal expression. The focus may, if desired, lie on a horizontal axis resting symmetrically on the vertical one. In many artistic contexts, and not least in architecture, mirror symmetry can be perceived as stable and powerful, such as an archway or a portal. The term *bilateral symmetry* is often used in biology to describe something *that is approximately* mirror-symmetric, such as a face or other living organisms, which are never perfectly symmetric.

**Symmetric balance:** Symmetry does not have to be mirrored exactly to be perceived as symmetric. In art, photography and graphic design, it is more common to create even weight distribution of objects around an axis, giving an optical perception of symmetry, *a symmetric balance*. It gives more freedom to create the desired expression as well as greater dynamic effect. Symmetric balance in a typographical composition tends to give a solemn, classic expression, and usually works best in small text boxes, like a classic title page in a book, a quote, a title, etc. Centred text in larger volumes may impair the legibility of the text.[90]

**2) Asymmetrical balance:** In asymmetrical balance, the goal is to balance visually different objects in a composition by means of shape, colour, placement, motion and eye-catcher. 'Which weighs more, a pound of feathers or a pound of lead? Of course, they both weigh a pound, but the amount or volume of each vary radically, This, then, is the essence of asymmetrical balance' (Pentak and Lauer, 2014, p. 96). Asymmetrical

While symmetry is present in the human body, in a leaf, in a tree, our surroundings are rarely mirror-symmetric, unless man-made, as in the case of design and architecture. Even then, we do not see full symmetry, unless we are personally in the centre, for example in front of a symmetric portal. This way, we can think that an asymmetrical composition can yield a more natural experience than a symmetric one.

balance is more informal than symmetric balance. In asymmetrical compositions, the entire surface is used more freely and more intuitively, and the elements are indirectly balanced with respect to an imaginary central axis. Using asymmetry can give more variation and tension in the composition, but can also be more demanding to work with. Balancing different objects on a surface can pose a greater challenge than repeating similar objects on either side of a centre. It can also be more engaging and challenging for the viewer to study an asymmetric image as opposed to a symmetric one, because our brain will intuitively compare the different sides and objects of the image and seek to find the balance.[91]

**Balance by colour and lightness:** On a light surface, a dark colour will be perceived as heavier than a light colour. Distributed around a central axis, creating balance will require less of the dark colour on one side than of the light colour on the other side. On a dark background, it will be the other way round: the bright colour will emerge and will be perceived as dominant, and the dark colour will merge into the background.

**Balance by texture and pattern:** An object with a pattern will attract our attention to a greater extent than an object with smooth structure. Balance between these two elements can most easily be achieved by reducing the size of the patterned object. A text box can be regarded as a pattern. The information in the pattern can be read, while the visual effect will be perceived as a smooth grey structure. Depending on layout, text box shape, font selection, dot size, and line spacing, the grey structure will vary in tone, density, and character, but it will still be perceived as a visual structure. In editorial page layouts, an area of 'texture' will balance photographs or graphics. (Pentak and Lauer, 2014, p. 100).

**Balance by shape:** Located on either side of an axis, an object with a complex shape will attract more attention than a smooth, familiar shape. Balance between these two elements can most easily be achieved by reducing the size of the object with a more complex shape.

**Balance by position and eye direction:**

- *Location*: In a composition, a large and a small object of the same colour and shade are balanced by placing the large object closer to the centre axis than the small object, or by placing the small object closer to the outer edge of the format. One example of this is one heavy and one light person on either side of a see-saw. In order to achieve balance, the heavier person will have to move closer to the centre of the see-saw.
- *Eye direction*: When we look at a picture with people as motif, we will intuitively look for the narrative in the picture. The people's eyes and eye direction will be a central part of the narrative and they will guide us in the direction of their gaze. The direction of the eye can be used to balance the image.
- *Direction and motion*: In the same way as with eye direction, directions and motion between elements of the composition can be consciously used to create balance.

**3) Radial symmetry:** In radial symmetry, all the elements surround or radiate from a midpoint. The term radial symmetry is used in biology for the symmetry of plants and animals, such as a starfish and a flower. The elements of radial symmetry may be organised symmetrically or asymmetrically depending on whether the focus is on the centre or away from the centre, and depending on whether the elements are organised

Fig. 4.56 **The illustration shows an example of radial symmetry, a type of symmetry naturally found in biology. © Grimsgaard, W. (2018).**

Tips for the designer

**A great way to test the balance of an asymmetrical composition is to hold it to a mirror to see it reversed. It will then often be easier to reveal bias to the composition that is otherwise 'invisible' to the eye (Pentak and Lauer, p. 104).**

**Balance and symmetry are factors that help to provide the experience of harmony. Factors that are important if you want to create something that is beautiful and attractive to people.**

91 Asymmetry: Jan Tschichold (1967): *Asymmetric Typography*. Available as PDF online. See also posters with asymmetrical composition from Tschichold's early years by searching for Tschichold posters.

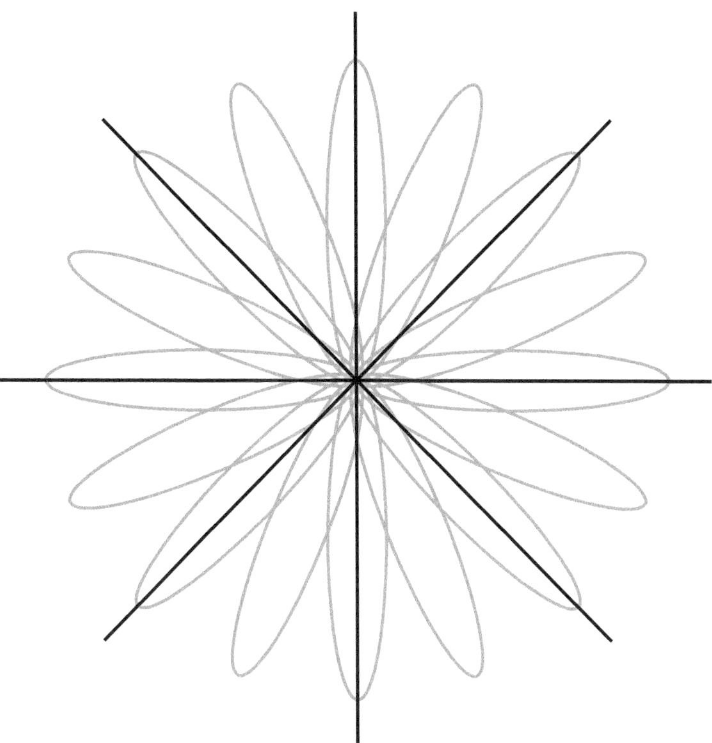

Fig. 4.56 Radial symmetry


1 Initiation
2 Insight
3 Strategy
4 Design
5 Production
6 Management

4.1 Design brief
4.2 Strategy><Design
4.3 Design methodology
4.4 Concept development
4.5 Design development
4.6 Design elements
4.7 Composition
4.8 Surface and format
4.9 Identity development

4.7.1 Perception
4.7.2 Principles of composition
4.7.3 Unity/whole
4.7.4 Focal point
4.7.5 Proportions
4.7.6 Balance
4.7.7 Rhythm

– Tips for creating balance


evenly or unevenly around the centre. Radial symmetry places a clear emphasis on a centre and gathers elements around it.

**4) Crystallographic balance (all-over balance):** Crystallographic balance is also called 'all-over' balance or mosaic, and is about creating balance in a pattern. One example of this can be found in compositions where there is repetition of almost identical elements on a surface, so that the whole is perceived as a pattern. Such composition lacks a clear focal point or eye catcher.

**5) Imbalance:** Our sense of gravity is something we consciously or unconsciously transfer to images by putting more weight on the bottom, giving a sense of stability and tranquillity. When the focus, weight and visual eye catcher are distributed higher up in the format, the image becomes more imbalanced.

- *Imbalance through absence of balance and centre of gravity*: When we talk about balance in an image, it is usually about horizontal balance, balance between the right and left sides of an image, around an imaginary horizontal axis. When the weight distribution between the right and left sides of the centre axis is uneven, imbalance is perceived. The absence of balance can be used deliberately to create intentional dynamic effects, tension, confusion, or motion (Pentak and Lauer, 2014, p. 90).

Symmetry: objects mirrored around an axis
Symmetric balance: Distribute objects on either side of a central axis so that it is perceived as balance.
Asymmetry: Create balance between visually different objects on a surface. This gives more variation and tension than symmetry.

## 4.7.7 Rhythm

Rhythm created through repetition and variation of approximately equal elements can stimulate the viewer's senses and provide an experience of direction and movement. The word rhythm is derived from Greek

| Selection of composition principles for surface and room | | |
|---|---|---|
| Principles of composition | Meaning | Devices |
| Unity/whole | Unity means that a composition is perceived as a whole.<br>A unified artistic style helps create a holistic expression. | Grouping: assembling items into a unity or a whole.<br>Repetition: repetition of object, shape, colour, texture, direction, angle, or anything else that provides a holistic experience. Similarity and congruency.<br>Related elements: uniform use of shape and colour. Uniform design language and congeniality.<br>Lines/grid: continuation of a line, edge, or direction from one element to another. |
| Focal point/eye catcher/ stop effect | Focal point is putting emphasis on a central element in a composition.<br>The focal point should attract attention and encourage the viewer to have a closer look. | Centring: placing the focus element in the centre.<br>Contrast: highlight an item using contrast in size, colour, and shape. Contrast is central in all compositions.<br>Isolation: isolate one element from the others.<br>Direction: create direction by placing elements or people's eyes, leading the attention towards the focal point.<br>Dominance: use of a single dominant, visually strong object as a focal point.<br>Absence of focal point: when there's no focal point, but an interesting whole instead, the viewer's attention is gradually directed towards the individual details in the composition. |
| Proportions/aspect ratio | Proportions are often used for describing comparable aspect ratios between different parts of a unit, or between different objects.<br>Aspect ratio in this context is about measurable sizes. | Aspect ratio: place an object with a known size, e.g. a matchbox, next to another object to indicate the actual size of the object.<br>Big and small: place a large object in the foreground and smaller ones in the background to create a focal point and a sense of perspective.<br>Out of proportion: make an object much smaller or much bigger in relation to its surroundings compared to real life.<br>Internal proportions: Test out the opportunities that lie in the aspect ratio of elements within a delimited surface or room.<br>The ideal proportions: consider how standardised proportions like the golden ratio can be used to create an experience of harmony or can serve as basis for creating a modular grid system. |
| Balance/symmetry/ Asymmetry | Balance is a state of equilibrium, as in the case of equal distribution of weight, quantity etc.<br>Balance creates a feeling of harmony and tranquillity. | Symmetry: the simplest form of balance we create through symmetry, a distribution of objects on each side of a central axis so that it is perceived as being in balance. Symmetric balance, mirror symmetry and bilateral symmetry.<br>Asymmetry: balance between visually different objects on a surface.<br>Radial symmetry: symmetry from a midpoint.<br>Crystallographic balance: *Balance in an irregular pattern.* |
| Rhythm | Rhythm is repetition of elements with minor changes. Visual rhythm can stimulate the viewer's senses and provide an experience of movement. | Form and repetition: Variety and repetition in dashes, colours, irregularities, light and darkness.<br>Patterns and sequences: Rhythm in the small irregularities or repetition of differences in a pattern.<br>Progressive rhythm: Objects, colours or texture in the repetition develop from small to larger or vice versa.<br>Polyrhythmic structures: Combination of multiple rhythmic repetitions in the same composition. |

Table 4.8 Composition principles

Fig. 4.57 Rhythm

and means flow or movement that takes place in a sequence of different time intervals. Usually, we associate rhythm with music we can hear or feel pulsating in our body, or music, the way we experience it in dance and poetry. Visual rhythm in an image or composition can stimulate the viewer's senses and provide an experience or sense of motion. This sense refers to movements in the eye of the beholder. The eye will move back and forth, and follow the repetition of elements, which could give a sense of rhythm. The use of repetition as a method is a key principle of composition in art and design for creating unity, such as, for example, the repetition of almost equal elements as in the case of a table or pattern. Good rhythm in a composition depends on the relationship between the individual elements building up in a consistent way, creating a pattern that is recognisable and that makes the composition vibrate and come to life. A mere repetition of elements of the same size can become monotonous and static. In the typography, rhythm is about the relationship between repeating elements, such as letters, words, lines, groups, titles, illustrations, dashes, ornaments, etc., where size, shape, strength, colour, and distance between the elements form a pattern.

Table 4.8 The table shows shows a selection of composition principles based on Pentak and Lauer (2014).

Fig. 4.57 Trees in a row can provide a natural experience of repetition and rhythm. (Photo: Sandstrom, H./unsplash.com)

Rhythm is naturally found in nature, as in night and day, the tide, and the planetary movements (Pentak and Lauer 2014). These rhythms occur in consecutive sequences in regular order. The term for this is *alternating rhythm* and is used in speech, poetry, and music to designate regular alternation or movement.

Tips for creating rhythm

**1) Form and repetition:** Repetition of shape, colour and texture, either separately or together, is a good starting point for creating repetition and rhythm, either in parts of a composition or used regularly throughout the entire composition. It can be created by variation and repetition between thick and thin lines, variation in waves and unevenness, contrast in colours and saturation, and alternation between light and dark, all of which are great ways of creating the experience of vibration, rhythm, and movement. The effect can also occur naturally, such as trees in a row and birds on a branch.

**2) Patterns and sequences:** By repetition of simple graphical elements, it is possible to create complex patterns. Rhythm is created in the small irregularities or in the repetition of differences, using 'non-figurative', abstract or geometric shapes. It is important for repetition and alternation to be predictable, otherwise the rhythm will become unclear. Even static sequences can create movement through the sensory impression or perception that occurs.

**3) Progressive rhythm:** Progressive rhythm means that objects, colours, or texture in the repetition evolve from smaller to larger or vice versa. This is called *progressive rhythm*.

**4) Polyrhythmic structures:** 'Polyrhythmic structures' is an expression for several different rhythms used in the same piece of music or a combination of several rhythmic repetitions in the same composition. Although the composition is built up of simple parts, the result can be a complex combination.

**5) Some other types of rhythms:** Sinus. Legato. Chopped uneven. Frequency.

Fig. 4.58 **The figure shows a two-dimensional surface. It has two coordinates x and y, with intersection in 0 (=Origo). The size of the surface is marked along the vertical and horizontal axes. The aspect ratio is x:y (based on matte.hiof.no).**

Surface vs. object vs. space

**A surface is a two-dimensional format, while objects and space can be both two-dimesional and three-dimensional. A room can be an open space, in a house, or in a box. A room has surfaces, on the inside and on the outside. A product also has surfaces, at the front and back. Space can also be *the perception* of space, as in writing, between the letters as well as inside them.**

## 4.8 Surface and format

The conscious use of surface and format is absolutely essential to design development and the same applies to knowledge of basic design elements and composition. The surface can be used to create identity, to convey information, and to create experience. Surface, object and space are different dimensions that are always present in design.

Generally, one could say that a graphic designer relates to *surfaces*, an industrial designer is concerned with the *object*, and an interior designer or architect creates solutions in *space*. The success factor often lies in the combination of the different areas of expertise, because in many contexts we work across surface, object and space. For example, an assignment to redesign a product in a grocery store could involve working on the shape of the product, the product label, and the exposure of the product in the room. In such assignments, it is necessary to create coherence across the aspect ratios and functions of the surfaces. Deliberate selection and use of surface and format are a natural part of the design process, and are done on the basis of goals, strategy and guides defined in the design brief. In this chapter we will look at the possibilities that lie in the design and application of surface and format.

## 4.8.1 Surface

1 Initiation
2 Insight
3 Strategy
4 Design
5 Production
6 Management

4.1 Design brief
4.2 Strategy><Design
4.3 Design methodology
4.4 Concept development
4.5 Design development
4.6 Design elements
4.7 Composition
4.8 Surface and format
4.9 Identity development

4.8.1 Surface
4.8.2 Format
4.8.3 Aspect ratios
4.8.4 The A series
4.8.5 The golden ratio
4.8.6 Golden rectangle
4.8.7 The golden spiral
4.8.8 Fibonacci
4.8.9 The rule of thirds

Choice of surface area is a natural part of the design development process. A surface can be paper, the front of a product, the wall of a room, or the façade of a building. When we talk about surfaces in a design project, it could be a matter of how it can be used visually and purposefully to convey a message, an identity, a brand, or an experience. All aircraft of type Boeing 737 are similar and all have a surface intended to satisfy aeronautical functions, but the surface also represents the possibility for an airline to create identity and make its aircraft stand out from competitor companies. For the industrial designer, it will always be about creating an airframe with proportions that provide the best possible flight characteristics. For the identity designer, the question will be which part of the aircraft's outer surfaces is most visible and exposes the identity elements best. Is it the top or bottom of the hull, or is it the tail? How a surface should be used as a profile and information carrier is a strategic choice.

A surface can be popularly described as the limitation of a body (Aubert, n.d.), object or item, measured in length and width. Surfaces can be defined differently, often with slightly different meanings, depending on their purpose and application. We then talk about the function and user properties of the surface, which should meet the intended demand. For example, it can be the surface that carries the profile of a company, product or service. The surface in that context can be the façade, shop window, car, uniform, business card, bottle, box, label, cap, PC screen, mobile phone display, newspaper, magazine, brochure, book, body, clothes, hats, and so on.

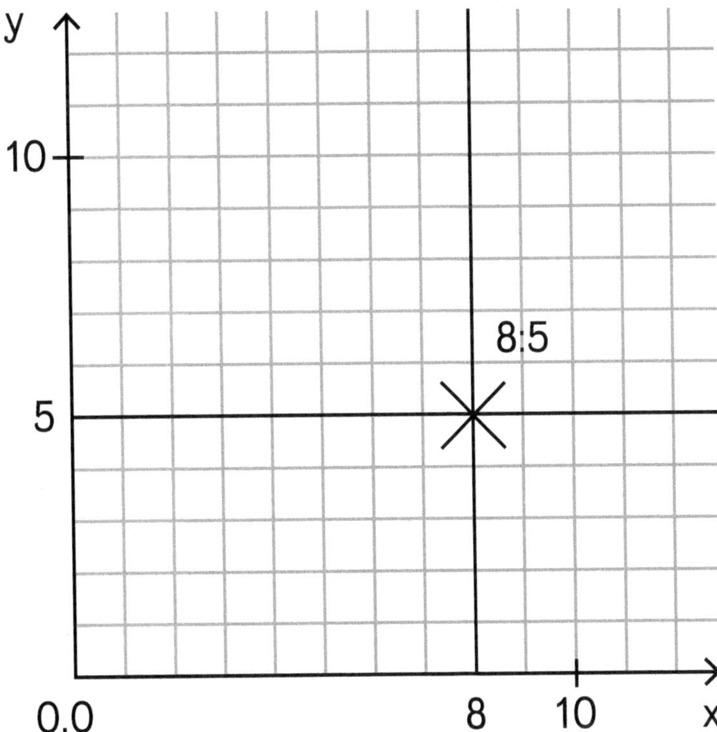


Fig. 4.58 Two-dimensional surface

## 2D and 3D surfaces

An image on a sheet of paper or a computer screen is two-dimensional (2D). A two-dimensional surface may be described using a two-dimensional Cartesian coordinate system,[92] a vertical axis and a horizontal axis, which may be used to define all points on the surface, expressed as oriented distances from the origin (0.0). A room has three dimensions (3D) and can be described in a three-dimensional Cartesian coordinate system using 3 coordinates, one of which describes the depth or perspective of the room. Drawing a three-dimensional room on a two-dimensional surface gives the perception of space, but the surface remains completely two-dimensional. An object has inner room, or volume, which is the content of the object. The volume is measured by multiplying the base surface (length times width) by height.

Fig. 4.59 The figure shows a three-dimensional surface, a spatial shape. It has three coordinates x, y and z. The depth of the room is described by the coordinate z. (based on matte.hiof.no).

Fig. 4.60 The figure illustrates that a white sheet also has information. The surface has different properties based, among other things, on our reading direction (which is culturally determined), here starting at the top left, and how we are used to view an image. Placement of elements on the left side of the sheet gives less dynamic (traditional expression), placement on the right side gives more dynamic (less traditional expression). Based on Rannem (2005).

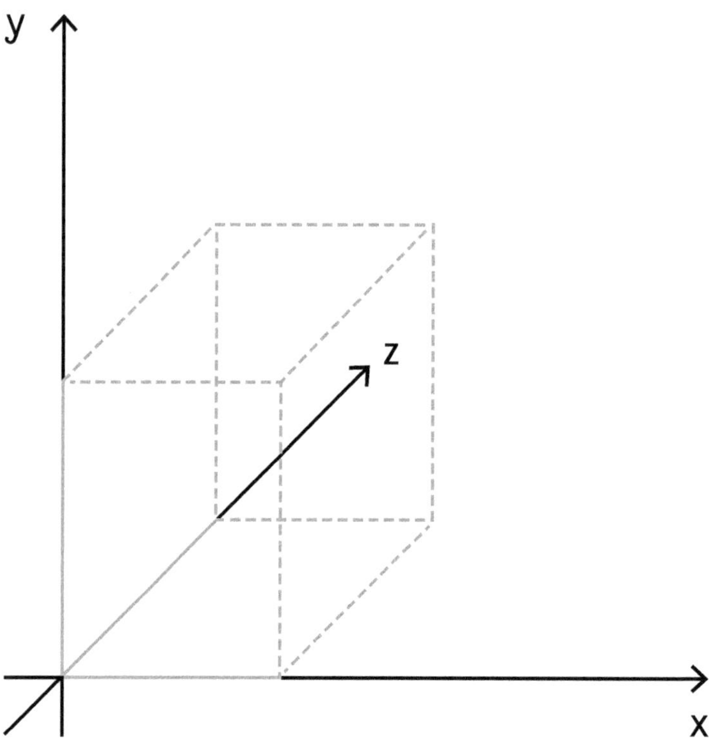


Fig. 4.59 Three-dimensional surface

## The white surface

A sheet of paper is a two-dimensional surface. A blank sheet of paper provides the freedom to unfold. Is an empty white paper surface really empty, or is there some kind of information in the empty white surface? One of the most distinguished artists of the 20th century, Wassily Kandinsky (1866–1944), talked about 'the breathing surface' ('Die Atmende Fläche'). To him, the surface was not just dead, flat paper. 'Kandinsky believed that the different parts of a surface had different symbolic and emotional value. The upper half is free, open, loose; the lower part is closed, bound, heavy. He also believed that the left side of the surface is open and free in about the same way as the top half, just not to the fullest extent, and that the right side is closed and bound almost like

92 'A Cartesian coordinate system in a plane is a coordinate system that specifies each point uniquely by a pair of numerical coordinates, which are the signed distances to the point from two fixed perpendicular oriented lines, measured in the same unit of length' (Cartesian coordinate system, n.d.).

1 Initiation
2 Insight
3 Strategy
4 Design
5 Production
6 Management

4.1 Design brief
4.2 Strategy><Design
4.3 Design methodology
4.4 Concept development
4.5 Design development
4.6 Design elements
4.7 Composition
4.8 Surface and format
4.9 Identity development

4.8.1 Surface
4.8.2 Format
4.8.3 Aspect ratios
4.8.4 The A series
4.8.5 The golden ratio
4.8.6 Golden rectangle
4.8.7 The golden spiral
4.8.8 Fibonacci
4.8.9 The rule of thirds

– 2D and 3D surfaces
– The white surface

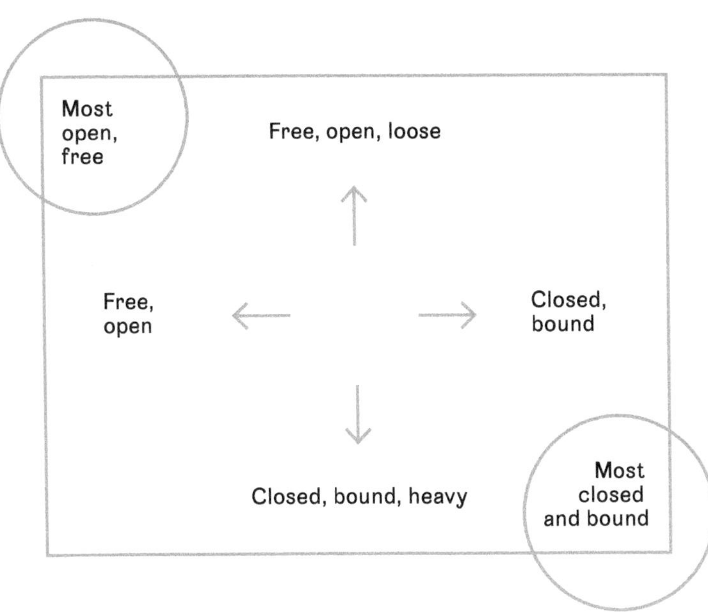


Fig. 4.60 Surface characteristics

the bottom half. The bottom right corner is the most bound and closed one, and the top left corner is the most open and free' (Rannem, 2005), see Figure 4.60.

The surface has optical midpoint, but this is not the geometric centre. When placing an element in the geometric centre, the optical experience will be that it is below the center of the format. To the eye, the optical centre is the midpoint. It is slightly above the geometric center. Try it: Take a blank A4 sheet of paper and put it in front of you. Put a cross in the centre of the sheet. Turn the sheet 180 degrees and check if the intersection is still in the middle. Take a ruler and check where it lies in relation to the geometric centre (Rannem, 2005, p. 181).

### 4.8.2 Format

The size and frame of a format constitute the limited framework for a two-dimensional design. The surface of a two-dimensional composition or layout is bound, it has shape, size and proportions; a format. The format plays a key role in everything developed by design, whether it is a matter of the format of a web page, a printed matter or a sign. In addition to serving as an information and identity bearer, the format will also implicitly convey an identity by virtue of the medium it represents. A book, newspaper, magazine, poster, sign, label, film, web page and various social media all have their genre identities. By that, a kind of perceived standard is meant, where the format is adapted to special considerations of purpose and function, and where the format is largely a consequence of the medium. Within a single medium there are also different genre identities, with distinctive expressions and features. Similarly, standard paper formats, packaging formats, and ad modules have fixed aspect ratios and features. Here there is also the possibility to create formats within the format.

> Surface and format
> Item = Product
> Room = Interior

One question that is relevant to ask is how the medium affects the content or the message. For example, we can use a book vs. a website as our starting point. What is the intrinsic identity, the intrinsic quality, the very ideology of a book form? What is the difference in terms of faithfulness between what you read in a book and what you read online? What is the authority of each medium and how does it affect the reader? Marshall McLuhan emphasised the role of format as a medium, in his 1967 book *The Medium is The Massage*.[93] The book was written at a time when the use of mass media and new technological developments were gathering momentum. In his book, McLuhan reflects on how the emergence of new technology transforms society, the individual's life and perception of reality, and how people are strongly influenced by the media and the formats we use to communicate. His reflection is just as relevant today.

How important is the identity of the format *in reality*, and to what extent does it characterise the content? Should the format be selected first, or should it come as a natural consequence of the content? Designer Aslak Gurholt Rønsen[94] has worked in various formats, both with large exhibitions and small book formats. He is reluctant to give the format too important a role. Instead, he is more concerned with what format the content needs. 'The format should be compatible with the content. Is it a textbook? Is it a book with pictures? What kind of format is suitable? How can the form of the book promote the content of the book? Basically, it is about designing the book from the inside out and not forcing it into a shape' (Gurholt Rønsen, 2015).

It is probably more common today to think format before content because one thinks about the medium first. This is the case, for example, with companies that decide that they need a website long before they have decided what they want to say on it. The essence should be, in the first place, what you want to convey, that is, what the message should be, and to whom it should be conveyed. This is the starting point for deciding which medium is best suited to deliver the message. Then comes choice of format. (3.8.8 Channels and media, 4.9.1 The identity principles: Communication surfaces).

Tips for the designer
Composition is something that takes place on a well-defined surface. The shape and size of the surface create possibilities and limitations. Read more in chapter 4.7 Composition.

Surface, format and proportions are interrelated. It is about purpose, function and identity.

### How to choose the format for press or print?

The format can present both opportunities and limitations. The designer is not always free to choose the format, and to some it may feel as a constraint, but others may view it as a challenge or an opportunity. Here are some tips based on an interview with graphic designer Lars Høie (2018).[95]

**What should govern format selection:** How do we get started when choosing format? Should the format be large or small? High or low? Wide or narrow? Should the format be selected based on medium and genre? Should the format be selected based on an idea? Should we start by determining the format and after that create the layout, or the other way round? Should we choose the format based on the medium, or let the content determine the format? A good idea would be to work both from the outside in, and from the inside out.

**The strategy:** The format is a communication surface. It is important to have a goal with what is to be communicated. Use the communication strategy and media strategy as a starting point. It does not need to be as comprehensive, but it should at least define the communication

93 Original title: *The Medium is The Massage*. The use of 'a' in 'message' was originally a typo. McLuhan adopted the term 'massage' to denote the effect of each medium on the human senses ('The Medium is The Massage,' n.d.).

94 From an interview Grafill did in 2015 of the award winning designer Aslak Gurholt cofounder of design studio Yokoland (yokoland.com). Grafill is the Norwegian organisation for visual communication.

95 Read also the interview with Lars Høie at designandstrategy.co.uk.

96 Michael Rock Designer as Author (1996): 2x4.org/ideas/22/designer-as-author/.

goals, the target groups and the channels and media through which they can best be met.

**Purpose:** What is the purpose? What should the outcome be? Should it be print or printed matter, is it web, video, audio, a performance? Is it supposed to be practical, information, advertising, experience, art? From a philosophical perspective, what should it be at all? It is important to really think through what the purpose is and what the problem is. What solves the problem? What tells the story best, or shows the idea? What do you have to say?

**Limitations:** What are the limitations? Designers who work for themselves have complete control and should set their own limits. Having infinite possibilities can also be inhibiting, but great possibilities open up for doing something that is unexpected and not so obvious, because one has that degree of freedom. When there is an assignment, there are often limitations related to content, genre, budget, and not least strategic directions for how the content should reach the target group and market. For the designer, there will always be a balance in how much he or she should be guided by limitations or guidelines in the project. From the client's standpoint, it can also be a good starting point to 'empower'; give more power to the designer, and think that design itself has value. From the client's standpoint, it is important to start from a position of trust and to consider that the design itself is content, and not only window dressing for the text. Michael Rock's[96] article 'The designer as author' (1996) has been read by many as an argument for the position that the designer should not and cannot ever be absent in the work. This is what many people have come to call 'graphic authorship', to recognise the designer's hand in the work, and that typo(graphic) gestures can be as important as the text or other content. With sufficient knowledge and understanding of the problem, the customers' situation and the market, the designer's intuitive approach is hardly coincidental.

**Target group:** If we use a book as an example, the practical choice of format, binding, typeface, etc., which is governed by budget and genre, will be just as important as the inherent quality of the format, binding, paper, typeface, and market-oriented approach: What sells or works best with a special target group in mind? If the choice is between hardcover or soft cover, price is a factor, but what the target group prefers is important, too. Those who go to the bookstore and are passionate about books often prefer soft covers and not hard ones as you might have thought, even though the latter are more expensive and perceived as being of higher quality. Typically, the traditional approach to format selection, which is governed by the people or target group being addressed and the relevant market, is used, together with practical and functional considerations. Sometimes, it can also be a good thing not to have a particular group in mind; it can bring forth new and unexpected solutions. Here, the content can contribute to the outcome via research and sketching, where the process leads to the format.

**Ergonomics:** The most important thing is ergonomics. What is it like to hold the book? What does a book that weighs five kilos say? A massive book says a lot in itself, but unless the purpose of the format is to be large and monumental, it should be manageable. It is essential how and where the book, magazine, report, brochure or program is to be read



People who are really passionate about books might for example prefer a quality softcover over a cheaply produced mass-market hardcover, even though the latter is typically more expensive and perceived as being of higher quality. – Lars Høie (2022).

(on the sofa, on the bus, at a concert), how it feels in one's hand, how the pages are to be turned, and how it is to be carried and stored. Paper and binding also play an essential role here. For example, landscape orientation will require stiffer paper and binding, if the printed matter is not to be seen as loose and cumbersome, and if it is not to be placed on a table when it is read. The form of the book, whether massive and monumental or nice and small, is in any case linked to its purpose: it is intended to convey content to a specific target group.

**Content:** It is natural to start with the content. What should the content be? How do you get hold of the content? Is it self-initiated or is it an assignment? Is it supposed to be information, advertising, narrative, academic, prose? The content also controls the style and not least the tone and genre set by the format. Olive oil and engine oil are both oils, but with two completely different purposes, and with two different genres. Is it going to be pictures with portrait orientation or pictures with landscape orientation? Take, for example, a sales brochure. What determines whether it should be small or large, portrait or landscape orientation? It is often the amount of text, the number of images, their shape, and the context in which the brochure is to work and be read. If the brochure has snowboard as its theme, photography of jumps in the air will require portrait orientation, but if we are talking about a brochure for sofas, it may be natural to choose landscape.

**Standard formats:** Digital printing technology, such as 'print on demand', allows more freedom than before when choosing formats and it is possible to do things that would not be possible otherwise. The development of books or printed matter in small editions or single copies, such as artist books, fanzines and ephemera,[97] opens up a remarkable number of possibilities, because it is something the designer makes on their own, compared to commercial projects with large editions and more limitations. Nevertheless, one should usually adhere to a number of constraints when choosing format in terms of genre, standard paper formats, etc. Standard paper formats can be trimmed-off A formats (A4, A3, A2, etc.), or used in an imposition context (multiple pages per sheet).

**The format as a starting point:** Even with strong guidelines for format selection, slight nuances a few centimetres in width or height will make a difference in terms of expression and experience, and in terms of grid and layout possibilities. Without an idea, there will be a great many possibilities in any case. One works slightly in the dark and the outcome can easily be more random than conscious. Testing out the format relatively quickly and separately from the rest can be a method, for example: Which one is the best to hold? Or the other way around: Which one is hardest to hold? Try it out right away by making quick dummies. This is a good approach if one has not drawn up a conceptual direction. Once the format has been determined, it is easier to get started with the grid and typographic system, and then to further break it down to the smallest components. If time and budget allow, it may be useful to start with several different formats to see how the content will fit.

**Idea as a starting point:** If you have a very specifically thought out idea, it determines in itself whether the format should be large and monumental or small and neat. This is in itself a decision that limits the choices.

Tips for the company

**The secret behind a holistic and functional grid system can be carefully calculated aspect ratios.**

> ***Format*** **plays a key role in everything developed by design, whether it is a matter of the format of printed matter, websites or signs.**
> ***Layout*** **is the directing on the surface. How the elements are disposed within the frames of the format.**

97 Ephemera: Temporary printed or written material, tightly bound to time, such as letters, postcards, programmes and tickets, which were not meant to last long or be stored, but which have since become collectibles.

Furthermore, the selection process can be broken down step by step with respect to the idea by breaking things down to the smallest components of design, seeing details and elements separately and gradually putting them together – possibly in a new way. Without a clear idea, a brochure may well become a brochure, but with a clear idea, the outcome might as well be a film (Lars Høie 2018).


1 Initiation
2 Insight
3 Strategy
4 Design
5 Production
6 Management

4.1 Design brief
4.2 Strategy><Design
4.3 Design methodology
4.4 Concept development
4.5 Design development
4.6 Design elements
4.7 Composition
4.8 Surface and format
4.9 Identity development

4.8.1 Surface
4.8.2 Format
4.8.3 Aspect ratios
4.8.4 The A series
4.8.5 The golden ratio
4.8.6 Golden rectangle
4.8.7 The golden spiral
4.8.8 Fibonacci
4.8.9 The rule of thirds

– Mathematical proportions


## 4.8.3 Aspect ratios

The conscious use of size and proportions is an important factor in visual design. Size is something that can be measured and expressed in numbers. Proportion is the comparable aspect ratio between things, such as size in relation to quantity, height, width, amount, number, distribution, and so on. Proportional means that the size increases or decreases in the same ratio, or that two sizes vary so that their ratio remains constant. Both size and proportions are important in terms of aesthetics and function. Regarding three-dimensional aspect ratios, many of the same basic principles apply to proportions as for two-dimensional formats.

When we talk about good proportions, we usually think of something that is perceived as harmonious and beautiful; a well-formed face, a beautiful building, or a great book. Some proportions appeal to the eye more than others and have occupied and fascinated mathematicians, musicians, artists, architects, and designers, regardless of cultures and borders for centuries. Many of these proportions are found in simple geometric figures such as triangles, squares, pentagons, hexagons, and octagons (Bringhurst, 1997), and in mathematical ratios such as the golden ratio and the Fibonacci sequence. By nature, many of these proportions are present in everything from the smallest microscopic molecules and crystals to plants and animals and our own anatomy. The fantastic thing is how wisely nature is set up. For in these proportions lies nature's genuine capacity for proportional modulability, something that makes nature a superior creator of solutions that are both practical and functional. A cone is beautiful in all its details, but it is also functional in design, because the seeds lie in a Fibonacci sequence, that is, the cone stores the maximum number of seeds, which in turn is essential for its task of propagating (4.8.8 Fibonacci). Here we will use some classic ratios and principles as an example of how sizes and proportions can be used intentionally, from the perimeter in a format to the grid system's smallest modules (4.7.2 Principles of composition, 4.7.5 Proportions).

### Mathematical proportions

The aspect ratio in a format is the ratio of the width to the height of the format. The aspect ratio of a two-dimensional figure is the ratio between the longest and the shortest side, between width and the height (Rouse, 2005) when the rectangle has landscape orientation. In mathematics, the ratio is expressed as two numbers separated by a colon, x:y (pronounced: x to y). The values x and y do not represent the actual width and height, but the 'ratio' of width to height. For example, 8:5, 16:10, and 1.6: 1 have the same aspect ratio ('Aspect Ratio,' n.d.).

'There are no rules, everything is tightly tied to each project' (Høie 2018).

*Rational numbers*: All rational numbers can be written as a ratio, a fraction, or a decimal number of a whole number (integer). Example: Ratio 1:2, fraction 1/2, recalculated 5/10 or decimal 0.5. In other words: 1:2 = 1/2 = 5/10 = 0,5. Rational numbers are symbolised by ℚ.
*Irrational numbers*: An irrational number is a real number that cannot be written as a fraction of two integers. There are a number of numerical ratios, a number of industrial standard sizes and a number of proportions, which include four irrational numbers of significant importance for the understanding and analysis of natural structures and processes (Bringhurst, 1996), for example:

Pi ($\pi$) = 3.14159... = the ratio of a circle's circumference to its diameter
$\sqrt{2}$ = 1.41421... = the diagonal of a square (A format)
$\phi$ = 1.61803... = the golden ratio

*Classic proportions*: Classic book design is a good starting point to talk about aspect ratios and proportions. Old book printing set the standard for much of what we perceive today as beautiful proportions. Old classical manuscripts and books from the Renaissance to modern times carry classical proportions as part of their identity. This does not mean that these proportions are reserved for book-design. In any design, creative and playful use of classic proportions can add something new and different to the design, while enriching it with aesthetic and functional qualities. Ratios from the old days were used for book formats and were often divisible in a way that was functional for the printing sheet. The perfect proportions from the European Middle Ages, which are still in use today, are the page proportions 2:3 (fifth) and 3:4 (fourth). Typographer and book-designer Jan Tschichold gave general advice on book formats: small books should be narrow, larger ones can be wide. The traditional octave format in 2:3 and the quarter-format in 3:4 he called 'husband and wife' - they are inextricably linked to each other in a functional relationship. If one folds (folds up) a 3:4 format, the new format becomes a 2:3-format (Rannem, 2008). The typical feature of several of the classic book formats is that the proportions alternate when folded in half. For example, a sheet with the proportions 5:8 produces two sheets with the proportions 4:5 when folded in half. If folded once again, it produces another sheet whose proportions are 5:8. In the same way, the proportion 1: 2 alternates with the ratio 1:1. In contrast, the format 1: $\sqrt{2}$ (A series) will retain its proportions when divided (Bringhurst, 1997, p. 147). See 4.8.4 A series.

*Format calculation based on aspect ratio*: An aspect ratio can be converted to actual size in the desired unit of measurement. The aspect ratio depends on whether the orientation is landscape or portrait. For example: You want to use the classic book format octave format (fifth), which has a size ratio of 2: 3. Let us say that the measure of the shortest

> Pure proportions, i.e. 1:2, 5:9, 2:3, 3:4 provide the best starting point for modular grid systems, which are proportional to the format.

Fig. 4.61 The figure shows Jan Tschichold's Van de Graaf canon, a reconstruction of a historical method that may have been used in book design to divide a page into pleasant proportions, also known as 'secret canon ', used in many medieval manuscripts and incunables. 'Canon' means rules or principles. Regardless of the size of the format, that is, the aspect ratio (width:height), this construction will result in a certain proportional size and placement of the page coverage on the format, which always gives the margin ratio 1/9 and 2/9 of the page size. This results in an inner margin that is half of the outer margin, and a margin ratio of 2:3:4:6 (inner:top:outer:bottom), when the aspect ratio is 2:3. Here is how to design a Van de Graaf canon: Make a sketch of the entire format. Draw a diagonal across the format 3) Draw a diagonal the other way. The point of intersection is the middle, 4) Draw a diagonal on each side starting from the margin and down in the opposite corner, 5) Draw a line from the intersection of the two diagonals up to the upper edge of the format.
Repeat section 5 on the left-hand side and draw diagonals across the sides from the outer points on each of the line segments. The intersections on each of the page formats make a corner on the two-page coverages, 7) The page coverage is drawn as shown in the figure. The result is a page coverage that is proportional to the aspect ratio/ format.

98 Already in the 1300s, Villard De Honnecourt arrived at a page coverage and margins calculation very similar to the principles shown in figure 4/64 His grid system made it possible to change the size of the page coverage, while retaining proportional size ratios on the margins.

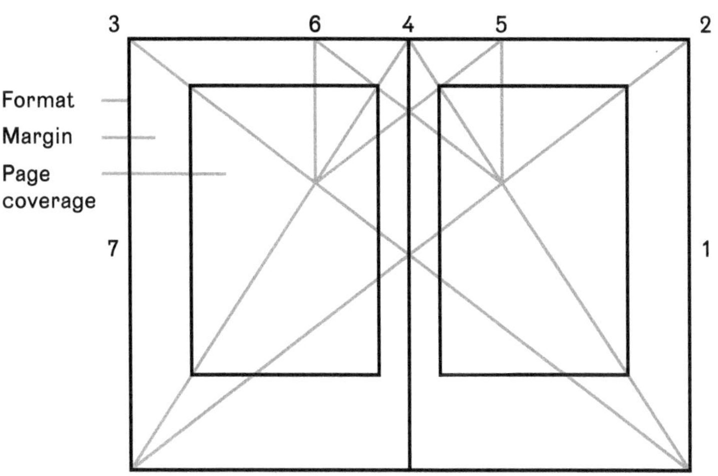


Fig. 4.61 Van de Graaf canon

1 Initiation
2 Insight
3 Strategy
4 Design
5 Production
6 Management

4.1 Design brief
4.2 Strategy><Design
4.3 Design methodology
4.4 Concept development
4.5 Design development
4.6 Design elements
4.7 Composition
4.8 Surface and format
4.9 Identity development

4.8.1 Surface
4.8.2 Format
4.8.3 Aspect ratios
4.8.4 The A series
4.8.5 The golden ratio
4.8.6 Golden rectangle
4.8.7 The golden spiral
4.8.8 Fibonacci
4.8.9 The rule of thirds

– Mathematical proportions

side is going to be 15 cm, and you want to figure out the measurement of the longest side. When you divide 15 by 2 and multiply by 3, you get 22.5. Length is 22.5. The size will then be 15 × 22.5 in the ratio 2:3. Optionally, you can multiply 15 times 3 and divide by 2, and you get the same result. This aspect ratio is a classic book format.

*Page coverage and margin construction*: There is a lot to learn from classic book design when it comes to choosing format, typed area and margins, whether it is design for print or digital media, where both functionality and aesthetics are essential. Few have been so concerned with creating greater awareness regarding the proportions of the book format as Jan Tschichold (Rannem, 2008). In the latter half of the 20th century, he popularised classical principles for book page construction based on the works of J. A. van de Graaf, Raúl M. Rosarivo, Hans Kayser and others[98] (Tschichold, Hartley and Marks, 1991, p. 46). These principles are equally relevant today for understanding the proportional and harmonious division of aspect ratios, whether the goal is to create a classic expression or use the principles in other contexts. Tschichold believed that one should stick to pure proportions, such as 1:2, 5:9, 2:3, 3:4 (Rannem/typografi.no) and other whole-number ratios, avoiding irrational numbers, like the golden ratio or what Tschichold called 5:8 'an approach to the golden ratio'. Pure proportions such as those he mentions are used as the basis for the construction of *The Van de Graaf canon* and Rosarivo's page proportions, see Figures 4.61 and 4.62. The most ideal aspect ratio for both of these construction methods is 2:3, but they can be used for any arbitrary aspect ratio to create a nice page coverage proportional to the format.

**Printing format:** A classic 2:3 book format is roughly equal to an A5. This format fits into a gross printing format in the old book-printing machines. The format was obtained based on the most economical use of the print format. Currently, format size is not associated with proportions in the same way. One has more freedom, but it has become all the more important to avoid wasting paper out of environmental considerations.

Further reading
The Best Dutch Book Designs: bestverzorgdeboeken.nl/en/.

2:3: Tscicholds van de Graaf canon can be used based on any format. The perfect format is the one based on the ratio 3, which also allows for a grid system in nine proportional parts horizontally and vertically, a so-called 'ninth'. The format can be drawn physically with a compass and ruler or in a drawing program using data. The result is a classic proportional page coverage and a grid system that is proportional to the format and the page coverage.

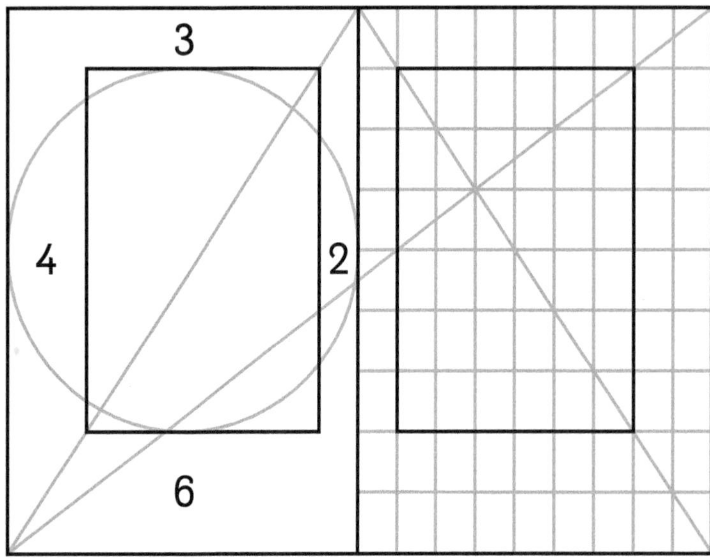


Fig. 4.62 The golden canon of page construction

2:3

Fig. 4.63 Aspect ratios

Fig. 4.62 The figure shows Tschichold's 'golden canon of page construction'. Jan Tschichold's example is a combination of the secret canon and Rosarivo's ninth. The secret canon is shown here on the left-hand side of the figure by a circle showing that the page coverage height is equal to the width of the format, and the result is a margin ratio of 2:3:4:6 (inner:top: outer:bottom), when the aspect ratio is 2:3, which is the starting point of the Van de Graf canon, as shown in the figure above. The right side of the Figure shows Rosarivo's construction by dividing the page into nine parts (ninth), based on page ratio 2:3, which, according to Tschichold, corresponded to a Van de Graaf canon.

Fig. 4.63 The aspect ratio 2:3 (approximately equal to format A5) was called the octave format or fifth in old book printing. This aspect ratio is the most ideal for constructing Tschichold's Van de Graaf canon, The secret canon and Rosarivo's ninth. See Figures 4.64 and 4.65.

Choosing formats that do not go up in the print sheet can mean poor utilisation of the print format and more paper cloak. An uneconomic exploitation of the surface may also mean a higher cost on the printed matter. It is therefore important to contact the printer when planning the format and choice of paper type in order to find out of the size of the gross format and its implications for format selection.

**Optimal optical perspective**

Old Greek architects counteracted the deformity that follows with visual perspective. Because Greek temples were buildings to stand over time, it was important that all parts were viewed in the correct size. Because objects look smaller when further away, Greek and Roman architects tried to counteract visual deception by adjusting the proportions. Objects further afield were enlarged to match the objects around them (Blankenbehler, 2014). For example, the architects made the pillars farthest away larger, even if it was mathematically incorrect, so that the pillars would be perceived as being of equal size. They adjusted the height of the pillars and the spacing between them, so that they would be perceived harmoniously and perfectly. The Greeks were more concerned with creating the perfect optical perspective than we are today. They had to deal with the rules of the time, which required them to spend time calculating and arriving at the optimal optical result.

99 An international standard is a technical standard developed by one or more international standards organisations. The most prominent such organisation is the International Organisation for Standardisation (ISO). ISO was founded 1947. The organisation develops and publishes worldwide technical, industrial and commercial standards. It is headquartered in Geneva, Switzerland and works in 165 countries (The International Organisation for Standardisation (ISO), n.d.). Other prominent international standards organisations include the International Telecommunication Union (ITU) and the International Electrotechnical Commission (IEC). Together, these three organisations formed the World Standards Cooperation alliance.

Paper for printing is available in a variety of standard sizes. Larger printed matter and books are printed on so-called printing sheets, with a number of 8, 16, 32 or optionally 12, 18 or 24 pages at a time, which are then folded, stapled and cut. Each of the 8, 16, or 32 pages is assembled in sets". The leaves are assembled into a book block, which is sewn and glued at the back. For example, a box size 17 × 24 cm requires an output format of 70 × 100 cm, providing 16 book pages on each side of the sheet (including space for cutting) (Rannem, 2004). Printing paper is available in a variety of standard stock formats that form the basis for the size of books and other printed matter (Rannem, 2012).


1 Initiation
2 Insight
3 Strategy
4 Design
5 Production
6 Management

4.1 Design brief
4.2 Strategy><Design
4.3 Design methodology
4.4 Concept development
4.5 Design development
4.6 Design elements
4.7 Composition
4.8 Surface and format
4.9 Identity development

4.8.1 Surface
4.8.2 Format
4.8.3 Aspect ratios
4.8.4 The A series
4.8.5 The golden ratio
4.8.6 Golden rectangle
4.8.7 The golden spiral
4.8.8 Fibonacci
4.8.9 The rule of thirds

– Mathematical proportions


**Classic book formats**

Here is an overview of classic book formats, based on page proportions, from the times when narrower format range applied. Many of these are inaccurate and no longer in use, but they give a good indication of the principle of how the printed sheet is folded and how this affects the formats and the number of book pages per printed sheet. Two book pages (spread) per sheet:

**Folio:** 2 sheets = 4 pages (approx. size A3), abbreviated f°. The biggest book format. The printed sheet is folded once to produce two sheets. (Aspect ratio 2:3.) Quarto: 4 sheets = 8 pages (approx. A4 or smaller), cf. 4°. The printed sheet is folded twice to produce four sheets. (Aspect ratio 3:4.)
**Octavo:** 8 sheets = 16 pages (approx. size A5 or smaller), (Lat. octo, eight; octavus, eighth, i.e. eighth size; also written 8vo or 8°). The printed sheet is folded three times to produce eight sheets. (Aspect ratio 2:3.)
**Duodecimo:** 12 sheets = 24 pages (approx. size A3: Of duodecim (lat.): twelve. The printed sheet is folded four times to produce 12 sheets. (Aspect ratio 3:4.)
**Sextodecimo:** 16 sheets = 32 pages (approx. size A3: Of sedecim (lat.): sixteen. The printed sheet is folded four times to produce 12 sheets. (Aspect ratio 2:3.) (Rannem, typografi.no)

*For page relationships in a book format, the old terms are 'minor' for the smallest part and 'major' for the largest part. Note: The octavo format in Norwegian is 'fifth' in English (Rannem).*

### 4.8.4 The A series

While the octavo and quarto formats were standard ratios in the old book printing days, The A series is an example of a standard paper size that is commonly used today. The A-size is one of more series in the ISO 216 standard, which is the international standard[99] for paper size. It is used across the world except in North America and parts of Central and South America, where paper sizes such as 'Letter' and 'Legal' are used. For many of us, the A4 or Letter, are paper sizes we use daily, not primarily because of its visual qualities, but mainly for its functional

Format crop example
Gross format (uncut): The gross size is 17.5 × 25 cm : 70 cm: 4 page widths = 17.5 cm/100 cm: 4 page heights = 25 cm
Net format (cropped): After the sheets are folded and assembled into a book block, it is cut 0.3 cm in the head, 0.7 cm in the lower edge and 0.5 cm in the outer edge. The net format is 17 × 24 cm (which is a widely used textbook format).

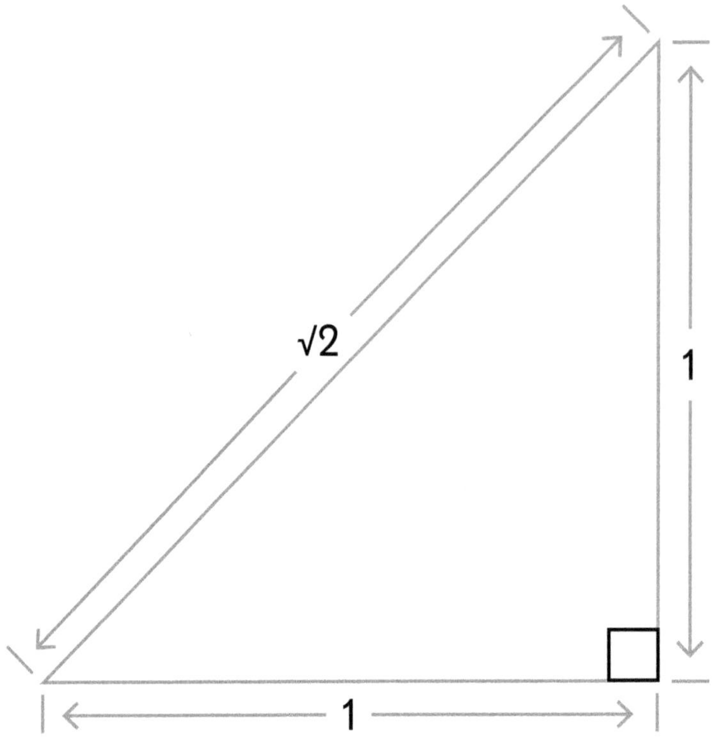


Fig. 4.64 Root-2 rectangle

ones. These paper formats have numbers of advantageous features for their use, such as in business printed matter, reports, public documents and the like where standardisation is of the utmost importance as far as paper, printers and binders are concerned.

We will take a closer look at the A series. Besides functional considerations, an A4 size or other sizes from the A series, is rarely the designer's first choice when choosing a paper format, because it is so common. Where it is still used, much can be done by choosing a dynamic shape on the typed area and being playful with the composition of

Fig. 4.65 Root-5 rectangle

Fig. 4.64 The figure shows the root-2 rectangle ('Square root of 2', n.d.). The long side of the A format is approximately 1.4142 times the short side. A root rectangle is a rectangle in which the ratio of the longer side to the shorter is the square root of an integer, such as √2, √3, etc. (C.H. Beck, 1990). A root rectangle is a rectangle in which the ratio of the longer side to the shorter is the square root of an integer, such as √2, √3, etc. (Skinner, 2006).

Fig. 4.65 The figure shows how a root-5 rectangle can be constructed by repeating the procedure as shown in the first rectangle. The ratio of the longitudinal side to the short side of a root-5 rectangle is the square root of five. Although the root-5 rectangle can be calculated based on the root-5 principle, it is not within the A series. The root-5 rectangle has one square and two golden ratio sections in it. The figure further shows how two golden ratios fit into a root-5 rectangle. This format can be found in frescoes and triptychs in old churches (Pentak and Laurer, p. 85).

Fig. 4.66 The figure shows the different sizes of the A format. As the figure shows, an A format is divisible by itself. The A format can be constructed by drawing a geometric arc from the left corner point of a square through the corner point lying diagonally to the right. Set a point in the extension of the side of the square, where the geometric arc intersects in the extension of the bottom line of the square. Extend the line from the square to the new point. Draw a corresponding line as an extension of the top line of the square. Connect the two extremes with a line, forming the right-hand side of the A4 format.

Tips for the designer

What is the format of an A4 sheet? If you are a designer, you would answer straight away.

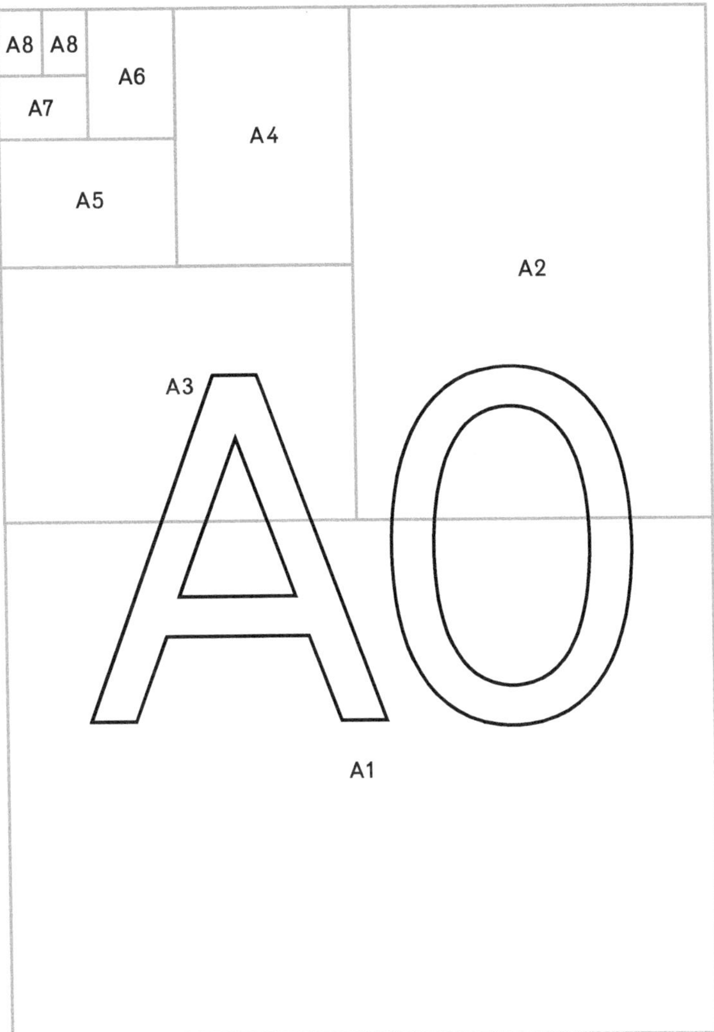


Fig. 4.66 The A format

elements on the surface. When used consciously, the A-size proportions can provide a functionally modulable grid system, because when dividing the format it retains its proportions. The ratio of the long side to the short side is constant. For example, an A4 sheet divided in two across the longitudinal side will produce two A5 sheets. Similarly, an A3 sheet is twice the size of an A4 sheet.

**Root-2 rectangle:** The A format is also called a root-2 rectangle because the ratio of the long side to the short side is the square root of 2. 'The short side of the rectangle relates to the long side as 1: √2 or as the side of the square to its diagonal (Lichtenberg 1785–1792). The aspect ratio is kept when the format is divided. This means that A5 is exactly similar to A4, but the area is half as large. The downscaling percentage of A4 to A5 format is 71%, while the upscaling of A4 to A3 is 141% (Rannem, 2008).

A4-size: 210mm × 297mm (8.27 inches × 11.7 inches). A0-size: It has an area of 1m2, and the dimensions are 841mm × 1189mm. It is the largest sheet of the A series. Letter: 8.5 × 11 inches. Legal: 8.5 × 14 inches. Tabloid: 11 × 17 inches. The North American paper sizes Letter, Legal and Tabloid are based on traditional formats with arbitrary aspect ratios.

### Format sizes and weight

The A format is a standard paper format series used in most countries around the world, and for most printers, binders and document formats. **The A series** (ISO 216)[100] is based on A0, which has an area of 1 $m^2$ (841 × 1189 mm). A4 has a surface of 1/16 $m^2$. The other formats are obtained by dividing the larger format across into two, such as A1 is 549 × 841 mm, exactly half of A0. A2 is 420 × 594 mm, half of A1, and so on. This proportional division is not self-evident when it comes to other formats, something one can test by dividing any other format into two equal parts at ratio 1:2. The new format will then be in 1:1 ratio (Rannem, 2008).
**The B series** (ISO 216) is slightly larger than the A format in order to cover a wider range of paper formats, where the A series does not suffice, such as for envelopes. The starting point for the B series is 1000 × 1414 mm, a format where the short side is exactly 1 metre.
**The C series** (ISO 269) is the international standard format for envelopes.
**Weight:** It says '80 grams' on A4 plain copy paper. This means 80 gram per square metre (g/m2), i.e. 80 grams per A0 sheet. An A4 copy sheet weighs 5 grams. To find the weight of any 80-gram sheet, one can use the following formula, where n denotes the size in the A series and m denotes the weight in grams: m=80/2n ('ISO 216,' n.d.) (See chapter 5.4.4 Paper properties).

| A series ISO 216 | | B series ISO 216 | | C series ISO 269 | |
|---|---|---|---|---|---|
| Format | Size (mm × mm) | Format | Size (mm × mm) | Format | Size (mm × mm) |
| A0 | 841 × 1189 | B0 | 1000 × 1414 | C0 | 917 × 1297 |
| A1 | 594 × 841 | B1 | 707 × 1000 | C1 | 648 × 917 |
| A2 | 420 × 594 | B2 | 500 × 707 | C2 | 458 × 648 |
| A3 | 297 × 420 | B3 | 353 × 500 | C3 | 324 × 458 |
| A4 | 210 × 297 | B4 | 250 × 353 | C4 | 229 × 324 |
| A5 | 148 × 210 | B5 | 176 × 250 | C5 | 162 × 229 |
| A6 | 105 × 148 | B6 | 125 × 176 | C6 | 114 × 162 |
| A7 | 74 × 105 | B7 | 88 × 125 | C7/6 | 81 × 162 |
| A8 | 52 × 74 | B8 | 62 × 88 | C7 | 81 × 114 |
| A9 | 37 × 52 | B9 | 44 × 62 | C8 | 57 × 81 |
| A10 | 26 × 37 | B10 | 31 × 44 | C9 | 40 × 57 |
| | | | | C10 | 28 × 40 |
| | | | | DL | 110 × 220 |

Table 4.9 The most common paper sizes

Table 4.9 The overview shows: The different sub-formats of the A format, based on the basic format A0. All A-size formats are based on A0, which has an area of 1 $m^2$. A4 has a surface of 1/16 $m^2$.

Fig. 4.67 The figure shows the structure of the golden ratio: On a line AC, draw a line CD perpendicular to AC. Let CD be half AC. Draw a line between AD. Let D be the centre of a circle with radius DC. The circle intersects AD in E. Let A be the centre of a circle with radius AE. This circle intersects AC in the golden ratio B. The golden ratio can also be constructed by constructing the golden rectangle, see next section. The golden rectangle and the golden spiral are both based on the golden ratio (based on kunstoghaandverk.org).

Fig. 4.68 The figure shows the golden ratio, which is based on the principle that the number ratio between two quantities shows how many times a value contains or exists within the other. Mathematically, this can be expressed as follows: If segment AB is divided into a point S so that the ratio of AB to AS is equal to the ratio of AS to BS, S is said to divide AB into the golden ratio. Calculated in numbers, the ratio of the long side to the short side of the golden ratio (phi – φ) is approximately 1:1.618. The long part of the line is 1.618 times longer than the short part, while the whole line is 1.618 times longer than the long part. A line of 1000 mm will be divided by the golden ratio if the longest section is 618 mm and the shortest section is 382 mm ('Golden ratio,' n.d.).

1 Initiation
2 Insight
3 Strategy
4 Design
5 Production
6 Management

4.1 Design brief
4.2 Strategy><Design
4.3 Design methodology
4.4 Concept development
4.5 Design development
4.6 Design elements
4.7 Composition
4.8 Surface and format
4.9 Identity development

4.8.1 Surface
4.8.2 Format
4.8.3 Aspect ratios
4.8.4 The A series
4.8.5 The golden ratio
4.8.6 Golden rectangle
4.8.7 The golden spiral
4.8.8 Fibonacci
4.8.9 The rule of thirds

– History behind the golden ratio


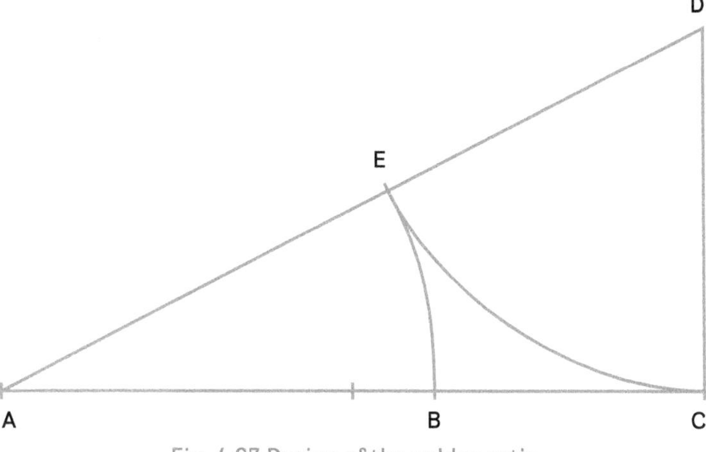


Fig. 4.67 Design of the golden ratio

### 4.8.5 The golden ratio

The golden ratio is a harmonious division of a line into two mutually proportional parts, one long and one short. According to classical theory, the same harmonious conditions are to be found naturally in plants, living organisms and in human anatomy. The relationship between the length from the shoulder to the fingertips and the length from the elbow to the fingertips, the knuckles of the hand and the length of the legs to the length from the knee to the toes are some of the examples of this (Hrant, 2014, p. 404). Ever since the ancient Greeks defined their mathematical theories of the golden ratio, these harmonious proportions and aesthetic qualities have captivated artists, architects, and designers. Deliberately or unconsciously, the golden ratio has been used in architecture and design for centuries, leaving many iconic models behind. One of the things that makes the golden ratio interesting to a designer today is the harmonic proportions and possibilities of proportional scaling.

Fig. 4.68 The golden ratio

The golden ratio is a proportional division of a line into two: a long and a short one. The ratio of the longest to the shortest part is equal to the ratio of the whole segment to the longest part (Hrant, 2014).

#### History behind the golden ratio

Among ancient Greeks, mathematicians such as Pythagoras and Hippasus have left their mark for posterity. Their mathematical theories paved the way for the Greek Euclid of Alexandria, the father of geometry, who was the first to define the golden ratio. Over 2,000 years ago, he said that a line is divided into the golden ratio if the whole line is in the same relation to the large section, as the large section is to the small one. The

100 ISO is an independent, non-governmental international organisation with a membership of 165 national standards bodies. Through its members, it brings together experts to share knowledge and develop voluntary, consensus-based, market-relevant international standards that support innovation and provide solutions to global challenges. ISO has published more than 19,000 international standards. (Iso.org, 'ISO 2016', n.d.) In addition to the A, B and C series, there are some help series with medium sizes D, E, F and G, former Swedish standards (SIS), which should cover the demand for more sizes.

$$\frac{a+b}{a}=\frac{a}{b}=\Phi$$

$$\Phi=\frac{1+\sqrt{5}}{2}\approx 1{,}618033989$$

Fig. 4.69 Phi

world's first book on the golden ratio was written by the mathematician Luca Bartolomeo de Pacioli in 1487. It was illustrated by the artist, scientist, and inventor Leonardo da Vinci (1452–1519). The book includes the great Roman architect Marcus Vitruvius Pollio and his ideas that an ideal human body fits perfectly into both a square and a circle. This was an idea later illustrated by Leonardo da Vinci in his famous drawing *The Vitruvian Man*. It was only in 1835 that the phrase '*golden ratio' (goldener Schnitt*) was presented in *the book Die Reine Elementar-Matematik* by Martin Ohm 1835 (Geelmuyden, 2013).

**A myth?**

'The golden ratio is total nonsense in design' (Brownlee, 2015). There are those who believe that the golden ratio is just a myth. The reason, among other things, is that if you have two objects (or a single object that can be split into two objects, like the golden rectangle), and if, after you do the maths, you get the number 1.6180, it's usually accepted that those two objects fall within the golden ratio. The problem, according to Brownlee, is that when you do the maths, the golden ratio does not come out to 1.6180. It comes out to 1.6180339887... And the decimal points go on forever.

### 4.8.6 Golden rectangle

Constructed from the principles of the golden ratio, the golden rectangle has the classic proportions often associated with natural beauty and harmony. Consciously used, the golden rectangle can be a good starting point for defining proportions for formats, objects and spaces that are proportionately scalable, perceived as aesthetic, and that provide a sense of quality and harmony. The aspect ratio of the golden rectangle can be repeated and expanded within the same number ratios, both vertically and horizontally. This provides an optimal starting point for creating an aesthetic and functional modular grid system, with similarity between the format's external proportions and the internal size ratios. The golden ratio can be found in many logo designs, including the logos of Toyota, Chevron, Nissan, National Geographic, even though this has probably not been the designer's intention. And if we take a look around us, we will probably discover a golden rectangle in a table, a book, a window, a vase. But it is not always intentional, because it might have been the designer's built-in talent for proportions that has led to the result being close to the golden ratio. The closer the ratio between the length and

Fig. 4.69 The figures above show ratios giving φ with the designation Phi. Phi or fi (Φ, φ, ϕ) is the 21st letter of the Greek alphabet ('Phi,' n.d.). In modern Greek, it corresponds to the Roman 'f'. φ is used as a symbol in a variety of theories and principles. In mathematics, art, design and architecture φ is an irrational number,[101] which corresponds/ symbolises the golden ratio: 1.61803398874989484 8204586834...

Fig. 4.70 The figure shows how to construct a golden rectangle. Draw a geometric arc from the midpoint of one side of the square to an opposite corner. Set a point, extending the side of the square where it cuts the geometric arc. Extend the line from the square to the new point. Draw a corresponding line as an extension of the opposite side of the square. Connect the two extremes with a line. The entire rectangle and the small rectangle inside it both have proportions like the golden rectangle, meaning that the proportions of the golden ratio are found in both the short and the long sides of the rectangle ('Golden rectangle,' n.d.).

Fig. 4.71 The figure shows the mathematical definition of the golden rectangle.

The golden ratio also has a long and strong tradition in typography and book production; writers and monks used it long before Gutenberg's time. The golden ratio can be used as ratio not only in format and page coverage, but also, for example, in the contrast in font size (Rannem/ typografi.no).

101 An irrational number means a number with infinitely many decimal places, which means that the number is neither a whole number, nor a fraction between two whole numbers.

1 Initiation
2 Insight
3 Strategy
4 Design
5 Production
6 Management

4.1 Design brief
4.2 Strategy><Design
4.3 Design methodology
4.4 Concept development
4.5 Design development
4.6 Design elements
4.7 Composition
4.8 Surface and format
4.9 Identity development

4.8.1 Surface
4.8.2 Format
4.8.3 Aspect ratios
4.8.4 The A series
4.8.5 The golden ratio
4.8.6 Golden rectangle
4.8.7 The golden spiral
4.8.8 Fibonacci
4.8.9 The rule of thirds

– History behind the golden ratio


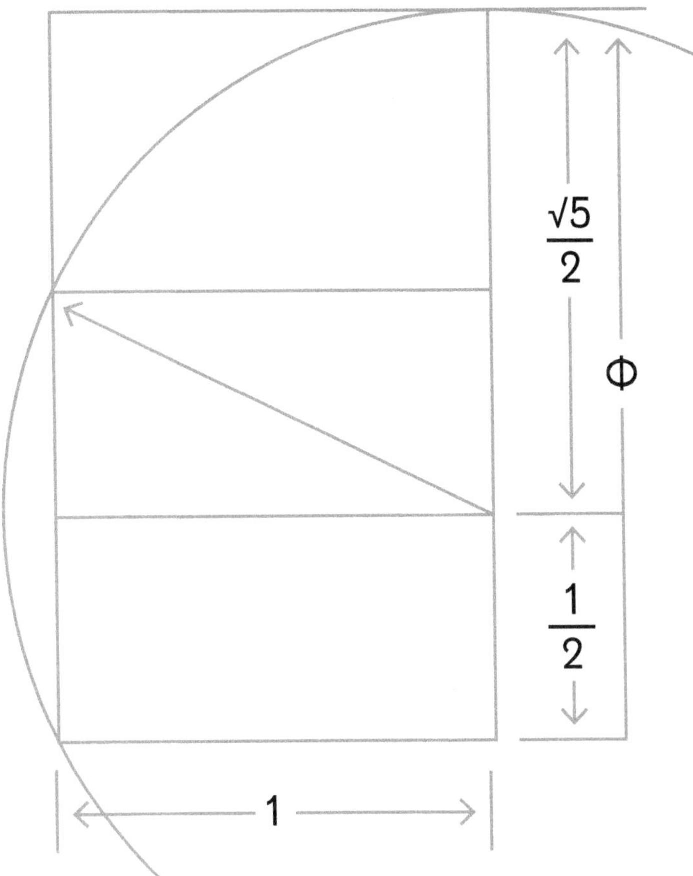


Fig. 4.70 The golden rectangle

width of the rectangle is to 1.618, the more certain you can be that the ratio is placed there intentionally (Geelmuyden, 2013).

The golden rectangle may be said to be the simplest shape based on the golden ratio (Geelmuyden, 2013), where the ratio between the long side and the short side approaches Φ (1: 1.618). In the golden rectangle, the short side of the rectangle is equal to the shortest part of the segment, while the long side is equal to the longest part of the segment. Both the short side and the long side have proportions like the golden ratio.

$$\sqrt{\left(\frac{1}{2}\right)^2} + \sqrt{\left(\frac{2}{2}\right)^2} = \sqrt{\left(\frac{5}{4}\right)^2} = \sqrt{\left(\frac{5}{2}\right)^2}$$

Φ will be

$$\sqrt{\left(\frac{1}{2}\right)^2} + \sqrt{\left(\frac{5}{2}\right)^2} = 1{,}618033988749894 82\ldots$$

Fig. 4.71 The golden rectangle

The Vitruvian man

Leonardo da Vinci's drawing from 1487 is claimed to be among the clearest examples of the golden ratio in art and human proportions. The drawing illustrates a man in a circle and a square, with four arms and four legs. The navel is the centre of the circle, dividing the man's height at the golden ratio. The horizontal lines on the chest are placed using the same ratio. The same applies to distance from the shoulder to the fingertips, and from the elbow to the fingertips as well. Similarly, the drawing illustrates several other conditions corresponding to the golden ratio (Geelmuyden, 2013, p. 10).

## 4.8.7 The golden spiral

The golden spiral is constructed based on the golden ratio principle. We find it in many places in nature, such as in a conch shell, in a wave, in the human ear. The golden spiral has an outer shape with the same proportions as the golden rectangle. The same proportions are repeated in all the rectangles from which the spiral is built, all the way into the core. The golden spiral is proportional both vertically and horizontally, and can be built from the outside in or from the inside out infinitely. Or put in another way: It can be divided into smaller golden rectangles or more golden rectangles can be added. (4.8.5 The golden ratio, 4.9.9 Grid system)

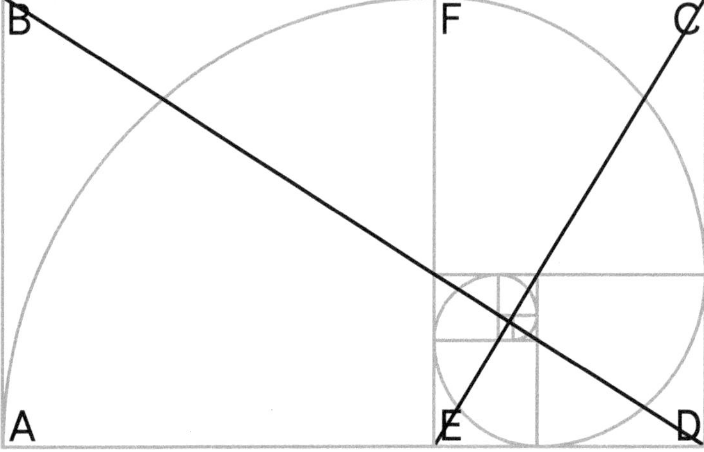


Fig. 4.72 The golden spiral

Fig. 4.73 The golden spiral in a snail's house

Fig. 4.72 The figure shows how to construct a golden spiral: Start by constructing a golden rectangle, as described in the previous section. Draw a square on the long side of the rectangle. This will be part of a new golden rectangle. Draw a new square along the long side of the new rectangle. This will be part of another new golden rectangle. Continue like this until the desired level of detail is achieved. Start drawing the spiral by creating a circle whose centre is the innermost left-hand corner of the innermost square. Draw a new circle with the innermost left-hand corner of the second innermost square as centre. Continue until the spiral is finished. The outer shape has the same proportions as the golden rectangle. The same applies to the inner rectangle as well, and to all the rectangles between the outer and the inner rectangle. The intersection of the diagonals is the centre of the spiral.[102]

Fig. 4.73 In nature, the golden spiral is omnipresent. The best example of that is a snail's shell. (Photo: Desayere, J./ unsplash.com)

Fig. 4.74 The figure shows a grid system of squares where all side lengths are consecutive Fibonacci numbers, 1, 1, 2, 3, 5, 8, 13, 21 and 34. Here is how the grid can be designed: Start by drawing two parallel squares. Draw a square using the width of the two squares. Then draw a new square using the length of the previous square and the side of the smallest square and so on. The grid system forms the basis for a Fibonacci spiral, which, in the same way as for the golden spiral, can be constructed by drawing circular arcs connecting the opposite corners of the squares and so on (Tiner, 2004).

102 There are several tutorials on YouTube on how to construct a golden spiral. For example: Arthur Geometry, 24 Dec 2015.

## 4.8.8 Fibonacci

The Fibonacci sequence is nature's very own logical numbering system. It is a principle that can also be used in design for creating logical modulable sequences and sizes. The Fibonacci number sequence is a series of irrational numbers, each number being the sum of the two preceding: 1, 1, 2, 3, 5, 8, 13, 21, 34, 55, 89, 144, 233, 377 ... Fibonacci numbers are found in many places in nature, such as in the way the branches of a tree, the petals of a flower, or the seeds of a cone are arranged. Take the sunflower, for example. The parts forming the flower lie in perfect spirals of 55, 34 and 21. This wise device by nature ensures a maximum number of seeds in the sunflower and maximum distribution of sunlight. The Fibonacci numbers can be used in

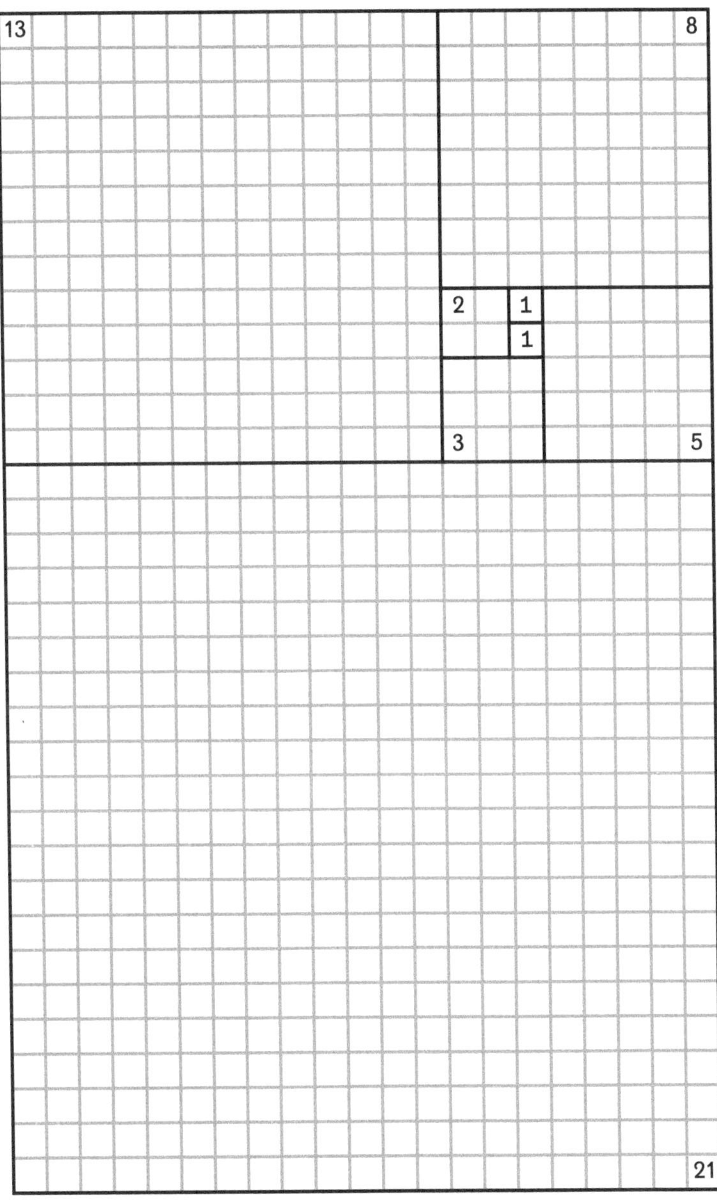


Fig. 4.74 Fibonacci

1 Initiation
2 Insight
3 Strategy
4 Design
5 Production
6 Management

4.1 Design brief
4.2 Strategy><Design
4.3 Design methodology
4.4 Concept development
4.5 Design development
4.6 Design elements
4.7 Composition
4.8 Surface and format
4.9 Identity development

4.8.1 Surface
4.8.2 Format
4.8.3 Aspect ratios
4.8.4 The A series
4.8.5 The golden ratio
4.8.6 Golden rectangle
4.8.7 The golden spiral
4.8.8 Fibonacci
4.8.9 The rule of thirds

Tips for the designer

The golden spiral can be a good starting point for constructing natural proportions and harmonic relationships between elements in any composition, whether it is a matter of a photo, a logo or a web page.

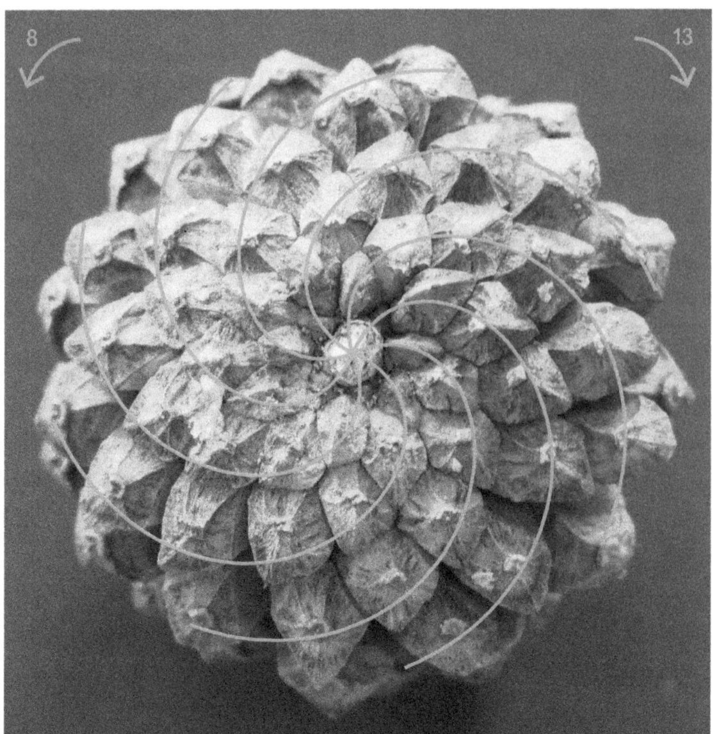


Fig. 4.75 Fibonacci in a cone

Fig. 4.75 The picture shows how the Fibonacci numbers can be read in the location of the seeds. Photo: Wanda Grimsgaard, 2022. © Grimsgaard, W. (2022).

Fig. 4.76 The figure shows the four intersecting points that appear in a rule of thirds composition. According to these principles, these four points have the most optimal focus within a composition. When positioning something at or near these points, the designer should decide which of the four points should be hierarchically the most important. Knowing the rule of thirds makes it easier for designers to consciously use those areas of the surface, which most easily attract the viewers' attention. The elements do not need to be placed directly at or within the points. The proximity is sufficient to draw attention to them (Elam, 2004, p. 13).

graphic design to construct grids or patterns in order to achieve similar structures and qualities that are found naturally in many plants and trees. The Fibonacci sequence was the inspiration for a solar panel development experiment conducted by the 13-year-old Aidan Dwyer in 2011.[103]

*Here is how the Fibonacci numbers work*: Each number is the sum of the previous two numbers. If you add the first two numbers 0 and 1, you get 1, you add 1 and 1, you get 2, and so the number sequence goes on infinitely. The conditions of the golden ratio can also be found in the infinite Fibonacci numbers. By dividing two numbers in the Fibonacci sequence, one gets close to the golden ratio. Example: 144:89≈1,6179≈1.618 (last decimal rounded off to 8). Proportion can also be expressed in the aspect ratio 21:34 (Rannem, 2008). The relationship between the golden ratio and the Fibonacci numbers can be explained by a calculation, which is both long and complex. The fascinating thing about the connection between the Fibonacci numbers and the golden ratio is that the two mathematical theories were probably defined independently of each other.[104]

### The story behind the Fibonacci Sequence

Filius Bonacci (1170–1250), originally called Leonardo Bonacci, was the originator of the Fibonacci Sequence. He used the Hindu-Arabic numerical system instead of the Roman one, which was common in Europe at the time for solving mathematical problems. One of the problems that fascinated him was: How many pairs of rabbits can a single pair of rabbits produce in one year if each pair gives life to a new pair of rabbits each month and each new pair of rabbits can start to reproduce when they are one month old, if no rabbits die? Fibonacci arrived at 377 pairs of rabbits

103 The experiment attracted a lot of media attention: ***13-Year-Old Designs Super-Effective Solar Array Based on the Fibonacci Sequence*** (Boyle, 2011). Sehgal (2011) writes in the article 'Blog Debunks 13-Year-Old Scientist's Solar Power Breakthrough' that according to the blog The Capacity Factor, this case was blown out of proportion by the media. Here there were shortcomings in the conducting of the experiment and cracks in theory.

104 Comparison of Fibonacci numbers and the golden ratio ('Golden ratio,' n.d.).

in one year and 39 million pairs of rabbits in three years. What he found out was that rabbit development follows a simple number sequence. This sequence, one of the world's simplest number sequences, was named the Fibonacci Sequence in the early 19th century by the mathematician Éduard Lucas (Geelmuyden, 2013).


1 Initiation
2 Insight
3 Strategy
4 Design
5 Production
6 Management

4.1 Design brief
4.2 Strategy><Design
4.3 Design methodology
4.4 Concept development
4.5 Design development
4.6 Design elements
4.7 Composition
4.8 Surface and format
4.9 Identity development

4.8.1 Surface
4.8.2 Format
4.8.3 Aspect ratios
4.8.4 The A series
4.8.5 The golden ratio
4.8.6 Golden rectangle
4.8.7 The golden spiral
4.8.8 Fibonacci
4.8.9 The rule of thirds

– The story behind the Fibonacci Sequence


**The Modulor Man**

The Modulor was devised by the Swiss-born French architect Le Corbusier (1887–1965), as a solution for harmonious standardisation of mass production based on mathematical foundations and human scale. The Modulor Man is based on the height of a human with one arm raised. Le Corbusier declared that the sequences of the Modulor create a measuring tool for harmonious design, a reference tool in designing new buildings. Among various metrics the Fibonacci sequence and the golden ratio are subtly included. 'While not being practical, it is considered by many scholars as a compelling marriage of mathematics and art' (Rozhkovskaya, 2019).

## 4.8.9 The rule of thirds

The rule of thirds is a guideline or 'rule of thumb' that applies to the composition of photo motifs, layout, films and paintings, and is well suited as basis for the development of a grid system when creating web pages and printed matter. The principle implies that a photo is intended to be divided into nine equal parts, two vertical and two horizontal, with equal distances between them. The main compositional elements should be placed along these lines or where they intersect. The grid system can be used when composing a motive to create greater dynamic in the image, including a more deliberate alignment of objects on the surface, conscious choice of focus point, as well as horizontal alignment.

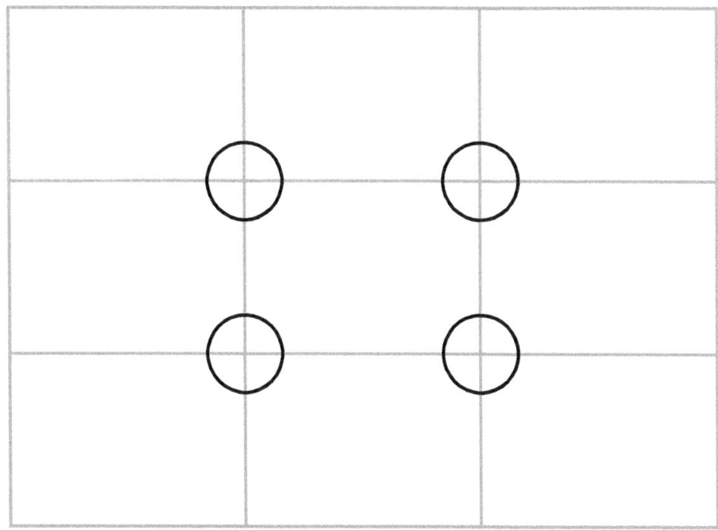

Fig. 4.76 The rule of thirds

Tips for the designer
**Identity and values are closely linked. Here you are at the intersection of strategy and design. Check out the chapters 3.2.5 Core values and 4.2.2 Visualise strategy.**

**The core values are the foundation for developing a visual identity.**

Identity is at the core of any design and strategic choice when it comes to how a company, a product, or a service will appear.

Identity is not just name, symbol, and logo. An object per se is identity, by virtue of its shape, colour, and material structure. Rooms and interiors are also identity, something experienced when entering a reception, a showroom or a trade fair stand. Surface is identity, too, whether a wall, a sign, a product, or a brochure, expressed through the shape, colour, structure, and message of the surface. What and how the company communicates is part of its identity. The same applies to the company's service, tone, attitudes, choices, actions and behaviour, see Figure 3.4 Corporate identity. The way the surroundings perceive the identity is essential when the company wants to take a position, create an image, be recognised, and build a brand. The heart of the identity are the core values, defined in the company's overall strategy (3.2 Overall strategy, 3.2.3 Core values).

Identity is about recognisability. Identity comes from *idem*, 'the same', which refers to aspects of a person, which are assumed to be more constant or unchangeable over time. Having identity can simply be described as being equal to oneself, identifiable by its feasibility (Rybakken, 2004). A recognisable visual identity is a competitive factor in any context in which a company, product, or service is to build a brand and convey its message, whether in commercial or non-profit context. In the struggle for people's attention, it is essential to give a company, a product, a garment, or a piece of furniture a distinctive character, something unique, something that can be recognised – a name, a logo, a colour, a shape, a wrapping, a message – which, with repeated use, creates recognisability and allows people to find it, recognise it, and make it a brand. The timeliness and value of the product are judged by its brand. The brand gives the character (Rybakken, 2004) and influences the value of the product or service the buyer perceives.

### Visual identity

The visual design and the presentation of the identity of a company, product, or service is called visual identity or profile. The term 'profile' of a company stems from the identification of a person. A person often has a characteristic and easily recognisable facial profile. In the past, the term 'profile' was used more frequently to describe the logo and overall visual image of a company. Today, it is more common to use the term 'visual identity' for the same. Names, logos, and symbols are key elements of identity, which, supported by colours, typography, patterns, graphic elements and visual forms, constitute a visual identity. A holistic and consistent use of the identity elements on different profile carriers produces the best foundation for building identity and brand awareness (4.9.2 Identity elements, 3.7.6 Brand assets).

### A strong identity

The visual identity of a company can be left to chance, or it can be planned consciously and consistently down to the smallest detail. The same applies to the company's products and services. The success factor lies in creating a holistic, consistent and credible identity, which is perceived the same way at all times, and which lives up to its promises. The strongest identity is the one that reflects the characteristics and values of the product, so that there is the best possible connection between the visible and inherent identity of the product (Rybakken, 2004). The same goes for a company. It does little good to have a great logo if the company's behaviour and actions give conflicting signals, or if the company's products or services do not meet expectations. For example, if the identity design expresses high quality, it is a promise that must be fulfilled. 'It can take 100 years to build up a good brand and 30 days to knock it down' (Naomi Klein 1999).

If the designer has fully comprehended the strategic foundation of the company or has participated in developing the strategy, the work on developing the visual profile will never be random. Then, the designer will know what the company does, for whom, where and why, what its goals and vision are, what its core values are, how the company would like to position and differentiate itself, what its desired reputation is and not least how the company's brand capital is intended develop over time. This insight will influence the choice of font, shape, colour, and other visual instruments when developing the visual identity. The main strategic basis for developing a company's visual identity is defined in its core values and value proposition. For products and services, also the brand position is crucial as a foundation. Basically, it is all about communication. Visual identity is communication. Therefore, having a communication strategy is absolutely essential (Table 3.2 Top 5 – strategic management tools, 3.2.5 Core values, 3.2.6 Value proposition, 3.7.3 Brand position, 3.8 Communication strategy).

1 Initiation
2 Insight
3 Strategy
4 Design
5 Production
6 Management

4.1 Design brief
4.2 Strategy><Design
4.3 Design methodology
4.4 Concept development
4.5 Design development
4.6 Design elements
4.7 Composition
4.8 Surface and format
4.9 Identity development

4.9.1 The identity principles
4.9.2 The identity elements
4.9.3 Logo
4.9.4 Symbol
4.9.5 Identity colours
4.9.6 Typography
4.9.7 Distinctive assets
4.9.8 Identity management
4.9.9 Grid system

### 4.9.1 The identity principles

When developing a visual identity, there are many things to consider. The identity principles are a useful starting point for clarifying key strategic issues and looking at the task in a larger context. In smaller projects, they can be used in a pre-project and for light strategy planning. In larger projects, they can be part of a broader strategic process and used in a design development plan (3.9 Design strategy). Here are the seven identity principles based on Rybakken (2004). The first thing to decide is: Who or what is the subject of the identity? Is it a matter of company, a product, or a service?

**1) Identity objectives:** Clarify which ambition, values, function, characteristics, benefits, and position should be expressed through identity. What are the actual communication needs? What impression should it leave? *Example*: Imagine that the identity object is a product, for example, a bottle of ketchup. What do we want to do with this ketchup, make it stand out more clearly, stand out better from the competition, be experienced as more modern or something else? (3.7.3 Brand position).

**2) Degree of interest:** Timeliness, season, trend, assumed demand? Interest affects accessibility. What interest is there for the object? Low interest? High interest? If it is a matter of volume products like holiday trips, electricity, gasoline, milk, bread, ketchup, it is all about catching

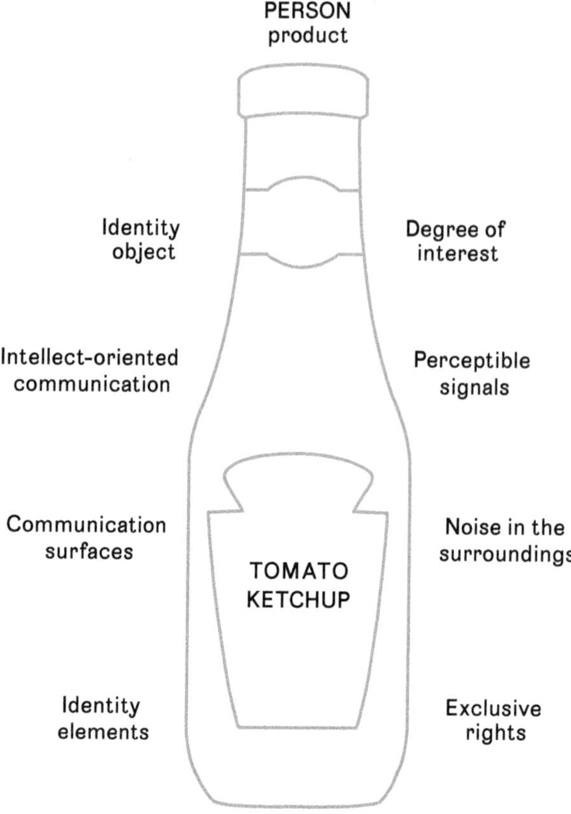


Fig. 4.77 Identity principles

Fig. 4.77 The figure shows the principles of identity. Here, as a starting point for developing the visual identity of a product. Based on Rybakken, 2004. © Grimsgaard, W. (2018).

Fig. 4.78 The figure shows how much more effective a short name is compared to a long one. Whether or not to take this into account depends on the task of the logo and where the logo is to be exposed. Should the logo be displayed primarily on a delivery truck, on a plane or at an online store? It is important to consider the physical shape of the surface when developing and selecting the name and logo. The physical shape of the communication surface may determine the length of a name or the perception quality of a logo. © Grimsgaard, W. (2018).

Fig. 4.79 The figure shows an example of communication surfaces for a product. © Grimsgaard, W. (2018).

Tips for the designer
**If we consider the exposure surfaces of a grocery product, the back or the label bottom will hardly be the surfaces that best expose the product information. For example, the bottom part of a product label is often hidden behind the edge of the shelf.**

> The logo is the label of the identity (Rybakken, 2004).

the eye. If it is a matter of an exclusive trip for mountain climbers to the Himalayas or niche products like HiFi speakers from Bang & Olufsen, it is all about capturing interest. We need to find out what triggers interest in order to send out signals that the interested party perceives. The visual identity should reflect the signals that trigger interest. Example: To some, ketchup is of great interest: 'I put ketchup on my ketchup' (Heinz). For most people, ketchup is used to spice up a meal, and is a must on sausages or hamburgers. In some seasons people eat more sausage or hamburger because of convenience, like during the barbecue season. Ketchup is easily available in all shops and most refrigerators. For many, ketchup is ketchup. How can we make people strive to find one favourite? (3.7.5 Brand identity, 3.7.9 Brand refresh, redesign, rebranding, 5.4.7 Green packaging).

**3) Intellect-oriented communication:** What are the characteristics of the target group's level of knowledge and understanding? It is important to ensure that elements of language, terminology, specialised knowledge, and logic conveyed through the visual identity meet the desired target group. Map communication needs. Who are we talking to? What tone, mood and style should we use in our language (tone-of-voice)? What should be said for others to understand what the product is and how it works? *Example*: Ketchup is a sauce, made from tomatoes, vinegar, sugar,

1 Initiation
2 Insight
3 Strategy
4 Design
5 Production
6 Management

4.1 Design brief
4.2 Strategy><Design
4.3 Design methodology
4.4 Concept development
4.5 Design development
4.6 Design elements
4.7 Composition
4.8 Surface and format
4.9 Identity development

4.9.1 The identity principles
4.9.2 The identity elements
4.9.3 Logo
4.9.4 Symbol
4.9.5 Identity colours
4.9.6 Typography
4.9.7 Distinctive assets
4.9.8 Identity management
4.9.9 Grid system

Fig. 4.78 Exposure on the surface

salt and spices. Tomatoes are healthy. Do we think ketchup is healthy? How should ketchup be communicated? 'No one grows ketchup like Heinz' (Heinz) (3.8.5 Communication platform; Tone-of-voice).

**4) Communication surfaces:** Which physical and perceptible communication surfaces are most important? For a courier company it can be the car, for an IT company it can be the website, for an airline it can be the hull or tail of the aircraft. What communication surfaces does a product have? Bottle, cork, label at the front, label at the back? The communication surfaces allow for identity and message exposure, and differentiation from competing products. It is necessary to know the character, possibilities and limitation of the surface. Also consider communication surfaces in digital and analog media. Which channels are important and what is possible with regard to budget? *Example*: The ketchup bottle communication surfaces are the bottle, cap, the labelling, front and

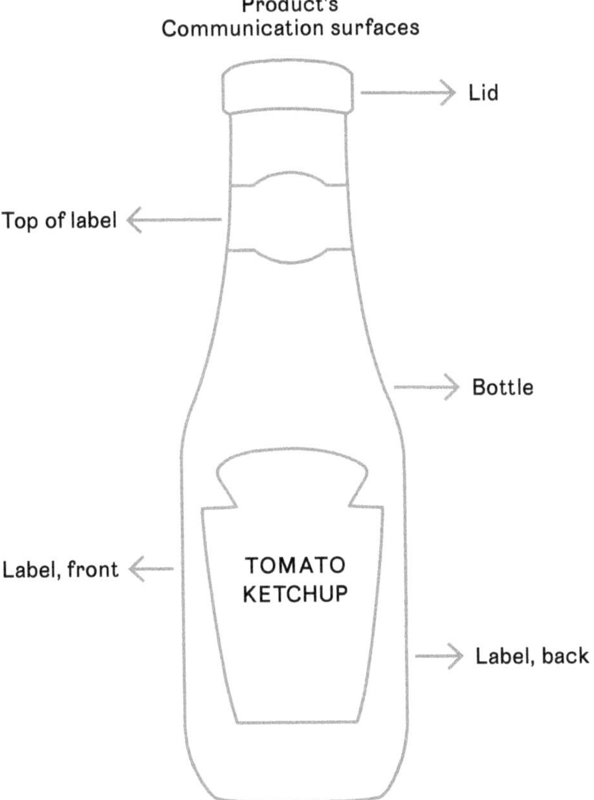


Fig. 4.79 Communication surfaces

Packaging design

Either the task is to make a new brand, extending or revitalising existing product lines, a success factor during the design process is to break down the packaging into individual elements, to assess and analyse the appearance of each element, to make the necessary changes, and test different ways of putting them together to achieve the desired effect (2.7.8 Visual analysis). Development of a prototype at various stages of the design process, as well as conducting instore testing and focus groups is crucial.

back, and the capsule at the top of the neck, see Figure 4.79. Which of the communication surfaces are more relevant and eye-catching? (3.8.8 Channels and media, 4.8 Surface and format).

Fig. 4.80 **The figure shows the most important identity elements for a company, product, or service. © Grimsgaard, W. (2018).**

**5) Perceptible signals:** What perceptible and subconscious signals are we responding to? Humans are designed to relate to, perceive and identify signals. Identifying which signals do what to us is crucial for reaching the target group. Example: Ketchup reminds us of the smell of freshly grilled sausages, a juicy hamburger, or crunchy fries. To many, ketchup is the finishing touch (3.7.6 Label elements, Figure 3.41 The Brand Sense Survey).

Tips for the designer
**Perceptible signals is the most important part of the communication, because much of what we surround ourselves with, we relate to in a purely sensory manner.**

**6) Noise:** What noise factors are important to consider? Noise is a subjective term for everything one does not want to hear, but it can also apply to anything one does not wish to see or anything that is an obstacle to what one wants to see. When you are looking for a specific product in a store, all the other products that prevent you from finding exactly the product you are looking for will be perceived as noise. The same is true in a market, in a jungle of signs, or in a vibrant urban environment. Similarity can also be perceived as noise because it is difficult to distinguish one product from the other. Products and companies with contemporary design and colours tend to be alike. Similarity as a result of trend, fashion and uniformity creates confusion. One must decide what will make one's product stand out from the others. To consciously place oneself in a noisy area, it is important to know who one is competing against. To call attention to ourselves in a noisy area, we can distinguish ourselves by doing the opposite of what others do. Success factors are preferably some unique distinctive features, combined with logical and simple communication and visible targeted exposure. Example: Red is the most used colour in the ketchup category. How to differ from the others? (3.7.3 Brand position, 3.7.2 Brand architecture).

**7) Exclusive rights:** Is there a free domain? Can the identity be protected to prevent others from imitating it? Aren't all ketchups the same? What really makes them different? Heinz is preservative free, based on sustainability and fair trade, the one with a special shape of the bottle and slightly higher quality. Can the shape of the bottle be patented? Can the name, logo, design or slogan be registered as a trademark? How about the content or concept, can it be legally protected? *Example*: First 'on' Marz. Heinz Marz Edition. Grown under Marz soil conditions (heinz.co.uk/marz-edition) (6.2 Legal protection, 6.2.3 Domain name).

> Heinz 'Marz' Edition. Ketchup made with tomatoes grown in Mars conditions. This limited edition launched November 8. 2021, was based on two years of research conducted by a team of astrobiologists at the Florida Institute of Technology's Aldrin Space Institute. Through the experiment they showed that tomatoes can be grown in more remote and harsh places on Earth, as well as off-planet. 'With regards to our own survival on this planet, one of the big questions is how do we grow in soils that are less than ideal,' (Dr Andrew Palmer, the Aldrin Space Institute). 'In space we have a saying, 'it's not about the food, it's about the sauce' (Mike Massimino, former NASA astronaut). Heinz are aiming for using 100% sustainably-sourced Heinz ketchup tomatoes by 2025 (Pearlman, 2021).

### 4.9.2 The identity elements

It is the identity elements together, which make up the visual identity, and that should help create recognition and build the brand. Their task is to visualise and communicate the main characteristics of a company, product or service in a clear, distinctive and recognisable manner. When we talk about identity related to company, product, or service, what we often think of as the most important elements of identity are the name, logo, symbol, colours, and typography. The way the different identity elements are positioned in relation to each other is also identity, what we here call *identity management*. That includes how text, photos and

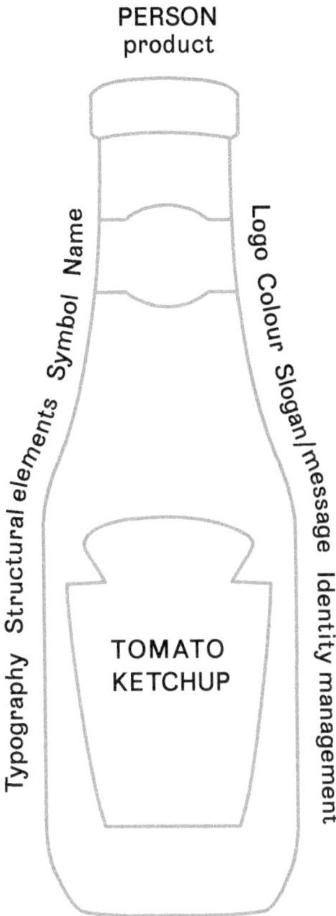


Fig. 4.80 Identity elements

illustrations are organised in a layout. A great deal is about shape, which itself is a very strong identity carrier, whether it is the matter of the shape of a graphic element, or the form of a product, an object, or a piece of furniture. The name is the most important identity element. Even when the name is not present, that is what we think about when we see identity elements that we associate with the brand. Choosing a name is a strategic move, anchored in the overall goal and strategy (3.7 Brand strategy, 3.7.6 Brand assets, 3.7.7 Brand name, 4.8 Surface and format).

Metaphorically speaking, the identity of a company, product, or service can be compared to that of a person. The face is the symbol, the voice is the typography, the hair, eyes, and skin colour are the colour palette, the logo corresponds to the appearance and attitude of the body. The person may also be in possession of so-called a fifth element or a distinctive brand asset. That is, a very typical feature, such as a unique colour of hair, a very special body shape, a characteristic smile, or the like. The *identity management* covers the entire person (2.2.2 PIPI workshop, 3.2.5 Core values). Here is an overview of the identity elements based on Rybakken (2004):

**Name:** What the person calls themselves, or what they are called. A company name, product name, brand name (3.7.7 Brand name).

**Signature:** The person's body, appearance, and main characteristics. A logo, logotype, monogram or brand (4.9.3 Logo).

**Symbol:** The person's face and other things that symbolise the person. A pictogram, emblem or symbol (4.9.4 Symbol).

The name is the most central; it is what one remembers, uses and refers to in all contexts.

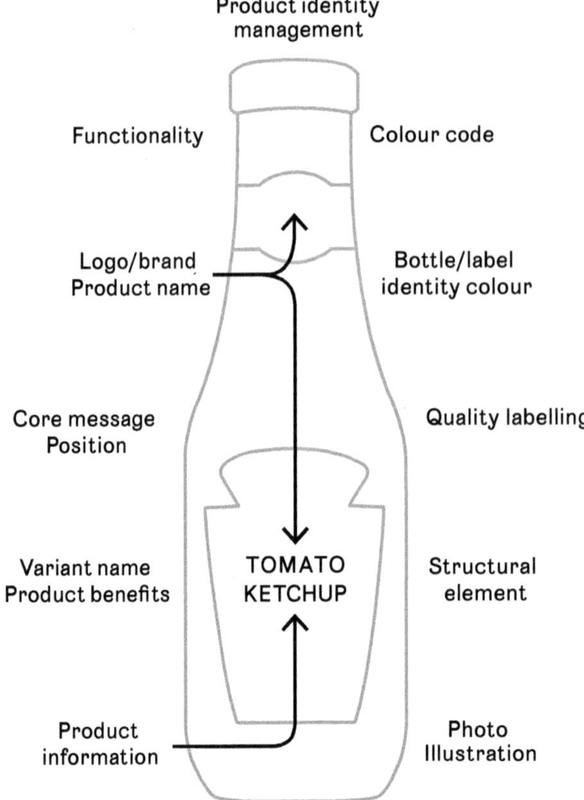


Fig. 4.81 Identity management

Fig. 4.81 The figure shows an example of identity management of a product. © Grimsgaard, W. (2018).

Fig. 4.82 The figure shows typical elements and designations included in the definition of a logo. © Grimsgaard, W. (2018).

Tips for the designer
While in the brand strategy we have talked about the strategic basis of the brand, we now mainly talk about the visual design. The success factor lies in the bridging of the two.

Logo is a term for a word mark, graphic mark, symbol, emblem or monogram used as public identification for a company, product, service or person, for recognition purposes, as well as brand building. Many use 'logo' as a term for a combination of word mark and symbol, or for a symbol alone. A slogan or tagline placed in combination with the logo may also be included as part of the logo, see Figure 4.82 Logo.

**Colour:** The colour of the person's hair, skin, eyes, and outfit. An identity colour used on a logo, symbol, graphic elements, or similar (4.9.5 Identity colours, 4.6.2 Colour, 5.5 Colour management).
**Distinctive assets:** The person's most typical characteristics, 'it' factor. A fifth element or structural element, a distinctive characteristic shape, pattern, material or a way of interacting with identity. The most distinctive brand assets (3.4.6 Distinctive asset-building strategy, 3.7.6 Brand assets, 4.9.7 Distinctive assets).
**Typography:** The person's ability to communicate and articulate combined with language, choice of words, tone of voice, dialect, etc. A marketing communication, tone-of-voice, slogan, information, message, and word choices, typeface, font, style, shape and congeniality (3.8.7 Communication development, 4.9.6 Typography).
**Identity direction:** The person's appearance, outfit and style. A layout of all elements, all the units to a whole, signalling the desired overall impression and experience of the identity (4.7 Composition, 4.8 Surface and format, 4.9.8 Identity management, 4.9.9 Grid system).

### 4.9.3 Logo

The logo is the visual design of the name of a company, product, or service, given a unique shape that expresses the values and characteristics that make up its identity. Conscious strategic anchoring and conscious use of fonts are prerequisites for success. The logo is the company's most central marketing element. It is always present; it can achieve recognition and esteem, and evolve into a brand over time. A brand is an asset, a value that can be measured in dollars and cents. The core values next to brand position and brand architecture provide the most important strategic directions for developing the logo, whether in terms of a new logo or a redesign (3.2.5 Core values, 3.7.3 Brand position, 3.7.2 Brand architecture).

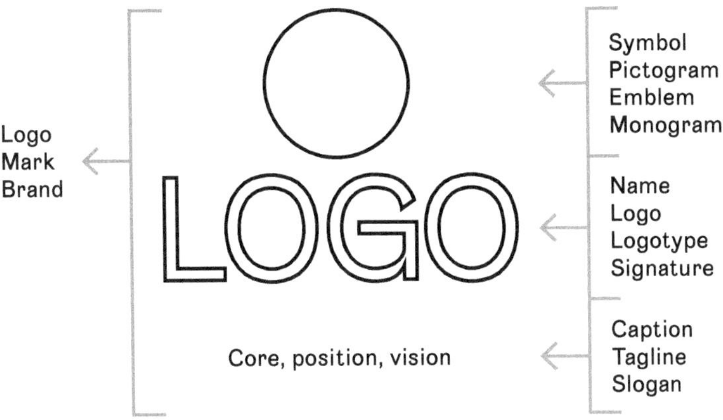


Fig. 4.82 Logo

### Logo vs. brand

Logo is an abbreviation of the English word logotype and comes originally from a compilation of the Greek terms λόγος (lógos) 'word, speech' and τύπος (túpos) 'imprint, mark'. A logo is also referred to as brand, trademark, word mark, graphic mark, logotype, symbol, icon, emblem, monogram, signature. This might be slightly confusing. In reality, there is a certain difference between a logo and a brand. *A logo* is a visual graphic or typographical element that identifies a company, product, or service, and contributes to differentiation and recognition. A logo is a trademark that can be registered under the Trademark Act, see 6.2 Legal protection. *A brand* is more than a logo. It is a combination of all the associations, values and attitudes that immediately come to one's mind in connection with the logo of a company, product or service. Such associations are built through the brand awareness, brand experience, and brand relationship the user or consumer establishes over time, based on a combination of influence and own experience with the company, product or service.

### The task of the logo

The task of the logo is to represent the name and reflect the main characteristics of a company, product or service in the most appealing, attractive and relationship-building way possible. 'Similarly to a person's signature, it should convey personality traits. Is it neat and clear or characterised by impatience? Is it powerful or quiet? A logo that stands alone can convey much between the lines; is it open and friendly, or timid and peculiar? Does it have monumental qualities or is it easy-going and intimate?' (Rybakken, 2004, p. 173). The logo should be charged with everything the company or product represents and wants to be perceived as, and its task is to bring out these associations in the recipient.

1 Initiation
2 Insight
3 Strategy
4 Design
5 Production
6 Management

4.1 Design brief
4.2 Strategy><Design
4.3 Design methodology
4.4 Concept development
4.5 Design development
4.6 Design elements
4.7 Composition
4.8 Surface and format
4.9 Identity development

4.9.1 The identity principles
4.9.2 The identity elements
4.9.3 Logo
4.9.4 Symbol
4.9.5 Identity colours
4.9.6 Typography
4.9.7 Distinctive assets
4.9.8 Identity management
4.9.9 Grid system

- Logo vs. brand
- The task of the logo
- The tip of the iceberg
- Requirements for a good logo
- Visual qualities of the logo
- Lettering
- Logo development

> 'A brand is a person's gut feeling about a product, service, or organisation' (Neumeier, 2005).

| Logo process | |
|---|---|
| Problem statement: | Identify the need or problem? Why a new logo? What task should the logo solve? (2.3 Problem statement). |
| Insight: | Conduct a workshop, a situational analysis, a visual analysis, case studies, observations, interviews, surveys, or anything else that provides sufficient insight (2.6 Survey). |
| Strategy: | Clarify core values and other strategic directions such as value proposition, brand position and design strategy (3.2.5 Core values, 3.2.6 Value proposition, 3.7.3 Brand position, 3.9 Design strategy). |
| Inspiration: | Use moodboards based on core values, case studies, font studies, literature, surveys, observations as inspiration for logo development (2.8.2 Moodboard). |
| Idea development: | Use brainstorming, creative workshop, the iterative method. Develop several conceptual directions. Select direction for further development (4.3.5 Iterative method, 4.4.5 Conceptual directions). |
| Design development: | Create hand and computer sketches to further develop the idea. Use moodboards of the core values as a platform. Test the logo on appropriate surfaces. Iterate (4.5 Design development). |
| Lettering: | Process or develop a font to bring out the idea, distinctiveness, and identity in the logo (4.9.6 Typography). |
| Detailing: | Gain deeper understanding of the origin, anatomy, and shape of the font. Work with inner shapes, outer shapes, line thickness, widths, heights, angles, corners, serifs, etc. Develop a grid to organise the details (4.9.9 Grid system). |
| Implementation: | Test the logo on different surfaces, profile carriers and in appropriate contexts during the process. Implement the logo on the selected surfaces (3.8.8 Channels and media, 4.8 Surface and format, 5.1 Implementation). |
| Identity management: | Compare elements in a unified manner on all surfaces to create a holistic expression (4.9.8 Identity management). |

Table 4.10 Logo process

Table 4.10 The table shows the main elements of a logo process. © Grimsgaard, W. (2018).

Fig. 4.83 The visual logo is just the tip of the iceberg. Behind the visual appearance of a logo is a rigorous process of strategic anchoring, insight into competitors, target groups and markets, goals, values, brand strategy, visual design and implementation on all surfaces. © Grimsgaard, W. (2018).

Tips for the designer

Logo development assumes that you examine both classical and newer typefaces, their inherent identity, origin and distinctiveness.

> Logo or wordmark is 'a freestanding acronym, company name, or product name that has been designed to convey a brand attribute or positioning' (Wheeler, 2018, p. 55).

## The tip of the iceberg

A logo is not just what you see. Behind is a rigorous process of strategic anchoring, insight into competitors, target groups and markets, development of brand strategy and visual design, implementation on all surfaces and so on. A logo affects everything the business is and stands for. It is the name and logo the company is known by, which one remembers, which one refers to, which is always present, which creates associations, at best pride, loyalty and relationships, among those who work in the company and those who buy the company's products or services. For a company whose ambition is to increase its competitiveness, gain awareness and build a brand, a rigorous logo process is crucial.

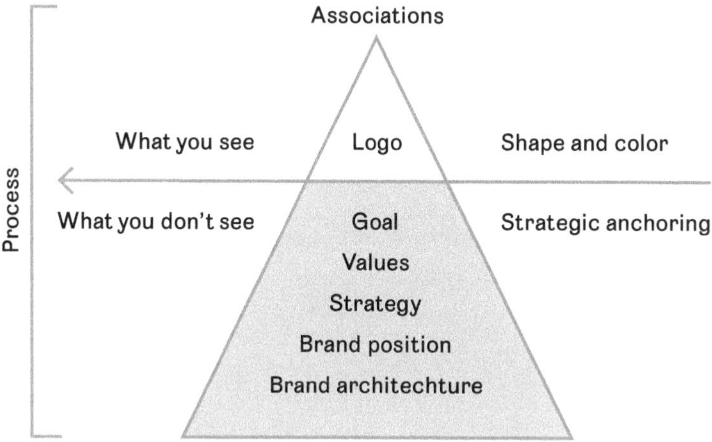


Fig. 4.83 Strategic anchoring

## Requirements for a good logo

What is a good logo? A good logo captures the attention, reflects the identity and key characteristics. It creates positive associations and long-term relationships, contributes to greater awareness, increased competitive power and a stronger position. A good logo is an important brand asset and a way to help differentiate the company from its competitors and communicate the essence of its brand to the market (Jason, 2016). Here are some general requirements for a good logo:

**Identity:** It should have a clear identity, which represents the core values.
**Unique:** It should have its own distinctive feature and a strong character. It should stand out and be easy to find.
**Association:** It should signal the characteristics, which trigger associations in the target group when they see the logo.
**Memorable:** It should be visible, clear, easily recognisable, and easy to remember.
**Visible and readable:** It should be visible and readable at a distance, in haste, in noise and in all sizes.
**Word mark/shape:** It should have a distinctive graphic shape, typographical word mark or figure.
**Position:** It should express and support the desired position in the way it stands out from its competitors.



> Logos are a tangible way to express some of the essence and characteristics of a brand with the help of a signature or a symbol but there is no way a logo can represent or illustrate everything about a brand (Jason, 2016).

**Simple shape:** It should have an interesting and aesthetically pleasing shape that works on different surfaces and in production.
**Black & White:** It should work without colours; in black and white.
**Consistent:** It should be possible to reproduce consistently at all times.
**Appealing:** It should be appealing, aesthetic and nice to look at. It should be perfect in every detail.

Tips for the designer
Multiple layers of information can make the logo richer and more visually appealing, but this should not be at the expense of the simplicity of the logo.

Tips for the company
The research article 'Guidelines for selecting or modifying logos' from 1998 can be an interesting read. Here, the authors Henderson and Cote develop guidelines to help leaders choose or change logos to achieve the company's image and goals. An empirical analysis of 195 logos, based on 13 design properties, identified logos that achieve high recognition. Available from: www.jstor.org/stable/1252158.

Does the logo signal a large company or a small company?

### Visual qualities of the logo

Here are ten criteria for assessing the visual qualities of a logo (based on Gernsheimer 2008):

**1) Distinctive:** The logo should be clear and differentiated and should be able to stand out in the crowd by virtue of its uniqueness. The logo should have a clear identity and distinctive character that highlights the attributes and characteristics of the company, product, or service.
**2) Sophisticated:** The logo should be nice to look at, refined and with aesthetic qualities. The conscious choice of font, colours, and motifs, combined with accurate details, and perfection, is key.
**3) Conceptual:** A logo that comes from an intelligent thought or idea can add a positive dimension, thereby adding value to the logo and enhancing the way it is perceived.
**4) Relevant:** Adding symbolic meaning to the logo as appropriate will make it easier for the logo to relate to what it is intended to represent, and thus will be perceived more easily as significant and right for the recipient. Excessively explicit relevance may limit the logo in cases where the company expands into new sectors.
**5) Flexible:** The logo should be flexible and versatile, which means that it should be suitable for use in different sizes and on different surfaces. It may be necessary to provide a fixed frame and background. The logo should be clear and readable, whether placed on a skyscraper, webpage or a ballpoint pen. It is important to test out the logo in different sizes during the development process e.g. to prevent typography or elements from merging when the logo is scaled down. The ideal solution is a logo that works in all sizes and contexts. In some cases, it may be necessary to develop a simplified version of the logo customised for shrinking below a certain size.
**6) Coherent/uniform:** The logo should have a coherent, uniform and consistent expression. All details, elements and devices should be as uniform as possible, in shape, style and colour. Uniform expression can be achieved by creating an optical perception of similarity in the design, both in small details such as serifs, and in larger shapes surrounding the symbol or logo.
**7) Attractive:** A logo that is nice to look at and attractive has a clear advantage when it comes to being preferred and remembered. What is perceived visually attractive is strongly linked to the style and trends of the time and may vary within different cultures and social status. The conscious application of basic principles of composition, proportions and balance can help give the logo universal appeal qualities.
**8) Legible and readable:**[105] Especially for a logo, it is of utmost importance to consider the factors that make the logo as readable as possible, such as font shape, letter spacing, and word spacing. This also includes choice of exposure sizes and consideration of the reader's distance to the logo.

105 Legibility is about making the text readable. Legibility is about a visual structure and a whole that make it easier to understand the relationship between elements, and thus the context of the text, which facilitates navigation (Rannem 2005: 121/129). Rannem refers to Ole Lund's doctoral thesis on the foundation of typographical knowledge, 1999. The thesis provides, among other things, thorough analysis and criticism of the history of legibility research.

When the typography is dominant in a logo, readability is important. The more legible the letters, the clearer the message becomes. When simplifying the letters of a logo, it is important to consider legibility. Sometimes joining two letters (ligatures) can harm legibility; other times it can strengthen it. Making the letters bolder can make the logo more visible but can also impair legibility because the outer and inner shapes become narrower.

**9) Memorable:** A frequently appearing logo will naturally be more easily remembered by the target group. Here, the readable and visual qualities of the logo, combined with knowledge and associations with the sender, will influence how memorable the logo is. If the logo belongs to a company, product, or service, which a person perceives as important to remember, this will affect the willingness to remember it. If the name is generic or ordinary, and thus more difficult to remember, a distinctive character could be added by giving the logo a unique visual form, possibly supported by a symbol, thus making it easier to remember.

**10) Long-lasting:** Unlike advertisements and brochures, a logo should last for decades. Developing a logo takes a lot of time, money, and resources, and is an investment in building public awareness and brand assets. A logo that lasts over time will achieve added value, such as being associated with something solid, safe, and firm by virtue of its durability.

**11) Redesign:** Constant modification of a logo may harm the recognition and values on which it is based. Nonetheless, it is necessary to redesign the logo from time to time so that it can retain its position and be perceived as timely. For a logo with which the audience is highly familiar, it is a matter of minor modifications to the logo, which are necessary to maintain the greatest possible recognisability among its audience. Redesign may also be advisable if a logo does not function according to expectations, for example if it is not capable of attracting the desired attention.

**A minimum of strategy**

Even if the logo should not cost very much and even if the time is scarce, the designer should take some strategic directions as basis. As a minimum, the designer should familiarise themselves with the company's goals and business strategy, clarify what the company does, what services or products it sells, to whom and where, and last, but not least, what it wants to achieve with what it does. The same applies if a logo is to be developed for a product or service. A crucial question will be: How do we find the identity? The answer lies in the core values. The core values are the essence of the identity and the platform for logo development. Therefore, they should be developed as a bare minimum, unless they already exist. Desired brand position is another factor that should be clarified, especially for companies competing in the market aiming at differentiating themselves from their competitors (3.1.3 TOP 5).

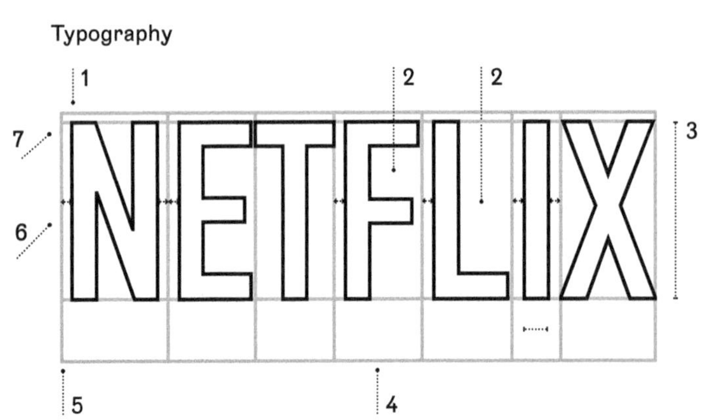


Fig. 4.84 a) Typography vs. lettering

**Typography: 1)** In typography all the units, font (letters), should be possible to combine, in any order. **2)** Between each symbol, there is optically equal amount of space. **3)** In order for each element to appear equally important, they share proportions, level of detail and thickness. **4)** Regardless of combination and quantity, they should form the same texture. This was Gutenberg's great invention. **5)** The letters are placed side by side, block by block, in order to form words and sentences. **6)** Equal shapes have exactly the same distance to the edges. **7)** The letters are placed on invisible squares.

Fig. 4.84 b) Typography vs. lettering

**Lettering: 1)** In lettering, the word is the unit, not every single letter. **2)** It is tempting to tie these together or move them further apart to avoid collisions. **3)** Since the letters should only work in this context, L can be made narrower, or I can be raised into the hollow space, or the problem can be solved by other means. **4)** Balance is achieved by adjusting different parts of the word. **5)** A curved baseline in combination with a straight top line can be made, which is impossible to obtain by typography, as shown in the other example. **6)** Some letters are larger than others (Frode Helland 2017).

Fig. 4.84 The figure at the top shows an example of typography, which involves the processing of fonts in running text and titles. Typography is about creating a pattern. The figure at the bottom shows examples of lettering, which involves customising text for a specific context, for example signature/logo. Lettering is about breaking a pattern and creating distinctiveness. The illustrations were developed by Frode Helland in 2017.

Tips for the designer
Multiple layers of information can make the logo richer and more visually appealing, but this should not be at the expense of the simplicity of the logo.

Tips for the designer
The logo should be tested on digital surfaces, such as web pages, app icons and 'profile pictures' on social media, to check if it is suitable for use here. The logo should also be tested on relevant analogue surfaces, such as prints (paper), signs (metal) and uniforms (textiles).

Tips for the designer
It may be necessary to investigate the level of familiarity the existing logo holds, using surveys or interviews, before determining the extent to which the logo can or should be changed.

106 See examples of redesign: underconsideration.com/brandnew.

### Lettering

The conscious selection and processing of fonts is central to the development of a logo. At the same time, there is a difference between the concepts of typography, font design, and lettering. Based on Helland (2017), these are:

*Font design* is the production of fonts, a laborious task that consists primarily of drawing letters, numbers, and characters, and then creating patterns with them. It should be possible to combine them in all possible ways, and should therefore appear optically equal – equal in size, equal in thickness, with equal level of detail, and with equal distance to the next letter – regardless of order and constellation.

*Typography* refers to the use of typefaces and text composition, including, among other things, smoothing, pinching, letter spacing, font selection, font size, line spacing, line width, and the use of different styles to communicate clearly. Typography is about, among other things, judging how well typographical font works as a pattern. *Lettering*, on the other hand, is tailored to one specific context, a static image formed by dynamic elements, as in a logo/signature. Good lettering is about creating dynamics by breaking the typographical pattern, creating distinctive attributes and distinctive features. For all these terms, it is about asking how well the typography, i.e. the use of fonts, actually serves the content (Helland, 2017).

### Logo development

Logo development is a laborious and time-consuming process. There is no one answer for either method or result. Knowledge of font and typography is essential. Just as important are strategic anchoring, sufficient insight, good and broad creative processes, use of iterative methods, good involvement of the client in the process, frequent testing of the logo along the way, and conscious work on the details in the final phase. Meanwhile, it is important to view the logo as a part of a holistic visual identity in interaction with other identity elements. It can, therefore, often be advantageous to develop logo and identity elements in parallel. Here are some tips for logo development:

**Clarify the needs and problem statement:** *Should a new logo be developed or a redesign*? This is not always clear from the start, and it is one of the questions the designer should address. In the case of redesign, a key question will be how much change may be made considering preserving recognisability. Is it the name or the word mark that people remember? If it is the name, one might be freer to change the design. Is the degree of recognition high or low? If low, should a brand-new solution be considered? If high, and the market budget big, would a brand-new design be an option, as Microsoft did in 2012 and Google in 2015. Or is it important to keep more or less of the knowledge, as for example Skype in 2014, Facebook in 2015, MasterCard in 2016, Fanta in 2017, Adobe Creative Cloud 2020, Toyota 2020, Burger King 2021?[106] (3.7.8 Brand perspective, 2.3 Problem statement, 3.7.9 Brand refresh, redesign, rebranding,).

**Gather the necessary insight:** *What do we need to know*? A situational analysis is a good starting point for clarifying the situation and finding out what one needs to know more about. It may also be necessary to implement visual analysis, observational studies, and target group

1 Initiation
2 Insight
3 Strategy
4 Design
5 Production
6 Management

4.1 Design brief
4.2 Strategy><Design
4.3 Design methodology
4.4 Concept development
4.5 Design development
4.6 Design elements
4.7 Composition
4.8 Surface and format
4.9 Identity development

4.9.1 The identity principles
4.9.2 The identity elements
4.9.3 Logo
4.9.4 Symbol
4.9.5 Identity colours
4.9.6 Typography
4.9.7 Distinctive assets
4.9.8 Identity management
4.9.9 Grid system

- Logo vs. brand
- The task of the logo
- The tip of the iceberg
- Requirements for a good logo
- Visual qualities of the logo
- Lettering
- Logo development

Further reading

– *Logo Modernism* (2015) by Jens Müller.
– *Made by James: The Honest Guide to Creativity and Logo Design* (2022) by James Martin.
– *Logo Design Love: A Guide to Creating Iconic Brand Identities* (2014) by David Airey

Tools tips

Check out Google Design. It is a directory of essential design tools and resources to keep your projects moving forward: design. google/resources/.

analysis, or other information that may provide the necessary insight. Insight is also needed in the creative process, for example through case studies, font studies, delving into old and new literature and magazines, internet search,[107] physical inspections and observations (2.7.1 Situational analysis, 2.6 Research, 2.6.3 Observation, 2.7.6 Target group analysis, 2.7.8 Visual analysis).

**Clarify areas of use and criteria:** *Where and how should the logo work?* Is there a need for large banners and signs? Is there a need for small sizes like favicon or app? For a courier car company it is important that the logo works well on the car, for a restaurant it should stand out well on the façade, while for an online store it should be easily noticeable on the website. Clarifying logo criteria can make it easier to create a logo that works optimally.

**Clarify goals and strategic anchoring:** *What strategic directions and objectives should be used as the basis for the development of the logo?* As part of logo development, one should familiarise oneself with existing goals and strategies, or contribute to their development. Business idea, core values, value proposition, brand position and brand narrative are among the most essential strategic benchmarks for developing a logo. The same applies to brand identity, tone-of-voice, and signal effect. A strategic process can be time-consuming and costly. Therefore, the scope of the strategy process should be considered in relation to the time and resources of the project. Sufficient time should be allocated for the design work and sufficient resources for the marketing of the new logo (3.2 Overall strategy, 3.7 Brand strategy, 3.8 Communication strategy).

**Clarify associations:** *Which associations should the logo evoke?* Clarify which associations should be linked with the logo visually and verbally. The core values, position and brand narrative are all good starting points for clarifying brand associations (3.2.5 Core values, 3.7.3 Brand position, 3.7.4 Brand story).

**Use a moodboard as inspiration:** *How to get started with logo development?* A good starting point is to visualise the identity and the core values. Feel free to start by creating a moodboard for each value word, either physically or on a computer. Use photos, shapes, patterns, fonts, colours, or physical materials that express the different values. Create a small colour chart based on the colours dominating in the pictures and implement in the moodboard. The mood, style, and expression of the moodboard can inspire the choice of typeface, shape, style, and colours, and can be combined with different ideas. Moodboards can also be developed for different idea concepts. (2.8.2 Moodboard).

**Idea and concept development:** *What idea should the logo be built on?* The best logos are those built on a clear idea. A good approach is to develop two to three conceptual directions for the logo. They should be presented to the client using moodboards, rough sketches, and verbal explanations. One or a combination of several directions is selected for further development and concretisation (4.3 Design methodology, 4.4 Concept development, 4.5 Design development).

Fig. 4.85 The figure shows examples of font and color selections based on type of business, purpose and strategic guidelines, such as core values and position. © Grimsgaard, W. (2018).

Table 4.11 Test the name in different typefaces, in capitals and lower-case letters, to get an impression of the word car. It is important that a logo gets a good word-picture. Test out classical typefaces against new ones. © Grimsgaard, W. (2018).

107 For example: Pinterest, Behance, Tumblr, Are.na, trendlist.org.
108 Pixel-based programs such as Adobe Photoshop are unsuitable for logo design.

**Font selection:** *Should you draw the font yourself or choose it?* A combination may be the answer. Font selection can be made by looking at typefaces from different eras, font libraries, and font foundries, and by studying online font design, case studies, and so on. A good start can be to set up the logo name in different typefaces and examine which typeface best highlight the values, attributes, and idea the logo should signal, see Figure 4.85 and Table 4.11. Also consider which typeface best contributes to providing a good word-mark (4.9.6 Typography: Font selection; Font identity; Font voice; Font anatomy.

Effective
(strong blue)
Safe
(warm yellow)
Competent
(black and white)


Fig. 4.85 Font and colour selection

The best typefaces are picked out. These can be the starting point for finding more typefaces. It is about searching deeply and looking for details that fit the look you wish to create. The best typefaces are tested in capital and lower-case letters, and different dot sizes. In such a process, one should go many rounds, printing, evaluating, adjusting, remain in the process and be patient, and spend time exploring the typical peculiarities of the different letters. It can be a special g or e that gives the writing personality and character, see Figures 4.95, 4.96, 4.97, 4.98, 4.99, 4.100, 4.101, 4.102 and 4.103.

One way to process the font manually is to print large-sized fonts and draw over on transparent paper. This way, one can work on adding or subtracting details to add distinctiveness to the naming sequence, in a simpler and freer way than starting on a computer immediately. In addition, you can make free hand sketches on the side. The hand sketches can be scanned onto data and drawn in vector graphics. Logos must be created as vector graphics e.g. in Adobe Illustrator in order to keep all details and qualities when magnified or reduced.[108] Remember to archive all stages so that it is possible to go back if necessary.

| Garamond | Baskerville | Bodoni | Futura | Gill | Helvetica | Mériva |
|---|---|---|---|---|---|---|
| Name | Name | Name | Name | Name | Name | Name |
| name | name | name | name | name | name | name |
| NAME | NAME | NAME | NAME | NAME | NAME | NAME |
| NamE | NamE | NamE | NamE | NamE | NamE | NamE |

Table 4.11 Testing out fonts

**Word image development (relief):** How can letters be modified to give them more distinctive features? Converting font to outline (in Adobe Illustrator) makes it easier to process the details, such as making the letters taller, wider, rounder, and adding or subtracting details so that one gets the appearance one is looking for. A good approach is trying out alternative modifications quickly, and avoid starting too early with time-consuming work on the details. A successful result depends on

1 Initiation
2 Insight
3 Strategy
4 Design
5 Production
6 Management

4.1 Design brief
4.2 Strategy><Design
4.3 Design methodology
4.4 Concept development
4.5 Design development
4.6 Design elements
4.7 Composition
4.8 Surface and format
4.9 Identity development

4.9.1 The identity principles
4.9.2 The identity elements
4.9.3 Logo
4.9.4 Symbol
4.9.5 Identity colours
4.9.6 Typography
4.9.7 Distinctive assets
4.9.8 Identity management
4.9.9 Grid system

- Logo vs. brand
- The task of the logo
- The tip of the iceberg
- Requirements for a good logo
- Visual qualities of the logo
- Lettering
- Logo development

A hall of shame

Examples of uncritical font modifications include redesigning the YouTube logo in 2017, which was criticised, among other things, for randomly cutting the corners of letters. According to Herrmann (2017) 'cutting off corners' has become 'a trend so big that it has got its own Tumblr feed as a hall of shame'. In his article 'The honest YouTube Sans reviews', he points out: '... consistency is key. It goes back to the roots of typefaces in writing, where the stroke endings were a result of the writing tool and the angle one would hold this tool' (Herrmann, 2017). Check out cuttingedgelogos.tumblr.com. See yourlogo-isnothardcore.tumblr.com how font modification has been carried out. It is about understanding the inherent identity and origins of the font. It can be helpful to study traditional font shape, similar to that found in classical typefaces, see Figure 4.116 Classic typefaces.

During the detailed work, it is important to note that each adjustment to the shape of a letter has consequences for the air inside and around it, and for the relationship with the letters next to it. Therefore, one should look at each letter and at the entire word-picture together and work to create consistency between the letters, balance the shapes relative to each other, and create even air (space) between the letters (4.9.6 Typography: Optical adjustment, Figure 4.107 Kerning, 4.108 Optically correct and 4.110 Overshoots).

**Choice off direction:** *Which option should be selected?* Select one or more draft logos for further elaboration and detail. Align with the strategic directions and requirements of the logo that are used as basis. Does the logo express the correct associations and desired position? Have the requirements for a good logo been met? (2.7.7 Brand analysis, Figure 2.31 Brand analysis internally/externally).

Fig. 4.86 **The figure shows a previous version of the Braun logo developed by Wolfgang Schmittel. The logo has been redesigned several times; the original and the initial wordmark Braun were designed by Will Münch in 1934.**

Tips for the designer

**Strategy check: Don't forget to check if your logo sketches fits with the core values of the company, product or service. If you have already made a moodboard of the core values, you can implement the logo drafts one by one to see how they correlates.**

**Detail checklist:**

**Colours:** Does the logo work in black and white? Do the colours provide the right associative experience? Should other colours be considered? Has the colour been assessed in relation to production and printing on relevant papers, fabrics, and other materials, with a view to production and colour management? What do the colours look like in current colour codes like CMYK, Pantone, NCS, RAL, HEX? Are there any major anomalies? Should other colour combinations be considered?

**Background:** Will the logo work on different backgrounds, such as photo or bright colours? Should the logo have a frame or a background field? Should guides be prepared for the backgrounds the logo should be used on? Comparison: How does the logo compare to pictograms and taglines? Has a sufficient number of alternative compositions been considered? Is the symbol too large or too small? Will the tagline also be readable in small size?

**Small/big:** Does the logo work in large size? Will the logo details tolerate being enlarged? Does the logo work in small size? How small can the logo be? Does the logo work at a distance?

**Context:** In what context should the logo be used? A good test to find out if it works is to place it on relevant surfaces, situations and contexts and assess how it works. At the same time, consideration should be given to how graphic elements, typography, colours, photographs, patterns etc. will support the logo and act as a holistic visual identity.

**What if?:** If you are wondering what to choose, what to do, and how, what happens if the logo gets a different typeface or a different colour. If you are wondering, then try! Think 'what if' – and TRY.

**Elaboration and detail.** *How to achieve a high level of detail?* In detailed work, it is necessary to zoom in strongly on the logo and get a close look at details such as serifs, arcs, and line thicknesses, to see how they can be further developed and refined. Equally important is to zoom out and look at the bigger picture. A good approach to controlling the details is by developing a grid. This can facilitate the work on aligning all letter heights, controlling overshoots, creating consistent thicknesses on stems and hairlines, perfecting geometric shapes, such as circles, ovals, rectangles, and so on. Grid system development should not be initiated too early. It can lead to touching up details prematurely and getting stuck. The grid system can be made simple or complex, see Figure 4.86. It may be useful to examine whether the logo can be adapted to size ratios that can also be used for formats and layouts in a modular grid system. The golden ratio is one example of proportions with such attributes. There are also several other mathematical proportions and numerical ratios that can be used for both the logo and the entire visual identity. A good approach is to explore the potential of the logo by looking at aspect ratios, angles, arcs, and line thicknesses, which can be rendered in a grid system (4.8.3 Aspect ratios, 4.9.9 Grid system).

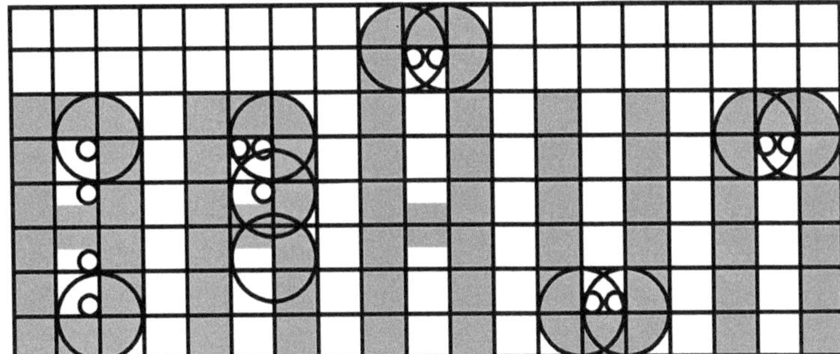

Fig. 4.86 Logo grid

**Testing and evaluation:** *When does testing and evaluation begin?* Testing and evaluation are done throughout the logo process in order to find out what works well and what does not, and thus plan the next step. The easiest test can be done by printing the logo in both large and small sizes (preferably on one and the same sheet); this makes it easier to examine how letter combinations and different details behave in different sizes. In large size it is easier to study the details. In small size it is easier to detect whether the letters grow together, whether lines are too narrow or too thick, and whether the legibility is good enough. By squinting at the logo in small size, you can more easily detect if it is too dense, if details are lost, and if it is legible enough. Eventually, it may be a good idea to test logo colours on prints and various types of paper and material. Testing out the draft logos in real situations allows you to quickly see what works and what does not. This can be done by implementing the logo on the mock-up of a sign, a uniform, a coffee cup, a web page, etc. Once the solution begins to take shape, there is time to create more elaborate examples and re-test these on current users or buyers to hear their views, for example in a focus group or an online or social media survey (5.2 Model, 2.6.4 Focus group, 2.6.1 Survey, 2.9 Testing and measuring).


1 Initiation
2 Insight
3 Strategy
4 Design
5 Production
6 Management

4.1 Design brief
4.2 Strategy><Design
4.3 Design methodology
4.4 Concept development
4.5 Design development
4.6 Design elements
4.7 Composition
4.8 Surface and format
4.9 Identity development

4.9.1 The identity principles
4.9.2 The identity elements
4.9.3 Logo
4.9.4 Symbol
4.9.5 Identity colours
4.9.6 Typography
4.9.7 Distinctive assets
4.9.8 Identity management
4.9.9 Grid system

- Logo vs. brand
- The task of the logo
- Strategic anchoring
- Requirements for a good logo
- Visual qualities of the logo
- Lettering
- Logo development


Further reading

*Principles of Logo Design: A Practical Guide to Creating Effective Signs, Symbols, and Icons* (2022) by George Bokhua.

**Relevant profile surfaces:** *Which exposure surfaces should the logo be implemented on*? If a communication strategy has been developed, relevant surfaces and profile carriers can be defined there. Examples are web pages, ads, social media, cars, uniforms, promotion materials, etc. (3.8.8 Channels and media: Communication mix).

**Design guidelines:** *How should the logo be placed on the surface*? Layout is also identity. How the logo is placed in relation to other identity elements, images and text contributes to creating a coherent expression and perceived identity. It is important for the visual identity to be used consistently on different profile carriers, so that the visual identity is appears as similar as possible each time it is displayed. This helps build up knowledge. This can be done, for example, by determining the fixed position of the logo on the surface, by deciding whether it should be centred, or at the right or left edge, and how much 'space' there should be around the logo (4.9.8 Identity management, 6.5 Design manual).

**Other identity elements:** *Is there a need for other identity elements*? A logo rarely conveys all the associations one wishes to communicate. What cannot be expressed through the logo can be conveyed through the surrounding identity elements, the text, the images, and the overall picture. The question is what should surround and support the logo to

Fig. 4.87 **The illustrations show the logo of the Bergen International Festival, which has been designed by Anti Bergen/Endre Berentzen. The grid system of the logo is explained in the video: Design – Bergen International Festival, available at Youtube.com**

**Logo classification**

There are a number of typical logo variants. Here is an overview of some of the most common ones, based on Rybakken (2004, p. 174).

**Calligraphic:** Calligraphy was traditionally done with brush and pen. Calligraphic logos resemble a signature and therefore inspire trust. For example: Ford and Coca-Cola.

**Pseudo-calligraphic:** This variant has calligraphic details, but is often more readable. Such logos signal artisan and tradition roots. For example: Ricola and Carlsberg.

**Typographic:** This variant is based on only one font, without any other devices. Such logos seem unpretentious, solid, and trustworthy. For example: Siemens and Peugeot.

**Accented:** These are typographical signatures with one or more minor peculiarities. They allow easier legal registration compared to just a typographical logo. For example: Dell.

**Formal:** These are typographical logos that are shaped with distinctive expressions and features, and that act more like a symbol. The specific values of a product can be more easily communicated in such a logo. For example: IBM. Illustrative: These are logos that visualise industry or product affiliation by a combination of typography and illustration. For example: Cotton and Vita Hjertego'.

**Integrated:** This category includes logos that are embedded in a geometric shape or framed. Such logos are consistent on different surfaces. For example: Harley Davidson.

**Combined:** Logos combining features and symbols in one and the same indivisible whole, where the symbol is never used alone. A particular industry, origin and values can be communicated more easily in one such logo. For example: Goodyear, Swatch and Converse.

100 **In 2018, Anti Bergen won the Design Effectiveness Awards (DBA) for this design (see 6.4.6 Design Effectiveness Awards).**

create the complete visual expression? During or after the development of the logo, one can start developing other identity elements such as symbols, colours, graphic elements, patterns and typography in order to create a holistic visual identity.

**Profile guidelines:** How to ensure consistent use of the logo and overall visual identity? Some guides for the use of logo and other identity elements should always be prepared. In smaller projects, this can be done easily on a page or two. In case of larger profiles, it will be necessary to develop design manuals (5.1 Implementation, 6.5 Design manual).

Fig. 4.87 Logo based on modular grid system

**A holistic visual identity:** The Bergen International Festival (Festspillene i Bergen) is one example of a logo and a holistic visual identity based on a clear idea and a modular grid. Details from the logo carry on in graphic elements and create room for playfulness, while preserving visual integrity.[109] See Figure 4.87 and check out the profile on Youtube.com: Design – Bergen International Festival.

## 4.9.4 Symbol

Symbol is one of the most central elements of an identity. It can act alone as a brand, along with a signature/logo, or as a graphic element. In the absence of symbolic meaning, pictograms may be a more accurate term to use than symbols. A symbol is a pictogram or a sign, charged with a meaning, symbolic meaning or association, which, to a larger or smaller group of people, has a common meaning that is agreed upon. A symbol is usually a visible sign, but it can also be a symbolic act, an abstract concept, or a mental performance. Some symbols are general in practical situations and in communication between people; others have a meaning only in the culture and context in which the symbol is used, while still others achieve iconic status. 'A symbol is basically a simplified way of saying something. A whole meaning, including thoughts, associations, and feelings, is framed by one symbol, a mark, or a sign' (Rybakken, 2004).

Many companies, products or services are recognised by their symbol alone, without their name or logo being in view. Such marks establish themselves in us as mental images. Examples of brands that are recognised by their symbol are Nike, Apple, and Lacoste. These symbols are charged with associations, which are carefully planned and built up over time, but which are also the result of the individual experience of the product. Wiedemann (2015) explains it this way: Once we see a symbol or mark, we record it in our memory as a film. We see a star in a special design, and we imagine a particular car. The star produces more mental images, about experiences we have had, about our dreams, and lifestyles, about luxury, and perhaps a very special drive we have felt. The star evokes the brand's symbolic meaning in us, the

1 Initiation
2 Insight
3 Strategy
4 Design
5 Production
6 Management

4.1 Design brief
4.2 Strategy><Design
4.3 Design methodology
4.4 Concept development
4.5 Design development
4.6 Design elements
4.7 Composition
4.8 Surface and format
4.9 Identity development

4.9.1 The identity principles
4.9.2 The identity elements
4.9.3 Logo
4.9.4 Symbol
4.9.5 Identity colours
4.9.6 Typography
4.9.7 Distinctive assets
4.9.8 Identity management
4.9.9 Grid system

Further reading

Check out the book: *Symbol* (2014) by Steven Bateman & Angus Hyland.

Fig. 4.88 Symbols

product concept, its performance, its surroundings, its communication, its prestige (Wiedemann, 2015, p. 8). It takes time and resources to incorporate symbolic meaning and associations into a stylised graphic figure or pictogram so that it is perceived as a symbol. When developing a new logo, it is therefore important not to overestimate the significance of the pictogram and believe that it can stand alone and act as a logo or brand without the name. The pictogram should be used together with the signature until it is incorporated and has acquired sufficient recognition to be able to trigger a memory of the name on its own.

If a pictogram is to serve as a symbol, it should be based not only on communicating the usefulness and function of the product or activity, but also on attributes and meta values that are not physically or rationally dependent. Meta values are thoughts, associations, experiences, feelings, and preferences - everything that in our mind surrounds a product, a service or a company that we cannot take or feel. Such meta values can be planned, communicated and visualised down to the smallest detail in order to build a desired association apparatus in the recipient. The symbol as visual mediator is an important brand asset because visual language helps us associate and understand the brand's culture and personality.

Fig. 4.89 Symbolic meaning

A symbol, pictogram, or icon is usually the simplification, abstraction, or stylisation of something known. Examples of symbols that are a simplification of something concrete, include the cross, the anchor, and the heart, each of which may have different symbolic meanings, but when juxtaposed, they all have the common symbolic meaning of 'faith, hope, and love.'[110]

Fig. 4.88 The cross, the anchor, and the heart, which are symbols of faith, hope, and love, are all stylised drawings of real objects. The sign of eternity and the yin-yang symbol are abstract symbols whose meaning we have learned. Through their meta values we understand and remember the meaning. Some symbols are also largely self-explanatory, such as the symbol of recycling.

Fig. 4.89 The symbols of women's and men's toilets can be designed in line with the visual identity, and they can contribute to a complete and conscious visual presentation. The figure shows how new symbolic meanings can be added to the original symbolic meaning.

Fig. 4.90 The figure shows from the left: a picture of an apple, an illustration of an apple (from the FRP logo), a stylisation of an apple, icon/ brand (the Apple logo). (The illustration is borrowed from Sidsel Lie, Grid branding: 'Verden vil ikonifiseres' 2017: 28, UIB).

110 Faith, Hope, and Love: Bible, 1 Corinthians 13:8–13.

1 Initiation
2 Insight
3 Strategy
4 Design
5 Production
6 Management

4.1 Design brief
4.2 Strategy><Design
4.3 Design methodology
4.4 Concept development
4.5 Design development
4.6 Design elements
4.7 Composition
4.8 Surface and format
4.9 Identity development

4.9.1 The identity principles
4.9.2 The identity elements
4.9.3 Logo
4.9.4 Symbol
4.9.5 Identity colours
4.9.6 Typography
4.9.7 Distinctive assets
4.9.8 Identity management
4.9.9 Grid system

- Stylisation
- Development of symbols
- Requirements for a good symbol/brand

Their meaning is easy to understand. No explanations are necessary. Other symbols may be more abstract, such as the sign of eternity and the yin-yang symbol, whose meaning we learn when it is explained to us.

Many of the familiar symbols and pictograms that we encounter appear daily in different ways, as we recognise them. Examples are pictograms for women's and men's toilets, see Figure 4.89. There are infinitely many ways to design these pictograms yet they still keep their symbolic meaning. In connection with the identity development of a restaurant or café, toilet signs can be designed in line with the restaurant's or the café's visual profile, so that they are part of the overall visual experience of the space. This can be done using the same style, colours and materials, or playing on typical associations at the place, its style and trend, theme, attire, or cheerful humour.

Fig. 4.90 Photo, illustration, stylisation, symbol

### Stylisation

Stylisation is a term for the reprocessing and abstraction of an organic or naturalistic shape into a simplified one, often as opposed to a realistic visual representation. The term stylisation is used, among other things, for symbols, flags, coats of arms/heraldry, house marks, seals, as well as in art, design and identities in various ways. Special features such as a special image, a distinctive sound, or smell can also be stylised and have a symbolic meaning. Historically, all fonts have originated from increasingly stylised imagery that gradually turns into characters. The most far-reaching stylisation results in the original figure being drawn only as a geometric shape (SNL, 2009), which is not recognisable as a motif if taken outside the context. Many symbols are based on the geometric original shapes circle, triangle, and square. A stylised spruce tree can take the form of a triangle. Colour and context will still make us perceive the shape of a spruce, see Figure 4.91 (4.6.1 Shape).

Stylisation can take place at different levels, from a simple illustration depicting any apple, to a stylisation that gives the apple a distinctive shape and symbolic meaning, as in Apple's apple symbol. Rob Janoff developed the symbol of Apple in 1977. He said he chose to illustrate that a piece of the apple had been taken, so that people would understand that it was an apple and not a cherry. 'The Apple logo symbolizes our use of their computers to obtain knowledge and, ideally, according to the human race' (Redding, 2014).

### Development of symbols

Developing a symbol requires good insight and strategic anchoring. Before the work on the visual development of the mark can begin, it is necessary to define what the task of the symbol should be, what the symbol should communicate, what associations it should trigger, and

Further reading
**Symbol by Pentagram Design Ltd (2014).**

what identity it should express. As with the development of a logo, core values are a central starting point. Work on the visual representation of symbols takes place through a thorough process of abstraction, simplification, and stylisation based on a concrete object or something abstract which should be explained through a visual shape. Stylisation requires knowledge of the object or abstract phenomenon to be stylised. For example, if the symbol is to represent a lion, which is very concrete, it is not enough to use as the basis the image one has in one's head of what a lion looks like. In order to create a good graphic figure, one must examine what is characteristic of the motif and what is important to emphasise in shape and expression in order for the idea and symbolic meaning to emerge. One must also consider the form of expression in case the symbol should be naturalistic or have a funny humorous shape, for example. In the same way as described when developing a logo, here, it is also necessary to create several ideas and work iteratively. This means diverging and converging, testing out on different surfaces and on relevant target groups, printing in small and large sizes, zooming in and working on the details, zooming out and working on the entirety.

Fig. 4.91 **The figure shows two stylised spruce trees. The starting point was a photo of a fir tree. The stylisation on the left is understandable regardless of the context. The figure on the right depends on a context in order for the geometric shape to be interpreted as a fir tree. © Grimsgaard, W. (2018).**

Tips for the designer

**Check out Pictogram-me on researchcatalogue.net. Pictogram-me is a project by Ashley Booth and Linda Lien (2010). The project aims to conduct visual research of different life experiences and perceptions using pictograms/symbols as common language and tools.**

**Explanation of terms:**

**Symbol:** A symbol is a sign, an object, an action, or something that has a deeper meaning, i.e. something that refers to or represents something other than itself, and that illustrates this in a concrete way. A symbol is often a visible or linguistic image of abstract concepts, ideas, and notions, and therefore symbols can also be called *types*. Symbols are used as practical aids in human communication, including writing and words. Symbols are often found in art, literature, and religion. The study of symbols is called semiotics, and the use of symbols is called *symbolic meaning*. *Symbolic* means 'in figurative sense' or 'figuratively'.

**Pictogram:** Pictogram is a simplified image, which symbolises a word, an object, or a concept. Modern pictograms are most often international and are used, among other things, on signs, in user manuals and computer programs to facilitate communication across different languages. The term 'pictogram' is used for characters and images displaying objects from reality, while ideograms are graphic symbols that are more abstract and less immediately understandable.

**Ideogram:** Pictograms can also be used to designate graphic symbols in pictographic fonts or ideograms, which are characters for an entire concept, that is, a word or an idea. For example, Korean, Japanese, and (a few) Chinese characters, ancient Egyptian hieroglyphics, and mathematical symbols as opposed to letters representing sounds. The letters in our alphabet also originate from simple pictograms.

**Icon:** The word 'icon' from the Greek word for 'image' can have several meanings, such as idol, data symbol and characteristic symbols or picture representations. Icon is also used for known symbolic brands, design objects, and architecture.

(Svendsen, 2021)

1 Initiation
2 Insight
3 Strategy
4 Design
5 Production
6 Management

4.1 Design brief
4.2 Strategy><Design
4.3 Design methodology
4.4 Concept development
4.5 Design development
4.6 Design elements
4.7 Composition
4.8 Surface and format
4.9 Identity development

4.9.1 The identity principles
4.9.2 The identity elements
4.9.3 Logo
4.9.4 Symbol
4.9.5 Identity colours
4.9.6 Typography
4.9.7 Distinctive assets
4.9.8 Identity management
4.9.9 Grid system

- Stylisation
- Development of symbols
- Requirements for a good symbol/brand


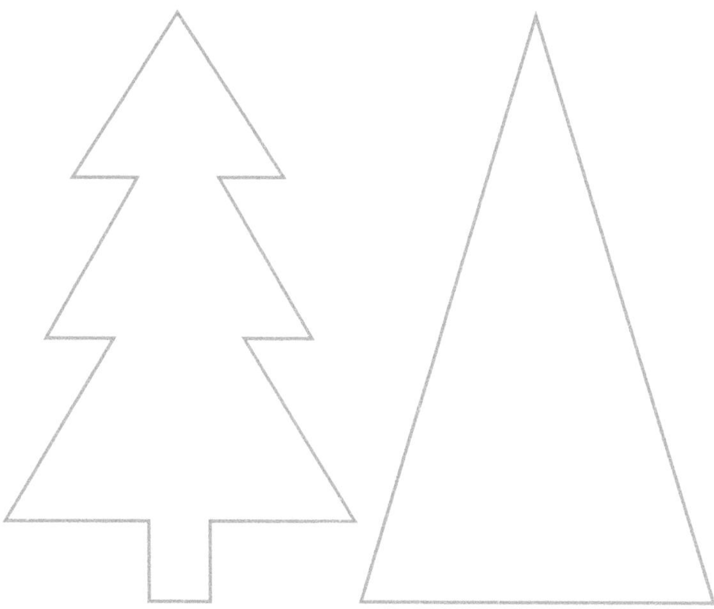

Fig. 4.91 Stylisation/abstraction

Development of the grid for the symbol can ensure more precise work in the details. Details are essential in order to achieve good stylisation and in order for the different details of the symbol to work well in all sizes. Symbols should often appear small because they are made for it thanks to their simplicity. Then, it is also important for details not to grow together or become unclear as the symbol size is decreased. At the same time, the details should appear accurate and with the right shape when the symbol is displayed in large size (4.9.3 Logo).

**Requirements for a good symbol/brand**

The aim is for the symbol to help create immediate recognition and perception of what the company or product is or does. The symbol should:

- be simple and unambiguous.
- work in black and white.
- be possible to scale up and down without quality loss.
- be possible to display in very small and in large size.
- be distinctive and differentiate itself from their competitors.
- be a simple shape that is easily recognisable.
- be possible to interpret the same way by other cultures if the symbol is to work internationally.
- appear clearly on different surfaces and backgrounds.
- be timeless, unless the task is to follow a specific trend.
- be unique, have an interesting shape and enough distinctiveness to be easy to remember.
- be modular? Can it be implemented on different surfaces? Does it work with and support the grid system, typography and other graphical elements included in the identity scheme?

In case of redesign: Be aware of the intrinsic value of the symbol. What characteristics are important to preserve? What is important to keep intact?

### 4.9.5 Identity colours

Determining an identity colour is a strategic choice that is made based on, among other things, core values, brand position and tone-of-voice.

Within all visual communication, colours are essential. Colours on a product, web page, shop or trade fair stand can help create identity and brand awareness, and are used as an effect in order to create eye-catchers, promote a message, and create differentiation. Equally important may be the significance of colour in creating a harmonious and aesthetic environment. Several colours have psychosomatic effects on us. Green lowers the heart rate, red stimulates the appetite, and yellow energises. The colours are directed at our emotions, instincts, and our mental association apparatus. We can distinguish among tens of thousands of colours. Yet, we associate only selected colours with brands, cultures, nationalities, politics, and other things worth remembering. When we think about the Kiwi food chain, we think of the bright green colour found in their logo, on their façade and on their website. Kiwi has taken ownership of the bright green colour, just as Coca-Cola owns red and IBM owns blue. In order for a colour to become an identity colour, it is important to use it as consistently as possible in all contexts, at the same amount of colour and with the same composition. It requires good planning and colour management (4.6.2 Colour, 5.5 Colour management).

#### Colour scheme

A good starting point for determining colour selection is to set up the requirements the colour should meet, based on the design brief and the strategic guides set for the assignment. In general, it is important to decide what the task of the font should be as an identity element or in the context of an assignment, what the target group is, what surfaces it should be used on, in what context it should be used, under what lighting conditions, and what duration it should have, and so on.

Insight is a key factor. It is necessary to find out which colours competitors use, which colours are used in the same industry or category, which colours are experienced traditionally, timely or trendy, which colours best match the target group, which colours best differentiate the company or product from competitors, which colours best express the identity and distinctiveness of the company or product, what these colours should signal, what associations they should trigger, what experience or mood they should create, what emotions they should bring about, and so on (3.4.6 Distinctive asset-building strategy, 3.9 Design strategy).

Given the wide range of colours we have to choose from, our linguistic colour designations are usually relatively limited. Red is used in the simplest sense for everything that looks like red, and the same applies to yellow and blue. But red is not just red, yellow is not just yellow, and blue is not just blue. There are countless shades to these colours. Choosing the right shade can be crucial to succeeding in creating the desired colour experience. At the same time, slight shades of a colour can fade out in different ways, preventing the colour from being perceived as consistent. This means that a colour can change in relation to its surrounding colours, on different surfaces, in different contexts, on different printers, on different fabrics, under different lighting conditions, etc. A few percent magenta too much in a blue colour can cause the colour to turn purple on a printout, on a screen, or on a projector with stronger

**Development of identity colours**

We are happy to divide identity colours into one primary colour, one or more secondary colours, and additional colours or colour codes. The primary or signal colour, as it may also be called, should help the company, product or service stand out.

Here is an example of a process for developing and selecting identity colours:

**Colour management:** Schedule colour management from the very beginning (5.5 Colour management).

**Basic colours:** Research some basic principles and rules concerning colour usage (4.6.2 Colour).

**Problem statement:** Based on the task the colour will have, the need it should cover, or the problem it should solve (2.3 Problem statement).

**Insight:** Examine which colours competitors use, which colours are most associated with the industry in question, the product category, the colour of the product, the taste, trends versus what is timeless, etc. (2.7.4 Competitor analysis).

**Target group:** Examine or analyse the target group's colour preferences (2.7.6 Target group analysis).

**Strategy:** Ensure anchoring in the company's strategy and goals. Core values, position and tone-of-voice are key strategic factors in colour selection (3.2.5 Core values, 3.7.1 Brand platform, 3.7.3 Brand position).

**Idea development:** Work broadly, intuitively, and without limitation with colours in the idea process. Use moodboards and create a colour palette based on the moodboards (4.4.4 Idea development), (2.8.2 Moodboard).

**Design development:** Work broadly with colours during the sketching process, too. Print frequently on different surfaces and with different colour combinations. When defining the design, it is time to work with colour pickers for different colour systems in order to find out which shades of the desired colour provide the best colour presentation for the purpose in question. Select primary, secondary, and any additional colours. Create colour maps that best place the main colour together with other colours (4.5 Design development).

**Production:** Contact printing houses and programmers in order to find out which shades of colour are best suited for web, print, interior, etc. Test out the colours of prints, on different surfaces and displays (Phase 5 – Production).

**Profile guides:** Enter the correct colour values for the current colour systems in a profile wizard (6.5 Design manual).

red rendering. For example, yellow paper can add extra yellow to a printing ink and cause a cool pastel blue to get an unwanted greenish tint. Ensuring consistent colour rendering requires good colour management and knowledge of different colour systems such as CMYK, PMS, NCS and RAL (5.5.3 Colour models, 5.5.9 Colour reference systems). Finding colours that work well across colour systems can be a challenging task. A valuable tool is to use physical colour pickers and check with printing houses, programmers etc., who will manage colour in the final run. The final run refers to the production or printing of different products, on different surfaces, and in different channels. Colours should also be tested on print, on different materials, on different screens, on different surfaces, in different contexts and under different lighting conditions, and not least on the different target groups or users.

Fig. 4.92 **The figure is based on Kissmetrics' 2010 analysis, which shows how colours affect customers in a buying situation. Graph 1) shows how appearance and colour affects the customers compared to other central factors. 2) shows that for 85% of all buyers, colour is the main reason they buy a special product. 3) shows that colour increases brand awareness by 80%. The survey has been conducted in the United States. The study is no one answer, but it can provide an indication of the importance of colour in marketing and branding. Factors such as one-to-one marketing and interaction when selling over the internet are factors that are likely to increasingly affect purchases, where colour may not be of foremost importance.**

### Symbolic meaning of colour

The significance of colour can vary widely across countries and cultures, which is important to consider if a visual design is to work internationally. Some colours are valid globally, like red and blue in politics, and stopping at a red light and driving on green. When choosing identity colours, it may be useful to know the symbolic meaning of the colours. There are many different theories.

Here are some examples based on Rybakken (2004):
**White:** Hides nothing, sacred, wedding dress (the West), grief (Asia), ghost, white flag (truce).
**Black:** Death, grief, the underworld (the West), north and winter (China). Associations towards evil magic.
**Red:** The colour of life. Blood, fire, passion. Love, danger, warning, stop signal. The devil is often depicted in red. A red card in football removes a player from the match.
**Orange:** Symbolises flames and overwhelming luxury. Japan and China > love and happiness.
**Brown:** Symbolises the earth and harvest > humility and decay.
**Yellow:** Symbolises gold, light, and the sun. Yellow is the most visible colour. In Islam > wisdom and good advice, pale yellow symbolises treachery and treason. In Egypt > envy and dishonour. In China > the sublime imperial colour.
**Green:** The colour of life, spring, youth, hope, and joy of life. Degradation, jealousy, poison. Islam > the sacred colour. Christianity > the colour of the Trinity. Eco-friendliness and ecology. Liberating colour > green prices, green wave, etc.
**Blue:** The colour of the sky and the sea. Symbolises silence, calmness, reflection, and intellect. Eternal, infinite and total nothing. Blue is the colour most people like.
**Purple:** Represents pride, greatness, and righteousness. The West > the power of the kingdom. The colour of Advent and Lent in Christianity.
**Pink:** The West > skin colour, sensuality, femininity. Traditional colour for little girls, as compared to pastel blue for little boys.
**Grey:** Associated with sadness and depression. As a nuance between white and black, it is the colour of meditation. Uncertainty and ambiguity are referred to as grey areas. In Christianity > the immortality of the soul.

### Colour influence

*How do colours affect buyers*? In a purchasing situation, colours are the strongest and most convincing factor, as demonstrated by a survey conducted by the analytical firm Kissmetics in 2010,[111] see Figure 4.92.

111 **Sources related to the survey: *The Effects of Store Environment on Shopping Behaviors: a Critical Review* (Lam, 2001).**

The survey showed that consumers place visual appearance and colour above other factors like sound, smell and texture. The survey also revealed other key factors that influence consumer behaviour, such as:

For those who buy goods from online stores, design, buzzwords and availability are factors that affect their urge to buy, while poor website navigation and consistently poor design are the predominant reasons why many choose not to buy a product. 42% of online buyers base their purchase on the overall design of the website. 52% of buyers do not return to the website for general aesthetic reasons. Here, too, time plays in, with 65% of online buyers choosing not to buy an item because the website is too slow. The survey also showed that words such as *sales* and *warranty* are sales-triggering words (Kissmetrics, 2010).

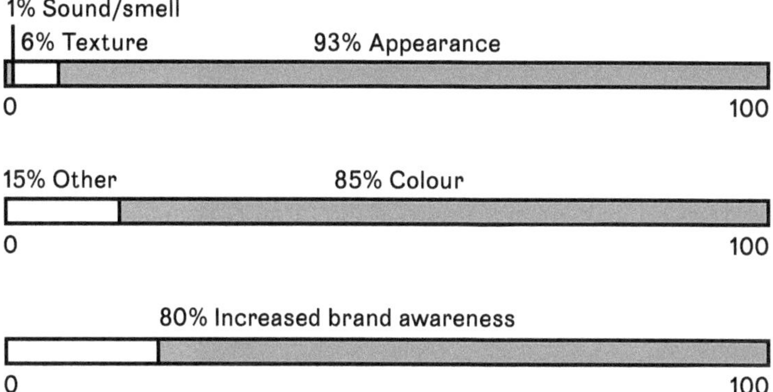


Fig. 4.92 The influence of colour in a buying situation

**The impact of colour on online purchases:** Kissmetics' survey (2010) showed how different colours affect online buyers in North America.
**Yellow:** Optimistic and youthful. Often used to get the attention of so-called window-shoppers, the ones who are outside browsing the shop window.
**Red:** Energy. Increases the heart rate. Creates haste. Frequently used in sales or final sales.
**Blue:** Creates a sense of credibility and security. Often used by banks and business enterprises.
**Green:** Associated with wealth. The easiest colour for the eye to relate to. Used in rest areas in stores.
**Orange:** Aggressive. Creates a call to action: subscribe, buy or sell.
**Pink:** Romantic and feminine. Used to promote products for girls and women.
**Black:** Powerful and slim. Used to market luxury products.
**Purple:** Used for soothing. Often seen on cosmetics and anti-ageing products (3.7.6 Brand assets: Brand Colour).

The Norwegian pilot study 'Sustainable Food Consumption in Nursing Homes: Less Food Waste with the Right Plate Color?' (Hansen, K.V. & Derdowski, L.A. 2020), showed how colored porcelain had a positive effect on food intake for people with dementia. Three different combinations of colors were tested in the research project. The porcelain factory Figgjo AS developed several combinations based on the study with the purpose of stimulating increased food intake. Many nursing homes have purchased the coloured porcelain and put it to use in their wards.

1 Initiation
2 Insight
3 Strategy
4 Design
5 Production
6 Management

4.1 Design brief
4.2 Strategy><Design
4.3 Design methodology
4.4 Concept development
4.5 Design development
4.6 Design elements
4.7 Composition
4.8 Surface and format
4.9 Identity development

4.9.1 The identity principles
4.9.2 The identity elements
4.9.3 Logo
4.9.4 Symbol
4.9.5 Identity colours
4.9.6 Typography
4.9.7 Distinctive assets
4.9.8 Identity management
4.9.9 Grid system

- Colour scheme
- Symbolic meaning of colour
- Colour influence

Less Food Waste with the Right Plate Colour?

The study explored the possibility of reducing food waste in Norwegian nursing homes by appraising how large this reduction could be as one replaces traditional dining white porcelain with plates with diverse color combinations. 'The results of the pilot study were extrapolated to the annual amount of food wasted at the national level. The findings indicate that, on average, 26% of food was thrown away when served on white plates compared to only 9% when served on one of the colored plate options tested. Nationally, approximately 992.6 tons of food per year could potentially be saved with only a single change, ultimately ameliorating the unsustainable food consumption problem among residents of nursing homes' (Hansen, K.V. & Derdowski, L.A. 2020).

### 4.9.6 Typography

Typography is about communication, about making text available in order to get the message across. At the same time, typography is also a strategic instrument for creating identity and is therefore included in this context as one of the key elements of identity. Here, we will look at some selected areas of typography, as a brief introduction to a large and complex subject area. Hopefully, this can arouse curiosity and inspire a desire to get to know better this exciting universe.

In our information society, where we are overwhelmed by information, most people hardly think about which typeface they are reading or how the text is typed. What they probably consciously or unconsciously notice is whether the text is easily accessible and easy to read, whether it has an aesthetic or appealing appearance, and whether it triggers associations with something familiar. If one or more of these factors are satisfied, it is hardly a coincidence. The conscious choice of fonts and text typing are essential for the information to reach the recipient, be it text on websites, smartphones, and e-readers, or in printed media such as books, magazines, and posters.

Øyvin Rannem (2005, p. 12) explains typography as follows: 'Typography is about arranging and presenting text through the use of fonts, possibly in combination with images. The text is created by a sender and is intended for a recipient, or a target audience. This means that the typographer conveys a message between two 'outside' parties, both with an assumed interest in the message arriving as it is intended.' Conscious use of typography is essential for creating a clear and holistic visual identity, and for creating visual communication that signals the intended mood, expression, and associations.

Typography in which the identity elements of a visual identity should function in conjunction with the logo and the other identity elements. A good starting point is to set up the requirements the font should meet, based on the design brief and the strategic guides set for the assignment. In general, it is important to decide what the task of the font should be, what the target group is, what surfaces it should be used on, in what context it should be used, under what lighting conditions it should be read, what duration it should have, and so on. Based on these guides, it may be a good idea to have a division into functional and emotional attributes, which the font should have. This is also good basis for testing the fonts. *Functional* attributes refer to the functions that should be performed for the font to be clear, legible, navigable, and usable on the relevant surfaces, in an information hierarchy, etc. *Emotional* attributes refer to the perception of form, style, and distinctiveness that should be safeguarded in order to trigger proper associations, and express the desired identity, and tone-of-voice (4.1 Design brief, 2.7.6 Target group analysis, 3.2.5 Core values, 3.7.3 Brand position, 3.8 Communication strategy, 3.8.5 Communication platform; Tone-of-voice).

#### Systematic process

When developing a typographic logo, the English term 'lettering' is often used (4.9.3 Logo: Lettering). When we talk about typography as part of a visual identity, we first of all think about how the font should

Fig. 4.93 The figure shows the most common terms used in connection with an editorial text image in a book. The same terms are used for digital surfaces. © Grimsgaard, W. (2018).

112 Body text designates the running text in a book, in printed matter, or on a web page, as opposed to, for example, headlines and captions.
113 Photo byline: The name of the photographer who has taken the photo. Often placed along the image border in small point size, such as 6 or 7 dots.
114 Column titles are short texts with information about the content of the text page, usually placed in the upper margin, i.e. at the top of the page above the page coverage or column. Usually used in academic books, catalogues, magazines, etc. (Rannem 2004: 228).
115 Text templates are named text styles that are predefined or user-defined. Working with text templates allows you to easily define fixed settings for titles, subtitles, body text, and so on.

be used in a text image or a layout. Traditionally, an editorial text image consists of a title, introduction, and body.[112] In addition, there may be titles in different levels, italicised text/quotes, captions, photo bylines,[113] etc. Page numbering (pagination) and column title[114] are also included in this image, see Figure 4.93. It is the context, the contrasts and the whole of the text image that contributes to its accessibility and legibility. *Typography* denotes the use of typefaces and composition of text, the art or procedure of arranging type (Helland, 2017).

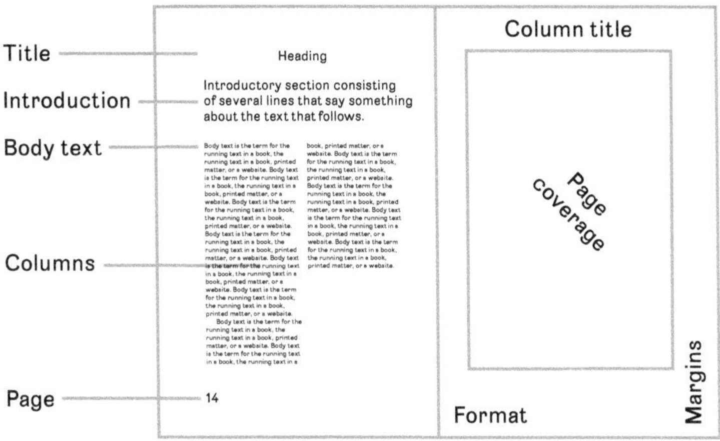


Fig. 4.93 Typographic layout

For the designer, the choice and use of font involves being aware of what should be communicated, what identity or idea the text should help express, what functional attributes are required in terms of legibility, what surfaces the text should work on and in what context. Whether it is a single text page that should be developed, many consecutive text pages or text templates,[115] a systematic approach is a must. It involves working with meticulous testing of typefaces, font sizes, line spacing, line width, page coverage, gap width, margins, grid systems and use of different styles (normal, bold, italics, etc.) for clear communication. Working with typography involves targeted planning and deliberate structuring of letters, words, and text on surfaces. Whether the communication task is to develop editorial media, profile a company or position a brand, the conscious selection and use of typeface is a success factor in making the content accessible. It is about the overall experience, where legibility, identity, and visual expression are central. It is also about how the identity and attributes of the typeface can be used to achieve the desired expression, as well as to strengthen the communication and message. Typography is about the big picture and the intricate details, about subtle undertones, about perception, and composition, about narrative, and dramatic effect. What one gains is knowledge of font history, the classical typefaces, font anatomy, and an alert look at new typefaces.

### Font selection

Font selection is something that happens in parallel with testing how the font will work in a word-picture, in a title, in a text, in a specific format, and in a larger whole of images, illustrations, and graphics. As important

1 Initiation
2 Insight
3 Strategy
4 Design
5 Production
6 Management

4.1 Design brief
4.2 Strategy><Design
4.3 Design methodology
4.4 Concept development
4.5 Design development
4.6 Design elements
4.7 Composition
4.8 Surface and format
4.9 Identity development

4.9.1 The identity principles
4.9.2 The identity elements
4.9.3 Logo
4.9.4 Symbol
4.9.5 Identity colours
4.9.6 Typography
4.9.7 Distinctive assets
4.9.8 Identity management
4.9.9 Grid system

- Systematic process
- Font selection
- Font selection principles
- Font identity
- Font voice
- Font anatomy
- Optical adjustment
- Font terminology
- Font history

**Typography is architecture**

Typography is the architecture in all processing of surfaces where text is to be used. Architecture in this context means the grid system and the principles underlying the organisation of text and images in a layout. 'Let the content be the first priority, and let the typographical choices be a suitable framework for this. Whatever the context' (Gürgens, 2017).

Fig. 4.94 Roman vs Sans serif

as choosing a font is using it consciously to create a system, structure, and style that solve the communication task.

When choosing a font, it is important to think about the task or role of the font; what is the purpose of the font. In most contexts, the font is to perform an important task of communicating content. Font per se cannot do this job alone. It is the typographing, the font processing on the surface, that determines how the text conveys the content. Typographing is largely about developing systems and principles for how the text should be used (4.9.9 Grid system).

When the purpose of the font is to work in running text and text fields, it could be an advantage to start by choosing a simple font family. For most projects, one font family[116] may be sufficient. A good start is to see if the font family has the all the necessary variations. For example, ultralight, light, normal, medium, bold, italic, italic light, italic bold, depending on what one needs. The font variants *normal* and *italics* can be a good starting point. Possibly limit to *normal* only, and create contrasts and dynamics using point size, line spacing, and composition. Using one font family, one can achieve great variety and homogeneity at the same time. In other words, many degrees and sizes, but only one

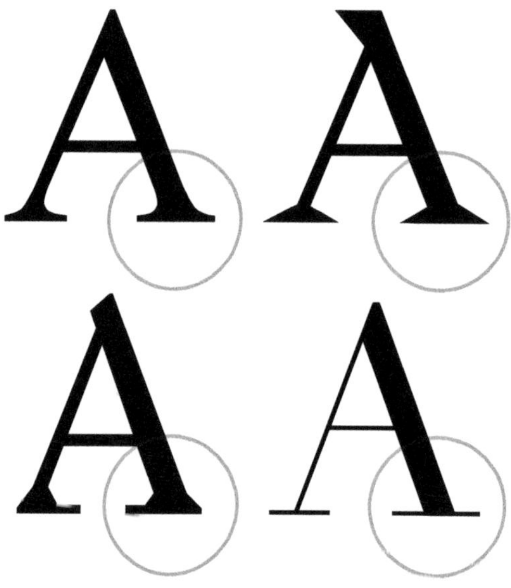
Fig. 4.95 Cut angle

Fig. 4.94 The figure shows examples of a Roman (Baskerville) font on the left and a Sans serif (Mériva) font on the right. The Roman font has clearer variation in line thickness, as we also see in early handwritten Roman script written with a larger pen and ink (calligraphy). A Sans serif usually has a uniform or optically equal line thickness. The contrast in the two main categories, Roman and Sans serif, varies for different typefaces and internally within the same typeface. Bodoni (regular and bold) and Garamond (regular and bold) are examples of typefaces with such variations.

Fig. 4.95 The figure shows how the line thickness and cut angle can vary in a Sans serif font. When selecting a font, it is important to look at how such details work in a typeface. It is equally important to assess resemblance to other identity elements, with a view to achieving a uniform visual expression. © W.G. (2018).

Fig. 4.96 The figure shows how serifs in a Roman typeface can vary in shape and character, something which can be used consciously to achieve the desired expression and identity on letters in a logo.

116 'A font family is a kind of standard set of letters, numbers and characters in several different font variants (normal and italic) and font weights (thin, bold, wide bold, narrow bold, etc.) and with a uniform design intended for typographical rendering. Examples of font families are Garamond, Helvetica, Palatino. In recent years, several font families have emerged that include both Sans serif and Roman.' (Rannem, 2005).

117 The profile was developed by Snøhetta design, and Magnus Rakeng for Avinor: avinor.no/profilmanual. The Avinor Sans profile typeface is available in three different weights: light, medium and bold, so it could meet different usage needs. The Kepler typeface has been selected as a secondary typeface for better readability with larger amounts of text.

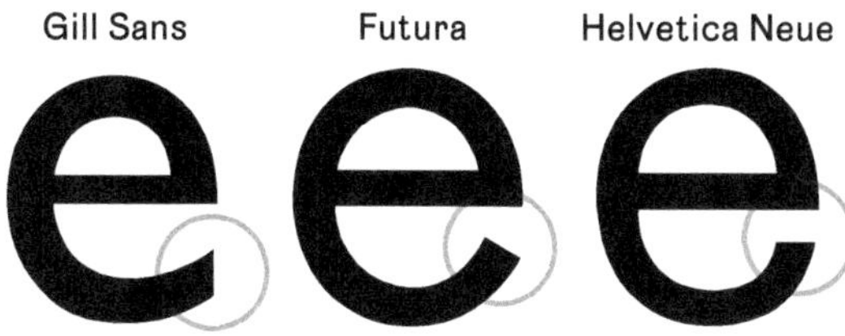


Fig. 4.96 Serifs

typographical culture. Choosing another typeface in addition is done because one needs another typeface, not just for the sake of doing it.

The reason for using a combination of two typefaces may be a need to have a primary typeface for titles and a secondary typeface for body text. This can contribute to creating the necessary contrast, texture, and logic in the text image, or a more interesting and distinctive expression. When selecting two primary typefaces, these are often selected to have distinct differences, but also family resemblance, when it comes to style. It is relatively common to use a combination of a Roman typeface, which is characterised by serifs, and a Sans serif typeface, which is characterised by lack of serifs, see Figure 4.94. Choosing two Roman typefaces or two San serif typefaces as an alternative may add too little contrast or be more difficult to combine. Thus, part of the point of having two typefaces is lost. In addition, using two almost identical typefaces can cause discord in the font picture. In some contexts, when intentionally and consciously done, it can work. An easy way to combine Roman and Sans serif is to choose a super family that includes both. The danger of doing so is that it can become too uniform and thus less interesting.

In some visual identities we see the use of the same typeface in both text and logo. This can work well if the logo is given a distinctive character, so that it is not perceived as generic (ordinary), or more as a title rather than as a logo. An example where this issue is considered to have been resolved well is Avinor's logo. It is based on the specially designed Avinor Sans[117] profile typeface, which also serves as the primary typeface in all Avinor applications.

### Font selection principles

According to Bringhurst (2004, p. 93), selecting and combining typefaces can succeed, provided that a few simple principles are followed:

- Select a font that fits both the task and the topic. *Elaboration*: It involves choosing a typeface that is suitable for the printed matter or website on which it will be used, and at the same time fits the theme. If the theme is racing bikes, a font with a high degree of ornamentation would hardly be suitable. It should rather employ a supple, strong and fast type.
- Select a font that can meet all emotional requirements. *Elaboration*: For example, requirements for shape, style and distinctiveness that should be addressed in order to trigger proper associations, and express the desired identity and tone-of-voice.
- Select fonts whose individual special features are in line with the text. *Elaboration*: Fonts have character, spirit, and personality. Typographers learn to distinguish between these attributes through years of working



**Roman + Sans serif**

When combining Roman and Sans serif, for a long time there has been an unwritten rule to use Roman typeface in the body text because it is easier to read in bulk text than Sans serif, while Sans serif is more suitable for titles. There is no evidence that Sans serif is less legible than Roman. On the contrary, they are more or less equally legible given that they, indeed, have a normal shape. Legibility depends on a number of factors, such as point size, line spacing, line width, etc.

with shape, and by studying and comparing the work of other designers, from the past and present.

- Consider the medium for which the font has originally been created. *Elaboration*: Is it created for a newspaper (Times), or for posters (Egyptienne).
- Select a font that is equipped with the technical attributes you need. *Elaboration*: Technical attributes represent functional requirements that should be met in order for the font to be clear, legible, navigable, and usable on the relevant surfaces and in an information hierarchy. If your text includes a lot of numbers, you may need a typestyle with a lot of number styles.[118] If you need a lot of weights, you may need a typeface with a large font family. Also, think about the kind of language support you need. Language does not only need letters, but should also have ligature support. The most common ligatures are: ff, fi, fl, ffi, ffl. An extreme example is fffl, used in the German word 'Sauerstoffflasche', which means oxygen tank (typography.com).
- Use what works best. *Elaboration*: If you have only one plain typeface available, which you believe to be neither optimal, nor of the quality you require, you can still resolve this as if that were your preferred typeface. In case of good typographing, which involves conscious use of point size, line spacing, kerning, line lengths, word splitting, and so on, attention should be paid to the quality of the composition, and not to the details of individual typefaces.
- Select typefaces with respect to use on digital surfaces, with a view to representation and legibility. Digital surfaces are often small, and there are many new typefaces that take this into account. The most important factors then are size and legibility.
- Select typefaces that are suitable for the paper you will be printing on, or paper that is suitable for the typeface you want to use. *Elaboration*: Most Renaissance and Baroque fonts were created for printing on robust uncoated paper for quite robust purposes. Most neoclassical typefaces were designed to be printed on coated paper, so the fine hairlines came into their own. Modern fonts generally 'withstand' both uncoated and coated paper.
- Select typefaces that will survive the printing process, and if possible, emerge stronger from it. *Elaboration*: Some typefaces have very delicate details, which in small point sizes only come into their own at very high high font resolution (dots per inch/dpi), and offset printing on high-quality coated paper. Other typefaces with simpler details can easily withstand lower resolution.
- Select types with historical origin and associations that are in harmony with your text. *Elaboration*: What we call classic typefaces is not a homogeneous group. They carry with them expressions from the time they were developed, e.g. Baskerville and Caslon, which were designed in England in the 18th century, have special features compared to fonts developed during the Renaissance, see Figure 4.116 Classic typefaces.

### Font identity

When we talk about fonts as identity elements, we mean the font used in titles, introductions, and running text, for example, on a website, in a magazine, or in a book. This font has a different purpose from the one used in the logo, although the same font can serve both purposes. One

Fig. 4.97 **The figure shows examples of some typefaces that to some may seem to have an inherent identity based on their origin, traditional use, or affiliation. This perception may change over time if we make new mental associations with the typeface. In general, how font is perceived is also related to colour and context. © Grimsgaard, W. (2018).**

Fig. 4.98 **The figure shows an example of how we can create a tone or a voice with/on the font.**

Typography nerds

**Typography nerds recognise typefaces by the details and know which font designer is behind them, what year they have been developed, what style or trend they represent and what history the fonts have. Such insight provides the best foundation for typeface selection.**

Further reading

**A film worth watching: *Helvetica* (2007), by Gary Hustwit.**

118 **For example: Text numbers/Old Style can be nice to use in running text because they have the same shape rhythm (ascenders (6, 8) or descenders (3, 4, 5, 7, 9), while others are at x-height (0, 1, 2). For this reason, they are well suited in lower case in running text).**

of the things often emphasised when choosing a font for a visual identity is creating a uniform expression. This means that there is a connection between the identity of the typeface and the shape expression in the other identity elements. At the same time, the opposite, great contrast in shape, style and expression, or even something completely wrong, can also work if done consciously. For example, if the identity should be ironic, informal, or unconventional.

Fig. 4.97 Font is identity

Many fonts have an inherent identity by virtue of their shape, origin, and how they have been used. Convention is a factor, how a font gets linked to something over time, without necessarily being a very obvious choice in the first place. It can affect our choice of font. We are happy to choose a calligraphic typeface for a diploma or an official invitation, an Egyptienne for Western posters, and a Roman typeface for books and newspapers, because it matches what we have seen in the past. Similarly, typefaces used in well-known brands will affect the way many designers choose to use fonts in their projects. We would hardly use the typeface Cochin, which is used in the luxury brand Dior, if we are creating a logo for an everyday, inexpensive product. The inherent identity of the font can be used consciously to best convey the content that should be communicated. It is about achieving congeniality (accordance) between the identity of the font and the content that the font should convey (4.7.3 Unity/whole: Congeniality).

### Font voice

We can clarify and dramatise the content of communication using typography in the same way we do when we speak. It is about the tone, the dialect, whether we are talking to children or adults, whether the voice is temperamental or calm, whether the theme is prose, news, or crime. We call this tone-of-voice. The tone of the font can be created by selecting the typeface and typographing that matches the drop in tone. For example, a 'light' typeface for light voice and 'bold' for dark voice, dense line spacing for dark text fields and open line spacing for light text fields, 'italics' for speed, 'spacing' for tranquillity, and calligraphy for elegance. There are many possibilities, and there is no one answer. By choosing the tone the communication and font should have, we can amplify the message or identity we want the font to express. Tone of voice is defined in the communication strategy or design strategy (3.8 Communication strategy).

*Quick* **Heavy** Mild

Fig. 4.98 The voice of the font


1 Initiation
2 Insight
3 Strategy
4 Design
5 Production
6 Management

4.1 Design brief
4.2 Strategy><Design
4.3 Design methodology
4.4 Concept development
4.5 Design development
4.6 Design elements
4.7 Composition
4.8 Surface and format
4.9 Identity development

4.9.1 The identity principles
4.9.2 The identity elements
4.9.3 Logo
4.9.4 Symbol
4.9.5 Identity colours
4.9.6 Typography
4.9.7 Distinctive assets
4.9.8 Identity management
4.9.9 Grid system

- Systematic process
- Font selection
- Font selection principles
- Font identity
- Font voice
- Font anatomy
- Optical adjustment
- Font terminology
- Font history


Font is identity. Identity is closely linked to values, one's roots one's choices, behaviour, attitudes and actions. This applies to us humans, to businesses and to their products and services. Choice of fonts is a strategic choice that should be based on properly defined core values (3.2.5 Core values).

Fig. 4.99 Double-storey 'a'

Fig. 4.100 Single-storey 'a'

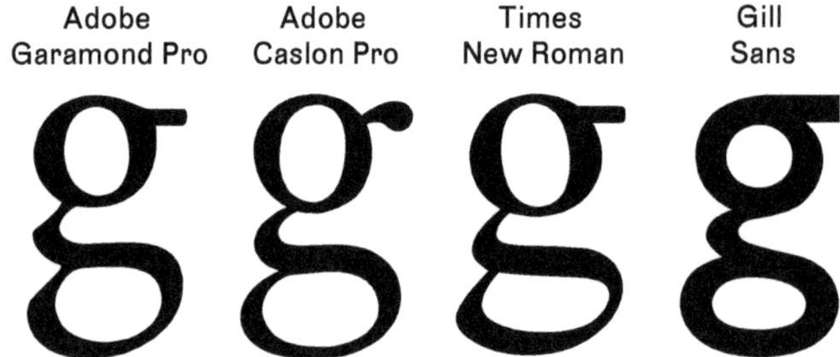


Fig. 4.101 Two-storey 'g'

Fig. 4.102 Single-storey 'g'

Fig. 4.99 Example of double-storey 'a' in different typefaces from different time periods. Notice how the variations in shape and details of the letters create distinctiveness. Note also how the anatomy of the letters rests on the same basic principles, regardless of their different cultural, historical and technological origin. At the same time, they still have markedly different expressions and identities. © Grimsgaard, W. (2018).

Fig. 4.100 The figure shows single-storey 'a' in different typefaces. These also have large variations, but a simpler expression compared to a double-storey 'a'. In addition to studying the details of the font, it is important to consider how it works in a word-picture, a title, or text body with different point sizes, line spacing and column widths. © Grimsgaard, W. (2018).

Fig. 4.101 The figure shows double-storey 'g' in different typefaces. Notice the variations in the details. © W.G. (2018).

Fig. 4.102 The figure shows single-storey 'g' in different typefaces, with clear distinctive features. © W.G. (2018).

Tips for designers

If you take an 'a' from ten different typefaces, increase size and put them side by side, you can study the distinctiveness of each one. There you will probably find subtle, distinctive, funny, elegant, or classic details, which can help create the desired expression or identity, or that something extra.

> The typographical details of the font affect how the font works in body text, titles or in a logo.

119 X height: the height of the minuscule (the lower-case letters), such as lowercase 'n' and lowercase 'x', i.e. the lowercase letters that do not have over- and underlengths.

## Font anatomy

There can be large variations between different font groups and within the same font groups. The differences can be distinctive and easily visible, or so small and subtle that one needs an in-depth study of each letter and a trained eye. The anatomy and distinctiveness of each font influences whether it works in a larger text field or whether it is best suited to stand alone and assert itself. A typeface that is wide with a large x-height may be better suited for bulk text than a typeface that is narrow with a low x-height.[119] Some typefaces have 'e' with a small eye, others with a large one. Some g's and a's have two storeys, some have one, some f's have high crossbar, others have a low one, some j's have long tail, others have short tails. Many typefaces may look quite similar at a first glance, but when you study them closely, you will find big differences in the smaller details, see Figures 4.99. 4.100, 4.101 and 4.102.

### Typography iteration

Font selection can be done using the iterative method: One starts by trying out typefaces, different font sizes, column widths and line spacings, printing out examples, testing legibility, learning what works and what does not, and using this to develop further in the next iteration. Here, it is important to be patient and persevering. Once the result is perceived as satisfactory, one should still do a few extra rounds. The process narrows towards the detail phase, which is all about remaining there until every last detail has been carefully considered and positioned. This is a time-consuming process, which needs to be tailored to the time and budget constraints of the assignment.

## Optical adjustment

Working with typography is a lot about working with millimetres, point sizes, and grid system calculations. The real goal is our eye, seeing what works optically right. 'Working with typography is basically working with a text message interface with the reader. The goal is to create an interface adapted to the human eye' (Rannem, 2005, p. 211). It is about combining technical precision with optical assessment. Here, we will look at some examples that may be useful to know when detailing and optically adjusting fonts.

**Form and counter-form:** Letters are both form and counter-form. It is the white versus the black and the black versus the white. With the black form we think of the form of the font, and with white we think of the inner form of the font. The black form cannot be changed without taking the white form into account. With white we also think of the air around, above, below and inside the letter, or the sheet on which the text is written or printed. These spaces, also called 'air' or 'space', influence how the font behaves in different contexts affects the legibility. Creating a good reading rhythm in the text is largely about conscious processing of the inner forms. 'It is in fact, the inner forms that we actually see and read. These are the ones that define the form of the whole letter and the whole text image' (Gürgens, 2017). Working with form and counter-form

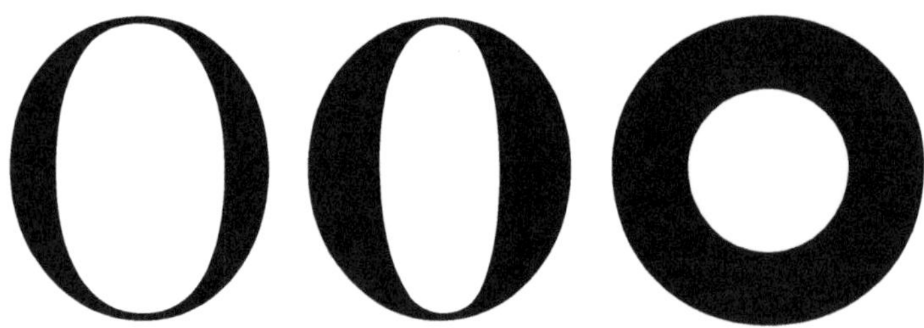

Fig. 4.103 Inner and outer form

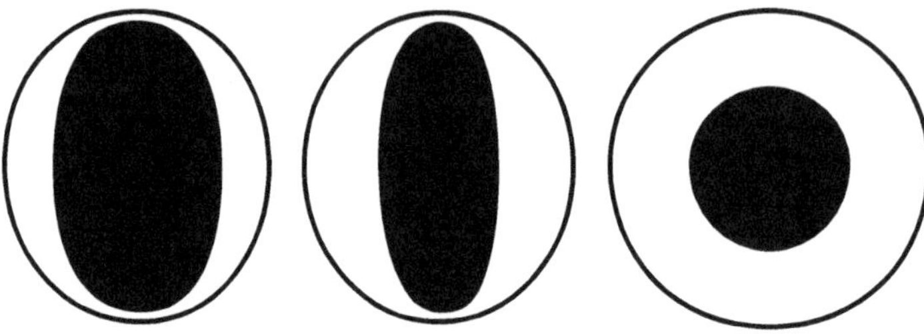

Fig. 4.104 Inner and outer form

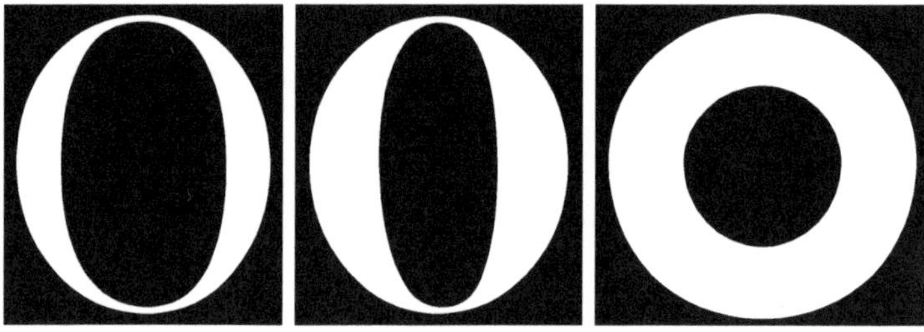

Fig. 4.105 Inner and outer form

Fig. 4.106 Inner and outer form

Fig. 4.103 The figure shows the letter in the typefaces Bodoni 72, Bodoni 72 bold, Futura bold, from left to right.

Fig. 4.104 The figure shows the inner form of the letter as black.

Fig. 4.105 The figure clarifies the relationship between inner and outer form. The three letters have approximately the same outer form, while it is the inner form that creates the major differences. The example is based on Noordzij (2005).

Fig. 4.106 The figure shows an example of the use of letter spaces. Too little letter space tears the letters apart from each other because parts of one letter connect to parts of another letter. This can then be perceived as flickering. Too large a letter space causes the word to fall apart. The middle row shows an example of optimal letter space, considering classic typographing and good legibility (based on Rannem 2005).

Fig. 4.107 The figure shows an example of letter spacing. There is usually a minimum gap between two round letters, a little more between a round and a straight letter, and maximum between a straight and another straight. The serifs are usually disregarded when kerning (adjusting letter spacing), but the serifs should not collide. One looks from stem to stem, from stroke to stroke. The starting point for adjustment should be the letters that collide the most. Adjust them, then adjust the whole word based on this. In other words, find the problem first. One can also regard the spaces between words as a glass of water, or as sand in an hourglass. How much water/sand is there? The point is to look at the volume. The inner form and outer form are volume. The volume inside the letters (shown here as white) should be as even as possible with the volume around (marked here as orange). © Grimsgaard, W. (2018).

is about perception, how we optically assess a text or the word-picture in terms of typographical qualities and legibility. 'The relationship between form and counter-form, which in writing constitutes the relationship between black and white, is the basis of our perception. (...) Different font types with their different constructions and their different line thicknesses can be compared to each other only considering the white of the word' (Noordzij, 2005, p. 15).

**Letter spacing:** 'In order for the text surface to have a calm and harmonious appearance without any black spots or white holes, there should be balance between the inner openings of the letters and the distance between the letters at the front and back. (...) The different widths and shapes of the letters mean that not all letters fit together equally well, which can create optically uneven letter spaces (e.g.: AV, HI, Tr, TL)', (Rannem, 2017). The distance between the letters when they are arranged in words is called letter spacing. In most quality fonts, the letter spacing is embedded in the letter's design, as part of the letter's width value. In case of unusual letter combinations, *condensing* (reduction of letter spacing) or *expanding* (increasing the letter space) may be necessary. The size of the word spaces has been gradually reduced over the past hundred years. In typography, today's norm is the breadth of a lower-case 'i'. The need for letter spacing is related to the inner structure of the letter. There should be a balance between the inner and outer spaces of the letters (Rannem, 2005, p. 150). For example, large internal openings will require large spaces. Some expressions for adjusting letter spacing:

- Kerning: adjusting the space between two letters.
- Expanding: increasing the letter space for several letters.
- Condensing: reducing the letter space for several letters.

Fig. 4.107 Kerning

**The font's DNA:** The distance between the letters is something most designers who work with fonts are aware of. It is about creating optical harmonic distance between the letters and good rhythm in the text. In a digital font, there is a default spacing between the letters. This distance is not random. In his article 'Hva er egentlig typografi' (2017), Frode Helland writes about the font's DNA. What is interesting is that the basic principles for creating the digital font are the same as for the lead types implemented by Gutenberg in the 16th century. As a font designer, he relates to each letter as part of a typographical system similar to what Gutenberg created. 'All letters have to fit into the typographical system – each individual element is built on the same DNA. Besides, each character is designed on an invisible square, and the distance to the edges – the air – is almost as important as the form itself. If I may, a brief history lesson: It was not first and foremost the printing press that was

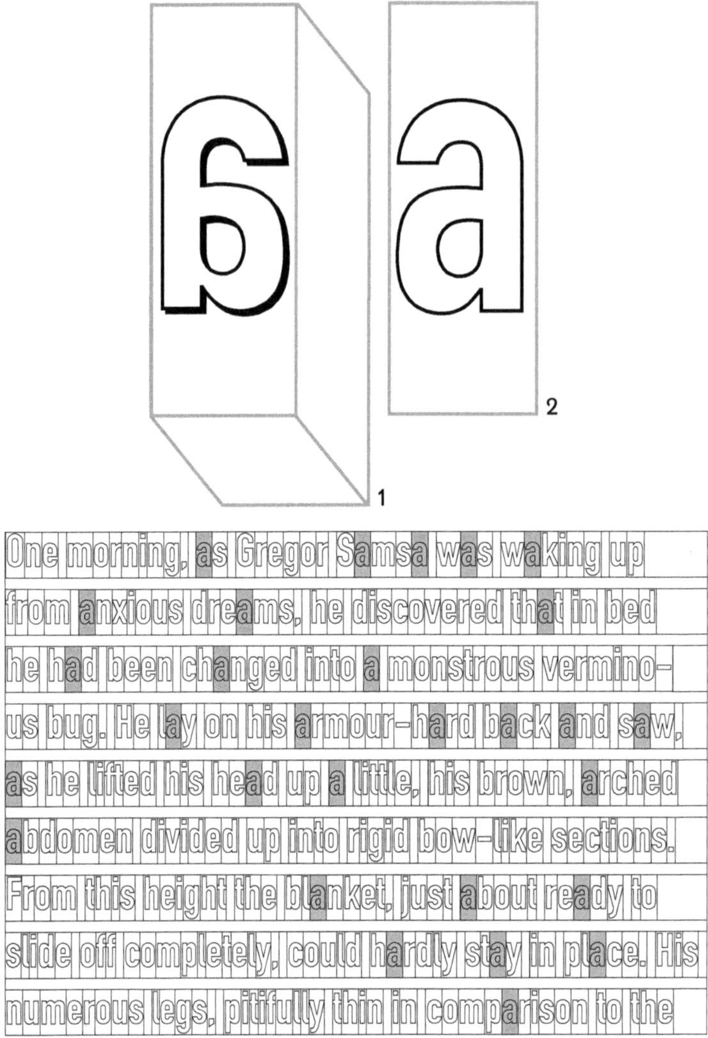


Fig. 4.108 The font's DNA

Fig. 4.108 **1) The figure shows a schematic representation of a lead type. An elevated relief of the lead type makes a mirrored impression on the paper. 2) Digital fonts operate with the same metaphor: Each character is defined on an invisible square (the illustration is based on Helland 2017). Here you can also observe how the letters form a texture on the page, which makes a big difference from the experience at micro-level. It is important to look at the texture of the letters, how they work in body text, in columns and longer sections, and not just look at the details of the isolated letters. As an example, one can examine how a one-storey 'a' works compared to a two-storey 'a' on the entire font picture.**

Fig. 4.109 **The figure shows optical alignment of a Roman italic. © Grimsgaard, W. (2018).**

Fig. 4.110 **Figures show examples of overshoots. Letters with round shapes, such as O, G and Q, have overshoots. This means that the arc goes slightly below the baseline and slightly opposite the accent line (or the centreline if it is a matter of a lower-case letter), in order for the letter to be perceived optically as being on a line. The same goes for letters that have a pointed shape, like A and V. The square on the left in the figure at the top shows a letter that does not usually have an overshoot, for example M, N and X. © Grimsgaard, W. (2018).**

Gutenberg's revolutionary invention, but rather the typeface. Typeface design is therefore a dynamic system built up of static elements. In short, mass production of font' (Helleand, 2017). Figure 4.108 shows a digital font compared to a lead type.

**Optical grid:** Optical adjustment is essential when working with typography. Some letters have so-called overshoots, which extend above or below the letter height line, such as the ltters O and G, and pointed letterforms like A and V, in order to to make them look optically aligned with other letters, see Figure 4.110. It is easy to imagine that italics have the same oblique position on all letters. If we go in and investigate further, it may turn out that the font designer has chosen different angles of the letters to ensure that they are optically perceived as having the same angle, see Figure 4.109. On the other hand it may be to create a liveliness to accentuate the formal contrast to the normal variant, which is the case with some historical italics.

120 **Anthropomorphism is the transfer of human qualities to non-human beings (gods, animals, things), especially in the notions people create about the divine. Common in the mythology and iconography in most religions (SNL, 2017).**

1 Initiation
2 Insight
3 Strategy
4 Design
5 Production
6 Management

4.1 Design brief
4.2 Strategy><Design
4.3 Design methodology
4.4 Concept development
4.5 Design development
4.6 Design elements
4.7 Composition
4.8 Surface and format
4.9 Identity development

4.9.1 The identity principles
4.9.2 The identity elements
4.9.3 Logo
4.9.4 Symbol
4.9.5 Identity colours
4.9.6 Typography
4.9.7 Distinctive assets
4.9.8 Identity management
4.9.9 Grid system

- Systematic process
- Font selection
- Font selection principles
- Font identity
- Font voice
- Font anatomy
- Optical adjustment
- Font terminology
- Font history

Fig. 4.109 Optically correct

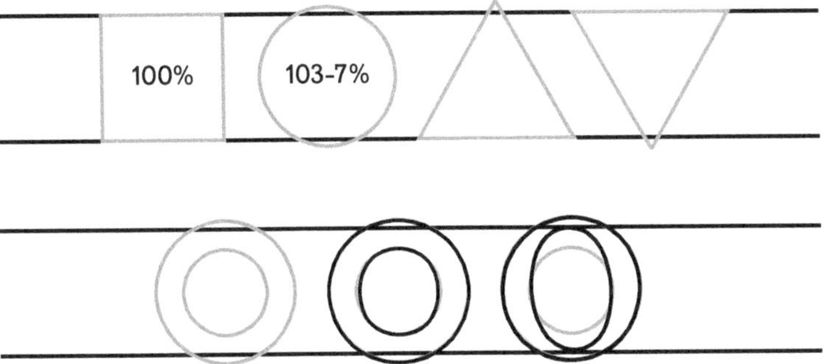


Fig. 4.110 Overshoots

**Letter axis:** When developing or processing fonts, it is necessary to understand the logic of font form. The key lies in studying the classic typefaces. Typical of many of the classic typefaces is that they mimic calligraphic writing techniques from different periods of font history, where the angle and pressure of the pen, together with the shape of the nib, determine the shape of the letter and the thickness of the stem and hairline, as well as the axis of the letter, see Figures 4.111 and 4.112. Many modern fonts are based on the same principles. If one understands the logic, one will have a greater chance of succeeding in the processing or development of fonts. It is also important in this context to know the background and history of the font, when it was developed, for what purposes it was used, and what associations it triggers, see Figure 4.113.

### Font terminology

In order to explain, justify and discuss the nuances of the different typefaces, it is a good idea to know the names of the letter parts and other typographical expressions. Several of the typographical expressions are taken from calligraphy such as *hairline*, others from book printing such as movement mirrors, body text and leading, and some expressions are anthropomorphic[120] such as *the eye* in lower-case 'e' (Rannem, 2005).

Fig. 4.111 Calligraphy

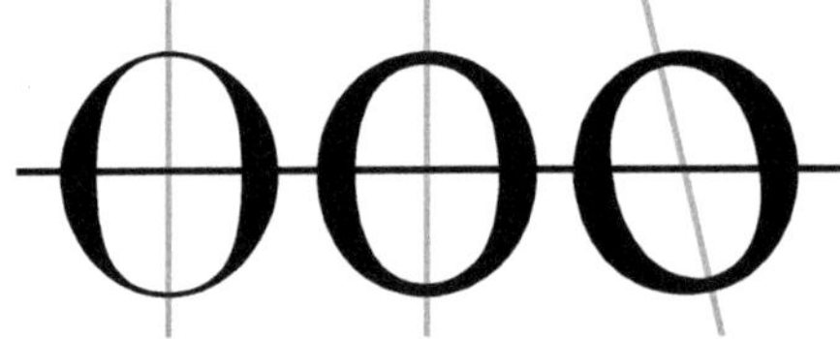

Fig. 4.112 Letter axis

Fig. 4.113 Font as identity element

Fig. 4.111 The figure shows how calligraphic font is formed according to the angle of the pen and the width of its nib. With a different nib thickness and pen angle, the result will be different. The wide pen naturally creates a thicker line down on the left and up on the right, as the pen is moved around. Calligraphic writing was the model for the first lead types.

Fig. 4.112 The figure shows examples of how different typefaces can have different axes. From the left: Didot, Times New Roman and Stanley. Axis is used primarily in typography for the main direction of the inner aperture, especially in round letterforms, such as minuscules b, c, d, e, o, p, q and capital letters C, D, G, O, Q. In calligraphy fonts, the aperture axis is the result of the angle of the pen nib. The angle may optionally be repeated in the design and composition of other elements to create a uniform expression. © Grimsgaard, W. (2018).

Fig. 4.113 The figure shows a typographic hand drawn logo containing calligraphic elements providing a characteristic, elevated expression of quality, handcraft and unique personality. By Strømme Throndsen Design for The Broth Company, 2020.

Fig. 4.114 The figure shows various font terms that can be used when it is necessary to understand, describe, or explain the geometry and optical position of the font on the line.

**Typographical terms:** Here is a small overview of some of the most common typographical terms:

**Font:** Font is currently widely used for writing, font families, font type, typeface, and type series.[121] Originally, font is an English term (fount) that means casting, linked to lead technology. At the time, it meant a complete set of all letters, numbers, and symbols in a degree within a particular typeface or font variant, such as 10 pt. Palatino (Rannem, 2004). Rannem uses *typeface* in the sense of form and *font* in the meaning of a technical part of a typeface.

**Point (pt):** Point is a typographic unit of lengths, used to specify the height of fonts, leading and column or any length. There are 12 points in a cicero. A cicero measures 4.5108 mm.[122] Points is also measures by inch. 1pt is also equal to 1/72th of an inch.

**Point (pt) vs. pixel (px):** 'Comparison of 1 pixel and 1 point depends on the resolution of the image. If the image is 72ppi (pixels per inch), then one point will equal exactly one pixel' (Singh, 2016). Px is a single square 'picture element' (hence pix-el), i.e. a single dot in an image. A 10x10

121 Series of type: the traditional term for a full set of letters in all degrees of a font, for example all degrees of Garamond normal.

122 Cicero is a typographical unit of measure developed by the Frenchman François A. Didot. It is used in all countries around the world except in Britain and the United States.

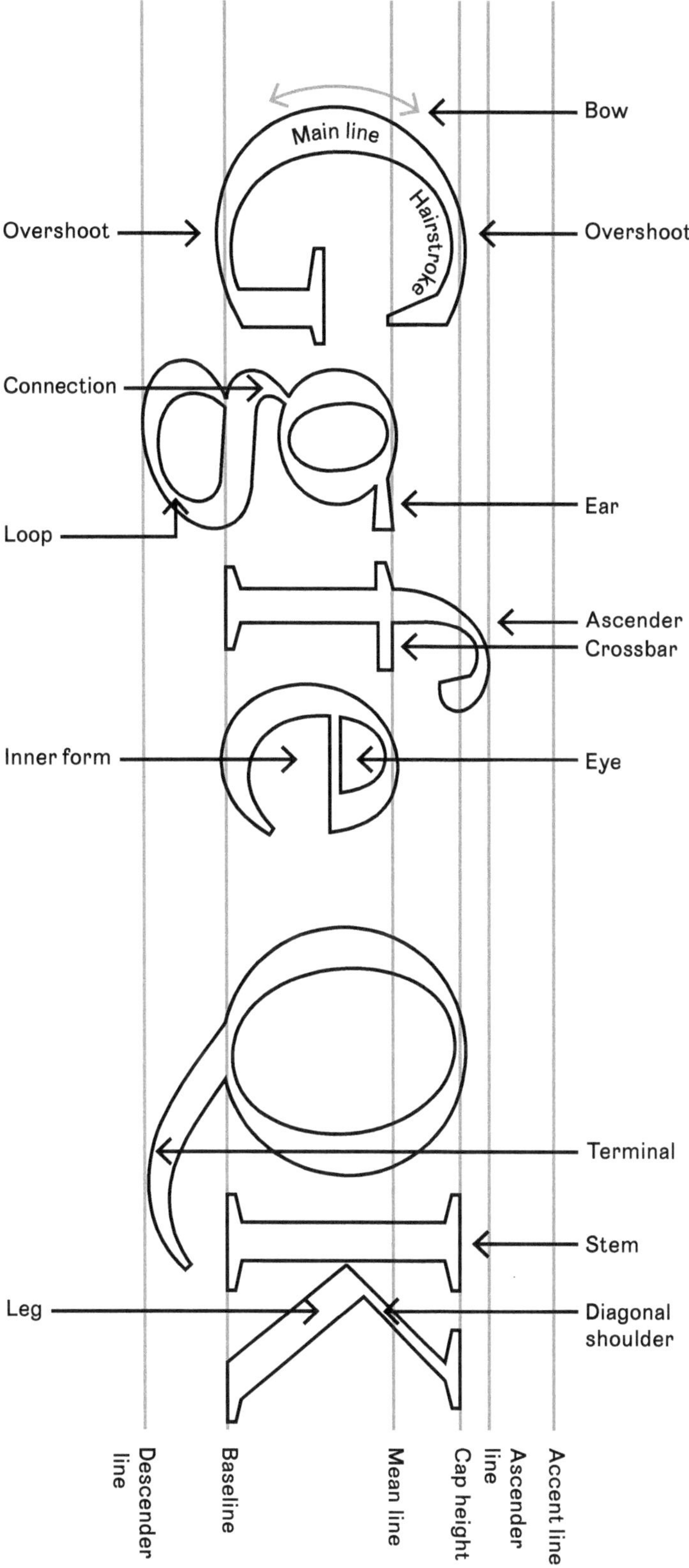


Fig. 4.114 Font terminology


1 Initiation
2 Insight
3 Strategy
4 Design
5 Production
6 Management

4.1 Design brief
4.2 Strategy><Design
4.3 Design methodology
4.4 Concept development
4.5 Design development
4.6 Design elements
4.7 Composition
4.8 Surface and format
4.9 Identity development

4.9.1 The identity principles
4.9.2 The identity elements
4.9.3 Logo
4.9.4 Symbol
4.9.5 Identity colours
4.9.6 Typography
4.9.7 Distinctive assets
4.9.8 Identity management
4.9.9 Grid system

- Systematic process
- Font selection
- Font selection principles
- Font identity
- Font voice
- Font anatomy
- Optical adjustment
- Font terminology
- Font history

image is made up of a set of pixels in a grid 10 wide by 10 high, totalling 100 pixels (Singh, 2016).

**Pica:** In Britain and the United States, font size, leading, and column height are specified in pica. A pica is 4.233 mm, approx. seven percent less than a cicero.

**Millimetre:** Metric unit of measure (mm). Some choose to use mm for paper formats, margins and column widths. Another approach is to choose mm only in format, and otherwise work in points (pt), as all fonts in the software today are defined in points.[123]

**Majuscule:** 'Big' letter. For example, capital 'S'. Monoalphabetic fonts with uniform height, like the Roman capital letters, are called majuscules. Originating from the Roman capitals (capitalis monumentalis), they are still found on Roman columns and monuments (Rannem, 2004).

**Minuscule:** 'Small' letter. For example, small 's'.

**Kerning:** For a word-picture to be perceived optically correct, the distance between letters can be adjusted by condensing (decreasing the distance) or expanding (increasing the distance).

**Page coverage:** The part of the paper format that can be covered by text and images, see Figure 4.93 Typographic layout.

**Text column:** Division of the text into columns within the page coverage.

**Column spacing:** The distance between the columns on the page coverage. The distance between the columns should not be less than the line height of the font being used (4.9.9 Grid system).

**Grid system:** Grid is a form of modular system for positioning of text and images. A standardisation of shape, size and position, often set up in a proportional modular system (4.8 Surface and format, 4.9.9 Grid system).

**Title:** A brief hint, description or symbolisation of content. There may be different title levels, such as main title, subtitle, intertitle, column title, etc. The title is essential for the reader to find their way through the article (Forfatterveiledning/SNL).

**Introduction:** A short introductory text to an article, chapter, or larger section. The introduction should introduce or summarise the matter, offer a 'taste' of what the matter is about, like a 'starter (petterandresen.no).

**Body type:** Running text whose size generally ranges from 8 to 12 pt.[124] The term body text or body matter comes from book printing and lead matter. Typographers' pay was calculated based on the number of lines they had set. The setting of the body was fast, and it was essentially how setters earned for their daily bread (Rannem, 2017).

**Title font:** Fonts that are generally larger than 12 pt.

**Initial:** An accent of an initial letter; the first letter of a section, chapter, article, etc.

**Ligature:** Ligature is a combination of two or more letters where the very letter images are linked in such a way that they become a whole from technical and design perspective (glyph).

**Column title:** short text with information about author, chapter title, book title, usually placed above the page coverage or column.

**Line length:** The length of the line of text in a body affects legibility. A rule of thumb is that the optimal line length is about 60 characters. This varies for digital and analogue surfaces, and for different typefaces. It should always be optically tested. Tests done by Tinker (1969, p. 86) showed that short and long lines are easier to read with slightly greater

Fig. 4.115 The figure shows some font terminologies that describe the different heights of the font.

123 Millimetres: If font should help define the surfaces from the very beginning, it will be the font size that will help define page coverage and column widths. In principle, this means defining everything within the page coverage in pt, and everything outside it in mm.

124 Different typefaces can have different x-height and overshoots. Eight-point font can have the same optical legibility as nine- or ten-point fonts.

125 This is because the text has completely regular (optical) word spacing, and word divisions can be largely avoided (Rannem, 2005, p. 128). Text that is centred or has a loose left edge is generally less legible.

126 The term 'leading' comes from the blank material used to make a distance between the lines in the lead type in former book prints. The need for line spacing depends on the shape of the font. Typefaces with high x height will generally need greater leading than lines with low x height. In a text column, long lines need more leading than short ones. Proper leading helps the reader get good context and read flow. For 10–12 pt fonts, normal legibility increases when line spacing is increased by two–three points, and decreases when line spacing is increased by four points or more.

127 Em was an important unit in the blank material used in lead types, including: en quad (half), drittel (one third) and slis (one quarter). Em is still used as a typographical unit of breadth on digital converters, and is also used as a starting point for font design (typografi&skrift)

128 Book printing is done at high pressure. Letterpress is the term also used today, see 5.6.1 Press techniques.

129 The Gutenberg Bible, also known as the 42-line Bible, the Mazarin Bible and B42, was completed by Johannes Gutenberg in Mainz, Germany, in 1455 ('Gutenberg Bible,' n.d.).

line spacing (Rannem, 2005, p. 128). Line alignment: There are four options here: Align (block/straight margins), loose right edge, loose left edge and centred. Text with a loose right edge may have an advantage over block alignment in terms of legibility.[125]
**Line spacing:** Line spacing or distance between two consecutive lines.

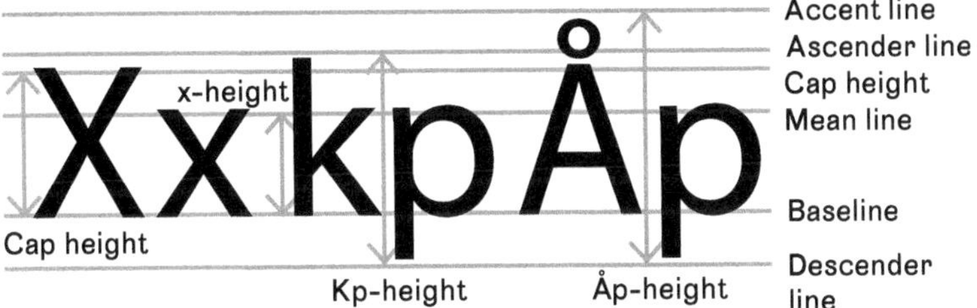


Fig. 4.115 Font terminology

**Leading:** Usually defined in points, but a distinction should be made between technical and optical distance. Selecting 9/12 pt (pronounced nine at twelve point) means using nine-point font with three-point leading.[126]
**Indentation:** Indents are used to mark a new section. The width should be assessed optically in relation to the width of the lines and the columns. Indent can be looped in the first line after a title and in the top line of a column. The indent should be clear. Half an em is the minimum. Em: Em is an old typographical term, which historically came from the width of M in lead type (em space). The point of the unit of measure is that M is a relative unit of width that varies according to the point size of the font. The width of the em is the same as the type body or height. In other words, the width of a ten-point em is ten points.[127]

### Font history

We cannot talk about typography without also talking about history because font *is* history. In Europe, typography as a subject emerged with book printing[128] and lead types in the 15th century. Johannes Gutenberg[129] established the printing technique as a time-saving way to produce books. The Gutenberg Bible was the first book printed with loose lead types.

Before book printing streamlined book production in Europe, book-making was a laborious and time-consuming work done by monks and professional writers who calligraphed book by book and page by page with pen and ink. It was also the shape of the calligraphic font that formed the basis of Gutenberg's first font alphabet cast in lead. It was a Gothic font, as strict and powerful as the power of the Church at the time. Religion and politics were two sides of the same coin, and rebellion against oppressive religious forces was also accompanied by waves of protest, and a need for freedom and openness. This influenced our way of thinking and writing, and led to more open and light forms of writing, which, combined with the possibilities offered by printing techniques and writing tools, evolved into new forms of writing. Thus, historical and social cycles through Gothic style, humanism, the Renaissance, Baroque, classicism, functionalism, modernism, post-modernism, combined with developments in printing techniques and eventually computer technology, have influenced font form and typography as a whole to this day.

The first book printers often cut and cast their types themselves as part of managing book printing and typesetting, and many of the typography expressions from the lead printing period are still used, such as page coverage, body type, capitals and minuscules. A printer's assistant in the 17th and 18th century could make a good living. Gradually, being a typographer evolved into a highly esteemed profession in Central Europe in the 19th and 20th century. One had classic role models from Baroque and neoclassicism, such as 16th-century Claude Garamond, 18th-century Giambattista Bodoni, and John Baskerville. The classical masters were followed by 20th century tone-setting font designers at a time marked by the various directions and fluctuations of modernism, such as the Swiss Max Miedinger and Adrian Frutiger, the German Jan Tschichold and Paul Renner, the Britons Eric Gill and Stanley Morison, and the American Herb Lubalin, to name a few.

In the 20th century, there was a development in printing technology from book printing to offset, allowing for higher speed and circulation of printed matter, while at the same time creating new opportunities for font development. Lead types and angle hooks were replaced by photo kit and paste-up. Font design and typography, began to find its way out of the printing houses and over to professional designers, and the typographers were reduced to 'providers'.

Many of the classic fonts from the previous centuries, developed from the 16th century to the end of the 19th century, live on in recreated versions. Many newer fonts are more or less inspired by the classics. Typefaces were drawn by hand until the 1990s, and many of today's font veterans have experienced the transition from handwriting to computer

Fig. 4.116 The figure shows a selection from the most common and most frequently used classic typefaces. As can be seen from the figure, these typefaces have been developed over hundreds of years and bear the characteristics of the writing style and printing technique used during the various periods. These classic fonts are just as topical today and are models for countless fonts developed in recent times.

Tips for the designer
Some type foundries to explore: Pangram Pangram, Good Type Foundry, Open Foundry, Grill Type, The Designers Foundry, Letters From Sweden, Monokrom Type Foundry, Klim Type Foundry, New Letters, Colophon, 205TF, R-Typography, Nova Type Foundry.

**Font history terminology**

**Johannes Gutenberg:** Inventor of modern book printing in Europe. Gutenberg's Bible was printed in 1455 and was among the very first printed books in Europe.
**Book printing:** Loose types of moulded were put together to form words, lines and entire print pages. The lead types were placed in a printing press, printing ink was applied and pressed against paper.
**Type:** Letterform cast in metal or cut in wood.
**Typeface:** Used for a special font or font family, such as Times New Roman, Helvetica, etc.
**Typography:** Typography of 'Typographie', French for printing (16th century), was a separate term for setting and printing text for a long time. Typographer was the title of book printers from the 16th century until the late 20th century. Most printing houses in Norway until around 1960–1970 were book printing houses. The great transition to offset did not arrive before that (Rannem, 2017). Today, typography is a central discipline in graphic design.
**Typographing:** Arranging and processing text, for example in an editorial layout.

Further reading
Check out online font tools:
Fonts in use:
https://fontsinuse.com/

My Fonts:
https://www.myfonts.com/

WhatTheFont.
Instant font identification:
https://www.myfonts.com/WhatTheFont/

Aldus (ca. 1490) Aldus Manutius
Garamond (1500) Claude Garamond
Caslon (1700) William Caslon
Baskerville (1700) John Baskerville
Bodoni (1700) Giambattista Bodoni
**Franklin Gothic (1904) Morris Fuller Benton**
**Gill Sans (1927) Eric Gill**
**Futura (1928) Paul Renner**
**Albertus (1932) Berthold Wolpe**
**Helvetica (1957) Max Miedinger**
**DIN (1995) Albert-Jan Pool**
**Gotham (2000) Tobias Frere-Jones**

Fig. 4.116 Classic typefaces



font design. In the mid-20th century, when corporate identity became the big trend in the business world, it gradually became quite common to create one's own font as part of the identity package. Font designers at that time, who received such assignments and provided many new font alphabets, included the German Erik Spiekermann, the Americans Carol Twombly, Jonathan Hoefler, Tobias Frere-Jones, and Zuzana Licko, as well as Emigre Fonts. From the later 'the cold-type era' in the 1960s to 1970s, typedesigners as Ed Benguiat, Herb Lubalin, Othmar Motter, Roger Excoffon etc. should be mentioned. An explosion of new expressions followed from the time when one was not bound to equally fixed technology! The Letraset vs. letterpress represented a whole new the selection of typefaces. In the digital age of the 21st century, digitisation influenced the development of newer fonts. Speaking of pixel fonts and early mac, Susan Kare along with Zuzana Licko were pioneers in early digital font design. Further, James Edmondson is an ingenious font designer and founder of Future Fonts that provides a new type of platform and distribution method for independent font designers.

### 4.9.7 Distinctive assets

A unique or distinctive identity element or shape can evolve to become the most recognisable brand asset. It can be a bearing idea, a visual detail that tickles one's stomach, a factor that helps create experience and commitment, the finishing touch and that little extra, which connects the outside world with the product or service in question. A distinctive identity element has many names, such as The fifth element, brand sense or distinctive brand asset.

- *The fifth element* is a visual element in addition to the traditional four elements: logo, colors, typography, and image. It can be a typographic compilation, a mascot, a pattern, the shape of a bottle, e.g. the typical shape of the Absolute Vodka bottle or the iconic shape of an old Coke bottle. We remember the brand name only by looking at the shape of the bottle. (4.2.6 The fifth element).
- *Brand sense* is a style, tone, and design expression, which produces an 'a-ha' response. No further explanations are needed to understand this. It is a convincing, inspiring, and unique idea that guides and unites all communication of the brand with its surroundings. It links the brand to the business strategy and is a springboard for communication work (Myhre, 2017).
- *Distinctive brand assets* are a characteristic shape, colour or sound, which immediately makes us think of the product or service it represents, even if we see or hear only fragments. The concept of distinctive brand assets was introduced by Jenni Romaniuk (2018). It involves choosing the one brand element that is most recognised by category shoppers and that clearly differentiates itself from the competitors in the same product or service category. The choice is made based on measurements of metrics among the customer group, which further provides a basis for a Distinctive Asset-building strategy (2.9.8 Mental availability measurements, 3.4.6 Distinctive asset-building strategy, 3.7.6 Brand assets).

**The purpose of identity management is to ensure that identity is perceived in the same way at any given moment and in any context, by placing identity elements consistently on all surfaces and formats.**

### 4.9.8 Identity management

Often, it is the first impression that counts or the first three seconds, during which one pays attention to the person or product. One takes in the big picture before the details. That is why the whole is so important. How elements are composed in relation to each other helps create distinctiveness and recognition. Composition is layout. Layout is identity. Identity is strategy. They are all connected. Always.

Earlier, we described identity as a person. It is a metaphor, which also applies to identity management; how the person is perceived as a whole. 'With the right management, we can combine the identity elements to create a complete person or a homogeneous identity' (Rybakken, 2004, p. 266). For a company or product, this means that identity is presented holistically and consistently, so that it is perceived in the same way as much as possible at any given moment. It is about directing the identity elements so that they appear as a whole, which is rendered in the same way on different profile carriers to the greatest extent possible. This also implies that the identity elements and the way they are directed have distinctive features that are easy to remember. Composition of identity elements is a central part of the perceived identity. It is about the size, aspect ratio, and location of the elements relative to each other (4.7 Composition, 4.8 Surface and format, 4.9.2 The identity elements, Figure 4.80).

Conscious composition of the identity elements can evoke attitude, disposition, temperament, mood, seriousness, etc. For example, placing elements on the left of a surface can be perceived as traditional, central placement can be perceived as solemn, random placement can be perceived as dynamical, but also inconsistent and messy, unless done intentionally. Composition is about how we build up and assemble the elements.

Consistent composition of identity elements means that the aspect ratio, composition, location, etc. are made as uniform as possible on all surfaces. Conscious identity management (or art direction) is central to creating a holistic and consistent visual identity. One example of that is the identity of Kiwi. Kiwi is recognised as a green colour, not only because of its colour, but because of how its colour is used on different surfaces in terms of the shape and size of the colour fields, and how they are aligned with other identity elements. Management is strategy. Kiwi uses the green colour to cover the entire surface, on walls, uniforms and shopping trolleys. That is how we recognise Kiwi. This is no accident. It is related to how they want to appear and be perceived compared to their competitors. It is about how they want to compete in the market. Should they focus on a niche market or on a broad market? Should they signal high or low prices? These issues are described in the competition strategy and brand position, and they give direction to the identity management. Identity management is the common thread (or the green thread, if you like) (3.4 Business strategy, 3.7.3 Brand position).

Once the direction has been determined, a profile guide or design manual is prepared as an aid for those in charge of commissioning the identity. It aims precisely to ensure consistent and comprehensive use of the identity elements (6.5 Design manual). The identity management should be adjusted over time in order to be perceived as trendy. Therefore, it is important to ensure that the identity framework is not too rigid. All identities should be reviewed/redesigned at regular intervals in order to be perceived as trendy. Some companies need to make frequent adjustments; for others, years may go by (Rybakken, 2004).

An effective way to create direction and structure is through the conscious use of grid systems, which we will look at in the next chapter (4.9.9 Grid system).

## 4.9.9 Grid system

The grid is a plan or principle for the composition of sound, motion, or visual elements. In visual design, it is largely about how text, images and graphic elements are arranged on a surface. It is a strategic matter related to functional and aesthetic considerations, and what expression, mood and style one wishes to convey.

The grid is an invisible net of vertical, horizontal, diagonal, and sometimes curved or round guides, which can be used to create structure and system in a composition of text, images, and graphic elements. The grid system is visible to the designer, but (usually) invisible in the finished design. Nevertheless, the beholder will use the experience of frames and lines that occur implicitly around and between the form elements to understand the whole and see connections. According to gestalt theory, we humans seek meaning in what we see by looking for parts in a context and putting them together mentally into a whole (4.7.1 Perception). This theory is also central to the principles of composition, which are largely based on the knowledge of perception (4.7.2 Principles of composition). Any composition is in principle based on a grid, intuitive or conscious, whether it is a few guides or a complex mathematically calculated grid. ‘A modular system ensures that the shape and size of the elements are either equal or clearly different and that they are positioned in relation

A grid can be perceived by many as limiting the room for action, with its frames and lines. In reality, the use of grids can offer greater freedom. A well-thought-out grid can help safeguard a desired uniform expression, while allowing for greater freedom and workflow.

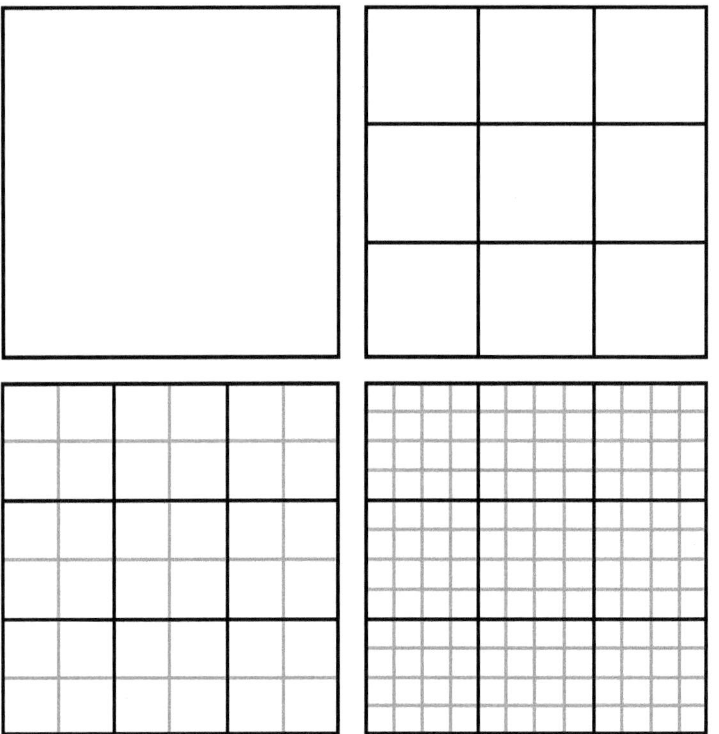

Fig. 4.117 Modular grid system

Fig. 4.117 The figure shows an example of a grid with various levels of detail, based on a square modulable aspect ratio. The level of detail of the grid system is assessed according to the task the grid system should contribute to solving. It is also assessed based on the size of the format.

Fig. 4.118 The picture shows the cover of the book *History of the Poster* by Müller-Brockmann (2004, p. 157). The book is a catalogue of selected posters designed by Josef Müller-Brockmann during the period from 1948 to 1981. The catalogue measures 21 × 21 cm and is a few millimetres thick. Next to each poster shown in the book is a production drawing or a grid system. The example is from the late 1940s, when Müller-Brockmann moved from his so-called illustrative period to constructivism. The grid here is perceived to a greater extent as an element of composition, unlike the example in Figure 4.117, where the modular system to a higher degree serves to organise text and images. The picture and text are based on Meister 2013 (Artwork: Josef Müller-Brockmann 'Weniger Laerm (Less Noise), 1960', © 2022. Digital image, The Museum of Modern Art, New-York/Scala, Florence).

to each other so that clear lines appear both vertically and horizontally. It allows the elements to have a neat relationship with each other; it creates order and overview' (Rannem, 2004, p. 190). A well-planned grid system could help simplify the work of implementing text and images, for example in a daily newspaper, a weekly newspaper, or on digital surfaces. For the designer, it can mean good systematic approach and workflow. For the user, a well-organised and aesthetically set typeface can mean good legibility and reading experience.

## Grid is history

The development and the use of grids stems from a need to create order and put things in a system. This need is inherent in us humans and can be traced far back in history. If we look at ancient ornaments, architecture, urban planning from ancient Greece, and paintings from the Renaissance, we will see examples of grid systems based on advanced mathematical calculations. Classic aspect ratios from the old days are also used in more recent times, such as the golden ratio and the Fibonacci sequence (4.8.5 The golden ratio, 4.8.8 Fibonacci). In music, too, notes and other musical elements were already put into a system by Pythagoras around 500 BCE, based on the ratio 3:2 (4.8.3 Aspect ratios). In the field of book art, the first experiment took place with page coverage in a grid system as early as the 14th century, when Villard De Honnecourt invented a system that made it easy to change the size of the page coverage while keeping the same margin ratio, see Figure 4.61 and 4.62.[130] Grid as a concept in modern design and typography discourse first became popular in Europe around World War I. Some early examples from this

130 Other historical examples of grid use (Müller-Brockmann, 2010, p. 158): The Vitruvian Man / Leonardo da Vinci (1487), a structure of Latin capital letters/ Johann Neudörffer (1660), alphabet for 7 × 9 matrix printer/ Olivetti (1972), 'Broadway Boogie Woogie' / Piet Mondrian (1872–1944), Modulor / Le Corbusier (1887–1965), 'Unité d'Habitation' / Le Corbusier (1887–1965).

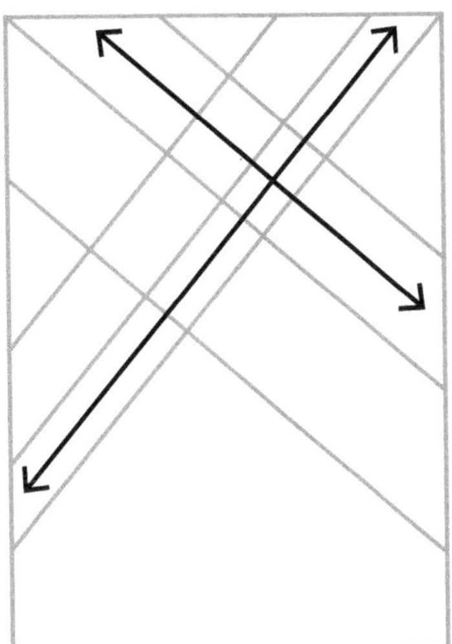

Fig. 4.118 Grid in layout


1 Initiation
2 Insight
3 Strategy
4 Design
5 Production
6 Management

4.1 Design brief
4.2 Strategy><Design
4.3 Design methodology
4.4 Concept development
4.5 Design development
4.6 Design elements
4.7 Composition
4.8 Surface and format
4.9 Identity development

4.9.1 The identity principles
4.9.2 The identity elements
4.9.3 Logo
4.9.4 Symbol
4.9.5 Identity colours
4.9.6 Typography
4.9.7 Distinctive assets
4.9.8 Identity management
4.9.9 Grid system

- Grid is history
- Grid is identity
- Grid system development
- Good legibility
- Grid system principles


period can be found among the constructivists in Russia and De Stijl in the Netherlands. The new schools, Bauhaus in Germany and Vkhutemas in the Soviet Union also became important institutions for typographical experimentation and the development of the new discourse. In the mid-1920s, the movement Die Neue Typografie also emerged, led by Jan Tschichold, among others. Very simply, one could say that the new currents broke with the traditional, or classic, approach based on symmetry, harmony, and toned-down instruments. Instead, they wanted a new design style with a more asymmetric approach in which grid systems, among other things, became important and more visible devices. This meant, for example, left text alignment, with a loose right edge, often placing the page coverage on the left or right in the format. Tschichold and other advocates of the new typography apparently argued in a scientific and objective way. At the same time, there was also a lot of disagreement about the new currents, and it should be mentioned that Tschichold later completely distanced himself from his previous view and went back to a more classical approach. Unfortunately, it did not take many years before both Bauhaus and Vkhutemas were shut down – in Germany because of the Nazis and in the Soviet Union because of Stalin. **Swiss style:** As one of the few neutral countries during both World War I and World War II, Switzerland was a meeting place for intellectual refugees from all over Europe, even as a great many leading designers emerged. The many official languages of Switzerland also contributed to unique problem statements that these designers wanted to solve using grid systems, among other things. To these designers, it was a matter of defining fixed design framework, where the placement of the various elements of the grid system was one of the most important tools for creating hierarchy, and thus order and clarity. The aim was to create an effective visual communication, based on the assumption that information presented in this way could not only be read more quickly and easily, but was also easier to understand and remember (Guity Novin, 2011).[131]

Especially after World War II, Switzerland became an important centre for the further development of this style, which eventually became

131 The Swiss style became very influential in the mid-20th century. What Müller-Brockmann emphasises and what characterises Swiss-style grids are grids divided into 4×8 or 4×10, 6×8, 6×12, and so on. It is a convenient method of division, based on the assumed number of columns the grid is to contain. For example, with a four-column grid, one cannot add up to a three-column grid.

known as Switzerland Typography, Swiss Style or International Typographic Style. It represented a thorough modernist project based on the belief in universal values, neutral idioms, and a quest to refine what they regarded as the objective of design. Famous practitioners of this style included, among others, Josef Müller-Brockmann, Armin Hofmann, Emil Ruder, Richard P. Lohse, Hans Neuburg, and Carlo Vivarelli. 'These innovative graphic designers saw design as part of industrial production and searched for anonymous, objective visual communication. They chose photographic images instead of illustrations, and fonts that were industrial, rather than those designed for books.' (guity-novin 2016). Figure 4.118 shows a work by Josef Müller-Brockmann[132] from a period he described as a transition from a focus on the subjective to a focus on the objective quality of design. With it, he would 'remove the designer's personality'[133] and focus on the objective quality of design. Müller-Brockmann, through his design work and publications, has become one of today's models when it comes to understanding the development and use of grid systems.

**Subjective vs. objective:** There are many conflicting views regarding subjectivity vs. objectivity in design. It is a matter of how much of the designer's subjective expression emerges in the design, as opposed to the objective; matter-of-factly, impartial, impersonal. It is also about how much power the designer has over the expression, for example co-authorship of a book. The main question is to what extent the designer/typographer's expression serves the content (passive) or is more active (with more driving force) as translator/designer in the process.[134] Rannem puts it this way: 'Form always sends a message, whether one likes it or not, whether one takes control of it or not. It is a message about the message itself, but also about the source of the message, about the sender. An advertisement brings a message about a product, but also about the person behind the product. The form of the advertisement should send the same message as the text, and everything should convey the message, which the advertiser wants to convey to the recipient with' (Rannem, 2004, p. 201).

### Grid is identity

Since a grid system is about organising elements, it has also a major impact on how the elements appear as a whole. Therefore, the grid can be a key factor when it comes to creating a perception of identity. Using the same grid principles to all profile carriers, the designer can create a holistic and consistent expression, communicating the desired identity. A grid may also have an inherent identity. We can easily imagine that a large format with many tall narrow text columns can work for a newspaper, while a small square format with a single text column is more suitable in a brochure (4.8.2 Format, 4.9.8 Identity management).

### Grid system development

When developing a grid system, the starting point, as in all projects, is a problem statement, strategic anchoring, alongside goals, requirements and framework related to the task and the type of text, which should be solved. Furthermore, it is necessary to provide an overview

Fig. 4.119 The figures show a reference from the book Bård Breivik – *I'd Love the Key to the Master Lock*.[135] The design by Rune Døli won the Most Beautiful Book of the Year award in 2017.[136] The grid system in the book is an example of a modular system with many modules, providing great variety in terms of image sizes, as is needed in this case. In a complex layout like this one, the grid system acts primarily as a functional and aesthetic way of organising the elements, compared to the example in Figure 4.118, which shows a grid used more as a composite element.

Subjectivity and objectivity

Read about typography, subjectivity and objectivity in the interview with Carl Gürgens. Available at designogstrategi.no.

132 Josef Müller-Brockmann, was a Swiss graphic designer and teacher, who has written a number of books on design and visual communication, including the book *Grid Systems in Graphic Design*, (1981, ed. 7, 2010), and *New Graphic Design* (1958–1965).

133 Josef Müller-Brockmann 1961, p. 9.

134 Among those who have expressed an opinion on the subject of public objectivity vs. subjectivity, is Michael Rock, who has a 'yes, but' attitude to this, Wim Crouwel and Jan van Toorn, or previous generations with Beatrice Warde (Crystal Goblet), for example. Each of them responds to different historical conditions.

135 Bård Breivik's *I'd Love the Key to the Master Lock* is published by Fagbokforlaget and Arnoldsche Art Publishers.

136 *Årets vakreste bøker (The Most Beautiful Books of the Year)* is an annual competition under the auspices of Grafill. grafill.no/avb.

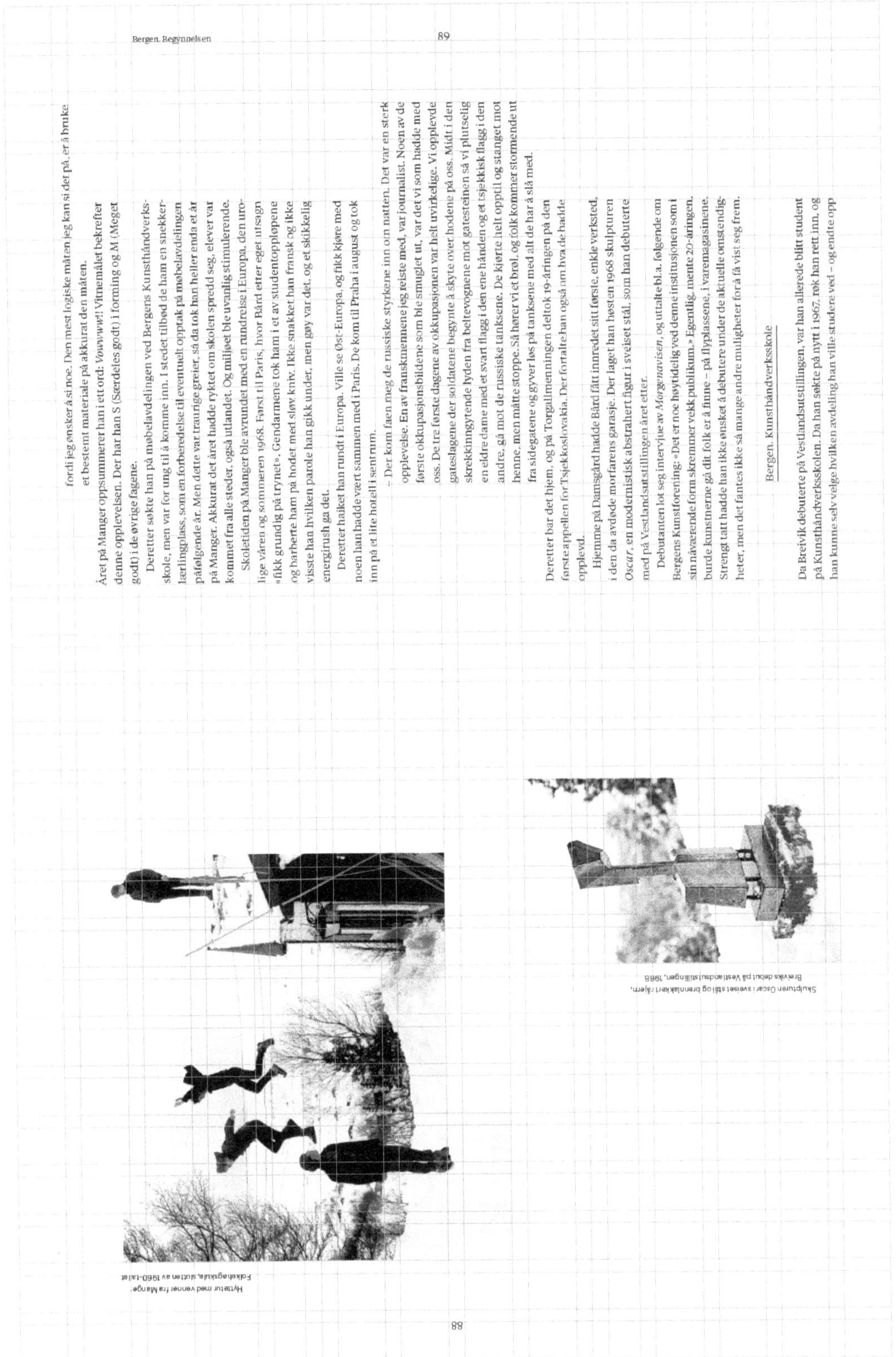

Fig. 4.119 Grid in layout

of the amount of text, type of photo and profile elements that should be implemented. Grid development requires thorough processes involving trial, testing and evaluation in multiple rounds. Among other things, it involves testing different typefaces, degrees, point sizes, line spacing, column widths, etc. Work is easier and more interesting if one has a clever idea and a plan before getting started. Precision in grid calculation and composition can be absolutely crucial for a successful result. If there are any inaccuracies in the grid system, they might propagate into various details and create disproportion and additional work.

There are many different ways to make grids. If there is mostly text in a layout, *a column grid* may be sufficient. In other words, the page is divided into columns, verticals and horizontals, or modules. If there are images in a layout, a modular system is more appropriate. Modular system is the division of pages into column widths and levels,

**Format selection:** What is the task of the format? Should it be printed, pressed in offset, displayed on a screen, or a combination of these? Is it to be read from a distance, up close, on a bus, on a plane, in an office or at home in the living room? Should it be carried in one's bag, pocket or in one's hand? Is it supposed to be on a shelf, lying on a table, sent by post, or handed out on the street? Should it be tall, wide, square, round, or random? Are there landscape images, portrait images, small images, or large images involved? Are there a few pictures or many pictures? Is there a lot of text or little text? Which paper supports the format? Can the sense of standard format be broken by choosing a more exciting format for the page coverage? (4.8 Surface and format).

**Font selection:** Should there be a lot of text or less text? What idea, style, and identity should the font express? (4.9.6 Typography: Font selection). The primary task of the text is to convey content to the reader, but text in a composition is not just verbal information. There are also fields or lines of texture, which form rectangles of tones in the composition. The conscious aspect ratio and position of the text fields are absolutely essential for creating a perception of order and uniform expression in the composition. 'The duality of the two roles of text makes the designer responsible for both readability and composition' (Elam, 2004, p. 5).

**Image selection:** The images should support the text and convey what the text does not say. Images can be photos, sketches, outlines, drawings, illustrations, graphic elements, patterns, etc. The images may carry the composition, if so desired. Clear and sharp, with good sectioning. Good image retouching can strengthen the image and the message. It is important to create contrasts, variation and dramatic effect when using images. Consistent image use can contribute to a perception of identity.

'You may often want to link multiple images to one larger image surface' (Rannem, 2004, p. 192). When placing an image at the top and bottom edge of the grid, it might be necessary to make optical adjustments so that the image should appear in the grid.

resulting in a set of squares or modules of uniform shape and size. The modules can be large and coarse if there are large images, or less coarse if there are many small ones. 'The more modules there are, the smaller each module will be. This offers greater variety in image size.' (Rannem, 2004, p. 192). How many columns you can have depends on the number of modules you have and how much you can play around. The level of detail of the grid system is assessed according to the task the grid system should contribute to solving. It is also assessed based on the size of the format. For example, a magazine will require a more complex grid system than a small label.

A grid can be calculated based on the outer proportions of the format down to the smallest point size in the text. The starting point can be any format or aspect ratio. It is also possible to set up a grid according to proportional size ratios, such as the classic size ratios 2:3 (fifth), 3:4 (fourth) or the golden ratio, or use standard formats as a starting point, such as the A format (4.8 Surface and format, 4.8.3 Aspect ratios, 4.8.4 The A series, 4.8.5 The golden ratio). There is no one answer on how to create a grid. It should be developed according to the needs and objectives of each assignment.

**Grid development tips**: Here are some simple tips based on Müller-Brockman (2010, p. 49):

- The problem statement should be clarified before work can begin.
- Requirements or questions regarding format, text and illustrations, typeface, printing method, and paper quality need to be clarified. In assignments, which allow great freedom, this can be clarified during the sketching process.
- The designer should know how much text and images to implement in the layout, and should have an idea of how to solve the problem.
- The designer begins problem solving by drawing many small sketches, the so-called free sketches. Small sketches make it easier to see a rough layout as a whole.
- The proportions on these sketches should be related to the final format, or to the formats that should be tested. Text fields can be shaded as grey fields, light grey for thin fonts and darker grey for bold fonts.
- In the sketching process, it is necessary to determine the number of columns on a page. Later in the sketching process, text can be sketched as lines, as realistically as possible in relation to the number of lines in the column. Eventually, sketches are developed on a computer, in parallel with testing different typefaces, in different degrees, point sizes, line spacing, columns, etc.
- Choosing one text column for text and illustration gives little freedom to reproduce the image in large, medium and small size.
- Two columns offer more possibilities by putting text in one column and illustrations in the other. As an additional option, two columns can be split into four in the same grid system.
- Three columns can also offer a variety of options for text and illustrations in different sizes. Three columns can also be split into six within the same grid system.
- Splitting into four or six columns is recommended when a lot of text and images are to be inserted into a page.

1 Initiation
2 Insight
3 Strategy
4 Design
5 Production
6 Management

4.1 Design brief
4.2 Strategy><Design
4.3 Design methodology
4.4 Concept development
4.5 Design development
4.6 Design elements
4.7 Composition
4.8 Surface and format
4.9 Identity development

4.9.1 The identity principles
4.9.2 The identity elements
4.9.3 Logo
4.9.4 Symbol
4.9.5 Identity colours
4.9.6 Typography
4.9.7 Distinctive assets
4.9.8 Identity management
4.9.9 Grid system

- Grid is history
- Grid is identity
- Grid system development
- Good legibility
- Grid system principles

Further reading
Check out the classic *Grid Systems in Graphic Design* (1996) by Josef Müller-Brockmann.

- Four columns can be further divided into 8, 16 or more columns.
- The number of columns, one, two or more, depends on the format of the printed matter and on the font size.
- The width of the column sets conditions for selection of font and point size. As a rule, the narrower the column is, the smaller the point size. If the column is too narrow and the font too large, there will be too few words on the line. It will then be difficult to read effortlessly from one line to the next.
- The format and size of the margins determine the size of the page coverage. The general aesthetic expression depends on the quality of the format's proportions, the size of the page coverage, and the selected typeface.
- Whether a text page as a whole is perceived harmonious and comfortable to read depends on the appearance of the font. It is about the font size, the length of the line, the line spacing, and the size of the margins.
- Problem statements differ, so the grid system needs to be recreated for each assignment in order to meet the challenges at hand. The design of a small newspaper ad is not as complex as that of a daily newspaper with ten or more columns, and many different elements and sections. Such assignments require a high degree of organisation, in order to create a logical system that caters for larger amounts of information elements with customised typography.

Tips for the designer

**To avoid binding to a grid system prematurely, it is a good idea to start with simple hand sketches or computer sketches. This way, one can work freely to arrive at the desired style and expression. If one starts drawing grids too early, it can easily become pointless. It is annoying to spend a lot of time customising a grid to find out that the columns are too narrow and that there is no room for all the text, or that the height format of the grid is not suitable for wide landscape images. Having said that, trial and error are also an important part of creating a grid system.**

### Good legibility

Whether the reader can read the content easily and comfortably depends to a significant extent on the length of the line, the choice of typeface, font size and line spacing. When legibility is optimal, the meaning of the text becomes clearer and 'fits' better. Here are some tips to ensure good legibility (based on Rannem, 2012, among others).

**Reading distance:**

- The reading distance to an outdoor billboard will naturally be greater than the reading distance in a book. Legibility should be assessed based on the distance in question. A 9 pt font is unlikely to be readable from a long distance.
- The normal reading distance for a book or magazine is 30–35 cm. For a screen, a little more.

**Line length:**

- Correct line length (column width) is important to allow the reader to relax and concentrate on the text.
- Lines that are too long are hard to read. It takes a lot for the reader to follow a horizontal line.
- If lines are too short, the eye is constantly forced to change line, which can tire the reader.
- A rule of thumb for the maximum number of characters on the line is 7 (–10) words per line or 60 characters per line.

**Line spacing:**

- Correct line spacing (leading) is one of the most important factors in achieving a harmonious and functional use of a typeface that is aesthetically pleasing and has optimal legibility.

137 **Excerpt from a compendium for teaching typography at the University of South-eastern Norway, 2017.**

- The line spacing (the vertical distance from line to line) should be suitable for the typeface. The typeface may vary in x- and y-height, up and down stroke, affecting the optical perception of line spacing. There is no one answer. One should test everything on case-by-case basis.
- A line spacing that is too close limits legibility because the eye also sees the line above and below. The reader gets distracted, uses more energy to stay focused on the line, and gets tired faster.
- However, if the line spacing is too open, the reader may have trouble linking it to the next line and thus get exhausted.
- Good line spacing guides the eye easily from one line to the other, providing optical rest and stability, and making it possible to absorb and remember what is being read.
- The default line spacing on a computer is often the minimum. The line spacing should be adjusted according to purpose, reading distance, desired expression, etc.

**Font size:**
- Both text that is too big and text that is too small can be demanding for the reader, who gets tired easily.
- 9/12 point (9 at 12 point) is regarded by many as an optimal ratio of point size to line spacing.

### Grid system principles

Here are some guiding principles for developing a modular grid, based on Swiss-style. The principles will work across platforms and formats provided that the same approach is used, written *by Carl Gürgens*.[137] (The interview with Gürgens available at designogstrategi.no.) The starting point is the establishment of a single grid system for an editorial. There is no absolute rule for how a grid should relate to, for example, font sizes, units of measurement, and formats, but it may be useful to follow some simple principles, which in turn can be carried forward in more complex and detailed systems. This explanation is a step-by-step formula for a relatively simple grid.

In most contexts, it will be necessary to create a grid, regardless of formats and proportions. When a grid has already been developed, as is the case for most editorial magazines and books, it can be used as a template. Then, it is useful to know how to best utilise such a template, so that the system responds to the needs it is intended to meet. The example used here is based on a page coverage, which initially includes several baselines and rows. This is to show how to create a grid that matches the font size and leading (line spacing from baseline to baseline), format, page coverage, and the need for format splitting, both vertically and horizontally.

Initially, there is a preset format, A4. Within it, I have a typeface that I have been working on in order to find the right pt size. The images to work with relate primarily to squares, so that my system will be based on a flexible grid, using a square grid as basis. The font to work with does an excellent job in 9/12 pt; 9 pt size and 12 pt line-spacing. The defined format then allows for a maximum number of baselines, including margins. I have estimated that with a slightly large margin at the bottom and less at the top I have to work within a limit of 714 pt. Where I have


1 Initiation
2 Insight
3 Strategy
4 Design
5 Production
6 Management

4.1 Design brief
4.2 Strategy><Design
4.3 Design methodology
4.4 Concept development
4.5 Design development
4.6 Design elements
4.7 Composition
4.8 Surface and format
4.9 Identity development

4.9.1 The identity principles
4.9.2 The identity elements
4.9.3 Logo
4.9.4 Symbol
4.9.5 Identity colours
4.9.6 Typography
4.9.7 Distinctive assets
4.9.8 Identity management
4.9.9 Grid system

- Grid is history
- Grid is identity
- Grid system development
- Good legibility
- Grid system principles

now set a 12 pt baseline, the total height will have to be divisible by 12. The closest number I get, which is divisible by 12, is 708. We will let this be our starting point to keep working.

Fig. 4.120 **The figure shows a page coverage with baseline that goes up in the page coverage.**

**1) New document**

- Set up the document in millimetres (mm). This is easier to convert to, for example, A formats and any specifications for printing houses because third-parties should only have to deal with the outer format in terms of units of measurement.
- InDesign Main Menu: File > New Document. Format: 210 × 297 mm (A4).

**2) Page coverage**

- Within the format, we first set the page coverage The page coverage is plotted using point size (pt). The unit of measure is important when creating a grid that relates to font sizes and line spacing.

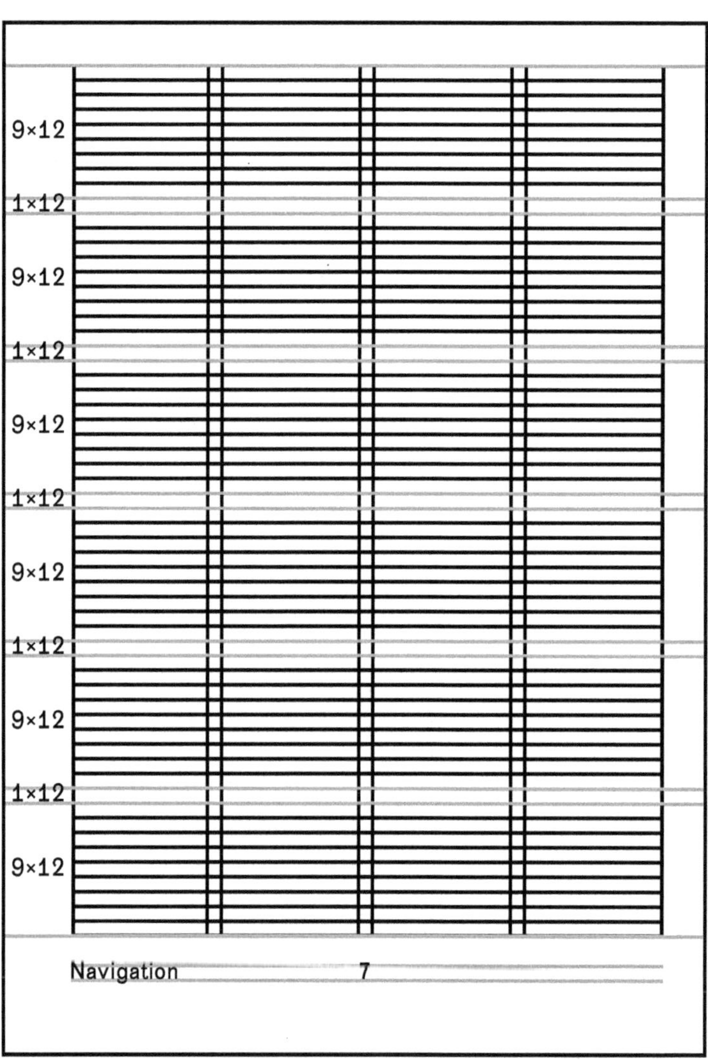


Fig. 4.120 Page coverage with baseline grid

- It is easier to work in pure numbers, given the grid calculation, and you will be able to use the system in a more logical way.
- Ensure that the page coverage is width × height (w × h) in whole points Here we use 500 × 708 pt as an example. Do not use decimals.
- Now think about where the page coverage should be positioned on the page, and consider this against what fixed elements are needed in the template. In this case, we leave plenty of space at the bottom, for navigation and page number (page numbering).
- NOTE! The margin size in this context should be in mm. The most important thing is for the page coverage itself to be in clear points
- InDesign Main Menu: Layout > Margins and columns.

**3) Baseline**

- My system is based on 9 pt size, and 12 pt leading. Baseline is the same size as the leading, i.e. 12 pt. We assume that the typeface DIN is the starting point for my assessment of font size and leading.
- The height of the page coverage should then correspond to 12 pt baseline:
- Calculation: 708 pt (page coverage height)/12 (leading) = 59.
- That means there are 59 baselines that can fit in within the page coverage Had this not been in whole numbers without decimals, one would have had to round up or down to a whole number of baselines so that it corresponds to the height. The height should be divisible by the pt size in the leading, so one ends up with a whole number. If the starting point is that one does not have a predefined height of the page coverage yet, then the baseline size should be used and then go up from there.
- InDesign Main Menu: Preferences > Grids.
- NOTE! Make sure that the first baseline starts where the page coverage starts.

**4) Sections/rows**

- In this context, we will use sections/rows to work with vertical division. This can pay off if, for example, one works a lot with photography, section divisions, and several hierarchies in typography. In this example, we are going to work with six parts. We put one baseline space for each section. This means that this space should also be included in the equation in order for it to fit in with the baselines. This can be done as follows:
- 59 – 5 (6 sections produce 5 baseline separators) = 54 (baselines)/6 (sections) = 9 (baselines).
- 54 baselines divided into six sections gives nine baselines per section. If this equation produces a whole number, the division will also add up with the baseline measures.
- InDesign Main Menu: Layout > Create Guides.
- NOTE! Work in Margins, not in Page.

**5) Columns**

- The desired number of columns can now be added.
- Here, we use six columns as an example. I want two, and then I have more flexibility to work with columns within the column itself.
- A good rule of thumb is for the distance in the division/gap distance (gutter) to be the same as the baseline. In this case, 12 pt. This is something assessed individually against the font size in the column; whether


1 Initiation
2 Insight
3 Strategy
4 Design
5 Production
6 Management

4.1 Design brief
4.2 Strategy><Design
4.3 Design methodology
4.4 Concept development
4.5 Design development
4.6 Design elements
4.7 Composition
4.8 Surface and format
4.9 Identity development

4.9.1 The identity principles
4.9.2 The identity elements
4.9.3 Logo
4.9.4 Symbol
4.9.5 Identity colours
4.9.6 Typography
4.9.7 Distinctive assets
4.9.8 Identity management
4.9.9 Grid system

- Grid is history
- Grid is identity
- Grid system development
- Good legibility
- Grid system principles

a larger font size would require larger gutter when the text covers multiple columns.
- InDesign Main Menu: Layout > Margins and Columns.

Fig. 4.121 The figure shows the solution to the exercise in Figure 4.37 Zeigarnik effect on page 401.

**6) Equation**
- Now, when we look at the equation, we see that the number of baselines inside the page coverage adds up to the height of the page coverage, so that the total height is the same.
- There are deviations, where the number of baselines, leading, format and sectioning do not match. Unfortunately/fortunately, the format can tell whether the numbers will work. This must be weighed well against the total height of the page coverage. If the figures do not add up, with correct use of grid equation, compromises/adjustments should be made in relation to the total height of the page coverage, or the unit of measurement in the baseline, for example, should be assessed.
- The most important thing in order to start using the grid is getting the page coverage and baselines to add up. One can eventually begin working on sectioning once one gets a slightly better grasp of system division and the need for a more detailed grid. This requires some training but will come more naturally as one starts to experience the importance and positive impact of a systematic approach.

Solution to Figure 4.37:

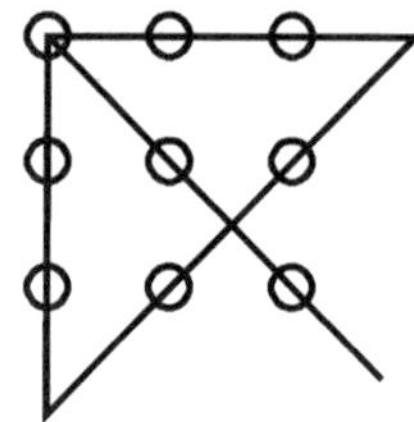

Fig. 4.121
The Zeigarnik effect

> There are several rules. They exist to ensure good readability, rhythm, balance, and a consistent and holistic expression. They are also meant to be broken, but this should be done consciously! Consciously means that nothing should be random! Every tiny dot or pixel should be justifiable. 'Learn the rules like a pro, so you can break them like an artist' (Pablo Picasso).

**Different approaches:**
**From the inside out:** Here one works with the architecture from the smallest unit of measure, and allows this to define the big lines. Let the baseline be the condition, and work upwards until you have figured out the page coverage and the grid system in general. Then let the grid determine the format, and also let margins be a large part of the overall systematic approach.
**Outside and in:** This example is based on a very similar approach as the one described above. When the format is defined, this is also more about defining which units of measurement one can work with. Both approaches work in their own way, and in most contexts there are always opportunities to work across these to approach a system.[138]
REMEMBER! Grids are specially designed for a format and the use of font sizes in this format. For this reason, different formats will rarely work optimally with the same grid.

138 Plugin: If one does not want to develop the grid system manually, there is an InDesign plugin that can be used as shortcut. It does a lot of the maths. There is a similar web solution. One should still know what happens and if it makes sense. There are also several other digital tools, such as Grid Calculator Pro.

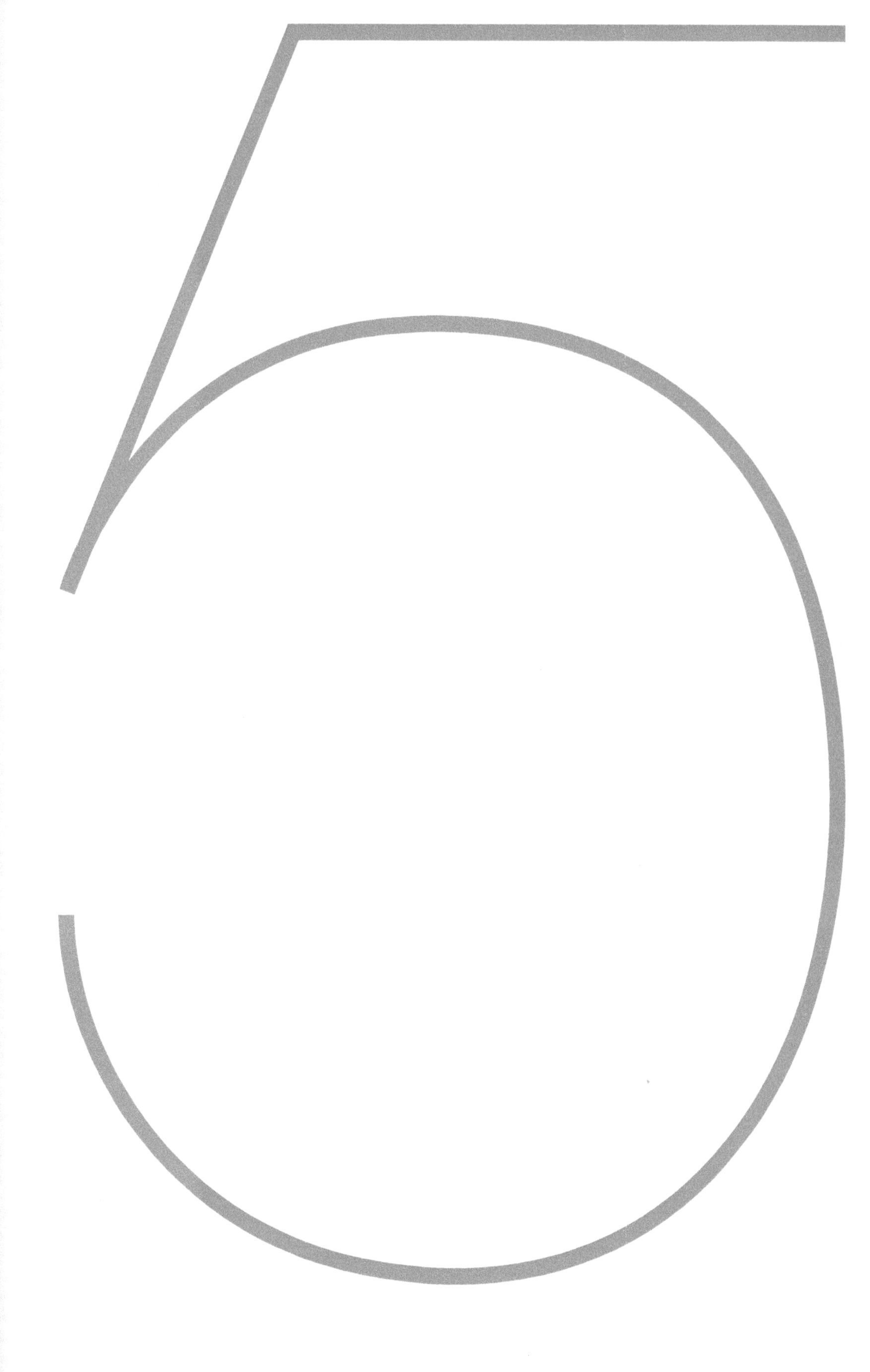

5.1 Implementation 532

5.2 Model 533
5.2.1 Dummy 534
5.2.2 Sketch model 535
5.2.3 Wireframe 535
5.2.4 Mockup 536
5.2.5 Prototype 536
5.2.6 Data model and simulation 538
5.2.7 Presentation model 538
5.2.8 Blueprint 539
5.2.9 Production model 539

5.3 Material selection 539
5.3.1 Materials 539
5.3.2 Functionality 540
5.3.3 Material insight 541
5.3.4 Material properties 541
5.3.5 Material life cycle 542
5.3.6 Product life cycle 543
5.3.7 Product life extension 543
5.3.8 Incorrect material selection 544
5.3.9 Sustainable materials 544

5.4 Paper and cartonboard 544
5.4.1 Paper 544
5.4.2 Paper construction 545
5.4.3 Paper production 545
5.4.4 Paper properties 546
5.4.5 Paper selection 548
5.4.6 Cartonboard 550
5.4.7 Green packaging 551
5.4.8 Packaging materials 553
5.4.9 Ecolabelling and certification 554

5.5 Colour management 556
5.5.1 Colour models 558
5.5.2 Colour gamut 559
5.5.3 Colour profiles 560
5.5.4 Select colour profile 562
5.5.5 Colour channels and tone depth 565
5.5.6 Workflow 566
5.5.7 File types 568
5.5.8 PDF for printing 569
5.5.9 Colour reference systems 572

5.6 Production for digital media 573

5.7 Production for printed media 575
5.7.1 Press techniques 576
5.7.2 Printing methods 577
5.7.3 Raster 578
5.7.4 Four colours (CMYK) 579
5.7.5 Printing inks 580
5.7.6 Printing effects 580

5.8 Installations and constructions 582

5.9 Quality assurance 583

Production is the fifth of six phases, and it is about realising and implementing the solution developed through the previous phases. Production involves making one or more products by mechanical, manual or digital means. It can be manufacturing a product, building an exhibition stand, printing a brochure, or programming an app. Production is something the designer often leaves to subcontractors, but production planning, follow-up and quality assurance is the designer's responsibility. This includes, among other things, choice of production technique, publishing solutions, and technology, choice of paper or other material, implementation and completion of design solution and output, as well as the conscious colour management and file format selection.

Production is something many put off until the project delivery deadline approaches. This might limit their options when it comes to choice of materials, manufacturing techniques, and software for digital output. There are many time-consuming factors in a production process, such as ordering paper for printed matter, using additional effects such as foiling or embossing, varnishing or finishing, which require drying, curing, etc. The time for production adjustments should also be taken into account in case something goes wrong. Murphy's law prevails in production processes, meaning 'Everything that can go wrong will.'[1] Therefore, production requires conscious follow-up and quality assurance in all stages. The key to success lies in careful planning and choice of production technique or manufacturing process and materials.

Production is inextricably linked to the problem or the need the assignment should help solve. The finished product is assessed based on whether or not it solves the problem and responds to the assignment. As the other phases of the design process, the production process should also be anchored in the company's overall strategy and goal. If the company has included sustainability as part of its strategy and ambition, this should influence its choice of production processes and the materials used, not least with a view to their durability and recycling potential. The designer can be an important driving force in influencing the company to develop products and services that meet the demand without harming life and environments (6.9 Sustainable management).

An efficient and targeted production process with optimal results and conscious material use requires careful planning and involvement of production and materials experts (5.3 Material selection: Material insight). Planning should start early in the design process as part of the insight phase and the idea process and follow the further progress of the design process up to production completion. The life cycle of the product should also be planned,[2] to consider things like maintenance, operation, upgrade, destruction and recycling.

> **Design templates**
> If design templates have been prepared, only text and images will have to be implemented. For example, a design template may consist of fixed design elements in a defined grid system with text size and line spacing pre-sets, and areas defined for images and illustrations.

## 5.1 Implementation

Guidelines and templates are created to show how design solutions should appear and be used. Usually, they are compiled in a design handbook. When realising the design in line with these conditions, we call it implementation. Implementation is also generally used for completion of a solution.

Implement, from the Latin 'implere' for 'fill up' (later 'employ'), is about completion and realisation, as opposed to constructing and designing. A design process usually results in a solution that should lead to some kind of change. The change does not happen by itself; it must be implemented. All types of change work have a description of *what* should be done. The implementation is about *how* this work should be put into effect, and is just as important (Øvregård, 2016). Several phases of a strategic design project may include something that needs to be implemented. For example, in the

1 The term originates from Air Force captain Edward A. Murphy, Jr. in the late 1940s at Edwards Air Force Base in southern California. His statement was transformed into Murphy's Law by the flight surgeon Stapp, who further stated: 'The only way to avoid catastrophe is to envision every possible scenario and plan against it' (Purtill, 2017).

2 Life cycle analysis is a method for creating an overall picture of a product's total environmental impact during its life cycle from raw material extraction, via production processes and use to waste management, including transport and energy use at all stages (5.3.6 Product life cycle).

strategy phase, implementation may involve initiating a new strategy in the company's organisation so that all employees acquire ownership of it and contribute to its realisation. During the design phase, it may be necessary to implement a new identity within the organisation so that everyone can identify with it and apply it consistently. In the design process, it can be a matter of making changes to a service and getting customers to adopt them, following a process where 'customer journey' is used as a method. In the context of design development, the term 'implementation' is most often used for placement of visual elements or content on relevant digital or analogue surfaces and in relevant contexts. In this connection, implementation can be understood in two ways.

- *Visual identity implementation*: Placing logo and other identity elements on relevant profile supports. It usually also involves the development of a brand guide and design templates, with guidelines for the placement of the identity elements (6.5 Design manual, 6.6 Design templates).
- *Content implementation*: Placing text, images, illustrations etc. in finished design templates according to given guidelines. The design templates will include predefined placement of the logo and other identity elements on relevant surfaces, such as websites, ads, newsletters, brochures, magazines, etc. The design template for a magazine usually allows some freedom to create different expressions within the set frames. In that case, implementation most often requires graphical software and is usually done by the designer. If the design template is a simple newsletter, the implementation job will be easier. In this case, it will be rather a mere production job, which a non-designer can do as well. If so, someone from the company, for example, can carry out the implementation work of placing text and images within the template.



## 5.2 Model

Model is used in this context as a generic term for prototype, mockup or dummy. During a design process, developing digital and physical models can provide good basis for testing and evaluating proposed solutions.

It can be easy to lose direction and focus on a project, while considering and trying different ideas and different options. One thing leads to another and before you know it, you spend a lot of time developing options and functions that do not solve the problem or respond to the assignment. Any errors, sneaking into the process, might take the project in the wrong direction and negatively affect the outcome. The causes can be many. For example, unclear communication between the designer and the client, unclear problem statement, or lack of insight, such as insufficient knowledge of the user and the user's needs. Nonetheless: A failed project is a waste of time and effort. By developing models in the course of the design process and testing the product or service on users, there is a greater chance for the result to be target-oriented and successful. This way, one can find out if the idea is user-friendly and appealing and make new improvements based on the feedback.

> Implementation
> One can view implementation as a type of change effort, a solution to be executed (Øvregård, 2016). Implementation is the realisation of an application, or execution of a plan, idea, model, design, specification, standard, algorithm, or policy ('Implementation,' n.d.).

Dummies, mockups and prototypes are different model concepts that can be linked to different stages of a development process, either digitally or physically. The terms are often interchangeable, and many use 'prototype' as a collective term. In general, one can say that a *dummy* is made early in the sketching process with whatever you have at hand. It is often created to explore different sketches, themes or concepts in the ideas phase, especially in terms of form and materiality. A dummy can also be more complex, such as a handmade copy of a finished hardbound book or magazine, with the correct paper, format, and weight, with or without text and images. A *mockup* is a term for a model of a full-size design, e.g. product or packaging, used by designers mainly for testing and obtaining feedback from users. At the same time, we can say that a mockup is a prototype if it provides at least one part of the functionality of a system and makes it possible to test the design (Vieru, 2009). The term *prototype*[3] is originally used for an early sample or model of a product built to test and evaluate a concept or a new design to enhance precision. Prototype is also referred to as a model that closely resembles the final result, e.g. a preliminary version of the product in order to demonstrate and test its function and design before the product is produced.

Creating a prototype can in some processes be called materialisation, the step between the formalisation and the evaluation of an idea (Soares, 2012).

In all phases of a design project, there may be a need to materialise ideas and solutions by developing models. The amount of time and resources that is spent will vary in the different phases of the project. In the idea phase, it is advisable to create rough models continuously in order to quickly assess and test out ideas. It is useful for assessing the idea, presenting it and testing it in relevant situations and on relevant users. In this way, one gets closer to a desired solution. When approaching a final solution, the model can be made in more detail considering production. At that stage, one has considered different aspects of the solution and is more confident about what it should look like. As a result, one can spend more time and resources on developing a final prototype and final testing.

In principle, development of models can be used in all forms of idea and design development, whether the aim is to develop a product, service, brand name, web page, advertisement or something else. The process will vary depending on the assignment type. The level of detail should preferably reflect the stage one is at. If models become too detailed and elaborate at an early stage, it can be difficult to move forward with new ideas.[4]

### 5.2.1 Dummy

To exemplify the design, e.g. of a logo and brand assets for a visual identity, it should be placed digitally in the correct poster format, brochure format, label, car, T-shirt etc. If the outcome is to be printed, then examples should be printed during the design process.

- *Print dummy*: Testing the design for printed matter on relevant surfaces and formats and printing it in the correct size is a useful thing to do several times during the design process. The print dummy can be assessed in the relevant context, which may be hanging the poster on a suitable wall surface outdoors or indoors, or sticking the logo on the car in question. This gives a more realistic idea of a visual design compared to a computer screen, making it easier to see what works and what does

3 Protype: From Ancient Greek, prōtótupos 'original; prototype', prefix meaning 'first; earliest' + túpos, 'blow, pressing; sort, type'.

4 The chapter about models are based on Lerdahl (2007), among others.

not, thus helping shorten the design process. It also makes it easier to test out the design on relevant users.

- *Paper dummy*: When designing a book, magazine, brochure or any other form of publication to be printed, it may be useful to make paper dummies. One starts early in the idea process to cut paper in the appropriate formats in order to test out different options. This way, one gets an impression of the formats and can assess them comparing them to each other. If one contact paper suppliers or printing houses, they will be able to make a full-fledged paper dummy with the correct format, desired number of pages, paper type and binding. It may be a good idea to order different formats and paper types, and assess them in relation to each other for the purpose (4.8 Surface and format).


1 Initiation
2 Insight
3 Strategy
4 Design
5 Production
6 Management

5.1 Implementation
5.2 Model
5.3 Material selection
5.4 Paper and cartonboard
5.5 Colour management
5.6 Production for digital media
5.7 Production for printed media
5.8 Installations and constructions
5.9 Quality assurance

5.2.1 Dummy
5.2.2 Sketch model
5.2.3 Wireframe
5.2.4 Mockup
5.2.5 Prototype
5.2.6 Data model and simulation
5.2.7 Presentation model
5.2.8 Blueprint
5.2.9 Production model


### 5.2.2 Sketch model

These are models created quickly, in small increments during the idea process, in order to give a visual impression of the idea in 3D form. To do so one needs malleable materials at one's disposal. For example, paper, cardboard, clay, Play-Doh, or easily mouldable foam. Such models can help give a concrete form to the ideas and initiate discussions, new associations, and new ideas. A sketch model can also be a simple hand sketch, such as of an information structure or the wireframe of a website or mobile application at an early stage of the development process.

- *Visual form model*: This model is made of foam or clay to give a visual impression of curves, shape and expression, when it is necessary to assess what the idea looks like in practice.
- *Extreme model*: This is an approach that allows greater freedom and involves using one's imagination and association skills to develop form. Such models are useful for exploring, provoking and challenging thoughts, without taking too much notice of criteria and function. The method can also be useful in making function models of a small part of the product, by moving from the extreme to cultivating one single function.

### 5.2.3 Wireframe

Wireframe is a sketch model that describes the structure of a website before the visual elements are designed, see Figure 5.1. The purpose is to be able to discuss, test and evaluate the structure and user interface without being distracted by graphical, visual elements. The wireframes show the overall layout of the websites and their framework as well as modules and components. Using wireframes, one can shape user-experience and visualise structure, navigation and content. This way, one can create a framework for what the final website will look like. 'Often, we use the "mobile first" methodology that prioritises wireframes for mobile devices to ensure mobile device users have the best possible experience of architecture and content. We then sketch accordingly for larger screens so that we see the whole' (A. Myhre 2017). A wireframe should show:

- The most important groups of content (what?)
- The information structure (where?)
- A description and visualisation of the user interface/interaction (how?)

Further reading
Digital sketch model: Proposing a hybrid visualisation tool combining affordances of sketching and CAD. Ranscombe, Charlie et al., 2019.

Wireframes are not just meaningless sets of grey boxes, although they may look just like that. They are the very backbone of the design and should include a representation of each of the most important parts of the final product (Treder, 2016).

Fig. 5.1 The figure shows examples of a wireframe (the figure is based on Akiko, 2022/ edrawsoft.com.). A wireframe is a rough sketch for a web page, a kind of prototype or mockup. It shows the structure of the web page. Frames and boxes indicate where text and images should be placed.

### 5.2.4 Mockup

Such a model is created in more detail to test out the idea in terms of technical possibilities, user characteristics and ergonomic needs, for example through user scenarios or user tests.

- *Physical mockups* may be useful during the early sketch phase in order to test out the design on relevant surfaces, and is well suited for testing out e.g. magazine or packaging design in a shop test.
- *Digital 3D Mockups* are well suited for screen presentation and printing, and can offer a fairly realistic experience of the final product. There is a variety of free online tools for the development of simple screen-based mockups, with the possibility of implementing visual identity on different profile supports. Its advantage is that it is easy to zoom in and out, see the big picture and the details, create using different perspectives and effects. The danger of using data modelling prematurely is that sketches can quickly look readier than they are, which may set limits on the further development process.
- *Web mockup* is a static design of a web page or application that features many of its final design elements but is not functional. It comes after a wireframe in the design process (Hufford, 2021). A further prototype can represent the user interface and information structure, visualise the content and demonstrate the basic interactive features e.g. that allows users to navigate from page to page and use functionality such as drop-down menus.
- *AR and VR mockups* are digital, virtual and augmented mockups[5] which can be created by using more advanced 3D computer graphics techniques, online tools, generators and animators. Virtual mockups can replace physical prototypes.

### 5.2.5 Prototype

A physical prototype is a model that shows what a shape, article or object looks like in practice and what it is like to touch and feel it. This is a good way of testing out an idea or finished solution, which makes it possible to get an impression of the idea, form and material. A digital prototype e.g. a web solution or software product prototype simulates user interface interaction in a manner similar to the end product. It will allow the user to experience content and interaction with the interface in a user test.

- *3D printing*: One limitation of computer models is that they cannot be touched, felt and tested in practice. The model drawn on a computer can be easily and quickly printed on a 3D printer to a physical, 3D shape. This makes it possible to test models quickly and to make adjustments, also called rapid prototyping. 3D printing is available in different quality and price ranges. An essential advantage of 3D printing is accuracy, as it is just as precise as the data file. Other advantages are that one can work with different materials and that it saves time. 3D printing can be used throughout the process and is particularly suitable in the final

Further reading
Check out the comprehensive coverage of prototype: wikipedia.org/wiki/Prototype.

5 'Virtual and Augmented Reality is being used to accelerate the product lifecycle across the concept, design, engineering, planning, assembly, marketing, and sales. Many of the virtual reality (VR) use cases are geared towards upfront definition and inspection whereas augmented reality (AR) use cases are more predominantly found in Assembly, Manufacturing & Service areas. Augmented Reality work instructions result in better understanding, improved quality and efficiency on the shop floor' (siemens.com).

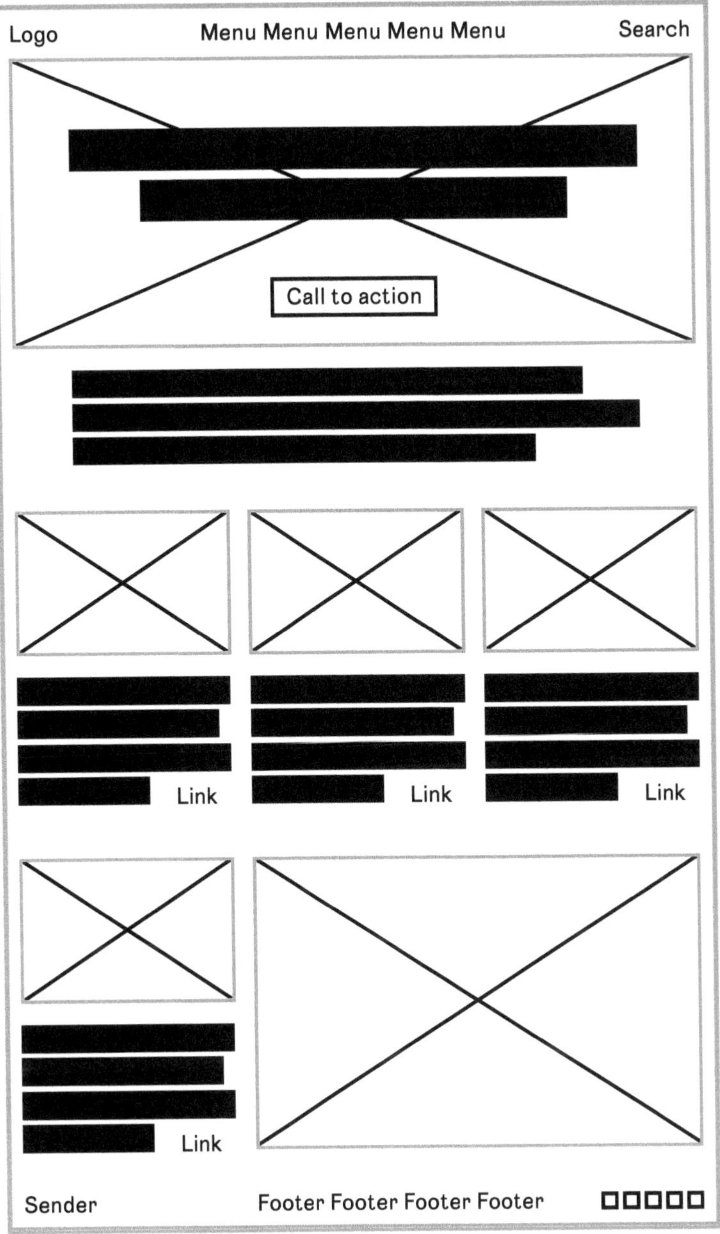


Fig. 5.1 Wireframe

1 Initiation
2 Insight
3 Strategy
4 Design
5 Production
6 Management

5.1 Implementation
5.2 Model
5.3 Material selection
5.4 Paper and cartonboard
5.5 Colour management
5.6 Production for digital media
5.7 Production for printed media
5.8 Installations and constructions
5.9 Quality assurance

5.2.1 Dummy
5.2.2 Sketch model
5.2.3 Wireframe
5.2.4 Mockup
5.2.5 Prototype
5.2.6 Data model and simulation
5.2.7 Presentation model
5.2.8 Blueprint
5.2.9 Production model

process where a high degree of precision is required. The models can also be cut into 3D models or shaped in clay, and rescanned to smooth out impurities on the surfaces. See also 5.6.2 Printing methods; 3D printing.

- *WOZ prototyping*: This is a design methodology used in rapid product development to improve user-experience, often used in agile software development and lean programming. WOZ prototyping requires developers to create a rudimentary model (sketch model) of the completed product. The prototype can be quite simple, using everyday objects to represent parts of the finished product or it may be a working model, capable of performing some – but not all – of the tasks the completed

'Thomas Edison thought the greatest benefit of prootyping was to learning what wouldn't work and (especially) why' (Neumeier, 2018).

product will perform. Once the prototype has been created, developers use role-playing to test how end users will interact with the product. After each iteration, anecdotal feedback (evidence) and data are collected and analysed to help improve the next development round. The testandlearn cycle is repeated until development is completed.[6]

- *Live prototyping*: This method is about physically trying out an idea, by simulating a situation. It could be an idea to redecorate an office, a new dish in a restaurant, a change of service, etc. A live prototype is about stress-testing a solution in real life. The prototype can be run from a few days to a few weeks. This provides an opportunity to learn how the solution works in practice and whether the idea is viable. More about this can be found in the interviews with Torbjørn Sitre and Birgitte Appelong (available at designandstrategy.co.uk).

**Fidelity**

Design fidelity refers to the level of details and functionality built into a prototype. There are three levels of fidelity: low, mid and high (Pacheco, cantina.co):

- *Low fidelity* prototypes consist of sticky notes and sketches, which is great for high-level brainstorming and collaboration.
- *Mid fidelity* prototypes are often called wireframes.
- *High fidelity* prototypes almost represent the finished product. Programs that are commonly used to create wireframe/prototypes and get others to user test them are for example Figma or Adobe XD.

### 5.2.6 Data model and simulation

- *Data Modelling* is used to 'document, define, organise, and show how the data structures within a given database, architecture, application, or platform are connected, stored, accessed, and processed within the given system and between other systems' (Knight, 2017).
- *Data simulation* is basically 'taking a large amount of data and using it to simulate or mirror real-world conditions to either predict a future instance, determine the best course of action or validate a model' (Robb, 2021).
- *3D data modelling* provides three-dimensional digital effects which makes it possible to quickly test out shape, technical principles and spatial structures, or to make animations used in films, video, videogames etc. 3D modelling is the process of creating a 3D representation of any surface or object by manipulating polygons, edges, and vertices in simulated 3D space (Slick, 2020).

### 5.2.7 Presentation model

A realistic model of a project which shows finished results or an end product. Its purpose is often to sell the project or serve as concept. In architecture, for example, it could be a prospectus of a construction project.

Further reading
- Service blueprint: servicedesigntools.org/tools/service-blueprint.
- *Service Blueprints: Definition* (Gibbons, 2017/Nielsen Norman Group).

6 The term Wizard of Oz prototyping is credited to the usability expert Dr. Jeff Kelley. The WOZ methodology requires three things: a script that provides directions for what is to take place, a person to play the role of the end user and a human 'wizard' that will perform tasks that will simulate the behaviour of the completed product. The person playing the end user may – or may not know – that they are playing a role or that the wizard's tasks are being performed manually by a human being instead of by a machine or computer program (Rouse, 2014).

## 5.2.8 Blueprint

Blueprint is a final print of the end result, a 'true copy'. In an offset printing process, the blueprint is the final contact copy of the film montage, used as a final review before printing plates are made. The term is also used for a drawing or detailed plan, for example in connection with architecture. In this context, the blueprint serves as a building plan, representing the final product – the house itself.

- *Service blueprint* is a diagram that visualises the entire process of service delivery. The purpose is to optimise how a business delivers a user-experience of a service, by listing all the activities that happen at each stage, performed by the different roles involved (4.3.12 Customer journey).

## 5.2.9 Production model

The purpose of the prototype made before manufacture is to demonstrate that the solution is working properly. It may have different levels of detail depending on the time and budget. The ideal situation is to create a prototype that is as close to the finished solution as possible. For 2D designs, the final prototype may be a sample print or a blueprint, which, for example, is printed on a high-quality printer. For 3D design, a final prototype from a 3D printer goes a long way.

## 5.3 Material selection

Knowledge of materials and how different materials work together is an important aspect throughout the design process. Understanding the material life cycle and sustainability impact is at the core alongside functionality, aesthetics, and costs.

Material selection is most relevant for the development of physical objects, products, goods, and printed items. Here, factors like technical characteristics, functionality, usability, aesthetic, sustainability and ethical factors are of key importance. Designers working on digital projects might also benefit from knowing different materials in order to be able to create the impression or illusion of materiality and tactility in a digital solution. When choosing materials, it is important to know how different materials work alone and/or together with other materials, and how this may be suitable for the purpose in question. This applies regardless of whether the material is wood, metal, fabric, glass, plastic, paper or digital. Quality, production methods, price and not least sustainability, are fundamental to consider.

### 5.3.1 Materials

It is important for a designer to keep an eye on technology and new materials or combination of materials emerging. With the immense focus on sustainability a lot of industries are exploring new ways of producing and reducing their carbon emissions. Examples of new material requirements



*The Story of Plastic*

***The Story of Plastic*** **was awarded a News and Documentary Emmy in the category of Outstanding Writing, 2021. The documentary has been highlighted as perhaps the most groundbreaking documentary in focusing on challenges with plastic. Deia Schlosberg, director of the film unpacks the full extent of the global plastic pollution crisis. The piece presents a timeline of the current environmental catastrophe, placing the onus on polluting corporations and debunking the idea that plastic recycling alone can solve the issue (Malloy, 2021). Available on YouTube, subtitled in 30 Languages.**

are materials for 3D printing, for both prototyping and manufacturing, and increasing demand of eco-friendly materials.[7] The requirements imposed on materials vary according to purpose, production technique, desired quality and lifespan, combined with the physical and visual characteristics one is looking for. The materials also set requirements. This means, among other things, conscious use, storage and maintenance, which is a prerequisite for achieving the desired result and durability (5.3.6 Product life cycle, 5.4.8 Packaging materials). 'Based on a designer's knowledge regarding technology and materials, a designer's focus is now more often than ever on new manufacturing techniques. This can be, for example, making very lightweight and strong products. Today you can cast a dining chair in carbon fibre (fibreglass chair reinforced with carbon fibre) that weighs 400 grams and can withstand 150 kilograms. In other words, the chair can withstand a fully grown adult, but when you lift it, you would not think this possible.' (Johansen, 2017).[8]

Material selection
Choose the material that is best suited to meet the requirements of a given:
- Application
- Function
- Performance
- Aesthetics
- Cost
- Maintenance
- Consistency
- Sustainability
- Availability
- Durability
- Climate

Or the other way around.

### 5.3.2 Functionality

The purpose of the product, and how it is used and manufactured, are amongst the most important factors that govern choice of material. One of the biggest challenges in product development is to be able to use resources to create functionality that adds value for end users. Therefore, it has become more and more common to use flexible techniques and the Lean mindset in product development (4.3.10 Lean and agile). In other words, you create the most important functions first. This first version of the product is often called Minimum Viable Product (MVP). When you see that the basic functionality works and gain experience

**Material insight example**

Wood is a living, usable material. It can be used to make paper, shape products, produce clothing etc. To get the most out of wood, one needs insight. For example, when building houses, boats or furniture, the quality of the wood should be assessed based on the size of the trees, their age, heart wood share, divisibility, trunk shape, crown shape, branch spacing and twisting. One also needs to consider the evenness and density of the tree rings, the ratio of summerwood to springwood, the forest terrain density and the tree habitat when looking for materials to meet different uses and functions. Materials are also defined in relation to compressive and tensile stress, surface properties, strength in relation to dimension, degradation, shrinkage and expansion. In addition comes the visual appearance, colour, tone and tactile experience. It may also be affected by the treatment of the wood in order to obtain the appearance, strength, properties and quality that are desirable for the purpose in question. The price of wood varies greatly, which has a lot to do with access, quality and the way the wood is processed – in other words, how many stages of processing it takes before the product goes to the manufacturer (ndla, 2017).

Further reading
'New perspectives on emerging advanced materials for sustainability' MacManus-Driscoll et al. (2020): doi.org/10.1063/5.0019300.

7 Today, materials can be customised for different purposes and specific applications. For example, about a hundred years ago, there were about 50 different materials in use in the building sector in Norway. Nowadays, there are at least 40,000 materials on the market (ndla, 2017).
8 The chapter is from an interview with interior designer Espen Johansen (2017).
9 When materials are combined with other materials, differences in the level of chemical reaction to moisture, salt, air or other materials may occur.

with what additional features users demand, you can add more features and refinements and evaluate materials. This procedure ensures that one would not spend time and money on unnecessary functionality and incorrect material selection.

1 Initiation
2 Insight
3 Strategy
4 Design
5 Production
6 Management

5.1 Implementation
5.2 Model
5.3 Material selection
5.4 Paper and cartonboard
5.5 Colour management
5.6 Production for digital media
5.7 Production for printed media
5.8 Installations and constructions
5.9 Quality assurance

5.3.1 Materials
5.3.2 Functionality
5.3.3 Material insight
5.3.4 Material properties
5.3.5 Material life cycle
5.3.6 Product life cycle
5.3.7 Product life extension
5.3.8 Incorrect material selection
5.3.9 Sustainable materials

### 5.3.3 Material insight

All materials serve a purpose. Materials are something you relate to physically. Therefore, a good way to get to know a material is to experiment with it and push its limits. That is how you get good at materials, because you get close to them. This is also useful when designing dummies and prototypes (5.2 Model). Equally important is professional knowledge of the material, such as how the material satisfies requirements concerning properties, technical and aesthetic functions, production costs and sustainability. The best thing is to seek the help of experts, so that as a designer you do not have to familiarise yourself with, or know everything. Those who know the materials can also help come up with new and exciting ways to use them. For example, when choosing foil for outdoor advertising, foiling of buses, cars, trains, planes etc., it is a must for the foil to stretch, shape, print on and wash. Graffiti should also be possible to remove. It should withstand temperature fluctuations, sunlight, weather, wind and so on. Materials will change over time. Things dry, bend and crack.

Successful material selection is about understanding the benefits and limitations of the material (ndla, 2017). Among other things, this means assessing several material properties to distinguish between different properties and areas of use. This includes, among other things:

- access to sources to effectively look for materials for specific purposes.
- knowledge of relevant materials and applications.
- insight into production processes and technical requirements.
- access to relevant material data and production characteristics.
- knowledge of relevant materials impact on climate and environment.

All materials have their properties and limitations. For example, you cannot make a concrete bench longer than two meters, because it will crack when it dries. Some materials become extremely costly if they have to be transported. It is essential to consider what is sustainable or ethically acceptable. For example, if you are going to order a marble plate from Malaysia, think about whether it is right to waste that much energy getting it here, when there are samples closer to you that might work just as well. You can afford to import it, but is it ethical of you to waste valuable energy transporting things? (E. Johansen 2017)

### 5.3.4 Material properties

Material characteristics are both visual and physical. We are often concerned with the visual characteristics, how the material visually fits the purpose. Physical characteristics are often just as important or even more so. One needs to understand how the product will be used, determine some key performance requirements and find suitable materials. It is crucial to consider how the material reacts to moisture, air, cold, salt, sunlight or any other situations to which the material could be exposed. Such factors may affect the lifespan and appearance of the material over time. The characteristics and durability of the material may differ in different contexts, such as outdoors and indoors, or how it behaves alone or in combination with other materials.[9] This is something one should acquaint oneself with and plan as early as possible. In selecting materials, it is also useful to learn about the origin, raw material, processing, maintenance, disposal, decomposition and recovery, and how the material impacts climate and environment.

## 5.3.5 Material life cycle

Materials have environmental impacts throughout their lifecycles. There has been a dramatic change in how businesses and society views the use of natural resources and environmental protection. *Material life cycle assessment*, *Life cycle thinking*, and *Sustainable materials management* are among many tools available.

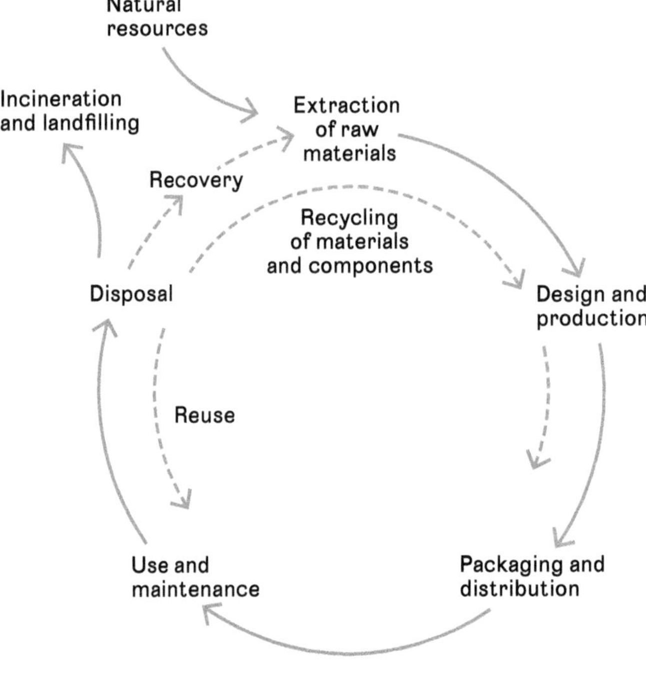


Fig. 5.2 Material life cycle

Fig. 5.2 The figure shows the major stages in a material's lifecycle, which are raw material acquisition, materials manufacture, production, use/reuse/maintenance, and waste management (EPA, n.d.) (the figure is based on lifecycle-initiative.org, What is life cycle thinking?)

Fig. 5.3 The illustration shows the product life cycle. Sales of a product increases and decreases over time. *Introduction*: a slow start, some products fail, others increase in sales. *Growth*: product upturn and take off, increased competition. *Maturity*: efforts to maintain market shares, market saturation starts. *Decline*: competing products emulate and supersede, consumer choose other products.

### Material life cycle assessment

Life cycle assessment (LCA) is a standardised, science-based tool for quantifying the environmental impacts of a product over its entire life cycle, from the extraction of raw materials to its end-of-life management (Origin, 2018). LCA is a standardised method through ISO 14040 and ISO 14044 standards (Deloitte Sustainability, 2020):[10]

- 1) a multi-step approach, considering potential impacts of a product all along its life-cycle.
- 2) a multi-criteria approach, taking a wide range of environmental issues into account e.g. climate change, water scarcity, air acidification, water eutrophication.

### Life Cycle Thinking

Life Cycle Thinking (LCT) is about going beyond the traditional focus on production site and manufacturing processes to include environmental, social and economic impacts of a product over its entire life cycle. The main goals of LCT are to reduce a product's resource use and emissions to the environment as well as improve its socio-economic performance through its life cycle. This may facilitate links between the economic, social and environmental dimensions within an organisation

Further reading
- *Better sustainable materials start with Origin* by Origin (2018): originmaterials.com
- *Origin Materials Life Cycle Assessment* by Origin (2018): originmaterials.com.
- *What is Life Cycle Thinking?* (2022): lifecycleinitiative.org
- *Life Cycle Analysis & Product Life Cycle*, by Youmatter (2019): youmatter.world.

10 *Deloitte LCA Report: Life Cycle Assessment of coproducts. Deloitte Sustainability*, June 22, 2020.
11 Life Cycle Initiative (lifecycleinitiative.org), hosted by UN environment programme
12 EPA, United States Environmental Protection Agency, epa.gov
13 Product lifecycle management (PLM) refers to the handling of a good as it moves through the typical stages of its product life: development and introduction, growth, maturity/stability, and decline (Kvilhaug 2021, Investopedia)

and through its entire value chain (Life Cycle Initiative 2022)[11] (2.7.3 Value chain analysis).

### Sustainable Materials Management

Sustainable materials management (SMM) is a systematic approach to using and reusing materials more productively over their entire life cycles. By examining how materials are used throughout their life cycle, an SMM approach seeks to (EPA 2021):[12]

- Use materials in the most productive way with an emphasis on using less.
- Reduce toxic chemicals and environmental impacts throughout the material life cycle.
- Assure we have sufficient resources to meet today's needs and those of the future.

## 5.3.6 Product life cycle

The traditional concept of Product life cycle (PLC) is the life of a product, which is the length of time from the product is introduced to the market until it's removed from the shelves. It concerns the life of a product with respect to business, commercial costs and sales measures. It is used by the management and marketers of the company as a tool in deciding when it is appropriate to increase advertising, reduce prices, expand to new markets, or redesign packaging. The concept is broken into four stages - introduction, growth, maturity, and decline (or renew).[13] Development of a product life cycle strategy, including marketing and brand stratey, can help extend the life cycle of the product in the market.

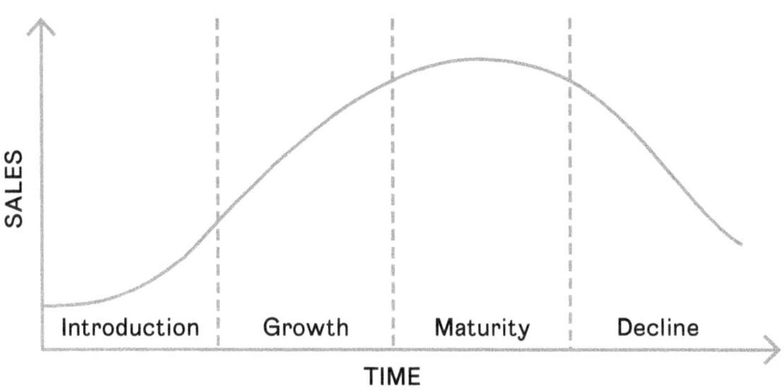


Fig. 5.3 Product life cycle

## 5.3.7 Product life extension

The concepts of *Product life extension* and *Product lifetime extension (PLE)* are part of the multifaceted solutions to create a circular economy. These are terms that describe or estimate the lifespan of a specific product or item, with the ultimate goal of maximising any given product's 'utilisation' rate and duration (Lee, 2019). Here lies the opportunity to create new business concepts or new products from recycled materials. The term should not be mixed up with product line extension which is when a company creates a new product in the same product line of an existing brand (3.7.8 Brand perspective, 6.9.3 Circular economy).



End of life product (EOL)
A product at the end of the product lifecycle.

End of sale (EOS)
A product is no longer for sale.

The time-frame
Depends on the market interest and the product's real life time.

Calculate your environmental impacts in minutes
One Click LCA is the #1 easy and automated life cycle assessment software that helps you calculate and reduce the environmental impacts of your building & infra projects, products and portfolio: oneclicklca.com

### 5.3.8 Incorrect material selection

A startling example of incorrect material selection occurred when designing packaging for a frozen fish product. The cardboard chosen for this purpose was not suitable for moisture and cold, nor did it have sufficient coating on the inside. The consequences were disastrous. The boxes became soft and thus difficult to stack and handle. The fish became less durable.

- Consequences of incorrect or poorly considered material selection: High manufacturing costs, complaints, liability for damages, defects in material, incorrect use of material, lack of information on how to use and maintain the material, etc.
- Lack of material competence can lead to: Failed production, shortened lifespan of the product, reduced product durability, higher production costs, higher maintenance costs, production loss, compensation claims for damages and clean-up after spillage.

Tips for the designer
**Paper can be used strategic to achieve good functionality, create a specific effect, express an identity, reinforce a message. Can also be used tactically to achieve good functionality, create a specific effect, express an identity, reinforce a message.**

> Paper can convey a feeling/tactility and add an extra dimension to the printed message (Arctic Paper, 2012).

### 5.3.9 Sustainable materials

Sustainable materials are 'materials used throughout our consumer and industrial economy that can be produced in required volumes without depleting non-renewable resources and without disrupting the established steady-state equilibrium of the environment and key natural resource systems' (Rutgers, 2010) (5.4.6 Cartonboard).

## 5.4 Paper and cartonboard

Paper is a material that consists of plant fibres, especially wood fibres, a thin, flat material for writing, drawing or printed matters, such as books, brochures and magazines. When thickness and weight increases one gets cartonboard, commonly used for packaging and book covers.

Awareness of the benefits of using paper and cardboard as materials is increasing, as it is biodegradable, easy to recycle, bio-based, reusable, versatile, flexible and one can print directly on paper. In the chapters that follow, we will first get acquainted with paper production, properties and concepts. Then we will talk about cartonboard as a sustainable alternative for use in packaging.

### 5.4.1 Paper

There are countless paper types to choose from, all with typical characteristics in terms of application, visual expression and tactile experience. Paper is used extensively in packaging, household, industrial and printing applications. Before the digital media took over most of advertising and information, it was big business for the paper industry to supply paper for printing newspapers, magazines, brochures, promotional materials, etc. Designers had shelves full of paper catalogues and new great paper samples kept coming in the mail. With the decrease in the use of printed

14 Chinese Cai Lun (Jingzhong) is traditionally considered the inventor of paper and the papermaking process ('Cai Lun,' n.d.).

15 The other tree parts are used instead as other raw materials or energy, which means that many modern paper mills are more than self-sufficient in terms of energy. Paper is an almost 100% natural product. There is currently tight control over the use of chemicals in paper production in order to avoid harm to the environment. These controls are carried out, among others, by local authorities and the EU via the REACH system. (REACH is a regulation adopted to improve the protection of human health and the environment from the risks that chemicals can cause (echa.europa.eu). Paper grades can also be tested for compliance with food contact as well as for safety of toys etc. (*Arctic Paper*, 2012, p. 10).

16 The paper mill Munkedal is especially known for the quality paper Munken. The Munken papers are premium uncoated fine papers and is the ideal choice for companies wishing to convey a genuine natural impression in their printed material. ... The mill is today one of the world's most environmentally-friendly paper mills – and practices sustainable production every day. (arcticpaper.com).

materials, paper played a less important role in the designer's everyday life. Yet paper remains an important material. At a time when you are overwhelmed with information and most of it is conveyed digitally, sharing something on paper can feel more exclusive and personal – holding a small pamphlet in your hand and feeling the texture of the paper against your fingertips, resting your eye on bright colours and great images, sitting quietly and reading the text, and experiencing the physical in contrast to the digital. Paper can be seductive; an uncoated paper, with its velvet soft surface, or a coated paper with its smooth glossy finish. There are many benefits to paper. Paper can replace plastic and other less sustainable materials, thus the sales situation for paper might be increasing in the future. This chapter on paper is based on the book Art Workshop (Arctic Paper, 2012), and on input from Erik Bakkelund (Arctic Paper).


1 Initiation
2 Insight
3 Strategy
4 Design
5 Production
6 Management

5.1 Implementation
5.2 Model
5.3 Material selection
5.4 Paper and cartonboard
5.5 Colour management
5.6 Production for digital media
5.7 Production for printed media
5.8 Installations and constructions
5.9 Quality assurance

5.4.1 Paper
5.4.2 Paper construction
5.4.3 Paper production
5.4.4 Paper properties
5.4.5 Paper selection
5.4.6 Cartonboard
5.4.7 Green packaging
5.4.8 Packaging materials
5.4.9 Ecolabelling and certification


### 5.4.2 Paper construction

The origin of paper dates to early ancient times when the Egyptians produced paper-like material from the papyrus plant. Papyrus is known as the first writing material. Papyrus scrolls have been found dating back to 3,000 BCE, but paper as we know it today is considered to have been invented by the Chinese Cai Lun in 105 BCE.[14] Paper today consists largely of plant fibres, especially cotton and cellulose fibres from various tree species, but also, flax and hemp. The cellulose fibres are released either chemically or mechanically. *The chemical method* involves boiling chips with chemical additives. Virtually all wood-containing substances are removed from the pulp,[15] except cellulose, hence the name woodfree paper. It provides strong and age-resistant paper. In *the mechanical method*, more than 95 percent of the tree volume is utilised, hence the name wood-containing paper. The cellulose is used for making pulp, to which fillers (limestone, clay, kaolin), water and chemicals (glue, starch, calcium carbonate, solids) are added. Chemicals are needed to make the paper, as well as to give the paper the desired properties, such as extra strength, better water repellence and the right colour shade. A paper made with fillers has better formation, higher opacity, better ink-setting properties, a smoother and more flexible surface – all of which make for better printing properties. Paper also contains a certain amount of moisture in the form of water, commonly between 3 to 7% of its weight. The final moisture level depends on what the paper is to be used for. Each paper type has a unique formula and its specific combination of ingredients and is produced to give them the desired properties.

### 5.4.3 Paper production

Paper is made in large paper mills. For instance, the paper machine in Munkedal, Sweden, is 80 metres long.[16] Papermaking usually starts by feeding the pulp into a long paper machine, where the pulp is sprayed onto a wire where the water is sucked out. In this process, the wood fibres orient themselves in the direction of the paper web. This way, the fibre direction is formed in the paper. Afterwards, the water is pressed out using a straining cloth. The pressure to which the paper is subjected affects the *bulk*, *stiffness*, *opacity*, *strength*, and *roughness* of the finished paper. After that, the fresh paper passes over heat rollers, which

Paper printing properties

**A paper made with fillers has better formation, higher opacity, better ink-setting properties, a smoother and more flexible surface – all of which make for better printing characteristics.**

further dry the paper. Finally, the paper is surface treated with a thin film of adhesive, usually starch, to give the surface extra strength and improve printability. At this stage, *the paper is called uncoated paper.*[17] Through further processing a thin layer of latex, clay, and some other substances can be applied to the paper to make the surface even more print friendly.[18] We are then talking about *coated paper*. Finally, the paper is wound onto large tambour reels, and then cut down into smaller reels or sheets, which are delivered for printing or other purposes. The entire process in the paper machine takes only 10 to 30 seconds.

Tips for the designer

**Correct fibre direction: You can check the fibre orientation of the paper by placing the sheet over a table edge. Across the fibre direction, the sheet will be less bendable. Another way is to run one's thumb and finger firmly along the edges of the paper. The edge that bends the most runs across the fibre direction.**

### 5.4.4 Paper properties

*Woodfree paper* properties include high strength and excellent performance. It is also age-resistant, which means, among other things, that it does not lose its structure over time or turn yellow nearly as fast as wood-containing paper. It is important, for example, when printing artworks, art catalogues or books to maintain consistent representation of colours of the image and the whiteness of the paper. A woodfree paper can fulfil the requirements of permanent paper, if it does not contain mechanical fibres. *Wood-containing paper* has good strength, good opacity and a natural feel to it, and is often considered a more environmentally friendly paper.[19] Wood-containing paper has a lifespan of up to 50 years, while woodfree paper has a lifespan of more than a hundred years. Lifespan also depends on storage conditions

**Coated and uncoated:** We usually talk about two main groups of paper: coated and uncoated. Uncoated paper has a rougher surface. Examples of uncoated paper are newsprint and paper commonly used in book production. Coated paper is treated with one or more layers of coating, usually chalk, clay, latex and binding agents, to give the paper certain printing properties. Examples of coated paper are magazine paper, and paper for art catalogues and art books. Coated paper is further divided into two main types; matte or glossy.[20]

**Bulk, grammage, thickness:** To determine paper bulk, grammage and thickness must be measured. Grammage, thickness and bulk are mathematically linked.

- *Bulk*[21] defines the ratio of paper thickness to its weight in cubic centimeters per gram. The formula for bulk is thickness (mm) x basis weight (g/m^2) x 1000.[22] A paper with *low bulk* is more compact and less airy than one with a *high bulk*. A low-bulk paper is therefore thin and heavy, while a high-bulk paper is light, airy and thick. High bulk drastically increases stiffness.[23]
- *Grammage (basis weight)* measures the weight of paper per unit area, in grams per square metre ($m^2$), for example 130 g/$m^2$. This means that an 80-gram A4 sheet does not weigh 80 grams. A so called 80-gram A4 sheet is based on the weight of the A0. A0 is exactly 1 square metre. An A4 sheet is exactly 1/16 square metres and weighs exactly 80/16 = 5 g. The ratio of the edge lengths of an A4 is 297/210, the root of 2 (4.8.4 The A series).
- *Thickness (caliper)* of the paper is measured in micrometres (μm) (one thousandth of a millimeter) and is indicated by the distance between the two surfaces of the paper. Thickness affects stiffness, stability, feel and thickness. For example, it will make a difference in multi-page printed matter, such as a book with hundreds of pages.

17 A paper that is uncoated, gives a different tactile experience than if it had been coated.
18 Print friendly is not always planet-friendly. Check out and make a conscious choice.
19 There are also wood-based papers that are made as a combination of wood-free and wood-containing, and have many of the qualities that a wood-free paper has.
20 There is also double-sided paper, which is coated on one side and uncoated on the other (Printbox.no).
21 'Bulk is a measurement of paper that often determines what type of printers can handle it' (Dombrower, 2017).
22 It gives the volume or compactness of a paper calculated in $cm^3/g$ (volume divided by weight). When the weight and volume of the paper are in $m^2$, the calculation will give the same result.
23 Bulk is in many cases a matter of cost. When setting up a mail campaign and choosing a paper with a slightly higher bulk and lower grammage, it is possible to save a lot of money in distribution costs. If one compares a paper with high and low bulk in terms of grammage ($m^2$), printing books, brochures, ads and the like, one will get more out of the paper and money if one chooses high bulk rather than low bulk.
24 Other similar methods of measuring paper surface roughness include Bekk, Sheffield and Parker Print. When measuring coated paper, the 'smoothness' is normally defined according to Parker Print Smoothness PPS.

**Roughness:** The paper surface has slight unevenness or roughness. Roughness of the paper defines a paper's deviation from a smooth surface. Roughness is expressed in ml/min, referring to the volume of air that passes between the paper surfaces in one minute, when a special measuring device is used. The target is called Bendtsen.[24] *Uncoated* paper has greater roughness than coated paper. To reduce roughness, the smooth paper is compressed in a calendar. There is a certain link between bulk and roughness, as a smooth, compressed paper will have a lower bulk. The same applies if the paper is *coated*; it gives a smoother paper and results in lower bulk, i.e., higher grammage compared to surface weight. Surface roughness also affects the colour rendition of the images in the printing process. The smoother the surface, the better the detail rendering.

**Brightness and shade:** Paper is produced in a wide range of brightness and shades, from white to natural, as well as coloured paper in many different variants. In production, various chemicals and dyes are added to the pulp to adjust the brightness and shade of the paper. The paper's optical parameters are often described as CIE whiteness, ISO brightness and shade.[25] When selecting paper from colour samples, it is important to study the paper in different light conditions and see different paper variants in relation to each other.[26]

**Opacity:** Opacity is a term for non-transparency. Opacity depends on how well the paper surface can scatter and absorb light. The higher a paper's opacity, the less translucent it is. A paper with 100 percent opacity is completely non-transparent. An example of low-opacity paper is tracing paper. The opacity of the paper can change in the printing process as printing ink penetrates the paper and reduces its opacity. This is especially important in double-sided printing, particularly on low-grammage paper, because images on one side can disturb the other.

**Porosity and absorption:** Porosity and absorption are two important factors where coated and uncoated paper differ. These two parameters influence the way paper absorbs the printing ink. Surface-sized paper is less porous and therefore absorbs less printing ink. In addition, the coating layer has a kind of filtering effect that keeps the colour pigment, together with some amount of ink binders, on top of the surface. When the colours remain on the outside surface, it gives high colour gloss. On uncoated paper, there is a bleeding effect (dot gain) where the colour dots (screen dots) grow when more colour pigments are absorbed in the paper, resulting in lower colour gloss (5.7.3 Raster, 5.7.4 Four colours).

**Fibre direction:** The direction the fibres orient to during paper production is simply called the paper's fibre direction or machine direction. The opposite direction is called cross direction. In the fibre direction, the paper will be stiffer and thereby harder to bend across. The correct fibre orientation of the paper is important in printed matter. A brochure with the wrong fibre direction feels less stable, and in a book, the pages feel stiff and are harder to open.

**Dimensions:** The paper is delivered from the paper mill to the printer on a roll or as large sheets in standard formats, which are delivered on pallets. Formats A and B are two different standards (4.8 Surface and format).



An 80-grams A4 sheet does not weigh 80 grams. A so called 80-grams A4 sheet is based on the weight of the A0. A0 is exactly 1 square metre. An A4 sheet is exactly 1/16 square metres and weighs exactly 80/16 = 5 g.

25 *Brightness* is expressed as a percentage of the amount of light of a certain wavelength, in the blue area of the daylight spectra, the 457 nm, that is reflected from the paper. Whiteness is measured over several wavelengths and it gives a value closer to what the eye actually perceives. Two papers with the same whiteness may have differences in yellow, red or green. To make the paper appear whiter, add a blue shade, and add a touch of yellow to a paper that should be as natural as possible. If optical brighteners have been added to a paper in order to increase its brightness, this can be verified by a UV lamp.

26 In the paper industry, D65 on the CIELAB scale is used as an illuminate for paper evaluation, and D50 for evaluating printing inks.

## 5.4.5 Paper selection

When the idea of making printed matter comes up, work begins to assess paper. Selecting paper is a targeted and strategic choice, which is linked to requirements and guidelines defined for the task. The deliberate choice of paper can strengthen the effect and purpose of the printed matter in many ways, or not thought through, it can have the opposite effect. There are two elements to consider; *the technical criteria* related to functionality, and *the subjective assessment*, related to how the paper fits with the idea and the desired solution. Overall, this means that the paper selection will be assessed based on visual appearance of the shade, tactile paper feel, how it can reproduce images, readability of text, paper lifespan and one's own experience of how the properties of the paper can best be used. Though, a given consideration should always be ethics and environment.

Tips for the designer
**The choice of paper quality will affect the effect of the printed matter in many ways and should therefore be considered thoroughly at an early stage in the design process.**

*Grammage* = thickness/bulk.
*Thickness* = grammage × bulk.
*Bulk* = thickness/grammage.

### Paper feeling

Paper feeling is the way the paper feels when you touch and hold it. Many do not reflect upon the fact that paper can feel hot or cold when touching it. Some paper surfaces draw heat from one's fingers, as is the case with coated paper, which has mineral surface. Uncoated paper is a wood fibre material and will therefore feel warmer. A smooth surface is often considered to give a more exclusive feel, whereas a rougher surface has a more tactile and natural feeling. A smooth surface often offers the best image rendering, while a rough surface can add a special touch to the image.

Stability, stiffness and the perceived thickness will all come from the actual *paper thickness*.[27] It will also give a different impression on how solid the printed matter feels. It is important to consider the thickness in relation to the size of the printed matter. A large format needs to be more rigid than a small format. In smaller books, care should be taken when choosing too thick/rigid paper, it can quickly become difficult to browse (self-closing). First impressions are important. Heavy or light? This must be considered in the context of the idea and objective of the printed matter. It is here that consideration of grammage, thickness and bulk can make a difference (5.4.3 Paper properties: Coated and uncoated; Bulk, grammage, thickness).

### Paper shade

The paper colour we see is a reflection of the light surrounding the paper. This means that the light conditions have a major impact on how we experience the paper. Therefore, it is important to assess where the printed matter should be read or used, and to test the paper in different light conditions, such as daylight, light from fluorescent tubes, incandescent light bulbs etc.

*White paper*: When choosing white paper, there are several considerations to think about. White paper is not only white, but can be off-white, white, natural or yellowish. White paper often has a bluish tone that can be perceived to have a somewhat colder expression compared to, for example, paper that is yellowish, creamier. White paper will give images more contrast, while cream-coloured paper can be perceived as more reader-friendly. Novels are often printed on cream-coloured paper.

Further reading
**– Find the right paper: monsterkamer.nl/en/.**
**– Designers about paper: monsterkamer.nl/en/katern/designers-about-paper/.**

27 A *high-bulk* paper has a greater thickness at a given grammage and will feel more stable and robust than a *low-bulk* paper.
28 The Green White Paper, 2014. antalis.com. Antalis is a global distributor of paper and packaging, with presence in 41 countries. antalis.co.uk.

*Text on paper*: Several studies have confirmed that black text with good contrast on yellowish paper makes it possible to keep concentration levels up for a longer period while reducing the strain on one's eyes. Specular reflections from paper cause major disturbances when reading.

### Image reproduction

In case of image reproduction in printed matter, there are several things to consider when selecting paper. Coated and uncoated paper will render images differently. As we have previously mentioned, the rough surface of uncoated paper will absorb more ink, in addition to the colour flowing out more by *dot gain*, among other things, compared to coated paper, where it remains more on the surface. Coated paper will give the images more shine, while uncoated paper can add interesting texture, softness or character to the images. Another consideration is the colour of the paper. A yellow-toned paper will give the image a warmer look, while a blue-toned paper will appear colder. At low opacity, the amount of shade in the images can cause the colours to penetrate the opposite side and become more visible there. To avoid breakthrough effects at low opacity, one can increase the paper grammage and thus increase the opacity.

### Lifespan of paper

As paper ages, it will turn yellow, and its strength and flexibility will decrease. In planning production, it is therefore important to consider how long the paper should stay fresh. An advertising brochure will not normally last very long, while a textbook or novel will perhaps be passed on to future generations. All paper turns yellow when exposed to light. Wood-containing paper can start yellowing after just a few days, while for a wood-free paper it can take significantly longer. In terms of paper strength, both paper quality and binding should be considered. The binding keeps the paper in place and therefore plays an important role. As a rule, woodfree paper is stronger than a wood-containing one; higher grammages are stronger than lower grammages and uncoated paper will be stronger than coated paper of the same grammage. Paper exposed to moisture will generally have a shorter lifespan.

### Environmental impact

Paper has multiple impacts on the environment throughout its lifecycle, such as extraction of raw materials, production, transformation, distribution, use and handling of waste. These are factors that need to be considered when determining the choice of paper. According to Antalis 'The green white paper',[28] the paper industry are making ongoing efforts to limit the environmental impact of the production process. 'The adoption of cogeneration as a source of energy (for example production which combines heat and electricity), and use of renewable energy sources (biomass), have both made a considerable contribution to reducing environmental impact. Going forward, all the players in the paper chain, including consumers, need to assimilate the notion of responsible management of this precious resource through their paper purchasing behaviour, their consumption patterns and the way in which they manage the resulting waste' (Antalis, 2014).



The paper manufacturer's paper dimensions reveal the fibre direction since the number given last indicates the direction of fibre, for example an A4 sheet with the dimensions 210 × 297, 297 will run along the fibre direction. The first number indicates the cross direction.

First and foremost paper has many environmental benefits, as it is a renewable, recyclable and biodegradable material.

Recycled paper is primarily used for newsprint or cardboard but is also found in some other grades of paper. In the recycling cycle, a distinction is made between virgin fibre, which is newly recycled, and cellulose fibre, which has been recycled several times and is therefore worn out. Virgin fibres kan be added to multiple recycled fibres to increase the capacity for reuse. Paper fibres can be recycled/reused 5 to 10 times. When the fibres are worn out, the paper can be burned to generate electricity or central heating for buildings. Paper profile: The environmental declaration for paper contains the most important environmental parameters, such as emissions to air and water, waste to landfill and purchased electricity. For certification and ecolabelling, see 5.4.9.

**Cartonboard (cardboard/consumer packaging) vs. cardboard (solid cardboard/book covers).**

### 5.4.6 Cartonboard

Cartonboard as a material is particularly suitable for a wide range of products, both food and non-food. The material has great advantages because it is based on wood fibre, which is a renewable and recyclable natural resource. In addition to its environmental properties such as recyclability and compostability, it is simple to produce and cost-effective due to its low weight (less material). This chapter is based on conversations with Eirik Faukland, manager of research and development at Moltzau Packaging AS.[29]

Cartonboard has been produced since the year 105 and is the world's most used packaging material. The basic production principles are the same today. However, there have been major changes in terms of producing, constructing, packaging design and printing techniques. The main suppliers of wood fibre for cartonboard are sustainably run forests in Scandinavia and similar in other regions of the world, that provide long, tough and strong fibre.[30]

Sustainable forest management can be explained as 'the stewardship and use of forests and forest lands in a way, and at a rate, that maintains their bio-diversity, productivity and their potential to fulfil, now and in the future, relevant ecological, economic and social functions, at local, national and global levels, and that does not cause damage to other ecosystems' (European Agreement, Helsinki, 1993).

With the world's cartonboard materials available today, there are basically 3 main groups:

**Chipboard:** Recycled material consisting of used fibres that may previously have been packaging, magazines, newspapers, etc. The quality is generally not approved for direct contact with food and is softer in its structure. You therefore need a significantly higher gram weight on this to get close to the strength of a virgin fibre-based cartonboard quality. (There are exceptions here.) Chipboard is the cheapest cartonboard quality.

**False carton:** Material consisting of new fibre (virgin) and is approved for direct contact with food. These folding board grades, which are produced by most raw board manufacturers, are the quality group most used in the world today. It meets very many 'normal' packaging requirements in the grocery industry and other industries worldwide.

29 Moltzau Packaging has a long history in the development and production of consumer packaging, moltzau.no.

30 Raw material for cartonboard does not come from the rain forest.

But if the requirements increase slightly in relation to logistics, tear strength, load-bearing capacity, and any moisture requirements, then there are homogeneous qualities.

**Homogen board:** First-class qualities that consist exclusively of virgin fibre. These qualities are distinguished by strong and tough fibres, often with selected types of wood for extra requirements for logistics and packaging machines, etc. The folding and punching properties of these qualities are the highest in the industry. Package logistics is also constantly evolving and often places very high demands on the mentioned properties.

- *Thickness/weight*: The thickness/weight of carton is defined in grams per square meter and is usually calculated from approx 180g–600g. Below 180g it is paper and above 600g it is solid cardboard (book cardboard).

One can distinguish between two main categories of cartonboard:

- *Graphic cartonboard* is used for everyday products that are not packaging, such as menus, brochure covers, writing pad covers, thinner paperback book covers, business cards, advertising products, etc. Compared to packaging cartonboard visually, the graphic cartonboard very often has a coated and glossy surface, often through-dyed or various forms of embossing, canvas embossing, elephant skin, etc.
- *Packaging cartonboard* is used for different types of packaging, such as for food and non-food. Packaging cartonboard sheets are double-sided, they can be: white/white, white/brown, brown/brown, white/grey, grey/grey or variants of these. Most grades are single-sided coated, a few are double-sided coated and still others may be completely uncoated.

### 5.4.7 Green packaging

There are two facilities on packaging: Food and non-food. Cartonboard packaging can replace plastic packaging on very many products. When choosing materials for packaging the fundamental requirements of packaging must be considered, which is mainly the protection and durability of the product. This to prevent the product from getting damaged and become unusable. The main functions of a packaging is to hold together, preserve, protect the product against adverse effects on the way from production to the end user, facilitate handling and use, inform and sell it. At the same time, the packaging must ensure that the contents - or parts of it - do not penetrate through the packaging. In other words, the right packaging helps to reduce wastage in product turnover and extend the life of the products. Used packaging should preferably proceed into the cycle as a renewable resource.

**Virgin fibres:** These are fibres from wood that is harvested for the first time. They have not been recycled.

- *White vs. brown cartonboard*: White cartonboard qualities of virgin fibres are often used for food packaging. That does not mean that white cartonboard material is cleaner than brown. Brown cartonboard can also consist of virgin fibre. Traditionally one associates white with purity, which is why the pharmaceutical industry uses almost exclusively white cartonboard for its products.



Antalis Green Star system™

'The Green Star System™ incorporates the vital information on the origin of the fibre and the manufacturing process and attributes each paper product a star rating from zero to five based on environmental performance. The Green Star System™ reflects the complexity of what it means to be an eco-responsible product which speaks to a technical audience, but simplifies the information in a rating system that can be understood by all audiences. As such, this self-explanatory system can be easily used by companies to select papers and to communicate about their environmental efforts with various stakeholders without any potential misunderstanding' (antalis.com).

- *Food packaging*: 100% virgin fibre is the most common. An option is virgin fibre on the inside (direct contact with the food must be virgin fibre), and chipboard on the outside. Simple chipboard qualities with PE coating can, in some cases also be used for food. PE (Polyethylene) is one of the most widely produced plastics in the world.
- *Virgin vs. recycled fibre?* Which is better? It depends on what it will be used for. For food is it undoubtedly virgin fibre. For none-food, such as boxes for nails and screws, both virgin and recycled fibre can be used, but virgin fibre will be more stable and robust. Any reuse of these boxes is possible for the consumer. Recycling of used material is impossible without the addition of virgin fibre from the forest.
- *Number of recycles*: The general rule has been that cardboard packaging can be recycled 5 to 7 times. Recent studies however conducted by Graz University of Technology in Austria, shows that 'Fibre-based packaging material – paper, board, cartonboard and folding boxes – can be recycled more than 25 times with little to no loss of integrity, according to latest, independent research' (technology.risiinfo.com).[31]

**Facts on recycling** (Mathias Hovet, 2022, Goods AS, goods.no)

- *Green Dot* usually says a rule of thumb for recycling is that if the object (in this case the paper bin) contains more than 80% of the main material, then it should be in this category. In the cartonboard recycling process, everything is cleaned, cut into small pieces, and separated. Plastic parts

| Packaging materials application areas, in order of priority | |
|---|---|
| Fibre: | Cartonboard: Consumer packaging<br>Solid cardboard: Packaging for fish<br>Corrugated cardboard: Transport packaging and display<br>Paper: Bags and similar |
| Glass: | Jams, cucumbers, foods, beverages. Can be recycled indefinitely. Limited possibilities of use. |
| Wood: | Pallets, gifts, packaging, games and toys. |
| Metal: | Foods, beverages (aluminium cans).<br>Protective layers in flexible packaging (plastic and aluminium), such as coffee, potato crisps, chocolate.<br>*Note: Metal will probably disappear. Laminate is worse than plastic, in the recycling process.* |
| Cellulose-acetate: | Can be used in combination with cardboard. Almost as transparent as plastic. Consists mainly of cellulose. |
| Plastic:[32] | PE (Polyethylene)/HDPE (High-Density Poly Ethylene)/LDPE (Low-Density Polyethylene): Tubes, foil, food and beverage containers, toys, and housewares.<br>PP (Polypropylene): Bags, sacks and similar.<br>PET (Polyethylene Terephthalate): Bottles and bowls.<br>EPS (Expanded PolyStyrene): A very lightweight white foam plastic material widely used in the export of fish and furniture.<br>EVOH (Ethylene vinyl alcohol): Used as a barrier layer that protects food and provides longer shelf life. |

Table 5.1 Packaging materials

Table 5.1 The table shows a list of different packaging materials, in priority order, starting with the most sustainable. Based on Faukland, E., Arctic Paper Norway (2022).

Tips for the company

When choosing packaging, the question is what is most important. It depends on what to make packaging for. If it is for food, food safety is most important. Ensuring that food does not deteriorate is also sustainability.

*Recycling* is using material from waste as a raw material to produce new goods or resources. *Upcycling* is the re-use of a material or object, but for a different purpose or in a different way from the original.

31 Graz, Austria, Jan. 13, 2022 (Press Release): 'Pro Carton announces study by Graz University of Technology in Austria proving that fibre-based packaging can be recycled over 25 times' (technology.risiinfo.com).

32 Bangladesh was the first country in the world to implement a ban on thin plastic bags in 2002, after it was found they played a key role in clogging drainage systems during disastrous flooding (Lindwall, 2020). According to a United Nations paper (2022) and several media reports, 77 countries in the world have passed some sort of full or partial ban on plastic bags (Buchholz 2021, Statista.com).

33 The information is based on: emballasjeforeningen.no.

will float up; the fibre will end up in the bottom and can be used as toilet paper or similar.

- Corrugated cardboard usually consists of one main part of recycled cardboard and one part of virgin fibre, which often has to do with the property of the virgin fibres.
- Printing method has nothing to say in itself, but chemical-free printing inks are preferable, e.g. algae ink, soy ink etc. This is not very widespread yet.
- Production from renewable energy: The packaging is produced with renewable *energy* from sources like water, wind or sun. This reduces the demand for fossil fuel.
- Whether plastic is more or less environmentally friendly depends on a number of factors that are difficult to predict without insight into the project. What plastic is it? What properties should it have? Is it recycled (correctly)?

### Sustainable packaging

When can you say that the packaging is environmentally friendly? It depends on the packaging. In order of priority: 1) Easy to recycle, 2) Reusable material type, 3) Efficient logistics, retail and transport packaging, 4) Proportion of recycled material, 5) Weight (quantity), 6) Easy to sort (empty, clean, compress, separate different parts as well (information). Choosing the optimal packaging material may require a good overview of the entire value chain and new studies in the area. Some simple advice (A. Fjelldal, Innoventi, 2022):

- Make sure that the packaging has a good degree of filling and does not use more material than necessary!
- Do not make residual waste.
- Use as few materials as possible and make it easy to separate them. One-material for the entire packaging is best.
- Avoid materials that are welded together by two different materials. These materials cannot be easily separated and are often burned, for example, cardboard with silver foil, plastic cover, etc.
- Make the packaging as flat as possible. This way it can be transported flat from the printing house to where the goods are packed. The less air in the truck, the better. It makes it super easy to understand that the packaging can be recycled. Tell people how to do it on the packaging with text and familiar symbols.
- Make sure the materials are easy to recognise, then it is easy to put them in the right bin.
- Designing consumer products with sustainability and recycling in mind! The front-end impacts choosing sustainable materials and constructions and examples of designing for end-of-life solutions.

## 5.4.8 Packaging materials

The five most common packaging materials are: Fibre (paper, cartonboard and cardboard), plastic (a variety of varieties), glass, metal and wood. Within the five main groups, there are many varieties, especially when it comes to plastic. Finding the right packaging is often about using the material that is best suited for the product in question.[33]



Further reading
Packaging design, materials, production, certification: index.goods.no

Circular economy
In a circular economy, it is important to keep the resources in circulation as long as possible, so that we get the most benefit and value out of them.

**Material innovation:** Research shows big potential for the use of seaweed as well as a demand for research to assure a successful use of this potential in various field such as active food packaging.[34]
**New solutions:** Packaging is constantly evolving in new directions. New materials, packaging solutions and requirements emerge. Companies invest large resources in coordinating finances, the environment, functionality, technology, packaging directives and product presentation so that optimal solutions are obtained. Changing demographic structures, societal views, health / hygiene regulations as well as increased trade, globalisation and competition constantly require new and better packaging solutions (based on Emballasjeforeningen).

### 5.4.9 Ecolabelling and certification

Certification of food packaging can show if the product is ethical, consumer-safe and complies with high environmental standards. Here is a list of some of the most common certifications for food packaging, retrieved from Index Goods, index.goods.no (2022).[35]

Table 5.2 The table shows list of some of the most common certifications for food packaging, retrieved from Index Goods, index.goods.no

| | |
|---|---|
| Estimated sign: | E-mark can be found on some prepacked products (food, drinks, cosmetics, cleaning) in Europe. Its use indicates that the prepackage has complied with the relevant European laws. |
| PEFC: | An organisation that works throughout the entire forest supply chain to promote good practice in the forest and to ensure that forest-based products are produced with respect for the highest ecological, social and ethical standards. pefc.org |
| Nordic Swan Ecolabel: | The official ecolabel of the Nordic countries. nordic-ecolabel.org |
| Food Safe: | The international symbol indicating that the material used in the product is considered safe for food contact. It's visualised as a wine glass and a fork. |
| FSC: | The label FSC (Forest Stewardship Council) provides information about the origin of the materials used to make the finished and labeled product. This is the original FSC. fsc.org. |
| FSC 100%: | A label indicating that all the materials used in the products are sourced from forests that have been audited by an independent third party to confirm they are managed according to FSC's rigorous social and environmental standards. fsc.org. |
| FSC MIX: | A label indicating that the products are made using a mixture of materials from FSC-certified forests, recycled materials, and/or FSC controlled wood. fsc.org. |
| FSC Recycled: | A label indicating that the products have been verified as being made from 100% recycled content (either post-consumer or pre-consumer reclaimed materials). fsc.org. |
| CE: | The letters 'CE' appear on many products traded on the extended Single Market in the European Economic Area (EEA). They signify that products sold in the EEA have been assessed to meet high safety, health, and environmental protection requirements. ec.europa.eu. |

34 'Seaweeds polysaccharides in active food packaging: A review of recent progress' Carina et al., 2021-04, Vol.110, p.559–572 doi.org/10.1016/j.tifs.2021.02.022
35 Goods As, is an award winning packaging design studio. 'We design consumer brands, retail and packaging for people and planet' (Goods As, goods.no).

| | |
|---|---|
| Universal Recycling Symbol: | An internationally recognised symbol used to designate recyclable materials. The recycling symbol is in the public domain and is not a trademark. |
| Asthma Allergy Nordic: | A collaboration between the asthma and allergy organisations in Norway, Sweden and Denmark. The label makes it easier for customers to find gentle products selected with care. asthmaallergynordic.com. |
| Ecolabel: | The EU Ecolabel is a label of environmental excellence that is awarded to products and services meeting high environmental standards throughout their life-cycle: from raw material extraction to production, distribution and disposal. ecolabel.eu. |
| Green Dot: | A non-profit company that provides financing for recycling of products around the world. The symbol doesn't mean that a product itself is recyclable, but that the company which produced the product has paid a recycling fee to Green Dot. pro-e.org/the-green-dot-trademark. |
| Fairtrade: | Changes the way trade works through better prices, decent working conditions and a fairer deal for farmers and workers in developing countries. fairtrade.net. |
| ISO Certifications: | A set of international standards issued by ISO (International Organization for Standardization) that help organisations ensure they meet customer and other stakeholder needs within statutory and regulatory requirements related to a product or service. |
| Certified B Corporation: | A new kind of business that balances purpose and profit. They are legally required to consider the impact of their decisions on their workers, customers, suppliers, community, and the environment. bcorporation.net. |
| 1% for the Planet: | A global movement inspiring businesses and individuals to support environmental solutions through annual memberships and everyday actions. Your donation is 1% of annual sales or salary. onepercentfortheplanet.org. |
| C2C certification: | Cradle to Cradle Certified® is the global standard for products that are safe, circular and responsibly made. |
| TCF and ECF: | Not bleached with chlorine gas. TCS (Total Chlorine Free) means completely chlorine-free. ECF (Elemental Chlorine Free) means that chlorine oxide is used in combination with, for example, oxygen and hydrogen peroxide. paper.co.uk/environment/ecf-tcf/. |
| C2C certification: | Cradle to Cradle Certified® is the global standard for products that are safe, circular and responsibly made. c2ccertified.org. |

Table 5.2 Ecolabelling and certification

**Product labelling/Ecolabelling:** Product declaration and information on durability and storage. Label for source sorting of packaging waste. Various forms of identity marking on the goods and traceability back to the various production stages and origin. Transparency helps the consumer choose products that are ethical, fair trade and sustainable. For production and distribution, barcodes are information carriers in logistics, transport, and sales of goods. In addition, much of the


1 Initiation
2 Insight
3 Strategy
4 Design
5 Production
6 Management

5.1 Implementation
5.2 Model
5.3 Material selection
5.4 Paper and cartonboard
5.5 Colour management
5.6 Production for digital media
5.7 Production for printed media
5.8 Installations and constructions
5.9 Quality assurance

5.4.1 Paper
5.4.2 Paper construction
5.4.3 Paper production
5.4.4 Paper properties
5.4.5 Paper selection
5.4.6 Cartonboard
5.4.7 Green packaging
5.4.8 Packaging materials
5.4.9 Ecolabelling and certification


Further reading
Managing Packaging Design For Sustainable Development (2016) by Hellström and Olsson DOI:10.1002/9781119151036

The tidyman symbol is present on many packaged items and is a reminder to the customer to dispose of the packaging in an appropriate manner. This does not mean that the item is recyclable.

labeling is designed for branding and marketing purposes. Make the material of the label the same as the packaging itself, for much easier recycling.

**Cradle-to-cradle**

It was in the 1970s, that people began to concentrate more on the environmental impact of the various products. In USA the growing mountain of garbage was a concern. That led to studies of the effects of different products on the environment and society, and the well-known concept *cradle-to-grave*, later referred to as *cradle-to-cradle* (C2C).[36] The concept refers to the product's life cycle from raw material via production, transport, consumption and to waste management. It implies that the product is 'sustainable and considerate of life and future generations, from the birth, or "cradle", of one generation to the next generation, versus from birth to death, or "grave", within the same generation' ('Cradle to cradle,' n.d.).

## 5.5 Colour management

The colours of the computer screen cannot be trusted. They may look quite different when viewed on print, video or other media. Colour management is about ensuring optimal and consistent rendering of colours across different colour systems. A colour captured by a camera may thus appear approximately the same on a computer screen, on a print-out, and on a print from a printing press.

Colour management means ensuring that the colours of a photo are displayed correctly on the screen and printed correctly. Colour management is important for several professions and affects those who produce cameras, computer equipment, digital printing machines, paper and screen media. Technically, the development of such media today is based on international colour management standards.[37] It allows for uniform colour reproduction between different devices (camera, monitor, scanner and print), but relies on the human factor to make this interact. The designer's task is to select the correct colour profiles and colour conversion methods early in the work process to ensure the desired colour rendering in the end result. It is about taking control of your own workflow, especially as documents are to be passed on, for example, to a printer. Improper colour rendering can have major consequences. It can lead to unwanted surprises and, in the worst-case scenario, to having to reprogram a website or to produce a printed matter over again. In some contexts, this can be costly for those responsible. In some cases, there is also no time to remanufacture, e.g. at fairs or other events that

Tips for nerds

All ICC-based colour profiles relate to CIELAB. The colour profile thus contains a conversion table from RGB or CMYK to CIELAB _and_ a conversion table from CIELAB to RGB or CMYK. E.g. The Adobe RGB icc profile contains a conversion table from RGB to CIELAB (used to convert colours from Adobe RGB to another colour space) _and_ a conversion table from CIELAB to Adobe RGB (used to convert colours from any other colour space to Adobe RGB. The conversion is done by our CMM, via 'Profile Connection Space' (this is CIELAB) to our destination colour space e.g. Adobe RGB.

Tips for the designer

If you plan to make large adjustments to a photo taken in RAW format or 16 bit RGB, it can be a practical solution to work with images in 16 bits per channel.

36 The cradle-to-cradle concept originates from Walter R. Stahel in his 1976 research report to the European Commission in Brussels *The Potential for Substituting Manpower for Energy*. McDonough and Braungart took the concept further and co-authored the book *Cradle to Cradle* (2002). Walter R. Stahel and Genevieve Reday also sketched the vision of an *economy in loops* (or *circular economy*) and its impact on job creation, economic competitiveness, resource savings and waste prevention. They published the book *Jobs for Tomorrow* 1982 (product-life.org n/d). 'In 1981, Stahel wrote the paper "The Product-Life Factor" and identified selling utilization instead of goods as the ultimate sustainable business model of a loop economy: selling utilisation enables to create sustainable profits without an externalisation of the costs of risk and costs of waste.' (product-life.org n/d).

37 For example, the ISO 12647 standards.

38 Colour management is offered as a separate subject in the bachelor in graphic design program at NTNU in Norway.

take place at specific times. In such cases, one may end up with a result that is not optimal.

Let us say that you have taken a photo of a beautiful flower in the garden and want to bring out all the nice shades of the original motif on your own computer screen. Similarly, you want the same colours to appear on millions of different screens over the internet. You want the same shades to be rendered correctly in a magazine people will read, or on a large poster that will hang on a wall. The reality is that every time the image of the flower is displayed on a new medium, digital platform or production stage, the image will relate to different colour profiles. In practice, this means that there is a potential risk that the colour shades might change at each stage (Gamborg, 2017). 'One example could be a picture of a metallic grey car from a major car manufacturer. If the car is silver-grey, problems with colour conversion can cause the car to appear light green or perhaps reddish in various newspapers, magazines or on screens. This potentially costs the car company large amounts of money since customers who contact the company based on the image they have seen in an ad do not recognise the product being sold. Those customers looking for a grey car will not be in touch' (Johansen, 2017). Completely independent of what settings are made, there will always be shade differences because different media reflect and handle colours differently and thus give colours different characters. Even different paper types or other materials affect the colour of the print. Nevertheless, a lot can be done using colour management to achieve the best possible colour reproduction between devices (camera, screen, scanner and print), different documents and stages of the work process up to the end result (print, web, video). This chapter on colour management is mainly based on interview with graphic designer Lars Christian Gamborg, and professional advice and input from Eivind Arnstein Johansen at NTNU Gjøvik.[38]

### Colour Management Module (CMM)

Screens display colours; scanners and cameras read colours; and printers render colours. Colour management is about eliminating factors that make colours behave differently and ensuring the best possible representation of colours on and between these different devices. Each computer has a Colour Management Module (CMM). We can say that CMM is the 'colour calculator' that converts colours from one colour gamut to another. Without CMM, there is no colour management. It converts different colour spaces and profiles to achieve the most accurate and consistent colour reproduction possible when colour conversion between different units and profiles is required. This does not mean that the designer is exempt from proper colour management. CMM basically does only what it is told to do by the designer. It is the designer's task to select the correct layout in Adobe applications to ensure correct colour rendering in one's own workflow all the way up to the end result (5.5.6 Workflow). It also involves selecting the correct input when converting colours to the colour spaces of different devices, see Table 5.3. In addition, it is beneficial to select drivers and profiles from the manufacturer who has manufactured the device being used, and not the one that comes with the operating system.



Tips for the designer

CMYK-based colour gamuts have far fewer shades than RGB. Therefore, it is important to preserve a larger colour gamuts as long as possible. If you have converted an image to a colour gamut with fewer shades, you will never get those shades back! (5.5.6 Workflow)

Tips for nerds

When we operate towards HDR screens with more intense primary colours (e.g. the Display P3 standard) or towards the UHD TV standard (Rec. 2020), we will be able to experience the phenomenon of 'banding', that colour gradients 'crack up' if we relates to only 8 bit colour depth per channel in RGB. The next natural step would be 16 bit colour depth. This would give approx. 65,000 tones per channel in RGB or 281 trillion colours (281 474 976 710 656). This requires large bandwidth when we often also have high-resolution screens. One compromise one has fallen on is 10 bit colour depth per channel. This gives 1024 tonal variations per channel in rgb which then gives us approx. 1 billion shades in total. As of HDMI 2.0, up to 12 bit colour depth per channel is supported, ie up to 68 billion colour shades in total.

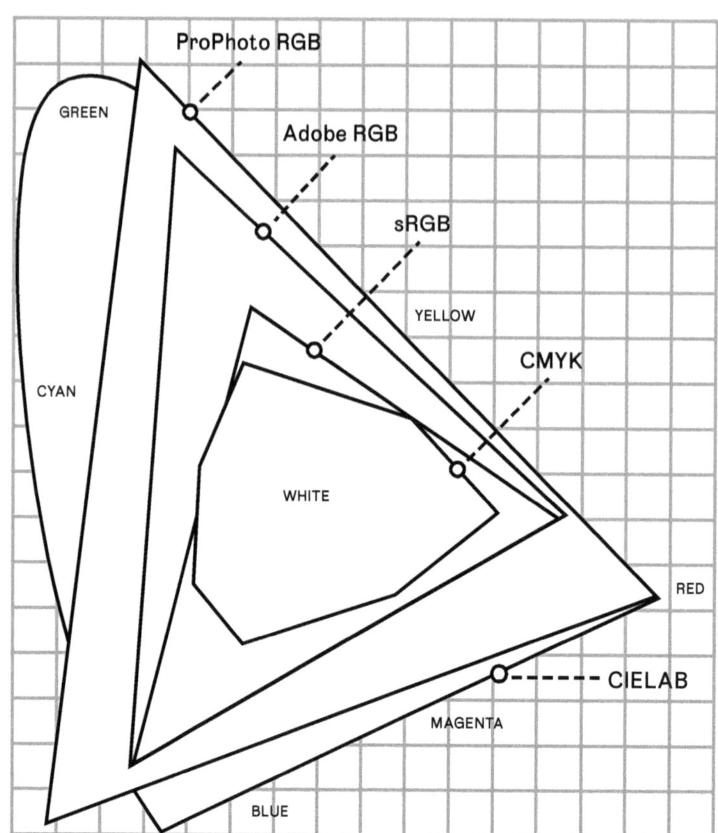


Fig. 5.4 CIELAB

Fig. 5.4 The figure shows a simplification of the international standard CIELAB and some of the most used colour gamuts. CIELAB is shown in the figure as a characteristic horseshoe shape. It contains all possible colours that can be represented. All standard colour gamuts and profiles are based on this. The figure shows the differences between some selected colour profiles. With so many different colour profiles, it is almost inevitable not to get nuance differences in a larger process that includes photography, design, and printing. CIELAB is based on the idea that there should be a correspondence between the perceived difference in hue and the numerically specified hue. CIELAB is the reference model for Pantone colours and ICC-based colour management. The figure is based on International Commission for Lighting (CIE) and International Colour Consortium (ICC).

## 5.5.1 Colour models

Colour perception is something created in one's brain when light of varying wavelengths reaches the eye. That is, when electromagnetic radiation with wavelengths within the visible part of the spectrum (from approximately 390 nanometres (nm) to 700 nm) strikes the rods and cones of the eye (4.6.2 Colour). There are two basic colour models that differ significantly from each other; subtractive colours (pigment colours) and additive colours (light colours). By mixing two pigment colours, for example yellow and red, we get the colour orange. This is called subtractive colour mixing, because colours on a paper consist of pigments and absorb (subtract) some wavelengths and reflect others, which are perceived by the eye. If all three primary colours yellow, red, and blue are mixed in equal parts, the eye perceives it as a shade of black.[39] Additive colour mixture works in a different way, or rather quite the opposite. Mixing all three light colours red, green and blue in equal parts, we end up with white light. By mixing coloured light, such as the basic colours red and green, the eye perceives it as yellow. Lighting in the interior, theatre and stage productions relate to the world of additive colour.

The designer moves between the two colour worlds (subtractive and additive) all the time. The screen we are working on relates to light colours, while what we print are pigment colours. It is not obvious that red in a subtractive colour mixture is equal to red in an additive colour

39 There are different sets of primary colours (or basic colours). Cyan, magenta and yellow are the primary colours used in offset printing.
40 It is also not obvious that the same proportion of red colour in two subtractive reproductions is the same if different pigments are used. The perception of colours on a substrate depends on the light source.
41 Pantone.com.
42 PMS is defined in CIEL* a *b* while NCS says nothing about the colour appearance, only about how the colour is mixed. This means that the same NCS colour will be perceived differently on different surfaces (ncscolour.no).
43 A colour gamut can be described according to a 3D mathematical model that consists of numerical values.
44 CIE 1931 XYZ and CIE 1931 RGB colour gamuts were established in 1931 by CIE (International Commission for Lighting) with a mandate from ISO (cie.co.at).

mixture.[40] In addition, the designer's subjective perception of colour is important too, and because colours are perceived in the brain, being able to perceive colours differently has always been a problem. Red for one person is not necessarily the same red for another. The use of colour systems makes it possible to agree on the same physical colour. For example, PMS (Pantone Matching Systems)[41] is a system used by the graphic industry, while NCS (Natural Colour System)[42] is a system used in the paint and interior decoration industry (see Table 5.7 Colour reference systems). When it comes to processing colours in a technical context, the question is how we can render colours consistently all the way. For example, it is about how a particular colour should be represented on a medium using light colours, such as video, TV and computer screens, and how it should be presented on paper, foil or other materials. In principle, one and the same colour must relate to widely differing physical rules and systems. To solve this, different standards have been defined (CIELAB and CIEXYZ), which can be used across technical devices such as cameras, screens, scanners and printers, since colours must change colour gamut and colour profiles (4.6.2 Colour: Basic colours, 4.9.5 Identity colours, 5.7 Production for printed media).

## 5.5.2 Colour gamut

A colour gamut describes the range of colours that can be perceived by the eye or rendered by reproduction within a given colour model, see Figure 5.4. A colour gamut is a theoretical way of organising colours, used in both analogue and digital contexts.[43] In those contexts, where there is a need to compare colours and render colours consistently, you need a common platform or reference system that describes colours independently of technical devices and human judgement. Therefore, the international organisations CIE[44] and ICC[45] have established a technical standard and developed colour models such as CIELAB (Lab colour) and CIEXYZ.[46] The standard is meant to help render colours in images as accurately as possible, regardless of system, program or medium. This is the very essence of the colour management process. Theoretically all possible colours that can be represented are often set at 16.7 million[47] (based on 8 bit RGB).[48] In principle it represents all the colours that can be perceived by the human eye, about 10 million. CIELAB is the international standard accepted today as an absolute colour gamut. There are different types of colour profiles that relate to CIELAB.[49]

### Out of gamut

In a workflow, it might be necessary to change the colour space or profile. Sometimes this may result in some shades falling outside what is possible to render within the spectrum of the new colour gamut or profile, see Fig. 5.4. In jargon, we say that there are colours that are 'out of gamut'. Every time colours are to be represented again, and where there may be a new colour gamut or new colour profile, there is a potential risk for some shades to end up outside the colour spectrum. This is a reality one has to deal with. Therefore, it is also important to ensure that the correct colour settings are set in the Adobe software (Photoshop, InDesign and Illustrator, Acrobat) and any other software



45 The ICC standard is established by the International Colour Consortium (ICC), and is based on CIELAB. ICC-based colour management relates to CIELAB. ICC profiles are colour profiles based on the ICC standard and CIE lab, adapted to different needs to help render colours in images as accurately as possible regardless of system, application or medium.
46 CIELAB and CIEXYZ, see also: wiki/Lab_colour_space.
47 Many colours cannot be represented. Among other things, it is possible to specify an intense laser-red colour that is also completely black. Such a colour is only theoretically possible and can not be reproduced on either screen or substrate.
48 8 bits gives 256 tones for R, G and B = 256 × 256 × 256 = 16.7 million rounded down.
49 Each time colours have to change colour gamut, the system goes via CIELAB/CIEXYZ and converts the colours to the new colour gamut. Switching back and forth to the same colour gamut can change colour values (Gamborg, 2018).

one wants to use, so that the program follows the correct colour profiles and performs the colour conversion correctly. The colour settings are set according to the settings best suited for the destination of the document being processed.

### 5.5.3 Colour profiles

Manufacturers of monitors, scanners, printers, digital cameras and so on each have their own way of describing and representing their colours. Therefore, they have also created colour profiles so that different colours and shades remain as correct as possible in workflow across systems and applications (5.5.6 Workflow).[50] The most common are sRGB, Adobe RGB and ProPhoto, but FOGRA39 and ISO Coated V2 are also used. These colour profiles are based on their own systems and purposes. In addition, they cover different parts of the visible colour spectrum. By visually comparing these colour gamuts, one will see how big the differences actually are, see Figure 5.4. As seen from the figure, the CMYK colour gamut is smaller than the various RGB colour gamuts, which means that a CMYK colour gamut can render fewer shades than an RGB colour gamut. In a graphical context, or when working with Adobe software, only RGB and CMYK colour models are considered.

At a printing house, consistent colour rendering will be achieved by calibrating, mapping and 'communicating with' all equipment such as software, computer screen, RIP and printing press using colour profiles.

| Colour model: | Colour gamut: | Colour profile: |
|---|---|---|
| Description of a physical/theoretical colour spectrum (visible colours) | Description of a particular colour model for a workspace | Description of colours in a particular colour gamut on a particular medium |
| Additive colour synthesis | RGB | sRGB (web)<br>AdobeRGB (1998) (print)<br>ProPhoto (photo) |
| Subtractive colour synthesis | CMYK | FOGRA27 (print)<br>FOGRA39 (print)<br>SWOP (print)<br>U.S. Web (print) |

Table 5.3 Colour model, colour gamut, colour profile

Table 5.3 The table shows the relationship between colour model, colour gamut and colour profile (Gamborg, 2017). (5.5.1 Colour models, 5.5.2 Colour gamut and 5.5.3 Colour profiles).

Tips for the designer
The Adobe RGB colour space has a wider range of colours than sRGB. An image saved with an Adobe RGB colour profile may appear to have less colour when viewed on the web, since web browsers use sRGB as the default colour space. Similarly, if you select the Adobe RGB colour space in Photoshop, then print to a printer that is set to sRGB, the printed colours show fewer colour shades compared to those on the screen.

#### Different colour profiles

**sRGB:** This is a profile based on an RGB colour gamut. In our digital everyday lives, all images in their original form are defined in RGB. sRGB is often set as a standard colour profile by manufacturers of cameras, scanners and software, and for displays or light-based media such as monitors, TV sets, computer screens, digital signboards.[51] [52]Most screen media today display colours in 8-bit (bpc), a total of 24-bit pitch depth. Image files from scanners and cameras may technically have greater colour depth, such as 16-bit or 32-bit per channel. This means that you cannot always rely on the screen to display all the shades the images actually have.

50 Often, the terms colour gamut and colour profile are used interchangeably because a colour profile represents the reproducible colours that make up a colour gamut, and the gamut is defined based on the colour profile one chooses. Alternatively, the term 'colour model' is used when we are not talking about specific colour gamuts, but rather about RGB and CMYK as two different ways of mixing colours. Note: The RGB colour gamut is associated with additive colour synthesis. sRGB, AdobeRGB and ProPhoto are all linked to the RGB gamut.

51 sRGB can be used in your own workflow unless the task requires switching to a larger and more suitable colour space, such as AdobeRGB.

52 The sRGB colour profile was jointly developed in 1996 by HP and Microsoft as a cross-platform for use on screens, printers and the Internet, and then standardised by IEC284 and CIE. IEC (International Electrotechnical Commission).

53 This does not mean that the printer's RIPs and printing machines do not support other profiles, but from a technical perspective, AdobeRGB is the profile that yields the best results.

Although sRGB supports 16-bit and 32-bit per channel, it is still optimised for screen media and web. As long as the screens are not designed to represent more colours than what the RGB colour profile already supports, that is the standard for screens we work with today. This applies to screens and not to the files themselves. Screen technology is constantly evolving, and there are already far more advanced screens with more bits per channel, with a completely different colour spectrum, such as HDR and WCG.

**Adobe RGB:** This is the recommended colour profile for use by designers working with both RGB images and vector-based elements in CMYK, and working with Adobe applications such as Photoshop, Illustrator and inDesign. AdobeRGB is an RGB colour gamut and colour profile developed by Adobe Systems, Inc. in 1998. It was designed to encompass most of the colours obtainable in CMYK colour printers converted from colours in RGB as shown on a computer screen. CMYK is the colour values used for press or print, known as four colours. Adobe RGB colours comprise approximately 50% of all visible colours specified in CIE colour spaces. Adobe RGB has a larger colour gamut than sRGB, which also includes some CMYK green shade values that sRGB does not support, see Figure 5.4. Today, AdobeRGB is an industry standard in the graphic business and a safe choice.[53]

**ProPhoto:** A profile intended for professional photographers, also known under the name ROMM RGB. It contains an even wider spectrum of colours than what Adobe RGB is able to represent. A professional photographer tends to keep colours as close to the motif or original as possible.

**eciRGB v2:** A profile that is better suited for a printing context.

**RGB and CMYK**

*RGB* consists of the basic colours red, green and blue. The RGB model is based on reflection of light and is given in values from 0 to 255, where 0 is no colour. When all RGB colours have a value of 0, this corresponds to completely black. RGB is a light-based colour gamut, an additive colour mixture. The more colour you add, the whiter it gets. Just like lighting and stage work, the more coloured light you blend in, the whiter you get on stage. The opposite happens in CMYK, which is a subtractive colour mixture: the more colour you add, the darker it gets, or more impure. So, they are actually opposing sciences.

*CMYK* stands for cyan, magenta, yellow and key colour (black). By adding different overlapping amounts of these basic colours, a large part of the colour spectrum can be reproduced in print. Black is used to add contrast and depth to images; that is why it is called key colour. Combining equal amounts of cyan, magenta and yellow gives a neutral grey/brown tone. For CMYK values, the degree of coverage is given as a percentage. When varying amounts of the four colours are printed in overlapping patterns, it provides an experience of continuous shades like in a photograph (polaristrykk.no) (4.6.2 Colour; Basic colours, 5.6.4 Four colours, 5.6.6 Printing inks).



Tips for the designer

Did you know that the mixture of red and blue in RGB to end up with magenta, similar to magenta in CMYK?

**FOGRA:** A CMYK colour profile that is actually intended for offset printing. It is available in both a coated and an uncoated variant. It was developed by the organisation FOGRA from Germany. This is the most common colour profile for CMYK in Norway and Europe.[54]
**ISO Coated v2:** A CMYK colour profile based on FOGRA39. The subvariant called 'ISO Coated v2 300%' has a maximum limit of 300% ink coverage when printed in offset. So CMYK has four colour channels, each of which has values from 0% to 100%. The profile should ensure that the total percentage coverage does not exceed 300%, without there being any visual difference.
**SWOP:** A colour profile intended for the US market is U.S. Web Coated (SWOP) v2. Other profiles (non-SWOP) intended for the US market are Coated GRACol 2006, US Newsprint (SNAP, 2007) and U.S. Sheetfed v2.
**Japan Color 2011:** A CMYK colour profile for the Japanese and Asian markets.

Choosing a colour profile
**If you are a beginner or when you are unsure what to use, it is best to stick to AdobeRGB for print and press, and sRGB for web and screen platforms. These are colour spaces/profiles that work best in all situations. The practical benefits of using profiles other than sRGB, AdobeRGB or ProPhoto are small, and visually the differences are minimal at best.**

### 5.5.4 Select colour profile

When dealing with colour profiles, it is important to distinguish between the device you are working on (camera, screen, scanner and print), different documents and stages of a work process, and the end result (web, video, print). In the workflow one distinguishes between the *original material* (such as a photo), the *working document* (used while designing), and the *final document* ready (for screen or press). The term *working space* is generally used to refer to the colour gamut associated with the working document. The colour profile that should be used for a working document depends on the final output to be created.

#### Original material

- *Photos*: Most photographers use AdobeRGB, while several professionals use ProPhoto RGB with 16 bit colour depth per channel to have a larger colour range in post-processing. Before converting a photo, most professional photographers often work in Camera RAW. Image data is not encoded against a given colour gamut here. Only when the image is exported for a digital use or printing process will the image data relate to a colour profile. sRGB[55] if the image is to be used on the web or in screen context, or Adobe RGB if the image is to be printed.

#### Working document

- *Internet and screen media*: sRGB colour is a safe choice of colour profile when designing for web and digital media. sRGB is standard in all computers and most computer software uses it as a focal point. Images displayed online always use sRGB.
- *Printed media*: AdobeRGB is a better choice when designing for print and press. AdobeRGB has a wider gamut than sRGB, see Figure 5.4 CIELAB. Adobe RGB is designed to be compatible with CMYK printers. If there are photos or illustrations where it is important to render many shades of colour, it is recommended to use RGB-based colour space because these generally support a wider colour gamut than CMYK-based colour spaces. On the other hand, when creating logos or graphic elements where it is often important for certain colours to

54 There are still new editions coming, but today many use FOGRA39, which has replaced the previous edition, FOGRA27.
55 Display P3 (DCI-P3) applies to many devices from most manufacturers, which is a larger screen colour gamut particularly relevant for newer Apple devices. To some extent, we can look at the DCI-P3 as 'the new sRGB' (Arnstein, 2021).
56 The term 'intent' is most commonly used about rendering intents (including Photoshop, Lightroom, RIP), which in turn concerns colour conversion methods. In other words, if we are converting colours from a large to a small colour gamut, we often end up with many colours that are not possible to reproduce in the new, 'small' colour space. Here, the rendering intent function comes to our rescue, and we can choose which compromise we are willing to make. Should we keep the ratio of colours, but then maybe lose some saturation? Or is it more important to keep the saturation in some colours at the expense of details that may disappear? (Arnstein, 2017).
57 FOGRA39 or the older edition FOGRA27.
58 The colour profile will here relate to the printing process, and whether one prints on matte or coated paper.

have a certain colour value, CMYK is recommended. This ensures that the correct colours and as much colour information as possible are retained until the end result.


1 Initiation
2 Insight
3 Strategy
4 Design
5 Production
6 Management

5.1 Implementation
5.2 Model
5.3 Material selection
5.4 Paper and cartonboard
5.5 Colour management
5.6 Production for digital media
5.7 Production for printed media
5.8 Installations and constructions
5.9 Quality assurance

5.5.1 Colour models
5.5.2 Colour gamut
5.5.3 Colour profiles
5.5.4 Select colour profile
5.5.5 Colour channels and tone depth
5.5.6 Workflow
5.5.7 File types
5.5.8 PDF for printing
5.5.9 Colour reference systems

- Colour settings
- Handling colour profiles in a design process


### Final document

When the design process is complete and one wants to create a *final document* for digital use or printing process, the program relates to an 'Output Profile Intent'.[56] Here, the final colour profile is selected. The choice of colour profile for final documents is based on where the visual design is intended to be used.

- *Internet and screen media*: sRGB or Display P3 may be best suited.
- *Printed media*: Check with the printing house. The final document sent out is converted to the colour profile that represents the printing process and the substrate that the printing house will use. Often the latest CMYK colour profile of FOGRA[57] is used as standard.[58] Essentially, a rule of thumb is to always use a colour gamut/profile that preserves as much information as possible and degrades as little colour as possible. Every time you convert colours to a new colour gamut, the colour quality will deteriorate. Therefore, colour conversions should be avoided for as long as possible and only converted to the correct display or print colour gamut when exporting the image for on-screen use or to a print file. Once you have chosen a colour profile with a smaller colour space, you may lose shades that you will never get back later. Therefore, many printing houses wish to receive the final document in an RGB profile, in order to convert it to CMYK in their *RIP*[59] themselves.
- *Working space:* The colour profiles (under Working space) in the *colour settings* of the Adobe package are set to let the application know which colour profile is preferred when using a document or element in either RGB or CMYK colour gamuts.

### Colour settings

It is the designer who should know what colour profile each job or document really needs. This is not something the program knows automatically. Photoshop, Illustrator and InDesign each have their own way of handling colour profiles.[60] InDesign is a layout application where the document itself does not have a colour profile. The individual images and elements one inserts (which have a colour profile) will apply and will be included when creating a PDF file later. Where an image does not have a colour profile, it will use default colour profiles from colour settings. In Photoshop and Illustrator this works differently. Here the *working document* is set to one fixed colour profile. All images and elements used in the working document will then be converted to the currently selected colour profile. This means that colour deterioration may occur.

The *colour settings* are usually set according to the American market, therefore, it is necessary to make sure that the settings remain as desired after any software updates. In the Adobe package, colour settings are available under the *Edit* menu (see Figure 5.5). In *Working spaces*, under the RGB option, it is recommended to use AdobeRGB.[61] For CMYK, use e.g. Fogra39 or PSO v3 based on Fogra51. Colour spaces and colour profiles can be configured individually for images in the

59 RIP (Raster Image Processing) converts the digital information so that it can be printed on a printer or used on a platesetter to prepare printing plates for offset printing. RIPs and platesetters fall under the term CTP (Computertoplate). A PDF file (ready-to-print) may contain images and elements with different colour profiles in both RGB and CMYK. A RIP will use the current colour profile of each item and read out the correct colour information considering what the printed matter is to be printed on.
60 Images or graphics imported to Photoshop and Illustrator will be converted to the colour profile set in the working space.
61 Cambridge in Colour: http://www.cambridgeincolour.com/tutorials/colour-space-conversion.htm.

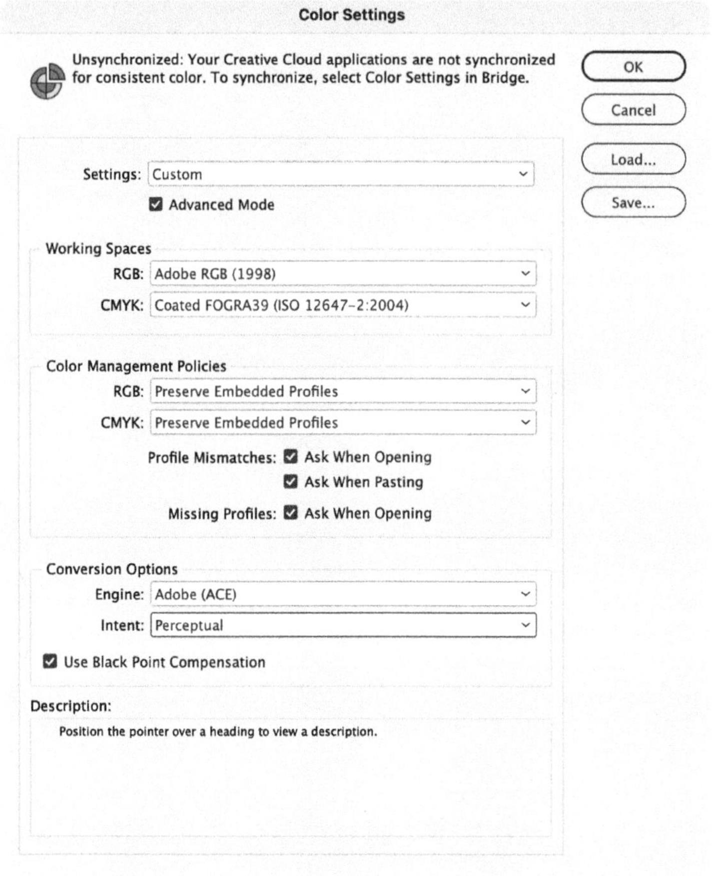

Color Settings

Unsynchronized: Your Creative Cloud applications are not synchronized for consistent color. To synchronize, select Color Settings in Bridge.

OK
Cancel
Load...
Save...

Settings: Custom
Advanced Mode

Working Spaces
RGB: Adobe RGB (1998)
CMYK: Coated FOGRA39 (ISO 12647-2:2004)

Color Management Policies
RGB: Preserve Embedded Profiles
CMYK: Preserve Embedded Profiles
Profile Mismatches: Ask When Opening
Ask When Pasting
Missing Profiles: Ask When Opening

Conversion Options
Engine: Adobe (ACE)
Intent: Perceptual
Use Black Point Compensation

Description:
Position the pointer over a heading to view a description.

Fig. 5.5 Colour settings

application. On *Conversion options* under the *Engine* option, the setting should be Adobe (ACE). This is the colour management module used to do the actual colour conversion between colour profiles. When converting between colour profiles, the *Intent* option tells the program what to do when colours fall outside the colour spectrum (Out of Gamut). It is recommended to use *Perceptual* as it tries to match colours as closely as possible to how our eye perceives them. You can read more about 'Colour Space Conversion' on cambridgeincolour.com.

### Handling colour profiles in a design process

In the design process, you often get original material in the form of photos from others with varying colour profiles. By default, Photoshop is set to give a warning when the file you open has a different colour gamut/colour profile than the profile in the *working space* of the application. For example, you may be working in AdobeRGB, while the file being imported is in sRGB. Initially, it is recommended to use the profile the image already has (*Keep built-in profiles*), it can be sRGB, FOGRA etc. although AdobeRGB is preferable.[62] This is to avoid further deterioration of the image. The more conversions you make, the more deterioration there will be. If the image is .jpg, it is a good idea to start by saving it as .tif, because .jpg is a compressed file format. If you receive images that do

Fig. 5.5 The figure shows what the colour settings look like in InDesign. They are more or less identical in Photoshop and Illustrator.

Tips for the designer
CMYK colour profiles used in different continents, such as America and Asia, have different values on dot gain. Dot gain has to do with how much the raster in a printing process should increase in size in connection with a tone transition. For example, if you use the wrong profile in another country, the raster may become darker or lighter than normal. Point increase is stated in a percentage increase of 50%. If you know that on a specific paper and printing press you experience e.g. 16% point increase (i.e. 50% raster in 'input' is measured at 66% on paper) this must be compensated for one place. This can be done either in the ICC profile or in RIP.

62 Linking an sRGB colour profile to an AdobeRGB colour space without converting colours can generate unwanted results.

63 Photos from the web are the ones we encounter most often, that do not contain a colour profile, and, consequently, sRGB should then be selected for correct colour rendering further in the process.

64 Point increase is stated in a percentage increase of 50%. If you know that on a specific paper and printing press you experience e.g. 16% dot pitch (i.e. 50% raster in 'input' is measured to 66% on paper) this must compensate. A picture must be 'developed' to an editable image format then e.g. at 16 bits per channel for editing. The point is, we do not normally edit image data in a RAW file directly. We can 'save' adjustments for interpreting a RAW file via e.g. Adobe Camera RAW, but here all adjustments will normally be stored in a separate XML-based XMP file with the same file name as the raw file. We like to say that adjustments are stored in a 'sidecar' file.res for a location. This can be done either in the ICC profile or in RIP.

*not* have a colour profile, the Photoshop dialogue box will define this as 'Untagged RGB'.[63] The image technically has some kind of colour gamut, but for some reason the colour profile itself is not associated with the file. Selection in the dialogue box is made based on one's current situation:

- Leave as it is (don't colour manage): this is not to be used under normal circumstances. One always wants to have a colour profile in one's photos.
- Assign working RGB: Use only if you are certain of what kind of colour gamut the image really has.
- Assign profile + convert document to working RGB: Use sRGB on images from cameras. 90% of all cameras are set to sRGB profile. On files from scanners (without a colour profile); use AdobeRGB, or the generic scanner profile.

### 5.5.5 Colour channels and tone depth

Tone depth can be compared to the number of colours in a colour palette. There is a technical concept of how many colours can be described in an RGB colour gamut. Where the *colour gamut/colour profile* determines the range of colour variations based on what the visible colour spectrum can represent, the tone depth is the number of colours or shades. The total tone depth (number of colours) of an image is determined by the tone depth of each colour channel (basic colour). Tone depth is measured in bits per channel and abbreviated as 'bpc'. The more bits, the more colours are present to create shades. The calculation is as follows: Colour channels × tone depth per channel (bpc) = Total tone depth (bits).

An RGB colour space has *three colour channels*, one per basic colour. A CMYK colour gamut has *four*. Nevertheless, CMYK colour gamuts have a smaller colour spectrum, see Figure 5.4. A tone depth of 8 bits per channel (bpc) in an RGB colour gamut is what is common for producing images and photos in natural colours ('true colour'). The total tone depth of an RGB colour gamut (which has three channels) will then be 24bit. If the image has a 24-bit colour gamut. Each colour channel has a value from 0 to 255. If you multiply all the colour combinations each of the basic colours can represent, you get a maximum number of the number of colours the colour gamut can represent, which is 16,777,216. Photoshop displays tone depth per channel on its documents. So, there is a difference in the colour spectrum range that colour gamuts cover, and the technical number of colours an RGB colour gamut has the capacity to display. The different RGB colour gamuts such as AdobeRGB and sRGB have different-sized colour spectra, as shown in Figure 5.4, but within each spectrum there are still 16,777,216 different colours and shades that can be displayed.

One cannot always rely on the screen to display all the shades the images actually have. You can convert an image from 8-bit to 16-bit or more, but you will never get more shades in the image than what the original already has. Different file types may have limitations on how many bits of colour they can accommodate. It is important to use the correct file format to get maximum colour rendering.


1 Initiation
2 Insight
3 Strategy
4 Design
5 Production
6 Management

5.1 Implementation
5.2 Model
5.3 Material selection
5.4 Paper and cartonboard
5.5 Colour management
5.6 Production for digital media
5.7 Production for printed media
5.8 Installations and constructions
5.9 Quality assurance

5.5.1 Colour models
5.5.2 Colour gamut
5.5.3 Colour profiles
5.5.4 Select colour profile
5.5.5 Colour channels and tone depth
5.5.6 Workflow
5.5.7 File types
5.5.8 PDF for printing
5.5.9 Colour reference systems

- Colour settings
- Handling colour profiles in a design process


Further reading

*New Colour Management Standards* by Livonia Print (2017): livoniaprint.lv/news/new-pre-press-standards.

Tips for the designer

In teamwork, it is important to have a common way of managing colour profiles in the situations described above. This saves time and reduces the risk of unwanted end results.

Camera Raw is not a format.[64] In practice, this means that image data from the camera's image chip is stored #directly#/raw in a raw format. This can be compared to a digital negative. Raw images have different file extensions depending on the camera manufacturer. Adobe has proposed a separate raw format with the extension DNG (Digital Negative).

## 5.5.6 Workflow

Workflow is about eliminating factors that make you work less efficiently. If unwanted results occur, finding the error is easier and takes less time if one already is in control of the workflow. Colour management is part of the workflow, ensuring consistent colour reproduction and desired end result. Proper set-up and use of software for proper application and technical understanding of different file types are significant factors. Additionally, creating a neat file structure on documents can provide a better overview of the project and thus a better workflow.

Working in a team, common rules and file structure are also important for creating a good workflow in the group. Everyone has different methods, thinks differently, and does things their way, so it is not uncommon to lose track, especially in teamwork. Increased stress before deadlines and unforeseen events are factors that can negatively affect the workflow.

### File structure

Whether working on one's own projects or in teams, it is a good idea to have a specific structure for the files one is working on. Grouping files as well as naming folders and files is good practice both for oneself, one's team and for the customers one works with. One gets a better overview, knows where to look and also separates the files from each other. Here there is no standard of how things should be done. There are many different ways to structure files and folders. One tip for structuring is to distinguish between *original files*, *work files* and *final documents*.

Naming files descriptively saves a lot of time in connection with subsequent use, since one avoids opening the file and checking. File and map structure can of course be expanded and customised. The more files and variants, the greater the need for a system. The whole point is to find a structure if you work alone, or a common structure if you are a team, that makes the work process easier and more transparent for everyone.

**File structure and naming:**

Original files:
Logo_Company_alt1_eng_CMYK
Logo_Company_alt1_eng_white negative
Logo_Company_alt1_eng_black
Logo_Company_alt1_eng_PMS

Logo_Company_alt1_no_CMYK
Logo_Company_alt1_no_white negative
Logo_Company_alt1_no_black
Logo_Company_alt1_no_PMS

Logo_Company_alt2_eng_CMYK
Logo_Company_alt2_eng_white negative
Logo_Company_alt2_eng_black
Logo_Company_alt2_eng_PMS

Work files:
Bcard_Mary Sharp_March 2022
Bcard_Tom Smart_March 2022

Final documents:
Bcard_Tom Smart_May 2022_proof
Bcard_Tom Smart_May 2022_print
Bcard_Tom Smart_May 2022_web

Fig. 5.6 Naming files

Fig. 5.6 The figure shows how to name files to get good structure and workflow. These are original files, work files and final documents. Original files are photos and similar material that the designer receives. Work files are design in process. Final documents are finished work, ready for use, web or print.

Fig. 5.7 a) The figure is an example of a file structure in a single project. Work files are added to the 'Business Cards' folder. Original files that you either create yourself or get from others, such as images, illustrations, text and fonts, are added to '01 Inbox'. Final documents are added to '02 Output'. Final documents can range from .pdf for printing or .jpg for web, so it is okay to gather them in one place.

Fig. 5.7 b) The figure shows an example of a file structure in a larger project. A client would like to have a design profile with graphical elements, images, logos and fonts. Since this is something often used on different printed matter and platforms, these can be gathered together under the 'customer' folder, for example as 'Design elements'.

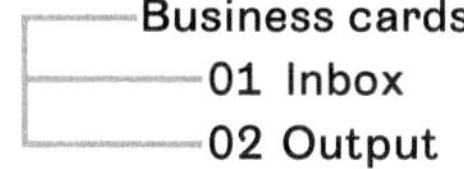


Fig. 5.7 a) File structure in a small project

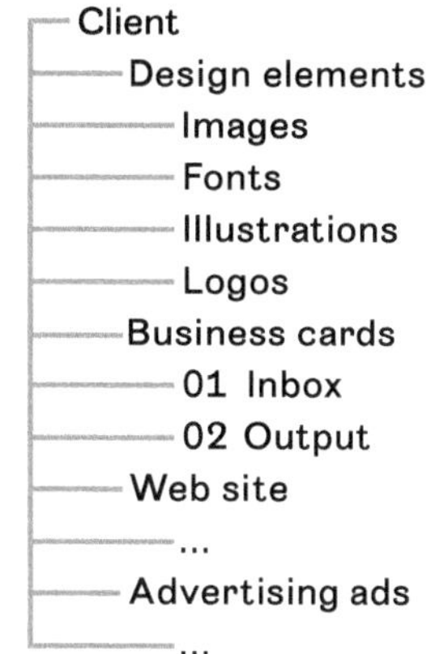


Fig. 5.7 b) File structure in a larger project

**Original files** are elements used in a layout and import into, for example, InDesign. They are often images, illustrations, logos and text that come from other sources or suppliers. A good habit is to leave the original intact or unchanged, while avoiding the use of destructive file types and working methods that 'destroy' the original. Then one also has the best starting point if the material is to be used for something else.

**Work files** or work file is the actual document one uses to 'stitch' the various elements together into a complete design. In addition, it is recommended to use InDesign, a program optimised for this type of work. Often, there is a need to create illustrations, logos or customise photos with effects, which in turn become new 'originals'. For this, either Illustrator or Photoshop are better suited. It is important to make sure that the 'original' being created has high enough resolution with the right colour gamut and profile.

**Final documents** can be files to be used on digital surfaces, such as web and screen media, and they can be print-ready files in PDF format. What a final document is and which file type it is first and foremost depends on the requirements of those who will receive the design or of the platform on which the design will be used. One should select a *file format* where all the necessary elements are included, and should ensure that those who receive the file see the same as what one sees.

**The end result:** Use the best starting point! The desired end result will never be better than the selected starting point. Therefore, it is important to retain as much information as possible for as long as possible and create a workflow with as few stages and changes along the way as possible. Sometimes one has to change the content along the way, for example by reducing the quality, but one should always leave the original intact. When it comes to image resolution, colour gamut and colour profiles, preserving the content as close to the original material as possible, for as long as possible, will achieve the best result.

### Design software tools

In a design process, it is important to use the right tools for the right job. A seasoned designer knows what tool to use at any time. The applications from the Adobe package, InDesign, Photoshop and Illustrator are used

1 Initiation
2 Insight
3 Strategy
4 Design
5 Production
6 Management

5.1 Implementation
5.2 Model
5.3 Material selection
5.4 Paper and cartonboard
5.5 Colour management
5.6 Production for digital media
5.7 Production for printed media
5.8 Installations and constructions
5.9 Quality assurance

5.5.1 Colour models
5.5.2 Colour gamut
5.5.3 Colour profiles
5.5.4 Select colour profile
5.5.5 Colour channels and tone depth
5.5.6 Workflow
5.5.7 File types
5.5.8 PDF for printing
5.5.9 Colour reference systems

- File structure
- Design software tools
- Pixel, raster, dot and vector

A final document is often intended for a particular application. Final documents for digital surfaces compressed or customised to a display medium (.jpg, .png, .gif) are often not suitable as original material for printing. When it comes to PDF for printing, it is important to check with the printing house to make sure that they receive the file the way they want.

here as examples. These programs are used across design disciplines, with emphasis on graphic processes leading up to a printed matter. Each of the three programs has its own applications, which sometimes overlap. Below is a brief overview of what sets them apart in a graphical process.

#### Pixel, raster, dot and vector

Graphical work can be divided into two groups; dot-based and vector-based graphics.

*Dot-based* graphics are also called pixel-based graphics or raster graphics. The essential thing here is that the content is built up of small dots or pixels. It includes camera photos or photos that have been scanned, and works developed in Adobe Photoshop. The end result depends on the resolution of the file.

*Vector-based* graphics are built up mathematically with dots, dashes and curves that can again be filled with colour or combined with effects. The advantage of pure vector graphics is that files become small and can be scaled infinitely without compromising their quality. Therefore, vector-based applications such as Adobe Illustrator are used to develop logos and graphical elements.

### 5.5.7 File types

Each file type, such as .jpg, is designed to serve a specific purpose or solve a technical challenge. Some file types also have limitations because the technology had not come this far. For example, Photoshop allows you to work with multiple layers. Saving this to .jpg will merge all layers into one layer. Where imported file types may have technical limitations, working documents will preserve the quality and all the technical capabilities of each application that is compatible with the file type. The file types .psd, .ai, and .indd can in some cases be used in their respective software, making the workflow more flexible. It is important to keep in mind that other software (not created by Adobe) does not support these file types as well. Alternatively, the files can be converted to other file types.

| Original files | Work files | Final documents |
|---|---|---|
| Files from cameras, scanners, logos and illustrations | Design process, layout | Intended use; web, print etc. |
| .raw, .tif, .jpg*, .eps, .ai | .indd, .psd, .ai, .eps, .tif | .jpg, .png, .pdf |

Table 5.4 Stages of a work process

*Lossy/destructive file type:* Some file types are designed to take up less space (file size) and/or are optimised for use on the web or on a screen medium. These are called destructive file types because they use a technique called lossy compression of the content to a minimum. It also means that shades deteriorate, disappear or get smoothed out. File types of this type are .jpg, .png. and .gif. Other file formats such as .tif can also be compressed, however, they use a different type of compression, 'lossless', which means that the visible content quality is not compromised.

Table 5.4 The figure shows different types of files and documents in a work process. One often works with the original material and work files in parallel, which end up in a final document. It is important to preserve as much quality and information as possible from source and original material to the final document. The division of the stages in the table, what is regarded as original material, working document and final document, and how file types are used is not an industry standard, but an example of good practice (the form has been developed by Lars Christian Gamborg).

Table 5.5 The table shows the characteristics of the three programs in a graphical workflow. The symbol (+) stands for 'good for', the symbol (–) stands for 'less good for'. Choosing the right software item for the different tasks in a work process can help create a better workflow (the form was developed by Lars Christian Gamborg).

| | Photoshop | InDesign | Illustrator |
|---|---|---|---|
| + | Pixel-based graphics<br>Image editing, photo<br>Digital photography productions<br>User Interface, websites<br>Animation | Primarily for layout, design<br>Multi-page, template page, large documents<br>Superior in typography and text management<br>True to Objects.<br>Photos and illustrations remain unchanged<br>Can cause bleeding/cut marks<br>Can export everything to 'package'<br>Manages multiple colour profiles | Vector/ dash-based<br>Font management<br>Scalable graphics (vector)<br>Logo and Illustrations |
| – | Dashes and text become pixels<br>Difficult for layout:<br>Large work files<br>Text, table, wraps, glyph<br>No bleed/cut marks<br>Layers become slightly opaque<br>Multi-page/template page/ autonumber<br>One solid colour profile | Weak vector management<br>Poor on photography. | Multi-page production is difficult<br>Table manager (text)<br>Text management – wrap.<br>No master page<br>No autonumber<br>Layout = Large work files<br>One solid colour profile |

Table 5.5 Choosing the right software



**Use of file formats**

Tips on which file formats work for different types of applications:

- *Internet and screen media*: Here one can use .jpg, .png, .svg. The .jpg file type is used for photo files. The .png file type is used for graphics and illustrations. The .svg file type is a vector-based file format intended for web and screen media.
- *Printed media*: .pdf format is the file format specifically designed to send printed matter with all fonts, text and graphics included in one file. It is a flexible format that has been an industry standard in the graphic business workflow for many years.
- *Other areas of application*: A final document may also be provided in .ai, .indd and .psd formats for example, if it is a design of original material, such as images, illustrations or logos. Either way, it should be noted that fonts are *not* included in the document. One either has to convert text into vector graphics or attach fonts when sending to others. Adobe's own working documents such as .ai, .indd and .psd can also be used directly as original material across various Adobe applications. When delivering the final document, it is also important to keep in mind that fonts and graphics linked to the document should be available except for PDFs.

## 5.5.8 PDF for printing

**What is a print-ready PDF?**: The PDF file type (Portable Document Format), as the name describes, is suitable for forwarding documents. A PDF is a so-called container file, a flexible file format suitable for use in many different contexts, from low-resolution files to proofreading and high-resolution to printing. You can include effects, audio and video that make the PDF suitable for presentation, screen media or the web. This means that it is not intended solely for the graphic industry and printing. When sending files to a printer or printing office, the printer explains how they want the PDF to be configured. Different printed matter may require different solutions for how to deliver files.

**How to create correct PDFs for printing?** PDFs received are not necessarily high-resolution. This should always be checked. The PDFs one creates are not automatically high-resolution and ready for printing either. They must be configured (PDF pre-set).[65] Today, it is no longer necessary to convert images or colours in PDFs to CMYK or other profiles. Many printing houses have equipment and RIPs designed to handle RGB profiles in a workflow. This is part of the principle of preserving as much information as possible for as long as possible. When you create a print-ready PDF, colour profiles from all objects (such as AdobeRGB from images) are included in the working document, plus an Output profile intent in the PDF itself. It tells the RIP that the document is intended to be printed. Conversion takes place in the RIP just before the document is printed. When pressed, objects and files with CMYK profiles that have CMYK values will be preserved and will remain unchanged in a workflow. This makes the use of CMYK values a safe solution for preserving certain colour values.

One should always check with the printing house first which PDF is pre-set or which profile is optimal to use. It is important to note that there may be printing houses requesting CMYK files. There may also be printed matter where there is a need to convert to CMYK before sending PDFs to the printing house. An example of this is logos and illustrations created in Illustrator, where it is particularly important to preserve the exact colour values.

Table 5.6 The table shows which file formats are recommended for which applications. The table shows best practices, although other applications can technically be used as well. Each of the formats has its technical limitations and possibilities about which information can be found on the Internet. *) Rather use .ai, .indd or .psd as a working document if possible. **) Many in the industry use .jpg or .pdf as original documents, but since the files are either compressed or may be intended for another original purpose, they are not always suitable.
.jpg and .pdf are not suitable for editing inside the files – although it is technically possible. The .eps format does not support colour profiles (not recommended). The PDF format is an adequate and better format for all cases where we would previously use .eps in the final document. In practice, the .ai-format is also a variant of PDF (the form has been developed by Lars Christian Gamborg).

**PDF preset**

There are several PDF presets in the Adobe package, which are intended to create print-ready PDFs for printing houses. Here is a selection with the most important differences.

| | |
|---|---|
| **PFD/X-1a** | Merges layers, transparency effect is lost.<br>RGB is being converted to CMYK.<br>CMYK values are preserved. |
| **PDF/X-3** | Merges layers, transparency effect is lost.<br>Supports RGB colour profiles on image files.<br>No colour conversion. |
| **PDF/X-4** | Supports RGB colour profiles on image files.<br>No colour conversion.<br>Supports transparent effect. |
| **Smallest File Size** | For screen and web. Images are scaled down.<br>Low resolution.<br>For proofreading. |

**Note:** In general, it is recommended to use PDF/X4 unless otherwise requested by the printing house.

65 Previously, it was common to convert images or colours in a PDF to CMYK (e.g. FOGRA27) in order to ensure that the colours were set up for an offset or digital printing method. Older RIPs were not designed to handle RGB profiles.

| File type | Graphic type | Purpose/ area of application | Original material | Working document | Final document |
|---|---|---|---|---|---|
| .indd | Layout | Layout and design. | Yes. Adobe package | Yes | No |
| .ai | Vector-based/ layout | Illustrations and logos. | Yes. Adobe package | Yes | No |
| .psd | Pixel-based | Photos and images. | Yes. Adobe package | Yes | No |
| .tif/ .tiff | Pixel-based | Press and print. Non-destructive file type. Keeps graphics and images unchanged. Options for teams. Supports vector graphics. | Yes | Yes | Yes (original material) |
| .eps | Vector-based/ layout | For use with illustrations, logos and vector-based graphics. Also supports image files. Vector graphics are scalable. | Yes | Yes * | Yes (original material) |
| .svg | Vector-based | Web/screen media. Scalable. Small file sizes. Supports pixel graphics. | Yes ** | Yes * | Yes (web/ screen) |
| .pdf | Container format | Transfer design/printing material from a designer to a printing house. Includes all elements; text, fonts, photos, illustrations etc. Flexible file format. | Yes ** | No | Yes (press, web and screen) |
| .jpg/ .jpeg | Pixel-based | Final document, for screen media and web. No layers. Compressed/destructive file format. Small files. | No ** | No | Yes (web/ screen) |
| .png | Pixel-based | Screens and internet. Non-destructive file format. Transparent layer. | No | Yes (web/screen) | Yes (web/ screen) |
| .gif | Pixel-based | Internet. Graphics and simple animation. Transparent layer. *NB! Obsolete file format.* | No | Yes (web/screen) | Yes (web/ screen) |

Table 5.6 File types used in the graphic business

## 5.5.9 Colour reference systems

Colour reference systems are arranged according to the perceptive appearance of the colour and attributes to which it is added, such as red, green or blue hue, colour brightness, saturation, etc. Different subject areas have given rise to different colour reference systems/colour maps.

| Colour reference: | Which principle is used as basis for the system: | Application: |
|---|---|---|
| Web colour | The system is based on hexadecimals. The value of a particular colour is determined based on a 6-digit number (with a # sign at the front). E.g. an RGB value for red becomes #ff0000. | Web colour is widely used in HTML languages on the web. Hexadecimal colours are 'ordinary' RGB, but given in a slightly different way. They comprise a secure system for rendering colours on the Internet. |
| RGB | The colour model is based on values from 0 to 255 for each of the three colour channels red, green, and blue. | Used in a variety of image and layout programs. It also serves as basis for rendering colours in an RGB colour gamut and on-screen medium. |
| CMYK | The colour model is based on the four different basic colours: cyan, magenta, yellow and black. Each parameter has a value from 0% to 100% coverage. | Used in a variety of image and layout programs. It also serves as basic colour model for printing and offset printing. |
| Pantone (PMS) | Pantone Matching System is a technical colour standard across different industries (based on subtractive colours). The system develops its own colours that can be mixed and rendered from 14 basic colours. | Used as printing colour in offset printing. Selected from colour catalogues in order to ensure correct colour rendering in connection with either colour raster or special colour (spot colour) on either coated or uncoated paper. |
| NCS | The colours in this system are a relation between yellow, red, blue and green and give the value in percent. The Swedish flag consists of: NCS 0580-Y10R (yellow) and NCS 4055-R95B (blue). The first two values define blackness and colourfulness. The next two values are the colour position between two of the four basic colours. | Often used in interior design and the paint industry. The colour system is originally from Sweden, but is also used in a number of other countries in Europe. |
| RAL | A system based on nine series of colours: yellow, orange, red, violet, blue, green, grey, brown, white/black. Within these series there are a number of shades. The colour code does not originate from any colour model. | Often used for foils, whether printed on foil or solid-coloured foil. The system is also used in interior decoration and metal colouring. |

Table 5.7 Colour reference systems

Table 5.7 Other colour systems such as DIN and Munsell are not included in the table because their area of use is limited. See also coloursystem.com (5.7.5 Printing inks).

Fig. 5.8 The figure shows UX design, frontend and backend in a web project. It starts with UX research, build wireframes, UX flow, prototypes, develop visual elements, and make sure that the design is human-centred and consistent with the product brand. Front-end developers work on functionalities, translate designs and pictures in code, make sure that interface elements bring the user to the right page, and that the data obtained from user/app interaction is saved and ready to be processed (eleken.co). Backend developers codes and adds utility to everything the front-end developer creates, maintaining, testing, debugging, and handle the core application logic, databases, data and application integration, API and other backend processes (The figure is based on Nashville software school, Eleken, 2022).

66 Center for digital media, thecdm.ca

A good digital media result is dependent on exceptional user-experience. The process of getting there is a combination of insight, strategy, design methodology, design, programming and other tools presented in the previous phases of the book.

Examples of digital media can be ecommerce, websites, mobile applications, social media, location based services, online gaming and more. Building digital media products requires teams of professionals with diverse skills, including technical skills, artistic skills, analytical and production coordination skills, with focus on creating the best user-experience (CDM)[66]

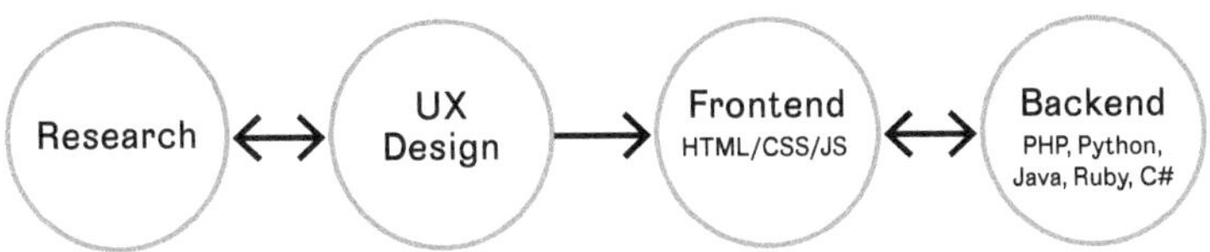


Fig. 5.8 Frontend and backend

*Frontend* and *backend* are terms commonly used in web and mobile app development. They need to communicate and operate effectively to improve a website's functionality across browsers and devices. To frontend and backend one could say that what a user sees on a website is the frontend, and behind the scenes functionality and stored data is the backend. When a web page loads, the backend retrieves the data from the database and displays it on the page, the frontend. This chapter briefly explains some key elements based on geeksforgeeks.org (2021) and conversations with Jonas Fredin (2022).

### Frontend

Frontend is the *client* side of an application, the part of a website that the user interacts with directly. It is the structure, design, behaviour, and content of everything seen in the browser. Key areas can be:

- Colours, typography, layout, spacing, images, text, graphs, tables, buttons, menus, everything a user can see and interact with is part of the front-end.
- *HTML, CSS, and JavaScript* are the main languages used for frontend development.
- *Responsiveness* is crucial to ensure that the application appears correctly on devices and performance is one of many keys to achieve good user-experience.

**Frontend languages:**

- *HTML, Hypertext Markup Language,* is the combination of hypertext and markup language. Hypertext defines the link between pages. The markup language defines the content with tags and attributes. In combination, HTML, defines the structure and hierarchy of a web page.

1 Initiation
2 Insight
3 Strategy
4 Design
5 Production
6 Management

5.1 Implementation
5.2 Model
5.3 Material selection
5.4 Paper and cartonboard
5.5 Colour management
5.6 Production for digital media
5.7 Production for printed media
5.8 Installations and constructions
5.9 Quality assurance

- Frontend
- Backend

Digital media
eCommerce
Games – console, online and mobile
Websites and mobile applications
Animation
Social media
Video
Augmented reality
Virtual reality
Data visualisation
Location-based services
Interactive storytelling

Printed media
Newspapers
Weeklies
Magazines
Brochures
Flyers
Hand outs
Billboards
Posters
Direct mail:
Letters and postcards
Print media selection (CDM).

- *CSS, Cascading Style Sheets,* is a language used to make an application presentable. CSS allows us to apply styles to elements which alters their default browser styling. Some browsers do not support all the features of CSS. Ideally an application should be more or less equal no matter what browser, phone or desktop is used. The problem with browsers like Google Chrome, Mozilla Firefox, Microsoft Edge, Safari, Opera and others, is that they interpret the standard differently. So, when a property is not supported nor performing satisfactorily, for example in an animation, JavaScript can be the solution. JavaScript has a completely different browser support than the latest features of CSS. An application that has been created in JavaScript can talk more easily to other types of services through API (application program interface), which is an interface that allows services and products to communicate with each other and leverage each other's data and functionality through a documented interface.
- *JavaScript*, or JS, is a scripting language often used to implement complex features on a web site, like interactive maps, heavy animations graphics and API calls. JS can also be used for simpler tasks e.g. to enhance the user-experience in areas where the browser lacks CSS support.

**Frontend frameworks and libraries:**

There are many different front-ends. Every front-end framework consists of the frontend languages HTML, CSS and JavaScript. Front-end frameworks often encourage a modular mindset, which can make production, collaboration and maintenance easier. Front-end frameworks such as Angular, React and Vue to name a few are in many areas trying to achieve the same, but they have their own syntax. What stack do you use? This is a question one often hears. The question means, which combination of technology do you use. Libraries can be used to simplify or add to a language.

Examples of widely used frameworks and libraries:

- *Angular* is a development platform built on TypeScript. It is a component-based framework for building scalable web applications.
- *Bootstrap* is a free and open-source tool collection for creating responsive websites and web applications. It is one of the most popular HTML, CSS, and JavaScript *framework* for developing responsive, mobile-first websites.
- *React.js* is an open-source, component-based JavaScript *library* maintained by Meta and a community of developers. It can be used as a base in the development of single-page applications and mobile apps.
- *SASS* is the most reliable, mature, and robust CSS extension language, with fully CSS-compatible syntax. It allows for the use of variables, nested rules, mixins, imports, and much more. It gives the developer more tools to build and to organise the stylesheets better.
- *Flutter* is an open-source UI development SDK-software development toolkit[67] managed by Google for building appealing, multi-platform applications for mobile (iOS, Android), web, and desktop from a single codebase.
- Other libraries and frameworks are Vue, Foundation, jQuery, Svelte, etc.

Tips for the designer

**Being a developer you will have to deal with many complex stuff and issues, such as API, Authentication, Design Patterns, MVC, Cache, Cookies, Sessions, JSON, Endpoints, Server, Hosting, Postman, CRUD, Curl... Not only will you be developing the apps but also you will be dealing with the backups and servers for hosting your application. Whatever technology you're choosing on the backend side, make sure that you implement the best practices on it (geeksforgeeks.org 2021).**

Tools tips

Design: material.io/design
Components: material.io/components
Develop: material.io/develop
Resources: material.io/resources
Material Design 3: m3.material.io

Further reading

Top 10 Best CSS Frameworks for Front-End Developers in 2022: hackr.io/blog/best-css-frameworks

67 SDK (software development toolkit) is a set of software tools and programs provided by hardware and software vendors that developers can use to build applications for specific platforms (whatis.techtarget.com).

68 APIs is a set of functions and procedures allowing the creation of applications that access the features or data of an operating system, application, or other service (API, n.d.).

### Backend

Backend, the server-side, is the part of the website that a user can not see and interact with.

- Data is arranged and stored in a database. The backend transfers data from the database to the client-side. It can also transfer data from the client-side and store it in the databse.
- Writing APIs,[68] creating libraries, and working with system components without user interfaces are included in the backend.
- JavaScript, C#, PHP, Python, Ruby, and Java are some of the main programming languages used.

**Backend languages:**

- *JavaScript* can be used as both frontend and backend programming languages.
- *C#* is a general-purpose programming language and widely used for competitive programming and as a backend language.
- *PHP* is a general-purpose scripting language designed for web development. One of the most popular content management system, WordPress, is written in PHP.
- *Python* is a general-purpose programming language. Its approach aims to help programmers write clear and logical code for both small- and large projects.
- *Node.js* is an open-source and cross-platform runtime environment for executing JavaScript code outside a browser. It is not a framework, nor a programming language. One often uses Node.js for building back-end services like APIs. It is suitable for large companies and has been used by big names such as Paypal, Uber, Netflix and Wallmart.
- *SQL* is designed for managing data held in a relational database.

**Backend frameworks:**

Software frameworks help developers make applications in a faster and more standardised way. Among the benefits are: time-saving, scalability, robustness, security and integrations. Examples of widely used frameworks:

- ExpressJS, Django, Ruby on Rails, Laravel, .NET, and more.

## 5.7 Production for printed media

A good print result is an interaction between paper, printing colours, printing machine and the person operating the printing process.

A good print result requires the designer to consciously choose paper or another material to be printed. Equally important is that the designer has good communication with the printing house about colour management and printing method, and to be present at the start of printing to ensure the best result. The choice of printing method depends on the quantity to be printed, cost, time, finishing and desired quality. Print media is physically printed media such as newspapers, magazines, posters and billboards and direct mail. Traditional press methods used today can



Further reading
Good Coding Practices For Backend Developers, 30 Apr, 2021: geeksforgeeks.org/good-coding-practices-for-backend-developers/?ref=rp

be traced back to the origins of book printing press in the 16th century. Even digital printing that came with computer technology is based on many of the same principles (4.9.6 Typography: Font history).

### 5.7.1 Press techniques

In general, graphic printing methods are all about press and colour. An *original* version of what is to be printed is converted into a printable form, called a printing plate, which is covered in ink and then pressed against formats of paper, cardboard, fabric, etc., so that they become exact reproductions of the original. This way one can multiply printed books, newspapers, magazines, packaging, T-shirts or other things. Today, many traditional printing methods are digitally controlled. In addition, there are many forms of completely digital reproduction methods, which we commonly call digital printing or just print (printing), such as photocopying, inkjet printing and laser printing, which work by transferring ink to paper using heat or static electricity (Woodford, 2018).

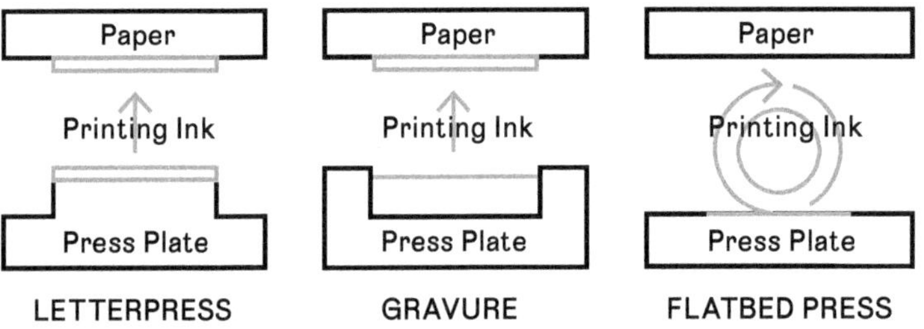


Fig. 5.9 Printing techniques

Fig. 5.9 The figure shows the principles of relief, gravure and flatbed printing. a) Relief printing means that the colour is rolled at the highest point of the printing form. b) Gravure is made by placing the colour in depressions in the printing plate. c) Flatbed printing means that the areas with printing ink are on the same plane as those without. This printing technique is used in offset.

Traditional printing methods can be divided into different main techniques depending on how the printing ink of the motif is transferred to the printing substrate (paper or other material). In addition, there are various mixing techniques. Here we will look at the main techniques of letterpress (relief), gravure (intaglio) and flatbed (planographic) printing, and then different printing methods based on these (based on Arctic Paper 2012, 'Graphic,' n.d., Woodford 2018):

**Letterpress:** In China there is relief printing dating back centuries before the birth of Christ. Press or relief printing is a common term for several graphic print techniques. Old-fashioned book printing using moulded lead types is relief printing, that also applies to woodblocks printing (xylography), linoleum block printing, potato printing and similar. The printing ink is rolled at the highest points of the printing mould, which are the press elements of the mould. In addition to lead types, the printing mould may be made of metal, rubber, plastics or cut plate.[69] The letterpress is a type of printing press based on the same principles as the one invented by Johannes Gutenberg in the 16th century.[70]

**Gravure:** Intaglio (gravure) printing was already used at the end of the 13th century and is considered the beginning of graphics in Europe. While in relief printing, colour is applied to elements protruding from the printing plate, a gravure is made by depositing colour in the plate

69 Cliché (from French: cliché) is originally a term derived from the art of book printing, where a cliché is a printing plate used to reproduce or multiply images. In everyday speech, cliché is rather a term for a fixed (trite) expression ('Cliché,' n.d.).

70 The flatbed press is a type of printing press based on the same principles as the printing press Johannes Gutenberg invented in the 16th century. In the simplest type of letterpress (flatbed press), the paper is supported on a flat metal plate, located under the printing plate holding a relief version of what is to be reproduced. The printing plate is covered with ink (by hand, brush or automated roller) before the paper is pressed tightly against it and then released. A classic letterpress is operated by hand, pressing one sheet at a time. This is time-consuming, which is why rotating cylinders are most often used instead of one or both surfaces; Flatbed cylinder press and Rotary webfed press (Woodford, 2018).

71 Lithography means 'stone writing', a method of printing from the surface of stones invented in 1798 by German actor and playwright Alois Senefelder. He took a large stone and drew a pattern on it with a wax crayon. Then he dipped the stone in water so that parts of the stone not covered in wax colour became wet. Next, he dipped the design in ink, so that the ink only adhered to the waxed parts of the stone and not the wet parts. The stone thus served as a printing plate, which he could press against paper to make a copy (Woodford, 2018).

depressions (engravings). The depressions are formed by etching the motif, or they are applied to the plate mechanically or by means of acids or other chemicals. The printing ink is rubbed onto the plate, while the highest part of the plate is wiped off (without colour). From there, the printing substrate (paper) is pressed against the printing plate and the motif is transferred by the printing ink, which pulls into the paper.[71]
**Flatbed printing:** Unlike relief printing and gravure, flat printing (planographic printing) has one plane. On the printing plate, the areas with printing ink are in the same plane as the areas without. One method of flatbed printing is lithography, which in the 19th century was the most widespread printing technique. Today, lithography is mostly used for printing art.[72]
Offset printing, is flatbed printing, based on the same printing principles as lithography. Read more about offset printing under 5.7.2 Printing methods.

## 5.7.2 Printing methods

There are different printing methods based on the printing techniques described in the previous section. Here are the most common ones:
**Offset printing:** This printing technique, development in 1875 by Robert Barclay for printing on tin and in 1904 by Ira Washington Rubel for printing on paper (Offset printing, n.d), has been the dominant printing technique for two centuries. In recent years, offset printing has been increasingly challenged by digital printing. There are several different offset techniques, but whatever the variation, all offset is based on the lithographic principle, which is an opposing relationship between grease and water. What is to be printed is transferred to a printing plate. This is done by exposing the printing plate to light so that it has areas that reject water but absorb colour, and other areas that do the opposite. The areas picking up colour consist of small raster dots to which the colour adheres (5.7.3 Raster). In the printing machine, the colour is transferred to a rubber cylinder, which then transfers the colour to the paper. The name 'offset' comes from the colour deposited mirrored on the canvas first, and then transferred to the paper (setoff). Since the printing plate is not in direct contact with the paper, low wear occurs. It therefore has a long durability, which is important when repeated printing is required (5.7.4 Four colours, 4.8 Surface and format, 4.8.3 Aspect ratios).
**Digital printing:** Digital printing is a reproduction technique in which digital images are rendered on different materials such as plain paper, photo paper, plastic foil or fabric. Unlike offset printing, digital printers use magnet, laser, ink (inkjet), instead of chemically treated printing plates. The toner that makes up the colour forms a thin layer on the outside of the paper, instead of pulling in like liquid ink. It allows for high resolution in the raster graphics. In the printing business, digital printing is often used to produce printed matter in small or medium print runs, and print-on-demand. Digital printing or just print is also used for digital printouts produced on inkjet printers, laser printers and photocopiers. The printing quality when using office printers and photocopiers is usually lower compared to what professional printing houses and printing offices can offer. Technically speaking, however, the method is the same (laser or ink).
**HP-indigo:** With HP Indigo one can self-mix custom colors off-press, or use Pantone licensed spot colours. HP-indigo has up to 7 ink stations on



72 'Copper stick is a gravure printing technique where the motif is cut into a copper printing plate using pointed tools. The technique is characterized by fine, sharp lines. The lines in the copper engraving line are delimited and have pointed beginning and end. The technique allows for thin lines and small details. By, among other things, parallel and cross hatching, one can obtain tints.' ('Engraving,'n.d.).

the press enable use of HP Indigo's wide digital color gamut including mixed spot colors and 6-color printing with special photo inks (digital-printing.hp.com).

**Silk-screen-printing:** This is a graphic printing method, which is part of the flatbed printing category, but instead of a printing plate a cloth (silk screen) is used. Silk-screen printing (serigraphy) is well suited to textiles, ceramics, glass, metal, plastics and most substrates in addition to paper, and is used for advertising prints on clothing, objects, posters and for more artistic purposes. The printing ink is transferred to the substrate through a tight, fine-mesh cloth. The motif is drawn on the cloth with varnish, like a template or stencil. This way, both dense and open sections are formed. The prints have even colour surfaces and clear lines, often in bright colours. The term silk screen printing is used both for the technique and for the prints. Silk screen printing originated in Japan and was used, among other things, for advertising posters in the United States in the early 20th century. From the 1930s silk screen prints were also used by visual artists, and are particularly associated with Andy Warhol and pop-art culture in the 1960s.

**Flexo printing:** This printing method, also called flexography or flexo, is a form of printing process using a flexible relief plate. It is essentially a modern version of the flatbed press that can be used for printing on almost any substrate, including plastics, metal films, cellophane and paper. It is widely used for printing on slippery surfaces for various types of food packaging, such as juice and milk cartons.

**Foil printing:** Foil printing (foil application) is the application of pressure to metallic or pigmented foil. The printing process takes place with a heated matrix depositing the motif on the foil. This leaves a permanent impression of the motif on the foil surface. Typical foil printing applications are for decorating windows, cars, buses and the like.

**3D printing:** While an inkjet printer prints text and images on a 2D surface, the 3D printer creates 3D artifacts based on predefined instructions.[73] 3D printing is an additive process because it prints by bonding or gluing the material together in a layered manner.[74] Like baking a cake, the principles of 3D printing usually involve a recipe, a set of ingredients, and a mechanism for gluing, hardening, or assembling them together. Unlike the way a cake is made, a 3D printer eliminates the need for intervention (physical intervention) by automating the forming process. The different technologies that make up 3D printing require different recipes and ingredients, because the processes may vary. Some processes, such as FDM (Fused Deposition Modeling), lay cords of plastic polymer layer-by-layer, while others, such as SLA (Stereolithography), are based on a liquid that reacts to light. There are also powder-based machines that spread layers on layers of fine-grained plastic, plaster or metal powder on a surface, which are then joined together. Paper sheets can also be cut, glued and stacked together to form a 3D object (Killi, 2017).[75]

### 5.7.3 Raster

A classic photo consists of a range of contiguous tones. These tones simply cannot be reproduced in print. Therefore, to make an image printable, it should be screened, i.e. divided into an array of microscopically small dots, called raster dots, or just raster. The dots in a screened

*Risography* is a brand of digital duplicators manufactured by the Riso Kagaku Corporation, that are designed mainly for high-volume photocopying and printing (wiki/Risograph, 2022).

73 The advantage of 3D printing is that it is possible to create a physical part from the 3D data file quickly and cost-effectively, and without the use of any casting tools. 3D printing is currently used, for example, in product development and industrial design, in architecture and other model making fields, as well as in orthopaedics and technical aids.

74 The terms describing this printing technology have changed over time, from 'rapid prototyping' to 'additive manufacturing and 3D printing', which largely reflects a focus on technology.

75 Steinar Killi, professor at the Oslo School of Architecture and Design (AHO), published a book in 2017 about 3D printing: *Additive Manufacturing: Design, methods, and processes*.

76 In a stochastic screen (FM screen), all dots are of the same size. They are very small (10–30 micrometres) and are placed randomly and with different frequencies in darker and lighter areas. A dark area has many dots, while a bright area has just a few. The advantage of a stochastic screen is that it can reproduce very fine details and eliminate the Moaré effect. A hybrid screen combines conventional and stochastic FM screen. The FM screen is used for the lighter tones, while the conventional screen is used for the dark tones. It allows for greater screen resolution and finer reproduction of details in print (Arctic Paper, 2012, p. 34). FM stands for Frequency Modulated.

77 For a good printing result, it must be compensated for. The compensation may be in the ICC profile (polaristrykk.no), see 5.5.2 Colour gamut.

image give the eye the illusion of continuous tones of different intensity, just like a 'normal' image. The raster dots are created in a RIP (Raster Image Processor) and then exposed to the printing plate. Conventional screen dots vary in size from 1 to 100%, creating a half-tone perception. A 5% dot is just a very small dot giving a hint of colour on the paper. 50% dots cover half of the paper surface and then give a mid-tone of colour. When the dots are at 100%, they have grown completely together, and one gets an all-over tint plate. It will not show any details, because details are only visible when there is space between the dots and the screen is open. In a conventional screen, the screen dots are arranged in lines and rows. Their density is called screen density and is normally measured in lines per inch (lpi) or lines per centimetre (l/cm). The denser the screen, the more detailed the image. When the ink dots representing each colour are printed on paper, they jointly make up the final image. The dots for each of the four colours (cyan, magenta, yellow and black/CMYK) are organised at specific angles. If there is an unwanted distortion of the angle, a pattern called Moaré is observed (Arctic Paper, 2012, p. 34). The alternatives to conventional screens are stochastic and hybrid screens.[76]



### 5.7.4 Four colours (CMYK)

In offset printing, one operates with four colours (CMYK), the so-called four-colour printing. The colours are transparent. Therefore, the paper shines through and is thus the fifth colour. A printing plate is made for each of the four colours. For the colours to be rendered correctly, the screen dots should be positioned at the correct angle (5.7.3 Raster). Therefore, on all print-ready originals there are several control lines and crosshairs of each printing ink at the edge of the printing sheets. When printing, these crosshairs are placed exactly on top of each other to avoid misalignment in the print, which can lead to a blurred result. During the printing process, a slight dot gain occurs, especially when the colour (from the screen dot) is transferred from the rubber blanket to the paper. The degree of dot gain depends on the paper quality, but also on other things such as screen type, screen density, printing press and printing ink. When using uncoated paper, it is most likely to have significant dot gain, with the colour seeping out into the porous paper. Therefore, uncoated paper is less suitable for achieving maximum photo reproduction of highest quality (5.4.4 Paper properties: Porosity and absorption, 5.4.5 Paper selection (Arctic Paper, 2012).

**Dot gain:** Dot gain can be divided into two categories; mechanical and optical. Mechanical dot gain occurs in the printing press when the colour is transferred from the printing plate to the rubber blanket and from the rubber blanket to the paper. The colour is transferred during printing and screen dots are enlarged as a result, among other things, of the colour 'bleeding out' in the paper. Optical dot gain is a visual 'disturbance' due to light reflection or lack thereof. This 'disturbance' varies in relation to the paper qualities being printed on. For example: If one has a 50% dot cover on a plate, one will normally have about 72% on print. Then we have a dot gain of 22%[77] (polaristrykk.no/teknisk informasjon/trykkteknisk/).

Further reading

The book *Additive Manufacturing: Design, Methods, and Processes*, Steinar Killi, 2017.

### 5.7.5 Printing inks

Deliberate lighting of colours, text, shape, object and space can help enhance experience and functionality.

The selected printing ink depends on the choice of printing method. The most common colour systems used for offset and digital printing are CMYK (four colours) and Pantone (spot colour), see 5.7.4 Four colours and 5.5.9 Colour reference systems; Figure 5.7. To find the correct colour code for a logo, for example, use a brand guide for the specific profile (6.5 Design Manual). If a new colour code is to be defined, the screen colour cannot be relied on. It is perfectly fine to work with the screen colours in the sketch process, but to define the printing ink one should use a physical colour selector/colour palette. CMYK values are defined in the Europa series,[78] while Pantone represents the colour system PMS.[79] In the PMS system there are also colour selectors showing which CMYK colour a Pantone colour represents. Conversion between CMYK and Pantone can also be done digitally. Here, there are several online applications that can be used,[80] but one should always cross-check with the physical colour palette. To ensure the best possible colour rendering from screen to print, the correct colour profile compatible with the printer's colour management tool should be selected. It should be done early in the design process.

CMYK for Cyan, Magenta, Yellow and Key (black) appears as small screen dots combined on the paper in different amounts. The colour is described with a percentage composition of the different colours. For example, Facebook Blue has the following CMYK values: 61% cyan, 41% magenta, 0% yellow, 40% black. Step 2: CMYK: 61, 41, 0, 40. The same colour values in RGB and HEX are: RGB: 59, 89, 152, Hex: #3b5998[81] (5.7.3 Raster, 5.7.4 Four colours).

Colour rendering from CMYK may vary depending on factors such as paper, temperature, saturation/ink level etc. Colours made with CMYK may also look a little blown out, but this also depends on the printing method and the printing substrate, paper, cardboard, plastic etc. Pantone colours can be used when one wants the colours to stand out. Pantone colours are pre-mixed and provide a more even and opaque colour because the colour is not mixed in the printing process like when using CMYK. Pantone colours also provide a more consistent colour rendering. For example, Pantone codes are written as follows: Pantone 286 (5.4 Paper and cartonboard, 5.7 Production for printed media).

### 5.7.6 Printing effects

You see the text stand out smooth from the matte paper. The effect arouses your interest. You let your fingertips slide over the text and feel the contrast between the smooth letters and the rough texture of the paper. The small effect excites your curiosity, and you want to know what more this printed matter can bring to you.

Varnish, embossing, punching and foiling are typical printing effects that can create that extra something. In the post-processing of a printed matter, i.e. after it comes out of the printing machine, different effects can be added or applied. Even if this is done after printing, it must be planned carefully in advance so that the print-ready file has the necessary information. The best thing is to talk to the printing house to decide how they want the original document delivered. Here is an

78 The Europa series of raster combinations for 4-colour printing (CMYK).
79 Pantone Matching System (PMS).
80 Conversion cmyk/pantone.com/colour- finder.
81 RGB colours are written with values from 0 to 255. For example: RGB: 59, 89, 152. RGB colours used on the web are often written as hexadecimals (HEX), which are easier for browsers to understand. They always start with a hashtag (#) followed by 3 or 6 letters and numbers, for example: Hex: #3b5998. More recently, RGB, RGBA (alpha-channel) and HSL have become more and more common on the web as well. They can then be written as rgb, rgba or hsl (Riktigspor.no 2016).
82 In offset printing process a cliché is an etched plate which is used to transfer an image to the paper.

overview of some effects that can be applied in post-processing (based on Arctic Paper, 2012, p. 100):

**Foil blocking:** Foil blocking involves adding a thin layer of foil to the paper with the help of heat and pressure. The plastic foil used usually comes in gold or silver and mother-of-pearl. Foil blocking and embossing can be performed in one and the same process.

**Embossing:** Embossing creates a relief (level difference) in the paper surface. The pattern is created in an embossing machine using clichés[82] or embossing plates. Positive embossing involves raising a section of the paper. Negative embossing means depressing. Sculpted embossing means that different levels are created. Paper quality plays an important role in embossing. The thicker and softer it is, the better. Coated paper is less suitable than uncoated paper. Bas-relief is an alternative embossing technique created using laser cutting.

**Varnishing:** One of the most common methods of surface treatment is coating and laminating. The most common is spot UV varnishing, full varnishing and protective varnishing and cover. Cover can be applied directly in the printing machine and is well suited to prevent the colour from coming off, i.e. being transmitted to other surfaces, fingers etc. Full varnishing means that the entire surface is varnished. Spot varnishing is applied only to sections of the paper, such as a logo or photo.

**Relief printing:** This method involves spraying a chemical powder over the ink on the sheet after the normal printing process. The sheet then goes into the heater where the printing ink and powder melt together and swell up into a relief. This effect is very suitable for narrow lines and texts. Embossing varnish is another method, which produces a similar effect. Embossing varnish is applied in silk screen printing according to the usual printing process.

**Lamination:** Laminating is a plastic film that can be melted or glued to the paper in the printing process, and similarly to painting it is a widely used method of protecting against dirt and abrasion. Matte, glossy and patterned laminates are available.

**Die cutting:** Die cutting is done using a metal die form. There are a number of standard shapes, but at the same time die forms can be custom-made according to one's needs. Die forms are used for labels and other printed matter that are to have a special shape, or for cutting a hole or window in packaging, for example. By unfolding a cardboard packaging, one can see how the shape/outline is cut.

**Punching:** If holes are necessary for punching of sheets for punching machines or other purposes, holes are made using a drill during post-processing.

**Perforation:** If tear edges on coupons etc. are required, it is common to choose perforation. Perforation is often performed on a flatbed press with a perforation rule or using a scoring tool.

**Grooving:** Grooving is done with a groove tool, which 'breaks' the paper fibres to make it easier to fold. This is a method that can also be done manually, for example when developing paper prototypes. Most people do not have a groove knife at their disposal. Instead, you can find a chubby bit that does not cut through the paper. For example, the tip of a pen without the pen itself. One should move the pen along the ruler at the edge of the tray. Then the sheet can be folded to the opposite side (see 5.2 Prototype).

A design challenge can be between a small pictogram on a business card and a large exhibition stand in the same project. In some contexts, there is a need for construction and assembly. It can be producing modular walls and furnishings for a trade fair, making furnishings for a store, or mounting posters for a campaign.

In a design project, production is what comes in the final phase when the solution is to be realised. The production phase may vary greatly depending on what is required in order to complete the solution. It may involve offset printing for magazines and posters, web programming, production of products, and physical assembly or construction. It can also in many contexts be a combination of print, digital, assembly and construction. Planning assembly and construction is something that should start early in the design process and includes services for which the designer often collaborates with subcontractors. Involving factors such as assembly and construction into the idea phase can be part of the solution proposal and contribute to smarter and more functional solutions.

Poor planning of the final phase of a project can be terribly costly. One example of this is when major changes need to be made. For instance, one may want to modify a fundamental structure if one wants a trade fair wall to be higher. Then the fitter will have to start from scratch. All changes propagate as a chain reaction, causing discrepancies elsewhere that need to be rectified. The earlier changes are made, the lesser the consequences will be. That is why it is important to have a positive conversation with the engineer as early as possible and throughout the process.

### Technical functionality and light

Technical functionality and light are factors that can strengthen a design solution if done intentionally, or weaken it, if inadequate. Design projects such as a trade fair stand, shop décor or outdoor advertising will often require lighting and technical installations, just as construction and assembly will be necessary, as we discussed in the previous section. These are services that the designer often buys from subcontractors. By involving experts early in the process, technical functionality and light can be factors to help strengthen the design solution. It is not always about something that needs to be resolved physically, but rather an awareness of considering light and functionality as part of the solution. In some projects, it can be less meaningful, in others it can be the idea and the experience itself. Light plays an important role.

Light is present in all visual design. Colours are only visible in light, and different light influences how we see the colour. Daylight renders colour differently compared to the light from a lamp. Text cannot be read without light, while proper lighting can accentuate the text. Light is therefore important in the development of information and signage design. If a sign is correctly positioned relative to the light sources in a room, it can help make the text on the sign more readable. It might be even more efficient to mount the light source optimally in relation to the sign.

Further reading
**Read more about light and space in the interview with Birgitte Appelong. Available at designandstrategy.co.uk.**

Light and shadow have an impact on how form is perceived and can help strengthen it. Similarly, light affects the experience of space, whether it is cold or hot light, whether it is direct or indirect, etc. For example, it is possible to create zones in a room using multiple light sources. During the day, a type of lighting can be used to highlight the room as large and open, while later in the day, general lighting can be dimmed, and smaller light sources can be used to create intimate zones in the room. Similarly, it is possible to light a home with different lighting moods during the day and control the light via a computer. One can pre-program different moods, and at the touch of a key one can change from one mood to the other (Appelong, 2017).



## 5.9 Quality assurance

Quality assurance is ultimately about ensuring that delivery is as good as promised.

'Simply put, quality is the ability to satisfy the customers' or user's requirements and expectations' (Gundersen and Halbo, n.d.). For a company, quality assurance is about ensuring that the products and services it delivers to its customers keep the quality promised. For the designer, quality assurance is all about the same thing. On the one hand, the designer should help ensure that the design solution does not promise more than what the product or service can deliver. On the other hand, the designer should ensure that the design work maintains the correct level of quality throughout the design process up to the result. This means that the final solution responds to the issue and the result satisfies the requirements, conditions and expectations that apply to the project.

The best starting point for quality assurance of a design project is agreeing on requirements concerning the quality of processes and results being expected. Secondly, that precise and sound objectives are defined, which are anchored in the overall objectives and strategy of the business (3.3 Goals and subgoals, 3.2 Overall strategy). The use of strategy as a management tool throughout the process is a prerequisite for ensuring targeted outcomes in all phases (Table 3.2 Top 5 – Strategic management tool). A project manager should be the one responsible for the delivery and quality of what is delivered. It can be a leader, middle manager, strategic counsellor, etc. In addition, there should be a project manager responsible for the project progress, finances and project management according to the signed agreements. Behind the project manager there is often a team specially assembled for the assignment in question, with the qualifications required to solve the task and deliver the quality expected. The project manager uses the team to quality assure the work in all phases of the project.

In smaller projects, the overall responsibility may lie with one person. Often the designer is responsible for both project management and implementation. Knowledge of the business, the situation and the surroundings is central to ensuring the quality of delivery, and then it is important that information is up-to-date and relevant (2.1 Understanding the company, 2.7.1 Situational analysis, 2.7.9 PESTLE analysis).

Understanding what the audience thinks, feels, and does is also essential for success (2.7.6 Target group analysis). Measurable targets are a good starting point for measuring and evaluating results along the way and after delivery to determine whether the result lives up to the quality requirement (3.3.6 Measurable goals).

Quality assurance is necessary in all phases of a project. Anything that can help give the most realistic impression of the result during the process and before realising it is important in order to ensure quality. Development of prototypes and implementation of user tests may be necessary to determine whether the project is progressing in the desired direction (5.2 Model, 2.9 Testing and measuring, 4.3.5 Iterative method). Quality assurance can also involve a paper dummy of a magazine to be designed, with the format, paper and binding intended, to find out if the paper is as perceived as expected. This is something the designer and design team can often deal with on their own, without involving an external test group. Another important quality assurance is colour management. A colour may appear differently on different devices such as cameras, printers, monitors. The colour displayed on the screen is probably not the same as the one displayed in print, unless good colour management is ensured. It can also be difficult to find colours that behave the same on different surfaces such as paper, interiors and textiles. Colour management is therefore central to any visual design (5.5 Colour management). Pressure start is also a form of quality assurance. Pressure start is necessary to produce larger printed matter to be printed in offset. This is done by the designer showing up at the printing house when they are going to start the printing process and giving the printer good guidance so that the result is according to intention and agreement. The designer follows up by printing the first pages to see that the colour saturation, colour value, and passport marks are correct compared to sample prints. This is one of several factors that can be adjusted in the printing process (5.7 Production for printed media).

The road to wisdom

**The road to wisdom?
–Well, it's plain and
simple to express:
Err
and err
and err again
but less
and less
and less.
Piet Hein[83]**

83 **Piet Hein (1905–1996) was a Danish poet and scientist.**

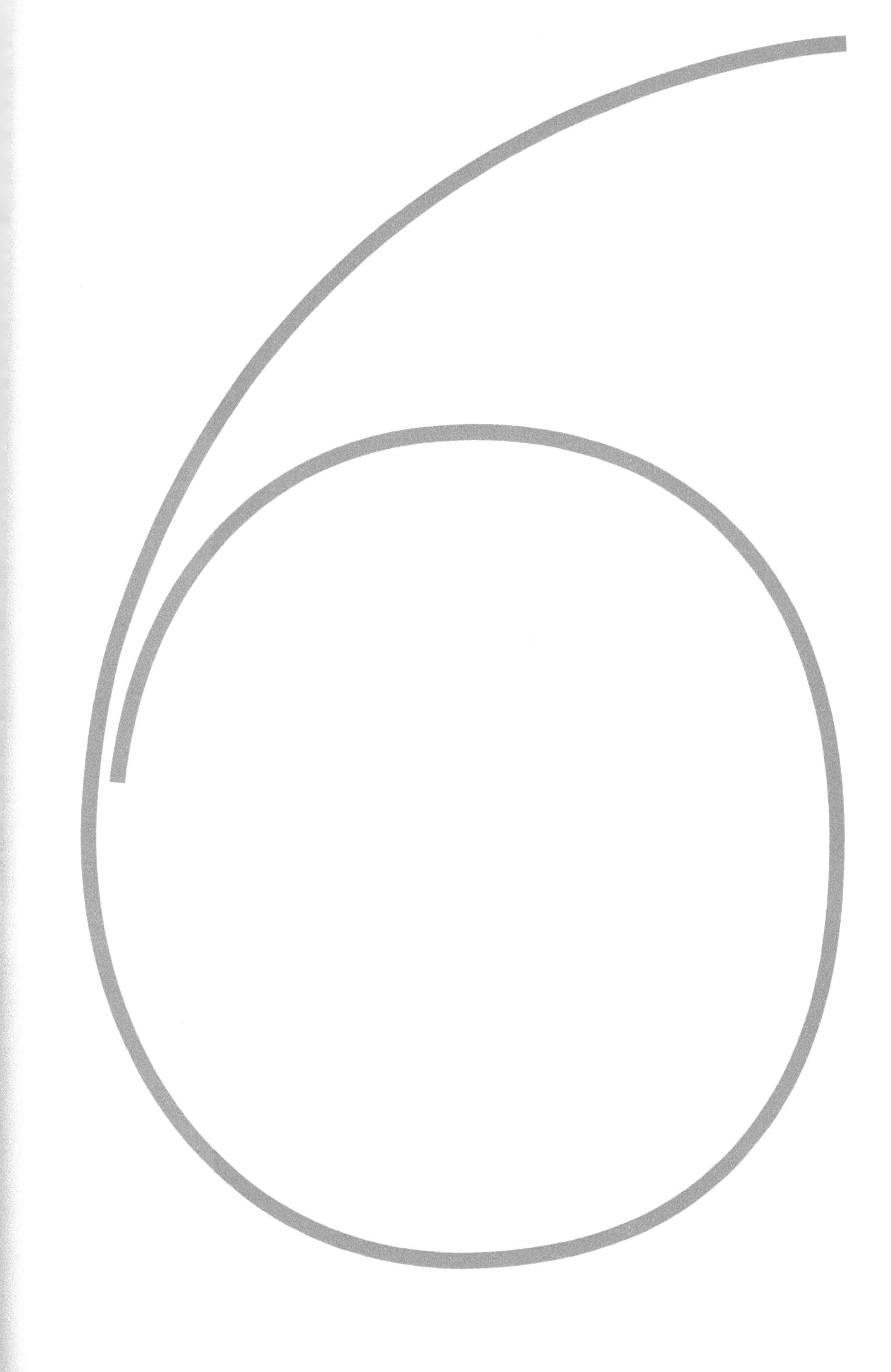

6.1 Intangible assets 588

6.2 Legal protection 590
6.2.1 Copyright 590
6.2.2 Trademark 591
6.2.3 Domain name 593
6.2.4 Company name 593
6.2.5 Exclusive rights in social media 594
6.2.6 Design rights 594
6.2.7 Patents 594
6.2.8 Counterfeiting 595
6.2.9 Marketing rights/ unfair competition 595

6.3 Design management 596

6.4 Design effect 597
6.4.1 Design ladder 598
6.4.2 The value of design 599
6.4.3 Design-driven company 600
6.4.4 Design impact awards 601
6.4.7 Visual impact 602
6.4.8 How to measure the design effect? 602

6.5 Design manual 604
6.5.1 Purpose and target group 604
6.5.2 Foundation 605
6.5.3 Scope 605
6.5.4 Digital design manual 605
6.5.5 Contents 606
6.5.6 Unbranding 611

6.6 Design templates 612

6.7 Operations manual 614

6.8 Further development 615

6.9 Sustainable management 615
6.9.1 Sustainability development 616
6.9.2 Corporate sustainability 616
6.9.3 Circular economy 617
6.9.4 Net zero 618
6.9.5 The trendsetters 618
6.9.6 Greenwashing 618
6.9.7 The designer's impact 619
6.9.8 High complexity 621
6.9.9 Sustainable font choice 622

Management is the sixth and last of all the phases in a strategic design process. It is about how the company can manage, control, and operate the assets created through a design project. Design templates and design manuals are necessary for ensuring the proper use of the design. Consistent design use helps build recognition, position, reputation, and proprietary brand. A brand represents an intangible asset, which, in contrast to tangible assets, is not so concrete and is difficult to evaluate. It is an asset that must be protected legally to avoid plagiarism. In addition, a brand is something that needs to be managed and developed in the long term, so that it retains its relevance and value. Sustainability management is a responsibility of both the company and the designer. That means incorporating the environmental and social costs of doing business into management and design decisions and focusing on long-term instead of short-term gains.

The term 'management' stands for control or administration. In this context, management refers to control and administration of the assets created through a design process. It is a responsibility that falls to the company's management and that requires expert design leadership. It is generally about protecting and preserving the design capital. This can be assets of a physical nature such as a designed object, an item, a building or another physical form, or of non-physical nature, the so-called intangible assets, e.g. company names, trademarks, designs, intellectual property and patents. In the next subchapters, we will look at various aspects of managing the design capital which is a task that is also about ensuring sustainability. In other words, design investments should be sustainable for the company, while not harming the environment and the people's health and well-being. Instead, design can be an important driving force when it comes to responsible life, environment and resource management.

Fig. 6.1 The figure shows how a brand is perceived. The symbol evokes associations in the recipient. The person sees the symbol and thinks the name, in this case Nike. Such associations can be worth millions. This is what we call intengible assets. A value that is difficult to measure. © Grimsgaard, W. (2018).

'Intellectual property (IP) refers to creations of the mind, such as inventions; literary and artistic works; designs; and symbols, names and images used in commerce' (WIPO, wipo.int/about-ip/en/).

## 6.1 Intangible assets

The intangible assets are often the most *valuable* assets a company owns and can be crucial for the survival of the company.

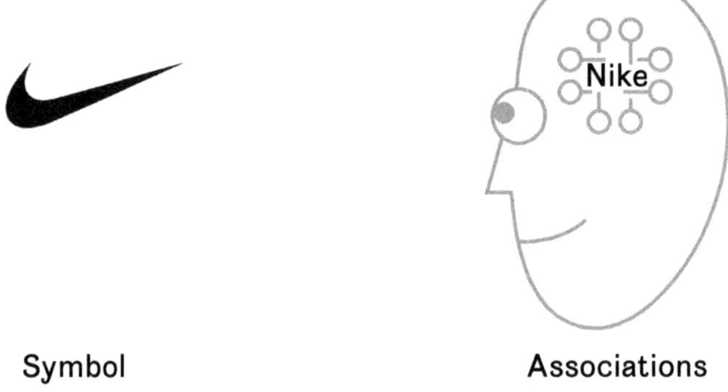


Fig. 6.1 Intangible assets

One way to evaluate a company's intangible assets is to assess what the company would be like without them. What is Coca-Cola without the name, the brand and the recognition? When a company is to be sold, it will be both the tangible and intangible assets that determine the price. It will not be buildings, machinery and equipment alone; it will also be things such as recognition, reputation and goodwill. It is often the intangible assets that count the most, and which mean that a company can be priced much higher than the actual physical assets. Intangible assets are difficult to put a monetary value on. There are different methods of assessing value, such as using the turnover of the company as a starting point and finding out how much of the company's current surplus comes from the intangible assets. One way of doing so is to make general comparisons with other companies of the same category, and on that basis assess how much of the company's turnover can be attributed to brand recognition and reputation.

Further reading
'Tangible vs. Intangible Assets: What's the Difference?' (Rudy, 2021): thebalance.com.

1 European Patent Office (EPO) press release 21.5.2019 Joint EPO-EUIPO study 2019.

**Industrial property rights (IP)**

*Intangible assets and rights*: 'Intangible assets are a collective term for assets that do not have a physical substance. IP is protected in law by, for example, patents, copyright and trademarks, which enable people to earn recognition or financial benefit from what they invent or create. By striking the right balance between the interests of innovators and the wider public interest, the IP system aims to foster an environment in which creativity and innovation can flourish' (WIPO). IP may include inventions, trademarks, designs, copyrights, production processes, procedures, databases, agreements, various types of intellectual property, know-how and trade secrets. Intangible rights are intangible assets which are derived from legal rights. The collective term includes industrial property rights (IP) and copyright ©. Industrial property rights mainly include patents, designs and registered or incorporated trademarks. They arise mainly by being registered after an application has been processed.

A study conducted 2019 by the European Patent Office (EPO) and the European Intellectual Property Office (EUIPO)[1] showed that 'Small and medium-sized enterprises (SMEs) that apply for patents, trade marks or designs have a greater probability of experiencing high growth than SMEs that do not' (European Patent Office 2019). The study also stated that firms with more than one intellectual property right are more likely to grow, and intellectual property rights use can identify future high growth firms early in their development (European Patent Office 2019).

**The most common intellectual property rights:** Patents protect new inventions which represent concrete solutions to a technical problem and where the solutions are also of a technical nature. The exclusive right is valid for up to 20 years. For pharmaceutical and plant products, the period of exclusivity can be extended to up to 25 years. Trademarks are used to identify goods and services. A trademark may consist of any kind of sign and will usually be reproduced graphically. A trademark usually consists of words and combinations of words, names, logos, letters, numbers and images, but may also consist of shapes, packaging, sound and motion. The trademark is granted for ten-year periods, and there is no limit to the number of years it can be renewed. Design rights protect the visual design of a product for up to 25 years. In addition to the protection of entire items and ornaments, parts of a product, graphic design, interior arrangements and web screens can be protected. Replacement parts can be renewed for five years. A copyright gives the creator of intellectual property the exclusive right to exploit artistic and creative works. Performances of works are also protected. Databases may be protected as copyright and protects the investment made in creating the database. A copyright arises automatically, without registration, at the moment a work is created. The work must be the result of an individual creative effort. The protection is linked to the author and lasts, as a general rule, for 70 years after the author's death.
Based on: Meld. St. 28 (2012–2013) regjeringen.no.

Design is something durable that is created, something that has a value. When a design, illustration or work of art is created, a right arises for the person who created it. The right can be sold to a company which will then exploit the rights.[2] The disposal of a right depends on several factors. First and foremost, it is a question of assessing the extent to which intellectual property has been created.

Fig. 6.2 © is the symbol for copyright, which means copy protection and authorship rights. In most countries there is no registration requirement. In the European Union, the subject matter of the copyright must be *an original work resulting from intellectual creation* in order to be protected. Similar requirements exist in other countries.

Fig. 6.3 The symbol ® means registered trademark. Use of the symbol is reserved for registered trademarks.

Fig. 6.4 TM stands for trademark and is a symbol used when a trademark is not registered or until the trademark is registered. TM is a signal to the market that it is to be understood as a trademark.

'All rights reserved'[4]

Legal protection is something that should be considered throughout the process. In all processes, intangible assets may arise along the way, so one should continuously assess what needs to be protected. If the company wishes to protect the intellectual property, there are many criteria that must be met, and which are important to consider during the development process itself. By being aware of the criteria, they can be safeguarded so that the intellectual property meets the requirements for legal protection and is thus protected from illegal copying and plagiarism. Companies that are concerned about protecting their intellectual property rights should have a strategy for doing so and a budget for implementing and maintaining the rights.

Most countries have national intellectual property offices with the power to register IP rights valid for the country in question. In addition there are some international bodies that handle IP applications for a group of countries. From a European perspective, the most important of these are the European Patent Office (EPO), which grants patents for almost all European countries and the EUIPO, which handles trademark and design registrations for the EU. The UN organisation WIPO facilitates the international patent application process through the PCT system, the international trademark system through the Madrid system and the international design system through The Hague system.

Most countries have a well-functioning patent agent profession that assists companies, entrepreneurs, inventors and creators in investigating, acquiring and safeguarding industrial and intellectual property rights. They can represent their clients before the national patent office and international bodies, and through good contacts with patent agencies in other countries they may assist clients in gaining protection worldwide. Many of them also offer technical and legal assistance.

This subchapter on legal protection is based on professional advice and input from the attorneys Arild Tofting and Thomas Hvammen Nicholson, in the company Protector IP.[3]

### 6.2.1 Copyright

The creator of creative works will be able to claim rights to copyright protection in most countries of the world. Examples of copyright protected subject matter includes writings of all kinds, musical works, cinematographic and photographic works, paintings, drawings, graphic

2 The EU and eventually Norway have removed the requirement for graphic reproduction. Digital files such as mp3 files, mp4 video files, etc. can now also be protected. But this is still not the case in large parts of the world.
3 Protector IP specialises in assisting large companies in optimising the use of their intangible assets in commercial activities.
4 The expression 'all rights reserved' has its origin in the Buenos Aires Convention of 1910, but no longer has any jurisdiction. It is nevertheless used by many rights holders.

and similar works of art, and handicraft objects. More and more, copyright protection is provided also for more functional works such as architecture and handicraft objects such as for example furniture. Under copyright law, the author's exclusive rights include making a permanent or temporary copy of the copyright, making it available to the public, translating, or adapting it. Copyright confers on its author the exclusive right to utilise and commercialise the work in question, a right which is transferable. In most jurisdictions, copyright protection is obtained when the work in question has been made publicly available. No registration is necessary. Further, under the Berne Convention for the Protection of Literary and Artistic Works which most countries in the world have ratified, a member state is obliged to provide the same protection for a work created abroad as for works created by its nationals. In most countries, copyright protection lasts for the lifetime of the author plus 70 years after his or her death.

Fig. 6.2 Copyright

Fig. 6.3 Registered trademark

Fig. 6.4 Trademark

## 6.2.2 Trademark

A trademark can consist of any sign that distinguishes the goods or services of one company from those of other companies. Examples of this are

- Word marks, such as a single words, several words, word compounds, slogans, names.
- Figures or figurative marks, such as letters, numbers, the product's shape, equipment and packaging.
- Combined marks, such as combinations of words and figurative elements.
- Non-traditional trademarks, for example motion marks (Nokia's grasping hands, Microsoft's screensaver), three-dimensional marks (a special packaging) or sound marks (jingles), for example, the sound of your laptop starting up, and from your telephone app, a vignette, or film clip.

Trademark vs. brand

A trademark is the name, symbol and pattern that identifies a product or service and its commercial origin. A brand is based on the network of associations we get when exposed to a trademark. Our perception of a brand is based on what we associate it with, noe som contributes to us wanting to buy it and pay more than what a similar product costs. This is brand equity and is among the company's intangible assets.

### Registered trademark

A trademark can be registered only if it is able to distinguish the goods and/or services of the company from those of others. This requires that the mark has sufficient distinctiveness and is not descriptive or generic. An exclusive right to use the trademark for goods and services is usually obtained by registration with the public registration authority (such as a a national trademark office or IP office). In many jurisdictions protection as a common law trademark may also be obtained as a result of extensive use of the mark. A trademark registration usually lasts for 10 years, and can be renewed for 10 years at a time. To secure the acquired right, the registered mark should also be actively used, if not it will often be liable to cancellation after several years of non-use.

### What if the name cannot be registered or protected?

In cases where a sign cannot be protected, it may instead be possible to register a combination of words and figurative elements. For example, giving the name a figurative shape, adding a pictogram symbol or other elements. It means adding something that makes the trademark distinctive as a whole.

### Management of registered trademarks

'Even if a trademark is protected by registration, considerable vigilance and commitment is required to ensure that the trademark maintains and increases its value as a distinctive feature' (Tysbo, 2013). Some simple advice on use and management:

- The trademark in use: the ® symbol should always be used. It is normally placed on the right-hand shoulder of the trademark.[5]
- Pending registration: use TM until registration is obtained.
- Avoid generic designations: A trademark can degenerate, i.e. become a generic product specification and may risk losing protection. Never use the trademark as a product name/generic designation.
- Create new product names: Create your own generic designations in addition to the trademark if the product is new and not previously known.
- Owner information: Refer to holder/originator where practical in marketing materials, web pages, and the like.
- Use the trademark as registered: Avoid the use of contracted forms, word combinations and puns.
- Keep the trademark separate: Avoid using several trademarks on the same packaging, as this defeats the purpose of the trademark.
- Use the trademark consistently: use the correct proportions, consistent colours, the correct pronunciation in the press, reference material and the like.
- Monitor the trademark: be present in social media and monitor for unwanted use/publicity of the trademark. Use professional consultants to monitor your trademark. This means checking on an ongoing basis whether identical or confusing trademarks are registered for other companies that may infringe your exclusive rights. Consider establishing an online brand protection procedure in order to take down any infringing use. Develop an IPR strategy.[6]
- Respond to infringements: contact legal counsel as soon as possible so that infringements can be identified and stopped. This includes establishing online brand protection procedures.

5 One should be careful to use (R) in jurisdictions where the mark is not registered, one must be careful to use it on the mark as it is registered and for the goods and services it is registered for.

6 IPR is an acronym for Intellectual Property Rights. IP stands for Intellectual property.

7 A top-level domain (TLD) is one of the domains at the highest level in the hierarchical Domain Name System (DNS) of the Internet after the root domain. Responsibility for management of most top-level domains (TLD) is delegated to specific organisations by the ICANN, an Internet multistakeholder community, which operates the Internet Assigned Numbers Authority (IANA), and is in charge of maintaining the DNS root zone. ('Cliché,' n.d.).

8 www.icann.org. ICANN is a non-profit public corporation with participants from around the world dedicated to keeping the internet secure, stable and interoperable. Through its role as coordinator of the Internet's naming systems, ICANN has an important influence on the expansion and development of the Internet.

- Trademark manual: Develop a design manual or profile guide that all employees, retailers and any licensees must use.
- Renew the registration: Remember to renew the registration prior the registration renewal date.

### 6.2.3 Domain name

All websites on the internet have an IP address, that points to a website's location, like some sort of GPS coordinates. The IP address is generally a set of numbers. 'A structure called the Domain Name System (DNS) translates those IP addresses into names that are (hopefully) simple to remember. Those names are called domain names' (mailchimp.com). A domain name is unique. When one owns a domain name, this is one's online identity and the address to post content online. For businesses a domain is a must-have for the outside world to find them, and is central to their brand building and positioning. A domain name can at best be the same as the brand name.

Domain names are broken up into two or three parts. Each part is separated by a dot. 'When reading right-to-left, the identifiers in domain names go from most general to most specific. The section to the right of the last dot in a domain name is the top-level domain (TLD)'[7] (cloudfare.com), such as .com, .net, .edu, .org, .gov and .mil., and for different countries like .it for Italy and, .ca for Canada and .no for Norway.

Registration of a domain name precludes others from registering an identical domain name as long as the registration is maintained but does not confer greater or different rights to the name than the applicant previously had. ICANN is an international company that oversees registered domains internationally, and which controls and monitors this industry[8] (3.7.6 Brand assets, 3.7.7 Brand name). Steps to buying a domain name (mailchimp.com):

1. Choose a reliable domain registrar
2. Find a domain availability checker tool
3. Choose the best domain name option
4. Purchase your domain name and complete its registration
5. Verify ownership of your new domain

Buying a domain from another person (mailchimp.com):

1. Find the owner's contact information
2. Negotiate a fair price
3. Complete the sale

### 6.2.4 Company name

A company name is the registered name of a company. In many jurisdictions, a company name and/or trade name may offer some protection against later names, trademarks and misuse, but the requirements for and extent of protection varies a lot. In addition, a company name protection will be limited to the country where it is registered/in use, whereas a trademark may be extended to many countries. Generally speaking, a trademark protection will offer substantially better protection compared to the protection of a company name.


1 Initiation
2 Insight
3 Strategy
4 Design
5 Production
6 Management

6.1 Intangible assets
6.2 Legal protection
6.3 Design management
6.4 Design effect
6.5 Design manual
6.6 Design templates
6.7 Operations manual
6.8 Further development
6.9 Sustainable management

6.2.1 Copyright
6.2.2 Trademark
6.2.3 Domain name
6.2.4 Company name
6.2.5 Exclusive rights in social media
6.2.6 Design rights
6.2.7 Patents
6.2.8 Counterfeiting
6.2.9 Marketing rights/ unfair competition

- Registered trademark
- What if the name cannot be registered or protected?
- Management of registered trademarks

### 6.2.5 Exclusive rights in social media

Nowadays, it is important to obtain the exclusive rights to a name or designation in social and digital media, such as for example a Facebook or Instagram account.

### 6.2.6 Design rights

The appearance and or shape of a product or part of a product may be protected through design registration (in some countries also called 'design patents'). A design registration can consist of:

- The shape and appearance of a product, for example, the design of a toothbrush, car, ship, telephone or a piece of furniture.
- Parts of the product, for example, the toothbrush head, the chair leg, the telephone keypad.
- The appearance of non-physical objects such as web screens, movable designs, typographic fonts and graphic symbols. (You cannot register computer program).
- An ornament, such as the decoration on a napkin or the design on textiles and wallpaper.
- An interior arrangement, such as a restaurant, café or shop interior.

Design registration is generally possible in most countries in the world. The requirements, procedures and costs for registration vary a great deal. Generally speaking designs will often have to fulfil the requirements of novelty and individual character. Also, technical solutions are usually not covered by a design registration. If you want protection for the technical solution, you have to apply for patent protection.

Design registration provides the propietor with the exclusive right to use the design. In Europe, a design registration has a maximum lifetime of 25 years, with renewals every five years. Design registrations are national rights, and it is necessary to file design applications in the countries where you want to register. In the EU it is possible to file one application for protection in all EU member states.

In Europe it is possible to apply for protection of several designs in the same class in one design application as a multiple registration. It is cheaper for the applicant to file a multiple application instead of separate applications for each design. In the EU, it is also possible to obtain unregistered design protection provided that the design is novel, has individual character and is not exclusively dictated by technical function. Such protection is awarded if the product was first made available to the public in the EU, and protection is for three years and limited to copies (=identical designs). It can be challenging to prove the validity of an unregistered design.

Tips for the designer

**During a name or logo process, it may be useful to consider contacting your national IP office or a local patent agency to have preliminary investigations carried out. This may include checking whether the name or logo is distinctive enough to be registered, and whether there are trademarks in your country or internationally that are similar. In many countries, the IP office may be able to help 'scan' the market to check whether there are similar trademarks in the same category.**

### 6.2.7 Patents

A patent is the protection of a new technical solution. Patents are granted for inventions that constitute a practical solution to problems, that are of a technical nature, have a technical effect and can be reproduced, and that can be industrially exploited. An idea cannot be

Further reading

Check out: How to Buy a Domain Name: Domain Registration Guide: mailchimp.com.

9 Most countries have the overriding Patent Act.

patented without explaining or showing how it can be put into practice. Nor can one obtain a patent for a business concept. Processes, products, devices and sometimes a new utilisation of a product can be patented. The Patent Act defines what can legally be patented.[9]

Applying for a patent is a solid sign of technological development, innovation and novelty in a company. A patent can provide an important competitive advantage because it gives the right to exploit the invention commercially. By being able to prove one's right to an invention, one also has a good starting point for negotiating the financing of development, and for entering into sales and licensing agreements. In this way, patent protection provides greater opportunities to secure investment and cover the costs of product development (The Patent Office).

A patent is valid for a limited period of time. A patent has a duration of 20 years from the date of filing of the application provided the renewal fees are paid.

### 6.2.8 Counterfeiting

Counterfeiting is a huge international problem. It involves the unauthorised copying of IP protected products, often by criminal organisations. There is no limit to the examples of pirated products infringing trademarks, designs, copyrights and patents. The classical example is that of clothes and handbags, but it may also consist of pharmaceutical products, cosmetics or more technical products, even spare parts for aeroplanes.

In addition to being a comprehensive social and economic problem as a driver of criminal and black economy, piracy is a problem for the owner of the trademark, design, or patent that is copied. Considerable work has often been put into developing the product and the goodwill value inherent in the product and its name. This value is diminished when counterfeit products come into circulation, which are often of a much lower quality than the genuine products, possibly even dangerous and harmful. In many jurisdictions, it is possible to cooperate with customs authorities in preventing counterfeits from entering the market.

### 6.2.9 Marketing rights/unfair competition

In addition to the protection obtained by patenting or registering a trademark or design, unwanted copying may in some countries and under specific circumstances be dealt with under unfair competition. This legal field is not harmonised, and practice varies a lot from country to country. Sometimes unfair competition may serve as a fallback option where other IP rights are missing, but claiming unfair competition can be quite challenging. In some countries, unfair competition may cover cases where the practice of one business is found in breach of honest business practices (bad faith), whereas in others such use may only qualify if a copied product for example is famous. Relying on unfair competition internationally can be very challenging, legally uncertain and expensive, and it is generally recommended to obtain registered rights such as trademarks, designs and patents instead.



Dangerous Fakes

The OECD-EUIPO report 'Dangerous Fakes. Trade in counterfeit goods that pose health, safety and environmental risks' (2022) shows data from customs seizures and other enforcement data and looks at how dangerous counterfeits can end up in the hands of consumers. Examples highlighted in the report:

– Perfumes, cosmetics, clothing, toys, automotive spare parts and pharmaceuticals, among the most common dangerous fakes.
– Substandard and counterfeit products can threaten consumers' health and, in some cases, lives.
– Online sales represent 60% of seizures of dangerous products destined for the EU.
– China and Hong Kong account for 75% of dangerous fakes seized.

Tips for the company
Check out: Grow, 'Tomorrow's design leaders': grow.empdl.com.

Simply put, design management is the business side of design (Design Management Institute, dmi.no).

Design management is a managerial role that involves responsibility and decision-making when it comes to how a company should develop and use design in its value creation.

Companies that have design managers on their staff are interested in using design as a key competitive factor and driver of innovation and see the use of design and design-driven processes as key tools for achieving success. Companies that have a design ambition as an overarching goal are often called design-driven companies. Design management is about leading design and innovation processes, product and service development, identity and brand building or other value creation, to help create user-friendly, profitable and sustainable outcomes. Design management involves the use of design methodology in product and service development, to deal with problem-solving, development and innovation. This includes the use of design thinking, systems thinking, user-centricity, problem solving, agile methods, co-creation, design sprint and iteration. Strategic anchoring is at the core, to ensure sustainable and targeted processes and results. That includes the use of strategic design process, design strategy and the ability to bridge strategy and design. Design management is also about leading the purchase of design services from external providers, to ensure good processes and targeted results. Managing the company's design capital, to secure intangible assets, such as brands and legal design rights, is at the core. Design management can take place internally in the company or on behalf of a company (2.1.2 Decision making).

Central to design management is the task of building an organisational culture with more design awareness. The organisational culture can be created through design management and the use of design methodology. De Mozota and Valade-Amland (2020) put it this way 'A more recent approach to design management is to consider it as a means of enhancing the ability of an organisation to take up new knowledge and embrace creativity on a strategic level and as an integrated element of organisational

**Design management tasks:**

- Lead design processes, to create user-friendly, profitable and sustainable solutions.
- Use design methodology, to create product and service innovation.
- Use strategic design processes, to ensure good targeted processes and results.
- Use design methodology in strategy and business development.
- Use systemic design to solve complex tasks.
- Lead the purchase of design services, to ensure the effect of the design investment.
- Manage design capital, to ensure intangible values of brands and design rights.

10 The Design Management Institute DMI, is an international membership organisation founded in 1975. The DMI facilitates transformational organisational change and design-driven innovation. (dmi.org).

11 As more research has been done on design management, studies has emerged that show that companies with a strong focus on the use of design gain increased competitiveness and impact from innovation.

and corporate culture, revealing its commonalities with concepts like design thinking and the emerging discipline of organisational design' (Borja and Valade-Amland 2020) (2.1.3 Organisational culture).

**Main responsibility areas:**

- *Externally*: Administration of the company's design investments provided by external (or internal) designers and design firms, such as corporate identity, product and service brands.
- *Internally*: Managing design operations internally within the company, using design methodology and design processes to solve business problems, create strategies, develop business concepts, products and services, create corporate culture, or tackle complex issues.

**Main approach:**
Use of design thinking methods, systemic design, user-driven techniques, experimentation and prototyping is 'proven valuable, whether for products or services development or for government policies, health care, and public service innovation' (Borja and Valade-Amland 2020). At a higher level, using design methodology and seeing people, systems, and environment in context can help solve complex economic, social, cultural and environmental problems.

Professionals who have roles as design managers in an organisation include design directors, design managers, design strategists, brand managers, leaders or decision makers. The Design Management Institute (DMI)[10] is an international member organisation for design management, linking design to business, to culture, to customers and to a changing world. DMI describes design management as the art and science of empowering design to enhance collaboration and synergy between design and the business side to improve the impact of design (dmi.org). As leading practitioners of design management, DMI members are actively engaged in design thinking and management of industrial design, graphic design, service design, environmental design, brand identity, fashion design, interface design, interior design, interaction design, architecture and engineering. They work for companies, design firms, educational institutions and the government.[11]

## 6.4 Design effect

### By measuring the effect of design investments, the designer and the company can plan further development and follow-up of design in a more targeted way.

The design project is completed, and the solution delivered. The results look great. The client is all smiles, and everyone is happy. The designer can breathe a sigh of relief and pat themselves on the back. But then it's time to ask questions: Did the solution meet the target? Did it address the problem? Did it solve the problem? Did the product stand out better on the shelf? Was the website navigation better? Was the package easier to open? Was information more accessible? Was the identity more recognisable? Did we reach a wider audience? Did we gain increased



Further reading
– 'Design: A business case. Thinking, leading, and managing' by design. Mozota and Valade-Amland, 2020.
– *The Handbook of Design Management* by Cooper, Rachel; Junginger, Sabine; Lockwood, Thomas 2011.
– *The Evolution of Design Management* by Rachel Cooper and Sabine Junginger, 2009, The Design Management Institute.

Design effect: The value of design is communicated by measuring effectiveness. Anti Bergen received the Design Effectiveness Awards 2018 for their success with a new brand identity for the Bergen International Festival which they developed in 2013. Visits increased by 108 per cent over four years.

awareness? Did we achieve the desired position? Did we increase our competitiveness? When can we expect to see the effect? How do we know it was the design that was the determining factor? What other factors might have influenced the outcome? It can be difficult to measure the effect of design separately, because often factors other than design also play a role. If we look at the whole process as a design-driven process, the overall effect can be measured.

The effect can be seen in both the short and long term, depending on the size and nature of the assignment, but it is difficult to isolate the effect of design because it is usually not clear that the effect is solely from design. A design project is rarely an isolated task, rather a part of a larger ambition, such as building a brand, positioning a product, increasing market share. It can take many years to gain recognition and build a brand. It can take many years to become a market leader if that is the goal. Therefore, it can take years to know whether a design project has been successful, whether it solved the problem and delivered on the objectives.

Goals such as increased recognition, increased competitiveness are qualitative goals that often pay off in the long run. Quantitative goals like increased sales, increased number of visits, increased number of searches, increased number of likes are factors that are simpler to measure. Such measures can also be considered symptomatic of qualitative factors such as awareness and recognition. We will look at some studies that have been carried out to determine the long-term effects of design.

### 6.4.1 Design ladder

In 2001, the Danish Design Center (DDC) wanted to measure the effects of design. This resulted in the development of the Danish Design Ladder, a tool to assess and illustrate the differences in how far companies have come in using design. The tool is based on the hypothesis that there is a positive correlation between higher earnings and an emphasis on the use of design methods in the early stages of development, and that giving design a more strategic position in the company's overall business strategy has an economic impact.[12] The four steps of the Danish Design Ladder (DDC, 2015) are presented in Figure 6.5:
Step 1) No design: Companies that do not use design.
Step 2) Design as styling: Companies that use design as styling.
Step 3) Design as a process: Companies that integrate design into the development process.
Step 4) Design as strategy: Companies that assess design as a key strategic element.

*The extended Danish Design Ladder:* The original ladder created in 2001 was a way of communicating how companies use and view design. But things have changed since then (Davies, 2019). In an article in *Medium*[13] 2016, Bryan Hoedemaeckers, a Director at Deloitte in Australia suggested two additional steps to the ladder: 'Systemic Change' and 'Culture', while David Pettigrew et al. in their conference paper, 2016[14] suggested extending the ladder by adding 'Organisational Transformation' and 'National Competitive Strategy'. Here are some additional steps, based on the rewritten version by Davies 2019: Step 5) Design as

Fig. 6.5 The figure shows the design ladder developed by the Danish Design Center in 2003. Results of surveys based on the design ladder, conducted in 2003 and 2007 gave the following results: 1) non-design: 15% in 2007 against 36% in 2003. 2) Design as styling: 17% in 2007 against 13% in 2003. 3) Design as process: 45% in 2007 against 35% in 2003. 4) Design as strategy: 21% in 2007 against 15% in 2003.

12 'When we speak of design, we mean design strategies, development and styling – everything that takes place prior to production or implementation of products (printed matter, sales fair stalls, web sites, interiors, etc.' DDC (Danish Design Centre).

13 'Are you getting the most out of design?' by Bryan Hoedemaeckers Nov 8, 2016, medium.com.

14 'A Design Innovation Adoption Tool for SMEs' Pettigrew et al., 2016, Conference: 20th DMI: Academic Design Management Conference, Design Management Institute, Boston.

15 'You use tools like roadmaps and diagrams to show where the business is today and where it needs to go and the steps leading to that change. It understands and appreciates things like "change management", "leadership", and "storytelling" in getting its strategy to stick. Multi-disciplined focus groups are used to check-in and monitor change progress. Each phase of change is considered and "designed"' (Davies, 2019).

16 'You use design to create desired behaviours in your people leveraging culture activities, training, learning and development, leadership and employee experience to get the whole organisation aligned around your core purpose. Design is embedded at every stage and there is space for innovation, ideas and leads through customer-centric brand thinking' (Davies, 2019).

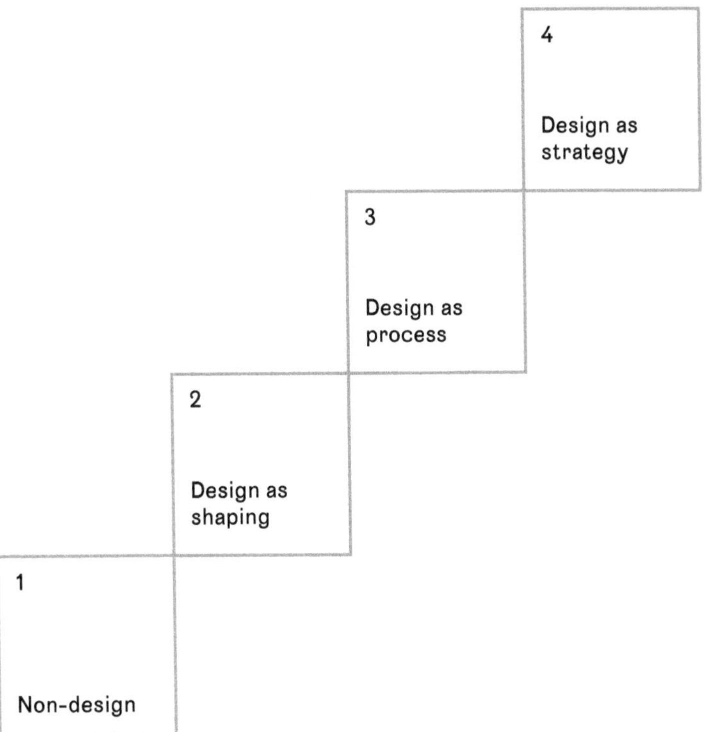


Fig. 6.5 The Danish design ladder

1 Initiation
2 Insight
3 Strategy
4 Design
5 Production
6 Management

6.1 Intangible assets
6.2 Legal protection
6.3 Design management
6.4 Design effect
6.5 Design manual
6.6 Design templates
6.7 Operations manual
6.8 Further development
6.9 Sustainable management

6.4.1 Design ladder
6.4.2 The value of design
6.4.3 Design-driven company
6.4.4 Design impact awards
6.4.7 Visual impact
6.4.8 How to measure the design effect?

change: Companies that use design to implement its strategy.[15] Step 6) Design as culture: Companies that use design to create, build and harness a great culture.[16]

## 6.4.2 The value of design

'The Economic Effects of Design'[17] is the title of a study based on the design ladder carried out by the Danish Design Centre in 2003. The study showed that design is good for business. Companies that work systematically with design have higher earnings and greater exports than those that do not use design. The economic effects are more pronounced in companies where design is firmly anchored in both internal and external design investments. A higher ranking on the design ladder is associated with a positive effect on gross income and a clear positive effect on exports.[18] The study results broke down the companies by percentage of design time: non-design (36 per cent), design as styling (13 per cent), design as process (35 per cent), design as strategy (15 per cent).

In 2007, the Danish Design Centre conducted the study 'Design Creates Values', based on the design ladder and the 2003 study. The percentage of companies not thinking about design at all had been reduced by more than half to 15 per cent in the four years between the studies. The percentage that understood design as a process had increased to 45 per cent, while a fifth, also an increase, had now integrated design as a key part of the business strategy, see Figure 6.5. In the report 'The Value of Design Factfinder' (Design Council, 2007), it is argued that the use and appreciation of design provides bottom-line benefits, and those

17 'The Economic Effects of Design', conducted by the National Agency for Enterprise and Hou sing for the Danish Design Centre.
18 The ladder is used in several different ways, example from: *Design ladder model: HCDI* – Human Centred Design Institute, Danish Design Ladder. Posted on 10 April 2013 by josephgiacomin.

who understand and act on this insight have a competitive advantage over the others. The report provides evidence of how businesses use and understand design, how design adds value to their products and how design affects their performance: 'Design can directly and significantly improve sales, profits, turnover and growth' (Design Council, 2007). A subsequent study 'The role and value of design',[19] carried out by the Design Council in 2015, reinforces this view.

This was also further proven in studies conducted by the Danish Design Centre in 2016 and 2018. According to the report: 'Design Delivers 2018: How design accelerates your business', studies conducted among 802 Danish companies showed that' Design has a positive impact on the bottom line of Danish companies that use design strategically. 79% express that design strengthens their brand. McKinsey's Business Value of Design series, is a comprehensive collection of reports and metrics that point to the value of design. An overview is gathered under the title: 'Design: Understand its value, measure it better, and lead the way' available online. 'Few today question whether design has an impact on business – especially given research showing that companies that excel at design grow revenues and shareholder returns at nearly twice the rate of their industry peers' (McKinsey & Company, 2021) (2.1.1 Value creation).

*The invisible forces*: In the study 'The dark matter of design: making the value and impact of design more visible', conducted by the Design Council in 2017,[22] the aim was to isolate the value of design and demonstrate the contribution design makes to the UK economy. The study uses the term 'dark matter',[23] which is a metaphor for the invisible forces in design. 'Much like the dark matter and energy which drives the expansion of the universe, good design and the process behind it can be invisible' (Stephen Miller, lead researcher).

### 6.4.3 Design-driven company

A design driven company views everything as design. Design is the practice of creating form, function and experience. The process of design can be applied to develop strategy, solve problems and create value (Spacey, 2017).

'Design is everything, because without it we have no business. (...) There is intense competition, and anyone can design a decent product. They can't all design great products. So, design is the differentiator' (Design Council, 2013).[20] The quote is taken from the 'Leading Business by Design Report' (2013). The report documents a survey on the effects of design as a mechanism for business growth and innovation.[21] The aim of the survey was to gather evidence on the effects of design by asking business leaders from different organisations how they use design and what benefits they derive from it. Interviews with business leaders from top companies such as Barclays, Diageo, Virgin Atlantic and Herman Miller led to three main findings:

1) Design is customer centred. The effect is greatest when design is closely linked to solving problems, especially customers' problems.
2) Design is most effective when it is culturally aligned. Design works best when it has strong support in the organisation, especially from upper management.

Tips for the designer

Strategy><Design: How can the choice of font, shape and colour reflect the company's goals and strategy?  See 4.2 Strategy><Design, Table 4.2. 

19 'The role and value of design', 'Working paper: Measuring and defining design', prepared by TBR's Creative and Cultural Team.

20 British Design Council (Design Council) The Design Council is a powerful organisation, recognised as a leading authority on the use of strategic design. 'We use design as a strategic tool to tackle major societal challenges, drive economic growth and innovation, and improve the quality of buildings in the environment. We are the UK Government's adviser on design' (designcouncil.org.uk).

21 The study entitled, 'Leading Business by Design: Why and how business leaders invest in design', was conducted by Warwick Business School for British Design Council: www. designcouncil. org: 'Leading Business by Design Report'.

22 www.designcouncil.org.uk/news-opinion/dark-matter-design-making-value-and-impact-design-more-visible.

23 Dark matter: 'In some cosmological theories nonluminous material which is postulated to exist in space and which could take either of two forms: weakly interacting particles (cold dark matter) or high-energy randomly moving particles created soon after the Big Bang (hot dark matter)' (Google.com).

24 DBA, Design Effectiveness Awards in the UK, awards design that has had a tangible and measurable impact on success. The jury is made up of business leaders who, working with clients and designers, assess the strategic and commercial value of the design to the business (http:// effectivedesign.org.uk/).

3) Design can add value to any organisation. Design can be useful for production and service-based organisations; small, medium or large. The report concluded, among other things, with: 'An increasing number of companies use design strategically – to differentiate themselves from competitors, to launch new brands and strengthen existing brands, and to make strategic choices. There is already considerable evidence that design is an agent of growth and innovation'.



### 6.4.4 Design impact awards

Today, there are numerous design competitions and prestigious awards that celebrate design. The vast majority judge the visual quality of design solutions without considering the objectives and strategic guides behind the task, and whether the design solution contributes to goal achievement. The impact of design lies in the achievement of goals, the creation of value and other effects of the design investment. From a brand building perspective, the design impact can, for example, be to do with increased awareness, brand recognition and sales. From a social perspective, the design impact can be to do with how the design solution affects people's social life, health and environment. 'We need different yardsticks to measure the impact of product design, service design, environmental design and the design of new cultures. Each of these possibilities can lead to change in a unique way' (Heller, 2017).

There are few design impact awards on a global basis. The reason may be that it requires a greater apparatus to assess design based on impact than to assess the visual solution in isolation. Assessing design impact is based on collecting data over several years, documented through measurements, case studies and reports. A well-established high impact award is the Design Effectiveness Awards (DBA).[24] The DBA celebrates the results of what happens when the designer and the company collaborate and combine design thinking and business understanding to create business growth (effectivedesign.org). In 2018, ANTI Bergen became the first Norwegian firm to receive an award in this competition, for a new brand identity for the Bergen International Festival, see Figure 4.87. The impact of the design was documented through a case study based on data from the four years that had passed since the launch of the new brand identity. 'The total number of attendees increased in this period by a staggering 108 per cent, and total income increased by 32 per cent. In a time when many large corporate sponsors spent less on funding, the festival managed to increase its sponsorship income by 59 per cent. The brand has consistently generated stronger and stronger results year after year, and no additional investment per attendee is required per year. The use of public funds became 27 per cent more efficient in just the first year' (Creative Forum, 2018). Tom Morgan, Strategic Director of ANTI Bergen: 'Design efficiency is no simple discipline, but we want to be at the forefront of increasing professionalism in this area in Norway. Our customers rely on us, and it is our responsibility to use creativity to help them achieve their goals. There is no recipe, but it is a matter of understanding business goals, and thinking and acting strategically through design. It is important for us that this is not the end point, but a step along the way in a process of continuous improvement' (Creative Forum, 2018).

*The IPA Effectiveness Awards* are advertising and marketing's most rigorous and coveted competition. Key effectiveness metrics is what matters (2.9.6 KPIs and metrics).

### 6.4.7 Visual impact

Tips for the company
Design that lasts, functions and is used over time – must be controlled.

The Norwegian brand Lofotprodukt, with a new brand identity and packaging design developed by Strømme Throndsen design. In less than six years, Lofotprodukt increased sales by as much as 300 per cent and went from being a local business in northern Norway to a nationwide fish food producer.

How can the use of visual effects help to achieve the desired effect? It goes without saying that text that is clear and easy to read gets the message across more easily, that a bright colour catches the eye more easily, and that a round shape is more appealing than an angular one. The choice of visual effects is a key factor in all visual design and brand building to create identity, awareness, recognition and functionality, and not least to appeal to emotions and associations. Recently marketers have begun to measure design in a new way, which puts design at the centre of the company's value assessment and branding, based on the theory of Romaniuk (2018). By measuring mental availability, the distinctive characteristics of the brand's design have become mentally attached to the category buyer and thus are more easily recognised and preferred in a buying situation (3.4.6 Distinctive asset-building strategy, 2.9.8 Mental availability measurements).

Often, colours and other visual elements are only part of many means of achieving the desired effect. Nevertheless, small details can have a big impact, something the successful Google employee Marissa Mayer was concerned about when she changed jobs in 2012 and started as the new CEO of the IT giant Yahoo.[25] When she started at Yahoo, it was already decided that the new email colour for Yahoo would be blue and grey. The idea was that users would be looking at Yahoo emails on their phones all day, so it was best to choose the most subtle contrasting colours possible. With her determined management style, she made the abrupt decision to change Yahoo's new identity colours from blue and grey to purple and yellow, which meant going in manually and changing colours in literally thousands of places, while still meeting a deadline for launching the new product. Although key employees of the company quit in protest, others supported her decision. The colour of the product may seem unimportant, but Mayer was obsessed with data, and the data showed that wasn't the case. On Yahoo's scale, with hundreds of millions of visitors per month, she showed that if you can change a colour slightly and affect performance by a factor of 0.01 per cent, it turns into millions of dollars (Carlson, 2015), which was not insignificant for a company that was trying to turn around a negative trend.[26]

25 Yahoo! Inc. is a US network provider, which is wholly owned by the US company Verizon Communications. Yahoo was one of the pioneers of the early Internet period in the 1990s and grew to become globally known for its web portal with several hundred million monthly visitors. Marissa Mayer was hired to reverse a negative trend in Yahoo, which would become a few intense years of upturns, downturns, and setbacks, mentioned in several articles and in the book *Marissa Mayer and the Fight to Save Yahoo!* by Nicholas Carlson (2015).

26 The colour purple was already part of Yahoo's identity from the moment Yang and Filo started the company in 1995. The colour came about by chance when Yang asked Filo to buy some grey paint for a wall. But as soon as the wall dried, the colour turned out to be lavender or purple. Yang and Filo's girlfriends at the time (now their wives) were in the office and spotted the purple wall. They thought it was very 'metrosexual' of them to choose purple. So, they went for purple. 'We were purple before it was cool to be purple', Yang stated (Swartz, 2017).

### 6.4.8 How to measure the design effect?

The choice of method for measuring design effect must be assessed in terms of the problem to be solved and the objective of the task. The customers' or user's experience of a product or service will always be holistic, taking into account the sum of design, product, content, technology, marketing and everything else involved in the realisation of the product. Therefore, it is critical at the beginning of a project to determine what outcomes one wants to achieve (Thelwell and Gothelf 2016). Many companies measure almost everything down to the smallest detail, and different types of companies measure their results in different ways. Designers need to understand which metrics are meaningful to their clients' businesses and be prepared to dive into and gain knowledge about them. It also requires that the company be willing to share information about its measurable goals and what results they expect. The designer and the company should talk about what impact the company sees for itself, and plan what needs to be measured and how, in order to demonstrate the effects of the design investment (Knapp, 2008).

Knapp (2008) points to two case studies that were able to document a clear design effect:

1) The British record company EMI group moved into new offices and immediately saw that absenteeism dropped considerably, despite the fact that that summer had been much warmer than normal. Technically, they should have seen an increase in absenteeism instead. In this case, designers were hired to create an environment people really wanted to be in. They designed a new cafeteria in the building that was so congenial that employees started having their meetings in-house instead of going out. They started bringing clients and vendors into the building more. As a result, the organisation also saw a big reduction in personnel costs. This allowed the designers to show solid figures – and a reduction in absenteeism and in personnel costs, both of which directly affect the company's bottom line.

2) The US investment firm Man Group saw a rise in share price following the launch of a new hedge fund because the design of the communications material was so clear that it made the subject more understandable to the market. In this case, it's not about choosing recycled paper or saving money on printing; it's about knowing what the company wants the results to be. This requires the designer to really understand the needs of their customers and how design can be used to generate the outcome their customers want.

Measuring the design effect can also be useful for making incremental improvements to a product or service that is already on the market. UX designers Thelwell and Gothelf (2016) at the software company Envato started to change the way they measure. Previously, they were most concerned with measuring how quickly they could get software out to customers and the design team's ability to help developers do so. Now they are more concerned with measuring the impact the software has on customers. The design team has started to measure against important business metrics that matter. So, everyone in the team – not just the designer – is working to improve the impact the design has on the customer. They focus on getting better results in the metrics in a 'sprint' every other week. 'A success factor or hypothesis is decided at the start of each sprint' (Thelwell and Gothelf 2016). For example:

- We measure the number of people who successfully register versus those who drop out. We have seen significant improvements since we developed new ways to register, for example during checkout or by reducing the number of steps.
- We are seeing an increase in conversion which reflects how we communicate the benefits of our software products, for example support.
- We are gradually reducing the webpage loading speed. We discovered a link between slow loading speed and high exit frequency. We believe this results in fewer purchases on these sites (2.9 Testing and measuring).



In the work of creating a design-driven corporate culture at IBM, continuous measurements are made by Doug Powell to find out the degree to which design and design thinking promote radical collaboration within the company and the quality and relevance of the innovation that collaboration generates. He uses the 'Net Promoter Score' to measure user sentiment (Heller, 2017).

## 6.5 Design manual

The design manual is a user guide that provides clear instructions for how the logo and other identity and design elements should appear on different profile carriers and exposure surfaces.

In all communication and brand building, having a strong visual identity can be an important competitive factor if you want to succeed. Recognition is the key factor, which requires the identity to be as consistent as possible in all contexts. Therefore, the designer must develop clear guides for how the identity should be used and clearly present them in a design manual. This is true whether it is an identity for the company or their products and services.

In the advertising and design industry of the 1970s, 80s and 90s, when large US companies jumped on the wave of developing corporate identities inspired by Paul Rand's logos for IBM, UPS, ABC, many large heavy design manuals of up to several hundred pages were developed. It was a great era for the advertising and design industry, which, in addition to developing visual identities, was also commissioned to create these ambitious design manuals. They were printed in offset and put into large binders and contained all the information on how the company's identity should be managed down to the smallest detail. Today, design manuals are primarily developed, distributed, and used digitally as a pdf or as interactive pages on the internet, while also usually including a print-friendly version.

Tips for the designer
*A collection of identity style guides from around the world*: www.logodesignlove.com/brand-identity-style-guides.

Tips for the designer
Examples of design handbooks: www.uber.design, skype-brand.pdf.

Tips for tools
Development of design manuals and templates: marcom.com, brandsystems.com, bynder.com.

> The designer should never deliver a visual identity without guides on how to use it.

### 6.5.1 Purpose and target group

A design manual is a document (often official) that the designer produces for the company after a visual identity or other design work has been developed. The purpose is to explain how the design should be used to ensure that it appears consistent and according to the intent. What one chooses to call a design manual varies. It can be a design manual, a brand manual, a profile manual, a profile guide, an identity guide, brand guidelines or something else. What is important is that the company and the designer agree on the purpose of the design manual and how it should serve as a guide for employees, collaborators, suppliers and others who will use the design. Some design manuals deal exclusively with the

> **Lack of consistency**
> When there are no rules for the use of a visual identity, each designer and each marketer will present their ideas in the manner they want. They will express their own personality rather than presenting the brand's identity. There is nothing wrong with variety, but there is a point where the variety can be too great. Different or conflicting design styles and communication methods could obscure the brand. It will also dilute brand identity and reduce brand credibility (Jani, 2017).

27 'Universal design means *designing* products, environments, programmes and services in such a way that they can be used by everyone, to the greatest extent possible, without the need for customization and a specific *design*' (Lid, 2015).

design aspect, while others also include the company's objectives, brand strategy and communication guidelines. Thorough design manuals will contain clear rules on how the company's *content creators* should write and design marketing and sales material. The content creators or content providers may be employees, designers, advertising, communications and media agencies, printers or others. These are the users of the design manual. 'A visual profile that must be well managed must ensure that each (initial) meeting with the users of the profile is introduced in a way that inspires insight and understanding, regardless of whether the user is an employee of the company or a collaborator. The design manual must take into account the need for functionality, flexibility and universal design,[27] and focus on the different needs of the users. Furthermore, all design elements and available files/templates must be clearly presented so that any intended user can easily and intuitively download and use them in a proper and appropriate manner' (A. Myhre, 2017).


1 Initiation
2 Insight
3 Strategy
4 Design
5 Production
6 Management

6.1 Intangible assets
6.2 Legal protection
6.3 Design management
6.4 Design effect
6.5 Design manual
6.6 Design templates
6.7 Operations manual
6.8 Further development
6.9 Sustainable management

6.5.1 Purpose and target group
6.5.2 Foundation
6.5.3 Scope
6.5.4 Digital design manual
6.5.5 Contents
6.5.6 Unbranding


## 6.5.2 Foundation

Any design solution or visual profile that is to form the basis of a design manual should start from a carefully thought-out brand and communication strategy, which is aligned with the company's overall objectives and strategy (3.7 Brand strategy, 3.8 Communication strategy, 3.2 Overall strategy, 3.3 Goals and subgoals). During the strategic and creative process, and the various decisions that are taken during it, it will be possible to evaluate and assess which elements should be the mainstay of the design and be given a place in the design manual (4.5 Design development, 4.9 Identity development). Furthermore, it is only after having had the opportunity to try out the design elements on actual exposure surfaces and in actual contexts that the final overall guidelines and rules can be set (A. Myhre, 2017). When this work is approved by the client, it means that the designer and the client agree on how the visual identity should appear in its final form and on different exposure surfaces. It forms the basis for the development of a design manual.

## 6.5.3 Scope

The size of a design manual can be anything from a one-page spread to booklets and large books. The amount of work that needs to be done is assessed based on the scope of the visual identity/design and the level of ambition, time, and resources of the assignment. A simple profile manual can be archived and distributed as a pdf. A larger and more comprehensive design manual can be included as a menu on the company's web or intranet page, possibly as a stand-alone web page with login. A compressed print version of the design manual, in a small handy format, can be useful for implementing the visual identity among the company's employees.

A brand guide can be particularly useful for new employees. Reading a manual will help them familiarise themselves with the rules of the brand much more quickly than by trial and error. It's more professional than someone correcting new employees for breaking a rule they didn't even know existed (Jani, 2017).

## 6.5.4 Digital design manual

'A digital brandguide is a single online destination dedicated to preserving and protecting your brand in a more cost-effective and sustainable way. It allows the marketing department to produce studio-standard marketing materials from bespoke templates, store, share and adapt them for their own markets and stay firmly educated on the brand's purpose, guidelines, and evolution. One of the biggest advantages of a digital design guide is that it is available and always updated 24/7' (Inki Annweiler, 2022). A digital design manual provides the means to easily share guidelines, design elements, downloadable templates for professional users in a user-friendly way (e.g. ready-made InDesign and Photoshop files), user-friendly Office templates for employees for routine use (e.g. PowerPoint and letter templates, etc.) and digital production solutions for generating templates and marketing materials that do not require graphic software or skills (6.6 Design templates). By developing a responsive solution, the design manual can also be made available to users on mobile and tablet devices. In a digital production solution, a simple direct contact for production at the printers or distribution out to the desired channels can also be included (A. Myhre, 2017).

Fig. 6.6 **The figure shows how guides for the logo can be visually simplified. In addition to the illustration, all guides for the use of the logo are described. For example: clear space around the logo, colour use in the logo, wrong colour use, minimum size of the logo, placement of the logo on surfaces, wrong use of the logo, logo in conjunction with other logos, applications of the logo, and others. © Grimsgaard, W. (2018).**

### 6.5.5 Contents

The contents of a design manual vary depending on the nature, size, needs and purpose of the company. We will highlight here some general principles. All guides should be presented with visual examples and short explanatory texts.

**1) Layout:** The design manual is an independent deliverable that the designer develops for the company and a separate item in the budget. Developing a design manual can be a complex task, requiring the designer to think about both the shape of the layout and a system for presenting the contents in addition to the actual contents. The design manual is in many contexts the content providers (users') first encounter with the profile in terms of actual use. The design manual should therefore itself signal the company's identity and behaviour. It should be neat, clear, and user-friendly for a wide range of users. A good manual is one that uses a type of language that is accessible to all, so that it can be understood even by a novice or someone with little or no experience in the field. The language and style should be clear and merely serve to help others understand and communicate how the design should be used. To have an intuitive, clear and user-friendly digital design manual, the contents of each category of elements and information should be arranged under its own title or tab. For example: introduction, identity elements, guidelines and templates for screens and digital surfaces, guidelines and templates for print, signage plan, uniform, image decoration and inspiration. Basic elements and templates should be able to be loaded down where this is described/explained and under its respective tab (Myhre, 2017).

**2) Introduction and anchoring:** Strategic anchoring and basic guidelines for the brand should be presented initially. How much to include here depends on the size of the project and the budget. At a minimum, it should include what is needed for the user of the design manual to understand the strategic guides. For example, the brand architecture can be important here, to explain whether it is a monolithic, sponsored, or individual identity, see Figure 3.30. Equally important is the brand hierarchy to explain the role of the brand in relation to other brands in the portfolio, see Figure 3.26 (3.7.2 Brand architecture). Examples of initial information:

- Introduction: a short text that says something about who, what and where the company is, possibly why, their products or services, and the purpose of the design manual.
- How to use the design manual: User guide, contact information and responsibilities.
- Table of contents: a structured, clear, and user-friendly system.
- Strategic anchoring: Anchoring in overall objectives and strategy. Positioning strategy, simple presentation of the brand hierarchy, and excerpts from the design and communication strategy. This could be, for example, the core values, value promise, and tone of voice.
- About the visual identity/design: overall idea of the concept.
- Legal use and practical information: legal rights to names, trademarks, domains, fonts, photos, illustrations or other.

Fig. 6.6 Logo guides

**3) Logo and logo use:** A logo/brand can consist of several elements, such as a name, symbol, and tagline, see Figure 4.77. The logo elements should be positioned in relation to each other so that they appear as a unified whole. It is equally important that the logo appear consistent (uniform, solid, coherent) on different surfaces. It is a question of establishing guides for how the logo should appear with other identity elements and in a composition with text, images, graphs and other elements (4.9.3 Logo).

There will normally be a need to enlarge and shape the logo on different profile carriers. In this context, it should be made clear that the logo must always keep the same proportions (size ratio). In addition, a minimum display size for the logo should be specified, as well as a minimum size for the use of the tagline in the logo. It is important that the tagline always be legible if it is to be included. If necessary, create a version of the logo

1 Initiation
2 Insight
3 Strategy
4 Design
5 Production
6 Management

6.1 Intangible assets
6.2 Legal protection
6.3 Design management
6.4 Design effect
6.5 Design manual
6.6 Design templates
6.7 Operations manual
6.8 Further development
6.9 Sustainable management

6.5.1 Purpose and target group
6.5.2 Foundation
6.5.3 Scope
6.5.4 Digital design manual
6.5.5 Contents
6.5.6 Unbranding

without the tagline that can be used when the logo is to be displayed in a small size. If a pictogram is to be included as part of the logo, it may be necessary to create custom guides for this. Explain the purpose of the pictogram, what it means to the brand, and how it is to be used in combination or in connection with the logo (4.9.4 Symbol). Guides for the logo:

- Main logo, any logo variants and interaction with other logos.
- Clear-space around the logo.
- Placement on formats (right left, centre, up, down, or other).
- Placement on other colours, images, textiles, materials.
- Acceptable adjustments (with or without tagline, symbol or other).
- Minimum permitted size.
- Examples of how the logo should not appear.
- Composition of the name, symbol, and tagline.
- Symbol(s) (pictogram, emblem, monogram) application and use.
- Consistent use of names, epithets, initials.

PROFIL COLOURS

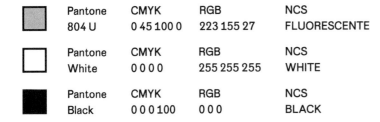

| | | | | |
|---|---|---|---|---|
| ■ | Pantone 804 U | CMYK 0 45 100 0 | RGB 223 155 27 | NCS FLUORESCENTE |
| □ | Pantone White | CMYK 0 0 0 0 | RGB 255 255 255 | NCS WHITE |
| ■ | Pantone Black | CMYK 0 0 0 100 | RGB 0 0 0 | NCS BLACK |

Fig. 6.7 Profile colours

Fig. 6.7 The figure shows an example of the presentation of colour systems and colour codes. See 5.5.10 Colour reference systems and Figure 5.6 for an explanation of colour systems. The colour scheme shown in the figure is the one used in this book. © Grimsgaard, W. (2018).

Fig. 6.8 The figure shows an example of the presentation of profile fonts and applications. Often the profile fonts are shown as entire alphabets for each typeface and degree, in addition to a small text describing the usage guides. The font choice, point sizes, and spacing shown in the figure are those used in this book. © Grimsgaard, W. (2018).

> Consistent identity perception on digital and analogue communication surfaces/profile carriers is a prerequisite for building recognition and brand.

**4) Profile colours and use of colours:** Consistent colour reproduction and use is an essential factor in building identity and recognition. Conscious colour management is necessary to ensure that the colour representation is as similar as possible when the colour is displayed on screens, prints, textiles, interiors or other (5.5 Colour management). It is therefore necessary to present the mixing ratio of the actual colours in the different colour systems that are currently used, such as RGB, CMYK, NCS and RAL, see Figures 5.8 and 6.7. Use physical colour selectors to find a colour mixture (colour code) for each colour which provides the most uniform representation of the colour across colour systems. In addition, it may be necessary to create a colour palette showing how the colours should be used in relation to each other and to what extent they should be used. How colours appear is what creates identity. If there are orange and green in the colour palette, it may be that these two colours should never appear next to each other or be used on text. White, black and shades of grey should also appear in the colour palette (4.9.5 Identity colours, 4.6.2 Colour). Colour guides:

- Colour palette: Composition and guides for the use of colours.
- Identity colours: Primary, secondary colours, signal colours, colour codes.
- Colour systems and colour codes: E.g., RGB, CMYK, NCS and RAL.
- Examples of how colours should not be used.

**5) Fonts and typography:** Define one or two primary typefaces that complement each other and any additional typefaces. Present the actual font(s) in the degrees to be used, for example normal, normal italic, medium, medium

28 For example, the illustrations in this book are made in monoline (same line thickness), only one colour (orange) is used in addition to black and the paper colour white, and the main font, point size and degree of the text in the illustrations.

italic or other. Clarify which rules apply and which typeface should be used on printed or digital surfaces. For example, how each of them should be used in titles, body text, captions, highlights and so on, as well as rules for the use of point size, colours and possibly also typography; line spacing, line width, hyphenation, grid system and so on (4.9.6 Typography). Provide information on licences and how to access the profile font(s). Font guides:

- Profile font 1: Degrees, application, usage guides.
- Profile font 2: Degrees, application, usage guides.
- System font(s) for use in e.g. Office templates.
- Rules for typography and use of the grid system.



PROFILE FONTS

8,5/12 pt **Mériva Medium is used for headings, text in figures, figure titles and figure numbering**

19/24 pt Domaine Text Light is used for the introduction of each phase

11/15 pt Domaine Text Light is used for introduction of main chapters

8,7/12 pt Domaine Text Light used for body text, in tables and text boxes. *Domaine Text Light Italic is used for highlighting*

7/9 pt Mériva Medium is used for navigation, figure explanations, fact boxes in the margin, little headers and footnotes

Fig. 6.8 Profile fonts

**6) Photo style:** Describe typical motif, cut, mood and style of choice of photo or photography. For example: a) Close-up of people, natural, eye contact, black and white; b) Close-up of food, fresh, colourful; c) Picture of people in a setting, talking to each other, happy mood. This can be elaborated and serve as a photo brief. Define how certain types of images should be used and edited. Describe in detail how images are to be obtained (rented, bought, own photo shoots or other). Are illustrations to be used in addition to or instead of pictures? Clarify the style, tone, colour and design of the illustrations.[28] This section will also include a brief for the photographer/illustrator. Guides for photos:

- Photo style 1
- Photo style 2
- Photo style 3

**7) Profile elements:** Profile elements can be graphic illustrations, patterns, structures, the shape of a package or other elements that form part of the visual identity. Present and explain each of the elements, why, where how and when to use them. Guides for profile elements:

- Design element 1
- Design element 2
- Design element 3

Toolbox
A design manual is a kind of toolbox that contains the different identity or brand elements that make up a visual profile.

**8) Layout principles and grid systems:** Many companies have a patchwork of different printed matter, advertisements, and websites, which have been created by chance when the need to communicate has arisen. Everything a company communicates out in the market and in the organisation says something about who they are. When this is done in a consistent manner, it helps to build identity and recognition. This involves defining a fixed identity regime for the composition of elements in the layout, be it web, brochures, magazines, postal printed matter (letterhead and envelopes) or other, to create a holistic expression that clearly identifies the originator.[29] The first step in the process is to follow the rules for the use of identity elements as explained in the previous sections. In addition, it is necessary to develop guides for the composition of elements on different profile carriers. The guides may include format, grid system, composition of elements (e.g. symmetric or asymmetric), and adaptation to digital and analogue surfaces. For example, a grid may include the size ratio of margins, typed area and columns, as well as fixed text templates and image proportions. The use of grids makes the work of implementing text and images much easier and helps to maintain a uniform look for all communication material. For more complex brands, the guidelines may also contain rules for implementation on analogue and digital profile carriers/templates, for example:[30]

- Digital media: Websites, web shops, social media, mobile advertising.
- Office material: Business cards, letterheads, envelopes, invoices, message blocks, folders, binders, stamps, stickers.
- Presentation material: PowerPoint templates, newsletters, email signatures.
- Image decoration: Company cars, event cars, vans.
- Signage: Shop facade signs, business facade signs, shop film.
- Advertising: Advertisements, magazines, posters, boards, adshells, brochures, flyers, TV/cinema.
- Event: Launch and conference material, invitations, brochures.
- Packaging design: Choice of material, tear-away, stickers, open/close mechanism, labelling.
- Shop material: Shelf posters, carrying bags, shop-in-shop material.
- Dress/uniform: Shirts, aprons, T-shirts, trousers.
- Trade fair/event material: Trade fair walls, tables, rollups, nameplates.
- Stadium advertising: Banners, posters, flyers.
- Sponsor material: Promotional merchandise, shakers, drink bottles, pens, T-shirts
- (3.8.8 Channels and media, Figure 3.52 Communication mix).

**9) Miscellaneous guides:** the contents of a design manual must be adapted to each project. Here are examples of other guides that can be used:

- Profile text: Slogans, brand narrative, quotes, boilerplate or others.
- Guides for printing and production: technical printing specifications (folding, stamping, cutting, etc.), other technical requirements.
- Paper and material selection: Specifications for the choice of paper, cardboard, textiles, film, and other materials.

**10) Inspiration:** This will provide inspiration for solving tasks and using and getting the most out of the profile elements. The inspiration section should include a good selection of examples that clearly demonstrate the system and present the features of the visual profile.

Unbrand

**The up-and-coming here are trying not to try too hard. They're using more of a toolbox than a framework.**

29 Acid test: If you remove the logo, will you still recognise the originator?
30 Check out Uber's Visual Identity on behance.net.
31 Max Ottignon is a creative and strategic director and one of the founders of Ragged Edge, a design firm focused on helping brands communicate in ways that are more meaningful, relevant, and useful to their consumers. See raggededge.com/opinion/Unbrand/, and itsnicethat.com: 'Throwing out the brand book: the power of unbranding' (Ottignon, 2017).
32 markettrack.com: 'What is branded content?' medium.com: 'Branded Content: The What, Why, When, and How'.
33 A meme is a cultural element in the form of an image, video, sentence, etc. that is transmitted via the Internet and often modified in a creative or humorous way (dictionary.com).

## 6.5.6 Unbranding

At a time when companies are increasingly looking outwards to understand user needs and draw users into their product and service development, empathy and collaboration with users comes naturally. This symbiosis leads to new ways of thinking about brand building. After half a century of large trendsetting companies managing their corporate branding by using design manuals that directed the use of the brand to the smallest detail, there are now companies that want to loosen up and put the user more at the centre. This means that the user has a greater opportunity to influence the brand, to interact with the brand and feel that it really belongs to them.

Unbranding has so far started to emerge to communicate with consumers. It challenges the rigid way of thinking about brand building, which involves the consistent use of brand elements on all exposure surfaces to create a holistic experience of the brand and in that way build recognition. According to Ottignon (2017),[31] this is no longer the way people want to work. This rigidity has its price, namely the individuality and passion of people who live and identify with their brand. Today's consumers don't just like being involved; they expect to be. In addition, unbranding places the people behind the brand at the forefront. An unbrand is designed with a flexibility that accommodates people's own expression, not the companies. It requires a much more fluid approach, allowing people to capture the spirit of the organisation in an infinite number of ways. It allows them to take ownership of the brand, without losing the essence of the core.

One example Ottignon cites is Google: Google is undeniably associated with its simple, distinctive logo, a bold use of colour and a semi-consistent use of typography. But instead of living by a set of guidelines, stakeholders are invited to make their own assessments based on a simple question: 'Does it feel Googly?' Many typical content brands[32] are adopting a type of unbranding strategy by letting the content dictate the look and feel, while the brand provides a recessive, unifying framework. MTV's identity is inspired by internet memes,[33] GIFs and videos supplied by viewers. MTV's brand developers give the creative team a toolbox instead of a style guide and make constant changes to the brand. The spirit remains the same, but the visual approach is fluid (Ottignon, 2017).

**Unbranding**

There are other ways of thinking than 'this is how it has been done and this is how it is frequently done'. In brand building towards young people, major brand builders like Nike, MTV and Vice have a brand building approach that involves people to a much greater extent. An interesting side here is that many of the large companies are no longer going to the big design firms, but to the younger ones who explore more and think outside the box, like Nike for example going to Hort and Mirko Borsche. As a result, they ended up with solutions they wouldn't have come up with otherwise (bureauborsche.com, www.hort.org.uk).



Further reading
No logo by Naomi Klein (2009).

There is, of course, another side to the coin. While MTV and Nike can do just about anything they want and still be recognised, new brands in general will need the consistent branding to build awareness before they can start with something like this? Anyway, with large enough access to the market, most things are possible. The New York-based branding agency Gretel developed a visual identity for the new TV channel Viceland in 2016, with a black and white colour palette and only one typeface (Helvetica bold). In an interview with Creative Review (2016),[34] Gretel explained that they were asked to create an identity that could express the tone and personality of each of Vice's shows without overshadowing the content. The shows had to fall into one of three categories: 'smart and curious', 'light and funny', and 'deep and dangerous'. The brand represents *the feeling of* VICE; it is blunt and raw. An exposed structure, a functional language without decoration, artwork, and veneer. The irony of such a low-tech, analogue approach is that it can easily adapt to almost any modern platform with the most basic tools (Steven, 2016).

Fig. 6.9 The figure shows examples of design templates for different profile carriers with fixed logo placement. © Grimsgaard, W. (2018).

## 6.6 Design templates

A design template is a standardised framework for advertisements, printed material, software solutions or anything else that needs to have a consistent visual design. It can be the fixed placement of logos and other identity elements, in addition to pre-determined formats, text templates, colour codes or other.

Design templates are an investment that contributes to simplifying and streamlining the development of communication materials, thus saving the company time and resources. The benefit, however, is first and foremost that the material produced by the company appears

**Design template for designers**

If a company has offices or shops that are spread out geographically, there will, for example, be a need to use local design firms and advertising agencies to develop advertising and shop materials. The usual approach is for the designer to develop an identity design, a design template for all material, and a design manual, which is distributed to the various local firms/agencies. These will be familiar with how the design manual and design template should be used.

**Design template for non-designers**

Often companies need to update their own communication and presentation material, such as newsletters and PowerPoint presentations. In this case, the designer can develop simple templates as a framework for implementing text and images in a layout, which does not require the user to have graphic software or design skills.

34 Creative Review: 'Gretel's "unbranded" branding for Vice TV channel, Viceland' (Steven 03/03/2016). Viceland is a multinational brand for a TV channel owned by Vice Media, launched 2016. viceland.com, gretelny.com.
35 Templates can be added for the Office suite. There are also a few web-based publishing solutions, which are offered for free or by subscription.

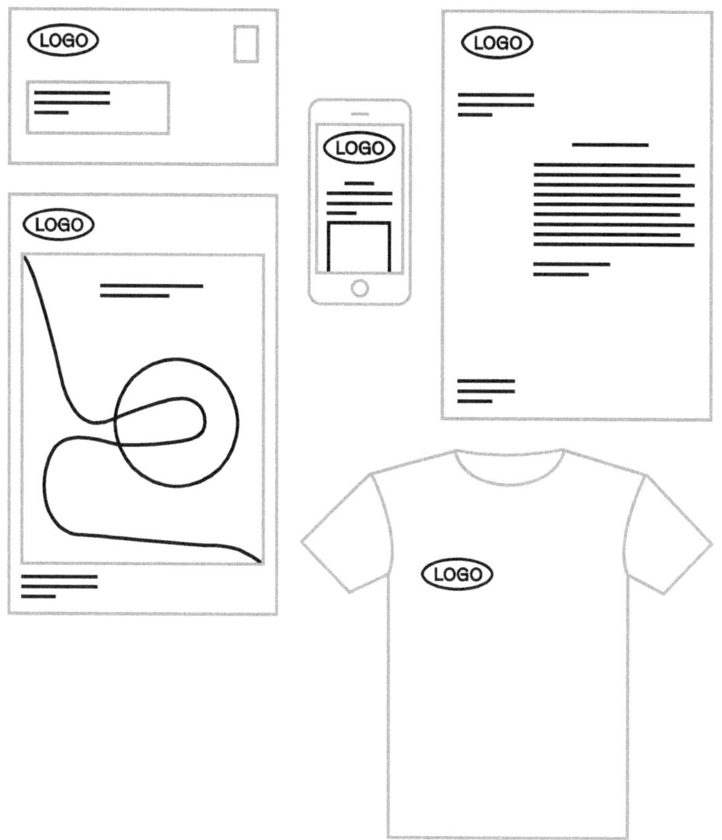


Fig. 6.9 Design templates

1 Initiation
2 Insight
3 Strategy
4 Design
5 Production
6 Management

6.1 Intangible assets
6.2 Legal protection
6.3 Design management
6.4 Design effect
6.5 Design manual
6.6 Design templates
6.7 Operations manual
6.8 Further development
6.9 Sustainable management

consistent and thus contributes to building recognition, which is an important competitive factor. There is a lot of communication material that the company's employees can easily produce themselves, without a designer as an intermediary. This requires the designer to have created design templates that can be used without the need for design skills or graphic software.[35] Examples of this are templates for the company's office and presentation material, such as letterheads, invoices, digital newsletters, PowerPoint presentations, websites and the like. Here the designer can define a layout with a fixed placement of the logo and other identity elements, as well as contact information and other standard text. These elements will be locked in the document so that they cannot be changed. In addition, the designer develops a standard for how text should be implemented. This means that titles and body text are defined in terms of point size, degree, column width, line spacing and so on. This is made available to the user as text templates. In addition, fixed borders are defined for the implementation of images, graphs and other elements. Design templates like this are made available to all employees of the company and require each user to follow the established guidelines.

The designer can also provide digital production solutions for the development of marketing material. Here the user can, by means of digitised templates, produce and order frequently used printed matter, such as simple brochures, direct advertising, ads and business cards. The templates can have different levels of editing options with regard to e.g. text, images and colours. Standardised information (such as addresses) can be entered automatically. Design templates can be linked to examples shown in the design manual (6.5 Design manual).

Some design templates are created for the designer. An example is a template for magazines. In this case, a creative process, design skills, and the use of graphic software will often be needed to create the content. Design templates in an editorial context will, for example, mean that the size of the format, fonts, grid system, typing area, margins, columns, point sizes, line spacing, hyphenation and so on are predefined in the template, as are the colour profile settings and technical specifications for print or other production (4.9.6 Typography, 5.5.3 Colour profiles).

Tips for the company
**The operations manual gives your employees the independence and security they need to operate in their jobs for maximum results (Inside eMyth, 2022).**

Operations manual
Company history
Vision/values
Position statement
Organisation/culture
Products/services
Systems/technology
Policies
Action plans

## 6.7 Operations manual

An operations manual is a form of user guide that provides instructions for the production, operation and maintenance of products, services, websites, software, technical equipment, installations or other items.

In a design assignment, there may be a need to develop an operation manual. Operations manuals is part of the company's optimising operational and maintenance practices, as a means of ensuring sustainable, safe and targeted business operations, in that what has been developed is taken care of, used, monitored, followed up and maintained over time. For example, it may be documentation of the technical structure, use and maintenance of a system. It could be instructions related to the processes and systems used to produce goods or provide services, or guidelines for the operation and servicing of equipment. It may be security procedures to help prevent failure or damage to equipment due to carelessness with equipment or faulty handling.

For an industrial designer or interior architect, there may be a need to adopt or develop guidelines for the assembly, disassembly and installation of lighting at an exhibition stand, showroom, shop, restaurant or other installation. For a web designer, there may be a need to provide instructions to the individual who will manage, for example, a website or web shop, including the use of different types of webpage templates, content templates, image formats and technical 'tricks' that are not built into the publishing system. In most places, IT and web operations are a completely different field managed by someone other than the web designer, and this is often where system responsibility lies. The operation of digital solutions and IT systems can be an extensive job, requiring procedures and guidelines for the maintenance of server farms, platforms, networks, software, ensuring data security, uptime, error reporting, troubleshooting and so on (Furu, 2018). Such information can be compiled in an operating manual to ensure the best possible quality of operations.

## 6.8 Further development

1 Initiation
2 Insight
3 Strategy
4 Design
5 Production
6 Management

6.1 Intangible assets
6.2 Legal protection
6.3 Design management
6.4 Design effect
6.5 Design manual
6.6 Design templates
6.7 Operations manual
6.8 Further development
6.9 Sustainable management

It's when the customers are pouring in, reputation is at its peak and sales are booming that the real work begins.

Long-term development and value creation is about preparing for growth and innovation, keeping focus, ensuring targeted strategic development, managing resources, motivating employees, keeping an eye on competitors, developing identity, sharpening communication and being visible and active in the market. In a competitive environment, there is always someone breathing down your neck in search of the same customers. If you rest on your laurels, you will quickly lose ground.

Coca-Cola is one of the world's biggest and most famous brands, a position it has held for a long time. Yet they continue to do expensive advertising and new products. They know that competitors like Pepsi are on their heels and are always looking for bigger market shares. The same goes for Apple or for Norwegian Tine. Revamping strategies, refining objectives, strengthening communications, further developing logos and packaging, and developing new products and services are key factors to both build position, maintain position and ensure increased competitiveness (3.7.8 Brand perspective, 3.4.5 Transient Advantage, 3.4 Business strategy, 3.7.3 Brand position).

## 6.9 Sustainable management

Design can be an important driving force for sustainable development, use and management of resources and for greater awareness of equality, human rights and ethics. Sustainability management is necessary in all phases of a design project. The responsibility lies with both the company, the designer and the user.

Sustainable management is needed to successfully maintain the quality of life on our planet. We are all stewards of the future of our environment. Sustainable management can be applied to all aspects of our lives. For the company, sustainable management is a way of governing that emphasises the concept of sustainability and takes into account economic, environmental and social impact when making management decisions. The three pillars economic viability, environmental protection and social equity, also known as people, planet, and prosperity are intrinsically interconnected. They need to be implemented and work in harmony for the company to achieve its sustainable goals. 'In using these industries, the ability of a system to thrive by maintaining economic viability and by limiting resource consumption to meet the needs of present and future generations is created' (MDPI, n.d.). (3.3.8 Sustainability goals).

Sustainable management looks beyond short-term profits and focuses on long-term gain by incorporating the environmental and social costs of doing business into management decisions. That means incorporating strategies for both sustainability and profitability in order

Further reading
– Concepts and Approaches for Sustainability Management
– Editors (view affiliations) Khai Ern Lee, 2020.

Sustainable design
Sustainability awareness should be included in the company's strategy; recognised, articulated, and defined before a design project is initiated, during the project, once the project is completed, and in the further follow-up and use of the assets created through the design process.

to achieve corporate growth and value creation in a more holistic way (Anaheim University, 2022). This applies to the application of sustainable practices in the processes of product development, production, packaging, design, commerce, society, agriculture, environment, personal life, and other fields which through sustainable management can be beneficial to present and future generations.

### 6.9.1 Sustainability development

The concept of sustainable development was launched in the report Our Common Future, also called the Bruntland Report, which defined sustainable development as 'development that meets the needs of the present without compromising the ability of future generations to meet their own needs' (World Commission on Environment and Development, 1987).[36]

The template for any policy, business practice, economy, people or society, is now the UN Sustainable Development Goals (SDG), available online at sdgs.un.org. The 17 SDGs were adopted by all United Nations Member States in 2015, with 169 targets to reach by 2030. The goals and targets are universal, meaning they apply to all countries around the world (sdgs.un.org). 'Reaching the goals requires action on all fronts-governments, businesses, civil society, and people everywhere all have a role to play' (IISD, n.d.)[37] (3.3.8 Sustainability goals).

### 6.9.2 Corporate sustainability

Corporate sustainability can be explained through the ESG criteria, which are the three pillars; environmental, social, and governance. These are frequently used criteria that investors emphasise when considering investing in a company. Thus, the company's ESG affects its perceived value. The main characteristics of the SDGs are based on Beattie (2021):

- *Environmental criteria* consider how business operations impact the environment (and vice versa). It may include energy use, waste, pollution, natural resource conservation or depletion, greenhouse gas emissions,

| Positive ESG criteria | |
|---|---|
| Environment | – Companies that put out carbon or sustainability reports<br>– Limits harmful pollutants and chemicals<br>– Seeks to lower greenhouse gas emissions<br>– Uses renewable energy sources |
| Social | – Companies that operate an ethical supply chain<br>– Supports LGBTQ rights and encourages diversity<br>– Has policies to protect against sexual misconduct<br>– Pays fair wages |
| Governance | – Companies that embrace diversity on their board<br>– Embraces corporate transparency<br>– Employs a CEO independent of the board chair |

Table 6.1 ESG criteria

Table 6.1 **The table shows what can be considered good ESG criteria for considering how a company performs as a steward of nature (Based on Trillum, 2021).**[38]

Tips for the company
**Rethink supply chain management.**

> In the broadest possible sense, sustainability refers to the ability of something to maintain or 'sustain' itself over time (Mollenkamp, 2021).

Further reading
As early as 2009 the Canadian David Berman, wrote the book 'Do Good Design: How Designers Can Change The World', with foreword by Erik Spiekermann.

36 Mother of Sustainable Development: 'Norway's first female Prime Minister Gro Harlem Brundtland was Director-General of the World Health Organization (WHO) from 1998 to 2003. She also chaired the Brundtland Commission which presented the Report on Sustainable Development in 1987' (Norway in the UN, n/d). The Commission was also called the Brundtland Commission after its leader Gro Harlem Brundtland.

37 IISD, International Institute for Sustainable Development, has over 150 full-time staff, plus more than 100 associates and consultants working around the world and across many disciplines. They are chemists, biologists, political scientists, lawyers, economists, researchers, reporters and communications experts, dedication to sustainable development.

38 Trillum ESG Criteria, trilliuminvest.com.

habitat destruction/preservation (or biodiversity), treatment of animals, climate change adaptation/risk management, product compliance and stewardship, issues related to its ownership of contaminated land, its disposal of hazardous waste, its management of toxic emissions, or its compliance with government environmental regulations.

- *Social criteria* examine how the organisation's operations affect its people and communities. It may include the business managers' relationships with employees, suppliers, customers, and the communities where they operate; their practice of diversity, equity, inclusion, human rights, fair trade and community investment. Workplace safety, hiring practices, consumer protection, training and education, are critical factors.
- *Governance* deals with how the company behaves and governs. Their leadership, transparency, ethics, and integrity, as well as corporate reputation (corruption, fraud, regulation), stakeholder engagement, internal system of controls, practices, and procedures. It also includes how they handle privacy and data security, executive compensation, donations and political lobbying, board diversity and structure and supply chain resilience.

No single company may pass every test in every category, so one need to decide what's most important to them.

### 6.9.3 Circular economy

In a circular economy, one eliminate waste and pollution, circulate products and materials, and regenerate nature. Circular economy is about expanding the cycle of products by involving sharing, leasing, reusing, repairing, recycling existing materials, preserving products for as long as possible, eliminating waste and pollution, and regenerating nature. 'A circular economy decouples economic activity from the consumption of finite resources. It is a resilient system that is good for business, people and the environment' (Ellen Macarthur Foundation n.d). According to the Ellen Macarthur Foundation, the circular economy is based on three principles, driven by design:

- Eliminate waste and pollution
- Circulate products and materials (at their highest value)
- Regenerate nature

Ellen Macarthur Foundation describes circular economy as two main cycles: 'The technical cycle and the biological cycle. In the technical cycle, products are kept in circulation in the economy through reuse, repair, remanufacture and recycling. In this way, materials are kept in use and never become waste. In the biological cycle, the nutrients from biodegradable materials are returned to the Earth, through processes like composting or anaerobic digestion. This allows the land to regenerate so the cycle can continue' (Ellen Macarthur Foundation n.d). Read more in the chapters 3.3.8 Sustainability goals, 3.4.3 Sustainability strategy, 3.5.2 Sustainable business model, 5.3.5 Material life cycle, 5.3.6 Product life cycle.



Further reading

- 'The Net-zero Transition: What it would cost, what it could bring' by McKinsey (2022).
- The McKinsey report, 'Net zero & ESG Strategy: Helping leaders and organisations rewrite the climate math equation' (2021).

### 6.9.4 Net zero

An increasing number of countries, organisations and businesses are committing to net zero emissions of greenhouse gases. 'Some are even moving beyond this, committing to transition to decarbonised and carbon-negative economies' (Design Council, 2022). In the report 'The Net-zero Transition: What it would cost, what it could bring' (2022), McKinsey look at what the economic transformation that a transition to net-zero emissions would entail. The study estimates the changes in demand, capital spending, costs, and jobs, to 2050, for sectors that produce about 85 percent of overall emissions and assess economic shifts for 69 countries. This report, as well as the McKinsey report 'Net zero & ESG Strategy: Helping leaders and organizations rewrite the climate math equation' (2021), will be of valuable help when recreating the business strategy.

### 6.9.5 The trendsetters

Corporate sustainability has become a crucial question in every business, big or small. Finding sustainable ways to deliver goods and services has become a competitive factor. Many corporate giants have named sustainability as a key priority moving forward and is at the forefront of sustainable bench-marking products. An early trendsetter was 'Adidas' launch of Adidas Parley[39] in 2015, a jogging shoe produced with recycled plastic waste from the sea, a contribution to help mitigate the amount of plastic that ends up in the ocean.[40] In doing so, they sent strong signals to their target groups, stakeholders and competitors. Their competitor Nike has stated that they are 'moving towards being a renewable energy-using company to reducing its waste entirely', by producing Recycled Material Sneakers. 'Move to zero is Nikes's journey towards zero carbon waste to help protect the future of sport' (Nike, 2022, nike.com/sustainability). They offer their customers to help reduce waste by cleaning and donating or recycling worn athletic shoes and apparel, through the concept of Reuse-A-Shoe.

It is not only the product's supply chain, material use and production that are the subject of a circular economy, but just as much the packaging. Packaging is closely linked to the product as it is intended to protect it, whether it is food safety or preventing damage to the product. Here, of course, is a race to arrive at eco-friendly materials, such as the Coca-Cola trialling of its first-ever paper bottle prototype June 2021, for the plant-based drink AdeZ, as part of the company's wider sustainability strategy[41] (3.3.8 Sustainability goals, 3.4.3 Sustainability strategy). These and many other major brands lead by example. The crucial factor here is to avoid falling into the greenwashing trap.

### 6.9.6 Greenwashing

There must be a holistic approach behind corporate sustainability, their sustainability goals, their value propositions and their sustainability efforts. They must live up to their sustainability goals in order to be taken seriously by customers and stakeholders. 'Business and governmental commitments to sustainability are increasingly common, though these

Fig. 6.10 The pyramid shows the eco-design pyramid, based on Goods (2022). It presents the design principles for sustainability. The designer can influence how to reduce consumption, reuse products, recycle materials, recover material for reuse, and dispose of waste for new purposes.

Tips for the company
Sustainable management entails incorporating the environmental and social costs of doing business into management and design decisions and focusing on long-term instead of short-term gains.

6 principles for sustainability (Thorn, 2022):
1. Circular economy
2. Energy savings
3. Sustainable material choices
4. Environmental product declaration (EPD)
5. Constant research and innovation
6. Corporate social responsibility

Further reading
*Beyond Net zero: A Systemic Approach,* by the Design Council (2021).

39 Adidas Parley is a collection of clothing and footwear originating from the collaboration of German multinational company Adidas and Parley for the Oceans, an organisation that addresses environmental threats towards the oceans, through plastic pollution ('Adidas Parley,' n.d.).
40 Adidas recreated three editions of their UltraBoost shoe, and a new version of their Adidas Originals shoe.
41 The prototype of the paper bottle for plant-based drink AdeZ, jointly developed by Danish startup Paboco and Coca-Cola, made its debut in Hungary, according to a press release sent to the *Budapest Business Journal.*

efforts encounter scepticism over corporate "greenwashing," which is the practice of providing a false impression to make a business seem more environmentally friendly than it is. Some evidence is accruing that investors are actively embracing green investments' (Mollenkamp, 2021).

Genuinely green products should explain the product's green claims in plain language and readable type and specify whether it refers to the product, the packaging, or just a portion of the product or package. The product marketing or advertising should not overstate an environmental attribute or benefit, and if the benefit is justified the claim of benefit should be substantiated (Kenton, 2022) (5.4.9 Ecolabelling and certification).


1 Initiation
2 Insight
3 Strategy
4 Design
5 Production
6 Management

6.1 Intangible assets
6.2 Legal protection
6.3 Design management
6.4 Design effect
6.5 Design manual
6.6 Design templates
6.7 Operations manual
6.8 Further development
6.9 Sustainable management

6.9.1 Sustainability development
6.9.2 Corporate sustainability
6.9.3 Circular economy
6.9.4 Net zero
6.9.5 The trendsetters
6.9.6 Greenwashing
6.9.7 The designer's impact
6.9.8 High complexity
6.9.9 Sustainable font choice


## 6.9.7 The designer's impact

We surround ourselves with design in everyday life, we see it, hold it, stand in it. Design affects us, our identity, lifestyle, attitudes, desires and needs, whether in the form of an object, a brand or as visual communication. Design can have a strong signalling effect and a power to influence. Therefore, the designer has a great responsibility for what is designed and communicated through design, in verbal, visual and material means, as well as the ethical backdrop and left footprints. Used consciously, design can be an impactful and powerful means to convey positive and appropriate sustainable attitudes, as part of the development of sustainable solutions.

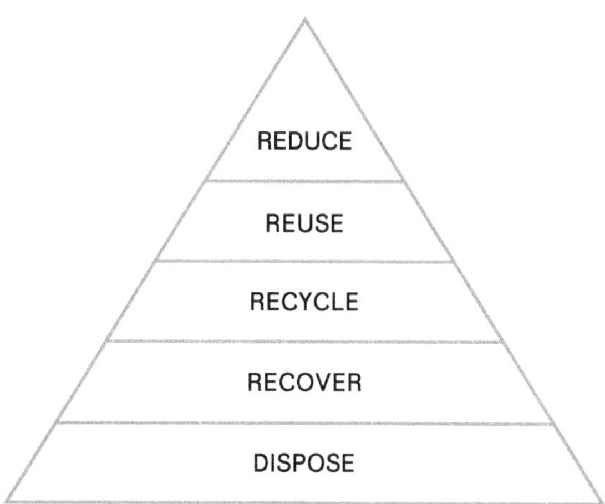


Fig. 6.10 The eco-design pyramid

Designers should acquire the necessary expertise on sustainability and be at the forefront of the field. They will then be able to use their expertise, methods and reasoning to influence their clients to make sustainable choices. For those companies that are at the forefront of sustainability development, the designer should be a natural partner throughout the entire value chain of a product or service development. Through a co-creation that includes the business, the designer and the user, one can create products and services that are user-friendly, environmentally friendly and recyclable.

Further reading
Check out The butterfly diagram at: ellenmacarthurfoundation.org/circular-economy-diagram.

Don't just do good design ... do good! (David Berman, 2008)

#### What does it mean to work sustainably?

Sustainability awareness follows the whole life cycle of a product: from raw materials, processing, distribution and sale to further recycling, reuse or destruction. It starts with the company being aware of who they buy their raw materials from and making sure that it does not involve crime, child labour or any other exploitation of people or the environment. Not least, it is about fair trade: making sure that those who sell raw materials or other goods are paid fairly, so that no one is exploited. It continues with the company taking responsibility for and planning where the waste ends up, so that it does not become a burden on nature, people or the environment. In the best case, the waste is reused in a new way, as part of a circular economy. The buyer and user of a product or service also have a responsibility themselves, by choosing businesses, products and services and are conscious of their role in a sustainable present and future.

**Sustainability should be a hygiene factor in any business, for any designer and in all phases of a design project.**

#### How can the designer make a difference?

The designer can make a difference by 'designing products with such high quality and materiality that circularity is almost not an issue. Take out services that reduce consumption by focusing on renting and reusing rather than owning. Design systems so we can scale up the changes and get them up to speed and get value chains to start talking to each other. The design subject has endless possibilities in this work. What it's about is that they are a new way of thinking about challenge, and if there is something we need more than ever, it is that we think new about challenges' (Bergan, 2022).

*Sustainable design management* means that the designer takes a conscious role and clear leadership in any assignment to ensure more sustainable design solutions, and includes sustainability in all phases of the design process.

#### Designing for circularity

Goods' (2022) appeal: Climate reports point to the need to set sustainability goals and for designers to think of sustainable solutions in all stages of a design project. The UN's sustainability goals are a common platform. What can the designer do? How can designers contribute? The designer can make a difference by designing for a circular economy and changing resource use. Consumption will never be sustainable - everything has a footprint. We as designers can take responsibility. Create the most sustainable consumer brand. We have to be curious and brave. We have to design for circularity. Know the consumer and the target group and how to understand communication and the balance between ethics and aesthetics. We must think: Yes, it should have a great effect and it should sell. As designers, we work towards material sustainability. We no longer just design for humans - we design for the planet. The call is: Limit global warming to 1.5 degrees. Do research, set good goals. Bring out what is important to the brand. If you dare to focus, you will be able to differentiate yourself. The danger is that everyone becomes too generic. Here are our suggestions (Goods, 2022):

1) Formulate the problems and solve them.
2) Do deep research. We have to get to know the whole business. We have to understand production and material selection, sales and

distribution and all departments. One has to understand the entire customer journey, the value chain and the supply chain. How is the picture today?

3) How to navigate 17 goals and 169 targets? Make realistic short-term moves and set long-term goals. You do not win the customer by talking about all the sustainability goals. You win by focusing on the sustainability concepts that are relevant to their brand and act on them.
4) Choose a focus. Everyone must understand the focus, why it is chosen. By focusing, the customers can understand the angle you create. That way you also build loyalty to the brand among the consumers. What is the focus? You must choose? Is it contents, materials, production, distribution or recycling? Remember to set realistic goals in the short term and ambitious goals in the long term.
5) The company's values are related to their behaviour, actions and promises. The values are defined in their overall strategy, their core values and value proposition. Suggest sustainable value propositions as the essence of the business model.
6) Main factors are Cost (economic), Footprint (environmental), Brand (social). Cost for the company. Real corporate ownership and real change take time to conceptualise, internally in the company and externally in the market. Build brand loyalty through real commitment and real change.
7) Develop ideas for solutions that make the use of sustainable materials possible. Work with sustainability and connect with the brand. Use as much recyclable material as possible. Think circular economy. Change resource use. Design for real change. Combine sustainability and brand building without compromising on quality and aesthetics.
8) Be aware of how you talk about sustainability. Sustainability has become a buzzword. Ensure clear communication about responsibility and choice of focus both internally and externally. Avoid using buzzwords without content. Tell the consumer what the material is made of. If there is plastic and paper together, where should I put this? Be sure to label; it's complex.

### 6.9.8 High complexity

Designers and non-designers across the globe face increasingly complex problems of social, economic and environmental character which need to be resolved. Complex problems or wicked problems are not easily solved, if at all (2.3.9 Wicked problems). Such tasks often include several interwoven problems and require a systemic approach to arrive at root causes, which needs to be addressed and solved by multidisciplinary teams (2.8.5 Giga mapping, 4.3.18 Systemic design). The report 'Beyond Net zero. A Systemic Design Approach' launched by the Design Council in April 2021, is a systemic design framework developed to help designers working on major complex challenges that involve people across different disciplines and sectors. 'It places our people and our planet at the heart of design' (Design Council, 2021). The framework is available in the publication, *Beyond Net zero: A Systemic Approach* (2021, p. 42–53).



> 'With environmental issues such as global warming, pollution and the depletion of natural resources threatening our very existence, corporations must learn to reduce, reuse and recycle in order to protect our planet while taking care of people and maximising profit' (Anaheim University 2022).

## 6.9.9 Sustainable font choice

Fig. 6.11 The figure shows two typefaces *Ryman Eco* and Ecofont Vera Sans which are both designed to use less printing ink.

Even small steps can make a big difference, not only in terms of saving the environment, but also in terms of saving money. One example is a scientific project that 14-year-old Suvir Mirchandani carried out in 2014. He was inspired by a desire to reduce paper use and ink for printing at his school. Suvir explained to CNN that ink is twice as expensive as the French perfume Chanel No. 5. Starting with the letters e, t, a, o and r, in the typefaces Garamond, Times New Roman, Century Gothic and Comic Sans, he measured how much ink was used for each letter. In addition, he measured the difference in weight. From this analysis, Suvir found that by using Garamond medium, which has thinner strokes, his school district could reduce ink consumption by 24 per cent, saving as much as £21,000 a year. He conducted the experiment on five pages printed by the US Government. Based on an estimated annual consumption of ink at a cost of £467 million, Suvir concluded that if the government used Garamond exclusively, it could save almost 30 per cent – or £136 million a year. In addition, it would mean significant savings on paper and postage (CNN, Stix 2014). Shortly after, Suvir's experiment was widely reported in the media; *The Independent* came up with a calculation showing that the claim was not completely on target. They concluded that the most sustainable way was to send as much as possible online[42] (Vincent, 2014).

The idea of ink-saving fonts was not entirely new. Ecofont Vera Sans (originally called Eco Sans) was developed in 2010 by SPRANQ in the Netherlands to reduce ink consumption in printing. Each character in the font contains small holes, reducing the amount of ink required by approximately 15 per cent compared to the Vera Sans font family on which Ecofont Sans is based. The font received a lot of attention and won several awards ('Ecofont,' n.d.).

Ryman Eco
Ecofont Vera Sans

Ryman Eco
Ecofont Vera Sans

Fig. 6.11 Sustainable font choice

In 2017, another font attracted attention: Ryman Eco, an environmentally sustainable font developed by the Monotype Type director Dan Rhatigan in collaboration with Grey London and the British stationery retailer Ryman. It uses on average 33 per cent less ink than standard fonts. The aim was to create the world's most attractive, sustainable font by finding the optimal balance between saving ink, legibility and attractiveness (Budrick 2017; rymaneco.co.uk; ultrasparky.org).[43] The font has been well received by environmentalists and the design community, although critics believe it is attractive but not sufficiently legible as body text.

Further reading
As early as 2009 the Canadian David Berman, wrote the book 'Do Good Design: How Designers Can Change The World', with a foreword by Erik Spiekermann. It was co-published with AIGA, the world's largest and oldest professional member organisation for designers with over 25,000 members.

42 '"Save $400m by switching fonts": Unfortunately it won't work for the US govern ment – or for you', James Vincent (1 April 2014).

43 *Ryman Eco* can be downloaded for free at rymaneco.co.uk. *Ecofont Vera Sans* can be downloaded at fonts4free.net/eco-font-vera-sans-font.html.

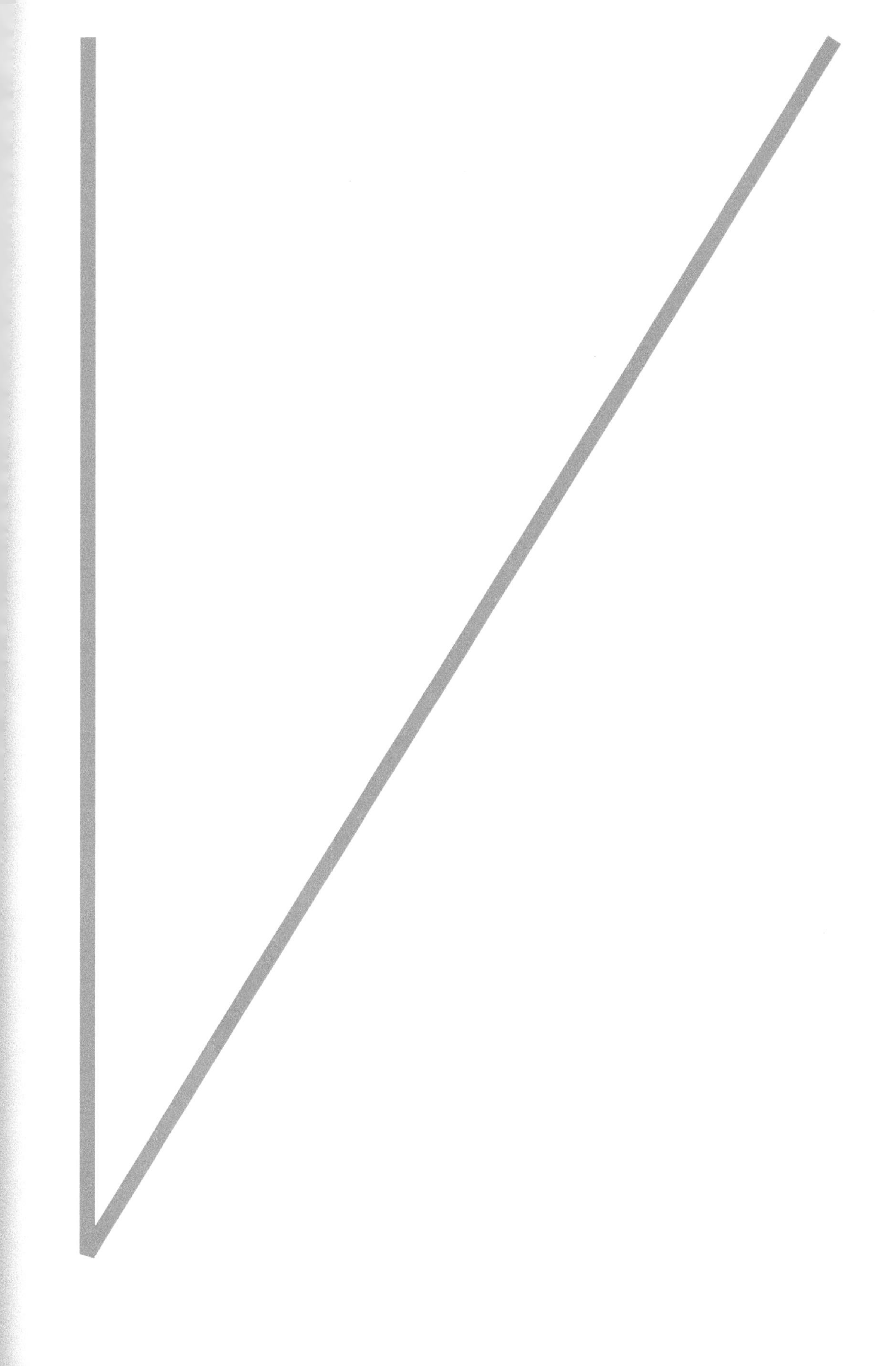

## Books and articles


16Personalities (n.d.). It's so incredible to finally be understood. *16personalities*. https://www.16personalities.com/

Aaker, D. A., & Keller, K. L. (1990). Consumer Evaluations of Brand Extensions. *Journal of Marketing, 54*(1), 27–41. https://doi.org/ https://doi.org/10.1177/002224299005400102

Ad Age, (2012). Interview of Haas, J. Avis's Marketing Director,

Adler, C. (2011). Ideas are overrated: startup guru Eric Ries' radical new theory. *Wired*. wired.com/2011/08/st-qareis/

Agile Alliance (2021). Manifesto for Agile Software Development. *Agile Alliance*. https://www.agilealliance.org/agile101/ the-agile-manifesto/

AIGA Standard Form of Agreement (2020). https://www.aiga.org/ resources/aiga-standard-form-of-agreement-for-design-services

Akre, J. & Scharning, H. S. (2016). *Prosjekthåndboka 3.0*. 3rd Edition. Oslo, Universitetsforlaget.

Akiko. (2022). Website Design Wireframe Examples. *Edraw*. https:// www.edrawsoft.com/website-design-wireframe-example.html

Albrighton, T. (31 August 2010). How to Define Your Brand's tone of voice. *ABC Copywriting*. abccopywriting.com/2010/08/31/ tone-of-voice-brand

Alizadeh, A., Moshabaki, A., Hoseini, S. H. K., Naiej, A. K. (2014). The Comparison of Product and Corporate Branding Strategy: a conceptual framework. *IOSR Journal of Business and Management* 16 (1), 14–24. C016141424.pdf

Altrichter, H., Feldman, A., Posch, P. & Somekh, B. (2008). *Teachers Investigate Their Work: An introduction to action research across the professions*. Routledge. p. 147 (2nd edition).

America's Leading Design Firm. New York: Currency Books.

Amor, J. (2016). Break Through the Noise: Optimize Share of Voice to Grow Market Share. *Linkedin*. https://www.linkedin.com/pulse/ break-through-noise-optimize-share-voice-grow-market-julie-amor-mha/?articleId=6148594699432181760

Amundsen, H. (2015). Pitch perfect! Seks tips for en vel-lykket pitch. hegnar.no. https://www. hegnar.no/Nyheter/Livsstil/2015/02/ Pitch-Perfect-Seks-tips-for-en-vellykket-pitch. https:// hildeamundsen. no/pitch/

Anaheim University. (2022). Sustainable Management. *Anaheim*. https://www.anaheim.edu/what-is-sustainable-management. html

Andersen, E. S., Grude, K. V., Haug, T. (2016). Målrettet prosjektstyring. NKI-Forlaget, Oslo

Anderson, D. J. (2010). *Kanban*. Blue Hole Press.

Andrew Chakhoyan, A. (2020). Strategic narrative: What it is and how it can help your company find meaning. *World Economic Forum*. https://www.weforum.org/agenda/2020/12/how-a-company-s-strategic-narrative-should-be-like-a-north-star/

Anholt, S. (1998). Nation-brands of the twenty-first century. *Journal of Brand Management, 5*, 395–406. https://link.springer.com/ article/10.1057/bm.1998.30

Annweiler, B. (2019). *Point of Purpose. How purposeful brands attract top employees, seduce customers, & fuel profit*. Noteworthy Books.

Antalis. (2014). The Green White Paper: Antalis green star system. *Antalis*. https://www.antalis.com/wp-content/uploads/2011/09/ AT-WHITE-PAPER-HQ.pdf

Anthony, S. D. A., Johnson, M. W., Sinfield, J. V., Altman, E. J. (2008). *Innovator's Guide to Growth – Putting Disruptive Innovation to Work*. Harvard Business School Press.

Anuupadhyay. (2021). Good Coding Practices for Backend Developers. *Geeksforgeeks*. https://www.geeksforgeeks.org/ good-coding-practices-for-backend-developers/?ref=rp

Arcalea. (2022). Share of Voice as a Strategic Accelerator. *Arcalea*. https://www.arcalea.com/blog/ share-of-voice-as-a-strategic-accelerator

Archer, L. B. (1979). Design as a Discipline. *Design Studies 1*(1), 18–20.

Archer, L. B. (1979). Whatever Became of Design Methodology? *Design Studies, 1*(1), 17–20.

Archer, L.B. (1965). *Systematic method for designers*. London: Council of Industrial Design.

ArcticPaper. (2012). Art workshop. The Munken Guide to Uncoated Paper. *ArcticPaper*. https://www.arcticpaper.com/ inspiration-news/articles/art-workshop/

Arnheim, R. (1969). *Visual Thinking*. University of California Press.

Asana.com. 5 steps to writing a clear project brief https://asana.com/ resources/project-brief.

Asimos, T. (2020). Content-first Approach to Redesigning Your Firm's Website. *CircleStudio*. https://www.circlesstudio.com/blog/ content-first-approach-redesigning-website/

Athuraliya, A. (2021). The Easy Guide to Creating an Effective Service Blueprint. *Creately*. https://creately.com/blog/diagrams/ what-is-a-service-blueprint/

Auh, S., Bell, S. J., McLeod, C. S., Shih, E. (2007). Co-Production and Customer Loyalty in Financial Services. *Journal of Retailing*. 83(3), p. 359–370. https://doi.org/10.1016/j.jretai.2007.03.001

Balaz, A. (2015). A Template for JTBD Interviews. *Job to be Done*. https://jtbd.info/ jobs-to-be-done-interview-template-30421972ab2a

Balmer, J. M. T., & Greyser, S.A. (n.d.). Revealing the corporation: An integrative framework. slideplayer.com.

Balmer, J. M. T & Soenen, G. B. (1999). The Acid Test of Corporate Identity Management™. *Journal of Marketing Management 15*(1), 69–92. DOI:10.1362/026725799784870441

Barnett, M. L (2006). Finding a Working Balance Between Competitive and Communal Strategies. *Journal of management studies. 43*(8), 1753–1773. doi.org/10.1111/j.1467-6486.2006.00661.x

Barney, J. B. (1991). Firm Resources and Sustained Competitive Advantage. *Journal of Management, 15*(5), 171–180.

Barney, J. B. (1995). Looking inside for Competitive Advantage *JSTOR, 9*(4), 49–61. https://www.jstor.org/stable/4165288

Barrett, S. (2019). The Key Differences between B2C & B2B Sales Market Segmentation. *SalesEssential*. https://www. salesessentials.com/2019/11/blog/the-key-differences-between-b2c-b2b-sales-market-segmentation/

Bason, C. (2017). Leading Public Design: How Managers Engage with Design to Transform Public Governance. *Copenhagen Business School. PhD Series 21.2017*.

Battie, A. (2021). The 3 Pillars of Corporate Sustainability. *Investopedia*. https://www.investopedia.com/articles/ investing/100515/three-pillars-corporate-sustainability.asp

Baytas, A. M. (2021). The Three Faces of Design Research. https:// www.designdisciplin.com/the-three-faces-of-design-research/

Beale, M. (2022). Why AI-Driven Innovation Should Be on Your Radar. *Itonics*. https://www.itonics-innovation.com/blog/ why-ai-driven-innovation

Beckman, S. L., & Barry, M. (2007). Innovation as a Learning Process: Embedding Design Thinking. *California Management Review, 50*(1), 23–56. DOI:10.2307/41166415

Beckman, S. L., & Barry, M. (2007). Innovation as a Learning Process: Embedding Design Thinking. *California Management Review, 50*, 25–56.

Bedrina, O. (n.d.) What Is a Storyboard and How Can You Make One for Your Video? *Wave.video*. https://wave.video/blog/ what-is-a-storyboard/

Beilock, S. (2019). How Diverse Teams Produce Better Outcomes. *Forbes*. https://www.forbes.com/sites/sianbeilock/2019/04/04/ how-diversity-leads-to-better-outcomes/

Belicove, M. E. (2013). Understanding Goals, Strategy, Objectives And Tactics In The Age Of Social. *Forbes*. https://www.forbes. com/sites/mikalbelicove/2013/09/27/understanding-goals-strategies-objectives-and-tactics-in-the-age-of-social/

Belludi, N. (2016). Inspirational Quotations by Pearl S. Buck (#638). *Right Attitudes*. https://www.rightattitudes.com/2016/06/26/ pearl-s-buck/

Bencini, G. (2021). User centered and environment centered design... why addressing needs means finding a business opportunity for sustainability. Medium. https://medium. com/sdi-service-design-innovation/user-centered-and-environment-centered-design-why-addressing-needs-means-finding-a-business-ba827a0d0317

Bergem, A. (2013). Slik lager du en service design blueprint for tjenesten din! *Sayitblogg*. https://no.pinterest.com/ pin/482940760036933968/

Bergen, M., & Peteraf, M. A. (2002). Competitor Identification and Competitor Analysis: A Broad-Based Managerial Approach. *Managerial and Decision Economics, 23*, 157–169. https://doi.org/ https://doi.org/10.1002/mde.1059

Berman, D. (2008). *Do Good Design* (1st ed.). New Riders Pub.

Beyer, C. (2020). Edmund Husserl. In *Stanford Encyclopedia of Philosophy*. https://plato.stanford.edu/entries/husserl/

Binet, L., & Field, P. (2013). The Long and the Short of it: Balancing Short and Long-Term Marketing Strategies (1st ed.). Institute of Practitioners in Advertising.

Birken, E. G., & Curry, B. (2021). Understanding Return On Investment (ROI). *Forbes advisor*. https://www.forbes.com/advisor/investing/roi-return-on-investment/

Birkigt, K., Stadler, M. M. (1986). *Corporate Identity, Grundlagen, Funktionen, Fallspielen*. Verlag Moderne Industrie.

Blekesaune. (n.d.). Kvalitative intervjuer og analyse av beretninger. https://docplayer.me/19582203-Forelesning-21-kvalitative-intervjuer-og-analyse-av-beretninger.html

Blenko, M. W., Mankins, M. C., Rogers, P. (2010). The Decision-driven Organization. *Harvard Business Review, 88(6)*, 54. https://hbr.org/2010/06/the-decision-driven-organization

Bocken, N. M. P., Short, S. W., Rana, P., Evans S. (2014). A literature and practice review to develop sustainable business model archetypes. *Journal of Cleaner Production, 65*, 42–56. https://doi.org/https://doi.org/10.1016/j.jclepro.2013.11.039

Bojukyan, E. (2022). 52 Video Marketing Statistics 2022. *Renderforest*. https://www.renderforest.com/blog/video-marketing-statistics

Bolano, A. (2018). List Of Geometric Shapes And Their Names. *Science Trends*. https://sciencetrends.com/list-of-geometric-shapes-and-their-names/

Booth, A., & Lien, L. (2010). Pictogram-me. *Researchcatalogue.net*. https://www.researchcatalogue.net/view/157238/296059

Borgdorff, H. (2006). *Amsterdam School of the Arts*. The_debate_on_research_in_the_arts.pdf

Boyle, R. (2011). 13-year-old designs super-efficient solar array based on the fibonacci sequence. *Popular Science*. https://www.popsci.com/technology/article/2011-08/13-year-old-designs-breakthrough-solar-array-based-fibonacci-sequence/

Bradford, A., & Weisberger, M. (2017). Deductive Reasoning vs. Inductive Reasoning. https://www.livescience.com/21569-deduction-vs-induction.html

Bradley, S. (2010). How To Use Space In Design. *Vanseo Design*. https://vanseodesign.com/web-design/design-space/

Braga, M. (2016). The Value of Design: An issue of vision, creativity and interpretation. DOI:10.21606/drs.2016.129. Conference: DRS2016. Brighton, 5, p. 1865–1881

Brain Quote. (n.d.) https://www.brainyquote.com/quotes/walt_disney_131670

Brand House (n.d.) Brand House Design. https://www.brandhouse.no/

BrandUniq. (2011). Points of Parity versus Points of Differentiation. https://branduniq.com/2011/points-of-parity-versus-points-of-differentiation/

Brenner, M. (2021). What is Content Marketing, Really? *Marketing insider group*. https://marketinginsidergroup.com/content-marketing/what-is-content-marketing/

Bringhurst, R. (1997). *The Elements of Typographic Style*. Hartley & Marks Publishers. https://readings.design/PDF/the_elements_of_typographic_style.pdf

Bringhurst, R. (2004). *The Elements of Typographic Style*. Hartley & Marks Publishers.

BritishDesignCouncil. (2021). A Systemic Approach. *Beyond Net Zero*, 42–53.

BritishDesignCouncil. (2021). *Beyond Net Zero*. https://www.designcouncil.org.uk/resources/guide/beyond-net-zero-systemic-design-approach

Bromley, D. B. (1995). *Reputation, Image, and Impression Management*. John Wiley & Sons. doi.org/10.1002/mar.4220120207

Brown, E. (2017). The Three Levels Of Design: Visceral, Behavioral And Reflective! *Designmantic*. https://www.designmantic.com/blog/interactive-media/3-levels-of-design/

Brown, T. (2009). *Change by Design: How design thinking transforms*

Bryman, A. (2012). *Social Research Methods* (4. ed.). Oxford University Press.

Brønn, P., & Ihlen, Ø. (2009). *Åpen eller innadvendt. Omdømmebygging for organisasjoner* (1st ed.). Gyldendal, Oslo.

Bubolz, M. M., Eicher, J. B., Evers, S. J., Sontag, M. S. (1980). A Human Ecological Approach to Quality of Life: *Social indicators research, 7*, 103–106.

Buchanan, R. (2001). Design Research and the New Learning. *Mit press journals. Design Issues, 17*(4): 3–23. Tilgjengelig fra: Design Research and the New Learning Hentet 26. mai 2018 fra: ida.liu.se/divisions/hcs/ixs/material/DesResMeth09/Theory/01-buchanan.pdf

Budapest Business Journal. (2021). Coca-Cola Testing Recyclable Paper Bottle in Hungary. *Bbj*. https://bbj.hu/economy/environment/recycling/coca-cola-testing-recyclable%C2%A0paper-bottle-in-hungary

Burgoon, J. K., Buller, D. B., White, C. H., Afifi, W., Buslig, L. S. (1999). The Role of Conversational Involvement in Deceptive Interpersonal Interactions. *Personality and Social Psychology Bulletin*. https://doi.org/https://doi.org/10.1177/0146167299025006003

Burgoon, J. K., Guerrero, L.K., Floyd, K. (2009). *Nonverbal Communication* (1st ed.). Routledge.

Burke, C. (2021). New Laws on alcohol advertising during sports and children's events come into force today. *Thejournal.ie*. https://www.thejournal.ie/new-laws-alcohol-advertising-sports-children-5598834-Nov2021/

Butterfield, J. (2022). Raison d'être In *Oxford Reference*.

Buxton, B. (2009). AEIOU. How to Think Outside the Box. *BusinessWeek*. https://billbuxton.com/BW%20Assets/08.%20Pencil.pdf

Canvasgeneration. (n/a). AEIOU Empathy Map. *canvasgeneration.com* https://www.canvasgeneration.com/canvas/aeiou-empathy-map/

Carps, K. (2017). Text Alignment in Web Design. *GuppyFish Web Design*. https://guppyfishweb.com/web-design/text-alignment-center/

Cartel Damage Claims (CDC). Cartel Damage Claims (CDC). www.carteldamageclaims.com/.

Carter, N., Bryant-Lukosius, D., DiCenso, A., Blythe, J., Neville, A. (2014). The use of triangulation in qualitative research. *Oncology Nursing Forum, 41*(5), 545–547.

Chaffey, D. (2016). *Digital Marketing: Strategy, Implementation and Practice*. (6th ed). Pearson

Chaffey, D., & Smith, P. R. (2008). *Emarketing Excellence, Planning and optimising your digital marketing* (3rd ed.). Oxford: Butterworth-Heinemann.

Charak, D. (2020). Why Triple Diamond is a Better Paradigm than the Double Diamond. *Dinker Charak*. https://www.ddiinnxx.com/why-triple-diamond-better-paradigm-than-double-diamond/

Checkland, P. (1981). *Systems Thinking. Systems Practice*. Chichester: John Wiley and sons.

Checkland, P. (2000). Soft Systems Methodology: A thirty year retrospective. *Systems Research and Behavioral Science, 17*(1), 11–58. https://doi.org/10.1002/1099-1743(200011)17:1+<::AID-SRES374>3.0.CO;2-O

Checkland, P., & Poulter, J. (2006). *Learning for Action: A short definitive account of soft systems methodology and its use, for practitioners, teachers and students*. Chichester: John Wiley and Sons.

Checkland, P., & Poulter, J. (2010). *Soft Systems Methodology*. London: Springer. 10.1007/978-1-84882-809-4_5

Cherry, K. (2020). How Applied Research Is Used in Psychology. *Verywell Mind*. https://www.verywellmind.com/what-is-applied-research-2794820#toc-basic-vs-applied-research

Cherry, K. (2021). The Trichromatic Theory of Color Vision. *ReoVeme*. https://no.reoveme.com/forstaa-trichromatic-theory-of-color-vision/

Chrisholm, J. (n.d.) What is co-design? Design for Europe. Hentet 29. mai 2018 fra designforeurope.eu/what-co-design http://designforeurope.eu/what-co-design

Chron Contributor. (2020). Line Extension vs. Brand Extension. *Chron*. https://smallbusiness.chron.com/line-extension-vs-brand-extension-36797.html

Chung, E. (2020). Generate Crazy Ideas With This Design Sprint Method. *UX Planet*. https://uxplanet.org/generate-crazy-ideas-with-this-design-sprint-method-c6a36a16c3d5

Churchman, C. W. (1967). Free for All: wicked problems. *Management Science, 4*, 141–146. https://doi.org/http://dx.doi.org/10.1287/mnsc.14.4.B141

CMI (Chr. Michelsen Institute) (2012). Henri Fayol (1841–1925). Planning, Organisation, Command, Coordination, Control Thinker, 016. https://www.managers.org.uk/~/media/Campus%20Resources/Henri%20Fayol%20%20Planning%20organisation%20command%20coordination%20and%20control.ashx

Coca-Cola Company (n.d.). https://www.coca-colacompany.com/
Collier, K. W. (2011). Agile Analytics: A Value-Driven Approach to Business Intelligence and Data Warehousing (Agile Software Development Series). *Addison-Wesley Professional*. https://www.amazon.com/Agile-Analytics-Value-Driven-Intelligence-Warehousing/dp/032150481X
Collins, J. (1994). BHAG. *Jim Collins*. https://www.jimcollins.com/concepts/bhag.html
Collins, J. (n.d.) BHAG. Excerpts from Built to Last (1994). https://www.jimcollins.com/concepts/bhag.html
Colman, H. L. (2014). *Organisasjonsidentitet*. Cappelen Damm Akademisk, Oslo
Compareyourfootprint. (2017). Measuring Key KPI's for Sustainability as a Business. *Compare your Footprint*. https://www.compareyourfootprint.com/measuring-key-kpis-sustainability-business/
Cook, M. L. (n.d.). Quotation. In *Goodreads*.
Copyrightlaws.com (2022). Introduction to international copyright law. https://www.copyrightlaws.com/introduction-international-copyright-law/
Council, B. D. (2005). What is the Framework for Innovation? Design Council's evolved Double Diamond. *Design Council*. https://www.designcouncil.org.uk/news-opinion/what-framework-innovation-design-councils-evolved-double-diamond
Creately. (2021). 5 Gap Analysis Tools to Identify and Close the Gaps in Your Business. *creately.com*. https://creately.com/blog/diagrams/gap-analysis-tools/#swot
Cross, N. (1982). Designerly Ways of Knowing *ScienceDirect*, *3*(4), 221–227. https://doi.org/https://doi.org/10.1016/0142-694X(82)90040-0
Crowe. (n.d.). Resources for Youth ESG Strategy. *Crowe*. https://www.crowe.com/insights/issues/esg-strategy
Cummings, S., & Angwin, D. (2015). *Strategy Builder: How to Create and Communicate More Effective Strategies*. Wiley.
Cuncic, A. (2021). Understanding Internal and External Validity. *Verywellmind*. https://www.verywellmind.com/internal-and-external-validity-4584479
Curtis, H. (2012). Hillman Curtis: The Original 'Digital Designer'. *Hatched*. https://hatchedlondon.com/hillman-curtis-the-original-digital-designer/
d.design. (n.d.). What to Do in Need Finding. *Hasso Plattner Institute of Design at Stanford University*. https://hci.stanford.edu/courses/dsummer/handouts/NeedFinding.pdf
d.studio (n.d.) Design processes. The University of British Columbia. dstudio.ubc.ca/research/toolkit/processes/
Dahl, H. (2013). Minerva livsstilsmodell. *Strategic Business Insights*. strategicbusinessinsights.com/vals/about.shtml
Dahlén, M. (2008). *Creativity Unlimited: Thinking inside the box for business innovation*. John Wiley & Sons.
Dalland, O. (2000). *Metode og oppgaveskriving for studenter*. Gyldendal akademisk, Oslo.
Danish Design Center (2015). The Design Ladder: Four steps of design https://issuu.com/dansk_design_center/docs/design-ladder_en
Davidoff, J. (2019). What is Values-Based Organizational Culture (VBOC), and Why is It Important? https://sparksuccess.com/what-is-values-based-organizational-culture-vboc-and-why-is-it-important/
Davies, M. (2019). The Danish Design Ladder. https://www.mrmattdavies.me/post/the-danish-design-ladder
Davies, S (2012). 6 differences between corporate brands and product brands. Daviesbdm.
Dawood, S. (2018). Pentagram's Natasha Jen: "Design is not a monster you 'unleash' to fix the world. *Design Week*. https://www.designweek.co.uk/issues/5-11-march-2018/
DDC (2018). Design Delivers 2018: How design accelerates your business. *DDC*. https://ddc.dk/design-delivers-2018-how-design-accelerates-your-business/
De Goey, H., Hilletoth, P., Eriksson, L. (2019). Design-Driven Innovation: A systematic literature review. *European Business Review*.
De Mozota, B., & Valade-Amland, S. (2020). *Design: A Business Case: Thinking, Leading, and Managing by Design* (1st ed.). Business Expert Press
Dearie, K. J. (2020). CCPA Privacy Policy. *Termly*. https://termly.io/resources/articles/ccpa-privacy-policy/
Deloitte. (2020). Creating human connection at enterprise scale. *DEL-5089_Emo2_White_Paper_v8.indd*. https://www2.deloitte.com/content/dam/Deloitte/global/Documents/Technology/gx-tech-creating-human-connection-at-enterprise-scale.pdf
DemandJump. (2020). Types of Market Trends: An Industry Trends Analysis. https://www.demandjump.com/blog/types-of-market-trends-an-industry-trends-analysis
Denning, S., (2020). Doing Agile Right: Transformation Without Chaos. Harvard Business Review Press.
Denny, J. (2020). What is an Algorithm? How the computers know what to do with data. *Business Standard*. https://www.business-standard.com/article/technology/what-is-an-algorithm-how-the-computers-know-what-to-do-with-data-120101700251_1.html
DesignCouncil. (2007). The Value of Design Factfinder. *British Design Council*. https://www.designcouncil.org.uk/sites/default/files/asset/document/TheValueOfDesignFactfinder_Design_Council.pdf
DesignCouncil. (2013). Leading Business by Design Report. *British Design Council*. https://www.designcouncil.org.uk/resources/report/leading-business-design
Design Council (2015) The Role and Value of Design. Working paper. designcouncil.org.uk
Design Council. (2017). The Dark Matter of Design: Making the value and impact of design more visible. *Design Council*. https://www.designcouncil.org.uk/news-opinion/dark-matter-design-making-value-and-impact-design-more-visible
Designmodo. (2022). Wireframing, Prototyping, Mockuping – What's the Difference? https://designmodo.com/wireframing-prototyping-mockuping/
Dixon-Fyle, S., Hunt, V., Prince, S., Dolan. K. (2020). *Diversity Wins: How inclusion matters*. McKinsey & Company. https://www.mckinsey.com/~/media/mckinsey/featured%20insights/diversity%20and%20inclusion/diversity%20wins%20how%20inclusion%20matters/diversity-wins-how-inclusion-matters-vf.pdf
DJ Team. (2020). Types of Market Trends: An Industry Trends Analysis. *Demand Jump*. https://www.demandjump.com/blog/types-of-market-trends-an-industry-trends-analysis
Dlrtoolkit. (n.d.). Fly On The Wall. *dlrtoolkit.com*. http://dlrtoolkit.com/fly-on-the-wall/
Doga, Design and Architecture Norway, https://doga.no/
Doga, Design and Architecture Norway. (2022). Hvordan kan design øke farten på det grønne skiftet? https://www.youtube.com/watch?v=DS2hJowOiB4
DOGA. (n.d.). Oslo Manifesto Home. *Oslo Manifesto*. https://www.oslomanifesto.com/
Drew, C. (2021). All 8 Models Of Communication, Explained! *Helpful Professor*. https://helpfulprofessor.com/communication-models/#google_vignette
Dube, N. (2021). Packaging and The Metaverse: AR, VR And Beyond. https://www.industrialpackaging.com/blog/packaging-and-the-metaverse
Duczek, M. (2021). Design for Innovation: Design Thinking and / or Design-driven Innovation. *Linkedin*. https://www.linkedin.com/pulse/design-innovation-thinking-design-driven-markus-duczek/?trk=public_profile_article_view
Eberle, R. F. (1971). *Scamper: Games for imagination development* (1 ed.). Buffalo.
Eby, K. (2021). Expert Tips for Writing a Project Description With Free Templates. *Smartsheet*. https://www.smartsheet.com/content/project-description
Egeland, J. N. (2016). Grafill 25 år: Intervju med Aslak Gurholt Rønsen *Grafill*. https://www.grafill.no/magasin/grafill-25-ar-intervju-med-aslak-gurholt-rnsen
Eggink, W. (2019). *Design research in Design education* https://www.researchgate.net/publication/334084615
Eleken. (2022). Hiring the Product Team. UI/UX Designer vs Front-end Developer. *Eleken*. https://www.eleken.co/blog-posts/ui-ux-designer-vs-front-end-developer
Ellen Macarthur Foundation. (n.d.). What is a circular economy? *Ellen Macarthur Foundation*.
Ensign, P. C. (2001). Value Chain Analysis and Competitive Advantage. *Journal of General Management*, *27*(1), 18–42. https://doi.org/https://doi-org.ezproxy2.usn.no/10.1177/030630700102700102

EPA, (n.d.). Sustainable Materials Management Basics. *EPA, United States Environmental Protection Agency*. https://www.epa.gov/smm/sustainable-materials-management-basics

EPO. (2019). Joint EPO-EUIPO study finds strong link between growth of SMEs and their use of Intellectual Property. *European Patent Office* https://www.epo.org/news-events/press/releases/archive/2019/20190521.html

EPO. (2021). The European Patent Convention. *European Patent Office* https://www.epo.org/law-practice/legal-texts/html/epc/2020/e/ar52.html

Eriksen, R. (2010). Lean eller agile, hva passer best for deg? *Soprasteria*. https://blog.soprasteria.no/blog/2010/05/24/lean-eller-agile/

Essam B. I., & Tina H. (2020) The impact of internal, external, and competitor factors on marketing strategy performance, *Journal of Strategic Marketing, 28*(7), 639–658, DOI: 10.1080/0965254X.2019.1609571

EthnoHub. (n.d.). AEIOU Framework. *help.ethnohub.com*. https://help.ethnohub.com/guide/aeiou-framework

European Parliament. (2021). Circular Economy: Definition, importance and benefits. *News European* Parliament.https://www.europarl.europa.eu/news/en/headlines/economy/20151201STO05603/circular-economy-definition-importance-and-benefits

Evans, S., Vladimirova, Holgado, M., van Fossen, K. Yang, M., Silva, E. A., Barlow, C. Y. (2017). Business Model Innovation for Sustainability: Towards a Unified Perspective for Creation of Sustainable Business Models. https://doi.org/DOI:10.1002/BSE.1939

Fangen, K. (2004). *Deltagende observasjon*. Fagbokforlaget, Bergen.

Faste, T., & Faste, H. (2012). *Demystifying 'Design research': Design is not research, research is design*. IDSA Education Symposium 2012, Boston.

Feigenbaum, E. (2017). Is There a Difference Between Organizational & Corporate Culture? *BizFluent*. https://bizfluent.com/info-8371893-there-between-organizational-corporate-culture.html

Findeli, A. (2010). Searching for Design~Research Questions: Some Conceptual Clarifications. https://www.researchgate.net/publication/235700600_Searching_for_DesignResearch_Questions_Some_Conceptual_Clarifications

Fletcher, A. (2001). *The Art of Looking Sideways*. London: Phaidon Press.

FO Future Orientation (2006). The Megatrends Matter Issue. *Copenhagen Institute for Future Studies*. https://www.yumpu.com/en/document/read/20465932/fo052006-the-megatrends-matter-issue-copenhagen-institute-for-

Fortune. (2021). 100 Best Companies to Work For. https://fortune.com/best-companies/2021/

Foskett, M. (2021). Font Size Conversion: Pixel-point-em-rem-percent. *Websemantics*. https://websemantics.uk/tools/font-size-conversion-pixel-point-em-rem-percent/

Fraser, H. M. A. (2009). Designing Business: New Models for Success. *Dmi:review, 20*(2), 56–65. https://doi.org/10.1111/j.1948-7169.2009.00008.x

Fraser, H. M. A. (2012). *Design Works: How to Tackle Your Toughest Innovation Challenges Through Business Design*. University of Toronto Press

Frayling, C. (1993/94). Research in Art and Design. *Royal College of Art Research*. researchonline.rca.ac.uk/384/3/frayling_research_in_art_and_design_1993.pdf

Frue, K. (2020). Create a PESTLE Analysis Template or Download One For Free. *https://pestleanalysis.com/pestle-analysis-template/*

Frue, K. (2020). PEST Analysis Ultimate Guide: Definition, Template, Examples. *Pestle Analysis*. Create a PESTLE Analysis Template or Download One For Free

Frue, K. (2020). PEST Analysis Ultimate Guide: Definition, Template, Examples. *Pestle Analysis*. https://pestleanalysis.com/pest-analysis/

Fugelsnes, E. (2003). Hjernen vil bedras. *Gemini.no*. https://gemini.no/2003/05/hjernen-vil-bedras/

Fällman, D. (2008). The Interaction Design Research Triangle of Design Practice. *Mit Press Journal 24*(3), 4–18.

Førsund, E. (2015). Hva er forskjellen på content marketing og inbound marketing?» *blogg.markedspartner.no*. https://blogg.markedspartner.no/hva-er-forskjellen-pa-content-marketing-og-inbound-marketing

Gartner. (2022). What Is Artificial Intelligence? *Gartner*. https://www.gartner.com/en/topics/artificial-intelligence

Geelmuyden, A. (2013). *Det gylne snitt. Nøkkelen til naturens og kunstens hemmeligheter* (1st ed.). Kagge Forlag.

Gestalt Institute of Cleveland. Generating powerful, positive change... https://www.gestaltcleveland.org/

Geyser, W. (2022). The Ultimate Influencer Marketing Blueprint for 2022. *Influencer Marketing Hub*. https://influencermarketinghub.com/influencer-marketing/

Geyti, S. (2011). Udvikling & Viden. *UCViden*. https://www.ucviden.dk/files/11153643/Introduktion_til_fokusgruppeinterview_som_metode_til_evaluering.pdf

Gibbons, S. (2017). Service Blueprints: Definition. *Nielsen Norman Group*. https://www.nngroup.com/articles/service-blueprints-definition/

Gisclard-Biondi, H. (2021). The Brand Platform, the Foundation of a Strong Brand Identity. https://www.appvizer.com/magazine/marketing/brand-management/brand-platform

Given, M. L. (2008). Rich Data. *The SAGE Encyclopedia of Qualitative Research Methods*. https://doi.org/https://dx.doi.org/10.4135/9781412963909

Gjoko, M. (2015). *Research for Designers* (1st ed.). SAGE Publications.

Goodman, M. (n.d.). Systems Thinking: What, why, when, where, and how? *Systems Thinker*. https://thesystemsthinker.com/systems-thinking-what-why-when-where-and-how/

GoodsAS. (n.d.). Goods Index. *Goods Index*. https://index.goods.no/

Gordon, J. (2021). Mintzberg's 5Ps of Strategy – Explained. *The Business Professor*. https://thebusinessprofessor.com/en_US/business-management-amp-operations-strategy-entrepreneurship-amp-innovation/mintzbergs-5ps-of-strategy

Gosh, I. (2021). Timeline: Key Events in U.S. History that Defined Generations. *Visual Capitalist*. https://www.visualcapitalist.com/timeline-of-us-events-that-defined-generations/

Gotsi, M. & Wilson, A. M. (2001). Corporate Reputation: Seeking a definition. *Corporate Communications: An International Journal, 6*(1), 24–30. https://doi.org/10.1108/13563280110381189

Govindarajan og Trible (2010). *The Other Side of Innovation. Solving the Execution Challenge*. Harvard Business Review Press

Graphic Gameplan: Leader's Guide – Strategic Visioning Guides Paperback – January 1, 1996 by The Grove Consultants International (Author): (Amazone)

Gray, D. (2017). Updated Empathy Map Canvas. https://medium.com/the-xplane-collection/updated-empathy-map-canvas-46df22df3c8a

Grimsgaard, W. (2018). *Design og strategi. Prosesser og metoder for strategisk utvikling av design*. Cappelen Damm Akademisk.

Grimsgaard, W., & Farbrot, A. (2020). Hvordan strategisk bruk av design kan øke merkeverdien. *Magma*, 59–67.

Grovetools Inc. Gameplan. https://grovetools-inc.com/collections/graphic-gameplan

Grow. (n.d.). Tomorrow's Design Learners. Grow. https://grow.empdl.com/#Education

GSA, U.S. General Services Administration (2021). Sustainable Design. *GSA*. https://www.gsa.gov/real-estate/design-construction/design-excellence/sustainability/sustainable-design

Guides, S. (2020). The 2020 Scrum Guide. *Scrum Guides*. https://scrumguides.org/scrum-guide.html#scrum-definition

Guity Novin. (2016). A History of Graphic Design. *Guity Novin*. guity-novin.blogspot.com/2011/07/chapter-42-swiss-grade-style-and-dutch.html

Guo, H. (2015, 6 April). When Change Is Constant: A Spiral UX Design Model. uxmatters.com/mt/archives/2015/04/when-change-is-constant-a-spiral-ux-design-model.php https://www.uxmatters.com/mt/archives/2015/04/when-change-is-constant-a-spiral-ux-design-model.php

Hager, P. J., Scheiber, H. J., Corbin, N. C. (1997). *Designing & Delivering: Scientific, Technical, and Managerial Presentations* (1 ed.). John Wiley & Sons.

Halogen (n.d.) System Oriented Design, *Halogen*. https://halogen.no/en/services/systems-oriented-design

Hanifan, O. (2021). What is audience engagement, and how do I do it? *Mentimeter*. https://www.mentimeter.com/blog/audience-energizers/what-is-audience-engagement-and-how-do-i-do-it

Hanlon, A. (2016). Digital Marketing Model: Lauterborn's 4 Cs. *Smart Insights*.
Hanlon, A. (2017). How to use the 7Ps Marketing Mix? *Smart Insights*. smartinsights.com/marketing-planning/marketing-models/how-to-use-the-7ps-marketing-mix/
Hanlon, A. (2021). The segmentation, targeting, positioning (STP) marketing model. *SmartInsight*. https://www.smartinsights.com/digital-marketing-strategy/customer-segmentation-targeting/segmentation-targeting-and-positioning/
Hanna, D., & Dempster, M. (2016). Looking at Levels of Measurement in Psychology Statistics. *Dummies*. https://www.dummies.com/article/body-mind-spirit/emotional-health-psychology/psychology/research/looking-at-levels-of-measurement-in-psychology-statistics-169542/
Hansen, K. V., & Derdowski, L. A. (2020). Sustainable Food Consumption in Nursing Homes: Less Food Waste with the Right Plate Color? *Sustainability, 12*(16), 6525 https://doi.org/10.3390/su12166525
Harbert Magazine. (2018). Doing well by doing good. *Auburn University*. http://harbertmagazine.auburn.edu/index.php/2018/03/21/doing-well-by-doing-good/
Harker, L. (2021). How to Prove Brand Performance to Your Boss. *Latana*. https://latana.com/post/prove-brand-performance/
Hasso Plattner Institute of Design at Stanford University, d.school (n.d.). What to do in Need Finding. https://hci.stanford.edu/courses/dsummer/handouts/NeedFinding.pdf
Hatched. (2012). Brands need to exceed the 'hygiene factors' if they want to succeed. *Hatched*. https://hatchedlondon.com/brands-need-to-exceed-the-hygiene-factors-if-they-want-to-succeed/
Haughey, D. (2014). A Brief History of SMART Goals. https://www.projectsmart.co.uk/smart-goals/brief-history-of-smart-goals.php
Hayes, A. (2021). Business. https://www.investopedia.com/terms/b/business.asp
Heald, E. (2015). 5 Easy Steps to Define and Use Your Brand Voice. *Contentmarket Institute*. https://contentmarketinginstitute.com/articles/define-brand-voice/
Heinz. (2022). *Heinz. Magic every day*. https://www.heinz.com/
Helgesen, T. (1998). *Markedskommunikasjon*. Cappelen Damm Akademisk.
Helgesen, T. (2004). *Markedskommunikasjon – prinsipper for effektiv informasjon og påvirkning*. Cappelen Damm akademisk.
Helland, F. (2017). Hva er egentlig typografi. *Grafill*. grafill.no/nyheter/hva-er-egentlig-typografi
Heller, C. (2017). Designing a Way to Measure the Impact of Design. *Stanford Social Innovation Review*. https://ssir.org/articles/entry/designing_a_way_to_measure_the_impact_of_design
Hellevik, O. (2015). Spørreundersøkelser. *De Nasjonale Forskningsetiske komiteene*. etikkom.no/fbib/introduksjon/metoder-og-tilnarminger/sporreundersokelser/
Hem, L. E. & Grønhaug, K (2002). 'Merkeelementer'. *Magma*. https://old.magma.no/merkeelementene
Hem, L.E; Grønhaug, K (2/2002). 'Merkeelementer'. *Magma*.
Herper, M. (2015). Rock Star Psychologist Steven Pinker Explains Why #TheDress Looked *Forbes*. https://www.forbes.com/sites/matthewherper/2015/02/28/psychologist-and-author-stephen-pinker-explains-thedress/
Herrmann, R. (2017). The Honest YouTube Sans Reviews. *Typography.guru*. https://typography.guru/journal/the-honest-youtube-sans-reviews-r52/
Hervik, S. (2017). Newtons metode. In *Store norske leksikon*.
Hoekman, R. Jr. (2016, 18 February). Negotiation 101: How To Sell Design Ideas To Skeptical Clients, 5 persuasive tactics for faster buy-in. Co.design. https://www.fastcompany.com/3056814/negotiation-101-how-to-sell-design-ideas-to-skeptical-clients
Hoem, J. (2015). Hva skiller Tesla-eierne fra andre bileiere? *Arkitekturnytt*. http://www.arkitekturnytt.no/2015/03/hva-skiller-tesla-eierne-fra-andre.html
Holck, P. (2009). Hjernebjelken. In *Store medisinske leksikon*.
Holston, D. (2011). *The Strategic Designer: Tools & techniques for managing the design process* (1st ed.). HOW Books.
Hookle. (2021). What is video marketing and why is it important for small businesses. *Hookle*. https://www.hookle.net/post/what-is-video-marketing-and-why-is-it-important-for-small-businesses
How to Write a GDPR Compliant Privacy Policy. https://www.websitepolicies.com/blog/gdpr-privacy-policy
Hrant, A. (2014). *Mathematics and History of the Golden Section*.
http://helenevenge.blogspot.com/2009/11/what-is-user-driven-innovation-and-what.html
http://www.pmarc.ed.ac.uk/people/ruudvanderweel.html
https://archive.nordes.org/index.php/n13/article/view/52
https://ellenmacarthurfoundation.org/topics/circular-economy-introduction/overview
https://mashable.com/2013/02/13/roi-social-media/?europe=true#UjrltP9BhsqW
https://www.daviesbdm.com/blog/6-differences-between-corporate-brands-and-product-brands/
https://www.ida.liu.se/divisions/hcs/ixs/material/DesResMeth09/Theory/01-buchanan.pdf
https://www.investopedia.com/terms/c/corporate-culture.asp
https://www.mdpi.com/journal/sustainability/sections/management_sustainability
https://www.smartinsights.com/marketing-planning/marketing-models/digital-marketing-model-lauterborns-4-cs/
Hubspot. (n.d.) What Is Inbound Marketing? *Hubspot*. https://www.hubspot.com/inbound-marketing
Hudson, E. (2021). How to Blend Web Analytics and Digital Marketing Analytics to Grow Better. *HubSpot*. https://blog.hubspot.com/marketing/digital-marketing-analytics
Hufford, B. (2021). What is a Mockup? *Clique*. https://cliquestudios.com/mockups/
Human Resource Management (n.d.) Whatishumanresource.com. https://www.whatishumanresource.com/
Hume, D. (1993). *Filosofi*. Pax.
Hume, David (January 2006). *An Enquiry Concerning Human Understanding*. Gutenberg Press.
Huque, D. (2022). Agile Strategy Management – Part I. Why 'Strategile' is the new Strategy Management! *Deloitte*. https://www2.deloitte.com/de/de/pages/technology/articles/agile-strategy-management.html
Husserl, E. (1986). Phänomenologie der Lebenswelt. *Reclam Philipp Jun., Germany*.
Hypebeast. (2021). Nike Steps Further Towards a Sustainable Future With New Recycled Material Sneakers. *Hypebeast*. https://hypebeast.com/2021/1/nike-sustainable-sneaker-air-max-90-am95-blazer-mid-zoom-type-af1-07-lv8-recycled
HyperCube. (2019). Rebrand vs. Redesign – Which One Do You Need. *HyperCube*. https://www.hypercube.co.nz/rebrand-vs-redesign-which-one-do-you-need/
IAIA, International Association for Impact Assessment (n.d.) Impact Assessment. *Iaia*. https://www.iaia.org/wiki-details.php?ID=4
Iconion (n.d.) The power of an Application Icons. *Iconion*. https://iconion.com/posts/the-power-of-an-application-icon-f.html
IDEO U (n.d.) Designing strategy. *IdeoU*. https://www.ideou.com/products/designing-strategy
IDEO U (n.d.). Strategic Planning: How to Get Started, with Roger Martin https://www.ideou.com/blogs/inspiration/strategic-planning-how-to-get-started
IDEO. (2009). Design Kit: The human-centered design toolkit. *Ideo*. ideo.com/post/design-kit
IDEO.org. Designkit. Available from: designkit.org
IKEA: 'To create a better everyday life for the many people' (ikea.com 2022)
Indeed. (2021) .What Is Competitive Positioning? *Indeed*. https://www.indeed.com/career-advice/career-development/competitive-positioning
Innovasjon Norge (2017). Skaper Innovasjon Norge verdier som står i forhold til innsatsen?
Innovasjon Norge (u.å.). Slik lager du forretningsmodell. Innovasjonnorge.no. innovasjonnorge.no/no/grunder/ideutvikling/slik-lager-du-en-forretningsmodell/
Insight One (n.d.) Mosaic. *Insightone*. https://www.insightone.no/mosaic/
Ioannidis, J. P. A. (2012). Why Science Is Not Necessarily Self-Correcting. *Sage*, *7*(6). https://doi.org/10.1177/1745691612464056
Ioannou, I., & Serafeim, G. (2019). Corporate Sustainability: A Strategy? *Harvard Business School Accounting & Management Unit Working Paper*. No. 19-065. https://ssrn.com/abstract=3312191 or http://dx.doi.org/10.2139/ssrn.3312191
Ioannou, I., & Serafeim, G. (2019). Yes, sustainability can be a strategy. *Harvard Business Review*. https://hbr.org/2019/02/yes-sustainability-can-be-a-strategy@

Isabelle, D., Horak, Kevin., McKinnon, S., Palumbo, C. (2020). Is Porter's Five Forces Framework Still Relevant? A Study of the capital/labour intensity continuum via mining and IT industries. *Technology innovation management review*, *10*(6).

Ivar Horneland Kristensen, CEO at Virke, citated from: Doga, Design and Architecture Norway. (2022). Hvordan kan design øke farten på det grønne skiftet? https://www.youtube.com/watch?v=DS2hJow0iB4

Jacobsen, D. I. (2005). *Hvordan gjennomføre undersøkelser? Innføring i samfunnsvitenskapelig metode.* (2nd ed.). Høyskoleforlaget, Kristiansand.

Jacobsen, D. I. (2005). *Kvalitative intervjuer og observasjon* uio.no/studier/emner/jus/afin/FINF4002/v12/Metode.kval.intervjuer.pdf

Jacobsen, D. I., Thorsvik, J. (2007). *Hvordan organisasjoner fungerer* (3rd ed.). Fagboklaget.

Jalil, M. (2021). AI-Driven Customer Segmentation Techniques for the Modern Age. *Lucrative*. https://www.lucrative.ai/customer-segmentation-techniques-for-today/

Jason. (2016). Brand vs. Logo: The Mystery Solved. *Gistbrands*. https://gistbrands.net/brand-vs-logo/

Jensen, T. A., & Tørdal, R. M. (2018). Dramaturgiske modeller og virkemidler. *NDLA*. https://ndla.no/subject:1:f7d7f164-fb40-4d21-9813-6a171603281d/topic:3:186479/topic:3:186487/resource:1:159249

Jensen, T. A., Tørdal, R. M. (2018). Dramaturgiske modeller. *NDLA*. https://ndla.no/nn/subject:1:f7d7f164-fb40-4d21-9813-6a171603281d/topic:3:186479/topic:3:186487/resource:1:159249

Johansson-Sköldberg, U., Woodilla, J., Çetinkaya, M. (2013). Design Thinking: Past, Present and Possible Futures. *Creativity and innovation management*. https://doi.org/10.1111/caim.12023

Johnson, M. (2016). *Branding In Five and a Half Steps* (1st ed). Thames and Hudson.

Jones, P. (2014). *Design Research Methods for Systemic Design: Perspectives from design education and practice* Relating Systems Thinking and Design 2014 https://www.researchgate.net/publication/289551227_Design_research_methods_for_systemic_design_Perspectives_from_design_education_and_practice

Jones, P. H. (2014). Systemic Design Principles for Complex Social Systems. *Translational Systems Science Series, Springer Verlag, 1*, 1–30. https://www.researchgate.net/publication/280921326_Systemic_Design_Principles_for_Complex_Social_Systems

Jones, P. (2019). Systemic Design Toolkit. Design dialogues. https://designdialogues.com/systemic-design-toolkit/

JovacoSolutions. (2016). The Analysis Phase of a Project: An Important Piece of Any Microsoft Dynamics 365 Implementation. *ERP SoftwareBlog*. https://www.erpsoftwareblog.com/2016/02/analysis-phase-project-important-piece-microsoft-dynamics-gp-implementation/

Jurevicius, O. (2013/2022). PEST & PESTEL Analysis. *Strategic Management Insight*. https://strategicmanagementinsight.com/tools/pest-pestel-analysis/

Jurevicius, O. (2021). VRIO Framework Explained. https://strategicmanagementinsight.com/tools/vrio/

Kalam, K. (2020). Market Segmentation, Targeting and Positioning Strategy Adaptation for the Global Business of Vodafone Telecommunication Company. *International Journal of Research and Innovation in Social Science (IJRISS) 4*, 427.

Kampanje (2017, 5 May). Design, hva er det godt for? *Kampanje*. https://kampanje.com/design/2017/05/--design-hva-er-det-godt-for/

Kanban (2021). *Kanban board*. kanbanize.com

Kanbanize Stand-up Meeting: The Definitive Guide for Holding Effective Stand-ups. Kanbanize.com.

Kapferer, J. N. (2012). *The New Strategic Brand Management: Advanced Insights & Strategic Thinking* (5th ed.). Kogan Page Publishers.

Kaplan, R. S., & Norton, D. P. (2004). *Strategy Maps: Converting intangible assets into tangible outcomes*. Harvard Business School Press.

Kappel, M. (2017). Find Your Customers with a Target Market Analysis. *Forbes*. https://www.forbes.com/sites/mikekappel/2017/01/09/find-your-customers-with-a-target-market-analysis/?sh=54359d756bab

Karagianni, K. (2018). Optimizing the UX Honeycomb. *UX Collective*. https://uxdesign.cc/optimizing-the-ux-honeycomb-1d10cfb38097

Karlsen, H. (2009). Ta kontroll over merkeleveransen. *Metro Branding as*. 16733052-Ta-kontroll-over-merkeleveransen.html

Kay, M. J. (2006). Strong brands and corporate brands. *European Journal of Marketing 40*(7/8), 742–760. https://doi.org/https://doi.org/10.1108/03090560610669973

Keating, G. (2021). How to choose the best marketing automation software in 2021. *Segment*. https://segment.com/blog/marketing-automation-software/

Keelson, S. A., & Polytechnic, T. (2012). A Quantitative Study of Market Orientation and Organizational Performance of Listed Companies: Evidence from Ghana. *International Journal of Management and Marketing Research*, *5*(3), 101–114.

Keller, K. L. (1998). Branding Perspectives on Social Marketing. *Advances in Consumer Research*, *25*, 299–302.

Keller, K. L. (2002). Branding and Brand Equity. *Marketing Science Institute*.

Keller, K. L. (2003). *Strategic Brand Management: Building, measuring, and managing brand equity*. Prentice Hall.

Keller, K. L. (2013). *Strategic Brand Management. Building, Measuring and Managing Brand Equity* (4th ed.). Pearson.

Kellerman, B. J., Gordon, P. J., Hekmat, F. (1995). Product and Pricing Courses are Underrepresented in Undergraduate Marketing Curricula. *Journal of Product & Brand Management*, *4*(1), 18–25.

Kelley, T. (2001). The Art of Innovation: Lessons in creativity from IDEO.

Kenny, G. (2014). Your Company's Purpose Is Not Its Vision, Mission, or Values. *Harvard Business Review*. https://hbr.org/2014/09/your-companys-purpose-is-not-its-vision-mission-or-values

Kenton, W. (2021). Research and Development (R&D). *Investopedia*. https://www.investopedia.com/terms/r/randd.asp

Killi, S. W. (2017). *Additive Manufacturing: Design, methods, and processes*. Pan Stanford.

Kim, W. C., & Mauborgne, R. (2005). Blue Ocean Strategy: How to Create Uncontested Market Space and Make Competition Irrelevant. *Harvard Business Review Press*, 7/118.

Kim, W. C., & Mauborgne, R. (2015). *Blue Ocean Strategy: How to Create Uncontested Market Space and Make Competition Irrelevant* (2nd ed.). Harvard Business Review Press.

Kim, W. C., & Mauborgne, R. (2004). Blue Ocean Strategy. *Harvard Business Review*. https://hbr.org/2004/10/blue-ocean-strategy

Kim, W. C., & Mauborgne, R. (2014). *The Blue Ocean Strategy: How To Create Uncontested Market Space and Make the Competition Irrelevant*. Harvard Business Review Press. https://helenescott.com/wp-content/uploads/2014/01/BookReportBlueOceanStrategy.pdf

Kissmetrics. (2010). How Colors Affect Conversions. *Kissmetrics*. https://blog.kissmetrics.com/wp-content/uploads/2013/04/how-colors-affect-conversion-rates.pdf

Klein, N. (1999). *No logo: Taking Aim at the Brand Bullies* (1st ed.). Knopf Canada.

Klein, N. (2009). No Logo, Media Education Foundation.

Kleon, A. (2014). Show Your Work!: 10 Ways to Share Your Creativity and Get Discovered. *Workman Publishing*.

Knapp, J. (2016). GV's Sprint Process in 90 Seconds. *YouTube*. https://www.youtube.com/watch?v=K2vSQPh6MCE

Knudsen, H., & Flåten, B. (2015). *Strategisk ledelse* (1st ed.). Cappelen Damm Akademisk.

Kolko, J. (2015). Design Thinking Comes of Age. *Harvard Business Review* (September), 66–71. https://hbr.org/2015/09/design-thinking-comes-of-age

Koskinen, I. Z., J., Binder, T., Redstrom, J., Wensveen, S. (2011). *Design Research Through Practice*. Morgan Kaufmann Publishers.

Kotler, P. (1967). *Marketing Management: Analysis, Planning, and Control*. Prentice-Hall.

Kotler, P. (2000). *Marketing Management: The Millennium Edition*. Person Prentice Hall.

Kotler, P. (2001). *Kotler On Marketing*. Simon & Schuster.

Kotler, P., & Keller, K. L. (2016). *Marketing Management* (15th ed.). Pearson.

Kumar, V. (2012). *101 Design Methods: A Structured Approach for Driving Innovation in Your Organization* (1st ed.). Wiley.

Kumar, Y. (2011). Agile Strategy Manifesto. *InfoQ*. https://www.infoq.com/articles/agile-strategy-manifesto/

Kunde, J. (2002). *Unik nå eller aldri* (1st ed.). Hegnar media.
Kvale, S., & Brinkmann, S. (2009). *Det kvalitative forskningsintervju* (2nd ed.). Gyldendal.
Kvale, S., & Brinkmann, S. (2015). *Det kvalitative forskningsintervju* (3rd ed.). Gyldendal.
Lafley, A. G., Martin, R., Ganser, L. J. (2014). *Playing to Win: How Strategy Really Works*. Harvard Business Review Press.
Landau, P. (2021). How to Create a Project Brief. *Projectmaker*. https://www.projectmanager.com/blog/create-a-project-brief
Lanzing, J. (1998). Concept Mapping: Tools for echoing the mind's eye. *Journal of Visual Literacy*. *18*(1), 1–14 (4). doi:10.1080/23796529.1998.11674524.
Larsen, G. (2006). Why Megatrends Matter. *Institute for Future Studies (CIFS)*, *5*. https://www.yumpu.com/en/document/view/20465932/fo052006-the-megatrends-matter-issue-copenhagen-institute-for-
Larsen, W. (2007). *En enkel metode* (1st ed.). Fagbokforlaget, Bergen.
LearningForSustainability (2022). Systemic Design. https://learningforsustainability.net/systemic-design/
Lee, B. B. (2008). The evolution of concepts of color vision. *National Library of Medicine*, *4*(4), 209–224. https://www.ncbi.nlm.nih.gov/pmc/articles/PMC3095437/
Leerberg, M. (2009). Design in the expanded field. Rethinking contemporary design. *Nordes, Nordic design research (3)*. https://archive.nordes.org/index.php/n13/article/view/52Leinslie, E., & Arntzen, K. O. (2018). Dramaturgi. In *Store norske leksikon*.
Lerdahl, E. (2017). *Nyskapning. Arbeidsbok i kreative metoder*. Gyldendal akademisk.
Lerdahl, E., & Finne, P. (2007). *Slagkraft*. Gyldendal akademisk.
Lewrick, M., Patrick Link, P., Leifer, L. (2018). *The Design Thinking Playbook: Mindful Digital Transformation of Teams, Products, Services, Businesses and Ecosystems* (1st ed.). Wiley.
Liberto, D. (2021). Social Sciences. *Investopedia*. https://www.investopedia.com/terms/s/social-science.asp
Lichtenberg, G. C. (1990). Briefwechsel, Band III (1785–1792), Verlag C. H. Beck.
Lie, S. (2017). Verden vil ikonifiseres. UiB Instituttet for design, visuell kommunikasjon 2017. N/A.
Liedtka, J. (2019). *The Designing for Growth Field Book: A Step-by-Step Project Guide* (2nd ed). Columbia Business School Publishing
Lien, L. B., Knudsen, E. S., Baardsen, T. Ø. (2016). *Strategiboken* (3rd ed.). Fagbokforlaget, Bergen.
Life Cycle Initiative. (n.d.). What is Life Cycle Thinking? *Life Cycle Initiative*. https://www.lifecycleinitiative.org/starting-life-cycle-thinking/what-is-life-cycle-thinking/
Lindblad, S. (2008). Lean – en filosofi. *forretningsprosess.no*. http://www.forretningsprosess.no/lean-en-filosofi/
London, B. (2017). How did this company crush their trade show? By nailing their customers' Elevator Rant. *Chieflistening officers*. http://www.chieflisteningofficers.com/2017/02/21/stop-using-trade-show-marketing-platitudes-lead-with-your-customers-elevator-rant/
Lorentzen, R., & Lund, J.F. (1998). *Strategiutvikling. Plan og ledelse* (3 ed.). Universitetsforlaget, Oslo.
Lotame. (2019). What is Data Analytics? *Lotame*. https://www.lotame.com/what-is-data-analytics/
Lovett, J. (1998). Original Design Overview: The elements of design. *John Lovett*. https://www.johnlovett.com/
Lucidchart. (n.d.). What is a Network Diagram. *lucidchart.com*. https://www.lucidchart.com/pages/network-diagram
Lundequist, J. (1992). *Introduktion till forskningsmetodiken*. Stockholm: Kungliga Tekniska Högskolan, Sektionen för Arkitektur. Forskarutbildningen.
Lydersen. (2006). First International Corporate Value Index 2006, by ECCO International Communications
Lynn, R. (2022). Agile vs Lean. *Planview*. https://www.planview.com/resources/articles/agile-vs-lean/
Lönngren, L., & Van Poeck, K. (2020). Wicked Problems: a mapping review of the literature. *International Journal of Sustainable Development & World Ecology*, *28*(6), 481–502 https://doi.org/10.1080/13504509.2020.1859415
Madsen, S. O. (2018). Mellem snak, handling, magt, skuespil og oversættelse – implementeringens dimensioner. Samfundslederskab i Skandinavien, *33*(1), 19–41. DOI: https://doi.org/10.22439/sis.v33i1.5539
Majaski, C. (2021). Mergers and Acquisitions: What's the Difference? *Investopedia*. https://www.investopedia.com/ask/answers/021815/what-difference-between-merger-and-acquisition.asp
Malamed, C. (2018). A Designer Addresses Criticism of Design Thinking. *Learning Solutions*. learningsolutionsmag.com/articles/a-designer-addresses-criticism-of-design-thinking
Mandel, N., & Johnson, E. J. (2002). When Web Pages Influence Choice: Effects of Visual Primes on Experts and Novices. *Journal of Consumer Research*, *29*(2). https://doi.org/DOI:10.1086/341573
Marcelo M. S., & Francesco R. (2012). *Advances in Usability Evaluation*. CRC Press, p. 482. ISBN 978-1-4398-7025-9.
MarketingAXBorders. (2020). Distinctive Brand Assets and Category Entry Points (CEPs). *Marketing AX Borders*. https://marketingacrossborders.blog/2020/02/24/distinctive-brand-assets-and-category-entry-points-ceps/
Martin, B., & Hanington, B. (2012). *Universal Methods of Design: 100 ways to research complex problems, develop innovative ideas, and design effective solutions* (O'reilly, Ed.). Rockport Publishers.
Martin, B., & Hanington, B. (2022). Directed Storytelling. *O'Reilly*. https://www.oreilly.com/library/view/universal-methods-of/9781592537563/xhtml/ch31.xhtml
Martin, R. L. (2017). Strategic Choices Need to Be Made Simultaneously, Not Sequentially. *Harvard Business Review*.
Martins, J. (2020). 5 steps to writing a clear project brief. *Asana*. https://asana.com/resources/project-brief
Martinsen, Ø. L. (2011). The Creative Personality: A Synthesis and Development of the Creative Person Profile. *Creativity Research Journal*, *23*(3), 185–202. https://doi.org/https://doi.org/10.1080/10400419.2011.595656
Mattick K., Johnston, J., De la Croix, A. (2018). How to...write a good research question. *The Clinical Teacher*, *15*, 104–108. https://doi.org/ https://doi.org/10.1111/tct.12776
Mauraya, A. (2012). Why Lean Canvas vs Business Model Canvas? *Continuous Innovation Blog*. https://blog.leanstack.com/why-lean-canvas-vs-business-model-canvas/
Maurya, A. (2012). *Running Lean: Iterate from Plan A to a Plan That Works* (2nd ed.). O'Reilly Media.
Maurya, A. (2012). Why Lean Canvas vs. Business Model Canvas? https://blog.leanstack.com/why-lean-canvas-vs-business-model-canvas/
McCarthy, E. J. (1960). *Basic Marketing: A managerial approach*. Richard D. Irwin, Inc.
McCarthy, & J., Wright, P. (2005). Putting 'felt-life' at the centre of human–computer interaction (HCI). *Springer*, *7*, 262–271. https://link.springer.com/article/10.1007/s10111-005-0011-y
McGrath, R. G. (2013). Competitive Strategy. Transient Advantage. *Harvard Business Review*. hbr.org/2013/06/transient-advantage
McKinsey & Company. (2018). The Business Value of Design. *McKinsey*. https://www.mckinsey.com/business-functions/mckinsey-design/our-insights/the-business-value-of-design
McKinsey & Company. (2021). Design: Understand its value, measure it better, and lead the way. *McKinsey*. https://www.mckinsey.com/featured-insights/themes/design-understand-its-value-measure-it-better-and-lead-the-way
McKinsey Sustainability. (2022). The Net-zero Transition: What it would cost, what it could bring. *McKinsey Sustainability*. https://www.mckinsey.com/business-functions/sustainability/our-insights/the-net-zero-transition-what-it-would-cost-what-it-could-bring
McLeod, S. (2020). Karl Popper – Theory of Falsification. *SimplyPsychology*. https://www.simplypsychology.org/Karl-Popper.html
MDPI. Sustainability, Sustainable Management. *MDPI, Sustainability*.
Miller, M. E., & Flowers, E. (2016). The difference between a journey map and a service blueprint. *Practical Service Design*. https://blog.practicalservicedesign.com/the-difference-between-a-journey-map-and-a-service-blueprint-31a6e24c4a6c
Mind tools content team (n.d.). Porter's Generic Strategies. *Mindtools*. https://www.mindtools.com/pages/article/newSTR_82.htm
Mintzberg, H. (1978). Patterns in Strategy Formation. *Management Science 24*(9), 934–948. http://www.jstor.org/stable/2630633.
Mintzberg, H. (1985). Of Strategies, Deliberate and Emergent. *Strategic Management Journal*, *6*(3), 257–272. https://doi.org/doi:10.1002/smj.4250060306

Mintzberg, H. (1987). The Strategy Concept I: five Ps for strategy. *California Management Review, 30*(1), 11–24. https://doi.org/https://doi.org/10.2307/41165263
Mintzberg, H. (1990). The Design School: Reconsidering the basic premises of strategic management. *Strategic Management Journal, 11*(3), 171–196. https://doi.org/doi:10.1002/smj.4250110302
Mollerup, P. (1998) *Design er ikke noe i seg selv*. Norsk Form, Oslo
Moreau, P. C., & Engeset M.G. (2016). The Downstream Consequences of Problem Solving Mindsets: How playing with LEGO influences creativity. *Journal of Marketing Research, 53*(1), 18–30.
Morganelli, M. (2020). What is Systems Thinking? *Southern New Hampshire University*. https://www.snhu.edu/about-us/newsroom/business/what-is-systems-thinking
Mosaic Personality Tasks (n.d.) Mosaictasks. *Mosaic*. https://www.mosaictasks.com/
Mosaic. (n.d.). Forbrukersegmentering. *InsightOne*. https://www.insightone.no/mosaic/
MSCI (n.d.). ESC Ratings. *MSCI*. https://www.msci.com/our-solutions/esg-investing/esg-ratings
Mulder, S., & Yaar, Z. (2006). *The User Is Always Right: A practical guide to creating and using personas for the web* (1st ed.). New Riders.
Munari, B. (1971). *Design as Art*. Pelican.
Murray, R. M. (2017). 'Design-Led Research Toolkit'. Parsons Transdisciplinary Design program, class of 2017. N.a.
Myersbriggs (n.d.). The Myers & Briggs Foundation. *Mbti*. https://www.myersbriggs.org/
Myklebust, I. (2016). Geometriske former. *NDLA*. https://ndla.no/nn/subject:1:9a925996-e067-42bc-aea0-f3fcb1d7c043/topic:3:192824/resource:1:162254
Müller-Brockmann, J. (1960). *Weniger Laerm (Less Noise)*. The Museum of Modern Art, NewYork/Scala, Florence NewYork/Scala, Florence.
NASA, G. R. C. (2022). Newton's Laws of Motion. https://www1.grc.nasa.gov/beginners-guide-to-aeronautics/newtons-laws-of-motion/
Nasa: 'To discover and expand knowledge for the benefit of humanity' (nasa.gov)
Nasjonalkolleksjon (n.d.) Riss. http://nasjonalkolleksjon.com/riss
Ndla. (2017). Materialer. *Ndla*. https://ndla.no/nb/subject:1:e4f1bd93-e941-4f7e-a150-1dd99a9ac419/topic:2:ff48ed85-dbc5-4b98-a3b2-4212fd341c1a/topic:2:e44fb5d1-ae7e-4e74-802e-a0ff04fc8426/resource:be1c6e98-c60f-4e57-9861-86f6c4b4dc4c
Neher, A. (1991). Maslow's Theory of Motivation. A Critique. *Journal of Humanistic Psychology, 31*(3).
Nenycz-Thiel, M., & Romaniuk, J. (2014). The real difference between consumers' perceptions of private labels and national brands. *Journal of Consumer Behaviour, 13*(4), 262–269. https://doi.org/https://doi-org.ezproxy1.usn.no/10.1002/cb.1464
Neumeier, M. (2005). *The Brand Gap* (2 ed.). New Riders.
Neumeier, M. (2006). *Zag: The Number One Strategy of High-Performance Brands*. Broché.
Neumeier, M. (2018). The Five Ps of Design Thinking. *Bobmorris.biz*. https://bobmorris.biz/marty-neumeier-on-the-five-ps-of-design-thinking
Nidumolu, R., Prahalad, C. K., & Rangaswami, M. R. (2009). Why sustainability is now the key driver of innovation. *Harvard business review, 87*(9), 56–64. DOI: 10.1109/EMR.2015.7123233
Nielsen. (2018). Sustainable shoppers buy the change they wish to see in the world. *Nielsen IQ*. https://nielseniq.com/global/en/insights/report/2018/sustainable-shoppers-buy-the-change-they-wish-to-see-in-the-world/
Nike (2022). To bring inspiration and innovation to every athlete in the world. *Nike*. https://about.nike.com/en
Nike: To bring inspiration and innovation to every athlete in the world (about.nike.com 2022)15
Noble, C. H. (1999). The Eclectic Roots of Strategy Implementation Research. *Journal of Business Research, 45*, 119–134. https://doi.org/http://dx.doi.org/10.1016/S0148-2963(97)00231-2
Noordzij, G. (2005). *The Stroke. Theory of Writing*. Hyphen Press
Nordby Lunde, H. (2008) Slik skriver du intervjuer. *Abc/nyheter*. https://www.abcnyheter.no/nyheter/2008/04/10/64456/slik-skriver-du-intervjuer
Norman, D. (1988). *The Psychology of Everyday Things* (1st ed.). Basic Books.
Norman, D. (2005). Human-Centered Design Considered Harmful. *Interactions 12*(4), 14–19. https://doi.org/DOI:10.1145/1070960.1070976
Norman, D. (2013). *The design of everyday things. Revised and expanded edition* (2 ed.). Basic Books.
Norman, D. (2019). HCD Harmful? A Clarification. *jnd.org*. https://jnd.org/hcd_harmful_a_clarification/
Norman, M. (2019). The 8-Question Framework for Successful Rebrands. *Medium*. https://medium.com/@meetmorg/the-8-question-framework-for-successful-rebrands-bc71ed8a987f
Næss, H. E., & Petersen, L. (2017). *Metodebok for kreative fag*. Universitetsforlaget.
O'Neal, B. (2009). Taking the Hocus Pocus Out of Market Segmentation. N/A.
O'Reilly, T. (n.d.) .The Lean Startup: The movement that is transforming how new products are built and launched. *Theleanstartup*. http://theleanstartup.com/
Odjick, D. (2021). Product Line Extensions: What They Are, Examples, and Tips for Forming Your Strategy. *Shopify*. https://www.shopify.co.uk/blog/product-line-extensions
OECD (n.d.). Frascati Manual 2015. *OECD*. https://www.oecd.org/publications/frascati-manual-2015-9789264239012-en.htm
OECD. (2015). *Frascati Manual*. https://www.oecd.org/publications/frascati-manual-2015-9789264239012-en.htm
Oetting, J. (2016). The 30 Best and Worst Rebrands of All Time *HubSpot*. https://blog.hubspot.com/agency/best-worst-rebrands-infographic
Olsen, L. E. (2004). Merkearkitektur: relasjoner og sammenhenger
Olsen, L. E. (2010). Det viktigste første problemet i praktisk posisjonering. *Magma*. https://old.magma.no/det-viktigste-foerste-problemet-i-praktisk-posisjonering
One Strategy. (2021). Differentiation Strategy. *Onestrategy*. https://onestrategy.org/differentiation-strategy/
Origin: John Heywood 1546. 'Head' here means 'mind', as opposed to heart or spirit. phrases.org.uk
Ormestad, H. (2015). Kraft: fysikk. In *Store norske leksikon*.
Orth, U. R., & Malkewitz, K. (2008). Holistic Package Design and Consumer Brand Impressions. *Journal of Marketing, 72*(3), 64–81. https://doi.org/10.1509/JMKG.72.3.064
Orton, K. (2017). Desirability, Feasibility, Viability: The Sweet Spot for Innovation. *Medium*. https://medium.com/innovation-sweet-spot/desirability-feasibility-viability-the-sweet-spot-for-innovation-d7946de2183c
Osborn, A. F. (1963). *Applied Imagination: Principles and Procedures of Creative Problem-solving* (3rd ed.). Charles Scribner's Sons.
Osterwalder, A. (2012). *Tools for Business Model Generation*. Stanford eCorner.
Osterwalder, A. (2014). *Value Proposition Design: How to create products and services customers want*. John Wiley and Sons.
Osterwalder, A., & Pigneur, Y. (2013). Designing Business Models and Similar Strategic Objects: The contribution of IS. *Journal of the Association for Information Systems 14*(5), 237–244.
Osterwalder, A., & Pigneur, Y. (2010). *Business Model Generation: A Handbook for Visionaries, Game Changers, and Challengers*. John Wiley & Sons.
Ottesen, O. (2005). *Strategisk ledelse av virksomhetens markedskommunikasjon: et helhetssyn for økt lønnsomhet*. Universitetsforlaget.
Ottinger, R. (2021). Create Sustainable Success with the 4 Types of Innovation. *Fresh Consulting*. https://www.freshconsulting.com/insights/blog/the-4-types-of-innovation/
Øvregård, M. O. (2020). Hva er implementering. https://www.uis.no/nb/laringsmiljosenteret/forskning/implementering-i-skole-og-barnehagekontekst#/
Packaging Europe. (2021). Exclusive: A behind the scenes look at Coca-Cola's paper bottle European trial. *Sustainable Packaging Summit*. https://packagingeurope.com/exclusive-a-behind-the-scenes-look-at-coca-colas-paper-bottle-european-trial/577.article
Paditar, M. (2017). Marketing Notes – Identifying and Analysing Competitors. *EnotesMBA*. https://www.enotesmba.com/2013/04/marketing-notes-identifying-and-analysing-competitors.html
Palmer, S. (1992). Common Region: A new principle of perceptual grouping. *Cognitive Psychology, 24*, 436–447.

Parekh, R. (2012; 27. august). After 50 Years, Avis Drops Iconic 'We Try Harder' – New Campaign Repositions Car-Rental Firm to Appeal to Busy Businessfolk. *AdAge*. https://adage.com/article/news/50-years-avis-drops-iconic-harder-tagline/236887
Patala, S., Jalkala, A., Keränen, J., Väisänen, S., Tuominen, V., Soukka, R. (2016). Sustainable Value Propositions: Framework and implications for technology suppliers. *Industrial Marketing Management*, *59*, 144–156. https://doi.org/https://doi.org/10.1016/j.indmarman.2016.03.001
Patentstyret (2016). Merkevare. *Patentstyret*. https://www.patentstyret.no/ord-og-uttrykk/merkevare/
Patton, M. Q. (1999). Enhancing the quality and credibility of qualitative analysis. *Management Science*, *34* (5 Pt 2), 1189–1189.
Pentak, S., & Lauer, D.A. (2015). *Design basics* (9th ed).
Percy, L., & Rosenbaum-Elliot, R. H. (2012). *Strategic Advertising Management* (4th ed.). Oxford University Press.
Petrány, M. (2014). Why Volvo Thinks It Can Eliminate All Deaths In Its Cars By 2020. *Jalopnik*. https://jalopnik.com/this-is-volvos-bold-plan-to-eliminate-all-deaths-in-its-1668747230
Pfeffer, J. (1977). The Ambiguity of Leadership. *The Academy of Management Review*, *2*(1), 104–112. https://doi.org/10.2307/257611
Pfeffer, J. (1991). Organization theory and structural perspectives on management, *Journal of Management*, *17*(4), 789–803. https://doi.org/10.1177/014920639101700411
Phillips., P. L. (2012). *Creating the Perfect Design Brief: How to manage design for strategic advantage* (2nd ed.). Allworth.
Picincu, A. (2018). Definition of Commercial Organization. https://bizfluent.com/about-5135762-definition-commercial-organization.html
Plumbe C., Kunur, M., Eikhaug, O., et al. (2010). *Innovating with People – The Business of Inclusive Design* (1st ed.). Norwegian Design Council (Doga), Oslo.
Polanyi, M. (1966/2009). The Tacit Dimension. *The University of Chicago Press Books*.
Porter, J. (2016). What companies have used Blue Ocean Strategy techniques and what were the results? *Quora*. quora.com/What-companies-have-used-Blue-Ocean-Strategy-techniques-and-what-were-the-results
Porter, M. E. (1979). How Competitive Forces Shape Strategy. *Harvard Business Review*. https://hbr.org/1979/03/how-competitive-forces-shape-strategy
Porter, M. E. (1985). *The Competitive Advantage: Creating and Sustaining Superior Performance*. Free Press.
Porter, M. E., & Kramer, M. R. (2011). Creating Shared Value, *Harvard Business Review*. https://hbr.org/2011/01/the-big-idea-creating-shared-value
Postma, C., Lauche, K., Stappers, P. J. (2009). Trialogues: A framework for bridging the gap between people research and design. *TuDelft*. https://repository.tudelft.nl/islandora/object/uuid%3Aa1172a2c-2550-4854-b895-51ddfb197fad
Postma, C., Lauche, K., Stappers, P. J. (2012). Social Theory as a thinking tool for empathic design. *Massachusetts Institute of Technology*, *28*(1), 30–49.
Postma, Z.-P., Daemen, Du (2012). Challenges of Doing Empathic Design: Experiences from Industry. *International Journal of Design*, *6*(1).
Prescott, B. (2012). Business Sense: Inbound Marketing. *Times Standard*. https://www.times-standard.com/2012/02/05/business-sense-inbound-marketing/
Product-life.org. (n.d.). The Product-Life Institute. http://www.product-life.org/
Proxy, Oxford Language
Purtill, C. (2017). Murphy's Law is totally misunderstood and is in fact a call to excellence. *Quartz*. https://qz.com/984181/murphys-law-is-totally-misunderstood-and-is-in-fact-a-call-to-excellence/
Qiany, S. (2020). How to choose an appropriate UX Research method. *UX Collective*. https://medium.com/user-experience-design-1/how-to-choose-an-appropriate-ux-research-method-14ef715a72a6
Questback (n.d.). Rocket fuel for curious organisations. *Questback*. https://www.questback.com/
Rabben, A. (2017, 5. september). Design, hva er det godt for? Kampanje.
Rajagopal, & Sanchez, R. J (2004). Conceptual analysis of brand architecture and relationships within product categories. *Journal of Brand Management*, *11*(3), 233–247
Ramamoorthy, A. (2021). How to Write a Target Market Analysis. *Wikihow*. https://www.wikihow.com/Write-a-Target-Market-Analysis
Rannem, Ø. (2005). *Typografi og skrift* (1 ed.). Abstrakt Forlag A/S.
Rannem, Ø. (2012). *Typografi og skrift* (2 ed.). Abstrakt Forlag A/S.
Redding, D. (2014). What Does The Apple Logo Mean?. *Magnetic State*. https://www.magneticstate.com/what-does-the-apple-logo-mean/
Refsum, G. (2004). Forskning og kunstnerisk utviklingsarbeid. Bidrag til en klargjøring av begrepene. https://www.refsum.no/wp-content/uploads/publications/Refsum_KHIO_aarbok2004.pdf
Regjeringen.no. (2012). Unike idear, store verdiar – om immaterielle verdiar og rettar (Meld. St. 28 (2012–2013). *Regjeringa.no*. https://www.regjeringen.no/no/dokumenter/meld-st-28-20122013/id722822/
Replicability-Index. (2019). Psychological Science is Self-Correcting. https://replicationindex.com/2019/03/04/psychological-science-is-self-correcting/
Ries, A., & Trout, J. (1986). *Positioning. The Battle for Your Mind* (1st ed.). McGraw Hill.
Rittel, H. W. J., & Webber M. M. (1973). Dilemmas in a general theory of planning. *Springer*. https://link.springer.com/article/10.1007/BF01405730
Robertson, G. (2013). How to figure out a brand concept that expresses your brand positioning. *Beloved Brands*. https://beloved-brands.com/brand-concept/
Robinson, A. (2018). Did Einstein Really Say That? *Nature*. https://www.nature.com/articles/d41586-018-05004-4
Robinson, R. E., Nitro, S. (2015). Building a Useful Research Tool: An Origin Story of AEIOU. *EPIC*. https://www.epicpeople.org/building-a-useful-research-tool/
Rock Content Writer. (2018). Brand Consistency: What is it and how to build a strong brand. *Rockcontent*. https://rockcontent.com/blog/brand-consistency/
RockContentWriter. (2020). How to Create a Global Content Marketing Strategy. *RockContent*. https://rockcontent.com/blog/global-content-marketing/
Rohrer, C. (2014). When to Use Which User-Experience Research Methods. *Nielsen Norman Group*. https://www.nngroup.com/articles/which-ux-research-methods/
Romaniuk, J. (2018). *Building Distinctive Brand Assets*. OUP Australia and New Zealand.
Romaniuk, J., & Sharp, B. (2022). *How Brands Grow*. Revised edition. Oxford.
Romm, J., & Paulen, A. (2014). Professional Applications of System Oriented Design (SOD): Developments in Practice. *OCAD University Open Research Repository*. http://openresearch.ocadu.ca/id/eprint/2107/1/Romm_WorkingPaper_2014.pdf
Roos, G., von Krogh, G., Roos, J., Fernström, L. (2014). *Strategi: en innføring*. Vigmostad & Bjørke AS.
Rosin, T. (2020). Kanban vs. Scrum: What's the difference in 2021? https://tinyurl.com/3zfuw266
Rossen, E. (2009). Informasjon. In *Store norske leksikon*.
Rotman Design Works. (2010). Introduction to Business Design – Rotman DesignWorks. In. Slideshare: RotmanDesignworks.
Rotman DesignWorks (n.d.) Introduction to Business Design. Slideshare. https://www.slideshare.net/alpeshmistry
Rouse, M. (2014). Wizard of Oz Prototyping. Techtarget.com. N/A.
Rozhkovskaya, N. (2019). Mathematical commentary on Le Corbusier's Modulor. *Nexus Network Journal* 22(4). DOI:10.1007/s00004-019-00469-w
Rudello, E. (2017). Inbound Marketing. *Slideshare*. https://www.slideshare.net/EnricoRudello/inbound-marketing-71411632
Rutgers. (2010). What Are Sustainable Materials? *Rutgers*.
Rybakken, B. (2004). *Visuell identitet* (1st ed.). Abstrakt forlag.
Samuelsen, B. M., Peretz, A., Olsen, L. E. (2010). *Merkevareledelse på Norsk 2.0* (1st ed.). Cappelen Damm AS.
Sander, K. (2019). Problem. *estudie.no*. https://estudie.no/hva-er-et-problem/
Sander, K. (2020). Induktiv og deduktiv studier. https://estudie.no/induktiv-deduktiv/
Sarkar, C., & Kotler, P. (2021). The Wicked 7. Can we solve the world's most urgent problems?

Schmidt, C. (2018). Through the decades, the Magic Kingdom has remained true to Walt Disney's vision. *AllEars*. https://allears.net/2018/02/19/through-the-decades-the-magic-kingdom-has-remained-true-to-walt-disneys-vision/

Schueller, S. (2021). What is Brand Experience? *Widen*. https://www.widen.com/blog/brand-experience

Schön, D. (1983). *The Reflective Practitioner: How professionals think in action*. (1st ed.). Basic Books.

Scott, H. The Six Principles of Blue Ocean Strategy (helenescott.com, blueoceanstrategy.com)

Sending A. et al. (2007). Driftsregnskap og budsjettering (2nd ed), Fagbokforlaget, Bergen.

Senge, P. M. (2006). *Fifth Discipline: The art and practice of the learning organization*. Crown, Illustrated edition

Sevaldson, B. (2010). Discussions and Movements in Design Research A systems approach to practice research in design. *Research by design, 3*(1).

Sevaldson, B. (2011). GIGA-Mapping: Visualisation for complexity and systems thinking in design. *NORDES, Nordic Design Research*.

Sevaldson, B. (2012). Systems Oriented Design for the Built Environment, in Design Innovation for the Built Environment. Research by Design and the Renovation of Practice. In M. Hensel (Ed.), *Oxon* (pp. 107–120). Routledge.

Sevaldson, B. (2013). *Systems Oriented Design: The emergence and development of a designerly approach to address complexity*. DRS Cumulus.

Sevaldson, B. (2019). Visualizing Complex Design: The Evolution of Gigamaps. In *Systemic Design* (pp. 243–269). Springer Japan.

Sevaldson, B., & Ryan, A. J. Relating Systems Thinking and Design I. Practical Advances in Systemic Design, *Form Academic, 7*(3). DOI: https://doi.org/10.7577/formakademisk.1233

Sharp, B. (2010). How Brands Grow: What Marketers Don't Know.

Sharp, B., & Romaniuk, J. (2019). How Brands Grow: Part 2: Emerging Markets, Services, Durables, New and Luxury Brands.

Shaw, R. (2015). 5 ways packaging can differentiate your brand. *Packaging Digest*. https://www.packagingdigest.com/packaging-design/5-ways-packaging-can-differentiate-your-brand

Sheppard, B., Kouyoumjian, G., Sarrazin, H. & Dore, F. (2018). The business value of design. *McKinsey Quarterly*. https://www.mckinsey.com/business-functions/mckinsey-design/our-insights/the-business-value-of-design

Shore, J. (2020). Where does blogging fit into your content marketing strategy? *Smartbug*. https://www.smartbugmedia.com/blog/where-does-blogging-fit-into-your-content-marketing-strategy

Siemens. (2022). Digital Mockup, Virtual & Augmented Reality. *Siemens*. https://www.plm.automation.siemens.com/global/en/industries/automotive-transportation/trucks-buses-specialty-vehicles/digital-mockup-virtual-augmented-reality.html

Sieniutycz, S. (2020). *Complexity and Complex Thermo-Economic Systems*. Elsevier Science Publishing Co. Inc.

Sigberg, T. (2019). Lean vs Agile vs Lean-Agile. *Medium*. https://medium.com/@thorbjorn.sigberg/lean-vs-agile-vs-lean-agile-c5d38a5406c6

Silva, T., & Marques, J. P. C. (2020). *Human-Centered Design for Collaborative Innovation* The ISPIM Innovation Conference, https://www.researchgate.net/publication/342038864

Simonsen, A. (2007). *Offentlig informasjons- og kommunikasjon-sarbeid. Mål og metoder*. (3rd ed.). Kommuneforlaget.

Simonsen, A. (2012). Kommunikasjonsstrategi – hvordan kan den se ut?. *Kommunikasjon.no*. n/a

Singh, C. (2016). Difference between point & pixel. *Linkedin*. https://www.linkedin.com/pulse/difference-between-point-pixel-charanjeet-singh/

Sitkin, S., Miller, C. C., Kelly, E. S., Lawless, M. W. (2010). The Paradox of Stretch Goals: Organizations in Pursuit of the Seemingly Impossible. *The Academy of Management Review 36*(3). https://doi.org/DOI:10.5465/AMR.2011.61031811

Skinner, S. (2006). *Sacred Geometry Deciphering the Code* (Vol. s). Sterling Publishing Company.

Skloot, G. (2022). What is Personality AI? *Crystal*. https://www.crystalknows.com/blog/what-is-personality-ai

Smith, G. (2015). 10 A/B testing tools to help improve conversions. *Mashable*. https://mashable.com/archive/ab-testing-tools#qvwzR0nGbaqh

Soegaard, M. & Friis, R. (2008). *Encyclopedia of Human-Computer Interaction*. Interaction Design Foundation.

Soegaard, M. & Friis Dam, R. (2008). The Interaction-Design.org Foundation

Spacey, J. (2017). 3 examples of design driven business. *Simplicable*. https://simplicable.com/new/design-driven

Spoelstra, J. (2013). Design thinking in het onderwijs. Folia.no. N/A.

Spradley, J. P. (1980). *Participant Observation* (1 ed.). Holt, Rinehart and Winston.

StackExchange (2022). Point vs Pixel: What is the difference? *StackExchange*. https://graphicdesign.stackexchange.com/questions/199/point-vs-pixel-what-is-the-difference

Starley, T. (2017, 5. januar). 'ROI—3 Incredible UX Case Studies!' mashable.com. https://mashable.com/2013/02/13/roi-social-media/#UjrltP9BhsqW+ https://mashable.com/2013/04/27/roi-definition/#gXfRz6bmbPqm

Stayman, D. (2015). How to Write Market Positioning Statements. *WCornell Impact*. https://ecornell-impact.cornell.edu/how-to-write-market-positioning-statements/

Steen Jensen, I. (2002). *Ona Fyr*. Dinamo.

Steen, M., Manschot, M., De Koning, N. (2011). Benefits of Co-design in Service Design Projects. IJDesign, 5(2). http://www.ijdesign.org/index.php/IJDesign/article/view/890/346

Stig og stein. Norgesmestere i design og ledelse av idéworkshopper! https://stigogstein.no/

Strain, M. (2015). 1983 to Today: A history of mobile apps. *The Guardian*. https://www.theguardian.com/media-network/2015/feb/13/history-mobile-apps-future-interactive-timeline

Strategic Business Insight: 'VALS'. http://strategicbusinessinsights.com/vals/

Strategyzer (n.d.). The Business Model Canvas. Your business model on one page. *Strategyzer*. strategyzer.com/canvas/business-model-canvas

Strategyzer. (n.d.). Business models. *Strategyzer*. https://www.strategyzer.com/expertise/business-models

Study.com (n.d.) Risk-Benefit Analysis: Definition & Example. Study.com. https://rb.gy/4y3mpa

Su, B. (2018). What is Cohort Analysis and How Should I Use it? *Medium*. https://medium.com/analytics-for-humans/what-is-cohort-analysis-and-how-should-i-use-it-3ac7c39c50dd

Superbra (n.d.) https://superbra.no/

Survey Monkey. (n.d.). *Survey Monkey*. https://www.surveymonkey.com/

SurveyMonkey. (2018). Spørreundersøkelsesmaler for markedsundersøkelser. *SurveyMonkeyInc*. https://no.surveymonkey.com/mp/market-research-survey-templates/

Sutherland, C. (2019). 5 Key Benefits of Organizational Development. https://explorance.com/blog/5-key-benefits-organizational-development/

Svartdal, F. (2017). Eksperiment. In *I Store norske leksikon*.

Svendsen, L. F. H. (2021). Symbol. In *Store norske leksikon*.

Sznel, M. (2020). The Time for Environment-Centered Design Has Come. *UX Collective*. https://uxdesign.cc/the-time-for-environment-centered-design-has-come-770123c8cc61

Szymańska, E. (2017). User-Driven Innovation – The Concept and Research Results. *Procedia Engineering, 182*, 694–700. DOI:10.1016/j.proeng.2017.03.182

Sørhøy, S. M., & Heir, W. (2017). Observasjon. *ndla.no*. ndla.no/nb/node/5472?fag=52

Tarver, E. (2021). Corporate Culture. *Investopedia*.

Tassi, R. (2009). Service Design Tools: Communication methods supporting design processes. *Service Design Tools*. https://servicedesigntools.org/

Taylor, M. D. (2006). *International Competition Law*. Cambridge University Press, UK. https://doi.org/https://doi.org/10.1017/CBO9780511494574

Taylor, Martyn D. (2006). *International Competition Law: A new dimension for the WTO?*. Cambridge University Press. p. 1.

Thagaard, Tove (1998). Systematikk og innlevelse. En innføring i kvalitativ metode. Bergen: Fagbokforlaget

The 16-Personality Test, based on the types of Jung, Myers, & Briggs (n.d.). *Crystal*. https://www.crystalknows.com/jung-myers-and-briggs-personality-test

The Coca-Cola Company. coca-colacompany.com

The Grove Consultants International, thegrove.com 'Grove Tools'. (January 1, 1996). https://grovetools-inc.com/collections/graphic-gameplan
The Grove Consultants International, thegrove.com Grove Tools (1996). 2021 from: https://grovetools-inc.com/collections/graphic-gameplan
TheConversation. (2020). *What is an algorithm? How computers know what to do with data*. https://theconversation.com/what-is-an-algorithm-how-computers-know-what-to-do-with-data-146665
TheLogoCreative. (2019). Rebrand vs Brand Refresh vs Redesign: 4 Signs That You Need to Update Your Logo. *The Logo Creative*. https://thelogocreative.medium.com/rebrand-vs-brand-refresh-vs-redesign-4-signs-that-you-need-to-update-your-logo-adf30948b9f6
Thorn. (2022). 6 principles for sustainability. *Thorn*. https://www.thornlighting.com/en/news/6-principles-for-sustainability
Thrive. (n.d.). Measuring what matters most. https://strive2thrive.earth/
Tiner, J. H. (2004). *Exploring the World of Mathematics: From Ancient Record Keeping to the Latest Advances in Computers*. New Leaf Publishing Group.
Traffis, C. (n.d.). Restrictive and Nonrestrictive Clauses—What's the Difference? *Grammarly blog*. https://www.grammarly.com/blog/using-that-and-which-is-all-about-restrictive-and-non-restrictive-clauses/?gclid=EAIaIQobChMIybuQ4ZbR9AIV4iitBh1OlwSfEAAYASAAEgJJz_D_BwE&gclsrc=aw.ds
Treder, M. (2016). Wireframing, prototyping, mockuping - What's
Trillum ESG Criteria. (2021). Active portfolios, global impact. *Trilluminvest*. https://www.trilliuminvest.com/documents/positive-negative-screens
Trott, P. (2017). *Innovation Management and New Product Development* (6th ed.). Pearson Education Limited.
Tschichold, J. (1967). *Asymmetric typography*. Reinhold Publishing.
Tschichold, J. (1991). *The Form of the Book: Essays on the morality of good design*. Hartley & Marks.
Tschichold, J. (2006). *The New Typography* (1st ed.). University of California Press.
Tschohl, J. (2012). Walk In Your Customers' Shoes: Doing So Will Give You the Information You Need To Grow Your Business. *Service Quality Institute*. https://customer-service.com/Walk-In-Your-Customers-Shoes-Doing-So-Will-Give-You-the-Information-You-Need-To-Grow-Your-Business/
United Nations. (2022). UN Climate Report: It's 'now or never' to limit global warming to 1.5 degrees. *UN News*. https://news.un.org/en/story/2022/04/1115452
UnitedNations. (2015). *The 17 goals. UN Sutainable goals (SDG)*. United Nations Department of Economic and Social Affairs. https://sdgs.un.org/goals
Van der Weel, R. (n.d.) Perception Movement Action.
Van Riel, C. (1996). *Principles of Corporate Communication* (2nd ed.). Prentice Hall.
Van Riel, C. (2010). Identiteit en imago; een inleiding in de corporate communication In M. Bouw (Ed.), (pp. 30–74). https://feb.studenttheses.ub.rug.nl/2007/1/MABouw.pdf
Van Riel, C., & Riel, B. C.M. (2002). *Identiteit en imago: grondslagen van corporate communication*. Academic Service
Van Vliet, V. (2011). Marketing mix, the 4p's (McCarthy). *ToolsHero*. https://www.toolshero.com/marketing/marketing-mix-4p-mccarthy/
Vanessa. (2022). What Are Internal & External Environmental Factors That Affect Business. *Mageplaza*. https://www.mageplaza.com/blog/what-are-internal-external-environmental-factors-that-affect-business.html
VanPatter, G. K., & Pastor, E. (2011). Next Design Geographies: Understanding design thinking 1,2,3,4.
VanPatter, G. K., & Pastor, E. (2013). *Innovation methods mapping, preview version*. Humantific for OPEN Innovation Consortium. Systemic Design Conference Oslo. https://issuu.com/humantific/docs/oslo_presentation_methodsmap
VanPatter, G. K., & Pastor, E. (2016). *Innovation methods mapping. Demystifying 80+ years of innovation process design*. Humantific Publishing.
Veal, R. (2021). How To Conduct User Experience Research Like A Professional. *CareerFoundry*. https://careerfoundry.com/en/blog/ux-design/how-to-conduct-user-experience-research-like-a-professional/
Vedeld, K., & Venheim, R. (2012). Formlikhet og kongruens. *Matematikk.org*. https://www.matematikk.org/artikkel.html?tid=155073
Venge, H. (2009). What is user-driven innovation - and what is not.
Verganti, R. & Öberga, Å. (2013). Interpreting and envisioning — A hermeneutic framework to look at radical innovation of meanings. *Industrial Marketing Management, 42*(1), 86–95. https://doi.org/10.1016/j.indmarman.2012.11.012
Verganti, R., (2008). Design, Meanings, and Radical Innovation: A Metamodel and a Research Agenda. *Journal of Product Innovation Management, 25*(5), 436–456. https://doi-org.ezproxy2.usn.no/10.1111/j.1540-5885.2008.00313.x
Verganti, R., (2009). *Design-driven Innovation: Changing the rules of competition by radically innovating what things mean*. Boston: Harvard Business Press.
Verganti, R., Vendraminelli, L., Lansiti, M. (2020). Innovation and Design in the Age of Artificial Intelligence. *Journal of Product Innovation Managemnent, 37*(3), 212–227. https://doi-org.ezproxy2.usn.no/10.1111/jpim.12523
Verma, P. (2017). The Blue Ocean Strategy: How To Create Uncontested Market Space and Make the Competition Irrelevant. *Linkedin*. https://www.linkedin.com/pulse/blue-ocean-strategy-how-create-uncontested-market-space-priyank-verma/?trk=public_profile_article_view
Vickers, J. (2011). Can induction be justified? In *The Stanford Encyclopedia of Philosophy*.
Vieru, T. (2009). KSC Gets Orion Mock-Up for Testing. *Softpedia News*. https://news.softpedia.com/news/KSC-Gets-Orion-Mock-Up-for-Testing-103300.shtml
Wagemans, J., Elder, J. H., Kubovy, M., Palmer, S. H., Peterson, M. A., Singh, M., von der Heydt, R. (2012). A Century of Gestalt Psychology in Visual Perception: I. Perceptual grouping and figure-ground organization. *National lLibrary of Medicine, 138*(6), 1172–1217. https://doi.org/doi: 10.1037/a0029333.
Ward, Andrew (2017). Enterprise UX Design: Unlocking ROI from the inside out. n drawbackwards.com. Retrieved March 15, 2022 from https://www.drawbackwards.com/blog/enterprise-ux-design-unlocking-roi-from-the-inside-out
Ward, M. R. & Lee, M. J. (2000). Internet shopping, consumer search and product branding, *Journal of Product & Brand Management, 9*(1), 6–20, https://doi.org/10.1108/10610420010316302
Ware, C. (2008). *Visual Thinking for Design* (1st ed.). Morgan Kaufmann
Warren, J (2016). Forget the 4 P's! What are the 4 C's of marketing? *Catmedia*. https://catmediatheagency.com/4-ps-of-marketing-strategy/
Wasson, C. (2000). Ethnography in the Field of Design *Human Organization. Social Science Premium Collection., 59*(4), 377–388.
Watkins, C. (2014). Hva er A/B-testing?, *Synlighetsbloggen*. N/A.
Wertheimer, M. (1923/1938). Untersuchungen zur Lehre von der Gestalt II. *Psychologische Forschung*, 4, 301–350. (Excerpts translated into English as 'Laws of Organization in Perceptual Forms' in W. D. Ellis (Ed.), *A Source Book of Gestalt Psychology*. New York: Hartcourt, Brace and Co., and as 'Principle of Perceptual Organization' in D. C. Beardslee & Michael Wertheimer (Eds.), *Readings in Perception*, Princeton, NJ: D. Van Nostrand Co., Inc.).
Westhagen et al. (2008). Prosjektarbeid. Gyldendal.
Westhagen, H., Faafeng, O., Hoff, K. G., Kjeldsen, T. & Røine, E. (2008). *Prosjektarbeid. Utviklings- og endringskompetanse* (opplag 6, 2016). Gyldendal.
Wettre, A., Sevaldson, B., Dudani, P. (2019). *Bridging Silos: A New Workshop Method for Training Silo Busting* Systemic Design Association, https://rsdsymposium.org/bridging-silos-a-new-workshop-method-for-training-silo-busting/
Wetzler, T. (2021). How to Create an App Icon: Essential insights and best practices. *Adjust*. https://www.adjust.com/blog/choosing-the-right-icon-for-your-app/
Wheeler, A. (2012). *Designing Brand Identity: An Essential Guide for the Whole Branding Team* (4th ed.). John Wiley and Sons.
Wheeler, A. (2017). *Designing Brand Identity* (5th ed.). John Wiley & Sons Inc.
White, M., & Morgan, A. (2006). Narrative Therapy with Children and Their Families. Adelaide, South Australia: Dulwich Centre Publications.

Wiik, T. (2015, 10. mars). 'Westhagens styringssløyfe' YouTube.com youtube.com/watch?v=j9hTzKhSSQc
Wildhagen, B. (2021). Combining Service and Systemic Design in Norway's Public Sector. *Service Design Network*. https://www.service-design-network.org/community-knowledge/combining-service-and-systemic-design-in-norways-public-sector
Wilkinson, S. (1998). Focus Group Methodology: A review. *International Journal of Social Research Methodology, 1*(3), 181–203.
Wilson, J. (2018). Five Reasons To Prioritize Sustainability In Your Brand Playbook. *Nielsen*. https://www.nielsen.com/eu/en/insights/article/2018/five-reasons-to-prioritize-sustainability-in-your-brand-playbook/
Wilson, M. (2014). Why VC firms are snapping up designers. *FastCompany*. https://www.fastcompany.com/3029639/why-vc-firms-are-snapping-up-designers
Wipo. (n.d.). IP. *World Intellectual Property Organization*. https://www.wipo.int/portal/en/index.html
Womack, J. P., & Jones, D.T. (1996). *Lean Thinking – Banish Waste and Create Wealth in your Corporation* (1st ed.). Free Press. https://www.mudamasters.com/en/lean-production/lean-thinking-jpwomack-dtjones-summary
Wong, J. (2016). The Four C's of Marketing. *Sales&Marketing*. https://www.business2community.com/marketing/four-cs-marketing-01459349
Woodford, C. (2018). How printing works. *Explain that stuff*. https://www.explainthatstuff.com/how-printing-works.html
Woodward, M. (2021). 16 Countries with GDPR-like Data Privacy Laws. *SecurityScorecard*. https://securityscorecard.com/blog/countries-with-gdpr-like-data-privacy-laws
Woodward, M. (2021). 16 Countries with GDPR-like Data Privacy Laws. *Security Scorecard*. https://securityscorecard.com/blog/countries-with-gdpr-like-data-privacy-laws
Wordstream. (2018). What Is a conversion rate? In *Wordstream.com*.
Working paper: Measuring and Defining Design. *British Design Council*. https://www.designcouncil.org.uk/sites/default/files/asset/document/value-design.pdf
Wright, G. (2021). What is RFM (Recency, Frequency, Monetary) analysis? *TechTarget*. https://www.techtarget.com/searchdatamanagement/definition/RFM-analysis
Wright, P., & McCarthy, J. (2005). The value of the novel in designing for experience. In Pirhonen, A., Saariluoma, P., Isomäki, H., Roast, C. (eds) *Future Interaction Design*. Springer, p. 9–30. https://doi.org/10.1007/1-84628-089-3_2
Wright, T. (2021). The 101 Most Inspiring Vision Statement Exam-ples We've Ever Seen! *Cascade*. https://www.cascade.app/blog/examples-good-vision-statements
Xie, H. Y., & Boggs, D. J. (2006). Corporate Branding versus Product Branding in Emerging Markets: A conceptual framework, Marketing Intelligence & Planning *Marketing Intelligence & Planning, 24*(4), 347–364. https://doi.org/https://doi.org/10.1108/02634500610672099
Y&R, Young & Rubicam. (2010). There Are Seven Kinds of People in the World. *Issuu*. https://issuu.com/youngandrubicam/docs/4cs
Yu, Jim (2013). Earned Media Rising – The Earned Media Ripple Effect. *Martech*. https://martech.org/earned-media-rising-the-earned-media-ripple-effect/
Zhel, M. (2016). The Beginner's Guide to a Sales Funnel. *Mailmunch*. mailmunch.co/blog/sales-funnel/
Zurb. (n.d.) Iteration. A cyclical process to improve the quality and function of design. *Zurb.com*.
Zwimpfer, M. (2001). *Visual Perception: Elementary Phenomena of Two-dimensional Perception. A Handbook for Artists and Designers* (2nd ed). Niggli
Øvregård, M. O. (2020). Hva er implementering. https://www.uis.no/nb/laringsmiljosenteret/forskning/implementering-i-skole-og-barnehagekontekst#/

## Encyclopedia

A snowball effect. (n.d.). In *Cambridge Dictionary* Retrieved March 15, 2022 from https://dictionary. cambridge.org/dictionary/english/a-snowball-effect
Adidas Parley. (n.d.). In *Wikipedia*. Retrieved March 15, 2022 from https://en.wikipedia.org/wiki/Adidas_Parley
Alan Bryman. (n.d.). In *Wikipedia*. Retrieved March 15, 2022 from https://en.wikipedia.org/wiki/Alan_Bryman
Alnes, J. H. (2017). Hypotetisk Deduktiv Metode. In *Store norske leksikon*.
API. (n.d.). In *Oxford Languages*.
Aspect Ratio. (n.d.). In *Wikipedia*. Retrieved March 15, 2022 from https://en.wikipedia.org/wiki/Aspect_ratio_(image)
Aubert, K. E. (n.d.). Flate (matematikk). In *Store Norske Leksikon*. Retrieved March 15, 2022 from https://snl.no/flate_-_matematikk
Aubert, K. E. (n.d.). Kongruens – geometri In *Store Norske Leksikon*. Retrieved March 15, 2022 from https://snl.no/kongruens_-_geometri
Aubert, K. E. (n.d.). Punkt (matematisk). In *Store Norske Leksikon*. Retrieved March 15, 2022 from https://snl.no/punkt_-_matematisk
Big data. (n.d.). In *OxfordReferences*. Retrieved March 15, 2022 from https://www.oxfordreference.com/search?q=Big+data&searchBtn=Search&isQuickSearch=true
Black Swan. (2022). In *Investopedia*. Retrieved March 15, 2022 from https://www.investopedia.com/terms/b/blackswan.asp
Bolierplate text. (n.d.). In *Wikipedia*. Retrieved March 15, 2022 from https://en.wikipedia.org/wiki/Boilerplate_text
Brainwriting. (n.d.). In *Wikipedia*. Retrieved March 15, 2022 from https://en.wikipedia.org/wiki/6-3-5_Brainwriting
Brand equity (n.d.) In *Lexico*. Retrieved March 15, 2022 from https://www.lexico.com/definition/brand_equity
Brand. (n.d.). In *Wikipedia*. Retrieved March 15, 2022 from https://en.wikipedia.org/wiki/Brand
Budget. (n.d.). In *CambridgeDictionary*. Retrieved March 15, 2022 from https://dictionary.cambridge.org/dictionary/english/budget
Cai Lun. (n.d.). In *Wikipedia*. Retrieved March 15, 2022 from https://en.wikipedia.org/wiki/Cai_Lun
Cartesian coordinate system. (n.d.). In *Wikiwand*. Retrieved March 15, 2022 from https://www.wikiwand.com/simple/Cartesian_coordinate_system
Cliché. (n.d.). In *Wikipedia*. Retrieved March 15, 2022 from https://en.wikipedia.org/wiki/Clich%C3%A9
Composition. (n.d.). In *Lexico*. Retrieved March 15, 2022 from https://www.lexico.com/definition/composition
Congruence. (n.d.). In *Your Dictionary*. Retrieved March 15, 2022 from https://www.yourdictionary.com/congruence
Consistent. (n.d.). In Merriam-Webster. Retrieved March 15, 2022 from https://www.merriam-webster.com/dictionary/consistent
Contextual inquiry. (n.d.). In *Wikipedia*. Retrieved March 15, 2022 from https://en.wikipedia.org/wiki/Contextual_inquiry
Copyright. (n.d.). In *Lexico*. Retrieved March 15, 2022 from https://www.lexico.com/definition/copyright
Cradle to cradle design. (n.d.). In *Wikipedia*. Retrieved March 15, 2022 from https://en.wikipedia.org/wiki/Cradle-to-cradle_design
Culture. (n.d.). In Merriam-Webster. Retrieved March 15, 2022 from https://www.merriam-webster.com/dictionary/culture
David E. Kelley. (n.d.). In *Wikipedia*. Retrieved March 15, 2022 from https://en.wikipedia.org/wiki/David_M._Kelley
Descriptive. (n.d.). In Merriam-Webster. Retrieved March 15, 2022 from https://www.merriam-webster.com/dictionary/descriptive
Design Research. (n.d.). In *Wikipedia*. Retrieved March 15, 2022 from
Ecofont. (n.d.). In *Wikipedia*. Retrieved March 15, 2022 from https://en.wikipedia.org/wiki/Ecofont
Ecosystem. (n.d.). In *Lexico*. Retrieved March 15, 2022 from *Lexico*. https://www.lexico.com/definition/ecosystem
Elevator pitch. (n.d.). In *Wikipedia*. Retrieved March 15, 2022 from https://en.wikipedia.org/wiki/Elevator_pitch
Engraving. (n.d.). In *Wikipedia*. Retrieved March 15, 2022 from https://en.wikipedia.org/wiki/Engraving
Euclid's Elements. (n.d.). In *Wikipedia*. Retrieved March 15, 2022 from https://en.wikipedia.org/wiki/Euclid%27s_Elements

Eureka. (n.d.). In *Wikipedia*. Retrieved March 15, 2022 from https://en.wikipedia.org/wiki/Eureka
Eye tracking. (n.d.). In *Wikipedia*. Retrieved March 15, 2022 from https://en.wikipedia.org/wiki/Eye_tracking
Favicon. (n.d.). In *Wikipedia*. Retrieved March 15, 2022 from https://en.wikipedia.org/wiki/Favicon
Form. (n.d.). In *Wikipedia*. Retrieved March 15, 2022 from https://en.wikipedia.org/wiki/Form
Gap analysis. (n.d.) In *Wikipedia*. Retrieved March 15, 2022 from https://en.wikipedia.org/wiki/Gap_analysis
Gestalt psychology. (n.d.). In *Britannica*. Retrieved March 15, 2022 from https://www.britannica.com/science/Gestalt-psychology
Gestalt. (n.d.). In *Lexico*. Retrieved March 15, 2022 from https://www.lexico.com/en/definition/gestalt
Golden ratio. (n.d.). In *Wikipedia*. Retrieved March 15, 2022 from https://en.wikipedia.org/wiki/Golden_ratio
Golden rectangle. (n.d.). In *Wikipedia*. Retrieved March 15, 2022 from https://en.wikipedia.org/wiki/Golden_rectangle
Graphics. (n.d.). In *Wikipedia*. Retrieved March 15, 2022 from https://en.wikipedia.org/wiki/Graphics
Gundersen, D. (n.d.). Jingle. In *Store norske leksikon*. Retrieved March 15, 2022 from https://snl.no/jingle
Gundersen, D., Halbo, L. (2018). Kvalitet. In *Store norske leksikon*. Retrieved March 15, 2022 from https://snl.no/kvalitet
Gutenberg Bible. (n.d.). In *Wikipedia*. Retrieved March 15, 2022 from https://en.wikipedia.org/wiki/Gutenberg_Bible
Hollywood model. (n.d.). In *Wikipedia*. Retrieved March 15, 2022 from https://no.wikipedia.org/wiki/Hollywood-modellen
https://en.wikipedia.org/wiki/Aspect_ratio
https://en.wikipedia.org/wiki/Design_research
https://en.wikipedia.org/wiki/Influencer_marketing
Hubspot. (n.d.). In *Wikipedia*. Retrieved March 15, 2022 from https://en.wikipedia.org/wiki/HubSpot
Human resources. (n.d.). In *Oxford Language Dictionaries*.
Hypothesis. (n.d.) In *Oxfordlearnerdictionaries*. Retrieved March 15, 2022 from https://www.oxfordlearnersdictionaries.com/definition/english/hypothesis
Hypothesis. (n.d.). In *Oxford Language Dictionaries*.
Implementation. (n.d.). In *Wikipedia*. Retrieved March 15, 2022 from https://en.wikipedia.org/wiki/Implementation
Implementere (n.d.) In *Wiktionary*. https://no.wiktionary.org/wiki/implementere
Influencer marketing. (n.d.). In *Wikipedia*. Retrieved March 15, 2022 from https://en.wikipedia.org/wiki/Influencer_marketing
International Organisation for Standardization (ISO). (n.d.). In *Wikipedia*. Retrieved March 15, 2022 from https://en.wikipedia.org/wiki/International_Organization_for_Standardization
ISO 216. (n.d.). In *Wikipedia*. Retrieved March 15, 2022 from https://en.wikipedia.org/wiki/ISO_216
Karl Popper. (n.d.). In *Wikipedia*. Retrieved March 15, 2022 from https://no.wikipedia.org/wiki/Karl_Popper
Konvergere. (n.d.). In *Store norske leksikon*. Retrieved March 15, 2022 from https://snl.no/konvergere
Liseter, I. M. og Rolstad.s, A. (2018, 24 April). Kravspesifikasjon. In *Store norske leksikon*. https://snl.no/kravspesifikasjon.
Metaverse. (n.d.). In *Lexico*. Retrieved March 15, 2022 from https://www.lexico.com/definition/metaverse
Michelin Guide. (n.d.). In *Wikipedia*. Retrieved March 15, 2022 from https://en.wikipedia.org/wiki/Michelin_Guide
Narrative. (n.d.). In Merriam-Webster. Retrieved March 15, 2022 from https://www.merriam-webster.com/dictionary/narrative
NGO. (n.d.). In *Lexico*. Retrieved March 15, 2022 from https://www.lexico.com/definition/ngo
Nude Descending a Staircase, No. 2. (n.d.). In *Wikipedia*. Retrieved March 15, 2022 from https://en.wikipedia.org/wiki/Nude_Descending_a_Staircase,_No._2
Offset printing (printing technique). (n.d). In *Encyclopaedia Britannica*. Retrieved Augusr 22, 2022 from https://www.britannica.com/technology/offset printing
Organization. (n.d.). In *Lexico*. Retrieved March 15, 2022 from https://www.lexico.com/definition/organization
Organization. (n.d.). In *Oxford Languages*.
PDCA. (n.d.). In *Wikipedia*. Retrieved March 15, 2022 from https://en.wikipedia.org/wiki/PDCA
Phenomenon. (n.d.). In Merriam-Webster. Retrieved March 15, 2022 from https://www.merriam-webster.com/dictionary/phenomenon
Phi. (n.d.). In *Wikipedia*. Retrieved March 15, 2022 from https://en.wikipedia.org/wiki/Phi
Pictogram. (n.d.). In *Wikipedia*. Retrieved March 15, 2022 from https://en.wikipedia.org/wiki/Pictogram
Pitch (n.d.). *In Lexico*. Retrieved March 15, 2022 from https://www.lexico.com/definition/pitch
Problematique. (n.d.). In *Lexico*. Retrieved March 15, 2022 from https://www.lexico.com/definition/problematique
Product backlog. (n.d.). In *Wikipedia*. Retrieved March 15, 2022 from https://en.wikipedia.org/wiki/Product_backlog
Promotion. (n.d.). In *Lexico*. Retrieved March 15, 2022 from https://www.lexico.com/definition/promotion
Proxy. (n.d.). In *Oxford Language Dictionaries*.
Proxy. (n.d). In *Cambridge Dictionary*. Retrieved March 15, 2022 from https://dictionary.cambridge.org/dictionary/english/proxy
Quintessence. (n.d.). In *Lexico*. Retrieved March 15, 2022 from https://www.lexico.com/en/definition/quintessence
Raison d'être Merriam-Webster, (n.d.) In *Meriam-Webster.com dictionary*. https://www.merriam-webster.com/dictionary/raison%20d%27%C3%AAtre
Registered trademark. (n.d.). In *Wikipedia*. Retrieved March 15, 2022 from https://en.wikipedia.org/wiki/Registered_trademark_symbol
Reputation. (n.d.). In *Wikipedia*. Retrieved March 15, 2022 from https://en.wikipedia.org/wiki/Reputation
Research. (n.d.). In *OxfordLearnersDictionaries*. Retrieved March 15, 2022 from https://www.oxfordlearnersdictionaries.com/definition/english/research_1
Risograph (n.d.). In *Wikipedia*. https://en.wikipedia.org/wiki/Risograph
Rouen Cathedral. (n.d.). In *Wikipedia*. Retrieved March 15, 2022 from https://en.wikipedia.org/wiki/Rouen_Cathedral
Sagdahl, M. S. (n.d.). Verdi. In *Store norske leksikon*. Retrieved March 15, 2022 from https://snl.no/verdi
Scientific. (n.d). In *Cambridge Dictionary*. Retrieved March 15, 2022 from https://dictionary.cambridge.org/dictionary/english/scientific
Scrum. (n.d.). In *Wikipedia*. Retrieved March 15, 2022 from https://no.wikipedia.org/wiki/Scrum
Social science. (n.d.). In Merriam-Webster. Retrieved March 15, 2022 from https://www.merriam-webster.com/dictionary/social%20science
Sony. (n.d.). In *Wikipedia*. Retrieved March 15, 2022 from https://no.wikipedia.org/wiki/Sony
Space X. (n.d.). In *Wikipedia*. Retrieved March 15, 2022 from https://no.wikipedia.org/wiki/SpaceX
Square root of 2. (n.d.). In *Wikipedia*. Retrieved March 15, 2022 from https://en.wikipedia.org/wiki/Square_root_of_2
Synectics. (n.d.). In *Wikipedia*. Retrieved March 15, 2022 from https://en.wikipedia.org/wiki/Synectics
Systemic design. (n.d.). In *Wikipedia*. Retrieved March 15, 2022 from https://en.wikipedia.org/wiki/Systemic_design
The fifth element. (n.d.). In *Wikipedia*. Retrieved March 15, 2022 from https://en.wikipedia.org/wiki/Fifth_Element
The Medium is The Massage. (n.d.). In *Wikipedia*. Retrieved March 15, 2022 from https://en.wikipedia.org/wiki/The_Medium_Is_the_Massage
The raison d'être of raison d'être. (n.d.) In *Lexico*. Retrieved March 15, 2022 from https://www.lexico.com/definition/raison_d'etre
Trademark. (n.d.). In *Wikipedia*. Retrieved March 15, 2022 from https://en.wikipedia.org/wiki/Trademark
Tranøy, K. E. (n.d.). Hypotese. In *Store norske leksikon*. Retrieved March 15, 2022 from https://snl.no/hypotese
Tranøy, K. E., Tjønneland, E. (n.d.). Analyse. In *Store norske leksikon*. Retrieved March 15, 2022 from https://snl.no/analyse
Trial and error. (n.d.). In Merriam-Webster. Retrieved March 15, 2022 from https://www.merriam-webster.com/dictionary/trial%20and%20error
Trichromacy. (n.d.). In *Wikipedia*. Retrieved March 15, 2022 from https://en.wikipedia.org/wiki/Trichromacy
Value proposition. (n.d.). In *Wikipedia*. Retrieved March 15, 2022 from https://en.wikipedia.org/wiki/Value_proposition
Vikøren, B. M. (2019). Markedsstrategi In *Store norske leksikon* Retrieved March 15, 2022 from https://snl.no/markedsstrategi

Vikøren, B. M., Pihl, R. Fokusgruppe In *Store norske leksikon* Retrieved March 15, 2022 https://snl.no/fokusgruppe
Virtual reality (VR). (n.d.). In *Lexico*. Retrieved March 15, 2022 from https://www.lexico.com/en/definition/virtual_reality
Zeigarnik. (n.d.). In *Wikipedia*. Retrieved March 15, 2022 from https://en.wikipedia.org/wiki/Bluma_Zeigarnik
Ørstavik, F. (n.d.). Innovasjon. In *Store norske leksikon*. Retrieved March 15, 2022 from https://snl.no/innovasjon

## Personal conversations, interviews and consultations

Appelong, B. Interior Architect, Designinstituttet, (2017)
Arnstein Johansen, E., Study Programme Director at design at NTNU (2017/2022)
Bakkelund, E., Advisor at Arctic Paper Norge AS, (2017)
Bendixen, A., Founding Partner at NSB Marketing Best Practice (2022)
Bergan, T. Senior Advicer Design at Design and Architecture Norway, Doga (2017/2022)
Brantenberg, Ina, Creative Leader/Partner at Tank (2022)
Brekke-Bjørkedal, A. Graphic Designer, Advicer at Oslo Municipality (2017)
Clausen, K. at Kaj Claussen Design AS, (2017)
Eide, E. Architect, Principal at Designinstituttet (2017)
Faukland, E., Creative Director at Moltzau Packaging AS (2022)
Feirud, L., Associate Professor at USN School of Business, University of South-Eastern Norway, USN (2017)
Fjelldal, A., Creative Director at Innoventi (2022)
Fredin, J., CTO and Senior Advisor at Mvh AS (2022)
Furu, N. Author and Partner at Webgruppen (2017/2022)
Gamborg, L. C. Graphic Designer (2017)
Gürgens, C., Senior Designer at Bold Scandinavia (2017/2022)
Hovet, M., Co-founder of Wanda, Heydays, Goods (2017/2022)
Hvammen Nicholson, T. Attorney at Law, Protector IP (2022)
Høie, L., Graphic Designer (2017/2022)
Johansen, E., Interior Designer (2017)
Karlsen, H. Head of Strategy Consulting at Compete Consulting Group AS (2017)
Kaspartu, E., Project manager digital innovation at Munch Museum (2017/2022)
Lien, L. Faculty of Fine Art, Music and Design at UIB, University of Bergen (2017)
Loe, M. Grimsgaard. Architect (2017)
Lysbakken, N., Lecturer at University of South-Eastern Norway and PhD fellow at The Oslo School of Architecture and Design
Madsen, S. O., Associate Professor at USN School of Business, University of South-Eastern Norway USN (2022)
Myhre, A. Client Director at Dinamo Design (2017/2022)
Olsen, L., Dean for Bachelor Programs/Professor of Marketing at BI Norwegian Business School (2022)
Opstad, B. Vice Dean at USN School of Business, University of South-Eastern Norway, USN (2017)
Rannem, Ø. Author, Typographer (2017)
Reenskaug, K., (2017), Head of Experience Strategy and Design Europe at Cognizant
Rekdal Nielsen, H., Co-founder and Creative Leader of Industrial Design at EGGS Design (2017/2022)
Sikkes, T. Assistant Professor at USN School of Business, University of South-Eastern Norway (2017)
Sitre, T. Consulting Director at Sopra Steria (2017/2022)
Skomsøy, G.A. Writer, consultant (2017)
Thorsen, D.E. Associate Professor at USN School of Business, University of South-Eastern Norway, USN (2017/2022)
Throndsen, M. Creative Director at Strømme Throndsen Design (2017/2022)
Thyness, J., Partner at Webgruppen (2017/2022)
Tofting, A., European Patent Attorney at Protector IP (2022).
Wildhagen, B. Senior Advicer Design at Design and Architecture Norway, Doga (2017/2022)
Winther, U. Communications Advisor/Secretary General at Norwegian Association Against Noise (2017/2022)

**A selection of interviews from 2017 and 2018 are available in short version at designandstrategy.co.uk**

## Illustration/model/photo loans

Morten Throndsen, creative director, Strømme Throndsen Design
Skule Storheill, Senior adviser Administration and IT at Nordic Innovation
Jonathan Romm, designer/advisor, Halogen
Frode Helland, font designer, Monokrom Skriftforlag
Anine Heitun, graphic designer, Graphic Designer at NYG Reklame
Sidsel Lie, partner/strategic advisor in design and brand, Grid design
Rune Døli, graphic designer, Graphic Designer at Modest
Endre Berentzen, executive creative director, founding partner, Anti Inc Bergen AS
The Museum of Modern Art, New York/Scala, Florence
Nina Furu og Jakob Thyness, Webgruppen

3D data modelling *538*
3D printing *536, 578*
3 Gears of Business Design *384*

# A

A/B testing *166*
A/B testing process *166*
a gap in the market *267*
abstract shapes *424*
ACCID workshop *139*
action plan *178, 331*
activity analysis *121*
administrative decisions *52*
AEIOU Empathy Map *98*
age and life cycle *130*
agile *372*
agile process management *39*
agile strategy *180, 222*
AI-driven Innovation *363*
ambition *34*
analogue media *328*
analyses *115*
analyses that provide insight *116*
analysis of competitors *123*
analysis of findings *154*
analysis of qualitative data *80*
analysis of quantitative data *81*
analysis process *117*
analysis/discussion *77*
app icon *282*
applied research *109*
AR and VR mockups *536*
argument *8*
artificial intelligence *132*
artistic research *112*
aspect ratios *455*
Audio Logo *288*
automated segmentation *132*
average tonality *170*

# B

B2B *130*
B2C *130*
baby boomers *131*
backend *575*
backend frameworks *575*
backend languages *575*
Balanced Scorecard *207*
baseline *527*
basic *421*
basic research *109*
basic research vs. applied research *109*
behavioural segmentation *132*
BHAG *203*
big hairy goals *203*
blue ocean strategy *215*
blueprint *539*
boilerplate *319*
bottom line results *208*
brainstorming *396*
brainstorming checklist *404*
brainstorming methods *402*
brainstorming process *396*
brand *246*
brand analysis *137*
brand analysis internally/externally *138*
brand analysis process *138, 139*
brand architecture *251*
brand assets *288*
brand categorisation *261*
brand character *284*
brand colour *283*
brand consistency *193*
brand extension *297*
brand goal and strategy *245*
brand hierarchy *258*
brand identity *140, 276*
brand levels *259*
brand management *249*
brand meaning *141*
brand name *289*
brand narrative *271*
brand narrative process *274*
brand perspective *296*
brand platform *251*
brand positioning *260*
brand redesign *299*
brand relationship *142, 279*
brand response *141*
brand strategies *257*
brand strategy *179, 245*
branded house strategy *254*
branding *248*
budget *30*
business concept *189*
business design *383*
business goals *202*
business idea *187*
business model *178, 225*
Business Model Canvas *227*
business model innovation *228*
business plan *178*
business strategy *178, 211*

# C

category entry points (CEPs) *170, 311*
channels and media *325*
chipboard *550*
choice of method *78*
choice of strategy *152*
choice of units *77, 79*
choice of values *194*
classic typefaces *515*
clear-space *608*
closed questions *93*
CMYK *557, 572, 580*
co-branding *254*
co-design *381*
coherent *488*
collaboration *32*
collaboration agreement *36*
collection of data *77*
colour *426*
colour channels *565*
colour gamut *559*
colour influence *496*
colour management *556*
colour management module (CMM) *557*
colour models *558*
colour profiles *560*
colour reference systems *572*
colour scheme *494*
colour settings *563, 564*
colour theories and systems *428*
column spacing *512*
column title *512*
columns *527*
communication audit *304*
communication channels *325*
communication development *321*
communication elements *318*
communication goals *309*
communication measurement *329*
communication mix *329*
communication platform *315*
communication process *322*
communication strategy *179, 300*
communication strategy development *301*
communication tasks *309*
company *50*
company name *593*
company's universe *54*
competition act *30*
competition analysis *123*
competition law *30*
competitive analysis *124*
competitive strategy *175, 178, 211*
competitor analysis *122*
competitor study *144*
competitors *123*
complex problem *161*
complex tasks *163*
composition *433*
computer sketches *416*
concept development *157, 390*
concept story *272*
conceptual directions *409*
concrete design *417*
concretised *412*
content marketing *238*
content marketing vs. inbound marketing *240*
content strategy *238*
context *64*
contract *31*
control loop *35*
converge *366*
conversion rate *167*
copyright *590*
core values *157, 178, 191*
corporate brand vs. product brand *246*
corporate communication *309*
corporate communication goals *309*
corporate identity *XII, 57, 192, 193*
corruption *69*
cost leadership *212*
counterfeiting *595*
cradle-to-cradle *556*
creative problem solving *392*
creativity *393*
critical success factors *169*
cultural anchoring *273*

current situation *202*
customer journey *160, 376*
customer journey process *378*
customer surveys *89*
customer workshop *159*
customer's needs *233*

# D

data analysis *80*
data collection *46*
data collection, advanced *76*
data collection, simplified *75*
data collection (Step 5) *80*
data interpretation *81*
data modelling *538*
data simulation *538*
decision areas *52*
decision making *51*
deductive (extensive) *111*
defining the problem *61*
delimitation of problem statement *63*
demographic segmentation *130*
descriptive or explanatory problem statement *66*
design *X, 339, 340*
design brief *179, 345*
design brief template *347*
design development *412*
design effect *597*
design elements *421*
design goal *334*
design impact *601*
design impact awards *601*
Design ladder *598*
design management *596*
design manual *604*
design methodology *354*
design platform *335*
design process *342, 345*
design research *49, 113*
design rights *594*
design sketches *413*
design software tools *567*
design sprint *368*
design sprint process *369*
design strategy *179, 213, 332*
Design strategy compass *333*
design strategy development *333*
design strategy vs. design brief *336*
design templates *612*
design thinking *374*
design-driven company *600*
design-driven innovation *361*
desired reputation *311*
desired situation *201*
detail checklist *486*
development of goals *204*
die cutting *581*
differentiation *213*
differentiation as a strategy *213*
digital brandguide *605*
digital design manual *605*
digital media *328*
digital printing *577*
digital strategy *178*
digital 3D mockups *536*
direct competitors *124*
disruptive innovation *360*
disruptive strategy *181*
distinctive asset-building strategy *219*
distinctive brand assets (DBAs) *169, 220, 352*
distortion methods *405*
diverge *366*
divergence and convergence *366*
domain name *281, 593*
dot gain *579*
dot-based graphics *568*
dramaturgy *274*
d.school's five-stage model *357*
dummy *533, 534*

# E

ecolabelling and certification *554*
ecological/environment *147*
economic *147*
Effect hierarchy model *323*
effectiveness measurements *330*
emotional attributes *199*
emotional design *359*
empathy *356*
empathy map *98*
empirical research *74*
endorsed identity *253*
endorser brand *255*
environmental *147*
environmental impact *549*
errors *365*
ethics *87*
examples of different surveys *89*
exclusive rights in social media *594*
experiment *106, 107*
experiment design *107, 108*
exploratory (unclear) problem statement *66*
external factors *151*
external validity *81*

# F

facts on recycling *552*
false carton *550*
falsification vs. verification *81*
fargesystemer *572*
favicon *283*
Fibonacci *467*
Fibonacci in a cone *468*
Fibonacci sequence *468*
fidelity *538*
file structure *566*
file types *568*
file types used in the graphic business *571*
final document *563, 567*
first and second levels *IX*
first position *266*
five forces *125*
five forces analysis *125*
Five Ps for strategy *180*
flatbed printing *577*
flexo printing *578*
focus *214*
focus group *102*
focus group process *103*
FOGRA *562*
foil printing *578*
font anatomy *505*
font history *514*
font identity *502*
font selection *499*
font terminology *509*
font voice *503*
fonts and typography *608*
food and non-food *551*
food packaging *552*
format *451*
format sizes and weight *462*
four colours *579*
framework *390*
Frascati manual *109*
frontend *573*
frontend frameworks and libraries *574*
frontend languages *573*
functional areas *52*
functional strategies *176*
functionality *540*
functional/operational strategies *179*
funnel *167*
future image *157*

# G

gameplan *37*
Gantt chart *25*
gap analysis *153*
gap analysis process *153*
GDPR *87*
gen Alpha *131*
gen X *131*
gen Y *131*
gen Z *131*
gender *131*
generalisation *81*
generalising ambition *83*
generalising or non-generalising *67*
generation *131*
geographical segmentation *131*
geometric shapes *422*
GIGA map *160, 350*
goal *178, 201*
goal achievement *208*
goal hierarchy *204*
goals as guideline *206*
goals as search area *206*
goals > consequence > measures *210*
goals for a design project *210*
golden rectangle *464*
good legibility *524*
graphic cartonboard *551*
graphic printing methods *576*
gravure *576*
green packaging *551*
grid in layout *519*
grid is history *518*
grid system *517*
grid system development *520*
grid system principles *525*
grid systems *610*
grooving *581*
group climate *36*
GV's Sprint Process *368*

# H

hand sketches *415*
hate and conflict *69*
HCD model *357*
health and livelihood *69*
high price or low price *268*
homogen board *551*
hourly rate *29, 31*
house of brands strategy *255*
how to use the book? *VIII*
HP-indigo *577*
hybrids *254*
hypothesis *62, 110*
hypothetical deductive method *111*

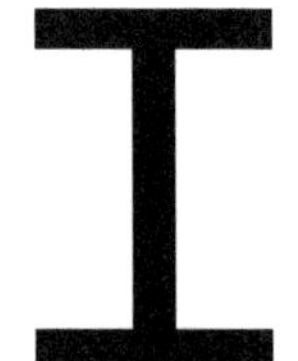

idea as a bridge *353*
idea development *398*
idea vs. concept *408*
idea work process *382*
identity *56*
identity colours *494*
identity development *470*
identity management *516*
identity rhombus *277*
IDEO HCD model *357*
image *56, 315*
image moodboard *156*
image reproduction *549*
image vs. reputation *312*
implementation *532*
implicit or explicit *63*
inbound marketing *239*
inbound vs. outbound *240*
inclusive and diverse *33*
incremental innovation *360*
indirect competitors *124*
induction and deduction *111*
inductive (intensive) *111*
industrial property rights (IP) *589*
inequality *69*
informants *79*
information hierarchy *143*
initial meeting *10*
initial preparations *5*
initial workshop *16*
initiation *3*
initiation of the project *346*
initiation process *4*
innovation *360*
innovation for marketig impact *361*
insight *44*
insight in all phases *45*
inspiration moodboard *159*
installation and construction *582*
intangible assets *588*
intangible assets and rights *589*
intellectual property rights *589*
intensive *111*
intensive vs. extensive research *81*
interactive media *327*
internal analysis *119*
internal and external factors *149*
Internal and external validity *81*
internal factors *150*
interpretation/ validation *77*
interview *90*
interview process *95*
invoice *29*
IP address *593*
ISO coated v2 *562*
iterative method *363*

kanban *371*
Kapferer's positioning prism *261*
Keller's brand equity model *140, 141*
kerning *507, 512*
key performance indicators *169*
KPIs and metrics *168*

# L

lamination *581*
layout principles *610*
Leading business by design report *600*
leading questions *92*
lean *373*
lean and agile *371*
Lean start-up *229*
legal *147*
legal protection *590*
letter axis *509*
letter spacing *507*
lettering *483*
letterpress *576*
life phase *130*
lifespan of paper *549*
ligature *512*
line extension *298*
line length *512, 524*
line spacing *524*
lines and dashes *425*
live prototyping *538*
logo *282, 476*
logo development *483*
logo guides *607*
logo process *478*
logo vs. brand *477*
long-term development *615*
long-term focus *299*
low-cost strategy *212*

majuscule *512*
management *587*
mapping *155*
mapping as a link *349*
mapping methods *156*
margins of error *86*
market segment *308*
market segmentation *129*
market strategy *178, 230, 232*
market surveys *89*
marketing communication *310*
marketing communication goals *310*
marketing funnel *167*
marketing mix *234*
marketing rights *595*
marketing tasks *231*
markets *230*
Maslow's hierarchy of needs *137*
mass communication *310*
mass media *325*
masterbrand *255*
material insight *541*
material life cycle *542*
material life cycle assessment *542*
material moodboard *159*
material properties *541*
material selection *539*
materials *539*
measurable goals *168*
measurable goals and objectives *208*
measure the design effect *602*
measurement *167*
measuring financial performance *169*
media channels *325*
media strategy *179*
meeting administration *13*
mega trends *146*
mental availability measurements *169*
message *318*
message strategy *321*
metaphors and analogies *407*
method selection *70, 78*
method triangulation *73*
metrics *168*
migration *69*
millimetre *512*
mind map *397*
Minerva method *134*
Minerva target group analysis *135*
minutes *15*
mission *178, 187*
mission statement *187*
mockup *533, 536*
model *533*
modular grid system *518*
monolithic identity *253*
moodboard *156, 349*
moodboard development *158*
multiple methods *73*

# N


name 281
name development 290
name types 292
naming process 293
narrative/story 201, 318
navigation XI
NCS 572
need-finding 378
needs analysis 154
niche or upstream 269
niche strategy 214
no competitors 124
non-participant observations 100
not valid and reliable 85
number of recycles 552


# O


objectives and key results (OKRs) 168
observation 97
observation process 101
offset printing 577
OKRs 168
open or concealed observation 99
open-ended questions 92
operating manual 614
optical adjustment 505
optical grid 508
organic shapes 424
organisation 53
organisational culture 53
organisational development 53, 54
organisational identity 57
original files 567
original material 562
out of gamut 559
overall goal 178, 206
overall strategy 175, 186
overall strategy and objectives 178


# P


package design XII
packaging 143, 284
packaging cartonboard 551
packaging materials 553
page coverage 526
paid, owned, earned attention 328
Pantone, PMS (special colour) 572, 580
paper 544
paper construction 545
paper feeling 548
paper production 545
paper properties 546
paper selection 548
paper shade 548
parent brand 253
participant observation 100
patents 594
PDF 568
PDF for printing 569, 570
PDF preset 570
perception 433
perception theory 434
perforation 581
performance 141
persona 157
personal media 327
personality 56, 191, 198
PESTLE analysis 146
phase structure VIII
phenomenon 62
phi 464
photo style 609
physical mockups 536
pica 512
PIPI workshop 56
pitch perfect 7
pixel, raster, dot and vector 568
planning 35
pluralistic identity 253
PMS 572
point (pt) vs. pixel (px) 510
points 426
points of differentiation 264
points of parity 264
political 147
population 69
Porter's five forces analysis 125
Porter's generic strategies 212
position 125
positioning 179, 233, 374
positioning analysis 125
positioning axis 126
positioning statement 270
potential competitors 124
presentation 6
presentation model 538
presentation of ideas 411
press techniques 576
price 30
price quotation 26
price request 28
price setup 28
primary colours 427
primary data 80
primary, secondary and tertiary colours 427
principles of composition 434
printing effects 580
printing ink 580
printing methods 577
problem 60
problem definition 61
problem of induction 111
problem solving 393
problem statement 58, 61, 76
problem statement analysis 65
problem statement delimitation 63
problem statement formulation 62
problem statement process 61
problem statement requirements 67
problem statement (Step 1) 76
product 143
product information 319
product labelling/ecolabelling 555
product life cycle 543
product lifetime extension 543
product positioning analysis 127
product strategy 179
production 531
production for digital media 573
production for printed media 575
production model 539
profile 56
profile colours 608
profile elements 609
profile font 609
profit 31
progress schedule 24
project brief 9
project brief template 9
project description 22, 23
promise 196, 197
protection of personal data 87
prototype 533, 536
prototyping of ideas 410
psychographic segmentation 132
pull in the same direction 203
punching 581
pure research 109
purpose 178
purpose statement 187

qual vs. quant goals 207
qualifications 33
qualitative data 80
qualitative goals 207
qualitative indicators 169
qualitative indicators and metrics 169
qualitative interview 90
qualitative KPI 169
qualitative method 70, 78
qualitative research 70, 79
qualitative vs. quantitative data 81
quality assurance 583
quality control 35
quantitative data 81
quantitative goals 207
quantitative method 71
quantitative methods 78
quantitative research 72, 79, 87
question design 88
question form 93
question formulation 86
questions 92
quotation 28, 30


# R


radical innovation 361
RAL 572
raster 578
rational attributes 199
R&D 109
reading distance 524
recipient 307

red vs. blue ocean strategy *216*
registered trademark *592*
registration of a domain name *593*
registration of names *293*
relief printing *581*
report *19*
report preparation *82*
repositioning *126, 270*
representative sample *85*
reputation *312*
reputation workshop *314*
requirements for a good logo *479*
research *74, 82*
research design (Step 2) *76*
research on the arts *112*
research process *74, 110*
research question *73*
research through design *48, 114*
research with big R vs. little r *47*
resource analysis *119*
respondent vs. informant *79*
respondents *79, 84*
response hierarchy *322*
RGB *560, 572*
RGB and CMYK *561*
risk *365*
risk of design process failure *163*
ROIs *208*
root-2 rectangle *460*
Rubin's vase *433*
rupture in the design process *163*

# S

salary *31*
sales funnel *167*
salience *140*
satisfaction survey *64, 65*
scamper *409*
scenario games *159*
scientific experiment *106*
scientific method *111*
scientific research *108*
second position *267*
secondary data *80*
sections/rows *527*
segmentation *232*
segmentation models *132*
select colour profile *562*
selection of respondents *88*
sense elements *286*
service blueprint *380*
service strategy *179*
shape *421*
shape vs. form *422*
share of market (SOM) *170*
share of voice/share of market *330*
share of voice (SOV) *170*
signal effect *317*
silk-screen-printing *578*
situation moodboard *157*
situational analysis *117*
situational analysis process *118*
situational study *55, 57*
situational study process *56*
sketch model *535*
sketch process *414*
sketch prototyping *416*
slogan *284*
slogan/tagline *318*
SMART goals *208*
social media *327*
social media sales funnel *168*
social media strategy *179*
social science *45, 48*
social sciences method *108, 112*
socio-cultural/social *147*
space *430, 431*
sprint *368*
stakeholder mapping *305*
stand up meetings *39*
standard text *319*
statement *411*
store study *144*
storyboard *159, 350*
storytelling *271*
STP marketing strategy *232*
strategic design *XI*
strategic design thinking *385*
strategic intent *178*
strategic management tool *181*
strategic process *181*
strategic use of design *XI*
strategic workshop *57, 182*
strategy *174*
Strategy><Design *348*
strategy as narrative *201*
strategy development *176, 177, 181*
strategy hierarchy *175*
strategy innovation *180*
strategy moodboard *157*
strategy on different levels *175*
strategy overview and definition of terms *178*
stretch goals *206*
stylisation *491*
sub-brand *254*
subgoals *201*
subjective vs. objective *520*
surface *449*
survey *82, 89*
survey categories *83*
survey form *84*
survey form structure *90*
survey process *88*
survey questions *86, 92*
sustainability goals *209*
sustainable business model *227*
sustainable font choice *622*
sustainable forest management *550*
sustainable management *615*
sustainable materials management *542*
sustainable packaging *553*
sustaining innovation *361*
SWOT analysis *148*
SWOT analysis process *151*
SWOT workshop *150*
symbol *282, 489*
symptom vs. problem *60*
system oriented design (SOD) *163, 389*
systematisation *349*
systemic design *386*
systems theory *388*
systems thinking *387*

# T

tacit knowledge *44*
target group *307*
target group analysis *129*
target group analysis process *134*
target market analysis *136*
targeting *233*
team *32*
team contract *40*
technological *147*
terms and conditions *28*
testing *164*
testing and measuring *164*
testing of ideas *410*
texture *430*
the A series *459*
the company *50*
the company's decision areas *52*
the company's functional areas *52*
the company's universe *54*
the consumer market *130*
the corporate market *130*
the dark matter of design *600*
the death of nature *69*
the distinctive asset grid *221*
the economic effects of design *599*
the emerging process *180*
the end result *567*
the fifth element *353, 516*
the four Cs *236*
the four orders of design *341*
the four Ps *234*
the golden ratio *463*
the golden spiral *466*
the Hollywood models *275*
the identity elements *474*
the identity principles *471*
the intersection *348*
the invisible forces *600*
the linear process *177*
the main characters of the book *X*
the Oslo Manifesto *210*
the Patent Act *595*
the phases of a design process *343*
the pre-war generation *131*
the research process *77*
the role and value of design *600*
the rule of thirds *469*
the share of voice rule *331*
the tip of the iceberg *479*
the value of design *599*
the value of design factfinder *599*
the wheel of competitive strategy *213*
the white surface *450*
the X factor *265*
thinking outside the box *401*
three-course menu *276*
three-direction principle *413*
time and motion *432*
time vs. costs *365*
tone depth *565*
tone of voice *316*
Top 5 – strategic management tool *182, 183*
total management in a company *52*
track and measure *169*
trademark *591*
transient advantage *217*
transient advantage strategy *218*
transient advantage workshop *219*
triangulation *73*
triple bottom line *209*
types of goals *206*

types of interviews *91, 95*
typographical terms *510*
typography *498*
typography iteration *505*

U

UBC's strategic design method (SDM) *385*
UN sustainable development goals *210*
unbranding *611*
unclear or clear problem statement *66*
understanding the company *50*
unfair competition *595*
units *64*
unity/whole *436*
use of colours *608*
use of file formats *569*
use of phases *XII*
user testing *165*
user-centricity *355*
user-driven innovation *361*
user-experience *358*
user-experience research *104*
UX *358*
UX research *104*
UX research methods *104*

valid and reliable *85*
validity and reliability *80*
value cabal *198*
value chain *122*
value chain analysis *121*
value creation *51*
value promise *199*
value proposition *178, 196*
Value proposition canvas *197*
value pyramid *198*
value-driven culture *193*
values *64*
Van de Graaf canon *457*
variables *64*
variables, units, values, context *81*
varnishing *581*
VAT *30*
vector-based graphics *568*
verbalisation and visualisation *410*
virgin fibres *551*
virgin vs. recycled fiber *552*
vision *178, 189*
visual analysis *142*
visual analysis process *144*
visual assets *336*
visual effect *602*
visual identity *470*
visualise brand architecture *351*
visualise brand position *351*
visualise name *352*
visualise sound, smell, taste, and emotion *351*
visualise strategy *350*
visualise values *350*
VRIO analysis *120*
VRIO model *119*

walking in the customer's shoes *160*
warm-up exercises *399*
web mockup *536*
web strategy *179*
what is design? *X*
where are we – where will we? *57*
white paper *548*
white vs. brown cartonboard *551*
wicked problems *68*
wicked 7 *69*
wireframe *535, 537*
Wizard of Oz experiment *108*
wood fiber *550*
work files *567*
workflow *566*
working document *562*
workshop *56*
workshop management *18*
workshop preparation *17*
workshop process *20, 182*
workshop report *19, 184*
workshop template *185*
WOZ prototyping *537*

Zeigarnik effect *401*
zero-point measurement *167*

Fig. 0.1 Phase structure VIII
Fig. 0.2 Linear and circular VIII
Fig. 0.3 The main characters of the book X
Fig. 0.4 Strategic design XI
Fig. 0.5 At the core XI
Fig. 0.6 Navigation XI
Fig. 1.1 Gantt chart 25
Fig. 1.2 Control loop 35
Fig. 1.3 Gameplan 37
Fig. 2.1 Data collection 47
Fig. 2.2 Design research 49
Fig. 2.3 The company 50
Fig. 2.4 Total management in a company 52
Fig. 2.5 The company's universe 54
Fig. 2.6 How do others see us? 57
Fig. 2.7 The problem and goal 60
Fig. 2.8 Problem statement delimitation 64
Fig. 2.9 The Wicked 7 69
Fig. 2.10 Empirical research 74
Fig. 2.11 Data collection, simplified 75
Fig. 2.12 Data collection, advanced 76
Fig. 2.13 Quantitative research 87
Fig. 2.14 Survey questions 92
Fig. 2.15 AEIOU Empathy Map 98
Fig. 2.16 A landscape of UX research methods 104
Fig. 2.17 Experiment design 107
Fig. 2.18 Design research process 114
Fig. 2.19 First research – then analyse 115
Fig. 2.20 Analysis process 117
Fig. 2.21 VRIO model 120
Fig. 2.22 Value chain 122
Fig. 2.23 Competitive analysis 124
Fig. 2.24 Five forces 125
Fig. 2.25 Repositioning 126
Fig. 2.26 Product positioning analysis 127
Fig. 2.27 Positioning analysis, business 128
Fig. 2.28 Segmentation principle 131
Fig. 2.29 Minerva target group analysis 135
Fig. 2.30 Maslow's hierachy of needs 137
Fig. 2.31 Brand analysis internally/externally 138
Fig. 2.32 ACCID 140
Fig. 2.33 Keller's Brand Equity Model 141
Fig. 2.34 Information hierarchy 143
Fig. 2.35 SWOT analysis 152
Fig. 2.36 Identifying the gap 153
Fig. 2.37 GAP analysis 154
Fig. 2.38 Using GIGA mapping 162
Fig. 2.39 Systematic use of GIGA maps 163
Fig. 2.40 User testing for the web 165
Fig. 2.41 Funnel 167
Fig. 3.1 Strategy 174
Fig. 3.2 Strategy hierarchy 175
Fig. 3.3 Business idea 188
Fig. 3.4 Corporate identity 193
Fig. 3.5 Value Proposition Canvas 197
Fig. 3.6 a) The value pyramid 199
Fig. 3.6 b) The value cabal 200
Fig. 3.7 Strategic narrative 201
Fig. 3.8 Desired situation 202
Fig. 3.9 Pull in the same direction 203
Fig. 3.10 Goal hierarchy 205
Fig. 3.11 Goals > Consequence > Actions 210
Fig. 3.12 The wheel of competitive strategy 213
Fig. 3.13 Porter's generic strategies 214
Fig. 3.14 Blue Ocean 217
Fig. 3.15 The wave of transient advantage 218
Fig. 3.16 Distinctive brand asset 220
Fig. 3.17 The distinctive asset grid 221
Fig. 3.18 Agile strategy framework 222
Fig. 3.19 Business model canvas 226
Fig. 3.20 Sustainable business model 228
Fig. 3.21 Lean start-up 229
Fig. 3.22 STP model 232
Fig. 3.23 The four Ps 235
Fig. 3.24 The four Cs 237
Fig. 3.25 Five steps to develop a content strategy 239
Fig. 3.26 Inbound marketing 240
Fig. 3.27 Digital strategy 243
Fig. 3.28 The company's brand value chain 248
Fig. 3.29 Brand identities 252
Fig. 3.30 Brand architecture 256
Fig. 3.31 Brand hierarchy 258
Fig. 3.32 Brand levels 259
Fig. 3.33 Kapferer's positioning rhombus 260
Fig. 3.34 Use situation for beverages 262
Fig. 3.35 The X factor 265
Fig. 3.36 The concept story 273
Fig. 3.37 The Hollywood model 275
Fig. 3.38 a) Identity prism 278
Fig. 3.38 b) Identity prism 278
Fig. 3.39 Brand assets 281
Fig. 3.40 Colour assets 283
Fig. 3.41 The Brand Sense Survey 286
Fig. 3.42 McDonald's 287
Fig. 3.43 Name test 289
Fig. 3.44 The FER model 300
Fig. 3.45 Stakeholder map 305
Fig. 3.46 Identity, image, reputation 313
Fig. 3.47 Reputation 313
Fig. 3.48 Brand image 315
Fig. 3.49 Signal effect 317
Fig. 3.50 Communication process 320
Fig. 3.51 Response hierarchy 323
Fig. 3.52 Communication mix 327
Fig. 3.53 Paid, owned, earned attention 329
Fig. 3.54 The share of voice rule 331
Fig. 3.55 Design strategy 332
Fig. 4.1 The four orders of design 341
Fig. 4.2 The phases of a design process 343
Fig. 4.3 Initiation of the project 346
Fig. 4.4 The big challenge 348
Fig. 4.5 Branding in five and a half steps 349
Fig. 4.6 Transfer by moodboard 349
Fig. 4.7 Customer journey 350
Fig. 4.8 Monolithic identity 351
Fig. 4.9 Visualise position 352
Fig. 4.10 Distinctive brand asset 353
Fig. 4.11 The fifth element 353
Fig. 4.12 IDEO HCD model 357
Fig. 4.13 Five-stage design thinking model 357
Fig. 4.14 UX model 359
Fig. 4.15 Innovation for marketing impact 361

Fig. 4.16 Iterative process 363
Fig. 4.17 Spiral UX model 364
Fig. 4.18 Time vs. costs 365
Fig. 4.19 Divergence and convergence 366
Fig. 4.20 Sections of divergence and convergence 367
Fig. 4.21 The Double Diamond 367
Fig. 4.22 GV's design sprint 368
Fig. 4.23 Scrum 370
Fig. 4.24 Agile 372
Fig. 4.25 Complementation 373
Fig. 4.26 Design thinking 375
Fig. 4.27 Customer journey 377
Fig. 4.28 Need-finding 379
Fig. 4.29 Service blueprint 381
Fig. 4.30 3 Gears of business design 384
Fig. 4.31 UBC's Strategic Design Method (SDM) 385
Fig. 4.32 Service system design process 387
Fig. 4.33 Systems thinking 388
Fig. 4.34 The big challenge 390
Fig. 4.35 The Creative Problem-Solving Process 393
Fig. 4.36 Analytical vs. Creative 394
Fig. 4.37 Zeigarnik effect 401
Fig. 4.38 Three-direction principle 413
Fig. 4.39 Two-dimensional basic shapes 423
Fig. 4.40 Use of basic shapes 423
Fig. 4.41 Three-dimensional basic shapes 424
Fig. 4.42 Abstraction 424
Fig. 4.43 Organic shapes 425
Fig. 4.44 Colour is influenced by surroundings 429
Fig. 4.45 Texture 430
Fig. 4.46 Whitespace 431
Fig. 4.47 Rubin's vase 432
Fig. 4.48 Illusion 435
Fig. 4.49 Gestalt theory 436
Fig. 4.50 Unity 437
Fig. 4.51 Similarity and congruency 438
Fig. 4.52 Line a) 439
Fig. 4.53 Lines b) 439
Fig. 4.54 Shape c) 440
Fig. 4.55 Proportions 442
Fig. 4.56 Radial symmetry 445
Fig. 4.57 Rhythm 447
Fig. 4.58 Two-dimensional surface 449
Fig. 4.59 Three-dimensional surface 450
Fig. 4.60 Surface characteristics 451
Fig. 4.61 Van de Graaf canon 457
Fig. 4.62 The golden canon of page construction 458
Fig. 4.63 Aspect ratios 458
Fig. 4.64 Root-2 rectangle 460
Fig. 4.65 Root-5 rectangle 460
Fig. 4.66 The A format 461
Fig. 4.67 Design of the golden ratio 463
Fig. 4.68 The golden ratio 463
Fig. 4.69 Phi 464
Fig. 4.70 The golden rectangle 465
Fig. 4.71 The golden rectangle 465
Fig. 4.72 The golden spiral 466
Fig. 4.73 The golden spiral in a snail's house 466
Fig. 4.74 Fibonacci 467
Fig. 4.75 Fibonacci in a cone 468
Fig. 4.76 The rule of thirds 469
Fig. 4.77 Identity principles 472
Fig. 4.78 Exposure on the surface 473
Fig. 4.79 Communication surfaces 473
Fig. 4.80 Identity elements 475
Fig. 4.81 Identity management 476
Fig. 4.82 Logo 477
Fig. 4.83 Strategic anchoring 479
Fig. 4.84 a) Typography vs. lettering 482
Fig. 4.84 b) Typography vs. lettering 482
Fig. 4.85 Font and colour selection 485
Fig. 4.86 Logo grid 487
Fig. 4.87 Logo based on modular grid system 489
Fig. 4.88 Symbols 490
Fig. 4.89 Symbolic meaning 490
Fig. 4.90 Photo, illustration, stylisation, symbol 491
Fig. 4.91 Stylisation/abstraction 493
Fig. 4.92 The influence of colour in a buying situation 497
Fig. 4.93 Typographic layout 499
Fig. 4.94 Roman vs Sans serif 500
Fig. 4.95 Cut angle 500
Fig. 4.96 Serifs 501
Fig. 4.97 Font is identity 503
Fig. 4.98 The voice of the font 503
Fig. 4.99 Double-storey 'a' 504
Fig. 4.100 Single-storey 'a' 504
Fig. 4.101 Two-storey 'g' 504
Fig. 4.102 Single-storey 'g' 504
Fig. 4.103 Inner and outer form 506
Fig. 4.104 Inner and outer form 506
Fig. 4.105 Inner and outer form 506
Fig. 4.106 Inner and outer form 506
Fig. 4.107 Kerning 507
Fig. 4.108 The font's DNA 508
Fig. 4.109 Optically correct 509
Fig. 4.110 Overshoots 509
Fig. 4.111 Calligraphy 510
Fig. 4.112 Letter axis 510
Fig. 4.113 Font as identity element 510
Fig. 4.114 Font terminology 511
Fig. 4.115 Font terminology 513
Fig. 4.116 Classic typefaces 515
Fig. 4.117 Modular grid system 518
Fig. 4.118 Grid in layout 519
Fig. 4.119 Grid in layout 521
Fig. 4.120 Page coverage with baseline grid 526
Fig. 4.121 The Zeigarnik effect 528
Fig. 5.1 Wireframe 537
Fig. 5.2 Material life cycle 542
Fig. 5.3 Product life cycle 543
Fig. 5.4 CIELAB 558
Fig. 5.5 Colour settings 564
Fig. 5.6 Naming files 566
Fig. 5.7 a) File structure in a small project 567
Fig. 5.7 b) File structure in a larger project 567
Fig. 5.8 Frontend and backend 573
Fig. 5.9 Printing techniques 576
Fig. 6.1 Intangible assets 588
Fig. 6.2 Copyright 591
Fig. 6.3 Registered trademark 591
Fig. 6.4 Trademark 591
Fig. 6.5 The Danish design ladder 599

Fig. 6.6 Logo guides 607
Fig. 6.7 Profile colours 608
Fig. 6.8 Profile fonts 609
Fig. 6.9 Design templates 613
Fig. 6.10 The eco-design pyramid 619
Fig. 6.11 Sustainable font choice 622

Table 0.1 First and second levels IX
Table 0.2 Example of use of phases XII
Table 2.1 Situational study 58
Table 2.2 Step 1 61
Table 2.3 Steps 1 and 2 63
Table 2.4 Satisfaction survey 65
Table 2.5 The research process 77
Table 2.6 Method selection 78
Table 2.7 Selection of survey form 84
Table 2.8 Examples of different surveys 89
Table 2.9 Question form 93
Table 2.10 Analyses that provide insight 116
Table 2.11 Visual analysis form 144
Table 2.12 PESTLE-analysis 147
Table 2.13 SWOT form 149
Table 3.1 Strategy overview and definition of terms 179
Table 3.2 Top 5 – strategic management tool 183
Table 3.3 Principles of agile strategy 184
Table 3.4 The Oslo Manifesto 209
Table 3.5 Red vs. Blue Ocean strategy 216
Table 3.6 Clarification of concepts 225
Table 3.7 Brand strategy process 247
Table 3.8 Brand platform 250
Table 3.9 Yoplait categorisation 263
Table 3.10 Points of parity vs. points of differentiation 265
Table 3.11 a) Name development 294
Table 3.11 b) Name development 295
Table 3.12 Communication strategy 302
Table 3.13 Tone of voice 316
Table 3.14 8 models of communication 324
Table 3.15 Communication mix 326
Table 4.1 The design process 345
Table 4.2 Visualise values 351
Table 4.3 Visualise sound, smell, taste, and emotion 351
Table 4.4 Design thinking vs. Lean mindset 373
Table 4.5 Creative problem solving 392
Table 4.6 Brainwriting 403
Table 4.7 Detail checklist 418
Table 4.8 Composition principles 446
Table 4.9 The most common paper sizes 462
Table 4.10 Logo process 478
Table 4.11 Testing out fonts 485
Table 5.1 Packaging materials 552
Table 5.2 Ecolabelling and certification 555
Table 5.3 Colour model, colour gamut, colour profile 560
Table 5.4 Stages of a work process 568
Table 5.5 Choosing the right software 569
Table 5.6 File types used in the graphic business 571
Table 5.7 Colour reference systems 572
Table 6.1 ESG criteria 616

## Planning tool

**Here is a short list that can be used when planning a project based on the phase structure of the book. See also Table 0.2.**

### PHASE 1 INITIATION

Initiation is about getting started on a design project, ensuring a good start to the project, clarifying which task is to be solved and defining clear framework and conditions.

Introduction: Basis for the project's content, scope and progress.

Initial preparations: The client defines qualifications needed for the assignment. The designer prepares a presentation of own expertise to get the assignment. Including: Preparation, presentation, and argumentation.

Project brief: When initiating a design project, the client develops a brief and clear description of the project to serve as a starting point for the first meeting with the designer. Including: Short introduction about the client and product or service, project, problem, objectives and task, target group, delivery, timeframe, budget framework and competence requirements.

Initial meeting: During the initial meeting, the client and the designer establish a common understanding of the assignment, the client's goal and level of ambition, the designer's qualifications and suitability, budget framework and delivery time. Including: Meeting administration, before the meeting, during the meeting, after the meeting.

Initial workshop: In an initial workshop, the designer and the client work together to clarify the assignment, the goal and strategic anchoring of the project. Including: Workshop purpose, preparations, invitations, facilities, management, execution, report and process.

Project description: The assignment is specified in a project description as basis for a price quotation and progress schedule. Including: Description of the project, the task to be solved, the goal of the assignment, the proposed work process divided into phases, progress schedule and price quotations.

Progress schedule: The designer draws up a progress schedule to get a good flow in the work process and ensure delivery according to the deadline. Including: Introduction, project name, date, short project description, timetable, tasks, presentations, production, interim deliverables, priorities, distribution of responsibilities and due date.

Price quotation: The designer prepares a price quotation that includes estimated time usage and resources, as well as relevant payment terms. Including: Price inquiry, price setup, terms and conditions, negotiation, and hourly rate.

Contract: The legal rights of the designer and the client are safeguarded by a contract signed by both parties. Including: Parties, delivery, price, complaint, legal ownership, obligations, liability, disputes, and signing.

Team collaboration: A good collaboration climate is a success factor for achieving good results. Including: Qualifications, level of ambition, goals and tasks, management, game plan and team contract.

### PHASE 2 INSIGHT

Insight is about acquiring the knowledge and understanding necessary to carry out a design project.

Introduction: How do we gain insight? When do we need insight? Insight into all phases, data collection and design research.

Understanding the company: Designers who understand the company have a good starting point for a fruitful dialogue with the client. Including: The company's universe, value creation, functional areas, decision making (strategic, administrative and operational aspects), organisational culture, products, services, organisation development, needs, markets, use of resources.

Situational study: It is necessary to know the current situation in order to develop goals and strategy. Including: Situational study process, workshops, content and report. Content: the company's problems, challenges, background, history, production, product development, target groups, segments, markets, organisation, alliance partners.

Problem statement: What problem should the project help to solve? How to arrive at a problem statement? Including: Problem definition, problem statement (Step 1) and (Step 2), problem statement formulation, problem statement delimitation (units, variables, values, context), problem statement analysis and requirements.

Method selection: The choice of method depends on what information can elucidate or help solve the problem statement. If one needs to go into depth, qualitative method should be selected. If necessary to generalise, quantitative method should be selected. Including: Qualitative method (interview, observation, document survey, studies), quantitative method (surveys, questionnaires), method triangulation (combination of quantitative and qualitative methods), research question (for surveys, scientific research and design research).

Research process: How to conduct a survey? Including: Problem statement, research design, choice of method, choice of units, data collection, data analysis and discussion, data interpretation and report preparation.

Research: The choice of research method is related to what one wants to get an answer to. Including: Survey, generalising ambition, respondents, representative sample, formulation of questions, ethics, personal protection, interview, interview forms, interview process, interview guide, interview subjects, good questions, bad questions, observation, focus group, UX research, experiment, scientific research, artistic research, design research.

Analyses: In an analysis, one dissolves a whole into smaller parts in order to investigate and research the different parts. Including: Situational analysis (internal factors and external factors), internal analysis (resource analysis, activity analysis, value chain analysis), competitor analysis, positioning analysis, target group analysis, brand analysis, visual analysis, PESTLE analysis, SWOT analysis and gap analysis.

Mapping: Different methods of mapping can be used to visualise research and analyses, to make data more available and easier to understand and use in the strategy and design process. Including: Mapping methods, moodboard, storyboard, customer journey and GIGA map.

Testing and measuring: Testing and measuring are needed in order to find out if the strategy, idea and solution work as desired and give the desired effect. Including: Zero-point measurement, funnel, user testing, A/B testing.

## PHASE 3 STRATEGY

**Strategy is about the strategic anchoring of a design process, the development of necessary goals and strategies, and the use of strategy as a management tool for the design process.**

Introduction: Strategy at various levels.

Strategy development: Different approaches to strategy development. TOP 5 as a minimum strategy and strategy management tool, the use of strategy workshop in the strategy development process. Including: Workshop preparations, process, report, and template.

Overall strategy: What should the company do and in what direction should it move? Including: Purpose, mission, business idea, vision, core values, and value proposition and values-based culture.

Goals and subgoals: Questions the business should be asked/ask itself: What is our desired situation? What do we wish to achieve? What should we do? What can we do? Including: Business goals, big hairy goals, development of goals, goal hierarchy, qualitative vs. quantitative goals, measurable goals, goal achievement, sustainable goals, goals for a design project.

Business strategy: How should the company compete in the market? Including: Competitive strategy, Porter's generic strategies (cost leadership, differentiation, focus), blue ocean strategy, transient advantage, distinctive asset-building strategy, agile strategy management. Has the right strategy been chosen?

Business model: Choise of business management platform and tool for realising the business idea and bringing it out to market. Including: Business model canvas, sustainable business model, business model innovation, lean start-up.

Market strategy: Which markets should the company invest in, who should they sell their products to and services, what should they achieve in different markets, how should they do it? Including: Markets, marketing tasks, STP marketing strategy, customer needs, the four Ps, the four Cs, content marketing, inbound marketing, digital strategy.

Brand strategy: Plan and management tools for brand development and brand building. Including: Brand strategy, brand platform, brand architecture, brand position, brand narrative and storytelling, brand identity, brand assets, brand name, brand perspective, brand redesign.

Communication strategy: What to communicate, to whom, when, where, why, and how. Including: Development of commutation strategy, communication audit, identify the target group, communication goals, desired reputation, communication platform, communication elements, communication development, channels and media, measurement and evaluation.

Design strategy: What consequences should the overall insight and strategy defined in the previous phases have for the design process and the solution? A strategic management tool for the development, implementation and application of design as a means of achieving the company's goals. Including: Design strategy development, process, content, design goal, operational strategy, design platform, design strategy vs. design brief.

## PHASE 4 DESIGN

**Design in this context is about developing design solutions based on the previous phases of initiating the project, gathering insight and developing strategy.**

Introduction: The design process, from problem understanding to final result, initiation and phase division.

Design brief: What is the assignment and design delivery? What goal should it fulfil? Including: Describe the design project, the task to be solved, the goal and scope of the assignment, level of ambition and strategic anchoring.

Strategy><Design: How to link strategy and design? Including: Mapping as a link, visualise strategy, visualise name, idea as a bridge builder, the fifth element and distinctive brand assets.

Design methodology: Which design methodology should be chosen to solve the problem and realise the goal? Including: Human-centred design, user-experience, emotional design, user-driven innovation, iterative method, divergence and convergence, sprint, scrum, lean and agile, design thinking, business design, co-design, idea work, customer journey, service blueprint, need-finding, systemic design, strategic design thinking.

Concept development: How to generate ideas and develop them further into clear concepts? Including: Foundation and framework, creative problem solving, brainstorming, idea development, conceptual directions, verbalisation and visualisation, prototyping and testing of ideas, presentation of ideas.

Design development: How to further develop and refine one or more conceptual directions to reach final solutions? Including: The three-direction principle, design sketches, concrete design, detailing, testing, evaluation, adjustment, completion and quality assurance.

Design elements: The fundamental design elements shape, colour and texture are the building blocks in all visual design. Including: Shape, colour, texture, space, time and movement.

Composition: How to compose visual elements to bring out the desired perception, message, and identity? Including: Perception, composition principles, unity and whole, focal point, proportions, balance, and rhythm.

Surface and format: How to use the surface and format to convey information, and create identity and experience?

Including: Surface, format, aspect ratio, the A series, the golden ratio, the golden rectangle, the golden spiral, fibonacci and the rule of thirds.

Identity development: How should the company and its products or services appear? How to create a visual identity anchored in the company's overall goal and strategy that is distinctive and appealing? Including: The identity principles, the identity elements, logo, symbol, identity colours, typography, the fifth element, identity management and grid systems.

## PHASE 5 PRODUCTION

**Production is about print, press, programming or other completion, conscious choice of paper and material, as well as finalisation of the design solution for production.**

Introduction: Murphy's law, success factor, follow-up and quality assurance.

Implementation: How to realise, complete and implement the solution? Including: Implementation of solutions, placement of visual elements and content on current digital and analogue surfaces.

Model: Dummies, mock-ups and prototypes are used in all phases of the design process to test ideas and design along the way and at the end. Including: Model, dummy, sketch model, wireframe, mockup, prototype, data model and simulation, blueprint, and production model.

Material selection: How to ensure the right choice of materials? Including: Materials, functionality, material insight, material properties, material life cycle, product life cycle, product life extension, environment and recycling.

Paper: How to choose paper, in terms of functionality, identity, message and sustainability? Including: Paper structure, paper production, paper properties, paper selection, environment and recycling.

Colour management: How to use colour management to get optimal and consistent colour representation? Including: Colour models, colour gamut, colour profiles, select colour profile, colour channels and tonal depth, colours for web, workflow, PDF for printing, colour reference systems.

Production for digital media: How to build digital media products, such as ecommerce, websites, mobile applications, social media, location based services, online gaming and more? Including: Frontend, languages, frameworks and libraries. Backend: languages and frameworks.

Production for printed media: Which printing technique should be selected for the printed matters? Including: Printing techniques, printing methods, raster, four colours, inks, and ink effects.

Installation and structure: How to start installation planning early in the process by integrating this into the idea and design development? This way, unnecessary changes and costs are avoided in the final phase.

Technical functionality and light: How to use lighting to strengthen the design solution, as well as to ensure that the technical functionality is handled by professional subcontractors?

Quality assurance: How to secure the promised quality throughout the project, thereby satisfying the customers' or the user's requirements and expectations?

## PHASE 6 MANAGEMENT

**Management is about how the company can manage, control and operate the assets created through a design project.**

Introduction: Values can be of physical nature such as a designed object, an item, a building, or another form of physical or non-physical nature, the so-called intangible assets.

Intangible assets: How will the company manage its intangible assets, such as knowledge, reputation, and goodwill? Including: Intangible values and rights.

Legal protection: To what extent has intellectual property been created, or other intangible assets, which can be protected? Including: Copyright, trademark, domain name, company name, social media exclusive rights, design law, patent, piracy, marketing rights.

Design management: Companies with design ambition as an overarching goal, the so-called design-driven enterprises, need design management that takes responsibility and decisions regarding how the enterprise will develop and use design in its value creation.

Effect measurement: Have measurable targets been defined? Can the effect of the design investment be measured in the short or long term? Including: The design ladder, the economic effect, the value of design, design-driven company, the invisible forces, design impact awards.

Design manual: How to create a design manual that ensures consistent use of design according to strategy and objectives, and that serves as a good tool for those who will use the design solution on different interfaces and in different contexts? Including: Purpose and target group, foundation, scope, digital design manual, content, unbranding.

Design templates: How to develop a standard framework for ads, printed matter, software solutions or other things that should have consistent visual design?

Operating manual: How to create good guidelines and instructions to ensure operation and maintenance of websites, software, technical equipment, installation, etc.?

Further development: How to manage continuous long-term strategic development and building of brand and other values created through the design process?

Sustainability: Are the UN Sustainable Development Goals safeguarded in the design process, through the development of ideas and designs, choice of method, materials, production process and the service life of the solution?